COMPREHENSIVE HANDBOOK
OF
PERSONALITY AND PSYCHOPATHOLOGY

COMPREHENSIVE HANDBOOK OF PERSONALITY AND PSYCHOPATHOLOGY

VOLUME 2
ADULT PSYCHOPATHOLOGY

Frank Andrasik
Volume Editor

Michel Hersen
Jay C. Thomas
Editors-in-Chief

John Wiley & Sons, Inc.

This book is printed on acid-free paper. ∞

Copyright © 2006 by John Wiley & Sons, Inc. All rights reserved.

Published by John Wiley & Sons, Inc., Hoboken, New Jersey.
Published simultaneously in Canada.

No part of this publication may be reproduced, stored in a retrieval system, or transmitted in any form or by any means, electronic, mechanical, photocopying, recording, scanning, or otherwise, except as permitted under Section 107 or 108 of the 1976 United States Copyright Act, without either the prior written permission of the Publisher, or authorization through payment of the appropriate per-copy fee to the Copyright Clearance Center, Inc., 222 Rosewood Drive, Danvers, MA 01923, (978) 750-8400, fax (978) 750-4470, or on the web at www.copyright.com. Requests to the Publisher for permission should be addressed to the Permissions Department, John Wiley & Sons, Inc., 111 River Street, Hoboken, NJ 07030, (201) 748-6011, fax (201) 748-6008, or online at http://www.wiley.com/go/permissions.

Limit of Liability/Disclaimer of Warranty: While the publisher and author have used their best efforts in preparing this book, they make no representations or warranties with respect to the accuracy or completeness of the contents of this book and specifically disclaim any implied warranties or merchantability or fitness for a particular purpose. No warranty may be created or extended by sales representatives or written sales materials. The advice and strategies contained herein may not be suitable for your situation. You should consult with a professional where appropriate. Neither the publisher nor author shall be liable for any loss of profit or any other commercial damages, including but not limited to special, incidental, consequential, or other damages.

For general information on our other products and services or for technical support, please contact our Customer Care Department within the United States at (800) 762-2974, outside the United States at (317) 572-3993 or fax (317) 572-4002.

Wiley also publishes its books in a variety of electronic formats. Some content that appears in print may not be available in electronic books. For more information about Wiley products, visit our web site at www.wiley.com.

Library of Congress Cataloging-in-Publication Data:

Comprehensive handbook of personality and psychopathology / Michel Hersen & Jay C. Thomas, editors-in-chief.
    p. ; cm.
    Includes bibliographical references.
    ISBN-13 978-0-471-47945-1 (cloth : alk. paper : set)
    ISBN-10 0-471-47945-4 (cloth : alk. paper : set) —
    ISBN-13 978-0-471-48837-8 (cloth : alk. paper : v. 1)
    ISBN-10 0-471-48837-2 (cloth : alk. paper : v. 1) —
    ISBN-13 978-0-471-48838-5 (cloth : alk. paper : v. 2)
    ISBN-10 0-471-48838-0 (cloth : alk. paper : v. 2) —
    ISBN-13 978-0-471-48839-2 (cloth : alk. paper : v. 3)
    ISBN-10 0-471-48839-9 (cloth : alk. paper : v. 3)
    1. Psychology, Pathological—Handbooks, manuals, etc. 2. Child psychopathology—Handbooks, manuals, etc. 3. Personality—Handbooks, manuals, etc. 4. Psychology—Handbooks, manuals, etc. I. Hersen, Michel. II. Thomas, Jay C., 1951–
    [DNLM: 1. Mental Disorders—therapy. 2. Personality. 3. Psychological Theory. WM 400 C737 2006] 1951–
RC456.C66 2006
618.92′89—dc22
                                                                                               2005043981

Printed in the United States of America.

10 9 8 7 6 5 4 3 2 1

Contents

Handbook Preface   ix

Preface to Volume 2   xi

Contributors   xiii

PART ONE
GENERAL ISSUES

1 DIAGNOSIS AND CLASSIFICATION   3
   James Langenbucher and Peter E. Nathan

2 RESEARCH CONSIDERATIONS: LATENT VARIABLE APPROACHES TO STUDYING THE CLASSIFICATION AND PSYCHOPATHOLOGY OF MENTAL DISORDERS   21
   Laura Campbell-Sills and Timothy A. Brown

3 BEHAVIORAL AND COGNITIVE INFLUENCES   36
   Arthur M. Nezu, Christine Maguth Nezu, and Elizabeth R. Lombardo

4 GENETIC INFLUENCES   52
   Kerry L. Jang

5 SOCIOCULTURAL INFLUENCES   67
   Dorothy Chin and Velma A. Kameoka

6 BIOLOGICAL INFLUENCES   85
   Beverly E. Thorn and Kristine L. Lokken

PART TWO
MAJOR DISORDERS AND PROBLEMS

7 GENERALIZED ANXIETY DISORDER   101
   Marilyn Holmes and Michelle G. Newman

8 PANIC AND AGORAPHOBIA   121
   Jasper A. J. Smits, Conall M. O'Cleirigh, and Michael W. Otto

9 SOCIAL ANXIETY DISORDER   138
   Meredith E. Coles and Betty Horng

10 SPECIFIC PHOBIAS   154
   Karen Rowa, Randi E. McCabe, and Martin M. Antony

11 **OBSESSIVE-COMPULSIVE DISORDER** 169
    David S. Riggs and Edna B. Foa

12 **POST-TRAUMATIC STRESS DISORDER** 189
    Richard A. Bryant

13 **MAJOR DEPRESSIVE DISORDER** 207
    Michael E. Thase

14 **DYSTHYMIA AND MINOR DEPRESSION** 231
    Karen B. Schmaling and Dolores V. Hernandez

15 **BIPOLAR DISORDER** 244
    Cory F. Newman

16 **SCHIZOPHRENIA** 262
    Kim T. Mueser, Elisa Bolton, and Susan R. McGurk

17 **ORGANIC MENTAL DISORDER** 278
    Drew Gouvier

18 **BORDERLINE PERSONALITY DISORDER** 299
    Timothy J. Trull, Stephanie D. Stepp, and Marika Solhan

19 **OTHER PERSONALITY DISORDERS** 316
    Kenneth N. Levy and Lori N. Scott

20 **ALCOHOL ABUSE AND DEPENDENCE** 337
    Marilyn J. Strada, Jennifer Karmely, and Brad Donohue

21 **DRUG ABUSE AND DEPENDENCE** 354
    Brad Donohue, Alisha M. Farley, and Samantha L. French

22 **GAMBLING AND IMPULSE DISORDERS** 370
    Alex Blaszczynski and Lia Nower

23 **EATING DISORDERS** 389
    Eric Stice, Joanne Peart, Heather Thompson-Brenner, Erin Martinez, and Drew Westen

24 **PSYCHOPHYSIOLOGICAL DISORDERS: HEADACHE AS A CASE IN POINT** 409
    Frank Andrasik

25 **SEXUAL DYSFUNCTION** 423
    Eric W. Corty

26 **SEXUAL DEVIATION** 436
    William D. Murphy and I. Jacqueline Page

27 **MARITAL DYSFUNCTION** 450
    Steven R. H. Beach, Charles Kamen, and Frank Fincham

PART THREE
TREATMENT APPROACHES

28 **PSYCHODYNAMIC PSYCHOTHERAPY**   469
Steven K. Huprich and Rachel A. Keaschuk

29 **COGNITIVE BEHAVIORAL TREATMENT**   487
Alisa R. Singer and Keith S. Dobson

30 **PSYCHOPHARMACOLOGICAL INTERVENTIONS**   503
Timothey C. Denko and Michael E. Thase

Author Index   519

Subject Index   535

Handbook Preface

Remarkably, the linkage between personality and psychopathology, although extensive, has not been underscored in the larger tomes on these subjects. In the last decade there have been many books on personality, adult psychopathology, and child psychopathology, but none seems to have related the three in an integrated fashion. In part, this three-volume *Comprehensive Handbook of Personality and Psychopathology* (CHOPP), with the first volume on *Personality and Everyday Functioning,* the second on *Adult Psychopathology,* and the third on *Child Psychopathology,* is devoted to remedying this gap in the literature. Another unique feature of CHOPP appears in the volumes on *Adult Psychopathology* and *Child Psychopathology,* where impact of adult and child psychopathology on family, work, school, and peers is highlighted, in addition to the relation of specific psychopathology to normal development. Given the marked importance of such impact, contributors were asked to delineate the negative impact of psychopathology on the individual's daily environments.

In light of the aforementioned features, we trust that CHOPP is timely and that it will be well received in many quarters in psychology. The work should stand as an entity as a three-volume endeavor. However, given the structure of each volume, we believe that it is possible to break up the set into individual volumes for relevant courses on personality, normal development, adult psychopathology, and child psychopathology.

Volume 1 (*Personality and Everyday Functioning*) contains 23 chapters divided into four parts (Foundations, Broad-Range Theories and Systems, Mid-Range Theories, and Special Applications). This volume is unique in that it encompasses both the broad theories of personality and those theories with a more limited range, known as mid-range theories. Broad-range theories were originally developed to explain the behavior of normal people in everyday situations. But it also is important to have a reference point for those individuals suffering from various sorts of psychopathology. Chapters in this section follow a general format where possible:

A. Statement of the Theory
B. Developmental Considerations
C. Biological/Physiological Relationships
D. Boundaries of the Theory
E. Evidence in Support of and against the Theory
F. Predictions for Everyday Functioning
   1. Family Life
   2. Work or School
   3. Retirement
   4. Recreation

Thus, Volume 1 sets the stage for Volumes 2 and 3 while at the same time standing on its own for understanding everyday life from the personality perspective.

Volume 2 (*Adult Psychopathology*) contains 30 chapters divided into three parts (General Issues, Major Disorders and Problems, Treatment Approaches). Volume 3 (*Child Psychopathology*) contains 27 chapters divided into three parts (General Issues, Major Disorders and Problems, Treatment Approaches). As previously noted, a unique feature in these volumes is mention of the impact of psychopathology on the family, work, school, and peers, often neglected in standard works. In both Volumes 2 and 3, most of the contributors have adhered to a relatively standard format for Part Two. In some instances, some of the authors have opted to combine sections.

A. Description of the Disorder
B. Epidemiology
C. Clinical Picture
D. Etiology
E. Course, Complications, and Prognosis
F. Assessment and Diagnosis
G. Impact on the Environment
   1. Family
   2. Work or School
   3. Peer Interactions
H. Treatment Implications

In addition, authors in Volume 3 include the sections Personality Development and Psychopathology and Implications for Future Personality Development. We trust that the relatively uniform format in Part Two of Volumes 2 and 3 will make for ease of reading and some interchapter comparisons within and across volumes.

Many individuals have worked very hard to bring this series of volumes to fruition. First, we thank our editor at John

Wiley, Tracey Belmont, for once again understanding the import and scope of the project and having confidence in our ability to execute in spite of interfering hurricanes, other natural events, and varied life events. Second, we thank our editors of the specific volumes for planning, recruiting, and editing. Third, we thank our eminent contributors for taking time out from their busy schedules to add yet one more writing task in sharing their expertise. Claire Huismann, our project manager at Apex Publishing, deserves special recognition for her extraordinary efforts, competence, and patience throughout the creation of this series. And finally, but hardly least of all, we thank all at John Wiley and Pacific University, including Carole Londeree, Linda James, Alison Brodhagen, Greg May, and Cynthia Polance, for their excellent technical assistance.

Michel Hersen and Jay C. Thomas
Forest Grove and Portland, Oregon

Preface to Volume 2

Volume 2 continues the themes articulated in the first volume of this series. It contains 30 chapters, divided into three parts. Part One includes chapters that discuss diagnosis and classification and pertinent research issues as well as separate chapters that discuss the behavioral, cognitive, genetic, sociocultural, and biological factors that influence development.

Part Two includes 21 chapters that cover a broad spectrum of disorders, including anxiety, mood, schizophrenia, organic, personality, substance use, eating, psychophysiological, sexual dysfunction and deviation, and marital dysfunction. These chapters continue the focus on the linkage of personality and psychopathology and how this impacts the individual's social unit (family and peers) and performance in work, school, and leisure settings. Although authors were asked to give equal weight to all of these specific impacts on the environment, the available literature demanded varied coverage, with authors left at times only to point out deficits in our current knowledge and future avenues for research. These chapters additionally provide descriptions of the disorders and the clinical picture; review epidemiology and etiological theories; discuss the typical course, complications, and prognosis; outline the approach to assessment and diagnosis; and review the literature bearing on treatment and the attendant implications.

Part Three includes three individual chapters, each focusing more in depth on the most current general treatment approaches for the conditions reviewed—psychodynamic, cognitive behavioral, and pharmacological.

A volume of this scope and size could not be possible without the eminent scholars who gave so generously of their time, in the face of multiple competing demands, to draft the copy you see here. It is equally true that a number of people worked just as diligently, behind the scenes, in order to produce this volume. My first word of thanks to the "behind-the-scenes crew" goes to the series editors, Michel Hersen and Jay C. Thomas, for affording me, and having the confidence in me, to serve as the volume editor and for providing assistance beyond that normally needed when Ivan the Terrible raised its ugly head. I thank Gayle Beck and Tim Brown for their wise consultation as I was selecting authors and topics. Prior to working on this volume, I felt I had a good handle on the editing process; however, working closely with Michel taught me that I had much to learn. I offer him my further thanks for teaching me so much more about the intricacies of successful editing. Final words of thanks are owed to Tracey Belmont and Isabel Pratt, both of John Wiley & Sons, for their patience, understanding, support, and flexibility; and to Claire Huismann, project manager at Apex Publishing, for her invaluable assistance, superb skills, and unflappable demeanor, all of which proved critical in getting this volume to the finish line in polished condition.

Frank Andrasik
Pensacola, Florida

Contributors

Frank Andrasik, PhD
University of West Florida
Pensacola, Florida

Martin M. Antony, PhD, ABPP
McMaster University
Hamilton, Ontario

Steven R. H. Beach, PhD
University of Georgia
Athens, Georgia

Alex Blaszczynski, PhD
University of Sydney
Sydney, Australia

Elisa Bolton, PhD
NH-Dartmouth Psychiatric Research Center
Concord, New Hampshire

Timothy A. Brown, PhD
Boston University
Boston, Massachusetts

Richard A. Bryant, PhD
University of New South Wales
Sydney, Australia

Laura Campbell-Sills, PhD
University of California, San Diego
La Jolla, California

Dorothy Chin, PhD
University of California, Los Angeles
Los Angeles, California

Meredith E. Coles, PhD
Binghamton University (SUNY)
Binghamton, New York

Eric W. Corty, PhD
Penn State Erie, The Behrend College
Erie, Pennsylvania

Timothey C. Denko, MD
University of Pittsburgh Medical Center
Pittsburgh, Pennsylvania

Keith S. Dobson, PhD
University of Calgary
Calgary, Alberta

Brad Donohue, PhD
University of Nevada, Las Vegas
Las Vegas, Nevada

Alisha M. Farley, BA
University of Nevada, Las Vegas
Las Vegas, Nevada

Frank Fincham, PhD
Florida State University
Tallahassee, Florida

Edna B. Foa, PhD
University of Pennsylvania School of Medicine
Philadelphia, Pennsylvania

Samantha L. French, BS
University of Nevada, Las Vegas
Las Vegas, Nevada

Drew Gouvier, PhD
Louisiana State University
Baton Rouge, Louisiana

Dolores V. Hernandez, MS
University of Texas at El Paso
El Paso, Texas

Marilyn Holmes, BA
Pennsylvania State University
University Park, Pennsylvania

Betty Horng, MA
Binghamton University (SUNY)
Binghamton, New York

Steven K. Huprich, PhD
Eastern Michigan University
Ypsilanti, Michigan

Kerry L. Jang, PhD
University of British Columbia
Vancouver, British Columbia

Charles Kamen, BS
University of Georgia
Athens, Georgia

Velma A. Kameoka, PhD
University of Hawaii at Manoa
Honolulu, Hawaii

Jennifer Karmely, MA
University of Nevada, Las Vegas
Las Vegas, Nevada

Rachel A. Keaschuk, MS
SUNY Upstate Medical University
Syracuse, New York

James Langenbucher, PhD
Rutgers, the State University of New Jersey
Piscataway, New Jersey

Kenneth N. Levy, PhD
Pennsylvania State University
University Park, Pennsylvania

Kristine L. Lokken, PhD
University of Alabama-Birmingham
Birmingham, Alabama

Elizabeth R. Lombardo, PhD, PT
Private Practice
Dallas, Texas

Erin Martinez, BA
University of Texas at Austin
Austin, Texas

Randi E. McCabe, PhD
McMaster University
Hamilton, Ontario

Susan R. McGurk, PhD
Dartmouth Medical School
Concord, New Hampshire

Kim T. Mueser, PhD
Dartmouth Medical School
Concord, New Hampshire

William D. Murphy, PhD
University of Tennessee Health Science Center
Memphis, Tennessee

Peter E. Nathan, PhD
University of Iowa
Iowa City, Iowa

Cory F. Newman, PhD
University of Pennsylvania, School of Medicine
Philadelphia, Pennsylvania

Michelle G. Newman, PhD
Pennsylvania State University
University Park, Pennsylvania

Arthur M. Nezu, PhD, ABPP
Drexel University
Philadelphia, Pennsylvania

Christine Maguth Nezu, PhD, ABPP
Drexel University
Philadelphia, Pennsylvania

Lia Nower, JD, PhD
University of Missouri-St. Louis
St. Louis, Missouri

Conall M. O'Cleirigh, PhD
University of Miami
Coral Gables, Florida

Michael W. Otto, PhD
Boston University
Boston, Massachusetts

I. Jacqueline Page, PsyD
University of Tennessee Health Science Center
Memphis, Tennessee

Joanne Peart, BA
Emory University
Atlanta, Georgia

David S. Riggs, PhD
University of Pennsylvania School of Medicine
Philadelphia, Pennsylvania

Karen Rowa, PhD
McMaster University
Hamilton, Ontario

Karen B. Schmaling, PhD, ABPP
University of North Carolina at Charlotte
Charlotte, North Carolina

Lori N. Scott, BA
Pennsylvania State University
University Park, Pennsylvania

Alisa R. Singer, MSc
University of Calgary
Calgary, Alberta

Jasper A. J. Smits, PhD
Southern Methodist University
Dallas, Texas

Marika Solhan, BS
University of Missouri-Columbia
Columbia, Missouri

Stephanie D. Stepp, MA
University of Missouri-Columbia
Columbia, Missouri

Eric Stice, PhD
University of Texas at Austin
Austin, Texas

Marilyn J. Strada, MA
University of Nevada, Las Vegas
Las Vegas, Nevada

Michael E. Thase, MD
University of Pittsburgh Medical Center
Pittsburgh, Pennsylvania

Heather Thompson-Brenner, PhD
Boston University
Boston, Massachusetts

Beverly E. Thorn, PhD
University of Alabama
Tuscaloosa, Alabama

Timothy J. Trull, PhD
University of Missouri-Columbia
Columbia, Missouri

Drew Westen, PhD
Emory University
Atlanta, Georgia

PART ONE
GENERAL ISSUES

CHAPTER 1

Diagnosis and Classification

JAMES LANGENBUCHER AND PETER E. NATHAN

A BRIEF OVERVIEW OF CONCEPTUAL UNDERPINNINGS

The craft of psychiatric diagnosis is essential to nearly all clinical, research, and policy endeavors involving mental health. For clinicians, diagnostic systems identify at-risk individuals for prevention services; select other cases for referral and brief treatment; in more serious cases they may suggest special courses of treatment that have been empirically tested; and of course they confer on third-party payers the responsibility to honor charges for that treatment. For scientists, well developed diagnostic systems protect the integrity of human research samples; provide an important heuristic function by suggesting systematic relationships among psychiatric illnesses; allow scientists (and practitioners) from disparate backgrounds to communicate via a consensual nomenclature; and enable epidemiologists to find illness base rates, risk/resilience indicators, and other facts in the data. For policymakers, these rewards of well developed diagnostic systems provide the tools to apportion health and other social resources wisely. But probably most importantly, well developed diagnostic systems provide nothing less than the essential structure for the storage and retrieval of new knowledge as it is gathered in the field (Blashfield & Draguns, 1976), in all ways essential to the scientific enterprise.

Though some diagnostic systems are dimensional or otherwise noncategorical, and will be discussed briefly later, most are categorical or, like *DSM-III, III-R,* and *IV,* "class-quantitative" (Strauss, 1975). Such systems permit additional nuance, such as severity ratings, codes for the presence/absence of special features, and so on, but they require, above all, diagnostic classification. This is so for, as Raven, Berlin, and Breedlove (1971) observed in a seminal monograph in the journal *Science,* "Man is by nature a classifying animal. ... Indeed, the very development of the human mind seems to have been closely related to the perception of discontinuities in nature" (p. 1210).

Raven and his colleagues used the term *folk taxonomy* to indicate the predisposition of subgroups, especially guildlike groups of craftsmen, to establish categorical nomenclatures (folk taxonomies) for classifying objects in nature that are of special interest to them. Thus, potters have extensive taxonomies of clay, stonecutters of hardness and grain, and so forth. In a classic monograph, the cognitive psychologist Eleanor Rosch (1973) extended this argument by observing that, across human cultures, there are nonarbitrary or "natural" categories that form around perceptually salient *natural prototypes.* Such natural categories could, of course, serve as the basis for the folk taxonomies described by Raven and his coauthors. Rosch explained the key attributes of natural categories: (1) they are nonarbitrary; (2) they are partitioned from continua; (3) they cannot, by use of normal language, be further reduced to simpler attributes; (4) they are easily learned by novices; (5) they serve as natural structures for the organization of more knowledge; and (6) they have indistinct boundaries, encompassing both clear-cut and marginal examples. So, not only do human beings naturally tend to categorize and classify things, as Raven and colleagues argue, Rosch would have it that human beings tend to categorize and classify things in roughly the same way, across cultures and, presumably, across historical eras. It seems a characteristically human thing to do.

In a more recent monograph, Lilienfeld and Marino (1995) extended a Roschian analysis to psychiatric diagnosis, arguing that major psychopathologic entities such as schizophrenia or bipolar illness are, like Roschian or natural prototypes, partitioned from the continuum of human behavior, irreducible to simpler concepts, understood analogously across cultures, have good and bad examples, and so on. This view complements the conceptualization of psychiatric diagnosis as a problem in *prototype categorization* (Cantor, Smith, French, & Mezzick, 1980). Cantor and her colleagues proposed that psychiatric diagnosis follows not a *classic categorization* model (universally accepted criteria, high agreement about class membership, and within-class homogeneity of members) but rather a *prototype categorization* model. Prototype categorization assumes (1) correlated—not necessarily pathognomonic—criteria for class membership, (2) high agreement among classifiers only when classifying cases that demonstrate most of the correlated criteria for class membership (disagreement is expected when cases have a marginal number of category features, or when they bear features from more than one category), and (3) heterogeneity of class membership, because criteria are only correlated, not pathognomonic.

Thus, whereas systems of psychiatric diagnosis have their critics—and many of their arguments will be reviewed later—there is nothing arcane, much less unprecedented, in the actions of a mental health professional who, encountering a new case, lifts a copy of the *DSM* from her desk, matches the properties of the new case to one or more of the *DSM* categories, and then uses the diagnostic result to select treatment, to make a referral, or to rule the case in or out of a research protocol. To the contrary, what the mental health professional is doing is as old, as honored, as universal, and as essentially human as the crafts themselves (Nathan & Langenbucher, 1999).

A BRIEF HISTORY OF DIAGNOSIS

Throughout the classical era, diagnoses were made on the basis of presumed etiology, as when Hippocrates rooted the illnesses he diagnosed (mania, melancholia, and paranoia) in various imbalances of black bile, yellow bile, blood, and phlegm (Zilboorg, 1941). Galen (A.D. 130–210), an influential Greek anatomist who lived more than 500 years later, took much the same view in his descriptions of both normal and abnormal sensations and perceptions as products of a spirit or vapor he called *pneuma psychikon*. Basing diagnostic assessments on such etiologic conceits changed only when the Swiss physician and natural philosopher Paracelsus (1490–1541) developed the concept of *syndromal diagnosis*. Paracelsus defined the syndrome as a group of signs and symptoms that co-occur in a common pattern and thereby, presumably, characterize a particular abnormality or disease state, but for which etiology is unknown, perhaps even unknowable. Syndromal diagnosis is epitomized today in the *DSM,* which continues its focus on the signs and symptoms of diseases, rather than their presumed etiologies, which are unnecessary for diagnostic purposes.

Typically, psychiatric illnesses are organized hierarchically, by the principles of descriptive similarity or shared symptom pictures. Thus, following Paracelsus, more comprehensive and better organized hierarchical classification systems were soon developed, first by Thomas Sydenham (1624–1689), an English physician for whom a childhood chorea is named, and a bit later by the French physician François de Sauvages (1706–1767). Shortly afterward, famed French hospital reformer Phillippe Pinel (1745–1826), pictured in almost every abnormal psychology textbook breaking the chains of the insane in Paris's Bicêtre and Salpêtrière hospitals, proposed a system that included melancholia, mania, mania with delirium, dementia, and idiotism. The appearance of this nomenclature coincided with the development of asylums for the insane, for which Pinel was partly responsible, and certainly contributed to both their humanity and their success. Building on this advance, both Pinel's system and the new availability of large numbers of diagnostically differentiated patients in asylums paved the way for the marked increase in efforts to categorize psychopathology during the nineteenth century.

The victims of serious, chronic psychopathology—what are today understood as organic mental disorders, severe developmental disabilities, dementia, schizophrenia, and bipolar disorder (Nathan, 1998; Spitzer, Williams, & Skodol, 1980)—were permanent residents of these asylums for the mentally ill. The study of their essential features accelerated when the German psychiatrist Karl Kahlbaum (1828–1899) discovered that understanding the premorbid course of *dementia praecox* (which today we call schizophrenia), and the factors that conferred risk for it, helped predict its outcome. The roots of modern syndromal classification, including the *Diagnostic and Statistical Manual of Mental Disorders,* can be traced to Kahlbaum and to fellow German taxonomists Griesinger and Hecker. But no figure in descriptive psychopathology stands taller than Emil Kraepelin (1856–1926), whose successive textbook editions at the end of the nineteenth and beginning of the twentieth centuries anticipated much of what modern-day diagnosticians would find familiar, including detailed medical and psychiatric histories of patients, mental status examination, emphasis on careful observation of signs and symptoms to establish diagnoses, and understanding the psychoses as largely diseases of the brain. Kraepelin's taxonomy of mental illness has a strikingly contemporary feel and includes many of the terms used today.

In the twentieth century, more and more mental health practice took place outside the mental asylums, to encompass the military services, private clinics and office practice, company-supported mental health and substance abuse services, and educational institutions at all levels. As a result, nosologies grew broader and increasingly complex in instruments published by the National Commission on Mental Hygiene/Committee on Statistics of the American Medico–Psychological Association in 1917 and the American Psychiatric Association/New York Academy of Medicine (1933). This was both fortunate and necessary, for during World

War II, unexpectedly, most psychological casualties resulted from nonpsychotic, acute disorders like substance abuse, depression, and the anxiety disorders, with extraordinarily high base rates among combat personnel. Clearly, the impact of these conditions on the war effort required development of a nomenclature that provided substantially greater coverage of these conditions so that they could be accurately identified, treated, and their sufferers returned to service.

A COMMON U.S. NOMENCLATURE: *DSM-I* AND *DSM-II*

Although the U.S. War Department worked hard to develop such a system in response to the flood of wartime psychiatric casualties, it was only in 1946 that representatives of the Veterans Administration, the War Department, and the civilian mental health community led by the American Psychiatric Association (APA) began to consider how to create a nomenclature that would meet their diverse needs. Their efforts led to the publication, in 1952, of the first edition of the APA's *Diagnostic and Statistical Manual of Mental Disorders (DSM-I)*.

The *DSM-I* (APA, 1952) was the first comprehensive syndromal system developed. As such, it was designed to offer mental health professionals a common diagnostic language through which to communicate about their patients and their research findings. Its appearance sparked a similar effort in Europe that ultimately caused the World Health Organization (WHO) to add a mental disorders section to the eighth edition of the *International Classification of Diseases (ICD-8;* WHO, 1967). Despite its promise, *DSM-I* (and *DSM-II* [APA, 1968], which closely resembled it) shared serious problems that markedly compromised their diagnostic reliability, validity, and utility.

Most obviously, the manuals contained relatively little textual material: The *DSM-I* contained 130 pages and fewer than 35,000 words; *DSM-II* was a mere four pages longer. As a consequence, these early efforts provided only brief descriptions of each syndrome, insufficient for reliable diagnoses. Moreover, the signs and symptoms of each syndrome were not empirically based. Instead, they represented the accumulated clinical wisdom of the small number of senior academic psychiatrists who staffed the *DSM* task forces. As a result, the diagnostic signs and symptoms that interested task force members were imperfectly related to the clinical experiences of mental health professionals working in public mental hospitals, mental health centers, and the like. Consequently, clinicians very often failed to agree with one another when assigning diagnoses based on *DSM-I* and *DSM-II*, whether they were presented with the same diagnostic information (*interclinician agreement;* Beck, Ward, Mendelson, Mock, & Erbaugh, 1962; Nathan, Andberg, Behan, & Patch, 1969) or they reevaluated the same patient after a period of time had passed (*diagnostic consistency;* Zubin, 1967).

Not surprisingly, the low reliability of *DSM-I* and *DSM-II* diagnoses affected both their validity and clinical utility. If clinicians could not agree on a diagnosis, they were unlikely to be able to validate it against other measures (Black, 1971), to have confidence in predictions of the future course of diagnosed disorders (Nathan, 1967), or to create the diagnostically homogeneous groups of patients necessary to spur substantive advances in etiological or treatment research (Nathan & Harris, 1980).

Just as predictably, the low reliability and validity of *DSM-I* and *DSM-II* diagnoses raised ethical concerns among practitioners and scholars. Psychiatrist Thomas Szasz (1960) created a national furor over what he considered the dehumanizing, stigmatizing consequences of psychiatric "labeling," ultimately concluding that the modern categories of psychiatric illness were mere "myths." Szasz's ideas gained empirical substance in 1973 when psychologist David Rosenhan published, in the world's most prestigious journal, *Science,* one of the most widely cited studies in psychiatry, "On Being Sane in Insane Places." At Rosenhan's behest, eight peers, friends, and graduate students presented for treatment to various psychiatric hospitals in northern California, complaining of "hearing voices." Auditory hallucinations are, of course, a "first-rank" symptom of schizophrenia (Schneider, 1959), and all eight pseudopatients were admitted to hospital. Immediately thereafter, they stopped complaining of the voices and denied any other symptoms of psychosis. Nonetheless, all were diagnosed as psychotic, and their subsequent behavior was construed in light of that label. Quite normal reactions they manifested, such as being wary of strange and perhaps menacing fellow patients, were characterized in chart notes and staff meetings as the products of paranoid and delusional processes. Summarizing his findings, Rosenhan concluded, "The normal are not detectably sane" (1973, p. 252), a damning assertion indeed. Clearly, psychiatric diagnosis had come as far as it possibly could as an "art" practiced in an arcane fashion by an elite group of the initiated. The time was ripe for its transformation into a science.

EMERGENCE OF THE NEO-KRAEPELINIAN TRADITION: *DSM-III* AND *DSM-III-R*

Antecedents

Beginning in the late 1960s, psychiatrist Robert Spitzer and colleagues at the New York State Psychiatric Institute developed several structured diagnostic interviews, including the Mental Status Schedule (Spitzer, Fleiss, Endicott, & Cohen, 1967) and the Psychiatric Status Schedule (Spitzer, Endicott, Fleiss, & Cohen, 1970), in an effort to begin to gather empirical data on diagnostic syndromes. Spitzer and his colleagues also developed computer programs called DIAGNO and DIAGNO-II that were designed to use the syndromal information gathered by the Mental Status Schedule to assign more reliable clinical diagnoses (Spitzer & Endicott, 1968, 1969).

Sharing a similar commitment to developing an empirically based, more reliable diagnostic system, researchers at Washington University in Saint Louis published an important article in 1972 (Feighner et al., 1972) that set forth explicit diagnostic criteria—the so-called Feighner criteria—for 16 major disorders. Their intent was to replace the vague and unreliable descriptions of *DSM-I* and *DSM-II* with systematically organized, empirically based diagnostic criteria, helping researchers to establish the diagnostically homogeneous and predictively valid experimental groups for which they had long striven in vain. The format of the Feighner criteria greatly influenced the format for diagnostic criteria adopted in *DSM-III*. A derivative of Feighner's work, the Research Diagnostic Criteria (RDC), developed jointly by the New York State Psychiatric Institute and Washington University groups (Spitzer, Endicott, & Robins, 1975), was published in 1975. Designed to permit empirical testing of the presumably greater reliability and validity of the Feighner criteria, the RDC criteria yielded substantially greater diagnostic reliability than the equivalent *DSM-II* disorders (Helzer, Clayton, et al., 1977; Helzer, Robins, et al., 1977), and so constituted a great step forward.

This work, rooted in the idea of psychiatric diagnosis as a rigorously developed and universally applied scientific tool, defined what came to be known as the *neo-Kraepelinian* school of U.S. psychiatry (Blashfield, 1984). Drawing largely from the groups that formulated the RDC—psychiatry faculty at the Washington University School of Medicine in Saint Louis and the Columbia University College of Physicians and Surgeons in New York—neo-Kraepelinian diagnostic research during the 1970s laid the groundwork for the revolutionary advances of *DSM-III*. Like Kraepelin himself, the neo-Kraepelinians endorsed the existence of a boundary between "pathological functioning" and "problems in living," viewed mental illness as the purview of medicine, and believed in the importance of applying the scientific method so that the etiology, course, prognosis, morbidity, associated features, family dynamics, predisposing features, and treatment of psychiatric illnesses could be elucidated more clearly.

Diagnostic Criteria

Five years after the RDC criteria were published, *DSM-III* appeared (APA, 1980), heralding substantial advances in the reliability, validity, and utility of syndromal diagnosis. Based in large part on the RDC, the inclusion in *DSM-III* of rigorously designed *diagnostic criteria* and, in an appendix, *diagnostic decision trees,* represented the new instrument's most significant advance. The criteria were designed to organize each syndrome's distinguishing signs and symptoms within a consistent format—they were, in scientific parlance, *operationalized,* so that each clinician who used them would define each sign and symptom the same way, and process the resulting diagnostic information in a consistent manner. This degree of detail in the diagnostic information available to *DSM-III*'s users contrasted sharply with the paucity of such detail in *DSM-I* and *DSM-II*.

Several structured and semistructured diagnostic interviews based on the *DSM-III*, very distant descendants of the Mental Status Schedule and the Psychiatric Status Schedule, were published around the time *DSM-III* appeared, in a related effort to enhance diagnostic reliability and, especially, to spur research. The best known of these was the NIMH Diagnostic Interview Schedule (DIS; Robins, Helzer, Croughan, & Ratcliff, 1981), a structured interview designed for nonclinician interviewers. The semistructured Structured Clinical Interview for *DSM-III* (SCID; Spitzer, 1983; Spitzer & Williams, 1986), designed for use by clinicians, was also published around the same time. These important, and in most ways unprecedented, new instruments provided the data-gathering structure both for major new epidemiologic efforts (e.g., Epidemiologic Catchment Area study [Regier et al., 1984], National Comorbidity Survey [e.g., Kessler, Sonnega, Bromet, Hughes, & Nelson, 1995; Kessler, Stein, & Berglund, 1998]) and for a host of clinical and preclinical studies, because they insured the internal validity of the research by helping ensure that the samples of human psychopathology were well characterized diagnostically. *DSM-III-R,* published in 1987, was a selective revision of *DSM-III* that retained the advances of the 1980 instrument and incorporated generally modest changes in diagnostic criteria that new clinical research (to a great extent dependent on findings produced by the application of the DIS and SCID to human research samples) suggested should be a part of the diagnostic system. It was in this way that diagnostic research "bootstrapped" its way from the dismal days of Rosenhan to the well-regarded science it is today, and its products, although not universally successful, have been impressive indeed.

Utility and Validity

DSM-III and *DSM-III-R* addressed their predecessors' disappointing diagnostic validity and utility in several ways (Spitzer et al., 1980). To begin with, both volumes are much larger than their predecessors, in part to accommodate inclusion of more than three times as many diagnoses, in part to provide detailed information on each syndrome along with its defining diagnostic criteria. The expansion of syndrome descriptions made it easier for clinicians to describe more precisely their patients' behavior, and to understand their suffering in the context of their milieu.

Another advantage of *DSM-III* and *DSM-III-R* was that they assessed patients along five dimensions, or axes: Psychopathology was diagnosed on Axes I and II; medical conditions impacting on the mental disorders were noted on Axis III; the severity of psychosocial stressors affecting the patient's behavior was noted on Axis IV; and the patient's highest level of adaptive functioning was noted on Axis V. The additional information available from multiaxial diagnosis was presumed to be more useful for treatment planning and disposition than the single diagnostic label available from *DSM-I* and *DSM-II*.

Reliability and Stability

A very substantial number of reliability studies of the *DSM-III* and *DSM-III-R* diagnostic criteria were published. Almost without exception, they pointed to much greater diagnostic stability and interrater agreement for these instruments than for their predecessors, *DSM-I* and *DSM-II*. Enhanced reliability was especially notable for the diagnostic categories of schizophrenia, bipolar disorder, major depressive disorder, and substance abuse and dependence; the reliability of the personality disorders, some of the disorders of childhood and adolescence, and some of the anxiety disorders has been less encouraging (e.g., Fennig et al., 1994; Klein, Ouimette, Kelly, Ferro, & Riso, 1994; Mattanah, Becker, Levy, Edell, & McGlashan, 1995), but this has been due to a variety of reasons, including conceptual underspecification (in the case of the personality disorders), and the inherently transitory of self-correcting nature (diagnostic stability problems) of some others (disorders of childhood and adolescence and some forms of anxiety).

Thus, despite these explicit efforts to enhance the diagnostic utility and validity of *DSM-III* and *DSM-III-R,* it did not prove easy to document the impact of these efforts. The absence of documented etiological mechanisms, with associated laboratory findings, by which the diagnoses of many physical disorders are confirmed—the "gold standard"—made establishing the construct validity of many *DSM-III* and *DSM-III-R* diagnoses difficult (Faraone & Tsuang, 1994). As noted later in this chapter, the same problem continues to stand in the way of attempts to validate *DSM-IV* diagnoses.

Although the *DSM-III* and *DSM-III-R* diagnostic criteria enhanced the instruments' diagnostic reliability, diagnostic stability continued to be an issue for diagnosticians because of changes in patient functioning over time. Thus, in a study of the six-month stability of *DSM-III-R* diagnoses in first-admission patients with psychosis, Fennig et al. (1994) reported that whereas affective psychosis and schizophrenic disorders showed substantial diagnostic stability, stability for subtypes of these conditions was less stable. Changes in patient functioning were seen as responsible for 43 percent of these diagnostic changes. In like fashion, Nelson and Rice (1997) reported that the one-year stability of *DSM-III* lifetime diagnoses of obsessive-compulsive disorder (OCD) turned out to be surprisingly poor: Of OCD subjects in the ECA sample they followed, only 19 percent reported symptoms a year later that met the OCD criteria. Mattanah and his colleagues (1995) reported that the diagnostic stability of several *DSM-III-R* disorders was lower for a group of adolescents two years after hospitalization than for the same diagnoses given adults. These and similar studies of diagnostic stability emphasized the extent to which diagnostic reliability is dependent not only on the validity of diagnostic criteria but on the inherent symptom variability of disorders over time as well.

Also, researchers using *DSM-III* and *DSM-III-R* diagnostic criteria undertook research during the years following their appearance to validate several of the manual's major diagnostic categories, including schizophrenia and major depressive disorder, despite the absence of a gold-standard criterion of validity. Our brief mention of validation studies includes only Kendler's familial aggregation and coaggregation research findings, both because they represent a particularly powerful approach to validation and because the findings generally mirror those found by others, but many others could be adduced.

When Kendler, Neale, and Walsh (1995) examined the familial aggregation and coaggregation of five hierarchically defined disorders—schizophrenia, schizoaffective disorder, schizotypal/paranoid personality disorder, other nonaffective psychoses, and psychotic affective illness—in siblings, parents, and relatives of index and comparison probands, they reported that although schizophrenia and psychotic affective illness could be clearly assigned to the two extremes of the schizophrenia spectrum, the proper placement of schizoaffective disorder, schizotypal/paranoid personality disorder, and other nonaffective psychoses could not be clearly made. In a companion report, Kendler and his coworkers (1995) found that probands with schizoaffective disorder differed significantly from those with schizophrenia or affective illness in lifetime psychotic symptoms as well as outcome and negative symptoms assessed at follow-up. Moreover, relatives of probands with schizoaffective disorder had significantly higher rates of schizophrenia than relatives of probands with affective illness.

Although Kendler's family research method validated only a portion of schizophrenic spectrum disorder diagnoses, he and his colleagues (Kendler et al., 1996; Kendler & Roy, 1995) were able by the same methods to strongly support the validity of the *DSM-III* major depression diagnostic syndrome. However, when Haslam and Beck (1994) tested the content and latent structure of five proposed subtypes of major depression, clear evidence for discreteness was found only for the endogenous subtype; the other proposed forms lacked internal cohesion or were more consistent with a continuous or dimensional account of major depression.

Criticisms

Although *DSM-III* and *DSM-III-R* represented major advances, they were widely criticized. This was particularly so for *DSM-III*, the first manual to truly shatter the mold in which prior nosologies had been cast. One major source of concern was that *DSM-III* incorporated more than three times the number of diagnostic labels in *DSM I*. Prominent clinical child psychologist Norman Garmezy (1978) expressed the concern that this proliferation of diagnostic labels would tempt clinicians to pathologize unusual but normal behaviors of childhood and adolescence, a criticism more recently directed at *DSM-IV* (Houts, 2002). In a similar vein, social workers Kirk and Kutchins (1992) accused the instrument's developers of inappropriately labeling "insomnia, worrying, restlessness, getting drunk, seeking approval, reacting to criticism, feeling sad, and bearing grudges . . . [as] possible signs of a psychiatric illness" (p. 12).

Thus, the definition of mental disorder developed for *DSM-III* (and retained in *DSM-III-R* and *DSM-IV*) has been criticized for being both too broad and encompassing of behaviors not necessarily pathological, and for offering poor guidance to clinicians who must distinguish between uncommon or unusual behavior and psychopathological behavior. Addressing these concerns, Spitzer and Williams (1982) defended the *DSM-III* approach (and by extension, the entire ensuing *DSM* tradition) by noting that the intention of the framers was to construct a nomenclature that would cast as wide a clinical net as possible, in order that persons suffering from even moderately disabling or distressing conditions would receive the help they needed.

But *overdiagnosis* was not the only rifle leveled at the *DSM* tradition. Schacht and Nathan (1977), Schacht (1985), and others questioned the frequent emphasis in *DSM-III* on disordered brain mechanisms in its discussions of etiology, as well as its apparent endorsement of pharmacological treatments in preference to psychosocial treatments for many disorders. In response, Spitzer (1983) noted that the *DSM-III* text simply reflected the state of knowledge of etiology and treatment. Similar concerns have been voiced about *DSM-IV* by Nathan and Langenbucher (1999).

DSM-III and its successors have also been criticized for their intentionally atheoretical, descriptive position on etiology. In a debate on these and related issues (Klerman, Vaillant, Spitzer, & Michels, 1984), these critics charged that an atheoretical stance ignored the contributions of psychodynamic theory to a fuller understanding of the pathogenesis of mental disorders, as well as to the relationship between emotional conflict and the ego's mechanisms of defense. But in the same debate, Spitzer questioned the empirical basis for the claim that psychodynamic theory had established the pathogenesis of many of the mental disorders. Clearly, these are matters on which much has still to be written and argued, as it surely will be.

THE PRESENT EMPIRICALLY BASED NOMENCLATURE: *DSM-IV*

The *DSM-IV* Process

The principal goal of the *DSM-IV* process was to create an empirically based nomenclature that improved in important ways on *DSM-III* and *DSM-III-R* (Frances, Widiger, & Pincus, 1989; Nathan, 1998; Nathan & Langenbucher, 1999; Widiger & Trull, 1993). To achieve this goal, a three-stage process was used. The process began with the appointment of 13 four- to six-person work groups of experts on the major diagnostic categories. Each work group began by undertaking systematic literature reviews designed to address unresolved diagnostic questions. When the literature reviews failed to resolve them, the work groups sought clinical data that might be capable of casting more light on outstanding questions; 36 reanalyses of existing patient data sets were ultimately completed. The work groups also designed and carried out 12 large-scale field trials involving more than seven thousand participants at more than 70 sites worldwide.

The *DSM-IV* development process is thoroughly chronicled in four *Sourcebooks* edited by Thomas Widiger and colleagues (Widiger et al., 1994, 1996, 1997, 1998). There, important literature reviews are archived and findings from data reanalyses and field trials are summarized. Most of the field trials contrasted the diagnostic sensitivity and specificity of alternative sets of existing diagnostic criteria, including those of *ICD-10, DSM-III-R,* and *DSM-III,* with one or more sets of new criteria, the *DSM-IV Options.* Many of the "options" explored the impact on diagnostic reliability of changes in the wording of criteria or the minimum number required to meet *diagnostic threshold* and permit formal diagnoses to be made.

Reliability and Validity

Most of the early data on the reliability and validity of *DSM-IV* diagnoses came from the field trials. Generally, the data suggested modest increases in the reliability of a few diagnostic categories (e.g., oppositional defiant disorder and conduct disorder in children and adolescents, substance abuse and dependence) and validity (e.g., autistic disorder; oppositional defiant disorder in childhood and adolescence). Unfortunately, they also reported no real progress in addressing the substantial reliability problems of the personality disorders, the sleep disorders, the disorders of childhood and adolescence, and some of the disorders within the schizophrenic spectrum. These continue to be thorny problems that scientists developing *DSM-V* are now hard at work to solve.

Because estimates of diagnostic reliability reflect, at least in part, the stability of the disorder's symptoms, a number of studies of *DSM-IV* symptom stability have been undertaken. To this end, Koenigsberg and his colleagues (2002) explored the instability of affective symptoms in borderline personality disorder; Mataix-Cols and his coworkers studied symptom stability in adult obsessive-compulsive disorder (2002), and Shea and her fellow investigators (2002) explored the short-term diagnostic stability of schizotypal, borderline, avoidant, and obsessive-compulsive personality disorders. It is not accidental that in all three instances the temporal stability of disorders with typically unstable symptom patterns was studied. Interestingly, in all three studies, the investigators found greater than anticipated symptom stability.

Of the relatively few very recent reliability studies appearing in the literature—their paucity reflects the substantial number of such studies already published in the *Sourcebooks,* as well as agreement among scholars and researchers that diagnostic reliability for most *DSM-IV* diagnostic categories is satisfactory—one reported good interrater agreement among experienced psychiatrists for *DSM-IV* diagnoses of bipolar II disorder (Simpson et al., 2002), whereas a second found "good to excellent reliability" for the majority of current and lifetime *DSM-IV* anxiety and mood disorder diagnoses (Brown, Di Nardo, Lehman, & Campbell, 2001). In addition, four recent pieces attested to the predictive validity of a diverse group of *DSM-IV* disorders. Kim-Cohen and her colleagues (2003) reported that between 25 percent and 60 percent of a large sample of British adults with a current psychiatric diagnosis had a history of conduct and/or oppositional defiant disorder, making the latter particularly predictive of adult disorder. Assessing psychiatric disorders in a random community sample of U.S. adolescents, Johnson, Cohen, Kotler, Kasen, and Brook (2002) found that depressive disorders during early adolescence were associated with elevated risk for the onset of eating disorders, and disruptive and personality disorders were independently associated with elevated risk for specific eating or weight problems. Yen and her colleagues (2003) reported that the diagnosis of borderline personality disorder (BPD) among patients in a more variegated group, when combined with a history of drug use, significantly predicted suicide attempts during a two-year follow-up; when BPD was controlled, a worsening in the course of major depressive disorder and of substance use disorders in the month preceding the suicide attempt was also a significant predictor of suicide. Following the five-year clinical course of almost 600 men and women with diagnoses of alcohol abuse or alcohol dependence, Schuckit and colleagues (2001) observed that the *DSM-IV* diagnosis of alcohol dependence predicted a chronic disorder with a relatively severe course, whereas *DSM-IV* alcohol abuse predicted a less persistent, milder disorder that did not usually progress to dependence. Results from these four studies support a growing consensus that the enhanced reliability of a number of *DSM-IV* diagnoses, reflecting more accurate diagnostic criteria, has led to their greater predictive validity.

In a thoughtful recent article that asked clinicians to distinguish between the concepts of diagnostic validity and diagnostic utility that also has relevance to the continuing dimensional/categorical controversy, Kendell and Jablensky (2003) observed that, despite historical assumptions to the contrary, little evidence demonstrates that most currently recognized mental disorders are separated by natural boundaries. Although these authors make the case that diagnostic syndromes should be regarded as valid only if they have been shown to be discrete entities with natural boundaries, they make a strong case for believing that many of these entities nonetheless possess high utility because they do provide valuable information on outcome, treatment response, and etiology. That is, with reference to the points with which we began this chapter, Kendell and Jablensky believe that *DSM-*

IV diagnoses are useful folk taxonomies in the sense described by Raven and colleagues, even if they do not meet the standard of natural prototypes described by Eleanor Rosch.

Gender and Cultural Bias

In response to the controversy surrounding *DSM-III-R*'s estimates that more women than men merit the diagnoses of histrionic PD and dependent PD, the *DSM-IV* text now avoids specifying gender prevalence rates for these disorders. *DSM-IV* has also added three PDs (schizoid, schizotypal, and narcissistic) to the three (paranoid, antisocial, and obsessive-compulsive) that *DSM-III-R* indicated were diagnosed more often in males than in females. In reviewing these changes, Corbitt and Widiger (1995) asked whether *DSM-IV* has unintentionally introduced diagnostic bias, in a laudable effort to combat it, by going beyond the modest empirical data on gender prevalence rates for the histrionic and dependent PDs.

Two recent studies examined the impact of ethnicity on rates of psychiatric disorders, in a continuing expression of interest in ethnicity and diagnosis stimulated in part by *DSM-IV*'s Appendix I. Minsky, Vega, Miskimen, Cara, and Escobar (2003) reported significantly higher rates of major depression for Latinos in a survey of differential diagnostic patterns among Latino, African American, and European American psychiatric patients drawn from a large behavioral health service delivery system in New Jersey. However, these authors were unsatisfied with the range of possible explanations for this unexpected finding. Canino and her colleagues (2004) examined rates of child and adolescent disorders in Puerto Rico, finding prevalence rates "that were generally comparable with those found in previous surveys" and broadly in line with previous surveys of children and adolescents on the U.S. mainland.

Criticisms

Although there is widespread agreement about the enhanced empirical base that underlies *DSM-IV*, many persons involved in the development of the instrument acknowledge limitations on full utilization of the extensive empirical database because of unavoidable, biased or misleading interpretations of the data (e.g., Kendler, 1990; Widiger & Trull, 1993). Responding to related criticisms that professional issues overshadowed scientific ones in the creation of *DSM-IV* (e.g., Caplan, 1991; Carson, 1991; Kirk & Kutchins, 1992), Widiger and Trull (1993) defended attention by the drafters of *DSM-IV* to issues of utility that sometimes preempted issues of validity, as when a valid diagnosis was de-emphasized because so few patients met its criteria. Nonetheless, even though the *DSM-IV* Task Force had to be sensitive to a variety of forensic, social, international, and public health issues, Widiger and Trull described the result as largely an empirically driven instrument. The *DSM* tradition, and the much enhanced approach to diagnostic inquiry it helped promulgate, has had impressive impact on how scientists conduct research and, thus, on how clinicians approach their patients.

TWO CRITICAL CASES OF DIAGNOSIS

Epidemiology: The CIDI in the NCS

Prior to the arrival in 1980 of a rule-guided diagnostic system, *DSM-III*, the basic fact of mental illness was appreciated, and some preliminary studies in psychiatric epidemiology—such as the New Haven Study (Hollingshead & Redlich, 1955) and the Midtown Manhattan Study (Srole, Langer, Michael, Opler, & Rennie, 1962)—were conducted. However, not even the best-informed scientist of the time knew much about how prevalent mental illnesses were, how they co-occurred, how they were concentrated in certain age ranges, what factors seemed to predispose to their presence and absence (e.g., risk and resiliency factors), and so on. Firm findings require reliable diagnoses, and these were impossible in the absence of rule-guided diagnostic systems like *DSM-III*. This gap in diagnostic methodology made investment in large-scale epidemiologic research by the U.S. government unattractive. Consequently, because health policymakers had little basis on which to make informed judgments, groups of underidentified persons affected by psychiatric conditions—PTSD patients, patients with mild depression, children with learning disorders, and so on—may well have suffered needlessly.

This situation changed with the development of the Epidemiologic Catchment Area study, which deployed an important tool, the structured diagnostic interview, for the first time in a large-scale epidemiologic study. The ECA involved face-to-face interviews of a stratified sample of more than 18,000 adult community respondents in five states during the early 1980s. Its goal was to establish the prevalence of a very wide range of mental and substance use disorders in the United States. This goal became possible with the development of the Diagnostic Interview Schedule, based on *DSM-III* diagnostic categories, and structured to permit specially trained non-mental-health professionals to interview and diagnose respondents reliably. The DIS was an early example of what became, during the late 1980s and 1990s, a large and sophisticated family of fully and semistructured or "guided" diagnostic interviews—including the CIDI (Robins et al.,

1988), SCID (Spitzer, Williams, Gibbon, & First, 1992), SADS (Endicott & Spitzer, 1978), PRISM (Hasin et al., 1996), and many others—developed by numerous independent research teams to facilitate both clinical and epidemiological research. It is true that most of these instruments require extensive interviewer training and can take several hours to complete, but they are designed to do something that was never before possible: to yield full knowledge of that respondent's psychiatric state and past history, formal diagnoses of illnesses that meet diagnostic threshold, and even the presence of individual symptom, symptom severity, symptom onset and offset patterns, and subclinical states.

Between September 1990 and February 1992, using a descendant of the DIS called the CIDI-UM, Kessler and colleagues undertook the successor to the ECA, the National Comorbidity Study (NCS). The NCS gathered data on demographics, psychiatric and health functioning, quality of life, and many other domains from a stratified national sample of more than 8,000 Americans aged 15 to 54 years. Like the ECA before it, the NCS dataset has generated scores of important epidemiologic and descriptive studies on issues as diverse as adolescent depression (Kessler, Avenevoli, & Merikangas, 2001), generalized anxiety disorder (Wittchen, Zhao, Kessler, & Eaton, 1994), symptom progression of alcohol dependence (Nelson, Little, Heath, & Kessler, 1996), and many others. Because of such studies, we now understand, within the limitations of our current concepts, how prevalent psychiatric illnesses are, how they onset, what genetic and other factors seem to predispose to them, and many other matters of crucial public concern. In fact, data derived from the NCS—and thus directly derived from the *DSM-IV* and the structured interviews it made possible—are constantly appealed to by mental health administrators and policymakers charged with assessing and predicting service and research requirements prior to distributing resources that are increasingly scarce and hard to come by.

Treatment Research: SCID in Randomized Trials

Prior to the 1980s, researchers charged with the design of clinical trials—say, studies of patients with recurrent major depression who could be used in the test of a new medication—suffered as a group from two important limitations: First, without a fairly long conversation with the doctor or diagnostic technician who admitted the subject to trial, no independent observer could have confidence that any particular case indeed met criteria for major depression as developed in *DSM-II;* and, second, no independent observer could have confidence that any particular case did not meet criteria for other psychiatric illnesses in addition to the illness of interest, perhaps much more serious ones, ones that would "wash out" the effects of treatment on the less severe illness. Subjects in such trials were typically deemed eligible for research on the basis of clinician judgment, chart review, and perhaps some narrow-band assessments directed at scaling the severity of the illness of interest, such as the Beck Depression Inventory (BDI; Beck, Ward, Mendelson, Mock, & Erbaugh, 1961), the State-Trait Anxiety Inventory (Speilberger, Gorsuch, & Lushene, 1970), and many others. It is inevitable that some, perhaps many, such cases did not suffer from the illness of interest at all and that a great many other such cases suffered from additional illnesses that confounded the results of the study. To use an analogy, it was as though chemists were charged with developing a new line of anticancer drugs while being blind to the identity of the powders and fluids on their workbenches and unsure of the illnesses from which their experimental subjects suffered.

But just as epidemiologic research was transformed by the availability of a host of fully structured and semistructured or "guided" diagnostic interviews in the 1980s, so, at the same time, did these same diagnostic interviews transform clinical research. Beginning in the 1980s with the development of the SCID, in particular, and continuing more vigorously now, editorial opinion governing the publication of clinical research involving psychiatric groups has required the administration of guided diagnostic interviews to prospective participants in order to protect the integrity of samples. It is difficult—impossible, in most venues—to publish treatment research results when participants have not been "SCID-ed," that is, thoroughly interviewed prior to trial enrollment by skilled diagnosticians using a diagnostic interview like the SCID or one of its close cousins. Is this without cost? No. Initial, preenrollment assessments regularly require hours, even days, to thoroughly characterize the prospective enrollee's history and current clinical state. But, is it worth it? We need cite nothing more than the recent development of *parity* between medical and mental health coverage (Goldman, Rye, & Sirovatka, 1999), a result based on the greater respect accorded research findings in the latter field to assert that it is surely so.

FUTURE DIRECTIONS

Although theoretical and methodological advances have driven forward much of the very clear advantages of *DSM-IV* over its predecessors, application of still other, emergent, research techniques are poised to do much to aid the understanding of, not only what psychiatric illnesses look like, but how they develop over time, what are their essential versus nonessential characteristics, how they might be further split into meaningful subgroups, and so on. Following, a few of the more promising techniques are briefly reviewed.

New Research Tools

As reviewed previously, the 1970s saw the emergence of an empirical, atheoretical approach to psychiatric diagnosis that blossomed in the work of the neo-Kraepelinian school of U.S. psychiatry. The neo-Kraepelinian movement argued that psychiatric diagnosis, like any branch of medicine, should be based solidly on empirical research (Compton & Guze, 1995). To fulfill this demand, and seeking a strong methodological and empirical base, diagnostic research in the 1970s came to borrow heavily from classical test theory (CTT), whereby such parameters as reliability, internal consistency, and predictive power grew in interest (Baldessarini, Finkelstein, & Arana, 1983). Precisely because of the nature of the methodological problems inherent in diagnostic research, researchers have been required to develop or import from other fields empirical approaches as well, such as epidemiologic concepts and methods, advanced quantitative approaches, and others.

The neo-Kraepelinians formed the core group whose work resulted in the *DSM-III* and later versions of the *DSM*. Their early and important contribution to diagnostic validation models (e.g., Robins & Guze, 1970) is one of the most widely cited papers in psychiatry. The Robins and Guze validation model proposed testing or *validating* diagnostic categories against five criteria: (1) clinical description (the degree to which the symptoms of the disorder cohere and logically connect); (2) laboratory studies (the degree to which the disorder can be seen to covary with physiological markers); (3) delimitation from other disorders (the degree to which the disorder can be distinguished from others, even though some features may overlap); (4) follow-up studies (the degree to which the disorder is stable across time); and (5) family studies (the degree of heritability of the disorder). To this basic model, Andreasen (1995), believing that psychiatry's neuroscience base is key to its future, added neurophysiological and neurogenetic tests. Contemporary validation efforts deploy a mix of clinical, epidemiological, genetic-familial, and neurobiological strategies, some of which will be reviewed in the following sections.

To fulfill the research needs of validation models such as this, a number of powerful advances in quantitative methods sharpened nosological research in the past quarter century. These included both traditional exploratory as well as confirmatory factor analysis (CFA; Cole, 1987; Jöreskog & Sörbom, 1989), to study the presumed internal coherence or unidimensionality of criterion arrays for such diagnoses as borderline personality (e.g., Sanislow et al., 2002) or somatization (Robbins, Kirmayer, & Hemami, 1997); cluster analysis (e.g., Ward, 1963), to discover in the data naturally occurring groups of respondents who may represent *subtype* manifestations of such disorders as mania (Dilsaver, Chen, Shoaib, & Swann, 1997), schizophrenia (Dollfus et al., 1996), or personality disorders (Morey, 1988); receiver/operator characteristic analysis (ROC; Murphy, Berwick, Weinstein, & Borus, 1987), to correct a shortcoming of the *DSM* tradition (the promulgation of clinical thresholds or "cut-points" for formal diagnosis arrived at by expert consensus rather than by quantitative means) by plotting sensitivity against specificity, thus suggesting optimally balanced diagnostic thresholds for such disorders as mania (Cassidy & Carroll, 2001), ADHD (Mota & Schachar, 2000) or traumatic grief (Prigerson et al., 1999), and others. Additional advanced quantitative methods will be reviewed in the following sections. The efforts of all have borne concrete benefits in many areas of research and service delivery.

Latent Class Analysis

Latent class analysis (LCA; McCutcheon, 1987) is a multivariate method that, like the earlier method of cluster analysis, finds structural relationships between cases in a dataset as a function of their status on a set of *manifest variables*. The assumption of users of LCA is that the manifest variables ". . . are imperfect indicators of an underlying latent variable with a finite number of mutually exclusive classes" (Peralta & Cuesta, 2002, p. 415). Whereas *latent profile analysis* is a variation on LCA in which continuous rather than categorical variables are used, LCA itself uses categorical variables, either Likert-type scores or, more commonly, binomial variables. As such, LCA is ideally suited to diagnostic research, where binomial variables—symptom present/absent—are of critical import, and is reviewed here.

Latent classes (they are referred to as *latent* because they are not directly observed, but inferred from the status of groups of cases on the *manifest variables*) fully structure the cases in a dataset with respect to the manifest variables. LCA uses maximum-likelihood estimates in an iterative way to produce model parameters, such as the number of latent classes, or the proportion of cases that fall into each latent class, that best model, or account for, the observed relationships between cases and between manifest variables. An advantage over older cluster analytic techniques is that LCA finds the ideal number of latent classes by testing goodness-of-fit for models with increasing numbers of classes, with the minimum number of latent classes still showing a significant fit by likelihood ratio chi-square (and other methods) being, in most cases, the preferred solution. LCA also produces, for each case, the probability of its proper fit within each latent class, though cases are classified into the class for which they have the greatest a posteriori probability of membership.

LCA has been of increasing interest to scientists interested in diagnostic issues, such as subtyping research. For instance, Peralta and Cuesta (2003) applied LCA to the abiding problem of psychotic disorders, which, as has been shown previously, have sometimes been difficult to parse adequately. With access to data on 660 psychiatric inpatients diagnosed by both *DSM-IV* and *ICD-10* criteria, Peralta and Cuesta entered 16 variables into the LCA procedure, including data on 15 symptoms (e.g., delusions, manic symptoms, acute versus gradual onset) and whether the data were derived from lifetime versus current (index episode) examination. The study's aims were actually quite ambitious, including a look at the concordance of *DSM* versus *ICD* diagnoses, to examine the relationship between case classifications made by *DSM/ICD* versus empirical LCA, and others. But a main intent was to determine, on the grounds of naïve empiricism, exactly how a large and heterogeneous group of mixed psychotic patients fall naturally into categories, irrespective of how *DSM* or *ICD* would classify them.

Though the patients as a group carried any of eight *DSM* diagnoses (any of seven, when diagnosed by *ICD*), the authors found that a fewer number—five categories—best modeled the data. These were (1) schizophrenia, which was characterized by disorganization, lack of insight, "negative" or "deficit" symptoms (e.g., poverty of speech, avolition), and residual symptoms; (2) psychosis, marked by delusions, hallucinations and lack of insight; (3) schizomanic/schizobipolar disorder, marked by disorganization, lack of insight, moderate depression, and acute onset; (4) schizodepression, with prominent negative, depressive, and residual symptoms; and (5) mixed psychosis, featuring typically moderate levels of many mixed symptoms. These results stand in marked contrast to the structure of *DSM* and *ICD*, with, historically, a fairly pronounced distinction, at the psychotic level of functioning, between illnesses featuring disorganized thought versus unregulated affect, and this area requires much more study. But it is fair to say that studies such as Peralta and Cuesta, using LCA and its associated methods, are certain to have increasing influence on how major sections of our diagnostic manuals are structured in the future.

Survival/Hazard Analysis

Whereas latent class analysis works well with an array of dichotomous indicator variables to describe samples in cross-section, other variables of interest to diagnostic research are neither dichotomous nor continuously scaled, but are rather *temporal* or time-dependent. That is, they have to do with the age of onset of an illness, the amount of time that elapses between the acquisition of the first symptom and the next, the length of latency to relapse after treatment, and so on. A family of techniques called *event-history analyses* or, more commonly, *survival/hazard analysis* (Cox & Oakes, 1984; Singer & Willett, 1991), can be applied to data such as these.

Basically, survival/hazard methods model the temporal pattern by which a group of respondents changes from one state (e.g., unaffected and symptom free) to another state (e.g., symptomatic or, more formally, diagnosable). These methods have the uncommon advantages of (1) being able to accommodate cases that have not yet experienced the outcome ("right-censored data"); (2) being able to show changes across time, rather than cross-sectionally; and (3) producing intuitive graphical plots of the data that may highlight obscure relationships (Langenbucher & Chung, 1995). Survival/hazard methods are therefore powerful tools for the nosologist, as well as for more applied clinical scientists, who may use survival/hazard methods to study relapse risk, to compare outcomes for different groups over time, and for many other purposes. In addition, advanced survival/hazard methods permit scientists to simultaneously input mediating or moderating variables that influence the survival function, just as covariates or moderating/mediating variables are used in more common multivariate routines.

Survival/hazard methods require the experimenter to define several parameters. First is the *anchor event*, the initial terminus of the *observation window* that "starts the clock," after which the *failure* or *index event* (such as the first occurrence of a symptom) can occur at any time for any particular respondent. That is, at least until the *censoring event* defines the final terminus of observation. The essence of the method is the analysis of the interval between the anchor event and the failure event or censoring event (whichever comes first), using dichotomous data (the failure has/has not occurred) for each discrete period of time during the observation window, until either the failure event occurs (rendering that case a failed or affected case) or the censoring event occurs (rendering that case "right-censored"). This ability of survival/hazard analysis to utilize data from right-censored cases makes it unique and powerful, because all other methods for describing temporality (e.g., mean time to relapse, comparing group means for time to relapse for two different treatment groups) use data only from fully expressed (uncensored) cases. This is because censored cases, those that have not yet experienced the index event, have an indeterminate value on the temporality variable, and so cannot be factored into the mean or average group value, though they may be less severe, or different in some other way, from cases in which the index event unfolds quickly. Thus, if the observation window is short and a large proportion of subjects are censored, only event-history analysis can take their information into account.

The basic product of event-history analysis is the "survival curve," based on a mathematical function that estimates the proportion of cases at each point in time after the anchor event that will have survived the onset of the failure event. The logarithmic transformation of the survival function is the *hazard function,* which estimates the probability of succumbing to the index or failure event during each discrete interval in the observation window. The most common technique of estimating the survival/hazard function uses Kaplan-Meier statistics to develop negatively decelerating survival curves decreasing from 100 percent survival at the anchor event to ever lower percentages surviving as the observation window marches forward. Survival curves with steep slopes at the early time points describe subject groups for whom the index event tends to occur relatively early; more gradual slopes indicate subject groups that tend to survive the onset of the event for a longer period. The log rank test and Wilcoxon tests are commonly used statistics for testing for between-group differences in survival/hazard functions, during the early and late periods of the observation window, respectively.

In an early application, Burke, Burke, Rae, and Regier (1991) used survival/hazard analysis to test whether major depression has become a serious concern for individuals at younger and younger ages—a matter of clinical, policy, and even social import. Using data from the ECA, the authors examined age of onset for unipolar depression (as well as for bipolar disorder, three classes of anxiety disorders, and alcohol/drug abuse and dependence) in four birth cohorts—6,566 individuals born before 1917; 4,432 individuals born between 1917 and 1936; 4,981 individuals born between 1937 and 1952; and 4,766 individuals born from 1953 to 1966—using survival/hazard methods. The anchor event was the respondent's birth, the failure event was first diagnosis of depression (or the other comparison disorders) in the respondent's lifetime as assessed by the DIS (the measure used by ECA interviewers), and the censoring event was age 30, selected by the researchers because of their interest in the early onset of depression. Separate survival/hazard functions were run for each birth cohort, and for each of the disorders tested. The data showed that there has indeed been a gradual shift across birth cohort to younger ages of onset for major depression, in particular increases in hazard in the late teens and twenties. Similar shifts were observed in age of onset for alcohol and drug abuse/dependence in the most recent cohorts, particularly those that came of age in the 1960s and '70s. Interestingly, there were no systematic cohort effects observed in the other comparison categories—bipolar disorder and anxiety disorders. The authors used the complex set of temporal analyses to speculate on social conditions as well as psychological variables that in the latter half of the twentieth century induced earlier and earlier onset of major depression and substance use disorders in Americans. The study is widely cited, and served as one of the sparks for an increasing attention to early-onset, even childhood, depression, in U.S. psychiatry.

IRT Analysis. Classical test theory (CTT), which had a pronounced effect on nosological methods in the 1970s and '80s, is now gradually being supplanted by item response theory (IRT; Embretson & Reise, 2000; Hambleton, Swaminathan, & Rogers, 1991) in the field of test development, though it has yet to see much employment in diagnostic research. That will likely change. Whereas IRT shares with CTT the assumption that a latent construct (such as *DSM-IV* alcohol dependence) is tapped by a set of items (such as *DSM-IV* criteria for alcohol dependence), it appears to have distinct advantages over CTT for understanding the behavior of diagnostic criteria. Because IRT models can provide a much more detailed picture of how well a criterion set functions than can methods based on CTT, their application to diagnostic measures should prove more and more valuable.

IRT assumes that a single latent construct is tapped by a set of items. This typically requires the preliminary step of confirmatory factor analysis to "... provide supporting 'evidence' that a data set is reasonably dominated by a single common factor" (Embretson & Reise, 2000). In diagnostic research, this requires administering a diagnostic interview like the SCID to a large sample of persons with varying degrees of illness or illness risk, noting for each subject which diagnostic criteria are met and which are not met, then exposing the group data to a confirmatory factor analysis routine like Mplus (Muthen & Muthen, 1998) to make sure that the diagnostic criteria tap only a single dimension of psychopathology (called a *latent trait* in the common IRT parlance). Binary IRT models can then be tested. The two-parameter model is most relevant to the situation in which psychiatric symptoms are queried dichotomously (symptom present/absent) by structured interview.

The two-parameter model run with IRT methods such as MULTILOG (Thissen, 1991) obtains two measures of the performance of each criterion. The first is the criterion's *threshold:* the point on the underlying dimension of psychopathology at which 50 percent of respondents endorse the item (i.e., report that they have the symptom). Threshold is therefore related to *item difficulty* in CTT. The second measure of a criterion's performance, *discrimination,* is an indicator of the degree of precision with which the criterion can distinguish between subjects with higher versus lower levels of psychopathology.

IRT methods offer several kinds of graphical output of interest to nosologists. An *item response curve* (IRC) is an S-shaped logistic function that shows the probability of endorsing the criterion at each level of the underlying psychopathology. Both threshold and discrimination are contained in the shape of the IRC, with low threshold criteria being located far to the left on the dimension of underlying psychopathology, high threshold criteria being located far to the right; and with poorly discriminating criteria showing a "lazy" or gradually ascending S-shaped curve, and highly discriminating criteria showing an abrupt, steep slope to the IRC. Each IRC can be transformed into an *item information curve* (IIC), in most cases a roughly bell-shaped curve that indicates the amount of psychometric information provided by the criterion at all points along the dimension of psychopathology. When criteria are combined into a common measure of the dimension of psychopathology, as they typically are in diagnostic practice and research, their IIC's are additive, and the functioning of the diagnostic criterion set as a whole can be indicated by its *test information curve* (TIC).

Once the information function of the criterion set is known, it is possible to examine how precisely the criterion set measures individuals at various ranges of the underlying dimension of psychopathology. If most or all criteria in a given set have the same or similar thresholds, the resulting TIC will be peaked, and the standard error plot will be U-shaped, indicating high measurement precision in a relatively narrow range of psychopathology (i.e., it is a *peaked test*). In comparison, if criterion thresholds are well distributed across the full range of psychopathology, the resulting test information curve will be relatively flat, indicating that measurement precision is more or less constant across the full range of the underlying dimension of psychopathology (i.e., it is an *equal-precise test,* and perhaps useful as a quasi-continuous measure of the latent trait).

In the first application of this type, Langenbucher et al. (2004) demonstrated the utility of IRT for evaluating the performance of criteria for diagnosing *DSM-IV* substance use disorders. Data on all 11 *DSM-IV* alcohol, cannabis, and cocaine symptoms were gathered from 372 adult addictions treatment subjects interviewed face-to-face with the CIDI-SAM. Mplus was used to test unidimensionality of the criteria, and MULTILOG was used to develop IRT parameters and graphical output. Two of the 11 criteria, "tolerance" and "legal problems," had very poor discrimination parameters (they failed to distinguish persons with many substance use symptoms from those with few symptoms) and fit poorly with a unidimensional factor model. Though they are included in the *DSM-IV* criteria for substance use disorders, they seem to measure something different from what the other criteria reflect, were dropped from subsequent analyses and should, the study argues, be dropped from any criterion list considered for *DSM-V,* an astonishing recommendation in the case of alcohol tolerance, given its central role in alcoholism assessment for nearly 60 years. The study showed that IRT can be used to identify diagnostic criteria with poor performance characteristics. Just as importantly, the study showed that IRT can be used to study the construct validity of *DSM-IV* diagnoses: The test information curves for the combined criteria showed only a single "peak" or area of precise information, suggesting that *DSM-IV* abuse and dependence criteria discriminate only "nondiagnosable" from "diagnosable" cases, with the best discrimination occurring at a moderate level of underlying psychopathology, equivalent to four criteria met (for alcohol), five met (for cannabis) or six met (for cocaine). This finding would appear to challenge the basic structure of this important set of *DSM-IV* categories, which purports to separate cases into undiagnosed, abuse, and dependence categories, with dependence commencing at a fairly mild level of involvement, any three or more of seven symptoms. IRT-based methods are obviously worthy of much more extensive application to symptom data, as the development process for *DSM-V* unfolds.

SUMMARY AND CONCLUSIONS

We have, in this chapter, explored the conceptual underpinnings of psychiatric diagnosis in the phenomena of *folk taxonomies* (Raven, Berlin, & Breedlove, 1971), *natural categories* (Rosch, 1973), and *prototype categorization* (Cantor et al., 1980). We developed the history of diagnosis from the earliest wonderings of Hippocrates, to Paracelsus's concept of *syndromal diagnosis,* to the contributions of Karl Kahlbaum and Emil Kraepelin, to the development of common but still naïve psychiatric nomenclatures in the years after World War II, all the way into a new empirical era with the arrival of the neo-Kraepelinian movement that delighted many while angering many of its critics (Rosenhan, 1973; Szasz, 1960). Along the way, we reviewed major findings on the reliability and validity of the diagnostic systems that have been constructed with such care and expense, on the development of new diagnostic interviews and how they have affected several branches of clinical science, particularly epidemiologic, treatment outcome, and descriptive psychopathology research. We introduced literature that is diverse, often conceptually difficult, and too often impossible to be meaningfully accessed by nonspecialists. This is particularly true of the more advanced quantitative methods that are, even now, just beginning to make their impacts felt, methods like *survival analysis, ROC analysis, latent class analysis,* and methods based in Item Response Theory, but to which we wanted to introduce the reader.

Nothing in these pages should be clearer than this: Diagnosis and classification of psychiatric illness is an evolving craft. It is as old as is attention to mental illness itself—taking a prominent place in the writings of Hippocrates, Galen, Paracelsus, and many other ancient scholars and scientists—but it is at the same time, purely on the basis of its growth as an empirical science, a young science, a work in progress not much more than a quarter-century old, since the neo-Kraepelinians first put pen to paper to formulate new research methods (Feighner et al., 1972; Robins & Guze, 1970; Spitzer et al., 1975), to describe the results of their new interviews (Spitzer et al., 1967, 1970), to show the promise of their new diagnostic manuals (APA, 1980, 1987, 1994), and to cast new light on matters as various as the prevalence of post-traumatic stress disorder (Kessler et al., 1995), the age of onset of major depression (Burke et al., 1991), the most predictive symptoms of alcohol dependence (Langenbucher et al., 2004), and many other issues.

Many, many crucial questions still remain, particularly concerning the personality disorders, the permeability of boundaries between disorders of thought and disorders of affect regulation, the most parsimonious ways to *subtype* major classes of psychiatric illness, and many others. The research participants are there, the empirical methods for gathering data through structured interviews are there, as are exciting, powerful new methods to partition and explain the data. Even looking back over the road so far traveled, it is difficult to disagree with Spitzer and Williams (1987), that the development of psychiatric classification systems in the last half-century—in America, this has been the *DSM* tradition—grew into one of the most prestigious forces in the maturation of the mental health system generally. This is a trend we fully expect to continue and intensify as the next decades unfold.

REFERENCES

American Psychiatric Association. (1933). Notes and comments: Revised classified nomenclature of mental disorders. *American Journal of Psychiatry, 90,* 1369–1376.

American Psychiatric Association. (1952). *Diagnostic and statistical manual of mental disorders.* Washington, DC: Author.

American Psychiatric Association. (1968). *Diagnostic and statistical manual of mental disorders* (2nd ed.). Washington, DC: Author.

American Psychiatric Association. (1980). *Diagnostic and statistical manual of mental disorders* (3rd ed.). Washington, DC: Author.

American Psychiatric Association. (1987). *Diagnostic and statistical manual of mental disorders* (3rd ed., rev.). Washington, DC: Author.

American Psychiatric Association. (1994). *Diagnostic and statistical manual of mental disorders* (4th ed.). Washington, DC: Author.

Andreasen, N. C. (1995). The validation of psychiatric diagnosis: New models and approaches. *American Journal of Psychiatry, 152,* 161–162.

Baldessarini, R., Finkelstein, S., & Arana, G. (1983). The predictive power of diagnostic tests and the effect of prevalence of illness. *Archives of General Psychiatry, 40,* 569–573.

Beck, A. T., Ward, C. H., Mendelson, M., Mock, J., & Erbaugh, J. (1961). An inventory for measuring depression. *Archives of General Psychiatry, 4,* 561–571.

Beck, A. T., Ward, C. H., Mendelson, M., Mock, J. E., & Erbaugh, J. K. (1962). Reliability of psychiatric diagnoses: II. A study of consistency of clinical judgments and ratings. *American Journal of Psychiatry, 119,* 351–357.

Black, S. (1971). Labeling and psychiatry: A comment. *Social Science and Medicine, 5,* 391–392.

Blashfield, R. K. (1984). *The classification of psychopathology.* New York: Plenum Press.

Blashfield, R. K., & Draguns, J. G. (1976). Toward a taxonomy of psychopathology. *British Journal of Psychiatry, 42,* 574–583.

Brown, T. A., Di Nardo, P. A., Lehman, C. L., & Campbell, L. A. (2001). Reliability of *DSM-IV* anxiety and mood disorders: Implications for the classification of emotional disorders. *Journal of Abnormal Psychology, 110,* 49–58.

Burke, K. C., Burke, J. D., Rae, D. S., & Regier, D. A. (1991). Comparing age of onset of major depression and other psychiatric disorders by birth cohorts in five US community populations. *Archives of General Psychiatry, 48,* 789–795.

Canino, G., Shrout, P. E., Rubio-Stipec, M., Bird, H. R., Bravo, M., Ramirez, R., et al.(2004). The *DSM-IV* rates of child and adolescent disorders in Puerto Rico. *Archives of General Psychiatry, 61,* 85–93.

Cantor, N., Smith, E. E., French, R. deS., & Mezzich, J. (1980). Psychiatric diagnosis as prototype categorization. *Journal of Abnormal Psychology, 89,* 181–193.

Caplan, P. J. (1991). How do they decide who is normal? The bizarre, but true, tale of the *DSM* process. *Canadian Psychology, 32,* 162–70.

Carson, R. C. (1991). Dilemmas in the pathway of the *DSM-IV. Journal of Abnormal Psychology, 100,* 302–7.

Cassidy, F., & Carroll, B. J. (2001). The clinical epidemiology of pure and mixed manic episodes. *Bipolar Disorders, 3,* 35–40.

Cole, D. A. (1987). Utility of confirmatory factor analysis in test validation research. *Journal of Consulting and Clinical Psychology, 55,* 584–594.

Compton, W. M., & Guze, S. B. (1995). The neo-Kraepelinian revolution in psychiatric diagnosis. *European Archives of Psychiatry and Clinical Neuroscience, 245,* 196–201.

Corbitt, E. M., & Widiger, T. A. (1995). Sex differences among the personality disorders: An exploration of the data. *Clinical Psychology: Science and Practice, 2,* 225–238.

Cox, D. R., & Oakes, D. (1984). *Analysis of survival data.* London: Chapman and Hall.

Dilsaver, S. C., Chen, R., Shoaib, A. M., & Swann, A. C. (1997). Phenomenology of mania: Evidence for distinct depressed, dysphoric, and euphoric presentations. *American Journal of Psychiatry, 156,* 426–430.

Dollfus, S., Everitt, B., Ribeyre, J. M., Assouly-Besse, F., Sharp, C., & Petit, M. (1996). Identifying subtypes of schizophrenia by cluster analyses. *Schizophrenia Bulletin, 22,* 545–555.

Embretson, S. E., & Reise, S. P. (2000). *Item response theory for psychologists.* Mahwah, NJ: Erlbaum.

Endicott, J., & Spitzer, R. L. (1978). A diagnostic interview: The Schedule for Affective Disorders and Schizophrenia. *Archives of General Psychiatry, 35,* 837–844.

Faraone, S. V., & Tsuang, M. T. (1994). Measuring diagnostic accuracy in the absence of a "gold standard." *American Journal of Psychiatry, 151,* 650–657.

Feighner, J. P., Robins, E., Guze, S. B., Woodruff, R. A., Winokur, G., & Munoz, R. (1972). Diagnostic criteria for use in psychiatric research. *Archives of General Psychiatry, 26,* 57–63.

Fennig, S., Kovasznay, B., Rich, C., Ram, R., Pato, C., Miller, A., et al. (1994). Six-month stability of psychiatric diagnoses in first-admission patients with psychosis. *American Journal of Psychiatry, 151,* 1200–1208.

Frances, A. J., Widiger, T. A., & Pincus, H. A. (1989). The development of *DSM-IV. Archives of General Psychiatry, 46,* 373–375.

Garmezy, N. (1978). Never mind the psychologists: Is it good for the children? *The Clinical Psychologist, 31,* 1–6.

Goldman, H. H., Rye, P., & Sirovatka, P. (1999). *Mental health: A report of the surgeon general.* (GPO No. 2004082500218). Washington, DC: U.S. Department of Health and Human Services.

Hambleton, R. K., Swaminathan, H., & Rogers, H. J. (1991). *Fundamentals of item response theory.* Newbury Park, CA: Sage.

Hartung, C. M., & Widiger, T. A. (1998). Gender differences in the diagnosis of mental disorders: Conclusions and controversies of *DSM-IV. Psychological Bulletin, 123,* 260–278.

Hasin, D. S., Trautman, K. D., Miele, G. M., Samet, S., Smith, M., & Endicott, J. (1996). *Psychiatric research interview for substance and mental disorders (PRISM).* New York: Research Assessment Associates.

Haslam, N., & Beck, A. T. (1994). Subtyping major depression: A taxometric analysis. *Journal of Abnormal Psychology, 103,* 686–692.

Helzer, J. E., Clayton, P. J., Pambakian, R., Reich, T., Woodruff, R. A., & Reveley, M. A. (1977). Reliability of psychiatric diagnosis: II. The test/retest reliability of diagnostic classification. *Archives of General Psychiatry, 34,* 136–141.

Helzer, J. E., Robins, L. N., Taibleson, M., Woodruff, R. A., Reich, T., & Wish, E. D. (1977). Reliability of psychiatric diagnosis: I. Methodological review. *Archives of General Psychiatry, 34* (Suppl. 328), 18–21.

Hollingshead, A. B., & Redlich, F. C. (1955). Social mobility and mental illness. *American Journal of Psychiatry, 112,* 179–185.

Houts, A. C. (2002). Discovery, invention, and expansion of the modern *Diagnostic and statistical manual of mental disorders.* In L. E. Beutler & M. L. Malik (Eds.), *Rethinking the DSM: A psychological perspective* (pp. 17–65). Washington, DC: American Psychological Association.

Johnson, J. G., Cohen, P., Kotler, L., Kasen, S., & Brook, J. S. (2002). Psychiatric disorders associated with risk for the development of eating disorders during adolescence and early adulthood. *Journal of Consulting and Clinical Psychology, 70,* 1119–1128.

Jöreskog, K., & Sörbom, D. (1989). *LISREL 7: Users reference guide.* Mooresville, IN: Scientific Software, Inc.

Kendell, R., & Jablensky, A. (2003). Distinguishing between the validity and utility of psychiatric diagnoses. *American Journal of Psychiatry, 160,* 4–12.

Kendler, K. S. (1990). Toward a scientific psychiatric nosology: Strengths and limitations. *Archives of General Psychiatry, 47,* 969–73.

Kendler, K. S., Eaves, L. J., Walters, E. E., Neale, M. C., Heath, A. C., & Kessler, R. C. (1996). The identification and validation of distinct depressive syndromes in a population-based sample of female twins. *Archives of General Psychiatry, 53,* 391–399.

Kendler, K. S., McGuire, M., Gruenberg, A. M., & Walsh, D. (1995). Examining the validity of *DSM-III-R* schizoaffective disorder and its putative subtypes in the Roscommon Family Study. *American Journal of Psychiatry, 152,* 755–764.

Kendler, K. S., Neale, M. C., & Walsh, D. (1995). Evaluating the spectrum concept of schizophrenia in the Roscommon Family Study. *American Journal of Psychiatry, 152,* 749–754.

Kendler, K. S., & Roy, M.-A. (1995). Validity of a diagnosis of lifetime major depression obtained by personal interview versus family history. *American Journal of Psychiatry, 152,* 1608–1614.

Kessler, R. C., Avenevoli, S., & Merikangas, K. R. (2001). Mood disorders in children and adolescents: An epidemiologic perspective. *Biological Psychiatry, 49,* 1002–1014.

Kessler, R. C., Sonnega, A., Bromet, E., Hughes, M., & Nelson, C. B. (1995). Posttraumatic stress disorder in the National Comorbidity Survey. *Archives of General Psychiatry, 52,* 1048–1060.

Kessler, R. C., Stein, M. B., & Berglund, P. (1998). Social phobia subtypes in the National Comorbidity Survey. *American Journal of Psychiatry, 155,* 613–619.

Kim-Cohen, J., Caspi, A., Moffitt, T. E., Harrington, H., Milne, B. J., & Poulton, R. (2003). Prior juvenile diagnoses in adults with mental disorder. *Archives of General Psychiatry, 60,* 709–717.

Kirk, S. A., & Kutchins, H. (1992). *The selling of DSM: The rhetoric of science in psychiatry.* Hawthorne, NY: Walter de Gruyter.

Klein, D. N., Ouimette, P. C., Kelly, H. S., Ferro, T., & Riso, L. P. (1994). Test-retest reliability of team consensus best-estimate diagnoses of Axis I and Axis II disorders in a family study. *American Journal of Psychiatry, 151,* 1043–1047.

Klerman, G. L., Vaillant, G. E., Spitzer, R. L., & Michels, R. (1984). A debate on *DSM-III. American Journal of Psychiatry, 141,* 539–553.

Koenigsberg, H. W., Harvey, P. D., Mitropoulou, V., Schmeidler, J., New, A. S., Goodman, M., et al. (2002). Characterizing affective instability in borderline personality disorder. *American Journal of Psychiatry, 159,* 784–788.

Langenbucher, J. W., & Chung, T. (1995). Onset and staging of *DSM-IV* alcohol dependence using mean age and survival/hazard methods. *Journal of Abnormal Psychology, 104,* 346–354.

Langenbucher, J., Labouvie, E., Sanjuan, P., Kirisci, L., Bavly, L., Martin, C., et al. (2004). Item Response Theory analysis of alcohol, cannabis and cocaine criteria in *DSM-IV. Journal of Abnormal Psychology, 113,* 72–80.

Lilienfeld, S. O., & Marino, L. (1995). Mental disorder as a Roschian concept: A critique of Wakefield's "harmful dysfunction" analysis. *Journal of Abnormal Psychology, 104,* 411–420.

Mataix-Cols, D., Rauch, S. L., Baer, L., Eisen, D. M., Goodman, W. K., Rasmussen, S. A., et al. (2002). Symptom stability in adult obsessive-compulsive disorder: Data from a naturalistic two-year follow-up study. *American Journal of Psychiatry, 159,* 263–268.

Mattanah, J. J. F., Becker, D. F., Levy, K. N., Edell, W. S., & McGlashan, T. H. (1995). Diagnostic stability in adolescents followed up 2 years after hospitalization. *American Journal of Psychiatry, 152,* 889–894.

McCutcheon, A. L. (1987). *Latent class analysis.* Thousand Oaks, CA: Sage.

Minsky, S., Vega, W., Miskimen, T., Cara, M., & Escobar, J. (2003). Diagnostic patterns in Latino, African American, and European American psychiatric patients. *Archives of General Psychiatry, 60,* 637–644.

Morey, L. C. (1988). The categorical representation of personality disorder: A cluster analysis of *DSM-III-R* personality features. *Journal of Abnormal Psychology, 97,* 314–321.

Mota, V. L., & Schachar, R. J. (2000). Reformulating attention-deficit/hyperactivity disorder according to signal detection theory. *Journal of the American Academy of Child & Adolescent Psychiatry, 39,* 1144–1151.

Murphy, J. M., Berwick, D. M., Weinstein, M. C., & Borus, J. F. (1987). Performance of screening and diagnostic tests: Application of receiver-operating characteristic analysis. *Archives of General Psychiatry, 44,* 550–555.

Muthen, B., & Muthen, L. (1998). *Mplus.* Los Angeles: Muthen.

Nathan, P. E. (1967). *Cues, decisions, and diagnoses.* New York: Academic Press.

Nathan, P. E. (1998). *DSM-IV* and its antecedents: Enhancing syndromal diagnosis. In J. W. Barron (Ed.), *Making diagnosis meaningful: New psychological perspectives* (pp. 3–27). Washington, DC: APA Books.

Nathan, P. E., Andberg, M. M., Behan, P. O., & Patch, V. D. (1969). Thirty-two observers and one patient: A study of diagnostic reliability. *Journal of Clinical Psychology, 25,* 9–15.

Nathan, P. E., & Harris, S. L. (1980). *Psychopathology and Society* (2nd ed.). New York: McGraw-Hill.

Nathan, P. E., & Langenbucher, J. W. (1999). Psychopathology: Description and classification. In J. T. Spence (Ed.), *Annual Review of Psychology* (Vol. 50, pp. 79–107). Palo Alto, CA: Annual Reviews.

Nelson, C. B., Little, R. J. A., Heath, A. C., & Kessler, R. C. (1996). Patterns of *DSM-III-R* alcohol dependence symptom progression in a general population survey. *Psychological Medicine, 26,* 449–460.

Nelson, E., & Rice, J. (1997). Stability of diagnosis of obsessive-compulsive disorder in the Epidemiologic Catchment Area study. *American Journal of Psychiatry, 154,* 826–831.

Peralta, V., & Cuesta, M. J. (2003). The nosology of psychotic disorders: A comparison among competing classification systems. *Schizophrenia Bulletin, 29,* 413–425.

Prigerson, H. G., Shear, M. K., Jacobs, S. C., Reynolds, C. F. III, Maciejewski, P. K., Davidson, J. R. T., et al. (1999). Consensus criteria for traumatic grief: A preliminary empirical test. *British Journal of Psychiatry, 174,* 67–73.

Raven, P. H., Berlin, B., & Breedlove, D. E. (1971). The origins of taxonomy. *Science, 174,* 1210–1213.

Regier, D. A., Myers, J. K., Kramer, M., Robins, L. N., Blazer, D. G., Hough, R. L., et al. (1984). The NIMH Epidemiologic Catchment Area program: Historical context, major objectives and study population characteristics. *Archives of General Psychiatry, 41,* 934–941.

Robbins, J. M., Kirmayer, L. J., & Hemami, S. (1997). Latent variable models of functional somatic distress. *Journal of Nervous & Mental Disease, 185,* 606–615.

Robins, E., & Guze, S. (1970). Establishment of diagnostic validity in psychiatric illnesses: Its application to schizophrenia. *American Journal of Psychiatry, 126,* 983–987.

Robins, L. N., Helzer, J. E., Croughan, J., & Ratcliff, K. S. (1981). National Institute of Mental Health Diagnostic Interview Schedule: Its history, characteristics, and validity. *Archives of General Psychiatry, 38,* 381–389.

Robins, L. N., Wing, J., Wittchen, H.-U., Helzer, J. E., Babor, T. F., Burke, J. D., et al. (1988). The Composite International Diagnostic Interview: An epidemiologic instrument suitable for use in conjunction with different diagnostic systems and in different cultures. *Archives of General Psychiatry, 45,* 1069–1077.

Rosch, E. R. (1973). Natural categories. *Cognitive Psychology, 4,* 328–350.

Rosenhan, D. L. (1973). On being sane in insane places. *Science, 179,* 250–258.

Sanislow, C. A., Grilo, C. M., Morey, L. C., Bender, D. S., Skodol, A. E., Gunderson, J. G., et al. (2002). Confirmatory factor analysis of *DSM-IV* criteria for borderline personality disorder: Findings from the Collaborative Longitudinal Personality Disorders Study. *American Journal of Psychiatry, 159,* 284–290.

Schacht, T. E. (1985). *DSM-III* and the politics of truth. *American Psychologist, 40,* 513–526.

Schacht, T. E., & Nathan, P. E. (1977). But is it good for the psychologists? Appraisal and status of *DSM-III*. *American Psychologist, 32,* 1017–1025.

Schneider, K. (1959). *Clinical Psychopathology.* New York: Grune & Stratton.

Schuckit, M. A., Smith, T. L., Danko, G. P., Bucholz, K. K., Reich, T., & Bierut, L. (2001). Five-year clinical course associated with *DSM-IV* alcohol abuse or dependence in a large group of men and women. *American Journal of Psychiatry, 158,* 1084–1090.

Shea, M. T., Stout, R., Gunderson, J., Morey, L. C., Grilo, C. M., McGlashan, T., et al. (2002). Short-term diagnostic stability of schizotypal, borderline, avoidant, and obsessive-compulsive personality disorders. *American Journal of Psychiatry, 159,* 2036–2041.

Simpson, S. G., McMahon, F. J., McInnis, M. G., MacKinnon, D. F., Edwin, D., Folstein, S. E., et al. (2002). Diagnostic reliability of Bipolar II disorder. *Archives of General Psychiatry, 59,* 736–740.

Singer, J., & Willett, J. (1991). Modeling the days of our lives: Using survival analysis when designing and analyzing longitudinal studies of duration and timing of events. *Psychological Bulletin, 110,* 268–290.

Speilberger, C. S., Gorsuch, R. L., & Lushene, R. E. (1970). *Manual for the State-Trait Anxiety Inventory.* Palo Alto, CA: Consulting Psychologists Press.

Spitzer, R. L. (1983). Psychiatric diagnosis: Are clinicians still necessary? *Comprehensive Psychiatry, 24,* 399–411.

Spitzer, R. L., & Endicott, J. (1968). DIAGNO: A computer program for psychiatric diagnosis utilizing the differential diagnostic procedure. *Archives of General Psychiatry, 18,* 746–756.

Spitzer, R. L., & Endicott, J. (1969). DIAGNO II: Further developments in a computer program for psychiatric diagnosis. *American Journal of Psychiatry, 125,* 12–21.

Spitzer, R. L., Endicott, J., Fleiss, J. L., & Cohen, J. (1970). The Psychiatric Status Schedule: A technique for evaluating psychopathology and impairment of role functioning. *Archives of General Psychiatry, 23,* 41–55.

Spitzer, R. L., Endicott, J., & Robins, E. (1975). *Research diagnostic criteria (RDC) for a selected group of functional disorders.* New York: New York State Psychiatric Institute.

Spitzer, R. L., Fleiss, J. L., Endicott, J., & Cohen, J. (1967). Mental Status Schedule: Properties of a factor-analytically derived scale. *Archives of General Psychiatry, 16,* 479–493.

Spitzer, R. L., & Williams, J. B. W. (1982). The definition and diagnosis of mental disorders. *Sage Annual Reviews of Studies in Deviance, 6,* 15–31.

Spitzer, R. L., & Williams, J. B. W. (1986). *Structured clinical interview for DSM-III.* New York: New York State Psychiatric Institute, Biometrics Research Department.

Spitzer, R. L., & Williams, J. B. W. (1987). Revising *DSM-III:* The process and major issues. In G. L. Tischler (Ed.), *Diagnosis and classification in psychiatry: A critical appraisal of DSM-III* (pp. 425–434). New York: Cambridge University Press.

Spitzer, R. L., Williams, J. B. W., Gibbon, M., & First, M. B. (1992). The structured clinical interview for *DSM-III-R* (SCID). I: History, rationale, and description. *Archives of General Psychiatry, 49,* 624–629.

Spitzer, R. L, Williams, J. B. W., & Skodol, A. E. (1980). *DSM-III:* The major achievements and an overview. *American Journal of Psychiatry, 137,* 151–164.

Srole, L., Langer, T. S., Michael, S. T., Opler, M. K., & Rennie, T. A. (1962). *Mental health in the metropolis: The Midtown Manhattan Study.* New York: McGraw-Hill.

Strauss, J. S. (1975). A comprehensive approach to psychiatric diagnosis. *American Journal of Psychiatry, 132,* 1193–1197.

Szasz, T. S. (1960). The myth of mental illness. *American Psychologist, 15,* 113–118.

Thissen, D. (1991). *MULTILOG user's guide—Version 6.* Chicago: Scientific Software, Inc.

Ward, J. H. (1963). Hierarchical grouping to optimize an objective function. *Journal of the American Statistical Association, 58,* 236–244.

Widiger, T. A., Frances, A. J., Pincus, H. A., First, M. B., Ross, R., & Davis, W. (Eds.). (1994). *DSM-IV sourcebook* (Vol. 1). Washington, DC: American Psychiatric Association.

Widiger, T. A., Frances, A. J., Pincus, H. A., Ross, R., First, M. B., & Davis, W. (Eds.). (1996). *DSM-IV sourcebook* (Vol. 2). Washington, DC: American Psychiatric Association.

Widiger, T. A., Frances, A. J., Pincus, H. A., Ross, R., First, M. B., & Davis, W. (Eds.). (1997). *DSM-IV sourcebook* (Vol. 3). Washington, DC: American Psychiatric Association.

Widiger, T. A., Frances, A. J., Pincus, H. A., Ross, R., First, M. B., Davis, W., et al. (Eds.). (1998). *DSM-IV sourcebook* (Vol. 4). Washington, DC: American Psychiatric Association.

Widiger, T. A., & Trull, T. J. (1993). The scholarly development of *DSM-IV*. In J. A. C. e Silva & C. C. Nadelson (Eds.), *International review of psychiatry* (pp. 59–78). Washington, DC: American Psychiatric Press.

Wittchen, H.-U., Zhao, S., Kessler, R. C., & Eaton, W. W. (1994). *DSM-III-R* generalized anxiety disorder in the National Comorbidity Survey. *Archives of General Psychiatry, 51,* 355–364.

World Health Organization. (1967). *International classification of diseases* (8th ed.). Geneva, Switzerland: Author.

World Health Organization. (1992). *International classification of diseases and related health problems* (10th rev.). Geneva, Switzerland: Author.

Yen, S., Shea, T., Pagano, M., Sanislow, C. A., Crilo, C. M., McGlashan, T. H., et al. (2003). Axis I and Axis II disorders as predictors of prospective suicide attempts: Finding from the Collaborative Longitudinal Personality Disorders study. *Journal of Abnormal Psychology, 112,* 375–381.

Zilboorg, G. (1941). *A history of medical psychology.* New York: Norton.

Zubin, J. (1967). Classification of behavior disorders. *Annual Review of Psychology, 18,* 373–406.

CHAPTER 2

Research Considerations: Latent Variable Approaches to Studying the Classification and Psychopathology of Mental Disorders

LAURA CAMPBELL-SILLS AND TIMOTHY A. BROWN

INTRODUCTION

Research in psychopathology covers a wide and varied range of content and methods. Perusal of any journal devoted to the study of psychopathology demonstrates this diversity: readers encounter articles on epidemiology, genetics, diagnosis and classification, psychophysiology, neuroimaging, development of assessment tools, experimental investigations of behavior, and many other topics. The research methods common to these content areas diverge substantially, and each subspecialty faces its own set of challenges in developing rigorous research design and data analytic approaches.

We have chosen to devote this chapter on research considerations to examining a methodological approach that has broad applicability to psychopathology research: structural equation modeling (SEM). Although SEM is not relevant to all domains of psychopathology research (e.g., it cannot be applied in small sample investigations), it has proven useful for evaluating wide-ranging hypotheses about the classification, course, and etiology of psychological disorders. Accurate classification, description, and causal models provide a foundation for any science, yet many questions remain regarding how to best classify and explain psychopathological phenomena. In this chapter, we present SEM as a "state-of-the-art" method for seeking answers to these crucial questions.

In the sections that follow, we briefly describe the procedures and advantages of SEM before moving to an overview of guidelines for maximizing some of this methodology's most important features (e.g., evaluation of model fit, modeling measurement error). We also explicate applications of SEM that have particular relevance for psychopathology but tend to be underutilized in applied research (e.g., construct validation techniques, measurement invariance testing). Finally, we identify common problems encountered with different SEM applications and recommend strategies for minimizing their impact. Readers are encouraged to refer to resources cited throughout the chapter for further examples and for explanations of technical aspects of SEM applications.

OVERVIEW OF STRUCTURAL EQUATION MODELING

Structural equation modeling (SEM) is increasingly used to address key questions in psychopathology research. In a recent introduction to a special section on SEM in the *Journal of Abnormal Psychology,* Tomarken and Baker (2003) reviewed the diverse areas that have been covered in this premiere psychopathology journal using SEM. Topics included (but were not limited to) assessment of construct validity, tests of etiological models, evaluation of genetic and environmental contributions to disorders, and modeling the course of symptoms over time. It is difficult to conceive of any other methodology currently in use that covers such vast conceptual territory.

SEM allows researchers to define latent constructs of interest (e.g., depression, neuroticism, impulsivity) by multiple, observable indicators (e.g., questionnaire scores, interviewer ratings, physiological responses). The direct relationships specified between observed measures (indicators) and their corresponding latent variables constitute the *measurement* component of an SEM model (along with the estimates and relationships among the indicator error variances; i.e., "error theory"). SEM also can be utilized to test causal models of the relationships among latent variables. The hypothesized relations among latent variables represent the *structural* component of an SEM model. Psychopathology research focused on construct or questionnaire validation might focus exclusively on evaluation of measurement models; whereas studies of etiological models of psychological disorders would also incorporate tests of structural models.

SEM can accommodate considerably more complex models of psychopathology than alternative data analytic methods (e.g., analysis of variance [ANOVA], multiple regression). For example, a single SEM analysis can incorporate multiple outcome variables and different types of nontautological relationships (e.g., indirect effects). Most constructs of interest in psychopathology research (e.g., psychological disorders) are conjectured to have multiple determinants (e.g., genetics, temperament, environmental factors) and to impact a variety of outcomes (e.g., work functioning, relationships). Therefore, SEM's capacity to simultaneously evaluate a complex array of relationships among multiple predictor and outcome variables allows researchers to reproduce the relationships among psychopathological constructs with greater verisimilitude.

SEM offers numerous other advantages over more traditional statistical approaches. For example, SEM helps psychopathology researchers surmount one of the major limitations of most investigations: imperfect measurement. Virtually no constructs studied in the field of psychopathology are free from measurement error. Nevertheless, traditional data analytic methods assume perfect reliability of all measures (i.e., it is assumed that the observed score is equal to the "true" score). In contrast, SEM allows researchers to examine the relationships among constructs of interest while adjusting for the effects of measurement error. The most common SEM approach to addressing measurement error is the use of multiple indicators to define each latent variable. However, even variables measured by single indicators can be adjusted for measurement error in an SEM model (cf. Bollen, 1989). Moreover, researchers may specify an error theory (e.g., modeling correlated error) that allows their models to approximate true relationships among variables even more closely.

Another benefit of SEM is the availability of statistics that assess the "goodness of fit" of the hypothesized model. In instances where the model is "overidentified" (i.e., the number of freely estimated parameters in the model is less than the number of elements—e.g., variances, covariances—of the input matrix), goodness-of-fit indexes provide a statistical evaluation of how well the hypothesized model accounts for the observed relationships in the data. The most common form of SEM analysis generates a predicted covariance matrix based on the resulting parameter estimates of the specified model (e.g., estimates from a path model A → B → C, would estimate the relationship between A and C as the product of the A → B and B → C paths). The predicted covariance matrix is compared to the sample (observed) covariance matrix. The residual covariance matrix reflects the discrepancies between the predicted and observed relationships (e.g., the observed relationship between A and C versus the relationship between A and C that is predicted by the A → B → C path model). In various manners, goodness-of-fit statistics summarize the degree of discrepancy between the observed and predicted matrices.

Another advantage of SEM is the ability to statistically compare hypothesized and competing models. Researchers are able to specify a model based on prior empirical evidence and theory, evaluate how well this hypothesized model fits the data, and compare its fit to that of plausible alternative models. This process improves upon the more common practice in psychopathological research in which models are assumed to be valid if they achieve statistical significance. With judicious use of SEM, a researcher can reasonably assert that his or her hypothesis produced a good-fitting model in which statistically significant relationships were observed, and that this model explained the data better than potentially viable alternative models.

As with any statistical technique, the utility of SEM depends on its proper application by psychopathology researchers. For example, not all models are testable in SEM. In order to be mathematically "identified," the hypothesized model must contain the same or a fewer number of freely estimated parameters (e.g., factor loadings, regressive paths) than the number of elements in the input matrices (e.g., indicator variances, covariances). If this number is equal, the model is "just-identified" (has zero df, where df = number of elements of input matrix minus the number of freely estimated parameters), and goodness-of-fit evaluation does not apply (i.e., the model can be tested, but goodness of fit is ensured to be perfect).[1] As noted previously, goodness of fit evaluation applies to overidentified solutions (i.e., models associated with dfs ≥ 1). "Underidentified" models cannot be tested in SEM. A solution may be underidentified mathematically (i.e., the number of estimated parameters exceeds the size of the input matrix, $df < 0$) or empirically (i.e., the model has $df ≥ 1$, but aspects of the specification and/or input matrix preclude the solution from obtaining a unique or valid set of parameter estimates). Complex model specifications (e.g., models with a large number of correlated errors, double-loading indicators, or bidirectional relationships) may often result in statistical or empirical underidentification.

Moreover, the sample data must satisfy the mathematical assumptions of the fitting function selected for the SEM analysis. The fitting function is the statistical algorithm used to estimate the model's parameter estimates (and standard errors) to minimize the difference between the observed and predicted matrices. The vast majority of SEM analyses are conducted with maximum likelihood (ML), the default estimator in most SEM software programs (e.g., LISREL, Jöreskog & Sörbom, 2001; Muthén & Muthén, 1998–2004). However, ML is not appropriate when the observed measures do not approximate normally distributed, interval-level qualities. Use of ML with ordinal or nonnormal data will result in erroneous estimates of standard errors (and significance tests of the parameter estimates) and goodness of fit. Alternative fitting functions should be used for nonnormal, continuous data (e.g., robust ML) or categorical data (e.g., weighted least squares).

In addition, as in any data analytic approach, SEM requires a sufficient sample size to ensure an acceptable level of statistical power and precision of the parameter estimates. In practice, various rules of thumb for sample size abound (e.g., minimum Ns such as 100 or 200; sufficiently high ratios between number of cases and indicators or freely estimated parameters). Adherence to such rules of thumb is limited by the fact that these guidelines do not generalize well to any given data set. Indeed, statistical power is influenced by a variety of aspects such as the size of the relationships among variables, study design (e.g., cross-sectional versus longitudinal data), normality, extent/patterns of missing data, and reliability of indicators. Recent releases of latent variable software programs now include more valid and straightforward approaches to determining appropriate sample size for a specific SEM study (e.g., Monte Carlo simulation; cf. Muthén & Muthén, 2002).

MAXIMIZING THE STRENGTHS OF STRUCTURAL EQUATION MODELING

Evaluation of model fit and modeling of error variance are two advantageous features of SEM. Although most researchers incorporate goodness-of-fit assessment and error modeling into their SEM studies, some important aspects of these basic SEM features are often neglected. In the following sections, we outline an approach to evaluation of model fit and error specification. The goals of this comprehensive approach are to maximize the technical strengths of SEM, more accurately model relationships among variables, and communicate SEM results in more meaningful terms.

Evaluation of SEM models: Overreliance on Goodness-of-Fit Statistics

Goodness-of-fit statistics are one of the most appealing aspects of SEM. They provide a seemingly straightforward way to judge the value of hypothesized models of psychopathology. Although goodness-of-fit statistics are necessary for evaluating SEM models, they are not sufficient for this endeavor. In fact, one of the most important aspects of model evaluation occurs before running any statistical analyses. It is imperative that researchers provide a compelling a priori justification for the hypothesized model (based on prior empirical evidence and theory) before undertaking SEM. Beyond justifying the proposed model on a substantive basis, researchers should adopt a thorough approach to assessing the acceptability of SEM solutions. Rather than relying strictly on goodness-of-fit statistics, researchers should examine overall model fit, possible localized areas of strain in the model, and magnitude and interpretability of the model's parameter estimates.

Overall Fit

Overall fit refers to how well the hypothesized model reproduces the relationships observed in the data. Goodness-of-fit statistics feature prominently in this aspect of model evaluation, in that they provide a summary of the degree of resemblance between the observed and predicted covariance matrices. One challenge for researchers is the selection of fit indexes, of which there are dozens (Hu & Bentler, 1999).

A reasonable recommendation for evaluation of overall model fit is to present a variety of indexes that represent three important domains of fit: (1) absolute fit, (2) fit taking into account model parsimony, and (3) comparative fit (Bollen, 1989; Jaccard & Wan, 1996). One example of an absolute fit index is the χ^2 statistic, which evaluates the null hypothesis that the difference between the observed (O) and predicted matrices (P) is zero. Although χ^2 is the "classic" fit index (i.e., it was the first fit statistic developed), its practical limitations include its oversensitivity to sample size (i.e., in large research data sets, model χ^2 is rarely nonsignificant) and the fact that it stringently tests for "perfect" fit (i.e., H_o: O = P). Nevertheless, model χ^2 is typically reported because of its tradition in SEM, because many other fit indexes use χ^2 in their calculation (e.g., Comparative Fit Index, Tucker-Lewis Index), and because it is useful for model revision and comparison (e.g., nested χ^2 difference testing; modification indexes/univariate Lagrange multipliers reflect χ^2 values with 1 df).

However, because of the limitations of χ^2, other absolute fit indexes should also be reported. One widely studied and well-behaved alternative to χ^2 is the standardized root mean square residual (SRMR). The SRMR reflects the average discrepancy between the correlations predicted by the model and the actual correlations observed in the data (cutoffs of close to .05 or .08 or lower have been suggested as being consistent with overall goodness of fit; cf. Hu & Bentler, 1999; Jaccard

& Wan, 1996). The Goodness-of-Fit Index (GFI) is another popular index of absolute fit (along with the Adjusted Goodness-of-Fit Index, AGFI, which adjusts for model parsimony). However, it is recommended that the GFI and AGFI not be used in the evaluation of overall fit in view of evidence of their poor performance in simulation studies (e.g., Hu & Bentler, 1998; Marsh, Balla, & McDonald, 1988).

A second class of fit indexes consists of those that invoke a penalty function for poor model parsimony. All other factors being equal, these fit indexes favor models that reproduce the observed correlations among variables with the fewest number of freely estimated parameters. An example of a goodness-of-fit index that takes into account model parsimony is the root mean square error of approximation (RMSEA; cutoffs of close to .06 or .08 or lower have been suggested as being consistent with overall goodness of fit; cf. Hu & Bentler, 1999; Jaccard & Wan, 1996). Because the distributional properties of the RMSEA are known, confidence intervals for its point estimate (90 percent is most common) and a significance test of close fit can be calculated to further foster the evaluation of overall goodness of fit.

The final type of fit that should be evaluated in SEM analyses entails comparing the fit of the hypothesized model to the fit of alternative models. Comparative fit indexes (also referred to as *incremental fit indexes;* e.g., Hu & Bentler, 1998) evaluate the fit of a user-specified solution in relation to a more restricted, nested baseline model. Typically, this baseline model is a "null" or "independence" model in which the covariances among all input indicators are fixed to zero (although no such constraints are placed on the indicators' variances). One such statistic is the Comparative-Fit Index (CFI; cutoffs of close to .90 or .95 or higher have been suggested as being consistent with overall goodness of fit; cf. Hu & Bentler, 1999; Jaccard & Wan, 1996). Another popular and generally well-behaved index falling under this category is the Tucker-Lewis Index (TLI; referred to as the Non-Normed-Fit Index in some programs). In addition, the TLI has features that compensate for the effect of model complexity (i.e., as does the RMSEA, the TLI includes a penalty function for adding freely estimated parameters that do not markedly improve the fit of the model). As with the CFI, the most widely accepted cutoffs for the TLI are close to .90 or .95 or higher.

Localized Points of Ill Fit

A model associated with goodness-of-fit indexes that fall within the conventional boundaries of good fit is promising; however, more analyses remain before it can be put forth confidently as a valid model. Even when all fit indexes point to good fit, there may be aspects of the data that are not reproduced accurately by the hypothesized model. This issue is important because even seemingly minor misspecifications can impact other parameter estimates. Thus, researchers should examine other statistical aspects of the results of their hypothesized models to detect possible localized points of strain (i.e., areas of ill fit). This process not only aids in improving models that meet conventional criteria for overall goodness of fit but provides a blueprint for revising models that fall short of that standard.

Commonly used statistical programs for SEM allow researchers to easily examine models for localized areas of ill fit. As noted earlier, the basis for SEM model assessment is the difference between predicted and observed covariance matrices. The residual covariance matrix summarizes these differences (i.e., it provides specific information about how well each variance and covariance was reproduced by the model's parameter estimates); however, it is challenging to interpret because it incorporates the full diversity of variable metrics in the model.

The residual matrix is much more straightforward to interpret when its values have been standardized (e.g., in LISREL, each fitted residual is divided by its estimated standard error). Standardized residuals approximate a normal distribution and thus can be interpreted in the manner of z scores (however, in the EQS software program, the term "standardized residual" is used in reference to the difference between observed and predicted correlation coefficients). Standardized residuals of ± 1.96 (indicating statistical significance at $p < .05$) reflect potential points of strain in the hypothesized model (i.e., significant observed covariance of indicators that has not been reproduced by the fitted model's parameter estimates). However, standardized residuals are influenced by sample size, and in large-sample studies many values may be higher than the criterion for statistical significance. Accordingly, researchers should pay closest attention to "stand out" standardized residuals and be mindful of the fact that values hovering around 2.0 may not substantively salient. Large positive standardized residuals indicate that a relationship between indicators is underestimated by the model. This suggests that the model may need to be respecified (e.g., add new freely estimated parameters such as factor cross-loadings) to reproduce the covariance of the indicators in question. In contrast, large negative standardized residuals imply that a relationship has been overestimated and that certain paths in the model may be unnecessary.

Modification indexes (MI; known as univariate Lagrange multipliers in EQS) provide another method for diagnosing areas of poor fit. Unlike standardized residuals, MIs relate areas of ill fit to particular matrices of the measurement and structural solution (e.g., in a multifactorial CFA solution, MIs are produced in LISREL to reflect specific potential cross-loadings and error covariances in the corresponding matrices, lambda and theta, respectively). MIs approximate how much the model χ^2 would decrease if a previously fixed or constrained parameter were freely estimated in the model. Because MIs reflect univariate χ^2 values, from a purely statistical perspective, the critical value (at $\alpha = .05$) of a MI is 3.84 (i.e., the critical value of χ^2 at 1 df; cf. χ^2's relationship to the z distribution, i.e., $z = 1.96^2 = 3.84$). In other words, if an MI is ≥ 3.84, this would indicate that freely estimating the parameter in question would result in a significant improvement ($p < .05$) in overall model fit. However, as with χ^2, MIs are inflated by sample size and thus this statistical cutoff should not be adhered to strictly. Strict adherence to this cutoff would frequently result in "overfitted" models that include parameters that, although perhaps improving overall fit, have negligible practical or clinical significance (i.e., are associated with modest effect sizes). Fortunately, SEM programs provide other data that help the investigator decide whether to pursue model adjustments. For example, expected parameter change (EPC) values provide information about the magnitude of change (i.e., size of the parameter estimate) that would be expected if a fixed or constrained parameter were freely estimated in the model. Investigators can examine EPC values to determine if freeing a path would lead to a substantive (or negligible) change in the model.

Both standardized residuals and modification indexes aid the researcher in identifying misspecifications in SEM models. However, they can lead to misleading models that capitalize on idiosyncratic sample features if used in the absence of a strong theoretical rationale. Methodologists have consistently warned against performing "specification searches," in which model development is guided by post hoc examination of fit statistics (MacCallum, 1986). A parameter should be freely estimated in a model only if it is conceptually plausible. This implies that in the majority of psychopathology studies, there should be only a small number of revisions that would be made to a hypothesized model based on elevated standardized residuals or modification indexes. However, in the event that a plausible relationship between variables or residuals was overlooked in the original model specification, fit diagnostics constitute useful tools for model improvement (Silvia & MacCallum, 1988).

Three other cautions should be noted. First, revising a hypothesized model by adding freely estimated paths increases the complexity of the model and risks underidentification (even if the overall model df is positive as in empirical underidentification), especially when multiple correlated errors or factor cross-loadings are involved (for further details, see Kenny, Kashy, & Bolger, 1998). Second, freeing one path may affect other relationships in the model; therefore, model adjustments must be undertaken one at a time. Jöreskog (1993) recommends freely estimating the parameter with the largest modification index and EPC, but only if this parameter can be interpreted substantively. If there is no meaningful explanation for that parameter, the parameter with the second largest modification index and EPC would be considered, and so on. Finally, respecifying parameters on the basis of fit diagnostics should be treated as an exploratory endeavor. Such solutions should be interpreted with caution and validated in independent samples whenever possible.

Evaluating the Strength and Interpretability of Parameter Estimates

If overall and localized fit are acceptable, model evaluation can proceed to interpreting the model's parameter estimates (e.g., factor loadings, regressive paths). An initial step in this process is to determine whether the parameter estimates make statistical and substantive sense. From a statistical perspective, the parameter estimates should not take on out-of-range values such as negative indicator error variances. Such values (commonly referred to as "offending estimates" or Heywood cases) imply problems with model specification or the input data (for further details, see Wothke, 1993). In addition, whereas a specified model may fit the data well, it may contain key parameter estimates (e.g., factor loadings, regressive paths) that have compromised utility in terms of their direction, size, or statistical significance. In other words, overall goodness of fit does not ensure that all parameter estimates are salient and interpretable. If hypothesized relationships are nonsignificant, of insignificant magnitude (i.e., statistically significant due to large sample size but so small that they are essentially meaningless; e.g., a factor loading of $< .10$ in a psychometric study), or in the opposite direction to prediction, then the acceptability of the specified model should be questioned. In some cases, revisions can be made to the hypothesized model (e.g., deletion of nonsignificant paths); however, these model respecifications should have a substantive basis and be treated with the same level of caution as post hoc addition of parameters.

Researchers must also consider the practical or clinical significance of the resulting parameter estimates. Examination of the proportion of variance in dependent (endogenous) variables accounted for by the predictor (exogenous) variables in the model helps to quantify practical or clinical significance. The squared multiple correlations for structural equations provide the variance in each endogenous variable that is accounted for by the hypothesized model. If a substantial amount of variance in the endogenous variables is left unexplained by the model, the researcher must question the model's practical or clinical significance. Specifically, the size and significance of direct (unmediated), indirect (mediated), and total effects should be provided (e.g., unstandardized parameter estimates, standard errors, z values). These effects convey the relative "importance" of each exogenous variable in the prediction of outcomes of interest. In addition, interpretation of unstandardized path coefficients can also convey important information about the nature of the effects if the latent variables' marker indicators were assessed using meaningful metrics. (For purposes of identification, latent variables must be provided a metric. When the unstandardized solution is of interest, this is accomplished by selecting a marker indicator for each latent variable whose units of measurement are passed on to the latent variable.)

Specifying Error in Structural Equation Models

One of the benefits of SEM is its capacity to account for measurement error and an error theory. The ability to model error does not substitute for use of psychometrically sound measures; however, the process of utilizing multiple indicators to define latent constructs allows for a "distillation" of true score variance (i.e., only the variance that is shared by all indicators is passed along to each latent variable). Moreover, in SEM it is possible to examine structural relationships (i.e., relationships among latent variables) that are refined by the removal of measurement error.

Measurement error may consist of random error and systematic error. When a researcher has no reason to believe that systematic error exists in his or her data set, a model is specified in which measurement error is estimated for each indicator, but all correlations between these residuals are set to zero. This type of model assumes that all covariance between indicators of the same latent variable can be explained by that underlying construct, and all covariance between indicators of disparate factors can be explained by factor intercorrelations (and the factor loadings of the respective factors). There are several circumstances under which researchers might suspect the possibility of nonrandom error. Some potential sources of systematic error include the use of the same mode of administration or scoring for some indicators but not others in the model (e.g., self-report questionnaires versus interviewer ratings), or similar wording on questionnaire items (e.g., use of a questionnaire that contains several reverse-worded items; very similar wording of two or more items).

Nonrandom error can be accommodated in SEM models through the specification of correlated errors (also called "residuals" or "uniquenesses"). Indeed, failure to accurately model nonrandom error can lead to poor model fit or faulty parameter estimates. For example, if two indicators of a factor have correlated error that is not specified in the model, this may result in elevated estimates of the factor loadings of these two indicators, and unduly lower factor loading estimates for other indicators that load on the same factor. In addition, omission of correlated errors can lead to specification of a model with spurious factors (e.g., inclusion of a "substantive" factor in a model that in fact represents a method effect).

This latter problem is illustrated by the divergent results obtained in psychometric studies when nonrandom error is specified versus omitted in measurement models. Methods such as exploratory factor analysis (EFA) do not allow for modeling of measurement error, and many applied investigators are unaware of the possible impact of measurement effects on EFA solutions. Analyses of two commonly used scales in psychopathology research, the Self-Esteem Scale (SES; Rosenberg, 1965) and the Penn State Worry Questionnaire (PSWQ; Meyer, Miller, Metzger, & Borkovec, 1990) have illustrated the impact of method effects on factor analytic solutions, and the ability of confirmatory factor analysis (CFA) to diagnose and accurately model method effects.

Both the SES and the PSWQ contain a combination of positively worded items (e.g., "I feel good about myself" from the SES; "I worry all the time" from the PSWQ) and negatively worded items (e.g., "At times I think I am no good at all" from the SES; "I never worry about anything" from the PSWQ). EFA studies of the SES and PSWQ consistently reported two-factor solutions (e.g., Fresco, Heimberg, Mennin, & Turk, 2002; Kaufman, Rasinski, Lee, & West, 1991), with one factor defined by the positively worded items (SES: "Positive Self-Evaluation"; PSWQ: "Worry Engagement") and the other by the negatively worded items (SES: "Negative Self-Evaluation"; PSWQ: "Absence of Worry"). Initial investigations of the latent structure of these questionnaires did not consider the possibility of a method effect arising from the differential item wording (i.e., response styles may differ for positively and negatively worded items).

Subsequent CFA studies (e.g., Brown, 2003; Marsh, 1996; Tomás & Oliver, 1999) questioned the theoretical basis and discriminant validity of the two-factor solutions of these questionnaires. For example, Brown (2003) questioned the conceptual value of a latent dimension of "absence of worry," especially given its large correlation (poor discriminant validity) with "worry engagement" ($r = .87$). The CFA investigators proposed alternate hypotheses that the true structures of the SES and PSWQ included a unitary substantive factor (e.g., worry, self-esteem) and a factor that represented a method effect. In both cases, CFA demonstrated the superiority of single-factor solutions where additional covariance of indicators was explained by correlated residuals between similarly worded items (e.g., Brown, 2003; Marsh, 1996; Tomás & Oliver, 1999). Not only were these unidimensional models preferable from a statistical perspective (i.e., better goodness of fit), but they were far more readily interpretable based on prior evidence and theory.

One underutilized application of CFA that can help researchers avoid the problem of spurious factors is "exploratory factor analysis within the CFA framework" (E/CFA; Jöreskog, 1969). E/CFA entails performing a CFA with all of the identifying restrictions used in EFA (i.e., fixing factor variances to 1, freely estimating factor covariances, specifying anchor items whose cross-loadings are fixed to zero). E/CFA is a useful precursor of CFA because it allows researchers to explore aspects of measurement models that are not available for inspection in EFA. Even though overall model fit will be identical in maximum likelihood EFA and E/CFA, the latter analysis provides information that is valuable to the development of realistic confirmatory solutions. For example, E/CFA provides standardized residuals, modification indexes, and z tests of primary and secondary loadings, which can signal the potential presence of cross-loading indicators and correlated residuals. For applications of this approach in clinical data sets, see Brown, White, and Barlow (2005) and Brown, White, Forsyth, and Barlow (2004).

APPLICATIONS OF SEM IN PSYCHOPATHOLOGY RESEARCH

Confirmatory factor analysis (CFA) was briefly mentioned previously as a technique for evaluating the latent structure of questionnaire items. More generally speaking, CFA is one type of SEM that focuses exclusively on the measurement properties (and not any structural aspects) of hypothesized models. CFA empirically evaluates the assumption that certain measured variables (e.g., responses on questionnaire items, endorsement of symptoms during a clinical interview) reflect the presence of underlying traits or syndromes (e.g., anxiety, psychosis, self-esteem). In addition to specifying sets of relationships between measured variables and hypothesized latent constructs, researchers using CFA estimate measurement error and model systematic error pertaining to model indicators. These features of CFA make it a particularly useful technique for validation of constructs and assessment tools relevant to psychopathology.

CFA and the Assessment of Construct Validity

Construct validation is an important endeavor in psychopathology research, but has been limited by researchers' tendencies to measure constructs in a cross-sectional manner using single measurement scales. In an attempt to improve upon existing conventions for construct validation, Campbell and Fiske (1959) proposed an approach called the multitrait-multimethod (MTMM) matrix. According to this approach, multiple traits (e.g., personality features, psychological disorders, behaviors) are each measured using several different methods (e.g., self-report questionnaires, interviewer ratings, observer ratings). The relationships between traits (T) and methods (M) are summarized in a symmetric correlation matrix ($T \times M$) that allows for assessment of convergent validity, discriminant validity, and method effects.

Various segments of an MTMM matrix can be visually examined to obtain information about measure reliability (the main diagonal; these values are actually inserted by the investigator in place of autocorrelations), convergent validity (the diagonals in heteromethod blocks), discriminant validity (the off-diagonal values of heteromethod blocks), and method effects (the off-diagonal values in monomethod blocks; for examples of MTMM matrices, see Campbell & Fiske, 1959). The general guidelines for interpretation of MTMM matrices are that reliability values should be greatest in magnitude, followed by strong correlations among methods measuring the same trait that reflect convergent validity. In contrast, measures of theoretically distinct constructs should not be highly correlated, even if they are assessed using the same method. Method effects are captured by the differences between correlations of distinct traits measured using the same method versus those same traits measured with different methods. Construct validity is supported when high convergent and discriminant validity are coupled with minimal method effects (Campbell & Fiske, 1959).

The MTMM matrix approach has been underutilized in the last two decades despite its superiority over more common methods of construct validation. However, interest in the MTMM matrix approach has been revitalized by the growing popularity of CFA. The procedures of CFA can readily accommodate the elements of the MTMM matrix. Furthermore, CFA improves upon the MTMM matrix by offering more objective criteria for the evaluation of construct validity as well as more refined measurement of key constructs (e.g., measurement error can be specified).

Two CFA methods have emerged as the preferred approaches for analysis of MTMM data. Figures 2.1 and 2.2 illustrate these two approaches for a hypothetical study attempting to validate the *DSM-IV* conceptualization of attention-deficit/hyperactivity disorder (American Psychiatric Association, 1994). In this model, three intercorrelated traits (inattention, hyperactivity, and impulsivity) are measured by three different methods (self-report inventory, clinical interview, and observer ratings).

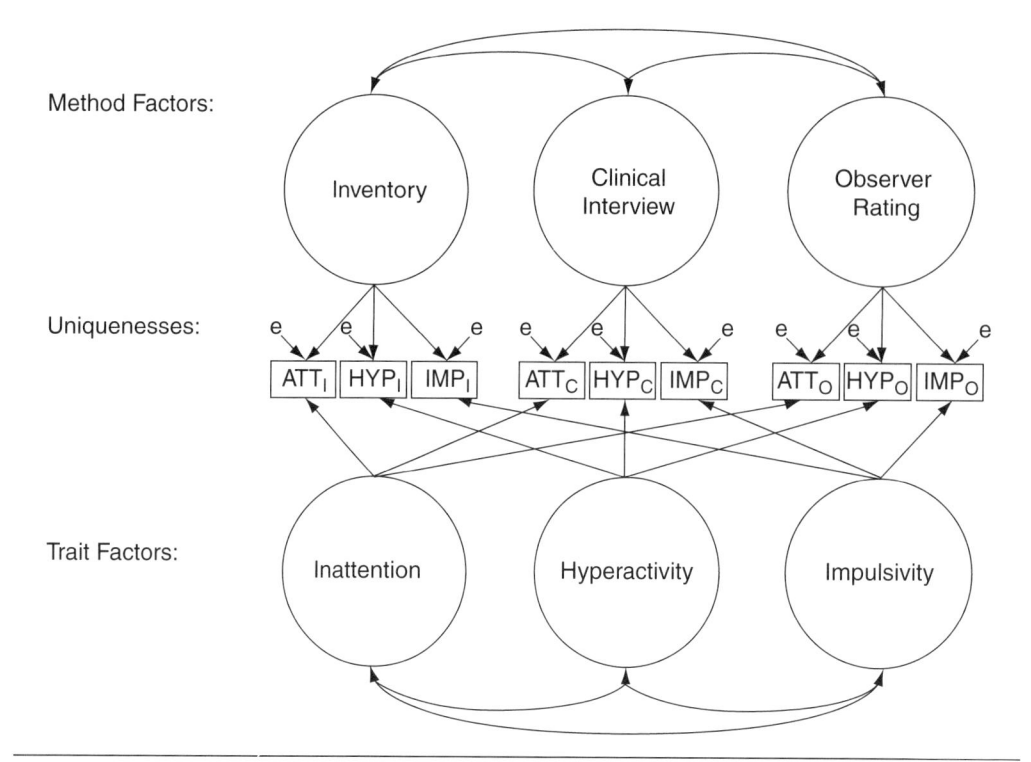

Figure 2.1 Correlated methods CFA model of attention-deficit/hyperactivity disorder. *Note.* ATT_I = self-report measure of inattention; ATT_C = clinical interview rating of inattention; ATT_O = observer rating of inattention; HYP_I = self-report measure of hyperactivity; HYP_C = clinical interview rating of hyperactivity; HYP_O = observer rating of hyperactivity; IMP_I = self-report measure of impulsivity; IMP_C = clinical interview rating of impulsivity; IMP_O = observer rating of impulsivity.

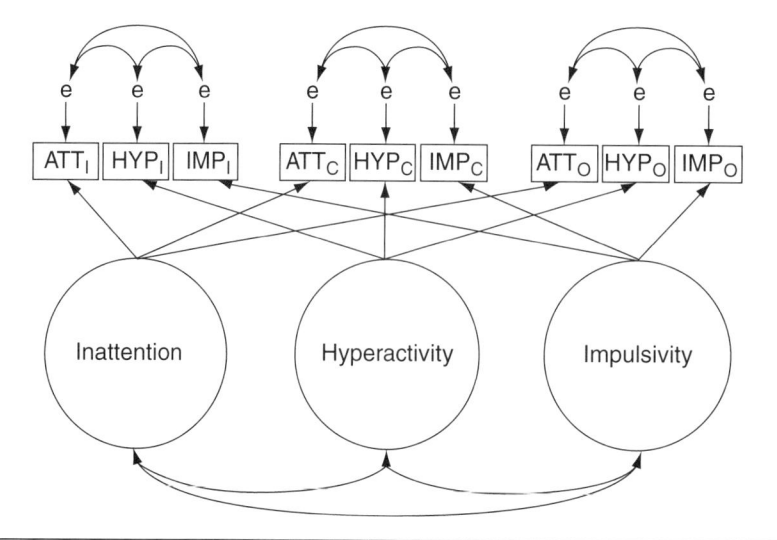

Figure 2.2 Correlated uniqueness CFA model of attention-deficit/hyperactivity disorder. *Note.* ATT_I = self-report measure of inattention; ATT_C = clinical interview rating of inattention; ATT_O = observer rating of inattention; HYP_I = self-report measure of hyperactivity; HYP_C = clinical interview rating of hyperactivity; HYP_O = observer rating of hyperactivity; IMP_I = self-report measure of impulsivity; IMP_C = clinical interview rating of impulsivity; IMP_O = observer rating of impulsivity.

The more traditional *correlated methods* approach depicted in Figure 2.1 is faithful to Campbell and Fiske's (1959) original conceptualization of MTMM matrices in that each indicator is literally considered to be a function of trait, method, and unique factors (Marsh, 1989; Marsh & Grayson, 1995; Widaman, 1985). Correlated methods models are defined by the following criteria: (1) for adequate identification, there must be at least three traits and three methods; (2) $T \times M$ indicators are used to define $T + M$ latent factors; (3) each indicator loads only on its corresponding trait factor and method factor; (4) factor correlations among traits and factor correlations among methods are freely estimated, but correlations among between trait and method factors are constrained to zero; and (5) indicator residuals are freely estimated but cannot be correlated with other indicator residuals.

An alternative approach to analyzing MTMM data is the correlated uniqueness CFA model (see Figure 2.2; Kenny, 1979; Marsh, 1989). Correlated uniqueness CFA models require two traits and two methods. Each indicator is permitted to load on just one trait factor, and the correlations among trait factors are freely estimated. Instead of defining method factors, correlated uniqueness models specify correlated residuals among indicators measured using the same method.

Interpretation of correlated methods and correlated uniqueness models is fairly straightforward. In both the correlated methods and correlated uniqueness approaches, convergent validity is reflected by the size and statistical significance of loadings of indicators on corresponding trait factors. Discriminant validity is indicated by relatively low correlations among trait factors. In correlated methods models, method effects are reflected by the loadings of indicators on corresponding method factors. In contrast, the size and statistical significance of residual covariances provide this information in correlated uniqueness models.

Methodologists have debated the relative merits of correlated methods versus correlated uniqueness approaches to analyzing MTMM data (e.g., Kenny & Kashy, 1992; Lance, Noble, & Scullen, 2002; Marsh & Grayson, 1995). One advantage of correlated methods models is that they follow directly from the original MTMM conceptualization in that the squared trait factor loading (trait effect), squared method factor loading (method effect), and residual (unique effect) of all indicators sum to 1.0. These parameters readily provide the investigator with information about the proportion of variance in an indicator accounted for by trait, method, and unique factors.

The major disadvantage of correlated methods models is that they are usually empirically underidentified, leading to solutions that fail to converge or contain invalid estimates. Marsh and Bailey (1991) reported that correlated methods models resulted in such improper solutions a disappointing 77 percent of the time. In contrast to the correlated methods approach, problems with empirical underidentification are rarely encountered with correlated uniqueness models (approximately 2 percent of the time; Marsh & Bailey, 1991). Correlated uniqueness models also can accommodate both unidimensional and multidimensional method effects, whereas correlated methods models are restricted to modeling method effects as unidimensional (i.e., all covariance associated with each assessment method must be explained by the single method factor). In practice, there may be a variety of circumstances that lead to multidimensional method effects (e.g., in addition to the mode of assessment, other aspects of measurement such as social desirability may affect some or all indicators in a model).

Correlated uniqueness models, on the other hand, are limited by their assumptions that correlations among methods and correlations between traits and methods are zero. When these assumptions do not hold, parameter estimates throughout the model may be biased (Kenny & Kashy, 1992; Marsh & Bailey, 1991). One way to minimize the bias introduced to correlated uniqueness models due to correlations among methods is by using assessment methods that are as independent as possible (Kenny & Kashy, 1992). Although both correlated methods and correlated uniqueness have strengths and weaknesses, the much greater likelihood of empirically underidentified solutions with correlated methods models causes many to favor the correlated uniqueness approach (e.g., Kenny & Kashy, 1992; Marsh & Grayson, 1995). However, the debate continues as some methodologists argue that the correlated methods model is theoretically and substantively superior, and that design and analytic remedies are increasingly available for its associated problems (e.g., Eid, Lischetzke, Nussbeck, & Trierweiler, 2003; Lance et al., 2002).

A final issue pertinent to construct validation is the inclusion of clinically meaningful background and distal variables in psychopathological models. Testing MTMM models in the CFA framework offers valuable information regarding the convergent and discriminant validity of constructs, as well as their susceptibility to method effects. However, construct validation can be extended in SEM to include tests of both predictive and incremental validity. For example, SEM models can be specified in which constructs of interest (e.g., reading comprehension; hopelessness) predict more distal and practically or clinically relevant variables (e.g., educational attainment; suicide attempts).

Inclusion of relevant background variables in SEM models also enhances assessment of construct validity. In particular, models validating newer constructs (e.g., negative cognitive bias) should include more well-established constructs that are conceptually similar (e.g., neuroticism). This allows the investigator to ensure that the potentially overlapping constructs have adequate discriminant validity. Moreover, if the newer construct adds to the prediction of clinically relevant outcome variables, incremental validity of that construct will be established.

Tests of Measurement Invariance and Population Heterogeneity

SEM readily lends itself to evaluation of interaction effects when moderator variables are categorical (e.g., gender, race, diagnosis). This approach often entails the analysis of measurement invariance and population heterogeneity; i.e., the degree of equivalence of an SEM solution across known groups (e.g., males and females). Investigators can use SEM techniques to evaluate two forms of measurement invariance: form equivalence (i.e., invariance of factor structure across groups) and parameter equivalence (i.e., equality of the model's parameter estimates, such as factor loadings and indicator intercepts, across groups). Population heterogeneity can be explored through invariance tests of factor means, variances, and covariances (e.g., Brown, 2003; Brown et al., 2004). For example, in psychopathology research, such approaches would be useful in determining the generalizability of *DSM* disorder constructs across relevant population subgroups (e.g., does the *DSM-IV* criteria set for major depressive disorder apply equally to males and females?). Two common methods for evaluating measurement invariance and population heterogeneity are Multiple-Groups Solutions (MGS; Byrne, Shavelson, & Muthén, 1989; Reise, Widaman, & Pugh, 1993) and Multiple Indicators Multiple Indicator Causes models (MIMIC; Muthén, 1989).

Researchers pursuing MGS should begin by verifying the adequacy of model fit within each subgroup. For example, a researcher interested in testing the potential moderating effects of gender on a model of post-traumatic stress disorder (PTSD) would run the measurement model separately in male and female samples. Assuming the model fits both sets of data well, the next step would be to test for form equivalence. Form equivalence is achieved when the factor structure (e.g., number of factors and pattern of factor loadings) is the same in all groups. Commonly used statistical programs allow the researcher to specify an overall model and to estimate it simultaneously in multiple groups. Output contains goodness-of-fit indexes and fit diagnostics for each group, as well as information about the degree to which each group contributed to overall model χ^2. When models are form equivalent, the fit statistics for all groups are within the range of adequate fit.

If form equivalence is established, the researcher may proceed to the evaluation of different types of parameter equivalence. These analyses typically begin with assessment of the invariance of factor loadings in which the unstandardized coefficients are held equal in all groups. In order to determine whether the restriction of equal loadings holds statistically, a nested χ^2 test is performed comparing the "equal factor loadings" model to the "form equivalent" model tested in the previous step. A model is "nested" under another model if it contains a subset of the original model's freed parameters (e.g., an equal form model in which factor loadings are freely estimated in each group versus an equal factor loading model in which factor loadings are constrained to equality across groups). The original model, with more freed parameters and fewer degrees of freedom, is often called the "parent" model (e.g., the equal form model). In contrast, the nested model contains fewer freely estimated parameters and more degrees of freedom (e.g., the equal loadings model). The χ^2 statistics associated with each model can be used to compare the fit of the parent and nested models (called a χ^2 difference test; χ^2_{diff}). The χ^2_{diff} test is evaluated for statistical significance using the difference in the degrees of freedom of the parent and nested models (although variations apply if an estimator other than ML is used). If the difference in χ^2 values is statistically significant, the nested model is considered to have degraded model fit and is rejected (e.g., the factor loadings are not equivalent across groups). If the χ^2 difference is nonsignificant, it can be concluded that constraining factor loadings to equality did not degrade model fit. This outcome would support the claim of invariance of factor loadings across groups.

The researcher can continue invariance tests in this fashion, placing increasingly restrictive equality constraints on the model for the multiple groups. Indicator intercepts, factor variances and covariances, residual variances and covariances, and factor means can be constrained to equality and tested against the previous model for comparative fit. For example, a model in which indicator intercepts are specified to be equal across groups would be compared to the "equal factor loadings" model using the nested χ^2 test. If none of the imposed constraints results in a degradation of model fit, then the researcher can assert that the model parameters are invariant across groups. If degradations in model fit do occur, then fit diagnostics can be inspected to determine which points in the model are moderated by group status.

MIMIC modeling (also known as CFA with covariates) constitutes a second approach for examining measurement invariance and population heterogeneity. As explained previously, MGS requires researchers to run simultaneous solutions with several groups. MIMIC modeling allows the researcher to add a covariate to his or her model and run a single analysis to test the impact of the covariate. MIMIC models, therefore, have several advantages over MGS models: they are more parsimonious, have smaller sample size requirements, and are simpler to conduct and interpret when more then two groups are being investigated. However, a major drawback of MIMIC models is that they only allow for invariance testing of two aspects of the solution; namely, factor means and indicator intercepts. This contrasts with the MGS approach, in which all aspects of measurement invariance can be tested.

As noted previously, potential moderating variables in MIMIC models are specified as covariates. Paths are estimated between covariates (e.g., gender) and latent factors in the model, as well as between covariates and indicators. The paths between covariates and latent factors test for population heterogeneity. If the path between the covariate and a latent factor is significant, this indicates that group differences exist for that variable. The interpretation of the path estimate will depend on the number of groups and how they have been dummy coded. For example, consider a model in which gender (dummy coded 0 and 1 for males and females, respectively) is predicted to influence scores on the avoidance cluster of PTSD symptoms. The researcher could examine the standardized parameter estimates, in which only latent dimensions are standardized and the metrics of observed variables (e.g., gender) are preserved (cf. completely standardized solutions, in which both observed and latent variables are standardized). Using the standardized solution, the researcher could interpret the parameter estimate of the path between gender and avoidance symptoms as reflecting the standard score difference between males and females on this dimension (in addition, the respective unstandardized path estimate could be interpreted as the magnitude of the group difference as reflected by the original metric of the marker indicator).

Direct paths from covariates to indicators (i.e., paths that are unmediated by latent factors) provide information about differential item (indicator) functioning. Significant paths between covariates and indicators reflect differences in indicator intercepts. Certain questionnaire items may behave differently across salient subgroups (e.g., by gender, age, or racial/ethnic groups). For example, in a recent psychometric study, an item on the Albany Panic and Phobia Questionnaire was found to function differently in male and female patients (Brown et al., 2005). Specifically, the intercept of an item from the Agoraphobia factor ("walking alone in isolated areas") was found to be noninvariant. Given that males and females would likely respond differently to this item regardless of agoraphobia status, this aspect of the scalar invariance analysis suggests that this item functions differently between sexes as an indicator of agoraphobic avoidance (i.e., even when the value of the underlying dimension of Agoraphobia is zero, females' observed scores on this item are higher than males' due to sex differences in the range of activities relating to personal safety). Hence, inclusion of this item may introduce bias against females (i.e., observed scores on the Agoraphobia may be artifactually elevated relative to males by this noninvariant item).

In summary, MGS and MIMIC models are somewhat underutilized applications of SEM that allow psychopathology researchers to test for group differences in measurement or structural SEM solutions. These approaches represent improvements over more traditional methods for evaluating the validity of psychopathological models across groups. In comparison with more standard practices of comparing group means on measures of psychopathology, measurement invariance testing in SEM examines differences between groups in a more refined and comprehensive manner (e.g., examining differences in factor structure, factor loadings, item functioning). Researchers are encouraged to consider the measurement invariance testing functions of SEM to assess the validity of their models and measures across demographic, diagnostic, and other important group distinctions.

Modeling Longitudinal Data in SEM: Latent Trajectory Models

Latent trajectory modeling (LTM) is an application of SEM that is tailored for the analysis of repeated measures or clustered data (Duncan, Duncan, Strycker, Li, & Alpert, 1999). Combining the use of longitudinal data with the modeling capabilities of SEM creates a particularly powerful method for testing causal hypotheses related to psychopathology. LTM is based on "the premise that a set of observed repeated measures taken on a given individual over time can be used to estimate an unobserved underlying trajectory that gives rise to the repeated measures" (Curran & Hussong, 2003, p. 527). Like other SEM techniques, LTM allows longitudinal researchers to test more complex models with greater statistical power than more traditional methodologies (e.g., repeated measures ANOVA).

Specifying an LTM model is relatively straightforward (see Figure 2.3 for an example). The central features of LTM are latent factors that represent the growth and intercept of the conjectured growth trajectory. Repeated measures are specified as indicators that load onto these latent factors. Initial values and slopes are allowed to vary across individuals, but all factor loadings are fixed in order to reflect the spacing of assessments and the hypothesized growth curve (e.g., lin-

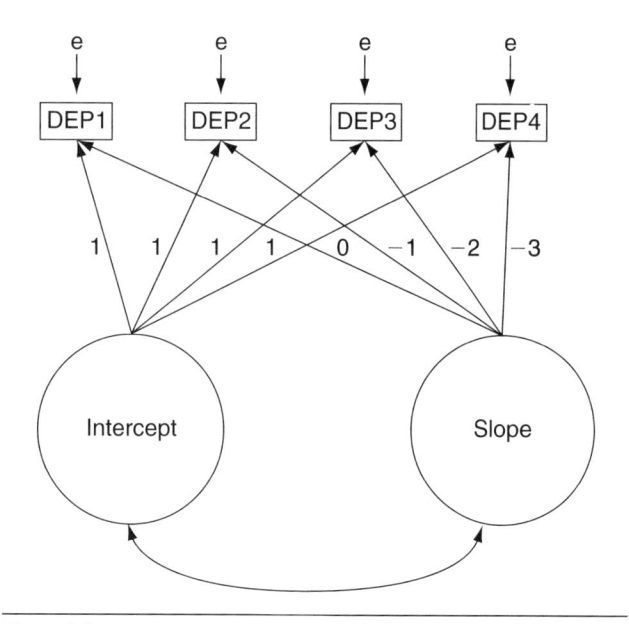

Figure 2.3 Linear unconditional LTM for depressive symptoms assessed throughout treatment at four equally spaced intervals. *Note.* DEP1 = measure of depressive symptoms taken at session one; DEP2 = measure of depressive symptoms taken at session four; DEP3 = measure of depressive symptoms taken at session eight; DEP4 = measure of depressive symptoms taken at session 12. Loadings of the repeated measure on the intercept factor are fixed to 1, and the predicted linear decrease in symptoms is modeled by setting the loadings on the slope factor to 0, −1, −2, and −3.

ear, quadratic, exponential). Moderator variables also may be specified as predictors of the growth trajectory, as long as the variance in the growth factor is not zero. LTM models that incorporate such moderator variables are called "conditional" growth models, and they can test the influence of specified factors on individual growth trajectories. Finally, distal outcome variables can be included in LTM analyses to determine if the specified growth trajectory predicts any relevant outcomes.

Parameters in LTM capture numerous variables of interest. For example, in a linear growth model, the mean and variance of the growth factor represent the mean slope of the repeated measures and the degree of variability of individual trajectories, respectively. Similarly, the mean and variance of the intercept factor convey information about the average value and degree of variability of initial values of the repeated measure.[2] The covariance between the growth and intercept factors reflects the relationship between initial values of the repeated measure and subsequent growth trajectories (e.g., individuals with lower initial values on a measure might have the steepest linear growth curve). Finally, the residual variances for each repeated measure represent the amount of variance in the repeated measure not explained by the growth curve.

Researchers can hypothesize various types of growth trajectories using LTM including polynomials, exponential functions, and "completely latent" functions (in which the shape of the trajectory is estimated from the data). If the hypothesized trajectory is consistent with patterns observed in the data, goodness-of-fit statistics will indicate adequate fit. In contrast, if change in the repeated measure is inconsistent with the specified trajectory, a poor-fitting model will result. As with other variants of SEM, researchers must have strong a priori justifications for their models before undertaking LTM. In addition, data often must be examined graphically prior to model fitting in order to determine if the hypothesized growth curve is reasonable.

A COMMON PROBLEM IN APPLIED SEM

The Problem of Equivalent Solutions

Equivalent solutions exist when different sets of model specifications produce identical covariance matrices and goodness-of-fit statistics in the same data set. Some examples of possible equivalent solutions are depicted in Figure 2.4. The models specify different structures to account for the relationships of six items from a questionnaire assessing obsessive-compulsive symptoms (four items that assess compulsive behaviors and two items that assess intrusive thoughts). The first diagram depicts a model in which compulsive behaviors and intrusive thoughts are considered separate but correlated factors with nonoverlapping indicators. The second model hypothesizes that one latent dimension (obsessive-compulsive disorder) explains the covariance among all six indicators, with additional covariance between the items assessing intrusive thoughts explained by correlated residuals. Finally, the third model posits that a higher-order factor (obsessive-compulsive disorder) underlies variance in two lower-order factors (compulsive behaviors and intrusive thoughts), which are defined by nonoverlapping indicators. As this figure demonstrates, solutions that diverge greatly in their conceptual implications are capable of producing identical statistical results.

The problem of equivalent solutions is frequently overlooked in applied CFA investigations. MacCallum, Wegener, Uchino, and Fabrigar (1993) found that equivalent solutions had been virtually ignored by researchers who published reports in the *Journal of Personality and Social Psychology,* even though the studies had a median number of 12 equivalent models. The number of equivalent solutions for any given model increases with model complexity. Relatively complex models with fewer *df* are more apt to have a large number of equivalent models that need to be considered as alternative interpretations of the observed patterns of covariation in the data. Fortunately, many equivalent solutions can be rejected on the basis of logic or theory (e.g., MacCallum et al., 1993). For example, a model that incorporates age as a predictor of executive functioning might have an equivalent solution in which executive functioning predicts age. Because this relationship is logically incoherent, the equivalent solution can be readily dismissed.

As Figure 2.4 shows, however, some equivalent solutions may be conceptually plausible. When this is the case, researchers should acknowledge the existence of the equivalent models in their reports and consider the evidence for each plausible model in their discussions (Tomarken & Waller, 2003). Subsequent studies should be designed to discriminate among equivalent models, with the ultimate goal of establishing one model as superior (e.g., via longitudinal investigations). Researchers seeking guidelines for the generation of equivalent CFA and SEM models are referred to Hershberger (1994), Lee and Hershberger (1990), or Stelzl (1986) for recommendations.

SUMMARY

This chapter presented SEM as a state-of-the-art method for examining key questions in psychopathology research. SEM has considerable advantages over more traditional data analytic methods and is uniquely suited to address a wide range of questions pertinent to psychopathology. We presented guidelines for some important practices in SEM, such as comprehensive evaluation of model fit and modeling of error theories. Applications of SEM that have particular relevance for psychopathology researchers also were highlighted. SEM provides a useful and powerful framework for assessment of construct validity, evaluation of measurement invariance, and analysis of longitudinal data. Although some methodological problems are encountered by SEM researchers, the impact of these problems can be minimized by rigorous approaches to study design and data analysis.

NOTES

1. Indeed, all forms of traditional data analysis (e.g., multiple regression, ANOVA) reflect just-identified statistical models.
2. Note that the loadings of the Slope latent factor of the LTM can be parameterized such that the Intercept reflects a time point other than the initial assessment (e.g., factor loadings of $-3\ -2\ -1\ 0$ would center the Intercept on the last assessment in the Figure 2.3 model).

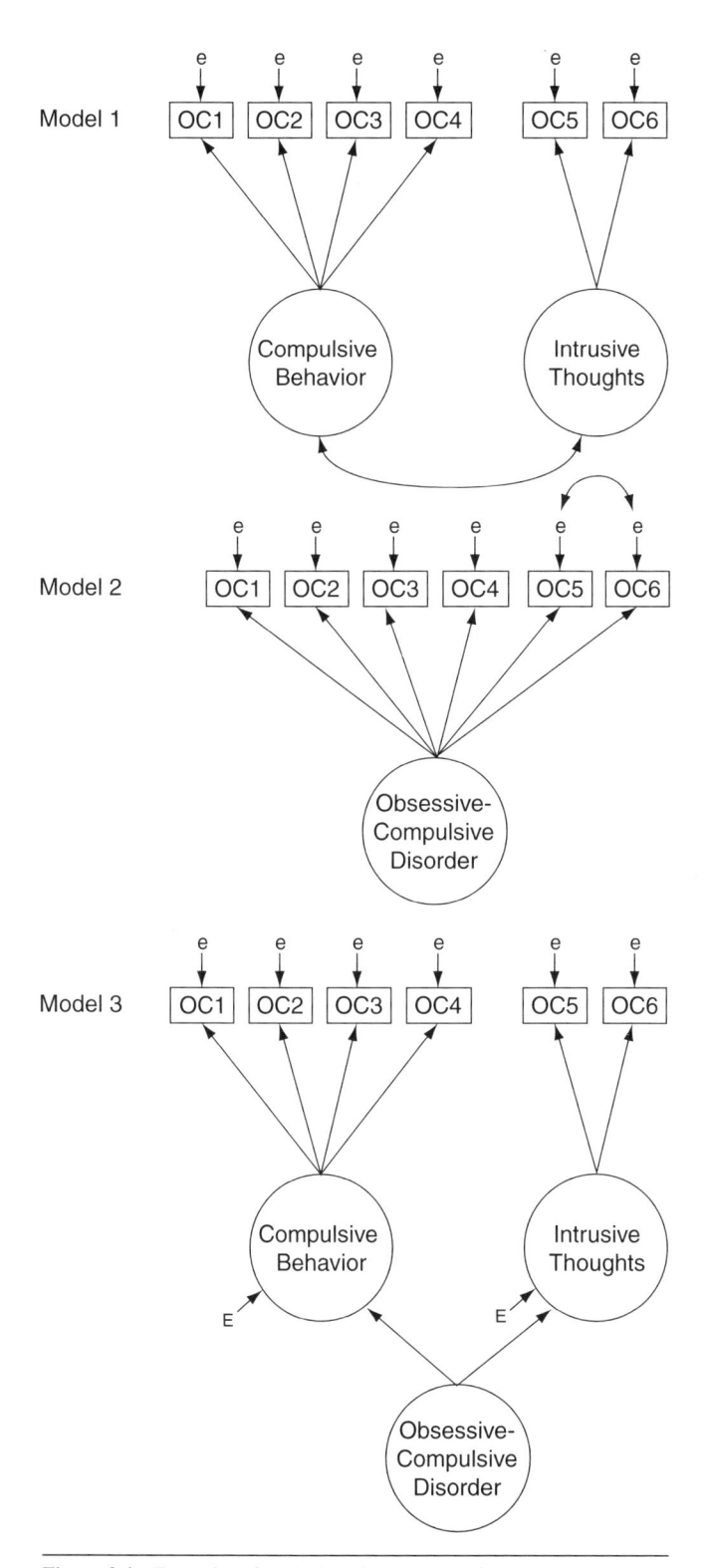

Figure 2.4 Examples of equivalent CFA models of obsessive-compulsive disorder. *Note.* OC1 = checking, OC2 = cleaning, OC3 = counting, OC4 = repeating, OC5 = aggressive thoughts/impulses, OC6 = blasphemous thoughts/impulses. In order for Model 3 to be identified, the two higher-order factor loadings (i.e., Obsessive-Compulsive Disorder → Compulsive Behavior, Obsessive-Compulsive Disorder → Intrusive Thoughts) must be constrained to equality.

REFERENCES

American Psychiatric Association. (1994). *Diagnostic and statistical manual of mental disorders* (4th ed.). Washington, DC: Author.

Bollen, K. A. (1989). *Structural equations with latent variables.* New York: Wiley.

Brown, T. A. (2003). Confirmatory factor analysis of the Penn State Worry Questionnaire: Multiple factors or method effects? *Behaviour Research and Therapy, 41,* 1411–1426.

Brown, T. A., White, K. S., & Barlow, D. H. (2005). A psychometric reanalysis of the Albany Panic and Phobia Questionnaire. *Behaviour Research and Therapy, 43,* 337–355.

Brown, T. A., White, K. S., Forsyth, J. P., & Barlow, D. H. (2004). The structure of perceived emotional control: Psychometric properties of a revised Anxiety Control Questionnaire. *Behavior Therapy, 35,* 75–99.

Byrne, B. M., Shavelson, R. J., & Muthén, B. (1989). Testing for the equivalence of factor covariance and mean structures: The issue of partial measurement invariance. *Psychological Bulletin, 105,* 456–466.

Campbell, D. T., & Fiske, D. W. (1959). Convergent and discriminant validation by the multitrait-multimethod matrix. *Psychological Bulletin, 56,* 81–105.

Curran, P. J. & Hussong, A. M. (2003). The use of latent trajectory models in psychopathology research. *Journal of Abnormal Psychology, 112,* 526–544.

Duncan, T. E., Duncan, S. C., Strycker, L. A., Li, F., & Alpert, A. (1999). *An introduction to latent variable growth curve modeling.* Mahwah, NJ: Erlbaum.

Eid, M., Lischetzke, T., Nussbeck, F. W., & Trierweiler, L. I. (2003). Separating trait effects from trait-specific method effects in multitrait-multimethod models: A multiple indicator CT-C($M-1$) model. *Psychological Methods, 8,* 38–60.

Fresco, D. M., Heimberg, R. G., Mennin, D. S., & Turk, C. L. (2002). Confirmatory factor analysis of the Penn State Worry Questionnaire. *Behaviour Research and Therapy, 40,* 313–323.

Hershberger, S. L. (1994). The specification of equivalent models before the collection of data. In A. von Eye & C. C. Clogg (Eds.), *Latent variables analysis* (pp. 68–105). Thousand Oaks, CA: Sage.

Hu, L., & Bentler, P. M. (1998). Fit indices in covariance structure modeling: Sensitivity to underparameterized model misspecification. *Psychological Methods, 3,* 424–453.

Hu, L., & Bentler, P. M. (1999). Cutoff criteria for fit indexes in covariance structure analysis: Conventional criteria versus new alternatives. *Structural Equation Modeling, 6,* 1–55.

Jaccard, J., & Wan, C. K. (1996). *LISREL approaches to interaction effects in multiple regression.* Thousand Oaks, CA: Sage.

Jöreskog, K. G. (1969). A general approach to confirmatory maximum likelihood factor analysis. *Psychometrika, 34,* 183–202.

Jöreskog, K. G. (1993). Testing structural equation models. In K. A. Bollen & J. S. Long (Eds.), *Testing structural equation models* (pp. 294–316). Newbury Park, CA: Sage.

Jöreskog, K., & Sörbom, D. (2001). LISREL 8.52 [Computer software]. Chicago: Scientific Software International.

Kaufman, P., Rasinski, K. A., Lee, R., & West, J. (1991). *National Education Longitudinal Study of 1988: Quality of the responses of eighth-grade students in NELS88.* Washington, DC: U.S. Department of Education.

Kenny, D. A. (1979). *Correlation and causality.* New York: Wiley.

Kenny, D. A., & Kashy, D. A. (1992). Analysis of the multitrait-multimethod matrix by confirmatory factor analysis. *Psychological Bulletin, 112,* 165–172.

Kenny, D. A., Kashy, D. A., & Bolger, N. (1998). Data analysis in social psychology. In D. T. Gilbert & S. T. Fiske (Eds.), *The handbook of social psychology* (Vol. 2, 4th ed., pp. 233–265). New York: McGraw-Hill.

Kline, R. B. (1998). *Principles and practices of structural equation modeling.* New York: Guilford Press.

Lance, C. E., Noble, C. L., & Scullen, S. E. (2002). A critique of the correlated trait-correlated method and correlated uniqueness models for multitrait-multimethod data. *Psychological Methods, 7,* 228–244.

Lee, S., & Hershberger, S. (1990). A simple rule for generating equivalent models in structural equation modeling. *Multivariate Behavioral Research, 25,* 313–334.

MacCallum, R. C. (1986). Specification searches in covariance structure modeling. *Psychological Bulletin, 100,* 107–120.

MacCallum, R. C., Wegener, D. T., Uchino, B. N., & Fabrigar, L. R. (1993). The problem of equivalent models in applications of covariance structure analysis. *Psychological Bulletin, 114,* 185–199.

Marsh, H. W. (1989). Confirmatory factor analyses of multitrait-multimethod data: Many problems and a few solutions. *Applied Psychological Measurement, 13,* 335–361.

Marsh, H. W. (1996). Positive and negative global self-esteem: A substantively meaningful distinction or artifactors? *Journal of Personality and Social Psychology, 70,* 810–819.

Marsh, H. W., & Bailey, M. (1991). Confirmatory factor analyses of multitrait-multimethod data: A comparison of the behavior of alternative models. *Applied Psychological Measurement, 15,* 47–70.

Marsh, H. W., Balla, J. R., & McDonald, R. P. (1988). Goodness-of-fit indices in confirmatory factor analysis: The effect of sample size. *Psychological Bulletin, 103,* 391–410.

Marsh, H. W., & Grayson, D. (1995). Latent variable models of multitrait-multimethod data. In R. H. Hoyle (Ed.), *Structural equation modeling: Concepts, issues, and applications* (pp. 177–198). Thousand Oaks, CA: Sage.

Meyer, T. J., Miller, M. L., Metzger, R. L., & Borkovec, T. D. (1990). Development and validation of the Penn State Worry Questionnaire. *Behaviour Research and Therapy, 28,* 487–495.

Muthén, B. O. (1989). Latent variable modeling in heterogeneous populations. *Psychometrika, 54,* 557–585.

Muthén, L. K., & Muthén, B. O. (1998–2004). Mplus 3.0 [Computer software]. Los Angeles: Author.

Muthén, L. K., & Muthén, B. O. (2002). How to use a Monte Carlo study to decide on sample size and determine power. *Structural Equation Modeling, 4,* 599–620.

Reise, S. P., Widaman, K. F., & Pugh, K. H. (1993). Confirmatory factor analysis and item response theory: Two approaches for exploring measurement invariance. *Psychological Bulletin, 114,* 552–566.

Rosenberg, M. (1965). *Society and the adolescent child.* Princeton, NJ: Princeton University Press.

Silvia, E. S., & MacCallum, R. C. (1988). Some factors affecting the success of specification searches in covariance structure modeling. *Multivariate Behavioral Research, 23,* 297–326.

Stelzl, I. (1986). Changing the causal hypothesis without changing the fit: Some rules for generating equivalent path models. *Multivariate Behavioral Research, 21,* 309–331.

Tomarken, A. J., & Baker, T. B. (2003). Introduction to the special section on structural equation modeling. *Journal of Abnormal Psychology, 112,* 523–525.

Tomarken, A. J., & Waller, N. G. (2003). Potential problems with "well fitting" models. *Journal of Abnormal Psychology, 112,* 578–598.

Tomás, J. M., & Oliver, A. (1999). Rosenberg's self-esteem scale: Two factors or method effects? *Structural Equation Modeling, 6,* 84–98.

Widaman, K. F. (1985). Hierarchically nested covariance structure models for multitrait-multimethod data. *Applied Psychological Measurement, 9,* 1–26.

Wothke, W. A. (1993). Nonpositive definite matrices in structural modeling. In K. A. Bollen & J. Scott Long (Eds.), *Testing structural equation models* (pp. 256–293). Newbury Park, CA: Sage.

CHAPTER 3

Behavioral and Cognitive Influences

ARTHUR M. NEZU, CHRISTINE MAGUTH NEZU, AND ELIZABETH R. LOMBARDO

INTRODUCTION

This chapter focuses on the influence of various behavioral factors regarding the etiopathogenesis of adult psychopathology. We adopt a broad definition of the term *behavioral* to encompass those major learning and cognitive processes that are traditionally invoked when describing cognitive-behavioral conceptualizations of a particular disorder (Nezu, Nezu, & Lombardo, 2004). Specifically, these entail the following broad categories: (1) *associative learning* (also termed *respondent, classical,* or *Pavlovian conditioning*); (2) *instrumental learning* (also termed *operant conditioning* or *Skinnerian conditioning*); (3) *imitative learning* (also termed *modeling* or *social learning theory*); and (4) *cognitive vulnerability factors.*

Beginning with associative learning, these general principles were established in the basic science laboratory and later applied to conceptualizing both "normal" and abnormal human behavior (Craighead, Craighead, & Illardi, 1995). Historically, these theories provided a departure from an understanding of psychopathology as individual, subjective, and difficult to study scientifically.

For each of the previous areas, we will provide a description of the process, how it influences either the development or maintenance of adult psychopathology, and examples of its influence on specific disorders.

ASSOCIATIVE LEARNING

Learning by association, or the pairing of two events, can be traced back to experiments in classical conditioning. Classical conditioning, also known as Pavlovian or respondent conditioning, is based upon the work, in part, of Ivan Pavlov, whose lifelong research in physiology and animal research culminated with his studies of the psychic reflex and conditioning (Pavlov, 1941). In the basic classical conditioning experimental paradigm, a stimulus is made to elicit a response that was not previously associated with that stimulus. Through repeated pairings of two stimuli, a conditioned stimulus comes to elicit a response (termed the *conditioned response*) that is similar to the one originally elicited by an unconditioned stimulus. In humans, an example of such a stimulus pairing is the experience of discomfort associated with sound of a dentist's drill. After repeated pairings, the sound of the drill by itself can elicit pain and discomfort.

The strength of the learned association depends upon the intensity of either the unconditioned or conditioned stimulus, as well as the order of stimulus presentation and time interval of the two stimulus pairings. For example, in the situation just described, if the sound of the dentist's drill is very loud, shrill, or unusual (intensity parameters) and it was introduced just prior to the experience of pain (order and time parameters), then the learned association between sound and pain is more likely to occur.

There are additional factors that influence the strength of a learned association, such as an individual's prior exposure or experience with one of the stimuli that was paired. For example, consider the individual who has heard a dentist's drill in several situations in which a response of pain did not result. He or she would be less likely to associate the sound of the drill with fear, arousal, or discomfort.

Experiments in classical conditioning also demonstrate that associative learning can occur when a previously conditioned stimulus is paired with a new conditioned stimulus. For example, research conducted by Staats and Staats (1959) revealed that emotional responses were reliably observed when people read neutral nonsense syllables that were paired with a word containing strong emotional connotation through previous conditioning (e.g., words such as *grief,* or *pain*). Referred to as *higher order conditioning,* this process has important implications for the development of psychopathology. Through higher order conditioning, emotions such as fear, anger, and sadness, as well as various attitudes and behavior, can all become conditioned responses to stimuli such as words, situations, or interactions with others through their association with other previously conditioned stimuli. The original unconditioned stimulus (i.e., the original stimuli that elicited physiologic arousal or pain) is no longer required.

Classical Conditioning and Anxiety Disorders

The first group of psychologists to rely on classical conditioning and the laws governing associative learning to explain human psychopathology focused their attention toward an explanation of anxiety disorders and phobias (e.g., Eysenck, 1960; Watson & Raynor, 1920; Wolpe, 1958). According to this view, anxiety reactions are the result of higher order conditioning of the autonomic nervous system to certain environmental events and situations. Fear reactions are particularly associable, in that many intense, fear-producing stimuli are available to be paired with a plethora of environmental phenomena. For example, post-traumatic stress disorder may result when individuals experience intense aversive events such as war, crime, child abuse, terrorism, or natural disaster. In such situations, environmental stimuli such as sounds, smells, and visual cues can all become conditioned stimuli as they are paired with interoceptive events.

Classical conditioning of autonomic reactivity can be found to make at least a partial contribution to the development of most anxiety disorders. These include specific phobias, as well as obsessive-compulsive disorder, agoraphobia, social phobia, and post-traumatic stress disorder (Nezu, Nezu, & Lombardo, 2004). In addition, higher order classical conditioning can be identified as being involved in the etiopathogenesis of anger problems, depression, and many interpersonal difficulties. For example, various environmental cues, such as a familiar song, a person's name, or other stimuli, may come to be associated with the experience of loss or sad mood. In most cases, however, in order to provide a full learning-based explanation of the disorder, additional types of learning should be posited to interact with classical conditioning.

Psychosomatics: A Contemporary Model of Classical Conditioning

Although classical conditioning was historically associated with the involuntary responses of the autonomic nervous system, as in the case of fear reactions, more recent models of classical conditioning have focused on its role in the development of psychosomatic disorders (Barker, 2001). Many studies support integrative explanatory models that link classical conditioning of both the autonomic and central nervous systems with the neuroendocrine and immune systems and environmental cues in such a way as to influence physiologic symptoms. These include studies of the classical conditioning aspects of psychoneuroimmunology (Ader & Cohen, 1993).

An example of this type of research was initially conducted by Robert Ader (e.g., Ader & Cohen, 1975). In a seminal experiment, rats were classically conditioned by giving them water that contained an immunosuppressant drug, cyclophosphamide, as well as saccharine. Thus, the cyclophosphamide was paired with saccharine. When the cyclophosphamide was removed, the sweetened water alone actually suppressed the rats' immune systems, as if they had been injected with the powerful immunosuppressant drug. Some rats were so immunocompromised that they died as a result of the sweetened water alone.

Additional research has linked previously neutral stimuli with psychosomatic reactions in asthma (Schmaling, Lehrer, Feldman, & Giardino, 2003), hypoglycemia (Stockhorst et al., 2004), allergic reactions, drug tolerance (Barker, 2001), medically unexplained symptoms (Nezu, Nezu, & Lombardo, 2001), and pain (Turk & Okiguji, 2003). Turk and Okiguji (2003) provide a clinical example of a pain patient who experiences increased pain during physical therapy. Through a classical conditioning paradigm, this patient comes to associate a negative emotional response to the presence of the physical therapist, treatment room, and other environmental cues associated with pain. Such negative emotional reactions can then lead to increased muscle tension and worsening of the pain, thus strengthening the association of physical therapy and pain.

Nonassociative Learning

There are times when a change in behavior occurs that is not the consequence of an association, but the result of an individual experiencing a single stimulus. Two examples of this form of learning are *habituation* and *sensitization*. Through habituation, the repeated presentation of a stimulus becomes nonrelevant and ignored. Common phenomena may include familiar household sounds, such as traffic noise for people accustomed to an urban environment. Sensitization occurs when repeated presentations of a stimulus are very intense and do not habituate easily. In such cases, the opposite effect can occur. Rather than a reduced responsiveness, the individual becomes sensitized to the stimulus and responds with a heightened or hypervigilant response. An example of how both processes can occur simultaneously involve mothers of small children in a nursery who become sensitized to their own child's cries, yet are habituated to the cries of other children, as they are able to discriminate between their own and other children.

One problem regarding habituation and sensitization as explanatory concepts of psychopathology is the difficulty in predicting how an individual will respond to a specific stimulus. The result of habituation or sensitization is dependent upon the intensity of the stimulus, the nature of the stimulus, the background conditions, and the individual's prior history with the stimulus (Barker, 2001; Overmeier & Seligman, 1967).

Nonassociative learning principles have been especially helpful regarding the understanding and treatment of anxiety disorders. One example, with regard to the treatment of phobias, is a procedure referred to as *in vivo exposure*. As part of this treatment, the therapist accompanies phobic individuals as they are placed in the presence (i.e., exposed to) of the phobic stimuli repeatedly and asked to refrain from avoidance or escape until the anxiety is habituated (Craighead & Craighead, 2003).

INSTRUMENTAL LEARNING

Instrumental learning, also known as operant or Skinnerian conditioning (named after B. F. Skinner who is considered to have conducted the seminal research in this area), refers to the acquisition and maintenance of voluntary or emitted behavior. In contrast to the autonomic nervous system and reflexive behavior that historically was the focus of classical conditioning, instrumental learning focuses on voluntary behavior assumed to be under the control of the central nervous system. Modification of behavior occurs as a function of the application of reinforcers or punishers (Skinner, 1953). Previous research by Thorndike (1932) established the scientific principles of behavior such as the *law of effect*, which proposed that an increase or decrease in the frequency of an emitted behavioral response is dependent upon its consequence. Later, the field of experimental analysis of behavior developed a more systematic refinement of the principles of operant conditioning.

Operant conditioning experiments support the law of effect in that overt actions and their immediate consequences "control" these actions. Further, signals or cues from the environment can inform an individual whether a particular response is likely to be reinforced or punished. Behavioral disorders, therefore, are viewed as a function of their consequences within a situational context. An operant or instrumental explanation of psychopathology focuses on identifying the controlling cues (antecedents) of the behavior under observation and the consequences of the behavior of concern.

Through this instrumental view, psychopathology is conceptualized in terms of behavioral problems. Behavioral excesses, such as destructive habits, alcohol abuse, aggression and violence, and panic attacks are undesirable behaviors currently maintained by environmental cues and consequences. Behavioral deficits, such as lack of communication skills, problem-solving skills, assertiveness skills, and decreases in enjoyment, activity, or pleasant events, are important behaviors that require instruction, shaping, or reinforcement. In other words, behavioral disorders are not viewed as psychological illnesses, but as phenomena that can be understood and treated according to the learning principles that are operative and functional.

Four phenomena are basic and important to the process of operant learning (Nemeroff & Karoly, 1991). They include the following: (1) *acquisition* of a response habit (learning that a response is followed by a specific consequence); (2) *extinction* of a response and consequence (learning that a response—consequence contingency no longer holds true); (3) *discrimination* (learning to identify stimuli or antecedent conditions when a consequence will or will not follow specific behavior); and (4) *generalization* (the process of continuing to engage in learned behaviors other than the original learning situation). With regard to psychopathology, an understanding of these processes provides an explanation for how symptoms and behavior problems are increased or maintained, and how adaptive coping behaviors may be fostered through behavior therapy interventions (Nezu, Nezu, & Lombardo, 2004).

As an illustration of an operant-based explanation of depression, for example, the following processes might occur. After experiencing an initial loss or failure, an individual engages in negative self-statements that are reinforced by a false sense of control and predictability over the events (i.e., acquisition). The person's predictions of failure or further loss can result in a decrease of pleasant and successful experiences (i.e., extinction of the belief that one's actions will result in a positive outcome). Any situations in which positive outcomes are possible are avoided in order to prevent further disappointment (i.e., discrimination). Even new situations are met with hopeless expectation of failure (i.e., generalization). Thus, depressive symptoms are engendered and maintained through operant processes.

Human learning of symptoms associated with psychopathology and behavioral disorders often involves combinations of operant, associative, and nonassociative learning, within a background of an individual's genetics, physiology, and social or cultural environment. Two examples of the complex integration of these various domains are provided in the following section.

Autoshaping and Automaintenance

Autoshaping refers to the occurrence and maintenance of behavior in the absence of observable reinforcement. *Auto-*

maintenance refers to the continuation or maintenance of a behavior in the absence of an observable contingency. As an example of these phenomena with regard to psychopathology, Barker (2001) provides a description of a type of stalking behavior. From an operant learning view, the stalker is never actually reinforced by a response for the person they are attracted to. In fact, the likely response of a person being stalked is to try to punish the behavior by preventing any kind of contact or access to them personally.

In a process similar to classical conditioning, an apartment, car, or favorite restaurant of the person being stalked becomes associated with the actual person to the extent that the site of these objects or places alone can elicit the stalker's arousal. However, classical conditioning does not explain the elaborate behavioral sequence of stalking that occurs and continues over time in the absence of access to the person being stalked. One hypotheses is that the stalker's sexual arousal sets into motion a type of automatic courting sequence (e.g., getting dressed, driving over to the apartment of the person he is attracted to, trying to be noticed by the object of his attraction). This sequence, over time, is reinforced and maintained by the experience of excitement and arousal (i.e., a consequence of the behavior). The behavior, therefore, is maintained through instrumental learning. The excitement experienced, however, is in response to objects, locations, or situations that that were the result of associative learning. Such behavioral learning interactions reveal that several different learning processes may be needed to explain the complexities of various behavior disorders. Another example of such as interaction can be found in Mowrer's two-factor theory of learning as described next.

Two-Factor Theory of Learning

Two-factor theory, originally proposed by Mowrer (1956, 1960), provides an explanation of how two forms of learning may explain how avoidance behavior can maintain strong anxiety patterns. Two-factor theory proposes one set of principles to explain one type of learning and a different set of principles to explain another type of learning within the context of the same behavioral phenomena. For example, with regard to avoidant behavior, classical conditioning occurs in the early stages of learned avoidance. One example might be the association made by a child who experiences a strong fear reaction when surprised by an aggressive and large barking dog. In such a case, the dog may act as a conditioned stimulus when paired with the arousal (unconditioned stimulus) that elicits fear (unconditioned response). In an attempt to escape, the child runs from the dog. This behavior results in a reduction of the fear and negative arousal. Thus, the child's avoidance behavior is negatively reinforced through removal of an aversive emotional experience (i.e., fear in this case).

In the future, whenever the child may experience any stimuli similar to the dog (stimulus generalization), this antecedent situation serves as a discriminative trigger for avoidance behavior. The reinforcing consequence of the avoidance behavior is a reliable decrease in anxiety. Thus, the first factor in Mowrer's two-factor theory is classical conditioning, which Mowrer referred to as *sign* learning. He referred to the second factor in his two-factor theory as *solution* learning, which essentially consists of instrumental or operant conditioning. Mowrer's work reveals how these two types of conditioning can be interrelated across a range of behavioral disorders and problems, especially phobias and obsessive-compulsive behaviors (Foa & Franklin, 2001).

SOCIAL LEARNING

A major concern voiced by Albert Bandura (1977), who is often considered as synonymous with social learning theory, regarding the explanatory power of operant approaches to human behavior, involved the inability of that approach to account for how new or novel behaviors are learned and how learning occurs in the absence of direct reinforcement or punishment of such behavior. A key component of Bandura's theory involved the role of *observational learning* (also termed *imitative* or *vicarious learning*), or learning by witnessing others' behavior. In other words, learning can occur vicariously; "most human behavior is learned observationally through modeling; from observing others one forms an idea of how new behaviors are performed, and on later occasions this coded information serves as a guide for action" (Bandura, 1977, p. 22). In this section, we focus on influences of observational learning regarding adult psychopathology.

General Principles of Modeling

According to social learning theory, certain features exist that increase the likelihood that imitative learning will actually occur. First, how the information is conveyed is important. Specifically, visually observed, rather than verbally instructed, behavior is more influential on learning. For example, consider the person who is trying to learn to play golf just by listening to someone describe it. In addition, particular characteristics of the model him- or herself can be influential. For example, models that are more respected, attractive, prestigious, and seen as competent or expert are more likely to induce learning. Those who invoke an emotional response, such as empathy, admiration, or sense of attachment, are also often more influential on the observer's learning. In addition, observers who can relate to the model (e.g., see themselves as similar) are more likely to perform the observed behaviors.

The specific effects of the model's behavior can further influence the performance of certain behaviors. Thus, activities that lead to more positive consequences are more likely to be performed. It is important to remember, however, that reinforcement is idiographic in nature. Thus, punishment can result after a certain behavior has occurred, and whereas one observer may see this aversive contingency as negative, another might identify the attention as reinforcing. In addition to the type of consequences, the timing of consequences can be important. For example, proximal rewards are often more reinforcing than distal incentives.

Finally, various characteristics of the observer him- or herself can affect learning. Optimal arousal level, which is classified as moderate intensity, can increase the likelihood that modeled behavior will be learned. Furthermore, observers with low self-esteem and diminished self-confidence are more likely to assume modeled behavior.

Effects of Modeling

Modeling can influence behavior in three key modes. First, observers can imitate certain observed behavior that they did not previously perform, such as children "parroting" their parents. Second, the performance of previously learned behaviors could be *inhibited or disinhibited* via observational learning. In other words, viewing a modeled action can result in increasing or decreasing the performance of that behavior. Last, modeling can "teach" novel or new behaviors. In other words, observers can apply what was learned from modeled behavior in one situation to similar situations. Such unique behaviors are more likely to occur if the learner expects positive outcomes, which are deemed valuable.

Observational Learning and Adult Psychopathology

Social learning principles have been invoked to explain the acquisition of certain psychological problems. The following presentations of the effects of observational learning on psychopathology may include references to children's behaviors. Although this volume is centered on adult psychopathology, many of the following disorders are affected by modeling during childhood.

Antisocial Behavior

Observational learning appears to influence antisocial behavior. Modeling of antisocial behavior can be achieved via direct or vicarious modeling. Directly modeled antisocial parental behavior is significantly related to conduct problems in children (Tapscott, Frick, Wootton, & Kruh, 1996) and conduct problems in childhood are often a precursor to full-blown antisocial personality disorder in adults.

The impact of vicarious modeling on violent behavior has been widely studied. Recently, for example, the role of the media has been gaining increased attention, with children who commit murder blame their viewing of television violence as the cause for such acts. Observational learning (e.g., watching a violent program) affects cognitions that induce aggressive behavior (Huesmann, 1997). Via modeling, observers learn that aggressive behavior can result in positive consequences, leading to the development of positive expectations about performing aggressive acts (e.g., stopping others from performing aggressive acts toward the aggressor, admiration from others, tension reduction).

A Congressional Public Health Summit, convened in 2000, reported that (1) exposure to violence desensitizes aggressive acts, resulting in greater acceptance of violence, as well as decreased empathy for the victim; (2) as a result of vicarious exposure to violence, violent behavior is viewed as an acceptable and effective manner of handling conflicts; and (3) children who observe violence on television are more likely to engage in acts of aggression. Furthermore, longitudinal studies demonstrate that childhood exposure to violence in the media predicts adult acts of aggression, in both males and females (Huesmann, Moise-Titus, Podolski, & Eron, 2003; Johnson, Cohen, Smailes, Kasen, & Brook, 2002). In addition to television media, video games and violent song lyrics depicting aggression often result in increased participant/listener aggressive thoughts and feelings of hostility (Anderson, Carnagey, & Eubanks, 2003; Funk, Baldacci, Pasold, & Baumgardner, 2004).

Anxiety

Vicarious experiences appear to influence the development and maintenance of anxiety disorders. Overall, anxiety behaviors, such as avoidance, can be learned via observational learning (Rapee, 2002). For example, a child who sees a parent shy away from social interactions may engage in social isolation him- or herself. Modeling also affects what is seen as "normal." For example, consider the young female patient who does not understand what is wrong with repeatedly rechecking the status of a locked door, explaining, "My father used to do that for hours each day."

Modeled behaviors have been documented as playing a significant role in the development of specific phobias, as well as social phobias (Mineka & Zinbarg, 1996). For example, the development of spider phobias has been found to be influenced by vicarious experiences (Kirkby, Menzies, Daniels, & Smith, 1995) and blood-injury-injection phobias can be acquired via observing others (Kleinknecht, 1994¹). Further, vicarious learning affects the frequency of panic attacks, whereby this relationship appears to be both direct and indirect, moderated by the effects of vicarious learning on anxiety sensitivity in general (Stewart et al., 2001).

With regard to PTSD, the impact of vicarious experiences with a traumatic event is well documented; note that criteria for a diagnosis of PTSD can be met without a direct encounter with the trauma. That is, vicarious exposure, either visually or auditorily (e.g., hearing about someone else's traumatic experiences) can result in full-blown PTSD. Such symptoms have been identified in international relief workers who themselves did not directly experience a trauma (Eriksson, Vande Kemp, Gorsuch, Hoke, & Foy, 2001), in partners of veterans with PTSD (Nelson & Wright, 1996), and in viewers of news broadcasts covering the September 11, 2001, terrorist attacks (Schlenger et al., 2002).

Depression

One of the strongest predictors of depression in children and adolescence is maternal depression (Beardslee, Versage, & Gladstone, 1998). Observational learning can play a role in this process. For example, modeling plays a key role in the development of learned helplessness (Breen, Vulcano, & Dyck, 1979) and other negative thoughts. Consider a young girl who observes her mother engaging in self-deprecating actions (e.g., repeatedly saying "I can't do anything right; I'm not good because I keep messing up"). The girl then internalizes such thoughts, developing a depressed mood, which eventually progresses into a mood disorder. Further, this depressed individual will engage in behavior that reflects her low self-esteem (e.g., she does not put effort into tasks because she expects failure). As a result, individuals coming into contact with her may react to this behavior (e.g., reprimand for poor effort and/or results), which further reinforces the individual's poor self-concept. Thus, a vicious cycle perpetuating the depressive symptoms and low self-esteem, originally instigated by observing her mother, is developed.

Eating Disorders

Eating disorders from both ends of the spectrum (i.e., overeating and undereating) have been shown to be influenced by observational learning. Regarding overeating, vicarious exposure to food via television advertisements prompts food consumption in both obese and lean children (Halford, Gillespie, Brown, Pontin, & Dovey, 2004). Observational learning can result in unrealistic expectations about body size, which may influence eating habits. Consider that the average U.S. woman is 5 feet, 4 inches, 145 pounds, and wears a size 11 to 14. In contrast, a Barbie doll, a childhood idol to many (relatively speaking), is 6 feet, 101 pounds, and a size 4. Thus, children grow up with their sense of the prototypical female as being something very different from reality. The emerging popularity of plastic surgery and use of airbrushing in magazine photographs to make models even thinner further contributes to unrealistic goals for women's bodies. In fact, merely watching thin women on television results in viewers' body dissatisfaction, regardless of their body size (Tiggemann & Slater, 2004).

Observational learning via the media further influences how people perceive persons with different body sizes. Overweight and obese women in television commercials are less attractive and less likely to be involved in romantic relationships (Greenberg, Eastin, Hofschire, Lachlan, & Brownell, 2003). This leads viewers to equate being fat with being disliked and socially ostracized. Conversely, due to media exposure, U.S. women of all ages often equate thin with being successful, attractive, and popular. Adolescent teenagers want to be thinner, despite their current size, and attribute this desire to media influences (Tiggemann, Gardiner, & Slater, 2000). This negative view of being overweight and positive view of being thin can influence individuals to engage in behaviors in an attempt to lose weight, such as anorexia nervosa and bulimia.

Substance Abuse

Substance abuse can also be influenced by observational learning. Vicarious experiences with alcohol appear to affect one's conceptualization of and perceptions about the effects (and, thus benefits) of alcohol (Goldman, 2002). Regarding smoking, it has been demonstrated that media outlets provide modeling for smoking behaviors, and media messages provide vicarious reinforcement for the act of smoking (Wakfield, Flay, Nichter, & Giovino, 2003).

COGNITIVE VULNERABILITY FACTORS

Partially in reaction to early behaviorists' lack of attention to mediational constructs (i.e., the "mind"), more and more psychologists during the last three decades of the twentieth century began to focus on the role of cognitive factors in human learning and psychopathology (Mahoney, 2003). Although there may be significant overlap between the consequent cognitive theories of psychopathology, a primary core proposition across these conceptual models involves the notion that cognitive activity affects behavior and emotion (Dobson, 2001). Cognitive models underscore the importance of mediational processes in determining the emergence and maintenance of emotional disturbance.

In reviewing the influence of cognitive factors on adult psychopathology, it is worthwhile to differentiate between cognitive deficiencies, cognitive distortions, and negative cognitive products. *Cognitive deficiencies* are absences or diminished skills in one's thinking processes, such as the failure to realize the consequences of one's actions due to deficient problem-solving skills. *Cognitive distortions* refer to errors in cognitive or informational processing, for example, misinterpretations of certain events based on dichotomous thinking. *Negative automatic thoughts,* although potentially being the product of either cognitive deficiencies or distortions, are discrete negative cognitions or thoughts, such as "I'm scared that I may die."

In this section, we review the influence on adult psychopathology of ineffective problem solving (cognitive deficiency), biased cognitive schemata and irrational beliefs (cognitive distortions), and negative thoughts (negative cognitive products).

Problem Solving

Problem solving is the cognitive-behavioral process by which a person attempts to identify or discover effective or adaptive solutions in order to cope effectively with stressful problems encountered during the course of living (D'Zurilla & Nezu, 1999; Nezu, 2004). Relevant problem-solving goals include altering the nature of the situation so that it no longer is problematic, changing one's reactions to such situations, or both. The outcome of this process is largely determined by two general, but partially independent, dimensions: (1) problem orientation, and (2) problem-solving style (D'Zurilla, Nezu, & Maydeu-Olivares, 2004).

Problem orientation is the set of relatively stable cognitive-affective schemata that represent a person's generalized beliefs, attitudes, and emotional reactions about problems in living and one's ability to successfully cope with such problems. One's problem orientation can be either positive or negative. A positive orientation involves the tendency to appraise problems as challenges, be optimistic in believing that problems are solvable, perceive one's own ability to solve problems as strong, and believe that successful problem solving involves time and effort. Conversely, a negative problem orientation is characterized by the tendency to view problems as threats, expect problems to be unsolvable, doubt one's own ability to solve problems successfully, and become frustrated and upset when faced with problems.

Problem-solving style refers to those core cognitive-behavioral activities that people engage in when attempting to cope with problems in living. *Rational problem solving* is the constructive problem-solving style that involves the systematic and planful application of the following four skills: (1) *problem definition and formulation* (the ability to understand the nature of problems, identify obstacles to goals, delineate realistic objectives, and perceive cause-effect relationships), (2) *generation of alternatives* (the ability to brainstorm multiple solution ideas), (3) *decision making* (the ability to identify potential consequences, predict the likelihood of such consequences, and conduct a cost-benefit analysis of the desirability of these outcomes), and (4) *solution implementation and verification* (the ability to carry out a solution plan optimally, monitor its effects, troubleshoot if the solution is not effective, and self-reinforce if the outcome is satisfactory).

In contrast to this rational approach, two additional problem-solving styles exist that are maladaptive in nature. The first is termed *impulsivity/carelessness,* and involves the generalized response pattern characterized by impulsive, hurried, and careless attempts at problem resolution. The second dysfunctional problem-solving style, *avoidance,* is characterized by procrastination, passivity, and overdependence on others to provide solutions. In essence, both styles can lead to ineffective or unsuccessful problem resolution, as well as increasing the possibility that such problems may worsen.

Problem Solving, Stress, and Psychopathology

According to a problem-solving model of stress (Nezu, 1987; Nezu & D'Zurilla, 1989; Nezu & Ronan, 1985), much of what is viewed as psychopathology can often be understood as ineffective and maladaptive coping behavior leading to various personal and social consequences, such as depression, anxiety, anger, interpersonal difficulties, and physical symptoms. Specifically, how people cope with stressful events (i.e., major negative life events, such as the loss of a loved one, as well as cumulative daily hassles or problems, such as frequent arguments with one's spouse) determines, in large part, the degree to which they will experience psychopathology and long-lasting psychological distress. Continued successful attempts at problem resolution can lead to a reduction or minimization of immediate emotional distress and a reduced likelihood of long-term negative affective states, such as depression and anxiety. Alternatively, if one's problem-solving coping skills are ineffective, or if extreme emotional distress impacts negatively on one's coping efforts, resulting in either reduced motivation, inhibition of problem-solving performance, or both, then the likelihood of long-term negative affective states will be increased. Further, such negative outcomes can lead to the exacerbation of existing problems and potentially the creation of new problems, which in turn can lead to additional stressful events. Consequently, how one copes with these problems can lead to either an escalation or attenuation of the stress process.

Relationship between Problem-Solving Deficits and Negative Affect

In a recent extensive review of the literature, Nezu (2004) found that, across various differing population samples of both clinical (e.g., depressed patients, veterans diagnosed with post-traumatic stress disorder) and nonclinical (e.g., college students, community residents) groups, and using various types of assessment tools (e.g., self-report and performance-based measures), a large body of studies identify strong associations between various social problem-solving variables and negative affect, specifically depression, anxiety, and worry. In particular, a negative problem orientation appears to be an especially strong predictor of depression and anxiety across various samples and measures of problem solving. Further, a significant number of studies found associations between deficient rational problem-solving skills and psychological distress.

In addition to those studies focusing on negative affect, problem-solving deficits have also been found to be significantly related to pessimism, poor self-esteem, feelings of hopelessness, increased suicidal risk, behavioral self-injury, schizophrenia, anger proneness, increased alcohol intake and substance risk taking, secondary physical complications (e.g., decubitus ulcers and urinary tract infections) among persons with spinal cord injuries, premenstrual and menstrual pain, physical health problems and symptoms among undergraduate college students, diminished life satisfaction among adults, and physical health problems among adult cancer patients (Nezu, 2004; Nezu, Wilkins, & Nezu, 2004).

Problem Solving as a Moderator of Stress

Nezu (2004) also reviewed the literature to determine the answer to the question of whether effective problem-solving ability leads to a reduction or minimization of immediate emotional distress and a reduced likelihood of experiencing long-term negative affective states, such as depression or anxiety. In general, several studies provide evidence that problem solving does function as a significant moderator of the relationship between stressful events and consequent psychological distress. For example, under similar levels of high stress, individuals with poor problem-solving skills have been found to experience significantly higher levels of psychological distress, such as depression (e.g., Cheng, 2001; Frye & Goodman, 2000; Nezu, Nezu, Saraydarian, Kalmar, & Ronan, 1986; Nezu & Ronan, 1988; Priester & Clum, 1993) and anxiety (Miner & Dowd, 1996; Nezu, 1986), as compared to individuals characterized by effective problem solving, suggesting that effective problem solving serves to attenuate the negative effects of stress. This conclusion is strengthened by the notion that this group of studies provides converging evidence for this hypothesis across varying subject samples (e.g., college undergraduates, adolescent and child populations, clinically depressed patients, adult cancer patients) and across differing measures of problem solving.

Consistent with the reciprocal nature of the problem-solving model of stress as it pertains specifically to depression (Nezu, 1987; Nezu, Nezu, & Perri, 1989), Dixon, Heppner, Burnett, Anderson, and Wood (1993), using a prospective design, found that ineffective problem solving was an important *antecedent* in predicting future depressive symptoms, as well as a *consequence,* in that the experience of depressive symptoms was also found to lead to temporary deficits in problem-solving ability. Moreover, Dixon (2000) provides evidence for a recovery function for problem solving, in that effective problem solvers are more likely to recover from a depressive episode than ineffective problem solvers.

Efficacy of Problem-Solving Therapy

Treatment approaches geared to enhance one's problem-solving abilities have been found to be an efficacious intervention regarding a wide range of clinical populations, psychological problems, and the distress associated with chronic medical disorders. These include unipolar depression, geriatric depression, distressed primary care patients, social phobia, agoraphobia, obesity, coronary heart disease, adult cancer patients, schizophrenia, mentally retarded adults with concomitant psychiatric problems, HIV risk behaviors, drug abuse, suicide, childhood aggression, and conduct disorder (for a review of the outcome literature, see Nezu, D'Zurilla, Zwick, & Nezu, 2004).

Biased Cognitive Schemata

Cognitive Therapy

Perhaps one of the most influential cognitive models of adult psychopathology is Beck's conceptualization of emotional disorders and its associated treatment approach, cognitive therapy, particular with regard to depression (Beck, 1976). In essence, a primary feature of his model focuses on the psychological importance of people's beliefs about themselves, their personal and social environment, and the future (i.e., the cognitive triad). To a large degree, the negative manner in which people (mis)interpret significant events in their lives is hypothesized to greatly influence the degree to which they will experience dysphoria and excessive anxiety. Depressed individuals, for example, typically view themselves as inadequate, worthless, and unlovable. They perceive their environment as generally overwhelming and fraught with obstacles that are insurmountable. The future is seen as hopeless, filled with loss and failure, and their ability to impact on the course of events is viewed as deficient. This is a distorted perspective, in that an objective review of the facts of their lives would likely show a more favorable picture; however, such individuals are prone to overestimate the negative factors and underestimate their own resources and abilities.

In addition, Beck (e.g., Beck, Rush, Shaw, & Emery, 1979) suggests that depressed patients characteristically engage in various cognitive distortions when encountering certain events that are different from those logical processes used by non-depression-prone people. These include (1) *arbitrary inference* (reaching conclusions that are not justified by available evidence), (2) *all-or-nothing thinking* ("black-or-white" thinking in extremes), (3) *overgeneralization* (drawing general conclusions on the basis of a single incident), (4) *selective abstraction* (attending to a particular detail while ignoring the whole context), (5) *magnification and minimization* (perceiving an event as far more important or far less important than it is), and (6) *personalization* (incorrectly attributing an external event to oneself).

Subsequent developments in cognitive models of psychopathology emphasize the role of early schemata developed during childhood as predisposing vulnerability factors (e.g., Young, 1999). In general, schemata are cognitive structures that screen, code, and evaluate the myriad of stimuli that humans are exposed to (Beck, 1976). Based on such schemata, individuals categorize and interpret experiences in an idiosyncratic fashion. "Pathological" schemata (or ones that predispose an individual to experience psychological disorders, such as depression, anxiety, and obsessions) are highly personalized and idiosyncratic and are triggered when an individual encounters a stressful situation. At that point, negative schemata "ascend" over positive ones, becoming the "filter" by which the person negatively interprets the meaning of the situation, as well as fostering a biased recall of similar events. In other words, such schemata predispose the depression-prone individual to view the negative aspects of a situation rather than the positive ones, remember negative events rather than positive ones, and perceive negative outcomes as being more probable than positive ones as a function of the event.

Young (1999) has developed a more formalized set of schemata that he terms *early maladaptive schemata*. He defines these as dysfunctional cognitive structures that are particularly stable and enduring, initially develop during childhood, and emerge throughout one's life. Essentially, such schemata are viewed by individuals as truths about themselves and their environment. They tend to be self-perpetuating, resistant to change, usually activated by a change in one's environment, particularly if negative (e.g., job loss), and generally associated with intense levels of affect when triggered. Such schemata are typically not in a person's conscious awareness and surface when a stressful event activates it, at which time the person interprets the situation through the filter of the schema.

Eighteen differing schemata have been hypothesized to exist by Young (1999) and are grouped according to the following five hypothesized domains: *disconnection and rejection* (expectation that one's need for security, safety, acceptance, and the like, will not be met in a predictable manner); *impaired autonomy and performance* (expectation that one cannot function independently or perform successfully); *impaired limits* (difficulties in making commitments to others and setting internal limits); *other-directedness* (excessive focus on the feelings and responses of others at the expense of one's own needs); and *overvigilance and inhibition* (excessive emphasis on suppressing one's spontaneous feelings or on meeting rigid internalized rules about one's performance and ethical behavior). These schemata usually result from an interaction between a child's innate temperament and various dysfunctional developmental experiences with family members and/or caretakers. Encountering a stressful life event (e.g., getting a divorce) can stimulate one of these schemata leading to the distorted interpretation of the meaning, impact, and outcome of the situation along the lines of the specific type of schema.

Not only has such a conceptualization served as the foundation of a cognitive formulation of depression (e.g., DeRubeis, Tang, & Beck, 2001), but it also has evolved as an explanatory model for personality disorders (Beck, Freeman, & Associates, 1990) and the positive and negative symptoms of schizophrenia (Rector & Beck, 2002). Moreover, cognitive therapy has been among the most extensively tested psychological interventions, particularly for depression, and found to be highly effective (J. Beck, 1995; Hollon, Haman, & Brown, 2002).

Irrational Beliefs

Somewhat similar in nature, but developed independently of cognitive therapy, is Ellis's rational emotive theory of psychological disorders. The related psychosocial intervention was originally termed *rational emotive therapy* (e.g., Ellis, 1962), but more recently entitled rational emotive behavior therapy (REBT; e.g., Ellis, 2003). As a primarily cognitive model, this theory basically states that abnormal emotional and behavioral disorders are maintained by the interpretations people apply to events in their lives. Drawing heavily from various philosophical perspectives, such as the first century philosopher, Epictetus ("people are disturbed not by things, but by the views they take of them"), rational emotive theory uses an ABC model to illustrate that when an event occurs, it serves to activate (A) certain beliefs (B) that can consequate (C) in various negative emotions and maladaptive behavior if such beliefs are irrational in nature.

Several of the various types of irrational or illogical beliefs that Ellis has described include the following categories: (1) *absolute thinking* (all-or-none, black-or-white thinking); (2) *catastrophizing* (perceiving minor situations as disastrous); (3) *low frustration tolerance* (inability to cope with minor inconveniences); (4) *overgeneralization* (drawing general conclusions based on the evidence of only one or two events); and (5) *personal worthlessness* (specific form of overgeneralization related to failure situations).

As can be seen, there is much overlap between Ellis's rational emotive theory of emotional disorders and Beck's cognitive model of psychopathology. However, one major difference lies in their associated clinical interventions. Specifically, Ellis's REBT tends to rely more on verbal persuasion in order to achieve philosophical conversion based on logic, whereas cognitive therapy (according to Beck), tends to emphasize a more collaborative relationship between patient and therapist, whereby the clinician uses the Socratic method to foster patients' identification and active disputation of their cognitive distortions based on scientific empiricism.

Attributions

Another cognitive vulnerability model of depression that has engendered substantial interest is hopelessness theory (Abramson, Metalsky, & Alloy, 1989). According to this model, individuals are likely to experience depression when they harbor generalized expectations that highly desired outcomes are unlikely to occur or that highly aversive outcomes are likely to occur, and that one cannot change such circumstances. At the core of this theory are *attributions* or inferences that individuals make when confronted with stressful events. These include *internal* (the reason why such negative events occurred is due to the person's deficiencies), *stable* (these negative events will continue over time), and *global* (the consequences of the event will be widespread) attributions about such events. In other words, when experiencing a negative life event, persons who attribute the cause of such an event to stable, global, and internal reasons are at high risk for developing a sense of hopelessness and feelings of depression. Research investigating such hypotheses generally provides evidence in support of this theory's major tenets (Abramson et al., 2002).

Negative Thoughts and Cognitions

As a function of the impact that Beck's cognitive therapy and other cognitive models had on the field in general, researchers and clinicians became more interested in understanding how a variety of cognitive factors influence the development and maintenance of adult psychopathology across a multitude of clinical disorders. Negative cognitions have been identified as important etiopathogenic features of many different adult disorders (Dobson & Hamilton, 2003). In this section, we describe the types of negative thoughts and cognitions that have been implicated across several of these major psychological disorders.

Specific Phobias

Dysfunctional beliefs about the meaning attached to a specific phobic object can serve to maintain one's phobic response and anxiety. Distortions may be the result of phobic-specific schemata that reinforce the perceived dangerous nature of the feared stimuli (e.g., "I may have a heart attack if I go near the water!"). Cognitive distortions may include certain informational biases (e.g., selective attention and memory bias), exaggeration of threat, and the probability of danger. Disconfirming evidence tends not to be sought or registered. Distorted thinking, including catastrophic thoughts about the consequences associated with contact with a feared stimulus, can instigate fear and avoidance. Early learning experiences can engender specific beliefs about the feared stimuli that lead to selective focus, evaluation, and coping strategies regarding the feared stimuli (Beck, Emery, & Greenberg, 1985).

Panic Disorder

Panic disorder is often characterized as "fear of fear" given that patients fear the recurrence of a panic attack. Such fear can develop as a result of catastrophic interpretations of physiological arousal (Beck et al., 1985; Clark, 1986). Specifically, *internal* (e.g., bodily sensations) or *external* (e.g., a place where escape is difficult) triggers stimulate the perception of threat. This perceived danger leads to apprehension, which stimulates somatic sensations (e.g., increased heart rate). The physiological arousal is interpreted as catastrophic, leading to greater anticipation of danger, and the sequence continues. Thus, a vicious, self-perpetuating cycle maintains the fear (Clark, 1986).

Ambiguous somatic symptoms are often interpreted as forecasting impending doom (Clark, Salkovskis, Öst, & Breitholtz, 1992). Catastrophic interpretations can take many forms. For example, heart palpitations may be interpreted as having a heart attack, dizziness as impending fainting, a lump in one's throat as choking to death, or mental blocking as going crazy (Hoffart, 1993). Beck (1988) proposed that catastrophic interpretations fall into three categories: biological (e.g., death, heart attack), mental (e.g., insanity), and behavioral (e.g., loss of control).

Generalized Anxiety Disorder (GAD)

Wells (1995) differentiated between two different types of worries in persons with GAD. Type 1 worry refers to worrying about external (e.g., threatening situations) and internal (e.g., somatic sensations) events. In contrast, Type 2 worry signifies metacognitions about worry. These metacognitions refer to one's perceptions about the function of thoughts and feelings about worrying. The two types of worry are related, in that Type 1 worry stimulates the schema of worry (i.e., Type 2), which, in turn, results in greater Type 1 worry (e.g., distress, negative affect, somatic symptoms). Pathological worry as seen in GAD is related to Type 2 worry (Wells & Carter, 1999).

Wells (1995, 2002) emphasizes the importance of metacognitions in perpetuating worry. Specifically, patients with GAD hold certain beliefs about the function of worry. Such beliefs may entail a negative appraisal about worry including disturbing performance, exaggerating the problem, and causing emotional distress (e.g., "I am going to go crazy with all of the worry"). However, beliefs may also be positive. Thus, schemata about worry may represent beneficial aspects of worry that include motivational influence, helping analytical thinking, helping prepare for a potentially negative event, and superstitious or magical thinking that worry will *prevent* the negative event from occurring (e.g., "if I worry, then bad things won't happen").

Social Anxiety

Dysfunctional beliefs are pervasive in social phobia and include extreme standards of perfectionism in social performance (e.g., "I can't show any signs of fear"), conditional beliefs of others' reactions (e.g., "If I mess up, everyone will not like me"), and negative beliefs about oneself (e.g., "I am no good"). Such beliefs can enhance the anxiety and anxious behaviors, thus perpetuating the patient's overall distress. Some researchers posit that dysfunctional beliefs are at the root of social phobia. For example, Beck et al. (1985) theorize that extreme standards of perfectionism in social performance, conditional beliefs of others' beliefs, and negative beliefs about oneself all contribute to a self-fulfilling prophecy. Clark and Wells (1995) further attribute the development of anxiety symptoms and maladaptive coping strategies (e.g., avoidance) to self-focused attention, coupled with unrealistically high standards for social performance and the expectation for negative evaluation from others. Such thoughts and behaviors increase the perception of threats, resulting in a cyclical maintenance of social phobia.

Another theory invoking a cognitive conceptualization proposes that social phobia develops because of a discrepancy between one's sense of self and others' expected standards (Rapee & Heimberg, 1997). According to this framework, the person with social phobia focuses on negative behaviors (e.g., sweating) and the perceived menacing environment, producing an idea of how one "should" act. A comparison is then made between this "should view" and the distorted view of the patient's self-perceived behavior.

Obsessive-Compulsive Disorder (OCD)

Although more than 80 percent of the population have had intrusive thoughts at one time (Salkovskis, 1985), OCD is not as common. What distinguishes individuals with OCD from nonclinical populations is their misinterpretation regarding the significance of the appraisal of the thoughts as threatening. This threatening appraisal causes both distress and subsequent attempts to decrease the distress.

The threatening appraisal of intrusive thoughts is centered on beliefs about both *responsibility* (e.g., "If I don't wash my hands, I could get my family sick") and *danger* (e.g., "There are noxious germs everywhere"). Salkovskis (1985) proposed that individuals with OCD have overactive schemata of responsibility (e.g., "It is my responsibility to protect myself and my loved ones") and danger (e.g., "It is highly likely that something bad will happen"), which influence their dysfunctional interpretation of intrusive thoughts. Thus, such individuals *overestimate* the probability of danger, their amount of responsibility for the predicted danger, and the consequences for being responsible.

This sense of responsibility for impending danger is key to a cognitive formulation of OCD and serves to differentiate OCD from other anxiety disorders. This appraisal of responsibility results in, and is enhanced by, selective attention of danger, adverse mood (e.g., distress, negative affect), and maladaptive coping strategies (e.g., overt neutralizing behaviors, avoidance, thought suppression) (Salkovskis, 1999; Salkovskis et al., 2000). As a consequence, a perpetuating system maintaining the OCD symptoms comes to exist.

Related to the appraisal of responsibility is the belief held by many with OCD that negative thoughts cause negative events. For example, the mother who has intrusive thoughts about hurting her child believes thinking about this injury will cause her to perform it. This phenomenon has been termed *thought-action fusion* (Amir, Freshman, Ramsey, Neary, & Brigidi, 2001).

Post-Traumatic Stress Disorder (PTSD)

Several theories regarding the role that dysfunctional beliefs play in PTSD have been developed. For example, Ehlers and Clark (2000) suggest that the individual with PTSD processes the traumatic experience based on the interpretation that threat continues to be present. This expectation of threat results in selective attention to threatening stimuli, cognitive intrusions, physiological arousal, psychological distress, and maladaptive coping skills (e.g., avoidance). Using a cognitive constructivist paradigm, McCann and Pearlman (1990) posit that traumatization can result in cognitive conflicts, which give rise to the intrusive thoughts, nightmares, arousal, and avoidance. Specifically, there is a disturbance of specific schema (e.g., safety, trust, independence, power, esteem, and intimacy) about themselves and others that differs from cognitive schema held prior to the trauma. Resick and Schnicke (1993) further conjecture that patients are often unable to effectively cognitively process the traumatic event within their available schema. As a result, maladaptive *assimilation* (i.e., understanding of the event is changed in order to fit into preexisting schemata) or *accommodation* (i.e., previous beliefs are modified to match the event) may ensue. Ineffective cognitive processing can result in thought intrusion, distress, and maladaptive coping.

Borderline Personality Disorder (BPD)

Core dysfunctional beliefs are self-maintaining because they structure patients' perceptions and interpretations of events and cause them to habitually react in ways that confirm their (inaccurate) beliefs. Patients with BPD frequently exhibit such negative core beliefs. For example, Arntz et al. (2002) developed a list of 20 common BPD assumptions based on the writings of Beck and colleagues (1990), as well as Young (1999). Such core beliefs reveal themes of aloneness, dependency, emptiness, "badness," interpersonal distrust, and vulnerability. In addition, the high prevalence of sexual abuse among persons diagnosed with BPD can further lead to cognitive target symptoms associated with trauma, such as fears, distrust, and dissociative symptoms (Soloff, Lynch, & Kelly, 2002).

Anger Problems

Dysfunctional cognitions and distortions involving blame, unfairness, and suspiciousness operate in anger experiences. For example, "He ruined my presentation by asking stupid questions; he probably wants to get me fired," is an example of how an individual who is prone to episodes of anger may think when confronted with a poor work performance. When this cognitive tendency represents a pervasive way of thinking, even benign situations may be interpreted within the context of a hostile schema (e.g., "Why are you asking me that, why are you always on my case?"). Although there are few empirical studies that support this association concerning adults, research with adolescents has strongly documented the relationship between hostile interpretations and aggressive behavior (Dodge, Price, Bacoworowski, & Newman, 1990). Such beliefs can enhance anger and arousal, increase the urge to verbally or physically attack the perceived perpetrator of one's well-being, and thus perpetuate a vicious cycle.

Deffenbacher and colleagues (e.g., Deffenbacher, Dahlen, Lynch, Morris, & Gowensmith, 2000), as well as Novaco (e.g., Robins & Novaco, 1999), suggest that extreme standards of judging others, suspiciousness concerning the insulting or harmful intent of others, rigid and righteous beliefs about how others "should" act, overgeneralization, and personalization, all can be strong cognitive factors that serve to maintain angry or aggressive episodes within the context of an overall systems approach to understanding the construct of anger.

Another theory invoking a cognitive conceptualization proposes that anger and aggression emerge as a way to resolve the discrepancy between one's high self-opinion or high self-esteem when confronted with the reality that such high self-esteem is not warranted or perceived by others (Bushman & Baumeister, 1998). Contrary to the popular myth that angry people have low self-esteem, this framework suggests that persons with high self-esteem, who are also highly narcissistic, are at significant risk for disorders related to anger.

CLOSING REMARKS

In this chapter, those behavioral and cognitive processes that are traditionally invoked when positing cognitive-behavioral formulations of psychopathology were discussed, especially in relation to their etiological impact on psychological disorders. In particular, we described how associative learning, instrumental learning, imitative learning, and cognitive vulnerability factors each influence the emergence and maintenance of adult psychopathology.

Elsewhere we have argued that most adult disorders are likely to be caused and/or maintained by multiple factors, including biological, interpersonal, and sociocultural variables, in addition to the previous cognitive and behavioral processes (Nezu & Nezu, 1989; Nezu, Nezu, & Lombardo, 2001, 2004). As such, in attempting to provide a comprehensive and meaningful model of the etiopathogenesis of a specific disorder, it is likely that one needs to invoke how such variables influence the disorder directly and indirectly in their interactions between each other. However, it was the purpose of the present chapter to elucidate specific behavioral and cognitive factors and their influence on adult psychopathology, rather than to provide a comprehensive model of any particular diagnostic entity.

REFERENCES

Abramson, L. Y., Alloy, L. B., Hankin, B. L., Haeffel, G. J., MacCoon, D. G., & Gibb, B. E. (2002). Cognitive vulnerability-stress models of depression in a self-regulatory and psychobiological context. In I. H. Gotlib & C. L. Hammen (Eds.), *Handbook of depression* (pp. 268–294). New York: Guilford Press.

Abramson, L. Y., Metalsky, G. I., & Alloy, L. B. (1989). Hopelessness depression: A theory-based subtype of depression. *Psychological Review, 96,* 358–372.

Ader, R., & Cohen, N. (1975). Behaviorally conditioned immunosuppression. *Psychosomatic Medicine, 37,* 333–340.

Ader, R., & Cohen, N. (1993). Immunomodulation by conditioning: Recent developments. *International Journal of Neuroscience, 71,* 231–249.

Amir, N., Freshman, M., Ramsey, B., Neary, E., & Brigidi, B. (2001). Thought-action fusion in individuals with OCD symptoms. *Behaviour Research and Therapy, 39,* 765–776.

Anderson, C. A., Carnagey, N. L., & Eubanks, J. (2003). Exposure to violent media: The effects of songs with violent lyrics on aggressive thoughts and feelings. *Journal of Personality & Social Psychology, 84,* 960–971.

Arntz, A., van den Hoorn, M. A., Cornelius, J., Verheul, R., van den Bosch, M. A., & de Bie, A. J. H. T. (2002). Reliability and validity of the borderline personality disorder severity index. *Journal of Personality Disorders, 17,* 45–59.

Bandura, A. (1977). *Social learning theory.* Englewood Cliffs, NJ: Prentice Hall.

Barker, L. (2001). *Learning and behavior: Biological, psychological, and sociological perspectives* (3rd ed.). Upper Saddle River, NJ: Prentice Hall.

Beardslee, W. R., Versage, E. M., & Gladstone, T. R. (1998). Children of affectively ill parents: A review of the past 10 years. *Journal of the Academy of Child and Adolescent Psychiatry, 37,* 1134–1141.

Beck, A. T. (1976). *Cognitive therapy and the emotional disorders.* New York: International Universities Press.

Beck, A. T. (1988). Cognitive approaches to panic disorder: Theory and therapy. In S. Rachman & J. D. Maser (Eds.), *Panic: Psychological perspectives* (pp. 91–109). Hillsdale, NJ: Erlbaum.

Beck, A. T., Emery, G., & Greenberg, R. L. (1985). *Anxiety disorders and phobias: A cognitive perspective.* New York: Basic Books.

Beck, A. T., Freeman, A., & Associates. (1990). *Cognitive therapy of personality disorders.* New York: Guilford Press.

Beck, A. T., Rush, A. J., Shaw, B., & Emery, G. (1979). *Cognitive therapy of depression.* New York: Guilford Press.

Beck, J. (1995). *Cognitive therapy: Basics and beyond.* New York: Guilford Press.

Breen, L. J., Vulcano, B., & Dyck, D. G. (1979). Observational learning and sex roles in learned helplessness. *Psychological Reports, 44,* 135–144.

Bushman, B., & Baumeister, R. (1998). Threatened egotism, narcissism, self-esteem, and direct and misplaced aggression: Does self-love or self-hate lead to violence? *Journal of Personality and Social Psychology, 75,* 219–229.

Cheng, S. K. (2001). Life stress, problem solving, perfectionism, and depressive symptoms in Chinese. *Cognitive Therapy and Research, 25,* 303–310.

Clark, D. M. (1986). A cognitive approach to panic. *Behaviour Research and Therapy, 24,* 461–470.

Clark, D. M., Salkovskis, P. M., Öst, L. G., & Breitholtz, E. (1992). Misinterpretation of body sensations in panic disorder. *Journal of Consulting and Clinical Psychology, 65,* 203–213.

Clark, D. M., & Wells, A. (1995). A cognitive model of social phobia. In R. G. Heimberg & M. R. Liebowitz (Eds.), *Social phobia: Diagnosis, assessment, and treatment* (pp. 69–93). New York: Guilford Press.

Craighead, W. E., & Craighead, L. W. (2003). Behavioral and cognitive psychotherapy. In G. Stricker & T. A. Widiger (Eds.), *Clinical psychology* (pp. 279–300). New York: Wiley.

Craighead, W. E., Craighead, L. W., & Illardi, S. S. (1995). Behavior therapies in historical perspective. In B. M. Bongar & L. E. Beutler (Eds.), *Comprehensive textbook of psychotherapy: Vol. 1. Theory & practice* (pp. 64–83). New York: Oxford University Press.

Deffenbacher, J. L., Dahlen, E. R., Lynch, R. S., Morris, C. D., & Gowensmith, W. N. (2000). An application of Beck's cognitive therapy to general anger reductions. *Cognitive Therapy and Research, 6,* 689–697.

DeRubeis, R. J., Tang, T. Z., & Beck, A. T. (2001). Cognitive therapy. In K. S. Dobson (Ed.), *Handbook of cognitive-behavioral therapies* (pp. 349–392). New York: Guilford Press.

Dixon, W. A. (2000). Problem-solving appraisal and depression: Evidence for a recovery model. *Journal of Counseling and Development, 78,* 87–91.

Dixon, W. A., Heppner, P. P., Burnett, J. W., Anderson, W. P., & Wood, P. K. (1993). Distinguishing among antecedents, concomitants, and consequences of problem-solving appraisal and depressive symptoms. *Journal of Counseling Psychology, 40,* 357–364.

Dobson, K. S. (Ed.). (2001). *Handbook of cognitive-behavioral therapies.* New York: Guilford Press.

Dobson, K. S., & Hamilton, K. E. (2003). Cognitive restructuring: Behavioral tests of negative cognitions. In W. O'Donohue, J. E. Fisher, & S. C. Hayes (Eds.), *Cognitive behavior therapy: Applying empirically supported techniques in your practice* (pp. 84–88). New York: Wiley.

Dodge, K. A., Price, J. M., Bacoworowski, J., & Newman, J. P. (1990). Hostile attribution biases in severely aggressive adolescents. *Journal of Abnormal Psychology, 99,* 385–392.

D'Zurilla, T. J., & Nezu, A. M. (1999). *Problem-solving therapy: A social competence approach to clinical intervention* (2nd ed.). New York: Springer.

D'Zurilla, T. J., Nezu, A. M., & Maydeu-Olivares, A. (2004). Social problem solving: Theory and assessment. In E. C. Chang, T. J. D'Zurilla, & L. J. Sanna (Eds.), *Social problem solving: Theory, research, and training* (pp. 11–27). Washington, DC: American Psychological Association.

Ehlers, A., & Clark, D. M. (2000). A cognitive model of post-traumatic stress disorder. *Behaviour Research and Therapy, 38,* 319–345.

Ellis, A. (1962). *Reason and emotion in psychotherapy.* New York: Lyle Stuart.

Ellis, A. (2003). Cognitive restructuring of the disputing of irrational beliefs. In W. O'Donohue, J. E. Fisher, & S. C. Hayes (Eds.), *Cognitive behavior therapy: Applying empirically supported techniques in your practice* (pp. 79–84). New York: Wiley.

Eriksson, C. B., Vande Kemp, H., Gorsuch, R., Hoke, S., & Foy, D. W. (2001). Trauma exposure and PTSD symptoms in international relief and development personnel. *Journal of Traumatic Stress, 14,* 205–219.

Eysenck, H. J. (1960). *Behavior therapy and the neuroses.* Oxford, England: Pergamon Press.

Foa, E. B., & Franklin, M. E. (2001). Obsessive-compulsive disorder. In D. H. Barlow (Ed.), *Clinical handbook of psychological disorders: A step-by-step treatment manual* (3rd ed., pp. 209–263). New York: Guilford Press.

Frye, A. A., & Goodman, S. H. (2000). Which social problem-solving components buffer depression in adolescent girls? *Cognitive Therapy and Research, 24,* 637–650.

Funk, J. B., Baldacci, H. B., Pasold, T., & Baumgardner, J. (2004). Violence exposure in real-life, video games, television, movies, and the Internet: Is there desensitization? *Journal of Adolescence, 27,* 23–39.

Goldman, M. S. (2002). Risk for substance abuse: Memory as a common etiological pathway. *Psychological Science, 10,* 196–198.

Greenberg, B. S., Eastin, M., Hofschire, L., Lachlan, K., & Brownell, K. D. (2003). Portrayals of overweight and obese individuals on commercial television. *American Journal of Public Health, 93,* 1342–1348.

Halford, J. C., Gillespie, J., Brown, V., Pontin, E. E., & Dovey, T. M. (2004). Food advertisements induce food consumption in both lean and obese children. *Obesity Research, 12,* 171.

Hoffart, A. (1993). Cognitive treatments of agoraphobia: A critical evaluation of theoretical basis and outcome evidence. *Journal of Anxiety Disorders, 7,* 75–91.

Hollon, S. D., Haman, K. L., & Brown, L. L. (2002). Cognitive-behavioral treatment of depression. In I. H. Gotlib & C. L. Hammen (Eds.), *Handbook of depression* (pp. 383–403). New York: Guilford Press.

Huesmann, L. R. (1997). Observational learning of violent behavior: Social and biosocial processes. In *Biosocial bases of violence. NATO ASI series: Series A. Life sciences* (Vol. 292, pp. 69–88). New York: Plenum Press.

Huesmann, L. R., Moise-Titus, J., Podolski, C. L., & Eron, L. D. (2003). Longitudinal relations between children's exposure to TV violence and their aggressive and violent behavior in young adulthood: 1977–1992. *Developmental Psychology, 39,* 201–221.

Johnson, J. G., Cohen, P., Smailes, E. M., Kasen, S., & Brook, J. S. (2002). Television viewing and aggressive behavior during adolescence and adulthood. *Science, 295,* 2468–2471.

Kirkby, K. C., Menzies, R. G., Daniels, B. A., & Smith, K. L. (1995). Aetiology of spider phobia: Classificatory differences between two original instruments. *Behaviour Research and Therapy, 33,* 955–958.

Kleinknecht, R. A. (1994). Acquisition of blood, injury, and needle fears and phobias. *Behaviour Research and Therapy, 32,* 817–823.

Mahoney, M. J. (2003). Minding science: Constructivism and the discourse of inquiry. *Cognitive Therapy and Research, 27,* 105–123.

McCann, I. L., & Pearlman, L. A. (1990). *Psychological trauma and the adult survivor: Theory, therapy, and transformation.* New York: Brunner/Mazel.

Mineka, S., & Zinbarg, R. (1996). Conditioning and ethological models of anxiety disorders: Stress-in-dynamic-context anxiety models. In D. A. Hope (Ed.), *Nebraska Symposium on Motivation: Vol. 43. Perspectives on anxiety, panic, and fear: Current theory and research in motivation* (pp. 135–210). Lincoln: University of Nebraska Press.

Miner, R. C., & Dowd, E. T. (1996). An empirical test of the problem solving model of depression and its application to the prediction of anxiety and anger. *Counseling Psychology Quarterly, 9,* 163–176.

Mowrer, O. H. (1956). Two-factor learning theory reconsidered, with special reference to reinforcement and the concept of habit. *Psychological Review, 63,* 114–128.

Mowrer, O. H. (1960). *Learning and behavior.* New York: Wiley.

Nelson, B. S., & Wright, D. W. (1996). Understanding and treating post-traumatic stress disorder symptoms in female partners of veterans with PTSD. *Journal of Marital & Family Therapy, 22,* 455–467.

Nemeroff, C. J., & Karoly, P. (1991). Operant methods. In F. H. Kanfer & A. P. Goldstein (Eds.), *Helping people change: A textbook of methods* (4th ed., pp. 122–160). New York: Pergamon Press.

Nezu, A. M. (1986). Negative life stress and anxiety: Problem solving as a moderator variable. *Psychological Reports, 58,* 279–283.

Nezu, A. M. (1987). A problem-solving formulation of depression: A literature review and proposal of a pluralistic model. *Clinical Psychology Review, 7,* 122–144.

Nezu, A. M. (2004). Problem solving and behavior therapy revisited. *Behavior Therapy, 35,* 1–33.

Nezu, A. M., & D'Zurilla, T. J. (1989). Social problem solving and negative affective states. In P. C. Kendall & D. Watson (Eds.), *Anxiety and depression: Distinctive and overlapping features* (pp. 285–315). New York: Academic Press.

Nezu, A. M., D'Zurilla, T. J., Zwick, M. L., & Nezu, C. M. (2004). Problem-solving therapy for adults. In E. C. Chang, T. J. D'Zurilla, & L. J. Sanna (Eds.), *Social problem solving: Theory, research, and training* (pp. 171–191). Washington, DC: American Psychological Association.

Nezu, A. M., & Nezu, C. M. (Eds.). (1989). *Clinical decision making in behavior therapy: A problem-solving perspective.* Champaign, IL: Research Press.

Nezu, A. M., Nezu, C. M., & Lombardo, E. R. (2001). Cognitive-behavior therapy for medically unexplained symptoms: A critical review of the treatment literature. *Behavior Therapy, 32,* 537–583.

Nezu, A. M., Nezu, C. M., & Lombardo, E. R. (2004). *Cognitive-behavioral case formulation and treatment design: A problem-solving approach.* New York: Springer.

Nezu, A. M., Nezu, C. M., & Perri, M. G. (1989). *Problem-solving therapy for depression: Theory, research, and clinical guidelines.* New York: Wiley.

Nezu, A. M., Nezu, C. M., Saraydarian, L., Kalmar, K., & Ronan, G. F. (1986). Social problem solving as a moderating variable between negative life stress and depression. *Cognitive Therapy and Research, 10,* 489–498.

Nezu, A. M., & Ronan, G. F. (1985). Life stress, current problems, problem solving, and depressive symptoms: An integrative model. *Journal of Consulting and Clinical Psychology, 53,* 693–697.

Nezu, A. M., & Ronan, G. F. (1988). Problem solving as a moderator of stress-related depressive symptoms: A prospective analysis. *Journal of Counseling Psychology, 35,* 134–138.

Nezu, A. M., Wilkins, V. M., & Nezu, C. M. (2004). Social problem solving, stress, and negative affective conditions. In E. C. Chang, T. J. D'Zurilla, & L. J. Sanna (Eds.), *Social problem solving: Theory, research, and training* (pp. 49–65). Washington, DC: American Psychological Association.

Overmeier, B., & Seligman, M. E. P. (1967). Effects of inescapable shock upon subsequent escape and avoidance responding. *Journal of Comparative and Physiological Psychology, 63,* 28–33.

Pavlov, I. P. (1941). *Conditioned reflexes and psychiatry.* New York: International.

Priester, M. J., & Clum, G. A. (1993). Perceived problem-solving ability as a predictor of depression, hopelessness, and suicide ideation in a college population. *Journal of Counseling Psychology, 40,* 79–85.

Rapee, R. M. (2002). The development and modification of temperamental risk for anxiety disorders: Prevention of a lifetime of anxiety? *Biological Psychiatry, 52,* 947–957.

Rapee, R. M., & Heimberg, R. G. (1997). A cognitive-behavioral model of anxiety in social phobia. *Behaviour Research and Therapy, 35,* 741–756.

Rector, N. A., & Beck, A. T. (2002). Cognitive therapy for schizophrenia: From conceptualization to intervention. *Canadian Journal of Psychiatry, 47,* 39–48.

Resick, P. A., & Schnicke, M. K. (1993). *Cognitive processing therapy for rape victims: A treatment manual.* Newbury Park, CA: Sage.

Robins, S., & Novaco, R. W. (1999). System conceptualization and treatment of anger. *Journal of Clinical Psychology/In Session: Psychotherapy in Practice, 55,* 325–337.

Salkovskis, P. M. (1985). Obsessional-compulsive problems: A cognitive-behavioural analysis. *Behaviour Research and Therapy, 23,* 571–583.

Salkovskis, P. M. (1999). Understanding and treating obsessive-compulsive disorder. *Behaviour Research and Therapy, 37* (Suppl. 1), S29–S52.

Salkovskis, P. M., Wroe, A. L., Gledhill, A., Morrison, N., Forrester, E., Richards, C., et al. (2000). Responsibility attitudes and interpretations are characteristic of obsessive compulsive disorder. *Behaviour Research and Therapy, 38,* 347–372.

Schlenger, W. E., Caddell, J. M., Ebert, L., Jordan, B. K., Rourke, K. M., Wilson, D., et al. (2002). Psychological reactions to terrorist attacks: Findings from the National Study of Americans' Reactions to September 11. *Journal of the American Medical Association, 288,* 581–588.

Schmaling, K. B., Lehrer, P. M., Feldman, J. M., & Giardino, N. D. (2003). Asthma. In A. M. Nezu, C. M. Nezu, & P. A. Geller (Eds.), *Health psychology* (pp. 99–120). New York: Wiley.

Skinner, B. F. (1953). *Science and human behavior.* New York: Macmillan.

Soloff, P. H., Lynch, K. G., & Kelly, T. M. (2002). Childhood abuse as a risk factor for suicidal behavior in borderline personality disorder. *Journal of Personality Disorders, 16,* 201–214.

Staats, C. K., & Staats, A. W. (1959). Meaning established by classical conditioning. *Journal of Experimental Psychology, 54,* 74–80.

Stewart, S. H., Taylor, S., Jang, K. L., Cox, B. J., Watt, M. C., Fedoroff, I. C., et al. (2001). Causal modeling of relations among learning history, anxiety sensitivity, and panic attacks. *Behaviour Research and Therapy, 39,* 443–456.

Stockhorst, U., Mahl, N., Krueger, M., Huenig, A., Schottenfield-Naor, Y. Huebinger, A., et al. (2004). Classical conditioning and the conditionability of insulin and glucose effects in healthy humans. *Physiology & Behavior, 81,* 375–388.

Tapscott, M., Frick, P. J., Wootton, J., & Kruh, I. (1996). The intergenerational link to antisocial behavior: Effects of paternal contact. *Journal of Child & Family Studies, 5,* 229–240.

Thorndike, E. L. (1932). *Fundamentals of learning.* New York: Columbia University Press.

Tiggemann, M., Gardiner, M., & Slater, A. (2000). "I would rather be size 10 than have straight A's": A focus group study of adolescent girls' wish to be thinner. *Journal of Adolescence, 23,* 645–659.

Tiggemann, M., & Slater, A. (2004). Thin ideals in music television: A source of social comparison and body dissatisfaction. *International Journal of Eating Disorders, 35,* 48–58.

Turk, D. C., & Okiguji, A. (2003). Pain management. In A. M. Nezu, C. M. Nezu, & P. A. Geller (Eds.), *Health psychology* (pp. 293–316). New York: Wiley.

Wakfield, M., Flay, B., Nichter, M., & Giovino, G. (2003). Role of the media in influencing trajectories of youth smoking. *Addiction, 98,* 79–103.

Watson, J. B., & Raynor, R. (1920). Conditioned emotional reactions. *Journal of Experimental Psychology, 3,* 1–14.

Wells, A. (1995). Meta-cognition and worry: A cognitive model of generalized anxiety disorder. *Behavioural and Cognitive Psychotherapy, 23,* 301–320.

Wells, A. (2002). Worry, metacognition, and GAD: Nature, consequences, and treatment. *Journal of Cognitive Psychotherapy, 16,* 179–192.

Wells, A., & Carter, K. (1999). Preliminary tests of a cognitive model of generalized anxiety disorder. *Behaviour Research and Therapy, 37,* 585–594.

Wolpe, J. (1958). *Psychotherapy by reciprocal inhibition.* Stanford, CA: Stanford University Press.

Young, J. E. (1999). *Cognitive therapy for personality disorders: A schema-focused approach* (3rd ed.). Sarasota, FL: Professional Resource Exchange.

CHAPTER 4

Genetic Influences

KERRY L. JANG

INTRODUCTION

Behavior does not exist in isolation. The focus of researchers and clinicians alike are the patterns of relationships between behaviors that are used to develop cohesive descriptions of individual disorders. The most consistent patterns have been formalized into diagnostic systems like the *Diagnostic and Statistical Manual for Mental Disorders* (e.g., *DSM-IV;* APA, 1994) and *International Classification of Disease* (e.g., *ICD-10;* WHO, 1992) as diagnostic categories. Even diagnoses do not lead a solitary existence. Antisocial personality disorder is frequently diagnosed with alcohol abuse and dependence; and the anxiety disorders, such as post-traumatic stress disorder (PTSD), is frequently diagnosed with depression. The observed covariation of disorders is referred to as *comorbidity,* which is defined as "... any distinct additional clinical entity that existed or that may occur during the clinical course of a patient who has the index disease under study" (Feinstein, 1970, pp. 456–457).

Comorbidity has become a central issue in psychopathology research. On the one hand, it is considered by many to be no more than a statistical artifact attributable to the problem of *criterion overlap* in which criteria used to diagnose one disorder are also used to define several others. For example, Mineka, Watson, and Clark (1998) suggest that the fact that sleep disturbances (i.e., hypersomnia or insomnia) are used to diagnose major depressive episode as well as generalized anxiety disorder (GAD) artifactually raises the co-occurrence of the disorders. On the other hand, comorbidity may be more than nuisance covariance that should be ignored or eradicated. Its presence could be an important indication that today's classification and diagnostic systems are lacking in parsimony (Krueger, 1999).

A potential resolution of this question may be possible with a determination of what causes comorbidity. One explanation for why criterion overlap exists is because it reflects the fact that two disorders share a common genetic basis—generically referred to as *pleiotropy*. Not only can two or more disorders be in a pleiotropic relationship, their relationship may also be influenced by the same environmental factors, such as chronic or acute exposure to events and experiences (e.g., loss of a cherished object or person whose impact is not limited to single behavior). It is important to note that the study of the etiological basis of comorbidity is not restricted to the relationship between two or more different disorders, but also between different forms of the same disorder.

For example, to what extent are normal shyness and social phobia caused by the same genetic and environmental factors? Are normal variations in mood related to depression and how? This raises the associated question of what causes normal forms of behavior to cross the threshold and develop into clinically significant and debilitating forms? From the perspective of geneticists, one possible hypothesis to investigate is whether the extreme behavior is attributable to alternate forms of an allele (e.g., dominant versus recessive forms of the genes controlling dopamine transport) or possibly to completely different genes altogether. Geneticists are also interested if nongenetic factors, such exposures to critical experiences, are responsible. Do these critical exposures have a direct effect on behavior? Or does exposure to critical environments somehow mediate gene function? On the other hand, do genes mediate exposure to specific kinds of environments that increase the risk for the development of the disorder? All of these questions fall under the purview of genetics.

From the perspective of geneticists, the study of psychopathology is a threefold task. The first task is to determine if and how much of a role genetics plays in the variability of a single disorder relative to the environment. This covers the search for the susceptibility gene itself to estimating the effect (indexed by the heritability coefficient, h^2) of all of the genes that contribute to individual differences in a disorder. The second task is to expand on the univariate results to the multivariate case to study the pleiotropic effect of any identified susceptibility genes with other disorders. Are the genes identified in schizophrenics also found among bipolar depressives? Do the effects of the genes causing individual differences on psychotic behavior also cause variability in mood? This task also encompasses studies of what lies at the interface of normal and abnormal behavior, for example are there specific genes and/or environmental influences for extreme forms of behavior?

Studying the genetic and environmental influences in common between or within disorders addresses only half of the research problem. The remainder is what differentiates disorders from one another and normal from abnormal forms. What are the genetic and environmental factors unique to each disorder? How do genetic and environmental influences act together in the development of disorder? Thus, the third task is to identify specific genetic and environmental factors that increase the risk for disorder, but also the mechanisms of gene-environment interplay. This chapter will review the behavioral methods used to undertake these three tasks illustrated by some recent examples from the literature and will discuss the impact of some findings and some of the limitations of methods discovered in their use.

THE METHODS OF BEHAVIORAL GENETICISTS

Pleiotropy comes in two different but closely interrelated forms. The first is *genetic pleiotropy* and the other is *statistical pleiotropy*. The goal of genetic pleiotropy is to identify the actual alleles that influence two or more conditions. Once a gene is linked to a specific disorder, the biochemistry associated with the gene becomes the focus to determine the intracellular mechanisms by which abnormal behavior is produced. Many of the researchers in this field of behavioral genetics are trained in medical genetics and other medical specialties. Their approach is to work from the "bottom up," with the fundamental unit of analysis being the gene and its variants.

It is not necessary to know the actual genes to study their effects—the influence genes have on creating individual differences in behavior relative to the influences of learning, experience, and environmental conditions. The study of genetic effects characterizes studies of statistical pleiotropy. The study of genetic effects is a "top down" approach that begins with recognized disorders (e.g., the symptoms and signs of mental illness) and uses genetically informative samples, such as twins or adoptees, to determine if individual differences in the disorder are due to genetic variations or changes in environmental conditions.

Genetic Pleiotropy

Studies of genetic pleiotropy begin by searching for the genes implicated in a disorder. One of the most familiar methods is *linkage analysis* that utilizes the known locations of genes as road signs (markers) for the disease gene to obtain an approximate idea of where it is located on a chromosome. For example, if the disease gene is suspected to be on a particular chromosome, a known gene on that chromosome is selected as a marker. The marker does not have to be involved with the disorder, just in close physical proximity to location where the disease gene is hypothesized to occupy. Common markers include the genes coding for blood groups.

Linkage Methods

According to Mendel's law of genetics, the transmission of genes from parent to offspring is random. Thus, if the disease and marker genes were far apart (e.g., on different chromosomes), the probability that they would be transmitted together from parent to offspring is zero. If the disease and marker genes were in close physical proximity, the probability of being transmitted together is greater than zero. A statistic called the *log probability ratio score* (LOD score) is used to estimate the actual likelihood that a disease and marker gene will be transmitted together in a high-risk family. This probability score is based on the frequency of the disorder (e.g., diagnosis of schizophrenia) and the frequency of the marker gene among family members whose psychiatric history has been traced across a number of generations of relations whose degree of genetic relatedness is known. LOD scores of 3.0 are traditionally considered the statistically significant threshold to indicate that the disease and marker genes are truly linked (for computational formulas, see King, Rotter, & Motulsky, 1992).

Linkage methods work best when the affected status of each member of a family can be assigned unequivocally. Any misdiagnosis (e.g., caused by poor assessment methods, uncertainty in diagnostic criteria, or the presence of a comorbid disorder) or missing data (e.g., affected status of a long-dead relative is unknown or members are unwilling to participate), even for a single person, can have a huge impact on the LOD score. Linkage methods are best suited for disorders caused by relatively few genes of large effect. Despite the volume of linkage research, for mental disorders, there have been relatively few replicable results (for detailed reviews, see McGuffin, Owen, & Gottesman, 2002), suggesting that psychopathology is truly multifactorial in nature—influenced by several genes of small effect (polygenic) in addition to a multitude of environmental factors.

Association Methods

Polygenic disorders are best approached using association methods that do not rely on the analysis of family pedigrees but rather simply test if the hypothesized disease gene is found in more affected than nonaffected individuals. The association of the disorder and the disease gene is indexed with a correlation coefficient (r). The basic approach of this method correlates the presence or absence of the hypothesized disease gene with presence or absence of a disorder in a sample of individuals. By using different types of correlation coefficients, quantitative data (e.g., scores on a mood rating scale that does not characterize behavior as simply *present* or *absent*) can be analyzed with equal ease. Association studies using quantitative data are referred to as *quantitative trait loci* or QTL analyses (for a detailed review of QTL methods, see Plomin, DeFries, Craig, & McGuffin, 2003).

Unlike linkage studies, association studies require that the gene selected for analysis (called a *candidate gene*) is actually involved in the disorder of interest. Candidate genes can be selected on the basis of predictions made by theory. For example, Cloninger and colleagues' (Cloninger, 1986; Cloninger, Svrakic, & Przybeck, 1993) Biosocial Model of Personality was used to select candidate genes for personality. This model hypothesized that each of the major personality domains they identified were controlled by genetically based monoamine neurotransmitter systems: serotonin for harm avoidance, dopamine for novelty seeking, and norepinephrine for reward dependence. As a result of this theory, one of the very first genetic associations in personality was found between the dopamine DRD4 gene and scores on measures of novelty seeking (Cloninger, Adolfsson, & Svrakic, 1996).

Candidates are also selected on the basis of results of biochemical studies showing that levels of specific neurotransmitters actually do in fact influence behavior. For example, Stein, Chartier, Kozak, King, & Kennedy (1998) selected the serotonin transporter (5HTT on chromosome 17) and receptor ($5HT_{2A}R$ on chromosome 13) genes as candidates for social phobia. These genes were selected because: (1) social phobia has been shown to be responsive to selective serotonin reuptake inhibitors (SSRIs) that cause changes in the 5-HTT gene; (2) generalized social phobia is frequently comorbid with major depressive episode, panic disorder, and obsessive-compulsive disorder (OCD), all of which have been the focus of intensive study via the serotonin system; and (3) social phobics have elevated scores on harm avoidance that has been associated with $5HT_{2A}R$ binding to blood platelets. In the absence of a suitable candidate, a *genome scan* can be conducted to identify possible susceptibility genes. This method systematically associates all of the genes (for example, 25 evenly spaced genes from every single chromosome) with disease status. The limitation of genome scans is that they require very large sample sizes of affected people and independent replications to reduce the number of false positives resulting from testing so many genes.

Genetic Comorbidity

Once the susceptibility gene for a disorder has been identified, the next step is to determine if it is implicated in another disorder. One way this is accomplished is to show that people who meet the criteria for two disorders possess the disease gene at significantly different frequencies compared to a matched control sample of unaffected individuals or individuals diagnosed with either one of the disorders. Another way is to demonstrate that the genes for one disorder are implicated in another. For example, recent reviews of bipolar depression have noted several significant linkages on chromosome 18p (see Gershon et al., 1998) as well as schizophrenia (see Gershon, 2000), and both disorders have also been linked to chromosome 13q (Detera-Wadleigh et al., 1999; Blouin et al., 1998). Gershon (2000) refers to these as *nonspecific psychopathology genes,* genes that are shared by families but do not coaggregate in families. Such genes challenge the validity of current diagnostic systems in suggesting that a general liability to psychopathology is inherited instead rather than specific disorders. The nature of this vulnerability is presently unclear, but if these genes exist their identification would lead to an understanding of the biology of susceptibility, new diagnostic tests for this vulnerability, and focus attention on the genetic and environmental factors that differentiate various manifestations of disorder.

Statistical Pleiotropy: Estimating Genetic Effect

The search for susceptibility genes has produced many tantalizing leads but replicable results have been elusive. Rutter (2002) discusses the fact that when reliable associations and linkages are found, it would a long time before knowledge of these genes would have any clinical impact because outside of knowing which gene(s) are implicated, little is known about what the gene actually does. Once the gene is identified, a great deal of work is required to determine which genes are switched on in particular cells to studies of protein interplay within cells, among other things (for a full discussion, see Rutter, 2002). However, not being able to find the specific genes does not preclude studying their effect on behavior and joint effects across multiple behaviors because whatever the genes are, they are still there and exerting an influence that can be readily measured.

A popular and powerful design to study genetic effects is the adoption study that compares adopted-away children and their biological parents. Because adopted-away children were raised apart from their biological parents, any similarities between them can only be due to the genes they share. Other popular methods compare the similarities between biological siblings, or parents and their offspring. These family designs are less powerful because they confound genetic and environmental effects. Siblings, for example, share both genes (50 percent) and the environments in which they were raised. However, these studies are extremely useful in identifying which disorders "run in families."

One of the most popular indexes of genetic effect is the heritability coefficient (h^2) that estimates the proportion (percent) of the observed variability in a disorder (or any measure of behavior) that is directly attributable to genetic differences between people. Estimates of h^2 are readily obtained by comparing the similarity (indexed by r) of monozygotic (MZ) to dizygotic (DZ) twins on a disorder of interest. A higher within-pair MZ correlation ($r_{MZ\ TWIN1.TWIN2}$) compared to the within-pair DZ correlation ($r_{DZ\ TWIN1.TWIN2}$) suggests that genetic influences are implicated because MZ twins share all of their genes in common whereas DZ twins share only approximately half. When $r_{MZ\ TWIN1.TWIN2} = r_{DZ\ TWIN1.TWIN2}$, no genetic influences are inferred because despite the twofold greater genetic similarity of MZ twins, their observed similarity is that of the DZ twins. A major assumption of the twin method is that the observed twin similarities are due to levels of genetic similarity only. The r_{MZ} could be spuriously inflated if MZ twins were treated more similarly than DZ twins (e.g., are dressed alike more often). Most twin studies test and correct their data to ensure that factors like "being dressed alike" or "spending more time together" does not contribute to twin similarity (for a discussion, see Boomsma, Martin, & Machin, 1997).

Just as genetic effects can be estimated, twin data also allow the direct estimation of environmental effects. These include the influence of common or shared family environment on a single variable (c^2) or on two variables (r_C) and nonshared family environmental effects (e^2 and r_E). Shared environmental influences distinguish the general environment of one family from another and influence all children within a family to the same degree (Rowe, 1994). A frequently used example of c^2 is total family income measured in dollars that affects each person within the family the same way and differentiates between families in a sample. Nonshared environmental influences are defined as any experience, milieu, or circumstance—virtually anything that causes children from the same family to be different from one another (see Heatherington, Reiss, & Plomin, 1994). Nonshared environmental influences are not solely random events (e.g., if one twin is involved in a motor vehicle accident and the other is not). It also includes experiences that systematically differentiate people from one another (e.g., one twin is systematically favored by parents over the other).

In the multivariate case, genetic effects in common to two variables—statistical pleiotropy—are indicated when the MZ cross-correlation (the correlation between one twin's score on one of the variables and the other twin's score on the other variable) exceeds the DZ cross-correlation. Statistical pleiotropy is indexed by the genetic correlation coefficient, r_G, which varies between -1.0 and $+1.0$ and is interpreted like any other correlation coefficient. The same indexes can be estimated to shared (r_C) and nonshared environmental (r_E) influences in common to two or more variables. The relationship between all these terms is neatly summarized by the equation:

$$r_{x.y} = (h_X \cdot h_Y \cdot r_G) + (c_X \cdot c_Y \cdot r_C) \\ + (e_X \cdot e_Y \cdot r_E) \qquad [\text{Equation 1}]$$

This expression states that the observed relationship between two measured variables, X and Y, ($r_{x.y}$) is a direct function of the degree to which genetic and environmental factors independently and jointly influence each. The ability to express the relationships between observed variables and their hypothesized causes in terms of mathematic equations permits the methods of statistical techniques, such as causal modeling (also known as path modeling or structural equation modeling) to be used not only estimate the magnitude of each term in the equation (e.g., h_X, r_E, etc.), but also tests if the hypothesized relationship between the terms is also true. For example, is $r_{x.y} = (h_X \cdot h_Y \cdot r_G) = (e_X \cdot e_Y \cdot r_E)$ [Equation 2] or is $r_{x.y} = (c_X \cdot c_Y \cdot r_C) + (e_X \cdot e_Y \cdot r_E)$ [Equation 3]? Figure 4.1 presents a path model version of Equation 2 to describe the relationship between three variables.

In the literature, Figure 4.1 is referred to as a *Cholesky* or *triangular decomposition*. The three boxes represent actual scores for three variables; for example, number of major depressive episodes, diagnosis of OCD, and anxiety. The first genetic component (G_1) estimates how much of the additive genetic variance is common to depression, OCD, and anxiety; the second genetic component (G_2) estimates how much is in common to OCD and anxiety; and finally the third component (G_3) estimates the genetic factors on anxiety only. The same effects are estimated for the nonshared environment factors (E_1, E_2, and E_3). The values of these paths are standardized to provide estimates of r_G and r_E between all three disorders. Note, too, that this path model can be used to analyze DNA data as discussed previously. For example, that G_1, G_2, and G_3 could represent the different forms of the serotonin transport genes. Jang et al. (2001) used such a model to show that the personality traits neuroticism and agreeable-

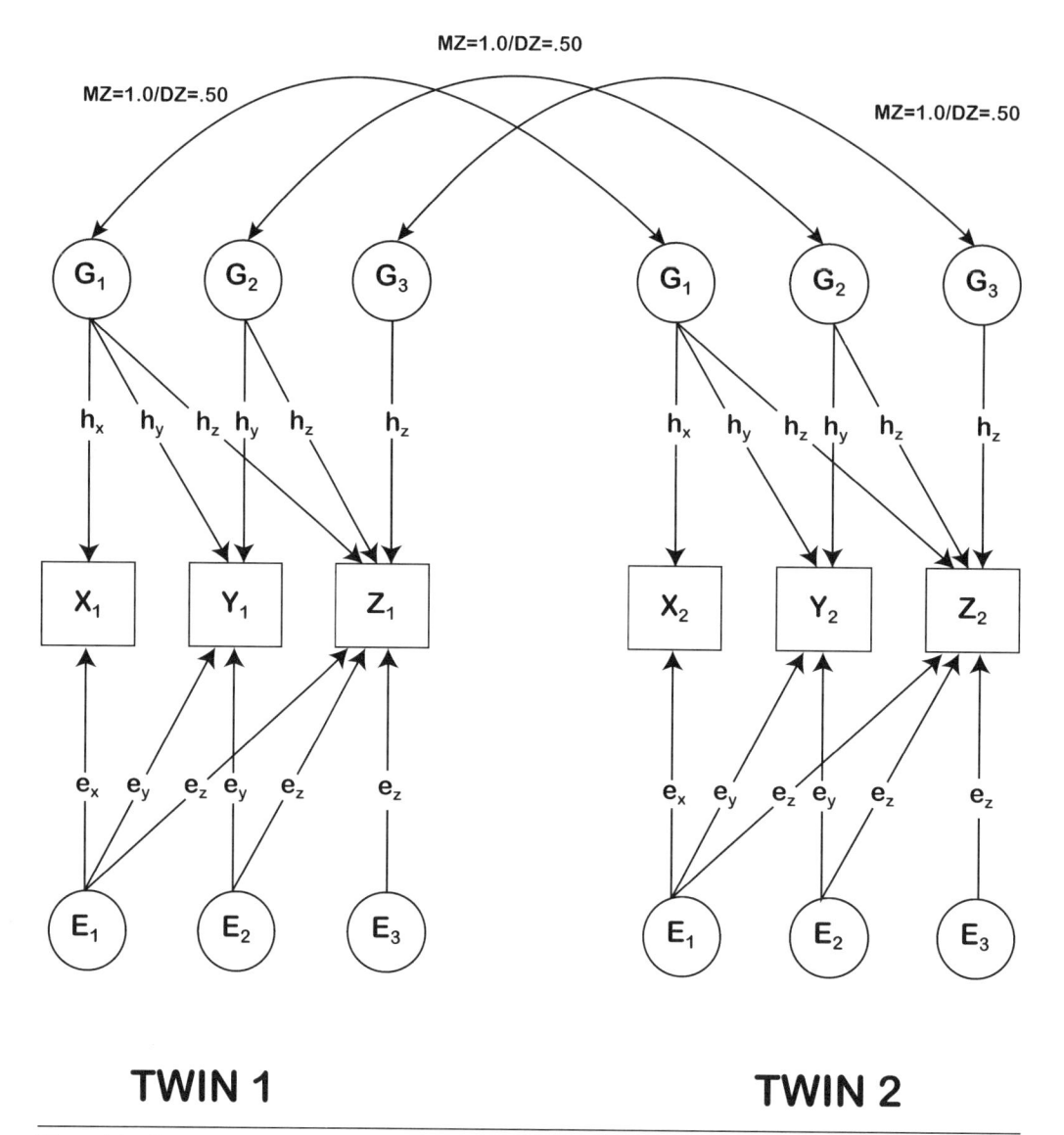

Figure 4.1 Cholesky decomposition. The general form of this path model is used to estimate genetic and environmental correlation coefficients. The labels G_1 to G_3 represent the genetic factors on each variable indexed by the paths marked h_x to h_z; similarly, the labels E_1 to E_3 represent the nonshared environmental factors on each variable indexed by the paths marked e_x to e_z. Common family environmental effects are not shown on this figure for clarity; MZ = monozygotic twins; DZ = dizygotic twins.

ness were influenced (in opposite directions) by variations in the 5-HTTLPR alleles.

Recent Applications

The literature in psychology and psychiatry abound with examples of this type of research. One application has been to understand the often observed relationship between substance use problems and antisocial personality. Grove et al. (1990) showed that this relationship had a genetic basis. The genetic correlation (r_G) between alcohol problems and childhood antisocial behavior was .54, and .75 with adult antisocial behavior. Some recent research (Jang, Vernon, & Livesley, 2000) has shown that narcissistic behavior, such as grandiosity ($r_G = .88$) and attention seeking ($r_G = .87$) as well as conduct disorder (e.g., failure to adopt social norms $r_G = .85$ and conduct problems $r_G = .78$) were more related to alcohol use problems than to sensation seeking aspects of antisocial personality such as recklessness ($r_G = .45$), impulsivity ($r_G = .45$), or stimulus seeking ($r_G = .33$).

This simple method has also been found to be useful to address diagnostic issues. For example, currently social phobia (*DSM* Axis I) and avoidant personality disorder (*DSM* Axis II) are classified and treated as separate disorders. However, family and community-based research suggests that social phobia is part of a continuum bounded by mild (i.e., normative) shyness at one end and avoidant personality disorder at the other (e.g., Tillfors, Furmark, & Ekselius, 2001), suggesting they represent the extremes of a single disorder. To test this hypothesis, Stein, Jang, and Livesley (2002) estimated the genetic correlations between the normal fear of being evaluated in public, a cognitive dimension central to social phobia, and traits delineating avoidant personality disorder (e.g., submissiveness, anxiousness, social avoidance).

The first set of analyses found that the fear was heritable ($h^2 = 48$ percent) with multivariate analyses showing that these genetic influences substantially overlapped with the genetic influences on avoidant personality disorder traits (r_Gs ranging from 0.78–0.80). The results show that the normal fear of being negatively evaluated in public is heritable and that many of the same genes that influence negative evaluation fears appear to influence a cluster of anxiety-related personality characteristics, supporting the growing consensus that social phobia on Axis I and avoidant personality disorder on Axis II are really classifying the same construct and that the argument that the division of Axis I and Axis II disorders, although heuristically convenient, is often not supported empirically (e.g., Widiger, 2003).

Normal and Abnormal Behavior

Widiger, Verheul, and van den Brink (1999) commented that there is little disagreement among personality disorder researchers that normal and abnormal personality are related but there is little agreement as to why they are related. Comments of this sort (e.g., what is the relationship between normal mood variation and clinical depression; or what is the relationship between nine diagnostic criteria and normal mood) are readily examined by computing estimates of r_G, r_C, and r_E. Personality research has used this approach extensively to test the validity of the *dimensional model of personality disorder* that states that personality disorder represents the extremes of normal personality function. This model has received some empirical support demonstrating that measures of normal and abnormal personality share a common genetic basis. For example, Jang and Livesley (1999) found several large genetic correlations, in predictable directions, between the NEO-PI-R (Costa & McCrae, 1992), a popular measure of normal personality, and a scale assessing traits delineating personality disorder. Between neuroticism and the personality disorder traits anxiousness, submissiveness, cognitive distortion, identity problems, and affective lability, the r_Gs ranged from .61 to .81. Not surprisingly, r_G between conscientiousness and compulsivity was .52; between extraversion and social avoidance was −.65; and between agreeableness and callousness and suspiciousness at −.65 and −.57, respectively. Markon, Krueger, Bouchard, and Gottesman (2002) reported similar findings between the scales of the Minnesota Multiphasic Personality Inventory and the Multidimensional Personality Questionnaire, a scale of normal range personality function (r_G range = .47 to .96). The most interesting aspect to both studies is that the environmental correlations between measures of normal and abnormal personality were uniformly low, suggesting that the environmental factors influencing normal and abnormal personality are unique, and that a role of the environment is to differentiate between normal and abnormal forms.

Because genetic and environmental correlations have the same properties as any other kind of correlation coefficient, they can be factored. This has been useful in examining the organization of symptoms or traits as a test of the dimensional model. For example, Livesley, Jang, and Vernon (1998) tested if the organization of traits delineating personality disorder was the same across a sample of personality-disordered patients and a normal control group. The dimensional model would be supported if the organization of traits were found to be the same across groups. Consistent with predictions made from the dimensional model, each group would possess the same traits and differ on them only in terms of how high or low they scored on the traits. A dimensional model would not be supported if the organization of traits were different, suggesting that the traits possessed by normal and abnormal populations are different. This study also estimated the genetic and environmental correlations between the traits using data from a twin sample. In this way, it is possible to test if the observed organization of traits reflects the underlying genetic and/or environmental organization.

The phenotypic correlations for the non twin samples and the phenotypic, genetic and environmental correlations in the twin sample between the traits were computed and factored. Four factors were extracted from each set of correlations and the congruency coefficients were extremely high, ranging from .94 to .98, providing support for the dimensional model. Moreover, the four factors extracted resembled four of the five major traits often found in studies of normal personality, lending further support. The four basic personality disorder traits are: (1) emotional dysregulation that resembles extreme aspects of normal trait neuroticism; (2) inhibition that resembles the negative end of extraversion; (3) dissocial behavior that forms the negative extreme of agreeableness; and (4) conscientiousness that resembles the extreme end of conscientiousness.

Only the normal personality trait openness to experience does not appear to have a corresponding pathological extreme.

The Structure of Comorbidity

Estimating r_G and r_E is just the beginning. Although they provide an index of why two or more variables are related, they say little about how disorders are organized. For example, are comorbid disorders always inherited together as part of a broad syndrome? Such an organization is shown in Figure 4.2, popularly known as a *common pathway model*. The figure is divided into three sections marked A, B, and C. Focusing attention on section B to start with, the boxes in the diagram contain the actual scores measured on a sample of people. These can be severity ratings on a set of symptoms of depression for example, or the presence or absence of different diagnoses (e.g., generalized anxiety disorder [GAD], alcohol dependence and major depressive episode). A proportion of the observed covariance of these variables is mediated by a higher order construct (marked P). The existence of this higher order construct is unmeasured and is inferred by the degree to which the measured variables appear together. This portion of Figure 4.2 is the same as a contemporary factor analysis model that extracts what is in common to a set of variables.

What makes Figure 4.2 special is the superimposing of genetic and environmental influences (sections A and C). In this figure, the addition of genetic and environmental effects transforms the construct P into a real entity that has a basis in biology. The genetic and environmental effect on P filters down to influence the variability of each of the measured variables. Note that the model allows for the each variable to be influenced by genetic and environmental factors that are unique to each. However, what is important is the fact that all variables are mediated to some extent by the common genetic and environmental factors. For psychiatric classification and treatment, this means that inheriting the risk for one variable automatically implies inheriting the risk for the remainder. Moreover, each symptom or disorder is simply an exemplar of P and each diagnosis represents a slightly different way of measuring the same thing.

The alternative to the common pathways model is one that does away with P and in so doing states that psychopathology is not inherited as a single genetically based syndrome. The basic form of this model is illustrated in Figure 4.3 and is commonly known as an *independent pathways model*. Like the common pathway model, the observed intercorrelation between observed variables is hypothesized to be due to the fact that each is directly influenced by genetic and experiential factors in common. This model allows for the possibility that inheriting the genes for one disorder does not automatically mean that a person has inherited the risk for all the others. As can be seen in Figure 4.3, two disorders may appear comorbid not because they share a common genetic basis (e.g., variables X and Z), but rather only because each shares a common genetic basis with a third variable on different genes (variable Y). This model shifts attention from the higher order construct to the individual disorders.

Comparing the relative fit of the common and independent pathway models has been used to address questions about the organization of common mental disorders. Nongenetic studies of the organization of mental disorder by Kreuger (1999) and Vollebergh et al. (2001) have found that the observed covariance of the ten most commonly diagnosed *DSM-III-R* mental disorders could be explained by three underlying factors (organized like the center portion of the diagram in Figure 2). The first factor, named *anxious misery* was defined by the comorbid relationship between major depressive episode, dysthymia, and GAD diagnoses. The second factor was called *fear* because of the close interrelationships between the phobia diagnoses (social, simple, and agoraphobia) and panic disorder. The third factor, named *externalizing disorder*, was defined by the covariance of the alcohol dependence, drug dependence, and antisocial personality disorder. An immediate implication of this organization is that it challenges the validity of the axial structure of *DSM* by suggesting the axes should be modified to reflect these factors, in contrast to the present system in which all but the personality disorders and mental retardation fall on a single axis (Krueger, McGue, & Iacono, 2001).

One of the first investigations of the genetic basis of this organization focused on the validating the Externalizing factor (Krueger et al., 2002). A sample of more than 600 twin pairs were assessed for alcohol dependence, drug dependence, adolescent antisocial behavior and conduct disorder to *DSM-III-R* criteria. They found that the covariance of these measures was a function of a single, genetically based higher order construct similar to that illustrated in Figure 4.2, suggesting that a broad syndrome is inherited. However, Kendler, Prescott, Myers, and Neale (2003) analyses suggested a genetically based higher order construct (e.g., akin to P as in Figure 4.2) was not required to explain the covariance. Their sample consisted of 5,600 twins interviewed on the rate of lifetime *DSM-III-R* diagnoses for major depression, GAD, adult antisocial behavior, conduct disorder, any phobia, *DSM-IV* alcohol dependence and drug abuse/dependence. They found that an independent pathways model, similar in form to that illustrated in Figure 4.3 that specified two genetic factors, two shared environmental factors, and two nonshared environmental factors directly influenced the covariance of

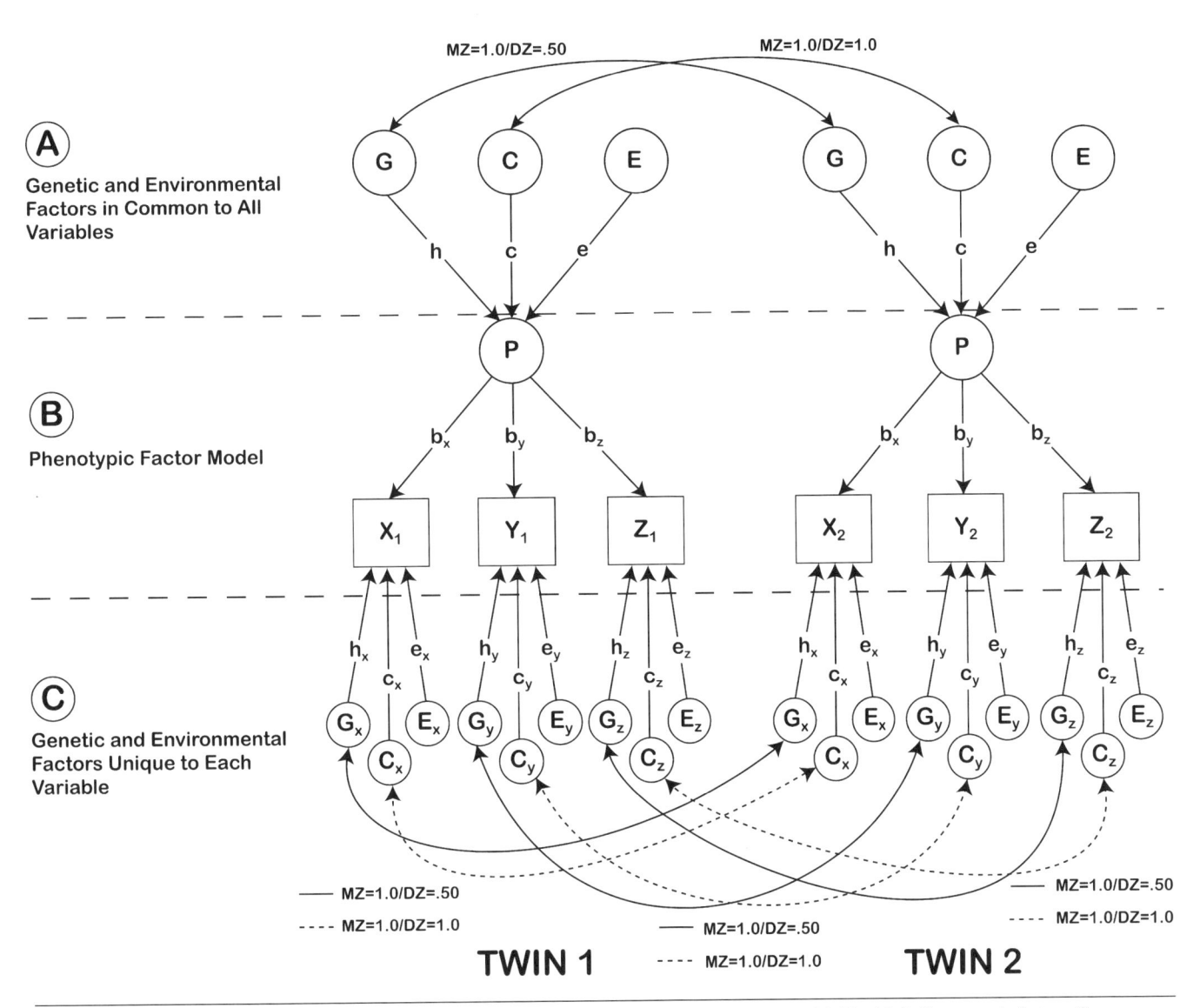

Figure 4.2 Common pathway model. The figure illustrates the general form of the common pathway model. The labels G = genetic factors, C = common family environmental factors, E = nonshared environmental factors; the influence of G, C, and E effects common and unique to each variable are indexed by the paths marked h to e, h_x to h_z, c_x to c_z, and e_x to e_z as appropriate; the paths marked b_x, b_y, and b_z represent the observed loadings of each variable on the latent factor P; MZ = monozygotic twins; DZ = dizygotic twins.

the different diagnoses. These results suggest that *anxious misery, fear,* and *externalizing disorder* are best conceptualized as simple descriptive labels to describe the pleiotropic effect of genes as opposed to veridical, genetically based entities.

So which is correct? Are syndromes inherited as a unitary entity or are they convenient names for frequently comorbid disorders that share a common genetic basis? These two studies highlight important strengths and weaknesses of the genetic models used to study comorbidity. On the one hand, the models explain why comorbidity exists and provides, in principle, the means to study the organization of variables. Conversely, they illustrate the phenomenon that two divergent models can provide an equally satisfactory explanation to the same data. A recent multivariate genetic analysis of behavioral disinhibition by Young, Stallings, Corley, Krauter, and Hewitt (2000) nicely illustrates this phenomenon. Levels of substance experimentation, novelty seeking, and *DSM-IV* symptom count for conduct disorder and attention-deficit/hyperactivity disorder (ADHD) were assessed on a sample of nearly 400 adolescent twin pairs. Multivariate genetic model-fitting analyses found that either a one-factor common pathways model or a one-genetic-factor independent pathway provided an equally good explanation of the covariance between these disorders. In the end, they selected the common pathways model because "... this is a more parsimonious

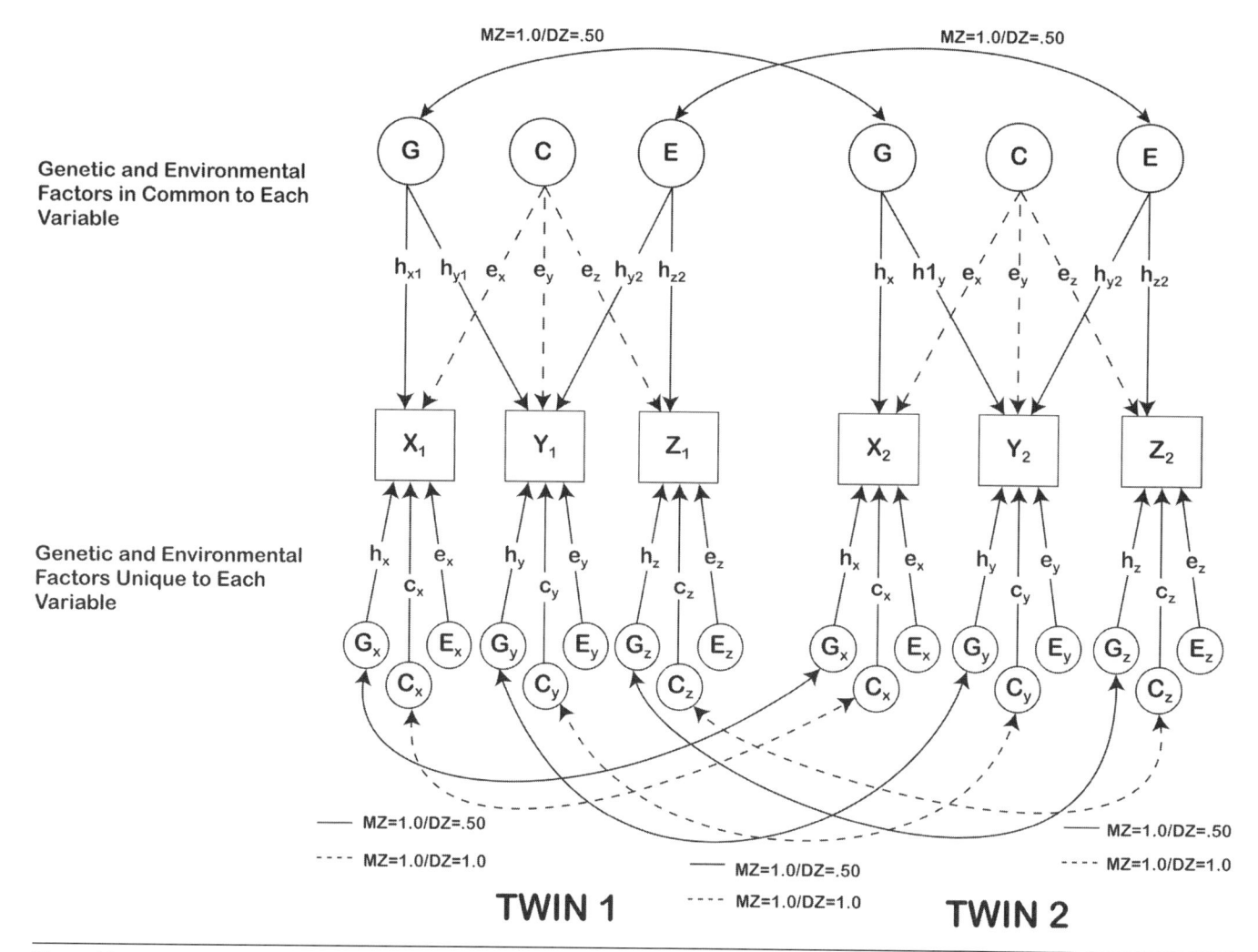

Figure 4.3 Independent pathway model. The figure illustrates the general form of the independent pathway model. The labels G = genetic factors, C = common family environmental factors, E = nonshared environmental factors; the influence of G, C, and E effects common and unique to each variable are indexed by the paths marked h to e, h_x to h_z, c_x to c_z, and e_x to e_z as appropriate; MZ = monozygotic twins; DZ = dizygotic twins.

model than the independent pathway model and shows no significant decrement in fit χ^2 difference test . . ." (pp. 690–691). One area of behavioral genetics that probably requires more attention is the development of criteria to guide selection between equally well-fitting models. Presently, when statistical guidance is lacking, the choice of model becomes (1) arbitrary, (2) based on one's own theoretical preferences, or (3) based on the principle of parsimony—the model with the fewest parameters is the simplest.

It should be pointed out that in the vast majority of studies, the choice between common or independent pathways model is clear and the use of these models has provided important new insights into psychopathology. For example, a question that is frequently discussed is whether all of the anxiety disorder diagnoses (the phobias, GAD, OCD, etc.) represent a cohesive set of disorders. Clinical research has shown that each of the individual disorders is frequently, but not always, comorbid with others. Moreover, some of the diagnoses such as GAD are more frequently comorbid with other disorders such major depression, questioning whether this diagnostic category should continue to exist. This question was addressed by Kendler et al. (1995), who found that the covariation of lifetime history of *DSM-III-R* phobia, GAD, panic, bulimia, major depression, and alcoholism could be explained by an independent pathways model that specified two additive genetic factors, one shared environmental factor, and one nonshared factor. The two genetic factors appeared to delineate two broad domains of anxiety disorder. The first genetic factor accounted for the largest proportion of heritable influence on phobia (33 percent), panic disorder (32 percent), and bulimia (29 percent) and in total accounted for less than 7 percent of the variance on the remaining disorders.

The second genetic factor was found to influence only GAD and major depression, accounting for 22 percent and 41 percent of the variance. This factor only accounted for 12 percent or less of the variance in the remaining four disorders. Alcoholism was little influenced by either genetic factor. Together, the common factors were found to account for only 7 percent of the variance on alcoholism, with 45 percent of the total variance attributable to alcohol specific genetic factors.

The shared environmental (c^2) factor accounted for 41 percent of the total variance across all disorders with the exception of bulimia, in which it accounted for approximately 2 percent. The single common nonshared environmental factor had the largest influences on GAD and depression, accounting for 38 percent and 34 percent of the total variance in each. Most of the nonshared environmental effects were found to be unique to each disorder, accounting for 29 percent to 49 percent of the total variance. These results clearly indicate that what is thought of as a genetically homogenous set of disorders is actually quite an etiologically diverse collection of conditions. A most interesting finding is that GAD has more in common with major depression than any of the other anxiety disorders, suggesting that its classification as an anxiety disorder is incorrect.

Gene-Environment Interplay
Gene-Environment Interaction: G × E

If ostensibly the same genes influence unique disorders such as GAD and major depression, what causes them to express and manifest as GAD, depression, or both? One explanation is the action of the environment. In many studies, environmental effects are often found to be largely unique to each disorder. For example, Roy, Neale, Pedersen, Mathe, and Kendler (1995) reported that despite finding a common genetic basis to GAD and major depression, major depression appears to be predominantly associated with "loss events" (e.g., death of a relative or loss of a job), whereas GAD was found to be primarily associated with "danger events" such as those that might elicit future crisis. Behavioral geneticists have long been occupied with identifying specific environmental effects, and excellent reviews of this research are provided by Turkheimer and Waldron (2000). Extensive meta-analysis of the environmental research on personality by Reiss, Neiderhiser, Heatherington, and Plomin (2000) describes one of the most ambitious studies ever conducted that attempts to identify environmental effects. Sadly, the main conclusion of these works is that identifying environmental effects has not been very successful. For example, Turkheimer and Waldron (2000) showed that that studies assessing family constellation variables accounted for only 1.1 percent of the variance on average; differences in maternal and paternal behavior fared slightly better at 2.3 percent and 1.6 percent, respectively; differences in sibling interaction accounted for on average 4.1 percent and differences in peer-teacher interactions a "sizeable" 9.1 percent on average. They conclude that environmental effects must be cumulative—that it may take many such small effects to accumulate and have a measurable effect on behavior (p. 91). Another explanation for the small effect of individual environmental stressors is that the nonshared environment does not have much effect that is independent of preexisting genetic factors, and what is important is the interplay of genetic and environmental factors that not only may increase liability to disorder but may also work to provide protection from development of psychopathology (Kendler & Eaves, 1986).

One of the mechanisms of interplay under active investigation is *gene-environment interaction* (Plomin, DeFries, & Loehlin, 1977). The usual design is to stratify a sample of probands into groups based on levels (usually the presence or absence) of a psychosocial stressor and show that each group is associated with particular polymorphisms implicated in the disorder of interest. One of the most dramatic examples of gene-environment interaction is the Caspi, McClay, and Moffitt (2002) study of antisocial behavior. Clinical research has identified family history of child abuse, specifically erratic, coercive, and punitive parenting as a major risk factor for the development of antisocial behavior in boys. However, this abuse is only a risk factor—there is little one to one correspondence as there are many abused children who do not develop antisocial behavior. This suggests the possibility that childhood abuse is the trigger that activates the development of antisocial behavior only in those children who had also inherited a genetic liability. In the case of antisocial behavior, the monoamine oxidase A gene (MAOA gene) was selected as the candidate because it has been associated with aggressive behavior in mice and some in some human studies.

For this study, 1,037 children were assessed at nine different ages for levels of maltreatment (no maltreatment, probable maltreatment, and severe maltreatment) and MAOA activity (low or high activity). They found that the effect of maltreatment was significantly weaker among males with high MAOA activity than those with low MAOA activity. Moreover, the probable and high maltreatment groups did not differ in MAOA activity, indicating that the genotype did not influence exposure to maltreatment. These results are a clear demonstration that the MAOA gene modifies the influence of maltreatment.

Another popular way gene-environment interaction is studied is with adoption data. Tienari et al. (2004) tested if the rate of schizophrenia spectrum disorder differed between children at high risk for this disorder (because their biological mothers were diagnosed with the disorder) compared to children at low risk for the disorder (no family history of the disorder) raised in adoptive family environments that differed in levels of functioning. Family functioning was defined as degree of *constriction* (e.g., range of affect, rigid family structure, passivity, apathy, lack of humor); *critical/conflictual* (e.g., criticism, parent-parent conflict, parent-child conflict, insecurity, lack of empathy, manifest anxiety, nonacknowledgment); and *boundary problems* (e.g., hierarchy, chaotic structure, individual and generational enmeshment, inadequate daily problem solving). The adoptive families were classified on these three dimensions (low versus high) and number of high versus low genetic risk adoptees diagnosed with schizophrenia spectrum disorder compared.

The results clearly showed that adoptees at high genetic risk are more sensitive to problems in the family environment in all domains than adoptees at low genetic risk. They also found that high-risk adoptees raised in highly functioning families have significantly fewer schizophrenia-spectrum outcomes than high genetic risk adoptees raised in dysfunctional adoptive families. These results suggest that healthy adoptive families provide a protective influence for high-risk individuals.

Another way gene-environment interaction has been identified is by showing that heritability estimates differ across environmental conditions. For example, Heath, Eaves, and Martin (1989) tested whether being married moderates the genetic basis to drinking habits. The study sample was conducted with nearly 2,000 female adult Australian same-sex twin pairs who were interviewed on the details of total weekly alcohol consumption. This consisted of reports measured in standard drink sizes (7 ounces in the case of beer, 4 ounces of wine, 1 ounce of spirits) for each day of the preceding seven-day week. Current marital status information was obtained: unmarried (single, separated, divorced or widowed) or married (married and living together). The twins were further subdivided into two age cohorts. The first consisted of younger adults (aged 30 years or younger) and the other of older adults (aged 31 years and older).

To test for gene-environment interaction effects, they estimated the magnitude of h^2_A, c^2, and e^2 conditional upon environmental exposure—married versus unmarried status. In a model that has no gene-environment interaction effects, estimates of h^2_A, c^2, or e^2 should not significantly differ between married and unmarried twins. If gene-environment interaction effects are present it is expected that estimates of h^2_A, c^2, or e^2 should vary significantly between married and unmarried twins. Their results showed that among females, marital status decreases genetic influences on alcohol consumption. In the younger adult cohort, $h^2_A = 60$ percent for unmarried twins compared to married twins for whom $h^2_A = 31$ percent. In the older adult cohort, h^2_A for unmarried twins was estimated at 76 percent whereas in married twins $h^2_A = 59$ percent. When the older and younger cohorts were combined, $h^2_A = 77$ percent for unmarried twins and 59 percent for married twins.

A potential problem with gene-environment interaction to be aware of is that the environmental variable used to stratify the sample that could be confounded with several other psychosocial stressors. For example, can estimates of maternal warmth be made independent of maternal care? Thus, any conclusions about the effect of a specific environmental stressor are limited to the extent that other potential moderators have been adequately controlled. Another issue to be aware of is that many stressors (e.g., levels of family conflict) cannot be simply categorized as present or absent. All families experience some level of conflict that varies from low to very high and simple contingency table designs potentially lose important information that can obscure the existence of interaction effects.

Fortunately, recent modifications to the path models (e.g., Dick, Rose, Viken, Kaprio, & Koskenvuo, 2001) used to estimate heritability is able to analyze continuously measured psychosocial variables (see Figure 4.4). In this model, the psychosocial/environmental experiences reported by each twin are represented by the triangles. The path M_a between A_{TWIN1}, A_{TWIN2} and the psychosocial variable M indexes gene-environment interaction because these influences directly moderate the effect of genetic influences, which is converted to h^2_A. This model is important because now the interplay of environments and experiences are directly estimated using variables that best reflect gradations in environmental effect.

This model is also important because it can estimate *experience by environmental interaction* (E × E). Just as genetic effects can be influenced by exposure to specific environmental effects, the environment can also be influenced by the occurrence of other nongenetic effects. For example, some people can live in extreme poverty but display no ill effects because the presence of another environmental factor such as an attentive mother that attends to the emotional needs of the child that cancels out the influence of poverty. These kinds of effects are estimated by the path M_c between the triangles and C_{TWIN1}, C_{TWIN2} indexes the degree to which the psychosocial stressors moderate the effect of shared environmental effects (c^2), and the path M_e between the triangles and E_{TWIN1}, E_{TWIN2} indexes the degree to which the psychosocial stressor moderates the effect of nonshared environmental effects (e^2).

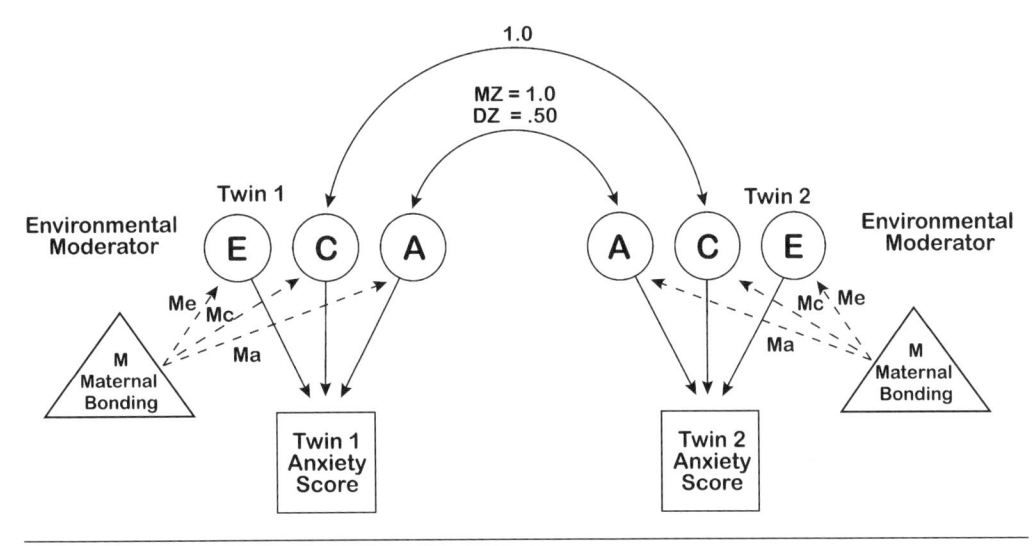

Figure 4.4 Sample gene environment interaction (G × E) model. A = genetic factors, C = common family environmental factors, E = nonshared environmental factors, M = environmental or psychosocial moderator variable. The influence of the moderator variables, M, is indexed by the paths M_a, M_c, M_e; MZ = monozygotic twins; DZ = dizygotic twins.

This kind of moderator model was used to study the effect of urban versus rural residency on alcohol use over two years (Rose, Dick, Viken, Pulkkinen, & Kaprio, 2001). Twins were assessed on a continuous measure of alcohol use (e.g., daily, couple of times a week, once a week, couple of times a month, about once a month, about once every two months, three to four times a year, once a year or less, I don't drink any alcohol). Heritability analyses showed that genetic factors influencing drinking patterns increased over the 30-month period. At age 16, 17, and 18.5 years, the h^2_A for drinking frequency was reported to account for 33 percent, 49 percent, and 50 percent, respectively, of the total variance; c^2 influences accounted for 37 percent, 20 percent, and 14 percent, respectively, with e^2 accounting for the remainder. When the estimates are crossed with area of residency, genetic factors assumed a larger role among adolescents residing in urban areas, whereas shared environmental influences were more important in rural settings.

Gene by Environment Correlation

Gene by environment correlation (r_{ge}) refers to the situation in which genetic factors influence the probability of exposure to adverse events (Plomin et al., 1977). On the face of it, the presence of r_{ge} could pose quite a problem for studies of gene-environment interaction because differences in environmental conditions may be influenced by genetically based factors.[1] It would be wrong to understand gene-environment correlation as mere statistical confound. From the perspective of psychopathology research, this phenomenon is important because it identifies which genetically based disorders influence the selection of environmental conditions or experiences conducive to its expression. For example, individuals high on the genetically based personality trait sensation seeking will prefer high-risk environments.

A good example of this kind of interplay is Kendler and Karkowski-Shuman's (1997) study testing if genetic risk factors for major depression increased the risk of experiencing a significant life event. A sample of 938 pairs of adult female twins was assessed for significant life events at two different times 17 months apart. The first step was to test each of the environmental variables to determine if they had a heritable basis. It is possible that genetically influenced depression can influence the frequency of endorsement of significant life events. Heritability analysis found that the life events: (1) serious marital problems, (2) divorce/breakup, (3) job loss, (4) serious illness, (5) major financial problems, and (6) trouble getting along with others in the person's interpersonal network had a significant heritable basis. They tested if the heritable effects on these environmental events is due in part the genetic factors underlying major depression that has influenced the person's risk for placing oneself in, or creating these situations, by estimating r_G between measures of depression and life events. They found significant associations with divorce/breakup ($r_G = 1.00$), serious illness ($r_G = .53$), and major financial problems ($r_G = .41$). These analyses showed that 10 percent to 15 percent of the impact of genes on the risk for major depression is mediated through significant life events.

Another example can be found with post-traumatic stress disorder (PTSD). Personality traits such as neuroticism have been implicated in influencing a person's risk for placing oneself in, or creating, potentially hazardous situations that lead to PTSD (e.g., Fauerbach et al., 2000). Other traits, such as sensation seeking, have been associated with increased risk for being a victim of rape (Kilpatrick, Resnick, Saunders, & Best, 1998). Recently, Koenen et al. (2002) reported that among males, preexisting conduct disorder (which might be considered an early manifestation of antisocial personality traits) was a risk factor for both trauma exposure and subsequent PTSD symptoms using data from male twins who served in the Vietnam War. The same mechanism applies to people in the general population. Jang, Stein, Taylor, Asmundson, and Livesley (2003) examined the relationship between a wide range of normal and abnormal personality traits and exposure to assaultive (e.g., getting beaten up, raped, robbed) and nonassaultive trauma (e.g., car accidents, natural disaster, death of close friend or relative). Multiple regression analysis identified that traits describing antisocial personality characteristics were most predictive of experiencing assaultive trauma and is was partially accounted for by a modest, but statistically significant genetic basis (r_G range = .14–.26). In contrast, personality factors were not implicated in exposure to nonassaultive trauma.

SUMMARY

The central question of psychopathology is comorbidity. So much of how disorders are classified, diagnosed, and understood is based on observations as to which normal behavior, symptoms and disorders occur together. Genetics research provides a form of "reality check" to these observations by testing if these relationships have a genuine biological-genetic basis. To study comorbidity, geneticists engage in a three-fold task. The first is to determine if existing disorders have a genetic basis. This involves research that tries to identify the actual genes (e.g., is the 5-HTTLPR gene controlling the transport of serotonin involved through linkage or association studies) to estimating the total effect of genes relative to the environment (estimating h^2, c^2, and e^2 effects) using adoption and twin studies.

Once these genes have been found or the magnitude of genetic effects estimated, the second task is to determine if they are simultaneously involved in other disorders. Multivariate genetic studies (e.g., r_G, common and independent pathways models) are used to estimate and make statements about the genetic and environmental basis and structure of any relationships. Many of these multivariate studies have shown that genetic factors account for the comorbidity of several disorders. However, they have also shown that most disorders are influenced by genetic and especially environmental factors unique to each disorder. As a result, the third task facing behavioral geneticists is to explicate the mechanisms by which genetic and environmental factors interact to produce different disorders from a common genetic liability, or abnormal forms of disorder from normal behavior. Two such mechanisms are under intense study—gene-environment interaction (environmental mediation of genetic effects) and gene-environment correlation (genetic mediation of environmental exposures/effects). Most investigations to date have sought to develop research designs that can detect and demonstrate these effects.

NOTE

1. Recently, Purcell (2002) developed a variant of the model shown in Figure 4.4 that tests for gene-environment interaction in the face of gene-environment correlation effects.

REFERENCES

American Psychiatric Association. (1987). *Diagnostic and statistical manual of mental disorders* (3rd ed., rev.). Washington, DC: Author.

American Psychiatric Association. (1994). *Diagnostic and statistical manual of mental disorders* (4th ed.). Washington, DC: Author.

Blouin, J. L., Dombroski, B. A., Nath, S. K., Lasseter, V. K., Wolyniec, P. S., Nestadt, G., et al. (1998). Schizophrenia susceptibility loci on chromosomes 13q32 and 8p21. *Nature Genetics, 20,* 70–73.

Boomsma, D. I., Martin, N. G., & Machin, M. A. (1997). A twin pronged attack on complex traits. *Science, 17,* 387–392.

Caspi, A., McClay, J., & Moffitt, T. (2002). Role of genotype in the cycle of violence in maltreated children. *Science, 297*(5582), 851–854.

Cloninger, C. R. (1986). A unified biosocial theory of personality and its role in the development of anxiety states. *Psychiatric Developments, 3,* 167–226.

Cloninger, C. R., Adolfsson, R., & Svrakic, N. M. (1996). Mapping genes for human personality. *Nature Genetics, 12,* 3–4.

Cloninger, C. R., Svrakic, D. M., & Przybeck, T. R. (1993). A psychobiological model of temperament and character. *Archives of General Psychiatry, 50,* 975–990.

Costa, P. T., & McCrae, R. R. (1992). *Revised NEO Personality Inventory (NEO-PI-R) and the NEO Five-Factor Inventory (NEO-FFI) professional manual.* Odessa, FL: Psychological Assessment Resources.

Detera-Wadleigh, S. D., Badner, J. A., Berrettini, W. H., Yoshikawa, T., Goldin, L. R., Turner, G., et al. (1999). A high-density genome scan detects evidence for a bipolar-disorder susceptibility locus on 13q32 and other potential loci on 1q32 and 18p11.2. *Proceedings of the National Academy of Sciences of the United States of America, 96,* 5604–5609.

Dick, D. M., Rose, R. J., Viken, R. J., Kaprio, J., & Koskenvuo, M. (2001). Exploring gene-environment interactions: Socioregional moderation of alcohol use. *Journal of Abnormal Psychology, 110,* 625–632.

Fauerbach, J. A., Lawrence, J. W., & Schmidt, C. W., Jr. (2000). Personality predictors of injury-related posttraumatic stress disorder. *Journal of Nervous & Mental Disease, 188*(8), 510–517.

Feinstein, A. R. (1970). The pretherapeutic classification of co-morbidity in chronic disease. *Journal of Chronic Disorders, 23,* 455–468.

Gershon, E. S. (2000). Bipolar illness and schizophrenia as oligogenic diseases: Implications for the future. *Biological Psychiatry, 47,* 240–244.

Gershon, E. S., Badner, J. A., Goldin, L. R., Sanders, A. R., Cravchik, A., & Detera-Wadleigh, S. D. (1998). Closing in on genes for manic-depressive illness and schizophrenia. *Neuropsychopharmacology, 18,* 233–242.

Grove, W. M., Eckert, E. D., Heston, L., Bouchard, T. J., Jr., Segal, N., & Lykken, D. T. (1990). Heritability of substance abuse and antisocial behavior: A study of monozygotic twins reared apart. *Biological Psychiatry, 27,* 1293–1304.

Heath, A. C., Eaves, L. J., & Martin, N. G. (1989). The genetic structure of personality: III. Multivariate genetic item analysis of the EPQ scales. *Personality and Individual Differences, 10,* 877–888.

Heatherington, E. M., Reiss, D., & Plomin, R. (1994). *The separate social worlds of siblings: The impact of nonshared environment on development.* Hillsdale, NJ: Erlbaum.

Jang, K. L., Dick, D. M., Taylor, S., Stein, M. B., Wolf, H., Vernon, P. A., et al. (2005). Psychosocial adversity and emotional instability: An application of gene-environment interaction models. *European Journal of Personality, 19,* 359–372.

Jang, K. L., Hu, S., Livesley, W. J., Angleitner, A., Riemann, R., Ando, J., et al. (2001). The covariance structure of neuroticism and agreeableness: A twin and molecular genetic analysis of the role of the serotonin transporter gene. *Journal of Personality and Social Psychology, 81*(2), 295–304.

Jang, K. L., & Livesley, W. J. (1999). Why do measures of normal and disordered personality correlate? A study of genetic comorbidity. *Journal of Personality Disorders, 13*(2), 10–17.

Jang, K. L., Stein, M. B., Taylor, S., Asmundson, G., & Livesley, W. J. (2003). Exposure to traumatic events and experience: Aetiological relationships with personality function. *Psychiatry Research, 120,* 61–69.

Jang, K. L., Vernon, P. A., & Livesley, W. J. (2000). Personality disorder traits, family environment, and alcohol misuse: A multivariate behavioural genetic analysis. *Addiction, 95,* 873–888.

Kendler, K. S., & Eaves, L. J. (1986). Models for the joint effect of genotype and environment on liability to psychiatric illness. *American Journal of Psychiatry, 143*(3), 279–289.

Kendler, K. S., & Karkowski-Shuman, L. (1997). Stressful life events and genetic liability to major depression: Genetic control of exposure to the environment? *Psychological Medicine, 27,* 539–547.

Kendler, K. S., Prescott, C. A., Myers, J., & Neale, M. C. (2003). The structure of genetic and environmental risk factors for common psychiatric and substance use disorder in men and women. *Archives of General Psychiatry, 60,* 929–937.

Kendler, K. S., Walters, E. E., Neale, M. C., Kessler, R. C., Heath, A. C., & Eaves, L. J. (1995). The structure of the genetic and environmental risk factors for six major psychiatric disorders in women. Phobia, generalized anxiety disorder, panic disorder, bulimia, major depression, and alcoholism. *Archives of General Psychiatry, 52,* 374–383.

Kilpatrick, D. G., Resnick, H. S., Saunders, B. E., & Best, C. L. (1998). Rape, other violence against women, and posttraumatic stress disorder. In B. P. Dohrenwend (Ed.), *Adversity, stress, and psychopathology* (pp. 161–176). London: Oxford University Press.

King, R. A., Rotter, J. I., & Motlusky, A. G. (Eds.). (1992). *The genetic basis of common diseases.* New York: Oxford University Press.

Koenen, K. C., Harley, R., Lyons, M. J., Wolfe, J., Simpson, J. C., Goldberg, J., et al. (2002). A twin registry study of familial and individual risk factors for trauma exposure and posttraumatic stress disorder. *Journal of Nervous & Mental Disease, 190*(4), 209–218.

Krueger, R. F. (1999). The structure of common mental disorders. *Archives of General Psychiatry, 56,* 921–926.

Krueger, R. F., Hicks, B. M., Patrick, C. J., Carlson, S. R., Iacono, W. G., & McGue, M. (2002). Etiologic connections among substance dependence, antisocial behavior, and personality: Modeling the externalizing spectrum. *Journal of Abnormal Psychology, 111,* 411–424.

Krueger, R. F., McGue, M., & Iacono, W. G. (2001). The higher-order structure of common *DSM* mental disorders: Internalization, externalization, and their connections to personality. *Personality & Individual Differences, 30*(7), 1245–1259.

Livesley, W. J., Jang, K. L., & Vernon, P. A. (1998). The phenotypic and genetic structure of traits delineating personality disorder. *Archives of General Psychiatry, 55*(10), 941–948.

Markon, K. E., Krueger, R. F., Bouchard, T. J., Jr., & Gottesman, I. I. (2002). Normal and abnormal personality traits: Evidence for genetic and environmental relationships in the Minnesota Study of Twins Reared Apart. *Journal of Personality, 70,* 661–694.

McGuffin, P., Owen, M. J., & Gottesman, I. J. (Eds.). (2002). *Psychiatric genetics and genomics.* Oxford, England: Oxford University Press.

Mineka, S., Watson, D., & Clark, L. A. (1998). Comorbidity of anxiety and mood disorders. *Annual Review of Psychology, 49,* 377–412.

Plomin, R., DeFries, J. C., Craig, I. W., & McGuffin, P. (Eds.). (2003). *Behavioral genetics in the postgenomic era.* Washington, DC: American Psychological Association.

Plomin, R., DeFries, J. C., & Loehlin, J. C. (1977). Genotype-environment interaction and correlation in the analysis of human behavior. *Psychological Bulletin, 84*(2), 309–322.

Purcell, S. (2002). Variance components models for gene-environment interaction in twin analysis. *Twin Research, 5,* 554–571.

Reiss, D., Neiderhiser, J. M., Heatherington, M., & Plomin, R. (2000). *The relationship code: Deciphering genetic and social influences on adolescent development.* Cambridge, MA: Harvard University Press.

Rose, R. J., Dick, D. M., Viken, R. J., Pulkkinen, L., & Kaprio, J. (2001). Drinking or abstaining at age 14? A genetic epidemiological study. *Alcoholism: Clinical and Experimental Research, 25,* 1594–1604.

Rowe, D. C. (1994). *The limits of family influence: Genes, experience, and behavior.* New York: Guilford Press.

Roy, M. A., Neale, M. C., Pedersen, N. L., Mathe, A. A., & Kendler, K. S. (1995). A twin study of generalized anxiety disorder and major depression. *Psychological Medicine, 25,* 1037–1049.

Rutter, M. (2002). Nature, nurture, and development: From evangelism through science toward policy and practice. *Child Development, 73,* 1–21.

Stein, M. B., Chartier, M. J., Kozak, M. V., King, N., & Kennedy, J. L. (1998). Genetic linkage to the serotonin transporter protein and 5HT2A receptor genes excluded in generalized social phobia. *Psychiatry Research, 81,* 283–291.

Stein, M. B., Jang, K. L., & Livesley, W. J. (2002). Heritability of social anxiety-related concerns and personality characteristics: A twin study. *Journal of Nervous and Mental Disease, 190*(4), 219–224.

Tienari, P., Wynne, L. C., Sorri, A., Lahti, I., Laksy, K., Moring, J., et al. (2004). Genotype-environment interaction in schizophrenia-spectrum disorder. *British Journal of Psychiatry, 184,* 216–222.

Tillfors, M., Furmark, T., & Ekselius, L. (2001). Social phobia and avoidant personality disorder as related to parental history of social anxiety: A general population study. *Behaviour Research and Therapy, 39*(3), 289–298.

Turkheimer, E., & Waldron, M. (2000). Nonshared environment: A theoretical, methodological, and quantitative review. *Psychological Bulletin, 126,* 78–108.

Vollebergh, W. A. M., Ledema, J., Bijl, R. V., de Graaf, R., Smitt, F., & Ormel, J. (2001). The structure and stability of common mental disorders: The NEMESIS Study. *Archives of General Psychiatry, 58,* 597–603.

Widiger, T. A. (2003). Personality disorder and Axis I psychopathology: The problematic boundary of Axis I and Axis II. *Journal of Personality Disorders, 17,* 90–108.

Widiger, T. A., Verheul, R., & van den Brink, W. (1999). Personality and psychopathology. In L. A. Pervin & O. P. John (Eds.), *Handbook of personality: Theory and research* (2nd ed., pp. 347–366). New York: Guilford Press.

World Health Organization. (1992). *The ICD-10 classification of mental and behavioral disorders: Clinical descriptions and diagnostic guidelines.* Geneva, Switzerland: Author.

Young, S. E., Stallings, M. C., Corley, R. P., Krauter, K. S., & Hewitt, J. K. (2000). Genetic and environmental influences on behavioral disinhibition. *American Journal of Medical Genetics, 96,* 684–95.

CHAPTER 5

Sociocultural Influences

DOROTHY CHIN AND VELMA A. KAMEOKA

In the past two decades, theory and research on the influences of psychopathology have focused upon genetic and biological influences, paralleling the rise of technology that enables the identification of genes responsible for physical and psychological disorder. Indeed, work on the Human Genome Project has thus far identified genes that influence alcoholism, schizophrenia, and bipolar disorder (Cowan, Kopnisky, & Hyman, 2002), and advances in brain imaging have pinpointed biological correlates for disorders ranging from Alzheimer's disease (Thompson, 2004) to antisocial behavior (Raine, 2002). It is now widely accepted that most, if not all, forms of psychopathology have some degree of genetic or biological influence, with the severest forms, such as schizophrenia, being fundamentally biologically determined (Bebbington, Walsh, & Murray, 1993). Even within this perspective, however, genetic and biological influences do not account for all of the variation in the prevalence or manifestation of psychopathology. It is equally accepted that social and cultural factors also influence the development and manifestation of psychopathology. The influence of sociocultural factors on psychopathology can be inferred by: (1) variation observed in the distribution of psychopathology as a function of sociocultural factors; (2) variation observed in the manifestation of psychopathology as a function of sociocultural factors; and (3) variation in the prognosis and course of a disorder as a function of sociocultural factors. Of course, the extent to which sociocultural factors influence psychopathology depends on the particular disorder under consideration. For example, the more severe disorders (e.g., schizophrenia) have been observed to be more biologically influenced and thus show less cross-cultural variation, whereas the less severe disorders (e.g., personality disorders) may be less biologically influenced and show greater cross-cultural variation (Marsella, 1980).

The goal of this chapter is to discuss the relationship between sociocultural factors and psychopathology in the context of key epistemological, theoretical, and methodological issues. The chapter is divided into three major sections. The first section highlights the major epistemological and methodological issues that influence sociocultural variation in psychopathology. In particular, we discuss two perspectives on psychopathology—the universality of disorders across cultures, or the *etic* perspective, and the cultural specificity and relativity of disorders, or the *emic* perspective. Within this context, we also discuss culturally relevant issues in assessment, diagnosis, and sampling. The second section critiques the current use of major sociocultural concepts and terms and highlights the need for greater clarity in defining and articulating sociocultural influences. Specifically, the concepts of race, culture, ethnicity, nationality, socioeconomic status, minority status, acculturation, and ethnic identity are delineated and their interrelationships discussed. The third section outlines the major conceptual frameworks and constructs that have been put forth to explain sociocultural variations in psychopathology, including individualism/collectivism, social stress and support, communication style, and beliefs and attitudes about mental health and illness. As the primary objective of this chapter is to provide the reader with a useful framework that illuminates the relationship between sociocultural influences and psychopathology, the treatment of these topics will be selective rather than comprehensive. Therefore, specific disorders will not be discussed in depth but will instead serve as examples illustrating key concepts and points. This approach is intended to complement the subsequent chapters in this volume, in which the etiology of specific disorders is discussed in detail.

EPISTEMOLOGICAL AND METHODOLOGICAL ISSUES INFLUENCING SOCIOCULTURAL VARIATION IN PSYCHOPATHOLOGY

Arguably, a sociocultural influence is suggested when the distribution, manifestation, or course of a disorder varies so-

---

Acknowledgment: The authors would like to thank Julie Gustafson and Marc Pincus for their assistance with this manuscript.

cially or culturally, for example, when the symptoms of depression differ markedly between two cultural groups. The presence of these variations, however, is difficult to establish owing to epistemological and methodological issues such as a lack of equivalence in concepts across cultures. For instance, Marsella (1980), in a review of depressive disorder across cultures, found that depression is viewed and experienced very differently cross-culturally. In some cultures such as in Malaysia, Borneo, and Africa, the concept of depression itself is not well represented (Marsella, 1980), whereas in others, the concept of depression markedly differs from that which prevails in Western nosological systems. In fact, the lack of cultural equivalence of the concept of depression renders cross-cultural epidemiological studies highly unreliable and difficult to interpret. That is, if the conception of *depression* is not the same across cultures, how can rates of the disorder be compared across cultures? Moreover, a lack of conceptual equivalence confounds a variation in prevalence with a variation in the manifestation of symptoms. For example, should the Chinese syndrome *shenjing shuaiuro*, characterized by dysphoric mood, anhedonia, weakness, and fatigue (Kleinman, 1982), be classified as depression, a cultural variant of depression, or a unique culture-bound syndrome? In a broader sense, to what extent can the concept of *depression* and, therefore, its manifestation be different and still be regarded as depression? And, if the symptoms are qualitatively different enough, do they constitute a unique culture-bound syndrome as opposed to variants of depressive disorder? These questions have important implications for the epidemiology of psychopathology across cultures because the prevalence of a particular disorder arrived at in cross-cultural studies depends on the particular perspective taken. The following subsections discuss in greater depth the relevant epistemological and methodological issues.

Etic versus Emic Perspectives

There are two major epistemological perspectives that impinge on the previously referenced questions—the *etic*, or the culturally universal, and the *emic*, or the culturally relative perspectives (Berry, 1969). The very notion that disorders have a universal, core structure or set of features can be traced back to Kraepelin (1904, cited in Draguns & Tanaka-Matsumi, 2003), who used the etic perspective in deriving cross-cultural estimates of dementia praecox. Thus, the etic approach forms the basis for cross-cultural epidemiological studies. In contrast, viewing a set of symptoms as comprising a culture-bound syndrome, without an eye toward fitting the symptoms into a universal classification system, represents the *emic* perspective. Occupying the middle ground of the etic-emic continuum is the view that a particular set of symptoms represents a cultural variant of a universal disorder. This middle view, called the *derived etic*, is the result of modifying the etic based on emic descriptions and etic interpretations of the disorder (Berry, 1969). Each of these epistemological perspectives has its unique problems and implications. For example, based on the etic perspective, epidemiological studies may miss cases that appear different but may not be, thereby counting only the proportion of cases that overlap significantly in symptoms and underestimating sociocultural influence on psychopathology. From an emic perspective, however, each cultural variant may be considered a unique syndrome, thus overestimating sociocultural influences.

These three perspectives—etic, derived etic, and emic—can be illustrated by examining the symptom manifestation of depression across cultures. A collaborative cross-cultural study on depression conducted in Canada, Iran, Japan, and Switzerland by the World Health Organization (WHO, 1983) found that the most basic and universal manifestations of depression are vegetative, somatic symptoms such as lethargy, inability to concentrate, anhedonia, fatigue, loss of sexual interest, and reduced appetite with or without weight loss, which were found among 76 percent of depressed patients. In addition, in a comparison of rates of depression across 10 nations, Weissman et al. (1996) found that insomnia and loss of energy were the most common symptoms across nations. These commonalities illustrate the etic perspective in viewing depression across cultures.

The derived etic perspective may be seen in the noted distinctions in depression symptomatology between Western and non-Western cultures. Although somatic symptoms are found in both Western and non-Western cultures, psychological and existential manifestations such as mood disturbance, self-depreciation, guilt, and despair are predominantly Western manifestations (Marsella, 1980; Prince, 1985; Ulusahin, Basoglu, & Paykel, 1994). Somatization was found to be higher in certain regions including China, Japan, India, Latin America, and Africa (Kirmayer, 1984; Kleinman, 1982). Indeed, based on comparative rates of symptoms worldwide, the tendency to view non-Western experiences of depression as "somaticizing" has been considered ethnocentric, as it is equally, if not more, likely that the Western experience represents the "psychologizing" of a predominantly physiological experience. In fact, Leff (1977) has noted that "only in Western cultures is depression articulated principally as an intrapsychic experience." The existence of sharp distinctions as well as similarities in depression symptomatology across cultures points to the utility of the derived etic perspective in order to arrive at a more accurate picture of the nature of depression worldwide.

Using the emic approach, syndromes that might be considered cultural variants of depression are viewed as unique culture-bound syndromes. For example, in India, "depression" is manifested as somatic complaints and agitation and anxiety (Teja, Narang, & Aggarwal, 1971), whereas "loss of vitality" and sleep disturbances are most common in Indonesia and feelings of sadness are often absent (Pfeiffer, 1968). From the emic perspective, viewing these culturally unique syndromes as simply "depression" is inaccurate and reductionistic (Kleinman, 1995).

Brain fag, categorized as a culture-bound syndrome in the *DSM-IV,* is an example of how a psychopathological syndrome can be understood from both universal and relativistic perspectives. The chief symptoms of brain fag are the inability to read and comprehend reading material, fatigue, sleepiness, and burning, crawling, "wormlike" sensations in the brain (APA, 1994). Brain fag afflicts high school and university students in response to school pressures and is found in sub-Saharan African countries. It is classified as a culture-bound syndrome because the dysfunction is seen as culturally unique, whose etiology and features arise from and are intimately tied to the cultural context (Prince, 1985). From the universal perspective, however, these signs are culturally congruent expressions of depression, in the context of cultures that experience many diseases involving heat (e.g., malaria, smallpox) and crawling sensations (e.g., hookworm, guinea worm) (Prince, 1985). Depressive experiences, then, are translated into these symptoms that represent familiar characteristics of illness in these cultures.

Similarly, *susto,* a disorder uniquely experienced by people in Mexico, Central America, and South America, is another example of a culture-bound syndrome. Referring to "soul loss" or "fright," in which a frightening event causes the soul to leave the body (APA, 1994), *susto* is characterized by weakness, loss of appetite, sleep disturbance, motor retardation, fear, loss of sex drive, and some anxiety indicators (e.g., sweating, racing heart; Marsella, 1980). From an etic perspective, *susto* can be readily categorized as a case of agitated depression, its expression congruent with strong cultural beliefs in the prominence and function of the soul.

Cross-cultural researchers have long called for the integration of emic and etic perspectives, highlighting its promise in bringing into focus the extent and nature of sociocultural variations (e.g., Davidson, Jaccard, Triandis, Morales, Diaz-Guerrero, 1976; Triandis, 1972). More recently, Draguns and Tanaka-Matsumi (2003) noted that greater integration is occurring "as etic research is informed by greater cultural sensitivity and emic studies become more objective, quantified, and rigorous" (p. 770). Empirical studies are currently underway in examining psychological disorders from both perspectives, including studies on depression and the culture-bound syndrome of *koro* (c.f., Draguns and Tanaka-Matsumi, 2003).

Assessment

Cross-cultural assessment depends on the ability to achieve validity and reliability of constructs, measures, items, and responses within and across cultures. To this end, cross-cultural psychologists have articulated a set of methodological principles, the center of which is the concept of equivalence. Equivalence refers to the extent to which a behavior, concept, or measurement procedure shares common meanings and relevance for culturally different groups (Kameoka, 1989; Marsella & Kameoka, 1989). Several types of equivalence have been delineated, including conceptual, functional, and norm equivalence. Conceptual equivalence refers to whether concepts have the same meaning across cultures. A lack of conceptual equivalence of depression across cultures was demonstrated by Tanka-Matsumi and Marsella (1976), who found that *yuutsu,* the term that is most equivalent to "depression" in Japanese, had different referents and connotations among Japanese nationals in comparison to the concept of depression among Americans. Similarly, Kinzie et al. (1982) found the concept of guilt to be associated with depression among Caucasian Americans but not Vietnamese Americans, demonstrating a lack of conceptual equivalence in depression between these groups. Functional equivalence refers to the degree of similarity between the functions and goals of behavior. If the antecedents, consequences, and correlates of a behavior are similar across cultures, the behavior is functionally equivalent (Frijda & Jahoda, 1966). Another type of equivalence concerns the quantitative aspects of psychological measurement, and includes metric equivalence (Van de Vijver & Poortinga, 1982), scalar equivalence, and item equivalence (Poortinga, 1975). These aspects of equivalence ensure that measurement instruments used across cultures have the same quantitative psychometric properties across cultures (Kameoka, 1985, 1989).

Among the various types of equivalence, the most relevant to our purposes here is norm equivalence. Norm equivalence refers to comparability in cultural norms for attitudes, beliefs, values, and behaviors (Marsella & Kameoka, 1989). Because cultural and social norms form the basis for judgments about normality and abnormality, it is imperative that norms are considered when comparing rates of psychopathology across cultures (Marsella & Kameoka, 1989). In the assessment endeavor, there are (at least) two sets of norms for appropriate behavior—the observer's and the subject's. If these two sets of standards differ substantially, judgments about psychopathology will vary not only according to actual symptomatology but differences between the sets of cultural norms as well. For example, Mann et al. (1992), using a standardized diagnostic system (ICD-9), asked mental health professionals in China, Indonesia, Japan, and the United States to evaluate and rate videotaped ADHD patients with respect to their hyperactive and disruptive behaviors. Not only was there a significant difference in ratings based on levels of hyperactivity, ratings were also significantly different between raters from different countries. Specifically, Chinese and Indonesian raters displayed a lower threshold for judging behaviors to be abnormal compared to Japanese and American raters. The basis for the cultural effect is evident when one examines the criteria for hyperactive-disruptive behaviors as proscribed in the ICD-9. In addition to items in the ICD-9 that are more objective, there are also items that call for judgments that are unavoidably based on cultural standards, including "difficulty remaining seated" and "fidgets too much." Even with phenomena that appear to be "objective," it may not be possible to set aside cultural frames of reference. For example, cultural groups who have little experience with pictorial representations have difficulty perceiving depth and distances shown in pictures (Derogowski, 1989).

Assessment is also predicated upon an interaction between the assessor and the assessed. This interaction is a complex process rendered even more complex in a cross-cultural context. The interaction between the observer and the subject is inevitably colored by each person's own cultural frame of reference and their perceptions of the other's cultural background in complex, interacting ways. To illustrate, in the WHO study on depression, guilt feelings were not expressed spontaneously by patients but were elicited by semistructured interviews asking about religious, social, and familial duties (WHO, 1983). Thus, other studies that found an absence of guilt (e.g., Singer, 1975) may not be tapping into the dimensions of guilt that have relevance and salience to these cultures. The mode of questioning also appeared to make a difference in responses. In semistructured interviews as compared to self-report questionnaires, patients disclosed greater feelings of guilt (WHO, 1983). Furthermore, in studies on ethnic matching between therapists and clients, Asian American, African American, Mexican American, Native American, and White patients had lower dropout rates and better outcomes with therapists of the same ethnicity (Sue, Fujino, Hu, Takeuchi, & Zane, 1991), suggesting the importance of cultural similarity in the therapist/client relationship. The underlying mechanism that may lead to better therapeutic outcomes, however, remains amorphous, as inter- and intracultural communication are processes that depend on many subtle factors such as empathy, social distance, and the existence and nature of stereotypes (Tanaka-Matsumi & Draguns, 1997).

Diagnosis

Diagnostic practices rely on cultural norms and standards for defining what is deviant and what is not. Some cultures are more tolerant of deviation from the norm whereas others insist on greater conformity (Edgerton, 1992). An example of the influence of cultural and social norms on diagnostic practices is how particular personality disorders are considered across cultures. Because personality disorders are long-standing patterns of behavior as opposed to acute syndromes, their diagnoses depend more on cultural conceptions of what constitutes a "normal" behavior pattern. Thus, social or cultural norms largely determine whether a personality pattern is "disordered" in a particular social or cultural context. According to Paris (1997), individualistic cultures (cultures that value autonomy and independence) will tolerate traits that are associated with autonomy, such as impulsivity and narcissism, mores so than traits associated with dependence. Conversely, collectivistic cultures (cultures that value interdependence and conformance) are less able to tolerate traits that isolate (e.g., schizoid) or differentiate (e.g., narcissism) the individual from the group or behaviors that conflict with group conformity and harmony (e.g., antisocial behavior). In the same vein, Lopez (1989) speculates that diagnoses reflect diagnosticians' beliefs about baselines rates and manifestations of the psychological disorder of interest in various populations.

Studies examining the diagnostic tendencies among psychiatrists in different countries have found significantly different rates of disorders across countries. In the U.S.–U.K. Diagnostic Project, diagnoses of schizophrenia and affective disorders among hospital admissions in New York and London were compared. Schizophrenia was found to be diagnosed significantly more frequently in the United States than in England, whereas depression was diagnosed more than twice as often among English patients than among U.S. patients (Cooper, Kendell, Gurland, Sartorius, & Farkas, 1969; Gurland et al., 1972). These differences disappeared, however, when a standardized diagnostic system, the ICD-8, was used. In another phase of the project in which videotaped interviews of patients were used as bases for making diagnoses, substantial cross-national agreement was found for typical cases; however, patients with mixed symptom profiles were more likely to elicit diagnoses of schizophrenia from American diagnosticians and affective disorders from British raters. Thus, these studies provide empirical support for cross-national agreement when standardized diagnostic criteria are used as well as the influence of cultural norms on diagnostic practices.

Sampling

The observation of sociocultural variations in psychopathology is affected by the sampling method used in cross-cultural epidemiological studies. One major methodological issue is whether studies use clinic-based samples or population-based samples. Clinic-based samples could be skewed by biases in diagnostic practices that vary cross-culturally, as noted earlier. Also, among patient samples, rates of a disorder could vary systematically due to cultural factors that influence whether treatment is sought. One such factor is the criterion by which people of different cultures use to determine the need for treatment. For example, Asians and Asian Americans tend to define illness by their capacity to maintain their work and familial obligations (Takeuchi & Uehara, 1996). As long as they can physically continue to work and fulfill social expectations, they do not consider themselves sick enough to seek treatment. This tendency may account for why Asian Americans have been found to underutilize mental health services relative to their proportion in the population (Abe & Zane, 1990). Other factors that systematically contribute to differences in patient samples across cultures include geographical access to services and economic resources. In addition, certain cultures may tolerate particular types of deviance more so than others (Paris, 1997), thus certain disorders may be overrepresented in patient samples in a particular culture and others underrepresented. Thus, using patient samples in studies that compare cross-cultural prevalence may indeed yield cross-cultural differences; however, these differences are likely to result from biased samples than from true differences in symptom prevalence or manifestation.

The use of nonpatient, population-based samples appears to avoid the biases that can occur in patient samples. In comparing prevalence rates of depression in studies using patient samples versus nonpatient samples, Marsella (1980) found that depression rates are more similar cross-culturally among nonpatient samples. This finding tentatively supports the argument that patient samples contain biases due to self-selection and differences in diagnostic practices. Epidemiological studies based on nonpatient samples, however, are not without methodological problems. For example, case identification may be based on different criteria in different cultures (Marsella, 1980), or on whether researchers emphasize similarities or differences in symptoms. Kleinman (1995) criticized the methodological strategy of the WHO depression studies due to its tendency to focus on similarities across cultures—an overreliance on the etic approach—which narrows the range of cases that are identified, thus underestimating cross-cultural variation. Furthermore, the person making the diagnosis may vary markedly, from psychiatrists and psychologists to relatively untrained interviewers (Dohrenwend & Dohrenwend, 1974). Thus, whereas nonpatient samples seem to be superior over patient samples in cross-cultural epidemiological studies on psychopathology, care must be taken to ensure that standards of cross-cultural equivalence are met and standardized procedures are used across cultures, while concurrently allowing for emic features to emerge and be documented.

DEFINING AND ARTICULATING SOCIOCULTURAL FACTORS

Various sociocultural factors have been studied in relation to their influence on psychopathology. These factors include culture, race, ethnicity, gender, religion, socioeconomic status (SES), acculturation, immigration, and minority status. As volumes have been written on how these factors might influence psychopathology, it is beyond the scope of this chapter to provide a comprehensive review of the literature on each factor. Of greater relevance and importance is the identification of key issues and problems underlying studies on these influences. In particular, a major problem in the empirical literature is the lack of clarity in how sociocultural factors are defined and operationalized. For example, culture has been variously conceptualized as nationality (e.g., WHO, 1983), knowledge of cultural values and language (e.g., Thomas, 1986), and ethnicity (e.g., Wildes & Emery, 2001). Furthermore, the use of the term *culture* as a predictor variable has been confounded with ethnicity, race, nationality, SES, acculturation, minority status, and even gender, which has been conceptualized as a *subculture* (Canales, 2000), obscuring the differences and implications of each. More often than not, studies that use this all-encompassing term do not explicitly define its relationship to other sociocultural factors. Thus, when a relationship between culture and psychopathology is found, it becomes extremely difficult to interpret what the findings mean. Furthermore, when a group of studies that use the term *culture* differently are taken together, it is almost impossible to draw any general conclusions about a cultural effect. The following sections critically examine research on sociocultural factors as they relate to psychopathology, focusing on culture, race, ethnicity, nationality, SES, minority status, acculturation, and ethnic identity. Although these factors are grouped into three sections based on conceptual similarities, it is understood that they all interrelate in significant ways. Selected research on these influences will be discussed in the context of conceptual and methodological issues, and suggestions will be offered for clarifying these constructs. Although gender and religion may influence psychopathology as well, the scope of this chapter precludes their discussion. The reader is referred to Frank (2000) for a review on the effects of gender and to Prince (1992) on the effects of religion.

Race, Culture, Ethnicity, and Nationality

The terms *race, culture, ethnicity,* and *nationality* are often used interchangeably in psychological research. Although these terms are related, certain distinctions exist that necessitate great care in their conceptualization, operationalization, and measurement. Of these terms, race is generally considered the least appropriate for psychological research, as it connotes a biological distinction that is, in actual usage, largely socially constructed (Alvidrez, Axocar, & Miranda, 1996), and neither the physical nor psychological features attributed to race are consistent or specific (Beutler, Brown, Crothers, Booker, & Seabrook, 1996). Ethnicity is used more often in psychological research as it obviates physical characteristics in favor of group identification based on a common ancestry, language, or nationality (Betancourt & Lopez, 1993). The concept of ethnicity, however, may be too broad to be meaningful because ethnic categories often encompass many diverse cultural groups. The concept of culture may be more meaningful. Among the dozens of varying definitions of culture that have been offered over the years (e.g., Herskovits, 1949; Marsella, 1980; Triandis, 1972), the most common and salient elements among them are: (1) culture has external, or tangible, referents (e.g., artifacts, institutions, activities, products), also referred to as material culture; (2) culture has internal, or intangible, referents (e.g., values, symbols, norms, language, customs, behaviors), also referred to as subjective culture; and (3) culture is transmitted and communicated inter- and intragenerationally. As such, culture may be the most appropriate construct to use in psychological research as it refers to substantive elements that vary and are measurable across cultures.

Among the various sociocultural influences of psychopathology, culture has received the most attention. Recent reviews of research on the relationship between culture and psychopathology include articles by Draguns and Tanaka-Matsumi (2003; Tanaka-Matsumi & Draguns, 1997), Tanaka-Matsumi (2001), and Lopez and Guarnaccia (2000). In psychopathology research, culture is often used interchangeably with nationality or ethnicity, the underlying assumption being that these constructs overlap considerably. In the WHO collaborative study on cultural variation of schizophrenia, incidence and symptomatology were assessed in China (Taiwan), Colombia, the Czech Republic, Denmark, India, Nigeria, Russia, Great Britain, and the United States (WHO, 1973, 1979, 1983). Cultural variation in incidence was found to be minimal, as rates were constant at 0.3 percent (Odejide, 1979), and a core set of symptoms was observed at all nine sites. These symptoms included restricted affect, poor insight, thinking aloud, poor rapport, incoherent speech, nonrealistic information, and bizarre or nihilistic delusions (Sartorius, Jablensky, Korten, & Ernberg, 1986). Although certain symptoms were fairly consistent across nations, the content of the symptoms—for example, what delusions were about—was found to differ. The similarities in rates prompted the investigators to suggest that schizophrenia is predominantly biologically influenced (Jablensky & Sartorius, 1988), although Kleinman (1995) criticized the studies' etically based methodology, which may have restricted the range of cases and therefore the symptoms that were observed.

It is noteworthy that the similarities and differences in schizophrenia symptoms worldwide are assumed to be due to culture. Although cultural differences obviously exist between countries in the WHO studies, other influences such as socioeconomic status may also exist. Indeed, in comparing the outcomes of patients in more industrialized and less industrialized countries, those in less developed countries exhibited better outcomes and lower relapse rates (Sartorius et al., 1986). Thus, this variation may not be based on culture as defined—that is, as a set of values, norms, and so forth that is transmitted generationally—but on economic conditions of a nation at a particular point in time. Nonetheless, lack of clarity in the conceptualization and operationalization of culture makes any interpretation of findings difficult, especially if, as in the case of depression as discussed earlier, "cultural" differences are found in incidence and prevalence.

In an article aptly entitled "Culture and Ethnicity: Maintaining the Distinction," Thomas (1986) sought to distinguish the two concepts. Thomas argued that cultural explanations may be erroneous when based on ethnic categories in multiethnic societies, unless the competence of members of a particular ethnic group in the group's language and cultural practices is also assessed (Thomas, 1986). In a comparative study of Maori and Pakeha (European) children in New Zealand, Thomas measured culture and ethnicity independently, with culture defined as knowledge of language and cultural practices, and found main effects for both ethnicity and culture in predicting children's achievement.

The concept of ethnicity has been acknowledged as "muddy" (Omi & Winant, 1994). The psychological literature does not typically distinguish between culture and ethnicity and often confuses the two. To wit, ethnicity has been referred to as "a social-psychological sense of peoplehood in which members of a group share a unique social and cultural heritage that is transmitted from one generation to another" (Sue, 1991). To examine ethnic differences in lifetime prevalence of mental disorders, the Epidemiologic Catchment Area (ECA) Study was conducted in five sites in the United States, including Los Angeles, California; New Haven, Connecticut; Baltimore, Maryland; St. Louis, Missouri; and Durham, North Carolina. Based on the Los Angeles sample and controlling for the effects of age, gender, marital status, education, income, and SES, it was found that Whites were more likely than Blacks to meet *DSM-III* (1980) criteria for depression, dysthymia, obsessive-compulsive disorder, drug and alcohol abuse and dependence, antisocial personality, and anorexia, and less likely to have phobia and somatization (Zhang and Snowden, 1999). Whites were more likely to have schizophrenia, obsessive-compulsive disorder, panic disorder, and drug use and dependence than Hispanics, and were more likely than Asians to have schizophreniform disorder, manic episodes, bipolar disorder, panic disorder, somatization, drug and alcohol dependence, and antisocial personality.

Although these findings suggest that psychological disorders are not uniformly distributed across ethnic groups, it is unclear what aspect of ethnicity explains these differences. The authors stated that "prevalence of mental disorders varies by ethnicity because of background cultural influences that can significantly modify experience and manifestation of mental disorders" (Zhang and Snowden, 1999, p. 135), thus suggesting that cultural variables underlie ethnic differences. Blacks, however, had lower prevalence rates in the other ECA study sites, prompting the authors to attribute this difference to the "sociopolitical scene" in Los Angeles during the early 1980s (Zhang & Snowden, 1999). Also, higher rates of immigration and extended family support were suggested as possible explanations for lower rates of mental disorders in Los Angeles as compared to the other sites. Thus, it appears that ethnicity is a proxy for a host of possible underlying social mechanisms including political circumstances, immigration, and the availability of family support in a geographic region, as well as cultural variables such as traditions and values.

The fact that each ethnic category actually comprises a multitude of diverse ethnic groups further obscures interpretation of the ECA findings. For example, the Asian category can encompass some 30 distinct ethnic groups, including Chinese, Japanese, Filipino, and Pacific Islanders (who were also included in the Asian category in the study), and Hispanics can encompass Mexicans, Central Americans, and South Americans, each group consisting of many ethnic subgroups that have distinct cultural traditions. In fact, when one considers the heterogeneity of these "ethnic" categories, any ethnic variation found may be viewed as artifacts based on an arbitrary system of distinction, because the underlying assumption that there are meaningful commonalities within each ethnic category is not easily supported.

The methodology used in the ECA study reflects an etic position, in which symptoms must conform to *DSM* criteria to be included as cases. Thus, as the authors noted, ethnically specific (emic) manifestations of disorders may not have been detected, and the findings do not reflect psychopathology in general but rather mental disorders as delineated and described in the *DSM*. A combined etic/emic methodology would better serve the goal of accurately assessing rates of psychopathology in culturally diverse populations.

Ethnic variations have also been suggested in eating disturbance and eating disorders. Studies on ethnic groups within the United States and between nationalities have found that White women in Western countries are more likely to develop dysfunctional eating attitudes and behaviors and to have a higher incidence of eating disorders than non-White and non-Western women (Crago, Shisslak, & Estes, 1996; Fitzgibbon et al., 1998; Pate, Pumariega, Hester, & Garner, 1992). A cultural explanation for the observed ethnic differences is consistent with data showing cultural historical trends toward a body ideal of thinness, including downward trends of body sizes of beauty pageant winners and *Playboy* centerfolds, paralleling the rise of eating disorders in the United States (Garfinkel & Garner, 1982). Sociocultural influences of eating disorder symptomatology appear so striking that some researchers have referred to eating disorders as culture-bound syndromes (Crago et al., 1996; Pate et al., 1993; Prince, 1985). In a meta-analysis of cross-ethnic studies on eating disturbance, Wildes and Emery (2001) found that of 35 studies that met criteria for inclusion, 11 included a measure of culture or acculturation. Based on the premise that the adoption of Western cultural values predisposes one to eating disturbances, measuring cultural values or acculturation independent of ethnicity is necessary to better understand the observed ethnic variations. Unfortunately, acculturation was defined and measured so differently among the studies (e.g., level of integration into a dominant culture versus level of identification with nondominant cultural groups versus cultural orientation) that no conclusions could be drawn regarding the effects of culture (Wildes & Emery, 2001). Nevertheless, these studies are laudable for distinguishing the concepts of ethnicity and culture.

SES and Minority Status

SES and minority status are conceptually different from race, culture, ethnicity, and nationality in that they are inherently relative terms. That is, inherent in the concept of socioeconomic position is stratification within a hierarchy of socioeconomic statuses, and meaning is derived from where one stands relative to others. Similarly, minority status is determined relative to some majority. Minority status refers to being a member of a social minority in terms of power. In the United States, social minorities are generally those that are also in the statistical minority but not always; for example, women are the statistical majority but are minorities in settings of power. Thus, a minority status effect would reflect the effects of unequal status in terms of power, and would be reflected in psychosocial outcomes such as prejudice and discrimination, differential access and treatment, and disenfranchisement and marginalization. It is important to note the difference between a minority status effect and a cultural effect; to illustrate, that Hispanic Americans are more likely to report greater stress due to discrimination and unequal access to resources is not a reflection of their culture but rather of their minority status in the United States. In other words, in their native countries, they would not experience the same levels of stress. This distinction is often lost in research on mental health and illness, which often refers to the stress experienced by a minority group as a cultural rather than a minority status effect. Minority status is implicated in the high rates of alcohol abuse among Native Americans, whose history of exploitation and marginalization in the United States is seen as an influencing factor (Sue, 1991). Minority status is also reflected in studies that compare ethnic groups in their native cultural settings and in settings in which they are minorities. For example, rates of psychosis among Black Caribbeans in the Caribbean are comparable to the rates among Whites in the United Kingdom, yet are markedly higher than those among Black Caribbeans in the United Kingdom (Sharpley, Hutchinson, McKenzie, & Murray, 2001).

Among the broad sociocultural constructs, SES has been perhaps the most misused in psychological research. Traditionally operationalized as some combination of education, income, and occupational status, SES typically serves as a proxy variable for factors ranging from poverty to job stress to dangerous neighborhoods. In reviewing studies that examine SES as a demographic predictor or covariate, two major conceptions of SES emerge: *SES as environment* and *SES as experience* (Chin, 1988). The idea of SES as environment focuses on external features associated with SES such as neighborhoods and communities, whereas the notion of SES as experience emphasizes internal processes such as stress and deprivation. Both of these conceptions are important in explicating any SES effect; however, unless the specific environmental or psychological variables of theoretical interest are directly measured, it remains difficult to interpret any SES effect.

SES is strongly correlated but not synonymous with race, ethnicity, and minority status (Goodnow, 1986; Williams & Collins, 1995). In psychopathology research, studies conducted on patient and nonpatient samples generally have found an inverse relationship between SES and psychopathology (Dohrenwend & Dohrenwend, 1974; Hollingshead & Redlich, 1958; Zigler & Glick, 1986). In the five-site Epidemiologic Catchment Area (ECA) study, those in the lowest socioeconomic status group were 2.5 times more likely to have one-month prevalence rates of a disorder, as assessed by the NIMH Diagnostic Interview Schedule, than those in the highest SES group, controlling for age, gender, race or ethnicity, and marital status (Regier et al., 1993). The effects of SES were even more evident for schizophrenia, in which the lowest SES individuals were more than eight times more likely to evidence the disorder than those in the highest SES group (Regier et al., 1993). This finding replicates previous studies that have shown schizophrenia to be more prevalent in lower SES groups (Beck, 1978; Dunham, 1976; Strauss, Bartko, & Carpenter, 1981). Whether this represents social causation—that events and experiences associated with low SES causes a higher rate of schizophrenia—or social selection—that schizophrenia causes a downward drift in social position—remains equivocal. The social causation hypothesis is consistent with the diathesis-stress model of schizophrenia, in which both biological vulnerability and environmental stress are postulated to cause the development of the disorder. Given that low socioeconomic status may be a proxy for more stressful life experiences, it seems probable that SES acts as a causal influence. Findings from empirical studies have been inconsistent, however. Some studies have supported the social selection hypothesis for schizophrenia (Dohrenwend et al., 1992), other studies have supported the hypothesis for certain types of schizophrenia but not others (Dunham, 1964), and yet others for both the social causation and social selection hypotheses (Clausen & Kohn, 1959; Wing, 1978).

The relationship between SES and other diagnostic categories has been demonstrated less consistently. Some studies have found a higher prevalence of depression among lower SES individuals (e.g., Gilman, Kawachi, Fitzmaurice, & Buka, 2003), whereas others have found the reverse (cf., Zigler & Glick, 1986). The varying rates of depression found among different social classes may be due to how depression is construed and measured. In studies using symptom rating scales as indexes for depression, greater symptomatology is evident in lower class individuals; however, when diagnostic criteria are used, higher rates of depression are found in middle- and upper-class individuals (Schwab, Brown, Holzer, & Sokolof, 1968; Weissman & Myers, 1978).

Another important consideration is the confounding of SES with race or ethnicity. A particular SES indicator may not be equivalent across race or ethnicity in terms of life circumstances. For example, at a given level of education Black Americans have less income than White Americans, and low-SES Blacks experience more crime and unemployment than Whites at the same SES level (Jaynes & Williams, 1989). Kessler and Neighbors (1986) stressed the importance of measuring the two constructs separately and testing for interactions between them. In a reanalysis of eight epidemiological studies, they found that when SES was controlled, the effect of race on psychological distress was nonsignificant. The interaction between race and SES, however, was significant, indicating that low-SES Blacks had higher rates of distress than did low-SES Whites (Kessler & Neighbors, 1986). When gender is considered as yet another factor, this finding changes, showing that low-SES White men had higher rates of psychiatric disorder than low-SES Black women (Williams, Takeuchi, & Adair, 1992).

Acculturation and Ethnic Identity

In contrast to the more macrolevel sociological constructs such as race, culture, and SES, acculturation and ethnic identity refer to more proximal psychosocial processes. Acculturation is defined as changes that occur either in a culture or an individual as a result of direct contact with another culture (Berry, Poortinga, Segall, & Dasen, 1992). At the individual level, acculturation is the process by which individuals learn about the customs, language, and rules for the behavior of a group of people (Corsini, 1987). Although contact between two cultures or two individuals of different cultures changes each, research in psychology has been more interested in the changes of individuals new to the dominant culture.

Two competing models of the acculturation process exist. The unidimensional model viewed the adoption of the new cultures as inevitably accompanied by the loss of the original culture, whereas the bidimensional model of acculturation posits two dimensions, the first indicating the extent to which an individual has integrated into the new culture and the second the extent to which he/she has retained elements of their original culture (Berry & Kim, 1988). The interaction of these two dimensions yields four modes of acculturation: (1) integration (or biculturalism), defined as the maintenance of one's native culture while simultaneously joining, participating in, and adopting aspects of the dominant culture; (2) assimilation, referring to the abandonment of one's native culture in favor of the dominant culture; (3) separation, in which one's native culture is maintained in favor of participating and integrating into the dominant culture; and (4) marginalization, in which the traditions and mores of one's native culture is abandoned yet no significant movement is made toward integrating into the new culture (Berry & Kim, 1988). Studies comparing the validity of unidimensional and bidimensional models have generally supported the bidimensional approach (e.g., Ryder, Alden, & Paulhus, 2000). Thus, the acquisition of values, attitudes, and behaviors of a new culture does not necessarily imply a loss of one's native culture.

In spite of the sophistication of theoretical models explicating the acculturation process, studies on the effects of acculturation on psychopathology have generally eschewed the multidimensional approach in favor of using proxy variables such as birthplace, length of residence in the United States, generational status, and language preference as indicators of acculturation. In an epidemiological study of Hispanics in the United States, higher acculturation, as indicated by nativity, parental nativity, and language preference, predicted more *DSM-III-R* (1987) disorders and substance abuse (Ortega, Rosenheck, Alegria, & Desai, 2000). This finding is consistent with the results of a large-scale study of Mexican immigrants, which showed that the lifetime prevalence rate for any disorder was 48.1 percent for U.S.-born Mexicans compared to 24.9 percent for immigrants (Vega et al., 1998). Also, short-term-stay immigrants, defined as less than 13 years residence in the United States, were found to have half the lifetime prevalence rate of immigrants living in the United States for more than 13 years. In contrast, other studies have reported a negative association between acculturation and psychopathology (e.g., Fabrega & Wallace, 1970) or no association (e.g., Ortega et al., 2000).

The inconsistency of results regarding the influence of acculturation may be due to the often simplistic manner by which it is operationalized, as described previously. The inappropriateness of using such proxy variables (e.g., generational status, birthplace, length of residence in the United States) as indicators of acculturation is underscored by Abe-Kim, Okazaki, and Goto (2001), who found that generational status cannot adequately capture the two dimensions of acculturation as posited in the bidimensional approach. Using multivariate analyses of covariance, they found that among a sample of Asian Americans, generational status predicted differences in some cultural indicators (e.g., individualism/collectivism) but not others (e.g., self-construal). The authors caution against the assumptions that group differences based on generational status are attributable to cultural-psychological effects and that immigrants are characterized by more traditionally Asian values compared to nonimmigrants.

Studies using the bidimensional model have produced more consistent results, with integrated individuals exhibiting the most positive psychological outcomes and marginalized individuals the poorest (Cuellar & Paniagua, 2000; Leiber, Chin, Nihara, & Mink, 2001; Sands & Berry, 1993). Another bidimensional model posits one dimension based on acculturation (high or low) and the second dimension on ethnic identity (high or low; Leiber et al., 2001). Ethnic identity refers to how one views oneself in terms of ethnicity, and is thus an aspect of one's broader identity (Phinney, 1990; Sue, Mak, & Sue, 1998). These two dimensions—acculturation and ethnic identity—though related, are conceptually distinct and independent. For example, one can view himself or herself as wholly Chinese while becoming integrated into a new sociocultural context. On the other hand, one's view of oneself may change significantly in the process of acculturation, during which "becoming" American occurs along with "acquiring" U.S. values, customs, and behaviors (Leiber et al., 2001). In a study of Chinese immigrants, the bicultural (high acculturation/high ethnic identification) group and the separated (low acculturation/high ethnic identification) group had significantly better psychological adjustment than the other groups (Lieber et al., 2001). This finding is consistent with the findings of Berry and Sam (1996) showing that assimilation and marginalization were associated with negative self-evaluation, depressive symptoms, and somatic symptoms. That separated groups fared better than assimilated groups is worth noting, as it calls into question assimilation as an adaptive acculturation strategy.

ELUCIDATING MECHANISMS UNDERLYING SOCIOCULTURAL VARIATIONS IN PSYCHOPATHOLOGY

In spite of the voluminous research linking various sociocultural factors with psychopathology, efforts to elucidate the mechanisms that explain the relationship have not kept pace. It has long been recognized that "macrolevel" variables such as culture and ethnicity must be translated into social and psychological processes in order for the relationship between these factors and psychopathology to be understood. Furthermore, very few theoretical frameworks have been advanced to specify the various conceptual levels that distinguish macrolevel from microlevel variables. Marsella and Yamada (2000) proposed three conceptual levels that capture key concerns in the field of culture and mental health: the individual, cultural, and sociopolitical levels. Each level consists of both negative and positive concerns. At the individual level are negative concerns such as distress and disorder and positive concerns such as health and adaptation. The cultural level includes concerns such as disintegration and dislocation on the negative side and organization and integration on the positive side. At the sociopolitical level are positive concerns such as colonization and oppression and negative concerns such as reconstruction and reform. This articulation of three widening spheres from the individual to the sociopolitical is helpful in clarifying the different conceptual levels at which constructs operate; however, it falls short of specifying how particular concerns at the individual level (e.g., distress) relate to concerns at the cultural and sociopolitical levels.

A more elaborated model that specifies the relationship between cultural characteristics and individual outcomes was proposed by Draguns and Tanaka-Matsumi (2003), who applied Hofstede's (2001) five cultural dimensions to notions of the self and psychological outcomes. Based on multivariate studies on work-related values in more than 40 countries worldwide, Hofstede identified five major dimensions that reliably differentiate cultures from one another: (1) individualism/collectivism; (2) power distance; (3) femininity/masculinity; (4) uncertainty avoidance; and (5) dynamism orientation (Hofstede, 1991, 2001). In relation to psychopathology, each of these dimensions has implications for views of the self as well as the nature of symptoms and issues that are expressed. For example, an individualistic culture fosters an independent self that, in turn, may lead to symptoms expressed as guilt, loneliness, and alienation should maladaptations occur.

Although the framework put forth by Draguns and Tanaka-Matsumi is an elegant and elaborate formulation of the relationship between culture and symptom manifestation, it does not address the influence of other sociocultural factors such as SES, ethnicity, and acculturation. An alternative conceptual framework is presented in Figure 5.1 for specifying social and psychological mechanisms that underlie the relationship between sociocultural factors and psychopathology outcomes. In order to have maximum heuristic value, a model or conceptual framework should add to the understanding of the phenomena of interest but at the same time be sufficiently parsimonious so as to illuminate and not obfuscate. As such, the present framework consists of two levels of constructs—the sociocultural and individual levels. The *sociocultural level* refers to macrolevel phenomena that may be conceptualized, measured, and analyzed at the cultural or social level. The *individual level* refers to microlevel phenomena that are experienced psychologically or behaviorally by individuals. Within each level are two types of variables. At the sociocultural level, the first type of variable is the *proxy variable* such as culture or SES, which is commonly used in studies as a predictor of psychopathology outcome, but which

Figure 5.1

	Sociocultural Level		**Individual Level**	
	Sociocultural Proxy Variable	Social/Cultural Characteristic	Psychological Experience	Psychopathology Outcome
Example 1:	Culture	Individualism / Collectivism	Independent Self-Construal / Interdependent Self-Construal	Depression Manifested as Existential Despair / Depression Manifested as Somatic Symptoms
Example 2:	SES	Resource Deprivation	Level of Stress	Level of Depression

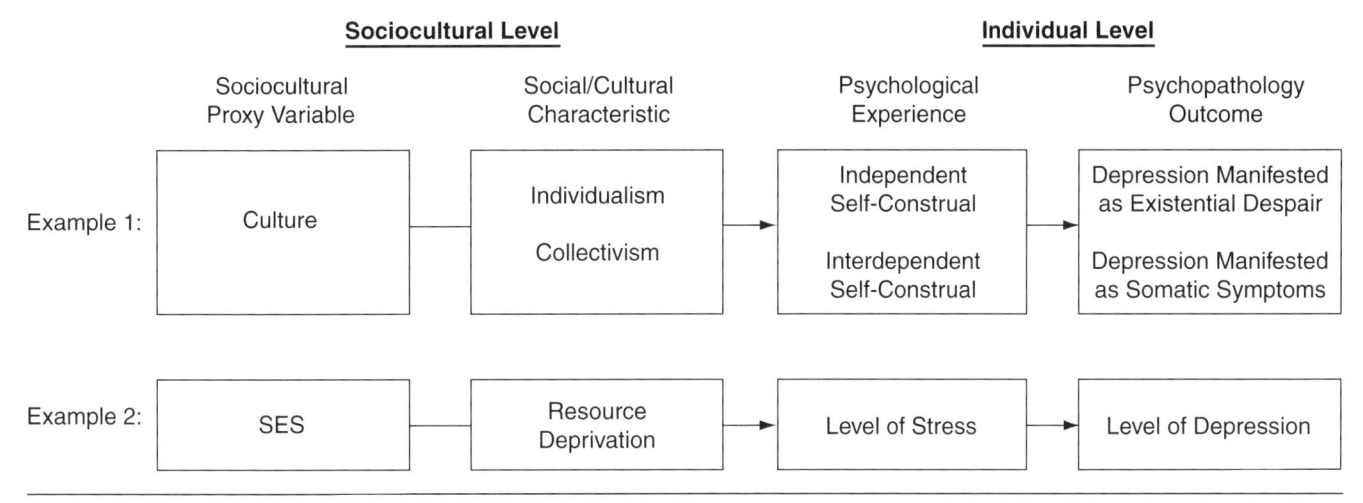

Figure 5.1 Conceptual framework for specifying social and psychological mechanisms underlying sociocultural-psychopathology relationship.

offers very little explanatory power. The second type of variable is the more meaningful *feature* or *characteristic* of the social or cultural context, which varies according to the associated proxy variable. At the individual level, the first type of variable is the psychological experience that serves as the link between the social or cultural characteristic and psychopathology outcome. The second type of individual-level variable is the psychopathology outcome itself.

In Example 1 in Figure 5.1, the influence of "culture" on psychopathology outcome is mediated by the following mechanism: culture is reflected in individualism or collectivism, which is associated with independent or interdependent self-construal, which in turn predicts whether depression is experienced and manifested as existential despair or somatic symptoms. An individual who views him/herself more independently is likely to experience depression as existential despair, whereas a person with an interdependent self-construal is likely to manifest somatic symptoms (Marsella, 1980). In Example 2, SES is reflected specifically in resource deprivation, which determines the level of stress one experiences and, in turn, one's level of depression. Using this bilevel framework as a guide, the mechanisms linking sociocultural factors that are currently too imprecisely construed to their respective psychopathology outcomes can be specified and the causal pathways tested. The following subsections discuss some promising cultural- and individual-level mechanisms proposed in the literature that are consistent with the framework presented in Figure 5.1.

Individualism/Collectivism

Individualism and collectivism are broad cultural orientations that have been found to reliably distinguish cultures from one another. In individualistic cultures, autonomy and independence is emphasized. Self-interest takes precedence over the interests of the group, and behavior is based on personal attitudes rather than group norms (Triandis, 2001). In contrast, collectivistic cultures emphasize interdependence within ingroups (family, tribe, nation, etc.). Behavior is shaped by group norms, and group harmony is valued above individual emotions or goals (Triandis, 2001). Much research has been conducted in the area of individualism/collectivism. Specifically, individualism/collectivism has been associated with psychological processes such as learning and reinforcement (Haruki et al., 1984), social perception (Bond & Forgas, 1984), social cognition (Berman, Murphy-Berman, & Singh, 1985), and self-construal (Markus & Kitayama, 1991). Individuals in individualistic cultures also differ from those in collectivistic cultures with respect to values and life experiences. Members of individualistic cultures exhibit higher achievement motivation, alienation, anomie, loneliness, value competition, pleasure, and social recognition, whereas people in collectivistic cultures appear to receive more and better social support, and value cooperation and harmony (Kagitcibasi & Berry, 1989).

Cross-cultural researchers have invoked individualism and collectivism to explain cultural variations in psychopathology. To explain the lower rates of depression among the Chinese, Lin and colleagues suggested that the Chinese collectivistic cultural orientation, which promotes tight family bonds and interrelationships, buffers the impact of negative events and provides greater social support in times of stress (Lin, 1985; Tseng, Lin, & Yee, 1995). A higher degree of collectivism may also explain the difference between industrialized and developing countries with respect to the course of schizophrenia. Among the nine countries that participated in the epidemiological study on schizophrenia conducted by the World Health Organization, patients in the less industrialized nations exhibited better prognoses and less relapse than those in the more prosperous, industrialized countries (Sartorius et al., 1986), possibly because developing countries may offer a greater sense of community and kinship than developed countries.

Collectivism and its social and psychological concomitants have been also hypothesized to explain cultural variation in rates and manifestations of depression. Specifically, Marsella (1980) evoked the *self-structure,* which may vary according to cultural orientation, and suggested a link to the different types of depression symptoms that prevail across cultures. For example, he noted that in some cultures in which an unindividuated self-structure predominates, along with a metaphorical language structure and an imagistic mode of experiencing reality, people develop *subjective epistemic orientations* that make it difficult to capture or express their internal states in objective, detached terms. Thus, members of these cultures would experience more somatic rather than affective, cognitive, or existential symptoms. For those in cultures that promote an individuated self-structure, along with an abstract language and a lexical mode of experiencing reality, an *objective epistemic orientation* is developed in which internal affective states can be pinpointed and labeled. Members of these cultures would experience depression as an affective, existential, and cognitive as well as somatic disturbance.

Marsella (1980) further suggested that these cultural differences in self-structure can explain why non-Western cultures have lower rates of suicide. Because a person with a subjective epistemic orientation does not experience a change in identity during the depressive state and does not label his or her experience as a psychological one, despair about the self is obviated and suicide does not result. On the other hand, a person with an objective epistemic orientation experiences illness as an essential change in the self, he or she experiences existential despair, and thus risk for suicide increases. Although Marsella did not specify which cultures have subjective versus objective epistemic orientations, it may be inferred that objective orientations are likely to be found in Western cultures.

Social Stress/Support

Social stress and support have been postulated as an underlying psychological mechanism linking broad sociocultural constructs, such as culture and SES, with individual psychopathology outcomes. In interpreting why SES may be inversely related to psychopathology, it has been suggested that those in the lower social classes experience more stressful and undesirable events (Strauss, 1979) and have less social support and fewer social networks (Billings, Cronkite, & Moos, 1983; Strauss, 1979; Zubin, Steinhauer, & Condray, 1992). Certainly, the diathesis-stress model of psychopathology suggests that stress is a significant environmental predictor of distress and disorder (Zuckerman, 1999). In a study of racial and ethnic differences in depression, Plant and Sachs-Ericsson (2004) found that the greater depressive symptoms experienced by ethnic minorities relative to Whites were mediated by difficulties meeting basic needs such as food, shelter, or clothing. Similarly, Ennis and colleagues found that stress that results from difficulties meeting daily needs is a stronger predictor of depressive symptoms than income level (Ennis, Hobfoll, & Schroeder, 2000). These findings highlight the importance of moving beyond the conventional indicators of SES such as income by examining chronic resource deficits and daily resource deprivation (Ennis et al., 2000; Hobfoll, 1998; Hobfoll, Johnson, Ennis, & Jackson, 2003).

Interestingly, Plant and Sachs-Ericsson (2004) noted that although the number of Asian participants was too small to be included in the main analyses, it appeared that the relationship between resources and depression would be different for Asians as compared to other minority groups. Specifically, it is possible that the collectivistic cultural orientation of most Asian groups buffers the deleterious effects of resource deprivation, perhaps through a greater sharing of resources or the provision of greater social and emotional support. This hypothesis is consistent with the lower rates of depression found in Asian cultures (Compton et al., 1991). Of course, SES and minority status should be controlled in studies examining the effects of culture, in which an adequate range of SES levels as well as minority (Asians in the United States) and majority status (Asians in Asian countries) are represented. It is only with such a design that the specific effects of the various sociocultural influences can be determined.

Acculturative stress may be viewed as a type of stress resulting from the acculturation process. Stress that stems from acculturation may lead to positive or negative consequences, depending on individual factors such as appraisal, self-efficacy, coping, and acculturation strategy, as well as environmental factors including circumstances of migration (Berry, 1998). Within this framework, much research has pinpointed acculturation strategy as a major predictor of psychological health and disorder, and has consistently found integration or biculturalism, to be associated with better mental health (cf. Berry, 1998).

Social stress and support have also been implicated in analyses of why higher suicide rates have been documented in certain places and time periods than others. Rates of suicide and admissions to psychiatric hospitals appear to increase during economic recessions and high unemployment (Williams & Collins, 1995). Social disintegration (Leighton,

1963) and rapid social transformation (Paris, 1991) have been postulated to lead to the breakdown of societal norms and family structures, triggering depression, alienation, social isolation, and hopelessness (Jilek-Aall, 1988; Desjarlais et al., 1995). The link between suicide and broad social change indicators is tenuous, however. Rapid social change does not always produce rises in suicide rates (Desjarlais, Eisenberg, Good, & Kleinman, 1995) nor does it necessarily produce increases in psychological states such as anomie (Durkheim, 1951) and hopelessness (Guthrie & Tanco, 1980). Methodological problems may contribute to inconsistencies in empirical findings. Concepts such as *social disintegration* and *rapid social change* may need to be defined more specifically in order to decrease the heterogeneity of a sample of societies that may be said to undergo such change. Moreover, the mediating mechanisms such as stress and social support, experienced by the individual, should be directly investigated as well.

Communication Style

Communication styles have been observed to differ across cultures. The anthropologist Edward T. Hall distinguished between "low context" and "high context" cultures with respect to communication (Hall, 1981). Members of low context cultures communicate more directly and literally, relying less on context to derive meaning from the communication. High context cultures communicate with more subtlety and nuance, and use the social context as a basis for interpreting verbal exchanges. For example, members of high context cultures rely on paralinguistic and nonverbal features such as posture and facial movements, as well as social etiquette such as receiving gifts and offering food, rather than direct verbal communication, to interpret the meaning of a particular exchange (Schweder, 1985).

This major difference in communication style has been raised as a critique of research on expressed emotion (EE) and its role in schizophrenia. Defined as criticism, hostility, and overinvolvement directed at a schizophrenic person by his or her family, EE has been associated with relapse and poorer prognoses for schizophrenic patients (Vaughn & Leff, 1976). A study of EE in Indian, Mexican, British, and Anglo families showed cultural differences, with the lowest levels of EE found in Indian families and the highest in Anglo families (Jenkins & Karno, 1992). Kleinman, however, questions whether the components of EE can be validly assessed in cultures in which communication is based not on direct verbal exchange, but rather on nonverbal aspects that are not part of the EE concept as defined (Kleinman, 1995). In other words, when taken out of its cultural context, can "hostility" be detected, given that cultures differ greatly on how emotions are expressed and perceived? This concern applies to any attempt to measure constructs using verbal means in cultures that communicate largely through nonverbal channels. The fact that different aspects of EE predict poor outcomes for different cultural groups further complicates the question. For example, Lopez et al. (1998) found that lack of family warmth predicted relapse in Mexican Americans, whereas criticism was related to relapse in Anglo-Americans. Given the different communication styles that exist among these cultural groups, the concepts of family warmth and criticism must first be established to be equivalent across cultural groups and then measured with reliability and validity within each group before these findings are fully understood.

Attitudes and Beliefs about Mental Health and Illness

The cultural and social construction of mental health and illness may determine illness behavior as well as responses to the behavior. More specifically, beliefs about what constitutes illness may shape the manifestation of a disorder. For example, the culture-bound syndromes of *brain fag* and *susto* may represent forms of depression consistent with cultural beliefs about illness. Thus, people within a particular culture share schemata about what discriminates illness from wellness based on what is prevalent and normative in their culture. Accordingly, they know which set of symptoms are acceptable for the sick role to be enacted.

Cross-cultural differences in conceptions of mental health and disease may also lead to the view that certain cultural groups "somaticize" more than others. The very idea of somatization assumes a separation of mind and body that is far from culturally universal. Indeed, the majority of cultures around the world may experience suffering as an integrated mind and body experience, and do not privilege the psychological aspects over the somatic (Lewis-Fernandez & Kleinman, 1994).

Definitions of mental health and illness are predicated upon the values of a culture and views of the self within cultures. For example, it has been found that Asians do not access mental health care until their symptoms are quite severe because they do not consider themselves ill until they can no longer fulfill their work and family obligations (Uehara, Takeuchi, & Smukler, 1994). Thus, their definition of illness is not based on subjective, internal states but rather on socially defined criteria. This definition is consistent with cultures that emphasize social reciprocity and construal of the self based on relationships with others. Furthermore, in Chinese culture, psychological symptoms do not justify help seeking (Cheung, 1989), further reducing the likelihood that treatment would be sought.

Similarly, beliefs about the causes of mental illness can vary cross-culturally, resulting in differences in the course and severity of the illness as well as help-seeking behavior (e.g., Narikiyo & Kameoka, 1992). Specifically, whether mental illness is believed to be internally or externally caused can determine how patients are treated within their families and cultures, thus either buffering or exacerbating the illness. For example, cross-cultural differences in expressed emotion may reflect beliefs about schizophrenia as being within or outside of an individual's control. If the predominant attribution is that it is within the individual's control, then high levels of criticism may ensue (Jenkins & Karno, 1992). The internal/external distinction is believed to vary across disorders as well. For example, when Mexican patients construe their illness as *ataque de nervios* rather than schizophrenia, they are more likely to receive sympathy and support because *nervios* is seen as a "legitimate" illness that is not under the individual's personal control (Jenkins, 1988). This construction of the disorder and the reactions it engenders is likely to have a positive effect on the course of schizophrenia. Again, the importance of culturally shared schema regarding what constitutes illness and the sick role and their relationship to illness manifestation and prognosis is underscored.

SUMMARY

Both universal and specific features of psychopathology have been found across cultural, ethnic, and social groups. In general, the wide range of sociocultural variation observed in the prevalence, manifestation, and course of psychological disorders points to the influence of sociocultural factors. The nature of this influence, however, is difficult to pinpoint owing to a host of epistemological, theoretical, and methodological issues. For instance, whether an etic, derived etic, or emic perspective is used in cross-cultural epidemiological studies affects the prevalence rates that are found. Moreover, the elucidation of sociocultural influence has suffered from a lack of clarity in the definition of sociocultural factors that are used to predict or correlate with psychopathology, such as culture, ethnicity, and socioeconomic status. Nevertheless, advances have been made in each of these domains in terms of their conceptual distinctions and how best to operationalize and measure them. A conceptual framework is presented in which proxy variables such as culture and SES are translated into meaningful cultural and social dimensions that relate to psychological experience. Specifically, some social and psychological processes that hold promise for explaining the sociocultural-psychopathology relationship include individualistic/collectivistic cultural orientation, social stress and support, communication style, and beliefs and attitudes about mental health and illness. When meaningful concepts are specified and measured at both cultural and individual levels, we can move beyond knowing that sociocultural factors influence psychopathology toward a deeper understanding of how and to what extent these factors influence psychopathology.

REFERENCES

Abe, J. S., & Zane, N. W. (1990). Psychological maladjustment among Asian and White American college students: Controlling for confounds. *Journal of Counseling Psychology, 37*(4), 437–444.

Abe-Kim, J., Okazaki, S., & Goto, S. G. (2001). Unidimensional versus multidimensional approaches to the assessment of acculturation for Asian American populations. *Cultural Diversity & Ethnic Minority Psychology, 7*(3), 232–246.

Alvidrez, J., Azocar, F., & Miranda, J. (1996). Demystifying the concept of ethnicity for psychotherapy researchers. *Journal of Consulting & Clinical Psychology, 64*(5), 903–908.

American Psychiatric Association. (1980). *Diagnostic and statistical manual of mental disorders* (3rd ed.). Washington, DC: Author.

American Psychiatric Association. (1987). *Diagnostic and statistical manual of mental disorders* (3rd ed., rev.). Washington, DC: Author.

American Psychiatric Association. (1994). *Diagnostic and statistical manual of mental disorders* (4th ed.). Washington, DC: Author.

Bebbington, P., Walsh, C., & Murray, R. (1993). The causes of functional psychosis. In C. G. Costello (Ed.), *Basic issues in psychopathology* (pp. 238–270). New York: Guilford Press.

Beck, J. C. (1978). Social influences on the prognosis of schizophrenia. *Schizophrenia Bulletin, 4*(1), 86–101.

Berman, J. J., Murphy-Berman, V., & Singh, P. (1985). Cross-cultural similarities and differences in perceptions of fairness. *Journal of Cross-Cultural Psychology, 16*(1), 55–67.

Berry, J. W. (1969). On cross-cultural comparability. *International Journal of Psychology, 4*(2), 119–128.

Berry, J. W. (1998). Acculturative stress. In P. B. Organista & K. M. Chun (Eds.), *Readings in ethnic psychology,* Florence, KY: Taylor & Francis/Routledge.

Berry, J. W., & Kim, U. (1988). Acculturation and mental health. In P. R. Dasen & J. W. Berry (Eds.), *Health and cross-cultural psychology: Toward applications. Cross-cultural research and methodology series, Vol. 10* (pp. 207–236). Thousand Oaks, CA: Sage.

Berry, J. W., Poortinga, Y. H., Segall, M. H., & Dasen, P. R. (1992). *Cross-cultural psychology: Research and applications.* New York: Cambridge University Press.

Berry, J. W., & Sam, D. (1996). Acculturation and adaptation. In J. W. Berry, M. H. Segall, & C. Kagitcibasi (Eds.), *Handbook of cross-cultural psychology: Vol. 3. Social behavior and applications* (pp. 291–326). Boston, MA: Allyn & Bacon.

Betancourt, H., & Lopez, S. R. (1993). The study of culture, ethnicity, and race in American psychology. *American Psychologist, 48*(6), 629–637.

Beutler, L. E., Brown, M. T., Crothers, L., Booker, K., & Seabrook, M. K. (1996). The dilemma of factitious demographic distinctions in psychological research. *Journal of Consulting & Clinical Psychology, 64*(5), 892–902.

Billings, A. G., Cronkite, R. C., & Moos, R. H. (1983). Social-environmental factors in unipolar depression: Comparisons of depressed patients and nondepressed controls. *Journal of Abnormal Psychology, 92*(2), 119–133.

Bond, M. H., & Forgas, J. P. (1984). Linking person perception to behavior intention across cultures: The role of cultural collectivism. *Journal of Cross-Cultural Psychology, 15*(3), 337–352.

Canales, G., (2000). Gender as subculture: The first division of multicultural diversity. In. I. Cuellar and F. A. Paniagua (Eds.), *Handbook of multicultural mental health* (pp. 64–76). San Diego, CA: Academic Press.

Cheung, F. M. C. (1989). The indigenization of neurasthenia in Hong Kong. *Culture, Medicine, and Psychiatry, 13,* 227–241.

Chin, D. (1988). *Disentangling the effects of socioeconomic status in developmental research.* Unpublished manuscript.

Clausen. J. A., & Kohn, M. L., (1959). Relation to schizophrenia to the social structure of a small city. In B. Pasamanick (Ed.), *Epidemiology of mental disorder* (pp. 69–94). Washington, DC: American Association for the Advancement of Science.

Compton, W. M., Helzer, J. E., Hwu, H. G., Yeh, E. K., McEvoy, L., Tipp, J. E., et al. (1991). New methods in cross-cultural psychiatry: Psychiatric illness in Taiwan and the United States. *American Journal of Psychiatry, 148*(12), 1697–1704.

Cooper, J. E., Kendell, R. E., Gurland, B. J., Sartorius, N., & Farkas, T. (1969). Cross-national study of diagnosis of the mental disorders: Some results from the first comparative investigation. *American Journal of Psychiatry, 125*(10, Suppl.), 21–29.

Cooper, J. E., Kendell, R. E., Guland, B. J., Sharpe, L., Copeland, J. R. M., & Simon, R. (1971). *Psychiatric diagnosis in New York and London.* London: Oxford University Press.

Corsini, R. J. (1987). *Concise encyclopedia of psychology.* Oxford, England: Wiley.

Cowan, W. M., Kopnisky, K. L., & Hyman, S. E. (2002). The Human Genome Project and its impact on psychiatry. *Annual Review of Neuroscience, 25,* 1–50.

Crago, M., Shisslak, C. M., & Estes, L. S. (1996). Eating disturbances among American minority groups: A review. *International Journal of Eating Disorders, 19*(3), 239–248.

Cuellar, I., & Paniagua, F. A. (2000). *Handbook of multicultural mental health.* San Diego, CA: Academic Press.

Davidson, A. R., Jaccard, J. J., Triandis, H. C., Morales, M. J., & Diaz-Guerrero, R. (1976). Cross-cultural model testing: Toward a solution of the etic-emic dilemma. *International Journal of Psychology, 11,* 1–13.

Derogowski, J. B. (1989). Real space and represented space: Cross-cultural perspectives. *Behavior and brain sciences, 12,* 51–73.

Desjarlais, R., Eisenberg, L., Good, B., & Kleinman, A. (1995). *World mental health: Problems and priorities in low-income countries.* London: Oxford University Press.

Dohrenwend, B. P., & Dohrenwend, B. S. (1974). Social and cultural influences on psychopathology. *Annual Review of Psychology, 25,* 417–452.

Dohrenwend, B. P., Levav, I., Shrout, P. E., Schwartz, S., Naveh, G., Link, B. G., et al. (1992). Socioeconomic status and psychiatric disorders: The causation-selection issue. *Science, 255* (5047), 946–952.

Draguns, J. G., & Tanaka-Matsumi, J. (2003). Assessment of psychopathology across and within cultures: Issues and findings. *Behaviour Research and Therapy, 41*(7), 755–776.

Dunham, H. W. (1964). Social class and schizophrenia. *American Journal of Orthopsychiatry, 34*(4), 634–642.

Dunham, H. W. (1976). Society, culture, and mental disorder. *Archives of General Psychiatry, 33*(2), 147–156.

Durkheim, E. (1951). *Suicide* (J. A. Spaulding & G. Simpson, Trans.). Glencoe, IL: Free Press.

Edgerton, R. B. (1992). *Sick societies: Challenging the myth of primitive harmony.* New York: Free Press.

Ennis, N. E., Hobfoll, S. E., & Schroeder, K. E. E. (2000). Money doesn't talk, it swears: How economic stress and resistance resources impact inner-city women's depressive mood. *American Journal of Community Psychology, 28*(2), 149–173.

Fabrega, H., Jr., Swartz, J. D., & Wallace, C. A. (1968). Ethnic differences in psychopathology. *Archives of General Psychiatry, 19*(2), 218–226.

Fabrega, H., Jr., & Wallace, C. A. (1970). Acculturation and psychiatric treatment: Study involving Mexican Americans. *British Journal of Social Psychiatry, 4,* 124–136.

Fitzgibbon, M. L., Spring, B., Avellone, M. E., Blackman, L. R., Pingitore, R., & Stolley, M. R. (1998). Correlates of binge eating in Hispanic, Black, and White women. *International Journal of Eating Disorders, 24*(1), 43–52.

Frank, E. (2000). *Gender and its effects of psychopathology.* Washington DC: American Psychiatric Press.

Frijda, N., & Jahoda, G. (1966). On the scope and methods of cross-cultural research. *International Journal of Psychology, 1*(2), 109–127.

Garfinkel, P. E., & Garner, D. M. (1982). Anorexia nervosa: A multidimensional perspective. New York: Brunner/Mazel.

Garner, D. M., Garfinkel, P. E., & Bemis, K. M. (1982). A multidimensional psychotherapy for anorexia nervosa. *International Journal of Eating Disorders, 1*(2), 3–46.

Gilman, S. E., Kawachi, I., Fitzmaurice, G. M., & Buka, S. L. (2003). Family disruption in childhood and risk of adult depression. *American Journal of Psychiatry, 160*(5), 939–946.

Goodnow, J. J. (1986). Cultural conditions and individual behaviours: Conceptual and methodological links. *Australian Journal of Psychology, 38*(3), 231–244.

Gurland, B., Fleiss, J., Sharpe, L., Roberts, P., Cooper, J., & Kendell, R. (1970). Cross-national study of diagnosis of mental disorders: Hospital diagnoses and hospital patients in New York and London. *Comprehensive Psychiatry, 11*(1), 18–25.

Gurland, B., Fleiss, J., Sharpe, L., Simon, R., Barrett, J., Copeland, J., et al. (1972). The mislabeling of depressed patients in New York state hospitals. In J. Zubin & F. Freyhan (Eds.), *Disorders of mood*. Baltimore: Johns Hopkins Press.

Guthrie, G., & Tanco, P. P. (1980). Alienation. In H. C. Triandis & J. G. Draguns (Eds.), *Handbook of cross-cultural psychology* (Vol. 6, pp. 9–59). Boston: Allyn & Bacon.

Hall, E. T. (1981). *Beyond culture*. Garden City, NY: Anchor Books.

Haruki, Y., Shigehisa, T., Nedate, K., Wajima, M., & Ogawa, R. (1984). Effects of alien-reinforcement and its combined type on learning behavior and efficacy in relation to personality. *International Journal of Psychology, 19*, 527–545.

Herskovits. M. (1949). *Man and his works*. New York: Knopf.

Hobfoll, S. E. (1998). Stress, culture, and community: The psychology and philosophy of stress. In *The Plenum series on stress and coping*. New York: Plenum Press.

Hobfoll, S. E., Johnson, R. J., Ennis, N., & Jackson, A. P. (2003). Resource loss, resource gain, and emotional outcomes among inner-city women. *Journal of Personality and Social Psychology, 84*(3), 632–643.

Hofstede, G. (1991). *Cultures and organizations: Software of the mind*. London: McGraw-Hill.

Hofstede, G. (2001). *Culture's consequences: Comparing values, institutions and organizations across nations* (2nd ed.). Thousand Oaks, CA: Sage.

Hollingshead, A. B., & Redlich, F. C. (1958). *Social class and mental illness: A community study*. Oxford, England: Wiley.

Jablensky, A., & Sartorius, N. (1988). Is schizophrenia universal? *Acta Psychiatrica Scandinavica, 78*(344, Suppl.), 65–70.

Jaynes, G. D., & Williams, R. M., Jr. (1989). *A common destiny: Blacks and American society*. Washington, DC: National Academy Press.

Jenkins, J. H. (1988). Conceptions of schizophrenia as a problem of nerves: A cross-cultural comparison of Mexican-Americans and Anglo-Americans. *Social Science & Medicine, 26*(12), 1233–1243.

Jenkins, J. H., & Karno, M. (1992). The meaning of expressed emotion: Theoretical issues raised by cross-cultural research. *American Journal of Psychiatry, 149*(1), 9–21.

Jilek-Aall, L. (1988). Suicidal behaviour among youth: A cross-cultural comparison. *Transcultural Psychiatric Research Review, 25*(2), 87–105.

Kagitcibasi, C., & Berry, J. W. (1989). Cross-cultural psychology: Current research and trends. *Annual Review of Psychology, 40*, 493–531.

Kameoka, V. A. (1985). Cross-validation of psychological measures in cross-cultural research: Analysis of linear structural relationships. In R. Diaz-Guerrero (Ed.), *Cross-national and national studies in social psychology* (pp. 57–68). Amsterdam: Elsevier.

Kameoka, V. A. (1989, August). *Measurement issues in theory testing across cultures*. Symposium presentation at the American Psychological Association Convention, New Orleans, LA.

Kessler, R. C., & Neighbors, H. W. (1986). A new perspective on the relationships among race, social class, and psychological distress. *Journal of Health & Social Behavior, 27*(2), 107–115.

Kinzie, J. D., Manson, S. M., Vihn, D. T., Tolan, N. T., Anh, B., & Pho, T. N. (1982). Development and validation of a Vietnamese-language Depression Scale. *American Journal of Psychiatry, 139*, 1276–1281.

Kirmayer, L. J. (1984). Culture, affect, and somatization: Parts 1 and 2. *Transcultural Psychiatric Research Review, 21*, 159–262.

Kleinman, A. (1982). Neurasthenia and depression: A study of somatization and culture in China. *Culture, Medicine & Psychiatry, 6*(2), 117–190.

Kleinman, A. (1995). Do psychiatric disorders differ in different cultures? The methodological questions. In N. R. Goldberger & J. B. Veroff (Eds.), *The culture and psychology reader* (pp. 631–651). New York: New York University Press.

Kohn, M. L., & Clausen, J. A. (1955). Social isolation and schizophrenia. *American Sociological Review, 20*, 265–273.

Leff, J. (1977). International variations in the diagnosis of psychiatric illness. *British Journal of Psychiatry, 131*, 329–338.

Leiber, E., Chin, D., Nihara, K., & Mink, I. T. (2001). Holding on and letting go: Identity and acculturation among Chinese immigrants. *Cultural diversity and Ethnic Minority Psychology, 7*(3), 247–261.

Leighton, A. H. (1963). *Psychiatric disorder among the Yoruba*. Ithaca, NY: Cornell University Press.

Lewis-Fernandez, R., & Kleinman, A. (1994). Culture, personality, and psychopathology. *Journal of Abnormal Psychology, 103*(1), 67–71.

Lin, T. Y. (1985). Mental disorders and psychiatry in Chinese cultures: Characteristic features and major issues. In W.-S. Tseng & D. Y. Wu (Eds.), *Chinese culture and mental health* (pp. 369–393). Orlando, FL: Academic Press.

Lopez, S. R. (1989). Patient variable biases in clinical judgment: Conceptual overview and methodological considerations. *Psychological Bulletin, 106,* 184–204.

Lopez, S. R., & Guarnaccia, P. J. J. (2000). Cultural psychopathology: Uncovering the social world of mental illness. *Annual Review of Psychology, 51,* 571–598.

Lopez, S. R., Nelson, K., Polo, A., Jenkins, J. H., Karno, M., & Snyder, K. (1998, August). Family warmth, attributions, and relapse in Mexican American and Anglo American patients with schizophrenia. Paper presented at the International Congress of Applied Psychology, San Francisco.

Lopez, S. R., Nelson, K., Snyder, K., & Mintz, J. (1999). Attributions and affective reactions of family members and course of schizophrenia. *Journal of Abnormal Psychology, 108,* 307–314.

Mann, E. M., Ikeda, Y., Mueller, C. W., Takahashi, A., Tao, K. T., Humris, E., et al. (1992). Cross-cultural differences in rating hyperactive-disruptive behaviors in children. *American Journal of Psychiatry, 149*(11), 1539–1542.

Markus, H. R., & Kitayama, S. (1991). Culture and the self: Implications for cognition, emotion, and motivation. *Psychological Review, 98*(2), 224–253.

Marsella, A. J. (1980). Depressive experience and disorder across cultures. In H. C. Triandis, & J. G. Draguns (Eds.), *Handbook of cross-cultural psychology: Psychopathology* (pp. 237–289). Honolulu, HI: Allyn & Bacon.

Marsella, A. J., & Kameoka, V. A. (1989). Ethnocultural issues in the assessment of psychopathology. In S. Wetzler (Ed.), *Measuring mental illness: Psychometric assessment for clinicians. The Clinical practice series, No. 8* (pp. 231–256). Washington, DC: American Psychiatric Association.

Marsella, A., & Yamada, A. M. (2000). Cultural and mental health: An introduction and overview of foundations, concepts, and issues. In I. Cuellar & F. Paniagua (Eds.), *Handbook of multicultural mental health* (pp. 3–24). San Diego, CA: Academic Press.

Narikiyo, T. A., & Kameoka, V. A. (1992). Attributions of mental illness and judgments about help-seeking among Japanese-American and White American students. *Journal of Counseling Psychology, 39,* 363–369.

Odejide, A. O. (1979). Cross-cultural psychiatry: A myth or reality. *Comprehensive Psychiatry, 20*(2), 103–109.

Omi, M., & Winant, H. (1994). *Racial formation in the United States: From the 1960's to the 1990's* (2nd ed.). New York: Routledge.

Ortega, A. N., Rosenheck, R., Alegria, M., & Desai, R. A. (2000). Acculturation and the lifetime risk of psychiatric and substance use disorders among Hispanics. *Journal of Nervous & Mental Disease, 188*(11), 728–735.

Paris, J. (1991). Personality disorders, parasuicide, and culture. *Transcultural Psychiatric Research Review, 28,* 25–39.

Paris, J. (1997). Social factors in the personality disorders. *Transcultural Psychiatry, 34*(4), 421–452.

Pate, J. E., Pumariega, A. J., Hester, C., & Garner, D. M. (1993). Cross-cultural patterns in eating disorders: A review. *Journal of the American Academy of Child and Adolescent Psychiatry, 31,* 802–808.

Pfeiffer, W. (1968). The symptomatology of depression viewed transculturally. *Transcultural Psychiatric Research Review, 5,* 102–142.

Phinney, J. S. (1990). Ethnic identity in adolescents and adults: Review of research. *Psychological Bulletin, 108*(3), 499–514.

Plant, E. A., & Sachs-Ericsson, N. (2004). Racial and ethnic differences in depression: The roles of social support and meeting basic needs. *Journal of Consulting & Clinical Psychology, 72*(1), 41–52.

Poortinga, Y. H. (1975). Some implications of three different approaches to intercultural comparison. In J. W. Berry & W. J. Lonner (Eds.), *Applied cross cultural psychology* (pp. 327–332). Amsterdam: Swets & Zeitlinger.

Prince, R. (1985). The concept of culture-bound syndromes: Anorexia nervosa and brain-fag. *Social Science & Medicine, 21*(2), 197–203.

Prince, R. H. (1992). Religious experience and psychopathology: Cross-cultural perspectives. In J. F. Schumaker (Ed.), *Religion and mental health* (pp. 281–290). London: Oxford University Press.

Raine, A. (2002, September). The biological bases of violence. Paper presented at the Neuropsychiatric Institute Grand Rounds, University of California, Los Angeles.

Regier, D. A., Farmer, M. E., Rae, D. S., Myers, J. K., Kramer, M., Robins, L. N., et al. (1993). One-month prevalence of mental disorders in the United States and sociodemographic characteristics: The Epidemiologic Catchment Area program. *Acta Psychiatrica Scandinavica, 88*(1), 35–47.

Ryder, A. G., Alden, L. E., & Paulhus, D. L. (2000). Is acculturation unidimensional or bidimensional? A head-to-head comparison in the prediction of personality, self-identity, and adjustment. *Journal of Personality & Social Psychology, 79*(1), 49–65.

Sands, E., & Berry, J. W. (1993). Acculturation and mental health among Greek-Canadians in Toronto. *Canadian Journal of Community Mental Health, 12,* 117–124.

Sartorius, N., Jablensky, A., Korten, A., & Ernberg, G. (1986). Early manifestations and first-contact incidence of schizophrenia. *Psychological Medicine, 16*(4), 909–928.

Schwab, J. J., Brown, J. M., Holzer, C. E., & Sokolof, M. (1968). Current concepts of depression: The sociocultural. *International Journal of Social Psychiatry, 14*(3), 226–234.

Schweder, R. A. (1985). Menstrual pollution, soul loss, and the comparative study of emotions. In A. Kleinman & B. Good (Eds.), *Culture and depression* (pp. 182–215). Berkeley: University of California Press.

Sharpley, M., Hutchinson, G., McKenzie, K., & Murray, R. M. (2001). Understanding the excess of psychosis among the African-Caribbean population in England. *British Journal of Psychiatry, 178*(40), 60–68.

Singer, K. (1975). Depressive disorders from a transcultural perspective. *Social Science and Medicine, 9*(6), 289–301.

Strauss, J. S. (1979). Social and cultural influences on psychopathology. *Annual Review of Psychology, 30,* 397–415.

Strauss, J. S., Bartko, J. J., & Carpenter, W. T. (1981). New directions in diagnosis: The longitudinal processes of schizophrenia. *American Journal of Psychiatry, 138*(7), 954–958.

Sue, S. (1991). Ethnicity and culture in psychological research and practice. In J. D. Goodchilds (Ed.), *Psychological perspectives on human diversity in America: The master lectures* (pp. 51–85). Washington, DC: American Psychological Association.

Sue, S., Fujino, D. C., Hu, L. T., Takeuchi, D. T., & Zane, N. W. (1991). Community mental health services for ethnic minority groups: A test of the cultural responsiveness hypothesis. *Journal of Consulting & Clinical Psychology, 59*(4), 533–540.

Sue, D., Mak, W. S., & Sue, D. W. (1998). Ethnic identity. In L. C. Lee & N. W. S. Zane (Eds.), *Handbook of Asian American psychology* (pp. 289–323). Thousand Oaks, CA: Sage.

Tanaka-Matsumi, J. (2001). Abnormal psychology and culture. In D. Matsumoto (Ed.), *The handbook or culture and psychology* (pp. 265–286). New York: Oxford University Press.

Tanaka-Matsumi, J., & Draguns, J. G. (1997). Culture and psychopathology. In J. Berry, M. H. Segall, & C. Kagitcibasi (Eds.), *Handbook of cross-cultural psychology: Vol. 3. Social psychology* (2nd ed., pp. 449–491). Boston: Allyn & Bacon.

Tanaka-Matsumi, J., & Marsella, A. J. (1976). Cross-cultural variations in the phenomenological experience of depression: I. Word association studies. *Journal of Cross-Cultural Psychology, 7*(4), 379–396.

Teja, J. S., Narang, R. L., & Aggarwal, A. K. (1971). Depression across cultures. *British Journal of Psychiatry, 119*(550), 253–260.

Thomas, D. R. (1986). Culture and ethnicity: Maintaining the distinction. *Australian Journal of Psychology, 38*(3), 371–380.

Thompson, P. (2004, April). Mapping brain changes in Alzheimer's disease, schizophrenia, and development. Paper presented at the Neuropsychiatric Institute Grand Rounds, University of California, Los Angeles.

Triandis, H. C. (1972). *The analysis of subjective culture.* New York: Wiley.

Triandis, H. C. (2001). Individualism-collectivism and personality. *Journal of Personality, 69*(6), 907–924.

Tseng, W.-S., Lin, T. Y., & Yee, E. (1995). Concluding comments. In T. Y. Lin, W.-S. Tseng, & E. Yee (Eds.), *Mental health in Chinese societies* (pp. 346–357). Hong Kong: Oxford University Press.

Uehara, E., Takeuchi, D., & Smukler, M. (1994). Effects of combining disparate groups in the analysis of ethnic differences: Variations among Asian American mental health service consumers in level of community functioning. *American Journal of Community Psychology, 22,* 83–99.

Ulusahin, A., Basoglu, M., & Paykel, E. S. (1994). A cross-cultural comparative study of depressive symptoms in British and Turkish clinical samples. *Social Psychiatry and Psychiatric Epidemiology, 29*(1), 31–39.

Van de Vijver, F. J., & Poortinga, Y. H. (1982). Cross-cultural generalization and universality. *Journal of Cross-Cultural Psychology, 13*(4), 387–408.

Vaughn, C. E., & Leff, J. P. (1976). The influence of family and social factors on the course of psychiatric illness: A comparison of schizophrenic and depressed neurotic patients. *British Journal of Psychiatry, 129,* 125–137.

Vega, W. A., Kolody, B., Aguilar-Gaxiola, S., Alderete, E., Catalano, R., & Caraveo-Anduaga, J. (1998). Lifetime prevalence of *DSM-III-R* psychiatric disorders among urban and rural Mexican Americans in California. *Archives of General Psychiatry, 55*(9), 771–778.

Weissman, M. M., Gland, R. C., Canino, G. J., Faravelli, C., Greenwald, S., Hwu, H. G., et al. (1996). Cross-national epidemiology of major depressive and bipolar disorder. *Journal of the American Medical Association, 276,* 293–299.

Weissman, M. M., & Myers, J. K. (1978). Affective disorders in a U.S. urban community: The use of Research Diagnostic Criteria in an epidemiological survey. *Archives of General Psychiatry, 35*(11), 1304–1311.

Wildes, J. E., & Emery, R. E. (2001). The roles of ethnicity and culture in the development of eating disturbance and body dissatisfaction: A meta-analytic review. *Clinical Psychology Review, 21*(4), 521–551.

Williams, D. R., & Collins, C. C. (1995). U.S. Socioeconomic and racial differences in health: Patterns and explanations. *Annual Review of Sociology, 21,* 349–386.

Williams, D. R., Takeuchi, D. T., & Adair, R. (1992). Socioeconomic status and psychiatric disorder among Blacks and Whites. *Sociological Forces, 71,* 179–194.

Wing, J. K. (1978). The social context of schizophrenia. *American Journal of Psychiatry, 135*(11), 1333–1339.

World Health Organization. (1973). *Report of the international pilot study of schizophrenia.* Geneva, Switzerland: Author.

World Health Organization. (1979). *Schizophrenia: An international follow-up study.* Geneva, Switzerland: Author.

World Health Organization. (1983). *Depressive disorders in different cultures: Report of the WHO collaborative study of standardized assessment of depressive disorders.* Geneva, Switzerland: Author.

Zhang, A. Y., & Snowden, L. R. (1999). Ethnic characteristics of mental disorders in five U.S. communities. *Cultural Diversity & Ethnic Minority Psychology, 5*(2), 134–146.

Zigler, E., & Glick, M. (1986). *A developmental approach to adult psychopathology.* Denver, CO: Wiley-Interscience.

Zubin, J., Steinhauer, S. R., & Condray, R. (1992). Vulnerability to relapse in schizophrenia. *British Journal of Psychiatry, 161*(18), 13–18.

Zuckerman, M. (1999). Vulnerability to psychopathology: A biosocial model. Washington, DC: American Psychological Association.

CHAPTER 6

Biological Influences

BEVERLY E. THORN AND KRISTINE L. LOKKEN

INTRODUCTION

For the most part, studying the biological influences of mental illness involves the study of brain-behavior relationships, or *psychobiology*. An explosion of research in this area has occurred over the past two decades, and our knowledge base continues to expand as increasingly sophisticated methodologies are developed within the neurosciences. The study of *brain-behavior relationships* is based on the following general areas of inquiry: (1) cellular neuroanatomy (e.g., neuronal shape, dendrites, axons, myelin); (2) cellular physiology (e.g., electrical conduction within the neuron); (3) neurochemical processes (e.g., chemical conduction between neurons); (4) developmental and structural neuroanatomy (e.g., lobes of brain, brain centers, and neural circuits); and (5) measurement of physiological processes of the brain (e.g., functional magnetic resonance imaging, or fMRIs).

Various theoretical foundations of brain-behavior relationships exist, and historically, most have revolved around whether the "mind" (sometimes called the *psyche* or the *soul*) is a nonphysiological process separate from the body. This mind-body dualistic notion was first proposed by Descartes in the fourteenth century, and predominated in medical thinking for the next 400 years. This notion promoted the view that mental illness was a separate and nonphysical phenomenon; however, this conceptualization is now considered obsolete.

An alternative (more "modern") view is that the brain is the "mind," and that emotional/behavioral illnesses are nothing more than abnormalities in brain circuitry, chemistry, or structure. Although this view has been vitally important in helping us to further understand the pathogenesis of many psychiatric disorders, the idea that mental illness is best represented by a "broken brain" is rather reductionistic, and implies that psychosocial and environmental variables have little importance in psychopathology. In fact, we know that these variables play a very important role in the expression of mental illness.

A diathesis-stress model of mental illness takes into account both organic predispositions toward a disorder (e.g., family history of depression and/or faulty brain development) and environmental events that could lead to the expression of the disorder (e.g., the stress associated with losing one's job and not being able to find another one). As you will read in various chapters of this book, there is good evidence that some mental disorders have a genetic predisposition or other biological underpinning that will put certain individuals at risk for developing the disorder. Certainly, there is plenty of evidence to support that the brain function in individuals with certain mental disorders, on the gross anatomical, cellular, or physiological level, is often aberrant. It is also the case that a predisposition (genetic or otherwise) does not guarantee that a disorder will be expressed. The diathesis-stress model of mental illness posits that when environmental events interact with a biological predisposition, psychopathological states can be triggered.

Perhaps the most representative view of brain-behavior relationships is that the brain is part of a transactional feedback loop with the rest of the body and with the environment external to the organism. The brain obtains information from the external environment, and it monitors the state of our internal organs. The brain sorts and integrates the input, ultimately determining one's behavioral response—psychopathological or otherwise. The brain, therefore, is ultimately responsible for dictating human behavior. However, there is also good evidence that behavioral/experiential events can serve to change the brain, both structurally and functionally. That is, our actions and the environment that we are in can alter our brain function, and thus also influence how we behave. Taken together, this means that the brain can modify behavior, but just as important, behavior can alter the brain. For example, we can change our brain chemistry simply by the act of engaging in physical exercise. Exercise can serve to function as a nonpharmacological antidepressive agent, as it has been found that regular exercise modifies the same neurochemical receptors in the brain that are changed following specific serotonin reuptake inhibitor (SSRI) treatment for depression (Dey, 1994; Dishman & Rod, 1997).

There is also evidence that engaging in psychotherapy can alter one's brain function. For example, in patients with obsessive-compulsive disorder (OCD), certain brain circuitry (i.e., frontal-subcortical circuitry) appears to function in an abnormal manner, with OCD symptoms associated with increased activation of this system (Saxena, Brody, Schwartz, & Baxter, 1998). When this regional brain activity was measured before and after successful treatment with psychotropic drugs or behavior therapy, it was found that improvement in OCD symptoms was correlated with a reduction in activity of this brain circuitry (Brody et al., 1998; Saxena et al., 1998). Of note, both behavioral therapy and pharmacotherapy produced similar brain activity changes, providing further evidence that changing our behavior alters our brain functioning.

This chapter provides an overview of psychobiology as it relates to psychopathology. In order to understand the evidence available about the biological underpinnings of psychopathology, the reader will need to understand the basics of neural anatomy and physiology, including the rudiments of neurochemistry. Because growing evidence suggests that neurodevelopmental processes are important in helping to explain psychopathology, we will also discuss the process of brain development, and how it can go awry. Present methodological techniques for studying the brain have increased our understanding of psychopathology tremendously, and we will also introduce the basics of these techniques in this chapter. Specific examples relevant to psychopathology will illustrate the points made in the various sections of the chapter.

CELLULAR ANATOMY AND PHYSIOLOGY

The nervous system comprises two types of unique cells: *neurons* and *neuroglia.* Neurons are the major source of information transmission within the nervous system, and because they are quite fragile, they require numerous support structures in order to function properly. Both neuroglia and a vascular filter known as the blood-brain barrier provide some of these critical protective functions. This section of the chapter introduces the structure and function of neurons, neuroglia, and the blood-brain barrier.

The Neuron

The neuron is the structural unit of the nervous system, and the central nervous system (CNS) contains billions of these cells. Although neurons come in many shapes and sizes, they have a common anatomical structure: a receiving end, called the *dendrite* (literally meaning "tree"); a reproductive/metabolic part, called the *soma* or *cell body;* and a component called the *axon,* which transmits its electrical message from one end of the neuron to the other. One neuron receives information from many transmitting neurons. Some of this information excites the membrane of the neuron, whereas some inhibits the membrane. In either case, there is a change in the electrical potential of the neuronal membrane as a result: If excitatory, the change is called an *excitatory postsynaptic potential* (EPSP), and if inhibitory, the change is called an *inhibitory postsynaptic potential* (IPSP). If the stimulation is sufficient, a rapid change in the electrical potential of the membrane of the neuron takes place via an event called an *action potential,* and, in the vernacular, the neuron is said to have *fired.* Once an action potential has taken place and the neuron has fired, the electrical charge is transmitted down the entire length of the axon to its terminal end.

The terminal end of the axon is usually referred to as the *terminal button(s),* where neurochemicals are released into a microscopic gap or cleft (the synapse), thereby communicating with the next neuron. What makes neurons different from other cells in the body is not so much their general anatomical structure, but rather their function in terms of cell-to-cell communication. Rather than being anatomically linked together, these cells communicate via neurochemical means. The main neurochemicals responsible for specific interneuronal communication are called *neurotransmitters,* although substances known as neuromodulators, and neurohormones, also play an important role in neurochemistry. Neurochemicals will be discussed in a later section of the chapter. At the receiving end of the neuron, specific receptors, literally imbedded in the neural cell membrane, work via a lock and key arrangement to receive messages from the transmitting cell. Specific neurons release specific, selective neurotransmitters, and receptors on the receiving cell (the "lock") are coded via their chemical structure to receive only specific neurotransmitters (the "key").

Perhaps the most unique aspect of neurons, and certainly one that we are only beginning to learn about, is the ability of these cells to change, in structure as well as function, which provides the avenue through which experience can actually modify the neuron, in short-term or lasting ways. We call this phenomenon neural plasticity, or the capacity of neurons to change their structure, their function, or even their chemical profile (Woolf & Salter, 2000). For example, there is good evidence that in people with schizophrenia, the brain makes more receptors for the neurotransmitter dopamine, a phenomenon called *receptor up-regulation* (Kestler, Walker, & Vega, 2001; Soares & Innis, 1999). Dopamine receptor up-regulation appears to be a compensatory process for what may be a brain development problem in people with a predisposition for schizophrenia. This example will be elaborated further as the chapter progresses.

Another illustration of neural plasticity comes from recent research in pain perception. There is now substantial evidence that the experience of pain changes the brain, a phenomenon specifically known as *central sensitization*. Tissue injury causes a short-term alteration in how the brain processes a painful stimulus, increasing the sensitivity of neurons to even mild pain signals. Once the tissue is healed, the hypersensitivity usually returns to normal. However, long-lasting alterations in neurons can also result from the experience of pain. These include such structural changes as an increase in the number of pain-sensitive receptors in the spinal cord, and a reduction in pain inhibitory processes within the brain following nerve injury (Woolf & Salter, 2000).

Neuroglia

Although there are many billions of neurons housed within the CNS, they make up only about half of its volume. The other half of the cell structure is made up of cells called *glia,* literally, the "glue" of the nervous system. Glial cells provide a structure for the more fragile neurons, insulate the neurons from one another, provide nutrients to neurons, and clean up neuronal debris, as well as form scar tissue in damaged areas of the CNS where neuronal death has occurred. Among the many functions of glia listed previously, these cells provide the fatty substance called *myelin,* which insulates many axons and results in a faster transmission of the message down the axon.

The importance of myelin in neuronal communication is highlighted in the well-known autoimmune disorder, multiple sclerosis (MS). Individuals with this disorder are often initially thought to have conversion disorder or depression, especially at early stages of the disease. Although people with MS can certainly be depressed and do have multiple unexplained and seemingly unrelated physical symptoms, the cause of their symptoms is actually the body attacking its own myelin, a process that causes irreversible damage to the cell-to-cell transmission at the spot the damage occurs. Immediate myelin damage can be detected on magnetic resonance images (MRIs), but once scar tissue has filled in the damaged spot, the MRI is no longer able to detect the damage, which further clouds the diagnostic picture. Unfortunately, the cell-to-cell transmission is lost permanently at that location, and in many cases, MS results in progressive debilitation of the individual (Feinstein, 1999).

The Blood-Brain Barrier

Another major protector of neurons in the brain is something called the *blood-brain barrier.* The brain has many blood vessels supplying it with oxygen and glucose, which is particularly important because neurons, which have a very high rate of metabolism, utilize a great deal of both. Without the blood-brain barrier the brain would be exposed to the many toxins that circulate in the bloodstream, and these substances would quickly kill the very delicate neurons, causing irreversible brain damage. The blood vessels immediately outside the brain, which make up the blood-brain barrier, have a unique feature: they are only semipermeable, thus not allowing certain chemical substances circulating in the body to enter the brain.

The clear importance of this brain filter is exemplified by lead poisoning, a condition once common in young children because household paints contained lead and very young children often ingest inedible substances. The chemical structure of lead allows it through the blood-brain barrier, and it is toxic to the brain, sometimes resulting in mental retardation (Beattie et al., 1975; Koller, Brown, Spurgeon, & Levy, 2004). Fortunately, lead is no longer used in household paints, but unfortunately, many toxic substances still pose danger to the brain because of their ingestion and ability to permeate the blood-brain barrier.

In addition to being a selective filter for many toxic substances, the blood-brain barrier has another unique property: In one particular location of the blood-brain barrier, an area near the brainstem center that controls vomiting (called the *area postrema*), the barrier is weaker, and allows substances to pass more readily there. This special function is adaptive because many toxic substances are ingested into the gastrointestinal tract. If the brain detects the substance and the vomiting reflex is activated, the organism may be able to rid itself of the substance before it does damage to the organs of the body. In point of fact, vomiting following ingestion of relatively large amounts of alcohol is the brain's way of trying to protect the body from a toxic dose of this substance. When the blood alcohol level reaches a certain point dangerous to the organism, the vomiting reflex is triggered. As it should be obvious from this reading, it is not prudent to continue drinking after vomiting from alcohol, yet individuals with substance abuse disorders often do just that!

NEUROCHEMICAL TRANSMISSION

Whereas transmission of information within the neuron is electrical, transmission of information between neurons is a chemical process. There are three important chemical messengers involved in neuronal communication: neurohormones, neuromodulators, and neurotransmitters. Neurohormones, like all hormones, are produced by endocrine glands within the body and released into the bloodstream. Cells in the nervous system with specific neurohormone receptors are influenced by these substances. Neuromodulators are chemical substances that are made and released within the nervous system, and they influence groups of neurons by diffusing into the synaptic areas of a small range of neurons. Thus, neuromodulators influence more than one neuron at a time. Neurotransmitters, on the other hand, are very specific and selective cell-to-cell communicators.

Neurotransmitters

At this writing, 11 neurotransmitters have been identified, but there may be more that have not yet been discovered. You may be familiar with such neurotransmitters as acetylcholine, serotonin, dopamine, and norepinephrine, because they have traditionally received the most study. Neurotransmitters are released into the synapse, the small space between the transmitting neuron's terminal buttons and the receiving neuron's dendrites. Recall that in an earlier section of this chapter we noted that the receiving neuron could obtain excitatory or inhibitory information from transmitting neurons. It was originally thought that neurotransmitters themselves were either excitatory or inhibitory, but we now know that excitation or inhibition of the receiving neuron depends upon the kind of receptor (the "lock") on the receiving neuron *and* the kind of transmitter (the "key") that is released into the synapse.

Although neurotransmitters are chemical substances, the effect they have on the receiving neuron is to open small pores or channels that permit charged particles (ions) to rush in (or out) of the intracellular fluid within the neuron. Depending upon what kind of channel is opened, the receiving neuron is either excited or inhibited. Note that the receiving neuron obtains information from multiple other neurons, and thus collects various chemical messages at the same time from along its dendrites. Therefore, multiple channels are opening along the membrane of the receiving neuron and causing small excitations or inhibitions depending upon what kind of ions are rushing in or out of the neuronal membrane. Only when the receiving neuron obtains a certain threshold of excitation does this neuron, in turn, transmit its electrical impulse down its axon to its terminal via an action potential, and ultimately release its neurotransmitter into the next synapse.

It is at the terminal that the electrical message within the neuron becomes a chemical message transmitted to another neuron. At the terminal, minute sacs of neurotransmitter have been stored and are resting at the surface of the neural membrane. When the action potential is received at the terminal, these sacs (or synaptic vesicles) burst open and their contents are spilled into the synapse. If the receiving neuron contains the matching receptor, the channels are opened, and the receiving neuron thus obtains its small excitatory or inhibitory electrical charge via the exchange of ions across the cell membrane.

Neurotransmitters are critically important to the smooth functioning of the nervous system, and malfunctioning neurotransmitter systems have been identified in various psychopathological states. For example, Alzheimer's disease (and related dementias) is associated with a loss of the acetylcholine (ACh)-producing neurons, with a resulting decrease in the neurotransmitter ACh in brain regions such as the cerebral cortex and the limbic system. The ACh-dependent tracts within these areas of the brain are responsible for the regulation of memory, behavioral responses, and emotional responsivity (Corey-Bloom, 2002; Robert, 2002). Another example of the importance of neurotransmitters on emotion and behavior involves the monoamine hypothesis of depression, which posits that a shortage of a group of neurotransmitters collectively known as the monoamines (specifically, norepinephrine and serotonin) is responsible for the symptoms of depression (Delgado, 2004). Many of the antidepressant medications work by increasing the availability of the brain monoamines. A third example of the relation between neurotransmitters and behavior is illustrated by the association of brain serotonin and aggression in human and nonhuman animals. For example, levels of serotonin have been found to correlate inversely with life history of aggression in individuals with personality disorders (Goveas, Csernansky, Coccaro, & Coccaro, 2004). Furthermore, in a prospective study of children with both disruptive behavior disorders and attention-deficit/hyperactivity disorder, lower levels of serotonin during childhood predicted a more severe progression of aggressive behaviors postpubertally, whereas higher childhood levels of serotonin predicted a reduction of aggressive behavior across time (Himelstein, 2003).

Neurons, and their respective neurotransmitters, are natural conservationists: After they are released into the synapse for cell-to-cell communication, neurotransmitters are usually taken back up into the transmitting neuron (a process called *reuptake*) and stored for another time. If a neurotransmitter is not taken back up into the cell, it is broken down by specific enzymes, which are present at the synapse. These processes terminate the immediate cell-to-cell communications between neurons, until another action potential travels down the transmitting neuron to cause release of another group of vesicles of neurotransmitters into the synapse. The frequency of neuronal firing determines the strength of the message transmitted to the receiving neuron.

Many of the *psychoactive* (also known as *psychotropic*) drugs that are now used in an effort to combat psychopathological states work via enhancing neurotransmitter release, blocking their reuptake, blocking (or enhancing) the enzymatic destruction of neurotransmitters, or blocking communication at the receiving end of the next neuron. Psychotropic drugs, by definition, work at the level of the CNS to influence one's mood and/or behavior. For example, many antidepressant drugs work to enhance the release and block the reuptake of serotonin, norepinephrine, or both. On the other hand, antianxiety drugs work via mimicking a naturally occurring neurotransmitter called *gamma-amino-butyric acid* (GABA), thus artificially stimulating GABA receptors in the brain. Antiepileptic drugs work via the same mechanism of action, that is, stimulating the GABA receptor. Some drugs designed to facilitate synaptic transmission of the neurotransmitter GABA, such as Gabapentin, were initially synthesized to prevent or reduce seizure activity in the brain. However, it is interesting to note that these drugs have been found to be useful in the treatment of other disorders, particularly, bipolar disorder (Julien, 2001). The reason behind the wide utility of GABA-ergic drugs is that GABA is generally an inhibitory neurotransmitter, and may thus slow the activity of several overly active circuits implicated in seizure disorder, anxiety states, or bipolar disorder.

It may come as a surprise to learn that antipsychotic drugs (antischizophrenic drugs) work by blocking specific dopamine receptors in the brain. Up to this point in the chapter, we implied that there appears to be a shortage of dopamine in individuals with schizophrenia, and that the brain compensates by making more dopamine receptors. Why, then, would an antipsychotic drug work by blocking these receptors? There are two important components in the explanation of the biological basis of schizophrenia, and they fit nicely within the diathesis/stress model of psychopathology. First, it appears that an individual predisposed to schizophrenia may experience faulty brain development. Groups of axons (called *tracts*) going from one area of the brain *(frontal cortex)* to another area of the brain *(nucleus accumbens)* are thus underdeveloped. These tracts synapse on dopamine-producing neurons in the nucleus accumbens, and these neurons are subsequently understimulated on a chronic basis. The dopamine receptors compensate by up-regulating the number of receptors. Although this compensatory action works while the individual is in a relatively quiescent, or stress-free state, when someone predisposed to schizophrenia confronts stressors, the nucleus accumbens, and the dopaminergic neurons subserved by this area, become overly active. Because there are more receptors available to respond to the extra outpouring of dopamine, the overactivation of the numerous dopamine receptors causes what are known as the positive symptoms of schizophrenia: the hallucinations and delusions. Blocking the overly activated dopamine receptors via antipsychotic drugs thus reduces the positive signs of schizophrenia. The *dopamine theory of schizophrenia* (as it is called), and the corresponding explanation, is quite complex and we will come back to it as the chapter goes along. Schizophrenia itself is covered in greater detail in Chapter 16.

THE NERVOUS SYSTEM

The nervous system has traditionally been divided into two parts: the *central nervous system* (CNS, the brain and spinal cord) and the *peripheral nervous system* (PNS, all nerve tissue outside the CNS). The PNS can be further divided into the *somatic nervous system* and the *autonomic nervous system*. The somatic nervous system serves as an informant between the body and the CNS, allowing the brain and spinal cord to communicate with the rest of the body via the cranial and spinal nerves. Afferent (incoming) sensory nerves convey external sensory information obtained by the sense organs to the CNS, whereas efferent (outgoing) motor nerves carry motor signals from the CNS to the body's muscles and glands.

Whereas the somatic nervous system provides feedback necessary for an individual to respond to the external environment, the autonomic nervous system is primarily concerned with the control of the body's internal environment, specifically regulation of the internal organs such as smooth muscle, cardiac muscle, and glands. The autonomic nervous system comprises two anatomically separate systems: the sympathetic nervous system and the parasympathetic nervous system. These two systems exert opposite effects on the internal organs, as the body constantly strives to maintain a homeostatic balance. The sympathetic division mobilizes energy for arousal by increasing blood flow to skeletal muscles and increasing heart rate and decreases nonessential activity such as gastric motility. The parasympathetic division, in contrast, works to conserve the body's energy. It is primarily responsible for facilitating vegetative responses by the organs and assisting the body in maintaining a relaxed state.

The sympathetic nervous system (SNS) is known as the "fight-or-flight" system, and its function is to mobilize the organism to fight for its life or flee from the enemy. In terms of evolutionary significance, the SNS is very adaptive in life-or-death emergencies and can mobilize us to great bursts of short-term strength and endurance. Everyone has heard of the example of a mother lifting a car off of her child when the car was crushing the child. This is the work of the SNS. Most present-day stressors are typically more chronic and less immediately life-threatening than the example given previously; yet, our SNS has not yet adapted to chronic lower level stressors of an industrialized society. Unfortunately, our SNS is often working overtime, generating a fight-or-flight response to many non-life-threatening stressors. Over time, the body's reaction to long-term activation by the SNS is a wearing down or a literal exhaustion of bodily functions. We believe this is the reason for the rise in stress-related disorders as diverse as essential hypertension, chronic pain, and malfunctions associated with the breakdown of the body's immune system, causing cancer and various autoimmune diseases. Psychopathological states are most assuredly influenced by the perception of stress, and the body's long-term reaction to stressors. This may be one reason why disorders with a clear physiological basis (e.g., heart disease) are so often co-morbid with mental disorders, such as depression (Mallack & Imperator, 2004).

As mentioned, the CNS is composed of the brain and the spinal cord. The brain has multiple subdivisions, but is generally broadly divided into the forebrain, the midbrain, and the hindbrain. Both the brain and the spinal cord are the most protected organs in the body, providing evidence of their valuable role in life sustaining functions. The spinal cord is protected by the vertebral column, and the brain is encased in the tough, bony skull. Further protection is provided by the meninges (three layers of tough connective tissue), the ventricular system (a series of hollow, interconnected chambers filled with cerebrospinal fluid that cushions the brain from shock and sudden changes of pressure), and the blood-brain barrier. Although the brain makes up less than 2 percent of the body, it uses 25 percent of the body's oxygen supply and more than 70 percent of the body's glucose supply. The brain receives its fuel supply of glucose and oxygen from the blood. Because the brain is unable to store glucose or oxygen, blood vessels must continually supply nutrients to the brain. Without immediate and continuous access to glucose and oxygen, the delicate neuron rapidly dies. This is precisely the process by which brain damage occurs following a stroke (also known as a cerebrovascular accident, or CVA). A blockage in one or more of the cerebral arteries may prevent the flow of oxygen and glucose to a particular brain region, thus killing the tissue. Alternatively, a rupture in a blood vessel within the brain can occur, which disrupts the transmission of oxygen and glucose, as well as contaminating the fragile neural tissue with blood. Depending on the location of the CVA, an individual experiencing a stroke can experience a variety of cognitive, behavioral, or emotional sequelae (Brown, Baird, & Shatz, 1986).

Neurodevelopment

In recent years, there has been mounting evidence of a link between neurodevelopmental alterations and the occurrence of specific psychiatric syndromes. Neurodevelopmental abnormalities can occur based on genetic heritability of a predisposition to a mental disorder. Although there is strong genetic evidence for many psychiatric disorders, heritability estimates are certainly not 100 percent, and often less than 50 percent. Thus, genetic inheritance is only part of the story, and highlights the ongoing dynamic interplay between genetic, biological, environmental, cognitive, and psychosocial factors.

An understanding of the development of the nervous system can help to make sense of its adult configuration. It can also provide an appreciation for the processes involved in normal development and how abnormal development can lead to susceptibility toward psychological disorders later in life.

Historically, the prenatal period of neural development was thought to be of little relevance to the occurrence of psychological disorders later in life. However, recent research indicates that what happens during the early stages of neural development may give us clues about the etiology of certain psychological processes. For example, Hirshfeld-Becker et al. (2004) found that prenatal stressors such as pregnancy and delivery complications increased a child's risk for anxiety disorders beyond that accounted for by parental psychopathology alone. Similarly, Allen, Lewinsohn, and Seeley (1998) reported a relationship between the number of negative prenatal and perinatal factors and risk for later psychopathology, and Wilcox and Nasrallah (1987) found perinatal distress to be a risk factor for chronic nonparanoid schizophrenia, independent of the genetic risk for the disorder.

Obviously, the effect of gross trauma on neural development is easily understood, as illustrated by the occurrence of hydrocephalus during infancy. Hydrocephalus occurs when there is an excessive accumulation of cerebrospinal fluid (CSF) in the brain secondary to a structural brain abnormality. The overabundance of CSF causes the ventricles of the brain to expand, thereby compressing the brain tissue. If not immediately corrected, hydrocephalus can have a devastating impact on the developing brain, and can lead to significant cognitive deficits (Willis, 1993).

The effect of more subtle interruptions in the timing or occurrence of developmental processes is less well understood and more difficult to research. To continue with the example of schizophrenia, recall that in individuals with schizophrenia there is evidence of an initial shortage of dopamine and subsequent dopamine receptor up-regulation (Kestler et al., 2001; Soares & Innis, 1999). It appears that during neural development the frontal cortex of people who may be predisposed to schizophrenia does not develop properly (a phenomenon called *hypofrontality*). As a result, the neuronal tract going from the underdeveloped frontal cortex and traveling to an area near the limbic system, called the *nucleus accumbens,* is also stunted. The ultimate effect at the level of the nucleus acumbens is a lowered supply of dopamine. Because the brain has the ability to change structurally as well as functionally, it makes more dopamine receptors at the level of the nucleus accumbens in an effort to compensate for the shortage. The apparent neurodevelopmental defect in the frontal lobe triggers the manufacture of additional dopamine receptors in the nucleus accumbens, which does not become a problem until the individual with a predisposition toward schizophrenia experiences emotional stress. At that point, a surge of dopamine release activates the available (and overabundant) dopamine receptors, causing the positive symptoms of schizophrenia. Thus, subtle neurodevelopmental alterations in the emergence of cortical circuitry can play a large role in the later development of psychiatric syndromes, such as schizophrenia. Although such developmental abnormalities can certainly predispose someone to developing a psychiatric syndrome, it will likely take the interaction of this biological predisposition with a certain set of environmental influences to actually trigger the onset of the disorder.

Neuroanatomy

The brain is the most amazing organ in the body. It is in essence what defines us as unique human beings. Through its capacity to engage in higher cortical thought, such as complex decision making, the human brain distinguishes us from other animals. The human brain is also the fundamental core of our distinct individual characteristics, such as personality traits and habits, and thus allows us to be uniquely different from one another. As a consequence, when things go awry in the development or functioning of the brain, various mental disorders can result.

At birth, the human brain weighs approximately 350 grams and nearly triples in size to a weight of more than 1,000 grams within the first year of life. The fully developed adult brain weighs approximately 1,400 grams (or 3 pounds), and it is estimated that the adult human brain houses between 10 billion and 100 billion neurons. This organ, which can be held in one hand, is responsible for integrating complex information and coordinating the body's actions, enabling us to move, think, remember, communicate, plan, and create. It is remarkable that the brain is able to function in as complex and precise a way as it does, and may be no surprise that the mounting evidence implicating CNS involvement in psychopathology has become much more explicit and convincing.

The human brain is primarily composed of two types of tissue: gray matter and white matter. Gray matter consists of areas where cell bodies of neurons (which are gray in color) predominate. The individual structures of the brain are primarily composed of gray matter. White matter consists of areas rich in axons covered in myelin (which is white in color). Myelinated axons connect cell bodies to one another and thus provide a means for the individual gray matter structures of the brain to communicate through white matter tracts or fiber pathways. When white matter is destroyed, as in the demyelinating disorder of multiple sclerosis, communication between individual structures of the brain is slowed or blocked. If the process of myelination is interrupted at some point in development, this could also cause faulty communication in the brain, and thus affect behavior. For example, disrupted myelination during neurodevelopment could result in slowed speed of response, reduced attention, and generally impaired information processing capacity, all of which have been implicated in various disorders, such as intellectual disabilities and developmental delays (Van der Knapp, Valk, Bakker, Schoonfeld, & Faberm, 1991).

As mentioned, the human brain is generally divided into three major divisions: the hindbrain, the midbrain, and the forebrain. The hindbrain consists of two major divisions: the *metencephalon* and the *myelencephalon.* The *cerebellum* and the *pons* are the two structures that make up the metencephalon. The cerebellum is primarily responsible for coordinating motor movements, and the pons serves to relay information from the rest of the brain to the cerebellum. The myelencephalon contains the *medulla oblongata,* which plays a major role in sustaining life functions such as respiration, blood pressure, and heart rate. The *midbrain* (also referred to as the *mesencephalon*) consists of two structures, the *tectum* and *tegmentum,* both of which play a large role in integrating sensory and motor information.

The *forebrain* is the largest area of the brain and is further divided into the *diencephalon* and the *telencephalon.* The diencephalon contains two important structures, the *thalamus* and the *hypothalamus.* The thalamus is a gray matter structure that is connected extensively with most other parts of the CNS through an intricate series of white matter tracts or nuclei. These tracts allow the thalamus to serve as a central relay station for the brain. The hypothalamus controls the autonomic nervous system and the endocrine system, controlling behaviors that are central to survival, such as the "fight-or-flight" system, eating, drinking, and mating.

The telencephalon is the area of the brain that is primarily responsible for the cognitive and behavioral functions unique to humans, and it is the area of the brain that is most implicated in the pathogenesis of certain psychological disorders. Thus the remainder of the discussion in this section will focus on this area of the brain. The telencephalon consists of the *cerebral cortex* (also called *neocortex* or *cerebrum*), the *basal ganglia,* and the *limbic system.* The basal ganglia are a collection of gray-matter structures, including the *caudate nucleus,* the *putamen,* the *globus pallidus,* and the *substantia nigra.* The basal ganglia are primarily involved it the control of movement. Damage to the basal ganglia has been implicated in the disease process of Parkinson's disease, a progressive degenerative movement disorder caused by the destruction of dopaminergic neurons in the substantia nigra. It is interesting to note that individuals with Parkinson's disease often experience depression to a greater degree than patients with other chronic diseases (Raskin, Borod, & Tweedy, 1990). Research continues to be conducted to figure out if there is a specific physiological basis for this phenomenon.

Two major structures of the limbic system include the *hippocampus* and the *amygdala,* although there are several more structures that make up this system. Both of these structures play a major role in emotional and memory functions. Damage to the hippocampus can produce memory loss, and it is this structure that is primarily affected in the disease process of Alzheimer's disease (AD). The hippocampus contains many neurons specific for producing the neurotransmitter, acetylcholine (ACh), and it has been speculated that drugs that interfere with the enzymatic deactivation of ACh by binding to the enzyme acetylcholinesterase (AChE), could serve as treatments for AD. Over the past 10 years, several drugs called AChE inhibitors, including such brand names as Cognex, Aricept, Exelon, and Reminyl, have been marketed for the treatment of AD (Ibach & Haen, 2004; Parihar & Hemnani, 2004). Although there is evidence that AChE inhibitors do provide some improvement in cognition, the overall benefits have been minimal, suggesting that AD is a far more complex brain disease (Bullock, 2004).

In addition to the aforementioned limbic system structures, an area of the cerebral cortex that is intimately involved with the limbic system is known as the *limbic cortex.* The limbic cortex is made up of gray matter (cell bodies) and forms a border between the cerebral cortex and the rest of the limbic system. The *cingulate gyrus* is housed within the limbic cortex, and dysfunctions within this area are linked to emotional disorders. Recall from an earlier section of the chapter that obsessive-compulsive disorder has been linked to overactivity in the frontal-subcortical circuitry of the brain (Brody et al., 1998; Saxena et al., 1998). Specifically, OCD has been linked to overactivity in the circuitry between the prefrontal lobe and the cingulate gyrus. Patients with severe and intractable OCD have been successfully treated with a procedure called *cingulotomy,* which is the surgical destruction of the connecting fiber bundles in this area.

Traditionally, it was thought that the limbic system also housed what was known as the "pleasure center" of the brain. Although the limbic system does play a large role in emotional response and reward learning, we know now that the experience of positive reinforcement in the brain involves a number of different brain mechanisms working together to produce synaptic changes that are pleasurable. An area of the brain called the *medial forebrain bundle* (a bundle of axons stretching from the midbrain through the hypothalamus to the basal forebrain) has been most reliably associated with the experience of pleasure. It is interesting to note that all natural reinforcers (e.g., food, water, sexual contact) produce a positive effect by stimulating the release of dopamine in the nucleus accumbens, which is located in the basal forebrain. Addictive drugs, such as cocaine and amphetamine, also work by triggering the release of dopamine in the nucleus accumbens (Di Ciano et al., 1995). This activation produces a euphoric, pleasurable effect, and thus serves to reinforce drug taking behavior. We will discover more about the effects of cocaine use and the limbic system later on in this chapter when we discuss specific methods of brain investigation.

The cerebral cortex is made up of gray matter and surrounds the left and right cerebral hemispheres, giving the brain its convoluted appearance of *gyri* (bulges) and *sulci* (grooves). The two hemispheres are connected by a bundle of white matter fibers called the *corpus callosum,* which allows for the exchange of information between the left and right hemispheres. There are four major divisions within each cerebral hemisphere, referred to as the *frontal, parietal, temporal,* and *occipital lobes.* Although these divisions of the cerebral hemispheres are somewhat arbitrary, the four lobes of the brain are associated with the primary and secondary processing of specific sensory or motor information.

The occipital lobe contains the primary visual cortex, and thus is mainly responsible for the processing of visual information. The parietal lobe principally serves to integrate cross-sensory information via the primary somatosensory cortex. The primary auditory cortex is located within the temporal lobe, and therefore influences this area of the brain to play a large role in receiving and interpreting auditory information; however, the temporal lobe also contributes to other types of behaviors, such as emotion, motivation, and memory. The frontal lobe is the largest lobe of the brain and houses both the primary motor cortex (which is concerned with initiating, activating, and performing motor activity), and an area called the *prefrontal cortex.* The prefrontal cortex is the area most associated with the unique individual personality characteristics and high level decision making that is specific to human beings. When there is damage to the prefrontal cortex, there can be devastating effects on our ability to organize, control, and manage behavior.

As described in the previous paragraph, localization of function for specific sensory-perceptual and motor processing exists to a certain extent in the human brain. However, complex mental functions (such as learning, memory, emotion, and executive function) do not wholly reside within the boundaries of a single lobe or structure of the brain, but rely on processing systems subserved by various regions of the brain. For example, given the central importance of the structures of the frontal lobe, it is connected to almost every other major region of the brain via a complex series of white matter tracts. These connections allow the frontal lobe to communicate with the rest of the brain, in order to serve as the final common pathway for behavioral functions and psychological dysfunctions.

An illustration of what happens when there is a breakdown in those connections has been provided through our ongoing explanation of the phenomenon of hypofrontality in the pathogenesis of schizophrenia. Let us elaborate on this further. We know that positive symptoms of schizophrenia (hallucinations and delusions) are ultimately associated with increased levels of dopamine production, whereas negative symptoms of schizophrenia (the absence of normal behaviors, such as poor initiation of behavior, flattened emotions, poverty of speech, and social withdrawal) have been functionally linked to developmental or degenerative processes that impair the frontal lobe (APA, 2000). Several investigators have suggested a connection exists between the occurrence of negative and positive symptoms, in that abnormal development of the prefrontal cortex leads to faulty neuronal connections between the frontal lobe and the mesolimbic system, and, therefore, also serves as the cause for mesolimbic dopamine hyperactivity (Weinberger, 1988). Because of the complex interconnections that exist between cortical regions, brain circuitry abnormalities can produce a wide range of cognitive and behavioral deficits.

METHODOLOGY

The human brain has the paradoxical capacity to study and understand itself. Over the past several decades, many exciting technological developments have enhanced our ability to learn about the workings of the human brain. Through the use of innovative tools designed to investigate the structure and function of the human brain, we may ultimately understand the mystery of why people think and act the way they do, and how certain dysfunctions of the brain can lead to psychopathological states.

Currently, there are many different research methodologies available for scientists to use to gather data about biological bases of behavior. Unfortunately, many of these tools can be complicated to use and laden with technical limitations. Thus, in order to examine human cognition and behavior in meaningful ways, it often requires a team of researchers from different disciplines to appropriately utilize and apply the results of such techniques. In addition to this, we are still in the very beginning stages of understanding how to fully make use of neuroscientific methods. Most of the research that has been conducted thus far has focused on statistical group differences, and has not yet been applied to understanding the behavior of individuals. A large number of confounding subject variables are inherent to the usage of neurobiological approaches in studying group differences, such as consideration of gender differences, age associated changes, the effects of neurotransmitters and neuromodulators, and the long-lasting influences of psychotropic or other medication on cell membranes.

Keeping these cautions in mind, we will begin this section by a discussion of long-standing techniques used to understand the localization of function, such as naturalistic or induced destruction of specific brain tissue. Next, we will discuss more contemporary imaging techniques. Imaging techniques can be divided into two broad categories: static and dynamic. Static imaging techniques, such as computerized tomography (CT) and magnetic resonance imaging (MRI), provide methods of taking a picture of the live brain, and thus are useful for understanding the brain's structure. Dynamic imaging methods, such as functional magnetic resonance imaging (fMRI) and positron-emission tomography (PET), provide measures of online brain activity, offering methods to study the function of the brain. When static and dynamic techniques are combined together, we are able to literally visualize how the brain works as a unit.

The reader is cautioned that the following is only a brief overview of a few of the most popular neuroimaging techniques. Even as you read this, groundbreaking research continues to be conducted to create novel, new methodologies and to invent innovative ways to use older neuroscientific research methods to examine the biological basis of behavior.

Brain Lesions

Prior to many of the technological advances of the twentieth century, there was really no way to examine the living human brain. Much of our early knowledge of brain-behavior relationships came from lesion studies conducted on animal models. A *lesion* is any type of wound or injury, so brain lesioning refers to the destruction of a certain part of the brain. Thus, an investigator would surgically induce a lesion in a specific area of an animal's brain, and then observe any subsequent changes in that animal's behavior. Although nonhuman animal research has been beneficial to our understanding of the human nervous system, devastating consequences can occur if the results of this research are inappropriately applied to humans. One such example is the application of human frontal lobe lesions ("lobotomies") to reduce emotional outbursts, after such results were achieved using chimpanzees as subjects. Between 1940 and 1954, more than 40,000 psychiatric patients underwent prefrontal lobotomies in an effort to treat "psychotic" behavior (in some cases, very loosely defined). As we now know, the prefrontal region is responsible for the initiation of behavior, so although this procedure may have reduced the expression of disruptive psychotic behavior, it caused many horrific side effects, including a profound disruption in the initiation of many behaviors and even patient death in some cases (Glidden, Zillmer, & Barth, 1990).

Another historical method of understanding brain-behavior relationships was to study individuals who experienced naturalistic brain damage and survived. You are probably already familiar with the case of Phineas Gage, who experienced a bizarre accident in 1848 while working as a foreman for the Rutland and Burlington Railroad. One day, as Gage and his crew were leveling uneven terrain by blasting, an accidental detonation sent a long metal rod shooting through Gage's forehead, landing 30 meters away from him. Amazingly, Gage survived the incident; however, he experienced a complete personality change after the accident. Prior to the accident, Gage had been regarded as a well balanced, hard-working, emotionally stable individual. After the accident, Gage's behavior was described as childish, irreverent, and capricious (Damasio, Grabowski, Frank, Galaburda, & Damasio, 1994). He had no sense of responsibility, he was impulsive, and he demonstrated very poor decision making ability. It is interesting, however, that Gage did not experience any changes in his intellect, speech, memory, or other such mental abilities. This was probably the first recorded case of injury to the frontal lobes resulting in enduring changes in personality and social behavior; however, it was not until 20 years after Gage's death that his skull was exhumed and an autopsy was conducted to determine the location of the brain damage.

As illustrated through the case of Phineas Gage, prior to the invention of imaging techniques, scientists and clinicians were limited to postmortem examination of an individual's brain in order to determine the type and location of the damage. Also, without the aid of imaging techniques, it was often difficult to know whether unusual cognitive and behavioral changes were attributable to brain injury or disease or due to other factors. Today, researchers continue to study the behavior of individuals with naturalistic brain damage. Through imaging and other diagnostic techniques, we are now better able to understand the cause and location of the cerebral damage and can therefore better apply it to behavioral outcome. However, it is important to take into consideration that direct interpretation of brain-behavior relationships can also be limited. First, a damaged brain may function very differently from a healthy brain and second, as we discussed earlier, we must be very cautious when relating function to specific structures or areas in the brain. We now know that there is no one-to-one relationship between brain structure and function, but rather brain functioning is an interrelated process with each region performing a function or set of functions that contributes to the performance of particular behaviors.

Brain Imaging Procedures: Computerized Tomography

Computed transaxial tomography, known as the CAT scan or CT scan, evolved from the initial X-ray of the head in the early 1970s. It is a radiological procedure that consists of passing a narrow X-ray beam through the brain at many different angles to obtain a number of two-dimensional images that can be converted into a three-dimensional image by a computer. The CT scan is able to provide a visual image of the structural features of the brain, and can indicate if there is damage to any region. A typical CT scan consists of black and white shadings, with the absorption of X-ray radiation varying with the density of each type of tissue. Bone is high-density tissue, as it absorbs a lot of radiation, and will show up as white in color. Cerebrospinal fluid and blood are low-density tissue; they absorb little radiation and show up as black in color. Radiation absorption of neural tissue lies between these two extremes, with gray matter showing up as darker in color and white matter as lighter in color. Neuroradiologists can examine the CT brain scan for any areas of abnormal hypodensity (too light in color, possibly indicating an old lesion in the gray matter), or hyperdensity (too dark in color, possibly indicating an abnormality such as a tumor or evidence of a cerebrovascular accident).

Because the ventricles contain cerebrospinal fluid, the size of the ventricles can be visualized easily on a CT scan. Ventricular enlargement is one of the most common brain structure abnormalities found in patients with psychiatric disorders. In fact, more than 75 percent of CT studies published examining abnormalities in the brain structure of schizophrenic patients have found significant group differences in ventricular size when brains of schizophrenic patients are compared to brains of control participants (Andreasen, 1995). Such results are neither specific nor diagnostic, meaning that ventricular enlargement is seen in many different types of disorders and might not be present in some individuals who have been diagnosed with schizophrenia. However, the robustness of this finding does suggest that most patients with schizophrenia, and patients with other psychiatric disorders, have likely experienced some type of brain insult (either during development or acquired later in life) that is related to their illness.

Magnetic Resonance Imaging

The medical application of magnetic resonance imaging (MRI) came about during the early 1970s and is used with increasing frequency today. It is so named because the technology involves the interaction between a large magnet (M) and radio waves of a specific resonance (R) to produce an image (I) of biological tissue, such as the brain. Biological tissue contains high concentrations of the hydrogen nucleus, generally in the form of water. MRI technology relies on the ability of the hydrogen nucleus to absorb radiofrequency energy in the presence of a strong magnetic field. The absorbed frequency provides an image that is characteristic of the element of interest and when the image is integrated in a computer it generates a series of pictures reflecting the hydrogen density in various regions throughout the brain or other anatomical structure. The images can be reconstructed in any plane, with horizontal (parallel to the ground), sagittal (perpendicular to the ground), and coronal (as seen from the front) being the three most common orientations.

MRI is considered to be superior to CT because it has the ability to provide images of greater anatomic resolution. Whereas CT can only distinguish between brain tissue, CSF, and blood, MRI can actually depict individual small brain structures in detail. In fact, MRI is so precise that it can visualize structures as small as 1 millimeter. MRI is also very sensitive to tissue alterations and is able to detect subtle changes such as the demyelination that occurs in multiple sclerosis. Because of this, MRI has not only become an important diagnostic tool for detecting disease processes, but it has also provided behavioral scientists with the capacity to link specific symptoms of disorders with respective underlying brain abnormalities. For example, MRI is a useful tool in the early diagnosis of Alzheimer's disease (AD), and reduced volume of the hippocampus has been consistently linked with the memory deficits that accompany AD (Pennanen et al., 2004). Other MRI studies examining brain functioning in schizophrenia have found that those patients who suffer from auditory hallucinations are more likely to have abnormalities in the superior temporal gyrus, the area of the brain most associated with auditory perception in healthy individuals (Levitan, Ward, & Catts, 1999).

Functional Magnetic Resonance Imaging

Whereas traditional MRI provides a method to study the structure of the brain through the use of magnetically altered hydrogen, the technique of functional MRI (fMRI) provides a method to study the function of the brain through monitoring changes in blood oxygenation. When we perform certain functions, such as processing visual information, engaging in memory tasks, or speaking, neurons in specific parts of the brain are activated and thus increase their use of oxygen. This increased use of localized oxygen causes a brief drop in the amount of oxygen in the blood, which subsequently alters the magnetic properties of the blood's water content (i.e., hydrogen molecules) and affects the MRI signal. Inferences of localization of function can be made by measuring the moment-to-moment MRI signal changes secondary to rising and falling oxygen levels. The data obtained during fMRI is then superimposed over structural MRI brain images, so that changes in activity can be attributed to specific brain structures. Using these two methods together allows for the precise mapping of brain function.

The combined use of MRI and fMRI provides a revolutionary way for researchers to examine how information is processed by the healthy human brain. By using information from control participants as a comparison, it also allows us to discover whether individuals with certain disorders process information differently. One such application of fMRI has been to examine how individuals with autism visually process facial information. Results of a study conducted by Schultz et al. (2000) found that individuals with autism showed increased activation in the region of the brain typically associated with the processing of objects (i.e., inferior temporal gyri) when they were shown pictures of human faces, and they showed less brain activation of the brain region typically associated with face processing (i.e., fusiform gyrus). These findings suggest that individuals with autism process faces as if they were objects, and they give us clues to possible underlying neural mechanisms associated with impaired social interaction that is present in autistic individuals.

Positron-Emission Tomography

Positron-emission tomography, or PET, also provides a dynamic way to measure brain function. PET requires the use of an expensive cyclotron to produce radioactive isotopes, which are then injected intravenously or inhaled by the patient. The radioactive tracers bind with glucose and travel to areas of the brain that are activated. As was discussed earlier, the brain is fueled by glucose, so when a specific area is actively engaged in neural processing it will take up a greater amount of glucose and thus a greater amount of the amalgamated radioactive tracers. PET provides a visual representation of the radionuclide uptake, showing "hot spots" of activity that can be detected and measured. These "hot spots" are portrayed by different color gradients, indicating different levels of brain activation. A variety of biochemical and physiological parameters can be obtained by using this method, including measurements of glucose and oxygen metabolism, blood flow, and receptor density of neurotransmitters.

PET imaging has been used to examine the brain substrates involved in cue-induced drug (cocaine) cravings, to further determine potential neural mechanisms underlying habitual drug use and relapse. Childress, Caldwell, Smith, and Swan (1999) used PET to measure and compare relative regional cerebral blood flow in detoxified male cocaine users versus cocaine-naive controls during two 25-minute videos: a nondrug-related nature travel log and a video containing images and sounds of the purchase, preparation, and use of crack cocaine. During the cocaine-related video, cocaine users experienced drug cravings, reported feeling a "druglike" euphoria simply from viewing the drug-related stimuli, and showed increased limbic system (specifically in the regions of the amygdala and the anterior cingulate) activation relative to that during the nondrug video. Cocaine-naive individuals denied the experience of cravings, showed no limbic activation when watching either video, and reported no signs or symptoms of a "druglike" high. The two structures that were activated in the cocaine users, the amygdala and the cingulate, are anatomically linked with the nucleus accumbens, the region most associated with the reinforcing properties of cocaine. These findings are consistent with the notion that the limbic system is involved in emotional response and reward learning. This study is also important, in that it suggests that individuals who are addicted to drugs can experience brain-related changes simply through the act of seeing stimuli related to their habit, providing further evidence of how experience and biology are inexplicably intertwined.

SUMMARY

This chapter has provided an overview of the biological basis of behavior and how it relates specifically to the pathogenesis of psychopathology. Biological conceptualizations are based on a foundation of knowledge in the areas of cellular neuroanatomy, cellular physiology, neurochemical processes, developmental and structural neuroanatomy, and such concepts have been reviewed. Several illustrations have been provided, with each implicating the role of CNS involvement in the development and maintenance of specific psychological disorders. Certainly there is compelling evidence implicating the role of genetics and biology in predisposing certain individuals to develop specific psychological disorders; however, the role of environment and personal behavior cannot be ignored. Thus, the most representative view of brain-behavior relationships has been discussed in terms of a transactional feedback loop, with the brain constantly monitoring and negotiating information received from the rest of the body, and the external environment.

This conceptualization emphasizes the role of the brain in determining one's behavioral output yet recognizes that behavioral/experiential events play a large role in altering our brain structure and function. Examples such as exercise mimicking the neurochemical effects of antidepressive agents, psychotherapy resulting in actual brain activity changes, and psychosocial stress acting as a precursor to psychopathological states serve to further exemplify this transactional feedback loop between the brain, behavior, and environment. It is virtually impossible to tease apart the separate contributions of biology and environment, as the two are so inextricably linked. This chapter has provided a basis for the hypothesis that environmental events ranging from teratogenic effects, stressful life experiences, or specific health behaviors can actually play a role in determining an individual's biological makeup and modifying one's neuronal circuitry.

An understanding of biological influences not only gives us insight into what can put someone at risk (putative factors) for a psychological disorder but can also give us clues as to what can serve as protective factors. Researchers are starting to discover how engaging in preventive health behaviors can ward off serious illness (mental and physical) and serve as neuroprotective agents.

There are many additional questions that remain unanswered in our quest to fully understand how biology influences psychopathology. Future research using biological concepts will facilitate the discovery of new methods of identifying, preventing, and treating mental illness.

REFERENCES

Allen, N. B., Lewinsohn, P. M., & Seeley, J. R. (1998). Prenatal and perinatal influences on risk for psychopathology in childhood and adolescence. *Development and Psychopathology, 10,* 513–529.

American Psychiatric Association. (2000). *Diagnostic and statistical manual of mental disorders* (4th ed., text rev.). Washington, DC: Author.

Andreasen, N. C. (1995). Symptoms, signs, and diagnosis of schizophrenia. *Lancet, 346,* 477–481.

Beattie, A. D., Moore, M. R., Goldberg, A., Finlayson, M. J. W., Mackie, E. M., Graham, F. F., et al. (1975). Role of chronic low level lead exposure in the etiology of mental retardation. *Lancet, 1,* 589.

Brodal, P. (1992). *The central nervous system: Structure and function.* New York: Oxford University Press.

Brody, A. L., Saxena, S., Schwartz, J. M., Stoessel, P. W., Maidment, K., Phelps, M. E., et al. (1998). FDG-PET predictors of response to behavioral therapy and pharmacotherapy in obsessive compulsive disorder. *Psychiatry Research: Neuroimaging, 84,* 1–6.

Brown, G., Baird, A. D., & Shatz, M. W. (1986). The effects of cerebrovascular disease and its treatment on higher cortical functioning. In I. Grant & K. M. Adams (Eds.), *Neuropsychological assessment of neuropsychiatric disorders.* New York: Oxford University Press.

Bullock, R. (2004). Future directions in the treatment of Alzheimer's disease. *Expert Opinion on Investigational Drugs, 13,* 303–314.

Childress, A. R., Caldwell, F., Smith, J., & Swan, N. (1999). Limbic activation during cue-induced cocaine craving. *American Journal of Psychiatry, 156,* 11–18.

Corey-Bloom, J. (2002). The ABC of Alzheimer's disease: Cognitive changes and their management in Alzheimer's disease and related dementias. *International Psychogeriatrics, 14*(Suppl. 1), 51–75.

Damasio, H., Grabowski, R., Frank, R., Galaburda, A. M., & Damasio, A. R. (1994). The return of Phineas Gage: Clues about the brain from the skull of a famous patient. *Science, 264,* 1102–1105.

Delgado, P. L. (2004). How antidepressant help depression: Mechanisms of action and clinical response. *The Journal of Clinical Psychiatry, 65*(Suppl. 4), 25–30.

Dey, S. (1994). Physical exercise as a novel antidepressant agent: Possible role of serotonin receptor subtypes. *Physiology & Behavior, 55,* 323–329.

Di Ciano, P., Coury, A., Depoortere, R. Y., Egilmez, Y., Lane, J. D., Emmett-Oglesby, M. W., et al. (1995). Comparison of changes in extracellular dopamine concentrations in the nucleus accumbens during intravenous self-administration of cocaine or d-amphetamine. *Behavioral Pharmacology, 6,* 311–322.

Dishman, R. K.(1997). Brain monoamines, exercise, and behavioral stress: Animal models. *Medicine & Science in Sports & Exercise, 29,* 63–74.

Feinstein, A. (1999). A clinical neuropsychiatry of multiple sclerosis. Cambridge, England: Cambridge University Press.

Glidden, R. A., Zillmer, E. A., & Barth, J. T. (1990). The long-term neurobehavioral effects of prefrontal lobotomy. *The Clinical Neuropsychologist, 4,* 301.

Goveas, J. S., Csernansky, J. G., & Coccaro, E. F. (2004). Platelet serotonin content correlates inversely with life history of aggression in personality disordered subjects. *Psychiatry Research, 126,* 23–32.

Himelstein, J. (2003). Serotonin and aggression in children with attention-deficit/hyperactivity disorder: A prospective follow-up study. *Dissertation Abstracts International, 63,* 4372B.

Hirshfeld-Becker, D. R., Biederman, J., Faraone, S. V., Robin, J. A., Friedman, D., Rosenthal, J. M., et al. (2004). Pregnancy complications associated with childhood anxiety disorders. *Depression and Anxiety, 19,* 152–162.

Huttenlocher, P. R. (1974). Dendritic development in neocortex of children with mental defect and infantile spasm. *Neurology, 24,* 203–210.

Huttenlocher, P. R., Levine, S., & Vevea, J. (1998). Environmental input and cognitive growth: A study using time period comparisons. *Child Development, 69,* 1012–1029.

Ibach, B., & Haen, E. (2004). Acetylcholinesterase inhibition in Alzheimer's disease. *Current Pharmaceutical Design, 10,* 231–251.

Julien, R. M. (2001). Barbiturates, general anesthetics, and antiepileptic drugs. In *A Primer of Drug Action* (9th ed., pp. 128–152). New York: Worth.

Kestler, L. P., Walker, E., & Vega, E. M. (2001). Dopamine receptors in the brains of schizophrenia patients: A meta-analysis of the findings. *Behavioral Pharmacology, 12,* 355–371.

Kolb, B., Forgie, M., Gibb, R., Gorny, G., & Rowntree, S. (1998). Age, experience and the changing brain. *Neuroscience and Biobehavioral Review, 22,* 143–159.

Koller, K., Brown, T., Spurgeon, A., & Levy, L. (2004). Recent developments in low-level exposure and intellectual impairment in children. *Environmental Health Perspectives, 112,* 987–994.

Levitan, C., Ward, P. B., & Catts, S. V. (1999). Superior temporal gyral volumes and laterality correlates of auditory hallucinations in schizophrenia. *Biological Psychiatry, 46,* 955–962.

Mallack, M., & Imperator, P. J. (2004). Depression and acute myocardial infarction. *Preventive Cardiology, 7*(2), 83–90.

Milunski, A., Jick, H., Jick, S. S., Bruell, C. L., MacLaughlin, D. S., Rothman, K. J., et al. (1989). Multivitamin/folic acid supplementation in early pregnancy reduces the prevalence of neural tube defects. *Journal of the American Medical Association, 262,* 2847.

Papalia, D., & Olds, S. (1992). *Human development* (5th ed.). New York: McGraw-Hill.

Parihar, M. S., & Hemnani, T. (2004). Alzheimer's disease pathogenesis and therapeutic interventions. *Journal of Clinical Neuroscience, 11,* 456–467.

Paus, T., Zijdenbos, A., Worsley, K., Collins, D., Blumenthal, J., Giedd, J., et al. (1999). Structural maturation of neural pathways in children and adolescents: In vivo study. *Science, 283,* 1908–1911.

Pennanen, C., Kivipelto, M., Tuomaninen, S., Hartikainen, P., Hanninen, T., Laakso, M. P., et al. (2004). Hippocampus and entorhinal cortex in mild cognitive impairment and early AD. *Neurobiology of Aging, 25,* 303–310.

Raskin, S. A., Borod, J. C., & Tweedy, J. (1990). Neuropsychological aspects of Parkinson's disease. *Neuropsychology Review, 1,* 185–221.

Robert, P. (2002). Understanding and managing behavioral symptoms in Alzheimer's disease and related dementias: Focus on rivastigmine. *Current Medical Research and Opinion, 18,* 156–171.

Saxena, S., Brody, A. L., Schwartz, J. M., & Baxter, L. R. (1998). Neuroimaging and frontal-subcortical circuitry in obsessive-compulsive disorder. *British Journal of Psychiatry, 173,* 26–37.

Schultz, R. T, Gauthier, I., Klin, A., Fulbright, R. K., Anderson, A. W., Volkmar, F., et al. (2000). Abnormal ventral temporal cortical activity during face discrimination among individuals with autism and Asperger syndrome. *Aropchives of General Psychiatry, 57,* 331–340.

Soares, J. C., & Innis, R. B. (1999). Neurochemical brain imaging investigations of schizophrenia. *Biological Psychiatry, 46,* 600–615.

Van der Knapp, M., Valk, J., Bakker, C., Schoonfeld, M., & Faberm, J. (1991). Myelination as an expression of the functional maturity of the brain. *Developmental Medicine and Child Neurology, 33,* 849–857.

Weinberger, D. R. (1988). Schizophrenia and the frontal lobe. *Trends in Neurosciences, 11,* 367–370.

Wilcox, J. A., & Nasrallah, H. A. (1987). Perinatal insult as a risk factor in paranoid and nonparanoid schizophrenia. *Psychopathology, 20,* 285–287.

Willis, K. E. (1993). Neuropsychological functioning in children with spina bifida and/or hydrocephalus. *Journal of Clinical Child Psychology, 22,* 247–265.

Woolf, C. J., & Salter, M. W. (2000). Neuronal plasticity: Increasing the gain in pain. *Science, 288,* 1765–1772.

PART TWO
MAJOR DISORDERS AND PROBLEMS

CHAPTER 7

Generalized Anxiety Disorder

MARILYN HOLMES AND MICHELLE G. NEWMAN

DESCRIPTION OF THE DISORDER AND CLINICAL PICTURE

Generalized anxiety disorder (GAD) has often been described as the "basic" anxiety disorder. This conceptualization is due in part to its early onset, persistent course, and resistance to change, as well as its gateway status to other anxiety disorders (Brown, Barlow, & Liebowitz, 1994). Furthermore, GAD's central and defining feature of uncontrollable worry is the primary element of anxiety. Individuals with GAD worry excessively about diverse subjects without a persistent focus on any one thing. It is the pervasive, uncontrollable quality of worry that makes it the hallmark of GAD and the true distinguishing feature of this disorder. Such constant, diffuse worrying leads to chronic feelings of anxiety. GAD might therefore be conceived as the absolute expression of high trait anxiety.

In order to understand GAD, then, it is important to understand the definition and nature of worry. By exploring the history of research into worry, a more complete picture of its meaning can be painted. In the 1970s, research into test anxiety first identified separate parts of the anxious experience. Cognitive and physiological aspects of anxiety were distinguished from one another. It was suggested that worry was the cognitive element of anxiety, and researchers defined worry as "a chain of thoughts and images, negatively affect-laden and relatively uncontrollable" (Borkovec, Robinson, Pruzinsky, & DePree, 1983). These authors argued that worry is closely tied to the fear process, as it involves attempts to mentally solve a problem when the outcome is uncertain and includes one or more negative possibilities. This view led to the conceptualization of worry as an attempt to evade perceived threat through cognitive avoidance (Borkovec, Metzger, & Pruzinsky, 1986).

In the wake of this conceptualization, researchers proceeded to investigate further the cognitive nature of worry and its distinction from anxiety. Research confirmed the cognitive quality of worry by demonstrating that it is functionally separate from somatic anxiety (Deffenbacher, 1986; Deffenbacher & Hazaleus, 1985). When worry is induced, participants show an absence of change in heart rate (Borkovec & Hu, 1990; York, Borkovec, Vasey, & Stern, 1987). Craske (1999) suggests that worry may be a cognitive planning stage in response to anticipated threat during which arousal is reduced. Worry, however, is unlikely to occur without anxiety, despite the fact that the two can be separated. Andrews and Borkovec (1988) found that by experimentally inducing a state of worry, a state of anxiety followed. Therefore, although theoretically there could be an adaptive function for worry (planning in order to cope with threat), Borkovec (1994) makes a distinction between preparatory coping and worry. Successful cognitive planning can be described as preparatory coping, but the anxiety-filled process of worrying does not involve effective, active problem solving or coping techniques (Borkovec et al., 1983). In fact, worry lengthens decision-making times (Metzger, Miller, Cohen, Sofka, & Borkovec, 1990) due to heightened evidence requirements (Tallis, Eysenck, & Mathews, 1991) and serves to incubate negative thought intrusions (Butler, Wells, & Dewick, 1995; Wells & Papageorgiou, 1995). It is as yet unclear, however, whether worry without anxiety exists in nature as a coping device.

Perhaps the most surprising finding from the research into worry, however, is that neither the process nor the effects of worry differ between normal and pathological worriers. For example, studies comparing the major topic areas of worry between those with GAD and controls, find that they do not differ (Craske, Rapee, Jackel, & Barlow, 1989; Roemer, Molina, & Borkovec, 1997). Similarly, studies show that when asked to worry, such worrying has the same physiological effect on nonworriers as it does on worriers. What then, distinguishes the worry found in GAD from normal worry? The major point of departure of pathological worry from normal worry comes with the frequency and uncontrollability of worry in GAD. Borkovec et al. (1983) found that in a college sample those with GAD reported that their worries were significantly more uncontrollable than those of nonanxious controls. In another study comparing worry between individuals with GAD and controls, those with GAD also reported significantly more difficulty controlling, stopping, and preventing their worries (Craske et al., 1989). Although these studies identified GAD participants based on *DSM-III-R* criteria, research indicates that individuals who meet criteria for GAD by *DSM-III-R* standards usually meet criteria according to *DSM-IV* as well (Abel & Borkovec, 1995). Results based on *DSM-III-R* criteria can therefore be considered generalizable to the current definition of GAD.

Various associated cognitive features common in GAD help to further illuminate the nature and function of worry in this disorder. Individuals with GAD generally view the world as a dangerous place, and in order to avoid possible danger, or to plan for ways to deal with the occurrence of danger, they feel that it is necessary to constantly scan their environment for cues of possible threat (Beck, Emery, & Greenberg, 1985). Because there is no actual present moment or physical danger, and the threat exists only in the future and in the mind, no behavioral avoidance is possible, and worry becomes the only conceivable coping strategy (Borkovec & Newman, 1998). Indeed, individuals with GAD tend to view worry as an adaptive coping strategy. They believe that worrying will help them problem solve and get ready for the negative event that they fear, and they often hold the superstitious belief that worrying about a negative event will help to prevent its occurrence (Borkovec & Roemer, 1995). Worry may, in fact, be negatively reinforced by alleviating perceptions of unpredictability and uncontrollability in the world and replacing them with feelings of readiness for any possibility (Craske, 1999). Perhaps due to this constant, heightened state of vigilance, or perhaps contributing to it, individuals with GAD tend to interpret ambiguous or neutral stimuli as negative or threatening and also show a bias toward threat cues, even when these cues are presented outside awareness (Mathews, 1990; Mathews & MacLeod, 1994).

Various physiological factors are associated with GAD as well. For example, GAD is associated with chronic vigilance, scanning, and muscle tension (Hoehn-Saric & McLeod, 1988; Lyonfields, Borkovec, & Thayer, 1995; Thayer, Friedman, & Borkovec, 1996). In addition, unlike other anxiety disorders, physiological activation is not a typical feature of GAD. In fact, whereas other anxiety disorders are associated with increased autonomic activation, people with GAD show a distinct pattern of autonomic inflexibility, i.e., a lack of autonomic reactivity (Hoehn-Saric, McLeod, & Zimmerli, 1989; Thayer et al., 1996). For example, Lyonfields, Borkovec, and Thayer (1995) found that analogue participants showed a lower baseline vagal tone and restricted variation in both vagal tone and heart rate between rest, aversive imagery, and worry states. Nonanxious participants on the other hand demonstrated a decrease in vagal tone from rest to imagery and a greater decrease with worry. Thayer and colleagues (1996) replicated these findings in GAD clients and controls using states of self-relaxation and worry. The persistent deficiency in vagal tone and the resulting autonomic inflexibility found in GAD are likely linked to chronic worrisome thinking, as demonstrated by the findings that worry physically reduces vagal tone in nonanxious controls. Interestingly, autonomic inflexibility has also been found in behaviorally inhibited children (Kagan & Snidman, 1990), which has been discussed as an associated childhood risk factor for GAD.

Low vagal tone and autonomic nonreactivity are likely interrelated with information processing difficulties found in GAD. For example, low vagal tone has been found to be related to poor concentration and distractibility in infants and adults (Porges, 1992; Richards, 1987). Several studies have also shown that worry strains the resources of working memory (Borkovec & Inz, 1990; Rapee, 1993). Furthermore, an inflexible information processing style is characteristic in those with GAD, especially in emotional processing.

GAD and worry are also associated with other information-processing dysfunctions. For example, individuals with GAD are more likely than nonanxious controls to interpret ambiguous information as threatening (Butler & Mathews, 1983). In addition, GAD participants show a bias for attending to threat cues, suggesting that they are hypervigilant about scanning their environment for potential danger (Mathews & MacLeod, 1985). Anxious children are also more likely to consider ambiguous cues as threatening and to rate the possible occurrence of threatening events more likely than nonanxious children (Chorpita, Albano, & Barlow, 1996). Further, individuals with GAD show a likely cognitive avoidance of threat words while at the same time demonstrating extensive processing of these words. This is reflected in their ability to recall fewer threat words than controls when using an attentional memory task, yet recall more threat words than controls when using an implicit, or automatic, memory task (Mathews, 1990; Mathews & MacLeod, 1994; Mathews, Mogg, May, & Eysenck, 1989; Mogg, Mathews, & Weinman, 1987). Consistent with these data, another study had people with GAD monitor their daily worry predictions and the rate at which their predicted outcomes actually occurred. The outcomes turned out better than expected 84 percent of the time. Of the remainder, clients coped better than expected in 78 percent of the cases. Thus, for only 3 percent of all worries did the core feared event ("The predicted bad event will occur, and I won't be able to cope with it") actually happen (Borkovec, Hazlett-Stevens, & Diaz, 1999). This suggests that GAD clients often fail to process the evidence that the world offers them.

PERSONALITY DEVELOPMENT AND PSYCHOPATHOLOGY

Several studies have examined personality correlates of GAD. Research suggests that children with GAD tend to be perfectionists, often redoing tasks if their performance is less than perfect. They may seek excessive approval and need disproportionate reassurance regarding their worries as well. Children with GAD may also be overly conforming and self-conscious and may have a negative self-image. Moreover, they are likely to report a high rate of such somatic complaints as feeling shaky and heart palpitations (Beidel, Christ, & Long, 1991; Masi, Mucci, Favilla, Romano, & Poli, 1999). Anxious children are described by parents and teachers as lacking social skills, shy, withdrawn, and lonely (Strauss, Lease, Kazdin, Dulcan, & Last, 1989). They are less liked by their peers and have trouble making friends (Strauss, Lahey, Frick, Fram, & Hynd, 1988). It is unclear whether these personality characteristics lead to GAD or whether they arise after the disorder is acquired. It is likely, however, that the relationship between these personality characteristics and the disorder exist in a cycle of interaction, each augmenting the other.

In fact, several theorists have suggested that fear and negative expectations about social situations can lead to problematic interpersonal behavior. Such behavior may pull for others to respond in ways that reinforce negative expectations and ultimately maintain a psychological disorder (Bandura, 1977; Safran & Segal, 1990; Strupp & Binder, 1984; Wachtel, 1994). For example, an individual who habitually worries that others will think badly of him may act overly intellectual in an attempt to gain self-confidence. His self-presentation might alienate others by appearing condescending, self-absorbed, or emotionally aloof, making others less interested in interacting with him in the future, hence confirming his fears. These patterns have been labeled negative interpersonal cycles by Safran and Segal (1990).

Indirect evidence suggests that negative interpersonal cycles may occur with GAD individuals thus leading to the maintenance of interpersonal worries. For example, there is extensive evidence that GAD patients fear and expect negative responses from others. The content of worry for GAD clients is more frequently about interpersonal fears than any other topic (Breitholtz, Johansson, & Öst, 1999; Roemer et al., 1997). Trait worry is also correlated more highly with social fears than with nonsocial fears (Borkovec et al., 1983; Ladouceur, Freeston, Fournier, Dugas, & Doucet, 2002). In addition, social anxiety disorder is the most frequent comorbid anxiety disorder to GAD (Borkovec, Abel, & Newman, 1995; Brawman-Mintzer et al., 1993; Brown & Barlow, 1992) and GAD is the most frequent comorbid disorder to social phobia (Turner, Beidel, Borden, Stanley, & Jacob, 1991). Experimental evidence also shows that GAD participants have a bias to social threat cues (MacLeod, Mathews, & Tata, 1986; Mathews & MacLeod, 1985; Mogg, Mathews, & Eysenck, 1992) and greater vigilance for and orientation to threatening faces relative to neutral faces compared to controls (Bradley, Mogg, White, Groom, & de Bono, 1999) and to controls or depressed participants (Mogg, Millar, & Bradley, 2000). A more recent experimental study found that compared to non-GAD participants, people with GAD had a more biased perception of their impact on other people, tending to either overestimate or underestimate the extent of their negative impact (Erickson & Newman, 2002).

In addition to data showing that GAD participants expect and worry about negative responses from others, studies suggest that they are likely to act on these fears using dysfunctional interpersonal behavioral patterns. For example, Axis II pathology (primarily characterized by chronic maladaptive relationship patterns) predicted greater odds of GAD in an epidemiological survey (Nestadt, Romanoski, Samules, Folstein, & McHugh, 1992). In addition, studies show a higher rate of personality pathology and lower social functioning in GAD than in panic disorder participants (Blashfield et al., 1994; Dyck et al., 2001) or compared to most other anxiety disorders (Reich et al., 1994; Sanderson, Wetzler, Beck, & Betz, 1994). Also, in a national comorbidity sample as well as a sample of more than 10,000 Australian subjects, GAD predicted increased odds of being separated or divorced (Hunt, Issakidis, & Andrews, 2002; Wittchen, Zhao, Kessler, & Eaton, 1994). There is also evidence that such marital problems are somewhat specific to GAD relative to other anxiety disorders. Wives with GAD have been found to be more dissatisfied with their marriages than wives with other anxiety disorders (McLeod, 1994), and spouses with GAD reported more conflictual marriages than spouses with agoraphobia (Friedman, 1990). Moreover, in a sample of 4,933 married couples, marital discord was independently and more strongly associated with GAD than major depression, mania, dysthymia, social phobia, simple phobia, agoraphobia, panic disorder, and alcohol dependence after controlling for demographic variables, comorbid disorders, and quality of other relationships (Whisman, Sheldon, & Goering, 2000). The latter study also found that GAD strongly predicted a lack of close friendships. Additional studies show that, compared to non-GAD participants, GAD women have more difficulty with emotional and interpersonal intimacy (Dutton, 2002) and that people with GAD approach their relationships with elevated hypervigilance, suspiciousness, and a tendency to feel easily slighted (Gasperini, Battaglia, Diaferia, & Bellodi, 1990). Further, parents with GAD had significantly higher rates of dysfunctional relationships with their spouses and children compared to parents without GAD (Ben-Noun, 1998). Moreover, Pincus and Borkovec (1994) found that compared to non-GAD persons, those with GAD had significantly greater interpersonal distress and interpersonal rigidity across different situations. They also found that mean scores of GAD individuals on five of eight Inventory of Interpersonal Problems Circumplex Scales (IIP-C; Alden, Wiggins, & Pincus, 1990) were significantly higher than psychiatric norms (based on 200 psychiatric clients of mixed diagnoses). Given that people with GAD worry predominantly about their relationships, their objective difficulty sustaining healthy relationships is likely to reinforce and maintain these worries. Taken together, findings suggest that relationship difficulties may contribute to the development or maintenance of GAD. As such, it is possible that changes in relationship difficulties may increment GAD treatment outcome.

Evidence exists that temperament may also play a role in the development of GAD. Kagan and coresearchers (Kagan, Snidman, & Arcus, 1998) have classified children as young as 21 months as behaviorally inhibited or uninhibited. Uninhibited children have adventure-seeking dispositions, whereas inhibited children show timidity and avoidance of novel and unfamiliar events. An inhibited temperament style could theoretically lead to hyperarousal to environmental stimuli, which could contribute to conditioned anxiety responses and make avoidance of such stimuli more reinforcing (Frick & Silverthorn, 2001). Research supporting this suggestion has revealed that infants showing behavioral inhibition to the unfamiliar are more likely to develop an anxiety disorder later in life (Hirshfeld et al., 1992).

EPIDEMIOLOGY

Precise prevalence estimates for GAD have been difficult to obtain, most likely due to definitional variations, considerable *DSM* criteria changes, and varying methods of assessment. Nevertheless, several studies examining prevalence are noteworthy, as they employ large representative samples and likely approximate actual prevalence rates.

Using *DSM-III* criteria with no diagnostic exclusions, the Epidemiologic Catchment Area study found an estimated one-year prevalence rate for GAD of 3.8 percent and a lifetime prevalence rate of 4.0 percent (Blazer, Hughes, George, Swartz, & Boyer, 1991). The National Comorbidity Study (NCS) used *DSM-III-R* criteria and found the prevalence rates for GAD to be 1.6 percent current and 5.1 percent lifetime. Twelve-month GAD prevalence rates from this study were near 3 percent (Kessler et al., 1994; Wittchen et al., 1994). The figures from the NCS most likely provide a close representation of prevalence estimates for GAD according to *DSM-IV* criteria as well because, as noted previously, most clients who meet *DSM-III-R* criteria also meet *DSM-IV* criteria for GAD (Abel & Borkovec, 1995). Finally, using *DSM-IV* criteria, the Australian National Survey of Mental Health and Well-Being found similar prevalence rates to the NCS, with 1 month at 2.8 percent and 12 months at 3.6 percent for GAD (Hunt et al., 2002).

The NCS prevalence estimates also reveal that GAD is somewhat more common in the general population than panic disorder, yet less common than social and simple (specific) phobia (Kessler et al., 1994). Moreover, GAD has been found to be among the most common comorbid conditions for other anxiety and mood disorders (Brown & Barlow, 1992). Nevertheless individuals with GAD report for mental health services relatively less often than do those with most other anxiety disorders, comprising only about 10 percent of anxiety disorder clients seeking such treatment (Kennedy & Schwab, 1997; Roy-Byrne, 1996). Indeed the NCS findings show that approximately half of its participants reported to primary care settings rather than mental health facilities when they sought treatment for GAD, and only about 12 percent of those patients were referred for psychotherapy treatment (Wittchen et al., 2002). Tellingly, among high medical utilizers in primary care settings, GAD prevalence rates rise to 22 percent (current) and 40 percent (lifetime; Katon et al., 1990).

To date, examinations of the association between sociodemographic features and an increased incidence of GAD have found gender to be the most highly correlated characteristic. As with many other anxiety disorders, GAD is much more common in women than in men. In both clinical (Woodman, Noyes, Black, Schlosser, & Yagla, 1999; Yonkers, Warshaw, Massion, & Keller, 1996) and community samples (Wittchen et al., 1994), GAD rates were found to be approximately double in women.

Other characteristics have also been established to be risk factors for GAD. The NCS found higher rates of GAD among homemakers and others not working outside the home and among those living in the Northeast as opposed to other regions of the country. However, no differences in the occurrence of GAD were found to be significantly linked to race, education, income, religion, and rural versus urban living. The Australian National Survey found being separated, divorced, or widowed and being unemployed were associated with GAD (Hunt et al., 2002).

GAD prevalence rates and associated sociodemographic considerations have also been studied in children. Overanxious disorder (the childhood version of GAD prior to *DSM-IV*) was found to have prevalence rates ranging from 3 percent to 12 percent in a review by Silverman and Ginsberg (1998) encompassing 10 studies published between 1987 and 1993. Surprisingly, despite a high correlation between gender and GAD in adults, no such reliable relationship has been found in children. For example, in a large community sample of children, Cohen et al. (1993) found no significant gender difference. And perhaps even more strikingly, other research has identified a greater incidence of childhood GAD in males—the exact opposite trend from that seen in adults (Anderson, Williams, McGee, & Silva, 1987).

ETIOLOGY

As is true for so many psychological disorders, no one simple pathway exists that leads to the emergence of GAD. Instead, a complex interlace of multiple factors—genetic, biological, environmental, and psychological—contributes to the development of this disorder. Perhaps the most straightforward examination of the etiology of any disorder comes from looking at genetic influence. Twin studies have revealed that GAD is moderately regulated by genetic factors, with about 30 percent of the variance due to heritability (Kendler, Neale, Kessler, Heath, & Eaves, 1992; Kendler et al., 1995). Research suggests that heritable traits (accounting for 30 percent to 50 percent of the variance) such as neuroticism, negative affectivity, and anxiety significantly correlate with anxiety and anxiety disorders (Brown, Chorpita, & Barlow, 1998; Clark, Watson, & Mineka, 1994; Trull & Sher, 1994; Zinbarg & Barlow, 1996). Furthermore, family studies have demonstrated that having a first-degree relative with GAD increases the likelihood of having the disorder (Noyes, Clarkson, Crowe, Yates, & McChesney, 1987), although caution in interpreting family studies is advisable, because it is impossible to tease out all environmental factors from genetic factors. Research examining genetic contributions to GAD suggests not that genetic factors specifically lead to GAD, but that heritability contributes to a general biological vulnerability to anxiety, upon which other factors act to manifest a distinct disorder (Barlow, 2002; Kendler, 1996; Kendler et al., 1995). The underlying genetic susceptibility for anxiety emerges as GAD only under circumstances in which biological, psychological, and environmental elements converge in appropriate patterns. Specifically, recent research indicates that dysfunctions in the areas of physiology, information processing, and interpersonal functioning interact in the development of GAD.

In addition to theories regarding the biological determinants of GAD, a review of the past decades of research into the development of anxiety disorders (Menzies & Clarke, 1995) found that much of the focus has been on conditioning and learning. Classical conditioning theory would suggest that a child would respond fearfully to a conditioned stimulus (CS) when it has been consistently paired with an aversive unconditioned stimulus (UCS). The CS then produces anxiety in the child, as he or she expects it to lead to that aversive event. By avoiding the CS, anxious behavior is reinforced (Mowrer, 1939). Furthermore, operant conditioning may be at work in the development and maintenance of anxiety, as parents have been shown to reward anxious behavior with extra attention, reassurance and assistance with avoidant behavior, thus positively reinforcing the anxiety (Ayllon, Smith, & Rogers, 1970). Social modeling may also be a strong contributing factor to learned anxious behavior (Bandura & Menlove, 1968). In fact, studies do show that children of parents with an anxiety disorder are more likely to be anxious compared to children of nonanxiety disordered parents (Muris, Steerneman, Merckelbach, & Meesters, 1996; Rosenbaum et al., 1988).

Although learning theories provide an important potential insight into the development and maintenance of anxiety disorders, attachment may play a role as well. In fact, Bowlby (1982) explicitly hypothesized that anxiety may be the direct result of certain aspects of an insecure attachment. He suggested that when an attachment figure is habitually unavailable to a child, the result is an insecure foundation from which the child approaches the world. Thus, the child develops mental models of the world as an unpredictable, uncontrollable, and dangerous place, tends to overestimate the likelihood and negativity of feared events, and underestimates his or her ability to cope with these events. Indeed, Bowlby's proposed model is consistent with what is known about the mental models of the world present in adults with GAD.

Research to date has provided support for the theory put forth by Bowlby (1982) that an insecure attachment is associated with anxiety disorders. For example, a prospective study found that anxious attachment in babies predicted the later development of anxiety disorders (Warren, Huston, Egeland, & Sroufe, 1997) and a retrospective study showed that anxious patients reported less parental care and more overprotection than matched controls (Parker, 1981). Moreover, participants classifying their parents as higher on protection and lower on care demonstrated significantly higher trait anxiety scores than those not classifying their parents in this manner (Parker, 1979). In regard to GAD per se, studies show that GAD persons score higher than non-GAD persons on role-reversed/enmeshed relationships (Cassidy, 1995; Cassidy & Shaver, 1999). These individuals may view the world as a dangerous place and as a result may feel that they have to anticipate and control danger for themselves and their parents. Persons with GAD were also more likely to report greater unresolved feelings of anger toward and vulnerability surrounding their primary caregivers when compared to individuals without GAD (Cassidy, 1995; Cassidy & Shaver, 1999). Some evidence also exists for the specificity of such attachment difficulties to GAD: a logistic regression found that retrospective reports of prior attachment difficulties predicted higher odds ratios for GAD than for panic disorder (Silove, Parker, Hadzi-Pavlovic, Manicavasagar, & Blaszczynski, 1991).

A possible factor that contributes to the maintenance of worry and GAD may be associated with its inflexible physiology described earlier. Borkovec has theorized that one of the functions of worrying by GAD individuals is to avoid uncomfortable emotions (Borkovec, Alcaine, & Behar, 2004). The theory further hypothesizes that such avoidance is enabled via the abstract verbal linguistic nature of worry and concomitant reduced imagery. As avoidance of a feared stimulus is likely to strengthen its anxious meaning (Fehr & Stern, 1970), such avoidance may be negatively reinforcing, thereby strengthening the associated fear and avoidance behavior.

Experimental evidence indeed shows that GAD and its cardinal characteristic of worry involve a predominance of verbal-linguistic thought and reduced imagery (Borkovec & Inz, 1990; East & Watts, 1994). During relaxation, nonanxious participants report a predominance of imagery whereas persons with GAD report equal amounts of thought and imagery. When participants shift to worrying, both GAD and nonanxious controls show a predominance of thought activity. Increased left cortical activation in GAD and control participants during worry compared to relaxation as well as greater activation in GAD participants compared to controls provides objective evidence of a predominance of thought (Carter, Johnson, & Borkovec, 1986; Heller, Nitschke, Etienne, & Miller, 1997).

In addition to evidence for the verbal-linguistic nature of worry and GAD, studies suggest that worrisome thought is more abstract and less concrete than nonworrisome thought in both nonclinical and GAD participants (Stöber & Borkovec, 2002; Stöber, Tepperwien, & Staak, 2000). When thought content is less concrete, concomitant imagery is less vivid and requires more effort to produce (Paivio, 1986).

The predominance of abstract thought over imagery is important to emotional processing because imagery is more closely tied to efferent command and to affect than is thought (Lang, 1985). Further, abstract verbal thought about feared stimuli leads to fewer and less salient images, which induce a much lower cardiovascular response than does a predominance of salient feared imagery (Vrana, Cuthbert, & Lang, 1986; Vrana, Cuthbert, & Lang, 1989). According to Foa and Kozak's (1986) emotional processing theory, such a lowered cardiovascular response to feared stimuli means that the full fear structure was not accessed and thus full emotional processing did not take place. In the absence of emotional processing, fear is maintained.

Experimental studies of the emotional impact of worrisome thought show inhibited emotional processing. Anxious participants who worry just prior to imaginal exposure to feared material show no cardiovascular response to that material. Those who think relaxing or neutral thoughts before imaginal exposure show strong cardiac arousal. Also, thinking relaxing thoughts prior to imaginal exposure leads to habituation over repeated images, whereas worrying before exposure does not (Borkovec & Hu, 1990; Peasley-Miklus & Vrana, 2000). A study of brain activity also showed that experimental manipulation of worry led to the suppression of affect at the level of the amygdala (Hoehn-Saric, Lee, McLeod, Resnik, & Wong, 2003). Further, the degree to which participants engage in worrisome thoughts, rather than thinking per se, predicts the degree of inhibited emotional processing (Borkovec, Lyonfields, Wiser, & Diehl, 1993; Freeston, Dugas, & Ladouceur, 1996). Moreover, although imagery of an aversive (unconditioned) stimulus can enhance a feared response to a previously conditioned stimulus (Davey & Matchett, 1994; Jones & Davey, 1990), worrying before imagining an aversive stimulus mitigates the impact of subsequent unconditioned stimulus imagery on skin conductance responses (Davey & Matchett, 1994), suggesting that worrying dampens emotional learning. Thus, it is possible that people with GAD use worrisome thinking as a means to maintain a distance from emotionally evocative material. In fact, there is evidence that verbal linguistic thought is used spontaneously by people to avoid emotional arousal associated with emotionally evocative stimulus materials (Tucker & Newman, 1981). Moreover, when GAD, nonworried anxious, and control participants were asked why they worried, in two separate studies the only item that discriminated the GAD group from the other two groups was "worry helps distract me from more emotional topics" (Borkovec & Roemer, 1995; Freeston, Rheaume, Letarte, Dugas, & Ladouceur, 1994). Higher levels of worry are also associated with less emotional clarity and more difficulty identifying and describing emotions (Turk, Heimberg, Luterek, Mennin, & Fresco, in press).

CLINICAL COURSE, COMPLICATIONS, AND PROGNOSIS

GAD, like many anxiety disorders, follows a chronic course, often quietly lingering even after successful treatment (Noyes et al., 1992; Yonkers et al., 1996). Many individuals with GAD cannot remember a time when they were not anxious and feel that they have had symptoms all of their lives. GAD does not usually appear out of the blue, but instead involves a slow, subtle, stealthy building of anxious symptoms. Individuals with the disorder generally report a gradual, insidious onset (Anderson, Noyes, & Crowe, 1984; Rapee, 1985) and an unremitting course (Noyes et al., 1992).

Perhaps in part due to this progressive beginning to the disorder, estimates of average age of onset are controversial and suggest a possible bimodal distribution. Some research has found that GAD has an earlier age of onset than other anxiety disorders (e.g., Noyes et al., 1992; Woodman et al., 1999). In the Epidemiological Catchment Area Study (using *DSM-III* criteria), GAD was most common among the youngest age group (Blazer et al., 1991). In keeping with this finding, earlier studies report that onset is usually in the midteens or early twenties (Anderson et al., 1984; Barlow, Blanchard, Vermilyea, Vermilyea, & Di Nardo, 1986; Rapee, 1985). In further support of early GAD onset, overanxious disorder (considered the childhood form of GAD) has relatively high prevalence estimates (Anderson et al., 1987). The early age of onset and chronic course of GAD have led many to speculate that GAD is a lifelong disorder. In fact, Rapee (1991) suggests that GAD might be considered a stable psychological trait or even a personality disorder, rather than a discreet disorder within an individual.

Other evidence, however, shows that there may be a second subgroup of GAD identified by late onset. The NCS found conflicting results compared to the Epidemiological Catchment Area Study, with estimates showing GAD having the highest prevalence ratings in those older than 45 years of age and the lowest prevalence ratings among those ages 15 to 24 (Wittchen et al., 1994). Brown (1999) suggests that the more stringent diagnostic criteria employed in *DSM-III-R* and *DSM-IV* studies removes the subclinical GAD diagnoses related to the disorder's gradual onset that earlier studies may have captured.

Recent research has further explored the possibility that there are two distinct subgroups of GAD specified by age of onset and the corresponding implications for course and treatment. Several studies have found confirming evidence that two subgroups of GAD are distinguishable based on age of onset and have examined differential effects on the course of the disorder. In a clinical sample of individuals with GAD, about two thirds of patients reported an early onset of symptoms (15 percent before age 10 and 85 percent between ages 10 and 19), whereas the rest of the patients reported a late onset (Hoehn-Saric, Hazlett, & McLeod, 1993). In a recent study attempting to clarify the age of onset and its correlates in GAD, Campbell, Brown, and Grisham (2003) found that most patients in their large clinical sample reported an onset of GAD by early adulthood, whereas a smaller number reported a later onset. These researchers found that early versus late onset had different meanings in several associated areas. Most patients with earlier-onset GAD reported that their symptoms arose without any precipitating stressors (however, a subgroup of the early-onset patients did report severe stressors surrounding the emergence of their disorder). Late-onset patients on the other hand were most likely to report that their GAD emerged during stressful times (Campbell et al., 2003; Hoehn-Saric et al., 1993). Early-onset GAD was also found to be associated with greater severity and higher levels of comorbidity in this study. Other research has associated early-onset GAD with a worse course of the disorder (Woodman et al., 1999); childhood problems with inhibited behavior, social and academic deficiencies, and difficult home environments; and current interpersonal difficulties and depression (Hoehn-Saric et al., 1993). However, as Brown (1999) points out, studies focusing on the impact of early versus late onset do not usually take into account duration of the disorder or the individual's current age.

Even without regard for onset subgroups, GAD is associated with high levels of comorbidity. In a study examining five different anxiety disorders, GAD was more often connected with a comorbid diagnosis than the four other disorders (Goisman, Goldenberg, Vasile, & Keller, 1995). Depressive disorders and anxiety disorders are the most commonly occurring comorbid diagnoses, specifically major depressive disorder (MDD), panic disorder, social phobia and simple phobia (Borkovec et al., 1995; Brawman-Mintzer et al., 1993; Noyes, 2001; Okasha et al., 1994; Sanderson, Beck, & Beck, 1990). The National Comorbidity Survey and the Midlife Development in the United States survey found that the majority of respondents who met criteria for GAD also met criteria for major depression (Kessler, DuPont, Berglund, & Wittchen, 1999). Interestingly, GAD is often temporally primary in relation to comorbid disorders, and most individuals with comorbid major depression report that their GAD preceded their depression (Kessler, Keller, & Wittchen, 2001). In a naturalistic study using a large sample, 39 percent of GAD patients had a comorbid diagnosis of depression at intake, a figure that increased to 74 percent at the eight-year follow-up. Of those with a singular diagnosis of GAD at intake, all but 1 of 20 patients went on to develop a comorbid disorder (Bruce, Machan, Dyck, & Keller, 2001).

Comorbidity correlates with greater impairment and worse prognosis when comparing GAD with and without comorbid diagnoses (Noyes, 2001). Nevertheless, results on the effects of comorbidity on prognosis of GAD have been mixed, perhaps in part due to the high incidence of comorbidity, leading to restricted variability. Some studies have found that Axis I comorbidity does not predict treatment outcome (e.g., Durham, Allan, & Hackett, 1997; Newman, Przeworski, & Borkovec, 2001; Yonkers, Dyck, Warshaw, & Keller, 2000). Specifically, comorbid social phobia, PTSD, and alcohol/substance abuse have not been found to predict treatment outcome (Bruce et al., 2001; Yonkers et al., 2000). Others, however, have found that comorbid diagnoses of MDD or panic disorder decrease the likelihood of remittance (Bruce et al., 2001). Noyes (2001) also found that comorbid diagnoses lead to a poorer response to both psychological and pharmacological treatments. Importantly, however, research has demonstrated that successful treatment of GAD leads to a reduction of comorbid disorders (Borkovec et al., 1995; Newman et al., 2001). Clearly further research into the connections between GAD and its frequent comorbid conditions would enhance our understanding of the disorder and its course.

Regardless of comorbid conditions, prognosis in general for GAD is not good. In a longitudinal study, the probability of naturalistic remission was only .15 at one year and .25 at two years (Yonkers et al., 1996). After participating in drug treatment studies, only 18 percent of those with GAD were in full remission at the five-year follow-up, compared with 45 percent of those with panic disorder (Woodman et al., 1999).

ASSESSMENT AND DIAGNOSIS

GAD is notoriously difficult to diagnose due to complexities in the interpretation of *DSM* criteria, symptom overlap with other disorders, questions regarding diagnostic threshold, and patient variability in reporting symptoms (e.g., Brown, Di Nardo, Lehman, & Campbell, 2001). Of all the anxiety disorders GAD is one of the least reliably diagnosed (Brown et al., 2001; Di Nardo, Moras, Barlow, Rapee, & Brown, 1993). In fact, some recommend the use of two independent structured interviews in order to obtain an accurate diagnosis (Borkovec & Newman, 1998; Borkovec & Whisman, 1996). In this section the diagnostic criteria for GAD and various assessment measures are discussed.

Since the initial inclusion of GAD in the third edition of the *Diagnostic and Statistical Manual of Mental Disorders* (*DSM-III;* American Psychiatric Association, 1980), research into worry has led to several important changes in the criteria for diagnosing GAD. In its third edition, the *DSM* divided the previously single category of anxiety neurosis into panic disorder and GAD. GAD at this point was simply a residual category, a diagnosis to be given only if no other anxiety disorder were diagnosed. GAD was defined by global anxiety and its associated symptoms of apprehensive expectation, vigilance, physical tension, and autonomic overactivity. At this early stage, however, there were apparent problems with the criteria for the disorder: Interrater reliability of GAD diagnosis (kappa = .47; Di Nardo, O'Brien, Barlow, Waddell, & Blanchard, 1983) was only fair, the one-month duration criterion resulted in overdiagnosis, and the residual status of the disorder led to confusion in diagnoses (Barlow, 2002).

The *DSM-III-R* (American Psychiatric Association, 1987) altered diagnostic criteria in response to these difficulties. GAD became a primary diagnosis, and worry (apprehensive expectation) was now its central defining feature. Its remaining symptoms were relegated to an 18-item list and recognized as associated symptoms. Nevertheless diagnostic reliability remained only fair (kappa = .57; Di Nardo et al., 1993).

Several further diagnostic revisions have followed. Comprehensive reviews of the empirical literature on GAD (e.g., Borkovec, Shadick, & Hopkins, 1991) led to the current *DSM-IV* definition. The earlier list of 18 associated symptoms has been reduced to 6 in recognition of Marten et al.'s (1993) research into the most reliably associated symptoms of GAD, and further research has supported the specific relevance of these 6 symptoms to GAD (Abel & Borkovec, 1995; Brawman-Mintzer et al., 1994; Brown, Marten, & Barlow, 1995). Perhaps most notably, the associated symptoms were changed so as to reflect central nervous system rather than autonomic nervous system activity, and recent research has indeed demonstrated that GAD is associated with reduced physiological arousal (Borkovec & Hu, 1990). Finally, and of central importance, the diagnostic criteria were further revised for the fourth edition to require that worry in GAD be perceived as difficult to control.

A diagnosis of GAD, according to the current *DSM-IV* criteria (American Psychiatric Association, 1994), requires excessive worry surrounding a number of events or situations, more days than not, lasting at least six months. The individual must experience the worry as difficult to control and must report at least three of six listed symptoms during most of their period of worrying. These symptom groups (restlessness, muscle tension, fatigue, difficulty concentrating, irritability, and sleep disturbance) are primarily associated with excessive psychophysiological arousal. Furthermore, in order for GAD to be diagnosed the *DSM-IV* requires that the associated worry must not be limited to aspects of another

Axis I disorder. For example, worry about being contaminated by germs (as in obsessive-compulsive disorder), would not be counted toward a diagnosis of GAD. Finally, the symptoms must cause clinically significant distress or functional impairment and not be due to the direct physiological effects of a substance or a general medical condition.

In a departure from earlier editions (*DSM III, DSM-III-R;* American Psychiatric Association, 1980, 1987), the *DSM-IV* (American Psychiatric Association, 1994) subsumes the childhood diagnosis of Overanxious Disorder under the category of Generalized Anxiety Disorder (GAD). The criteria for GAD are thought to describe adequately the disorder in children as well as adults (Tracey, Chorpita, Douban, & Barlow, 1997).

Taken separately, several of these criteria have substantial diagnostic overlap with other anxiety and mood disorders. The listed psychophysiological symptoms, for example, are not unique to GAD and are commonly reported in other anxiety disorders as well (Barlow et al., 1986). Moreover, the associated symptoms of GAD are almost identical to symptoms associated with depression. This symptom criterion alone cannot distinguish individuals with a diagnosis of GAD from those with depressive disorders (Brown et al., 1995). Only in conjunction with the other criteria do these symptoms signify GAD specifically. GAD's worry criterion has some overlap with other disorders as well. Naturally, worry regarding specific events, activities, or situations occurs in other anxiety and mood disorders (Barlow, 1988, 2002). Clearly, there are subtleties in the diagnostic criteria and symptom picture of GAD that need to be taken into consideration during assessment.

Useful assessment tools for GAD include both those designed to diagnose according to *DSM* criteria and those aimed more at appraising and understanding associated symptoms, features, and characteristics. Also, although not reviewed here, measures designed to assess for comorbid disorders are especially important when a diagnosis of GAD is determined, as evidenced by findings discussed earlier. Commonly used assessment tools for diagnosing GAD and examining its associated features discussed in the following paragraphs include interview-based instruments and self-report measures.

The Anxiety Disorder Schedule for *DSM-IV* (ADIS-IV; Brown, Di Nardo, & Barlow, 1994) and the Lifetime Version of this scale (ADIS-IV-L; Di Nardo, Brown, & Barlow, 1994) are the most widely used interview tools for assessment of GAD. Along with determining current and lifetime GAD, the ADIS-IV-L also assesses GAD onset, remission, and temporal sequence of comorbid anxiety disorders. Moreover it provides diagnoses of other anxiety, mood, and substance abuse disorders that often co-occur with GAD. In a departure from standard *DSM-IV* diagnostic methods, both the ADIS-IV and ADIS-IV-L examine symptom intensity for associated and core features of GAD, even when diagnostic criteria are not fully met, in an assumption that emotional disorders exist along a continuum (cf. Brown et al., 1998; Brown et al., 2001; Ruscio, Borkovec, & Ruscio, 2001). Assessing for dimensional severity not only captures subclinical levels of a disorder, but is also useful for assessing change in treatment outcome studies (Borkovec, Newman, Pincus, & Lytle, 2002; Brown & Barlow, 1995). Interrater reliability of the ADIS-IV diagnoses for GAD (kappa = .67; Brown et al., 2001) is good.

The Structured Clinical Interview for *DSM-IV* Axis I Disorders (SCID-IV; First, Spitzer, Gibbon, & Williams, 1996) is a second widely used diagnostic interview used to assess for GAD along with other Axis I disorders. However, unlike the ADIS-IV, its scope is limited strictly to assessing *DSM-IV* criteria.

Although many self-report measures have been designed to assess different aspects of GAD, few exist with the function of diagnosing this disorder. One such diagnostic self-report tool is the Generalized Anxiety Disorder Questionnaire IV (GADQ-IV; Newman, Zuellig, et al., 2002). This 21-item, Likert-scaled measure screens for GAD based on *DSM-IV* criteria as standardized against the ADIS-IV (Brown, Di Nardo, et al., 1994). The GADQ-IV has good psychometric properties, with a specificity of 89 percent, a sensitivity of 83 percent, 92 percent of participants maintaining a stable diagnosis for two-week test-retest reliability, and a good rate of agreement between the GADQ-IV and the ADIS-IV (kappa = .65; Newman, Zuellig, et al., 2002). As suggested by its designers, this measure is particularly useful as an initial screening device for GAD, in order to rule out those not meeting criteria before a more costly structured interview is administered.

Although not specifically intended to be diagnostic, the Penn State Worry Questionnaire (PSWQ; Meyer, Miller, Metzger, & Borkovec, 1990) is a widely used measure designed to determine the frequency and intensity of pathological worry. Because it measures a traitlike tendency to worry, the PSWQ is often used as a screening device for GAD. Factor analysis shows that this 16-item self-report device measures a unidimensional construct (Meyer et al., 1990). The PSWQ also has high internal consistency ($\alpha = .91$), good test-retest reliability, and sensitivity to change in response to psychotherapy (Borkovec & Costello, 1993; Meyer et al., 1990). Molina and Borkovec (1994) provide a review of the strong psychometric properties of the PSWQ in both clinical and nonclinical populations. This measure also shows discriminant ability between GAD and PTSD and among presence, absence, and subthreshold *DSM-III-R* GAD criteria (Meyer et al., 1990).

Other reliable and valid measures in common use include those for assessing different aspects of worry and anxiety. For example, the Meta-Cognitions Questionnaire (MCQ; Cartwright-Hatton & Wells, 1997) examines positive and negative beliefs about worry. Similarly, the Why Worry Scale (Freeston et al., 1994) assesses reasons people worry, and the Consequences of Worrying Questionnaire (CWQ; Davey, Tallis, & Capuzzo, 1996) assesses the consequences of worrying. The Reactions to Relaxation and Arousal Questionnaire (RRAQ; Heide & Borkovec, 1983) measures anxiety associated with relaxation, and the Intolerance of Uncertainty Scale (IU; Freeston et al., 1994) measures attempts to control the future, difficulty dealing with uncertainty, and reactions to ambiguous events.

More general measures of anxiety are also used to assess different aspects of GAD. For example, the State-Trait Anxiety Inventory (STAI; Spielberger, Gorsuch, Lushene, Vagg, & Jacobs, 1983) is often used to examine changes in trait anxiety in GAD treatment outcome studies. In its Tension/Stress subscale, the Depression, Anxiety, and Stress Scales (Lovibond & Lovibond, 1995) assesses anxious arousal, problems relaxing, irritability, and becoming agitated quickly. Individuals with GAD have been shown to have significantly higher scores on this subscale compared to those with panic disorder, social phobia, and specific phobia (Brown, Chorpita, Korotitsch, & Barlow, 1997).

IMPACT ON ENVIRONMENT

The overall picture for GAD is one of significant psychosocial impairment, with family life, peer interactions, and work all negatively affected. In the Epidemiological Catchment Area study (ECA), 38 percent of ECA subjects with GAD and 71 percent of outpatients with GAD characterized their emotional health as only fair to poor (Massion, Warshaw, & Keller, 1993). Other recent studies have confirmed the severe disability and poor quality of life associated with GAD (Maier, Gansicke, Freyberger, & Schnaier, 2000; Sanderson & Andrews, 2002; Stein, 2001). Such disability has been found to be comparable to disability from depression (Wittchen, Carter, Pfister, Montgomery, & Kessler, 2000). Furthermore, research shows that significant disability similar to what would be expected from chronic medical illnesses can result from cases in which chronic anxiety is not successfully treated (Fifer et al., 1994).

One area of particular distress for individuals with GAD is close personal relationships. GAD negatively affects both peer and family relationships. The disorder is associated with high marital discord and a lack of close friendships (Pincus & Borkovec, 1994; Sanderson et al., 1994; Whisman et al., 2000). Also, in a national comorbidity sample as well as a sample of more than 10,000 Australian subjects, GAD predicted increased odds of being separated or divorced (Hunt et al., 2002; Wittchen et al., 1994). Further evidence suggests such marital problems are somewhat specific to GAD relative to other anxiety disorders. Wives with GAD have been found to be more dissatisfied with their marriages than wives with other anxiety disorders (McLeod, 1994), and spouses with GAD reported more conflictual marriages than spouses with agoraphobia (Friedman, 1990). Moreover, in a sample of 4,933 married couples, marital discord was independently and more strongly associated with GAD than major depression, mania, dysthymia, social phobia, simple phobia, agoraphobia, panic disorder, and alcohol dependence after controlling for demographic variables, comorbid disorders, and quality of other relationships (Whisman et al., 2000). Additional studies show that compared to non-GAD participants, GAD women have more difficulty with emotional and interpersonal intimacy (Dutton, 2002). Compared to agoraphobic patients and their spouses, GAD patients and their spouses report that there is greater conflict and less cohesion in their families (Friedman, 1990). Finally, parents with GAD report significantly greater dysfunction in their families compared to those without GAD (Ben-Noun, 1998). The poor quality of peer and family relationships found in those with GAD can be associated with several personality and interpersonal problems typically found in the disorder.

Given that people with GAD approach their relationships with elevated hypervigilance, suspiciousness, and a tendency to feel easily slighted (Gasperini et al., 1990), it is not surprising that they have high levels of interpersonal problems. As noted earlier, negative interpersonal cycles may occur with GAD individuals, thus leading to the maintenance of interpersonal problems and worries.

Restricted emotional expression (a common trait for those with GAD) may also contribute to the poor close relationships associated with the disorder. Research has demonstrated that high levels of emotional disclosure predict being liked and are necessary for the development of close relationships (Collins & Miller, 1994; Dindia, 2000). Yet clinical observations suggest that individuals with GAD have restricted affect, empathy, and spontaneity and avoid displaying emotional vulnerability (Newman, 2000b; Newman, Castonguay, Borkovec, & Molnar, 2004). Several lines of research also support the idea that people with GAD have difficulty expressing emotion. For example, compared to nonanxious individuals, both GAD analogues and clients report a greater intensity of emotional experience and greater difficulty labeling emotions (Abel, 1994; Brown, Di Nardo, et al., 1994; Mennin, Turk, Fresco, & Heimberg, 2000; Turk et al., in press; Yamas, Hazlett-Stevens, & Borkovec, 1997). Furthermore, because worry inhibits emotional processing (Borkovec & Hu, 1990; Borkovec et al., 1993; Peasley-Miklus & Vrana, 2000), it has been conceived as motivated avoidance of emotional imagery and associated physical sensations (Borkovec & Inz, 1990). This avoidance of emotion likely leads to the "opposite" of emotional disclosure found in those with GAD (Borkovec, Roemer, & Kinyon, 1995).

Along with problems relating to close relationships, GAD also has a negative impact on work. The anxiety associated with GAD is debilitating, causing many with the disorder to be unable to go to work. For example, the ECA survey found that 27 percent of ECA subjects with GAD and 25 percent of outpatients with GAD were receiving disability payments, and only about 50 percent worked full-time. Of those who were working, 38 percent had missed at least one week of work in the past year due to their anxiety (Massion et al., 1993). It is likely that both extreme worry and the interpersonal apprehension and rigidity common to GAD lead to difficulty excelling in the workplace as well. Indeed, the ECA survey also found a strong correlation between both occupational status and income and GAD. GAD was associated with a threefold greater likelihood of working at a low occupational level and a more than twofold likelihood of earning less than $10,000 per year. Another recent study found that the role impairment in those with pure GAD (without comorbidity) *is comparable to that of major depression* (Kessler, Stang, Wittchen, Stein, & Walters, 1999).

TREATMENT IMPLICATIONS

Although substantial gains in GAD treatment have been made over the years, it remains the least successfully treated of the anxiety disorders (Brown, Barlow, et al., 1994). Nevertheless, cognitive behavioral treatment (CBT) for GAD has been found to be generally effective against the disorder (for a review, see Newman, Castonguay, Borkovec, & Molnar, 2004). The symptoms of GAD are believed to arise from consistent, spiraling, rigid patterns of interaction between cognitive, imaginal, and physiological responses to continuously perceived threat (Barlow, 1988; Borkovec & Inz, 1990; Newman & Borkovec, 2002). Cognitive behavioral therapy contains elements designed to target each of these cognitive, imaginal, and physiological response systems (Newman, 1999; Newman & Borkovec, 1995). The client learns techniques in CBT with the aim of developing a more flexible and relaxed lifestyle leading to a reduction in their anxiety. The specific interventions in CBT include self-monitoring, stimulus control, relaxation, self-control desensitization, and cognitive therapy. Several recent chapters provide a more complete review of CBT for GAD (Borkovec & Newman, 1998; Newman, 2000a; Newman & Borkovec, 2002).

Clients in CBT first learn self-monitoring and early cue detection. They are taught to pay attention to internal (and, with less emphasis, external) cues that signal that they are becoming anxious. Because of the spiraling nature of anxiety in GAD, it is important for clients to learn their early warning signs and stop their worry early before it reaches uncontrollable levels. Self-monitoring helps to identify triggers and patterns specific to the anxious experience of each individual client. Once clients are aware of their anxiety cues, elements of CBT designed to intervene at early stages of anxiety and worry can be employed.

Stimulus control is the next element of CBT that clients learn to utilize. GAD clients worry across numerous situations, a habit that leads to many cues (both internal and external) that trigger their anxiety. In order to lessen the association between worry and these cues, clients are asked to schedule in a specific 30-minute worry period each day and to purposefully put off worrying at other times until the appointed time. This procedure provides the client with a sense of control over their worry, thus targeting the prominent feature of uncontrollable worry indicative of GAD.

The physiological aspects of GAD are also targeted in therapy. Diaphragmatic breathing and progressive muscle relaxation (PMR) are helpful methods of addressing the autonomic rigidity common to the disorder. Diaphragmatic breathing teaches clients that breathing from the chest activates the sympathetic autonomic nervous system, thus leading to physiological sensations indicating anxiety. Breathing from the diaphragm, on the other hand, stimulates the parasympathetic nervous system and produces physiological sensations of deep relaxation. Clients can actively switch to breathing from the diaphragm as soon as they detect the first cues of their anxiety. This simple breathing technique offers clients a better sense of control over their somatic anxious sensations. PMR is another helpful method of relaxation. Clients are taught to systematically tense and then release 16 distinct muscle groups. As the technique is mastered, the muscle groups are gradually reduced to only four, and finally clients are able to relax their muscles without first tensing them at all. During PMR, clients focus on a calming mantra or image in order to aide the relaxation process. The goals of relaxation are to increase adaptive behavior and to focus the client's attention on the present moment. Applied relaxation (AR) can further help clients to reach these goals by requiring them to use relaxation techniques throughout the day whenever they detect anxiety cues.

Imaginal exposure is another important element in the treatment of GAD. Whereas worry impedes emotional processing, imagery assists the process. Self-control desensitization (SCD) uses imagery as a form of exposure to anxiety problems in which no specific phobic object exists (Goldfried, 1971). First clients use PMR to relax, and then they imagine themselves in an anxiety-provoking situation until they feel symptoms of anxiety. Next the clients imagine themselves coping effectively with the situation and thus relax the anxiety away. SCD teaches clients to use their CBT coping strategies when they notice anxious cues.

Another important element of CBT is cognitive therapy (CT). CT is based on the premise that emotions depend on the way an individual interprets different situations. People with GAD tend to negatively interpret ambiguous or neutral stimuli (Mathews, 1990; Mathews & MacLeod, 1994). They also often vastly misjudge the probability of a core feared event occurring, as evidenced by the finding in the Penn State GAD project that this event occurred in only 3 percent of all worries. Therefore, CT may be a particularly important element of treatment for GAD. Cognitive therapy teaches clients to reinterpret stimuli in a more accurate, positive light based on actual evidence from their environment.

Although CBT has been shown to be effective in treating GAD, on average only about 50 percent of clients show clinically significant change at follow-up (Borkovec & Newman, 1998; Newman, 2000b). Some authors suggest that by introducing interpersonal and experiential elements into the now-standard CBT package for GAD, more of the core elements of the disorder would be addressed, thus leading to higher rates of therapeutic change (e.g., Newman, 2000b; Newman et al., 2004). In fact, these researchers have developed a therapy that integrates present-moment awareness and interpersonal concerns into a CBT package in order to focus on these specific difficulties associated with GAD (Newman, Castonguay, & Borkovec, 2002).

Pharmacological treatment has also been used effectively to treat GAD, however, its effects have not been found to be as high as those found with CBT, particularly when clients have comorbid depression (Gould, Otto, Pollack, & Yap, 1997). Three classes of drugs are commonly used to treat GAD, those being benzodiazepines, azapirones, and antidepressants. Benzodiazepines such as diazepam have historically been the most widely used medication for anxiety. They have been shown to produce short-term alleviation of GAD symptoms; however, full remission is rare, and relapse after treatment is common (Schweizer & Rickels, 1996).

Benzodiazepines target the somatic symptoms of GAD and have not been found to be particularly effective against the cognitive symptoms such as worry (e.g., Pourmotabbed, McLeod, Hoehn-Saric, Hipsley, & Greenblatt, 1996). Furthermore, benzodiazepines have been shown less effective when depressive symptoms are present (Gould et al., 1997), which presents an important consideration in light of high rates of comorbidity. A further drawback of benzodiazepines includes serious side effects such as anterograde amnesia (Lucki, Rickels, & Geller, 1986), sedation (Shader & Greenblatt, 1993), and psychomotor dysfunction (Pourmotabbed et al., 1996). Finally, benzodiazepines can be addictive (Moller, 1999) and often produce withdrawal symptoms after long-term treatment (Rickels, Case, Schweizer, Swenson, & Fridman, 1986; Schweizer & Rickels, 1998). Abecarnil, a new type of partial benzodiazepine agonist that has recently been developed, seems to produce fewer withdrawal symptoms while still reducing anxiety effectively compared to placebo in some studies (Lydiard, Ballenger, & Rickels, 1997). Further research is needed, however, as other studies have failed to show a significant difference between abecarnil and placebo (e.g., Rickels, DeMartinis, & Aufdembrinke, 2000).

Azapirones such as buspirone and antidepressants such as impramine (a tricyclic antidepressant) and paroxetine (a selective serotonin reuptake inhibitor) are also used to treat GAD. These drugs have fewer side effects and dependence risk than benzodiazepines and target cognitive symptoms of anxiety rather than somatic symptoms. Although these improvements are hopeful, there is a strong likelihood of relapse once use of the drug is discontinued, and due to the chronicity and early onset of GAD, drug therapy is often problematic for this disorder (Schweizer & Rickels, 1996).

Few studies to date exist regarding factors predictive of treatment outcome for GAD (Newman, Crits-Christoph, Connelly, & Erickson, in press). Expectancy ratings at the start of treatment have been found to predict outcome in some studies (Borkovec & Costello, 1993; Borkovec & Mathews, 1988) but not in others (Borkovec et al., 2002; Ladouceur et al., 2000). Similarly, whereas some studies found no relationship between credibility and outcome (Borkovec & Costello, 1993; Borkovec & Mathews, 1988), others found credibility ratings significantly predicted outcome (Borkovec et al., 2002). Also, Borkovec and colleagues found a negative relationship between anxiety experienced during relaxation and treatment outcome (Borkovec et al., 1987; Borkovec & Mathews, 1988). Finally, Borkovec, Newman et al. (2002) identified several dimensions of interpersonal problems reported both at the start of treatment and at follow-up as negative predictors of outcome.

SUMMARY

This chapter has provided an overview of generalized anxiety disorder (GAD), including a clinical picture of the disorder and sections on personality development, etiology, course and prognosis, epidemiology, assessment and diagnosis, impact on the environment, and treatment. The nature and function of worry were discussed, including cognitive findings regarding information processing dysfunctions such as the tendency of those with GAD to interpret ambiguous/neutral stimuli as negative. These difficulties are related to the view held by individuals with GAD that the world is a dangerous place and the belief that worry is a positive coping strategy. Also, emotion avoidance theory was discussed based on findings of inflexible physiological characteristics of those with GAD. Worry reduces physiological arousal and thus may be negatively reinforced, with the negative consequence of precluding emotional processing. Next, personality correlates of the disorder were detailed, and development in terms of negative interpersonal cycles was discussed, along with various accounts of etiology. The development and maintenance of GAD is linked to attachment theory, the verbal-linguistic nature of worry, and emotional processing dysfunction. Prevalence of GAD and risk factors such as gender and marital status were noted in the next section. The early onset, chronic course, and the frequently comorbid nature of GAD were highlighted as well. Possibilities of a bimodal age of onset and its implications were also discussed. Current assessment and diagnosis tools such as the GADQ-IV were outlined, and diagnostic criteria were given. Finally, various treatment strategies such as cognitive behavioral techniques and pharmacological interventions were reviewed.

REFERENCES

Abel, J. L. (1994, November). *Alexithymia in an analogue sample of generalized anxiety disorder and non-anxious matched controls.* Paper presented at the 28th annual meeting of the Association for Advancement of Behavior Therapy, San Diego, CA.

Abel, J. L., & Borkovec, T. D. (1995). Generalizability of *DSM-III-R* generalized anxiety disorders to proposed *DSM-IV* criteria and cross-validation of proposed changes. *Journal of Anxiety Disorders, 9,* 303–315.

Alden, L. E., Wiggins, J. S., & Pincus, A. L. (1990). Construction of circumplex scales for the Inventory of Interpersonal Problems. *Journal of Personality Assessment, 55,* 521–536.

American Psychiatric Association. (1980). *Diagnostic and statistical manual of mental disorders* (3rd ed.). Washington, DC: Author.

American Psychiatric Association. (1987). *Diagnostic and statistical manual of mental disorders* (3rd ed., rev.). Washington, DC: Author.

American Psychiatric Association. (1994). *Diagnostic and statistical manual of mental disorders* (4th ed.). Washington, DC: Author.

Anderson, D. J., Noyes, R., & Crowe, R. R. (1984). A comparison of panic disorder and generalized anxiety disorder. *American Journal of Psychiatry, 141,* 572–575.

Anderson, J. C., Williams, S. M., McGee, R., & Silva, P. A. (1987). *DSM-III* disorders in preadolescent children: Prevalence in a large sample from the general population. *Archives of General Psychiatry, 44,* 69–76.

Andrews, V. H., & Borkovec, T. D. (1988). The differential effects of inductions of worry, somatic anxiety, and depression on emotional experience. *Journal of Behavior Therapy and Experimental Psychiatry, 19,* 21–26.

Ayllon, T., Smith, D., & Rogers, M. (1970). Behavioral management of school phobia. *Journal of Behavior Therapy and Experimental Psychiatry, 1,* 125–138.

Bandura, A. (1977). *Social learning theory.* Oxford, England: Prentice Hall.

Bandura, A., & Menlove, F. L. (1968). Factors determining vicarious extinction of avoidance behavior through symbolic modeling. *Journal of Personality and Social Psychology, 8,* 99–108.

Barlow, D. H. (1988). *Anxiety and its disorders: The nature and treatment of anxiety and panic.* New York: Guilford Press.

Barlow, D. H. (Ed.). (2002). *Anxiety and its disorders: The nature and treatment of anxiety and panic* (2nd ed.). New York: Guilford Press.

Barlow, D. H., Blanchard, E. B., Vermilyea, J. A., Vermilyea, B. B., & Di Nardo, P. A. (1986). Generalized anxiety and generalized anxiety disorder: Description and reconceptualization. *American Journal of Psychiatry, 143,* 40–44.

Beck, A. T., Emery, G., & Greenberg, R. L. (1985). *Anxiety disorders and phobias: A cognitive perspective.* New York: Basic Books.

Beidel, D. C., Christ, M. A., & Long, P. J. (1991). Somatic complaints in anxious children. *Journal of Abnormal Child Psychology, 19,* 659–670.

Ben-Noun, L. (1998). Generalized anxiety disorder in dysfunctional families. *Journal of Behavior Therapy and Experimental Psychiatry, 29,* 115–122.

Blashfield, R., Noyes, R., Reich, J., Woodman, C., Cook, B. L., & Garvey, M. J. (1994). Personality disorder traits in generalized anxiety and panic disorder patients. *Comprehensive Psychiatry, 35,* 329–334.

Blazer, D. G., Hughes, D. C., George, L. K., Swartz, M. S., & Boyer, R. (1991). Generalized anxiety disorder. In L. N. Robins & D. A. Regier (Eds.), *Psychiatric disorders in America* (pp. 180–203). New York: Free Press.

Borkovec, T. D. (1994). The nature, functions, and origins of worry. In G. C. L. Davey & F. Tallis (Eds.), *Worrying: Perspectives on theory, assessment and treatment* (pp. 5–33). Oxford, England: Wiley.

Borkovec, T. D., Abel, J. L., & Newman, H. (1995). Effects of psychotherapy on comorbid conditions in generalized anxiety disorder. *Journal of Consulting and Clinical Psychology, 63,* 479–483.

Borkovec, T. D., Alcaine, O., & Behar, E. S. (2004). Avoidance theory of worry and generalized anxiety disorder. In R. Heimberg, D. Mennin, & C. Turk (Eds.), *The nature and treatment of generalized anxiety disorder* (pp. 77–108). New York: Guilford Publication.

Borkovec, T. D., & Costello, E. (1993). Efficacy of applied relaxation and cognitive-behavioral therapy in the treatment of generalized anxiety disorder. *Journal of Consulting and Clinical Psychology, 61,* 611–619.

Borkovec, T. D., Hazlett-Stevens, H., & Diaz, M. L. (1999). The role of positive beliefs about worry in generalized anxiety disorder and its treatment. *Clinical Psychology and Psychotherapy, 6,* 126–138.

Borkovec, T. D., & Hu, S. (1990). The effect of worry on cardiovascular response to phobic imagery. *Behaviour Research and Therapy, 28,* 69–73.

Borkovec, T. D., & Inz, J. (1990). The nature of worry in generalized anxiety disorder: A predominance of thought activity. *Behaviour Research and Therapy, 28,* 153–158.

Borkovec, T. D., Lyonfields, J. D., Wiser, S. L., & Diehl, L. (1993). The role of worrisome thinking in the suppression of cardiovascular response to phobic imagery. *Behaviour Research and Therapy, 31,* 321–324.

Borkovec, T. D., & Mathews, A. M. (1988). Treatment of nonphobic anxiety disorders: A comparison of nondirective, cognitive, and coping desensitization therapy. *Journal of Consulting and Clinical Psychology, 56,* 877–884.

Borkovec, T. D., Mathews, A. M., Chambers, A., Ebrahimi, S., Lytle, R., & Nelson, R. (1987). The effects of relaxation training with cognitive or nondirective therapy and the role of relaxation-induced anxiety in the treatment of generalized anxiety. *Journal of Consulting and Clinical Psychology, 55,* 883–888.

Borkovec, T. D., Metzger, R. L., & Pruzinsky, T. (1986). Anxiety, worry, and the self. In L. M. Hartman & K. R. Blankstein (Eds.), *Perception of self in emotional disorder and psychotherapy* (Vol. 11, pp. 219–260). New York: Plenum Press.

Borkovec, T. D., & Newman, M. G. (1998). Worry and generalized anxiety disorder. In A. S. Bellack, M. Hersen (Series Eds.), & P. Salkovskis (Vol. Ed.), *Comprehensive clinical psychology: Vol. 6. Adults: Clinical formulation and treatment* (pp. 439–459). Oxford, England: Pergamon Press.

Borkovec, T. D., Newman, M. G., Pincus, A. L., & Lytle, R. (2002). A component analysis of cognitive-behavioral therapy for generalized anxiety disorder and the role of interpersonal problems. *Journal of Consulting and Clinical Psychology, 70,* 288–298.

Borkovec, T. D., Robinson, E., Pruzinsky, T., & DePree, J. A. (1983). Preliminary exploration of worry: Some characteristics and processes. *Behaviour Research and Therapy, 21,* 9–16.

Borkovec, T. D., & Roemer, L. (1995). Perceived functions of worry among generalized anxiety disorder subjects: Distraction from more emotionally distressing topics. *Journal of Behavior Therapy and Experimental Psychiatry, 26,* 25–30.

Borkovec, T. D., Roemer, L., & Kinyon, J. (1995). Disclosure and worry: Opposite sides of the same emotional processing coin. In J. Pennebaker (Ed.), *Emotion, disclosure and health* (pp. 47–70). Washington, DC: American Psychological Association.

Borkovec, T. D., Shadick, R. N., & Hopkins, M. (1991). The nature of normal and pathological worry. In R. M. Rapee & D. H. Barlow (Eds.), *Chronic anxiety: Generalized anxiety disorder and mixed anxiety-depression* (pp. 29–51). New York: Guilford Press.

Borkovec, T. D., & Whisman, M. A. (1996). Psychosocial treatment for generalized anxiety disorder. In M. R. Mavissakalian & R. F. Prien (Eds.), *Long-term treatments of anxiety disorders* (pp. 171–199). Washington, DC: American Psychiatric Association.

Bowlby, J. (1982). *Attachment and loss: Vol. 1. Attachment* (2nd ed.). New York: Basic Books.

Bradley, B. P., Mogg, K., White, J., Groom, C., & de Bono, J. (1999). Attentional bias for emotional faces in generalized anxiety disorder. *British Journal of Clinical Psychology, 38,* 267–278.

Brawman-Mintzer, O., Lydiard, R. B., Crawford, M. M., Emmanuel, N., Payeur, R., Johnson, M., et al. (1994). Somatic symptoms in generalized anxiety disorder with and without comorbid psychiatric disorders. *American Journal of Psychiatry, 151,* 930–932.

Brawman-Mintzer, O., Lydiard, R. B., Emmanuel, N., Payeur, R., Johnson, M., Roberts, et al. (1993). Psychiatric comorbidity in patients with generalized anxiety disorder. *American Journal of Psychiatry, 150,* 1216–1218.

Breitholtz, E., Johansson, B., & Öst, L. G. (1999). Cognitions in generalized anxiety disorder and panic disorder patients: A prospective approach. *Behaviour Research and Therapy, 37,* 533–544.

Brown, T. A. (1999). Generalized anxiety disorder and obsessive-compulsive disorder. In T. Millon, P. H. Blaney, & R. D. Davis (Eds.), *Oxford textbook of psychopathology* (pp. 114–143). London: Oxford University Press.

Brown, T. A., & Barlow, D. H. (1992). Comorbidity among anxiety disorders: Implications for treatment and *DSM-IV*. *Journal of Consulting and Clinical Psychology, 60,* 835–844.

Brown, T. A., & Barlow, D. H. (1995). Long-term outcome in cognitive-behavioral treatment of panic disorder: Clinical predictors and alternative strategies for assessment. *Journal of Consulting and Clinical Psychology, 63,* 754–765.

Brown, T. A., Barlow, D. H., & Liebowitz, M. R. (1994). The empirical basis of generalized anxiety disorder. *American Journal of Psychiatry, 151,* 1272–1280.

Brown, T. A., Chorpita, B. F., & Barlow, D. H. (1998). Structural relationships among dimensions of the *DSM-IV* anxiety and mood disorders and dimensions of negative affect, positive affect, and autonomic arousal. *Journal of Abnormal Psychology, 107,* 179–192.

Brown, T. A., Chorpita, B. F., Korotitsch, W., & Barlow, D. H. (1997). Psychometric properties of the Depression Anxiety Stress Scales (DASS) in clinical samples. *Behaviour Research and Therapy, 35,* 79–89.

Brown, T. A., Di Nardo, P. A., & Barlow, D. H. (1994). *Anxiety Disorders Interview Schedule for DSM-IV.* San Antonio, TX: Psychological Corp.

Brown, T. A., Di Nardo, P. A., Lehman, C. L., & Campbell, L. A. (2001). Reliability of *DSM-IV* anxiety and mood disorders: Implications for the classification of emotional disorders. *Journal of Abnormal Psychology, 110,* 49–58.

Brown, T. A., Marten, P. A., & Barlow, D. H. (1995). Discriminant validity of the symptoms constituting the *DSM-III-R* and *DSM-IV* associated symptom criterion of generalized anxiety disorder. *Journal of Anxiety Disorders, 9,* 317–328.

Bruce, S. E., Machan, J. T., Dyck, I., & Keller, M. B. (2001). Infrequency of "pure" GAD: Impact of psychiatric comorbidity on clinical course. *Depression and Anxiety, 14,* 219–225.

Butler, G., & Mathews, A. (1983). Cognitive processes in anxiety. *Advances in Behaviour Research and Therapy, 5,* 51–62.

Butler, G., Wells, A., & Dewick, H. (1995). Differential effects of worry and imagery after exposure to a stressful stimulus: A pilot study. *Behavioural and Cognitive Psychotherapy, 23,* 45–56.

Campbell, L. A., Brown, T. A., & Grisham, J. R. (2003). The relevance of age of onset to the psychopathology of generalized anxiety disorder. *Behavior Therapy, 34,* 31–48.

Carter, W. R., Johnson, M. C., & Borkovec, T. D. (1986). Worry: An electrocortical analysis. *Advances in Behaviour Research and Therapy, 8,* 193–204.

Cartwright-Hatton, S., & Wells, A. (1997). Beliefs about worry and intrusions: The Meta-Cognitions Questionnaire and its correlates. *Journal of Anxiety Disorders, 11,* 279–296.

Cassidy, J. A. (1995). Attachment and generalized anxiety disorder. In D. Cicchetti & S. Toth (Eds.), *Rochester Symposium on Developmental Psychopathology: Emotion, cognition, and representation* (Vol. 6, pp. 343–370). Rochester, NY: University of Rochester Press.

Cassidy, J. A., & Shaver, P. R. (Eds.). (1999). *Handbook of attachment: Theory, research, and clinical applications.* New York: Guilford Press.

Chorpita, B. F., Albano, A. M., & Barlow, D. H. (1996). Cognitive processing in children: Relation to anxiety and family influences. *Journal of Clinical Child Psychology, 25,* 170–176.

Clark, L. A., Watson, D., & Mineka, S. (1994). Temperament, personality, and the mood and anxiety disorders. *Journal of Abnormal Psychology, 103,* 103–116.

Cohen, P., Cohen, J., Kasen, S., Velez, C. N., Hartmark, C., Johnson, J., et al. (1993). An epidemiological study of disorders in late childhood and adolescence: I. Age- and gender-specific prevalence. *Journal of Child Psychology and Psychiatry and Allied Disciplines, 34,* 851–867.

Collins, N. L., & Miller, L. C. (1994). Self-disclosure and liking: A meta-analytic review. *Psychological Bulletin, 116,* 457–475.

Craske, M. G. (1999). *Anxiety disorders: Psychological approaches to theory and treatment.* Boulder, CO: Westview.

Craske, M. G., Rapee, R. M., Jackel, L., & Barlow, D. H. (1989). Qualitative dimensions of worry in *DSM-III-R* generalized anxiety disorder subjects and nonanxious controls. *Behaviour Research and Therapy, 27,* 397–402.

Davey, G. C. L., & Matchett, G. (1994). Unconditioned stimulus rehearsal and the retention and enhancement of differential "fear" conditioning: Effects of trait and state anxiety. *Journal of Abnormal Psychology, 103,* 708–718.

Davey, G. C. L., Tallis, F., & Capuzzo, N. (1996). Beliefs about the consequences of worrying. *Cognitive Therapy and Research, 20,* 499–520.

Deffenbacher, J. L. (1986). Cognitive and physiological components of test anxiety in real-life exams. *Cognitive Therapy and Research, 10,* 635–644.

Deffenbacher, J. L., & Hazaleus, S. L. (1985). Cognitive, emotional, and physiological components of test anxiety. *Cognitive Therapy and Research, 9,* 169–180.

Di Nardo, P. A., Brown, T. A., & Barlow, D. H. (1994). *Anxiety Disorders Interview Schedule for DSM-IV: Lifetime Version (ADIS-IV-L).* San Antonio, TX: Psychological Corp.

Di Nardo, P. A., Moras, K., Barlow, D. H., Rapee, R. M., & Brown, T. A. (1993). Reliability of *DSM-III-R* anxiety disorder categories: Using the Anxiety Disorders Interview Schedule–Revised (ADIS-R). *Archives of General Psychiatry, 50,* 251–256.

Di Nardo, P. A., O'Brien, G. T., Barlow, D. H., Waddell, M., & Blanchard, E. B. (1983). Reliability of *DSM-III* anxiety disorder categories using a new structured interview. *Archives of General Psychiatry, 40,* 1070–1074.

Dindia, K. (2000). Sex differences in self-disclosure, reciprocity of self-disclosure, & self-disclosure and liking: Three meta-analyses reviewed. In S. Petronio (Ed.), *Balancing the secrets of private disclosures* (pp. 21–35). Mahwah, NJ: Erlbaum.

Durham, R. C., Allan, T., & Hackett, C. A. (1997). On predicting improvement and relapse in generalized anxiety disorder following psychotherapy. *British Journal of Clinical Psychology, 36,* 101–119.

Dutton, S. S. (2002). Marital relationship functioning in a clinical sample of generalized anxiety disorder clients. *Dissertation Abstracts International, 62,* 4216B.

Dyck, I. R., Phillips, K. A., Warshaw, M. G., Dolan, R. T., Shea, M. T., Stout, R. L., et al. (2001). Patterns of personality pathology in patients with generalized anxiety disorder, panic disorder with and without agoraphobia, and social phobia. *Journal of Personality Disorders, 15,* 60–71.

East, M. P., & Watts, F. N. (1994). Worry and the suppression of imagery. *Behaviour Research and Therapy, 32,* 851–855.

Erickson, T., & Newman, M. G. (2002, November). *Emotional expression in GAD analogues based on an emotional disclosure task.* Paper presented at the 36th Annual Meeting of the Association for Advancement of Behavior Therapy, Reno, NV.

Fehr, F. S., & Stern, J. A. (1970). Peripheral physiological variables and emotion: The James-Lange theory revisited. *Psychological Bulletin, 74,* 411–424.

Fifer, S. K., Mathias, S. D., Patrick, D. L., Mazonson, P. D., Lubeck, D. P., & Buesching, D. P. (1994). Untreated anxiety among adult primary care patients in a health maintenance organization. *Archives of General Psychiatry, 51,* 740–750.

First, M. B., Spitzer, R. L., Gibbon, M., & Williams, J. B. W. (1996). Structured Clinical Interview for *DSM-IV* Axis I disorders: Patient edition (SCID-I/P, Version 2.0). New York: Biometrics Research Dept., New York State Psychiatric Institute.

Foa, E. B., & Kozak, M. J. (1986). Emotional processing of fear: Exposure to corrective information. *Psychological Bulletin, 99,* 20–35.

Freeston, M. H., Dugas, M. J., & Ladouceur, R. (1996). Thoughts, images, worry, and anxiety. *Cognitive Therapy and Research, 20,* 265–273.

Freeston, M. H., Rheaume, J., Letarte, H., Dugas, M. J., & Ladouceur, R. (1994). Why do people worry? *Personality and Individual Differences, 17,* 791–802.

Frick, P. J., & Silverthorn, P. (2001). Psychopathology in children. In H. E. Adams & P. B. Sutker (Eds.), *Comprehensive handbook of psychopathology* (3rd ed., pp. 881–920). New York: Kluwer Academic/Plenum Publishers.

Friedman, S. (1990). Assessing the marital environment of agoraphobics. *Journal of Anxiety Disorders, 4,* 335–340.

Gasperini, M., Battaglia, M., Diaferia, G., & Bellodi, L. (1990). Personality features related to generalized anxiety disorder. *Comprehensive Psychiatry, 31,* 363–368.

Goisman, R. M., Goldenberg, I., Vasile, R. G., & Keller, M. B. (1995). Comorbidity of anxiety disorders in a multicenter anxiety study. *Comprehensive Psychiatry, 36,* 303–311.

Goldfried, M. R. (1971). Systematic desensitization as training in self-control. *Journal of Consulting and Clinical Psychology, 37,* 228–234.

Gould, R. A., Otto, M. W., Pollack, M. H., & Yap, L. (1997). Cognitive behavioral and pharmacological treatment of generalized anxiety disorder: A preliminary meta-analysis. *Behavior Therapy, 28,* 285–305.

Heide, F. J., & Borkovec, T. D. (1983). Relaxation-induced anxiety: Paradoxical anxiety enhancement due to relaxation training. *Journal of Consulting and Clinical Psychology, 51,* 171–182.

Heller, W., Nitschke, J. B., Etienne, M. A., & Miller, G. A. (1997). Patterns of regional brain activity differentiate types of anxiety. *Journal of Abnormal Psychology, 106,* 376–385.

Hirshfeld, D. R., Rosenbaum, J. F., Biederman, J., Bolduc, E. A., Faraone, S. V., Snidman, N., et al. (1992). Stable behavioral inhibition and its association with anxiety disorders. *Journal of the American Academy of Child and Adolescent Psychiatry, 31,* 103–111.

Hoehn-Saric, R., Hazlett, R. L., & McLeod, D. R. (1993). Generalized anxiety disorder with early and late onset of anxiety symptoms. *Comprehensive Psychiatry, 34,* 291–298.

Hoehn-Saric, R., Lee, J. S., McLeod, D. R., Resnik, S., & Wong, D. F. (2003). *The effect of worry on rCBF in non-anxious subjects.* Unpublished manuscript.

Hoehn-Saric, R., & McLeod, D. R. (1988). The peripheral sympathetic nervous system: Its role in normal and pathological anxiety. *Psychiatric Clinics of North America, 11,* 375–386.

Hoehn-Saric, R., McLeod, D. R., & Zimmerli, W. D. (1989). Somatic manifestations in women with generalized anxiety disorder: Psychophysiological responses to psychological stress. *Archives of General Psychiatry, 46,* 1113–1119.

Hunt, C., Issakidis, C., & Andrews, G. (2002). *DSM-IV* generalized anxiety disorder in the Australian National Survey of Mental Health and Well-Being. *Psychological Medicine, 32,* 649–659.

Jones, T., & Davey, G. C. L. (1990). The effects of cued USC rehearsal on the retention of differential "fear" conditioning: An experimental analogue of the "worry" process. *Behaviour Research and Therapy, 28,* 159–164.

Kagan, J., & Snidman, N. (1990). Temperamental contributions to human development: The biological characteristics of infants influence their initial behavior to unfamiliar contexts. *Research and Clinical Center for Child Development, 59*–70.

Kagan, J., Snidman, N., & Arcus, D. (1998). Childhood derivatives of high and low reactivity in infancy. *Child Development, 69,* 1483–1493.

Katon, W., Von Korff, M., Lin, E., Lipscomb, P., Russo, J., Wagner, E., et al. (1990). Distressed high utilizers of medical care: *DSM-III-R* diagnoses and treatment needs. *General Hospital Psychiatry, 12,* 355–362.

Kendler, K. S. (1996). Major depression and generalised anxiety disorder same genes, (partly) different environments—Revisited. *British Journal of Psychiatry, 168,* 68–75.

Kendler, K. S., Neale, M. C., Kessler, R. C., Heath, A. C., & Eaves, L. J. (1992). Generalized anxiety disorder in women: A population-based twin study. *Archives of General Psychiatry, 49,* 267–272.

Kendler, K. S., Walters, E. E., Neale, M. C., Kessler, R. C., Heath, A. C., & Eaves, L. J. (1995). The structure of the genetic and environmental risk factors for six major psychiatric disorders in women: Phobia, generalized anxiety disorder, panic disorder, bulimia, major depression, and alcoholism. *Archives of General Psychiatry, 52,* 374–383.

Kennedy, B. L., & Schwab, J. J. (1997). Utilization of medical specialists by anxiety disorder patients. *Psychosomatics: Journal of Consultation Liaison Psychiatry, 38,* 109–112.

Kessler, R. C., DuPont, R. L., Berglund, P., & Wittchen, H. U. (1999). Impairment in pure and comorbid generalized anxiety disorder and major depression at 12 months in two national surveys. *American Journal of Psychiatry, 156,* 1915–1923.

Kessler, R. C., Keller, M. B., & Wittchen, H. U. (2001). The epidemiology of generalized anxiety disorder. *Psychiatric Clinics of North America, 24,* 19–39.

Kessler, R. C., McGonagle, K. A., Zhao, S., Nelson, C. B., Hughes, M., Eshleman, S., et al. (1994). Lifetime and 12-month prevalence of *DSM-III-R* psychiatric disorders in the United States: Results from the National Comorbidity Survey. *Archives of General Psychiatry, 51,* 8–19.

Kessler, R. C., Stang, P., Wittchen, H. U., Stein, M., & Walters, E. E. (1999). Lifetime comorbidities between social phobia and mood disorders in the U.S. National Comorbidity Survey. *Psychological Medicine, 29,* 555–567.

Ladouceur, R., Dugas, M. J., Freeston, M. H., Leger, E., Gagnon, F., & Thibodeau, N. (2000). Efficacy of a cognitive-behavioral treatment for generalized anxiety disorder: Evaluation in a controlled clinical trial. *Journal of Consulting and Clinical Psychology, 68,* 957–964.

Ladouceur, R., Freeston, M. H., Fournier, S., Dugas, M. J., & Doucet, C. (2002). The social basis of worry in three samples: High school students, university students, and older adults. *Behavioural and Cognitive Psychotherapy, 30,* 427–438.

Lang, P. J. (1985). Cognition in emotion: Concept and action. In C. E. Izard, J. Kagan, & R. B. Zajonc (Eds.), *Emotions, cognition, and behavior* (pp. 192–226). New York: Cambridge University Press.

Lovibond, P. F., & Lovibond, S. H. (1995). The structure of negative emotional states: Comparison of the Depression Anxiety Stress Scales (DASS) with the Beck Depression and Anxiety Inventories. *Behaviour Research and Therapy, 33,* 335–343.

Lucki, I., Rickels, K., & Geller, A. M. (1986). Chronic use of benzodiazepines and psychomotor and cognitive test performance. *Psychopharmacology, 88,* 426–433.

Lydiard, R., Ballenger, J. C., & Rickels, K. (1997). A double-blind evaluation of the safety and efficacy of abecarnil, alprazolam, and placebo in outpatients with generalized anxiety disorder. *Journal of Clinical Psychiatry, 58,* 11–18.

Lyonfields, J. D., Borkovec, T. D., & Thayer, J. F. (1995). Vagal tone in generalized anxiety disorder and the effects of aversive imagery and worrisome thinking. *Behavior Therapy, 26,* 457–466.

MacLeod, C., Mathews, A., & Tata, P. (1986). Attentional bias in emotional disorders. *Journal of Abnormal Psychology, 95,* 15–20.

Maier, W., Gansicke, M., Freyberger, H. J., & Schnaier, J. A. (2000). Generalized anxiety disorder (ICD-10) in primary care from a cross-cultural perspective: A valid diagnostic entity? *Acta Psychiatrica Scandinavica, 101,* 29–36.

Marten, P. A., Brown, T. A., Barlow, D. H., Borkovec, T. D., Shear, M. K., & Lydiard, R. B. (1993). Evaluation of the ratings comprising the associated symptom criterion of *DSM-III-R* generalized anxiety disorder. *Journal of Nervous and Mental Disease, 181,* 676–682.

Masi, G., Mucci, M., Favilla, L., Romano, R., & Poli, P. (1999). Symptomatology and comorbidity of generalized anxiety disorder in children and adolescents. *Comprehensive Psychiatry, 40,* 210–215.

Massion, A. O., Warshaw, M. G., & Keller, M. B. (1993). Quality of life and psychiatric morbidity in panic disorder and generalized anxiety disorder. *American Journal of Psychiatry, 150,* 600–607.

Mathews, A. (1990). Why worry? The cognitive function of anxiety. *Behaviour Research and Therapy, 28,* 455–468.

Mathews, A., & MacLeod, C. (1985). Selective processing of threat cues in anxiety states. *Behaviour Research and Therapy, 23,* 563–569.

Mathews, A., & MacLeod, C. (1994). Cognitive approaches to emotion and emotional disorders. *Annual Review of Psychology, 45,* 25–50.

Mathews, A., Mogg, K., May, J., & Eysenck, M. (1989). Implicit and explicit memory bias in anxiety. *Journal of Abnormal Psychology, 98,* 236–240.

McLeod, J. D. (1994). Anxiety disorders and marital quality. *Journal of Abnormal Psychology, 103,* 767–776.

Mennin, D. S., Turk, C. L., Fresco, D. M., & Heimberg, R. G. (2000, November). *Deficits in the regulation of emotion: A new direction for understanding generalized anxiety disorder.* Paper presented at the 34th Annual meeting of the Association for Advancement of Behavior Therapy, New Orleans, LA.

Menzies, R. G., & Clarke, J. C. (1995). The etiology of phobias: A nonassociative account. *Clinical Psychology Review, 15,* 23–48.

Metzger, R. L., Miller, M. L., Cohen, M., Sofka, M., & Borkovec, T. D. (1990). Worry changes decision making: The effect of negative thoughts on cognitive processing. *Journal of Clinical Psychology, 46,* 78–88.

Meyer, T. J., Miller, M. L., Metzger, R. L., & Borkovec, T. D. (1990). Development and validation of the Penn State Worry Questionnaire. *Behaviour Research and Therapy, 28,* 487–495.

Mogg, K., Mathews, A., & Eysenck, M. (1992). Attentional bias to threat in clinical anxiety states. *Cognition and Emotion, 6,* 149–159.

Mogg, K., Mathews, A., & Weinman, J. (1987). Memory bias in clinical anxiety. *Journal of Abnormal Psychology, 96,* 94–98.

Mogg, K., Millar, N., & Bradley, B. P. (2000). Biases in eye movements to threatening facial expressions in generalized anxiety disorder and depressive disorder. *Journal of Abnormal Psychology, 109,* 695–704.

Molina, S., & Borkovec, T. D. (1994). The Penn State Worry Questionnaire: Psychometric properties and associated characteristics. In G. C. L. Davey & F. Tallis (Eds.), *Worrying: Perspectives on theory, assessment and treatment* (pp. 265–283). Oxford, England: Wiley.

Moller, H. J. (1999). Effectiveness and safety of benzodiazepines. *Journal of Clinical Psychopharmacology, 19,* 2S–11S.

Mowrer, O. H. (1939). A stimulus-response analysis of anxiety and its role as a reinforcing agent. *Psychological Review, 46,* 553–566.

Muris, P., Steerneman, P., Merckelbach, H., & Meesters, C. (1996). The role of parental fearfulness and modeling in children's fear. *Behaviour Research and Therapy, 34,* 265–268.

Nestadt, G., Romanoski, A. J., Samules, J. F., Folstein, M. F., & McHugh, P. R. (1992). The relationship between personality and *DSM-III* Axis I disorders in the population: Results from an epidemiological survey. *American Journal of Psychiatry, 149,* 1228–1233.

Newman, M. G. (1999). The clinical use of palmtop computers in the treatment of generalized anxiety disorder. *Cognitive and Behavioral Practice, 6,* 222–234.

Newman, M. G. (2000a). Generalized anxiety disorder. In M. Hersen & M. Biaggio (Eds.), *Effective brief therapies: A clinician's guide* (pp. 157–178). San Diego, CA: Academic Press.

Newman, M. G. (2000b). Recommendations for a cost-offset model of psychotherapy allocation using generalized anxiety disorder as an example. *Journal of Consulting and Clinical Psychology, 68,* 549–555.

Newman, M. G., & Borkovec, T. D. (1995). Cognitive-behavioral treatment of generalized anxiety disorder. *The Clinical Psychologist, 48,* 5–7.

Newman, M. G., & Borkovec, T. D. (2002). Cognitive behavioral therapy for worry and generalized anxiety disorder. In G. Simos (Ed.), *Cognitive behaviour therapy: A guide for the practising clinician* (pp. 150–172). New York: Taylor & Francis.

Newman, M. G., Castonguay, L. G., & Borkovec, T. D. (2002, June). *Integrating cognitive-behavioral and interpersonal/emotional processing treatments for generalized anxiety disorder: Preliminary outcome findings.* Paper presented at the Society for Psychotherapy Research, Santa Barbara, CA.

Newman, M. G., Castonguay, L. G., Borkovec, T. D., & Molnar, C. (2004). Integrative psychotherapy. In R. Heimberg, D. Mennin, & C. Turk (Eds.), *Generalized anxiety disorder: Advances in research and practice* (pp. 320–350). New York: Guilford Press.

Newman, M. G., Crits-Christoph, P., Connelly, M. B., & Erickson, T. (in press). Participant factors in the treatment of anxiety disorders. In L. G. Castonguay & L. E. Beutler (Eds.), *Effective Principles of Change.* New York: Oxford University Press.

Newman, M. G., Przeworski, A., & Borkovec, T. D. (2001, November). *The effect of psychotherapy for GAD on comorbid Axis I conditions.* Paper presented at the 35th Annual Meeting of the Association for Advancement of Behavior Therapy, Philadelphia, PA.

Newman, M. G., Zuellig, A. R., Kachin, K. E., Constantino, M. J., Przeworski, A., Erickson, T., et al. (2002). Preliminary reliability and validity of the Generalized Anxiety Disorder Questionnaire-IV: A revised self-report diagnostic measure of generalized anxiety disorder. *Behavior Therapy, 33,* 215–233.

Noyes, J., Russell. (2001). Comorbidity in generalized anxiety disorder. *Psychiatric Clinics of North America, 24,* 41–55.

Noyes, R., Clarkson, C., Crowe, R. R., Yates, W. R., & McChesney, C. M. (1987). A family study of generalized anxiety disorder. *American Journal of Psychiatry, 144,* 1019–1024.

Noyes, R., Woodman, C., Garvey, M. J., Cook, B. L., Suelzer, M., Chancy, J., et al. (1992). Generalized anxiety disorder vs. panic disorder: Distinguishing characteristics and patterns of comorbidity. *Journal of Nervous and Mental Disease, 180,* 369–379.

Okasha, A., Bishry, Z., Khalil, A. H., Darwish, T. A., Seif El Dawla, A., & Shohdy, A. (1994). Panic disorder: An overlapping or independent entity? *British Journal of Psychiatry, 164,* 818–825.

Paivio, A. (1986). *Mental representations: A dual coding approach.* New York: Oxford University Press.

Parker, G. (1979). Reported parental characteristics in relation to trait depression and anxiety levels in a non-clinical group. *Australian and New Zealand Journal of Psychiatry, 13,* 260–264.

Parker, G. (1981). Parental representation of patients with anxiety neurosis. *Acta Psychiatrica Scandinavica, 63,* 33–36.

Peasley-Miklus, C., & Vrana, S. R. (2000). Effect of worrisome and relaxing thinking on fearful emotional processing. *Behaviour Research and Therapy, 38,* 129–144.

Pincus, A. L., & Borkovec, T. D. (1994, June). *Interpersonal problems in generalized anxiety disorder: Preliminary clustering of patients' interpersonal dysfunction.* Paper presented at the Annual Meeting of the American Psychological Society, New York.

Porges, S. W. (1992). Autonomic regulation and attention. In B. A. Campbell, H. Hayne, & R. Richardson (Eds.), *Attention and information processing in infants and adults* (pp. 201–223). Hillside, NJ: Erlbaum.

Pourmotabbed, T., McLeod, D. R., Hoehn-Saric, R., Hipsley, P., & Greenblatt, D. J. (1996). Treatment, discontinuation and psychomotor effects of diazepam in women with generalized anxiety disorder. *Journal of Clinical Psychopharmacology, 16,* 202–207.

Rapee, R. M. (1985). Distinctions between panic disorder and generalised anxiety disorder: Clinical presentation. *Australian and New Zealand Journal of Psychiatry, 19,* 227–232.

Rapee, R. M. (1991). Generalized anxiety disorder: A review of clinical features and theoretical concepts. *Clinical Psychology Review, 11,* 419–440.

Rapee, R. M. (1993). The utilisation of working memory by worry. *Behaviour Research and Therapy, 31,* 617–620.

Reich, J., Perry, J. C., Shera, D., Dyck, I., Vasile, R., Goisman, R. M., et al. (1994). Comparison of personality disorders in different anxiety disorder diagnoses: Panic, agoraphobia, generalized anxiety, and social phobia. *Annals of Clinical Psychiatry, 6,* 125–134.

Richards, J. E. (1987). Infant visual sustained attention and respiratory sinus arrhythmia. *Child Development, 58,* 488–496.

Rickels, K., Case, W. G., Schweizer, E. E., Swenson, C., & Fridman, R. B. (1986). Low-dose dependence in chronic benzodiazepine users: A preliminary report on 119 patients. *Psychopharmacology Bulletin, 22,* 407–415.

Rickels, K., DeMartinis, N., & Aufdembrinke, B. (2000). A double-blind, placebo-controlled trial of abecarnil and diazepam in the treatment of patients with generalized anxiety disorder. *Journal of Clinical Psychopharmacology, 20,* 12–18.

Roemer, L., Molina, S., & Borkovec, T. D. (1997). An investigation of worry content among generally anxious individuals. *Journal of Nervous and Mental Disease, 185,* 314–319.

Rosenbaum, J. F., Biederman, J., Gersten, M., Hirshfeld, D. R., Meminger, S. R., Herman, J. B., et al. (1988). Behavioral inhibition in children of parents with panic disorder and agoraphobia: A controlled study. *Archives of General Psychiatry, 45,* 463–470.

Roy-Byrne, P. P. (1996). Generalized anxiety and mixed anxiety-depression: Association with disability and health care utilization. *Journal of Clinical Psychiatry, 57,* 86–91.

Ruscio, A. M., Borkovec, T. D., & Ruscio, J. (2001). A taxometric investigation of the latent structure of worry. *Journal of Abnormal Psychology, 110,* 413–422.

Safran, J. D., & Segal, Z. V. (1990). *Interpersonal process in cognitive therapy.* New York: Basic Books.

Sanderson, K., & Andrews, G. (2002). Prevalence and severity of mental health related disability and relationship to diagnosis. *Psychiatric Services, 53,* 80–86.

Sanderson, W. C., Beck, A. T., & Beck, J. (1990). Syndrome comorbidity in patients with major depression or dysthymia: Prevalence and temporal relationships. *American Journal of Psychiatry, 147,* 1025–1028.

Sanderson, W. C., Wetzler, S., Beck, A. T., & Betz, F. (1994). Prevalence of personality disorders among patients with anxiety disorders. *Psychiatry Research, 51,* 167–174.

Schweizer, E., & Rickels, K. (1996). The long-term management of generalized anxiety disorder: Issues and dilemmas. *Journal of Clinical Psychiatry, 57*(Suppl. 7), 9–12.

Schweizer, E., & Rickels, K. (1998). Benzodiazepine dependence and withdrawal: A review of the syndrome and its clinical management. *Acta Psychiatrica Scandinavica, 393*(Suppl.), 95–101.

Shader, R. I., & Greenblatt, D. J. (1993). Use of benzodiazepines in anxiety disorders. *New England Journal of Medicine, 328,* 1398–1405.

Silove, D., Parker, G., Hadzi-Pavlovic, D., Manicavasagar, V., & Blaszczynski, A. (1991). Parental representations of patients with panic disorder and generalised anxiety disorder. *British Journal of Psychiatry, 159,* 835–841.

Silverman, W. K., & Ginsburg, G. S. (1998). Anxiety disorders. In M. Hersen & T. H. Ollendick (Eds.), *Handbook of child psychopathology* (3rd ed., pp. 239–268). New York: Plenum Press.

Spielberger, C. D., Gorsuch, R. L., Lushene, R., Vagg, P. R., & Jacobs, G. A. (1983). *Manual for the State-Trait Anxiety Inventory STAI (Form Y).* Palo Alto, CA: Mind Garden.

Stein, D. J. (2001). Comorbidity in generalized anxiety disorder: Impact and implications. *Journal of Clinical Psychiatry, 62,* 29–34.

Stöber, J., Tepperwien, S., & Staak, M. (2000). Worrying leads to reduced concreteness of problem elaborations: Evidence for the avoidance theory of worry. *Anxiety, Stress and Coping: An International Journal, 13,* 217–227.

Stöber, J. B., & Borkovec, T. D. (2002). Reduced concreteness of worry in generalized anxiety disorder: Findings from a therapy study. *Cognitive Therapy and Research, 26,* 89–96.

Strauss, C. C., Lahey, B. B., Frick, P., Fram, C. L., & Hynd, G. W. (1988). Peer social status of children with anxiety disorders. *Journal of Consulting and Clinical Psychology, 56,* 137–141.

Strauss, C. C., Lease, C. A., Kazdin, A. E., Dulcan, M. K., & Last, C. G. (1989). Multimethod assessment of the social competence of children with anxiety disorders. *Journal of Clinical Child Psychology, 18,* 184–189.

Strupp, H. H., & Binder, J. L. (1984). *Psychotherapy in a new key.* New York: Basic Books.

Tallis, F., Eysenck, M., & Mathews, A. (1991). Elevated evidence requirements and worry. *Personality and Individual Differences, 12,* 21–27.

Thayer, J. F., Friedman, B. H., & Borkovec, T. D. (1996). Autonomic characteristics of generalized anxiety disorder and worry. *Biological Psychiatry, 39,* 255–266.

Tracey, S. A., Chorpita, B. F., Douban, J., & Barlow, D. H. (1997). Empirical evaluation of *DSM-IV* generalized anxiety disorder criteria in children and adolescents. *Journal of Clinical Child Psychology, 26,* 404–414.

Trull, T. J., & Sher, K. J. (1994). Relationship between the Five-Factor Model of personality and Axis I disorders in a nonclinical sample. *Journal of Abnormal Psychology, 103,* 350–360.

Tucker, D. M., & Newman, J. P. (1981). Verbal versus imaginal cognitive strategies in the inhibition of emotional arousal. *Cognitive Therapy and Research, 5,* 197–202.

Turk, C. L., Heimberg, R. G., Luterek, J. A., Mennin, D. S., & Fresco, D. M. (in press). Delineating emotion regulation deficits in generalized anxiety disorder: A comparison with social anxiety. *Cognitive Therapy and Research.*

Turner, S. M., Beidel, D. C., Borden, J. W., Stanley, M. A., & Jacob, R. A. (1991). Social phobia: Axis I and II correlates. *Journal of Abnormal Psychology, 100,* 102–106.

Vrana, S. R., Cuthbert, B. N., & Lang, P. J. (1986). Fear imagery and text processing. *Psychophysiology, 23,* 247–253.

Vrana, S. R., Cuthbert, B. N., & Lang, P. J. (1989). Processing fearful and neutral sentences: Memory and heart rate change. *Cognition and Emotion, 3,* 179–195.

Wachtel, P. L. (1994). Cyclical processes in personality and psychopathology. *Journal of Abnormal Psychology, 103,* 51–54.

Warren, S. L., Huston, L., Egeland, B., & Sroufe, L. A. (1997). Child and adolescent anxiety disorders and early attachment. *Journal of the American Academy of Child and Adolescent Psychiatry, 36,* 637–644.

Wells, A., & Papageorgiou, C. (1995). Worry and the incubation of intrusive images following stress. *Behaviour Research and Therapy, 33,* 579–583.

Whisman, M. A., Sheldon, C. T., & Goering, P. (2000). Psychiatric disorders and dissatisfaction with social relationships: Does type of relationship matter? *Journal of Abnormal Psychology, 109,* 803–808.

Wittchen, H. U., Carter, R. M., Pfister, H., Montgomery, S. A., & Kessler, R. C. (2000). Disabilities and quality of life in pure and comorbid generalized anxiety disorder and major depression in a national survey. *International Clinical Psychopharmacology, 15,* 319–328.

Wittchen, H. U., Kessler, R. C., Beesdo, K., Krause, P., Hofler, M., & Hoyer, J. (2002). Generalized anxiety and depression in primary care: Prevalence, recognition, and management. *Journal of Clinical Psychiatry, 63*(Suppl. 8), 24–34.

Wittchen, H. U., Zhao, S., Kessler, R. C., & Eaton, W. W. (1994). DSM-III-R generalized anxiety disorder in the National Comorbidity Survey. *Archives of General Psychiatry, 51,* 355–364.

Woodman, C. L., Noyes, R., Jr., Black, D. W., Schlosser, S., & Yagla, S. J. (1999). A 5-year follow-up study of generalized anxiety disorder and panic disorder. *Journal of Nervous and Mental Disease, 187,* 3–9.

Yamas, K., Hazlett-Stevens, H., & Borkovec, M. (1997, November). *Alexithymia in generalized anxiety disorder.* Paper presented at the 31st Annual meeting of the Association for Advancement of Behavior Therapy, Miami, FL.

Yonkers, K. A., Dyck, I. R., Warshaw, M., & Keller, M. B. (2000). Factors predicting the clinical course of generalised anxiety disorder. *British Journal of Psychiatry, 176,* 544–549.

Yonkers, K. A., Warshaw, M. G., Massion, A. O., & Keller, M. B. (1996). Phenomenology and course of generalised anxiety disorder. *British Journal of Psychiatry, 168,* 308–313.

York, D., Borkovec, T. D., Vasey, M., & Stern, R. (1987). Effects of worry and somatic anxiety induction on thoughts, emotion and physiological activity. *Behaviour Research and Therapy, 25,* 523–526.

Zinbarg, R. E., & Barlow, D. H. (1996). Structure of anxiety and the anxiety disorders: A hierarchical model. *Journal of Abnormal Psychology, 105,* 181–193.

CHAPTER 8

Panic and Agoraphobia

JASPER A. J. SMITS, CONALL M. O'CLEIRIGH, AND MICHAEL W. OTTO

DESCRIPTION OF THE DISORDER AND CLINICAL PICTURE

Paula, a 26-year-old married woman is sitting on the sofa watching her favorite television show. Suddenly, without warning, her heart starts pounding and she is overcome by a feeling of impending doom. This feeling is quickly followed by a hot flush as she becomes frightened about what is happening to her. Her breath quickens, and she finds that she is laboring to catch her breath. She wonders if she is having a heart attack or other medical emergency, and these fears intensify as she finds herself becoming increasingly dizzy. With her hands shaking, she reaches for the phone and dials 911.

Ever since a similar episode at the grocery store a few months ago, Paula has been feeling increasingly unsafe outside her home. She has canceled many social activities in the last few months, and last month she decided to quit her part-time job, and now she only leaves the house with her husband. Last night, she did not sleep well because she was worried that this was going to happen; her husband had indicated that he had to stay late for work. Now, as the ambulance arrives at her house, her symptoms lessen, but she remains concerned about her physical condition. At the hospital, the results of the medical tests again show no signs of any physical abnormality. Her relief is only short lived as she quickly becomes consumed by the thought of whether she will survive the next episode.

Panic disorder is characterized by unexpected panic attacks coupled with persistent apprehension surrounding the attacks. A panic attack is defined as the sudden onset of intense fear that reaches its peak within 10 minutes. Along with the peak in fear, a panic attack includes a significant increase in physiological arousal that results in the experience of least four symptoms (*DSM-IV*; American Psychiatric Association, 1994).[1] The panic-related apprehension manifests in one or more of the following ways: (1) persistent worry about future attacks; (2) unrealistic concern about the consequences of having a panic attack (e.g., heart attack, losing sanity, social embarrassment); or (3) changes in behavior to cope with the fear of panic (e.g., avoidance of situations that may trigger an attack; American Psychiatric Association, 1994).

Literally, agoraphobia refers to fear of the market place. The *DSM-IV* (American Psychiatric Association, 1994), however, defines agoraphobia as the anxiety and avoidance associated with places or situations from which escape might be difficult (or embarrassing). Commonly reported agoraphobic situations include being outside the home alone, being in a crowd, and public transportation. Driven by the concern of having a panic attack or paniclike symptoms, agoraphobia is generally considered a complication of panic disorder (Goisman et al., 1993). However, agoraphobia is sometimes present in individuals without a history of panic or panic disorder (Andrews & Slade, 2002). A close examination of the phenomenology of agoraphobia without panic disorder (AWOPD) leads to the conclusion that it is perhaps best viewed on a continuum with uncomplicated panic disorder and panic disorder with agoraphobia. Specifically, most AWOPD sufferers experience limited symptom attacks and report catastrophic cognitions associated with agoraphobia (e.g., Andrews & Slade, 2002).

Panic disorder is associated with significant psychiatric comorbidity. Approximately 70 percent of patients with panic disorder have at least one comorbid psychiatric disorder (Brown & Barlow, 1992). Drawing from the National Comorbidity Survey (NCS), a representative sample of the U.S. population between ages 15 and 54, Magee and colleagues found co-occurrence of anxiety disorders in three of four panic disorder sufferers, with social anxiety disorder as the most frequently reported anxiety disorder (46 percent; Magee, Eaton, Wittchen, McGonagle, & Kessler, 1996). The comorbidity between anxiety disorders and depression has been well documented (Kessler et al., 1996; Merikangas et al., 1996). Fifty-six percent of panic disorder sufferers in the NCS study reported symptoms consistent with major depression (Roy-Byrne et al., 2000). Other Axis-I disorders that often co-occur with panic disorder are alcohol (24 percent), and drug disorders (18 percent; Markowitz, Weissman, Ouellette, Lish, & Klerman, 1989).

Results from several lines of research suggest that panic disorder seems to precede the onset of comorbid affective or substance use disorders. First, retrospective age-at-onset reports show that the onset of anxiety disorders typically occurs at an earlier age compared to depression or substance use disorders (Magee et al., 1996; Merikangas et al., 1998). Second, data from these cross-sectional studies suggest that the onset of anxiety disorders significantly predicts the subsequent onset of depression and substance use disorders (Kessler et al., 1998; Warner et al., 1995). Third, prospective studies show that those suffering from panic disorder at baseline are at an increased risk of developing alcohol disorders (Zimmermann et al., 2003) or major depression disorder (Wittchen, Kessler, Pfister, & Lieb, 2000) during a four to five year follow-up period.

In addition to Axis-I disorder comorbidity, many panic disorder sufferers show Axis-II psychopathology (Brooks, Baltazar, & Munjack, 1989; Sanderson, Wetzler, Beck, & Betz, 1994). Using a structured clinical interview, Renneberg, Chambless, and Gracely (1992) found that 56 percent of an outpatient sample of panic disorder patients had at least one personality disorder. Diagnoses of cluster C were most prevalent (44 percent of the sample), with avoidant personality disorder as the single most frequent Axis II diagnosis (32 percent).

Compared to the general population, patients with panic disorder have higher rates of chronic medical conditions. For example, in a study of 195 primary care patients, Katon et al. (1986) found hypertension in 13.6 percent of panic disorder patients, compared to 4.4 percent of normal controls. Several studies have linked mitral valve prolapse to panic disorder, with comorbidity rates up to 40 percent (e.g., Liberthson, Sheehan, King, & Weyman, 1986; Matuzas, Al-Sadir, Uhlenhuth, & Glass, 1987). In addition to elevated rates of cardiovascular disease, evidence exists for an association between panic disorder and respiratory disorders (Goodwin, Jacobi, & Thefeld, 2003; Karajgi, Rifkin, Doddi, & Kolli, 1990). Other medical conditions that are more frequently observed in patients suffering from panic disorder include thyroid dysfunction (Simon, Blacker, et al., 2002) and migraine headaches (Rogers et al., 1994; Swartz, Pratt, Armenian, Lee, & Eaton, 2000).

PERSONALITY DEVELOPMENT AND PSYCHOPATHOLOGY

Crucial to the development of prevention strategies for psychopathology is the study of risk factors. The question whether there are certain qualities observable early in life that predispose children to the later development of panic disorder has led to research on personality characteristics and their relationship to the onset of anxiety disorders. Two personality traits that have been given much attention with respect to panic disorder are *behavioral inhibition* and *anxiety sensitivity*.

Described by Kagan and associates (Kagan, Snidman, Arcus, & Reznick, 1994), behavioral inhibition refers to a temperamental trait that is characterized by a tendency to be cautious, quiet, and behaviorally reserved in unfamiliar situations. A series of longitudinal studies completed in the 1980s demonstrated the tendency to either approach or withdraw (behavioral inhibition) in novel situations is a relatively stable trait during childhood throughout adolescence (Caspi & Silva, 1995; Garcia Coll, Kagan, & Reznick, 1984). The association between behavioral inhibition and panic disorder with agoraphobia has been observed in studies comparing children of individuals suffering from panic disorder and agoraphobia (with or without comorbid depression) to the offspring of parents with depression or other psychiatric disorders. These studies have consistently demonstrated higher rates of behavioral inhibition among children of parents with panic disorder and agoraphobia compared to children of parents without panic disorder and agoraphobia or major depressive disorder (Battaglia et al., 1997; Manassis, Bradley, Goldberg, Hood, & Swinson, 1995; Rosenbaum et al., 1988). Recent data suggest that the link between parental panic disorder and childhood behavioral inhibition is mostly accounted for by the comorbidity of parental panic disorder and major depression (Rosenbaum et al., 2000). Specifically, Rosenbaum et al. found the largest proportion of behavioral inhibition in children with parents who had panic disorder plus major depression, and found no differences in rates between the offspring of parents with uncomplicated depression only and the offspring of parents with uncomplicated panic disorder and agoraphobia.

Do children with behavioral inhibition then go on to develop panic disorder? To date, there is only little support for this hypothesis. Using retrospective self-report questionnaires tapping behavioral inhibition during childhood, Reznick, Hegeman, Kaufman, & Woods (1992) found higher rates among adult panic disorder patients compared to control adults. However, they reported similar findings for adults suffering from depression. Longitudinal studies, which have followed children from early infancy to early adulthood, generally suggest that behavioral inhibition may be related to the subsequent development of anxiety related disorders but lacks specificity as a risk factor for panic disorder (Biederman et al., 1993; Caspi, Moffitt, Newman, & Silva, 1996; Eaton, Kessler, Wittchen, & Magee, 1994; Schwartz, Snidman, &

Kagan, 1999). Further longitudinal study of children at risk is needed to confirm whether early BI is linked with later onset of panic disorder (Rosenbaum et al., 1993).

Another well-studied personality characteristic is anxiety sensitivity. Anxiety sensitivity refers to the tendency to respond fearfully to anxiety-related sensations (Reiss, Peterson, Gursky, & McNally, 1986). McNally (2002) emphasizes that anxiety sensitivity is different from trait anxiety, which denotes a tendency to respond with anxiety to stressors in general, and not a specific fear of anxiety. Anxiety sensitivity is an enduring trait. Weems, Hayward, Killen, and Taylor (2002) followed 2,365 adolescents with varying degrees of anxiety sensitivity over the span of four years and found little fluctuation in anxiety sensitivity. This pattern has also been observed in adult samples.

Several lines of research have provided evidence linking anxiety sensitivity to panic disorder. First, descriptive studies show that panic disorder patients score significantly higher on the Anxiety Sensitivity Index (ASI; Reiss et al., 1986) compared to psychiatric and nonpsychiatric controls (Taylor, Koch, & McNally, 1992; Telch, Jacquin, Smits, & Powers, 2003). Second, following a laboratory challenge that induces anxiety-related symptoms (e.g., voluntary hyperventilation or inhalation of CO_2 enriched air), panic disorder patients respond with greater anxiety and panic compared to psychiatric and nonpsychiatric controls (Gorman et al., 1994; Papp et al., 1997; Telch et al., 2003). Furthermore, anxiety sensitivity is a predictor of the level of emotional responding to these challenges, with those who score high on the ASI reporting greater anxiety and more panic (Brown, Smits, Powers, & Telch, 2003; Rapee, Brown, Antony, & Barlow, 1992). Third, successful treatment of panic disorder is associated with a decrease in scores on the ASI (Penava, Otto, Maki, & Pollack, 1998; Simon et al., 2004), and improvement in emotional responding to laboratory challenges (Schmidt, Trakowski, & Staab, 1997). Moreover, preliminary evidence suggests that panic disorder symptom improvement following cognitive-behavioral treatment is mediated by changes in fear of anxiety-related sensations (Smits, Powers, Cho, & Telch, 2004).

Although these studies underscore that anxiety sensitivity is implicated in the maintenance of panic disorder, they provide no evidence for anxiety sensitivity as a risk factor of panic disorder. As McNally (2002) points out, anxiety sensitivity can only qualify as a risk factor for panic disorder if it is observed in people with no history of panic. Several studies have now demonstrated that anxiety sensitivity can be present without a prior experience with panic (Asmundson & Norton, 1993; Donnell & McNally, 1989). For example, Asmundson and Norton (1993) administered the anxiety sensitivity index to a large sample of college students and found that 70 percent of the students with high anxiety sensitivity had never experienced an unexpected panic attack, and 45 percent had never experienced a situational panic attack.

Are people who exhibit high anxiety sensitivity at risk for developing panic disorder? This question was first addressed by Maller and Reiss (1992) in a three-year follow-up study with a small sample of college students with no history of panic attacks. They found that the ASI scores at baseline predicted the frequency and intensity of panic attacks during the follow-up period. Moreover, participants high in anxiety sensitivity were five times more likely to develop an anxiety disorder. Schmidt, Lerew, and Jackson (1997) evaluated approximately one thousand cadets during the first and last weeks of basic cadet training. Anxiety sensitivity predicted the development of spontaneous panic attacks, even after controlling for a history of panic attacks and trait anxiety. Spontaneous panic attacks were experienced in approximately 20 percent of high anxiety sensitivity individuals versus only 6 percent in the remainder of the sample.

Several prospective studies since have confirmed that people who score high on the ASI are at greater risk for developing naturally occurring panic attacks compared to those who score low on the ASI (Hayward, Killen, Kraemer, & Taylor, 2000; Schmidt, Lerew, & Jackson, 1999). However, as Schmidt et al. (1999) correctly note, anxiety sensitivity only accounts for a small amount of unique variance in panic occurrence (2 percent), suggesting that anxiety sensitivity provides, at best, only a partial explanation of the development unexpected panic attacks. More importantly, it remains unclear whether the increased risk of spontaneous panic observed in individuals with high anxiety sensitivity translates to an increased risk for panic *disorder*. Further longitudinal research is needed.

EPIDEMIOLOGY

Estimates of incidence and prevalence rates for panic and agoraphobia come from large-scale survey studies with samples representative of the general adult population. Results vary across studies, and depend on point in time and geographical location in which the study was conducted.

Results are suggestive of a recent increase in the number of people with lifetime occurrence of panic attacks. Goodwin (2003) found a significant higher prevalence of panic attacks among the respondents in a survey conducted in 1995 (12.7 percent; Midlife Development in the United States Survey; Wang, Berglund, & Kessler, 2000), compared to those in the

1980 survey (5.3 percent; Epidemiologic Catchment Area Program study; Eaton et al., 1984).

Based on the National Comorbidity Survey (NCS) conducted in 1995, Eaton and colleagues determined the annual rate of panic disorder in the United States at 1 per 100 (i.e., 1 percent incidence; Eaton et al., 1994). Further, the lifetime prevalence rate for panic disorder was estimated at 3.5 percent (Kessler et al., 1994). Weissman et al. (1997) found comparable incidence rates in nine other countries around the world (Canada, Puerto Rico, France, West Germany, Italy, Lebanon, Korea, Taiwan, and New Zealand). However, prevalence rates were lower than observed in the NCS study, ranging from 0.4 percent in Taiwan, where psychiatric illness is generally low, to 2.9 percent in Italy.

Approximately 50 percent of panic disorder sufferers meet criteria for panic disorder with agoraphobia (Eaton et al., 1994). Findings from the NCS study further showed that agoraphobia without panic disorder was at least as common as panic disorder. Specifically, Kessler et al. (1994) estimated the lifetime prevalence rate of agoraphobia without panic disorder at 5.3 percent. According to NCS data, panic disorder is more common in women (5 percent) than in men (2 percent; Eaton et al., 1994; Kessler et al., 1994). This 2.5:1 female-to-male ratio has also generally been observed in other countries (Weissman et al., 1997). Results of small-scale studies with outpatient samples further suggest that women may be more likely to have panic disorder with agoraphobia (Yonkers et al., 1998), and more severe forms of agoraphobia (Turgeon, Marchand, & Dupuis, 1998).

Although present in children, the onset of panic disorder occurs usually in the early to middle 20s. The NCS study yielded a mean onset age of 25.5 years in the United States (Eaton et al., 1994). Weissman et al. (1997) found that the age of onset occurs later in Germany (35.5 years) and Korea (32.1 years).

ETIOLOGY

Neurobiology

Several approaches have helped advance the understanding of the neurobiology of panic disorder. Family and twin studies have increased the knowledge with respect to the influence of heredity on the development of panic disorder. Family studies have consistently shown increased rates of panic disorder in first-degree relatives of those with a present diagnosis of panic disorder (i.e., probands) compared to first-degree relatives of controls (Fyer et al., 1996; Maier, Lichtermann, Minges, Oehrlein, & Franke, 1993). In their meta-analysis of family and twin studies for anxiety disorders, Hettema, Neale, and Kendler (2001) estimated the aggregate risk of panic disorder in relatives of probands at 10 percent, compared to 2.1 percent in comparison relatives. Twin studies have enabled us to make inferences regarding the relative contribution of genetics to the familial transmission of panic disorder. Hettema et al. (2001) found that twin studies showed greater concordant rates for monozygotic (MZ) than for dizygotic (DZ) twins, yielding a heritability estimate of 0.43. Hettema et al. (2001) concluded that genetic components account for significant variance in the development of panic disorder.

Recently, Stein, Jang, and Livesley (1999) argued that it is unlikely that the *disorder* has a familial basis. Instead, they suggested that it may be psychological risk factors such as anxiety sensitivity that are transmitted. Preliminary findings are consistent with this hypothesis, as concordant rates for anxiety sensitivity were greater in MZ than DZ twins (Stein et al., 1999).

Laboratory challenge studies such as inhalation of carbon-dioxide enriched air have advanced the understanding of the neural events that occur during panic attacks. As mentioned previously, these studies have consistently demonstrated that panic disorder sufferers respond with greater fear and panic to respiratory arousal compared to control participants (e.g., Gorman et al., 1994; Griez, Lousberg, & van den Hout, 1987; Papp et al., 1997). Klein (1993) has interpreted these findings as consistent with his suffocation alarm theory, which posits that panic disorder patients have a hypersensitive respiratory control system, causing them to respond with suffocation alarms following an increase in CO_2 levels. In their review of the literature, Gorman and colleagues (Sinha, Papp, & Gorman, 2000) concluded that results of the study of respiratory functioning in panic disorder fail to support the suffocation alarm theory. Instead, the authors (Gorman, Kent, Sullivan, & Coplan, 2000; Sinha et al., 2000) propose that the enhanced responding to biological challenges is perhaps best explained by a hypersensitive fear network, which includes the amygdala, the hippocampus, and the medial prefrontal cortex. Gorman and colleagues base their hypothesis on findings from carefully designed basic experiments, which have demonstrated that these structures play a central role in the acquisition and maintenance of fear in animals (LeDoux, 1998).

Neuroimaging studies have examined the neural circuits of panic disorder patients both during baseline, when panic disorder patients characteristically experience anticipatory anxiety, as well as following a laboratory challenge, which typically provokes panic. Studies are still limited in number. Findings indicate that anticipatory anxiety observed in panic disorder patients is reflected by increased hippocampal activity (Boshuisen, Ter Horst, Paans, Reinders, & den Boer, 2002; Nordahl et al., 1990; Reiman, Raichle, Butler, Herscovitch, & Robins, 1984). Panic attacks following laboratory challenges have been associated with reduced activity in cortical regions (Stewart, Devous, Rush, Lane, & Bonte, 1988; Woods et al., 1988) and greater activation in motor and insular striatal regions (Reiman et al., 1989). Interestingly, Benkelfat et al. (1995) also observed these deviations in healthy controls who experienced panic following the challenge. It is, therefore, unclear whether these findings reflect pathological anxiety or simply fear processing in general.

Learning Theory

The learning theory as a model for the etiology of fear and avoidance has its origins in Pavlov's empirical work (Pavlov, 1927). Pavlov started his famous work on classical conditioning studying the digestion systems of dogs. He found that a novel stimulus (the sound of a bell) could elicit a reflex (saliva) after repeated pairing with a natural eliciting stimulus (food). He used the term unconditioned response (UR) to refer to the reflex response. Similarly, the stimulus naturally eliciting the UR was referred to as the unconditioned stimulus (US). The novel stimulus was termed the conditioned stimulus (CS) as it came to yield the reflex response after repeated pairing with the US. Likewise, the response that was elicited by the CS was referred to as the conditioned response (CR).

In his two-factor theory, Mowrer (1939) outlined the two processes involved in the acquisition of avoidance behavior. First, fear is elicited through classical conditioning. Thus, a previously innocuous stimulus is conditioned (CS) to elicit a fear response (CR). Second, this link between the CS and the CR implies that termination of the CS is associated with fear reduction, a negatively reinforcing response. This negative reinforcing quality of fear reduction drives the termination of the CS. Thus, Mowrer states that avoidance is a learned response, acquired to terminate the CS and the associated fear response.

Original conditioning theories of panic disorder (Eysenck & Rachman, 1965) explained (unexpected) panic attacks or agoraphobia as learned responses (CRs) to *external* stimuli (e.g., shopping malls, driving, social events). In other words, after pairing with a panic attack, any event or situation could effectively become a CS, always triggering panic and agoraphobic behavior when encountered. Goldstein and Chambless (1978) revised this notion, emphasizing the role of *interoceptive* conditioning in the acquisition and maintenance of panic disorder. The authors described panic disorder as a product of "fear of fear," in which benign *internal* sensations associated with early stages of panic (e.g., heart racing) become CS to (unexpected) panic attacks.

Bouton, Mineka, and Barlow (2001) recently integrated empirical findings and proposed a modified learning theory of the development and maintenance of panic disorder. Following classical conditioning principles, the authors propose that at the onset of panic disorder is exposure to a panic attack experienced in the absence of a legitimate threat (i.e., a false alarm). The experience of a false alarm allows for the conditioning of both anxiety and panic to cues (external, internal, or both) associated with the early stages of the attack. As a result, the experience of anxiety or exposure to cues associated with panic will elicit subsequent panic attacks, and as explained by Mowrer's (1939) two-factor theory, will result in agoraphobia. As evidence in support of their theory, the authors refer to studies that have shown that a significant percentage of panic disorder sufferers indicate having experienced a false alarm immediately preceding the onset of the disorder (Craske, Miller, Rotunda, & Barlow, 1990; Öst & Hugdahl, 1983). Similarly, most patients report that their panic attacks are preceded by anxiety, and that the intensity of this anxiety is positively associated with the intensity of panic (Basoglu, Marks, & Sengun, 1992).

Cognitive Theory

The cognitive approach to anxiety disorders posits that the tendency to make faulty threat forecasts is crucial to the development and maintenance of pathological anxiety (Beck, Emery, & Greenberg, 1985). Based on this assumption, Clark (1986) proposes that catastrophic misinterpretations of benign bodily sensations are at the core of panic disorder. At first glance, this notion seems identical to the anxiety sensitivity perspective mentioned earlier. However, the anxiety sensitivity perspective refers to the tendency to merely respond fearfully to anxiety, whereas the cognitive perspective holds that panic disorder suffers fear anxiety because they mistake the sensations for something else (McNally, 2002). Specifically, Clark (1986) hypothesizes that when presented with a situation that elicits bodily sensations (e.g., exercise results in heart racing), a panic disorder sufferer will forecast specific imminent threat (e.g., I will have a heart attack), and therefore experience a panic attack. The specific threat forecast is thought to be logically linked to the nature of the bodily sensations. For example, cardiac and respiratory sensations are likely viewed as precursors of *physical* catastrophes (e.g., heart attack, suffocation), and vestibular sensations are typically interpreted as indicators of *mental* catastrophes (e.g., losing control, going crazy). The model that Clark presents is cyclical. Catastrophic thoughts associated with arousal are thought to heighten overall anxiety and consequently bodily sensations, which in turn strengthen catastrophic thoughts, thereby ultimately causing recurrence of panic. A consequence is agoraphobia and the use of safety behaviors (e.g., carrying rescue medication, avoiding aerobic exercise) to reduce the likelihood of catastrophic outcomes. Such behavior is hypothesized to maintain the distorted beliefs, because it does not allow the individual to collect disconfirmatory evidence (i.e., the individual will not come to see that bodily sensations are not dangerous; Salkovskis, Clark, & Gelder, 1996). Evidence consistent with the cognitive model comes from several sources. First, studies that have employed diaries show that panic disorder patients identify the anticipation of mental or physical catastrophes as thoughts experienced prior or during panic episodes (Rachman, Levitt, & Lopatka, 1987; Westling & Öst, 1993). Second, when presented with descriptions of ambiguous autonomic sensations, panic patients are more likely to report thoughts of impending physical or mental disaster compared to other anxiety disorder patients and nonpatients (Clark et al., 1997). Moreover, the strength of belief in these thoughts is associated with greater anxiety and panic following laboratory challenges that induce actual arousal (Zvolensky & Eifert, 2001). Finally, cognitive therapy, which results in reductions in catastrophic thinking (Clark et al., 1997), has demonstrated efficacy in the treatment of panic disorder (Clark et al., 1994).

COURSE, COMPLICATIONS, AND PROGNOSIS

The understanding of the course of panic disorder with agoraphobia facilitates the development of interventions designed to prevent the onset of the disorder, and the development of treatments that will produce more potent and durable effects. This understanding comes from a number of sources, including retrospective reports from anxiety patients, naturalistic longitudinal studies, and long-term follow-up treatment studies.

Although the onset of panic disorder typically occurs in early adulthood, evidence exists that most panic disorder patients exhibit anxiety during childhood and adolescence. Specifically, Otto, Pollack, Rosenbaum, Sachs, and Asher (1994) found that 55 percent of a sample of panic disorder outpatients reported having suffered from at least one anxiety disorder during childhood. The most common anxiety disorders were social phobia and overanxious disorder (36 percent, and 31 percent, respectively), followed by avoidant disorder (20 percent), separation anxiety disorder (19 percent), and agoraphobia (16 percent). In general, panic disorder with agoraphobia in adulthood seemed to naturally follow unsuccessful or untreated childhood anxiety disorders. Otto and colleagues further found that patients with a history of childhood anxiety disorders presented with more severe psychopathology, including more avoidance behavior and greater levels of depression (Pollack et al., 1996).

Naturalistic prospective studies have demonstrated that the course of panic disorder, especially in the presence of agoraphobia, is typically chronic and characterized by frequent relapses following periods of remission. Over the course of eight years, the Harvard Anxiety Research Program (HARP) conducted repeated short-interval interviews with panic disorder patients with or without agoraphobia who were treated naturalistically in different settings. Results revealed that the duration of the illness prior to intake was on average more than 10 years (Keller et al., 1994). Moreover, the HARP study demonstrated that patients receiving pharmacotherapy were generally undertreated, and relatively few patients received cognitive-behavioral therapy (Goisman et al., 1993). Patients with uncomplicated panic disorder were more likely to have achieved remission status during the eight-year period compared to patients with panic disorder with agoraphobia (Yonkers, Bruce, Dyck, & Keller, 2003). Specifically, the cumulative probability for *remission* was 76 percent for women and 69 percent of men with uncomplicated panic disorder, and 39 percent for women and 35 percent for men who had initially presented panic disorder with agoraphobia. These sex differences were not significant (Yonkers et al., 2003).

Most patients reported recurrence of symptoms, especially during the first two years (Yonkers et al., 1998). Moreover, the cumulative probability for *relapse* across the eight-year period for women with uncomplicated panic disorder was threefold the rate for men (64 percent and 21 percent, respectively; Yonkers et al., 2003). The cumulate probability of relapse for complicated panic disorder did not differ between women and men (50 percent and 42 percent, respectively; Yonkers et al., 2003). The high relapse rates have been underscored by findings of the Massachusetts General Hospital Longitudinal Study of Panic Disorder (Pollack et al., 1990). Predictors of relapse in this study included indexes of severity of illness at intake (i.e., panic attacks, avoidance, disability) and elevated anxiety sensitivity (Pollack et al., 1990).

As indicated previously, most patients in the HARP study were undertreated. This leads to the question whether the course of panic disorder would be different if patients would receive adequate treatment. This question can be addressed by randomized controlled clinical trials that have included long-term follow-up assessments. Roy-Byrne and Cowley (1994–1995) reviewed 16 controlled pharmacotherapy trials that examined panic disorder status one year to seven years following treatment initiation. In general, the presence of agoraphobia, major depression, and personality disorders at intake were associated with poorer outcome. Although panic-free rates were reported in 30 percent to 80 percent of patients, few patients reached panic disorder–free status. Specifically, 50 percent of patients remained functionally impaired, and approximately 70 percent maintained their avoidance behaviors. These results show that, despite initial improvements with adequate pharmacotherapy, panic disorder remains a chronic illness. It should be noted that this review was conducted prior to the use of serotonin reuptake inhibitors (SSRIs). However, there are no data to date suggesting that treatment with SSRIs results in better acute outcomes for panic disorder than older antidepressants (Otto, Tuby, Gould, McLean, & Pollack, 2001).

Follow-up assessments in trials investigating the efficacy of cognitive-behavioral treatments (CBT) have been conducted up to two years after treatment initiation. Some data suggest a more favorable long-term course for patients who receive CBT. Specifically, studies have shown that approximately 75 percent of patients remain panic free over a two-year period, and 50 percent to 70 percent of patients report no recurrence of functional impairment or agoraphobia (Brown & Barlow, 1995; Clark et al., 1994). However, Brown and Barlow (1995) found that only one out of five patients sought no additional treatment to maintain their improved status. Taken together, these findings suggest that when provided with adequate dosages of either treatment modality, patients do experience acute clinical improvements, but many need additional treatment to sustain those improvements over the long term.

ASSESSMENT AND DIAGNOSIS

Regardless of the theoretical orientation or treatment perspective the priorities for assessment are to generate reliable information on the presence or absence of the disorder during diagnosis, the individual profile of the disorder during treatment planning including symptom presentation and severity, the individual response during treatment, and the outcomes of the course of treatment. Shear and Maser (1994) provide recommendations for both diagnostic and symptom assessment in panic disorder in the areas of frequency of panic attacks, anticipatory anxiety, phobic fear and avoidance, and global impairment. Assessment instruments in each of these areas are reviewed in the following section.

Diagnosis of Panic Disorder

The priority for the diagnosis of panic disorder is fundamentally to assess for the absence or presence of the disorder with or without agoraphobia and secondarily to assess for the presence of other comorbid conditions that may impact the course or treatment of panic disorder. Diagnostic assessment is most often undertaken through standardized structured interviews that assess for each of the *DSM-IV* symptoms and allow for the collection of reliable information. The most commonly used structured interview assessment for panic disorder in treatment outcome studies is the Structured Clinical Interview for *DSM* (Spitzer, Williams, Gibbon, & First, 1992). The next most commonly used structured interview for the assessment of panic is the Anxiety Disorders Interview Schedule-Revised (ADIS-R; Di Nardo, Brown, & Barlow, 1994). The ADIS-R is designed for diagnostic assessment and also includes clinician-rated severity indexes for panic disorder including distress and disability and fear and avoidance ratings across a range of common agoraphobic situations. Both the SCID and ADIS have been demonstrated to possess acceptable psychometric properties (Brown, Di Nardo, Lehman, & Campbell, 2001; Williams et al., 1992).

Panic Frequency

It has been suggested that daily assessment of panic attacks is essential for the study or treatment of panic disorder (Shear & Maser, 1994). Panic diaries (self-report tracking of panic symptoms) are often used to accomplish this. To be comprehensive, patients could be provided with a diary that prompts them to record the frequency and duration and severity of panic episodes. In addition, panic diaries can include information as to whether the panic attack was with full or limited symptoms and whether it was situationally cued or "unexpected." Otto, Penava, and Pollack (1998) recommend that care is taken to ensure that patients and treaters agree on definitions of symptoms. This is particularly important to help distinguish anticipatory anxiety from limited or full panic attacks. It has also been recommended, because of high variability in frequency of panic attacks across days or even weeks, that prolonged baseline monitoring of two weeks to one month be undertaken to obtain more representative estimates of pretreatments levels of panic (Shear & Maser, 1994).

Panic-Related Fears

The tendency to respond fearfully to anxiety-related symptoms is central to the classical learning theory (Bouton et al., 2001) and cognitive theory (Clark, 1986) conceptualizations of panic disorder and underscores its importance in the assessment and treatment of panic. Two self-report questionnaires that assess panic-related fears are described in the following sections.

Anxiety Sensitivity Index (ASI)

The ASI (Peterson & Reiss, 1987) is a 16-item self-report instrument that assesses the patient's tendency to respond fearfully to anxiety related symptoms. The scale comprises statements about the negative consequences of anxiety and patients are required to endorse each item on a Likert scale ranging from very little (0) to very much (4). The ASI has favorable reliability and validity (Telch, Shermis, & Lucas, 1989). The ASI distinguishes healthy controls from patients with panic disorder and/or agoraphobia and is sensitive to clinical improvement (McNally, 2002).

Body Sensations Questionnaire (BSQ)

The BSQ (Chambless, Caputo, Bright, & Gallagher, 1984) is a 17-item self-report questionnaire, like the ASI, that assesses fear of body sensations. Each item represents a body sensation (e.g., heart palpitations) and is rated on a Likert scale from 1 (not frightened or worried by this sensation) to 5 (extremely frightened by this sensation). The BSQ has high internal consistency and moderate test-retest reliability, discriminated patients, with panic disorder from health controls, and is sensitive to treatment-related changes (Chambless et al., 1984).

Agoraphobic Avoidance

As panic disorder typically presents with agoraphobia and impairment associated with avoided panic-related situations, comprehensive assessment should include assessment of agoraphobic avoidance. Three measures are briefly described.

Fear Questionnaire (FQ)

The FQ (Marks & Mathews, 1979) is a 15-item self-report questionnaire that requires patients to rate the degree to which they would avoid particular situations with a higher score indicating higher levels of avoidance. In addition to a total score, three subscales can be calculated: agoraphobia (FQ-Ag), social phobia (FQ-Soc), and avoidance of situations related to blood/injury phobia (FQ-BI). The BQ is one of the most widely used self-report measures in treatment outcome studies of agoraphobia (Mavissakalian, 1986) and has adequate test-retest reliability (Michelson & Mavissakalian, 1983).

Mobility Inventory (MI)

The MI (Chambless, Caputo, Jasin, Gracely, & Williams, 1985) is a seven-item self-report measure that assesses avoidance in a variety of situations. The scale has high internal consistency and good test-retest reliability, is sensitive to change during treatment, and distinguishes patients with agoraphobia from patients with social phobia (Chambless et al., 1985).

Behavioral Avoidance Tests (BATs)

BATs provide a measure of avoidance that does not rely on patient self-report and so is not vulnerable to the bias of that methodology. BATs typically require patients to walk a course that includes exposure to standard agoraphobic situations (e.g., crowded shopping center, crowded bus). Patients are required to walk the course alone until they complete the course or experience unendurable anxiety. The level of anxiety and the degree of completion provide a measure of avoidance. BATs can incorporate standardized courses that may be too limited or idiosyncratic courses more tailored to the patient's avoidance profile (de Beurs, Lange, & Van Dyck, 1992).

Assessment of quality of life in psychiatric patients has attracted considerable interest recently and there are a growing number of instruments available to document the distress and impairment associated with mental illness and the impact of treatment. Quality of life has been shown to be associated with severity of psychological symptoms in panic disorder (Simon, Otto, et al., 2002; Telch, Schmidt, Jaimez, Jacquin, & Harrington, 1995) and has been used as a secondary outcome in psychological interventions to treat panic (e.g., Telch et al., 1995).

Medical Outcome Study Short Form-36 (SF-36)

The SF-36 is a brief, self-report instrument that assesses health related quality of life or functional impairment. It is made up of eight subscales that assess limitations in physical, social, and usual activities, pain, vitality, mental health, and general health perceptions as a result of physical or emotional problems (Ware & Sherbourne, 1992). It is scored from 0 to 100 with higher scores indicating greater health and has been used to document impairment in patients with panic disorder (Sherbourne, Wells, & Judd, 1996).

IMPACT ON ENVIRONMENT

Considerable research has focused on the impact of panic disorder on the environment in which the patient lives and works. Findings reveal that panic disorder is associated with significant impairments in quality of life, comparable to those suffering from major depression (Candilis et al., 1999). Approximately one-third of panic disorder patients indicate poor emotional and physical health (Massion, Warshaw, & Keller, 1993). In addition to emotional and health suffering, panic disorder often contributes to significant impairment in occupational functioning. For example, Massion et al. (1993) reported a fourfold rate of unemployment (relative to the national average) among patients with panic disorder, and found increased rates of financial dependency (e.g., receiving disability or welfare).

The increased utilization of medical services among panic disorder patients is perhaps not surprising. According to the NCS, panic disorder patients report not only a greater number of visits to outpatient mental health clinics, but also higher utilization of specialists such as cardiologists, neurologists, and primary care physicians (Leon, Olfson, & Portera, 1997). Leon et al. (1997) estimated the mean expenditure for a panic episode at $3,393.

How does panic disorder affect social functioning? Work by Chambless and colleagues suggests that patients suffering from panic disorder with agoraphobia may be more dependent and nonassertive, and, therefore, ineffective in resolving interpersonal conflicts (Chambless, Hunter, & Jackson, 1982; Goldstein & Chambless, 1978). Consequently, it has been suggested that panic disorder with agoraphobia may be associated with greater marital distress (Hafner & Minge, 1989). To address this hypothesis, Arrindell and Emmelkamp (1986) administered self-report questionnaires tapping marital adjustment and intimacy to couples with a female panic disorder with agoraphobia spouse, couples with a nonphobic female psychiatric spouse, maritally distressed couples, and happily married couples. Results revealed that panic disorder patients describe their marriages as less satisfactory than happily married couples but no more satisfactory than maritally distressed couples. Recently, Chambless et al. (2002) argued that such conclusion is premature when based on merely self-report questionnaires. Therefore, they collected observational measures of marital interaction in addition to the traditional in sample of married couples with a female agoraphobic spouse and control couples. The results were consistent with previous reports, as clinical couples reported more distress on self-report questionnaires. Moreover, they displayed more negative nonverbal behavior and had longer periods of negative interactions.

TREATMENT IMPLICATIONS

Treatment Approaches

Two treatment modalities for panic disorder have received intensive evaluation in controlled treatment trials: cognitive-behavior therapy (CBT) and pharmacotherapy. Of pharmacologic agents for panic disorder, studies indicate benefit following treatment with serotonin selective reuptake inhibitors (SSRIs), tricyclic antidepressants, benzodiazepines, and monoamine oxidase inhibitors (Lydiard, Brawman-Mintzer, & Ballenger, 1996). These medications appear to attenuate the anxiety elicited by phobic cues, helping patients end cycles of anticipatory anxiety and avoidance. However, improvements from medications may be lost when medications are discontinued, although rates of relapse appear to be reduced when medication treatment is maintained for a longer period (e.g., six months) before discontinuation (Mavissakalian & Perel, 1993).

As compared to pharmacotherapy, CBT for panic disorder is designed to help patients identify the internal and external cues that trigger their panic, and utilize alternative emotional and behavioral responses to these cues. Common treatment components include (1) psychoeducation concerning the nature and physiology of panic and anxiety; (2) cognitive restructuring designed to teach patients how to identify and correct faulty threat perceptions that contribute to their panic and anxiety; (3) interoceptive exposure to the physical symptoms of panic designed to reduce the patients' fear of harmless bodily sensations associated with physiological activation; (4) in vivo exposure to target agoraphobic avoidance, and (5) breathing retraining to assist patients to control hyperventilation or relaxation techniques to help reduce anxious arousal (Margraf, Barlow, Clark, & Telch, 1993). Of these strategies, there is evidence that relaxation training and breathing retraining may not provide additive benefit to core information, exposure, and cognitive-restructuring interventions (Schmidt et al., 2000).

Treatment Efficacy

The efficacy of pharmacotherapy, cognitive-behavior therapy and the combination of these treatment modalities has been examined in numerous randomized controlled clinical trials. Summary of these trials in meta-analytic reviews indicate that both CBT and pharmacotherapy offer greater benefit than control conditions (e.g., waiting list, pill placebo, or psychosocial placebo), and that CBT is at least as effective as pharmacologic alternatives (Clum, Clum, & Surls, 1993; Gould, Otto, & Pollack, 1995). For example, Gould et al. compared the efficacy of pharmacological, cognitive-behavioral, and combined pharmacological and cognitive-behavioral treatments, conducted between 1974 and 1994, in a meta-analysis of 43 controlled studies that included 76 treatment interventions. A comparison of these treatments revealed an advantage of CBT alone over medication and the combination treatment (effects sizes [ES], 0.88, 0.47, and 0.56, respectively). In addition, the smallest average attrition rates were associated with CBT, suggesting that it is better tolerated (was associated with lower study dropout rates) than pharmacotherapy alone or pharmacotherapy in combination with CBT. The Gould et al. (1995) meta-analysis also provided evidence for greater longevity of treatment gains with CBT. As compared to CBT, pharmacotherapy often requires ongoing treatment to maintain treatment gains; it is this quality of CBT that makes the treatment a particularly cost-effective treatment option (see following paragraph).

Meta-analytic reviews, by their nature, provide a particularly broad summary of findings across different research centers, populations, and research methods. Accordingly, meta-analytic reviews are open to criticisms that estimates of treatment effects may be unduly influenced by differences in study methods and populations. Given this concern, it is particularly noteworthy when meta-analytic results are replicated in the context of a single study that takes into account differences between site and populations. For example, Barlow, Gorman, Shear, and Woods (2000) examined the relative efficacy of five treatment conditions: (1) CBT, (2) Imipramine, (3) Imipramine plus CBT, (4) CBT plus placebo, or (5) pill placebo. All active treatments were found to be effective immediately following treatment, with a modest advantage of the combination treatment. Nonetheless, the long-term effects of combined treatment were inferior to CBT alone following medication discontinuation, suggesting that some of the benefits of CBT achieved while taking medication fade when medication is discontinued (Barlow et al., 2000). These findings are consistent with results reported by (Marks et al., 1993), a finding that may be explained by state-dependent (context) learning effects (see Otto, Smits, & Reese, 2005).

Fortunately, there is evidence that some of the beneficial effects of CBT on a long-term course can be maintained if CBT is reinstated/ongoing at the time of medication discontinuation. Brief CBT conducted during and after the course of taper appears to be effective in aiding benzodiazepine taper, reducing residual panic symptoms, and leading to longer-term maintenance of treatment gains (Bruce, Spiegel, & Hegel, 1999; Otto et al., 1993; Spiegel, Bruce, Gregg, & Nuzzarello, 1994). In terms of context effects, ensuring that CBT extends to the posttaper period appears to ensure longer-term maintenance of "safety" learning in the medication-free context.

Effects on Quality of Life

In addition to examining the short and long-term efficacy of interventions to treat panic disorder, several studies have evaluated the effect of treatments for panic disorder on patients' quality of life. Telch et al. (1995) found that participants who had received a 12-session CBT showed more improvement in domains such as work functioning, social functioning, and family functioning compared to wait-listed controls. These gains were maintained at six-month follow-up. Improvement in quality of life is not restricted to CBT treatments. Jacobs, Davidson, Gupta, and Meyerhoff (1997) and Rapaport, Pollack, Wolkow, Mardekian, and Clary (2000) found that panic patients treated with medication showed significantly greater increases in quality of life indexes than patients treated with placebo. Interestingly, improvements in quality of life were directly related to improvements in panic symptoms (Jacobs et al., 1997).

Predictors of Clinical Response

There is considerable variability in patients' response to treatment. The occurrence of treatment nonresponse and relapse suggests that there may be individual differences factors that moderate the efficacy of existing interventions. Cowley, Flick, and Roy-Byrne (1996) conducted follow-up interviews with panic disorder patients up to 60 months after completion of treatment. Consistent with previous findings (e.g., Warshaw, Massion, Shea, Allsworth, & Keller, 1997), they found that baseline level of agoraphobia was the strongest predictor of overall improvement. Also, comorbid psychopathology (major depression or Axis II comorbidity) at baseline was predictive of poorer treatment outcome. However, there is also evidence that panic patients with and without comorbid depression show similar response to CBT (McLean, Woody, Taylor, & Koch, 1998; Tsao, Lewin, & Craske, 1998). There is also evidence that CBT for panic disorder can have a beneficial impact on comorbid conditions as well, with evidence of sustained improvements in comorbid conditions over follow-up intervals (Tsao et al., 1998).

Schmidt and Telch (1997) examined the relationship between perceived physical health and clinical response to treatment with panic patients. Immediately following cognitive-behavioral treatment, 71 percent of patients who perceived their physical health as good met recovery criteria, compared with only 35 percent of those who perceived their health as poor. These differences in response rates were maintained at six-month follow-up.

Adherence to treatment has also been shown to impact treatment outcomes in patients being treated for panic disorder. Schmidt and Woolaway-Bickel (2000) reported that therapist's ratings of treatment compliance and therapist ratings of the quality of the participant's work predicted a more favorable response to treatment.

These results provide some good initial evidence that may account for the observed variability in response to treatment. The presence of additional psychopathology and adherence to treatment procedures significantly impact treatment outcome and may provide legitimate targets for modifications to CBT technology.

Treatment Effectiveness

There is a paucity of research examining whether efficacy data from panic treatments delivered in the context of randomized clinical trials can be generalized to "real world" clinical practice. Fortunately, initial results are promising. For example, Wade, Treat, and Stuart (1998) compared the results of a 15-session CBT protocol in a community mental heath center (CMHC) to the results of two CBT efficacy studies. Both acute treatment outcomes and longer-term follow-up findings observed in the CMCH sample were comparable to those observed in controlled efficacy studies (Stuart, Treat, & Wade, 2000). These results further encourage the application of manualized treatments and the translation of research findings from academic centers to practice procedures in community clinics.

Efforts are also underway to translate advances in the conceptualization and treatment of panic disorder into prevention efforts. For example, researchers have investigated whether the modification of identified risk factors can prevent the onset of panic disorder. Using the presence of anxiety sensitivity as a marker of risk, Gardenswartz and Craske (2001) randomized individuals at risk to either a five-hour workshop or waiting list. The procedural components of the workshop were borrowed from contemporary CBT packages. At six months following the intervention, 1.8 percent of those attending the prevention workshop developed panic disorder compared to only 13.6 percent of participants assigned to waiting list. These results are promising, and encourage the further development of prevention programs for individuals at risk for onset of panic disorder.

Cost-Effectiveness

In addition to treatment efficacy, tolerability, and effectiveness, treatment costs should be an important consideration when evaluating utility of a treatment. In their meta-analyses of interventions for panic disorder, Gould et al. (1995) estimated the expenses for CBT relative to those for pharmacological treatment. They reported that Imipramine and group-administered CBT were the most cost-effective interventions with a total cost, over a 12-month period, of approximately $600 for Imipramine and group CBT, compared to a total yearly cost of approximately $1,400 for individual CBT.

Otto, Pollack, and Maki (2000) extended the previous analysis by Gould et al. (1995) allowing for the possibility that previous estimates might have been colored by the controlled conditions evident in clinical trials (e.g., sample characteristics, manualized treatment). Using an outpatient clinic sample, the average visit costs, medication costs, and alternative treatment costs per person were calculated for both the acute treatment phase as well as for a one-year interval. Group CBT was the most cost-effective intervention for the acute phase ($518) as well as for a one-year interval ($523). Pharmacological treatment emerged as more cost-effective than individual CBT during the acute phase (costs $839 and $1,357, respectively). However, the cost for individual CBT was 59 percent of the cost for pharmacological treatment for a one-year interval.

Otto et al. (2000) also estimated cost-benefit ratios for each treatment modality. The cost-benefit ratio was calculated by dividing the total cost of the intervention by the change in clinical status as measured by the clinical global improvement scale. A similar pattern of results emerged indicating superiority for group CBT for both the acute phase and one-year interval.

CONCLUDING COMMENTS

Panic disorder is a prevalent, debilitating, and chronic disorder that emerges, on average, in the third decade of life. Panic disorder and agoraphobia are associated with substantial impairments in role functioning and quality of life. Fortunately, considerable advances have been made in the conceptualization and treatment of this disorder, and it is clear that pharmacologic and cognitive-behavioral treatments offer beneficial outcomes to patients. These treatments are acceptable to patients and offer comparable acute outcome, although CBT may offer advantages in terms of longer-term maintenance of treatment gains without the need for ongoing medication. In addition to attempts to refine existing treatments and identify new treatment approaches, researchers are also investigating strategies for preventing the onset of panic disorder. With these advances, the future holds the promise of more optimal approaches to the treatment of patients with panic disorder.

NOTE

1. The *DSM-IV* lists the following symptoms: a feeling of imminent danger or doom; the need to escape; palpitations; sweating; trembling; shortness of breath or a smothering feeling; a feeling of chok-

ing; chest pain or discomfort; nausea or abdominal discomfort; dizziness or lightheadedness; a sense of things being unreal, depersonalization; a fear of losing control or "going crazy"; a fear of dying; tingling sensations; chills or hot flushes.

REFERENCES

American Psychiatric Association. (1994). *Diagnostic and statistical manual of mental disorders* (4th ed.). Washington, DC: Author.

Andrews, G., & Slade, T. (2002). Agoraphobia without a history of panic disorder may be part of the panic disorder syndrome. *Journal of Nervous and Mental Disease, 190,* 624–630.

Arrindell, W. A., & Emmelkamp, P. M. (1986). Marital adjustment, intimacy and needs in female agoraphobics and their partners: A controlled study. *British Journal of Psychiatry, 149,* 592–602.

Asmundson, G. J., & Norton, G. R. (1993). Anxiety sensitivity and its relationship to spontaneous and cued panic attacks in college students. *Behaviour Research and Therapy, 31,* 199–201.

Barlow, D. H., Gorman, J. M., Shear, M. K., & Woods, S. W. (2000). Cognitive-behavioral therapy, imipramine, or their combination for panic disorder: A randomized controlled trial. *JAMA, 283,* 2529–2536.

Basoglu, M., Marks, I. M., & Sengun, S. (1992). A prospective study of panic and anxiety in agoraphobia with panic disorder. *British Journal of Psychiatry, 160,* 57–64.

Battaglia, M., Bajo, S., Strambi, L. F., Brambilla, F., Castronovo, C., Vanni, G., et al. (1997). Physiological and behavioral responses to minor stressors in offspring of patients with panic disorder. *Journal of Psychiatric Research, 31,* 365–376.

Beck, A. T., Emery, G., & Greenberg, R. (Eds.). (1985). *Anxiety disorders and phobias: A cognitive perspective.* New York: Basic Books.

Benkelfat, C., Bradwejn, J., Meyer, E., Ellenbogen, M., Milot, S., Gjedde, A., et al. (1995). Functional neuroanatomy of CCK4-induced anxiety in normal healthy volunteers. *American Journal of Psychiatry, 152,* 1180–1184.

Biederman, J., Faraone, S. V., Hirshfeld-Becker, D. R., Friedman, D., Robin, J. A., & Rosenbaum, J. F. (2001). Patterns of psychopathology and dysfunction in high-risk children of parents with panic disorder and major depression. *American Journal of Psychiatry, 158,* 49–57.

Biederman, J., Rosenbaum, J. F., Bolduc-Murphy, E. A., Faraone, S. V., Chaloff, J., Hirshfeld, D. R., et al. (1993). A 3-year follow-up of children with and without behavioral inhibition. *Journal of the American Academy of Child and Adolescent Psychiatry, 32,* 814–821.

Boshuisen, M. L., Ter Horst, G. J., Paans, A. M., Reinders, A. A., & den Boer, J. A. (2002). rCBF differences between panic disorder patients and control subjects during anticipatory anxiety and rest. *Biological Psychiatry, 52,* 126–135.

Bouton, M. E., Mineka, S., & Barlow, D. H. (2001). A modern learning theory perspective on the etiology of panic disorder. *Psychological Review, 108,* 4–32.

Brooks, R. B., Baltazar, P. L., & Munjack, D. J. (1989). Co-occurrence of personality disorders with panic disorder, social phobia, and generalized anxiety disorder: A review of the literature. *Journal of Anxiety Disorders, 3,* 259–285.

Brown, M., Smits, J. A. J., Powers, M. B., & Telch, M. J. (2003). Differential sensitivity of the three ASI factors in predicting panic disorder patients' subjective and behavioral response to hyperventilation challenge. *Journal of Anxiety Disorders, 17,* 583–591.

Brown, T. A., & Barlow, D. H. (1992). Comorbidity among anxiety disorders: Implications for treatment and *DSM-IV*. *Journal of Consulting and Clinical Psychology, 60,* 835–844.

Brown, T. A., & Barlow, D. H. (1995). Long-term outcome in cognitive-behavioral treatment of panic disorder: Clinical predictors and alternative strategies for assessment. *Journal of Consulting and Clinical Psychology, 63,* 754–765.

Brown, T. A., Di Nardo, P. A., Lehman, C. L., & Campbell, L. A. (2001). Reliability of *DSM-IV* anxiety and mood disorders: Implications for the classification of emotional disorders. *Journal of Abnormal Psychology, 110,* 49–58.

Bruce, T. J., Spiegel, D. A., & Hegel, M. T. (1999). Cognitive-behavioral therapy helps prevent relapse and recurrence of panic disorder following alprazolam discontinuation: A long-term follow-up of the Peoria and Dartmouth studies. *Journal of Consulting and Clinical Psychology, 67,* 151–156.

Candilis, P. J., McLean, R. Y., Otto, M. W., Manfro, G. G., Worthington, J. J., III, Penava, S. J., et al. (1999). Quality of life in patients with panic disorder. *Journal of Nervous and Mental Disease, 187,* 429–434.

Caspi, A., Moffitt, T. E., Newman, D. L., & Silva, P. A. (1996). Behavioral observations at age 3 years predict adult psychiatric disorders: Longitudinal evidence from a birth cohort. *Archives of General Psychiatry, 53,* 1033–1039.

Caspi, A., & Silva, P. A. (1995). Temperamental qualities at age three predict personality traits in young adulthood: Longitudinal evidence from a birth cohort. *Child Development, 66,* 486–498.

Chambless, D. L., Caputo, G. C., Bright, P., & Gallagher, R. (1984). Assessment of fear of fear in agoraphobics: The body sensations questionnaire and the agoraphobic cognitions questionnaire. *Journal of Consulting and Clinical Psychology, 52,* 1090–1097.

Chambless, D. L., Caputo, G. C., Jasin, S. E., Gracely, E. J., & Williams, C. (1985). The Mobility Inventory for Agoraphobia. *Behaviour Research and Therapy, 23,* 35–44.

Chambless, D. L., Fauerbach, J. A., Floyd, F. J., Wilson, K. A., Remen, A. L., & Renneberg, B. (2002). Marital interaction of agoraphobic women: A controlled, behavioral observation study. *Journal of Abnormal Psychology, 111,* 502–512.

Chambless, D. L., Hunter, K., & Jackson, A. (1982). Social anxiety and assertiveness: A comparison of the correlations in phobic and college student samples. *Behaviour Research and Therapy, 20,* 403–404.

Clark, D. M. (1986). A cognitive approach to panic. *Behaviour Research and Therapy, 24,* 461–470.

Clark, D. M., Salkovskis, P. M., Hackmann, A., Middleton, H., Anastasiades, P., & Gelder, M. (1994). A comparison of cognitive therapy, applied relaxation and imipramine in the treatment of panic disorder. *British Journal of Psychiatry, 164,* 759–769.

Clark, D. M., Salkovskis, P. M., Öst, L. G., Breitholtz, E., Koehler, K. A., Westling, B. E., et al. (1997). Misinterpretation of body sensations in panic disorder. *Journal of Consulting and Clinical Psychology, 65,* 203–213.

Clum, G. A., Clum, G. A., & Surls, R. (1993). A meta-analysis of treatments for panic disorder. *Journal of Consulting and Clinical Psychology, 61,* 317–326.

Cowley, D. S., Flick, S. N., & Roy-Byrne, P. P. (1996). Long-term course and outcome in panic disorder: A naturalistic follow-up study. *Anxiety, 2,* 13–21.

Craske, M. G., Miller, P. P., Rotunda, R., & Barlow, D. H. (1990). A descriptive report of features of initial unexpected panic attacks in minimal and extensive avoiders. *Behaviour Research and Therapy, 28,* 395–400.

de Beurs, E., Lange, A., & Van Dyck, R. (1992). Self-monitoring of panic attacks and retrospective estimates of panic: Discordant findings. *Behaviour Research and Therapy, 30,* 411–413.

Di Nardo, P., Brown, T., & Barlow, D. (1994). Anxiety Disorders Interview Schedule for *DSM-IV.* Albany, NY: Graywind Publications.

Donnell, C. D., & McNally, R. J. (1989). Anxiety sensitivity and history of panic as predictors of response to hyperventilation. *Behaviour Research and Therapy, 27,* 325–332.

Eaton, W. W., Holzer, C. E., Von Korff, M., Anthony, J. C., Helzer, J. E., George, L., et al. (1984). The design of the Epidemiologic Catchment Area surveys: The control and measurement of error. *Archives of General Psychiatry, 41,* 942–948.

Eaton, W. W., Kessler, R. C., Wittchen, H. U., & Magee, W. J. (1994). Panic and panic disorder in the United States. *American Journal of Psychiatry, 151,* 413–420.

Eysenck, H. J., & Rachman, S. (Eds.). (1965). *The causes and cures of neurosis.* London: Routledge & Kegan Paul.

Fyer, A. J., Mannuzza, S., Chapman, T. F., Lipsitz, J., Martin, L. Y., & Klein, D. F. (1996). Panic disorder and social phobia: Effects of comorbidity on familial transmission. *Anxiety, 2,* 173–178.

Garcia Coll, C., Kagan, J., & Reznick, J. S. (1984). Behavioral inhibition in young children. *Child Development,* 1005–1019.

Gardenswartz, C., & Craske, M. G. (2001). Prevention of panic disorder. *Behavior Therapy, 32,* 725–737.

Goisman, R. M., Rogers, M. P., Steketee, G. S., Warshaw, M. G., Cuneo, P., & Keller, M. B. (1993). Utilization of behavioral methods in a multicenter anxiety disorders study. *Journal of Clinical Psychiatry, 54,* 213–218.

Goldstein, A. J., & Chambless, D. L. (1978). A reanalysis of agoraphobia. *Behavior Therapy, 9,* 47–59.

Goodwin, R. D. (2003). The prevalence of panic attacks in the United States: 1980 to 1995. *Journal of Clinical Epidemiology, 56,* 914–916.

Goodwin, R. D., Jacobi, F., & Thefeld, W. (2003). Mental disorders and asthma in the community. *Archives of General Psychiatry, 60,* 1125–1130.

Gorman, J. M., Kent, J. M., Sullivan, G. M., & Coplan, J. D. (2000). Neuroanatomical hypothesis of panic disorder, revised. *American Journal of Psychiatry, 157,* 493–505.

Gorman, J. M., Papp, L. A., Coplan, J. D., Martinez, J. M., Lennon, S., Goetz, R. R., et al. (1994). Anxiogenic effects of CO2 and hyperventilation in patients with panic disorder. *American Journal of Psychiatry, 151,* 547–553.

Gould, R. A., Otto, M. W., & Pollack, M. H. (1995). A meta-analysis of treatment outcome for panic disorder. *Clinical Psychology Review, 15,* 819–844.

Griez, E. J. L., Lousberg, H., & van den Hout, M. A. (1987). CO2 vulnerability in panic disorder. *Psychiatry Research, 20,* 87–95.

Hafner, R. J., & Minge, P. J. (1989). Sex role stereotyping in women with agoraphobia and their husbands. *Sex Roles, 20,* 705–711.

Hayward, C., Killen, J. D., Kraemer, H. C., & Taylor, C. B. (2000). Predictors of panic attacks in adolescents. *Journal of the American Academy of Child and Adolescent Psychiatry, 39,* 207–214.

Hettema, J. M., Neale, M. C., & Kendler, K. S. (2001). A review and meta-analysis of the genetic epidemiology of anxiety disorders. *American Journal of Psychiatry, 158,* 1568–1578.

Jacobs, R. J., Davidson, J. R., Gupta, S., & Meyerhoff, A. S. (1997). The effects of clonazepam on quality of life and work productivity in panic disorder. *American Journal of Managed Care, 3,* 1187–1196.

Kagan, J., Snidman, N., Arcus, D., & Reznick, J. S. (1994). *Galen's prophecy: Temperament in human nature.* New York: Basic Books.

Karajgi, B., Rifkin, A., Doddi, S., & Kolli, R. (1990). The prevalence of anxiety disorders in patients with chronic obstructive pulmonary disease. *American Journal of Psychiatry, 147,* 200–201.

Katon, W., Vitaliano, P. P., Russo, J., Cormier, L., Anderson, K., & Jones, M. (1986). Panic disorder: Epidemiology in primary care. *Journal of Family Practice, 23,* 233–239.

Keller, M. B., Yonkers, K. A., Warshaw, M. G., Pratt, L. A., Gollan, J. K., Massion, A. O., et al. (1994). Remission and relapse in subjects with panic disorder and panic with agoraphobia: A prospective short-interval naturalistic follow-up. *Journal of Nervous and Mental Disease, 182,* 290–296.

Kessler, R. C., McGonagle, K. A., Zhao, S., Nelson, C. B., Hughes, M., Eshleman, S., et al. (1994). Lifetime and 12-month prevalence of *DSM-III-R* psychiatric disorders in the United States: Results from the National Comorbidity Survey. *Archives of General Psychiatry, 51*(1), 8–19.

Kessler, R. C., Nelson, C. B., McGonagle, K. A., Liu, J., Swartz, M., & Blazer, D. G. (1996). Comorbidity of *DSM-III-R* major depressive disorder in the general population: Results from the US National Comorbidity Survey. *British Journal of Psychiatry, 30,* 17–30.

Kessler, R. C., Stang, P. E., Wittchen, H. U., Ustun, T. B., Roy-Burne, P. P., & Walters, E. E. (1998). Lifetime panic-depression comorbidity in the National Comorbidity Survey. *Archives of General Psychiatry, 55,* 801–808.

Klein, D. F. (1993). False suffocation alarms, spontaneous panics, and related conditions: An integrative hypothesis. *Archives of General Psychiatry, 50,* 306–317.

LeDoux, J. (1998). Fear and the brain: Where have we been, and where are we going? *Biological Psychiatry, 44,* 1229–1238.

Leon, A. C., Olfson, M., & Portera, L. (1997). Service utilization and expenditures for the treatment of panic disorder. *General Hospital Psychiatry, 19,* 82–88.

Liberthson, R., Sheehan, D. V., King, M. E., & Weyman, A. E. (1986). The prevalence of mitral valve prolapse in patients with panic disorders. *American Journal of Psychiatry, 143,* 511–515.

Lydiard, R. B., Brawman-Mintzer, O., & Ballenger, J. C. (1996). Recent developments in the psychopharmacology of anxiety disorders. *Journal of Consulting and Clinical Psychology, 64,* 660–668.

Magee, W. J., Eaton, W. W., Wittchen, H. U., McGonagle, K. A., & Kessler, R. C. (1996). Agoraphobia, simple phobia, and social phobia in the national comorbidity survey. *Archives of General Psychiatry, 53,* 159–168.

Maier, W., Lichtermann, D., Minges, J., Oehrlein, A., & Franke, P. (1993). A controlled family study in panic disorder. *Journal of Psychiatric Research, 27*(Suppl. 1), 79–87.

Maller, R. G., & Reiss, S. (1992). Anxiety sensitivity in 1984 and panic attacks in 1987. *Journal of Anxiety Disorders, 6,* 241–247.

Manassis, K., Bradley, S., Goldberg, S., Hood, J., & Swinson, R. P. (1995). Behavioural inhibition, attachment and anxiety in children of mothers with anxiety disorders. *Canadian Journal of Psychiatry. Revue Canadienne de Psychiatrie, 40,* 87–92.

Margraf, J., Barlow, D. H., Clark, D. M., & Telch, M. J. (1993). Psychological treatment of panic: Work in progress on outcome, active ingredients, and follow-up. *Behaviour Research and Therapy, 31,* 1–8.

Markowitz, J. S., Weissman, M. M., Ouellette, R., Lish, J. D., & Klerman, G. L. (1989). Quality of life in panic disorder. *Archives of General Psychiatry, 46,* 984–992.

Marks, I. M., & Mathews, A. M. (1979). Brief standard self-rating for phobic patients. *Behaviour Research and Therapy, 17,* 263–267.

Marks, I. M., Swinson, R. P., Basoglu, M., Kuch, K., Noshirvani, H., O'Sullivan, G., et al. (1993). Alprazolam and exposure alone and combined in panic disorder with agoraphobia: A controlled study in London and Toronto. *British Journal of Psychiatry, 162,* 776–787.

Massion, A. O., Warshaw, M. G., & Keller, M. B. (1993). Quality of life and psychiatric morbidity in panic disorder and generalized anxiety disorder. *American Journal of Psychiatry, 150,* 600–607.

Matuzas, W., Al-Sadir, J., Uhlenhuth, E. H., & Glass, R. M. (1987). Mitral valve prolapse and thyroid abnormalities in patients with panic attacks. *American Journal of Psychiatry, 144,* 493–496.

Mavissakalian, M. (1986). The Fear Questionnaire: A validity study. *Behaviour Research and Therapy, 24,* 83–85.

Mavissakalian, M., & Perel, J. M. (1993). Clinical experience in maintenance and discontinuation of imipramine therapy in panic disorder with agoraphobia. *Archives of General Psychiatry, 49,* 318–323.

McLean, P. D., Woody, S., Taylor, S., & Koch, W. J. (1998). Comorbid panic disorder and major depression: Implications for cognitive-behavioral therapy. *Journal of Consulting and Clinical Psychology, 66,* 240–247.

McNally, R. J. (2002). Anxiety sensitivity and panic disorder. *Biological Psychiatry, 52,* 938–946.

Merikangas, K. R., Angst, J., Eaton, W., Canino, G., Rubio-Stipec, M., Wacker, H., et al. (1996). Comorbidity and boundaries of affective disorders with anxiety disorders and substance misuse: Results of an international task force. *British Journal of Psychiatry, 30,* 58–67.

Merikangas, K. R., Stevens, D. E., Fenton, B., Stolar, M., O'Malley, S., Woods, S. W., et al. (1998). Co-morbidity and familial aggregation of alcoholism and anxiety disorders. *Psychological Medicine, 28,* 773–788.

Michelson, L., & Mavissakalian, M. (1983). Temporal stability of self-report measures in agoraphobia research. *Behaviour Research and Therapy, 21,* 695–698.

Mowrer, O. H. (1939). A stimulus response theory. *Psychological Review, 46,* 553–565.

Nordahl, T. E., Semple, W. E., Gross, M., Mellman, T. A., Stein, M. B., Goyer, P., et al. (1990). Cerebral glucose metabolic differences in patients with panic disorder. *Neuropsychopharmacology, 3,* 261–272.

Öst, L. G., & Hugdahl, K. (1983). Acquisition of agoraphobia, mode of onset and anxiety response patterns. *Behaviour Research and Therapy, 21,* 623–631.

Otto, M. W., Penava, S. A., & Pollack, M. H. (1998). Diagnostic and symptom assessment of panic disorder. In J. F. Rosenbaum and M. H. Pollack (Eds.), *Diagnostic and symptom assessment of panic disorder* (pp. 323–340). New York: Marcel Dekker.

Otto, M. W., Pollack, M. H., & Maki, K. M. (2000). Empirically supported treatments for panic disorder: Costs, benefits, and stepped care. *Journal of Consulting and Clinical Psychology, 68,* 556–563.

Otto, M. W., Pollack, M. H., Rosenbaum, J. F., Sachs, G. S., & Asher, R. H. (1994). Childhood history of anxiety in adults with panic disorder: Association with anxiety sensitivity and comorbidity. *Harvard Review of Psychiatry, 1,* 288–293.

Otto, M. W., Pollack, M. H., Sachs, G. S., Reiter, S. R., Meltzer-Brody, S., & Rosenbaum, J. F. (1993). Discontinuation of benzodiazepine treatment: Efficacy of cognitive-behavioral therapy for patients with panic disorder. *American Journal of Psychiatry, 150,* 1485–1490.

Otto, M. W., & Reilly-Harrington, N. (1999). The impact of treatment on anxiety sensitivity. In S. Taylor (Ed.), *Anxiety sensitivity: Theory, research, and treatment of the fear of anxiety* (pp. 321–336). Mahwah, NJ: Erlbaum.

Otto, M. W., Smits, J. A. J., & Reese, H. E. (2005). Combined pharmacotherapy and cognitive behavior therapy for mood and anxiety disorders in adults: Review and analyses. *Journal of Clinical Psychology: Science and Practice, 12,* 72–86.

Otto, M. W., Tuby, K. S., Gould, R. A., McLean, R. Y., & Pollack, M. H. (2001). An effect-size analysis of the relative efficacy and tolerability of serotonin selective reuptake inhibitors for panic disorder. *American Journal of Psychiatry, 158,* 1989–1992.

Papp, L. A., Martinez, J. M., Klein, D. F., Coplan, J. D., Norman, R. G., Cole, R., et al. (1997). Respiratory psychophysiology of panic disorder: Three respiratory challenges in 98 subjects. *American Journal of Psychiatry, 154,* 1557–1565.

Pavlov, I. P. (1927). *Conditioned reflexes.* London: Oxford University Press.

Penava, S. J., Otto, M. W., Maki, K. M., & Pollack, M. H. (1998). Rate of improvement during cognitive-behavioral group treatment for panic disorder. *Behaviour Research and Therapy, 36,* 665–673.

Peterson, R. A., & Plehn, K. (1999). Measuring anxiety sensitivity. In S. Taylor (Ed.), *Anxiety sensitivity: Theory, research, and treatment of the fear of anxiety* (pp. 61–81). Mahwah, NJ: Erlbaum.

Peterson, R. A., & Reiss, R. S. (1987). *Anxiety Sensitivity Index.* Palos Heights, IL: International Diagnostic Systems.

Pollack, M. H., Otto, M. W., Rosenbaum, J. F., Sachs, G. S., O'Neil, C., Asher, R., et al. (1990). Longitudinal course of panic disorder: Findings from the Massachusetts General Hospital Naturalistic Study. *Journal of Clinical Psychiatry, 51*(Suppl. A), 12–16.

Pollack, M. H., Otto, M. W., Sabatino, S., Majcher, D., Worthington, J. J., McArdle, E. T., et al. (1996). Relationship of childhood anxiety to adult panic disorder: Correlates and influence on course. *American Journal of Psychiatry, 153,* 376–381.

Rachman, S., Levitt, K., & Lopatka, C. (1987). Panic: The links between cognitions and bodily symptoms—I. *Behaviour Research and Therapy, 25,* 411–423.

Rapaport, M. H., Pollack, M., Wolkow, R., Mardekian, J., & Clary, C. (2000). Is placebo response the same as drug response in panic disorder? *American Journal of Psychiatry, 157,* 1014–1016.

Rapee, R. M., Brown, T. A., Antony, M. M., & Barlow, D. H. (1992). Response to hyperventilation and inhalation of 5.5% carbon dioxide-enriched air across the *DSM-III-R* anxiety disorders. *Journal of Abnormal Psychology, 101,* 538–552.

Reiman, E. M., Raichle, M. E., Butler, F. K., Herscovitch, P., & Robins, E. (1984). A focal brain abnormality in panic disorder, a severe form of anxiety. *Nature, 310,* 683–685.

Reiman, E. M., Raichle, M. E., Robins, E., Mintun, M. A., Fusselman, M. J., Fox, P. T., et al. (1989). Neuroanatomical correlates of a lactate-induced anxiety attack. *Archives of General Psychiatry, 46,* 493–500.

Reiss, S., Peterson, R. A., Gursky, D. M., & McNally, R. J. (1986). Anxiety sensitivity, anxiety frequency and the prediction of fearfulness. *Behaviour Research and Therapy, 24,* 1–8.

Renneberg, B., Chambless, D. L., & Gracely, E. J. (1992). Prevalence of SCID-diagnosed personality disorders in agoraphobic outpatients*1. *Journal of Anxiety Disorders, 6,* 111–118.

Reznick, J. S., Hegeman, I. M., Kaufman, E. R., & Woods, S. W. (1992). Retrospective and concurrent self-report of behavioral inhibition and their relation to adult mental health. *Development & Psychopathology, 4,* 301–321.

Rogers, M. P., White, K., Warshaw, M. G., Yonkers, K. A., Rodriguez-Villa, F., Chang, G., et al. (1994). Prevalence of medical illness in patients with anxiety disorders. *International Journal of Psychiatry in Medicine, 24,* 83–96.

Rosenbaum, J. F., Biederman, J., Bolduc-Murphy, E. A., Faraone, S. V., Chaloff, J., Hirshfeld, D. R., et al. (1993). Behavioral inhibition in childhood: A risk factor for anxiety disorders. *Harvard Review of Psychiatry, 1,* 2–16.

Rosenbaum, J. F., Biederman, J., Gersten, M., Hirshfeld, D. R., Meminger, S. R., Herman, J. B., et al. (1988). Behavioral inhibition in children of parents with panic disorder and agoraphobia: A controlled study. *Archives of General Psychiatry, 45,* 463–470.

Rosenbaum, J. F., Biederman, J., Hirshfeld-Becker, D. R., Kagan, J., Snidman, N., Friedman, D., et al. (2000). A controlled study of behavioral inhibition in children of parents with panic disorder and depression. *American Journal of Psychiatry, 157,* 2002–2010.

Roy-Byrne, P. P., & Cowley, D. S. (1994–1995). Course and outcome in panic disorder: A review of recent follow-up studies. *Anxiety, 1,* 151–160.

Roy-Byrne, P. P., Stang, P., Wittchen, H. U., Ustun, B., Walters, E. E., & Kessler, R. C. (2000). Lifetime panic-depression comorbidity in the National Comorbidity Survey: Association with symptoms, impairment, course and help-seeking. *British Journal of Psychiatry, 176,* 229–235.

Salkovskis, P. M., Clark, D. M., & Gelder, M. G. (1996). Cognition-behaviour links in the persistence of panic. *Behaviour Research and Therapy, 34,* 453–458.

Sanderson, W. C., Wetzler, S., Beck, A. T., & Betz, F. (1994). Prevalence of personality disorders among patients with anxiety disorders. *Psychiatry Research, 51,* 167–174.

Schmidt, N. B., Lerew, D. R., & Jackson, R. J. (1997). The role of anxiety sensitivity in the pathogenesis of panic: Prospective evaluation of spontaneous panic attacks during acute stress. *Journal of Abnormal Psychology, 106,* 355–364.

Schmidt, N. B., Lerew, D. R., & Jackson, R. J. (1999). Prospective evaluation of anxiety sensitivity in the pathogenesis of panic: Replication and extension. *Journal of Abnormal Psychology, 108,* 532–537.

Schmidt, N. B., & Telch, M. J. (1997). Nonpsychiatric medical comorbidity, health perceptions, and treatment outcome in patients with panic disorder. *Health Psychology, 16,* 114–122.

Schmidt, N. B., Trakowski, J. H., & Staab, J. P. (1997). Extinction of panicogenic effects of a 35% CO2 challenge in patients with panic disorder. *Journal of Abnormal Psychology, 106,* 630–638.

Schmidt, N. B., & Woolaway-Bickel, K. (2000). The effects of treatment compliance on outcome in cognitive-behavioral therapy for panic disorder: Quality versus quantity. *Journal of Consulting and Clinical Psychology, 68,* 13–18.

Schmidt, N. B., Woolaway-Bickel, K., Trakowski, J., Santiago, H., Storey, J., Koselka, M., et al. (2000). Dismantling cognitive-behavioral treatment for panic disorder: Questioning the utility of breathing retraining. *Journal of Consulting and Clinical Psychology, 68,* 417–424.

Schwartz, C. E., Snidman, N., & Kagan, J. (1999). Adolescent social anxiety as an outcome of inhibited temperament in childhood. *Journal of the American Academy of Child & Adolescent Psychiatry, 38,* 1008–1015.

Shear, M. K., & Maser, J. D. (1994). Standardized assessment for panic disorder research: A conference report. *Archives of General Psychiatry, 51,* 346–354.

Sherbourne, C. D., Wells, K. B., & Judd, L. L. (1996). Functioning and well-being of patients with panic disorder. *American Journal of Psychiatry, 153,* 213–218.

Simon, N. M., Blacker, D., Korbly, N. B., Sharma, S. G., Worthington, J. J., Otto, M. W., et al. (2002). Hypothyroidism and hyperthyroidism in anxiety disorders revisited: New data and literature review. *Journal of Affective Disorders, 69,* 209–217.

Simon, N. M., Otto, M. W., Korbly, N. B., Peters, P. M., Nicolaou, D. C., & Pollack, M. H. (2002). Quality of life in social anxiety disorder compared with panic disorder and the general population. *Psychiatric Services, 53,* 714–718.

Simon, N. M., Otto, M. W., Smits, J. A. J., Colette Nicolaou, D., Reese, H. E., & Pollack, M. H. (2004). Changes in anxiety sensitivity with pharmacotherapy for panic disorder. *Journal of Psychiatric Research, 38,* 491–495.

Sinha, S., Papp, L. A., & Gorman, J. M. (2000). How study of respiratory physiology aided our understanding of abnormal brain function in panic disorder. *Journal of Affective Disorders, 61,* 191–200.

Smits, J. A. J., Powers, M. B., Cho, Y., & Telch, M. J. (2004). Mechanism of change in cognitive-behavioral treatment of panic disorder: Evidence for the fear of fear mediational hypothesis. *Journal of Consulting and Clinical Psychology, 72,* 646–652.

Spiegel, D. A., Bruce, T. J., Gregg, S. F., & Nuzzarello, A. (1994). Does cognitive behavior therapy assist slow-taper alprazolam discontinuation in panic disorder? *American Journal of Psychiatry, 151,* 876–881.

Spitzer, R. L., Williams, J. B., Gibbon, M., & First, M. B. (1992). The Structured Clinical Interview for *DSM-III-R* (SCID): I. History, rationale, and description. *Archives of General Psychiatry, 49,* 624–629.

Stein, M. B., Jang, K. L., & Livesley, W. J. (1999). Heritability of anxiety sensitivity: A twin study. *American Journal of Psychiatry, 156,* 246–251.

Stewart, R. S., Devous, M. D., Sr., Rush, A. J., Lane, L., & Bonte, F. J. (1988). Cerebral blood flow changes during sodium-lactate-induced panic attacks. *American Journal of Psychiatry, 145,* 442–449.

Stuart, G. L., Treat, T. A., & Wade, W. A. (2000). Effectiveness of an empirically based treatment for panic disorder delivered in a service clinic setting: 1-year follow-up. *Journal of Consulting and Clinical Psychology, 68,* 506–512.

Swartz, K. L., Pratt, L. A., Armenian, H. K., Lee, L. C., & Eaton, W. W. (2000). Mental disorders and the incidence of migraine headaches in a community sample: Results from the Baltimore Epidemiologic Catchment area follow-up study. *Archives of General Psychiatry, 57,* 945–950.

Taylor, S., Koch, W. J., & McNally, R. J. (1992). How does anxiety sensitivity vary across the anxiety disorders? *Journal of Anxiety Disorders, 6,* 249–259.

Telch, M. J., Jacquin, K., Smits, J. A., & Powers, M. B. (2003). Emotional responding to hyperventilation as a predictor of agoraphobia status among individuals suffering from panic disorder. *Journal of Behavior Therapy and Experimental Psychiatry, 34,* 161–170.

Telch, M. J., Schmidt, N. B., Jaimez, T. L., Jacquin, K. M., & Harrington, P. J. (1995). Impact of cognitive-behavioral treatment on quality of life in panic disorder patients. *Journal of Consulting and Clinical Psychology, 63,* 823–830.

Telch, M. J., Shermis, M. D., & Lucas, J. A. (1989). Anxiety sensitivity: Unitary personality trait or domain-specific appraisals? *Journal of Anxiety Disorders, 3,* 25–32.

Tsao, J. C., Lewin, M. R., & Craske, M. G. (1998). The effects of cognitive-behavior therapy for panic disorder on comorbid conditions. *Journal of Anxiety Disorders, 12,* 357–371.

Turgeon, L., Marchand, A., & Dupuis, G. (1998). Clinical features in panic disorder with agoraphobia: A comparison of men and women. *Journal of Anxiety Disorders, 12,* 539–553.

Wade, W. A., Treat, T. A., & Stuart, G. L. (1998). Transporting an empirically supported treatment for panic disorder to a service clinic setting: A benchmarking strategy. *Journal of Consulting and Clinical Psychology, 66,* 231–239.

Wang, P. S., Berglund, P., & Kessler, R. C. (2000). Recent care of common mental disorders in the United States: Prevalence and conformance with evidence-based recommendations. *Journal of General Internal Medicine, 15,* 284–292.

Ware, J. E., Jr., & Sherbourne, C. D. (1992). The MOS 36-item short-form health survey (SF-36): I. Conceptual framework and item selection. *Medical Care, 30,* 473–483.

Warner, L. A., Kessler, R. C., Hughes, M., Anthony, J. C., & Nelson, C. B. (1995). Prevalence and correlates of drug use and dependence in the United States: Results from the National Comorbidity Survey. *Archives of General Psychiatry, 52,* 219–229.

Warshaw, M. G., Massion, A. O., Shea, M. T., Allsworth, J., & Keller, M. B. (1997). Predictors of remission in patients with panic with and without agoraphobia: Prospective 5-year follow-up data. *Journal of Nervous and Mental Disease, 185,* 517–519.

Weems, C. F., Hayward, C., Killen, J., & Taylor, C. B. (2002). A longitudinal investigation of anxiety sensitivity in adolescence. *Journal of Abnormal Psychology, 111,* 471–477.

Weissman, M. M., Bland, R. C., Canino, G. J., Faravelli, C., Greenwald, S., Hwu, H. G., et al. (1997). The cross-national epidemiology of panic disorder. *Archives of General Psychiatry, 54,* 305–309.

Westling, B. E., & Öst, L. G. (1993). Relationship between panic attack symptoms and cognitions in panic disorder patients. *Journal of Anxiety Disorders, 7,* 181–194.

Williams, J. B. W., Gibbon, M., First, M. B., Spitzer, R. L., Davis, M., Borus, J., et al. (1992). The Structured Clinical Interview for *DSM-III-R* (SCID) II: Multi-site test-retest reliability. *Archives of General Psychiatry, 49,* 630–636.

Wittchen, H. U., Kessler, R. C., Pfister, H., & Lieb, M. (2000). Why do people with anxiety disorders become depressed? A prospective-longitudinal community study. *Acta Psychiatrica Scandinavica, 406,* 14–23.

Woods, S. W., Koster, K., Krystal, J. K., Smith, E. O., Zubal, I. G., Hoffer, P. B., et al. (1988). Yohimbine alters regional cerebral blood flow in panic disorder. *Lancet, 2,* 678.

Yonkers, K. A., Bruce, S. E., Dyck, I. R., & Keller, M. B. (2003). Chronicity, relapse, and illness—Course of panic disorder, social phobia, and generalized anxiety disorder: Findings in men and women from 8 years of follow-up. *Depression and Anxiety, 17,* 173–179.

Yonkers, K. A., Zlotnick, C., Allsworth, J., Warshaw, M., Shea, T., & Keller, M. B. (1998). Is the course of panic disorder the same in women and men? *American Journal of Psychiatry, 155,* 596–602.

Zimmermann, P., Wittchen, H. U., Hofler, M., Pfister, H., Kessler, R. C., & Lieb, R. (2003). Primary anxiety disorders and the development of subsequent alcohol use disorders: A 4-year community study of adolescents and young adults. *Psychological Medicine, 33,* 1211–1222.

Zvolensky, M. J., & Eifert, G. H. (2001). A review of psychological factors/processes affecting anxious responding during voluntary hyperventilation and inhalations of carbon dioxide-enriched air. *Clinical Psychology Review, 21,* 375–400.

CHAPTER 9

Social Anxiety Disorder

MEREDITH E. COLES AND BETTY HORNG

DESCRIPTION OF THE DISORDER AND CLINICAL PICTURE

Social phobia (i.e., social anxiety disorder) is characterized by "a marked and persistent fear of social or performance situations in which embarrassment may occur" (American Psychiatric Association, 1994, p. 411). For example, individuals with this disorder frequently fear social gatherings, meeting unfamiliar people, formal and informal performance situations, and/or being assertive (Rapee, 1995). Although the nature of the feared situations may vary, exposure to such situations customarily elicits a rapid anxiety response. In feared situations, individuals with social phobia often experience physical symptoms such as racing heart, sweating, and trembling, and nearly half experience situationally bound panic attacks (Jack, Heimberg, & Mennin, 1999). In addition, although persons with the disorder typically recognize the excessive nature of their fears, they are still likely to avoid engaging in the feared situations or endure the situations with extreme distress. This cycle of fear, avoidance, and distress, serves to produce marked disruptions in activities of daily living (see for example, Schneier et al., 1994). The *Diagnostic and Statistical Manual of Mental Disorders* (4th ed., APA, 1994) highlights that social phobia is likely to produce impairment in normal routines, occupational functioning, academic functioning, social activities, and relationships.

As suggested previously, although fear of social situations is at the core of social phobia, the feared situations vary. Research has shown that the most commonly feared situation is public speaking (Holt, Heimberg, Hope, & Liebowitz, 1992; Stein & Deutsch, 2003). Other commonly feared situations include speaking in meetings or classes, talking with strangers, entering a room where others are seated, talking with authority figures, and making eye contact with strangers (Stein & Deutsch, 2003). Most individuals with social phobia fear multiple social situations. For example, studying a large community sample of individuals with social phobia, Stein, Torgrud, and Walker (2000) found the mean number of social fears reported to be 4.8 (standard deviation = 2.4), and that more than 90 percent of the sample endorsed fears of multiple social situations. Given this variability in the number of social situations feared, the *DSM* instructs diagnosticians to specify the diagnosis as "'generalized,' if the fears include most social situations" (APA, 1994, p. 417). Practical definitions of the term *generalized* have varied; however, there is generally support for the reliability and validity of distinguishing patients based on the breadth of their fears (see Heckelman & Schneier, 1995; Mannuzza et al., 1995).

In addition to the types of situations that elicit social anxiety, there are clinical features of the disorder that also accompany and maintain this fear, such as the focus on physiological and cognitive components. As mentioned earlier, exposure to feared situations in social phobia frequently provokes rapid physiological responses (e.g., rapid heart rate, sweating). Although the reactions of anxious patients are generally similar across diagnoses, there is evidence to suggest that individuals with social phobia are more likely than individuals with panic disorder to report stammering, blushing, twitching (Solyom, Ledwidge, & Solyom, 1986), and dry mouth (Reich, Noyes, & Yates, 1988). Symptoms can be circumscribed for some individuals with social phobia; however, Jack et al. (1999) found that the symptoms were substantial enough to meet criteria for a situationally bound panic attack in nearly half of their sample of social phobia patients. Further, their results showed that the presence of these situationally bound panic attacks was associated with greater avoidance of social situations, larger impairment, and decreased hope about the future. Clearly, physiological arousal plays an important role in social phobia.

Biased cognitive content and processes are also important clinical features of social phobia. Regarding cognitive content, research has demonstrated that individuals with social phobia are characterized by elevated levels of negative self-focused thoughts as assessed by both self-statement questionnaire (Glass, Merluzzi, Biever, & Larsen, 1982) and thought-listing methods (Hofmann, Moscovitch, Kim, &

Taylor, in press; Stopa & Clark, 1993). Research has shown that individuals with social phobia are characterized by increased self-focused attention (Hope, Heimberg, & Klein, 1990) and elevated levels of public self-consciousness (Bruch, Gorsky, Collins, & Berger, 1989). In addition, there is robust evidence that individuals with social phobia rate their own performance more negatively than do observers (Rapee & Lim, 1992). Further, individuals with social phobia demonstrate judgment and interpretation biases. For example, they estimate negative social events as more likely than control subjects (Foa, Franklin, Perry, & Herbert, 1996; Lucock & Salkovskis, 1988; McManus, Clark, & Hackmann, 2000), rate the cost of negative social events as greater (Foa et al., 1996; McManus et al., 2000), and are more likely to interpret ambiguous social events negatively (Amir, Foa, & Coles, 1998; Stopa & Clark, 2000). Finally, individuals with social phobia demonstrate a bias to allocate their attention toward socially threatening information (for a review, see Heinrichs & Hofmann, 2001).

Typically, social anxiety disorder is associated with other clinical symptoms and syndromes. Studying a community sample, the Epidemiological Catchment Area (ECA) study (Schneier, Johnson, Hornig, Liebowitz, & Weissman, 1992) found that 69 percent of individuals meeting criteria for social phobia also met criteria for at least one additional lifetime psychiatric diagnosis. Studies using treatment-seeking samples have estimated that nearly 50 percent of patients with social phobia received one or more secondary Axis I diagnoses (Brown, Campbell, Lehman, Grisham, & Mancill, 2001; Turner, Beidel, Borden, Stanley, & Jacob, 1991). Studies indicate that the most commonly diagnosed comorbid conditions include generalized anxiety disorder, simple phobia, major depressive disorder, and dysthymic disorder (Brown, Campbell, et al., 2001; Turner et al., 1991). Social phobia is also associated with alcohol abuse and dependence, with estimated rates of alcoholism in patients with social phobia ranging from 16 percent to 36 percent (for a review, see Heckelman & Schneier, 1995).

In addition to the Axis I correlates, social phobia is also frequently associated with the presence of Axis II diagnoses, particularly avoidant personality disorder. Estimates vary based on which version of the *DSM* criteria are used and the breadth of social phobia concerns; however, the data suggest that at least 25 percent of patients with social phobia also meet criteria for avoidant personality disorder (for a recent review, see Rettew, 2000). Given the high rates of comorbidity between these two disorders much has been written about the overlap in their definitions. Most broadly, the majority of research suggests that the two disorders differ qualitatively, not quantitatively, with individuals reporting generalized and severe social anxiety most likely to have comorbid avoidant personality disorder (Rettew, 2000). In addition to avoidant personality disorder, research has also shown that social phobia is associated with elevated rates of obsessive-compulsive personality disorder (OCPD). Turner et al. (1991) found that 13.2 percent of patients with social phobia met criteria for OCPD.

PERSONALITY DEVELOPMENT AND PSYCHOPATHOLOGY

An important issue in understanding social phobia is clarifying its relationship with the personality characteristic of shyness. Due to the apparent similarity of social anxiety and shyness, much has been written about their relationship. For example, Turner, Beidel, and Townsley (1990) highlighted the similarities in cognitive, behavioral, and somatic symptoms, noting that both conditions include fear of negative evaluation, avoidance of social situations, and elevated autonomic arousal. Both conditions have also been associated with social skills deficits, such as poor eye contact (see Chavira, Stein, & Malcarnem, 2002). Beyond symptom presentation, empirical data shows that social phobia occurs at elevated rates in individuals who are highly shy (Chavira et al., 2002; Heiser, Turner, & Beidel, 2003). For instance, Chavira et al. (2002) found that 49 percent of their elevated shyness group met criteria for social phobia compared to only 18 percent of their low shyness group. In addition to these cross-sectional relationships, longitudinal data has shown that shy temperament predicts later problems with anxiety. Specifically, shy temperament in early life (from infancy onward) has been shown to predict a higher incidence of anxiety problems in early adolescence (Prior, Smart, Sanson, & Oberklaid, 2000).

Although social phobia and shyness have similar characteristics, it is also important to consider their differences. First, it is important to note that the two conditions differ dramatically in their prevalence, with shyness being much more common (for a discussion, see Chavira et al., 2002). For example, Heiser et al. (2003) found that 82 percent of their elevated shyness group did not meet criteria for social phobia. In addition, the presence of shyness in childhood does not equate to later social phobia. For example, focusing on children who consistently showed shy/inhibited temperament, only 27 percent developed subsequent anxiety problems in early adolescence (Prior et al., 2000). Social phobia also appears to differ from shyness by resulting in additional impairment beyond shyness alone. For example, Chavira et al. (2002) found that highly shy individuals with social phobia reported greater impairment in work or school and social functioning than highly shy individuals without social phobia. Finally, data suggest that social phobia may be associated with a more chronic course than shyness (see Chavira et al., 2002).

In addition to examining the relationship of social phobia to shyness in particular, studies have broadly studied the personality characteristics of individuals with social phobia. Numerous studies have found social phobia to be associated with the personality characteristics of increased harm avoidance and decreased self-direction (Chatterjee, Sunitha, Velayudhan, & Khanna, 1997; Marteinsdottir, Tillfors, Furmark, Andenberg, & Ekselius, 2003; Pelissolo et al., 2002). Also, two studies showed that social phobia is associated with decreased cooperation (Chatterjee et al., 1997; Marteinsdottir et al., 2003). Finally, single studies have found social phobia to be associated with decreased persistence, self-transcendence (Marteinsdottir et al., 2003), novelty seeking (Chatterjee et al., 1997), socialism, and social desirability (Marteinsdottir, Furmark, Tillfors, Fredrikson, & Ekselius, 2001). In addition, one study (Marteinsdottir et al., 2001) found elevated anxiety traits, indirect aggression, irritability, and detachment in individuals with social phobia. Most broadly, these findings suggest that individuals with social phobia are characterized by avoidant personality traits. However, more research is needed to replicate these findings and clarify the role of personality features in social phobia.

It is also worth considering whether the high comorbidity between social phobia and avoidant personality disorder provides additional information about the personality characteristics and development of individuals with social phobia. As discussed earlier in this chapter, at least 25 percent of patients with social phobia also meet criteria for avoidant personality disorder (for a review, see Rettew, 2000). Of most relevance to the current discussion are findings that social phobia and avoidant personality disorder are not associated with different personality traits. For example, Marteinsdottir et al. (2003) found very few differences in the personality traits of individuals with social phobia with and without comorbid avoidant personality disorder. Similarly, comparing patients with social phobia to healthy controls, Fahlen (1995) found that individuals with social phobia had deviations in personality traits (higher ratings of avoidant social behavior and general depressive-anxious traits). From this, he concluded that there is no support for distinguishing the Axis I and Axis II diagnoses (social phobia & avoidant personality disorder) based on the presence of deviant personality traits. Although the debate regarding the comparability between social phobia and avoidant personality disorder remains, it appears that both disorders are similarly characterized by deviations in personality.

Finally, any discussion of personality development and social phobia would not be complete without considering behavioral inhibition. A component of temperament, behavioral inhibition comprises a constellation of behaviors including withdrawal, avoidance, shyness, and fear of unfamiliar objects or people (Kagan & Snidman, 1991), and a physiological component (high heart rate and increased salivary cortisol; see Hayward, Killen, Kraemer, & Taylor, 1998). Clinical observations reveal similarities between children with behavioral inhibition and social anxiety: Both exhibit avoidance of social situations, show exaggerated sympathetic arousal (Neal & Edelmann, 2003), and demonstrate extended speech latencies (Beidel, Turner, & Morris, 1999). In addition, there is a growing body of empirical data linking behavioral inhibition and social anxiety (see Neal & Edelmann, 2003). In a sample of 269 young children (ages 2 to 6), Biederman et al. (2001) found that the prevalence of social phobia/avoidant personality disorder was significantly greater in children identified as behaviorally inhibited than noninhibited children (17 percent versus 5 percent, respectively). Further, college students with elevated levels of social anxiety retrospectively report higher levels of behavioral inhibition than students with low anxiety and students with elevated levels of generalized anxiety (Mick & Telch, 1998). Additionally, a prospective link has also been established between behavioral inhibition and social anxiety. For example, the presence of behavioral inhibition prior to age 31 months has been shown to be associated with elevated rates of generalized social anxiety at age 13 (Schwartz, Snidman, & Kagan, 1999). Finally, using a four-year prospective design, Hayward et al. (1998) found that high school students who demonstrated certain characteristics of behavioral inhibition (i.e., high fearfulness and social avoidance) developed social phobia at a rate more than four times greater than students who did not exhibit either component of behavioral inhibition.

EPIDEMIOLOGY

Within the United States, social phobia is considered the third most common psychological disorder, following major depressive disorder and alcohol dependence (Kessler et al., 1994; Moutier & Stein, 1999). The two largest epidemiological studies conducted in the United States are the Epidemiologic Catchment Area (ECA) Study, which utilized *DSM-III* criteria, and the National Comorbidity Survey (NCS), which utilized *DSM-III-R* criteria (see Kessler et al., 1994; Schneier et al., 1992). The ECA assessed a limited range of social fears within the assessment of simple phobias, and produced a lifetime prevalence rate of 2.4 percent for social phobia (Schneier et al., 1992). In contrast, using a more comprehensive assessment and following *DSM-III-R* criteria, the NCS showed a lifetime prevalence rate of 13.3 percent for social phobia (Kessler et al., 1994; Magee, Eaton, Wittchen, McGonagle, & Kessler, 1996). Much has been written about the discrepancy between these two estimates, with possible explanations including differences in the diagnostic criteria applied and the assessment measures used (e.g., see Wittchen & Fehm, 2001). Recently, Narrow, Rae, Robins, and Regier (2002) reexamined data from the ECA and NCS studies applying an additional clinical significance criterion. These authors estimated the prevalence of distressing symptoms that led to seeking professional help/medication or that interfered with daily functioning. Interestingly, after application of this additional clinical significance criterion the ECA and NCS produced similar one-year prevalence rates for social phobia (1.7 percent and 3.7 percent, respectively, compared to initial rates of 1.7 percent and 7.4 percent). Overall, these findings suggest that differences in diagnostic criteria used, assessment measures, and emphasis on clinical significance, may impact observed prevalence rates.

After the publication of the ECA and NCS papers, a number of studies have utilized *DSM-IV* criteria to examine the prevalence of social phobia worldwide (for a review, see Wittchen & Fehm, 2001). As summarized by Wittchen and Fehm (2001), studies utilizing community samples in Germany, France, and Canada have yielded remarkably consistent lifetime prevalence rates for social phobia: 7.3 percent, 7.3 percent, and 7.2 percent, respectively. Estimates of 12-month prevalence rates using *DSM-IV* criteria in Australia, Italy, and Germany, have also converged on similar estimates ranging from 2.3 percent to 4.0 percent (see Lampe, Slade, Issakidis, & Andrews, 2003; Wittchen & Fehm, 2001).

Demographically, numerous community surveys have demonstrated that social anxiety disorder is more prevalent among females than males (Kessler et al., 1994; Lampe et al., 2003; Magee et al., 1996; Moutier & Stein, 1999; Schneier et al., 1992). However, data from more than 10,000 participants in Australia suggested that the gender ratio may vary by age (Lampe et al., 2003). Epidemiologic studies have also reported social phobia to be more common among younger individuals (Lang & Stein, 2001; Magee et al., 1996; Schneier et al., 1992). For example, Lampe et al. (2003) found that the odds of having social phobia in their age 55 and older group were one-third of that for their age 35 to 54 group, and Stein et al. (2000) found that persons with social phobia were likely to be less than age 40. Finally, existing data suggest that individuals with social anxiety tend to be not married (i.e., widowed, divorced, or separated), single, and/or never married (Lampe et al., 2003; Magee et al., 1996; Schneier et al., 1992) and are less likely to have completed high school (Stein et al., 2000).

ETIOLOGY

Generally, theoretical conceptualizations of social phobia have focused primarily on the maintenance of the disorder, and less on etiology. Models of social phobia have been developed from a variety of theoretical approaches. However, the most prominent are the cognitive-behavioral models. In this section, first, the most influential cognitive-behavioral models that briefly address etiology will be reviewed. Following after, the literature on the etiology of social phobia will be discussed.

Arguably the two most significant models of social phobia are those of Clark and Wells (1995) and Rapee and Heimberg (1997). Based in cognitive-behavioral conceptualizations of psychopathology, both models begin with the assumption that individuals with social phobia highly value being positively evaluated by others. Clark and Wells (1995) state that the core of the disorder not only includes this desire to be positively appraised by others but also marked insecurity about one's ability to achieve a favorable impression. Similarly, Rapee and Heimberg's model (1997) begins from the assumption that individuals with social phobia assume that others are critical and that being positively evaluated by others is valued. Both models then build from this fear of negative evaluation in proposing that biased processing of information in social situations leads to elevated levels of social anxiety. For example, the models propose that elevated social anxiety is associated with biased perceptions of the self as a social object, or as if seen by the audience. Clark and Wells (1995) posit that this biased information processing prohibits socially anxious individuals from fully processing information during social situations, that associated safety behaviors negate possible disconfirmatory evidence, and that the individuals' impressions of themselves is used as the basis for predicting others' reactions. Similarly, Rapee and Heimberg (1997) propose that information-processing biases such as preferential allocation of attention to threatening information, and overestimates of the probability and cost of negative evaluation, drive exacerbated levels of social anxiety. Finally, both models emphasize that the focus on the self as a social object is associated with physiological, cognitive, and behavioral reactions.

Empirical data support these two cognitive-behavioral models. On a basic level, data have shown that individuals with social phobia overestimate the probability and cost of being negatively evaluated in social situations (Foa et al., 1996; McManus et al., 2000). Research has also demonstrated that individuals with heightened social anxiety tend to interpret ambiguous social information in a threatening manner (Amir et al., 1998; Stopa & Clark, 2000). Further, numerous studies have shown that individuals with social phobia rate their performance in social situations as significantly worse than ratings from independent observers (e.g., see Rapee & Lim, 1992; Stopa & Clark, 1993). In addition, research has shown that when recalling anxiety-provoking social situations, individuals with social phobia tend to view themselves as if from an external point of view, as if observing oneself (Coles, Turk, Heimberg, & Fresco, 2001; Wells, Clark, & Ahmad, 1998). Finally, there is a great deal of support for the proposal that individuals with social phobia preferentially allocate their attention to threatening information. Computer-based tasks have also provided evidence that individuals with social phobia tend to focus on threat words (and not neutral or physical threat words), as compared to nonanxious controls (Asmundson & Stein, 1994). Additionally, role-play tasks have shown that individuals with elevated social anxiety are more accurate at, and sensitive to, detecting negative audience behaviors than nonanxious controls (Veljaca & Rapee, 1998). In summary, research largely supports the cognitive-behavioral proposal that individuals with social phobia are characterized by biased processing of social information.

Although the models of Clark and Wells (1995) and Rapee and Heimberg (1997) mainly focus on the maintenance of social anxiety, they also cover, in less detail, the etiology of the disorder. Clark and Wells (1995) speak very briefly on the etiology of social phobia, proposing that behavioral predispositions interact with learning experiences to produce a series of dysfunctional beliefs. These dysfunctional beliefs, such as excessively high social standards and conditional beliefs regarding social evaluation, are hypothesized to be activated in social situations and thereby lead the individual to perceive social situations as dangerous, regardless of the objective dangerousness of the situation. Rapee and Heimberg (1997) devote more attention to the etiology of social phobia, presenting an integrative model combining genetic and environmental influences. For example, based on their review of the literature, Rapee and Heimberg (1997) propose that genetic factors may predispose individuals to have a general bias to preferentially allocate attention to threatening information and environmental influences then impact which specific cues are attended to. Following from this conceptualization, Rapee and Heimberg focus on the impact of family factors (such as encouraging avoidance) in conferring vulnerability to social anxiety.

In addition to these two models, past literature has addressed the etiology of social phobia (Hudson & Rapee, 2000; Neal & Edelmann, 2003; Ollendick & Hirshfeld-Becker, 2002; Stein, Chavira, & Jang, 2001). Encouragingly, there is great consistency in the constructs identified as relevant to the etiology of this disorder. The majority of reviews have converged on concluding the importance of both biological and environmental family influences, peer influences, and temperament on the development of social phobia. Support for genetic vulnerability to social phobia comes from twin studies demonstrating the heritability of this disorder (e.g., Kendler, Karkowski, & Prescott, 1999) and family studies showing that social phobia aggregates in families (for reviews, see Hudson & Rapee, 2000; Stein et al., 2001). Review of the literature also suggests that the impact of family goes beyond heritability, with data supporting a role of child rearing practices in the development of social phobia. For example, social phobia is clearly related to parenting styles of overcontrol, rejection, and lack of warmth (see Hudson & Rapee, 2000; see also Lieb et al., 2000). A lack of family experiences with social situations, via upbringing discouraging social interaction and encouraging social isolation, has been linked to social phobia, as well (see Neal & Edelmann, 2003). Finally, research has demonstrated that socially anxious parents model anxious responding and avoidance for their children (see Hudson & Rapee, 2000). In addition to the impact from family members, data also suggest peer relationships may influence the development of shyness and social phobia. One study showed that peer isolation in second grade predicted teacher's ratings of shyness in fifth grade (Hymel, Rubin, Rowden, & LeMare, 1990). Finally, as reviewed earlier in this chapter, there is also strong support for the role of temperament, particularly behavioral inhibition, in the development of social phobia.

In summary, social phobia is likely to be multidetermined, influenced by genetic contributions, family and peer influences, and temperament (see Ollendick & Hirshfeld-Becker, 2002). To date, no one specific vulnerability factor has been identified that is necessary or sufficient to determine the presence of the disorder. It is also important to note that the majority of existing data are correlational, thereby prohibiting the ability to draw causal conclusions. Finally, the specificity of these vulnerabilities to social phobia in particular remains to be seen.

COURSE, COMPLICATIONS, AND PROGNOSIS

Empirical findings suggest that social phobia typically onsets in adolescence and follows a chronic course (Lang & Stein, 2001). In the Epidemiologic Catchment Area Survey (ECA) social phobia was reported to characteristically onset between ages 0 and 5 and around age 13. Further, nearly half of the individuals with social phobia reported having social phobia their entire life, or prior to age 10 (Schneier et al., 1992). Reviewing the literature, Wittchen and Fehm (2001) noted the mean age of onset in clinical samples to be between 13 and 24 and between 10 and 16.6 in epidemiologic samples. Finally, numerous papers suggest that onset of social phobia after age 25 is rare (see Wittchen & Fehm, 2001).

In addition to the early age of onset, social phobia is a chronic disorder. Indeed, numerous epidemiologic and clinical studies have shown a mean illness duration of 20 years (see Moutier & Stein, 1999). For example, Reich, Goldenberg, Goisman, Vasile, and Keller (1994) found their sample of individuals with social phobia to report a mean illness duration of 18 years. Other studies have found even longer estimates, with survival analyses suggesting a median illness length of 25 years (DeWit, Ogborne, Offord, & MacDonald, 1999). In addition, longitudinal studies show that natural remission from social phobia is rare. In an eight-year naturalistic longitudinal prospective study of the course of social phobia, only about one-third of subjects were found to remit from their social phobia (Yonkers, Dyck, & Keller, 2001). Based on results of a five-year longitudinal study, Wittchen, Nelson, and Lachner (1998) concluded that regardless of some fluctuations in severity (particularly during adolescence) few individuals with social phobia experience spontaneous and stable remission.

The negative impact of social phobia is further heightened by its association with numerous comorbid conditions such as major depression, other anxiety disorders, and substance abuse disorders (see Wittchen & Fehm, 2001). Comorbidity in individuals with social phobia is very common, with estimates ranging between 50 percent and 80 percent of individuals having at least one comorbid condition (Wittchen & Fehm, 2001). For example, research has shown that between 78 percent and 81 percent of individuals with social phobia have at least one comorbid diagnosis (respectively, Lampe et al., 2003; Magee et al., 1996). Further, the large majority of evidence suggests that social phobia precedes the onset of other conditions. Social phobia has been demonstrated to herald the onset of major depression, generalized anxiety disorder, and alcohol abuse (Lampe et al., 2003). Similarly, data analyses from the National Comorbidity Survey indicated that social phobia was the primary diagnosis in approximately two-thirds of cases (as cited in Wittchen & Fehm, 2001). In addition, data suggests that social phobia may also be associated with increased incidence of medical difficulties, such as peptic ulcer disease and increased utilization of outpatient medical services (Davidson, Hughes, George, & Blazer, 1993).

Given that social phobia is typically chronic and is associated with the development of comorbid conditions, researchers have begun to examine predictors of course. However, this body of research is limited to a small number of studies that have often provided contradictory evidence. Further, the individual studies have typically studied unique potential predictors, thereby prohibiting comparisons across studies. However, a few directions can be taken from the existing literature. Some research has suggested that age of onset, comorbid disorders, and global functioning may influence the course of social phobia (DeWit et al., 1999; Yonkers et al., 2001). However, other research has appeared to contradict these findings. Review of the literature suggests that some of the apparent inconsistencies may be explained by subtle differences in the definition of the variables. For example, Reich et al. (1994) reported that age of onset did not significantly predict the course of social phobia over a period of 65 weeks. However, when focusing on onset prior to age 7 compared to after age 13, DeWit et al. (1999) found onset prior to age 7 resulted in a particularly chronic course of the disorder. Similarly, Reich et al. (1994) failed to find a relationship between baseline global functioning and course. However, when conducting analyses including gender as a variable, Yonkers et al. (2001) found that women with poor baseline functioning were least likely to experience a remission.

The impact of comorbid conditions on the course of social phobia still remains unclear. Yonkers et al. (2001) found that patients with social phobia who were not in remission at 6 months were more likely to have agoraphobia than patients in remission, suggesting that comorbidity is related to increased chronicity. However, Reich et al. (1994) did not find relationships between course of social phobia and lifetime history of anxiety disorders or cross-sectional comorbidity of anxiety or depressive disorders. Interestingly, one study examining the impact of comorbid personality disorders suggested that avoidant personality disorder is unique in predicting the course of social phobia. Specifically, the presence of avoidant personality disorder predicted 41 percent lower likelihood of remission from social phobia after five years (Massion et al., 2002). Other research suggests that the presence of past suicide attempts in women (Yonkers et al., 2001) and the presence of lifetime or current alcohol abuse or dependence (Massion et al., 2002) may be predictive of lower rates of social phobia remission. Finally, using survival analyses, DeWit et al. (1999) found results suggesting that distal childhood circumstances (e.g., number of siblings, size of childhood town), disorder attributes (e.g., number of symptoms), and physical and mental health status (e.g., chronic health problems or comorbid major depression prior to onset) were significant predictors of recovery.

ASSESSMENT AND DIAGNOSIS

The accurate assessment and diagnosis of social phobia relies on the selection of a comprehensive assessment battery. Assessment often begins with use of a structured or semistructured diagnostic interview to obtain information about the patient's symptoms and formulate diagnostic impressions (McNeil, Ries, & Turk, 1995). Supplementary assessment methods such as clinician-administered scales, self-report questionnaires, and behavioral assessment tests, are also frequently employed. These measures allow the clinician to assess the severity of symptoms and associated impairment, while also developing an understanding of the nature of the problems (e.g., identifying specific feared social situations, the breadth of concerns, and severity of symptoms). Thorough assessment enables clinicians to accurately diagnose patients and plan appropriate intervention. A brief overview of selected assessment measures for understanding social phobia is provided in the following section.

Diagnostic Assessment

Many diagnostic instruments are available (e.g., the Structured Clinical Interview for *DSM-IV;* SCID-I/P; First, Spitzer, Gibbon, & Williams, 1996). However, the majority of such measures do not target anxiety disorders or social anxiety disorder. This section highlights measures that are designed for the assessment of anxiety and social anxiety specifically.

Anxiety Disorders Interview Schedule for DSM-IV: *Lifetime Version (ADIS-IV-L)*

The Anxiety Disorders Interview Schedule for *DSM-IV:* Lifetime Version (ADIS-IV-L; Di Nardo, Brown, & Barlow, 1994) is a semistructured diagnostic interview designed to provide thorough assessment of anxiety disorders and other Axis I conditions (e.g., mood, somatoform, and substance use disorders; Brown, Di Nardo, Lehman, & Campbell, 2001). Strengths of the ADIS-IV-L include the following: It focuses on anxiety disorders, it provides both cross-sectional and longitudinal perspectives, and it allows the clinician to develop both continuous severity ratings and categorical diagnoses. In addition, the ADIS-IV-L has been shown to have strong psychometric properties and is widely used in anxiety disorders treatment and research. In a large study of the reliability of ADIS-IV-L diagnoses, Brown, Di Nardo, et al. (2001) found good to excellent interrater reliability for most diagnoses. With respect to social phobia, the interrater reliability for dimensional ratings of fear of social situations, avoidance of social situations, and overall clinical severity, were strong ($r = .86, .86, \& .80$, respectively). In addition, diagnostic reliability for the presence or absence of social phobia was strong for both current and lifetime diagnoses (kappa = .77 & .70, respectively).

Social Phobia Diagnostic Questionnaire (SPDQ)

A promising new instrument is the SPDQ (Newman, Kachin, Zuellig, Constantino, & Cashman-McGrath, 2003), a self-report measure screening for the diagnosis of social phobia based on *DSM-IV* criteria. The SPDQ was modeled after the social anxiety section in the ADIS-IV (Newman et al., 2003) and contains 25 items assessing the presence or absence of social fears (7 items) and levels of fear and avoidance (18 items). Preliminary analyses using an undergraduate sample revealed strong psychometric properties for the SPDQ, with the questionnaire demonstrating high specificity (85 percent) and sensitivity (82 percent) and a moderate level of agreement with the ADIS-IV (Kappa = .66; Newman et al., 2003). Additionally, the measure contained high internal consistency (alpha = .92) and split-half reliability ($r = .89$), as well as retest reliability (two-week interval; Kappa = .63; Newman et al., 2003). Finally, the authors also reported evidence suggesting that the SPDQ has good convergent and discriminant validity. The measure has yet to be evaluated with a clinical sample of individuals with social phobia but is promising for use in the identification of social phobia according to the *DSM-IV.*

Clinician Administered Measures

Liebowitz Social Anxiety Scale (LSAS)

The LSAS (Liebowitz, 1987) is a clinician-rated measure of an individual's level of fear and avoidance in social interaction and performance situations (11 and 13 items, respectively). Respondents verbally rate their anxiety and avoidance during the past week on a Likert-type scale from 0 to 3, with higher scores indicative of greater severity. The clinician can then modify scores based on clinical judgment. Heimberg et al. (1999) reported strong support for the psychometric properties of the LSAS using a sample of 382 individuals with social phobia. Internal consistency was strong for both the subscales (alphas = .81–.92) and total score (alpha = .96). Further, the LSAS total score was moderately to strongly correlated with other measures of social anxiety ($r = .52–.73$), and more modestly correlated with measures of general anxiety and depression (Heimberg et al., 1999). Finally, recent efforts have been devoted to examining the utility of the LSAS as a self-report measure (LSAS-SR; see Baker, Heinrichs, Kim, & Hofmann, 2002; Fresco et al., 2001).

Findings suggest that the psychometric properties of the LSAS are very similar when administered by a clinician or as a self-report questionnaire with clear instructions.

Self-Report Symptom Measures

Self-report measures enable clinicians to get a sense of the client's thoughts, behaviors, and physiological reactions to the feared social situations. Representative measures that have good psychometric properties, are widely used, and are readily available are reviewed in the following sections. For a more comprehensive list of social anxiety measures along with detailed descriptions see Orsillo (2001).

Social Avoidance and Distress (SADS) and Fear of Negative Evaluation (FNE) Scales

The SADS and FNE are companion scales developed by Watson and Friend (1969) to measure distress and avoidance in social situations (e.g., "I try to avoid situations which force me to be very sociable") and anxiety related to the anticipation of negative cognitive appraisals from others (e.g., "I am often afraid that I may look ridiculous or make a fool of myself"), respectively. The SADS contains 28 items and the FNE contains 30 items in which respondents report whether each statement describes them, using a true-false format. The SADS and FNE have shown sufficient retest reliability over a one-month interval in a student sample ($r = .78$ and $.68$, respectively, Watson & Friend, 1969) and strong internal consistency in both student (alphas = $.94-.96$; Watson & Friend, 1969) and clinical samples (alpha = $.94$; Oei, Kenna, & Evans, 1991). In addition, analyses examining the validity of the FNE and SADS have shown that they are significantly correlated with measures of anxiety and social-evaluative anxiety but less strongly related to achievement anxiety (Watson & Friend, 1969). Finally, there is mixed evidence regarding the ability of the SADS and FNE to discriminate between social phobia and other anxiety disorders (Oei et al., 1991; Turner, McCanna, & Beidel, 1987).

Brief Fear of Negative Evaluation (BFNE) Scale

The BFNE (Leary, 1983) is an abbreviated version of the FNE scale (Watson & Friend, 1969), created to provide a more concise measure of an individual's fear of negative appraisals from others. In addition, the sensitivity of the measure was increased by changing the item response format from true-false (FNE) to a 5-point Likert-type rating (BFNE). Eight items are scored as rated and five items are reverse scored. The 12-item BFNE is highly correlated with the original 30-item FNE ($r = .96$) and has been shown to have good retest reliability over four weeks ($r = .75$) in a student sample (Leary, 1983). In addition, the BFNE has been shown to be significantly correlated with other measures of social anxiety in both nonclinical and clinical samples (Leary, 1983; Weeks et al., in press). Further, in individuals with social phobia, the BFNE was found to be significantly more strongly correlated with another measure of social anxiety than a measure of depressive symptoms (Weeks et al., in press). In addition, Weeks et al. (in press) also found the BFNE to be sensitive to treatment-induced changes from cognitive-behavioral group therapy. Finally, of note, findings in individuals with social phobia suggest that the BFNE can be further shortened to only the eight non-reverse-scored items and yield even stronger psychometric properties (Weeks et al., in press).

Social Interaction Anxiety Scale (SIAS) and Social Phobia Scale (SPS)

The SIAS and SPS, created by Mattick and Clarke (1998), are self-report measures specifically designed to assess two features of social anxiety. The SIAS measures the degree to which situations involving social interaction are distressing, such as the respondent's perceived inability to converse with other people (e.g., "I have difficulty talking with other people") and the respondent's anxious feelings about being in social interaction situations (e.g., "I feel I'll say something embarrassing when talking"). The SPS assesses the extent to which the respondent is distressed by performance situations or situations in which the respondent would be observed and scrutinized. The SPS taps both the respondents' concerns that other people will notice their anxious behaviors (e.g., "I worry I'll lose control of myself in front of other people") and discomfort in anticipation of being faced with certain observed/performance situations (e.g., "I would find it difficult to drink something if in a group of people"). Both measures contain 20 items in which respondents rate how characteristic each statement is of them on a Likert-type scale from 0 to 4 (Mattick & Clarke, 1998). Scores are summed to create total scores in which higher scores represent increased severity.

Both scales have strong internal consistency in individuals with social phobia (alpha = $.89$ for SPS and $.93$ for SIAS), other clinical groups (e.g., agoraphobia and simple phobia), and in nonclinical samples (Mattick & Clarke, 1998). Further, the retest reliability of these measures over 4 to 12 weeks is strong ($r = .91-.93$ for SPS and $.92$ for SIAS). In addition to their strong reliability, the validity of the scales is supported by results showing that the scales can differentiate individuals with social phobia from other clinical and nonclinical groups, and findings that both measures are significantly correlated with other measures of social anxiety (i.e., r = .54–.69 for SPS and .66–.74 for SIAS). Finally, the SIAS and SPS are sensitive to treatment changes (Mattick & Clarke, 1998).

Other Assessment Methods

Behavioral Assessment Tests (BATs)

In addition to clinician-administered and self-report measures of social anxiety it can be extremely helpful to utilize BATs. Most simply, BATs are social situations that are role-played in the laboratory or therapy setting (e.g., conversing with strangers or delivering an impromptu speech; McNeil et al., 1995; Orsillo & Hammond, 2001). BATs are powerful in that they are direct assessment techniques that enable clinicians to observe clients' overt behaviors or reactions to anxiety-provoking social situations. Clinicians are provided a unique opportunity to observe the client in action, and can use BATs to assess levels of anxiety over time, social skills, and behavioral reactions such as avoidance (McNeil et al., 1995; Orsillo & Hammond, 2001). In addition, clients can be asked to report their automatic thoughts and physical symptoms throughout the BATs (McNeil et al., 1995).

IMPACT ON ENVIRONMENT

The majority of research examining the impact of social phobia on the lives of individuals affected by it has focused on two areas: quality of life and disability. *Quality of life* refers to the degree of perceived life satisfaction and enjoyment of life whereas *disability* refers to the level of functional impairment or difficulties attributed to a disorder (Hambrick, Turk, Heimberg, Schneier, & Liebowitz, 2003; Wittchen & Fehm, 2001). For the current discussion, the impact of social anxiety on both quality of life and disability will be discussed.

Social phobia is often quite debilitating and negatively impacts many areas of the individuals' lives. Overall findings suggest that quality of life and impairment in functioning tends to be more severe for individuals experiencing generalized social anxiety and/or individuals that have comorbid conditions (Stein & Kean, 2000; Wittchen, Fuetsch, Sonntag, Muller, & Liebowitz, 1999). Research examining the impact of social anxiety on interpersonal functioning, marital functioning, occupational functioning, and educational attainment will be briefly reviewed. However, it is noteworthy that the majority of existing research has examined the relationship between social anxiety and general functioning, with far less research studying the impact of the disorder on specific areas of functioning.

Individuals with social phobia frequently report difficulties in their relationships with others. Specifically, individuals with social phobia endorse impaired interpersonal functioning and decreased satisfaction in areas involving dating and romantic relationships, friendships, family relationships, and other social relationships, as a result of their symptoms (Davila & Beck, 2002; Schneier et al., 1994; Walker & Kjernisted, 2000; Wittchen et al., 1999). With respect to friendships, Schneier et al. (1994) suggested that although individuals with social anxiety maintained close friendships with a few people, they were dissatisfied with their number of friends and desired to have more. Similarly, Davidson, Hughes, et al. (1993) found that individuals with social phobia were less likely than controls to report unimpaired subjective social support and unimpaired instrumental support. Further, they found that higher levels of social anxiety were significantly related to the anxious interpersonal styles of avoidance of expressing strong emotions, desire to avoid and actual avoidance of conflict, lack of assertiveness, fear of rejection, and overreliance on significant others. Finally, Eng, Coles, Heimberg, and Safren (2005) found that individuals with social phobia reported decreased satisfaction with their social functioning and interpersonal relationships.

Other research has demonstrated that social anxiety is associated with decreased satisfaction with, and increased impairment in, marital relationships specifically (Schneier et al., 1994; Stein & Kean, 2000; Walker & Kjernisted, 2000; Wittchen et al., 1999). Individuals with social phobia are less likely to be married than individuals without social phobia (Magee et al., 1996; Schneier et al., 1992; Walker & Kjernisted, 2000). For example, Wittchen and Beloch (1996) and Davidson, Hughes, et al. (1993) found that only 37 percent and 47 percent of individuals with social phobia were married compared to 57 percent and 59 percent of controls, respectively. In addition, Davidson, Hughes, et al. (1993) found that the presence of comorbid conditions and social phobia further reduced the likelihood of being married (50 percent of participants with one comorbid diagnosis were married, and 43 percent of participants with two or more comorbid diagnoses were married). Consistent with findings from clinical samples, correlational analyses in a community sample showed that higher levels of social anxiety corresponded to lower levels of couple marital adjustment, poorer satisfaction with the relationship in general, the extent to which the couple shares activities, and the degree to which the couple agreed on important relationship issues (Filsinger & Wilson, 1983). Finally, Hart, Turk, Heimberg, and Liebowitz (1999) found that in comparison to individuals with social phobia who were married, individuals with social phobia who were single reported significantly more fear and avoidance of both performance and social interaction situations and were more likely to meet criteria for a comorbid mood disorder and avoidant personality disorder.

In addition to the interpersonal difficulties, social phobia negatively impacts occupational functioning, as well (Schneier, 1994; Wittchen et al., 1999). For instance, individuals with social phobia are more likely than nonanxious individuals to be unemployed or underemployed (Bruch, Fallon, & Heimberg, 2003; Walker & Kjernisted, 2000; Wittchen et al., 1999). Further, previous findings suggest that social anxiety may be the cause of this occupational impairment. Wittchen et al. (1999) found that individuals with social anxiety who were unemployed frequently attributed their lack of employment to their social anxiety. In addition, the impact of social phobia is still evident even when employment is secured. Specifically, research has shown that individuals with social anxiety who were employed reported performing below their ability and having decreased work productivity in comparison to control samples (Schneier et al., 1994; Wittchen et al., 1999). Also, Bruch et al. (2003) found that socially anxious individuals reported that they perceived their supervisors would evaluate their level of dependability as being lower compared to a nonanxious sample. Social anxiety may impair individuals from advancing in their career, as well (Bruch et al., 2003; Wittchen et al., 1999).

Furthermore, social anxiety has a negative impact on educational attainment and academic functioning. For example, Wittchen and Beloch (1996) found that more than half of their sample of 65 individuals with social phobia retrospectively reported that their social anxiety had caused impairment in their education and career development. Further, Davidson, Hughes, et al. (1993) found that social phobia was associated with numerous school difficulties. For example, in comparison to individuals without social phobia those with the disorder reported an increased likelihood of having repeated a grade (38.6 percent versus 25.4 percent) and were more likely to report that their grades had been generally low (14.5 percent versus 8.1 percent). Also, Monroe, Borzi, and Burrell (1992) found that students high in communication apprehension, an internal cognitive state generated by fear of communicating with others, are more likely to drop out of high school prematurely and that 25 percent of students leaving school early cited communication apprehension as the primary reason for leaving school. Similarly, in an anxiety disorder sample, VanAmeringen, Mancini, and Farvolden (2003) found that 61.2 percent of patients who had left school prematurely met criteria for generalized social phobia, compared to 44.7 percent of the patients who had completed school.

TREATMENT IMPLICATIONS

The most empirically supported therapeutic approach for the treatment of social phobia available today is cognitive behavioral therapy (CBT). CBT is grounded in the belief that individuals' patterns of thinking and behaving serve to maintain their anxiety and is focused on decreasing avoidance of social situations through exposure to feared situations and modifying maladaptive self-talk with the use of cognitive restructuring (see Heimberg, 2002). In addition, CBT often includes social skills training and/or relaxation training. Although it remains debatable whether combining interventions (e.g., exposure and cognitive restructuring versus exposure only) improves outcomes beyond each intervention alone (Turk, Coles, & Heimberg, 2002), it is clear that CBT is efficacious for treating social phobia (Otto & Safren, 2001).

The efficacy of CBT is well documented for social phobia (for a review, see Heimberg, 2002). Controlled studies have demonstrated the superiority of CBT incorporating exposure and cognitive restructuring compared to waiting-list controls (e.g., DiGiuseppe, McGowan, Sutton-Simon, & Gardner, 1990; Hope, Heimberg, & Bruch, 1995), an active psychotherapy control (education-support control; Heimberg et al., 1998), pill placebo alone (Heimberg et al., 1998), and pill placebo plus self-exposure (Clark et al., 2003). Heimberg et al. (1998) also documented that group CBT lead to greater changes than both psychotherapy and medicine controls on the proportion of patients classified as responders, clinician ratings of severity and social avoidance, self-reported levels of social avoidance, and ratings of satisfaction with one's performance in a role-played social situation.

In addition to controlled research supporting the *efficacy* of CBT for social phobia, there is recent support for the *effectiveness* of this approach. A recent study of 217 patients with a primary diagnosis of social phobia supported the effectiveness of CBT (exposure plus cognitive restructuring) in community treatment clinics (Lincoln et al., 2003). This study was unique in that patients were not preselected in any way (based on comorbidity, age, etc.), services were provided in community treatment clinics, subjects were not required to agree to randomization, and services were provided by therapists of varying experience. Results after the completion of therapy showed that reliable change was found for 56 percent of patients on social anxiety scores, 41 percent of patients on related fears and avoidance, 48 percent of patients on general impairment, and 41 percent of patients on depression.

Additionally, studies have also documented the maintenance of gains from CBT across follow-up periods between six months (e.g., Heimberg et al., 1990) through approximately five years (Heimberg, Salzman, Holt, & Blendell,

1993). For example, patients with social phobia who have completed group CBT are more likely than patients completing an education-support control to maintain their gains over a six-month follow-up (Heimberg et al., 1990). Also, studying the maintenance of gains over 4.5 to 6.25 years, Heimberg et al. (1993) found that 89 percent of patients who had completed group CBT were assigned severity ratings below the clinical threshold at the long-term follow-up assessment. Further, a recent comparison of group CBT to the medication phenelzine (Liebowitz et al., 1999) showed that over a six-month, treatment-free, follow-up period, patients previously treated with the group therapy were less likely to relapse than patients who had been treated with phenelzine. Finally, numerous meta-analyses examining the efficacy of CBT in individuals with social phobia have supported the long-term maintenance of gains (see Heimberg, 2002). Results of one meta-analysis (Taylor, 1996) suggested that patients who have previously completed CBT may even experience additional improvements across treatment-free follow-ups.

Numerous pharmacological approaches have also been documented to be efficacious for the acute treatment of social phobia (Blanco, Anita, & Liebowitz, 2002). In support, a recent meta-analysis of published placebo-controlled treatment trials for social phobia revealed that the majority of medications tested had moderate to large effect sizes, and that most were significantly better than placebo (Blanco et al., 2003). Medications for treatment of social phobia are generally from four classes: selective serotonin reuptake inhibitors (SSRIs), irreversible nonselective monoamine oxidase inhibitors (MAOIs), reversible MAOIs (RIMAs), and benzodiazepines. Each class will be reviewed, with emphasis placed on the SSRIs given their use as first-line pharmacological treatment (Ameringen & Mancini, 2001; Blanco et al., 2002; Walker & Kjernisted, 2000).

There is a great deal of support for the use of SSRIs as first-line treatment of social phobia (Walker & Kjernisted, 2000). A large advantage of the SSRIs is their low incidence of significant side effects and their high tolerability. Controlled trials have been published using sertraline, fluvoxamine, and paroxetine in the treatment of social phobia. Two controlled trials have demonstrated response rates at or greater than 50 percent for patients treated with sertraline over 10 to 20 weeks, compared to placebo response rates of 9 percent to 29 percent (Katzelnick et al., 1995; VanAmeringen et al., 2001). Similar results have been found in two controlled trials of fluvoxamine, with response rates between 43 percent and 46 percent for fluvoxamine and between 7 percent and 23 percent for placebo (see Blanco et al., 2002). Additionally, two controlled trials of paroxetine showed strong support for its efficacy in treating social phobia, documenting response rates of 55 percent and 66 percent for the paroxetine groups, compared to 24 percent and 32 percent for the placebo groups (Walker & Kjernisted, 2000). Finally, from their meta-analysis of placebo-controlled trials, Blanco et al. (2003) advocated that SSRIs be utilized as first-line treatment for social phobia given their efficacy and high safety and tolerability.

Among the MAOIs, phenelzine has been most extensively evaluated. Blanco et al. (2002) reviewed four placebo-controlled studies of phenelzine, reporting responder rates between 30 percent and 69 percent and that two of the trials documented phenelzine's superiority compared to placebo. Also, based on a meta-analysis of placebo-controlled trials, Blanco et al. (2003) reported that phenelzine was among the medications with the largest effect sizes. However, despite its documented efficacy, phenelzine is not typically utilized as a first-line treatment due to the need for dietary restrictions associated with the drug and common side effects (e.g., orthostatic hypotension).

Reversible MAOIs (RIMAs), such as moclobemide and brofaromine, were developed in an attempt to maintain the efficacy of MAOIs while reducing side effects and improving safety (Blanco et al., 2002). The efficacy of moclobemide has produced mixed results (Walker & Kjernisted, 2000). Three published placebo-controlled trials have assessed the efficacy of brofaromine, a RIMA that also alters serotonin reuptake (Walker & Kjernisted, 2000). Response rates ranged from 50 percent to 80 percent of brofaromine patients, compared to between 14 percent and 23 percent of placebo patients (Blanco et al., 2002). However, brofaromine is not commercially available in the United States.

Three benzodiazepines, alprazolam, bromazepam, and clonazepam, have been the focus of double-blind trials for the treatment of social phobia (Blanco et al., 2002). In the only controlled trial of alprazolam (Gelernter et al., 1991), 38 percent of patients were responders at week 12 but experienced significantly less improvement on work and social disability than phenelzine patients. In the only controlled trial of bromazepam, Versiani, Nardi, Figueria, Mendlowicz, and Marques (1997) found an 84 percent response rate in the bromazepam group, compared to a 20 percent response rate in the placebo group at week 12. Similar results were found in a 10-week controlled trial of clonazepam (Davidson, Potts, et al., 1993) that had a 78 percent response rate in the clonazepam group, compared to a 20 percent response rate in the placebo group. Although there is data to suggest that benzodiazepines can reduce social anxiety, the number of controlled trials is limited, there appears to be variability in the efficacy of these drugs, and their use raises concerns regarding potential dependence and withdrawal (Blanco et al., 2003).

SUMMARY AND CONCLUSIONS

In conclusion, social phobia is a chronic disorder that typically begins early in life and results in substantial impairment. In addition, social phobia is common worldwide. Encouragingly, CBT and pharmacotherapy can reduce symptoms. However, these interventions typically reduce symptoms, but do not eliminate them. Further, the efficacy of medication beyond acute treatment trials remains to be seen. Conceptualizations of social phobia have improved dramatically over the past 20 years, however, much work remains. Three important areas for future efforts are: (1) developing theoretical models that comprehensively address both the etiology and maintenance of social phobia, (2) identifying reliable predictors of the course of social phobia, and (3) identifying variables that are useful in matching individual patients to the specific treatment that would produce the best outcomes for them.

REFERENCES

American Psychiatric Association. (1994). *Diagnostic and statistical manual of mental disorders* (4th ed.). Washington, DC: Author.

Ameringen, M., & Mancini, C. (2001). Pharmacotherapy of social anxiety disorder at the turn of the millennium. *Psychiatric Clinics of North America, 24*, 783–803.

Amir, N., Foa, E. B., & Coles, M. E. (1998). Negative interpretation bias in social phobia. *Behaviour Research and Therapy, 36*, 945–957.

Asmundson, G. J. G., & Stein, M. B. (1994). Selective attention for social threat in patients with generalized social phobia: Evaluation using a dot-probe paradigm. *Journal of Anxiety Disorders, 8*, 107–117.

Baker, S. L., Heinrichs, N., Kim, H., & Hofmann, S. G. (2002). The Liebowitz Social Anxiety scale as a self-report instrument: A preliminary psychometric analysis. *Behaviour Research and Therapy, 40*, 701–715.

Beidel, D. C., Turner, S. M., & Morris, T. L. (1999). Psychopathology of childhood social phobia. *American Academy of Child and Adolescent Psychiatry, 38*, 643–650.

Biederman, J., Hershfeld-Becker, D. R., Rosenbaum, J. F., Herot, C., Friedman, D., Snidman, N., et al. (2001). Further evidence of association between behavioral inhibition and social anxiety in children. *American Journal of Psychiatry, 158*, 1673–1679.

Blanco, C., Antia, S. X., & Liebowitz, M. R. (2002). Pharmacotherapy of social anxiety disorder. *Biological Psychiatry, 51*, 109–120.

Blanco, C., Schneier, F. R., Schmidt, A., Blanco-Jerez, C., Marshall, R. D., Sanchez-Lacay, A., et al. (2003). Pharmacological treatment of social anxiety disorder: A meta-analysis. *Depression and Anxiety, 18*, 29–40.

Brown, T. A., Campbell, L. A., Lehman, C. L., Grisham, J. R., & Mancill, R. B. (2001). Current and lifetime comorbidity of the *DSM-IV* anxiety and mood disorders in a large clinical sample. *Journal of Abnormal Psychology, 110*, 585–599.

Brown, T. A., Di Nardo, P. A., Lehman, C. L., & Campbell, L. A. (2001). Reliability of *DSM-IV* anxiety and mood disorders: Implications for the classification of emotional disorders. *Journal of Abnormal Psychology, 110*, 49–58.

Bruch, M. A., Fallon, M., & Heimberg, R. G. (2003). Social phobia and difficulties in occupational adjustment. *Journal of Consulting Psychology, 50*, 109–117.

Bruch, M. A., Gorsky, J. M., Collins, T. M., & Berger, P. A. (1989). Shyness and sociability reexamined: A multicomponent analysis. *Journal of Personality and Social Psychology, 57*, 904–915.

Chatterjee, S., Sunitha, T. A., Velayudhan, A., & Khanna, S. (1997). An investigation into the psychobiology of social phobia: Personality domains and serotonergic function. *Acta Psychiatrica Scandinavica, 95*, 544–550.

Chavira, D. A., Stein, M. B., & Malcarnem V. L. (2002). Scrutinizing the relationship between shyness and social phobia. *Journal of Anxiety Disorders, 16*, 585–598.

Clark, D. M., Ehlers, A., McManus, F., Hackmann, A., Fennell, M., Campbell, H., et al. (2003). Cognitive therapy versus fluoxetine in generalized social phobia: A randomized placebo-controlled trial. *Journal of Consulting & Clinical Psychology, 71*, 1058–1067.

Clark, D. M., & Wells, A. (1995). A cognitive model of social phobia. In R. G. Heimberg, M. R. Liebowitz, D. A. Hope, & F. R. Schneier (Eds.), *Social phobia: Diagnosis, assessment and treatment* (pp. 69–93). New York: Guilford Press.

Cloitre, M., & Shear, M. K., (1995). Psychodynamic perspectives. In M. B. Stein (Ed.), *Social phobia: Clinical and research perspectives* (pp. 163–188). Washington, DC: American Psychiatric Press.

Coles, M. E., Turk, C. L., Heimberg, R. G., & Fresco, D. M. (2001). Effects of varying levels of anxiety within social situations: Relationship to memory perspective and attributions in social phobia. *Behaviour Research and Therapy, 39*, 651–665.

Cox, B. J., & Swinson, R. P. (1995). Assessment and measurement. In M. B. Stein (Ed.), *Social phobia: Clinical and research perspectives* (pp. 261–292). Washington, DC: American Psychiatric Press.

Davidson, J. R., Hughes, D. L., George, L. K., & Blazer, D. G. (1993). The epidemiology of social phobia: Findings from the Duke Epidemiological Catchment Area Study. *Psychological Medicine, 23*, 709–718.

Davidson, J. R. T., Potts, N., Richichi, E., Krishnan, R., Ford, S. M., Smith, R., et al. (1993). Treatment of social phobia with clonazepam and placebo. *Journal of Clinical Psychopharmacology, 13,* 423–428.

Davila, J., & Beck, J. G. (2002). Is social anxiety associated with impairment in close relationships? A preliminary investigation. *Behavior Therapy, 33,* 427–446.

DeWit, D. J., Ogborne, A., Offord, D. R., & MacDonald, K. (1999). Antecedents of the risk of recovery from *DSM-III-R* social phobia. *Psychological Medicine, 29,* 569–582.

DiGiuseppe, R., McGowan, L., Sutton-Simon, K., & Gardner, F. (1990). A comparative outcome study of four cognitive therapies in the treatment of social anxiety. *Journal of Rational-Emotive and Cognitive-Behavior Therapy, 8,* 129–146.

Di Nardo, P. A., Brown, T. A., & Barlow, D. H. (1994). *Anxiety Disorders Interview Schedule for DSM-IV: Lifetime version (ADIS-IV-L).* San Antonio, TX: Psychological Corp.

Eng, W. E., Coles, M. E., Heimberg, R. G., & Safren, S. A. (2005). Domains of life satisfaction in social anxiety disorder: Relation to symptoms and response to cognitive-behavioral therapy. *Journal of Anxiety Disorders, 19,* 143–156..

Fahlen, T. (1995). Personality traits in social phobia: I. Comparisons with healthy controls. *Journal of Clinical Psychiatry, 56,* 560–568.

Filsinger, E. E., & Wilson, M. R. (1983). Social anxiety and marital adjustment. *Family Relations, 32,* 513–519.

First, M. B., Spitzer, R. L., Gibbon, M., & Williams, J. (1996). *Structured Clinical Interview for DSM-IV Axis I Disorders-Patient Edition (SCID-I/P, Version 2.0).* New York: Biometrics Research Department, New York State Psychiatric Institute.

Foa, E. B., Franklin, M. E., Perry, K. J., & Herbert, J. D. (1996). Cognitive biases in generalized social phobia. *Journal of Abnormal Psychology, 105,* 433–439.

Fresco, D. M., Coles, M. E., Heimberg, R. G., Liebowitz, M. R., Hami, S., Stein, M. B., et al. (2001). The Liebowitz Social Anxiety Scale: A comparison of the psychometric properties of self-report and clinician-administered formats. *Psychological Medicine, 31,* 1025–1035.

Gelernter, C. S., Uhde, T. W., Cimbolic, P., Arnkoff, D. B., Vittone, B. J., Tancer, M. E., et al. (1991). Cognitive behavioral and pharmacological treatment of social phobia: A controlled study. *Archives of General Psychiatry, 48,* 938–945.

Glass, C. R., Merluzzi, T. V., Biever, J. L., & Larsen, K. H. (1982). Cognitive assessment of social anxiety: Development and validation of a self-statement questionnaire. *Cognitive Therapy and Research, 6,* 37–55.

Hambrick, J. P., Turk, C. L., Heimberg, R. G., Schneier, F. R., & Liebowitz, M. R. (2003). The experience of disability and quality of life in social anxiety disorder. *Depression and Anxiety, 18,* 46–50.

Hart, T. A., Turk, C. L., Heimberg, R. G., & Liebowitz, M. R. (1999). Relation of marital status to social phobia severity. *Depression and Anxiety, 10,* 28–32.

Hayward, C., Killen, J. D., Kraemer, H. C., & Taylor, C. B. (1998). Linking self-reported childhood behavioral inhibition to adolescent social phobia. *Journal of the American Academy of Child and Adolescent Psychiatry, 37,* 1308–1316.

Heckelman, L. R., & Schneier, F. R. (1995). Diagnostic issues. In R. G. Heimberg, M. R. Liebowitz, D. A. Hope, & F. R. Schneier (Eds.), *Social phobia: Diagnosis, assessment, and treatment* (pp. 3–20). New York: Guilford Press.

Heimberg, R. G. (2002). Cognitive-behavioral therapy for social anxiety disorder: Current status and future directions. *Biological Psychiatry, 51,* 101–108.

Heimberg, R. G., Dodge, C. S., Hope, D. A., Kennedy, C. R., Zollo, L. J., & Becker, R. E. (1990). Cognitive-behavioral group treatment of social phobia: Comparison to a credible placebo control. *Cognitive Therapy and Research, 14,* 1–23.

Heimberg, R. G., Hope, D. A., Rapee, R. M., & Bruch, M. A. (1988). The validity of the social avoidance and distress scale and the fear of negative evaluation scale with social phobic patients. *Behaviour Research and Therapy, 26,* 407–410.

Heimberg, R. G., Korner, K. J., Juster, H. R., Safren, S. A., Brown, E. J., Schneier, F. R., et al. (1999). Psychometric properties of the Liebowitz Social Anxiety Scale. *Psychological Medicine, 29,* 199–212.

Heimberg, R. G., Liebowitz, M. R., Hope, D. A., Schneier, F. R., Holt, C. S., Welkowitz, L. A., et al. (1998). Cognitive-behavioral group therapy versus phenelzine in social phobia: 12-week outcome. *Archives of General Psychiatry, 55,* 1133–1141.

Heimberg, R. G., Salzman, D. G., Holt, C. S., & Blendell, K. A. (1993). Cognitive-behavioral group treatment for social phobia: Effectiveness at five-year follow-up. *Cognitive Therapy and Research, 17,* 325–339.

Heinrichs, N., & Hofmann, S. G. (2001). Information processing in social phobia: A critical review. *Clinical Psychology Review, 21,* 751–770.

Heiser, N. A., Turner, S. M., & Beidel, D. C. (2003). Shyness: Relationship to social phobia and the other psychiatric disorders. *Behaviour Research and Therapy, 41,* 209–221.

Hofmann, S. G., Moscovitch, D. A., Kim, H., & Taylor, A. N. (in press). Changes in self-perception during treatment of social phobia. *Journal of Consulting and Clinical Psychology.*

Holt, C. S., Heimberg, R. G., Hope, D. A., & Liebowitz, M. R. (1992). Situational domains of social phobia. *Journal of Anxiety Disorders, 6,* 63–77.

Hope, D. A., Heimberg, R. G., & Bruch, M. A. (1995). Dismantling cognitive-behavioral group therapy for social phobia. *Behaviour Research and Therapy, 33,* 637–650.

Hope, D. A., Heimberg, R. G., & Klein, J. F. (1990). Social anxiety and the recall of interpersonal information. *Journal of Cognitive Psychotherapy: An international quarterly, 4,* 185–195.

Hudson, J., & Rapee, R. M. (2000). The origins of social phobia. *Behavior Modification, 24,* 102–129.

Hymel, S., Rubin, K. H., Rowden, L., & LeMare, L. (1990). Children's peer relationships: Longitudinal prediction of internalizing and externalizing problems from middle to late childhood. *Child Development, 61,* 2004–2021.

Jack, M. S., Heimberg, R. G., & Mennin, D. S. (1999). Situational panic attacks: Impact on distress and impairment among patients with social phobia. *Depression and Anxiety, 10,* 112–118.

Kagan, J., & Snidman, N. (1991). Temperamental factors in human development. *American Psychologist, 46,* 856–862.

Katzelnick, D. J., Kobak, K. A., Greist, J. H., Jefferson, J. W., Mantle, J. M., & Serlin, R. C. (1995). Sertraline for social phobia: A double-blind, placebo-controlled crossover study. *American Journal of Psychiatry, 152,* 1368–1371.

Kendler, K. S., Karkowski, L. M., & Prescott, C. A. (1999). Fears and phobias: Reliability and heritability. *Psychological Medicine, 29,* 539–553.

Kessler, R. C., McGonagle, K. A., Zhao, S., Nelson, C. B., Hughes, M., Eshleman, S., et al. (1994). Lifetime and 12-month prevalence of *DSM-III-R* psychiatric disorders in the United States: Results from the National Comorbidity Survey. *Archives of General Psychiatry, 51,* 8–19.

Lampe, L., Slade, T., Issakidis, C., & Andrews, G. (2003). Social phobia in the Australian National Survey of Mental Health and Well-Being (NSMHWB). *Psychological Medicine, 33,* 637–646.

Lang, A. J., & Stein, M. B. (2001). Social phobia: Prevalence and diagnostic threshold. *Journal of Clinical Psychiatry, 62,* 5–10.

Leary, M. R. (1983). A brief version of the fear of negative evaluation scale. *Personality and Social Psychology Bulletin, 9,* 371–375.

Lieb, R., Wittchen, H., Hofler, M., Fuetsch, M., Stein, M. B., & Merikangas, K. R. (2000). Parental psychopathology, parenting styles, and the risk of social phobia in offspring: A prospective-longitudinal community. *Archives of General Psychiatry, 57,* 859–866.

Liebowitz, M. R. (1987). Social phobia. *Modern Problems in Pharmacopsychiatry, 22,* 141–173.

Liebowitz, M. R., Heimberg, R. G., Schneier, F. R., Hope, D. A., Davies, S., Holt, C. S., et al. (1999). Cognitive-behavioral group therapy versus phenelzine in social phobia: Long-term outcome. *Depression and Anxiety, 10,* 89–98.

Lincoln, T. M., Rief, W., Hahlweg, K., Frank, M., vonWitzleben, I., Schroeder, B., et al. (2003). Effectiveness of an empirically supported treatment for social phobia in the field. *Behaviour Research and Therapy, 41,* 1251–1269.

Lucock, M. P., & Salkovskis, P. M. (1988). Cognitive factors in social anxiety and its treatment. *Behaviour Research and Therapy, 26,* 297–302.

Magee, W. J., Eaton, W. W., Wittchen, H., McGonagle, K. A., & Kessler, R. C. (1996). Agoraphobia, simple phobia, and social phobia in the National Comorbidity Survey. *Archives of General Psychiatry, 53,* 159–168.

Mannuzza, S., Schneier, F. R., Chapman, T. F., Liebowitz, M. R., Klein, D. F., & Fyer, A. J. (1995). Generalized social phobia: Reliability and validity. *Archives of General Psychiatry, 52,* 230–237.

Marteinsdottir, I., Furmark, T., Tillfors, M., Fredrikson, M., & Ekselius, L. (2001). Personality traits in social phobia. *European Psychiatry, 16,* 143–150.

Marteinsdottir, I., Tillfors, M., Furmark, T., Andenberg, U. M., & Ekselius, L. (2003). Personality dimensions measured by the Temperament and Character Inventory (TCI) in subjects with social phobia. *Nordic Journal of Psychiatry, 57,* 29–35.

Massion, A. O., Dyck, I. R., Shea, M. T., Phillips, K. A., Warshaw, M. G., & Keller, M. B. (2002). Personality disorders and time to remission in generalized anxiety disorder, social phobia and panic disorder. *Archives of General Psychiatry, 59,* 434–440.

Mattick, R. P., & Clarke, J. C. (1998). Development and validation of measures of social phobia scrutiny fear and social interaction anxiety. *Behaviour Research and Therapy, 36,* 455–470.

McManus, F., Clark, D. M., & Hackmann, A. (2000). Specificity of cognitive biases in social phobia and their role in recovery. *Behavioural and Cognitive Psychotherapy, 28,* 201–209.

McNeil, D. W., Ries, B. J., & Turk, C. L. (1995). Behavioral assessment: Self-report, physiology, and overt behavior. In R. G. Heimberg, M. R., Liebowitz, D. A. Hope, & F. R. Schneier (Eds.), *Social phobia: Diagnosis, assessment, and treatment* (pp. 202–231). New York: Guilford Press.

Mick, M. A., & Telch, M. J. (1998). Social anxiety and history of behavioral inhibition in young adults. *Journal of Anxiety Disorders, 12,* 1–20.

Monroe, C., Borzi, M. G., & Burrell, R. D. (1992). Communication apprehension among high school dropouts. *School Counselor, 39,* 273–280.

Moutier, C. Y., & Stein, M. B. (1999). The history, epidemiology, and differential diagnosis of social anxiety disorder. *Journal of Clinical Psychiatry, 60*(Suppl. 9), 4–8.

Narrow, W. E., Rae, D. S., Robins, L. N., & Regier, D. A. (2002). Revised prevalence estimates of mental disorders in the United States. *Archives of General Psychiatry, 59,* 115–123.

Neal, J., & Edelmann, R. J. (2003). The etiology of social phobia: Toward a developmental profile. *Clinical Psychology Review, 23,* 761–786.

Newman, M. G., Kachin, K. E., Zuellig, A. R., Constantino, M. J., & Cashman-McGrath, L. (2003). The social phobia diagnostic questionnaire: Preliminary validation of a new self-report diagnostic measure of social phobia. *Psychological Medicine, 33,* 623–635.

Oei, T. P., Kenna, D., & Evans, L. (1991). The reliability, validity, and utility of SAD and FNE for anxiety disorder patients. *Personality and Individual Differences, 12,* 111–116.

Ollendick, T. H., & Hirshfeld-Becker, D. R. (2002). The developmental psychopathology of social anxiety disorder. *Biological Psychiatry, 51,* 44–58.

Orsillo, S. M. (2001). Measures for social phobia. In M. M. Antony, S. M. Orsillo, & L. Roemer (Eds.), *Practitioner's guide to empirically based measures of anxiety* (pp. 165–187). New York: Kluwer Academic/Plenum.

Orsillo, S. M., & Hammond, C. (2001). Social phobia: A brief overview and guide to assessment. In M. M. Antony, S. M. Orsillo, & L. Roemer (Eds.), *Practitioner's guide to empirically based measures of anxiety* (pp. 159–164). New York: Kluwer Academic/Plenum.

Otto, M. W., & Safren, S. A. (2001). Mechanisms of action in the treatment of social phobia. In S. G. Hofmann & P. M. DiBartolo (Eds.), *From social anxiety to social phobia: Multiple perspectives* (pp. 391–407). Boston: Allyn & Bacon.

Pelissolo, A., Andre, C., Pujol, H., Yao, S. N., Servant, D., Braconnie, A., et al. (2002). Personality dimensions in social phobics with or without depression. *Acta Psychiatrica Scandinavica, 105,* 94–103.

Prior, M., Smart, D., Sanson, A., & Oberklaid, F. (2000). Does shy-inhibited temperament in childhood lead to anxiety problems in adolescence? *Journal of the American Academy of Child and Adolescent Psychiatry, 39,* 461–468.

Rapee, R. M. (1995). Descriptive psychopathology of social phobia. In R. G. Heimberg, M. R. Liebowitz, D. A. Hope, & F. R. Schneier (Eds.), *Social phobia: Diagnosis, assessment, and treatment* (pp. 41–66). New York: Guilford Press.

Rapee, R. M., & Heimberg, R. G. (1997). A cognitive-behavioral model of anxiety in social phobia. *Behaviour Research and Therapy, 35,* 741–756.

Rapee, R. M., & Lim, L. (1992). Discrepancy between self and observer ratings of performance in social phobics. *Journal of Abnormal Psychology, 101,* 727–731.

Reich, J., Goldenberg, I., Goisman, R., Vasile, R., & Keller, M. (1994). A prospective, follow-along study of the course of social phobia: II. Testing for basic predictors of course. *Journal of Nervous & Mental Disease, 182,* 297–301.

Reich, J., Noyes, R., & Yates, W. (1988). Anxiety symptoms distinguishing social phobia from panic and generalized anxiety disorders. *Journal of Psychopathology and Behavioral Assessment, 10,* 287–299.

Rettew, D. C. (2000). Avoidant personality disorder, generalized social phobia, and shyness: Putting the personality back into personality disorders. *Harvard Review of Psychiatry, 8,* 283–297.

Schneier, F. R., Heckelman, L. R., Garfinkel, R., Campeas, R., Fallon, B. A., Gitow, A., et al. (1994). Functional impairment in social phobia. *Journal of Clinical Psychiatry, 55,* 322–331.

Schneier, F. R., Johnson, J., Hornig, C. D., Liebowitz, M. R., & Weissman, M. M. (1992). Social phobia: Comorbidity and morbidity in an epidemiologic sample. *Archives of General Psychiatry, 49,* 282–288.

Schwartz, C. E., Snidman, N., & Kagan, J. (1999). Adolescent social anxiety as an outcome of inhibited temperament in childhood. *Journal of American Academy of Child and Adolescent Psychiatry, 38,* 1008–1015.

Solyom, L., Ledwidge, B., & Solyom, C. (1986). Delineating social phobia. *British Journal of Psychiatry, 149,* 464–470.

Stein, M. B., Chavira, D. A., & Jang, K. L. (2001). Bringing up bashful baby: Developmental pathways to social phobia. *Psychiatric Clinics of North America, 24,* 661–675.

Stein, M. B., & Deutsch, R. (2003). In search of social phobia subtypes: Similarity of feared social situations. *Depression and Anxiety, 17,* 94–97.

Stein, M. B., & Kean, Y. M. (2000). Disability and quality of life in social phobia: Epidemiologic findings. *American Journal of Psychiatry, 157,* 1606–1613.

Stein, M. B., Torgrud, L. J., & Walker, J. R. (2000). Social phobia symptoms, subtypes, and severity: Findings from a community survey. *Archives of General Psychiatry, 57,* 1046–1052.

Stopa, L., & Clark, D. M. (1993). Cognitive processes in social phobia. *Behaviour Research and Therapy, 31,* 255–267.

Stopa, L., & Clark, D. M. (2000). Social phobia and interpretation of social events. *Behaviour Research and Therapy, 38,* 273–283.

Taylor, S. (1996). Meta-analysis of cognitive-behavioral treatment for social phobia. *Journal of Behavior Therapy and Experimental Psychiatry, 27,* 1–9.

Turk, C. L., Coles, M. E., & Heimberg, R. G. (2002). Psychological treatment of social phobia. In D. J. Stein & E. Hollander (Eds.), *Textbook of anxiety disorders.* Washington, DC: American Psychiatric Press.

Turner, S. M., Beidel, D. C., Borden, J. W., Stanley, M. A., & Jacob, R. G. (1991). Social phobia: Axis I and II correlates. *Journal of Abnormal Psychology, 100,* 102–106.

Turner, S. M., Beidel, D. C., & Larkin, K. T. (1986). Situational determinants of social anxiety in clinic and nonclinic samples: Physiological and cognitive correlates. *Journal of Consulting and Clinical Psychology, 54,* 523–527.

Turner, S. M., Beidel, D. C., & Townsley, R. M. (1990). Social phobia: Relationship to shyness. *Behaviour Research and Therapy, 28,* 497–505.

Turner, S. M., McCanna, M., & Beidel, D. C. (1987). Validity of the social avoidance and distress and fear of negative evaluation scales. *Behaviour Research and Therapy, 25,* 113–115.

VanAmeringen, M. A., Lane, R. M., Walker, J. R., Bowen, R. C., Chokka, P. R., Goldner, E., et al. (2001). Sertraline treatment of generalized social phobia: A 20-week, double-blind, placebo-controlled study. *American Journal of Psychiatry, 158,* 275–281.

VanAmeringen, M., Mancini, C., & Farvolden, P. (2003). The impact of anxiety disorders on educational achievement. *Journal of Anxiety Disorders, 17,* 561–571.

Veljaca, K. A., & Rapee, R. M. (1998). Detection of negative and positive audience behaviours by socially anxious subjects. *Behaviour Research and Therapy, 36,* 311–321.

Versiani, M., Nardi, A. E., Figueria, I., Mendlowicz, M., & Marques, C. (1997). Double-blind placebo controlled trial with bromazepam in social phobia. *Journal Brasileiro de Psiquiatria, 46,* 167–171.

Walker, J. R., & Kjernisted, K. D., (2000). Fear: The impact and treatment of social phobia. *Journal of Psychopharmacology, 14*(2, Suppl. 1), S13–S23.

Watson, D., & Friend, R. (1969). Measurement of social-evaluative anxiety. *Journal of Consulting and Clinical Psychology, 33,* 448–457.

Weeks, J. W., Heimberg, R. G., Fresco, D. M., Hart, T. A., Turk, C. L., Schneier, F. R., et al. (in press). Empirical validation and psychometric evaluation of the Brief Fear of Negative Evaluation Scale in patients with social anxiety disorder. *Psychological Assessment.*

Wells, A., Clark, D. M., & Ahmad, S. (1998). How do I look with my minds eye: Perspective taking in social phobic imagery. *Behaviour Research and Therapy, 36,* 631–634.

Wittchen, H. U., & Beloch, E. (1996). The impact of social phobia on quality of life. *International Clinical Psychopharmacology, 11,* 15–23.

Wittchen, H., & Fehm, L. (2001). Epidemiology, patterns of comorbidity, and associated disabilities of social phobia. *Psychiatric Clinics of North America, 24,* 617–641.

Wittchen, H., Fuetsch, M., Sonntag, H., Muller, H., & Liebowitz, M. (1999). Disability and quality of life in pure and comorbid social phobia: Findings from a controlled study. *European Psychiatry, 14,* 118–131.

Wittchen, H., Nelson, G. B., & Lachner, G. (1998). Prevalence of mental disorders and psychosocial impairments in adolescents and young adults. *Psychological Medicine, 28,* 109–126.

Yonkers, K. A, Dyck, I. R, & Keller, M. B. (2001). An eight-year longitudinal comparison of clinical course and characteristics of social phobia among men and women. *Psychiatric Services, 52,* 637–643.

CHAPTER 10

Specific Phobias

KAREN ROWA, RANDI E. MCCABE, AND MARTIN M. ANTONY

DESCRIPTION OF THE DISORDER AND CLINICAL PICTURE

Specific phobias are characterized by excessive or unreasonable fear that is cued by the presence or anticipation of encountering a particular object or situation (American Psychiatric Association [APA], 2000). Some examples of objects or situations feared by people with specific phobias include animals, heights, blood, injections, enclosed places, and flying. Although phobias are among the most treatable of the anxiety disorders (e.g., Öst, 1989), untreated specific phobias can cause significant levels of impairment in people's lives. For example, individuals may turn down promotions that involve travel (due to fear of flying) or put their health at risk by avoiding necessary medical procedures (for fear of injections or surgery).

According to the text revision of the fourth edition of the *Diagnostic and Statistical Manual of Mental Disorders* (*DSM-IV-TR;* APA, 2000), there are five types of specific phobias, including animal, situational, blood-injection-injury (BII), natural environment, and other types. Examples of common phobias from each type are presented in Table 10.1, and many others have been described (e.g., the Web site www.phobialist.com lists more than 500 types of fears). The decision to distinguish different types of phobias arises from research suggesting that each type has distinct features. For example, phobia types differ with respect to age of onset, physiological response (e.g., fainting, panic attacks), fear of physical sensations, and patterns of comorbidity (e.g., Antony, Brown, & Barlow, 1997a). A recent study on a diagnostically "pure" sample of individuals with specific phobias (i.e., no lifetime anxiety comorbidity and no specific phobias from types other than the identified type) found a later age of onset for situational phobias as compared to animal and BII phobias, a higher rate of unexpected panic attacks for situational as compared to nonsituational phobias, and a greater focus on physical symptoms than on harm or catastrophe in BII phobias (Lipsitz, Barlow, Mannuzza, Hofmann, & Fyer, 2002).

Despite several differences between phobia types, some researcher have argued that distinguishing between phobia types may not be either meaningful or useful (e.g., Antony et al., 1997a). First, some phobias do not fall neatly into a particular type. For example, it is unclear whether a fear of bridges is a situational type or a natural environment type (e.g., heights). Antony and Barlow (2002) also question whether naming the type communicates any more relevant information about the phobia than simply naming the phobia itself. Indeed, providing a diagnosis of "specific phobia, elevators" provides immediate, useful information whereas "specific phobia, situational type" is less informative. Finally, some factor analytic studies suggest that three subtypes may be more accurate as natural environment and situational fears tend to load on the same factor (Fredrikson, Annas, Fischer, & Wik, 1996).

Comorbidity

Comorbidity rates for specific phobias differ, depending on whether a specific phobia is identified as the principal diagnosis (i.e., the problem causing the most distress and interference) or a specific phobia is identified as an additional diagnosis and another disorder is the primary problem. As a primary diagnosis, specific phobias have lower rates of current comorbidity compared to other primary anxiety or mood disorders (e.g., Brown, Campbell, Lehman, Grisham, & Mancill, 2001). However, specific phobias are common co-

TABLE 10.1 Specific Phobia Types in *DSM-IV-TR*

Phobia type	Examples
Animal type	Insects, snakes, spiders, dogs, cats, birds, fish, mice
Natural-environment type	Heights, being near water, storms
Blood-injection-injury type	Seeing blood, receiving an injection, having blood drawn, watching surgery
Situational type	Tunnels, bridges, elevators, flying, driving, enclosed spaces
Other type	Choking, vomiting, loud sounds, costumed characters

morbid diagnoses when another mood or anxiety disorder is the principal diagnosis. Sanderson, Di Nardo, Rapee, and Barlow (1990) found that specific phobias were the most commonly diagnosed additional problem in individuals with anxiety disorders.

When multiple specific phobias exist in the same individual, they tend to cluster within types. Having a specific phobia of one type (e.g., animal type) makes it more likely that an individual will have another specific phobia of the same type (Öst, 1992) rather than another type (e.g., natural environment).

Gender Differences

Research consistently suggests that certain specific phobias (animals, lightning, enclosed spaces, and darkness) are more common in women than in men (Curtis, Magee, Eaton, Wittchen, & Kessler, 1998; Fredrikson et al., 1996; Goisman et al., 1998), whereas gender differences in prevalence are smaller for phobias of heights, flying, injections, and dentists.

There is much speculation about the reason for gender differences in phobias (see Antony & Barlow, 2002). One possibility that has received some support is the idea that men may underreport levels of fear. In a nonclinical study, Pierce and Kirkpatrick (1992) asked women and men first to report whether specific fears are present and then to complete the fear survey again on a later date, under the pretense that actual fear levels could be ascertained by various physiological means. Whereas women's fear ratings did not change over the two testing periods, men's self-reported fear levels significantly increased when they believed their actual levels of fear could be assessed. Gender differences may also arise from women presenting for treatment more readily than men. Although this explanation can help explain gender differences in studies conducted in treatment settings, it does not explain the consistent gender differences seen in epidemiological studies.

Age Differences

Studies suggest that the prevalence of specific phobias varies across the life span. Older adults (mean age of 53 years) rated phobias of storms and heights as more prevalent and rated these stimuli as causing greater fear than did younger adults (mean age of 29; Fredrikson et al., 1996). Older women rated some fears as stronger than did younger women (e.g., deep water, high places, strange dogs; Kirkpatrick, 1984). Studies also suggest that prevalence rates increase across the life span and then decline later in life, especially for men (e.g., Kirkpatrick, 1984).

Cultural Differences

Although there are many similarities in the content of specific phobias and fears across cultures, prevalence rates tend to vary. For example, fears and phobias are more prevalent in African Americans (Brown, Eaton, & Sussman, 1990) and Mexican Americans born in the United States (Karno et al., 1989) in comparison to Caucasian Americans. Nigerian and Kenyan children reported greater fear ratings than did children from the United States, Australia, and China (Ingman, Ollendick, & Akande, 1999), and fear ratings were especially elevated for Christian children from these African countries as compared to Muslim children.

Studies conducted outside of North America suggest that certain phobias are present in other countries, but direct comparisons of prevalence rates within and outside of North America have not been conducted. For example, da Motta et al. (2000) found an extremely high prevalence of phobias in a Brazilian epidemiological study.

Despite some clear differences, important similarities across cultural groups have also been reported. For example, fear content appears to be fairly consistent across cultures (e.g., Neal, Lilly, & Zakis, 1993) and individuals from Western and Asian countries agree about which animals constitute a disgust-relevant category (Davey et al., 1998).

EPIDEMIOLOGY

The lifetime prevalence of specific phobias appears to be approximately 11 percent according to results from the Epidemiological Catchment Area study (ECA; Eaton, Dryman, & Weissman, 1991) and the National Comorbidity Survey (NCS; Kessler et al., 1994). Smaller studies have found a wide range of prevalence estimates, from less than 1 percent (Faravelli, Guerrini Degl'Innocenti, & Giardinelli, 1989) to almost 20 percent (Fredrikson et al., 1996). Differences in assessment methods and diagnostic criteria probably contribute to these differences. For example, in the Faravelli et al. (1989) study, diagnostic decisions did not allow for multiple diagnoses to be made, meaning that the diagnosis of specific phobias may have been made much less frequently than if comorbidity was allowed. Data from the NCS (Curtis et al., 1998) found that prevalence rates for specific fears and phobias varied depending on phobia type, with phobias of animals and heights being the most frequently diagnosed.

Prevalence rates suggest that specific phobias are a common clinical problem, but significant fears that do not meet diagnostic criteria for specific phobias are even more prevalent. A survey of 2,000 randomly selected participants from primary care settings revealed high rates of specific fears in this group (Birchall, 1996). Although many fears listed may be related to other psychiatric difficulties (e.g., fear of closed spaces may be associated with panic disorder), it is clear that there is a high rate of phobia-relevant fears in a primary care population. For example, almost 24 percent of respondents reported being moderately fearful of injections or minor surgery. Similarly, Curtis et al. (1998) reported high rates of specific fears in the general population.

COURSE, COMPLICATIONS, AND PROGNOSIS

Physiological Responses to Cues

The most common physiological response to a phobic cue is a panic attack or paniclike symptoms. Antony et al. (1997a) found that a significant proportion of participants experienced a panic attack during a Behavioral Approach Test (BAT). The breakdown of panic attacks by phobia type was as follows: blood-injection-injury, 50 percent; heights, 47 percent; driving, 36 percent; and animals, 20 percent.

One type of specific phobia is associated with a unique reaction that is unparalleled across other phobia types or across the anxiety disorders, in general. BII phobias are associated with a diphasic response in which heart rate and blood pressure initially increase then abruptly decrease (see Page, 1994). This response is often accompanied by fainting (e.g., Curtis & Thyer, 1983). Approximately 70 percent of individuals with blood phobias and 56 percent of those with injection phobias demonstrate the diphasic response (Öst, 1992). In nonclinical samples, between 10 percent and 14 percent of undergraduates reported a history of fainting due to blood or injury cues (Kleinknecht, 1988). The fainting response appears to be equivalent across genders (Kleinknecht, Kleinknecht, & Thorndike, 1997).

Fainting is not a universal response in individuals with BII phobias. Öst (1992) found that 30 percent of individuals with blood phobias and 44 percent of individuals with injection phobias did not report a history of fainting. Fainting may also sometimes occur outside the context of a BII phobia. Some individuals may faint in response to blood cues despite not reporting a blood phobia (Kleinknecht & Lenz, 1989). Thus, fainting may not be the result of having a BII phobia, but rather a BII phobia may intensify or be maintained by fears concerning fainting.

Age of Onset and Course

Phobias have a mean age of onset of approximately 15 years (Magee, Eaton, Wittchen, McGonagle, & Kessler, 1996), but this varies with the particular phobia. Generally, animal and blood-injection-injury phobias tend to have an earlier age of onset (i.e., childhood; Öst, 1987) than do other types of phobias, though some studies have not replicated this finding with respect to animal phobias (e.g., Goisman et al., 1998). On the other hand, situational phobias and height phobias tend to begin in adolescence or adulthood (Öst, 1987). Studies reporting age of onset should be interpreted cautiously, however, due to differences in how various studies coded answers of "as long as I can remember" when participants were asked about specific phobia onset. Some studies exclude these participants, some select a standard age (e.g., 5 years old) to code these responses, and other studies ask participants to provide a best estimate.

Few studies have asked participants about the age of fear onset (i.e., the age when the fear began, but full criteria for a specific phobia were not met). One exception is a study by Antony et al. (1997a), which found an average difference of nine years between fear onset and phobia onset. Thus, distinguishing between fear onset and phobia onset is an important consideration for future research and this issue provides another reason to be cautious when interpreting prior studies on age of onset.

IMPACT ON ENVIRONMENT

When impairment associated with a specific phobia is mild, affected individuals can continue to live productive lives and appear relatively unaffected by their disorder. However, impairment associated with a specific phobia may also be in the moderate to severe range, having a significant impact on people's lives and leading to high levels of disruption at work, in relationships, and in other areas of functioning.

Although a number of studies have investigated the impairment and economic burden of a broad range of anxiety disorders, scant research has examined these issues in individuals diagnosed with a primary specific phobia. Further, some of the existing research has mixed groups of people with specific phobias and other anxiety disorders, limiting conclusions that can be drawn for specific phobias. Across the anxiety disorders, in general, research suggests significant social, occupation, and economic burden. For example, Greenberg et al. (1999) estimated the annual economic burden of the anxiety disorders for 1998 as $63.1 billion. Much of this cost for most anxiety disorders is attributed to decreased productivity at work, though having a diagnosis of a specific phobia was not associated with significant lost productivity.

Studies examining specific phobias as a distinct diagnostic category have found that a diagnosis of a specific phobia is associated with significant use of the health care system (Chartier, Walker, & Kjernisted, 2000; Kessler et al., 1999), high functional impairment (Magee et al., 1996), and impaired social functioning (Schonfeld et al., 1997). For example, Chartier et al. (2000) found that having a specific phobia was linked with increased odds of visiting one's general practitioner more than three times in the past year, visiting an emergency room, and seeking help of any kind. Further, Woodruff-Borden, Brothers, Lasch, Jeffery, and Butterman (1997) found that two of five individuals with specific phobias in their sample also endorsed significant suicidal ideation, a rate that was consistent with that of other anxiety disorders. Of course, one must be cautious when interpreting these results due to the small number of participants in this study, and further research on suicidal ideation in specific phobia is warranted.

In addition to functional impairment, some authors have focused on quality of life in the anxiety disorders. Mogotsi, Kaminer, and Stein (2000) highlight subjective variables such as life satisfaction and general well-being as indicators of quality of life. From their review, it is clear that minimal research has addressed quality of life issues in specific phobia, and they point out that research is virtually nonexistent on topics such as the impact of anxiety disorder on caregivers' quality of life.

Thus, research seems to support clinical impressions that the impairment from specific phobias can range from mild to severe. It is clear that the impairment from specific phobias is often less significant than that of other anxiety disorders (e.g., Greenberg et al., 1999). In fact, it is often the case that people's symptoms meet all diagnostic criteria for a specific phobia except the impairment criterion (e.g., Antony et al., 1994; Romano, Tremblay, Vitaro, Zoccolillo, & Pagani, 2001), and in these cases a diagnosis of specific phobia is not assigned.

ETIOLOGY

There has been much interest in and debate about the origins of specific fears and phobias. Current perspectives implicate genetic factors (e.g., Kendler, Myers, Prescott, & Neale, 2001), conditioning models (e.g., Rachman, 1977), and possible nonassociative factors (e.g., Poulton & Menzies, 2002). Although the debate about the viability of these theories has yet to be resolved, we will review each of these perspectives, in turn.

Conditioning models have their roots in Mowrer's two-stage model of fear development (1939). Essentially, this model postulates that neutral stimuli (e.g., animals, storms) become associated with aversive stimuli (e.g., pain or fear-evoking stimuli) through a classical conditioning process. For example, dental phobia may develop when going to the dentist (a neutral stimulus) becomes associated with pain (an aversive stimulus). Once this connection is established, phobias are maintained by operant conditioning. That is, avoidance of the feared stimuli allows the individual to minimize his or her fear reaction, and therefore the fear is maintained by negative reinforcement.

Though appealing, Mowrer's theory could not explain some important observations, including the fact that individuals with phobias often cannot identify a specific conditioning experience and that many individuals who have had traumatic conditioning experiences do not go on to develop phobias (e.g., Di Nardo et al., 1988). For extensive reviews of the shortcomings of this model see Davey (1992) and Rachman (1991). Thus, Mowrer's initial ideas were expanded upon by Rachman (1977), who highlighted three pathways to the development of fears. These pathways include (1) *direct conditioning,* which, like Mowrer's model, refers to a stimulus becoming associated with a fear reaction though a traumatic experience; (2) *vicarious acquisition,* which involves witnessing someone else have a fearful reaction or upsetting experience involving the feared stimulus; and (3) *informational pathways,* which involve learning that a particular stimulus is dangerous through information transmitted by others (e.g., on television, during conversations, while reading, etc.).

There is support for Rachman's model. For example, many individuals can recall incidents that correspond to these pathways to phobia acquisition (e.g., Menzies & Clarke, 1993b; Merckelbach, Arntz, Arrindell, & de Jong, 1992) and a recent study of childhood dental fear found that objectively difficult dental experiences (e.g., number of tooth extractions) had a small but significant relation with indices of dental fear (Ten Berge, Veerkamp, & Hoogstraten, 2002).

Despite this evidence, there are several critiques of the conditioning perspective. First, many studies of phobia onset have not included appropriate comparison groups. When nonphobic controls are included in studies, results suggest that conditioning events are equally prevalent in phobic and nonphobic individuals (e.g., Menzies & Parker, 2001; Merckelbach et al., 1992). Second, studies concerning Rachman's pathways to fear contain a number of methodological issues that may have contaminated results, including employing retrospective accounts of fear onset that are subject to a number of reporting biases, using questionnaires that ask only about conditioning-based modes of onset, and inconsistencies in methodology (e.g., sometimes asking about multiple causes and other times only asking about the primary cause of phobia onset; Poulton & Menzies, 2002).

It is clear that conditioning accounts of phobia acquisition, though still useful and appealing, cannot explain the broad realm of phobia onset. There are a number of other factors that should be considered. For example, Menzies and colleagues (e.g., Menzies & Clarke, 1995b; Poulton & Menzies, 2002) propose adding a fourth, nonassociative pathway to Rachman's three pathways to fear development. These authors suggest that some fears may be innately present from a young age without any conditioning experiences at all. Biologically relevant fears (e.g., water or heights) have evolved through natural selection to be innately fear provoking. For most individuals, these fears extinguish through normal developmental processes. For others, these fears either (1) never go away or (2) become reactivated following a nonspecific stressful period in their lives.

Although there is some compelling evidence to support a nonassociative model of fear acquisition (e.g., see Poulton & Menzies, 2002), authors have expressed a number of concerns with this model. For example, some authors argue that evolutionary explanations of current phenomena run the risk of not being falsifiable (e.g., Davey, 2002) and that it is dangerous to assume that the lack of an identifiable associative history indicates a nonassociative history (e.g., Kleinknecht, 2002). It is clear that a nonassociative pathway has created interest and debate about the multiple origins of specific phobias, and further research on these ideas should prove useful in our understanding of the etiology of phobias.

In addition to psychological theories of phobia development, researchers have acknowledged various biological and genetic influences. To explain the nonrandom distribution of human phobias, Seligman (1971) proposed that individuals are "prepared" or predisposed to learn associations between certain stimuli and a fear response. Stimuli that are more likely to become phobic objects are those that have implications for survival. For example, Cook and Mineka (1989) found that monkeys developed a fear of snakes through observing other monkeys responding fearfully to snakes, but the same result could not be replicated with flowers as the phobic stimuli. Theoretically, fear of flowers is harder to induce because monkeys are not "prepared" to be fearful of this stimulus. Although the preparedness hypothesis has received some empirical support, its broad applicability is in dispute (e.g., see Merckelbach & de Jong, 1996). Further, some authors have argued, similar to arguments made against the nonassociative pathway to fear, that evolutionary explanations are based on what is plausible, not on what is provable (McNally, 1995).

A number of twin studies have examined the extent to which genetic factors predispose individuals to specific phobias. Generally, these studies suggest that there is a genetic contribution to the development of specific phobias, though this contribution is best described as a general predisposition that may manifest itself in a number of different ways (Kendler et al., 2001). More specifically, a twin study examining genetic transmission of phobias found heritability estimates of 47 percent for animal phobias, 59 percent for blood-injection-injury phobias, and 46 percent for situational phobias (Kendler, Karkowski, & Prescott, 1999). However, other studies have found no genetic component in the development of natural environment and situational fears (e.g., Skre, Onstad, Torgersen, Lygren, & Kringlen, 2000).

In summary, it seems clear that there are a number of pathways to the development of a specific phobia. Although conditioning theories were once the predominant explanation for phobia onset, genetic and evolutionary explanations also merit consideration. Further, evidence from genetic studies suggests that individuals often inherit general tendencies that may culminate in specific fears. It is to these general tendencies that we now turn.

PERSONALITY DEVELOPMENT AND PSYCHOPATHOLOGY

Research described earlier appears to implicate genetically based personality traits as important precursors to the development of specific phobias. What are these various personality traits and how might they contribute to fear development? One possibility is the construct of behavioral inhibition, or the tendency of individuals to withdraw from or overreact to novel situations. This construct, most commonly discussed in reference to shyness and social anxiety, has also been implicated in anxiety disorders more generally (e.g., Rosenbaum et al., 1993). With respect to specific phobias, Biederman et al. (1990) found that children who scored high on behavioral inhibition at 21 months of age were at higher risk for the development of multiple specific phobias at 7 or 8 years of age than were less inhibited children. Thus, behavioral inhibition may be one temperamental variable that increases a child's risk for anxiety disorders in general, though it may have more limited explanatory power for explaining the onset of particular fears.

Another heritable personality construct that appears to be related to phobia onset is neuroticism (i.e., the tendency to experience negative emotion). The tripartite model of anxiety and depression (Clark & Watson, 1991) proposes that neuroticism underlies both of these conditions and research clearly links neuroticism to a variety of mood and anxiety disorders (see Clark, Watson, & Mineka, 1994). In the case of specific phobias, research suggests that neuroticism is related to animal phobias, situational phobias, and BII phobias (Arrindell, 2000), to fear in general (e.g., Neiger, Atkinson, & Quarrington, 1981), as well as to specific phobias in a heterogeneous anxiety population (Watson, Clark, & Carey, 1988). Taylor (1998) argues that neuroticism is part of a hierarchical model of fears. Drawing from factor analytic studies, Taylor suggests that there are at least three levels in the hierarchical structure of fears, and neuroticism forms the highest and most general of these levels.

Neuroticism may exert its influence on the development of specific phobias through a relationship with response style to phobic stimuli. Wilson, Kumari, Gray, and Corr (2000) showed that individuals with high levels of neuroticism demonstrated a greater startle response to arousing film clips than did those with low levels of neuroticism, whereas those with low neuroticism showed a greater startle response when faced with disgust eliciting clips. The authors suggested that neuroticism may facilitate an escape response when fear is the predominant response and a blunting response in the presence of disgusting cues where escape is not necessary or feasible. Other authors have argued that neuroticism may actually account for both disgust sensitivity and the fear response, though evidence is equivocal for this contention (see Woody & Teachman, 2000).

Disgust sensitivity, itself, is a trait that has been implicated in the etiology and phenomenology of certain specific phobias, especially animal phobias and BII phobias. Early studies operationalized disgust sensitivity as an individual's willingness to eat contaminated foods, though later studies expanded upon this definition to include disgust reactions to phobic-specific stimuli. For example, disgust sensitivity is elevated in BII fears and phobias in relation to both general (e.g., rotting food) and phobia-specific (e.g., wounds) indicators of disgust (Sawchuk, Lohr, Tolin, Lee, & Kleinknecht, 2000; Tolin, Lohr, Sawchuk, & Lee, 1997).

In addition, disgust sensitivity has been shown to be elevated in people with spider phobias on both questionnaire measures of disgust (e.g., Merckelbach, de Jong, Arntz, & Schouten, 1993) and physiological indicators of disgust (e.g., de Jong, Peters, & Vanderhallen, 2002). When exposed to fear producing stimuli, spider phobic individuals appear to have mixtures of fear and disgust reactions (Tolin et al., 1997). One study did not find differences in disgust sensitivity among spider phobics, other phobics, and controls (Thorpe & Salkovskis, 1998), though procedural differences between studies may account for this discrepant finding (see Woody & Teachman, 2000).

Studies suggest that scores reflecting global disgust sensitivity do not change following successful treatment, though phobia-specific disgust reactions do (de Jong, Andrea, & Muris, 1997; Smits, Telch, & Randall, 2002). In addition, disgust sensitivity also does not interfere with the effects of treatment (Merckelbach et al., 1993). Further research is necessary to untangle the precise role that disgust sensitivity plays in development and maintenance of specific phobias.

Anxiety sensitivity (i.e., one's beliefs that the physical sensations of fear and anxiety are dangerous) may contribute to the phobic response in certain types of specific phobias. Individuals with situational phobias may be especially concerned with the physical sensations of fear, focusing on the consequences of anxiety and panic attacks when encountering the phobic stimulus (Antony et al., 1997a). Research generally supports this notion, demonstrating that individuals with phobias from the situational type score higher on the Anxiety Sensitivity Index (ASI; Peterson & Reiss, 1993) than do individuals with animal phobias and BII phobias (Antony et al., 1997a). Further, anxiety sensitivity interacts with expected anxiety when predicting avoidance behavior in claustrophobic situations (Valentiner, Telch, Petruzzi, & Bolte, 1996). Individuals with phobias from the situational type also tend to respond more strongly to panic induction challenges (e.g., Verburg, Griez, & Meijer, 1994), though some studies have not found significant differences between specific phobia types (e.g., Antony, Brown, & Barlow, 1997b).

Individuals with specific phobias also appear to demonstrate some biases in attention and memory for phobic stimuli, though the literature contains some inconsistencies. Results suggest that spider phobic individuals pay more attention to threat-related words (e.g., Kindt & Brosschot, 1997; Lavy & van den Hout, 1993) and safety stimuli (Thorpe & Salkovskis, 1998) than do control participants. On the other hand, some studies have found that participants spend less time looking at threat-related pictures (e.g., Tolin, Lohr, Lee, & Sawchuk, 1999), whereas other studies have found participants take longer (i.e., greater interference) on a Stroop naming task when pictorial stimuli were used (Constantine, McNally, & Hornig, 2001).

Findings are also equivocal for studies examining memory for threat-relevant information. Although some studies suggest that phobic participants show no difference in recall or recognition to threat-relevant information compared to control participants (e.g., Thorpe & Salkovskis, 2000; Watts, Trezise, & Sharrock, 1986), other studies examining more specific aspects of memory suggest that phobic participants display memory bias for threat-relevant words. For example, individuals with spider phobia demonstrated enhanced memory for threat-relevant as compared to nonthreat-relevant stimuli (Wessel & Merchelbach, 1998). Phobic participants reported greater difficulty than did control participants in remembering peripheral details about the experimental situation (e.g., objects in the room) when in the presence of a live spider; however, the groups did not differ in memory for central details (e.g., color of the spider; Wessel & Merckelbach, 1997).

Recent research has begun to investigate automatic aspects of memory related to phobic stimuli. The Implicit Associations Test (IAT; Greenwald, McGhee, & Schwartz, 1998) is designed to measure the associations individuals have for phobic stimuli, even when these associations are outside of conscious awareness. Spider-fearful individuals implicitly associate spiders with negative constructs like *afraid* and *disgusting* (de Jong, van den Hout, Rietbroek, & Huijding, 2003; Teachman, Gregg, & Woody, 2001). Interestingly, both spider-fearful and nonfearful participants demonstrated negative implicit associations with spiders, suggesting that nonfearful individuals can suppress these negative associations whereas spider-phobic individuals cannot (de Jong et al., 2003).

Finally, research has consistently demonstrated that individuals with specific phobias have distorted thinking about a number of phobic stimuli (e.g., Cavanagh & Davey, 2003; Kent, 1985; Menzies & Clarke, 1995a), especially when the phobic individual faces high danger and low safety situations (Wright, Holborn, & Rezutek, 2002). For example, Cavanagh and Davey (2003) found that spider-fearful individuals could generate more reasons than nonfearful controls about why spiders were harmful. Individuals tend to assume that there is a high correlation between their feared stimulus and feared outcome (e.g., de Jong, Merckelbach, & Arntz, 1995). Individuals also show perceptual distortions about feared objects (e.g., Rachman & Cuk, 1992) and react with increased fear to fearful information about objects (Muris, Bodden, Merckelbach, Ollendick, & King, 2003). Spider-fearful individuals also generated more fearful and vivid spider images than did nonfearful individuals, with associated bodily reactions (e.g., uncomfortable skin sensations; Pratt, Cooper, & Hackmann, 2004).

ASSESSMENT AND DIAGNOSIS

Assessment plays a number of important roles with regard to management of specific phobias, including obtaining information to develop a diagnostic conceptualization, identifying key physical, cognitive, and behavioral targets to guide treatment planning and selection of treatment interventions, and monitoring progress and outcome. This section provides an overview of assessment procedures for specific phobias (for more comprehensive reviews, see Antony, 2001b; McCabe & Antony, 2002; McCabe, Antony, & Ollendick, in press).

Diagnostic Features

According to the *DSM-IV-TR* (APA, 2000), the central feature of a specific phobia is an excessive and persistent fear of a specific situation or object (e.g., heights, seeing blood, animals or insects, enclosed places). To establish a diagnosis of a specific phobia, the individual must display insight into the excessive or unreasonable nature of the fear. However, the presence of insight is not required to make a diagnosis of a specific phobia in children. In addition, due to the transient nature of many childhood fears, a fear must be present for at least six months before a diagnosis of specific phobia can be assigned in those younger than age 18. Given that fears are normative and often adaptive, a fear must lead to significant distress or impairment in functioning to warrant a diagnosis of specific phobia. Finally, to assign a diagnosis of specific phobia, the symptoms must not be better accounted for by another mental disorder. For example, an individual who develops a fear of enclosed places and flying after having a panic attack in an airplane might receive a diagnosis of panic disorder and agoraphobia (PDA) if all of the required features of PDA are present rather than a diagnosis of specific phobia, situational type.

The diagnostic conceptualization is based on a comprehensive assessment that is ideally multimodal, including a combination of clinical interview, relevant symptom-specific questionnaires, and behavioral assessment. A semistructured interview, such as the Anxiety Disorders Interview Schedule for *DSM-IV* (ADIS-IV; Brown, Di Nardo, & Barlow, 1994; Di Nardo, Brown, & Barlow, 1994) or the Structured Clinical Interview for *DSM-IV* (SCID-IV; First, Spitzer, Gibbon, & Williams, 1996) can improve the reliability of the diagnosis (Summerfeldt & Antony, 2002).

Clinical Interview

Once the presence of a specific phobia is detected using general screening questions (e.g., "Are there any specific situations or objects that you are very afraid of, such as flying, heights, the dentist, enclosed places, seeing blood or getting a needle, or certain animals or insects?"), a comprehensive clinical interview should focus on collecting relevant information in the following areas:

- Fear: intensity of fear upon exposure to the situation or object, physical reactions associated with the fear response (e.g., panic symptoms, fainting), the degree to which the

fear is excessive or out of proportion to the actual level of danger, the degree to which the fear is distressing or impairing to everyday functioning, and the etiology of the fear
- Behavior: behavioral reactions associated with the fear, overt and subtle avoidance
- Cognition: beliefs associated with the fear, level of insight into the excessiveness of the fear
- Environmental context: factors that may influence fear level (e.g., for snake phobia, factors may include the size of the snake, movement, color, sound, distance, etc.), associated medical problems (e.g., a person with diabetes who has a fear of needles), family factors (e.g., support, symptom accommodation)
- Treatment history: which treatments have worked in the past and which have not worked

Following the initial assessment, it may also be useful to obtain information from significant others (e.g., family member, teacher) who may be able to provide additional relevant details. This should occur with the permission of the patient, ideally with the patient present during the interview.

It is important for the clinician to be aware that the assessment process itself may be quite anxiety provoking. For example, just saying the word *snake* may induce fear in a patient who avoids snakes. Thus, it is important for the clinician to remain sensitive to the patient's fear level. Strategies that are helpful for reducing discomfort during the assessment include letting the patient know at the outset that he or she may experience some fear and discomfort due to the focus of the questions and periodically checking in on the patient's comfort level and the pacing of the assessment.

Self-Report Measures

Self-report measures are used to provide additional detail about the individual's fear and typically assess the severity of the fear and avoidance. For example, there are well established scales for measuring a variety of fears including fear of spiders (e.g., Fear of Spiders Questionnaire; Szymanski & O'Donohue, 1995) and heights (e.g., Acrophobia Questionnaire [AQ]; Cohen, 1977), among others. There are also measures available to screen for a wide range of specific fears (e.g., Fear Survey Schedule III [FSS-III]; Wolpe & Lang, 1964). For an extensive review of adult measures, see Antony (2001a) or McCabe and Antony (2002). For a review of child measures, see Ollendick, Davis, and Muris (in press).

In addition, it is useful to assess other variables that are associated with the specific phobia including fear of arousal-related physical symptoms (e.g., Anxiety Sensitivity Index [ASI]; Peterson & Reiss, 1993) and disgust sensitivity (e.g., Disgust Scale; Haidt, McCauley, & Rozin, 1994; Disgust Emotion Scale; Kleinknecht, Tolin, Lohr, & Kleinknecht, 1996).

Self-monitoring records also provide useful data for assessment and treatment planning. They involve having the individual record specific aspects of the fear (e.g., frequency, intensity, situational context or triggers, physiological response, cognitions, and behaviors) on a daily basis, or whenever the fear is triggered.

Behavioral Assessment

Behavioral assessment is an important component of the overall assessment because individuals may not always be aware of the subtle cues (i.e., specific contextual factors) that affect their fear and avoidance. Also, they may overreport the amount of fear that they typically experience in a phobic situation (e.g., Klieger, 1987), and they may have difficulty articulating specific details about their fear in an interview situation. The most common mode of behavioral assessment for specific phobia is a Behavioral Approach Test (BAT). The BAT involves exposing the individual to the phobic stimulus in a controlled manner (e.g., a snake phobic is presented with a snake on one side of the room and asked to come as close to it as possible) so that the clinician can assess the fear (e.g., including fear intensity using a scale ranging from 0 to 100, anxious thoughts, physical symptoms, behavioral responses) in the real-life situation. In addition, psychophysiological assessment (e.g., measurement of heart rate) can provide useful information over and above the patient's subjective report (Yartz & Hawk, 2001).

TREATMENT IMPLICATIONS

Despite the arguments that conditioning models of phobia onset may not explain the development of all phobias, therapeutic-outcome studies are clear that exposure to feared stimuli is an effective treatment for phobias (for a review, see Antony & Barlow, 2002). In the case of blood and injection phobias, applied muscle tension (Öst & Sterner, 1987) should also be considered, particularly for patients who have a history of fainting. Applied muscle tension involves having patients repeatedly tense all the muscles of their bodies while engaged in exposure to blood or injection cues. The muscle tension exercises lead to a temporary increase in blood pressure and thereby prevent fainting upon exposure to blood or medical procedures.

The duration of exposure treatment for specific phobia treatment may be brief, with studies suggesting that even one long session of therapist-assisted exposure is helpful (Öst, Brandburg, & Alm, 1997). The necessity for therapist involvement is unclear, with results suggesting that individuals do less well when given self-help materials to complete on their own but do very well when using these materials in a clinical setting or when working with a therapist (Öst, Salkovskis, & Hellström, 1991).

Scant research has investigated group versus individual treatment of specific phobias, but results of one study suggest that group treatment can be just as effective as individual treatment (Öst, 1996). However, group treatment may be less practical for specific phobias than it is for other anxiety disorders, given the effectiveness of single session treatment. It may be easier for clinicians to provide a session of treatment for each client than to wait and accumulate multiple clients with the same specific fear. Additionally, research has shown that individuals do not benefit as much from watching someone being treated, even in person, as they do from engaging in exposure themselves (Menzies & Clarke, 1993a).

A number of factors have been shown either to enhance or detract from the outcome of exposure treatment. Many studies suggest that variables that enhance fear reduction in the short term may not be as effective at helping to generalize or maintain results in the long term. For example, massed exposure (i.e., daily rather than weekly exposure sessions) appears to enhance fear reduction during exposure treatment for anxiety disorders (e.g., Foa, Jameson, Turner, & Payne, 1980). However, studies examining the benefits of an expanding spaced exposure schedule (starting with sessions close together and gradually increasing the interval between sessions) have yielded inconsistent findings (Lang & Craske, 2000; Rowe & Craske, 1998a).

Further, Rowe and Craske (1998b) found that using multiple spiders during exposure for spider phobia led to less fear reduction than consistently using one spider. However, using multiple spiders enhanced the generalizability of exposure. In addition, reliance of safety behaviors during exposure seems to hamper outcomes. Powers et al. (2002) found that allowing people with claustrophobia concerns to engage in safety behaviors (e.g., medications, distraction) during exposure interfered with fear reduction during exposure.

Studies on the effect of distraction during exposure have yielded mixed results. Some studies have found that distraction interferes with exposure, especially during high intensity exposure (Rodriguez & Craske, 1995). However, other studies have found no effects of distraction on exposure outcome (Antony, McCabe, Leeuw, Sano, & Swinson, 2001) or have found that distraction may enhance the effects of exposure (Johnstone & Page, 2004). Johnstone and Page (2004) had spider phobic individuals complete exposure while having either a relevant (i.e., discussing the spider or current anxiety levels) or irrelevant (i.e., discussing school or vacations) conversation with the experimenter. Individuals undergoing distracted exposure had significantly greater reductions on self-reported fear and improved performance on a behavioral task. These results are perplexing in light of the emotional processing model of fear reduction (Foa & Kozak, 1986), which suggests that attention to the feared stimulus is necessary for fear reduction. It is possible that minimal levels of attention are necessary for emotional processing to occur, such that maintaining visual contact with the feared stimulus is adequate.

In spite of the proven efficacy of exposure treatments for specific phobias, some fears may return. Research suggests that the fear response is more likely to return when individuals are tested in a different context from that in which treatment took place (Mineka, Mystkowski, Hladek, & Rodriguez, 1999). For example, Mystkowski, Mineka, Vernon, and Zinbarg (2003) gave spider fearful individuals either placebo or caffeine during treatment and at follow-up. Results indicated that return of fear was greatest for individuals whose treatment and follow-up states were incongruent.

Technology in the Treatment of Specific Phobias

In recent years, clinicians have begun to use various technological advances in the treatment of specific phobias. One significant advance is the use of virtual reality to treat various fears including fears of flying, spiders, and heights. Studies on the effectiveness of virtual reality are now being conducted and generally indicate that exposure via virtual reality is an effective way to treat phobias. Case reports and preliminary studies have found that virtual reality is an effective treatment for fears of spiders (St-Jacques & Bouchard, 2002) and driving fears (Wald & Taylor, 2000). Randomized controlled studies also suggest that virtual reality treatment is more effective than wait-list control for height fears (Krijn et al., 2004) and fear of flying (Rothbaum, Hodges, Smith, Lee, & Price, 2000). However, some studies have found that in vivo exposure is still superior to virtual reality (e.g., Dewis et al., 2001), others have found the approaches to be equivalent (e.g., Emmelkamp et al., 2002; Rothbaum, Hodges, Anderson, Price, and Smith, 2002). Very few studies have examined the long-term effectiveness of virtual reality treatment. Rothbaum et al. (2002) found strong follow-up results for the treatment of fear of flying, with the majority of individuals treated with either virtual reality or standard exposure having taken a flight during a 12-month follow-up period. On the other hand, Maltby, Kirsch, Mayers, and Allen (2002) found that the superiority for virtual reality exposure over an attention-placebo group treatment disappeared at six-month follow-up. However, participants in the Maltby et al. (2002) study were a mixed group in terms of diagnoses, which included specific phobia of flying, panic disorder, or agoraphobia. Therefore, it is difficult to make conclusions about the outcome of virtual reality treatment for specific phobias, specifically, from this study.

Research also suggests that computer-administered or assisted behavioral treatments are helpful in the treatment of a number of phobias (Coldwell et al., 1998; Marks, Kenwright, McDonough, Whittaker, & Mataix-Cols, 2004). For example, Marks et al. (2004) found that computer-guided self-exposure for individuals with specific phobias or panic disorder worked just as well as therapist-guided exposure, with close to 50 percent improvement on outcome measures at posttreatment and one-month follow-up.

The Use of Medication to Treat Specific Phobias

Pharmacotherapy is generally thought to be ineffective for treatment of specific phobias. However, little research has been conducted to assess the utility of medications for specific phobias. A few relevant studies have examined the use of benzodiazepines and beta-blockers alone or in combination with behavioral treatments for specific phobias and in general have found that drugs do not contribute much to the treatment of specific phobias (for a review, see Antony & Barlow, 2002). However, one problem with the research to date is that it has not taken into account differences between specific phobia types. For example, as discussed earlier, phobias of the situational type appear to share more features with panic disorder than with the other specific phobia types. Medications that are effective for panic disorder may prove to be effective for situational phobias. One small placebo-controlled, double-blind pilot study found that paroxetine was superior to placebo in reducing anxiety and fear levels in individuals with different types of specific phobia (Benjamin, Ben-Zion, Karbofsky, & Dannon, 2000). There have also been several case study reports indicating the usefulness of selective serotonin reuptake inhibitors in the treatment of specific phobia including fluvoxamine for storm phobia (Balon, 1999) and fluoxetine for driving phobia (Abene & Hamilton, 1998).

Other Treatment Options for Specific Phobias

Although exposure treatments are the most commonly used treatment for specific phobias, researchers are also studying Eye Movement Desensitization and Reprocessing (EMDR) therapy and cognitive therapy for phobias. The research generally suggests that EMDR does lead to decreased in subjective fear ratings among people with specific phobias, but not in measures of avoidance or physiological indices. In addition, improvements appear to be due to the imaginal exposure inherent in this procedure rather than eye movements (for a review, see Antony & Barlow, 2002). Similarly, cognitive strategies may lead to fear reduction for specific phobias, but the long-term benefits are still in question (for reviews, see Antony & Barlow, 2002; Craske & Rowe, 1997).

SUMMARY

Specific phobia is a common problem that has received a great deal of empirical attention. As a result, our understanding of the nature, assessment, and treatment of phobias is strong. As with all psychological problems, however, more research is necessary to fully understand the phenomenology, etiology, and impact of this disorder. For example, after years of research on conditioning models, there is still controversy about the pathways to phobia development. Although the new ideas have in some ways increased confusion about etiology, they have also provoked intense debate among researchers and clinicians that may lead to new and innovative lines of research. Further, the high prevalence of specific fears and phobias appears to have fostered an impression that specific phobias do not have a significant impact in terms of functional impairment, economic burden, and quality of life. Although their impact may not be as extensive as that of other anxiety disorders, further research is necessary to investigate these variables in "clean" samples of people with specific phobias as well as in comorbid groups. From clinical experience, it is clear that specific phobias have the potential to cause severe impairment in people's lives.

REFERENCES

Abene, M. V., & Hamilton, J. D. (1998). Resolution of fear of flying with fluoxetine treatment. *Journal of Anxiety Disorders, 12,* 599–603.

American Psychiatric Association. (2000). *Diagnostic and statistical manual of mental disorders* (4th ed., text rev.). Washington, DC: Author.

Antony, M. M. (2001a). Measures for specific phobia. In M. M. Antony, S. M. Orsillo, & L. Roemer (Eds.), *Practitioner's guide to empirically based measures of anxiety* (pp. 133–158). New York: Kluwer Academic/Plenum.

Antony, M. M. (2001b). Specific phobia: A brief overview and guide to assessment. In M. M. Antony, S. M. Orsillo, & L. Roemer (Eds.), *Practitioner's guide to empirically based measures of anxiety* (pp. 127–132). New York: Kluwer Academic/Plenum.

Antony, M. M., & Barlow, D. H. (2002). Specific phobias. In D. H. Barlow (Ed.), *Anxiety and its disorders: The nature and treatment of anxiety and panic* (2nd ed). New York: Guilford Press.

Antony, M. M., Brown, T. A., & Barlow, D. H. (1997a). Heterogeneity among specific phobia types in *DSM-IV*. *Behaviour Research and Therapy, 35,* 1089–1100.

Antony, M. M., Brown, T. A., & Barlow, D. H. (1997b). Response to hyperventilation and 5.5% CO_2 inhalation of subjects with types of specific phobia, panic disorder, or no mental disorder. *American Journal of Psychiatry, 154,* 1089–1095.

Antony, M. M., McCabe, R. E., Leeuw, I., Sano, N., & Swinson, R. P. (2001). Effect of exposure and coping style on in vivo exposure for specific phobia of spiders. *Behaviour Research and Therapy, 39,* 1137–1150.

Antony, M. M., Moras, K., Meadows, E. A., Di Nardo, P. A., Utech, J. E., & Barlow, D. H. (1994). The diagnostic significance of the functional impairment and subjective distress criterion: An illustration with the *DSM-III-R* anxiety disorders. *Journal of Psychopathology and Behavioral Assessment, 16,* 253–263.

Arrindell, W. A. (2000). Phobic dimensions IV: The structure of animal fears. *Behaviour Research and Therapy, 38,* 509–530.

Balon, R. (1999). Fluvoxamine for phobia of storms. *Acta Psychiatrica Scandinavica, 100,* 244–246.

Benjamin, J., Ben-Zion, I. Z., Karbofsky, E., & Dannon, P. (2000). Double-blind placebo-controlled pilot study of paroxetine for specific phobia. *Psychopharmacology, 149,* 194–196.

Biederman, J., Rosenbaum, J. F, Hirshfeld, D. R., Faraone, S. V., Bolduc, E. A., Gersten, M., et al. (1990). Psychiatric correlates of behavioral inhibition in young children of parents with and without psychiatric disorders. *Archives of General Psychiatry, 47,* 21–26.

Birchall, H. M. (1996). Just how common are common fears? *Anxiety, 2,* 303–304.

Brown, D. R., Eaton, W. W., & Sussman, L. (1990). Racial differences in prevalence of phobic disorders. *Journal of Nervous and Mental Disease, 178,* 434–441.

Brown, T. A., Campbell, L. A., Lehman, C. L., Grisham, J. R., & Mancill, R. B. (2001). Current and lifetime comorbidity of the *DSM-IV* anxiety and mood disorders in a large clinical sample. *Journal of Abnormal Psychology, 110,* 585–599.

Brown, T. A., Di Nardo, P. A., & Barlow, D. H. (1994). *Anxiety Disorders Interview Schedule for DSM-IV (ADIS-IV).* Boulder, CO: Graywind Publications.

Cavanagh, K., & Davey, G. (2003). Access to information about harm and safety in spider fearful and nonfearful individuals: When they were good they were very very good but when they were bad they were horrid. *Journal of Behavior Therapy and Experimental Psychiatry, 34,* 269–281.

Chartier, M., Walker, J., & Kjernisted, K. (2000, March). *Health care utilization and anxiety disorders.* Poster presented at the Anxiety Disorders Association of America Conference, Washington, DC.

Clark, L. A., & Watson, D. (1991). Tripartite model of anxiety and depression: Psychometric evidence and taxonomic implications. *Journal of Abnormal Psychology, 100,* 316–336.

Clark, L. A., Watson, D., & Mineka, S. (1994). Temperament, personality, and the mood and anxiety disorders. *Journal of Abnormal Psychology, 103,* 103–116.

Cohen, D. C. (1977). Comparison of self-report and overt-behavioral procedures for assessing acrophobia. *Behavior Therapy, 8,* 17–23.

Coldwell, S. E., Getz, T., Millgrom, P., Prall, C. W., Spadafora, A., & Ramsay, D. S. (1998). CARL: A LabView 3 computer program for conducting exposure therapy for the treatment of dental injection fear. *Behaviour Research and Therapy, 36,* 429–441.

Constantine, R., McNally, R. J., & Hornig, C. D. (2001). Snake fear and the pictorial emotional Stroop paradigm. *Cognitive Therapy and Research, 25,* 757–764.

Cook, M., & Mineka, S. (1989). Observational coding of fear to fear-relevant versus fear-irrelevant stimuli in rhesus monkeys. *Journal of Abnormal Psychology, 98,* 448–459.

Craske, M. G., & Rowe, M. K. (1997). A comparison of behavioral and cognitive treatments for phobias. In G. C. L. Davey (Ed.), *Phobias: A handbook of theory, research, and treatment.* New York: Wiley.

Curtis, G. C., Magee, W. J., Eaton, W. W., Wittchen, H.-U., & Kessler, R. C. (1998). Specific fears and phobias: Epidemiology and classification. *British Journal of Psychiatry, 173,* 212–217.

Curtis, G. C., & Thyer, B. A. (1983). Fainting on exposure to phobic stimuli. *American Journal of Psychiatry, 140,* 771–774.

da Motta, W. R., de Lima, M. S., de Oliveira Soares, B. G., Paixão, N. R., & Busnello, E. D. (2000, May). *An epidemic of phobic disorders in Brazil? Results from a population-based cross-sectional survey.* Poster presented at the American Psychiatric Association Conference, Chicago, IL.

Davey, G. C. L. (1992). Classical conditioning and the acquisition of human fears and phobias: A review and synthesis of the literature. *Advances in Behaviour Research and Therapy, 14,* 29–66.

Davey, G. C. (2002). "Nonspecific" rather than "nonassociative" pathways to phobias: A commentary on Poulton and Menzies. *Behaviour Research and Therapy, 40,* 151–158.

Davey, G. C., McDonald, A. S., Hirisave, U., Prabhu, G. G., Iwawaki, S., Jim, C. I., et al. (1998). A cross-cultural study of animal fears. *Behaviour Research and Therapy, 36,* 735–750.

de Jong, P. J., Andrea, H., & Muris, P. (1997). Spider phobia in children: Disgust and fear before and after treatment. *Behaviour Research and Therapy, 35,* 559–562.

de Jong, P. J., Merckelbach, H., & Arntz, A. (1995). Covariation bias in phobic women: The relationship between a priori expectancy, on-line expectancy, autonomic responding, and a posteriori contingency judgment. *Journal of Abnormal Psychology, 104,* 55–62.

de Jong, P. J., Peters, M., & Vanderhallen, I. (2002). Disgust and disgust sensitivity in spider phobia: Facial EMG in response to spider and oral disgust imagery. *Journal of Anxiety Disorders, 16,* 477–493.

de Jong, P. J., van den Hout, M. A., Rietbroek, H., & Huijding, J. (2003). Dissociations between implicit and explicit attitudes toward phobic stimuli. *Cognition and Emotion, 17,* 521–545.

Dewis, L. M., Kirkby, K. C., Martin, F., Daniels, B. A., Gilroy, L. J., & Menzies, R. G. (2001). Computer-aided vicarious exposure versus live graded exposure for spider phobia in children. *Journal of Behavior Therapy and Experimental Psychiatry, 32,* 17–27.

Di Nardo, P., Brown, T. A., & Barlow, D. H. (1994). *Anxiety Disorders Interview Schedule for DSM-IV.* Boulder, CO: Graywind Publications.

Di Nardo, P. A., Guzy, L. T., Jenkins, J. A., Bak, R. M., Tomasi, S. F., & Copland, M. (1988). Etiology and maintenance of dog fears. *Behaviour Research and Therapy, 26,* 241–244.

Eaton, W. W., Dryman, A., & Weissman, M. M. (1991). Panic and phobia. In L. N. Robins and D. A. Regier (Eds.), *Psychiatric disorders in America: The Epidemiologic Catchment Area Study* (pp. 155–179). New York: Free Press.

Emmelkamp, P. M., Krijn, M., Hulsbosch, A. M., de Vries, S., Schuemie, M. J., & van der Mast, C. A. (2002). Virtual reality treatment versus exposure in vivo: A comparative evaluation in acrophobia. *Behaviour Research and Therapy, 40,* 509–516.

Faravelli, C., Guerrini Degl'Innocenti, B., & Giardinelli, L. (1989). Epidemiology of anxiety disorders in Florence. *Acta Psychiatrica Scandinavica, 79,* 308–312.

First, M. B., Spitzer, R. L., Gibbon, M., & Williams, J. B. W. (1996). *Structured Clinical Interview for Axis I DSM-IV Disorders–Patient Edition (SCID-I/P Version 2.0).* New York: Biometrics Research Department, New York State Psychiatric Institute.

Foa, E. B., Jameson, J. S., Turner, R. M., & Payne, L. L. (1980). Massed versus spaced exposure sessions in the treatment of agoraphobia. *Behaviour Research and Therapy, 18,* 333–338.

Foa, E. B., & Kozak, M. J. (1986). Emotional processing of fear: Exposure to corrective information. *Psychological Bulletin, 99,* 20–35.

Fredrikson, M., Annas, P., Fischer, H., & Wik, G. (1996). Gender and age differences in the prevalence of specific fears and phobias. *Behaviour Research and Therapy, 26,* 241–244.

Goisman, R. M., Allsworth, J., Rogers, M. P., Warshaw, M. G., Goldenberg, I., Vasile, R. G., et al. (1998). Simple phobia as a comorbid anxiety disorder. *Depression and Anxiety, 7,* 105–112.

Greenberg, P. E., Sisitsky, T., Kessler, R. C., Finkelstein, S. N., Berndt, E. R., Davidson, J. R. T., et al. (1999). The economic burden of anxiety disorders in the 1990s. *Journal of Clinical Psychiatry, 60,* 427–435.

Greenwald, A. G., McGhee, D. E., & Schwartz, J. L. K. (1998). Measuring individual differences in implicit cognition: The Implicit Association Test. *Journal of Personality and Social Psychology, 74,* 1464–1480.

Haidt, J., McCauley, C., & Rozin, P. (1994). Individual differences in sensitivity to disgust: Scale sampling seven domains of disgust elicitors. *Personality and Individual Differences, 16,* 701–713.

Ingman, K. A., Ollendick, T. H., & Akande, A. (1999). Cross-cultural aspects of fears in African children and adolescents. *Behaviour Research and Therapy, 37,* 337–345.

Johnstone, K. A., & Page, A. C. (2004). Attention to phobic stimuli during exposure: The effect of distraction on anxiety reduction, self-efficacy and perceived control. *Behaviour Research and Therapy, 42,* 249–275.

Karno, M., Golding, J. M., Burnam, M. A., Hough, R. I., Escobar, J. I., Wells, K. M., et al. (1989). Anxiety disorders among Mexican Americans and non-Hispanic Whites in Los Angeles. *Journal of Nervous and Mental Disease, 177,* 202–209.

Kendler, K. S., Karkowski, L. M., & Prescott, C. A. (1999). Fear and phobias: Reliability and heritability. *Psychological Medicine, 29,* 539–553.

Kendler, K. S., Myers, J., Prescott, C. A., & Neale, M. C. (2001). The genetic epidemiology of irrational fears and phobias in men. *Archives of General Psychiatry, 58,* 257–265.

Kent, G. (1985). Cognitive processes in dental anxiety. *British Journal of Clinical Psychology, 24,* 259–264.

Kessler, R. C., McGonagle, K. A., Zhao, S., Nelson, C. B., Hughes, M., Eshleman, S., et al. (1994). Lifetime and 12-month prevalence of *DSM-III-R* psychiatric disorders in the United States: Results from the National Comorbidity Survey. *Archives of General Psychiatry, 51,* 8–19.

Kessler, R. C., Shanyang, Z., Katz, S. J., Kouzis, A. C., Frank, R. G., Edlund, M., et al. (1999). Past-year use of outpatient services for psychiatric problems in the National Comorbidity Survey. *American Journal of Psychiatry, 156,* 115–123.

Kindt, M., & Brosschot, J. F. (1997). Phobia-related cognitive bias for pictorial and linguistic stimuli. *Journal of Abnormal Psychology, 106,* 644–648.

Kirkpatrick, D. R. (1984). Age, gender and patterns of common intense fears among adults. *Behaviour Research and Therapy, 22,* 141–150.

Kleinknecht, R. A. (1988). Specificity and psychosocial correlates of blood/injury fear and fainting. *Behaviour Research and Therapy, 26,* 303–309.

Kleinknecht, R. A. (2002). Comments on non-associative fear acquisition: A review of the evidence from retrospective and longitudinal research. *Behaviour Research and Therapy, 40,* 159–163.

Kleinknecht, R. A., Kleinknecht, E. E., & Thorndike, R. M. (1997). The role of disgust and fear in blood and injection-related fainting symptoms: A structural equation model. *Behaviour Research and Therapy, 35,* 1075–1087.

Kleinknecht, R. A., & Lenz, J. (1989). Blood/injury fear, fainting and avoidance of medically-related situations: A family correspondence study. *Behaviour Research and Therapy, 27,* 537–547.

Kleinknecht, R. A., Tolin, D. F., Lohr, J. M., & Kleinknecht, E. E. (1996, November). *Relationships between blood injury fears, disgust sensitivity, and vasovagal fainting in two independent samples.* Paper presented at the meeting of the Association for Advancement of Behavior Therapy, New York.

Klieger, D. M. (1987). The Snake Anxiety Questionnaire as a measure of ophidophobia. *Educational and Psychological Measurement, 47,* 449–459.

Krijn, M., Emmelkamp, P. M. G., Biemond, R., de Wilde de Ligny, C., Schuemie, M. J., & van der Mast, C. A. P. G. (2004). Treatment of acrophobia in virtual reality: The role of immersion and presence. *Behaviour Research and Therapy, 42,* 229–239.

Lang, A. J., & Craske, M. G. (2000). Manipulations of exposure-based therapy to reduce return of fear: A replication. *Behaviour Research and Therapy, 38,* 1–12.

Lavy, E., & van den Hout, M. (1993). Selective attention evidenced by pictorial and linguistic Stroop tasks. *Behavior Therapy, 24,* 645–657.

Lipsitz, J. D., Barlow, D. H., Mannuzza, S., Hofmann, S. G., & Fyer, A. J. (2002). Clinical features of four *DSM-IV* specific phobia subtypes. *Journal of Nervous and Mental Disease, 190,* 471–478.

Magee, W. J., Eaton, W. W., Wittchen, H. U., McGonagle, K. A., & Kessler, R. C. (1996). Agoraphobia, simple phobia, and social phobia in the National Comorbidity Survey. *Archives of General Psychiatry, 53,* 159–168.

Maltby, N., Kirsch, I., Mayers, M., & Allen, G. J. (2002). Virtual reality exposure therapy for the treatment of fear of flying: A controlled investigation. *Journal of Consulting and Clinical Psychology, 70,* 1112–1118.

Marks, I. M., Kenwright, M., McDonough, M., Whittaker, M., & Mataix-Cols, D. (2004). Saving clinicians' time by delegating routine aspects of therapy to a computer: A randomized controlled trial in phobia/panic disorder. *Psychological Medicine, 34,* 9–17.

McCabe, R. E., & Antony, M. M. (2002). Specific and social phobias. In M. M. Antony & D. H. Barlow (Eds.), *Handbook of assessment, treatment planning, and outcome evaluation: Empirically supported strategies for psychological disorders* (pp. 113–146). New York: Guilford Press.

McCabe, R. E., Antony, M. M., & Ollendick, T. H. (in press). Assessment of specific phobias. In V. E. Caballo (Ed.), *Handbook of cognitive-behavioral assessment of psychological disorders.* Madrid, Spain: Piramide.

McNally, R. J. (1995). Preparedness, phobias, and the Panglossian paradigm. *Behavioral and Brain Science, 18,* 303–304.

McNally, R. J., & Steketee, G. S. (1985). The etiology and maintenance of severe animal phobias. *Behaviour Research and Therapy, 23,* 431–435.

Menzies, R. G., & Clarke, J. C. (1993a). A comparison of in vivo and vicarious exposure in the treatment of childhood water phobia. *Behaviour Research and Therapy, 31,* 9–15.

Menzies, R. G, & Clarke, J. C. (1993b). The etiology of fear of heights and its relationship to severity and individual response patterns. *Behaviour Research and Therapy, 31,* 355–365.

Menzies, R.G, & Clarke, J. C. (1995a). Danger expectancies and insight in acrophobia. *Behaviour Research and Therapy, 33,* 215–221.

Menzies, R. G, & Clarke, J. C. (1995b). The etiology of phobias: A non-associative account. *Clinical Psychology Review, 15,* 23–48.

Menzies, R. G., & Parker, L. (2001). The origins of height fear: An evaluation of neoconditioning explanations. *Behaviour Research and Therapy, 39,* 185–199.

Merckelbach, H., Arntz, A., Arrindell, W. A., & de Jong, P. J. (1992). Pathways to spider phobia. *Behaviour Research and Therapy, 30,* 543–546.

Merckelbach, H., & de Jong, P. J. (1996). Evolutionary models of phobias. In G. C. L. Davey (Ed.), *Phobias: A handbook of description, treatment, and theory.* Chichester, England: Wiley.

Merckelbach, H., de Jong, P. J., Arntz, A., & Schouten, E. (1993). The role of evaluative learning and disgust sensitivity in the etiology and treatment of spider phobia. *Advances in Behaviour Research and Therapy, 15,* 243–255.

Mineka, S., Mystkowski, J. L., Hladek, D., & Rodriguez, B. I. (1999). The effects of changing contexts on return of fear following exposure therapy for spider fear. *Journal of Consulting and Clinical Psychology, 67,* 599–604.

Mogotsi, M., Kaminer, D., & Stein, D. J. (2000). Quality of life in the anxiety disorders. *Harvard Review of Psychiatry, 8,* 273–282.

Mowrer, O. H. (1939). Stimulus response theory of anxiety. *Psychological Review, 46,* 553–565.

Muris, P., Bodden, D., Merckelbach, H., Ollendick, T. H., & King, N. (2003). Fear of the beast: A prospective study on the effects of negative information on childhood fear. *Behaviour Research and Therapy, 41,* 195–208.

Mystkowski, J. L., Mineka, S., Vernon, L. L., & Zinbarg, R. E. (2003). Changes in caffeine state enhance return of fear in spider phobia. *Journal of Consulting and Clinical Psychology, 71,* 243–250.

Neal, A. M., Lilly, R. S., & Zakis, S. (1993). What are African American children afraid of? A preliminary study. *Journal of Anxiety Disorders, 7,* 129–139.

Neiger, S., Atkinson, L., & Quarrington, B. (1981). A factor analysis of personality and fear variables in phobic disorders. *Canadian Journal of Behavioural Sciences, 13,* 336–348.

Ollendick, T. H., Davis, T. E., III, & Muris, P. (in press). The treatment of specific phobias in children and adolescents. In P. M. Barrett and T. H. Ollendick (Eds.), *Handbook of interventions that work with children and adolescents: From prevention to treatment.* London: Wiley.

Öst, L. G. (1987). Age of onset in different phobias. *Journal of Abnormal Psychology, 96,* 223–229.

Öst, L. G. (1989). One-session treatment for specific phobias. *Behaviour Research and Therapy, 27,* 1–7.

Öst, L. G. (1992). Blood and injection phobia: Background and cognitive, physiological, and behavioral variables. *Journal of Abnormal Psychology, 101,* 68–74.

Öst, L. G. (1996). One-session group treatment for spider phobia. *Behaviour Research and Therapy, 34,* 707–715.

Öst, L. G., Brandberg, M., & Alm, T. (1997). One versus five sessions of exposure in the treatment of flying phobia. *Behaviour Research and Therapy, 35,* 987–996.

Öst, L. G., Salkovskis, P. M., & Hellström, K. (1991). One-session therapist directed exposure vs. self-exposure in the treatment of spider phobia. *Behavior Therapy, 22,* 407–422.

Öst, L. G., & Sterner, U. (1987). Applied tension: A specific behavioral method for treatment of blood phobia. *Behaviour Research and Therapy, 25,* 25–29.

Page, A. C. (1994). Blood-injury phobia. *Clinical Psychology Review, 14,* 443–461.

Peterson, R. A., & Reiss, S. (1993). *Anxiety Sensitivity Index Revised test manual.* Worthington, OH: IDS Publishing.

Pierce, K. A., & Kirkpatrick, D. R. (1992). Do men lie on fear surveys? *Behaviour Research and Therapy, 30,* 415–418.

Poulton, R., & Menzies, R. G. (2002). Non-associative fear acquisition: A review of the evidence from retrospective and longitudinal research. *Behaviour Research and Therapy, 40,* 127–149.

Powers, M. B., Smits, J. A. J., Ngoc Bui, T., Harness, A., Caudwell, J., Barera, P., et al. (2002, November). *The effect of safety-behavior availability or utilization on claustrophobic fear reduction: A treatment study.* Poster presented at the Association for Advancement of Behavior Therapy Conference, Reno, NV.

Pratt, D., Cooper, M. J., & Hackmann, A. (2004). Imagery and its characteristics in people who are anxious about spiders. *Behavioural and Cognitive Psychotherapy, 32,* 165–176.

Rachman, S. (1977). The conditioning theory of fear-acquisition: A critical examination. *Behaviour Research and Therapy, 15,* 375–387.

Rachman, S. (1991). Neoconditioning and the classical theory of fear acquisition. *Clinical Psychology Review, 11,* 155–173.

Rachman, S., & Cuk, M. (1992). Fearful distortions. *Behaviour Research and Therapy, 30,* 583–589.

Rodriguez, B. I., & Craske, M. G. (1995). Does distraction interfere with fear reduction during exposure? A test among animal-fearful subjects. *Behavior Therapy, 26,* 337–349.

Romano, E., Tremblay, R. E., Vitaro, F., Zoccolillo, M., & Pagani, L. (2001). Prevalence of psychiatric diagnoses and the role of perceived impairment: Findings from an adolescent community sample. *Journal of Child Psychology and Psychiatry and Allied Disciplines, 42,* 451–461.

Rosenbaum, J. F., Biederman, J., Bolduc-Murphy, E. A., Faraone, S. V., Chaloff, J., Hirshfeld, D. R., et al. (1993). Behavioral inhibition in childhood: A risk factor for anxiety disorders. *Harvard Review of Psychiatry, 1,* 2–16.

Rothbaum, B. O., Hodges, L., Anderson, P. L., Price, L., & Smith, S. (2002). Twelve-month follow-up of virtual reality and standard exposure therapies for the fear of flying. *Journal of Consulting and Clinical Psychology, 70,* 428–432.

Rothbaum, B. O., Hodges, L. F., Smith, S., Lee, J. H., & Price, L. (2000). A controlled study of virtual reality exposure therapy for the fear of flying. *Journal of Consulting and Clinical Psychology, 68,* 1020–1026.

Rowe, M. K., & Craske, M. G. (1998a). Effects of an expanding-spaced vs. massed exposure schedule on fear reduction and return of fear. *Behaviour Research and Therapy, 36,* 701–717.

Rowe, M. K., & Craske, M. G. (1998b). Effects of varied-stimulus exposure training on fear reduction and return of fear. *Behaviour Research and Therapy, 36,* 719–734.

Sanderson, W. C., Di Nardo, P. A., Rapee, R. M., & Barlow, D. H. (1990). Syndrome comorbidity in patients diagnosed with a *DSM-III-R* anxiety disorder. *Journal of Abnormal Psychology, 99,* 308–312.

Sawchuk, C. N., Lohr, J. M., Tolin, D. F., Lee, T. C., & Kleinknecht, R. A. (2000). Disgust sensitivity and contamination fears in spider and blood-injection-injury phobias. *Behaviour Research and Therapy, 38,* 753–762.

Schonfeld, W. H., Verboncoeur, C. J., Fifer, S. K., Lipschutz, R. C., Lubeck, D. P., & Buesching, D. P. (1997). The functioning and well-being of patients with unrecognized anxiety disorders and major depressive disorder. *Journal of Affective Disorders, 43,* 105–119.

Seligman, M. E. P. (1971). Phobias and preparedness. *Behavior Therapy, 2,* 307–320.

Skre, I., Onstad, S., Torgersen, S., Lygren, S., & Kringlen, E. (2000). The heritability of common phobic fear: A twin study of a clinical sample. *Journal of Anxiety Disorders, 14,* 549–562.

Smits, J. A. J., Telch, M. J., & Randall, P. K. (2002). An examination of the decline in fear and disgust during exposure-based treatment. *Behaviour Research and Therapy, 40,* 1243–1253.

St-Jacques, J., & Bouchard, S. (2002, November). *Effectiveness of a virtual reality exposure for children and adolescents with arachnophobia.* Paper presented at the meeting of the Association for Advancement of Behavior Therapy, Reno, NV.

Summerfeldt, L. J., & Antony, M. M. (2002). Structured and semistructured diagnostic interviews. In M. M. Antony & D. H. Barlow (Eds.), *Handbook of assessment, treatment planning, and outcome evaluation: Empirically supported strategies for psychological disorders* (pp. 3–37). New York: Guilford Press.

Szymanski, J., & O'Donohue, W. (1995). Fear of Spiders Questionnaire. *Journal of Behavior Therapy and Experimental Psychiatry, 26,* 31–34.

Taylor, S. (1998). The hierarchic structure of fears. *Behaviour Research and Therapy, 36,* 205–214.

Teachman, B. A., Gregg, A. P., & Woody, S. R. (2001). Implicit associations for fear-relevant stimuli among individuals with snake and spider fears. *Journal of Abnormal Psychology, 110,* 226–235.

Ten Berge, M., Veerkamp, J. S. J., & Hoogstraten, J. (2002). The etiology of childhood dental fear: The role of dental and conditioning experiences. *Journal of Anxiety Disorders, 16,* 321–329.

Thorpe, S. J., & Salkovskis, P. M. (1998). Studies on the role of disgust in the acquisition and maintenance of specific phobias. *Behaviour Research and Therapy, 36,* 877–893.

Thorpe, S. J., & Salkovskis, P. M. (2000). Recall and recognition memory for spider information. *Journal of Anxiety Disorders, 14,* 359–375.

Tolin, D. F., Lohr, J. M., Lee, T. C., & Sawchuk, C. N. (1999). Visual avoidance in specific phobia. *Behaviour Research and Therapy, 37,* 63–70.

Tolin, D. F., Lohr, J. M., Sawchuk, C. N., & Lee, T. C. (1997). Disgust and disgust sensitivity in blood-injection-injury and spider phobia. *Behaviour Research and Therapy, 35,* 949–953.

Valentiner, D. P., Telch, M. J., Petruzzi, D. C., & Bolte, M. C. (1996). Cognitive mechanisms in claustrophobia: An examination of Reiss and McNally's expectancy model and Bandura's self-efficacy theory. *Cognitive Therapy and Research, 20,* 593–612.

Verburg, C., Griez, E., & Meijer, J. (1994). A 35% carbon dioxide challenge in simple phobias. *Acta Psychiatrica Scandinavica, 90,* 420–423.

Wald, J., & Taylor, S. (2000). Efficacy of virtual reality exposure therapy to treat driving phobia: A case report. *Journal of Behaviour Therapy and Experimental Psychiatry, 31,* 249–257.

Watson, D., Clark, L. A., & Carey, G. (1988). Positive and negative affect and their relation to anxiety and depressive disorders. *Journal of Abnormal Psychology, 97,* 346–353.

Watts, F. N., Trezise, L., & Sharrock, R. (1986). Processing of phobic stimuli. *British Journal of Clinical Psychology, 25,* 253–259.

Wessel, I., & Merckelbach, H. (1997). The impact of anxiety on memory for details in spider phobics. *Applied Cognitive Psychology, 11,* 223–231.

Wessel, I., & Merckelbach, H. (1998). Memory for threat-relevant and threat-irrelevant cues in spider phobics. *Cognition and Emotion, 12,* 93–104.

Wilson, G. D., Kumari, V., Gray, J. A., & Corr, P. J. (2000). The role or neuroticism in startle reactions to fearful and disgusting stimuli. *Personality and Individual Differences, 29,* 1077–1082.

Wolpe, J., & Lang, P. J. (1964). A Fear Survey Schedule for use in behaviour therapy. *Behaviour Research and Therapy, 2,* 27–30.

Woodruff-Borden, J., Brothers, A. J., Lasch, K. H., Jeffery, S., & Butterman, J. (1997, November). *Suicidality across the anxiety disorders: Frequency and specificity.* Poster presented at the Association for Advancement of Behavior Therapy Conference, Miami Beach, FL.

Woody, S. R., & Teachman, B. A. (2000). Intersection of disgust and fear: Normative and pathological views. *Clinical Psychology: Science and Practice, 7,* 291–311.

Wright, L. M., Holborn, S. W., & Rezutek, P. E. (2002). An experimental test of stimulus estimation theory: Danger and safety with snake phobic stimuli. *Behaviour Research and Therapy, 40,* 911–922.

Yartz, A. R., & Hawk, L. W. (2001). Psychophysiological assessment of anxiety: Tales from the heart. In M. M. Antony, S. M. Orsillo, & L. Roemer (Eds.), *Practitioner's guide to empirically based measures of anxiety* (pp. 25–30). New York: Kluwer Academic/Plenum.

CHAPTER 11

Obsessive-Compulsive Disorder

DAVID S. RIGGS AND EDNA B. FOA

DESCRIPTION OF THE DISORDER AND CLINICAL PICTURE

The behaviors and symptoms that characterize what is now known as obsessive-compulsive disorder (OCD) have been recognized for centuries in many cultures (for a review, see Pitman, 1994), and the syndrome was first described as a medical/mental problem by Esquirol in 1838. Over the years, the characterization of the obsessive-compulsive syndrome has changed somewhat, but core elements have remained fairly stable. It has long been recognized that obsessive-compulsives experience both intrusive thoughts, ideas that generate distress, and repetitive behaviors that are carried out compulsively. The current diagnostic definition of OCD retains these dual manifestations although a person can be diagnosed with OCD if he or she manifests either obsessions or compulsions. According to the *DSM-IV* (American Psychiatric Association, 1994), OCD is characterized by recurrent obsessions defined as "persistent ideas, thoughts, impulses, or images that are experienced as intrusive and inappropriate and cause marked anxiety or distress" (p. 418) and by compulsions defined as "repetitive behaviors . . . or mental acts . . . the goal of which is to prevent or reduce anxiety or distress" (p. 418).

The *DSM-IV* definition of OCD is similar to earlier conceptualizations, but it incorporates several important ideas that were not included in previous models of the disorder. It retains the *DSM-III-R* view that emphasized the functional relationship between obsessions and compulsions, i.e., compulsions are performed in order to prevent harm or decrease distress associated with obsessions (Foa & Tillmanns, 1980). There is strong empirical support for this view. For example, in the *DSM-IV* field study on OCD, 90 percent of participants reported that their compulsions aim to either prevent harm associated with their obsessions or reduce obsessional distress (Foa et al., 1995). Data from the field study also indicated that almost all (about 98 percent) of individuals with OCD manifest both obsessions and compulsive rituals (including behavioral and mental rituals). More than 90 percent reported overt behavioral rituals (Foa et al., 1995). The *DSM-IV* introduced the idea that compulsions can be manifested by either overt behaviors (e.g., repeated washing) or mental rituals (e.g., silently repeating prayers) and that both function to reduce obsessional distress, prevent feared harm, or restore safety. Thus, the old distinction between obsessions as mental events and compulsions as behavioral events is no longer valid: all obsessions are mental events, but compulsions may be behavioral or mental.

Earlier conceptualizations of OCD required that individuals acknowledge their obsessions and compulsions as senselessness or excessive. However, this view has been challenged and it has become clear that not all OCD sufferers have insight into the senseless nature of their symptoms. Indeed, a minority of people with OCD contend that their obsessions and rituals are completely rationale. Therefore, it has been argued that a continuum of "insight" or "strength of belief" more accurately depicts the clinical presentation of OCD than the previously view that all obsessive-compulsives recognize the senselessness of their obsessions and compulsions (Kozak & Foa, 1994). At present, individuals who evidence obsessions and compulsions but do not recognize their senselessness receive the diagnosis of OCD "with poor insight." However, clinical observations suggest that obsessive-compulsives' insight into their own difficulties may fluctuate across time and situations. Thus, patients may recognize the senselessness of their symptoms when discussing them as part of an evaluation, but when confronted with the feared situation, they lose this insight. Other factors such as mood, presence of other people, and stress may also impact on insight. The importance of the patients' insight into their OCD symptoms is highlighted by the finding that individuals with poor insight may be less responsive to exposure and ritual prevention, a first line treatment for OCD (Foa, Abramowitz, Franklin, & Kozak, 1999).

OCD Subtypes

Although the *DSM-IV* does not formally distinguish between subtypes of OCD (except for identifying those with poor insight), many OCD classification schemes categorize obsessive-compulsives according to the topography of the ritualistic activity (i.e., compulsions). However, whereas few obsessive-compulsives manifest only one type of ritual (e.g., washing), most manifest multiple obsessions and compulsions (e.g., washing, checking and repeating). The predominant ritual may be used to classify an individual with OCD (e.g., as a washer, a checker, a repeater), but because typical presentations include multiple forms of rituals, it is more common to classify symptoms rather than individuals. Thus, a patient may be described as having washing and repeating rituals.

Relying on compulsions to classify OCD subtypes is likely due to the relative ease of observing overt compulsions. However, it is important to note that topographically similar behaviors may be functionally related to different obsessive fears. Thus, one patient may wash compulsively to remove germs and prevent illness whereas another may wash to ensure that he has no semen on his hands that might cause him to impregnate a woman inadvertently. Therefore, though it may be useful to classify OCD patients on the basis of their rituals, it is important to identify their obsessions as well to ensure a full understanding of the function of the ritual.

Ritualistic washing is the most common compulsion and is typically performed to decrease discomfort associated with obsessional fears about germs or diseases. For example, individuals who fear contact with "AIDS germs" clean themselves excessively in order to prevent either contracting AIDS themselves or spreading it to others. In addition (or alternatively) to washing themselves excessively, some washers will clean their environment to excess. Ritualistic washing may involve multiple repetitions, radical cleansers (e.g., bleach, alcohol), or ritualized patterns of washing. For some washers, there is no fear of contracting an illness or spreading it to others. Instead, the state of being contaminated or unclean generates extreme discomfort without a feared consequence. Here, too, the washing rituals serve to decrease this distress.

Another common compulsion is repetitive checking. Patients typically check to assure themselves that a feared catastrophe will not happen or has not happened. Because there are many potential feared catastrophes, obsessive-compulsives check a wide variety of things. Some of the most commonly reported checks include making sure that doors are locked, faucets are off, electrical appliances are off (and/or unplugged), that one hasn't lost important possessions (e.g., keys, wallet), and that one has not hit a pedestrian while driving. Thus, individuals who fear that a burglar will enter their home, take their valuables, and possibly harm their family will repeatedly check doors and windows to decrease this fear. Similarly, compulsive checkers who fear that they might run over a pedestrian and fail to notice it will repeatedly retrace their driving route to search for possible victims. This same person may check news reports to make sure that no hit-and-run accidents were reported.

Other rituals such as repeating, ordering, and counting may serve to prevent disasters much as checking does, but often the mechanism through which they operate is more superstitious or magical. These rituals tend to lack the logical connection to the feared consequence seen in checkers. For example, it is logical (if excessive) to check the windows many times if one fears a burglary, but it is illogical to count the letters in words repeatedly to prevent a loved one's death in a motor vehicle accident. Notably, many repeaters, orderers, and counters perform their rituals just to reduce distress or to ensure that things "feel right," rather than to prevent a feared disaster.

Repeating and counting, and to a lesser extent checking in the form of reviewing may manifest as mental rituals with little or no observable behavior associated with them. Repeaters may find themselves repeating words, sounds, songs, prayers, or images in an attempt to "undo" an obsessive thought or image. Similarly, counters may count silently rather than aloud. Reviewers will find themselves replaying actions in their mind to assure themselves that they actually completed the action or completed it correctly. Individuals with mental rituals often describe them as automatic or uncontrollable in part because they tend to be very brief (e.g., a single word or phrase), though sometimes they must be repeated for a prolonged time to reduce distress.

Hoarders are another class of obsessive-compulsives that involves the accumulation of excessive amounts of material. Hoarding is atypical in that many hoarders engage in little compulsive activity, but are perhaps better characterized as avoidant. Instead of going to great lengths to collect materials to save, many hoarders simply avoid discarding items they encounter in everyday life (e.g., newspapers, string) for fear of not having them available in the future. There are, of course, hoarders who do compulsively accumulate certain materials (e.g., subscribing to multiple newspapers, downloading excessive amounts of information from the Internet, buying many "copies" of an item). Over long periods of time, consistent avoidance of discarding can result in overwhelming accumulations, even in the absence of active gathering rituals. Hoarded material can vary from items of some monetary value (e.g., complete sets of *Sports Illustrated* magazines) to those that are worthless (e.g., chicken bones, empty milk containers). A diagnosis of OCD is more complicated when the hoarded material is "collectible" or potentially valuable. In these cases, the diagnosis relies more on the distress associated with the loss or failure to obtain the collectible object, or by the functional impairment resulting from the collection and associated activities (e.g., oven filled with comic books, failure to go to work in order to tend to collection).

In pediatric OCD, the most common compulsions are washing and cleaning followed by checking, counting, repeating, touching, and straightening (Swedo, Rapoport, Leonard, Lenane, & Cheslow, 1989). The obsessions that correspond to these rituals are fear of contamination, harm to self, harm to a familiar person, and symmetry/exactness urges. As with adult OCD sufferers, most children and adolescents present with more than one type of ritual. In almost all cases, children's symptoms are driven by one or more dysphoric affects, including anxiety, fear, doubt, or disgust. However, some rituals are performed in response to rudimentary urges and feelings of having to get it to feel "just right," which some have labeled sensory incompleteness. The child's developmental stage may influence the OCD presentation: for example, clinical experience suggests that children are more likely to experience "magical" or superstitious OCD perhaps because children tend to be more magical in their thinking in general than are adults.

EPIDEMIOLOGY

Once thought to be rare, it is now estimated that approximately 2.5 percent of the adult population has OCD at some point in their lifetimes (Karno, Golding, Sorenson, & Burnam, 1988; Rasmussen & Eisen, 1992; Sasson, et al., 1997). Incidence rates over a 12-month period have been estimated at 0.7 percent (Andrews, Henderson, & Hall, 2001), and current incidence rates for OCD range from 0.5 percent to 1.6 percent (Andrews et al., 2001; Rasmussen & Eisen, 1992). Recent epidemiological studies of OCD among children and adolescents suggest similar lifetime prevalence rates in these populations (e.g., Flament et al., 1988; Valleni-Basile et al., 1994). Studies suggest that slightly more than half of the adults with OCD are female (Rasmussen & Tsuang, 1986), but among pediatric clinical samples boys outnumber girls almost two to one (e.g., Hanna, 1995; Swedo et al., 1989).

ETIOLOGY

Over the years, several theoretical accounts have been put forth to account for the etiology and maintenance of OCD. Dollard and Miller (1950) proposed Mowrer's (1939, 1960) two-stage theory for the acquisition and maintenance of fear and avoidance behavior to explain OCD symptoms. According to this theory, a previously neutral object, event or situation may come to elicit fear after being paired with, or experienced with, an event that by its nature causes anxiety and distress. Distress can be conditioned to mental events (e.g., thoughts) as well as to physical events (e.g., bathrooms, electrical appliances). Once fear is acquired, escape or avoidance patterns develop to reduce fear, and are maintained by the negative reinforcement of fear reduction. In the case of OCD, passive-avoidance strategies, such as those used by phobics, are not sufficient to control distress because the situations that evoke fear are not easily avoided. Therefore, compulsions, or active avoidance strategies, develop and are maintained by their success in reducing fear and alleviating distress.

It has been acknowledged that Mowrer's theory does not adequately account for fear acquisition (Rachman & Wilson, 1980), but it is consistent with observations about the maintenance of compulsive rituals. That is, compulsions appear to be, at least in part, maintained by the fact that they reduce the anxiety and distress arising from the obsessions (e.g., Roper & Rachman, 1976; Roper, Rachman, & Hodgson, 1973). Evidence in support of this formulation includes psychophysiological studies showing significant increases in heart rate and skin conductance in response to obsessional thoughts or exposure to feared (e.g., contaminated) objects (Boulougouris, Rabavilas, & Stefanis, 1977; Hodgson & Rachman, 1972; Hornsveld, Kraaimaat, & van Dam-Baggen, 1979). Importantly, performance of a ritual following the provocation of an urge to ritualize typically resulted in a decrease of anxiety (Hodgson & Rachman, 1972; Hornsveld et al., 1979; Roper & Rachman, 1976; Roper et al., 1973).

Cognitive theorists have argued that OCD is founded in ideas of exaggerated negative consequences (Carr, 1974; McFall & Wollersheim, 1979). These models suggest that obsessional content typically exaggerates common concerns (e.g., health, death, religion, etc.) combined with erroneous beliefs regarding the need to be perfect, the "magical" power of rituals, and that failure should be punished. However, clinical observations suggest that mistaken evaluation of danger and the idea that self-worth is connected with being perfect are typical of all anxiety disorders. Thus, these theories do not address the characteristics that distinguish OCD from other disorders.

Salkovskis (1985) offered a more thorough cognitive analysis of OCD. He proposed that intrusive thoughts interact with the person's belief system such that the obsession leads to negative automatic thoughts. These thoughts focus largely on issues of responsibility and self-blame. Compulsions, behavioral or cognitive, are seen as attempts to reduce responsibility and prevent blame. Salkovskis further proposed that five assumptions are specifically characteristic of OCD: (1) thinking of an action is analogous to its performance; (2) failing to prevent (or failing to try to prevent) harm to self or others is morally equivalent to causing the harm; (3) responsibility for harm is not diminished by extenuating circumstances; (4) failing to ritualize in response to an idea about harm constitutes an intention to harm; and (5) one should exercise control over one's thoughts (Salkovskis, 1985, p. 579). An interesting implication of this theory is that whereas the obsessive intrusions may be seen by the patient as unacceptable, the automatic thoughts and the mental and overt rituals that they prompt will be acceptable.

Foa and Kozak (1985) hypothesized that OCD, and anxiety disorders in general, reflect impairments in emotional memory networks. These impairments reflect the presence of erroneous estimates of threat, high negative valences for the feared consequences, and excessive responses to the feared stimuli. Foa and Kozak suggested that obsessive-compulsives are distinguished from other anxiety-disordered individuals by an additional problem in the mechanisms underlying information processing. Specifically, they proposed that obsessive-compulsives have impairments in the processes or rules for interpreting threat or harm. Thus, obsessive-compulsives often conclude that a situation is dangerous because they lack evidence of safety. In contrast, non-OCD persons tend to conclude that a situation is safe unless there is clear evidence of danger. For example, in order to feel safe, an OCD sufferer requires a guarantee that the toilet seat is safe (uncontaminated by germs) before sitting on it, whereas a person without OCD would assume that the toilet seat is clean and safe unless there was something particular about it indicating danger, such as visible brown spots on the seat. Because complete assurance of safety is unattainable, rituals that are performed to reach complete safety will inevitably fail. That is, no amount of rituals can guarantee that the situation is truly safe; thus, the ritual must be repeated.

There is evidence to support the role of cognitive difficulties in OCD, but the specific deficits or impairments are not yet clearly delineated. OCD is associated with indecisiveness (Summerfeldt, Huta, & Swinson, 1998), and persistent doubt about the accuracy of memories for actions that could cause harm (Rachman & Hodgson, 1980; Reed, 1976). Some studies have identified general memory deficits in OCD, particularly in nonverbal memory (Tallis, Pratt, & Jamani, 1999; Zitterl et al., 2001), but a number of studies have failed to find hypothesized memory deficits (e.g., Brown, Kosslyn, Breiter, Baer, & Jenike, 1994; Constans, Foa, Franklin, & Mathews, 1995; Foa, Amir, Gershuny, Molnar, & Kozak, 1997; McNally & Kohlbeck, 1993; Radomsky & Rachman, 1999; Tolin et al., 2001). One study found that obsessive-compulsives had a better memory for threat-related than for neutral actions, a difference that was not apparent in the comparison sample (Constans et al., 1995). Studies of obsessive-compulsives have consistently found that, compared to nonanxious controls, obsessive-compulsives report less *confidence* in their memory judgments (Brown et al., 1994; Foa et al., 1997; MacDonald, Antony, MacLeod, & Richter, 1997; McNally & Kohlbeck, 1993; Tolin et al., 2001; Zitterl et al., 2001). Several studies found that obsessive-compulsives require more information before arriving at a decision (Goodwin & Sher, 1992; Milner, Beech, & Walker, 1971; Volans, 1976). One recent study found that the need for additional information is driven, at least in part, by feelings of distress suggesting that perceptions of risk can influence the degree to which obsessive-compulsives are unsure of decisions that they are making (Foa et al., 2003).

The prevailing biological model of OCD hypothesizes that abnormal serotonin metabolism is expressed in OCD symptoms. The efficacy of serotonin reuptake inhibitors (SRIs) for OCD as compared to nonserotonergic compounds and to pill placebo (PBO) has provided a compelling argument for this hypothesis (Zohar & Insel, 1987). Also, significant correlations between clomipramine (CMI) plasma levels and improvement in OCD have been found, leading researchers to suggest that serotonin function mediates obsessive-compulsive symptoms and lending further support to the serotonin hypothesis (Insel et al., 1983; Stern, Marks, Mawson, & Luscombe, 1980). However, studies that directly investigated serotonin functioning in obsessive-compulsives are inconclusive. For example, studies that examined serotonin platelet uptake failed to differentiate obsessive-compulsives from controls (Insel, Mueller, Alterman, Linnoila, & Murphy, 1985; Weizman et al., 1986). Also inconsistent with the serotonin hypothesis are findings that clomipramine, a nonselective serotonergic medication, appears to produce greater reductions in OCD symptoms than selective serotonin reuptake inhibitors such as fluoxetine, fluvoxamine, and sertraline (Greist, Jefferson, Kobak, Katzelnick, & Serlin, 1995).

COURSE, COMPLICATIONS, AND PROGNOSIS

Onset of the disorder typically ranges from early adolescence to young adulthood, with males generally developing symptoms at a younger age. Modal onset in males is between 13 and 15 years old, and in females it is between 20 and 24 years old (Rasmussen & Eisen, 1990). Notably, cases of OCD have been documented in much younger children, even as young as age 2 (Rapoport, Swedo, & Leonard, 1992). The disorder usually develops gradually, but more acute onset has been reported in some cases. One study reported that obsessive-compulsives with a relatively early onset to their symptoms (younger than 15) had a more gradual onset of symptoms, whereas those whose symptoms began after age 15 were more likely to report a sudden onset of symptoms (Millet et al., 2004). Early onset cases also reported more obsessions and more compulsions (particularly repeating, counting and tapping rituals) than did the late onset participants. Finally, those with early onset OCD were more likely to report motor and verbal tics and less likely to report depression than were obsessive-compulsives with later onset of symptoms.

A subset of pediatric patients suffer from a similar clinical course of illness now referred to as pediatric autoimmune neuropsychiatric disorders associated with strep (PANDAS), in which patients experience dramatic onset OCD and/or tic symptoms following strep infection (Swedo et al., 1998). Notably, these symptoms in PANDAS are often followed with periods of relative symptom quiescence once the infection is successfully treated. If the child is reinfected with strep, the OCD symptoms often reoccur as well.

If untreated, OCD is typically a chronic disorder. Over time, the symptoms may wax and wane in severity, but they rarely remit without treatment. However, other patterns are possible with approximately 10 percent of obsessive-compulsives reporting episodic and deteriorating courses (Rasmussen & Eisen, 1989). Most obsessive-compulsives suffer for years before seeking treatment with one study finding that patients presented for psychiatric treatment an average of more than seven years after the onset of their symptoms (Rasmussen & Tsuang, 1986). In another study, almost two-thirds of the sample (63 percent) had not sought treatment for OCD despite having symptoms lasting about 16 years on average (Mayerovitch et al., 2003).

Associated Disorders

OCD commonly occurs with other mental health symptoms including depression, anxiety, worry, and phobic avoidance (e.g., Rasmussen & Eisen, 1992; Sasson et al., 1997; Tukel, Polat, Ozdemir, Askut, & Turksoy, 2002). Indeed, it is more common for OCD to co-occur with another psychiatric disorder than to be the sole complaint (Pigott, L'Heureux, Dubbert, Bernstein, & Murphy, 1994; Sasson et al., 1997; Tukel et al., 2002). The most commonly reported Axis I comorbid disorder is depression with as many as two-thirds of obsessive-compulsives having comorbid depression (Crino & Andrews, 1996; Rasmussen & Eisen, 1992; Sasson et al., 1997; Tukel et al., 2002). Other comorbid Axis I diagnoses include simple phobia, social phobia, dysthymia, and substance use disorders, each of which has been reported in about 10 percent to 20 percent of obsessive-compulsive samples (Crino & Andrews, 1996; Mayerovitch et al., 2003; Rasmussen & Eisen, 1992; Sasson et al., 1997). Among obsessive-compulsives with additional Axis I diagnoses, it is common to find multiple problems. For example, Mayerovitch et al. (2003) assessed comorbid Axis I diagnoses in a sample of 172 obsessive-compulsive samples from the adult population of Edmonton, Canada, and found that 24 percent of the sample had one additional diagnosis, 24 percent had two additional diagnoses, and 32 percent of the sample had three or more diagnoses in addition to OCD. Similarly, in a sample of 147 patients being treated for OCD in an outpatient clinic, Tukel et al. (2002) found that about 26 percent had one comorbid disorder, 28 percent had two additional disorders, and 14 percent had three or more Axis I diagnoses in addition to the OCD.

There are fewer studies examining the co-occurrence of personality (Axis II) disorders with OCD than those examining Axis I disorders, and to the best of our knowledge, no epidemiological studies have examined the question of Axis II comorbidities. Further, sampling and methodological differences among the existing clinical studies make it difficult to draw firm conclusions about the rate of Axis II comorbidity among obsessive-compulsives. Several studies have documented overall rates of personality disorders in about 33 percent of obsessive-compulsives seeking treatment (Black, Noyes, Pfohl, Goldstein, & Blum, 1993; Samuels et al., 2000; Steketee, Chambless, & Tran, 2001; Tenney, Schotte, Denys, van Megan, & Westenberg, 2003). Other studies document significantly higher rates of Axis II disorders with estimates as high as 85 percent (Black et al., 1993; Joffe, Swinson, & Regan, 1988), and one study found only 9 percent of obsessive-compulsives with a personality disorder (Crino & Andrews, 1996). Of obsessive-compulsives diagnosed with a personality disorder, about two-thirds are diagnosed with one or more of the anxious or cluster C disorders (avoidant, dependent, obsessive-compulsive) with smaller proportions (10 percent to 30 percent) meeting criteria for a cluster A or B disorder (Denys et al., 2003; Samuels et al., 2000; Steketee et al., 2001).

ASSESSMENT AND DIAGNOSIS

A number of assessment instruments have been developed to diagnose and/or measure the severity of OCD. These instruments vary in form (i.e., interview versus self-report) and focus (i.e., documenting symptoms versus identifying treatment targets). One of the most commonly used instruments is the Yale-Brown Obsessive Compulsive Scale (Y-BOCS). The Y-BOCS provides three continuous severity scores (obsessions, compulsions, total) based on five items assessing the severity of obsessions and five parallel items assessing the severity of compulsions. However, the items assess the severity of interference and distress associated with the OCD symptoms rather than the severity of the symptom themselves. The Y-BOCS has excellent psychometric properties (Goodman, Price, Rasmussen, Mazure, et al., 1989) and has demonstrated sensitivity to treatment response. However, estimates of discriminant validity are poor (Taylor, 1995). The Y-BOCS also includes an extensive checklist that provides information about the content of the obsessions and compulsions. This information can be quite useful clinically, but the size and nature of the checklist makes it difficult to summarize the nature and severity of specific content areas.

In addition to the Y-BOCS, interview-based assessment instruments for OCD are included in broader standardized assessment interviews including the Standardized Clinical Interview for *DSM-IV* (SCID), the Mini International Neuropsychiatric Interview (MINI), and the Anxiety Disorders Interview Schedule (ADIS). Each of these diagnostic interviews has well-established psychometric properties and has been widely used in both research and clinical settings. The primary drawback to these instruments is that they are time consuming to administer and, except for the ADIS, do not provide estimates of severity.

Several self-report instruments designed to assess OCD symptom severity have been developed. The Obsessive-Compulsive Inventory (OCI; Foa, Kozak, Salkovskis, Coles, & Amir, 1998) is a questionnaire that assesses symptom severity in each of five types of compulsions (washing, checking, hoarding, ordering, and mental neutralizing) as well as obsessing and doubting. The OCI total score and subscales have good internal consistency, reliability and validity (Foa, Kozak, et al., 1998). The response of the OCI to treatment has not yet been examined. Recently, a short version of the OCI (18 items versus 42 items) was developed and found to have satisfactory psychometric properties (Foa, Franklin, & Moser, 2002).

The Leyton Obsessional Inventory (LOI) is a card-sort task that has shown good reliability and validity estimates (Cooper, 1970; Taylor, 1995). Several studies suggest that the LOI is less sensitive to treatment changes than are other similar measures (Allen & Rack, 1975; Ananth, Solyom, Bryntwick, & Krishnappa, 1979) and the card-sort procedure can be cumbersome. A questionnaire version of the LOI, the Lynfield Obsessional/Compulsive Questionnaire (LOCQ) has been developed, but its psychometric properties have not been established (Allen, 1977; Allen & Tune, 1975).

The Maudsley Obsessive-Compulsive Inventory (MOCI; Hodgson & Rachman, 1977) is a questionnaire with good internal validity and reliability (Rachman & Hodgson, 1980). The MOCI provides severity estimates for the total score and four empirically derived subscales, washing, checking, slowness, and doubting. The Padua Inventory (PI; Sanavio, 1988) is another questionnaire that assesses obsessions and compulsions. Like the MOCI, the PI has four subscales, impaired mental control, contamination, checking, and loss of control of actions. Internal consistency and reliability are satisfactory. Both the MOCI and the PI have been used in research and clinical settings, but each fails to assess specific areas of OCD symptomatology (e.g., hoarding, neutralizing).

Two additional questionnaire measures focus specifically on obsessions or on compulsions. The Compulsive Activity Checklist (CAC), originally developed as the Obsessive-Compulsive Interview Checklist (Marks, Hallman, Connolly, & Philpott, 1977), focuses specifically on washing and checking compulsions. It has adequate psychometric properties (Freund, Steketee, & Foa, 1987) and appears responsive to treatment (Foa, Steketee, Grayson, Turner, & Latimer, 1984). In contrast, the Obsessive Thoughts Questionnaire (OTC; Cottraux, 1989) focuses on obsessions. Internal consistency and reliability estimates were satisfactory, and a factor analysis revealed two distinct factors: perfectionism and pathological responsibility (Cottraux, 1989).

Diagnostic Issues

The high rates of comorbidity present among individuals with OCD may make diagnosis, and particularly differential diagnosis, difficult. As mentioned previously, many obsessive-compulsives experience significant depression, but it is also the case that many people with depression experience ruminations that may resemble obsessions, but do not warrant a diagnosis of OCD. The primary distinction between obsessions and depressive ruminations has to do with the individual's reaction to them. Because depressive ruminations tend to be congruent with the person's depressed mood, there is rarely much attempt to suppress or ignore them. In contrast, obsessive-compulsives work incessantly to suppress the obsessive thoughts. This distinction may be obscured by the presence of cognitive or mental compulsions that obsessive-compulsives typically do not try to suppress. However, because these thoughts function to reduce distress (by their nature as a compulsive ritual), they tend to be incongruent with depressed moods.

Recently, a number of authors have noted the comorbidity between OCD and post-traumatic stress disorder (PTSD; Becker, 2002; de Silva & Marks, 1999; Gershuny, Baer, Wilson, Radomsky, & Jenkie, 2003; Jenike, 2001; Kimble, 2000; Pitman, 1993). Although the rate of co-occurrence of these two disorders appears somewhat greater than chance (Breslau, Davis, Andreski, & Peterson, 1991; Brown, Campbell, Lehman, Grisham, & Mancill, 2001; Slade & Andrews, 2002), it is not clear whether this reflects a shared mechanism or simply an overlap in symptoms (Huppert et al., in press). Both disorders are characterized by intrusive, unwanted, distressing thoughts. However, in the case of PTSD, these thoughts are typically recollections of the traumatic event that precipitated the symptoms, whereas obsessions are almost always fears of things that might occur in the future. Individuals with PTSD may also develop repetitive behaviors or routines designed to avoid or prevent a future trauma. Some of these may appear topographically similar to compulsive rituals. For example, after being raped at home one might routinely check the doors and windows prior to going to bed to ensure that an intruder will not gain easy entry. In contrast to compulsions though, the behaviors seen in PTSD tend to be thematically linked to the prior trauma and are only rarely associated with dramatic increases in distress if they are interrupted or have the sense of urgency seen in obsessions.

The potential presence of additional anxiety disorders means that a clinician must strive to determine whether the distress that the patient is reporting arises from obsessional fears or other phobic stimuli. Also, avoidance strategies adopted to manage anxiety due to a simple phobia or panic disorder may be repeated in an almost ritualistic manner, complicating the diagnostic question. Patients with post-traumatic stress disorder (PTSD) will report intrusive recollections of their trauma that elicit fear and distress. Similarly, depressive rumination about unpleasant events or life problems may mimic obsessions. In some cases (e.g., simple phobia) these difficulties may reflect the shortcomings in the specificity of the current diagnostic criteria; in other cases (e.g., PTSD) the diagnostic difficulty may reflect phenomenologically similar symptoms with distinct etiologies.

Generalized anxiety disorder (GAD) is characterized by excessive worry that can often seem obsessional. Such worries are distinguished from obsessions in OCD in that the worries typically are excessive concerns about real-life problems. These worries are usually experienced as appropriate given the patient's current circumstances. An example is excessive worry about the possibility of being fired or about possible financial problems. In contrast, obsessions tend to be unrealistic fears (e.g., "If I don't touch the door five times my mother will die") and the obsessions are experienced as inappropriate or ego dystonic. In cases in which the obsessional fear reflects a realistic danger (e.g., "If I eat without washing my hands I will become ill") the obsessive-compulsive, like the person with GAD, will tend to exaggerate the likelihood of the consequence.

As mentioned previously, individuals with OCD may have additional phobias. It is also the case that many obsessive-compulsives will avoid situations much as a phobic would. For example, a person who obsesses about germs may avoid petting dogs and thus appear to be dog phobic. However, the dog phobic is afraid about being bitten by the dog, whereas the obsessive-compulsive person is afraid of catching a disease. Because of this, obsessive fears will not be limited to a single type of object (e.g., dogs) but will instead manifest across a wide range of situations. This also means that passive-avoidance or escape behaviors are less likely to work for obsessive-compulsive who instead develop active rituals to reduce distress. Thus, the obsessive-compulsive, but not the phobic individual, will exhibit ritualistic behavior.

Other diagnostic complications arise with disorders such as hypochondriasis and body dysmorphic disorder (BDD). In both cases, individuals manifest worries about having a physical malady (illness in the case of hypochondriasis and a physical defect in BDD) that may rise to the level of obsessiveness. Some obsessive-compulsives will also manifest fears about their physical health (particularly in the case of contamination fears) or appearance; this often couples with checking rituals and seeking reassurance from others that function to reduce distress. Such rituals may also be present in persons that carry a diagnosis of BDD or hypochondriasis, including the tendency to repeatedly seek consultation and testing from physicians. When obsessions or compulsions that are not directly related to the physical concern are also present in the same person, it is probably appropriate to diagnose him/her as having OCD (Riggs & Foa, 1993). However, differentiating between OCD and these two disorders is often difficult.

Ritualized and repetitive motor behaviors can occur in Tourette's syndrome and related tic disorders. It is also the case that a subgroup of obsessive-compulsives, particularly those who develop OCD at an early age, also suffer from a tic disorder. In most cases, the differentiation of the disorders is based on the function of the behaviors. In OCD, the rituals function to lessen the distress associated with the obsession. In contrast, in tic disorders, the behaviors do not reduce distress but are generally perceived as involuntary and unintentional. Some patients with tic disorders do report that completing the movement reduces a sense of stress or that resisting the urge will increase tension, but this feeling tends not to be associated with any feared consequences as is typical of OCD.

As mentioned previously, the issue of how strongly an obsession is held varies across patients. In some cases, obsessive-compulsives may present with obsessive beliefs that they hold so strongly that they appear delusional, leading to the possibility that they should be diagnosed with delusional disorder or schizophrenia. Typically, obsessions of delusional intensity can be distinguished from delusional disorder by the presence of associated rituals that are almost always present in obsessive-compulsives but usually not in patients with delusional disorder. Like schizophrenic delusions, obsessions seen in OCD may appear quite bizarre. For example, one patient feared that he might accidentally leave parts of his body behind when he left a room. However, even when obsessions are bizarre and reach delusional intensity, obsessive-compulsives rarely manifest other symptoms of schizophrenia such as prominent hallucinations, thought insertion/projections, flat or inappropriate affect, or loosening of associations. It should be remembered though that some individuals will meet criteria for both diagnoses.

IMPACT ON ENVIRONMENT

As might be expected given the chronic nature of OCD as well as the common delay in obtaining treatment, the disorder is associated with impairments in general functioning and quality of life (Hollander, Kwon, Stein, & Broatch, 1996; Sorensen, Kirkeby, & Thomsen, 2004). Problems include disruptions of academic endeavors (Sorensen et al., 2004), employment (Leon, Portera & Weissman, 1995; Sorenson et al., 2004), and difficulties in marital and other interpersonal relationship difficulties (Emmelkamp, de Haan, & Hoogduin, 1990; Riggs, Hiss. & Foa, 1992). Adolescents identified as having OCD (Flament et al., 1988) reported in a subsequent follow-up study that they had withdrawn socially to prevent contamination and to conserve energy for obsessive-compulsive behaviors (Flament et al., 1990). Despite the apparent impact of OCD on functioning and quality of life, there have been few studies of these problems.

The area of functioning that has received the most attention in the literature is family and relationship functioning (e.g., Black, Gaffney, Schlosser, & Gabel, 1998; Bressi & Guggeri, 1996; Emmelkamp et al., 1990; Riggs et al., 1992; Steketee & Pruyn, 1998). This reflects the recognition that families in which one member has OCD often have to accommodate to the obsessive-compulsive's symptoms in order to help manage his or her anxiety (Calvocoressi et al., 1995; Shafran, Ralph, & Tallis, 1995); this accommodation has been associated with more severe family disruption (Calvocoressi et al., 1995). OCD can disrupt different aspects of family functioning. For example, Livingston-van Noppen, Rasmussen, Eisen, and McCartney (1990) found that more than half of the families assessed with the Family Assessment Device (FAD; Miller, Epstein, Duane, & Keitner, 1985) scored in the unhealthy range in at least one of the assessed areas (i.e., family problem solving, communication, roles, affective responsiveness, affective involvement, behavior control, global functioning). Compared to control families, these OCD families were more likely to indicate problems in all of these areas except communication.

Marital relationships may also suffer when one partner has OCD. Across several studies, up to 50 percent of the marriages of obsessive-compulsives are rated as distressed or unhappy (Chambless & Steketee, 1999; Emmelkamp et al., 1990; Kringlen 1965; Riggs et al., 1992). However, one study reported that the relationships of obsessive-compulsives were generally happy (Balslev-Olesen & Geert-Jorgensen, 1989). Whether these disruptions in marital and family functioning reflect a consequence of the OCD or if the disturbance in family functioning serves to exacerbate the OCD symptoms is not yet clear. However, two studies have found that the successful treatment of OCD symptoms improves marital quality, at least among patients whose relationships were distressed prior to treatment (Emmelkamp et al., 1990; Riggs et al., 1992).

There are few studies that have focused on the impact of OCD on employment and education. The results of these studies suggest that obsessive-compulsives have lower rates of employment, lower earnings, less education, and more reliance on disability payments than are people without a mental illness and individuals with an anxiety disorder other than OCD (Knapp, Henderson, & Patel, 2000). For example, in the Epidemiological Catchment Area Survey (Karno et al., 1988), 45 percent of men and 68 percent of women with OCD indicated that they were not employed, compared to 21 percent of men and 46 percent of women without an Axis I disorder. A similar rate was found among obsessive-compulsives in the British Psychiatric Morbidity Surveys (Foster, Meltzer, Gill, & Hinds, 1996, cited in Knapp et al., 2000); only 48 percent were employed. In a review of obsessive-compulsives treated in various trials, Steketee (1997) concludes that there are generally moderate to severe problems in workplace functioning.

TREATMENT IMPLICATIONS

Until the middle of the 1960s, OCD was considered to be refractory to treatment: neither psychodynamic psychotherapy nor a wide variety of pharmacotherapies had proven successful in ameliorating OCD symptoms. Early case reports employing exposure procedures (e.g., systematic desensitization, paradoxical intention, imaginal flooding, satiation) also yielded generally unimpressive results, as did several operant-conditioning procedures aimed at blocking or punishing obsessions and compulsions (e.g., thought stopping, aversion therapy, covert sensitization; for a review, see Foa, Franklin, & Kozak, 1998).

A dramatic shift occurred when Victor Meyer (1966) reported on two patients treated successfully with a behavioral program that included prolonged exposure to obsessional cues and strict prevention of rituals (EX/RP). This treatment program was subsequently found to be very successful in 10 of 15 cases and partly effective in the remainder; after five years only 2 of 15 patients in this open clinical trial had relapsed (Meyer & Levy, 1973; Meyer, Levy, & Schnurer, 1974). Another prognostic shift occurred with the finding that the tricyclic clomipramine (Anafranil) was effective in reducing OCD symptoms (e.g., Fernandez-Cordoba & Lopez-Ibor Alino, 1967). Subsequent research aimed at further developing these treatments and determining their relative efficacy. In the three decades following these initial reports, the efficacy of two treatments has been established: cognitive behavioral therapy by EX/RP and pharmacotherapy with serotonin reuptake inhibitors (SRIs).

Review of the OCD Treatment Outcome Literature

Exposure and Ritual Prevention (EX/RP)

Exposure and response (ritual) prevention (EX/RP) has proven to be a highly effective form of intervention for OCD (for a comprehensive review, see Franklin & Foa, 2002) and is considered the psychosocial treatment of choice for this disorder (March, Frances, Carpenter, & Kahn, 1997). Through exposure to feared stimuli and voluntary abstinence from compulsive rituals these programs are thought to promote habituation to feared thoughts and situations and to provide information that disconfirms mistaken beliefs held by the patients (Foa & Kozak, 1986).

Most contemporary EX/RP programs include two forms of exposure designed to prompt obsessional distress. The first, in vivo exposure has patients directly confront the feared object or situation. In imaginal exposure, the second type of exposure, patients imagine the consequences that they fear will occur should they fail to complete compulsive rituals (e.g., refraining from compulsive praying now will result in demonic possession at some time in the future). In most EX/RP programs, exposure exercises, whether in vivo or imaginal, are conducted in a graduated manner, with moderately distressing situations and thoughts confronted prior to more upsetting ones. The order of exposures is usually based on the patient's predicted level of distress prior to beginning treatment, but it may change as treatment progresses.

Ritual prevention is somewhat of a misnomer in that therapists do not actually prevent patients from engaging in rituals. Instead, therapists encourage patients to refrain from rituals on their own. Ideally, the patient will refrain from all rituals during the period of treatment, including when exposure exercises are conducted during treatment sessions, during additional exposures prescribed as homework, and when the urge to ritualize arises spontaneously. To encourage patients to refrain from their rituals, therapists will typically provide an explicit rationale and clear instructions for ritual prevention. They will also encourage attempts at stopping rituals and verbally reinforce successful abstinence. Patients are typically asked to record violations of ritual abstinence and to discuss them with the therapist. The therapist can then reinforce successful ritual prevention and, when necessary, help the patient to develop strategies to more successfully refrain from rituals in the future.

Numerous uncontrolled and controlled studies offer empirical support for the efficacy of EX/RP. The most compelling evidence for the efficacy of EX/RP comes from randomized controlled trials (RCTs) that have demonstrated its superiority compared to various control treatments, including relaxation (Fals-Stewart, Marks, & Schafer, 1993; Marks, Hodgson, & Rachman, 1975), pill placebo (Foa et al., in press), and anxiety management training (Lindsay, Crino, & Andrews, 1997). On the whole, the evidence indicates clearly that EX/RP produces substantial and clinically meaningful symptom reductions at posttreatment and that these reductions persist over time. In a review of EX/RP studies, Foa and Kozak (1996) found that an average of 83 percent of treatment completers were classified as responders (using the individual studies' varied definitions) immediately after treatment, and 76 percent of patients who evaluated for long-term outcome (mean follow-up interval of 29 months) were rated as responders. The effects of EX/RP appear to be very robust: they are largely consistent across different sites and procedural variations. Notably, two recent studies that have examined the effectiveness of EX/RP outside the context of controlled research trials suggest that its benefits are not limited to the highly selected patient samples that participate in randomized controlled trials (RCTs; Franklin, Abramowitz, Kozak, Levitt, & Foa, 2000; Rothbaum & Shahar, 2000).

Several meta-analytic studies (e.g., Abramowitz, 1996; Cox, Swinson, Morrison, & Lee, 1993; van Balkom et al., 1994) detected large effect sizes (≥ 1.0) for EX/RP in adults with OCD. Although variations in EX/RP treatment procedures are common across outcome studies, the effects of the treatment appear largely resilient to variations in factors such as frequency and length of sessions, but the core components of EX/RP appear important. Programs that incorporate both exposure and ritual prevention yield better outcome than treatment with either exposure or ritual prevention alone (Foa et al., 1984). Based on a meta-analysis of 38 trials, Abramowitz (1996) concluded that: (1) therapist-assisted exposure was more effective than self-exposure; (2) studies that included strict ritual prevention instructions yielded greater improvement than those with partial or no ritual prevention instructions; and (3) imaginal and in vivo exposure in combination was superior to in vivo exposure alone.

Pharmacotherapy

A comprehensive review of the OCD pharmacotherapy literature is beyond the scope of this chapter, but such reviews are available elsewhere (e.g., for adult OCD, see Dougherty, Rauch, & Jenike, 2002; for pediatric OCD, see March, Franklin, Nelson, & Foa, in press; Thomsen, 2002). To summarize, it appears that the tricyclic antidepressant clomipramine (e.g., Clomipramine Collaborative Group, 1991; DeVeaugh-Geiss, Landau, & Katz, 1992) and the serotonin reuptake inhibitors fluoxetine (e.g., Geller et al., 2001; Tollefson et al., 1994), sertraline (e.g., Greist et al., 1995; March et al., 1998), fluvoxamine (e.g., Goodman, Price, Rasmussen, Delgado, et al., 1989; Riddle et al., 2001), paroxetine (e.g., Wheadon, Bushnell, & Steiner, 1993) and, more recently, citalopram (e.g., Montgomery, Kasper, Stein, Hedegaard, & Lemming, 2001) are superior to pill placebo. Meta-analytic studies indicate that SSRI medications are, on the whole, associated with large effect sizes when used to treat OCD (Cox et al., 1993; van Balkom et al., 1994). However, on average the groups treated with medication in these trials still met the criteria for study inclusion, which suggests that even though medications are efficacious, the typical patient treated with SRI monotherapy still has substantial residual symptoms.

In addition to residual symptoms, SRI treatment for OCD raises other concerns. Some patients experience significant side effects, up to one-third of patients treated with SRIs do not respond to the medication and, especially with younger patients, concerns are emerging about the long-term implications of remaining on an SRI. Despite these concerns, there are a number of appealing aspects to SRI treatment for OCD. Among these are the relative availability of SRIs (as compared to EX/RP), the ease of administering the treatment (for both the physician and patient), and the fact that it has proven highly effective for at least some OCD patients even if treatment response is neither universal nor complete. A course of SRI should be recommended as first treatment for clinically impaired OCD patients who decide that EX/RP is either too difficult, too expensive, unavailable within a reasonable distance from their homes, or who do not believe they are ready to commit to a course of EX/RP.

EX/RP versus Pharmacotherapy with Serotonin Reuptake Inhibitors (SRIs)

The first study comparing EX/RP to medication was conducted by Marks and his colleagues (Marks, Stern, Mawson, Cobb, & McDonald, 1980; Rachman et al., 1979). Using a complex experimental design, 40 patients were randomly assigned to receive either clomipramine or pill placebo (PBO) for four weeks followed by six weeks of inpatient psychological treatment (daily 45-minute sessions). At the end of the six-week psychosocial treatment, patients were discharged from the hospital. Medication was tapered after week 36 and discontinued by week 40. Patients were followed for a year after drug discontinuation. Results suggested that, compared to placebo, clomipramine produced significant improvements in mood and rituals only in those patients who were initially depressed. EX/RP was associated with greater reductions in rituals, but not with improvements in mood. Unfortunately, the design did not allow for a direct comparison of clomipramine and exposure alone across the same time period.

Cottraux et al. (1990) compared the efficacy of fluvoxamine (FLU) with EX/RP. Patients were assigned to one of three conditions: FLU with antiexposure instructions, FLU + EX/RP, and pill placebo (PBO) with EX/RP. EX/RP treatment was provided in weekly outpatient sessions. For the first 8 weeks, treatment included self-exposure between sessions and imaginal exposure during sessions. The following 16 weeks included therapist-guided exposure and ritual prevention. Treatment continued for 24 weeks, after which EX/RP was stopped and medication was tapered over 4 weeks. At posttreatment (week 24), results revealed a reduction in ritual duration of 42 percent in the FLU + antiexposure group, 46 percent in the FLU + EX/RP group, and 25 percent in the PBO + EX/RP group. At six-month follow-up, reductions in ritual duration were: FLX + antiexposure 42 percent, FLX + EX/RP 45 percent, and PBO + EX/RP 35 percent.

Hohagen et al. (1998) randomly assigned 58 patients to FLU + EX/RP or PBO + EX/RP. In both conditions, EX/RP involved a three-week assessment period followed by a four-week regimen of lengthy (three-hour minimum) thrice-weekly sessions. Analyses were conducted on a subset of patients (n = 49), with nine outliers dropped in order to equate the two groups on baseline Y-BOCS severity. Both groups improved significantly and comparably on compulsions, but patients who received fluvoxamine with EX/RP were significantly better at posttreatment on obsessions than those who received placebo. Additional analyses indicated that patients who suffered from secondary depression also fared better if they were receiving active medication along with EX/RP.

A recently completed study aimed at providing a clear comparison of the efficacy of CMI, intensive EX/RP, and their combination (Foa et al., in press). In this study, an EX/RP program that included an intensive phase (15 two-hour sessions conducted over three weeks) and follow-up phase (six brief sessions delivered over eight weeks) was compared to CMI, EX/RP + CMI, and pill placebo (PBO). Results suggest that all active treatments are superior to PBO, that EX/RP is more efficacious than CMI in completers, and that the combination of the two treatments is not superior to EX/RP alone. However, the design adopted in this study may not have been appropriate for promoting an additive effect because the EX/RP program was largely completed before the effects of CMI could be realized.

In summary, there is ample evidence for the efficacy of both SRI pharmacotherapy and EX/RP treatments. However, information about their relative efficacy is scarce because most of the few studies that addressed this issue are plagued with design and procedural deficiencies. The data do not support the unequivocal statement that combined treatment is generally superior to EX/RP alone. Despite this, many experts advocate combined treatment as the treatment of choice for OCD (e.g., Greist, 1992). It should be noted that clinically there might be circumstances when combined treatment may be preferable. For example, patients who have significant psychiatric comorbidity such as major depressive disorder might benefit from combined treatment because the medication also ameliorates symptoms of the other disorder that can attenuate CBT compliance (e.g., lack of motivation). The data clearly indicate that combined treatment does not interfere with EX/RP alone, and thus patients who are already receiving SRI need not discontinue their medication in order to fully benefit from EX/RP (Franklin, Abramowitz, Bux, Zoellner, & Feeny, 2002).

Cognitive Therapy

Cognitive approaches have been brought to bear in treating OCD, sometimes as formal protocols designed to be alternatives to EX/RP and sometimes less formally, as part of EX/RP programs. As discussed elsewhere (e.g., Foa et al., 2002; Franklin et al., 2002), EX/RP therapists typically aim at changing OCD-related cognitions, but these changes are brought about through the EX/RP procedures and informal cognitive discussions. Thus far studies of cognitive therapy for OCD have yielded some positive findings (e.g., Freeston et al., 1997), and studies comparing cognitive therapies to EX/RP have generally failed to find an advantage of one over the other (e.g., van Balkom et al., 1998), with the exception that group EX/RP may be superior to group CT (McLean et al., 2001).

An early study of cognitive therapy for OCD yielded no differences between a combination of Self-Instructional Training plus EX/RP versus EX/RP alone (Emmelkamp, van der Helm, van Zanten, & Plochg, 1980). In a second study, Emmelkamp, Visser, and Hoekstra (1988) randomly assigned patients to one of two treatments: EX/RP or Rational Emotive Therapy (RET), another cognitive approach. Treatment consisted of 10 sessions (60 minutes each) conducted over eight weeks; patients in both conditions were also given homework assignments. Both groups were improved at posttreatment with the RET group showing about a 40 percent improvement and the EX/RP group 51 percent improvement. A primary difficulty lies in the treatment procedure itself: sessions were only 60 minutes in length, held approximately once per week, did not include therapist-assisted exposure, included only two homework assignments per week, and seems to have employed a more gradual response prevention than is typically recommended. This truncated treatment program may have been responsible for the inferior outcome of EX/RP compared to other studies (e.g., Foa, Kozak, Steketee, & McCarthy, 1992).

In a further examination of the relative efficacy of cognitive therapy and EX/RP for OCD, van Balkom et al. (1998) randomly assigned patients to: (1) cognitive therapy for weeks 1 to 16; (2) EX/RP for weeks 1 to 16; (3) fluvoxamine for weeks 1 to 16 plus cognitive therapy in weeks 9 to 16; (4) fluvoxamine for weeks 1 to 16 plus EX/RP in weeks 9 to 16; and (5) wait-list for weeks 1 to 8. Behavioral experiments (exposures) were not included in the cognitive treatment until after session 6 (week 8). Conversely, in the first six EX/RP sessions care was taken by the therapist to specifically avoid any discussion of disastrous consequences. Cognitive therapy focused primarily on themes of danger overestimation and inflated personal responsibility as suggested by Salkovskis (1985). EX/RP included self-exposure, with patients determining the speed at which they worked through the fear hierarchy. Sessions in both treatment conditions lasted for 45 minutes. Results indicated that all active treatments were superior to wait-list at week 8. After 8 weeks of cognitive therapy without behavioral experiments and EX/RP without discussion of disastrous consequences, Y-BOCS reductions of 15 percent and 25 percent were observed for cognitive therapy and EX/RP, respectively. At posttreatment, all active treatments improved significantly on almost all measures and no differences emerged among the treatment groups. The authors suggest that the lack of observed differences between the combined conditions and the monotherapies suggests that clinicians should start with either cognitive therapy or EX/RP alone rather than with combination treatments.

More research is clearly needed to determine whether there is an advantage to using one treatment over the other with certain OCD subtypes (e.g., those with feared consequences versus those without), and much more needs to be learned about the mechanisms by which the treatments exert their influence. Clinically we focus of exposure exercises and ritual prevention instructions, yet we include informal cognitive interventions in therapy, particularly when they can be used to reinforce the EX/RP interventions. For example, therapists discuss cognitive risk factors (e.g., thought suppression, thought-action fusion) to explain the maintenance of OCD symptoms and encourage patients to use "positive self-talk" to encourage themselves when they confront feared situations and refrain from ritualizing. We also conduct informal discussions about the absence of the anticipated harm despite exposure and ritual prevention (e.g., "You refrained from checking your stove every day this week and yet the house has not burned down—what do you make of it?") to help patients challenge their beliefs. Our clinical stance is to use such methods to support and enhance EX/RP rather than to replace it. The possibility remains that CT is a viable alternative to EX/RP when patients refuse EX/RP, fail to comply with EX/RP procedures, or fail to benefit significantly even after a complete course.

Predictors of Treatment Outcome and Maintenance of Gain

Identifying divergent outcomes for patient subgroups and identifying change mechanisms are important secondary goals of treatment outcome studies (March & Curry, 1998). However, in the literature examining treatment for OCD such efforts are infrequent. One of the primary limiting factors on such research is the difficulty involved in accruing the very large samples needed to adequately examine various predictors. In addition, as the identification of outcome predictors is never the primary aim, studies are not designed specifically to address these questions. Accordingly, the literature is replete with inconsistent findings, null results, or studies with clear methodological problems that make it impossible to clearly delineate factors that would lead to specific treatment recommendations. Finally, because of the relative recency of pharmacological and cognitive treatments for OCD, most of what we know about predicting treatment outcome relies on studies of EX/RP; data on predictors of the effects of medication and cognitive therapy are largely unavailable.

The most studied predictor of response to EX/RP is comorbid depression, which is important clinically because of the high rate of depression in patients with OCD. Some studies have found that higher depression levels prior to treatment were related to less improvement and poorer outcome (e.g., Keijsers, Hoogduin, & Schaap, 1994; Steketee et al., 2001), others have found little or no effect (Mataix-Cols, Marks, Greist, Kobak, & Baer, 2002; O'Sullivan, Noshirvani, Marks, Monteiro, & Lelliott, 1991; Steketee, Eisen, Dyck, Warshaw, & Rasmussen, 1999). One potential reason for these disparate findings may be the assumption that there is a linear relationship between depressive and OCD symptoms. One study that grouped patients according to their initial levels of depression found that only patients who were severely depressed were less likely to respond to EX/RP; patients who were not depressed, mildly depressed, or moderately depressed responded equally well (Abramowitz, Franklin, Street, Kozak, & Foa, 2000). Similar effects were also found when the diagnosis of depression was considered. OCD patients who were nondepressed fared better than those diagnosed with co morbid depression both at posttreatment and follow-up (Abramowitz & Foa, 2000). Importantly, although they did not fare as well as the other groups, even the severely depressed patients in Abramowitz et al. (2000) improved significantly with EX/RP. Some studies that examined combining EX/RP and pharmacotherapy have found the combination works better than EX/RP alone in depressed individuals (Hohagen et al., 1998) and helped reduce depression (Marks et al., 1980; Rachman et al., 1979). Therefore, it may be appropriate to use combined treatment with obsessive-compulsives with comorbid severe depression.

It has been thought that personality psychopathology might hinder improvement with EX/RP; however, there has been little research examining this. The total number of comorbid personality diagnoses that obsessive-compulsives had was not predictive of treatment outcome in several studies (de Haan et al., 1997; Dressen, Hoekstra, & Arntz, 1997). However, in another study, patients with no personality pathology benefited most EX/RP (Fals-Stewart & Lucente, 1993). When examining the personality clusters, it appears that different personality traits may affect treatment outcome differently. In one study, high levels of dependent traits were associated with better outcome but high levels of passive-aggressive traits were associated with worse outcomes (Steketee et al., 2001). In another study, histrionic/borderline traits were associated with successful treatment outcome at posttreatment, but a loss of gains by follow-up (Fals-Stewart

& Lucente, 1993). With regard to schizotypal traits, one study found such traits to be associated with markedly poorer outcome (Minichiello, Baer, & Jenike, 1987). However, other studies have suggested that this relationship is not as strong as originally thought (Dressen et al., 1997; Fals-Stewart & Lucente, 1993; Steketee et al., 2001).

Some studies found that initial OCD symptom severity had no effect on posttreatment outcome (de Araujo, Ito, & Marks, 1996), but others have found initial severity to be a predictor of posttreatment outcome (Basoglu, Lax, Kasvikis, & Marks, 1988; Keijsers et al., 1994; Mataix-Cols et al., 2002). Studies that included follow-up assessments found no effects of initial symptom severity on follow-up symptom levels (Basoglu et al., 1988; O'Sullivan et al., 1991). The patient's insight, or lack of insight, into his or her OCD (i.e., the degree to which patients are convinced that their feared outcomes will occur if they do not engage in rituals) was found related to outcome (Foa et al., 1999). Patients with poor insight were more severe at posttreatment than those with better insight. Similarly, Basoglu et al. (1988) found that high fixity of beliefs, a measure of poor insight, was predictive of poorer outcome.

REFERENCES

Abramowitz, J. S. (1996). Variants of exposure and response prevention in the treatment of obsessive-compulsive disorder: A meta-analysis. *Behavior Therapy, 27,* 583–600.

Abramowitz, J. S., Foa, E. B. (2000). Does major depressive disorder influence outcome of exposure and response prevention for OCD? *Behavior Therapy, 31*(4), 795–800.

Abramowitz, J. S., Franklin, M. E., Filip, J. C., & Foa, E. B. (2000). Spacing of sessions in the treatment of OCD. In *Proceedings for the 34th annual meeting of the Association for the Advancement of Behavior Therapy.* New York: AABT.

Abramowitz, J. S., Franklin, M. E., & Foa, E. B. (in press). Empirical status of cognitive methods in the treatment of OCD. In M. H. Freeston & S. Taylor (Eds.), *Cognitive approaches to treating obsessions and compulsions: A clinical casebook.* Mahwah, NJ: Erlbaum.

Abramowitz, J. S., Franklin, M. E., Street, G. P., Kozak, M. J., & Foa, E. B. (2000). The effects of pre-treatment depression on cognitive-behavioral treatment outcome in OCD clinic outpatients. *Behavior Therapy, 31,* 517–528.

Allen, J. J. (1977). The measurement of obsessionality: First validation studies of the Lynfield Obsessional/Compulsive Questionnaire. *Journal of International Medical Research, 5,* 12–15.

Allen, J. J., & Rack, P. H. (1975). Changes in obsessive-compulsive patients as measured by the Leyton inventory before and after treatment with clomipramine. *Scottish Medical Journal, 20* (Suppl. 1), 41–44.

Allen, J. J., & Tune, G. S. (1975). The Lynfield obsessional-compulsive questionnaire. *Scottish Medical Journal, 20,* 25–28.

American Psychiatric Association. (1994). *Diagnostic and statistical manual of mental disorders.* (4th ed.). Washington, DC: Author.

Ananth, J., Solyom, L., Bryntwick, S., & Krishnappa, U. (1979). Chlorimipramine therapy for obsessive-compulsive neurosis. *American Journal of Psychiatry, 136*(5), 700–701.

Andrews, G., Henderson, S., & Hall, W. (2001). Prevalence, comorbidity, disability and service utilization. *British Journal of Psychiatry, 178,* 145–153.

Balslev-Olesen, T., & Geert-Jorgensen, E. (1989). The prognosis of obsessive-compulsive disorder. *Acta Psychiatrica Scandinavica, 34,* 232–241.

Basoglu, M., Lax, T., Kasvikis, Y., & Marks, I. M. (1988). Predictors of improvement in obsessive-compulsive disorder. *Journal of Anxiety Disorders, 2*(4), 299–317.

Beck, A. T. (1976). *Cognitive therapy and the emotional disorders.* New York: International Universities Press.

Beck, A. T., Ward, C. H., Mendeleson, M., Mock, J., & Erbaugh, J. (1961). An inventory for measuring depression. *Archives of General Psychiatry, 4,* 561–571.

Becker, C. B. (2002). Integrated behavioral treatment of comorbid OCD, PTSD, and borderline personality disorder: A case report. *Cognitive and Behavioral Practice, 9,* 100–110.

Black, D. W., Gaffney, G. R., Schlosser, S., & Gabel, J. (1998). The impact of obsessive-compulsive disorder on the family: Preliminary findings. *Journal of Nervous & Mental Disease, 186,* 440–442.

Black, D. W., Noyes, R., Pfohl, B., Goldstein, R. B., & Blum, N. (1993). Personality disorder in obsessive-compulsive volunteers, well comparison subjects, and their first-degree relatives. *American Journal of Psychiatry, 150,* 1226–1232.

Boulougouris, J. C., Rabavilas, A. D., & Stefanis, C. (1977). Psychophysiological responses in obsessive-compulsive patients. *Behaviour Research and Therapy, 15,* 221–230.

Breslau, N., Davis, G., Andreski, P., & Peterson, E. (1991). Traumatic events and posttraumatic stress disorder in an urban population of young adults. *Archives of General Psychiatry, 48,* 216–222.

Bressi, C., & Guggeri, G. (1996). Obsessive-compulsive disorder and the family emotional environment. *New Trends in Experimental & Clinical Psychiatry, 12,* 265–269.

Brown, H. D., Kosslyn, S. M., Breiter, H. C., Baer, L., & Jenike, M. A. (1994). Can patients with obsessive-compulsive disorder discriminate between percepts and mental images? A signal detection analysis. *Journal of Abnormal Psychology, 103,* 445–454.

Brown, T. A., Campbell, L. A., Lehman, C. L., Grisham, J. R., & Mancill, R. B. (2001). Current and lifetime comorbidity of the

DSM-IV anxiety and mood disorders in a large clinical sample. *Journal of Abnormal Psychology, 110,* 585–599.

Calvocoressi, L., Lewis, B., Harris, M., Goodman, W. K., Trufan, S. J., McDougle, C. J., et al. (1995). Family accommodation in obsessive compulsive disorder. *American Journal of Psychiatry, 152,* 441–443.

Carr, A. T. (1974). Compulsive neurosis: A review of the literature. *Psychological Bulletin, 81,* 311–318.

Chambless, D. L., & Steketee, G. (1999). Expressed emotion and behavior therapy outcome: A prospective study with obsessive-compulsive and agoraphobic outpatients. *Journal of Consulting and Clinical Psychology, 67,* 658–665.

Clomipramine Collaborative Group. (1991). Clomipramine in the treatment of patients with obsessive-compulsive disorder. *Archives of General Psychiatry, 48,* 730–738.

Constans, J., Foa, E. B., Franklin, M. E., & Mathews, A. (1995). Memory for actual and imagined events in OC checkers. *Behaviour Research and Therapy, 33*(6), 665–671.

Cooper, J. (1970). The Leyton Obsessional Inventory. *Psychological Medicine, 1*(1), 48–64.

Cottraux, J. (1989). Behavioral psychotherapy for obsessive-compulsive disorder. *International Review of Psychiatry, 1,* 227–234.

Cottraux, J., Mollard, E., Bouvard, M., Marks, I., Sluys, M., Nury, A. M., et al. (1990). A controlled study of fluvoxamine and exposure in obsessive-compulsive disorder. *International Clinical Psychopharmacology, 5,* 17–30.

Cox, B. J., Swinson, R. P., Morrison, B., & Lee, P. S. (1993). Clomipramine, fluoxetine, and behavior therapy in the treatment of obsessive-compulsive disorder: A meta-analysis. *Journal of Behavior Therapy and Experimental Psychiatry, 24*(2), 149–153.

Crino, R. D., Andrews, G. (1996). Obsessive-compulsive disorder and Axis I comorbidity. *Journal of Anxiety Disorders, 10*(1), 37–46.

de Araujo, L. A., Ito, L. M., & Marks, I. M. (1996). Early compliance and other factors predicting outcome of exposure for obsessive-compulsive disorder. *British Journal of Psychiatry, 169*(6), 747–752.

de Araujo, L. A., Ito, L. M., Marks, I. M., & Deale, A. (1995). Does imagined exposure to the consequences of not ritualising enhance live exposure for OCD? A controlled study: I. Main outcome. *British Journal of Psychiatry, 167*(1), 65–70.

De Haan, E., Hoogduin, K. A. L., Buitelaar, J. K., & Keijsers, G. P. J. (1998). Behavior therapy versus clomipramine for the treatment of obsessive-compulsive disorder in children and adolescents. *Journal of the American Academy of Child and Adolescent Psychiatry, 37,* 1022–1029.

De Haan, E., van Oppen, P., van Balkom, A. J. L. M., Spinhoven, P., Hoogduin, K. A. L, & Van Dyck, R. (1997). Prediction of outcome and early vs. late improvement in OCD patients treated with cognitive behaviour therapy and pharmacotherapy. *Acta Psychiatrica Scandinavica, 96*(5), 354–361.

de Silva, P., & Marks, M. (1999). The role of traumatic experiences in the genesis of obsessive-compulsive disorder. *Behaviour Research and Therapy, 37,* 941–951.

DeVeaugh-Geiss, J., Landau, P., & Katz, R. (1989). Treatment of obsessive compulsive disorder with clomipramine. *Psychiatric Annals, 19*(2), 97–101.

DeVeaugh-Geiss, J., Moroz, G., Biederman, J., Cantwell, D. P., Fontaine, R., Greist, J. H., et al. (1992). Clomipramine hydrochloride in childhood and adolescent obsessive-compulsive disorder: A multicenter trial. *Journal of the American Academy of Child and Adolescent Psychiatry, 31*(1), 45–49.

Dollard, J., & Miller, N. E. (1950). *Personality and psychotherapy: An analysis in terms of learning, thinking and culture.* New York: McGraw-Hill.

Dougherty, D. D., Rauch, S. L., & Jenike, M. A. (2002). Pharmacological treatments for obsessive compulsive disorder. In P. E. Nathan & J. M. Gorman (Eds.), *A guide to treatments that work* (2nd ed., pp. 387–410). London: Oxford University Press.

Dressen, L., Hoekstra, R., & Arntz, A. (1997). Personality disorders do not influence the results of cognitive and behavior therapy for obsessive compulsive disorder. *Journal of Anxiety Disorders, 11*(5), 503–521.

Eichstedt, J. A., & Arnold, S. L. (2001). Childhood-onset obsessive-compulsive disorder: A tic-related subtype of OCD? *Clinical Psychology Review, 21,* 137–158.

Ellis, A. (1962). *Reason and emotion in psychotherapy.* New York: Lyle Stuart.

Emmelkamp, P. M. G., & Beens, H. (1991). Cognitive therapy with obsessive-compulsive disorder: A comparative evaluation. *Behaviour Research and Therapy, 29,* 293–300.

Emmelkamp, P. M. G., de Haan, E., & Hoogduin, C. A. L. (1990). Marital adjustment and obsessive-compulsive disorder. *British Journal of Psychiatry, 156,* 55–60.

Emmelkamp, P. M. G., van der Helm, M., van Zanten, B. L., & Plochg, I. (1980). Treatment of obsessive-compulsive patients: The contribution of self-instructional training to the effectiveness of exposure. *Behaviour Research and Therapy, 18,* 61–66.

Emmelkamp, P. M. G., Visser, S., & Hoekstra, R. J. (1988). Cognitive therapy vs. exposure in vivo in the treatment of obsessive-compulsives. *Cognitive Therapy and Research, 12,* 103–114.

Fals-Stewart, W., Lucente, S. (1993). An MCMI cluster typology of obsessive-compulsives: A measure of personality characteristics and its relationship to treatment participation, compliance and outcome in behavior therapy. *Journal of Psychiatric Research, 27*(2), 139–154.

Fals-Stewart, W., Marks, A. P., & Schafer, J. (1993). A comparison of behavioral group therapy and individual behavior therapy in treating obsessive-compulsive disorder. *Journal of Nervous and Mental Disease, 181*(3), 189–193.

Fernandez-Cordoba, E., & Lopez-Ibor Alino, J. (1967). Monochlorimipramine in mental patients resisting other forms of treatment. *Actas Luso-Espanolas de Neurologia y Psiquitria, 26*(2), 119–147.

Flament, M. F., Koby, E., Rapoport, J. L., Berg, C. J., Zahn, T., Cox, C., et al. (1990). Childhood obsessive-compulsive disorder: A prospective follow-up study. *Journal of Child Psychology and Psychiatry and Allied Disciplines, 31*(3), 363–380.

Flament, M. F., Whitaker, A., Rapoport, J. L., Davies, M., Zaremba, C., Kalikow, K., et al. (1988). Obsessive compulsive disorder in adolescence: An epidemiological study. *Journal of the American Academy of Child and Adolescent Psychiatry, 27*(6), 764–771.

Foa, E. B., Abramowitz, J. S., Franklin, M. E., & Kozak, M. J. (1999). Feared consequences, fixity of belief, and treatment outcome in OCD. *Behavior Therapy, 30*, 717–724.

Foa, E. B., Amir, N., Gershuny, B., Molnar, C., & Kozak, M. J. (1997). Implicit and explicit memory in obsessive-compulsive disorder. *Journal of Anxiety Disorders, 11*, 119–129.

Foa, E. B., Franklin, M. E., & Kozak, M. J. (1998). Psychosocial treatments of obsessive compulsive disorder. In R. Swinson, M. Antony, S. Rachman, & M. Richter (Eds.), *Obsessive-compulsive disorder: Theory, research, and treatment* (pp. 258–276). New York: Guilford Press.

Foa, E. B., Franklin, M. E., & Moser, J. (2002). Context in the clinic: How well do CBT and medications work in combination? *Biological Psychiatry, 51*, 989–997.

Foa, E. B., & Goldstein, A. (1978). Continuous exposure and complete response prevention in the treatment of obsessive-compulsive neurosis. *Behavior Therapy, 9*, 821–829.

Foa, E. B., & Kozak, M. J. (1985). Treatment of anxiety disorders: Implications for psychopathology. In A. H. Tuma & J. D. Maser (Eds.), *Anxiety and the anxiety disorders* (pp. 421–452). Hillsdale, NJ: Erlbaum.

Foa, E. B., & Kozak, M. J. (1986). Emotional processing of fear: Exposure to corrective information. *Psychological Bulletin, 99*, 20–35.

Foa, E. B., & Kozak, M. J. (1996). Psychological treatment for obsessive-compulsive disorder. In M. R. Mavissakalian & R. F. Prien (Eds.), *Long-term treatments of anxiety disorders* (pp. 285–309). Washington, DC: American Psychiatric Press.

Foa, E. B., Kozak, M. J., Goodman, W. K., Hollander, E., Jenike, M., & Rasmussen, S. (1995). DSM-IV field trial: Obsessive-compulsive disorder. *American Journal of Psychiatry, 152*(1), 90–94.

Foa, E. B., Kozak, M. J., Salkovskis, P. M., Coles, M. E., & Amir, N. (1998). The validation of a new obsessive-compulsive disorder scale: The Obsessive-Compulsive Inventory. *Psychological Assessment, 10*(3), 206–214.

Foa, E. B., Kozak, M. J., Steketee, G. S., & McCarthy, P. R. (1992). Treatment of depressive and obsessive-compulsive symptoms in OCD by imipramine and behavior therapy. *British Journal of Clinical Psychology, 31*(3), 279–292.

Foa, E. B., Liebowitz, M. R., Kozak, M. J., Davies, S. O., Campeas, R., Franklin, M. E., et al. (in press). Treatment of obsessive compulsive disorder by exposure and ritual prevention, clomipramine, and their combination: A randomized, placebo-controlled trial. *American Journal of Psychiatry.*

Foa, E. B., Mathews, A., Abramowitz, J. S., Amir, N., Przeworski, A., Riggs, D. S., et al. (2003). Do patients with obsessive-compulsive disorder have deficits in decision-making? *Cognitive Therapy and Research, 27*, 431–445.

Foa, E. B., Steketee, G., Grayson, J. B., Turner, R. M., & Latimer, P. (1984). Deliberate exposure and blocking of obsessive-compulsive rituals: Immediate and long-term effects. *Behavior Therapy, 15*(5), 450–472.

Foa, E. B., Steketee, G. S., & Milby, J. B. (1980). Differential effects of exposure and response prevention in obsessive-compulsive washers. *Journal of Consulting and Clinical Psychology, 48*, 71–79.

Foa, E. B., Steketee, G., Turner, R. M., & Fischer, S. C. (1980). Effects of imaginal exposure to feared disasters in obsessive-compulsive checkers. *Behaviour Research and Therapy, 18*, 449–455.

Foa, E. B., & Tillmanns, A. (1980). The treatment of obsessive-compulsive neurosis. In A. Goldstein & E. B. Foa (Eds.), *Handbook of behavioral interventions: A clinical guide* (pp. 416–500). New York: Wiley.

Franklin, M. E., Abramowitz, J. S., Bux, D. A., Jr., Zoellner, L. A., & Feeny, N. C. (2002). Cognitive-behavioral therapy with and without medication in the treatment of obsessive-compulsive disorder. *Professional Psychology: Research & Practice, 33*(2), 162–168.

Franklin, M. E., Abramowitz, J. S., Kozak, M. J., Levitt, J., & Foa, E. B. (2000). Effectiveness of exposure and ritual prevention for obsessive compulsive disorder: Randomized compared with non-randomized samples. *Journal of Consulting and Clinical Psychology, 68*, 594–602.

Franklin, M. E., & Foa, E. B. (2002). Cognitive behavioral treatments for obsessive compulsive disorder. In P.E. Nathan & J. M. Gorman (Eds.), *A guide to treatments that work* (2nd ed., pp. 387–410). London: Oxford University Press.

Franklin, M. E., Kozak, M. J., Cashman, L., Coles, M., Rheingold, A., & Foa, E. B. (1998). Cognitive behavioral treatment of pediatric obsessive compulsive disorder: An open clinical trial. *Journal of the American Academy of Child and Adolescent Psychiatry, 37*, 412–419.

Freeston, M. H., Ladouceur, R., Gagnon, F., Thibodeau, N., Rhéaume, J., Letarte, H., et al. (1997). Cognitive-behavioral treatment of obsessive thoughts: A controlled study. *Journal of Consulting & Clinical Psychology, 65*(3), 405–413.

Freund, B., Steketee, G. S., & Foa, E. B. (1987). Compulsive Activity Checklist (CAC): Psychometric analysis with obsessive-compulsive disorder. *Behavioral Assessment, 9*(1), 67–79.

Geller, D. A., Hoog, S. L., Heiligenstein, J. H., Ricardi, R. K., Tamura, R., Kluszynski, S., et al. (2001). Fluoxetine treatment for obsessive-compulsive disorder in children and adolescents:

A placebo-controlled clinical trial. *Journal of the American Academy of Child and Adolescent Psychiatry, 40*(7), 773–779.

Gershuny, B. S., Baer, L., Wilson, K. A., Radomsky, A. S., & Jenike, M. A. (2003). Connection between symptoms of obsessive-compulsive disorder and posttraumatic stress disorder: A case series. *Behaviour Research and Therapy, 41,* 1029–1041.

Goodman, W. K., Price, L. H., Rasmussen, S. A., Delgado, P. L., Heninger, G. R., & Charney, D. S. (1989). Efficacy of fluvoxamine in obsessive-compulsive disorder: A double-blind comparison with placebo. *Archives of General Psychiatry, 46,* 36–44.

Goodman, W. K., Price, L. H., Rasmussen, S. A., Mazure, C., Fleischmann, R. L., Hill, C. L., et al. (1989). The Yale-Brown Obsessive Compulsive Scale: I. Development, use, and reliability. *Archives of General Psychiatry, 46,* 1006–1011.

Goodwin, A. H., & Sher, K. J. (1992). Deficits in set-shifting ability in nonclinical compulsive checkers. *Journal of Psychopathology & Behavioral Assessment, 14*(1), 81–92.

Greist, J. H. (1992). An integrated approach to treatment of obsessive compulsive disorder. *Journal of Clinical Psychiatry, 53,* 38–41.

Greist, J. H., Jefferson, J. W., Kobak, K. A., Katzelnick, D. J., & Serlin, R. C. (1995). Efficacy and tolerability of serotonin transport inhibitors in obsessive-compulsive disorder: A meta-analysis. *Archives of General Psychiatry, 52,* 53–60.

Hanna, G. L. (1995). Demographic and clinical features of obsessive-compulsive disorder in children and adolescents. *Journal of the American Academy of Child and Adolescent Psychiatry, 34*(1), 19–27.

Hiss, H., Foa, E. B., & Kozak, M. J. (1994). Relapse prevention program for treatment of obsessive-compulsive disorder. *Journal of Consulting and Clinical Psychology, 62*(4), 801–808.

Hodgson, R., & Rachman, S. (1972). The effects of contamination and washing in obsessional patients. *Behaviour Research and Therapy, 10*(2), 111–117.

Hodgson, R., & Rachman, S. (1977). Obsessional compulsive complaints. *Behaviour Research and Therapy, 15,* 389–395.

Hohagen, F., Winkelman, G., Rasche-Rauchale, H., Hand, I., Konig, A., Munchau, N., et al. (1998). Combination of behaviour therapy with fluvoxamine in comparison with behaviour therapy and placebo: Results of a multicentre study. *British Journal of Psychiatry, 173,* 71–78.

Hollander, E., Kwon, J. H., Stein, D. J., & Broatch, J. (1996). Obsessive-compulsive and spectrum disorders: Overview and quality of life issues. *Journal of Clinical Psychiatry, 57*(8), 3–6.

Hornsveld, R. H., Kraaimaat, F. W., & van Dam-Baggen, R. M. (1979). Anxiety/discomfort and handwashing in obsessive-compulsive and psychiatric control patients. *Behaviour Research and Therapy, 17*(3), 223–228.

Huppert, J. D., Moser, J. S., Gurshuny, B. S., Riggs, D. S., Spokas, M., Filip, J., et al. (in press). The relationship between obsessive-compulsive and posttraumatic stress symptoms in clinical and non-clinical samples. *Journal of Anxiety Disorders.*

Insel, T. R., & Akiskal, H. S. (1986). Obsessive-compulsive disorder with psychotic features: A phenomenologic analysis. *American Journal of Psychiatry, 143*(12), 1527–1533.

Insel, T. R., Mueller, E. A., Alterman, I., Linnoila, M., & Murphy, D. L. (1985). Obsessive-compulsive disorder and serotonin: Is there a connection? *Biological Psychiatry, 20*(11), 1174–1188.

Insel, T. R., Murphy, D. L., Cohen, R. M., Alterman, I. S., Kilts, C., & Linnoila, M. (1983). Obsessive-compulsive disorder: A double-blind trial of clomipramine and clorgyline. *Archives of General Psychiatry, 40,* 605–612.

Jenike, M. A. (2001). A 45-year-old woman with obsessive-compulsive disorder. *Journal of the American Medical Association, 285,* 2121–2128.

Joffe, R. T., Swinson, R. P., & Regan, J. J. (1988). Personality features of obsessive-compulsive disorder. *American Journal of Psychiatry, 145*(9), 1127–1129.

Karno, M., Golding, J. M., Sorenson, S. B., & Burnam, M. A. (1988). The epidemiology of obsessive-compulsive disorder in five U.S. communities. *Archives of General Psychiatry, 45*(12), 1094–1099.

Keijsers, G. P. J., Hoogduin, C. A. L., & Schaap, C. P. D. R. (1994). Predictors of treatment outcome in the behavioural treatment of obsessive-compulsive disorder. *British Journal of Psychiatry, 165*(6), 781–786.

Kimble, M. O. (2000). The case of Howard. *Cognitive and Behavioral Practice, 7,* 118–122.

Knapp, M., Henderson, J., & Patel, A. (2000). Costs of obsessive-compulsive disorder: A review. In M. Maj, N. Sartorius, A. Okasha, & J. Zohar (Eds.), *Obsessive-compulsive disorder: WPA series evidence and experience in psychiatry* (pp. 253–299). New York: Wiley.

Kozak, M. J., & Foa, E. B. (1994). Obsessions, overvalued ideas, and delusions in obsessive-compulsive disorder. *Behaviour Research and Therapy, 32*(3), 343–353.

Kozak, M. J., & Foa, E. B. (1996). Obsessive compulsive disorder. In V. B. V. Hasselt & M. Hersen (Eds.), *Sourcebook of psychological treatment manuals for adult disorders* (pp. 65–122). New York: Plenum Press.

Kozak, M. J., Liebowitz, M. R., & Foa, E. B. (2000). Cognitive behavior therapy and pharmacotherapy for OCD: The NIMH-Sponsored Collaborative Study. In W. Goodman, M. Rudorfer, & J. Maser (Eds.), *Obsessive compulsive disorder: Contemporary issues in treatment.* Mahwah, NJ: Erlbaum.

Kringlen, E. (1965). Obsessional neurotics. A long-term follow-up. *British Journal of Psychiatry, 111*(477), 709–722.

Lang, P. J. (1979). A bio-informational theory of emotional imagery. *Psychophysiology, 16*(6), 495–512.

Lelliott, P. T., Noshirvani, H. F., Basoglu, M., Marks, I. M., & Monteiro, W. O. (1988). Obsessive-compulsive beliefs and treatment outcome. *Psychological Medicine, 18,* 697–702.

Leon, A. C., Portera, L., & Weissman, M. M. (1995). The social costs of anxiety disorders. *British Journal of Psychiatry, 166* (Suppl. 27), 19–22.

Lindsay, M., Crino, R., & Andrews, G. (1997). Controlled trial of exposure and response prevention in obsessive-compulsive disorder. *British Journal of Psychiatry, 171,* 135–139.

Livingston-van Noppen, B., Rasmussen, S. A., Eisen, J., & McCartney, L. (1990). Family function and treatment in obsessive-compulsive disorder. In M. A. Jenike, L. Bear, & W. E. Minichiello (Eds.), *Obsessive-compulsive disorder: Theory and treatment.* Chicago: Year Book Medical Publishers.

MacDonald, P. A., Antony, M. M., MacLeod, C. M., & Richter, M. A. (1997). Memory and confidence in memory judgments among individuals with obsessive compulsive disorder and nonclinical controls. *Behaviour Research and Therapy, 35*(6), 497–505.

March, J. S., Biederman, J., Wolkow, R., Safferman, A., Mardekian, J., Cook, E. H., et al. (1998). Setraline in children and adolescents with obsessive-compulsive disorder: A multicenter randomized controlled trial. *JAMA: Journal of the American Medical Association, 280*(20), 1752–1756.

March, J. S., & Curry, J. F. (1998). Predicting the outcome of treatment. *Journal of Abnormal Child Psychology, 26*(1), 39–51.

March, J. S., Frances, A., Carpenter, D., & Kahn, D. (1997). The Expert Consensus Guideline Series: Treatment of obsessive compulsive disorder [Special issue]. *The Journal of Clinical Psychiatry, 58*(Suppl. 4).

March, J. S., Franklin, M. E., Nelson, A. H., & Foa, E. B. (in press). Cognitive-behavioral psychotherapy for pediatric obsessive-compulsive disorder. *Journal of Clinical Child Psychology.*

March, J. S., Mulle, K., & Herbel, B. (1994). Behavioral psychotherapy for children and adolescents with obsessive-compulsive disorder: An open trial of a new protocol-driven treatment package. *Journal of the American Academy of Child and Adolescent Psychiatry, 33,* 333–341.

Marks, I. M., Hallman, R. S., Connolly, J., & Philpott, R. (1977). *Nursing in behavioural psychotherapy.* London: Royal College of Nursing.

Marks, I., Hodgson, R., & Rachman, S. (1975). Treatment of chronic obsessive-compulsive neurosis by in vivo exposure. *British Journal of Psychiatry, 127,* 349–364.

Marks, I. M., Lelliott, P. T., Basoglu, M., Noshirvani, H., Monteiro, W., Cohen, D., et al. (1988). Clomipramine, self-exposure and therapist-aided exposure for obsessive-compulsive rituals. *British Journal of Psychiatry, 152,* 522–534.

Marks, I. M., Stern, R. S., Mawson, D., Cobb, J., & McDonald, R. (1980). Clomipramine and exposure for obsessive-compulsive rituals—I. *British Journal of Psychiatry, 136,* 1–25.

Mataix-Cols, D., Marks, I. M., Greist, J. H., Kobak, K. A., & Baer, L. (2002). Obsessive-compulsive symptom dimensions as predictors of compliance with and response to behaviour therapy: Results from a controlled trial. *Psychotherapy & Psychosomatics, 71*(5), 255–262.

Mayerovitch, J. I., du Fort, G. G., Kakuma, R., Bland, R. C., Newman, S. C., & Pinard, G. (2003). Treatment seeking for obsessive-compulsive disorder: Role of obsessive-compulsive disorder symptoms and comorbid psychiatric diagnoses. *Comprehensive Psychiatry, 44*(2), 162–168.

McDougal, C. J., Epperson, C. N., Pelton, G. H., Wasylink, S., & Price, L. H. (2000). A double-blind, placebo-controlled study of risperidone addition in serotonin reuptake inhibitor-refractory obsessive-compulsive disorder. *Archives of General Psychiatry, 57,* 794–801.

McFall, M. E., & Wollersheim, J. P. (1979). Obsessive-compulsive neurosis: A cognitive behavioral formulation and approach to treatment. *Cognitive Therapy and Research, 3,* 333–348.

McLean, P. D., Whittal, M. L., Thordarson, D. S., Taylor, S., Soechting, I., Koch, W. J., et al. (2001). Cognitive versus behavior therapy in group treatment of obsessive-compulsive disorder. *Journal of Consulting and Clinical Psychology, 69*(2), 205–214.

McNally, R. J., & Kohlbeck, P. A. (1993). Reality monitoring in obsessive-compulsive disorder. *Behaviour Research and Therapy, 31*(3), 249–253.

Mehta, M. (1990). A comparative study of family-based and patients-based behavioural management in obsessive-compulsive disorder. *British Journal of Psychiatry, 157,* 133–135.

Meyer, V. (1966). Modification of expectations in cases with obsessional rituals. *Behaviour Research and Therapy, 4,* 273–280.

Meyer, V., & Levy, R. (1973). Modification of behavior in obsessive-compulsive disorders. In H. E. Adams & P. Unikel (Eds.), *Issues and trends in behavior therapy* (pp. 77–136). Springfield, IL: Charles C. Thomas.

Meyer, V., Levy, R., & Schnurer, A. (1974). The behavioural treatment of obsessive-compulsive disorders. In H. R. Beech (Ed.), *Obsessional states* (pp. 233–258). London: Methuen.

Miller, I. W., Epstein, N. B., Duane, S., & Keitner, G. I. (1985). The McMaster Family Assessment Device: Reliability and validity. *Journal of Marital & Family Therapy, 11*(4), 345–356.

Millet, B., Kochman, F., Gallarda, T., Krebs, M. O., Demonfaucon, F., Barrot, I., et al. (2004). Phenomenological and comorbid features associated in obsessive-compulsive disorder: Influence of age of onset. *Journal of Affective Disorders, 79,* 241–246.

Milner, A. D., Beech, H. R., & Walker, V. J. (1971). Decision processes and obsessional behaviour. *British Journal of Social & Clinical Psychology, 10*(1), 88–89.

Minichiello, W. E., Baer, L., & Jenike, M. A. (1987). Schizotypal personality disorder: A poor prognostic indicator for behavior therapy in the treatment of obsessive-compulsive disorder. *Journal of Anxiety Disorders, 1*(3), 273–276.

Montgomery, S. A., Kasper, S., Stein, D. J., Hedegaard, K. B., & Lemming, O. M. (2001). Citalopram 20 mg, 40 mg, and 60 mg are all effective and well tolerated compared with placebo in obsessive-compulsive disorder. *International Clinical Psychopharmacology, 16*(2), 75–86.

Mowrer, O. H. (1939). A stimulus-response analysis of anxiety and its role as a reinforcing agent. *Psychological Review, 46,* 553–565.

Mowrer, O. H. (1960). *Learning theory and behavior.* New York: Wiley.

O'Sullivan, G., Noshirvani, H., Marks, I., Monteiro, W., & Lelliott, P. (1991). Six-year follow-up after exposure and clomipramine therapy for obsessive compulsive disorder. *Journal of Clinical Psychiatry, 52*(4), 150–155.

Pato, M. T., Zohar-Kadouch, R., Zohar, J., & Murphy, D. L. (1988). Return of symptoms after discontinuation of clomipramine in patients with obsessive-compulsive disorder. *American Journal of Psychiatry, 145*(12), 1521–1525.

Piacentini, J. (1999). Cognitive behavioral therapy of childhood OCD. *Child and Adolescent Psychiatric Clinics of North America, 8,* 599–617.

Pigott, T. A., L'Heureux, F., Dubbert, B., Bernstein, S., & Murphy, D. L. (1994). Obsessive compulsive disorder: Comorbid conditions. *Journal of Clinical Psychiatry, 55,* 15–28.

Pigott, T. A., L'Heureaux, F., Rubenstein, C. S., Bernstein, S. E., Hill, J. L., & Murphy, D. L. (1992). A double-blind, placebo-controlled study of trazodone in patients with obsessive-compulsive disorder. *Journal of Clinical Psychopharmacology, 12,* 156–162.

Pigott, T. A., & Seay, S. (1998). Biological treatments for obsessive compulsive disorder: Literature review. In R. Swinson, M. Antony, S. Rachman, & M. Richter (Eds.), *Obsessive-compulsive disorder: Theory, research, and treatment* (pp. 298–326). New York: Guilford Press.

Pitman, R. K. (1993). Posttraumatic obsessive-compulsive disorder: A case study. *Comprehensive Psychiatry, 34,* 102–107.

Pitman, R. (1994). Obsessive compulsive disorder in Western history. In E. Hollander, J. Zohar, D. Marazziti, & B. Olivier (Eds.), *Current insights in obsessive compulsive disorder* (pp. 3–10). New York: Wiley.

Rabavilas, A. D., Boulougouris, J. C., & Stefanis, C. (1976). Duration of flooding sessions in the treatment of obsessive-compulsive patients. *Behaviour Research and Therapy, 14,* 349–355.

Rachman, S., Cobb, J., Grey, S., McDonald, B., Mawson, D., Sartory, G., et al. (1979). The behavioural treatment of obsessional-compulsive disorders, with and without clomipramine. *Behaviour Research and Therapy, 17,* 467–478.

Rachman, S., & Hodgson, R. (1980). *Obsessions and compulsions.* Englewood Cliffs, NJ: Prentice Hall.

Rachman, S. J., & Wilson, G. T. (1980). *The effects of psychological therapy.* Oxford, England: Pergamon Press.

Radomsky, A. S., & Rachman, S. (1999). Memory bias in obsessive-compulsive disorder (OCD). *Behaviour Research and Therapy, 37*(7), 605–618.

Rapoport, J. L., Swedo, S. E., & Leonard, H. L. (1992). Childhood obsessive compulsive disorder. 144th Annual Meeting of the American Psychiatric Association: Obsessive compulsive disorder: Integrating theory and practice (1991, New Orleans, Louisiana). *Journal of Clinical Psychiatry, 53*(4, Suppl.), 11–16.

Rasmussen, S. A., & Eisen, J. L. (1989). Clinical features and phenomenology of obsessive compulsive disorder. *Psychiatric Annals, 19*(2), 67–73.

Rasmussen, S. A., & Eisen, J. L. (1990). Epidemiology of obsessive compulsive disorder. *Journal of Clinical Psychiatry, 51*(2, Suppl.), 10–13.

Rasmussen, S. A., & Eisen, J. L. (1992). The epidemiology and clinical features of obsessive compulsive disorder. *Psychiatric Clinics of North America, 15,* 743–758.

Rasmussen, S. A., & Tsuang, M. T. (1986). Clinical characteristics and family history in *DSM-III* obsessive-compulsive disorder. *American Journal of Psychiatry, 143*(3), 317–322.

Reed, G. F. (1976). Indecisiveness in obsessional-compulsive disorder. *British Journal of Social & Clinical Psychology, 15*(4), 443–445.

Riddle, M. A., Reeve, E. A., Yaryura-Tobias, J. A., Yang, H. M., Claghorn, J. L., Gaffney, G., et al. (2001). Fluvoxamine for children and adolescents with obsessive-compulsive disorder: A randomized, controlled, multicenter trial. *Journal of the American Academy of Child and Adolescent Psychiatry, 40,* 222–229.

Riggs, D. S., & Foa, E. B. (1993). Obsessive compulsive disorder. In D. H. Barlow (Ed.), *Clinical handbook of psychological disorders: A step-by-step treatment manual* (2nd ed., pp. 189–123). New York: Guilford Press.

Riggs, D. S., Hiss, H., & Foa, E. B. (1992). Marital distress and the treatment of obsessive compulsive disorder. *Behavior Therapy, 23*(4), 585–597.

Roper, G., & Rachman, S. (1976). Obsessional-compulsive checking: Experimental replication and development. *Behaviour Research and Therapy, 14,* 25–32.

Roper, G., Rachman, S., & Hodgson, R. (1973). An experiment of obsessional checking. *Behaviour Research and Therapy, 11,* 271–277.

Roper, G., Rachman, S., & Marks, I. (1975). Passive and participant modelling in exposure treatment of obsessive-compulsive neurotics. *Behaviour Research and Therapy, 13,* 271–279.

Rothbaum, B. O., & Shahar, F. (2000). Behavioral treatment of obsessive-compulsive disorder in a naturalistic setting. *Cognitive and Behavioral Practice, 7,* 262–270.

Salkovskis, P. M. (1985). Obsessional compulsive problems: A cognitive behavioral analysis. *Behaviour Research and Therapy, 23,* 571–583.

Samuels, J., Nestadt, G., Bienvenu, O. J., Costa, P. T., Jr., Riddle, M. A., Liang, K. Y., et al. (2000). Personality disorders and normal personality dimensions in obsessive-compulsive disorder. *British Journal of Psychiatry, 177,* 457–462.

Sanavio, E. (1988). Obsessions and compulsions: The Padua Inventory. *Behaviour Research and Therapy, 26,* 169–177.

Sasson, Y., Zohar, J., Chopra, M., Lustig, M., Iancu, I., & Hendler, T. (1997). Epidemiology of obsessive-compulsive disorder: A world view. *Journal of Clinical Psychiatry, 58*(12), 7–10.

Shafran, R., Ralph, J., & Tallis, F. (1995). Obsessive-compulsive symptoms and the family. *Bulletin of the Menninger Clinic, 59*(4), 472–479.

Slade, T., & Andrews, G. (2002). Exclusion criteria in the diagnostic classifications of *DSM-IV* and *ICD-10:* Revisiting the co-occurrence of psychiatric syndromes. *Psychological Medicine, 32,* 1203–1211.

Sorensen, C. B., Kirkeby, L., & Thomsen, P. H. (2004). Quality of life with OCD: A self-reported survey among members of the Danish OCD Association. *Nordic Journal of Psychiatry, 58*(3), 231–236.

Stampfl, T. G., & Levis, D. J. (1967). Essentials of implosive therapy: A learning-theory-based psychodynamic behavioral therapy. *Journal of Abnormal Psychology, 72,* 496–503.

Steketee, G. (1993). Social support and treatment outcome of obsessive compulsive disorder at 9-month follow-up. *Behavioural Psychotherapy, 21*(2), 81–95.

Steketee, G. (1997). Disability and family burden in obsessive-compulsive disorder. *Canadian Journal of Psychiatry, 42*(9), 919–928.

Steketee, G., Chambless, D. L., & Tran, G. Q. (2001). Effects of Axis I and II comorbidity on behavior therapy outcome for obsessive-compulsive disorder and agoraphobia. *Comprehensive Psychiatry, 42*(1), 76–86.

Steketee, G., Eisen, J., Dyck, I., Warshaw, M., & Rasmussen, S. (1999). Predictors of course in obsessive-compulsive disorder. *Psychiatry Research, 89*(3), 229–238.

Steketee, G. S., Foa, E. B., & Grayson, J. B. (1982). Recent advances in the treatment of obsessive-compulsives. *Archives of General Psychiatry, 39,* 1365–1371.

Steketee, G., & Pruyn, N. A. (1998). Families of individuals with obsessive-compulsive disorder. In R. P. Swinson, M. M. Antony, S. Rachman, & M. A. Richter (Eds.), *Obsessive-compulsive disorder: Theory, research, and treatment* (pp. 120–140). New York: Guilford Press.

Stern, R. S., Marks, I. M., Mawson, D., & Luscombe, D. K. (1980). Clomipramine and exposure for compulsive rituals: II. Plasma levels, side effects and outcome. *British Journal of Psychiatry, 136,* 161–166.

Summerfeldt, L. J., Huta, V., & Swinson, R. P. (1998). Personality and obsessive-compulsive disorder. In R. P. Swinson, M. M. Antony, S. Rachman, & M. A. Richter (Eds.), *Obsessive-compulsive disorder: Theory, research, and treatment* (pp. 79–119). New York: Guilford Press.

Swedo, S. E., Leonard, H. L., Garvey, M., Mittleman, B., Allen, A. J., Perlmutter, S., et al. (1998). Pediatric autoimmune neuropsychiatric disorders associated with streptococcal infections: Clinical description of the first 50 cases. *American Journal of Psychiatry, 155,* 264–271.

Swedo, S. E., Rapoport, J. L., Leonard, H. L., Lenane, M., & Cheslow, D. (1989). Obsessive-compulsive disorder in children and adolescents: Clinical phenomenology of 70 consecutive cases. *Archives of General Psychiatry, 46*(4), 335–341.

Tallis, F., Pratt, P., & Jamani, N. (1999). Obsessive compulsive disorder, checking, and non-verbal memory: A neuropsychological investigation. *Behaviour Research and Therapy, 37*(2), 161–166.

Taylor, S. (1995). Assessment of obsessions and compulsions: Reliability, validity, and sensitivity to treatment effects. *Clinical Psychology Review, 15,* 261–296.

Tenney, N. H., Schotte, C. K. W., Denys, D. A. J. P., van Megan, H. J. G. M., & Westenberg, H. G. M. (2003). Assessment of *DSM-IV* personality disorders in obsessive-compulsive disorder: Comparison of clinical diagnosis, self-report questionnaire, and semi-structured interview. *Journal of Personality Disorders, 17,* 550–561.

Thomsen, P. H. (2002). Pharmacological treatment of pediatric obsessive compulsive disorder. *Expert Review in Neurotherapeutics, 2,* 549–554.

Tolin, D. F., Abramowitz, J. S., Brigidi, B. D., Amir, N., Street, G. P., & Foa, E. B. (2001). Memory and memory confidence in obsessive-compulsive disorder. *Behaviour Research and Therapy, 39*(8), 913–927.

Tollefson, G. D., Rampey, A. H., Potvin, J. H., Jenike, M. A., Rush, A. J., Dominguez, R. A., et al. (1994). A multicenter investigation of fixed-dose fluoxetine in the treatment of obsessive-compulsive disorder. *Archives of General Psychiatry, 51,* 559–567.

Tukel, R., Polat, A., Ozdemir, O., Aksut, D., & Turksoy, N. (2002). Comorbid conditions in obsessive-compulsive disorder. *Comprehensive Psychiatry, 43,* 204–209.

Valleni-Basile, L. A., Garrison, C. Z., Jackson, K. L., Waller, J. L., McKeown, R. E., Addy, C. L., et al. (1994). Frequency of obsessive-compulsive disorder in a community sample of young adolescents. *Journal of the American Academy of Child and Adolescent Psychiatry, 33*(6), 782–791.

van Balkom, A., J., L. M., de Haan, E., van Oppen, P., Spinhoven, P., Hoogduin, K. A. L., & van Dyk, R. (1998). Cognitive and behavioral therapies alone versus in combination with fluvoxamine in the treatment of obsessive-compulsive disorder. *Journal of Nervous and Mental Disease, 186,* 492–499.

van Balkom, A. J. L. M., van Oppen, P., Vermeulen, A. W. A., van Dyck, R., Nauta, M. C. E., & Vorst, H. C. M. (1994). A meta-analysis on the treatment of obsessive compulsive disorder: A comparison of antidepressants, behavior, and cognitive therapy. *Clinical Psychology Review, 5,* 359–381.

Volans, P. J. (1976). Styles of decision-making and probability appraisal in selected obsessional and phobic patients. *British Journal of Social & Clinical Psychology, 15*(3), 305–317.

Watts, F. N. (1973). Desensitization as an habituation phenomenon: II. Studies of interstimulus interval length. *Psychological Reports, 33,* 715–718.

Weizman, A., Carmi, M., Hermesh, H., Shahar, A., Apter, A., Tyano, S., et al. (1986). High-affinity imipramine binding and serotonin uptake in platelets of eight adolescent and ten adult obsessive-compulsive patients. *American Journal of Psychiatry, 143*(3), 335–339.

Wever, C., & Rey, J. M. (1997). Juvenile obsessive-compulsive disorder. *Australian and New Zealand Journal of Psychiatry, 31,* 105–113.

Wheadon, D. E., Bushnell, W. D., & Steiner, M. (1993, December). *A fixed dose comparison of 20, 40 or 60 mg paroxetine to placebo in the treatment of OCD.* Paper presented at the annual meeting of the American College of Neuropsychopharmacology, Honolulu, HI.

Zitterl, W., Urban, C., Linzmayer, L., Aigner, M., Demal, U., Semler, B., et al. (2001). Memory deficits in patients with *DSM-IV* obsessive-compulsive disorder. *Psychopathology, 34* (3), 113–117.

Zohar, J., & Insel, T. R. (1987). Drug treatment of obsessive-compulsive disorder. *Journal of Affective Disorders, 13*(2), 193–202.

CHAPTER 12

Post-Traumatic Stress Disorder

RICHARD A. BRYANT

Post-traumatic stress disorder (PTSD) is an anxiety condition that has attracted much attention in recent years. Much of this interest arises from the need to understand how people respond to terrorism, war, and other forms of trauma. Equally important is the recognition that PTSD offers insight into human fear because it exemplifies extreme fear reactions. This chapter reviews the course of psychological adaptation after trauma, describes the major models of PTSD, outlines the evidence for these models, and discusses treatment options for the disorder. PTSD, perhaps more than any other anxiety disorder, has often been associated with practices that lack scientific rigor. Recognizing the need for evidence-based understanding and management of PTSD, this chapter aims to synthesize our current knowledge that is based on sound scientific study of people affected by trauma.

DESCRIPTION OF THE DISORDER AND CLINICAL PICTURE

PTSD was introduced as a psychiatric disorder in the third edition of the *Diagnostic and Statistical Manual of Mental Disorders* (*DSM-III;* American Psychiatric Association [APA], 1980). To satisfy the criteria for PTSD (see Table 12.1) in the current version of *DSM-IV* (APA, 1994), one must initially be exposed to an event that involves actual or threatened harm to oneself or others, and the individual need not respond with fear, helplessness, or horror. The current definition stipulates that the traumatic event needs to be significantly threatening because there is a dosage relationship between the severity of a traumatic event and the likelihood of PTSD development (March, 1993). Accordingly, traumatic events, such as war, rape, assault, severe motor vehicle accidents, and natural disasters comprise a large proportion of precipitants of PTSD. If the stressor criterion is satisfied, one must also display three clusters of symptoms: (1) repeatedly reexperiencing the traumatic experience (e.g., intrusive recollections of the event, nightmares); (2) avoidance of activities and stimuli reminiscent of the trauma and emotional numbing (e.g., difficulty experiencing positive emotions); and (3) elevated arousal (e.g., exaggerated startle reflex, insomnia).

PERSONALITY DEVELOPMENT AND PSYCHOPATHOLOGY

The documented finding that only a minority of trauma survivors develop PTSD raises the issue about variables that increase risk for PTSD development. Most research on vulnerability factors for PTSD has been conducted by retrospectively collecting data after trauma exposure, and consequently the findings needed to be interpreted cautiously. Although many factors are associated with PTSD development, the failure to assess these factors before trauma exposure often precludes researchers from delineating between factors that pose a risk for PTSD and factors that are a result of trauma exposure or PTSD. Factors associated with PTSD development can be categorized as occurring prior to the trauma, being associated with the traumatic event itself, or factors occurring in the environment after the trauma.

Pretrauma Risk Factors

In terms of preexisting risk factors, cross-sectional studies indicate that prior psychological disturbance (Breslau, Davis, Andreski, & Peterson, 1991; Smith, North, McCool, & Shea, 1990), family history of psychological disorders (Breslau et al., 1991; Davidson, Swartz, Storck, Krishnan, & Hammett, 1985), abusive childhoods (Bremner, Southwick, Johnson, Yehuda, & Charney, 1993; Breslau, Chilcoat, Kessler, & Davis, 1999; Engel et al., 1993; Nishith, Mechanic, & Resick, 2000), female gender (Riggs, Rothbaum, & Foa, 1995), and a history of family instability (King, King, Foy, & Gudanowski, 1996) are predictive of PTSD development. There is also evidence that lower intelligence is associated with greater PTSD symptom severity (McNally & Shin, 1995; Silva et al.,

TABLE 12.1 *DSM-IV* Diagnostic Criteria for Post-Traumatic Stress Disorder

A. The person has been exposed to a traumatic event in which both of the following were present:
   (1) The person experienced, witnessed, or was confronted with an event or events that involved actual or threatened death or serious injury or a threat to the physical integrity of self or others.
   (2) The person's response involved intense fear, helplessness, or horror.
   (Note: In children, this may be expressed instead by disorganized or agitated behavior.)

B. The traumatic event is persistently reexperienced in one (or more) of the following ways:
   (1) Recurrent and intrusive distressing recollections of the event, including images, thoughts, or perceptions.
   (Note: In young children, repetitive play may occur in which themes or aspects of the trauma are expressed.)
   (2) Recurrent distressing dreams of the event.
   (Note: In children, there may be frightening dreams without recognizable content.)
   (3) Acting or feeling as if the traumatic event were recurring (includes a sense of reliving the experience, illusions, hallucinations, and dissociative flashback episodes, including those that occur on awakening or when intoxicated).
   (Note: In young children, trauma-specific reenactment may occur.)
   (4) Intense psychological distress at exposure to internal or external cues that symbolize or resemble an aspect of the traumatic event.
   (5) Physiological reactivity on exposure to internal or external cues that symbolize or resemble an aspect of the traumatic event.

C. Persistent avoidance of stimuli associated with the trauma and numbing of general responsiveness (not present before the trauma), as indicated by three (or more) of the following:
   (1) Efforts to avoid thoughts, feelings, or conversations associated with the trauma.
   (2) Efforts to avoid activities, places, or people that arouse recollections of the trauma.
   (3) Inability to recall an important aspect of the trauma.
   (4) Feeling of detachment or estrangement from others.
   (5) Restricted range of affect (e.g., unable to have loving feelings).
   (6) Sense of a foreshortened future (e.g., does not expect to have a career, marriage, children, or a normal life span).

D. Persistent symptoms of increased arousal (not present before the trauma), as indicated by two (or more) of the following:
   (1) Difficulty falling or staying asleep.
   (2) Irritability or outbursts of anger.
   (3) Difficulty concentrating.
   (4) Hypervigilance.
   (5) Exaggerated startle response.

E. Duration of the disturbance (symptoms in Criteria B, C, and D) is more than 1 month.

F. The disturbance causes clinically significant distress or impairment in social, occupational, or other important areas of functioning.

Specify if:
   Acute: if duration of symptoms is less than 3 months.
   Chronic: if duration of symptoms is 3 months or more.

Specify if:
   With Delayed Onset: if onset of symptoms is at least 6 months after the stressor.

Note. Reprinted with permission from the *Diagnostic and Statistical Manual of Mental Disorders* (4th ed.). Copyright 1994 by the American Psychiatric Association.

2000; Vasterling, Brailey, Constans, Borges, & Sutker, 1997; Vasterling et al., 2002). It is possible that people with higher intelligence can process the trauma in more adaptive ways or possess superior coping skills that lead to greater adaptation after trauma.

Peritraumatic Risk Factors

Not surprisingly, one of the major predictors of PTSD is the nature of the traumatic event itself. In general, the more one is exposed to threat, and the one is exposed to grotesque or distressing events, the more likely one is to develop PTSD (Brewin, Andrews, & Valentine, 2000; March, 1993). Associated with the objective definition of the stressor, there is also evidence that the more a person perceives the experience to be threatening, the more likely they will develop PTSD. Distress or perceived threat has predicted PTSD severity in combat veterans (King, King, Gudanowski, & Vreven, 1995), torture survivors (Basoglu, Paker, Ozmen, Tasdemir, & Sahin, 1994), burn victims (Perry, Difede, Musgni, Frances, & Jacobsberg, 1992), assault survivors (Kilpatrick, Saunders, Amick-McMullan, & Best, 1989), and accident survivors (Blanchard et al., 1995; Ehlers, Mayou, & Bryant, 1998; Schnyder, Moergeli, Klaghofer, & Buddeberg, 2001). The higher the distress or perceived threat, the more severe PTSD symptoms were likely to be.

Researchers have also tested whether symptom severity in the period shortly after trauma exposure predicts later PTSD. Symptom severity in the first few days following the trauma fails to predict later PTSD (e.g., Shalev, 1992), whereas symptom severity measured from one to two weeks post-trauma onward correlates highly with subsequent symptom severity (e.g., Harvey & Bryant, 1998; Koren, Arnon, & Klein, 1999; Murray, Ehlers, & Mayou, 2002; Shalev, Freedman, Peri, Brandes, & Sahar, 1997).

Much attention has focused on the predictive power of initial dissociative reactions. One meta-analysis has indicated that peritraumatic dissociation was the single best predictor of ($r = .35$) of PTSD among the trauma-exposed (Ozer, Best, Lipsey, & Weiss, 2003). For example, one study of survivors of motor vehicle accidents, terrorist attacks, and other traumatic events found that a sense that what was happening was unreal (derealization) and a sense of time distortion (things happening in slow motion) predicted who met criteria for PTSD six months later (Shalev, Peri, Canetti, & Schreiber, 1996). Depersonalization, emotional numbing, motor restlessness, and a sense of reliving the trauma predicted later PTSD among survivors of motor vehicle accidents (Harvey & Bryant, 1998). However, Murray et al. (2002) found that although peritraumatic dissociation predicted PTSD six months after a motor vehicle accident, persistent dissociation at four weeks was a more powerful predictor. Moreover, another study found that after initial symptom severity is controlled for, peritraumatic dissociation failed to predict later PTSD symptoms (Marshall & Schell, 2002). That is, whereas peritraumatic dissociation appears to be associated with subsequent PTSD, it is not linearly related to subsequent disorder. It is possible that dissociation is related to other reactions that are strongly predictive of PTSD (Bryant, 2003).

Consistent with cognitive models of PTSD (Ehlers & Clark, 2000), there is evidence that appraisal of the stressor and of one's reactions to the stressor influence whether chronic PTSD develops. There is evidence that people with acute stress disorder (ASD) exaggerate both the probability of future negative events occurring and the adverse effects of these events (Smith & Bryant, 2000; Warda & Bryant, 1998a). Catastrophic appraisal of symptoms (e.g., "my flashbacks must be a sign of madness") or about oneself following the trauma increase risk for PTSD (Dunmore, Clark, & Ehlers, 2001; Ehlers et al., 1998; Engelhard, van den Hout, Arntz, & McNally, 2002; Murray et al., 2002). Relatedly, the nature of attributions about the trauma shortly after the event apparently influences longer-term functioning. Prospective studies indicate that attributing responsibility to another person (Delahanty et al., 1997) and attributions of shame (Andrews, Brewin, Rose, & Kirk, 2000) in the acute phase are associated with later PTSD.

Posttrauma Risk Factors

Regarding risk factors associated with the posttrauma environment, there is evidence that self-reported levels of low social support are associated with PTSD (e.g., Boscarino, 1995; Brewin et al., 2000; Keane, Scott, Chavoya, Lamparski, & Fairbank, 1985). There is also evidence that use of avoidant coping strategies after trauma that involves active disengagement of trauma reminders is associated with longer-term PTSD (Bryant & Harvey, 1995a). This may not be a surprising finding, however, because avoidance is inherent in the PTSD definition.

The most robust method for identifying risk factors of PTSD is to assess factors before trauma exposure, and then assess people after they have been exposed to trauma. This is an expensive and difficult approach because researchers typically do not know which individuals are going to be exposed to trauma. One approach that has been adopted in recent years has been to assess cohorts who are high-risk for trauma exposure (e.g., military personnel emergency service personnel) prior to their exposure tom traumatic events. There is evidence that precombat school problems, lower arithmetic aptitude, and lower heart rate predict PTSD in military personnel (Pitman, Orr, Lowenhagen, Macklin, & Altman, 1991). Several researchers have found that personality variables measured before deployment to war zones, such as Hypochondriasis, Psychopathic Deviate, Paranoia, Femininity (Schnurr, Friedman, & Rosenberg, 1993) and negativism (similar to neuroticism; Bramsen, Dirkzwager, & van der Ploeg, 2000) predicted PTSD. Two studies have also found that lower predeployment intelligence test scores predicted PTSD in men who subsequently entered combat zones (Kaplan et al., 2002; Macklin et al., 1998).

Family and genetic studies are pointing toward the role of genetic contributions to post-traumatic stress reactions. Adult children of Holocaust survivors with PTSD show a greater prevalence of PTSD to their own traumatic events compared to adult children of Holocaust survivors without PTSD (Yehuda, McFarlane, & Shalev, 1998). Recent twin studies are indicating the role of genetic contribution, given the increased prevalence of PTSD in monozygotic compared with dizygotic twins (True et al., 1993). Using magnetic resonance imaging to study monozygotic co-twins, Gilbertson et al. (2002) found that Vietnam veterans with PTSD were characterized by smaller hippocampi than were Vietnam veterans without PTSD, but that the co-twins of those with PTSD (but who had not served in Vietnam) had hippocampi that were just as small. These findings suggest that small hippocampal volume may constitute a vulnerability factor for PTSD among people exposed to trauma. Indeed, contrary to some views (e.g., Bremner, 2002), traumatic stress does not seem to shrink the hippocampus of people exposed to trauma; rather, small hippocampi may be best conceptualized as a risk factor for PTSD.

There is also evidence that people's capacity for conditioning may be a risk factor for PTYSD development. One study compared startle responses in pairs of Vietnam combat veterans and their non-combat-exposed monozygotic twins (Orr et al., 2003). This study found evidence of more slowly habituating skin conductance startle responses in veterans with PTSD and their non-combat-exposed co-twins, compared to veterans without PTSD and their non-combat-exposed co-twins. This finding suggests that more slowly habituating skin conductance responses to startle stimuli may represent a pretrauma vulnerability factor for PTSD (Orr et al., 2003). Another study found that skin conductance and eyeblink EMG startle responses before trauma exposure in a cohort of firefighter trainees predicted acute stress reactions after subsequent trauma exposure (Guthrie & Bryant, 2005).

EPIDEMIOLOGY

Population studies have shown that many American adults have been exposed to traumatic stressors, as defined by *DSM*.

The National Comorbidity Survey indicated that 60.7 percent of randomly sampled adults reported exposure to a traumatic stressor (Kessler, Sonnega, Bromet, Hughes, & Nelson, 1995). A study of adults living in Detroit found that 89.6 percent reported exposure to a traumatic stressor (Breslau et al., 1991). Despite the frequency of exposure to potentially traumatizing events, relatively few people actually develop PTSD. For example, the National Comorbidity Survey found that only 20.4 percent of the women and 8.2 percent of the men ever developed PTSD (Kessler et al., 1995). Similarly, the Detroit study found that only 13 percent of the women and 6.2 percent of the men had developed PTSD (Breslau et al., 1991). These studies indicate that the normative response following trauma exposure is to adapt to the experience and to not develop PTSD. More severe traumas tend to result in more severe PTSD. Yehuda (2002) found that interpersonal violence leads to more PTSD than impersonal trauma. For example, across studies PTSD developed in 55 percent of rape victims but in only 7.5 percent of accident victims.

ETIOLOGY

Cognitive Models of Post-Traumatic Stress Disorder

Cognitive models of PTSD posit that the development and maintenance of PTSD rely heavily on two processes: (1) maladaptive appraisals of the trauma and its aftermath and (2) disturbances in autobiographical memory that involve impaired retrieval and strong associative memory (Ehlers & Clark, 2000). According to this perspective, trauma memories are often encoded in a fragmented manner because of the elevated arousal that occurs at the time of trauma. It is proposed that the difficulty in organizing these memories into a coherent narrative can impede adaptive processing of the experience, and can limit the extent to which the traumatic experience can be placed in a context of other nontraumatic memories that the person may retrieve. It is also proposed that the manner in which people appraise the traumatic event, their responses to it, and their environment after the trauma are pivotal in terms of perpetuating the individual's sense of threat or negative mood. Cognitive models hold that networks of mental representations are established that encompass stimuli, responses, and meanings that are associated with trauma, and that these networks of fear-related representations can be readily activated by many triggers.

Cognitive theories predict that individuals with PTSD are likely to have a bias toward searching for and identifying threatening information because these events are more strongly represented in their fear networks. Consistent with this prediction, there is much evidence that individuals with PTSD display slower color-naming of threat words (Bryant & Harvey, 1995b; Cassiday, McNally, & Zeitlin, 1992; Foa, Feske, Murdock, Kozak, & McCarthy, 1991; Harvey, Bryant, & Rapee, 1996; McNally, Kaspi, Riemann, & Zeitlin, 1990) and are drawn to threat in dot-probe (Bryant & Harvey, 1997) and eye-tracking (Bryant, Harvey, Gordon, & Barry, 1995) paradigms.

There is also evidence that people with PTSD are deficient in recalling specific positive memories. McNally and colleagues found that Vietnam veterans with PTSD have deficits in retrieving specific positive memories (McNally, Lasko, Macklin, & Pitman, 1995; McNally, Litz, Prassas, Shin, & Weathers, 1994). There is also evidence that overgeneral retrieval of autobiographical memories shortly after trauma exposure is predictive of subsequent PTSD (Harvey, Bryant, & Dang, 1998). It appears that difficulty in retrieving positive personal memories from one's past may hinder people's ability to consider the traumatic experience in the context of prior positive or safe memories.

There is also evidence that people with PTSD may manage trauma-related information differently from other trauma survivors. The most common finding is that people with PTSD have a tendency to be avoidant of distressing material. People with ASD findings use avoidant cognitive strategies to manage their trauma memories (Guthrie & Bryant, 2000; Warda & Bryant, 1998b). There is also some evidence that individuals with ASD tend to avoid aversive information. One study employed a directed forgetting paradigm that required ASD, non-ASD, and non-trauma-exposed control participants to read a series of trauma-related, positive, or neutral words, and after each presentation participants were instructed to either remember or forget the words (Moulds & Bryant, 2002). The finding that ASD participants recalled fewer trauma-related to-be-forgotten words than non-ASD participants suggests that they have an aptitude for forgetting aversive material. In a similar study that employed the list method form of directed forgetting, which indexes retrieval patterns, ASD participants displayed poorer recall of to-be-forgotten trauma words than non-ASD participants (Moulds & Bryant, in press). These findings suggest that people with ASD possess a cognitive style that avoids awareness of aversive or distressing information. Avoidance of distressing information or memories may be associated with psychopathological responses because it may lead to impaired processing of trauma-related memories and affect. In contrast, studies of more chronic PTSD suggest the disorder is not characterized by avoidant tendencies. Using a directed forgetting paradigm, one study found that adult survivors of childhood sexual abuse with PTSD did not display recall deficits for trauma-related words that they were instructed to remember (McNally, Metzger, Lasko, Clancy, & Pitman, 1998). This finding is comparable to studies of patients with borderline personality disorder, which is also characterized by severe trauma histories, which have not found enhanced directed forgetting effects (Cloitre, Cancienne, Brodsky, Dulit, & Perry, 1996; Korfine & Hooley, 2000).

Biological Theories of Post-Traumatic Stress Disorder

Biological models have focused on fear conditioning and progressive neural sensitization in the weeks after trauma as possible explanations of the genesis and maintenance of PTSD (Kolb, 1987; Pitman, Shalev, & Orr, 2000). Fear conditioning involves the application of classical conditioning principles to trauma. Specifically, when a traumatic event (unconditioned stimulus) occurs, people typically respond with fear (unconditioned response). It is argued that the strong fear elicited by the trauma will lead to strong associative conditioning between the fear and the events surrounding the trauma. As reminders of the trauma occur (conditioned stimuli), people then respond with fear reactions (conditioned response). It has been hypothesized that extreme sympathetic arousal at the time of a traumatic event may result in the release of stress neurochemicals (including norepinephrine and epinephrine) into the cortex, mediating an overconsolidation of trauma memories (Cahill & McGaugh, 1996; Pitman, 1988, 1989). It is possible that sensitization occurs as a result of repetitive activation by trauma reminders and re-experiencing symptoms, elevating sensitivity of limbic networks (Post, Weiss, & Smith, 1995), and that as time progresses these responses become increasingly conditioned to trauma-related stimuli (LeDoux, Iwata, Cicchetti, & Reis, 1988).

Much preclinical research elucidated the neural underpinnings of fear conditioning (Davis, 1992; LeDoux, 1995; LeDoux, 1998). Brain structures activated during aversive conditioning procedures are highly preserved across species, thus inferences about neural structures implicated in human fear and anxiety can be extrapolated from preclinical studies (LeDoux, 1996). The amygdala has been implicated in the processing of the emotional significance of stimuli (LeDoux, 1998) and there is now converging evidence from a variety of experimental techniques demonstrating a crucial role of the amygdala in the acquisition and expression of conditioned fear (Davis, 2000). Specifically, peripheral sensory signals are projected to the lateral nucleus of the amygdala via convergent thalamic and sensory cortical pathways (LeDoux, Farb, & Milner, 1991; LeDoux, Farb, & Ruggiero, 1990; Li, Stutzmann, & LeDoux, 1996). LeDoux (1995) has proposed that the amygdala may be activated by rapid but rudimentary thalamic sensory inputs suggestive of threat to the organism, and it may be subsequently inhibited if slower, more detailed cortical inputs indicate the stimulus is harmless. The lateral nucleus of the amygdala sends projections to the central nucleus of the amygdala, which controls the behavioral, autonomic, and endocrine responses to aversive environmental stimuli via efferent projections to brainstem, limbic, and hypothalamic nuclei (LeDoux, 1995). Projections to the locus coeruleus, which releases norepinephrine, have been implicated in the control of heart rate, blood pressure, and behavioral arousal (Cedarbaum & Aghajanian, 1978). Projections from the central nucleus of the amygdala to the hypothalamic paraventricular nucleus (Champagne, Beaulieu, & Drolet, 1998; Gray, Carney, & Magnuson, 1989; Roozendaal, Koolhaas, & Bohus, 1992) may mediate neuroendocrine regulation of stress reactions involving the hypothalamic-pituitary-adrenal axis (HPA; Davis, 2000; LeDoux, 1995). Consequently, biological models of PTSD have hypothesized amygdala-mediated fear conditioning to underlie the pathogenesis of this disorder (Charney, Deutch, Krystal, Southwick, & Davis, 1993; Kolb, 1987).

In support of these proposals, there is evidence that people who eventually develop PTSD display elevated resting heart rates in the initial week after trauma (Bryant, Harvey, Guthrie, & Moulds, 2000; Shalev et al., 1998; see also Blanchard, Hickling, Galovski, & Veazey, 2002). There is also evidence that lower cortisol levels shortly after trauma may predict subsequent PTSD (Delahanty, Raimonde, & Spoonster, 2000; McFarlane, Atchison, & Yehuda, 1997). Cortisol may act as an "antistress" hormone that regulates initial activation of cortisol to restore equilibrium, and lower cortisol levels may reflect an incapacity to lower arousal following trauma (Yehuda, 1997). The importance of increased arousal in the acute phase is also indicated by the prevalence of panic attacks in people ASD (Bryant & Panasetis, 2001; Nixon & Bryant, 2003).

Numerous studies have tested the fear conditioning model by indexing psychophysiological responses to stimuli that are associated with the traumatic experience. Studies have found that combat-relevant audiovisual cues evoke larger increases in heart rate in Vietnam veterans with PTSD compared to nonveteran male controls (Blanchard, Kolb, Pallmeyer, & Gerardi, 1982) and veteran controls without PTSD (Blanchard, Kolb, Gerardi, Ryan, & Pallmeyer, 1986; Pallmeyer, Blanchard, & Kolb, 1986). This heightened physiological reactivity appears to be specific to trauma-related stimuli. Psychophysiological studies have also explored the responses of individuals with PTSD using their own recollections of the trauma as the eliciting stimulus. When individuals with PTSD have employed script-driven imagery to recall past traumatic events, they have consistently produced larger psychophysiological responses, including heart rate, skin conductance and facial electromyogram (EMG), compared with individuals with a similar trauma history without PTSD. This pattern has been found in Vietnam veterans (Pitman, Orr, Forgue, de Jong, & Claiborn, 1987), Korean and World War II veterans (Orr, Pitman, Lasko, & Herz, 1993), female victims of childhood sexual abuse (Orr et al., 1998), victims of terrorist attacks and other civilian traumas (Shalev, Orr, & Pitman, 1993; Shalev, Peri, Gelpin, Orr, & Pitman, 1997), breast cancer patients (Pitman et al., 2001), and survivors of motor vehicle accidents (Blanchard, Hickling, Buckley, et al., 1996). Notably, elevated psychophysiological reactivity does not appear to be the result of having an anxiety disorder per se, because psychophysiological reactivity is not elevated in combat veterans with a non-PTSD anxiety disorder (Pitman et al., 1990).

Current models propose that PTSD symptomatology occurs when the amygdala is hyperresponsive to fear-related stimuli, and there is a concomitant lack of "top-down" inhibition from the medial prefrontal cortex (Rauch et al., 2000). This view is supported by evidence that reduced activation in the medial prefrontal regions in PTSD patients has been reported in some (e.g., Bremner et al., 1999; Liberzon et al., 1999; Rauch et al., 2000; Shin et al., 2004), but not all (e.g., Gilboa et al., 2004), brain imaging studies.

COURSE, COMPLICATIONS, AND PROGNOSIS

There is much evidence of a broad array of stress reactions in the initial weeks after trauma exposure. There are reports of high rates of emotional numbing (Feinstein, 1989; Noyes, Hoenk, Kuperman, & Slymen, 1977), reduced awareness of one's environment (Berah, Jones, & Valent, 1984, Hillman, 1981), derealization (Cardeña & Spiegel, 1993; Freinkel, Koopman, & Spiegel, 1994; Noyes & Kletti, 1976, 1977; Sloan, 1988), depersonalization (Cardeña & Spiegel, 1993; Freinkel et al., 1994; Noyes et al., 1977; Sloan, 1988), intrusive thoughts (Cardeña & Spiegel, 1993; Feinstein, 1989; Sloan, 1988), avoidance behaviors (Bryant & Harvey, 1996; Cardeña & Spiegel, 1993; North, Smith, McCool, & Lightcap, 1989), insomnia (Cardeña & Spiegel, 1993; Feinstein, 1989; Sloan, 1988), concentration deficits (Cardeña & Spiegel, 1993; North et al., 1989), irritability (Sloan, 1988), and autonomic arousal (Feinstein, 1989; Sloan, 1988). Despite the prevalence of acute stress reactions, the majority of these stress responses are transient. For example, whereas 94 percent of rape victims displayed sufficient PTSD symptoms two weeks posttrauma to meet criteria (excluding the one-month time requirement), this rate dropped to 47 percent 11 weeks later (Rothbaum, Foa, Riggs, Murdock, & Walsh, 1992). In another study, 70 percent of women and 50 percent of men were diagnosed with PTSD at an average of 19 days after an assault; the rate of PTSD at four-month follow-up dropped to 21 percent for women and zero for men (Riggs et al., 1995). Similarly, half of a sample meeting criteria for PTSD shortly after a motor vehicle accident had remitted by six months and two-thirds had remitted by one year posttrauma (Blanchard, Hickling, Barton, et al., 1996). Even following the terrorist attacks on New York City in 2001, there was a steady decline in people reporting PTSD reactions in the months after the attacks. Galea et al. (2002) surveyed residents of New York City five to eight weeks after the attacks and found that 7.5 percent of a random sample of adults living south of 110th Street in Manhattan had developed PTSD, and of those living south of Canal Street, 20 percent had PTSD. In February 2002, Galea's group did a follow-up study on another group of adults living south of 110th Street and found that only 1.7 percent of the sample had PTSD related to the attacks (Galea, Boscarino, Resnick, & Vlahov, in press).

In recognition of the common transient stress reactions that occur after trauma exposure, *DSM-IV* stipulated that PTSD could only be diagnosed at least one month after a trauma. This time frame was established in recognition of the likelihood that many stress reactions would have abated within this time. In addition, *DSM-IV* introduced the acute stress disorder (ASD) diagnosis to describe stress reactions that occur in the initial month after a trauma (Harvey & Bryant, 2002). One goal of the diagnosis was to describe initial traumatic stress reactions that occur in the initial month after trauma exposure because it was felt that there was a need to describe reactions occurring in the initial month. A second goal was to identify people who shortly after trauma exposure would subsequently develop PTSD (Koopman, Classen, Cardeña, & Spiegel, 1995). *DSM-IV* stipulates that ASD can occur after a fearful response to experiencing or witnessing a threatening event (Cluster A). The requisite symptoms to meet criteria for ASD include three dissociative symptoms (Cluster B), one reexperiencing symptom (Cluster C), marked avoidance (Cluster D), marked anxiety or increased arousal (Cluster E), and evidence of significant distress or impairment (Cluster F). The disturbance must last for a minimum of two days and a maximum of four weeks (Cluster G) after which time a diagnosis of PTSD should be considered. The primary difference between the criteria for ASD and PTSD is the time frame and the former's emphasis on dissociative reactions to the trauma. ASD refers to symptoms manifested during the period from two days to four weeks posttrauma, whereas PTSD can only be diagnosed from four weeks. The diagnosis of ASD requires that the individual has at least three of the following: (1) a subjective sense of numbing or detachment, (2) reduced awareness of one's surroundings, (3) derealization, (4) depersonalization, or (5) dissociative amnesia.

The ASD diagnosis was largely influenced by the notion that dissociative reactions are a pivotal mechanism in posttraumatic responses. This proposal builds on Janet's (1907) early suggestion that mental representations of traumatic experiences that were excessively aversive were split from awareness to reduce distress; although this dissociation allegedly led to short-term relief, it purportedly resulted in a loss of mental functioning because mental resources were not available for other processes. This perspective was given much attention in recent years (van der Kolk & van der Hart, 1989) and provided the theoretical basis for dissociation playing a pivotal role in the ASD diagnosis. It was argued that dissociative responses in the aftermath of trauma would lead to impaired processing of trauma memories, and this would lead to ongoing PTSD (Spiegel, 1996).

There are now 12 prospective studies of adults that have prospectively assessed the relationship between ASD in the initial month after trauma, and development of subsequent PTSD (Brewin, Andrews, Rose & Kirk, 1999; Bryant & Harvey, 1998; Creamer, O'Donnell, & Pattison, 2004; Difede et al., 2002; Harvey & Bryant, 1998, 1999, 2000; Holeva, Tarrier, & Wells, 2001; Kangas, Henry, & Bryant, 2005; Murray et al., 2002; Schnyder et al., 2001; Staab, Grieger, Fullerton, & Ursano, 1996). In terms of people who meet criteria for ASD, a number of studies have found that approximately three-quarters of trauma survivors who display ASD subsequently develop PTSD (Brewin et al., 1999; Bryant & Harvey, 1998; Difede et al., 2002; Harvey & Bryant, 1998, 1999, 2000; Holeva et al., 2001; Kangas et al., 2005; Murray et al., 2002). Compared to the expected remission of most people who display initial post-traumatic stress reactions, these studies indicate that the ASD diagnosis is performing reasonably well in predicting people who will develop PTSD. The predictive utility of the ASD diagnosis is less encouraging when one considers the proportion of people who eventually developed PTSD and who initially displayed ASD. In most studies, the minority of people who eventually developed PTSD initially met criteria for ASD. That is, whereas the majority of people who develop ASD are at high risk for developing subsequent PTSD, there are many other people who will develop PTSD who do not initially meet ASD criteria. It appears that a major reason for people who are at high risk for PTSD not meeting ASD criteria is the requirement that three dissociative symptoms be displayed. In one study, 60 percent of people who met all ASD criteria except for the dissociation cluster met PTSD criteria six months later (Harvey & Bryant, 1998), and 75 percent of these people still had PTSD two years later (Harvey & Bryant, 1999). This pattern suggests that emphasizing dissociation as a critical factor in predicting subsequent PTSD leads to a neglect of other acute stress reactions that also represent a risk for development of chronic PTSD.

It is important to note that PTSD is only one of an array of mental health problems that can arise after trauma exposure. Trauma survivors are at increased risk for the development of major depression, panic disorder, generalized anxiety disorder, and substance abuse relative to people who have not experienced trauma (Kessler et al., 1995). They are also at risk for developing more somatic symptoms and physical illnesses, particularly hypertension, asthma, chronic pain syndromes and other psychosomatic illnesses (Boscarino, 1996).

ASSESSMENT AND DIAGNOSIS

There is an increasing range of diagnostic tools available to assess PTSD (for a review, see Wilson & Keane, 2004). Two structured clinical interviews stand out as the most highly regarded in terms of their psychometric properties and clinical use. The Clinician-Administered PTSD Scale (Blake et al., 1995). This interview indexes the severity and frequency of each PTSD symptom, as defined by *DSM-IV*, as well as indexing trauma exposure and associated trauma responses, such as guilt and dissociation. Considerable research has validated the decision rules by which a diagnosis of PTSD can be made on the CAPS (Weathers, Ruscio, Keane, 1999), and this research has underscored the reliability of diagnostic decisions made on the basis of the CAPS (Weathers, Keane, & Davidson, 2001). The other primary structured clinical interview is the PTSD Symptom Scale-Interview (PSS-I; Foa, Riggs, Dancu, & Rothbaum, 1993). This interview also asks the respondent about all *DSM-IV* criteria for PTSD and the interviewer makes a decision on a 0 to 3 Likert scale on the severity of each symptom. Direct comparisons of the CAPS and the PSS-I indicate that they perform equally well, although there is some evidence that the PSS-I requires less time to administer (Foa & Tolin, 2000). There is also a range of self-report measures available to assess PTSD. The Post-Traumatic Stress Diagnostic Scale (PDS; Foa, Cashman, Jaycox, & Perry, 1997) is a self-report version of the PSS-I that indexes the severity of each *DSM-IV* criteria for PTSD. This scale has excellent psychometric properties, and provides both a diagnostic decision and a severity scale. Other well-respected self-report measures include the Davidson Trauma Scale (Davidson, Book, et al., 1997) and the PTSD Checklist, Civilian Version (PCL-C; Weathers & Ford, 1996).

In terms of ASD, there are currently three major measures that have adequate psychometric properties. The first measure to be developed was the Stanford Acute Stress Reaction Questionnaire (SASRQ). The current version of the SASRQ (Cardeña, Koopman, Classen, Waelde, & Spiegel, 2000) is a 30-item self-report inventory that encompasses each of the ASD symptoms. The Acute Stress Disorder Interview (ASDI; Bryant, Harvey, Dang, & Sackville, 1998) is a structured clinical interview that is based on *DSM-IV* criteria. The ASDI possesses good internal consistency ($r = .90$), test-retest reliability ($r = .88$), sensitivity (91 percent), and specificity (93 percent) relative to independent clinician diagnosis of ASD. The ASDI has been used in a range of prospective studies that have identified recently trauma-exposed people who subsequently develop PTSD (Bryant & Harvey, 1998; Harvey & Bryant, 1998, 1999, 2000). The Acute Stress Disorder Scale (ASDS; Bryant, Moulds, & Guthrie, 2000) is a self-report inventory that is based on the same items described in the ASDI. The major limitation of all these measures of ASD is that reliance on meeting the dissociative criteria of ASD tends to result in neglect of people who are at high risk for developing PTSD.

IMPACT ON ENVIRONMENT

There is strong evidence that PTSD results in increased stress on family members of the PTSD patient. For example, the report of the President's Commission on Mental Health (1978) indicated that 38 percent of marriages of Vietnam veterans terminated within six months of returning from Vietnam. The National Vietnam Veterans Readjustment Study found that approximately one third of male veterans engaged in partner violence in the previous year (Jordan et al., 1992). Numerous studies of veterans' wives and partners indicate that those who live with a veteran with PTSD often suffer emotional detachment from the husband, battering, increased responsibility for the husband's well-being, frustration of sexual needs, insomnia, somatic problems, and poor social support (Dirkzwager, Bramsen, Adèr, & van der Ploeg, 2005; Jordan et al., 1992; Solomon, Kotler, & Mikulincer, 1988; Solomon et al., 1992). One of the most worrying statistics is the high prevalence of domestic violence among partners of veterans with PTSD (Jordan et al., 1992). It appears that veterans with PTSD are more likely to engage in partner violence if they are depressed, drug dependent, and were exposed to more atrocities during war experience (Casey et al., 2005).

There are several explanations for these findings. It is possible that partners of those with PTSD suffer chronic stress because they are frequently exposed to the anger, emotional outbursts, and detachment of the PTSD sufferer. Alternately, some partners may experience "secondary traumatization," in which the partner identifies with the traumatic experiences of the PTSD sufferer. That is, after hearing stories of traumatic experiences and witnessing the PTSD patient's symptoms, a partner may become attuned to similar triggers and develop stress reactions as well.

Similarly, there is convergent evidence that children can suffer stress reactions when a parent has PTSD. In a study of children of veterans with and without PTSD, it was found that children of PTSD veterans perceived higher levels of family dysfunction (Davidson & Mellor, 2001). Some evidence indicates that emotional numbing and avoidance are the primary symptoms that contribute to impaired parenting in those with PTSD (Ruscio, Weathers, King, & King, 2002). Focusing largely on offspring of Holocaust survivors, a number of studies have indexed the possibility of transgenerational effects of PTSD. Specifically, these studies have hypothesized that being reared by a parent with PTSD may lead to PTSD because of secondary traumatization. In a series of studies, Yehuda and colleagues have reported that children of Holocaust survivors with PTSD are more likely to develop PTSD themselves (Yehuda, Halligan, & Bierer, 2001; Yehuda, Schmeidler, Wainberg, Binder-Brynes, & Duvdevani, 1998). Interestingly, tentative evidence exists that this link may be stronger in maternal PTSD, raising the possibility of in utero effects of stress on the fetus (Yehuda et al., 2001).

As a result of the documented effect of PTSD on partners and children, there is increasing attention to the need for treatment programs for the families of people with PTSD. These programs tend to teach families education about PTSD, skills to cope with the effects of PTSD symptoms on the family, self-protection, and self-help groups (Nelson & Wright, 1996). Veteran and civilian agencies frequently offer these services to reduce possible adverse mental health consequences of living with someone with PTSD.

TREATMENT IMPLICATIONS

Pharmacological Therapy

Study of pharmacological interventions for PTSD is relatively recent (see Friedman, 2000; Friedman, Davidson, Mellman, & Southwick, 2000; Pearlstein, 2000). The first medication approved by the U.S. Food and Drug Administration (FDA) for treating PTSD was the SSRI sertraline. Two 12-week randomized clinical trials of sertraline versus placebo indicated significant symptom reduction in response to sertraline (Brady et al., 2000; Davidson, Londborg, et al., 1997). These findings support small studies that have also reported efficacy with the SSRI, fluoxetine in which civilian, but not veteran, subjects responded successfully to the SSRI (Marshall, Beebe, Oldham, & Zaninelli, 2001; van der Kolk et al., 1994). Three studies with SSRIs also suggest that therapeutic efficacy is associated with reduction of autonomic dysregulation, indicated by heart rate variability (Cohen, Kotler, Matar, Kaplan, 2000) and by elimination of elevated reactivity to script-driven imagery, assessed by increases in blood pressure and heart rate (Tucker et al., 2001). Overall, these reports suggest that SSRIs are an effective class of medications for patients with PTSD.

In terms of early intervention, there is promising evidence from attempts to limit fear conditioning by reducing epinephrine shortly after trauma exposure. On the premise that propranolol abolishes the epinephrine enhancement of conditioning (Cahill, Prins, Weber, & McGaugh, 1994), one pilot study attempted to prevent PTSD by administering propranolol (a-adrenergic blocker) within six hours of trauma exposure (Pitman et al., 2002). Although propranolol did not result in reduced PTSD relative to a placebo condition, patients receiving propranolol displayed less physiological reactivity to trauma reminders three months later. This outcome suggests that propranolol administration shortly after trauma exposure may limit fear conditioning that may contribute to subsequent PTSD development. Supporting this possibility, another study that administered propranolol within hours of trauma exposure found that it led to less PTSD six weeks later than placebo (Vaiva et al., 2003). These recent developments point to the possibility of secondary prevention of PTSD through limiting fear-conditioning responses in the immediate aftermath of trauma exposure.

PSYCHOLOGICAL THERAPY FOR PTSD

The psychological treatment of choice for PTSD is cognitive behavior therapy (CBT) and typically comprises psychoeducation, anxiety management, stress inoculation, cognitive restructuring, imaginal and in vivo exposure, and relapse prevention (for reviews, see Bryant & Friedman, 2001; Foa & Meadows, 1997; Harvey, Bryant, & Tarrier, 2003). Psychoeducation comprises providing information about common symptoms following a traumatic event, legitimizes the trauma reactions, and establishes a rationale for treatment. Anxiety management techniques aim to provide individuals with coping skills to assist them to gain a sense of mastery over their fear, to reduce arousal levels, and to assist the individual when engaging in exposure to the traumatic memories. Anxiety management approaches often include stress inoculation training that follows Meichenbaum's (1975) program of psychoeducation, relaxation skills, thought stopping, and self-talk. Prolonged imaginal exposure requires the individual to vividly imagine the trauma for prolonged periods. Prolonged exposure typically occurs for at least 50 minutes, and is usually supplemented by daily homework exercises. Variants of imaginal exposure involve requiring clients to repeatedly write down detailed descriptions of the experience (Resick & Schnicke, 1992) and implementing exposure with the assistance of virtual reality paradigms implemented via computer-generated imagery (Rothbaum et al., 2001). Most exposure treatments supplement imaginal exposure with in vivo exposure that involves live graded exposure to the feared trauma-related stimuli. Other variants to exposure approaches include earlier work on systematic desensitization (Wolpe, 1958) and eye movement desensitization and reprocessing (Shapiro, 1995). Cognitive restructuring, which is based on the premise that maladaptive appraisals underpinning the maintenance of PTSD (Ehlers & Clark, 2000), involves teaching patients to identify and evaluate the evidence for negative automatic thoughts as well as helping patients to evaluate their beliefs about the trauma, the self, the world, and the future in an evidence-based manner. The duration of CBT for PTSD is typically 9 to 12 sessions.

Efficacy of CBT in the Treatment of PTSD

One of the earliest well-controlled studies of CBT randomly assigned assault survivors who had PTSD to either prolonged exposure, stress inoculation training, supportive counseling, or a wait-list control group (Foa, Rothbaum, Riggs, & Murdock, 1991). Whereas stress inoculation training resulted in greater gains than supportive counseling or wait-list control at posttreatment, the prolonged exposure condition led to greater reduction in PTSD symptoms at three-month follow-up. The authors interpreted these findings as indicating that whereas stress inoculation training led to short-term symptom reduction, prolonged exposure resulted in longer-term benefits because the fear networks were activated and modified. Foa and colleagues subsequently replicated this study in a design that randomized 96 assault victims to prolonged exposure, stress inoculation training, the combination of prolonged exposure and stress inoculation training, and a wait-list control condition (Foa et al., 1999). The three active treatments were associated with reduced PTSD and depression relative to controls. The intention-to-treat analysis indicated that prolonged exposure was superior to stress inoculation training, and the combined treatment.

In an adaptation of CBT, Resick and colleagues have proposed cognitive processing therapy (CPT) as a structured combination of exposure and cognitive therapy that is based on five major cognitive themes that are suggested to be central to rape victims' cognitive schema (Resick & Schnicke, 1992). One of the features of their approach is that exposure is achieved through repeatedly writing out the trauma narrative. In a study that compared CPT with prolonged exposure (PE) and a waiting minimal-attention condition, intention-to-treat analyses indicated that active treatments were comparably efficacious and superior to the wait-list condition. The efficacy of CBT has been reported in a range of other well-controlled studies (Blanchard et al., 2003; Ehlers et al., 2003; Fecteau & Nicki, 1999; Glynn et al., 1999; Keane, Fairbank, Caddell, & Zimering, 1989; Marks, Lovell, Noshirvani, Livanou, & Thrasher, 1998; Tarrier et al., 1999). Interestingly, these studies have not found that combining different components of CBT leads to better outcome than providing the single components. For example, providing cognitive restructuring as well as exposure does not lead to better outcome than providing exposure alone (Foa et al., 1999; Marks et al., 1998; Resick, Nishith, Weaver, Astin, & Fever, 2002). In contrast, Bryant and colleagues did find that imaginal exposure and cognitive restructuring randomly led to better outcome than exposure alone (Bryant, Moulds, Guthrie, Dang, & Nixon, 2003). It should be noted that this study differed from previous studies, however, because it did not include in vivo exposure.

The efficacy of treating PTSD with CBT has led researchers to attempt secondary prevention of PTSD by applying CBT to high-risk trauma survivors shortly after trauma exposure. Foa and colleagues provided a brief cognitive behavioral treatment program to sexual and nonsexual assault victims shortly after the assault and compared outcomes with matched participants who received repeated assessments. Each participant received four sessions, and was then assessed by blind assessors at two months posttreatment and five months follow-up. At five months there were no differences between the groups, although the CBT group was less depressed. Another approach has attempted to focus on individuals who are at high risk for developing PTSD by focusing on people who meet criteria for ASD. In an initial treatment study of ASD participants, Bryant and colleagues randomly allocated motor vehicle accident (MVA) or nonsexual assault survivors with ASD to either CBT or supportive counseling (Bryant, Harvey, Dang, Sackville, & Basten, 1998). Both interventions consisted of five 1.5-hour weekly individual therapy sessions. At the six-month follow-up, there were fewer participants in the CBT group (20 percent) who met diagnostic criteria for PTSD compared to supportive counseling control participants (67 percent). In a subsequent study that dismantled the components of CBT, 45 civilian trauma survivors with ASD were randomly allocated to five sessions of either (1) CBT (prolonged exposure, cognitive therapy, anxiety management), (2) prolonged exposure combined with cognitive therapy, or (3) supportive counseling (Bryant, Sackville, Dang, Moulds, & Guthrie, 1999). This study found that at the six-month follow-up, PTSD was observed in approximately 20 percent of both active treatment groups compared to 67 percent of those receiving supportive counseling. A further study randomly allocated civilian trauma survivors ($N = 89$) with ASD to either CBT, CBT plus hypnosis, or supportive counseling (Bryant, Moulds, Guthrie, & Nixon, 2005). The hypnosis component was provided immediately prior to imaginal exposure in an attempt to facilitate emotional processing of the trauma memories. In terms of treatment completers, more participants in the supportive counseling condition (57 percent) met criteria for PTSD at the six-month follow-up than those in the CBT (21 percent) or CBT plus hypnosis (22 percent) condition. Interestingly, participants in the CBT plus hypnosis condition reported greater reduction of reexperiencing symptoms at posttreatment than those in the CBT condition. This finding suggests that hypnosis may facilitate treatment gains in ASD participants. Finally, a recent study replicated the original Bryant et al. (1998) study with a sample of ASD participants ($N = 24$) who sustained mild traumatic brain injury following MVAs (Bryant, Moulds, Guthrie, & Nixon, 2003). Following five sessions of CBT, fewer participants receiving CBT (8 percent) met criteria for PTSD at the six-month follow-up compared to those receiving supportive counseling (58 percent).

CONCLUDING COMMENT

Our understanding of PTSD has grown markedly in recent years. The complimentary approaches of cognitive and biological models have resulted in new insights into the diverse mechanisms underpinning the development and maintenance of PTSD. As clinical and basic research into PTSD becomes more integrated, it is probable that our treatment approaches will be enhanced by modifying those biological and cognitive variables that contribute to successful adaptation after trauma exposure.

REFERENCES

American Psychiatric Association. (1980). *Diagnostic and statistical manual of mental disorders* (3rd ed.). Washington, DC: Author.

American Psychiatric Association. (1994). *Diagnostic and statistical manual of mental disorders* (4th ed.). Washington, DC: Author.

Andrews, B., Brewin, C. R., Rose, S., & Kirk, M. (2000). Predicting PTSD in victims of violent crime: The role of shame, anger and blame. *Journal of Abnormal Psychology, 109,* 69–73.

Basoglu, M., Mineka, S., Paker, M., Livanou, M., & Gok, S. (1997). Psychological preparedness for trauma as a protective factor in survivors of torture. *Psychological Medicine, 27,* 1421–1433.

Basoglu, M., Paker, M., Ozmen, E., Tasdemir, O., & Sahin, O. (1994). Factors related to long-term traumatic stress responses in survivors of torture in Turkey. *Journal of the American Medical Association, 272,* 354–363.

Beck, A. T., Rush, A. J., Shaw, B. F., & Emery, G. (1979). *Cognitive therapy of depression.* New York: Guilford Press.

Berah, E. F., Jones, H. J., & Valent, P. (1984). The experience of a mental health team involved in the early phase of a disaster. *Australian and New Zealand Journal of Psychiatry, 18,* 354–358.

Blake, D. D., Weathers, F. W., Nagy, L. M., Kaloupek, D. G., Gusman, F. D., Charney, D. S., et al. (1995). The development of a clinician administered PTSD scale. *Journal of Traumatic Stress, 8,* 75–90.

Blanchard, E. B., Hickling, E. J., Barton, K. A., Taylor, A. E., Loos, W. R., & Jones-Alexander, J. (1996). One-year prospective follow-up of motor vehicle accident victims. *Behaviour Research and Therapy, 34,* 775–786.

Blanchard, E. B., Hickling, E. J., Buckley, T. C., Taylor, A. E., Vollmer, A. J., & Loos, W. R. (1996). Psychophysiology of posttraumatic stress disorder related to motor vehicle accidents: Replication and extension. *Journal of Consulting & Clinical Psychology, 64,* 742–751.

Blanchard, E. B., Hickling, E. J., Devineni, T., Veazey, C. H., Galovski T. E., Mundy, E., et al. (2003). A controlled evaluation of cognitive behavioral therapy for posttraumatic stress in motor vehicle accident survivors. *Behaviour Research and Therapy, 41,* 79–91.

Blanchard, E. B., Hickling, E. J., Galovski, T., & Veazey, C. (2002). Emergency room vital signs and PTSD in a treatment seeking sample of motor vehicle accident survivors. *Journal of Traumatic Stress, 15,* 199–204.

Blanchard, E. B., Hickling, E. J., Mitnick, N., Taylor, A. E., Loos, W. R., & Buckley, T. C. (1995). The impact of severity of physical injury and perception of life threat in the development of post-traumatic stress disorder in motor vehicle accident victims. *Behaviour Research and Therapy, 33,* 529–534.

Blanchard, E. B., Kolb, L. C., Gerardi, R. J., Ryan, P., & Pallmeyer, T. P. (1986). Cardiac response to relevant stimuli as an adjunctive tool for diagnosing post-traumatic stress disorder in Vietnam veterans. *Behavior Therapy, 17,* 592–606.

Blanchard, E. B., Kolb, L. C., Pallmeyer, T. P., & Gerardi, R. J. (1982). A psychophysiological study of post traumatic stress disorder in Vietnam veterans. *Psychiatric Quarterly, 54,* 220–229.

Boscarino, J. A. (1995). Post-traumatic stress and associated disorders among Vietnam veterans: The significance of combat exposure and social support. *Journal of Traumatic Stress, 8,* 317–336.

Boscarino, J. A. (1996). Posttraumatic stress disorder, exposure to combat, and lower plasma cortisol among Vietnam veterans: Findings and clinical implications. *Journal of Consulting and Clinical Psychology, 64,* 191–201.

Brady, K., Pearlstein, T., Asnis, G. M., Baker, D., Rothbaum, B., Sikes, C. R., et al. (2000). Efficacy and safety of sertraline treatment of posttraumatic stress disorder: A randomized controlled trial. *Journal of the American Medical Association, 283,* 1837–1844.

Bramsen, I., Dirkzwager, A. J. E., & van der Ploeg, H. M. (2000). Predeployment personality traits and exposure to trauma as predictors of posttraumatic stress symptoms: A prospective study of former peacekeepers. *American Journal of Psychiatry, 157,* 1115–1119.

Bremner, J. D. (2002). *Does stress damage the brain?* New York: Norton.

Bremner, J. D., Southwick, S. M., Johnson, D. R., Yehuda, R., & Charney, D. S. (1993). Childhood physical abuse and combat-related posttraumatic stress disorder in Vietnam veterans. *American Journal of Psychiatry, 150,* 235–239.

Bremner, J. D., Staib, L. H., Kaloupek, D., Southwick, S. M., Soufer, R., & Charney, D. S. (1999). Neural correlates of exposure to traumatic pictures and sound in combat veterans with and without posttraumatic stress disorder: A positron emission tomography study. *Biological Psychiatry, 45,* 806–816.

Breslau, N., Chilcoat, H. D., Kessler, R. C., & Davis, G. C. (1999). Previous exposure to trauma and PTSD effects of subsequent trauma: Results from the Detroit Area Survey of Trauma. *American Journal of Psychiatry, 156,* 902–907.

Breslau, N., Chilcoat, H. D., Kessler, R. C., Peterson, E. L., & Lucia, V. C. (1999). Vulnerability to assaultive violence: Further specification of the sex difference in post-traumatic stress disorder. *Psychological Medicine, 29,* 813–821.

Breslau, N., Davis, G. C., Andreski, P., & Peterson, E. (1991). Traumatic events and posttraumatic stress disorder in an urban population of young adults. *Archives of General Psychiatry, 48,* 216–222.

Brewin, C. R., Andrews, B., Rose, S., & Kirk, M. (1999). Acute stress disorder and posttraumatic stress disorder in victims of violent crime. *American Journal of Psychiatry, 156,* 360–366.

Brewin, C. R., Andrews, B., & Valentine, J. D. (2000). Meta-analysis of risk factors for posttraumatic stress disorder in trauma-exposed adults. *Journal of Consulting and Clinical Psychology, 68,* 748–766.

Bryant, R. A. (2003). Early predictors of posttraumatic stress disorder. *Biological Psychiatry, 53,* 789–795.

Bryant, R. A., & Friedman, M. (2001). Medication and non-medication treatments of posttraumatic stress disorder. *Current Opinion in Psychiatry, 14,* 119–123.

Bryant, R. A., & Harvey, A. G. (1995a). Avoidant coping style and post-traumatic stress following motor vehicle accidents. *Behaviour Research and Therapy, 33,* 631–635.

Bryant, R. A., & Harvey, A. G. (1995b). Processing threatening information in post traumatic stress disorder. *Journal of Abnormal Psychology, 104,* 537–541.

Bryant, R. A., & Harvey, A. G. (1996). Initial post-traumatic stress responses following motor vehicle accidents. *Journal of Traumatic Stress, 9,* 223–234.

Bryant, R. A., & Harvey, A. G. (1997). Attentional bias in post-traumatic stress disorder. *Journal of Traumatic Stress, 10,* 635–644.

Bryant, R. A., & Harvey, A. G. (1998). Relationship of acute stress disorder and posttraumatic stress disorder following mild traumatic brain injury. *American Journal of Psychiatry, 155,* 625–629.

Bryant, R. A, Harvey, A. G., Dang, S., & Sackville, T. (1998). Assessing acute stress disorder: Psychometric properties of a structured clinical interview. *Psychological Assessment, 10,* 215–220.

Bryant, R. A., Harvey, A. G., Dang, S. T., Sackville, T., & Basten, C. (1998). Treatment of acute stress disorder: A comparison of cognitive behavior therapy and supportive counseling. *Journal of Consulting and Clinical Psychology, 66,* 862–866.

Bryant, R. A., Harvey, A. G., Gordon, E., & Barry, R. (1995). Eye-movement and electrodermal responses to threat stimuli in post-traumatic stress disorder. *International Journal of Psychophysiology, 20,* 209–213.

Bryant, R. A., Harvey, A. G., Guthrie, R., & Moulds, M. (2000). A prospective study of acute psychophysiological arousal, acute stress disorder, and posttraumatic Stress disorder. *Journal of Abnormal Psychology, 109,* 341–344.

Bryant, R. A., Moulds, M., & Guthrie, R. (2000). Acute Stress Disorder Scale: A self-report measure of acute stress disorder. *Psychological Assessment, 12,* 61–68.

Bryant, R. A., Moulds, M. L., Guthrie, R. M., Dang, S. T., & Nixon, R. D. V. (2003). Imaginal exposure alone and imaginal exposure with cognitive restructuring in treatment of posttraumatic stress disorder. *Journal of Consulting and Clinical Psychology, 71,* 706–712.

Bryant, R. A., Moulds, M. L., Guthrie, R., & Nixon, R. D. V. (2003). Treating acute stress disorder after mild brain injury. *American Journal of Psychiatry, 160,* 585–587.

Bryant, R. A., Moulds, M. L., Guthrie, R., & Nixon, R. D. V. (2005). The additive benefit of hypnotherapy and cognitive behavior therapy in treating acute stress disorder. *Journal of Consulting and Clinical Psychology, 73.* 334–340.

Bryant, R. A., Moulds, M. A., & Nixon, R. (2003). Cognitive behaviour therapy of acute stress disorder: A four-year follow-up. *Behaviour Research and Therapy, 41,* 489–494.

Bryant, R. A., & Panasetis, P. (2001). Panic symptoms during trauma and acute stress disorder. *Behaviour Research and Therapy, 39,* 961–966.

Bryant, R. A., Sackville, T., Dang, S. T., Moulds, M., & Guthrie, R. (1999). Treating acute stress disorder: An evaluation of cognitive behavior therapy and counselling techniques. *American Journal of Psychiatry, 156,* 1780–1786.

Cahill, L., & McGaugh, J. L. (1996). Modulation of memory storage. *Current Opinion in Neurobiology, 6,* 237–242.

Cahill, L., Prins, B., Weber, M., & McGaugh, J. L. (1994). B_ Adrenergic activation and memory for emotional events. *Nature, 371,* 702–704.

Cardeña, E., Koopman, C., Classen, C., Waelde, L. C., & Spiegel, D. (2000). Psychometric properties of the Stanford Acute Stress Reaction Questionnaire (SASRQ): A valid and reliable measure of acute stress. *Journal of Traumatic Stress, 13,* 719–734.

Cardeña, E., & Spiegel, D. (1993). Dissociative reactions to the San Francisco Bay Area earthquake of 1989. *American Journal of Psychiatry, 150,* 474–478.

Casey, T., Pless, A. P., Stalans, L. J., Koenen, K. C., King, L. A., & King, D. W. (2005). Risk factors for partner violence among a national sample of combat veterans. *Journal of Consulting and Clinical Psychology, 73,* 151–159.

Cassiday, K. L., McNally, R. J., & Zeitlin, S. B. (1992). Cognitive processing of trauma cues in rape victims with post-traumatic stress disorder. *Cognitive Therapy and Research, 16,* 283–295.

Cedarbaum, J. M., & Aghajanian, G. K. (1978). Afferent projections to the rat locus coeruleus as determined by a retrograde tracing technique. *Journal of Comparative Neurology, 178,* 1–16.

Champagne, D., Beaulieu, J., & Drolet, G. (1998). CRFergic innervation of the paraventricular nucleus of the rat hypothalamus: A tract-tracing study. *Journal of Neuroendocrinology, 10,* 119–131.

Charney, D. S., Deutch, A. Y., Krystal, J. H., Southwick, S. M., & Davis, M. (1993). Psychobiologic mechanisms of posttraumatic stress disorder. *Archives of General Psychiatry, 50,* 294–305.

Cloitre, M., Cancienne, J., Brodsky, B., Dulit, R., & Perry, S. W. (1996). Memory performance among women with parental abuse histories: Enhanced directed forgetting or directed remembering? *Journal of Abnormal Psychology, 105,* 204–211.

Cohen, H., Kotler, M., Matar, M., & Kaplan, Z. (2000). Normalization of heart rate variability in post traumatic stress disorder patients following fluoxetine treatment: Preliminary results. *Israel Medical Association Journal, 2,* 296–301.

Creamer, M. C., O'Donnell, M. L., & Pattison, P. (2004). The relationship between acute stress disorder and posttraumatic stress disorder in severely injured trauma survivors. *Behaviour Research and Therapy, 42,* 315–328.

Davidson, A. C., & Mellor, D. J. (2001). The adjustment of children of Australian Vietnam veterans: Is there evidence for the transgenerational transmission of war-related trauma? *Australian and New Zealand Journal of Psychiatry, 35,* 345–351.

Davidson, J. R. T., Book, S. W., Colket, J. T., Tupler, L. A., Roth, S., David, D., et al. (1997). Assessment of a new self-rating scale of post-traumatic disorder. *Psychological Medicine, 27,* 153–106.

Davidson, J. R. T., Rothbaum, B. O., van der Kolk, B. A., Sikes, C. R., & Farfel, G. M. (2001). Multicenter double-blind comparison of sertraline and placebo in the treatment of posttraumatic stress disorder. *Archives of General Psychiatry, 58,* 485–492.

Davidson, J., Swartz, M., Storck, M., Krishnan, R. R., & Hammett, E. (1985). A diagnostic and family study of posttraumatic stress disorder. *American Journal of Psychiatry, 142,* 90–93.

Davis, M. (1992). The role of the amygdala in fear and anxiety. *Annual Review of Neuroscience, 15,* 353–375.

Davis, M. (2000). The role of the amygdala in conditioned and unconditioned fear and anxiety. In J. P. Aggleton (Ed.), *The amygdala* (pp. 213–287). New York: Oxford University Press.

Davis, M., & Myers, K. M. (2002). The role of glutamate and gamma-aminobutyric acid in fear extinction: Clinical implications for exposure therapy. *Biological Psychiatry, 52,* 998–1007.

Delahanty, D. L., Herberman, H. B., Craig, K. J., Hayward, M. C., Fullerton, C. S., Ursano, R. J., et al. (1997). Acute and chronic distress and posttraumatic stress disorder as a function of responsibility for serious motor vehicle accidents. *Journal of Consulting and Clinical Psychology, 65,* 560–567.

Delahanty, D. L., Raimonde, A. J., & Spoonster, E. (2000). Initial posttraumatic urinary cortisol levels predict subsequent PTSD symptoms in motor vehicle accident victims. *Biological Psychiatry, 48,* 940–947.

Difede, J., Ptacek, J. T., Roberts, J. G., Barocas, D., Rives, W., Apfeldorf, W. J., et al. (2002). Acute stress disorder after burn injury: A predictor of posttraumatic stress disorder. *Psychosomatic Medicine, 64,* 826–834.

Dirkzwager, A. J. E., Bramsen, I., Adèr, H., & van der Ploeg, H. M. (2005). Secondary traumatization in partners and parents of Dutch peacekeeping soldiers. *Journal of Family Psychology, 19,* 217–226.

Dunmore, E., Clark, D. M., & Ehlers, A. (1999). Cognitive factors involved in the onset and maintenance of posttraumatic stress disorder (PTSD) after physical or sexual assault. *Behaviour Research and Therapy, 37,* 809–829.

Ehlers, A., & Clark, D. (2000). A cognitive model of posttraumatic stress disorder. *Behaviour Research and Therapy, 38,* 319–345.

Ehlers, A., Clark, D. M., Hackmann, A., McManus, F., Fennell, M., Herbert, C., et al. (2003). A randomized controlled trial of cognitive therapy, self-help, and repeated assessment as early interventions for PTSD. *Archives of General Psychiatry, 60,* 1024–1032.

Ehlers, A., Mayou, R. A., & Bryant, B. (1998). Psychological predictors of chronic PTSD after motor vehicle accidents. *Journal of Abnormal Psychology, 107,* 508–519.

Engel, C. C., Jr., Engel, A. L., Campbell, S. J., McFall, M. E., Russo, J., & Katon, W. (1993). Posttraumatic stress disorder symptoms and precombat sexual and physical abuse in Desert Storm veterans. *Journal of Nervous and Mental Disease, 181,* 683–688.

Engelhard, I., van den Hout, M. A., & Arntz, A. (2001). Posttraumatic stress disorder after pregnancy loss. *General Hospital Psychiatry, 23,* 62–66.

Engelhard, I. M., van den Hout, M. A., Arntz, A., & McNally, R. J. (2002). A longitudinal study of "intrusion-based reasoning" and posttraumatic stress disorder after exposure to a train disaster. *Behaviour Research and Therapy, 40,* 1415–1424.

Fecteau, G., & Nicki, R. (1999). Cognitive behavioural treatment of posttraumatic stress disorder after motor vehicle accident. *Behavioural and Cognitive Psychotherapy, 27,* 201–215.

Feinstein, A. (1989). Posttraumatic stress disorder: A descriptive study supporting *DSM III-R* criteria. *American Journal of Psychiatry, 146,* 665–666.

Foa, E. B., Cashman, L., Jaycox, L., & Perry, K. (1997). The validation of a self-report measure of posttraumatic stress disorder: The posttraumatic diagnostic scale. *Psychological Assessment, 9,* 445–451.

Foa, E. B., Dancu, C. V., Hembree, E. A., Jaycox, L. H., Meadows, E. A., & Street, G. P. (1999). A comparison of exposure therapy, stress inoculation training, and their combination for reducing posttraumatic stress disorder in female assault victims. *Journal of Consulting and Clinical Psychology, 67,* 194–200.

Foa, E. B., Feske, U., Murdock, T. B., Kozak, M. J., & McCarthy, P. R. (1991). Processing of threat-related information in rape victims. *Journal of Abnormal Psychology, 100,* 156–162.

Foa, E. B., Hearst-Ikeda, D., & Perry, K. J. (1995). Evaluation of a brief cognitive-behavioral program for the prevention of chronic PTSD in recent assault victims. *Journal of Consulting and Clinical Psychology, 63,* 948–955.

Foa, E. B., & Meadows, E. A. (1997). Psychosocial treatments for posttraumatic stress disorder: A critical review. *Annual Review of Psychology, 48,* 449–480.

Foa, E. B., Riggs, D. S., Dancu, C. V., & Rothbaum, B. O. (1993). Reliability and validity of a brief instrument for assessing posttraumatic stress disorder. *Journal of Traumatic Stress, 6,* 459–473.

Foa, E. B., Rothbaum, B. O., Riggs, D. S., & Murdock, T. B. (1991). Treatment of posttraumatic stress disorder in rape victims: A comparison between cognitive-behavioral procedures and counseling. *Journal of Consulting and Clinical Psychology, 59,* 715–723.

Foa, E. B., & Tolin, D. F. (2000). Comparison of the PTSD Symptom Scale-Interview Version and the Clinician-Administered PTSD Scale. *Journal of Traumatic Stress, 13,* 181–191.

Freinkel, A., Koopman, C., & Spiegel, D. (1994). Dissociative symptoms in media witnesses of an execution. *American Journal of Psychiatry, 151,* 1335–1339.

Friedman, M. J. (2000). A guide to the literature on pharmacotherapy for PTSD. *PTSD Research Quarterly, 11,* 1–7.

Friedman, M. J., Davidson, J. R. T., Mellman, T. A., & Southwick, S. M. (2000). Pharmacotherapy. In E. B. Foa, T. M. Keane, & M. J. Friedman (Eds.), *Effective treatments for posttraumatic stress disorder: Practice guidelines from the International Society for Traumatic Stress Studies* (pp. 84–105). New York: Guilford Press.

Galea, S., Ahern, J., Resnick, H., Kilpatrick, D., Bucuvalas, M., Gold, J., et al. (2002). Psychological sequelae of the September 11 terrorist attacks. *New England Journal of Medicine, 346,* 982–987.

Galea, S., Boscarino, J., Resnick, H., & Vlahov, D. (in press). Mental health in New York City after the September 11 terrorist attacks: Results from two population surveys. In R. W. Manderscheid & M. J. Henderson (Eds.), *Mental health, United States, 2002.* Washington, DC: U.S. Government Printing Office.

Gilbertson, M. W., Shenton, M. E., Ciszewski, A., Kasai, K., Lasko, N. B., Orr, S. P., et al. (2002). Smaller hippocampal volume predicts pathologic vulnerability to psychological trauma. *Nature Neuroscience, 5,* 1242–1247.

Gilboa, A., Shalev, A. Y., Laor, L., Lester, H., Louzoun, Y., Chisin, R., et al. (2004). Functional connectivity of the prefrontal cortex and the amygdala in posttraumatic stress disorder. *Biological Psychiatry, 55,* 263–272.

Glynn, S. M., Eth, S., Randolph, E. T., Foy, D. W., Urbaitis, M., Boxer, L., et al. (1999). A test of behavioural family therapy to augment exposure for combat-related posttraumatic stress disorder. *Journal of Consulting and Clinical Psychology, 67,* 243–251.

Gray, T., Carney, M., & Magnuson, D. (1989). Direct projections from the central amygdaloid nucleus to the hypothalamic paraventricular nucleus: Possible role in stress induced adrenocorticotropin release. *Neuroendocrinology, 50,* 433–446.

Guthrie, R., & Bryant, R. A. (2000). Attempted thought suppression over extended periods in acute stress disorder. *Behaviour Research and Therapy, 38,* 899–907.

Guthrie, R. M., & Bryant, R. A. (2005). Acoustic startle response in firefighters before and after trauma exposure. *American Journal of Psychiatry, 162,* 283–290.

Harvey, A. G., & Bryant, R. A. (1998). The relationship between acute stress disorder and posttraumatic stress disorder: A prospective evaluation of motor vehicle accident survivors. *Journal of Consulting and Clinical Psychology, 66,* 507–512.

Harvey, A. G., & Bryant, R. A. (1999). The relationship between acute stress disorder and posttraumatic stress disorder: A 2-year prospective evaluation. *Journal of Consulting and Clinical Psychology, 67,* 985–988.

Harvey, A. G., & Bryant, R. A. (2000). Two-year prospective evaluation of the relationship between acute stress disorder and posttraumatic stress disorder following mild traumatic brain injury. *American Journal of Psychiatry, 157,* 626–628.

Harvey, A. G., & Bryant, R. A. (2002). Acute stress disorder: A synthesis and critique. *Psychological Bulletin, 128,* 892–906.

Harvey, A. G., Bryant, R. A., & Dang, S. T. (1998). Autobiographical memory in acute stress disorder. *Journal of Consulting and Clinical Psychology, 66,* 500–506.

Harvey, A. G., Bryant, R. A., & Rapee, R. (1996). Supraliminal and subliminal processing of threat-related material in post-traumatic stress disorder. *Cognitive Therapy and Research, 20,* 613–623.

Harvey, A. G., Bryant, R. A., & Tarrier, N. (2003). Cognitive behaviour therapy of posttraumatic stress disorder. *Clinical Psychology Review, 23,* 501–522.

Hillman, R. G. (1981). The psychopathology of being held hostage. *American Journal of Psychiatry, 138,* 1193–1197.

Holeva, V., Tarrier, N., & Wells, A. (2001). Prevalence and predictors of acute stress disorder and PTSD following road traffic accidents: Thought control strategies and social support. *Behavior Therapy, 32,* 65–83.

Janet, P. (1907). *The major symptoms of hysteria.* New York: McMillan.

Jordan, B. K., Marmar, C. R., Fairbank, J. A., Schlenger, W. E., Kulka, R. A., Hough, R. L., et al. (1992). Problems in families of male Vietnam veterans with posttraumatic stress disorder. *Journal of Consulting and Clinical Psychology, 60,* 916–926.

Kangas, M., Henry, J. L., & Bryant, R. A. (2005). The relationship between acute stress disorder and posttraumatic stress disorder following cancer. *Journal of Consulting and Clinical Psychology, 73,* 360–364.

Kaplan, Z., Weiser, M., Reichenberg, A., Rabinowitz, J., Caspi, A., Bodner, E., et al. (2002). Motivation to serve in the military influences vulnerability to future posttraumatic stress disorder. *Psychiatry Research, 109,* 45–49.

Keane, T. M., Fairbank, J. A., Caddell, J. M., & Zimering, R. T. (1989). Implosive (flooding) therapy reduced symptoms of PTSD in Vietnam combat veterans. *Behavior Therapy, 20,* 245–260.

Keane, T. M., Scott, W. O., Chavoya, G. A., Lamparski, D. M., & Fairbank, J. (1985). Social support in Vietnam veterans with posttraumatic stress disorder: A comparative analysis. *Journal of Consulting and Clinical Psychology, 53,* 95–102.

Kessler, R. C., Sonnega, A., Bromet, E., Hughes, M., & Nelson, C. B. (1995). Posttraumatic stress disorder in the National Comorbidity Survey. *Archives of General Psychiatry, 52,* 1048–1060.

Kilpatrick, D. G., Saunders, B. E., Amick-McMullan, A., & Best, C. L. (1989). Victim and crime factors associated with the development of crime-related post-traumatic stress disorder. *Behavior Therapy, 20,* 199–214.

King, D. W., King, L. A., Foy, D. W., & Gudanowski, D. M. (1996). Prewar factors in combat-related posttraumatic stress disorder: Structural equation modeling with a national sample of female and male Vietnam veterans. *Journal of Consulting and Clinical Psychology, 64,* 520–531.

King, D. W., King, L. A., Gudanowski, D. M., & Vreven, D. L. (1995). Alternative representations of war zone stressors: Relationships to posttraumatic stress disorder in male and female Vietnam veterans. *Journal of Abnormal Psychology, 104,* 184–196.

Kolb, L. C. (1987). A neuropsychological hypothesis explaining post-traumatic stress disorder. *American Journal of Psychiatry, 144,* 989–995.

Koopman, C., Classen, C., Cardeña, E., & Spiegel, D. (1995). When disaster strikes, acute stress disorder may follow. *Journal of Traumatic Stress, 8,* 29–46.

Koopman, C., Classen, C., & Spiegel, D. (1994). Predictors of posttraumatic stress symptoms among survivors of the Oakland/Berkeley, Calif., firestorm. *American Journal of Psychiatry, 151,* 888–894.

Koren, D., Arnon, I., & Klein, E. (1999). Acute stress response and posttraumatic stress disorder in traffic accident victims: A one-year prospective, follow-up study. *American Journal of Psychiatry, 156,* 367–373.

Korfine, L., & Hooley, J. M. (2000). Directed forgetting of emotional stimuli in borderline personality disorder. *Journal of Abnormal Psychology, 109,* 214–221.

LeDoux, J. E. (1995). Setting "stress" into motion: Brain mechanisms of stimulus evaluation. In M. J. Friedman, D. S. Charney, & A. Y. Deutch (Eds.), *Neurobiological and clinical consequences of stress: From normal adaptation to post-traumatic stress disorder* (pp. 125–134). Philadelphia: Lippincott-Raven.

LeDoux, J. E. (1996). *The emotional brain: The mysterious underpinnings of emotional life.* New York: Simon & Schuster.

LeDoux, J. (1998). Fear and the brain: Where have we been, and where are we going? *Biological Psychiatry, 44,* 1229–1238.

LeDoux, J. E., Farb, C. R., & Milner, T. A. (1991). Ultrastructure and synaptic associations of auditory thalamo-amygdala projections in the rat. *Experimental Brain Research, 85,* 577–586.

LeDoux, J. E., Farb, C., & Ruggiero, D. A. (1990). Topographic organization of neurons in the acoustic thalamus that project to the amygdala. *Journal of Neuroscience, 10,* 1043–1054.

LeDoux, J. E., Iwata, J., Cicchetti, P., & Reis, D. J. (1988). Different projections of the central amygdaloid nucleus mediate autonomic and behavioral correlates of conditioned fear. *Journal of Neuroscience, 8,* 2517–2529.

Li, X. F., Stutzmann, G. E., & LeDoux, J. E. (1996). Convergent but temporally separated inputs to lateral amygdala neurons from the auditory thalamus and auditory cortex use different postsynaptic receptors: In vivo intracellular and extracellular recordings in fear conditioning pathways. *Learning & Memory, 3,* 229–242.

Liberzon, I., Taylor, S. F., Amdur, R., Jung, T. D., Chamberlain, K. R., & Minoshima, S. (1999). Brain activation in PTSD in response to trauma-related stimuli. *Biological Psychiatry, 45,* 817–826.

Lichstein, K. L., Riedel, B. W., & Grieve, R. (1994). Fair tests of clinical trials: A treatment implementation model. *Advances in Behaviour Research and Therapy, 16,* 1–29.

Macklin, M. L., Metzger, L. J., Litz, B. T., McNally, R. J., Lasko, N. B., Orr, S. P., et al. (1998). Lower pre-combat intelligence is a risk factor for posttraumatic stress disorder. *Journal of Consulting and Clinical Psychology, 66,* 323–326.

March, J. S. (1993). What constitutes a stressor? The "Criterion A" issue. In R. J. Davidson & E. B. Foa (Eds.), *Posttraumatic stress disorder: DSM-IV and beyond* (pp. 37–54). Washington, DC: American Psychiatric Press.

Marks, I., Lovell, K., Noshirvani, H., Livanou, M., & Thrasher, S. (1998). Treatment of posttraumatic stress disorder by exposure and/or cognitive restructuring: A controlled study. *Archives of General Psychiatry, 55,* 317–325.

Marshall, G. N., & Schell, T. L. (2002). Reappraising the link between peritraumatic dissociation and PTSD symptom severity: Evidence from a longitudinal study of community violence survivors. *Journal of Abnormal Psychology, 111,* 626–636.

Marshall, R. D., Beebe, K. L., Oldham, M., & Zaninelli, R. (2001). Efficacy and safety of paroxetine treatment for chronic PTSD: A fixed-dose, placebo-controlled study. *American Journal of Psychiatry, 158,* 1982–1988.

McFarlane, A. C., Atchison, M., & Yehuda, R. (1997). The acute stress response following motor vehicle accidents and its relation to PTSD. In R. Yehuda & A. C. McFarlane (Eds.), *Psychobiology of posttraumatic stress disorder* (pp. 433–436). New York: New York Academy of Sciences.

McNally, R. J. (2003). *Remembering trauma.* Cambridge, MA: Belknap Press.

McNally, R. J., Bryant, R. A., & Ehlers, A. (2003). Psychological debriefing and its alternatives: A critique of early intervention for trauma survivors. *Psychological Science in the Public Interest, 4,* 45–79.

McNally, R. J., Kaspi, S. P., Riemann, B. C., & Zeitlin, S. B. (1990). Selective processing of threat cues in posttraumatic stress disorder. *Journal of Abnormal Psychology, 99,* 396–402.

McNally, R. J., Lasko, N. B., Macklin, M. L., & Pitman, R. K. (1995). Autobiographical memory disturbance in combat-related posttraumatic stress disorder. *Behaviour Research and Therapy, 33,* 619–630.

McNally, R. J., Litz, B. T., Prassas, A., Shin, L. M., & Weathers, F. W. (1994). Emotional priming of autobiographical memory in post-traumatic stress disorder. *Cognition and Emotion, 8,* 351–367.

McNally, R. J., Metzger, L. J., Lasko, N. B., Clancy, S. A., & Pitman, R. K. (1998). Directed forgetting of trauma cues in adult survivors of childhood sexual abuse with and without posttraumatic stress disorder. *Journal of Abnormal Psychology, 107,* 596–601.

McNally, R. J., & Shin, L. M. (1995). Association of intelligence with severity of posttraumatic stress disorder symptoms in Vietnam combat veterans. *American Journal of Psychiatry, 152,* 936–938.

Meichenbaum, D. (1975). Self-instructional methods. In F. H. Kanfer & A. P. Goldstein (Eds.), *Helping people change* (pp. 357–391). New York: Pergamon Press.

Moulds, L. M., & Bryant, R. A. (2002). Directed forgetting in acute stress disorder. *Journal of Abnormal Psychology, 111,* 175–179.

Moulds, M. L., & Bryant, R. A. (in press). Retrieval inhibition of traumatic stimuli in acute stress disorder. *Journal of Traumatic Stress.*

Murray, J., Ehlers, A., & Mayou, R. A. (2002). Dissociation and post-traumatic stress disorder: Two prospective studies of road traffic accident survivors. *British Journal of Psychiatry, 180,* 363–368.

Nelson, B. S., & Wright, D. W. (1996). Understanding and treating post-traumatic stress disorder symptoms in female partners of veterans with PTSD. *Journal of Marital & Family Therapy, 22,* 455–467.

Nishith, P., Mechanic, M. B., & Resick, P. A. (2000). Prior interpersonal trauma: The contribution to current PTSD symptoms in female rape victims. *Journal of Abnormal Psychology, 109,* 20–25.

Nixon, R., & Bryant, R. A. (2003). Peritraumatic and persistent panic attacks in acute stress disorder. *Behaviour Research and Therapy, 41,* 1237–1242.

North, C. S., Smith, E. M., McCool, R. E., & Lightcap, P. E. (1989). Acute postdisaster coping and adjustment. *Journal of Traumatic Stress, 2,* 353–360.

Noyes, R., Hoenk, P. R., Kuperman, S., & Slymen, D. J. (1977). Depersonalization in accident victims and psychiatric patients. *Journal of Nervous and Mental Disease, 164,* 401–407.

Noyes, R., Jr., & Kletti, R. (1976). Depersonalization in the face of life-threatening danger: A description. *Psychiatry, 39,* 19–27.

Noyes, R., Jr., & Kletti, R. (1977). Depersonalization in response to life-threatening danger. *Comprehensive Psychiatry, 18,* 375–384.

Orr, S. P., Lasko, N. B., Metzger, L. J., Berry, N. J., Ahern, C. E., & Pitman, R. K. (1998). Psychophysiologic assessment of women with posttraumatic stress disorder resulting from childhood sexual abuse. *Journal of Consulting & Clinical Psychology, 66,* 906–913.

Orr, S. P., Metzger, L. J., Lasko, N. B., Macklin, M. L., Hu, F. B., Shalev, A. Y., et al. (2003). Physiologic responses to sudden, loud tones in monozygotic twins discordant for combat exposure: Association with posttraumatic stress disorder. *Archives of General Psychiatry, 60,* 283–288.

Orr, S. P., Pitman, R. K., Lasko, N. B., & Herz, L. R. (1993). Psychophysiological assessment of posttraumatic stress disorder imagery in World War II and Korean combat veterans. *Journal of Abnormal Psychology, 102,* 152–159.

Ozer, E. J., Best, S. R., Lipsey, T. L., & Weiss, D. S. (2003). Predictors of posttraumatic stress disorder and symptoms in adults: A meta-analysis. *Psychological Bulletin, 129,* 52–73.

Pallmeyer, T. P., Blanchard, E. B., & Kolb, L. C. (1986). The psychophysiology of combat-induced post-traumatic stress disorder in Vietnam veterans. *Behaviour Research and Therapy, 24,* 645–652.

Pearlstein, T. (2000). Antidepressant treatment of posttraumatic stress disorder. *Journal of Clinical Psychiatry, 61,* 40–43.

Perry, S., Difede, J., Musgni, G., Frances, A. J., & Jacobsberg, L. (1992). Predictors of posttraumatic stress disorder after burn injury. *American Journal of Psychiatry, 149,* 931–935.

Pitman, R. K. (1988). Post-traumatic stress disorder, conditioning, and network theory. *Psychiatric Annals, 18,* 182–189.

Pitman, R. K. (1989). Post-traumatic stress disorder, hormones, and memory. *Biological Psychiatry, 26,* 221–223.

Pitman, R. K., Lanes, D. M., Williston, S. K., Guillaume, J. L., Metzger, L. J., Gehr, G. M., et al. (2001). Psychophysiologic assessment of posttraumatic stress disorder in breast cancer patients. *Psychosomatics, 42,* 133–140.

Pitman, R. K., Orr, S. P., Forgue, D. F., Altman, B., de Jong, J. B., & Herz, L. R. (1990). Psychophysiologic responses to combat imagery of Vietnam veterans with posttraumatic stress disorder versus other anxiety disorders. *Journal of Abnormal Psychology, 99,* 49–54.

Pitman, R. K., Orr, S. P., Forgue, D. F., de Jong, J., & Claiborn, J. M. (1987). Psychophysiologic assessment of posttraumatic stress disorder imagery in Vietnam combat veterans. *Archives of General Psychiatry, 44,* 970–975.

Pitman, R. K., Orr, S. P, Lowenhagen, M. J., Macklin, M. L., & Altman, B. (1991). Pre-Vietnam contents of posttraumatic stress disorder veterans' service medical and personnel records. *Comprehensive Psychiatry, 32,* 416–422.

Pitman, R. K., Sanders, K. M., Zusman, R. M., Healy, A. R., Cheema, F., Lasko, N. B., et al. (2002). Pilot study of secondary prevention of posttraumatic stress disorder with propranolol. *Biological Psychiatry, 51,* 189–192.

Pitman, R. K., Shalev, A. Y., & Orr, S. P. (2000). Posttraumatic stress disorder: Emotion, conditioning and memory. In M. D. Corbetta & M. Gazzaniga (Eds.), *The new cognitive neurosciences* (2nd ed.). New York: Plenum Press.

Post, R. M., Weiss, S. R. B., & Smith, M. (1995). Sensitization and kindling: Implication for the evolving neural substrates of post-traumatic stress disorder. In M. J. Friedman, D. S. Charney, A. Y. Deutch (Eds.), *Neurobiological and clinical consequences of stress: From normal adaptation to posttraumatic stress disorder.* Philadelphia: Lippincott-Raven.

President's Commission on Mental Health. (1978). Report to the President. *Mental health problems of Vietnam-era veterans* (Vol. 3). Washington, DC: Government Printing Office.

Rauch, S. L., Whalen, P. J., Shin, L. M., McInerney, S. C., Macklin, M. L., Lasko, N. B. et al. (2000). Exaggerated amygdala response to masked fearful vs. happy facial stimuli in posttraumatic stress disorder: A functional MRI study. *Biological Psychiatry, 47,* 769–776.

Resick, P. A., Nishith, P., Weaver, T. L., Astin, M. C., & Feuer, C. A. (2002). A comparison of cognitive-processing therapy with prolonged exposure and a waiting condition for the treatment of posttraumatic stress disorder in female rape victims. *Journal of Consulting and Clinical Psychology, 70,* 867–879.

Resick, P. A., & Schnicke, M. K. (1992). Cognitive processing therapy for sexual assault victims. *Journal of Consulting and Clinical Psychology, 60,* 748–756.

Riggs, D. S., Rothbaum, B. O., & Foa, E. B. (1995). A prospective examination of symptoms of posttraumatic stress disorder in victims of nonsexual assault. *Journal of Interpersonal Violence, 10,* 201–213.

Roozendaal, B., Koolhaas, J. M., & Bohus, B. (1992). Central amygdaloid involvement in neuroendocrine correlates of conditioned stress responses. *Journal of Neuroendocrinology, 4,* 46–52.

Rothbaum, B., Foa, E., Riggs, D., Murdock, T., & Walsh, W. (1992). A prospective examination of post-traumatic stress disorder in rape victims. *Journal of Traumatic Stress, 5,* 455–475.

Rothbaum, B. O., Hodges, L. F., Ready, D., Graap, K., Alarcon, R. D., & Renato, D. (2001). Virtual reality exposure therapy for Vietnam veterans with posttraumatic stress disorder. *Journal of Clinical Psychiatry, 62,* 617–622.

Ruscio, A. M., Weathers, F. W., King, L. A., & King, D. W. (2002). Male war-zone veterans' perceived relationships with their children: The importance of emotional numbing. *Journal of Traumatic Stress, 15,* 351–357.

Schnurr, P. P., Friedman, M. J., & Rosenberg, S. D. (1993). Premilitary MMPI scores as predictors of combat-related PTSD symptoms. *American Journal of Psychiatry, 150,* 479–483.

Schnyder, U., Moergeli, H., Klaghofer, R., & Buddeberg, C. (2001). Incidence and prediction of posttraumatic stress disorder symptoms in severely injured accident victims. *American Journal of Psychiatry, 158,* 594–599.

Shalev, A. Y. (1992). Posttraumatic stress disorder among injured survivors of a terrorist attack: Predictive value of early intrusion and avoidance symptoms. *Journal of Nervous and Mental Disease, 180,* 505–509.

Shalev, A. Y., Freedman, S., Peri, T., Brandes, D., & Sahar, T. (1997). Predicting PTSD in trauma survivors: Prospective evaluation of self-report and clinician-administered instruments. *British Journal of Psychiatry, 170,* 558–564.

Shalev, A. Y., Freedman, S., Peri, T., Brandes, D., Sahar, T., Orr, S. P., et al. (1998). Prospective study of posttraumatic stress disorder and depression following trauma. *American Journal of Psychiatry, 155,* 630–637.

Shalev, A. Y., Orr, S. P., & Pitman, R. K. (1993). Psychophysiologic assessment of traumatic imagery in Israeli civilian patients with posttraumatic stress disorder. *American Journal of Psychiatry, 150,* 620–624.

Shalev, A. Y., Peri, T., Canetti, L., & Schreiber, S. (1996). Predictors of PTSD in injured trauma survivors: A prospective study. *American Journal of Psychiatry, 153,* 219–225.

Shalev, A. Y., Peri, T., Gelpin, E., Orr, S. P., & Pitman, R. K. (1997). Psychophysiologic assessment of mental imagery of stressful events in Israeli civilian posttraumatic stress disorder patients. *Comprehensive Psychiatry, 38,* 269–273.

Shalev, A. Y., Sahar, T., Freedman, S., Peri, T., Glick, N., Brandes, D., et al. (1998). A prospective study of heart rate response following trauma and the subsequent development of posttraumatic stress disorder. *Archives of General Psychiatry, 55,* 553–559.

Shapiro, F. (1995). *Eye movement desensitization and reprocessing: Basic principles, protocols, and procedures.* New York: Guilford Press.

Shin, L. M., Orr, S. P., Carson, M. A., Rauch, S. L., Macklin, M. L., Lasko, N. B., et al. (2004). Regional cerebral blood flow in the amygdala and medial prefrontal cortex during traumatic imagery in male and female Vietnam veterans with PTSD. *Archives of General Psychiatry, 61,* 168–176.

Silva, R. R., Alpert, M., Munoz, D. M., Singh, S., Matzner, F., & Dummitt, S. (2000). Stress and vulnerability to posttraumatic stress disorder in children and adolescents. *American Journal of Psychiatry, 157,* 1229–1235.

Sloan, P. (1988). Post-traumatic stress in survivors of an airplane crash-landing: A clinical and exploratory research intervention. *Journal of Traumatic Stress, 1,* 211–229.

Smith, E. M., North, C. S., McCool, R. E., & Shea, J. M. (1990). Acute postdisaster psychiatric disorders: Identification of persons at risk. *American Journal of Psychiatry, 147,* 202–206.

Smith, K., & Bryant, R. A. (2000). The generality of cognitive bias in acute stress disorder. *Behaviour Research and Therapy, 38,* 709–715.

Solomon, Z., Kotler, M., & Mikulincer, M. (1988). Combat-related posttraumatic stress disorder among second-generation Holocaust survivors: Preliminary findings. *American Journal of Psychiatry, 145,* 865–868.

Solomon, Z., Laor, N., & McFarlane, A. C. (1996). Acute posttraumatic reactions in soldiers and civilians. In B. A. van der Kolk, A. C. McFarlane, & L. Weisaeth (Eds.), *Traumatic stress: The effects of overwhelming experience on mind, body, and society* (pp. 102–114). New York: Guilford Press.

Solomon, Z., Waysman, M., Levy, G., Fried, B., Mikulincer, M., Benbenishty, R., et al. (1992). From front line to home front: A study of secondary traumatization. *Family Process, 31,* 289–302.

Spiegel, D. (1996). Dissociative disorders. In R. E. Hales & S. C. Yudofsky (Eds.), *Synopsis of psychiatry* (pp. 583–604). Washington, DC: American Psychiatric Press.

Staab, J. P., Grieger, T. A., Fullerton, C. S., & Ursano, R. J. (1996). Acute stress disorder, subsequent posttraumatic stress disorder and depression after a series of typhoons. *Anxiety, 2,* 219–225.

Tarrier, N., Pilgrim, H., Sommerfield, C., Faragher, B., Reynolds, M., Graham, E., et al. (1999). A randomised trial of cognitive therapy and imaginal exposure in the treatment of chronic posttraumatic stress disorder. *Journal of Consulting and Clinical Psychology, 67,* 13–18.

True, W. R., Rice, J., Eisen, S. A., Heath, A. C., Goldberg, J., Lyons, M. J., et al. (1993). A twin study of genetic and environmental contributions to liability for posttraumatic stress disorder. *Archives of General Psychiatry, 50,* 257–264.

Tucker, P., Smith, K. L., Marx, B., Jones, D., Miranda, R., & Lesngraf, J. (2000). Fluvoxamine reduces physiologic reactivity to trauma scripts in posttraumatic stress. *Journal of Clinical Psychopharmacology, 20,* 367–372.

Tucker, P., Zaninelli, R., Yehuda, R., Ruggiero, L., Dillingham, K., & Pitts, C. D. (2001). Paroxetine in the treatment of chronic posttraumatic stress disorder: Results of a placebo-controlled, flexible-dosage trial. *Journal of Clinical Psychiatry, 62,* 860–868.

Vaiva, G., Ducrocq, F., Jezequel, K., Averland, B., Lestavel, P., Brunet, A., et al. (2003). Immediate treatment with propranolol decreases posttraumatic stress disorder two months after trauma. *Biological Psychiatry, 54,* 947–949.

van der Kolk, B. A., Dreyfuss, D., Michaels, M., Shera, D., Berkowitz, R., Fisler, R. E., et al. (1994). Fluoxetine in posttraumatic stress disorder. *Journal of Clinical Psychiatry, 55,* 517–522.

van der Kolk, B. A., & van der Hart, O. (1989). Pierre Janet and the breakdown of adaptation in psychological trauma. *American Journal of Psychiatry, 146,* 1530–1540.

Vasterling, J. J., Brailey, K., Constans, J. I., Borges, A., & Sutker, P. B. (1997). Assessment of intellectual resources in Gulf War veterans: Relationship to PTSD. *Assessment, 1,* 51–59.

Vasterling, J. J., Duke, L. M., Brailey, K., Constans, J. I., Allain, A. N., Jr., & Sutker, P. B. (2002). Attention, learning, and memory performances and intellectual resources in Vietnam veterans: PTSD and no disorder comparisons. *Neuropsychology, 16,* 5–14.

Warda, G., & Bryant, R. A. (1998a). Cognitive bias in acute stress disorder. *Behaviour Research and Therapy, 36,* 1177–1183.

Warda, G., & Bryant, R. A. (1998b). Thought control strategies in acute stress disorder. *Behaviour Research and Therapy, 36,* 1171–1175.

Weathers, F. W., & Ford, J. (1996). Psychometric properties of the PTSD Checklist (PCL-C, PCL-S, PCL-M, PCL-PR). In B. H. Stamm (Ed.), *Measurement of stress, trauma, and adaptation* (pp. 250–252). Lutherville, MD: Sidran Press.

Weathers, F. W., Keane, T. M., & Davidson, J. R. (2001). Clinician-Administered PTSD Scale: A review of the first ten years of research. *Depression and Anxiety, 13,* 132–156.

Weathers, F. W., Ruscio, A. M., & Keane, T. M. (1999). Psychometric properties of nine scoring rules for the Clinician-Administered Posttraumatic Stress Disorder Scale. *Psychological Assessment, 11,* 124–133.

Wilson, J. P., & Keane, T. M. (Eds.). (2004). *Assessing psychological trauma and PTSD.* New York: Guilford Press.

Wolpe, J. (1958). *Psychotherapy by reciprocal inhibition.* Stanford, CA: Stanford University Press.

Yehuda, R. (1997). Sensitization of the hypothalamic-pituitary-adrenal axis in posttraumatic stress disorder. *Annals of the New York Academy Science, 821,* 57–75.

Yehuda, R. (Ed.). (1999). *Risk factors for posttraumatic stress disorder.* Washington, DC: American Psychiatric Press.

Yehuda, R. (2002). Post-traumatic stress disorder. *New England Journal of Medicine, 346,* 108–114.

Yehuda, R. (2002, March). The lessons of 9-11. Address delivered at the meeting of the Anxiety Disorders Association of America, Austin, TX.

Yehuda, R., Halligan, S. L., & Bierer, L. M. (2001). Relationship of parental trauma exposure and PTSD to PTSD, depressive and anxiety disorders in offspring. *Journal of Psychiatric Research, 35,* 261–270.

Yehuda, R., & McFarlane, A. C. (1995). Conflict between current knowledge about posttraumatic stress disorder and its original conceptual basis. *American Journal of Psychiatry, 152,* 1705–1713.

Yehuda, R., McFarlane, A. C., & Shalev, A. Y. (1998). Predicting the development of posttraumatic stress disorder from the acute response to a traumatic event. *Biological Psychiatry, 44,* 1305–1313.

Yehuda, R., Schmeidler, J., Wainberg, M., Binder-Brynes, K., Duvdevani, T. (1988). Vulnerability to posttraumatic stress disorder in adult offspring of Holocaust survivors. *American Journal of Psychiatry, 155,* 1163–1171.

CHAPTER 13

Major Depressive Disorder

MICHAEL E. THASE

Depressive disorders have plagued humanity for at least as long as people have been able to record their experiences in writing. This should not be surprising because one's mood is the expression of subjective well-being, a state that is continually challenged by threats, losses, frustrations, setbacks, and disappointments that, in aggregate, make periods of suffering an almost inevitable consequence of human existence. Across history, depressive disorders have been attributed to be the result of forces as varied as excessive black bile (the origin of the term *melancholia*), demonic possession, and introjected unconscious drives (see Jackson, 1986). Despite such diverse models of presumed causation, however, the depressive syndromes described in the Bible and in Burns's seventeenth-century classic *The Anatomy of Melancholia* are very much like those that afflict people at the start of the twenty-first century. Although the core syndrome of depression has not changed much across centuries, knowledge about the depressive disorders has grown dramatically, and in the past several decades there has been considerable progress with respect to more accurate methods of assessment and classification, development of more reliably effective and better tolerated treatments, and more sophisticated methods of studying the biological, psychological, and social underpinnings of the depressive disorders. This chapter will review the status of this area circa March 2005.

DESCRIPTION OF THE DISORDER AND CLINICAL PICTURE

Also sometimes referred to in the popular press as "clinical depression," the condition known as major depressive disorder (MDD) is the most common of the mood disorder diagnoses codified in the fourth edition of the American Psychiatric Association's *Diagnostic and Statistical Manual* (*DSM-IV*; American Psychiatric Association, 1994). The MDD diagnosis describes a syndrome of persistently depressed mood (variably described as sad, dejected, low, down, or "blue") or a loss of interest or pleasure in most activities, and at least four common symptoms that have been manifest for at least two weeks. In addition to mood and hedonic capacity, the common symptoms of depression span domains of cognitive (i.e., pessimism, suicidal ideation, and difficulty concentrating), neurovegetative (i.e., disturbances of sleep, appetite, and libido), and behavioral (i.e., psychomotor retardation or agitation) functioning. The symptoms must be present most of the time over the two-week period. The thresholds that define the lower boundary of the syndrome are clearly arbitrary and, in practice, most people have been symptomatic for a number of months or even years before presenting for treatment and are suffering from a number of symptoms well above the minimum number.

The most common parallel to MDD in everyday life is bereavement. During the weeks or even months following the death of a loved one, many of the symptoms of depression are commonly experienced; even suicidal thoughts ("I don't want to go on living without her") are not out of the ordinary. Because of the universality of this reaction, however, the diagnosis of MDD is not made unless there is gross functional impairment or markedly disturbed behavior (i.e., psychosis or intense suicidality) or the length of the bereavement is unusually prolonged.

A major depressive disorder is distinguished from other more transient states of sadness by the duration, intensity and pervasiveness of the symptoms. The *DSM-IV* criteria also include the following caveats: (1) the syndrome causes clinically significant distress or impairment in social, vocational, or other important areas of functioning; (2) the syndrome is not the direct physiological consequence of a drug or general medical condition; and (3) there is no history of manic or hypomanic episodes. In the first case, if there is no significant impairment, the diagnosis of *adjustment disorder with depressed mood* may be more appropriate. When the depressive syndrome is clearly associated with an illness (such as hypothyroidism or lupus) or a consequence of a medication (such as an antihypertensive or an oral contraceptive), diagnoses such as *mood disorder* due to a *general medical condition* and *substance-induced mood disorder* should be used. In the third case, the diagnosis of *bipolar affective disorder* should be used when the person experiencing the major depressive episode has a history of euphoric mood swings (see Chapter 15).

DEPRESSIVE SUBTYPES

Major depressive disorder is a very heterogeneous condition. Although it should not be thought of as a specific disease, physicians and other health care professionals sometimes use terms such as depressive illness metaphorically, because of the potentially serious nature of the condition. The current state of classification can be contrasted to general internal medicine, where more general syndromal terms, such as pneumonia or renal failure, are still used, but as a way station toward identification of more specific disease states (i.e., pneumococcal pneumonia or acute glomerulonephritis resulting from an autoimmune reaction to a bacterial antibody). More precise pathophysiological specification of depressive states continues to be a topic for research, but it is unlikely that specific, etiologically based classifications will be identified in the foreseeable future.

MDD thus is best conceptualized as a biopsychosocial disorder. As such, the MDD classification is the "home" of an incredibly diverse group of syndromal presentations. For example, the same diagnosis may apply to both a sluggish, irritable adolescent who reports overeating and sleeping 14 hours a day and an emaciated, agitated elder with marked insomnia and the delusional belief that God is punishing him/her for past sins.

The heterogeneity of MDD is partly accounted for in *DSM-IV* by use of multiaxial case formulation (see the section "Assessment and Diagnosis") and descriptive subtypes (known in current jargon as *course or episode specifiers*). There are eight specifiers currently in use (see Table 13.1). One describes the longitudinal course of the disorder, specifically, whether there have been past episodes of MDD. At least 70 percent of people who experience a first episode of MDD will experience subsequent or recurrent episodes (Keller & Boland, 1998). The *single episode versus recurrent* distinction has important prognostic implications because, once a pattern of recurrent MDD has been established, the "well interval" between episodes typically diminishes. In fact, after only the third lifetime episode of MDD, the probability that a fourth episode will occur within, say three to five years, may exceed 80 percent without preventive therapy (Frank & Thase, 1999). Although not formally used in *DSM-*

TABLE 13.1 Specifiers of MDD According to *DSM-IV-TR*

Specifer	Key features
Single/recurrent	Approximately 80% of depressions run a recurrent course
With melancholic features	Nonreactive mood, anhedonia, weight loss, guilt, psychomotor retardation or agitation, morning worsening of mood, early-morning awakening
With atypical features	Reactive mood, oversleeping, overeating, leaden paralysis, interpersonal rejection sensitivity
With psychotic features	Hallucinations or delusions
With catatonic features	Catalepsy (waxy flexibility), catatonic excitement, negativism or mutism, mannerisms or stereotypes, echolalia or echopraxia. This subtype is not commonly seen in clinical practice.
With chronic pattern	Two years or more with full criteria for MDE
With seasonal pattern	Regular onset and remission of depressive episodes during a particular season (usually fall/winter onset)
With postpartum onset	Onset of depressive episode within four weeks postpartum

Source: American Psychiatric Association. (2000). *Diagnostic and statistical manual of mental disorders* (4th ed., text rev.). Washington, DC: Author.

IV, the term *unipolar depression* is essentially a synonym for MDD recurrent subtype.

The remaining specifiers are used to describe the depressive *episode.* This first of these pertains to syndromal severity, which also has important prognostic and treatment implications (Thase, 2000). The *DSM-IV* diagnosis of MDD includes a semiquantitative coding of severity, ranging from full and partial remission through mild, moderate, severe (nonpsychotic), and severe (psychotic) presentations. At least 10 percent of MDD episodes are psychotic, meaning that the depressed person is experiencing hallucinations or expressing delusions (Schatzberg & Rothschild, 1992). The psychotic features of MDD, which often go unrecognized (Mulsant et al., 1997), have ominous prognostic implications: psychotic depressive episodes do not respond as well to standard antidepressant therapies and convey increased risks of suicide and disability (Schatzberg & Rothschild, 1992).

The second episode specifier categorically describes the duration of the current depressive episode. The term *chronic* is used when the episode has persisted in full syndromal intensity for at least two years. This is in contrast to dysthymic disorder, which is defined by a similar duration of symptoms at subsyndromal intensity. Once a pattern of chronicity develops, the chances of spontaneous remission diminish to an almost negligible level (i.e., on the order of 5 percent per six-month interval; Keller & Boland, 1998) and the various social and vocational complications of depression mount (see the section "Impact on Environment"). In practice, it is often difficult to distinguish a chronic episode of MDD from recurrent episodes of MDD superimposed on antecedent dysthymic disorder (so-called "double depression") or a pattern of recurrent MDD with incomplete remission between discrete depressive episodes. In fact, there is a strong empirical rationale to group these three forms of chronic depression together (McCullough et al., 2000).

Two episode specifiers, *with melancholic features* and *with atypical features*, are arguably more important from a historical perspective than they are to current practice. In current usage, *melancholia* refers to the classical presentation of more severe depressive episodes, particularly as manifest in mid- and later life. Melancholic features include pervasive anhedonia, lack of mood reactivity, a "distinct quality" of mood disturbance (i.e., unlike sadness or grief), diurnal mood variation (i.e., regularly worse in the morning), early morning awakening, psychomotor disturbance, significant weight loss, and excessive or inappropriate guilt.

Although melancholia was first included in the third edition of the *DSM* (*DSM-III;* American Psychiatric Association, 1980), it is the direct descendant of one of the older models of dichotomous classification, commonly known as *endogenous depression*. As suggested by the name, endogenous depressive episodes have long been presumed to have a more clear-cut biomedical causality than other forms of depression (Rush & Weissenburger, 1994). The choice of a historically referent name, *melancholia,* to describe this classical subform in the current nomenclature reflects, in part, recognition that a dichotomous, etiologically based model of depression is overly simplistic.

Atypical depression is the best-recognized form of nonendogenous depression. First described in the 1950s, atypical depression is defined by preserved mood reactivity, interpersonal sensitivity, and the predominance of so-called reverse neurovegetative features (i.e., "leaden" anergia, oversleeping, and overeating; Stewart, McGrath, Rabkin, & Quitkin, 1993). When compared to melancholia, atypical depressive episodes have an earlier age of onset and tend to have a more chronic and less episodic course (Parker et al., 2002). This subtype of depression was initially validated by patients' relatively favorable response to the monoamine oxidase inhibitors (MAOIs) in comparison to therapies of first choice at the time, the tricyclic antidepressants (TCAs) and electroconvulsive therapy (ECT; Stewart et al., 1993). Although this presentation may well have seemed atypical to hospital-based psychiatrists in the 1950s, it is now clear that reverse neurovegetative features are quite common in more representative groups of depressed people, particularly among younger women (Levitan et al., 1997; Sullivan, Neale, & Kendler, 2002). The availability of a newer generation of therapeutics has lessened the importance of this classification (see, for example, Thase & Kupfer, 1996).

One specifier, *with postpartum onset,* is applicable only to depressed women. This subtype is used when the depressive episode begins within four weeks of childbirth. Not to be confused with the more ubiquitous "baby blues," this is a potentially severe (and sometimes psychotic) form of depression that can threaten the life of the infant as well as the mother (Spinelli, 2004). Careful monitoring and vigorous treatment thus are indicated.

The sixth episode specifier, *with seasonal pattern,* refers to the tendency for some patients to regularly suffer depressive episodes in the fall and winter or, less commonly, the spring and summer. Both seasonal patterns appear to be more common in patients with bipolar disorder than patients with recurrent MDD. The fall-winter pattern is of particular interest because reverse neurovegetative features predominate and phototherapy (i.e., exposure to 30 to 60 minutes of bright, full spectrum light each morning) can have significant antidepressant effects (see Kennedy, Lam, Nutt, & Thase, 2004).

The final specifier, *with catatonic features,* is used to describe the rarest form of depression. *Catatonia* refers to a markedly disturbed psychomotor state characterized by catalepsy ("waxy" flexibility) or stupor and extreme negativity (e.g., a catatonic individual may stand in one position for hours). More common in schizophrenia than depression, other catatonic features include periods of excessive and apparently purposeless motor activity, echolalia, and echopraxia. MDD with Catatonic Features is a very severe condition and hospitalization and involuntary treatment are usually necessary.

CHANGES IN REGIONAL CEREBRAL METABOLISM

Advances in radiographic methods used to visualize the living brain, principally by positron emission tomography (PET) and functional magnetic resonance imaging (fMRI), have permitted another way of describing MDD. The most widely replicated changes in functional cerebral activity include: (1) increased blood flow and neuronal activity in limbic structures, including the amygdala; (2) decreased blood flow and neuronal activity in the dorsolateral prefrontal cortex; and (3) reduced volume of the anterior cingulated and hippocampus (Drevets, 2000; Liotti & Mayberg, 2001). Figure 13.1 presents a composite image derived from the PET scans of depressed people and matched controls that illustrates several of these changes in regional cerebral metabolic activity. In simple terms, these changes reflect that more severely depressed people are neurobiologically primed to affectively

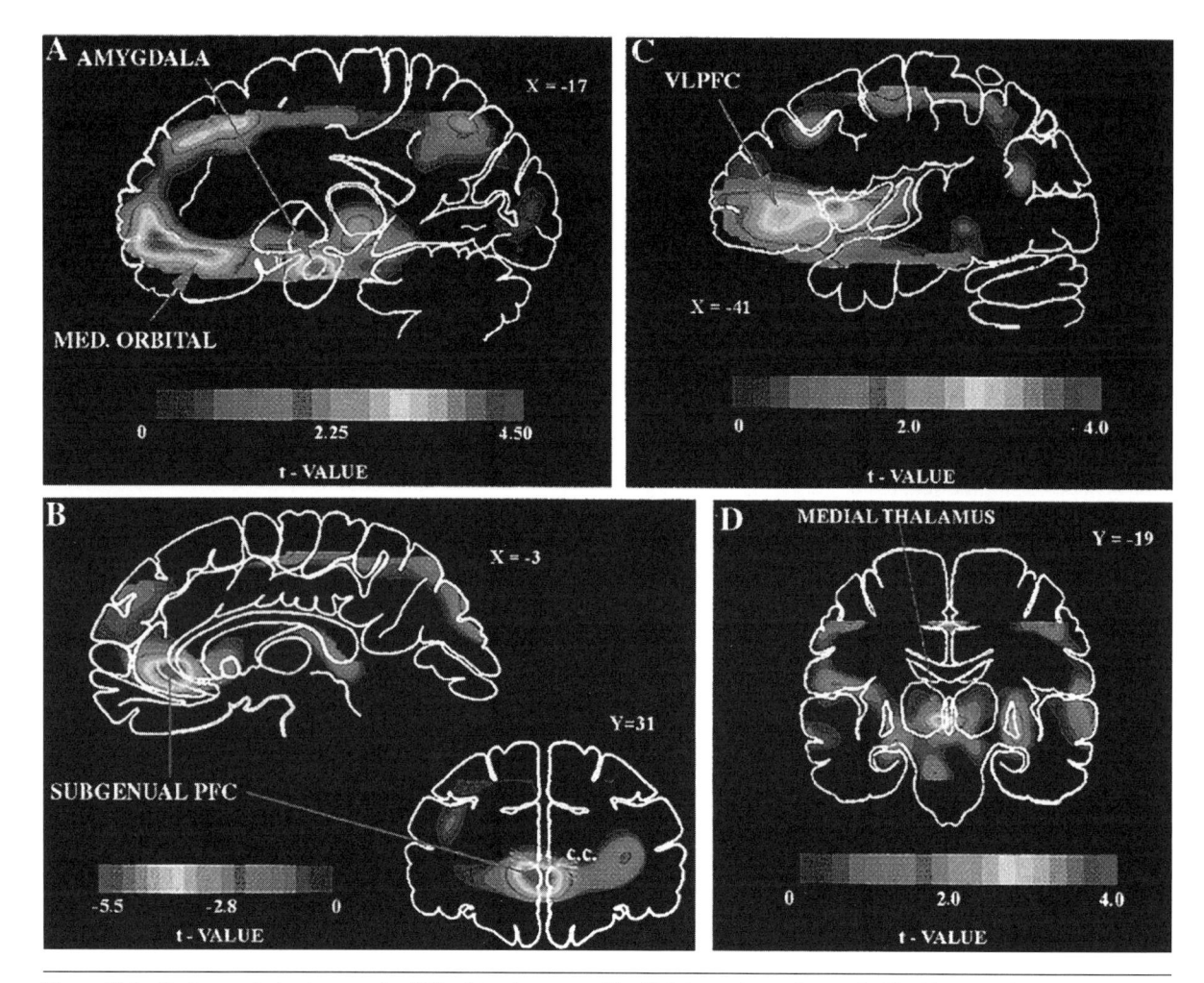

Figure 13.1 Positron emission tomography (ET) subtraction scans of familial depression and a matched healthy control group. *Source:* Drevets, 1998.

charged cognition and have relatively diminished capacity to inhibit these experiences with executive methods of cognitive control. This type of abnormal distribution in cerebral resources appears to be more common among individuals with a family history of depression and elevated levels of the stress-related hormone cortisol (Drevets et al., 2002).

With respect to structural changes, in one study, the reduction hippocampal volume was correlated with lifetime duration of untreated depression (Sheline, Gado, & Kraemer, 2003). However, in another study of people experiencing their first lifetime episode, hippocampal volume changes already were apparent and were not correlated with the length or severity of the depressive episode (Frodl et al., 2002). As hippocampal volume is both partially under genetic control (Lyons, Yang, Sawyer-Glover, Moseley, & Schatzberg, 2001; Sullivan, Pfefferbaum, Swan, & Carmelli, 2001) and is reduced by prolonged exposure to high levels of the stress hormone cortisol (Sapolsky, 2000), the contribution of both nature and nurture in the pathophysiology of depression is underscored.

COMORBIDITY

Another aspect of the heterogeneity of MDD is comorbidity. The imperfect nature of the current nomenclature is reflected by the fact that a large majority of people with MDD also meet criteria for other mental disorder diagnoses. In *DSM-IV,* comorbidities are classified on Axis I (principal psychiatric syndromes), Axis II (personality and developmental disorders), and Axis III (general medical illnesses). MDD is particularly common among those with antecedent anxiety disorders, substance abuse disorders, eating disorders, and personality disorders, as well as general medical disorders (Grant et al., 2005; Hettema, Prescott, & Kendler, 2003; Regier et al., 1990; Roose, Glassman, & Seidman, 2001;

Shea, Widiger, & Klein, 1992). Among the anxiety disorders, agoraphobia, generalized anxiety disorders, and post-traumatic stress disorder have the highest comorbidity with MDD and there is evidence of shared genetic vulnerability (Kendler, 2001; Roy, Neale, Pedersen, Mathe, & Kendler, 1995). Approximately 40 percent to 50 percent of depressed people meet criteria for one or more personality disorder (Shea, Widiger, et al., 1992). Lifetime rates of depression among alcoholics and substance abusers are similarly high (Grant et al., 2005; Regier et al., 1990). One often overlooked comorbidity is with nicotine dependence. People with MDD are about twice as likely as the general U.S. population to smoke cigarettes (Grant, Hasin, Chou, Stinson, & Cawson, 2004) and have a significantly harder time quitting than other smokers (Laje, Berman, & Glassman, 2003). Patients with general medical disorders such as hypertension, diabetes, arthritis, chronic pain syndromes, and heart disease also have at least twice the lifetime risk of developing depression; risks are even higher with some malignancies and endocrine disorders (Bair, Robinson, Katon, & Kroenke, 2003; Kennedy et al., 2004; Roose et al., 2001). Comorbid depressive disorders tend to be more severe, chronic, and less responsive to standard forms of therapy (Reich & Green, 1991; Roose et al., 2001; Shea, Wideger, et al., 1992).

Several common correlates of MDD are not included in the nomenclature, but are nevertheless important. Most depressed patients have significant anxiety, even if they do not meet criteria for a comorbid anxiety disorder (Fava et al., 2004). Typically, the anxiety associated with depression is best described as generalized, although panic attacks, obsessions, and phobic features also can occur solely within a depressive episode. A second common feature is somatization, including (but not limited to) increased pain perception (Bair et al., 2003; Kroenke, 2003). This helps to explain why depressed people are such high utilizers of medical resources.

PERSONALITY DEVELOPMENT AND PSYCHOPATHOLOGY

There has been interest in the relationship between personality traits and depression proneness dating to antiquity (Jackson, 1986). Contemporary models of psychopathology focus on stress-diathesis relationships, with personality being one prominent aspect of diathesis (i.e., vulnerability). From this standpoint, individuals with particular personality traits may be more sensitive to particular kinds of stress or may become depressed following exposure to less severe stressors than individuals with lower diathesis levels. It must be kept in mind, however, that the cognitive/affective components of a depressive state inflate ratings of negative personality dimensions and that the experience of an early onset, chronic depression might scar or alter personality (see, e.g., the discussion by Klein et al., 2002).

Contemporary approaches to personality focus on two broad components, temperament, which is considered to be heritable, and character, which is considered to be the product of social learning. In Eysenck's (1970) model of personality, a depressive temperament resulted from a high level of neuroticism in combination with a low level of extraversion. More recently, Clark and Watson (1999) posited that it is a low level of positive affectivity in the combination with a high level of neuroticism that defines depressive temperament.

Among these dimensions, neuroticism (defined by a high level of emotionality and increased physiological reactivity) has received the most extensive study. Consistent with a temperament (as opposed to a characterological vulnerability), neuroticism is highly heritable (Kendler, Aggen, Jacobson, & Neale, 2003). Although neuroticism conveys broad vulnerability and is hardly specific to depression (see, e.g., Kendler, Neale, Kessler, Heath, & Eaves, 1993), several longitudinal studies have documented that elevated neuroticism levels are predictive of the onset of a first lifetime episode of major depressive disorder (Hirschfeld et al., 1989; Kendler et al., 1993; Kendler, Kuhn, & Prescott, 2004; Kreuger, 1999). This increased vulnerability appears to be mediated by three complications of neuroticism: (1) provocation of greater levels of life stress (Kendler, Gardner, & Prescott, 2003); (2) amplification of the effects of stress (Kendler, Kuhn, & Prescott, 2004); and (3) poorer interpersonal relationships (Kendler, Gardner, & Prescott, 2002). The latter complication reflects that observation that individuals with high levels of neuroticism elicit and maintain lower levels of social support and, hence, miss out on the "antidepressant" effects of close, confiding relationships.

The approach of Cloninger (1987; Cloninger, Bayon, & Svrakic, 1998) evaluates four traits (novelty seeking, harm avoidance, reward dependence, and persistence) and three character dimensions (self-directedness, cooperativeness, and self-transcendence). Harm avoidance, which overlaps substantially with neuroticism, has been repeatedly associated with depressive symptoms, as has low levels of low levels of self-directedness and cooperativeness (reviewed by Klein et al., 2002). Prospective studies have not yet linked these personality dimensions with increased risk of first lifetime episodes of depression.

The personality dimension of interpersonal dependency has figured prominently in psychodynamic models of depression (Chodoff, 1972). Although some ratings of interpersonal dependency are somewhat state-dependent and typically higher in women than men, high levels of interpersonal dependence are predictive of the onset of a first lifetime episode of depression (Sanathara, Gardner, Prescott, & Kendler, 2003). A related construct, sociotrophy, is employed by researchers following Beck's (1987) cognitive model of psychopathology. There is some evidence that individuals with high levels of sociotrophy may be more likely to relapse if stressed by an interpersonal loss, whereas individuals with higher levels of autonomy may be more vulnerable to setbacks in achievement domains (Hammen, Ellicott, Gitlin, & Jamison, 1989; Segal, Vella, Shaw, & Katz, 1992). Given the impact of depression on self-confidence and assertiveness, it is not surprising that ratings of sociotrophy are elevated during depressive episodes and tend to decline with successful treatment (see Klein et al., 2002). The role of sociotrophy in vulnerability to the first onset of depression has not yet been established (Coyne & Whiffen, 1999).

Ratings of another personality trait, obsessionality, are elevated in some studies of depressed patients (see Klein et al., 2002). In contrast to neuroticism and sociotrophy/interpersonal dependency, obsessionality does not appear to be state dependent. Obsessionality is, however, correlated with other traits, including autonomy and perfectionism (Coyne & Whiffen, 1999). High levels of obsessionality do not appear to have ominous prognostic implications, but may be weakly predictive of favorable response to antidepressant medications that enhance serotoninergic neurotransmission (Anseau, Troisfontaines, Papart, & von Frenckell, 1991) and poorer response to cognitive therapy (Barber & Muenz, 1996).

Two temperamental traits, positive affectivity and behavioral inhibition, have been studied in children as risk factors for subsequent risk of depression. *Behavioral inhibition,* which may be thought of as a developmental precursor of neuroticism and harm avoidance, refers to higher levels of fearfulness and apprehension and lower levels of approach in novel situations (Kagan, Resnick, & Snidman, 1988). Low levels of *positive affectivity* and higher levels of behavioral inhibition have been observed in the young children of parents with a history of depression (Rosenbaum, Biederman, & Hirshfeld-Becker, 2000; Schwartz, Wright, Shin, Kagan, & Rauch, 2003). High levels of behavioral inhibition in infants and toddlers appear to predict increased risk to both depression and anxiety disorders in adolescence and adulthood, a vulnerability possibly mediated by increased central nervous system responses to threat and novelty (Schwartz et al., 2003).

Another pathway by which traits such as dependency and neuroticism may predispose to depression is by priming cognitive and affective neural circuits, particularly in response to adversity (Segal, Williams, Teasdale, & Gemar, 1996).

This may explain why patterns of negative thinking, including dysfunctional attitudes and a depressogenic attributional style, begin to emerge as risk factors for depression during adolescence (Abramson et al., 2002; Garber & Horowitz, 2002).

EPIDEMIOLOGY

The point prevalence and lifetime incidence of MDD in the United States has been the focus of study of three large epidemiologic studies (Kessler, Chiu, Demler, Merikangas, & Walters, 2005; Kessler, McGonagle, Swartz, Blazer, & Nelson, 1993; Weissman et al., 1988). At any given time, approximately 3 percent to 5 percent of adults meet criteria for a current episode of MDD, with a lifetime incidence of as high as 16 percent. The one-year prevalence rates for children and adolescents are 1 percent and 8 percent, respectively (Lewinsohn & Essau, 2002). In the United States, depression rates are somewhat higher among African Americans and lower among Asians (Kessler, 2002). Rates of MDD are roughly comparable in industrialized European countries, Canada, and Australia, although lower rates of depression are typically observed in Asian and African countries (see Table 13.2; Demyttenaere et al., 2004; Weissman et al., 1996). Female sex, living in an urban setting, and poverty appear to be universal sociodemographic risk factors for depression (Kessler, 2002).

Depression is approximately twice as common in women as in men, a finding that is evident in virtually all countries and regions of the world (Weissman et al., 1996). Similar gender differences are seen in rates of two related conditions, dysthymic disorder and generalized anxiety disorder, which reflect a broader relationship between gender and psychopathology. However, men and women have relatively similar rates of bipolar affective disorder, which indicates that females do not have a uniformly increased vulnerability to all mood disorders. Further, the gender difference in rates of MDD may be partly estrogen dependent: rates of depression are comparable among elementary schoolgirls as boys, with rates increasing in young women coincident with the onset of menarche (Nolen-Hoeksema & Girgus, 1994). A careful review of the various risk factors suggest that the higher rate of depression in women is attributable to a combination of biological (i.e., depressions related to reproductively related events such as childbirth, oral contraceptive use, and menopause), psychological (i.e., women's greater tendency to use emotion-focused ways of coping, such as rumination), and social-cultural (differences in economic power and victimization; Nolen-Hoeksema, 2002).

TABLE 13.2 Lifetime and Annual Rates and Onset Age for Major Depression, Ages 18 to 64 Years

	Annual rate/ 100 (SE)†	Lifetime rate/100 (SE)				Mean age at onset, y (SE)
		Overall	Females	Males	F/M ratio	
United States	3.0 (0.18)	5.2 (0.24)	7.4 (0.39)	2.8 (0.26)	2.6 (0.11)	25.6 (0.30)
Edmonton, Alberta	5.2 (0.45)	9.6 (0.60)	12.3 (0.93)	6.6 (0.73)	1.9 (0.13)	24.8 (0.52)
Puerto Rico	3.0 (0.49)	4.3 (0.59)	5.5 (0.91)	3.1 (0.72)	1.8 (0.29)	29.5 (1.19)
Paris, France	4.5 (0.65)	16.4 (1.16)	21.9 (1.80)	10.5 (1.39)	2.1 (0.16)	29.2 (0.52)
West Germany‡	5.0 (1.13)	9.2 (1.50)	13.5 (2.46)	4.4 (1.56)	3.1 (0.39)	29.7 (1.18)
Florence, Italy	. . .	12.4 (1.33)	18.1 (2.16)	6.1 (1.40)	3.0 (0.26)	34.8 (1.12)
Beirut, Lebanon	. . .	19.0 (1.76)	23.1 (2.63)	14.7 (2.25)	1.6 (0.19)	25.2 (1.00)
Taiwan	0.8 (0.09)	1.5 (0.12)	1.8 (0.19)	1.1 (0.16)	1.6 (0.17)	29.3 (1.04)
Korea	2.3 (0.22)	2.9 (0.24)	3.8 (0.38)	1.9 (0.29)	2.0 (0.18)	29.3 (0.88)
Christchurch, New Zealand	5.8 (0.70)	11.6 (0.96)	15.5 (1.51)	7.5 (1.14)	2.1 (0.18)	27.3 (0.53)

Note. Figures standardized to U.S. age and sex distribution.
† Ellipses indicate data not available.
‡ Data from former Federal Republic of Germany (West Germany) based on ages 26 to 64 years.
Source: American Psychiatric Association. (2000). *Diagnostic and statistical manual of mental disorders* (4th ed., text rev.). Washington, DC: Author.

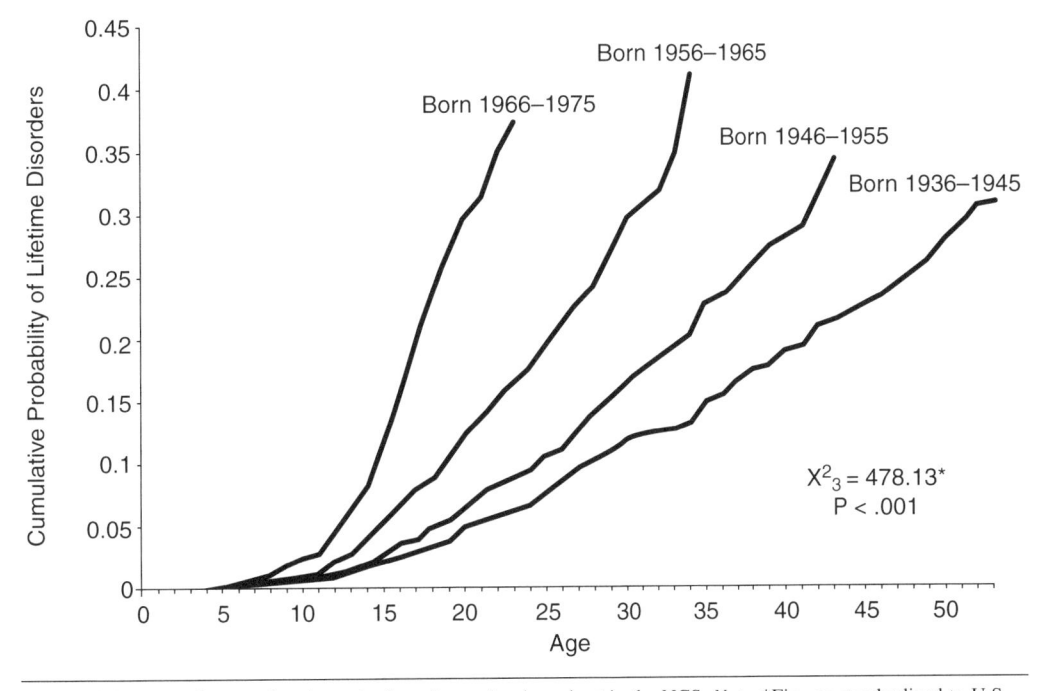

Figure 13.2 Age of onset of major and minor depression by cohort in the NCS. *Note.* *Figures standardized to U.S. age and sex distribution. From Kessler, 2002. ($X^2_3 = 478.13^*$, $P < .001$)

The average age of onset of a first lifetime episode of MDD is now about 30 years of age (Kessler, 2002). There has been a marked shift in both age of first onset and lifetime risk of depression across the last four generations born in the twentieth century (Klerman & Weissman, 1989; Wittchen, Knauper, & Kessler, 1994). In fact, the age cohort born between 1966 and 1975 already has reached about the same lifetime risk as the generation born between 1936 and 1945 (see Figure 13.2). This apparent epidemic no doubt reflects temporal differences in symptom reporting as well as the tendency for older individuals to "forget" more remote episodes, particularly the milder ones. Nevertheless, it does seem likely that rates of depression are indeed higher than ever before.

Rates of MDD in patients seeking treatment in primary care settings tend to be about twice that seen in the general population (Depression Guideline Panel, 1993; Katon & Schulberg, 1992). As noted before, this trend largely reflects the fact that depressed people often seek relief for both the specific and nonspecific (i.e., aches and pains, fatigue, gastrointestinal disturbances) aspects of the disorder. In fact, as the number of unexplained physical symptoms reported by a primary care patient increases, so does the probability of an otherwise undetected depressive disorder (Kroenke, 2003). Even higher rates are detected in medical hospitals and among certain high-risk groups such as nursing home residents (Katon & Schulberg, 1992). Primary care practices have thus become an important venue for screening for depression. Unfortunately, simply detecting the existence of depressive disorder does not ensure that it will be properly treated. At any given time, no more than 50 percent of depressed people are receiving any form of treatment, and, among those receiving any form of treatment, only about one-third are receiving an adequate level of care as defined by contemporary practice guidelines (Hirschfeld et al., 1997).

ETIOLOGY

The description of MDD as a biopsychosocial condition explicitly recognizes the multiple known sources of vulnerability, as articulated 30 years ago in the "final common pathway" model of Akiskal and McKinney (1975). In this section, two broad and (perhaps surprisingly) interrelated etiological factors, life stress and heredity, will be emphasized. Where pertinent, links to the psychologic and biologic correlates of depressive states will be highlighted.

Approximately 80 percent of people with MDD report experiencing an adverse life event prior to the onset of the episode (Mazure, 1998). Given such a clear link, the role of stress as a provocative factor has received extensive study. In traditional psychodynamic models, the breaking of an attachment bond in adult life, whether by death or rejection by a romantic partner, may provoke reexperiencing of earlier unresolved conflicts, such as the death or loss of a parent through divorce. The resulting psychic energy mobilized by the conflict must be dealt with indirectly, typically through the defense of introjection (i.e., "aggression turned inward").

One problem hampering research on the relationship between life stress and the onset of depression has been difficulties in reliably quantifying the severity of the adverse life events. The scientific study of life stress has been greatly facilitated by the methods developed by Brown and Harris (1978, 1989), which apply standardized assessments of the context and severity of stressful life events. In this regard, the personally "toxic" aspects of stress are linked to perceived levels of threat, entrapment, and humiliation (Brown & Harris, 1989; Kendler, Hettema, Butera, Gardner, & Prescott, 2003). Research utilizing more rigorous assessments of life events has helped to clarify the significance of adversity in relation to the onset and symptom expression of depressive episodes (Brown, Harris, & Hepworth, 1994; Frank, Anderson, Reynolds, Ritenour, & Kupfer, 1994).

Contemporary approaches examine the impact of life stress in relation to interdependent biological, psychological, and social processes. Animal studies have been instrumental in documenting the proximal and remote effects of stressors as diverse as pain (i.e., electric foot shock), crowding, foraging demands, changes in social dominance rankings, and maternal separation. Recent work documents that even brief periods of maternal separation early in life can cause long-standing changes in central nervous system stress responses (Ladd, Huot, Thrivikraman, Nemeroff, & Plotsky, 2004). Interestingly, such potentially permanent changes are partly mediated by the maternal animal's behavior immediately following the separation (Huot, Gonzalez, Ladd, Thrivikraman, & Plotsky, 2004). Conversely, studies of adult animals document that high levels of sustained stress can cause a behavioral state of "learned helplessness" associated with significant alterations of central nervous functions mediated by the classic monoamines serotonin (5-HT), norepinephrine (NE), and dopamine (DA; Weiss & Simpson, 1988; Willner, 1997). The ability of stress, both during critical developmental periods and, if severe and protracted, during adulthood to elicit changes in monoamine function is critical because these very neural systems have long been implicated in both the pathophysiology of depression and the mechanism(s) of action of antidepressant medications (Thase, Jindal, & Howland, 2002).

In addition to disturbances of monoaminergic function, the effects of stress and early adversity on the integrity of the hypothalamic-pituitary-adrenocortical (HPA) axis, the brain's principal modulator of stress responses, has also been a topic of intense investigation (Holsboer, 2000; Nemeroff, 2004). During acute stress, the HPA axis is activated instantaneously by the hypothalamic neuropeptide corticotrophin releasing factor (CRF; Nemeroff, 2004). Unlike the "normal" phasic HPA response to acute stress, however, elevated levels of the adrenocorticoid hormone cortisol (in plasma, cerebrospinal fluid, urine, and saliva) may persist indefinitely in more severe depressive states. There is evidence that sustained elevations of cortisol are associated with changes in both brain structure and function, perhaps mediated by suppression of another important neuropeptide, brain derived neurotrophic factor (BDNF; Duman, 2004). One mechanism underlying dysregulation of HPA function in depression is impairment of inhibitory feedback mechanisms; an abnormality moderated by the effects of aging and illness characteristics such as symptom severity, psychosis, and episode recurrence (Holsboer, 2000; Thase et al., 2002).

Returning to the importance of stress during critical developmental periods, increased rates of depression have been associated with loss of a parent (through either death or divorce) and more subtle forms of parental neglect, as well as more horrific forms of physical and sexual abuse. Of note, results of animal studies indicate that even relatively short-lived exposure to high levels of stress in utero can result in lasting alternations in central nervous system stress responses (Graham, Heim, Goodman, Miller, & Nemeroff, 1999). The depressogenic effects of early adversity span biological, psychological, and social functioning in areas as diverse as the security of intimate attachments, regulation of stress response, and development of negative self-schemata (Goodman, 2002; Graham et al., 1999; Hooley & Gotlib, 2000; Nemeroff, 2004). Importantly, the enduring neurobiologic effects of severe early trauma can greatly accelerate the both the development and magnitude of HPA dysfunction in depression (Heim, Plotsky, & Nemeroff, 2004).

Although it also has long been known that depression runs in families, until the past decade the relative contributions of nature and nurture were difficult to disentangle. The contribution of genetic factors is best estimated by comparing the concordance of depression between monozygotic and same-sex dizygotic twins. Studies examining the concordance of depression among twins reared apart, although rare, have provided a second useful source of information.

Early studies suggested a very high level of concordance of depression among monozygotic twins, whether raised together or apart, although serious methodological limitations lessened confidence in the findings (see Farmer, 1996). Modern studies using standardized diagnostic assessments and karyotypic confirmation of the mono- versus dizygotic genetic classification indicate that about 40 percent to 50 percent of the risk of MDD is heritable (Kendler, Neale, Kessler, Heath, & Eaves, 1992; McGuffin, Katz, & Rutherford, 1991; Sullivan et al., 2000). For example, in the study of McGuffin and colleagues (1991), the rate of concordance was 53 percent for monozygotic twin pairs and 28 percent for dizygotic twin pairs. In fact, rates of inheritance for dizygotic twins are, on average, not much greater than for same-sex siblings (Wallace, Schneider, & McGuffin, 2002). Generally, siblings and parents (first-degree relatives) have about twice the risk of depression as in the general population and heritability appears to be comparable for women and men (Wallace et al., 2002).

Heritability is greater for more severe depressive episodes, for recurrent episodes, and for younger ages of onset (Malhi, Moore, & McGuffin, 2000; Weissman et al., 2005). Conversely, late-onset episodes of MDD (i.e., after age 60) may be less heritable (Maier et al., 1991). The latter finding suggests that factors linked to medical status, particularly vulnerability to subcortical vascular disease (Steffens, Taylor, & Krishnan, 2003), gain greater importance with aging.

Interestingly, heritability includes not only the predisposition to depression per se, but also the likelihood to encounter certain depressogenic life events (Kendler, Karkowski, & Prescott, 1999; Thapar, Harold, & McGuffin, 1998). Likewise, adequate social support, which has a powerful protective effect against the onset of MDD in the face of adversity, also shows heritability (Wade & Kendler, 2000).

Now that level of inherited risk has been reliably quantified, research aimed at identifying specific vulnerability genes can be intensified. To date, genes that code for products involved in the neurotransmission of the classical monoamines (especially 5-HT and NE) and regulation of the HPA axis have received the most intensive study (see, e.g., Garlow, Boone, Li, Owens, & Nemeroff, 2005; Malhi et al., 2000; Zubenko et al., 2004). The leading candidate so far has been the serotonin transporter gene, which is located on chromosome 17 (see Mahli et al., 2000). Specifically, a polymorphism in the transcriptional control region of this gene has been identified, with less functional short (*s*) and more functional long (*l*) forms of the gene. The short form is less functional than the more common long form. Of note, about 5 percent to 7 percent of the U.S. population has the *s/s* genotype and about one third have the heterozygous (*s/l*) genotype (Malhi et al., 2000). Research indicates that, although the *s* polymorphism does not cause depression per se, individuals with two copies (*s/s*) of this polymorphism are more emotionally responsive to threatening cues (Hariri et al., 2005) and are more likely to become depressed in the context of adverse life events (Caspi et al., 2003; see Figure 13.3). By contrast, individuals with the *l/l* genotype appeared to be relatively immune to the depressogenic effects of severe stress.

An interactive model of risk referred to as episode sensitization or kindling helps to further clarify the relationship between recent life stress and heredity. The kindling model postulates that adverse life events have a greater role early in the course of illness, with the progressively greater likelihood that subsequent episodes of depression will develop more autonomously (i.e., without environmental provocation; Post, 1992). Support for this model has emerged from a pair of studies by Kendler, Thornton, and Gardner (2000, 2001). They found that individuals at high genetic risk (i.e., an affected monozygotic twin sibling) had a stably high risk of depression onset, regardless of number of past episodes or recent life stresses. By contrast, for individuals at low genetic risk (i.e., a monozygotic twin with no history of depression) the roles of life stress and lifetime episodes of depression

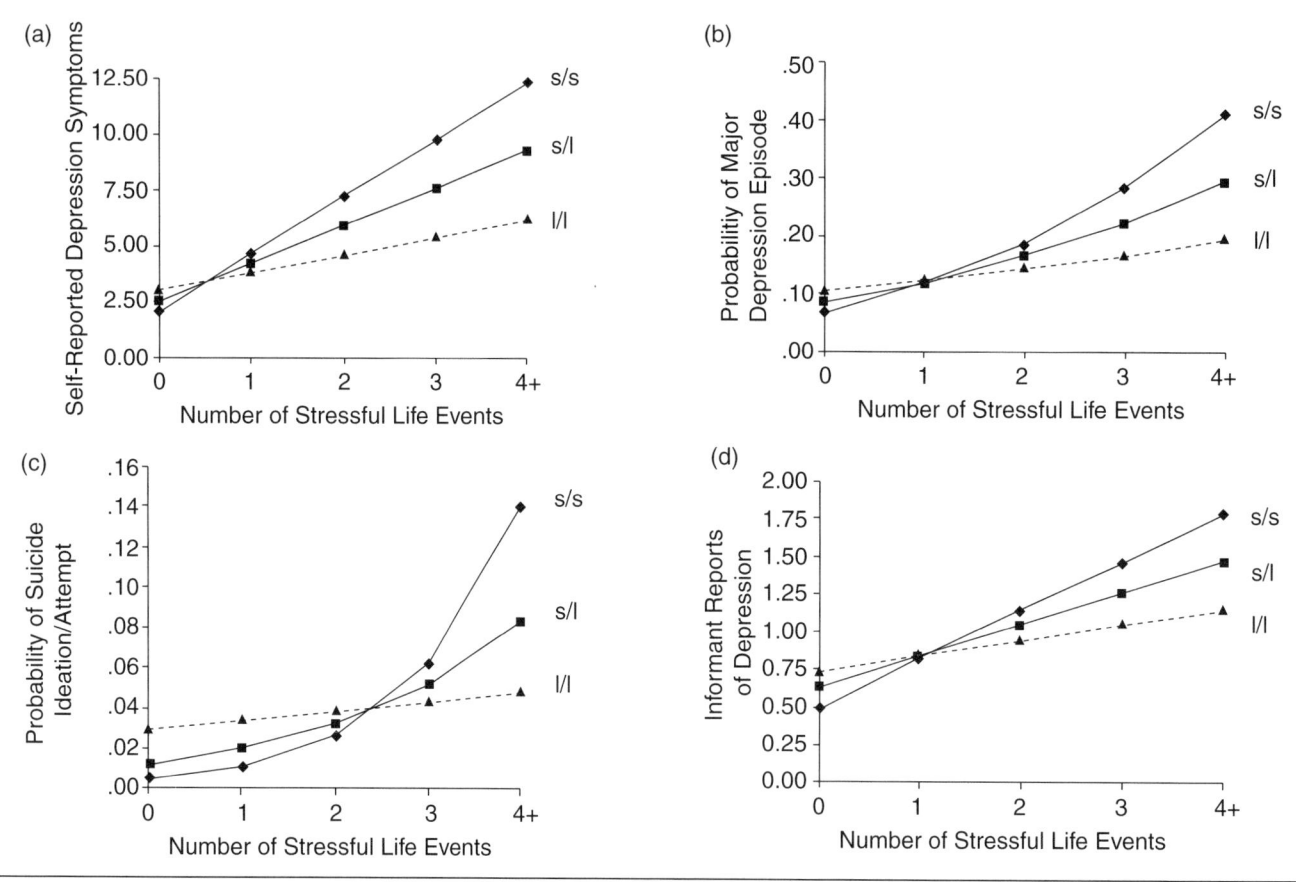

Figure 13.3 Relationship of serotonin transporter genotype, adverse life events, and risk of depression. Results of multiple regression analyses estimating the association between number of stressful life events (between ages 21 and 26 years) and depression outcomes at age 26 as a function of 5-HT T genotype. Among the 146 s/s homozygotes, 43 (29 percent), 37 (25 percent), 28 (19 percent), 15 (10 percent), and 23 (16 percent) study members experienced zero, one, two, three, and four or more stressful events, respectively. Among the 435 s/l heterozygotes, 141 (32 percent), 101 (23 percent), 76 (17 percent), 49 (11 percent), and 68 (16 percent) experienced zero, one, two, three, and four or more stressful events. Among the 264 l/l homozygotes, 79 (29 percent), 73 (28 percent), 57 (21 percent), 26 (10 percent), and 29 (11 percent) experienced zero, one, two, three, and four or more stressful events. (A) Self-reports of depression symptoms. The main effect of 5-HT TLPR (i.e., an effect not conditional on other variables) was marginally significant ($b = -0.96$, SE $= 0.52$, $t = 1.86$, $P = 0.06$), the main effect of stressful life events was significant ($b = 1.75$, SE $= 0.23$, $t = 7.45$, $P < 0.001$), and the interaction between 5-HT TLPR and life events was in the predicted direction ($b = -0.89$, SE $= 0.37$, $t = 2.39$, $P = 0.02$). The interaction showed that the effect of life events on self-reports of depression symptoms was stronger among individuals carrying an s allele ($b = 2.52$, SE $= 0.66$, $t = 3.82$, $P < 0.001$ among s/s homozygotes, and $b = 1.71$, SE $= 0.34$, $t = 5.02$, $P < 0.001$ among s/l heterozygotes) than among l/l homozygotes ($b = 0.77$, SE $= 0.43$, $t = 1.79$, $P = 0.08$). (B) Probability of major depressive episode. The main effect of 5-HT TLPR was not significant ($b = -0.15$, SE $= 0.14$, $z = 1.07$, $P = 0.29$), the main effect of life events was significant ($b = 0.37$, SE $= 0.06$, $z = 5.99$, $P < 0.001$), and the G × E was in the predicted direction ($b = -0.19$, SE $= 0.10$, $z = 1.91$, $P = 0.056$). Life events predicted a diagnosis of major depression among s carriers ($b = 0.52$, SE $= 0.16$, $z = 3.28$, $P = 0.001$ among s/s homozygotes, and $b = 0.39$, SE $= 0.09$, $z = 4.24$, $P < 0.001$ among s/l heterozygotes) but not among l/l homozygotes ($b = 0.16$, SE $= 0.13$, $z = 1.18$, $P = 0.24$). (C) Probability of suicide ideation or attempt. The main effect of 5-HT TLPR was not significant ($b = -0.01$, SE $= 0.28$, $z = 0.01$, $P = 0.99$), the main effect of life events was significant ($b = 0.51$, SE $= 0.13$, $z = 3.96$, $P < 0.001$), and the G × E interaction was in the predicted direction ($b = -0.39$, SE $= 0.20$, $t = 1.95$, $P = 0.051$). Life events predicted suicide ideation or attempt among s carriers ($b = 0.48$, SE $= 0.29$, $z = 1.67$, $P = 0.09$ among s/s homozygotes, and $b = 0.91$, SE $= 0.25$, $z = 3.58$, $P < 0.001$ among s/l heterozygotes) but not among l/l homozygotes ($b = 0.13$, SE $= 0.26$, $z = 0.49$, $P = 0.62$). (D) Informant reports of depression. The main effect of 5-HT TLPR was not significant (b $= -0.06$, SE $= 0.06$, t $= 0.98$, $P = 0.33$), the main effect of life events was significant ($b = 0.23$, SE $= 0.03$, $t = 8.47$, $P < 0.001$), and the G × E was in the predicted direction ($b = -0.11$, SE $= 0.04$, $t = 2.54$, $P < 0.01$). The effect of life events on depression was stronger among s carriers ($b = 0.39$, SE $= 0.07$, $t = 5.23$, $P < 0.001$ among s/s homozygotes, and $b = 0.17$, SE $= 0.04$, $t = 4.51$, $P < 0.001$ among s/l heterozygotes) than among l/l homozygotes ($b = 0.14$, SE $= 0.05$, $t = 2.69$, $P < 0.01$). Note. From Caspi et al., 2003.

with inversely correlated. Whereas a recent negative life event figured prominently in the risk of onset of the initial lifetime episodes of depression, less stress was no longer a risk factor by the time the individual had experienced a fifth or sixth lifetime episode. Indeed, the highly recurrent or kindled subjects with no family history of depression had acquired the same vulnerability to depression onset as the group at high genetic risk.

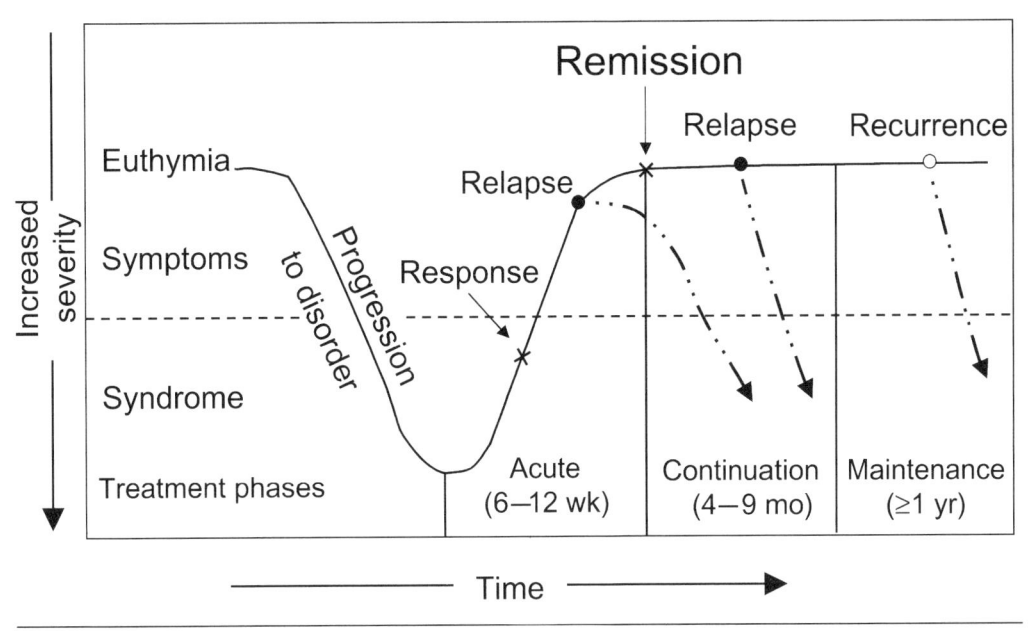

Figure 13.4 Clinical outcomes and phases of treatment of episodic major depressive disorder. *Note.* From Kupfer, 1991.

COURSE, COMPLICATIONS, AND PROGNOSIS

The course of an episode of MDD is commonly described by five outcomes, each coincidentally beginning with the letter R: response, remission, recovery, relapse, and recurrence (Frank et al., 1991; Keller, 2003; see Figure 13.4). The first and most proximal outcome, *response,* describes a significant reduction in symptom severity. In treatment studies, a 50 percent reduction in severity on a standardized rating scale is typically used as the operational definition of response. The second outcome, *remission,* describes a more complete or higher grade of response. Remission represents a level of improvement such that the person has no more signs and symptoms of depression than someone who has never been ill. Ideally, remission is accompanied by resolution of the functional impairment associated with the depressive episode. The term *recovery* is used when there has been a period of sustained remission; conceptually, recovery demarks the end of the depressive episode. There is no consensus regarding the appropriate duration of remission before declaring recovery: proposed durations range from two months to nine months. *Relapse* describes an exacerbation of the index depressive episode after a response but before recovery has been achieved. A *recurrence* is distinguished from a relapse only by definition: a recurrence can occur only after recovery. So defined, relapse conceptually represents the reemergence of the index depressive episode, whereas recurrence is conceptually viewed as a new episode of illness.

Once thought to be a generally self-limiting group of conditions (and insensitively referred to as "the common cold of mental disorders"), MDD is now known to be a highly recurrent and potentially chronic and disabling condition. As noted earlier, relatively few people suffer only a single lifetime episode and, with each new episode of MDD there are renewed risks of chronicity, disability, and suicide. Once an individual has experienced at least three lifetime episodes, the probability of recurrence is quite high, perhaps up to 80 percent within five years without preventive treatment. And for each new episode, there is approximately a 10 percent risk of chronicity (Keller et al., 1992).

MDD runs a variable course and, for many, the episodes are short lived. For example, typically, 50 percent to 60 percent of depressive episodes will remit within six months (Boland & Keller, 2002). The probability of spontaneous remission is not uniform, however, and decreases dramatically after the first six to eight weeks. Thus, unless there is a clear-cut history of brief but infrequent episodes of MDD, treatment can be expected to both reduce suffering and improve the proximal course of the disorder (as compared to the natural history) by accelerating the time to remission.

Once remission is achieved, in naturalistic follow-up studies there is about a 20 percent risk of relapse across one year (Boland & Keller, 2002). Relapse rates are higher for those with more severe index episodes and greater levels of comorbidity (including dysthymia). Perhaps the greatest risks of relapse are the result of incomplete remission and premature termination of an antidepressant therapy (Keller, 2003). The latter is because antidepressants do not "cure" the depressive disorder but, rather, suppress illness activity. Consequently, complete remission has become the standard outcome for the acute phase of therapy and, when effective, antidepressants should be continued for six to nine months of continuation phase therapy (American Psychiatric Association, 2000; Depression Guideline Panel, 1993; Frank & Thase, 1999). Incompletely remitted patients may face the same risk of relapse when a time-limited course of psychotherapy is ended (Jarrett et al., 2001; Thase et al., 1992).

About 20 percent of all depressive episodes persist for two years or longer. The risk of chronicity is directly related to the duration of the depressive episode prior to the start of the study period. For example, after one year of persistent MDD, there is a 67 percent risk that the depression will last for at least another year (Keller et al., 1992). Similarly, although the chance that a depressive episode will last for five years or longer is only about 10 percent at the outset, a patient who has already been depressed for two years has a 60 percent chance of remaining depressed for five full years (Keller & Boland, 1998).

Suicide, the eighth leading cause of death among adults living in the United States, is the most dreaded outcome of an episode of MDD. Psychological autopsy studies indicate that approximately two-thirds of those who complete suicide have a depressive disorder. Typically, people who complete suicide are either receiving no treatment or have received only low, inadequate levels of care in the weeks preceding their demise. In older follow-up studies of hospitalized depressed patients (including a high proportion suffering from more severe/psychotic episodes of MDD), about 15 percent ultimately died by suicide (see, e.g., Guze & Robins, 1970). More recent studies of broader, more representative groups of depressed patients suggest that lifetime suicide rates are lower, but still range between 5 percent and 7 percent (Bostwick & Pankratz, 2000; Inskip, Harris, & Barraclough, 1998). Suicide rates are higher among men (especially older White males), psychotic features, people with chronic incapacitating illnesses, prior serious suicide attempts, and alcoholism or other forms of substance abuse. The major reason for the gender difference in suicide rates is that men are more likely to use more lethal means than women (i.e., gunshot, hanging, or jumping versus overdose of medication or wrist-cutting).

ASSESSMENT AND DIAGNOSIS

The full *DSM-IV* case formulation makes use of a multiaxial coding system. In addition to the three axes described earlier,

TABLE 13.3 *DSM-IV-TR* **Criteria for the Diagnosis of Major Depressive Episode**

A. Five (or more) of the following symptoms have been present during the same two-week period and represent a change from previous functioning; at least one of the symptoms is either (1) depressed mood or (2) loss of interest or pleasure:
  1. Depressed mood most of the day or nearly every day, as indicated by either subjective report (e.g., feels sad or empty) or observation made by others (e.g., appears tearful). Note: In children and adolescents, can be irritable mood.
  2. Markedly diminished interest or pleasure in all, or almost all, activities most of the day or nearly every day (as indicated by either subjective account or observation made by others).
  3. Significant weight loss when not dieting or weight gain (e.g., a change of more than 5% of body weight in a month) or decrease or increase in appetite nearly every day. Note: In children, consider failure to make expected weight gains.
  4. Insomnia or hypersomnia nearly every day.
  5. Psychomotor agitation or retardation nearly every day (observable by others; note merely subjective feelings of restlessness or being slowed down).
  6. Fatigue or loss of energy nearly every day.
  7. Feelings of worthlessness or excessive or inappropriate guilt (which may be delusional) nearly every day (not merely self-reproach or guilt about being sick).
  8. Diminished ability to think or concentrate, or indecisiveness, nearly every day (either by subjective account or as observed by others).
  9. Recurrent thoughts of death (not just fear of dying), recurrent suicidal ideation without a specific plan, or a suicide attempt or a specific plan for committing suicide.
B. The symptoms do not meet criteria for a mixed episode.
C. The symptoms cause clinically significant distress or impairment in social, occupational, or other important areas of functioning.

Source: American Psychiatric Association. (2000). *Diagnostic and statistical manual of mental disorders* (4th ed., text rev.). Washington, DC: Author.

Axis IV is used to rate Global Assessment of Functioning and Axis V is used to record pertinent life stresses.

The *DSM-IV* criteria for a major depressive episode are summarized in Table 13.3. As noted at the outset of this chapter, the diagnosis of MDD is made when there is no history of mania or hypomania and the episode is not better explained as a consequence of alcoholism, substance abuse, an untoward reaction to a medication, or a general medical disorder. The diagnosis of MDD thus depends on obtaining a history and conducting an evaluation that permits identifying the necessary features of the syndrome in tandem with excluding pertinent alternate considerations.

In practice, the criteria of the *DSM-IV* are typically reviewed, checklist style, after completion of an unstructured diagnostic interview. Standards of practice for the length of this "intake" evaluation vary widely, though it is hard to imagine reaching this diagnosis with certainty after less than a 30-minute interview. On occasion, even two hours does not suffice! The results of field trials indicate that the *DSM-IV* criteria can be reliably applied by psychiatrists and psychologists, with test-retest and interrater reliabilities in excess of 80 percent (Keller et al., 1995).

Given the association between general medical illnesses and depression, a medical history, a review of current medications (and, when pertinent, the temporal sequence between medication changes and the onset or worsening of depression), and a review of systems should be included as part of all diagnostic evaluations. When indicated, this basic information should be supplemented by a physical examination and appropriate laboratory tests.

For the purposes of research, semistructured interviews have been developed; both the Structured Clinical Interview for *DSM-IV* Axis I disorders (SCID; Spitzer, Williams, Gibbon, & First, 1992) and the briefer MINI International Neuropsychiatric Interview (Sheehan et al., 1998) are capable of yielding an even greater level of reliability (i.e., kappa values >0.9 for MDD) and have become the standard of practice for methodologically rigorous investigations. These assessments have essentially replaced earlier interviews such as the Schedule for Affective Disorders and Schizophrenia (Endicott & Spitzer, 1978) and the Diagnostic Interview Schedule (DIS; Robins, Helzer, & Ratcliff, 1981). The advantage of these semistructured approaches is that skilled nondoctoral raters, including social workers and psychiatric nurses, can be trained to a level of reliability that matches that of doctoral staff. A briefer interview, the PRIME-MD (Spitzer et al., 1994), serves a similar purpose for studies conducted in primary care.

As important as the need for accurate diagnosis, efficient and reliable ongoing assessment of outcome by quantifying syndromal (symptom) severity is necessary to ensure that treatment is effective or, if not, that changes in the treatment plan can be made in a timely manner. For decades, the self-report Beck Depression Inventory (BDI; Beck & Steer, 1984; Beck, Ward, Mendelson, Mock, & Erbaugh, 1961) has both been widely used and, all in all, largely met the need. One of the major shortcomings of the BDI, namely inadequate coverage of the full *DSM-IV* syndromal criteria, was largely rectified with the development of the BDI-II (see, e.g., Beck, Steer, & Brown, 1996). The BDI-II contains 21 four-point (i.e., 0 to 3) items, resulting in a score range of 0 to 63. Most people who are not depressed score 10 or less; most people with MDD score 20 and higher. Scores higher than 35 are considered indicative of severe depression. The major drawback of the BDI-II is that it has been copyrighted and the holder of copyright requires that clinicians purchase copies of the test. As older forms of the BDI are not protected by this copyright, "bootleg" copies of the venerable rating scale abound. The remaining criticism of the BDI-II is, like its ancestor, that experts believe that the scale gives too much weight to the cognitive symptoms of depression versus the neurovegetative symptoms.

Several additional useful self-report assessments include the Zung Depression Rating Scale, the Center for Epidemiological Studies Depression (CES-D) Scale, and the depression subscale of the Minnesota Multiphasic Personality Inventory (MMPI-D; see Nezu, Maguth Nezu, McClure, & Zwick, 2002). All are valuable and, at the end of the day, the practice of serially monitoring patient outcomes is much more important than the choice of a particular rating scale.

The most commonly used clinician rating scale is the Hamilton Depression Rating Scale (HAM-D; Hamilton, 1960). The original scale consists of 17 items, with some scored on a 3-point scale and others on a 5-point scale. A total score of ≤ 7 is typical for nondepressed individuals and, hence, is often used to define the threshold for remission. Most depressed people score ≥ 14 points, with additional thresholds of ≥ 20 and ≥ 25 representing moderate and severe depression, respectively. Like the BDI, the HAM-D has good psychometric properties and has ably served the field for more than four decades. And like the BDI, incomplete coverage of the *DSM-IV* symptoms of MDD and idiosyncratic weighting of particular symptom clusters are somewhat problematic.

To address the several problems associated with the BDI and HAM-D, Rush and colleagues (Rush, Gullion, Basco, Jarrett, & Trivedi, 1996; Rush et al., 2003; Trivedi et al., 2004) developed the Inventory of Depressive Symptoms (IDS). Not only does the IDS include full coverage of (and equal weighting for) the *DSM-IV* symptom criteria for MDD, but it is also available in both self-report and clinician-rated forms. Psychometric studies have confirmed the utility of both forms of the IDS. More recently, an attenuated or quick version (the Q-IDS) has been developed and found to have acceptable psychometric characteristics (Rush et al., 2003).

IMPACT ON ENVIRONMENT

MDD is one of the world's greatest public health problems because it is common, often goes undetected and/or untreated, and is associated with considerable disability. In fact, a survey conducted under the auspices of the World Health Organization concluded that MDD was the fourth greatest cause of global illness burden in 1990 and projected depression will become the world's second greatest public health problem by 2020 (Murray & Lopez, 1996).

Beyond the inestimable costs of human suffering, tens of billions of dollars are lost each year as a result of diminished productivity absenteeism, disability, and premature death (Greenberg et al., 2003; Greenberg, Stiglin, Finkelstein, &

Berndt, 1993). Depression is the greatest single source of diminished productivity and sick days in the workplace (Kessler & Frank, 1997; Simon et al., 2001), with depression costing the average worker to use more than two sick days per month (Wang et al., 2004).

The cost of treating depression pales in comparison to the other costs of the illness (Simon et al., 2001). In Greenberg et al.'s studies, only about 15 percent of the billions lost because of depression were attributable to treatment expenses (Greenberg et al., 1993, 2003). Further, there is evidence that effective treatment reduces the level of impairment associated with depression such that the cost of care is largely, if not completely, offset (Simon et al., 2001).

The effects of depression in the home are arguably even more significant than in the workplace (Joiner, 2002). Depression is associated with high rates of marital discord and divorce (Gotlib & Whiffen, 1989). Having a depressed spouse or parent increases the risk of depression throughout the household (Joiner, 2002). The children of depressed parents also suffer from greater difficulties in the classroom and peer-group relations (Ellis & Garber, 2000; Hammen, Shih, & Brennan, 2004; Kane & Garber, 2004). Depressed people tend to be less assertive, have less gratifying peer and friendship relations, and have difficulties engaging in reciprocally reinforcing interactions with others (Segrin, 2000).

Depression has an effect on quality of life that is greater than most common chronic medical conditions, surpassed only by the disability resulting from congestive heart failure and recent myocardial infarction (Wells et al., 1989). Depression not only is more likely to occur among those with chronic medical illnesses but it also complicates the management and course of these diseases (Roose et al., 2001) and increases mortality risks from other causes in addition to suicide (Cuijpers & Schoevers, 2004). For example, even minor depressive symptoms increase the chance of dying following a myocardial infarction or stroke, is associated with poorer control of hypertension and diabetes, and greater functional impairment in chronic painful conditions such as arthritis.

TREATMENT IMPLICATIONS

Most episodes of MDD respond to treatment with either psychotherapy or antidepressant medication, either singly or in combination. Combined treatment is probably most clearly indicated for patients with more severe, recurrent, and complex forms of MDD. For example, in one study of patients with chronic forms of MDD, the combination of psychotherapy and pharmacotherapy resulted in a 75 percent remission rate at week 12, as compared to approximately 50 percent remission rates for the groups receiving either psychotherapy or pharmacotherapy alone (Keller et al., 2000). For patients with milder, uncomplicated depressive episodes, the advantage of combining modalities is less clear cut (Thase et al., 1997). Although comparably effective in groups of patients, psychotherapy and pharmacotherapy probably treat only partially overlapping patient groups (Thase, 2001). When choosing between psychotherapy and pharmacotherapy options, factors such as insurance coverage and availability of a skilled psychotherapist are relevant. When all other factors are equal, patient preference should determine which form of treatment is selected first.

Psychotherapy

Some practice guidelines favor use of the newer forms of psychotherapy, including cognitive behavior therapy (CBT) and interpersonal therapy (IPT; Depression Guideline Panel, 1993; Kennedy et al., 2004). This is because these depression-focused therapies are generally time limited (i.e., beneficial effects should be apparent within two to three months) and they have been better studied than more traditional and longer-term models of psychodynamic psychotherapy. In fact, in randomized controlled trials, CBT and IPT generally have been found to be as effective as standard antidepressant medications; both types of intervention yield intent-to-treat response rates of about 45 percent to 55 percent (Hollon, Thase, & Markowitz, 2002; Thase, 2001). Although acknowledging the dearth of controlled studies, the American Psychiatric Association's practice guideline (2000) also notes the extensive clinical experience using more traditional models of therapy with depressed patients.

Although IPT and CBT share a number of common features, they differ in both strategy and tactics. IPT focuses on one or more of the areas of interpersonal difficulty that commonly characterize the depressed person's interpersonal world, including role transitions, role disputes, unresolved grief, and social deficits such as loneliness (see Klerman, Weissman, Rounsaville, & Chevron, 1984). CBT focuses on the interrelationship of distorted negative thinking and maladaptive behaviors in maintaining depressive states (see Beck, Rush, Shaw, & Emery, 1979). Whereas IPT follows a medical illness management model and is more traditionally conversational in its tactical focus, CBT sessions are more structured and incorporate specific assignments both during and between sessions.

Only a few controlled studies have directly compared IPT and CBT and, to date, no consensus about comparative efficacy has emerged. There is some evidence that CBT may have more enduring effects that protect against relapse (Evans et al., 1992; Simons, Murphy, & Levine, 1986), relapse (Paykel et al., 1999), and recurrence (Fava, Rafanelli, Grandi, Conti, & Belluardo, 1998). However, in the only controlled study directly comparing these therapies to employ a longer-term follow-up phase, no such advantage was observed (Shea, Elkin, et al., 1992).

Both CBT and IPT have been adapted as group therapies. Although clearly less popular than individual therapy, group therapy offers a potentially great advantage in terms of cost-effectiveness (Depression Guideline Panel, 1993). This may be particularly true in settings and regions in which there is a shortage of psychotherapists. Other types of psychotherapy with evidence of efficacy for MDD include problem-solving therapy (a briefer model of therapy utilizing cognitive and behavior interventions; Mynors-Wallis, Gath, Day, & Baker, 2000) and various forms of time-limited couples therapy (see, e.g., Beach & Jones, 2002).

Pharmacotherapy

More than 25 antidepressant medications are available worldwide, with most falling into two classes: the older tricyclic antidepressants (TCAs) and the newer selective serotonin reuptake inhibitors (SSRIs; see Table 13.4). For treatment of psychotic depression, antidepressants are routinely combined with antipsychotic medications (also see Chapter 30). For more than a decade, the SSRIs have been considered to be the first line of antidepressant pharmacotherapy throughout most of the world. There are five SSRIs approved by the U.S. Food and Drug Administration (FDA) for treatment of depression: fluoxetine (Prozac and others), sertraline (Zoloft), paroxetine (Paxil and Paxil CR), citalopram (Celexa), and escitalopram (Lexapro); a sixth SSRI, fluvoxamine (Luvox), was only approved for treatment of obsessive compulsive disorder. Many of the SSRIs also have FDA approval for the treatment of various other disorders, including all of the *DSM-IV* anxiety disorders.

The SSRIs and the previous standard of efficacy, the TCAs, are generally comparably effective, although several members of the older class may be more effective for the most severely depressed patients (Anderson, 1998). The SSRIs supplanted the TCAs largely because of their superior tolerability, greater safety (especially in overdose), and relative simplicity of administration (Thase & Kupfer, 1996). Unlike the TCAs, all of the SSRIs can be started at a therapeutic dose and are relatively safe in overdose as large as a one-month supply of medication. The major shortcoming of the SSRIs has been higher retail cost, but this disadvantage has largely dissipated as members of this class have lost patent protection.

Other newer antidepressants include bupropion (Wellbutrin XL), which enhances norepinephrine and dopamine neurotransmission, the tetracyclic compound mirtazapine, which enhances both norepinephrine and serotonin through complex mechanism, and the so-called serotonin-norepinephrine reuptake inhibitors (SNRIs), venlafaxine (Effexor XR) and duloxetine (Cymbalta), which more directly enhance serotonin and norepinephrine neurotransmission. Because of the potential for a broader spectrum of effects, the SNRIs may have an efficacy advantage as compared to the SSRIs (Smith, Dempster, Glanville, Freemantle, & Anderson, 2002; Thase, Entsuah, & Rudolph, 2001). However, this potential benefit is not universally recognized (American Psychiatric Association, 2000; Burke, 2004) and, even if true, must be balanced against the potential for broader spectrum of side effects.

Recent controversy has emerged regarding the safety of antidepressant therapy in youth, culminating in the decisions of the FDA and several other regulatory agencies to issue warnings. Specifically, in meta-analyses of controlled studies of antidepressants in children and adolescents, a small (about 2 percent greater than in the placebo group) but reliable increase in the risk of suicidal ideation, agitation, and related forms of behavioral activation was observed (Gunnell, Saperia, & Ashby, 2005; Licinio & Wong, 2005). Although the emergence of suicidal ideation early in the course of antidepressant therapy has been described for decades, the issue is more salient for treatment of youth because the benefits of pharmacotherapy have not been as well established (Brent, 2004; Wong, Besag, Santosh, & Murray, 2004). Epidemiological studies provide some reassurance, as rates of completed suicide have actually decreased since the introduction of the newer antidepressants (Gibbons, Hur, Bhaumik, & Mann, 2005; Grunebaum, Ellis, Li, Oquendo, & Mann, 2004; Isacsson, Holmgren, & Ahlner, 2005; Olfson, Shaffer, Marcus, & Greenberg, 2003). Perhaps ironically, one of the most rigorous studies of treatment of depressed adolescents, a multicenter trial sponsored by the National Institute of Mental Health, was published in the midst of this controversy (March et al., 2004). In the TADS trial, response rates after 12 weeks of therapy were as follows: placebo, 35 percent; CBT alone, 43 percent; fluoxetine alone, 61 percent; CBT plus fluoxetine combined, 71 percent. Although patients in all four treatment arms experienced reductions in suicidal thinking, the greatest improvement was observed in the group receiving the combination of CBT and fluoxetine.

Antidepressants are not habit-forming and, with rare exception, do not have mood-elevating effects for nondepressed people. The emergence of mood elevation during antidepressant treatment is strong evidence that a bipolar disorder has been uncovered. The principal side effects of the SSRIs in-

TABLE 13.4 Commonly Used Antidepressants

Class	Brand Name	Usual dose (mg/day)	Prominent side effects*
MAOIs			Dry mouth, constipation, nausea, nervousness, difficulty sleeping or daytime drowsiness, tremor (shakiness), blurred vision, increased sweating, fatigue, and muscle jerks (neurologic myoclonus); less commonly headaches, urinary retention, appetite change with weight gain or loss, memory problems, and sexual side effects; especially problematic are orthostatic hypotension (sudden drop in blood pressure upon standing that causes a person to feel dizzy or faint) and hypertensive crisis (potentially life-threatening increase in blood pressure following ingestion of certain foods or medications)
Irreversible			
Isocarboxazid	Marplan	15–30	
Phenelzine	Nardil	45–90	
Tranylcypromine	Parnate	30–60	
Reversible			
Moclobemide	Not yet approved for use in the United States	300–600	
TCAs			Anticholinergic side effects (dry mouth, constipation, difficulty urinating, blurred vision, memory impairment, and confusion); less commonly difficulty sleeping, headaches, tremor (shakiness), appetite change with weight gain, and sexual side effects; especially problematic are orthostatic hypotension (see MAOIs) and cardiac arrhythmias for people with heart problems (can be lethal in overdose for anyone)
Tertiary amines†			
Amitriptyline	Elavil	100–300	
Clomipramine	Anafranil	100–250	
Doxepin	Sinequan	100–300	
Imipramine	Tofranil	100–300	
Trimipramine	Surmontil	100–300	
Secondary amines†			
Desipramine	Norpramin	100–300	
Nortriptyline	Aventyl	50–200	
Protriptyline	Vivactil	15–60	
Tetracyclics†			
Amoxapine	Ascendin	100–400	
Maprotiline	Ludiomil	100–225	
SSRIs			Nausea, diarrhea, insomnia, nervousness, muscle jerks, and especially sexual side effects; less commonly headaches, tremor (shakiness), motor restlessness (akathisia), daytime drowsiness, and vomiting
Citalopram	Celexa	20–60	
S-citalopram	Lexapro	10–20	
Fluoxetine	Prozac	20–60	
Fluvoxamine	Luvox	50–300	
Paroxetine	Paxil	20–50	
Sertraline	Zoloft	50–200	
Others			
NE reuptake inhibitor			
Reboxetine	Not yet approved for use in the United States	8–10	Anticholinergiclike side effects (see TCAs) and insomnia
Mixed reuptake inhibitors			
Bupropion (DA, NE)	Wellbutrin	300–400	Nausea, vomiting, insomnia, headaches, and seizures
Venlafaxine (5-HT, NE)	Effexor	75–225	Nausea, diarrhea, nervousness, increased sweating, dry mouth, muscle jerks, and sexual side effects; less commonly vomiting, insomnia or daytime drowsiness, headaches, tremor (shakiness), and increased blood pressure
Duloxetine	Cymbalta	60–80	Similar to venlafaxine (although risk of increased blood pressure appears to be lower)
5-HT modulators			
Nefazodone	Serzone	150–300	Orthostatic hypotension (see MAOIs), headaches, daytime drowsiness, visual disturbances, and liver damage (in rare instances)
Trazodone	Desyrel	75–300	Orthostatic hypotension (see MAOIs), sedation, and priapism
NE and 5-HT modulator			
Mirtazapine	Remeron	15–45	Weight gain and daytime drowsiness

Note. MAOIs = monoamine oxidase inhibitors; TCAs = tricyclic antidepressants; SSRIs = selective serotonin reuptake inhibitors; NE = norepinephrine; 5-HT = serotonin; DA = dopamine.
* For MAOIs, TCAs, and SSRIs, side effects for the entire class are shown; for the other antidepressants, side effects for each agent are shown separately.
† Tertiary amines, secondary amines, and tetracyclics are structurally related compounds, which collectively can be grouped together as tricyclics.
Source: American Psychiatric Association. (2000). *Diagnostic and statistical manual of mental disorders* (4th ed., text rev.). Washington, DC: Author.

clude gastrointestinal disturbances such as nausea and diarrhea, insomnia, and sexual dysfunction. The TCAs also have anticholinergic side effects (including dry mouth, constipation, and blurry vision), antihistaminic side effects (including increased appetite, sedation, and weight gain), and cardiovascular side effects (such as tachycardia, orthostatic hypotension, and the potential to adversely affect heart rhythms). Venlafaxine and duloxetine tend to have an intermediate side effect burden (i.e., greater than SSRIs and less than TCAs).

The herbal remedy Saint-John's-wort also is used as an antidepressant. However, despite evidence of efficacy from smaller studies employing active comparators such as the TCA amitriptyline, two large placebo-controlled studies conducted in the United States failed to demonstrate a significant antidepressant effect (Hypericum Depression Trial Study Group, 2002; Shelton et al., 2001). Beyond uncertain efficacy, two additional drawbacks of this herbal therapy include problems with standardization (it is considered by the FDA to be a dietary supplement, not a drug, and as a result the amount of the active ingredient, hypericum, may vary across commercial products) and the potential for drug-drug interactions (including reducing the effects of birth control pills).

It is difficult to predict which depressed patient will respond to which specific antidepressant. The classes of antidepressants are not interchangeable, and a poor response or intolerable side effects with one medication do not preclude a good response to another. The interested reader is referred elsewhere for a comprehensive review of the evidence pertaining to alternate strategies for treatment resistant depression (Thase, 2004). After nonresponse to one type of antidepressant, the clinician may try a second medication within the same class, switch to a dissimilar class, or try to augment response with a second agent (e.g., lithium, buspirone, thyroid hormone, or an atypical antipsychotic). An otherwise seldom-used class of antidepressants, the MAOIs, can be particularly effective even when several trials of newer medications have been ineffective (Thase, Trivedi, & Rush, 1995).

When antidepressant treatment is effective, an improvement should be apparent within four to six weeks. An effective course of antidepressant medication should be followed by six to nine months of continuation phase therapy to prevent relapse. Said another way, discontinuation of an effective antidepressant medication within the first few months of response at least doubles the risk of relapse. After the third lifetime episode of MDD, a longer, perhaps even indefinite course of maintenance phase pharmacotherapy is recommended for prevention of recurrent episodes (American Psychiatric Association, 2000; Depression Guideline Panel, 1993; Frank & Thase, 1999).

When multiple trials of antidepressant medication are not effective, the oldest proven treatment for depression, electroconvulsive therapy (ECT), still provides a powerful alternative (American Psychiatric Association, 2000; UK ECT Review Group, 2003). ECT typically requires a course of 6 to 12 treatments, typically administered every other day. Treatment effects depend on induction of a series of cerebral seizures, with either high energy unilateral (nondominant) or bilateral electrode placement. In contemporary practice, ECT bears little resemblance to its depiction in movies such as *Frances* or *One Flew over the Cuckoo's Nest*. Patients receive general anesthesia, oxygen, and deep muscle relaxation, and are carefully monitored to ensure that the course of treatment is both adequate and safe. Nevertheless, confusion and transient amnesia are still common short-term side effects. Relapse following a successful course of ECT is unfortunately common and vigorous pharmacotherapy is needed after successful treatment to lessen the risk of relapse (see, e.g., Sackeim et al., 2001).

SUMMARY

Major Depressive Disorder (MDD) is the most common of the *DSM-IV* mood disorders; at any time about 4 percent to 5 percent of adults living in the United States are suffering from an episode of MDD, with a lifetime prevalence of as high as 16 percent. Twice as common in women as men, MDD represents a heterogeneous group of syndromes affecting mood, affect, cognition, neurovegetative functions, and overt behavior. The heterogeneity of MDD is partly addressed in *DSM-IV* through use of descriptive illness subtypes. MDD also is highly comorbid with anxiety and substance abuse disorders. Not only do chronic general medical disorders increase the risk of developing MDD, but depression worsens the course and mortality of these diseases. Vulnerability to depression is partly mediated by temperamental factors, such as neuroticism and social inhibition. Life stress, both current and during critical developmental periods, is an important etiologic factor, as is heredity. In fact, through multiple mechanisms, up to 50 percent of the vulnerability to MDD is mediated by genetic factors. The course of MDD is marked by high rates of recurrence and significant risks of periods of chronicity and disability. Ultimately up to 6 percent of people with more severe and recurrent forms of MDD will die by suicide. Effective treatments include psychotherapies such as CBT and IPT and antidepressant medications such as the SSRIs, SNRIs, and TCAs. Patients with more severe, complex, and chronic depressions have better outcomes when treated with both modalities.

REFERENCES

Abramson, L. Y., Alloy, L. B., Hankin, B. L., Haeffel, G. J., MacCoon, D. G., & Gibb, B. E. (2002). Cognitive vulnerability—Stress models of depression in a self-regulatory and psychobiological context. In I. H. Gotlib and C. L. Hammen (Eds.), *Handbook of depression* (pp. 268–294). New York: Guilford Press.

Akiskal, H. S., & McKinney, W. T., Jr. (1975). Overview of recent research in depression. Integration of ten conceptual models into a comprehensive clinical frame. *Archives of General Psychiatry, 32,* 285–305.

American Psychiatric Association. (1980). *Diagnostic and statistical manual of mental disorders* (3rd ed.). Washington, DC: Author.

American Psychiatric Association. (1994). *Diagnostic and statistical manual of mental disorders* (4th ed.). Washington, DC: Author.

American Psychiatric Association. (2000). Practice guideline for the treatment of patients with major depressive disorder (revision). *American Journal of Psychiatry, 157,* 1–45.

Anderson, I. M. (1998). SSRIs versus tricyclic antidepressants in depressed inpatients: A meta-analysis of efficacy and tolerability. *Depression and Anxiety, 7*(Suppl.), 11–17.

Ansseau, M., Troisfontaines, B., Papart, P., & von Frenckell, R. (1991). Compulsive personality as predictor of response to serotoninergic antidepressants. *British Medical Journal, 303,* 760–761.

Bair, M. J., Robinson, R. L., Katon, W., & Kroenke, K. (2003). Depression and pain comorbidity: A literature review. *Archives of Internal Medicine, 163,* 2433–2445.

Barber, J. P., & Muenz, L. R. (1996). The role of avoidance and obsessiveness in matching patients to cognitive and interpersonal psychotherapy: Empirical findings from the treatment for depression collaborative research program. *Journal of Consulting and Clinical Psychology, 64,* 951–958.

Beach, S. R. H., & Jones, D. J. (2002). Marital and family therapy for depression in adults. In I. H. Gotlib & C. L. Hammen (Eds.), *Handbook of depression* (pp. 422–440). New York: Guilford Press.

Beck, A. T. (1987). Cognitive models of depression. *Journal of Cognitive Psychotherapy: An International Quarterly, 1,* 5–37.

Beck, A. T., Rush, A. J., Shaw, B. F., & Emery, G. (1979). *Cognitive therapy of depression: A treatment manual.* New York: Guilford Press.

Beck, A. T., & Steer, R. A. (1984). Internal consistencies of the original and revised Beck Depression Inventory. *Journal of Clinical Psychology, 40,* 1365–1367.

Beck, A. T., Steer, R. A., & Brown, G. K. (1996). *Manual for the BDI-II.* San Antonio, TX: Psychological Corp.

Beck, A. T., Ward, C. H., Mendelson, M., Mock, J., & Erbaugh, J. (1961). An inventory for measuring depression. *Archives of General Psychiatry, 4,* 561–571.

Boland, R. J., & Keller, M. B. (2002). Course and outcome of depression. In I. H. Gotlib & C. L. Hammen (Eds.), *Handbook of depression* (pp. 43–60). New York: Guilford Press.

Bostwick, J. M., & Pankratz, V. S. (2000). Affective disorders and suicide risk: A reexamination. *American Journal of Psychiatry, 157,* 1925–1932.

Brent, D. A. (2004). Treating depression in children: Antidepressants and pediatric depression—The risk of doing nothing. *New England Journal of Medicine, 351,* 1598–1601.

Brown, G. W., & Harris, T. O. (1978). *Social origins of depression.* London: Tavistock.

Brown, G. W., & Harris, T. O. (1989). *Life events and illness.* New York: Guilford Press.

Brown, G. W., Harris, T. O., & Hepworth, C. (1994). Life events and endogenous depression: A puzzle reexamined. *Archives of General Psychiatry, 51,* 525–534.

Burke, W. J. (2004). Selective versus multi-transmitter antidepressants: Are two mechanisms better than one? *Journal of Clinical Psychiatry, 65*(Suppl. 4), 37–45.

Caspi, A., Sugden, K., Moffitt, T. E., Taylor, A., Craig, I. W., Harrington, H., et al. (2003). Influence of life stress on depression: Moderation by a polymorphism in the 5-HTT gene. *Science, 301,* 386–389.

Chodoff, P. (1972). The depressive personality. *Archives of General Psychiatry, 27,* 666–677.

Clark, L. A., & Watson, D. (1999). Temperament: A new paradigm for trait psychology. In L. A. Pervin & O. P. John (Eds.), *Handbook of personality: Theory and research* (pp. 399–423). New York: Guilford Press.

Cloninger, C. R. (1987). A systematic method for clinical description and classification of personality variants: A proposal. *Archives of General Psychiatry, 44,* 573–588.

Cloninger, C. R., Bayon, C., & Svrakic, D. M. (1998). Measurement of temperament and character in mood disorders: A model of fundamental states as personality types. *Journal of Affective Disorders, 51,* 21–32.

Coyne, J. C., & Whiffen, V. E. (1999). Issues in personality as diathesis for depression: The case of sociotropy-dependency and autonomy-self-criticism. *Psychological Bulletin, 118,* 358–378.

Cuijpers, P., & Schoevers, R. A. (2004). Increased mortality in depressive disorders: A review. *Current Psychiatry Report, 6,* 430–437.

Demyttenaere, K., Bruffaerts, R., Posada-Villa, J., Gasquet, I., Kovess, V., Lepine, J. P., et al. (2004). WHO World Mental Health Survey Consortium: Prevalence, severity, and unmet need for treatment of mental disorders in the World Health Organization World Mental Health Surveys. *Journal of the American Medical Association, 291,* 2581–2590.

Depression Guideline Panel. (1993). *Clinical Practice Guideline number 5: Depression in primary care: Vol. 2. Treatment of major depression* (Rep. No. 93–0551). Rockville, MD: U.S. Department of Health and Human Services Agency for Health Care Policy and Research.

Drevets, W. C. (1998). Functional neuroimaging studies of depression: The anatomy of melancholia. *Annual Review of Medicine, 49,* 341–361.

Drevets, W. C. (2000). Functional anatomical abnormalities in limbic and prefrontal cortical structures in major depression. *Progress in Brain Research, 126,* 413–431.

Drevets, W. C., Price, J. L., Bardgett, M. E., Reich, T., Todd, R. D., & Raichle, M. E. (2002). Glucose metabolism in the amygdala in depression: Relationship to diagnostic subtype and plasma cortisol levels. *Pharmacology, Biochemistry & Behavior, 71,* 431–447.

Duman, R. S. (2004). Depression: A case of neuronal life and death? *Biological Psychiatry, 56,* 140–145.

Ellis, B. J., & Garber, J. (2000). Psychosocial antecedents of variation in girls' pubertal timing: Maternal depression, stepfather presence, and marital and family stress. *Child Development, 71,* 485–501.

Endicott, J., & Spitzer, R. L. (1978). A diagnostic interview: The Schedule for Affective Disorders and Schizophrenia. *Archives of General Psychiatry, 35,* 837–844.

Evans, M. D., Hollon, S. D., DeRubeis, R. J., Piasecki, J. M., Grove, W. M., Garvey, M. J., et al. (1992). Differential relapse following cognitive therapy and pharmacotherapy for depression. *Archives of General Psychiatry, 49,* 802–808.

Eysenck, H. J. (1970). The classification of depressive illnesses. *British Journal of Psychiatry, 117,* 241–250.

Farmer, A. (1996). The genetics of depressive disorders. *International Review of Psychiatry, 8,* 372.

Fava, G. A., Rafanelli, C., Grandi, S., Conti, S., & Belluardo, P. (1998). Prevention of recurrent depression with cognitive behavioral therapy: Preliminary findings. *Archives of General Psychiatry, 55,* 816–820.

Fava, M., Alpert, J. E., Carmin, C. N., Wisniewski, S. R., Trivedi, M. H., Biggs, M. M., et al. (2004). Clinical correlates and symptom patterns of anxious depression among patients with major depressive disorder in STAR*D. *Psychological Medicine, 34,* 1299–1308.

Frank, E., Anderson, B., Reynolds, C. F., III, Ritenour, A., & Kupfer, D. J. (1994). Life events and the RDC endogenous subtype: A confirmation of the distinction using the Bedford College methods. *Archives of General Psychiatry, 51,* 519–524.

Frank, E., Prien, R. F., Jarrett, R. B., Keller, M. B., Kupfer, D. J., Lavori, P. W., et al. (1991). Conceptualization and rationale for consensus definitions of terms in major depressive disorder: Remission, recovery, relapse, and recurrence. *Archives of General Psychiatry, 48,* 851–855.

Frank, E., & Thase, M. E. (1999). Natural history and preventative treatment of recurrent mood disorders. In C. H. Coggins, E. W. Hancock, & L. J. Levitt (Eds.), *Annual review of medicine: Selected topics in the clinical sciences* (pp. 453–468). Palo Alto, CA: Annual Reviews.

Frodl, T., Meisenzahl, E. M., Zetzsche, T., Born, C., Groll, C., Jager, M., et al. (2002). Hippocampal changes in patients with a first episode of major depression. *American Journal of Psychiatry, 159,* 1112–1118.

Garber, J., & Horowitz, J. H. (2002). Depression in children. In I. H. Gotlib & C. L. Hammen (Eds.), *Handbook of depression* (pp. 510–540). New York: Guilford Press.

Garlow, S. J., Boone, E., Li, W., Owens, M. J., & Nemeroff, C. B. (2005). Genetic analysis of the hypothalamic corticotropin-releasing factor system. *Endocrinology, 146,* 2362–2368.

Gibbons, R. D., Hur, K., Bhaumik, D. K., & Mann, J. J. (2005). The relationship between antidepressant medication use and rate of suicide. *Archives of General Psychiatry, 62,* 165–172.

Goodman, S. H. (2002). Depression and early adverse experiences. In I. H. Gotlib & C. L. Hammen (Eds.), *Handbook of depression* (pp. 245–267). New York: Guilford Press.

Gotlib, I. H., & Whiffen, V. E. (1989). Depression and marital functioning: An examination of specificity and gender differences. *Journal of Abnormal Psychology, 98,* 23–30.

Graham, Y. P., Heim, C., Goodman, S. H., Miller, A. H., & Nemeroff, C. B. (1999). The effects of neonatal stress on brain development: Implications for psychopathology. *Development and Psychopathology, 11,* 545–565.

Grant, B. F., Hasin, D. S., Chou, S. P., Stinson, F. S., & Cawson, D. A. (2004). Nicotine dependence and psychiatric disorders in the United States: Results from the national epidemiologic survey on alcohol and related conditions. *Archives of General Psychiatry, 61,* 1107–1115.

Grant, B. F., Hasin, D. S., Stinson, F. S., Dawson, D. A., Chou, S. P., Ruan, J. W., et al. (2005) Co-occurrence of 12-month mood and anxiety disorders and personality disorders in the U.S.: Results from the national survey on alcohol and related conditions. *Journal of Psychiatric Research, 39,* 1–9.

Greenberg, P. E., Kessler, R. C., Birnbaum, H. G., Leong, S. A., Lowe, S. W., Berglund, P. A., et al. (2003). The economic burden of depression in the United States: How did it change between 1990 and 2000? *Journal of Clinical Psychiatry, 64,* 1465–1475.

Greenberg, P. E., Stiglin, L. E., Finkelstein, S. N., & Berndt, E. R. (1993). The economic burden of depression in 1990. *Journal of Clinical Psychiatry, 54,* 405–418.

Grunebaum, M. F., Ellis, S. P., Li, S., Oquendo, M. A., & Mann, J. J. (2004). Antidepressants and suicide risk in the United States, 1985–1999. *Journal of Clinical Psychiatry, 65,* 1456–1462.

Gunnell, D., Saperia, J., & Ashby, D. (2005). Selective serotonin reuptake inhibitors (SSRIs) and suicide in adults: Meta-analysis of drug company data from placebo controlled, randomised controlled trials submitted to the MHRA's safety review. *British Medical Journal, 330,* 385.

Guze, S. B., & Robins, E. (1970). Suicide and primary affective disorders. *British Journal of Psychiatry, 117,* 437–438.

Hamilton, M. (1960). A rating scale for depression. *Journal of Neurology, Neurosurgery, and Psychiatry, 23,* 56–62.

Hammen, C., Ellicott, A., Gitlin, M., & Jamison, K. R. (1989). Sociotropy/autonomy and vulnerability to specific life events in patients with unipolar depression and bipolar disorders. *Journal of Abnormal Psychology, 98,* 154–160.

Hammen, C., Shih, J. H., & Brennan, P. A. (2004). Intergenerational transmission of depression: Test of an interpersonal stress model in a community sample. *Journal of Consulting and Clinical Psychology, 72,* 511–522.

Hariri, A. R., Drabant, E. M., Munoz, K. E., Kolachana, L. S., Mattay, V. S., Egan, M. F., et al. (2005). A susceptibility gene for affective disorders and the response of the human amygdala. *Archives of General Psychiatry, 62,* 146–152.

Heim, C., Plotsky, P. M., & Nemeroff, C. B. (2004). Importance of studying the contributions of early adverse experience to neurobiological findings in depression. *Neuropsychopharmacology, 29,* 641–648.

Hettema, J. M., Prescott, C. A., & Kendler, K. S. (2003). The effects of anxiety, substance use and conduct disorders on the risk of major depressive disorder. *Psychological Medicine, 33,* 1423–1432.

Hirschfeld, R. M., Keller, M. B., Panico, S., Arons, B. S., Barlow, D., Davidoff, F., et al. (1997). The National Depressive and Manic-Depressive Association consensus statement on the undertreatment of depression. *Journal of the American Medical Association, 277,* 333–340.

Hirschfeld, R. M. A., Klerman, G. L., Lavori, P., Keller, M. B., Griffith, P., & Coryell, W. (1989). Premorbid personality assessments of first onset of major depression. *Archives of General Psychiatry, 46,* 345–350.

Hollon, S. D., Thase, M. E., & Markowitz, J. C. (2002). Treatment and prevention of depression. *Psychological Science in the Public Interest, 3,* 39–77.

Holsboer, F. (2000). The corticosteroid receptor hypothesis of depression. *Neuropsychopharmacology, 23,* 477–501.

Hooley, J. M., & Gotlib, I. H. (2000). A diathesis-stress conceptualization of expressed emotion and clinical outcome. *Journal of Applied and Preventive Psychology, 9,* 135–151.

Huot, R. L., Gonzalez, M. E., Ladd, C. O., Thrivikraman, K. V., & Plotsky, P. M. (2004). Foster litters prevent hypothalamic-pituitary-adrenal axis sensitization mediated by neonatal maternal separation. *Psychoneuroendocrinology, 29,* 279–289.

Hypericum Depression Trial Study Group. (2002). Effect of *Hypericum perforatum* (St John's wort) in major depressive disorder: A randomized controlled trial. *Journal of the American Medical Association, 287,* 1807–1814.

Inskip, H. M., Harris, E. C., & Barraclough, B. (1998). Lifetime risk of suicide for affective disorder, alcoholism and schizophrenia. *British Journal of Psychiatry, 172,* 35–37.

Isacsson, G., Holmgren, P., & Ahlner, J. (2005). Selective serotonin reuptake inhibitor antidepressants and the risk of suicide: A controlled forensic database study of 14,857 suicides. *Acta Psychiatrica Scandinavica, 111,* 286–290.

Jackson, S. W. (1986). *Melancholia and depression from Hippocratic times to modern times.* New Haven, CT: Yale University Press.

Jarrett, R. B., Kraft, D., Doyle, J., Foster, B. M., Eaves, G. G., & Silver, P. C. (2001). Preventing recurrent depression using cognitive therapy with and without a continuation phase: A randomized clinical trial. *Archives of General Psychiatry, 58,* 381–388.

Joiner, T. E. (2002). Depression in its interpersonal context. In I. H. Gotlib & C. L. Hammen (Eds.), *Handbook of depression* (pp. 295–313). New York: Guilford Press.

Kagan, J., Resnick, J. S., & Snidman, N. (1988). Biological bases of childhood shyness. *Science, 240,* 167–171.

Kane, P., & Garber, J. (2004). The relations among depression in fathers, children's psychopathology, and father-child conflict: A meta-analysis. *Clinical Psychology Review, 24,* 339–360.

Katon, W., & Schulberg, H. (1992). Epidemiology of depression in primary care. *General Hospital Psychiatry, 14,* 237–247.

Keller, M. B. (2003). Past, present, and future directions for defining optimal treatment outcome in depression: Remission and beyond. *Journal of the American Medical Association, 289,* 3152–3160.

Keller, M. B., & Boland, R. J. (1998). Implications of failing to achieve successful long-term maintenance treatment of recurrent unipolar major depression. *Biological Psychiatry, 44,* 348–360.

Keller, M. B., Klein, D. N., Hirschfeld, R. M., Kocsis, J. H., McCullough, J. P., Miller, I., et al. (1995). Results of the *DSM-IV* mood disorders field trial. *American Journal of Psychiatry, 152,* 843–849.

Keller, M. B., Lavori, P. W., Mueller, T. I., Endicott, J., Coryell, W., Hirschfeld, R. M., et al. (1992). Time to recovery, chronicity, and levels of psychopathology in major depression: A 5-year prospective follow-up of 431 subjects. *Archives of General Psychiatry, 49,* 809–816.

Keller, M. B., McCullough, J. P., Klein, D. N., Arnow, B., Dunner, D. L., Gelenberg, A. J., et al. (2000). A comparison of nefazodone, the cognitive behavioral-analysis system of psychotherapy, and their combination for the treatment of chronic depression. *New England Journal of Medicine, 342,* 1462–1470.

Kendler, K. S. (1996). Major depression and generalised anxiety disorder: Same genes, (partly) different environments—Revisited. *British Journal of Psychiatry, 168,* 68–75.

Kendler, K. S. (2001). Twin studies of psychiatric illness: An update. *Archives of General Psychiatry, 58,* 1005–1014.

Kendler, K. S., Aggen, S. H., Jacobson, K. C., & Neale, M. C. (2003). Does the level of family dysfunction moderate the impact of genetic factors on the personality trait of neuroticism? *Psychological Medicine, 33,* 817–825.

Kendler, K. S., Gardner, C. O., & Prescott, C. A. (2002). Toward a comprehensive developmental model for major depression in women. *American Journal of Psychiatry, 159,* 1133–1145.

Kendler, K. S., Hettema, J. M., Butera, F., Gardner, C. O., & Prescott, C. A. (2003). Life event dimensions of loss, humiliation, entrapment, and danger in the prediction of onsets of major depression and generalized anxiety. *Archives of General Psychiatry, 60,* 789–796.

Kendler, K. S., Karkowski, L. M., & Prescott, C. A. (1999). Causal relationship between stressful life events and the onset of major depression. *American Journal of Psychiatry, 156,* 837–841.

Kendler, K. S., Kuhn J. W., & Prescott, C. A. (2004). The interrelationship of neuroticism, sex, and stressful life events in the prediction of episodes of major depression. *American Journal of Psychiatry, 161,* 621–636.

Kendler, K., Neale, M., Kessler, R., Heath, A., & Eaves, L. (1992). Major depression and generalized anxiety disorder. *Archives of General Psychiatry, 49,* 716–722.

Kendler, K. S., Neale, M. C., Kessler, R. C., Heath, A. C., & Eaves, L. J. (1993). A longitudinal twin study of personality and major depression in women. *Archives of General Psychiatry, 50,* 853–862.

Kendler, K. S., Thornton, L. M., & Gardner, C. O. (2000). Stressful life events and previous episodes in the etiology of major depression in women: An evaluation of the "kindling" hypothesis. *American Journal of Psychiatry, 157,* 1243–1251.

Kendler, K. S., Thornton, L. M., & Gardner, C. O. (2001). Genetic risk, number of previous depressive episodes, and stressful life events in predicting onset of major depression. *American Journal of Psychiatry, 158,* 582–586.

Kennedy, S. H., Lam, R. W., Nutt, D. J., & Thase, M. E. (2004). *Treating depression effectively: Applying clinical guidelines.* London: Martin Dunitz.

Kessler, R. C. (2002). Epidemiology of depression. In I. H. Gotlib & C. L. Hammen (Eds.), *Handbook of depression* (pp. 23–42). New York: Guilford Press.

Kessler, R. C., Chiu, W. T., Demler, O., Merikangas, K. R., & Walters, E. E. (2005). Prevalence, severity, and comorbidity of 12-month *DSM-IV* disorders in the National Comorbidity Survey Replication. *Archives of General Psychiatry, 62,* 617–627.

Kessler, R. C., & Frank, R. G. (1997). The impact of psychiatric disorders on work loss days. *Psychological Medicine, 27,* 861–873.

Kessler, R. C., McGonagle, K. A., Swartz, M., Blazer, D. G., & Nelson, C. B. (1993). Sex and depression in the National Comorbidity Survey I: Lifetime prevalence, chronicity, and recurrence. *Journal of Affective Disorders, 29,* 85–96.

Klein, D. F., Thase, M. E., Endicott, J., Adler, L., Glick, I., Kalali, A., et al. (2002). Improving clinical trials: American Society of Clinical Psychopharmacology recommendations. *Archives of General Psychiatry, 59,* 272–278.

Klerman, G. L., & Weissman, M. M. (1989). Increasing rates of depression. *Journal of the American Medical Association, 261,* 2229–2235.

Klerman, G. L., Weissman, M. M., Rounsaville, B. J., & Chevron, E. S. (1984). *Interpersonal psychotherapy of depression.* New York: Basic Books.

Krishnan, K. R. R., Hays, J. C., & Blazer, D. G. (1997). MRI-defined vascular depression. *American Journal of Psychiatry, 154,* 497–501.

Kroenke, K. (2003). Patients presenting with somatic complaints: Epidemiology, psychiatric comorbidity and management. *International Journal of Methods and Psychiatric Research, 12,* 34–43.

Krueger, R. F. (1999). Personality traits in late adolescence predict mental disorders in early adulthood: A prospective-epidemiological study. *Journal of Personality, 67,* 39–65.

Kupfer, D. J. (1991). Long term treatment of depression. *Journal of Clinical Psychiatry, 52*(Suppl. 5), 28–34.

Ladd, C. O., Huot, R. L., Thrivikraman, K. V., Nemeroff, C. B., & Plotsky, P. M. (2004). Long-term adaptations in glucocorticoid receptor and mineralocorticoid receptor mRNA and negative feedback on the hypothalamo-pituitary-adrenal axis following neonatal maternal separation. *Biological Psychiatry, 55,* 367–375.

Laje, R. P., Berman, J. A., & Glassman, A. H. (2001). Depression and nicotine: Preclinical and clinical evidence for common mechanisms. *Current Psychiatry Reports, 3,* 470–474.

Levitan, R. D. (2000). Treatment of atypical depression with cognitive therapy. *Archives of General Psychiatry, 57,* 1084.

Levitan, R. D., Lesage, A., Parikh, S. V., Goering, P., & Kennedy, S. H. (1997). Reversed neurovegetative symptoms of depression: A community study of Ontario. *American Journal of Psychiatry, 154*(7), 934–940.

Lewinsohn, P. M, & Essau, C. A. (2002). Depression in adolescents. In I. H. Gotlib & C. L. Hammen (Eds.), *Handbook of depression* (pp. 541–559). New York: Guilford Press.

Licinio, J., & Wong, M. L. (2005). Depression, antidepressants and suicidality: A critical appraisal. *National Reviews Drug Discovery, 4,* 165–171.

Liotti, M., & Mayberg, H. S. (2001). The role of functional neuroimaging in the neuropsychology of depression. *Journal of Clinical and Experimental Neuropsychology, 123,* 121–136.

Lyons, D. M., Yang, C., Sawyer-Glover, A. M., Moseley, M. E., & Schatzberg, A. F. (2001). Early life stress and inherited variation in monkey hippocampal volumes. *Archives of General Psychiatry, 58,* 1145–1151.

Maier, W., Lichtermann, D., Minges, J., Heun, R., Hallmayer, J., & Klingler, T. (1991). Unipolar depression in the aged: Determinants of familial aggregation. *Journal of Affective Disorders, 23,* 53–61.

Malhi, G. S., Moore, J., & McGuffin, P. (2000). The genetics of major depressive disorder. *Current Psychiatry Reports, 2,* 169.

March, J., Silva, S., Petrycki, S., Curry, J., Wells, K., Fairbank, J., et al. (2004). Fluoxetine, cognitive-behavioral therapy, and their combination for adolescents with depression: Treatment for Adolescents with Depression Study (TADS) randomized controlled trial. *Journal of the American Medical Association, 292,* 807–820.

Mazure, C. M. (1998). Life stressors as risk factors in depression. *Clinical Psychology, Science and Practice, 5,* 291–313.

McCullough, J. P., Klein, D. N., Keller, M. B., Holzer, C. E. I., Davis, S. M., Kornstein, S. G., et al. (2000). Comparison of *DSM-III-R* chronic major depression and major depression superimposed on dysthymia (double depression): Validity of the distinction. *Journal of Abnormal Psychology, 109,* 419–427.

McGuffin, P., Katz, R., & Rutherford, J. (1991). Nature, nurture and depression: A twin study. *Psychological Medicine, 21,* 329–335.

Monroe, S. M., & Hadjiyannakis, K. (2002). The social environment and depression: Focusing on severe life stress. In I. H. Gotlib & C. L. Hammen (Eds.), *Handbook of depression* (pp. 314–340). New York: Guilford Press.

Mulsant, B. H., Haskett, R. F., Prudic, J., Thase, M. E., Malone, K. M., Mann, J. J., et al. (1997). Low use of neuroleptic drugs in the treatment of psychotic major depression. *American Journal of Psychiatry, 154,* 559–561.

Murray, C. J. L., & Lopez, A. D. (1996). Evidence-based health policy: Lessons from the Global Burden of Disease Study. *Science, 274,* 740–741.

Mynors-Wallis, L. M., Gath, D. H., Day, A., & Baker, F. (2000). Randomised controlled trial of problem solving treatment, antidepressant medication, and combined treatment for major depression in primary care. *British Medical Journal, 320,* 26–30.

Nemeroff, C. B. (2004). Early-life adversity, CRF dysregulation, and vulnerability to mood and anxiety disorders. *Psychopharmacology Bulletin, 38,* 14–20.

Newport, D. J., Heim, C., Owens, M. J., Ritchie, J. C., Ramsey, C. H., Bonsall, R., et al. (2003). Cerebrospinal fluid corticotropin-releasing factor (CRF) and vasopressin concentrations predict pituitary response in the CRF stimulation test: A multiple regression analysis. *Neuropsychopharmacology, 28,* 569–576.

Nezu, A. M., Maguth Nezu, C., McClure, K. S., & Zwick, M. L. (2002). Assessment of depression. In I. H. Gotlib & C. L. Hammen (Eds.), *Handbook of depression* (pp. 61–85). New York: Guilford Press.

Nolen-Hoeksema, S. (2002). Gender differences in depression. In I. H. Gotlib & C. L. Hammen (Eds.), *Handbook of depression* (pp. 492–509). New York: Guilford Press.

Nolen-Hoeksema, S., & Girgus, J. S. (1994). The emergence of gender difference in depression in adolescence. *Psychological Bulletin, 115,* 443.

Olfson, M., Shaffer, D., Marcus, S. C., & Greenberg, T. (2003). Relationship between antidepressant medication treatment and suicide in adolescents. *Archives of General Psychiatry, 60,* 978–982.

Parker, G., Roy, K., Mitchell, P., Wilhelm, K., Malhi, G., & Hadzi-Pavlovic, D. (2002). Atypical depression: A reappraisal. *American Journal of Psychiatry, 159,* 1470–1479.

Paykel, E. S., Scott, J., Teasdale, J. D., Johnson, A. L., Garland, A., Moore, R., et al. (1999). Prevention of relapse in residual depression by cognitive therapy: A controlled trial. *Archives of General Psychiatry, 56,* 829–835.

Post, R. M. (1992). Transduction of psychosocial stress into the neurobiology of recurrent affective disorder. *American Journal of Psychiatry, 149,* 999–1010.

Quitkin, F. M., Stewart, J. W., McGrath, P. J., Tricamo, E., Rabkin, J. G., Ocepek-Welikson, K., et al. (1993). Columbia atypical depression: A subgroup of depressives with better response to MAOI than to tricyclic antidepressants or placebo. *British Journal of Psychiatry, 163,* 30–34.

Regier, D. A., Farmer, M. E., Rae, D. S., Locke, B. Z., Keith, S. J., Judd, L. L., et al. (1990). Comorbidity of mental disorders with alcohol and other drug abuse. Results from the Epidemiologic Catchment Area (ECA) Study. *Journal of the American Medical Association, 264,* 2511–2518.

Reich, J. H., & Green, A. I. (1991). Effect of personality disorders on outcome of treatment. *Journal of Nervous and Mental Disease, 179,* 74–82.

Robins, L. N., Helzer, J. E., & Ratcliff, K. S. (1981). National Institute of Mental Health Diagnostic Interview Schedule. Its history, characteristics, and validity. *Archives of General Psychiatry, 38,* 381–389.

Roose, S. P., Glassman, A. H., & Seidman, S. N. (2001). Relationship between depression and other medical illnesses. *Journal of the American Medical Association, 286,* 1687–1690.

Rosenbaum, J. F., Biederman, J., & Hirshfeld-Becker, D. R. (2000). A controlled study of behavioral inhibition in children of parents with panic disorder and depression. *American Journal of Psychiatry, 157,* 2002–2010.

Roy, M. A., Neale, M. C., Pedersen, N. L., Mathe, A. A., & Kendler, K. S. (1995). A twin study of generalized anxiety disorder and major depression. *Psychological Medicine, 25,* 1037–1049.

Rush, A. J., Gullion, C. M., Basco, M. R., Jarrett, R. B., & Trivedi, M. H. (1996). The Inventory of Depressive Symptomatology (IDS): Psychometric properties. *Psychological Medicine, 26,* 477–486.

Rush, A. J., Trivedi, M. H., Ibrahim, H. M., Carmody, T. J., Arnow, B., Klein, D. N., et al. (2003). The 16-item Quick Inventory of Depressive Symptomatology (QIDS), Clinician Rating (QIDS-C), and Self-Report (QIDS-SR): A psychometric evaluation in patients with chronic major depression. *Biological Psychiatry, 54,* 573–583.

Rush, A. J., & Weissenburger, J. E. (1994). Melancholic symptom features and *DSM-IV. American Journal of Psychiatry, 151,* 489–498.

Sackeim, H. A., Haskett, R. F., Mulsant, B. H., Thase, M. E., Mann, J. J., Pettinati, H. M., et al. (2001). Continuation pharmacotherapy in the prevention of relapse following electroconvulsive therapy: A randomized controlled trial. *Journal of the American Medical Association, 285,* 1299–1307.

Sanathara, V. A., Gardner, C. O., Prescott, C. A., & Kendler, K. S. (2003). Interpersonal dependence and major depression: Aitiological inter-relationship and gender differences. *Psychological Medicine, 33,* 927–931.

Sapolsky, R. M. (2000). Glucocorticoids and hippocampal atrophy in neuropsychiatric disorders. *Archives of General Psychiatry, 57,* 925–935.

Schatzberg, A. F., & Rothschild, A. J. (1992). Psychotic (delusional) major depression: Should it be included as a distinct syndrome in *DSM-IV? American Journal of Psychiatry, 149,* 733–745.

Segal, Z. V., Vella, D. D., Shaw, B. F., & Katz, R. (1992). Cognitive and life stress predictors of relapse in remitted unipolar depressed patients: Test of the congruency hypothesis. *Journal of Abnormal Psychology, 101,* 26–36.

Segal, Z. V., Williams, J. M., Teasdale, J. D., & Gemar, M. (1996). A cognitive science perspective on kindling and episode sensitization in recurrent affective disorder. *Psychological Medicine, 26,* 371–380.

Segrin, C. (2000). Social skills deficits associated with depression. *Clinical Psychology Review, 22,* 379–403.

Shelton, R. C., Keller, M. B., Gelenberg, A., Dunner, D. L., Hirschfeld, R., Thase, M. E., et al. (2001). Effectiveness of St. John's wort in major depression: A randomized controlled trial. *Journal of the American Medical Association, 285,* 1978–1986.

Shwartz, C. E., Wright, C. I., Shin, L. M., Kagan, J., & Rauch, S. L. (2003). Inhibited and uninhibited infants "grown up": Adult amygdalar response to novelty. *Science, 300*(5627), 1952–1953.

Shea, M. T., Elkin, I., Imber, S. D., Sotsky, S. M., Watkins, J. T., Collins, J. F., et al. (1992). Course of depressive symptoms over follow-up: Findings from the National Institute of Mental Health Treatment of Depression Collaborative Research Program. *Archives of General Psychiatry, 49,* 782–787.

Shea, M. T., Widiger, T. A., & Klein, M. H. (1992). Comorbidity of personality disorders and depression: Implications for treatment. *Journal of Consulting and Clinical Psychology, 60,* 857–868.

Sheehan, D. V., Lecrubier, Y., Sheehan, K. H., Amorim, P., Janavs, J., Weiller, E., et al. (1998). The Mini-International Neuropsychiatric Interview (M.I.N.I.): The development and validation of a structured diagnostic psychiatric interview for *DSM-IV* and *ICD-10. Journal of Clinical Psychiatry, 59*(Suppl. 20), 22–33.

Sheline, Y. I., Gado, M. H., & Kraemer, H. C. (2003). Untreated depression and hippocampal volume loss. *American Journal of Psychiatry, 160,* 1516–1518.

Simon, G. E., Barber, C., Birnbaum, H. G., Frank, R. G., Greenberg, P. E., Rose, R. M., et al. (2001). Depression and work productivity: The comparative costs of treatment versus nontreatment. *Journal of Occupational and Environmental Medicine, 43,* 2–9.

Simons, A. D., Murphy, G. E., & Levine, J. L. (1986). Relapse after treatment with cognitive therapy and/or pharmacotherapy: Results after one year. *Archives of General Psychiatry, 43,* 43–48.

Smith, D., Dempster, C., Glanville, J., Freemantle, N., & Anderson, I. (2001). Efficacy and tolerability of venlafaxine compared with selective serotonin reuptake inhibitors and other antidepressants: A meta-analysis. *British Journal of Psychiatry, 180,* 396–404.

Spinelli, M. G. (2004). Maternal infanticide associated with mental illness: Prevention and the promise of saved lives. *American Journal of Psychiatry, 161,* 1548–1557.

Spitzer, R. L., Williams, J. B., Gibbon, M., & First, M. B. (1992). The Structured Clinical Interview for *DSM-III-R* (SCID): I. History, rationale, and description. *Archives of General Psychiatry, 49,* 624–629.

Spitzer, R. L., Williams, J. B. W., Kroenke, K., Linzer, M., deGruy, F. V., III, Hahn, S. R., et al. (1994). Utility of a new procedure for diagnosing mental disorders in primary care: The prime-MD 1000 study. *Journal of the American Medical Association, 272,* 1749–1756.

Steffens, D. C., Taylor, W. D., & Krishnan, K. R. (2003). Progression of subcortical ischemic disease from vascular depression to vascular dementia. *American Journal of Psychiatry, 160,* 1751–1756.

Stewart, J. W., McGrath, P. J., Rabkin, J. G., & Quitkin, F. M. (1993). Atypical depression: A valid clinical entity? *Psychiatric Clinics of North America, 16,* 479–495.

Sullivan, E. V., Pfefferbaum, A., Swan, G. E., & Carmelli, D. (2001). Heritability of hippocampal size in elderly twin men: Equivalent influence from genes and environment. *Hippocampus, 11,* 754–762.

Sullivan, P. F., Neale, M. C., & Kendler, K. S. (2000). Genetic epidemiology of major depression: Review and meta-analysis. *American Journal of Psychiatry, 157,* 1552–1562.

Sullivan, P. F., Prescott, C. A., & Kendler, K. S. (2002). The subtypes of major depression in a twin registry. *Journal of Affective Disorders, 68,* 273–284.

Thapar, A., Harold, G., & McGuffin, P. (1998). Life events and depressive symptoms in childhood: Shared genes or shared adversity? A research note. *Journal of Child Psychology & Psychiatry, 39,* 1153–1158.

Thase, M. E. (2000). Treatment of severe depression. *Journal of Clinical Psychiatry, 61,* 17–25.

Thase, M. E. (2001). Depression-focused psychotherapies. In G. O. Gabbard (Ed.), *Treatment of psychiatric disorders* (3rd ed., pp. 1181–1227). Washington, DC: American Psychiatric Press.

Thase, M. E. (2004). Therapeutic alternatives for difficult-to-treat depression: A narrative review of the state of the evidence. *CNS Spectrums, 9,* 808–821.

Thase, M. E., Entsuah, A. R., & Rudolph, R. L. (2001). Remission rates during treatment with venlafaxine or selective serotonin reuptake inhibitors. *British Journal of Psychiatry, 178,* 234–241.

Thase, M. E., Greenhouse, J. B., Frank, E., Reynolds, C. F., III, Pilkonis, P. A., Hurley, K., et al. (1997). Treatment of major depression with psychotherapy or psychotherapy-pharmacotherapy combinations. *Archives of General Psychiatry, 54,* 1009–1015.

Thase, M. E., Jindal, R. D., & Howland, R. H. (2002). Biological aspects of depression. In I. H. Gotlib & C. L. Hammen (Eds.), *Handbook of depression* (pp. 192–218). New York: Guilford Press.

Thase, M. E., & Kupfer, D. J. (1996). Recent developments in the pharmacotherapy of mood disorders. *Journal of Consulting and Clinical Psychology, 64,* 646–659.

Thase, M. E., Simons, A. D., McGeary, J., Cahalane, J. F., Hughes, C., Harden, T., et al. (1992). Relapse after cognitive behavior therapy of depression: Potential implications for longer courses of treatment? *American Journal of Psychiatry, 149,* 1046–1052.

Thase, M. E., Trivedi, M. H., & Rush, A. J. (1995). MAOIs in the contemporary treatment of depression. *Neuropsychopharmacology, 12,* 185–219.

Trivedi, M. H., Rush, A. J., Ibrahim, H. M., Carmody, T. J., Biggs, M. M., Suppes, T., et al. (2004). The Inventory of Depressive Symptomatology, Clinician Rating (IDS-C) and Self-Report (IDS-SR), and the Quick Inventory of Depressive Symptomatology, Clinician Rating (QIDS-C) and Self-Report (QIDS-SR) in public sector patients with mood disorders: A psychometric evaluation. *Psychological Medicine, 34,* 73–82.

UK ECT Review Group. (2003). Efficacy and safety of electroconvulsive therapy in depressive disorders: A systematic review and meta-analysis. *Lancet, 361,* 799–808.

Wade, T. D., & Kendler, K. S. (2000). The relationship between social support and major depression: Cross-sectional, longitudinal, and genetic perspectives. *Journal of Nervous and Mental Disease, 188,* 251–258.

Wallace, J., Schneider, T., & McGuffin, P. (2002). Genetics of depression. In I. H. Gotlib & C. L. Hammen (Eds.), *Handbook of depression* (pp. 169–191). New York: Guilford Press.

Wang, P. S., Beck, A. L., Berglund, P., McKenas, D. K., Pronk, N. P., Simon, G. E., et al. (2004). Effects of major depression on moment-in-time work performance. *American Journal of Psychiatry, 161,* 1885–1891.

Weiss, J. M., & Simpson, P. E. (1988). Neurochemical and electrophysiological events underlying stress-induced depression in an animal model. *Advances in Experimental and Medical Biology, 245,* 425–440.

Weissman, M. M., Bland, R. C., Canino, G. J., Faravelli, C., Greenwald, S., Hwu, H. G., et al. (1996). Cross-national epidemiology of major depression and bipolar disorder. *Journal of the American Medical Association, 276,* 293–299.

Weissman, M. M., Leaf, P. J., Tischler, G. L., Blazer, D. G., Karno, M., Bruce. M. L., et al. (1988). Affective disorders in five United States communities. *Psychological Medicine, 18,* 141–153.

Weissman, M. M., Wickramaratne, P., Nomura, Y., Warner, V., Verdeli, H., Pilowsky, D. J., et al. (2005). Families at high and low risk for depression: A 3-generation study. *Archives of General Psychiatry, 62,* 29–36.

Wells, K. B., Hays, R. D., Burnam, M. A., Rogers, W., Greenfield, S., & Ware, J. E., Jr. (1989). Detection of depressive disorder for patients receiving prepaid or fee-for-service care: Results from the medical outcomes study. *Journal of the American Medical Association, 262,* 3298–3302.

Willner, P. (1997). Validity, reliability and utility of the chronic mild stress model of depression: A 10-year review and evaluation. *Psychopharmacology (Berl), 134,* 319–329.

Wittchen, H. U., Knauper, B., & Kessler, R. C. (1994). Lifetime risk of depression. *British Journal of Psychiatry, 165*(Suppl. 26), 16–22.

Wong, I. C., Besag, F. M. C., Santosh, P. J., & Murray, M. L. (2004). Use of selective serotonin reuptake inhibitors in children and adolescents. *Drug Safety, 27,* 991–1000.

Zubenko, G. S., Maher, B. S., Hughes, H. B., III, Zubenko, W. N., Stiffler, S., & Marazita, M. L. (2004). Genome-wide linkage survey for genetic loci that affect the risk of suicide attempts in families with recurrent, early-onset, major depression. *American Journal of Medical Genetics Part B: Neuropsychiatric Genetics, 129B,* 47–54.

CHAPTER 14

Dysthymia and Minor Depression

KAREN B. SCHMALING AND DOLORES V. HERNANDEZ

DESCRIPTION OF THE DISORDER AND CLINICAL PICTURE

The current psychiatric nosological and diagnostic systems such as the fourth edition of the *Diagnostic and Statistical Manual of Mental Disorders* (*DSM-IV;* American Psychiatric Association [APA], 1994) and the tenth edition of the *International Classification of Diseases* (*ICD-10;* World Health Organization, 1992) place the depressive disorders among the larger class of mood disorders. Generally, mood disorders can be categorized into those that emphasize the dysphoric end of the mood spectrum, also known as unipolar disorders, those that emphasize the euphoric end of the mood spectrum, and those that include both. The focus of this chapter is on the chronic (dysthymic disorder) and minor unipolar disorders. Within the depressive disorders, dysthymic disorder (DD) and minor depressive (MD) disorders have been the focus of much less attention than major depressive disorder (MDD). For example, a PubMed search using the term *major depression* will result in more than 11,000 matches, whereas the terms *dysthymia* or *minor depression* will result in about one-tenth the number of matches (approximately 1,100 and 1,900, respectively). Although the relative emphasis on MDD is intuitively compelling—it is generally regarded as a more acute, and therefore disabling, disorder—there are many reasons to be concerned about the appearance of DD or clinically significant depressive symptoms. MDD and DD/MD overlap in terms of symptoms, and DD/MD often occurs before the onset of MDD, simultaneously with it, and may characterize interepisode status. For these reasons, throughout the discussion that follows, when data specific to DD/MD are lacking, the literature on MDD is used to inform our understanding of DD/MD. But this phenomenon of the relative emphasis on MDD in the literature is not well justified based on extant empirical evidence regarding the impact of DD and MD, as we will discuss.

DSM-IV and *ICD-10* Diagnostic Criteria

According to the *DSM-IV,* DD is characterized by at least two years of depressed mood for the majority of the time, accompanied by two or more of the following symptoms during the same period: poor appetite or overeating; insomnia or hypersomnia; low energy or fatigue; low self-esteem; poor concentration or difficulty making decisions; or feelings of hopelessness (APA, 1994). It has been noted that there is sparse evidence that the vegetative symptoms included among the DD criteria are central and essential features of the syndrome (Gwirtsman, Blehar, McCullough, Kocsis, & Prien, 1997). As we will discuss in a later section, the vegetative symptoms among the DD diagnostic criteria are key to its discrimination from depressive personality disorder (DPD). An alternative set of diagnostic criteria for DD has been proposed for further study in *DSM-IV.* The alternative criteria set does not include two of the vegetative symptoms in the current *DSM-IV* criteria (appetite/eating and insomnia/hypersomnia criteria) and adds anhedonia, social withdrawal, guilt and brooding, irritability or excess anger, and decreased activity, productivity, or effectiveness to the criteria set.

It is important to assess and characterize the onset of DD as compared to any major depressive episodes. Dysthymia should predate the onset of a major depressive episode (MDE) by at least two years, after which time an MDE may be superimposed on dysthymia. If an MDE precedes the development of dysthymia, the person should evidence full remission of the MDE for at least two months before the onset of dysthymia. If these conditions are not met, an MDD in partial remission or chronic MDD may be more appropriate characterizations of the patient's symptoms.

Like the *DSM-IV,* the foremost and "essential feature" of DD in *ICD-10* is long-standing depressed mood (World Health Organization, 1992). Associated features include fatigue, lack of interest or pleasure, insomnia, brooding, complaining, and low self-esteem. In short, the *DSM-IV* and *ICD-10* criteria for DD are similar.

Dysthymic Disorder Specifiers

In addition to meeting the basic diagnostic criteria for DD, there are three diagnostic specifiers in the *DSM-IV* that are important to identify as they may have important implications for the course of the disorder and its outcome. The *Early Onset* specifier is used for persons whose DD symptoms appeared to begin before 21 years of age. The *Late Onset* specifier is used for persons whose DD symptoms began after 21 years of age. The *With Atypical Features* specifier is used if in the most recent two years of the disorder there is evidence of mood reactivity (mood improves in response to positive events) and there are two or more of the following symptoms: significant weight gain or increase in appetite (DD diagnostic criteria emphasize appetite increase whereas MDE diagnostic criteria emphasize actual weight gain), hypersomnia, leaden paralysis, or interpersonal rejection sensitivity to the extent that social or occupational impairment result.

As most persons with DD will develop episodes of major depression, and each episode of major depression increases the likelihood of subsequent episodes of major depression, an early onset of DD bodes ill for a chronic and disabling course of illness (e.g., Kovacs, Akiskal, Gatsonis, & Parrone, 1994). In addition, it appears particularly difficult to discriminate early-onset DD with DPD or other personality disorders. Stated otherwise, early-onset DD is likely to be associated with multiple Axis I and II comorbid conditions. Although research on the effects of the presence of atypical features on illness course and treatment outcomes has been limited, there is some evidence that atypical features are associated with a more chronic course accompanied by greater functional impairment than illness with non-atypical features (e.g., Agosti & Stewart, 2001).

Minor Depressive Disorder

MD is a set of diagnostic criteria proposed for further study in the *DSM-IV*. MD is characterized by depressive symptoms of the same duration as MDD (two weeks or longer), but has fewer symptoms (two to four symptoms, whereas MDD requires the concurrent presence of five or more) and clinically significant distress or impairment that is less than the distress or impairment associated with MDD. Among accepted diagnoses in the *DSM-IV* nomenclature, symptoms that meet criteria for MD would be appropriately labeled as depressive disorder not otherwise specified (NOS) unless the symptoms occur in response to a psychosocial stress, in which case adjustment disorder with depressed mood would be the more appropriate diagnosis.

Differential Diagnosis

As indicated previously, MDD is characterized by more symptoms that are considered more severe than those observed among persons with DD or MD. Adjustment disorder with depressed mood is characterized by a set of symptoms that begin within three months of a stressor and last no longer than six months after the end of the stressor. Depressive symptoms that persist long after the termination of a stressor may be better characterized as DD, MD, or other depressive disorder, depending on the nature, severity, and number of symptoms.

For both DD and MD, it is important to exclude other conditions or the use of substances that could account for the symptoms, such as schizophrenia, certain medical conditions such as hypothyroidism or pancreatic cancer, or the use of alcohol or sedatives.

Functional Status

An important part of the clinical picture of DD/MD is the morbidity and functional decrements associated with these disorders. DD is distinguished from MDD by the lack of clearly demarcated episodes of severe depressive symptoms seen in the former condition. Partially because of its insidious onset and long-term course, persons with DD may appear relatively "adjusted" to their condition—that is, appear to live with their symptoms more easily than persons with MDD. However, large studies of functional status have revealed that persons with DD have poorer status in several realms of functioning than do persons with MDD. For example, studies using the Medical Outcomes Study Short Form-36, a widely used 36-item self-report measure of functional status in eight domains, have found that persons with DD scored significantly below the normal range across all functional arenas, including measures of physical functional status, that were lower (worse) than persons with MDD on all measures except role (emotional) functioning (Hays, Wells, Sherbourne, Rogers, & Spritzer, 1995). Furthermore, at two-year follow-up, persons with DD at the index evaluation had worse outcomes than persons with MDD (Wells, Burnam, Rogers, Hays, & Camp, 1992). In the Hays et al. (1995) study, persons with "subthreshold depression," who may have met *DSM-IV* criteria for depression NOS or MD, also scored below the normal range on all realms of functional status. Patients with depression NOS had lengths of illness, and levels of symptoms and functional status that were as long and impaired as patients with MDD (Furukawa et al., 2000). Two years later, their functional status was better than persons with DD or

MDD, but below the normal range, and about one-quarter had developed incident cases of MDD.

Taken together, this literature suggests that clinicians should be alert for DD/MD, and intervene in a timely fashion to curtail the negative consequences of these conditions as much as possible.

PERSONALITY DEVELOPMENT AND PSYCHOPATHOLOGY

The associations between temperament, personality traits, personality disorders, and DD/MD have been issues of considerable interest, particularly as DD/MD and depressive personality disorder (DPD) may be components in a spectrum of depressive disorders. Temperament may be defined as a set of innate tendencies, including characteristic behavioral and mood arousal and reactivity levels. Personality traits are thought to be shaped over time by temperament ←→ environment interactions. Personality disorders are characterized by long-standing and pervasive dysfunctional intra- and interpersonal patterns.

Relevant typologies include Cloninger's (1987) three factor model of harm avoidance, reward dependence, and novelty seeking. Although sometimes referred to as a personality typology, Cloninger's model may be closer to a typology of temperament because, consistent with the notion that temperament has genetic/biological components, Cloninger and others have suggested that these three factors have unique associations with different biological substrates (i.e., neurotransmitters and, by association, psychiatric disorders). Harm avoidance, putatively associated with serotonin, includes tendencies to be inhibited, shy, withdrawn, and timid. Harm avoidance and neuroticism have been strongly associated with depressive disorders including DD and DPD (Lyoo, Gunderson, & Phillips, 1998), shown to decrease in response to treatment for DD (Dunner et al., 1996; Hellerstein, Kocsis, Chapman, Stewart, & Harrison, 2000), and predicted poor response to treatment for DD (Abrams et al., 2004).

A review of major personality theories is beyond the scope of this article, so the focus here is on typologies of personality that have been examined vis-à-vis persons with DD/MD. The Five-Factor Model of Costa and McRae (1991) includes neuroticism, extraversion, openness, agreeableness, and conscientiousness. Of particular importance in our understanding of DD/MD is neuroticism: individuals high on neuroticism are characterized by tendencies to experience a variety of negative emotions, maladjustment, and emotional instability. The concept of neuroticism is similar to that of negative affectivity (Watson & Clark, 1984). Not surprisingly, then, neuroticism is particularly associated with depressive disorders (Klein & Santiago, 2003; McCullough et al., 1994; Watson & Clark, 1984). Among persons with DD, poorer outcomes have been associated with high neuroticism in naturalistic studies (Hayden & Klein, 2001) and treatment outcome studies (Katon et al., 2002) and also among those with MD (Oxman et al., 2001).

Personality disorders are characterized by the presence of a pervasive pattern of dysfunctional intra- and interpersonal behaviors that occur in a variety of contexts. The proposed diagnostic criteria for DPD in the *DSM-IV* include a pervasive pattern of five or more depressive cognitions and behaviors: dejected, gloomy, cheerless, and/or unhappy usual mood; self-concept reflects inadequacy, worthlessness, and/or low self-esteem; self-critical, self-derogatory, and/or blaming; brooding and worrying; negativistic, critical, and judgmental toward others; pessimistic; feeling guilty and remorseful (APA, 1994). In terms of the differential diagnosis of DPD and DD, the *DSM-IV* emphasizes cognitive content, interpersonal and intrapsychic traits in DPD. By contrast, DD diagnostic criteria emphasize appetite, sleep, energy, and cognitive functioning symptoms—classic vegetative symptoms typically associated with Axis I depressive disorders. Dysphoria, poor self-esteem, and hopelessness or pessimism are symptoms that overlap between DPD and DD. DPD should not be used if the symptoms are better accounted for by DD, for example, if the appetite, sleep, and energy symptoms prevail in the clinical picture.

At least one longitudinal study of women with and without DPD with no comorbid Axis I or II disorders found that women with DPD were significantly (more than 4.5 times) more likely to develop DD than women without DPD over a three-year follow-up; the groups did not differ in the likelihood of developing major depression (Kwon et al., 2000). This study (Kwon et al., 2000) and others (e.g., Phillips et al., 1998) have identified persons who meet DPD criteria without DD or other depressive disorders, suggesting an ability to make meaningful distinctions between DPD and DD. However, the *DSM-IV* notes that the distinction between DPD and DD may not be valid or useful. Some investigators have found "modest overlap" (e.g., Klein & Shih, 1998; McDermut, Zimmerman, & Chelminski, 2003), whereas others have found few or no clinically significant differences between the disorders (e.g., Bagby & Ryder, 1999). The degree of overlap versus distinctiveness between DPD, DD, and other depressive disorders, and the clinical utility of these distinctions, is an issue for future research. Given that both DPD and DD require symptoms that address physical, cognitive, and interpersonal realms, it is logically appealing that persons who appear to meet criteria for both disorders are likely to be more globally impaired than persons with one or the other disorder.

The co-occurrence of DD and other personality disorders appears to be common, particularly with cluster B (dramatic-emotional) or C (anxious-fearful) personality disorders and among those with DD with early onset (e.g., Garyfallos et al., 1999). The overlap of an early-onset and chronic Axis I disorder such as DD and an Axis II disorder is not surprising. One or more common factors may underlie the development of DD/MD and the cluster B or C disorders, including shared biological or genetic, temperamental, or environmental events (e.g., Klein & Schwartz, 2002).

EPIDEMIOLOGY

The *DSM-IV* places the lifetime prevalence of dysthymic disorder at 6 percent, and the six-month point prevalence at 3 percent (APA, 1994). The *DSM-IV* does not give prevalence estimates for depressive disorder NOS or the proposed minor depressive disorder, probably because of the inherent variability in the former, which would make reliable prevalence estimates difficult, and the provisional nature of the latter, which is linked with limited focused research (APA, 1994).

Population-based prevalence estimates for DD and other psychiatric disorders are generally based on a few large studies, such as the National Comorbidity Study (NCS) and the Epidemiological Catchment Area Study (ECA). The NCS placed the lifetime prevalence of DD at 6.4 percent and the 12-month point prevalence at 2.5 percent, with women being nearly twice as likely as men to meet diagnostic criteria (Kessler et al., 1994). A more recent population-based survey of younger adults aged 17 to 39 years obtained similar lifetime prevalence estimates for DD of 6.2 percent (Jonas, Brody, Roper, & Narrow, 2003). In more selected populations, such as primary care, the prevalence increases. For example, Browne et al. (1999) found a 5.1 percent point prevalence for DD in primary care.

Although prevalence estimates for clinically significant depressive symptoms are not as frequently reported, the ECA data revealed a lifetime prevalence of 23.1 percent of its participants for depressive symptoms (symptoms in two of the four *DSM-III* depressive symptom groups; Johnson, Weissman, & Klerman, 1992), and a 41 percent six-month prevalence of one or more depressive symptoms (Crum, Cooper-Patrick, & Ford, 1994).

In addition to women being more likely than men to meet criteria for DD/MD, like other depressive disorders, DD appears to be more prevalent among younger adults than among older adults (e.g., Weissman, Leaf, Bruce, & Florio, 1988).

Studies of the prevalence of depressive disorders among racial and ethnic groups have largely focused on major depression. The prevalence of DD/MD is likely to be folded into a category termed *other depression,* so data from such categories cannot be considered as direct and "clean" prevalence estimates as methods that specifically assessed for the presence of DD/MD. For example, in both population-based and mental health outpatient studies, African Americans appear to be less likely to have lifetime affective disorders than non-Latino Whites (Kessler et al., 1994; Minsky, Vega, Miskimen, Gara, & Escobar, 2003, respectively), with Latinos being somewhat but not significantly less likely to have depressive disorders than non-Latinos.

Taken together, these studies suggest that DD and depressive symptoms are very common, with more than one in four adults experiencing DD or clinically significant depressive symptoms at one or more times in their life, and women generally being about twice as likely as men to experience clinically significant depressive symptoms and DD or MD.

ETIOLOGY

In this section, we review briefly the major models of the etiology of psychiatric disorders as they relate to DD/MD: biological/genetic contributions; cognitive-behavioral models; and interpersonal/psychodynamic models. It should again be noted that none of these major models has explicated a specific variant regarding the etiology of DD/MD, but the following descriptions are generally applicable to the spectrum of unipolar depressive disorders.

Biological-Genetic Factors

Like other depressive disorders, there is evidence for family histories and genetic contributions of depressive disorders in DD/MD (Akiskal et al., 1980; Klein et al., 1995), especially among persons with early onset DD compared to late-onset DD (for a review, see Klein & Santiago, 2003; see also Devanand et al., 1994, 2004). Klein et al. (1995) found significantly higher rates of MDD among first-degree relatives of persons with DD compared to control participants without psychiatric disorders. In addition, there was evidence that DD may aggregate in families: DD was significantly more likely among first-degree relatives of DD probands than first-degree relatives of persons with MDE or nonpsychiatric controls (Klein et al., 1995). Finally, there is an extensive literature on the degree of heritability of MDD, for which at least 40 percent is typically attributable to genetic factors (see meta-analysis by Sullivan, Neale, & Kendler, 2000), but studies have not specifically examined the heritability of DD/MD.

We discussed earlier Cloninger's typology in which harm avoidance tendencies are putatively linked to serotonin and depressive disorders. However unlike MDD, abnormalities of serotonergic functioning have not been consistently found in DD (for a review, see Riso, Miyatake, & Thase, 2002).

Cognitive-Behavioral Models

According to cognitive models of depression, dysfunctional interpretations of life events give rise to negative moods. Depressives' characteristic interpretations may be dominated by pessimism and hopelessness (e.g., Abramson, Metalsky, & Alloy, 1989) or other negative views that are global, stable, and internal (e.g., "I'm an unlovable person so I will never succeed or be happy"; Beck, 1967).

Behavior theories of depression posit that decreased reinforcement in the environment brings on and maintains depressive symptoms through inactivity and avoidance that further decreases opportunities for reinforcement (e.g., Ferster, 1973; Martell, Addis, & Jacobson, 2001).

Interpersonal and Psychodynamic Factors

Coyne (1976) suggested that interactions with a depressed person are inherently aversive because of the depressed person's unhappiness. Significant others may try to "cheer up" the depressed individual, which may be experienced as invalidating and only serve to escalate the depressive person's expressions of depressed mood and depressive cognitions. In time, significant others may withdraw and avoid the depressed person when they cannot successfully improve their mood, leading the depressed individual to be correct in their predictions about being unlovable and rejected by others.

Psychodynamic views of depression emphasize intrapsychic factors related to pre-Oedipal fixations thought to result from inconsistent parenting, with depressive symptoms being related internalized anger and disappointments (e.g., Becker, 1974).

COURSE, COMPLICATIONS, AND PROGNOSIS

Course, Prognosis, and Outcomes

DD/MD may be first recognized in childhood or adolescence, as suggested by the inclusion of the *With Early Onset* specifier in the *DSM-IV.* Longitudinal data are limited on the course of clinically significant depressive symptoms, DD, MD, and symptom precursors to the development of new onset (incident) cases of DD/MD. Different precursors may be identified for DD and MD. As the majority of DD begins in early adulthood, biological, personality/temperamental, and childhood environmental events would need examination. MD may herald the beginning of a chronic condition such as DD or may resolve in a relatively short period of time.

Depressive symptoms are generally prodromal and predictive of the development of DD (e.g., Horwath, Johnson, Klerman, & Weissman, 1992). Naturalistic, longitudinal studies of the course of DD/MD, once recognized, are rare. In one sample of participants with DD, about 40 percent of individuals recovered after 30 months (i.e., had several weeks of few or no symptoms; Klein et al., 1998) and the percentage of persons who recovered reached 50 percent after five years (Klein, Schwartz, Rose, & Leader, 2000). These studies reinforce the nature of DD as a chronic condition.

Although because of its apparent similarity to major depression one might expect MD to evidence a shorter and remitting course than DD, the extant data suggest otherwise. Among persons with depressive symptoms, a minority (26 percent) had symptom remission in a six-year follow-up; most participants had chronic depressive symptoms or developed depressive disorders (Beekman et al., 2002).

The scant longitudinal data suggest that persons with depressive symptoms, DD, and MD are not likely to recover. Rather, depressive symptoms, DD, and MD precede and predict the persistence of these conditions, or the development of new or additional conditions, such as depressive symptoms preceding DD, and DD preceding the onset on MDD.

Complicating Features

At least two potentially complicating features of DD and MD warrant comment: the presence of hopelessness and suicidal ideation or attempts; and the paradoxical problems associated with the chronicity of DD, such as adjustment to its presence. In addition, the prevalence and effects of comorbid personality disorders, which we discussed in an earlier section, is a significant complicating feature.

Unlike MDD, the diagnostic criteria for DD do not include suicidal ideation or attempts; hopelessness is among the diagnostic criteria for DD. Hopelessness has been linked repeatedly to completed suicide, suicidal attempts, and suicidal ideation among psychiatric patients (e.g., Beck, Brown, Berchick, Stewart, & Steer, 1990). More recent population-based studies also support the predictive value of hopelessness in reference to suicidal behavior. For example, Kuo, Gallo, and Eaton (2004) found that people who expressed hopelessness were more than 10 times more likely to evidence suicidal behavior 13 years later, after controlling for depressive and substance use disorders, suggesting that the symptom of hopelessness is significant in itself. These data suggest that monitoring hopelessness among patients with DD and other disorders is clinically indicated.

As noted previously, because of the chronicity of DD, patients may learn to live with and to some extent tolerate its presence. However, this "adjustment" is not functional or positive—these patients suffer with relatively poor functioning in multiple realms in life. As MD may predispose to DD, MD and DD appear to be components of a spectrum of acute and chronic depressive disorders that are predicted to be the leading cause of disability and global disease burden by the year 2020 (Murray & Lopez, 1997).

ASSESSMENT AND DIAGNOSIS

In an earlier section we reviewed the *DSM-IV* and *ICD-10* diagnostic criteria for DD and the proposed criteria for MD. In this section we focus on methods to apply the diagnostic criteria and characterize DD/MD symptoms and their severity, including interview and rating methods. A consensus conference sponsored by the National Institute of Mental Health (NIMH) resulted in recommendations regarding the standardized assessment of DD (Gwirtsman et al., 1997) and will be referenced as appropriate in the following section.

Interview methods of psychiatric diagnostic assessment vary in their degree of structure, the population in which they are most appropriate for use, and level of interviewer expertise required (clinician versus lay interviewer). For example, the widely used Structured Interview for *DSM-IV* (SCID; First, Spitzer, Gibbon, & Williams, 1995) is meant to be administered by a trained clinician and is more appropriate for use in a mental health population in which the presence of one of more psychiatric disorders is likely and the primary task is discriminating among them. On the other hand, the Composite International Diagnostic Interview (CIDI; Robins et al., 1988) was designed to be administered by a layperson and is more appropriate for use in a community or population-based study that has the primary goal of detecting psychiatric disorders and the secondary goal of identifying the diagnoses that are present. However, the concordance between clinician diagnoses and diagnoses generated by structured interviews administered by lay or automated interviewers has not always been in the acceptable range. For example, the concordance for DD as measured by kappa was only .48 between automated CIDI and clinician-administered semistructured interview, the Schedules for Clinical Assessment in Neuropsychiatry (Brugha, Jenkins, Taub, Meltzer, & Bebbington, 2001).

The NIMH assessment conference resulted in the recommendation that the use of semistructured diagnostic interviews administered by clinical professionals was essential. Especially in a mental health population, the use of a skilled diagnostician is sensible as DD/MD may be among the spectrum of depressive disorders with chronic and/or relapsing/remitting features and somewhat fluid boundaries among the disorders. Discriminating the characteristics of DD from among other depressive disorders is challenging.

Rating scale methods (self- and clinician-rated) for monitoring symptom severity and illness course in DD/MD have received relatively little attention in comparison to the efforts and resulting literature regarding the ability of questionnaires to detect MDD. And, aside from a few notable exceptions, questionnaires specific to DD/MD have not been developed. Rather, depressive symptom rating scales' ranges have been adapted for DD/MD at different levels than are applied for MDD. Among clinician-rated scales, the Hamilton Rating Scale for Depression (HAM-D; Hamilton, 1967) was deemed as essential by the NIMH consensus conference (Gwirtsman et al., 1997), with the further specific recommendation that the longer versions of the HAM-D be used rather than the common 17-item version (e.g., the 25-item version; Thase, Carpenter, Kupfer, & Frank, 1991). Additional recommendations were made in the NIMH consensus conference for self- and clinician-rated depressive symptom scales to use for monitoring symptom status over time. These scales include those that have been the focus of much research in MDD, such as the 21-item self-rated Beck Depression Inventory (BDI; Beck, Ward, Mendelson, Mock, & Erbaugh, 1961), and those that have been developed specifically for DD, such as the 20-item clinician-rated Cornell Dysthymia Scale (Mason et al., 1993).

Efforts have been made to characterize remission, recovery, relapse, and recurrence, and define scores on self- and clinician-rated scales that would reflect patients' clinical status for patients with DD (Gwirtsman et al., 1997), similar to efforts that have been made with MDD (Frank et al., 1991). Using the 17-item HAM-D, there is agreement in how recovery is defined both for MDD and DD in these consensus documents (i.e., asymptomatic for six or more months), and remission is asymptomatic for two weeks to six months for MDD and four or more weeks for DD. However, there is slight divergence on how being asymptomatic would be reflected in the HAM-D scores. For example, patients recovered from MDD should have HAM-D scores of 7 or less (Frank et al., 1991), but patients recovered from DD should have HAM-D scores of 6 or less (Gwirtsman et al., 1997).

The lack of recognition of depression in primary care settings has received a good deal of attention in recent years because of the medical utilization, morbidity, and ensuing costs associated with depressive symptoms and disorders. There is some evidence that MD is recognized even less often than MDD or DD (e.g., Hunter, Hunter, West, Kinder, & Carroll, 2002), which goes unrecognized by primary care physicians in about half of cases (e.g., Wells et al., 1989). Furthermore, case-finding instruments are not as sensitive in detecting MD or MDD, compared to detecting MDD alone (Williams, Pignone, Ramirez, & Stellato, 2002). Recent recommendations regarding the systematic application of screening and case-finding instruments for depressive disorders in primary care (Pignone et al., 2002) become especially important for DD/MD given their underrecognition and undertreatment.

IMPACT ON ENVIRONMENT

Social Environment

The early social environment may be among the predisposing or contributing factors to the later development of depressive disorders. Among the social factors worthy of further examination are attachment and parenting style, and adverse events in childhood, including parental death, divorce, and abuse.

The classic assessment of attachment based on John Bowlby's theory, is developmental psychologist Mary Ainsworth's "strange situation" task, which involves the separation of an infant from his or her mother, and observing the infant's reactions when reunited with the mother as indicative of general internalized models of interpersonal relationships. Adult attachment inventories (e.g., Griffin & Bartholomew, 1994) classify adults into four attachment styles: secure, preoccupied, dismissing, and fearful. We are only aware of one study that has examined adult attachment styles among persons with DD/MD: West and George (2002) found preoccupied attachment to be most frequently associated with women with DD. Among adolescents, DPD-like traits also were associated with preoccupied attachment styles (Rosenstein & Horowitz, 1996). Preoccupied attachment is characterized by a negative self-view coupled with emotional dependence on others for approval, and is associated with inconsistently available parenting.

The level of childhood adversity and the degree of chronicity of depression may be associated in a cumulative dose-response-type fashion (Klein & Santiago, 2003), with some evidence that persons with chronic depressive disorders had poorer relationships with their parents than persons with MDD (Alnaes & Torgersen, 1989), which may be particularly true for persons with early-onset DD (Lizardi et al., 1995).

In adulthood, persons with DD are less likely to be partnered than the general population (e.g., Johnson et al., 1992; Judd, Paulus, Wells, & Rapoport, 1996; Weissman et al., 1988). DD also has been associated with more constrained social networks with fewer supportive others (Judd et al., 1996; McCullough et al., 1994). Fewer social supports and significant others would be consistent with an interpersonal model of depression that specifically posits that interactions with depressed persons are aversive and over time are associated with avoidance and rejection by nondepressed persons (Coyne, 1976). Finally, as there is some degree of heritability associated with all depressive disorders, the offspring of parents with DD/MD are more likely to have a depressive disorder than children of parents without depressive disorders (Bell et al., 2004): the presence of MD/DD confers some risk of depressive illness to the offspring.

Work and Economic Environments

Persons with DD/MD are more likely to have low incomes (Weissman, et al., 1988) and financial problems (Judd et al., 1996) than persons without psychiatric disorders. Relatedly, the rate of unemployment is high and social-vocational adjustment is low compared to nonpsychiatric controls (21 percent unemployment in the DD sample; Evans et al., 1996). Subnormal role functioning also is characteristic of DD/MD, as described previously (see DeLisio et al., 1986).

TREATMENT IMPLICATIONS

As described in the previous section on etiology, biological/genetic, cognitive-behavioral, and interpersonal/psychodynamic approaches may be considered the theoretical perspectives that have received the most attention in the depressive disorders. As these models of the etiology, maintenance, and exacerbation of depressive disorders also inform intervention strategies, we will summarize the methods and efficacy of the primary approaches to treatment associated with each of these models.

In recent years there have been systematic efforts to document extant efficacy for specific psychotherapies of specific disorders. As DD and MD may be considered phenomenologically similar to MDD and part of a spectrum of depressive disorders, it makes sense to first examine the extent that efficacious treatments for MDD have been tested for their efficacy with DD/MD, given the greater attention to MDD. The psychotherapy treatments for MDD that have been determined to be well-established (i.e., two or more trials utilizing between-group designs demonstrating statistically superior efficacy of the treatment being tested to placebo or other psychological treatment, or equivalent efficacy to an already established treatment, or a large series of single case experiments using good experimental designs and comparing the intervention to another treatment, all using a treatment manual, clearly defined client samples, and done by two or more investigators) are behavior therapy (e.g., Martell et al., 2001), cognitive therapy (CT; Beck, Rush, Shaw, & Emery, 1979), and interpersonal therapy (IPT; Chambless et al., 1998; Klerman, Weissman, Rounsaville, & Chevron, 1984).

Cognitive and Interpersonal Treatments (versus Medications)

Briefly, CT (Beck et al., 1979) is based on the notion that dysfunctional interpretations of events result in depressed mood; conversely, the modification of cognitions will result in less depressed mood. IPT (Klerman et al., 1984) focuses on current relationship patterns and problems, and through improving social functioning, decreases depressive symptoms. The best-known study of the efficacy of CT and IPT for MDD (compared with imipramine, a tricyclic antidepressant, and placebo) was the NIMH Treatment of Depression Collaborative Research Program (TDCRP), which enrolled 250 patients into these four conditions. To summarize the relevant results, the active treatments and placebo were similarly effective in reducing depressive symptoms for less severely depressed patients; among more severely depressed patients, IPT and imipramine were superior to CT and placebo and no significant differences were found between CT and placebo (Elkin et al., 1995). Based in large part on the TDCRP results, practice guidelines for the treatment of MDD (e.g., APA, 2000) generally recommend antidepressant medications as the first line of treatment, and recommend psychotherapy only for patients with depression of mild-to-moderate severity. A number of methodological concerns about the TDCRP, including variability between the sites, inadequate CT training and implementation, and other issues have been expressed (e.g., Jacobson & Hollon, 1996) that should mitigate professionals from uncritically excluding CT from the treatment armamentarium for MDD.

Intervention studies of IPT or CT in DD are few. In a sample of 31 patients with DD, a 16-week trial of CT versus fluoxetine (a selective serotonergic reuptake inhibitor [SSRI]) showed no statistically significant differences in outcome between the treatments, although more patients dropped out of treatment in the fluoxetine condition (33 percent) than the CT condition (9 percent; Dunner et al., 1996). Although the data were not analyzed based on all patients enrolled (i.e., an intent-to-treat approach), it is possible that given the greater apparent acceptability of CT to the patients in this study, CT may have demonstrated superior outcomes had an intent-to-treat analysis strategy been undertaken. Sertraline (a SSRI) alone or sertraline plus group CT were more effective in reducing depressive symptoms than was CT plus placebo; this latter group did not improve significantly more than placebo alone (Ravindran et al., 1999).

De Mello, Myczcowisk, and Menezes (2001) randomly assigned 35 patients with DD to either moclobemide (a monoamine oxidase inhibitor) plus IPT or moclobemide plus clinical management. Similar to the Dunner et al. (1996) study, fewer patients in the de Mello et al. (2001) study who received psychotherapy dropped out of treatment (38 percent) than those receiving clinical management (58 percent). Both groups responded similarly well to treatment, and there was a statistically nonsignificant trend for the patients who received moclobemide plus IPT to have fewer symptoms and better functioning over time (they were followed to 48 weeks) than patients who received moclobemide alone. In the largest trial of DD to date, Browne et al. (2002) randomly assigned 707 primary care patients with DD to sertraline, 10 sessions of IPT, or both. At the end of the six-month acute treatment phase, patients who received sertraline alone or sertraline and IPT had significantly fewer depressive symptoms than patients who received IPT alone. This pattern of outcomes was maintained at the two-year uncontrolled follow-up, and persons who received IPT alone were least likely to be retained over the follow-up period.

Behavioral Treatments (versus Medications)

As with other behaviorally informed views of depression, behavioral activation (BA; Martell et al., 2001) is based on the notion that depression results from decreased reinforcement in the environment (e.g., Ferster, 1973) and is maintained by depressed patients' characteristic inactivity and avoidance that further decreases opportunities for reinforcement. BA was developed as an elaborated version of the behavioral component of CT. To date, the efficacy of BA has only been examined with major depressive disorder. In a large study of 241 patients with MDD that compared CT, between 10 mg and 50 mg of paroxetine, behavioral activation (BA), and placebo (e.g., Dimidjian et al., 2004), nearly 44 percent of participants assigned to paroxetine did not complete 16 weeks of treatment, compared to 13 percent and 16 percent in CT and BA, respectively. After 16 weeks of treatment, using an intent-to-treat analytic approach, patients who received BA or paroxetine had greater decreases in depressive symptoms than patients who received CT. BA demonstrated comparable efficacy to paroxetine among moderately to severely depressed patients and had greater acceptability (treatment retention and lack of side effects). Although only tested in patients with MDD to date, BA holds much promise as a treatment, and is similar to other behavioral treatments that have been tested in DD/MD, as we will review.

Based on a similar emphasis on the role of inactivity and avoidance of life problems in the etiology, maintenance, and exacerbation of depression, problem-solving therapy (PST) also is designed to help patients systematically identify and address problems, and increase social and physical activity. Problem-solving therapy for primary care (PST-PC; Mynors-Wallis, Gath, Lloyd-Thomas, & Tomlinson, 1995) is a structured behavioral treatment that emphasizes skills training and practice in identifying problems, possible solutions, mapping out action plans to address the problems, and generally increasing activity levels. In randomized controlled trials utilizing patients with MDD, it has been found to be more effective than placebo (Mynors-Wallis et al., 1995), and to obtain similar reductions in depressive symptoms as amitriptyline (Mynors-Wallis et al., 1995) or fluvoxamine or paroxetine (Mynors-Wallis, Gath, Day, & Baker, 2000). Of 92 patients with MD, there were no significant differences in depressive symptoms among participants who received 6 visits of PST-PC over 11 weeks compared to those who received between 10 mg and 40 mg of paroxetine or placebo at posttreatment. However, in an uncontrolled 14-week follow-up after treatment ended, participants who received PST-PC had significantly less depressive symptoms than participants who received paroxetine or placebo (Schmaling, Dimidjian, Katon, & Sullivan, 2002). In an effectiveness trial, 138 patients 60 years of age or older with MD or DD were randomly assigned to treatment as usual or an intervention that included PST-PC and recommendations for antidepressant medications to participants' primary care physicians if indicated (Ciechanowski et al., 2004). During the active treatment phase, the number of participants using antidepressants did not differ between the treatment conditions, but at 6- and 12-month follow-ups, the participants who received PST-PC were more likely to show a significant (50 percent) reduction in depressive symptoms and have improvements in quality of life measures than participants who received treatment as usual.

Treatments Developed for Chronic Depression

Some researchers would argue that DD has important distinctions from MDD, so new or modified treatments must be developed and tested for DD and other chronic depressions that are specific to their characteristics. A major figure in the development of a treatment specific for DD is James McCullough, Ph.D. As reflected in his serial case study publications (1984, 1991), McCullough developed a treatment for dysthymia, the cognitive-behavioral analysis system of psychotherapy (CBASP). CBASP is based on the notion that dysthymic patients' interactions with others are unskillful. CBASP (for the treatment and skills training manuals, see, respectively, McCullough, 1999, 2001) was subsequently tested in a very large (N = 681) trial comparing it with nefazodone, or both, in the treatment of chronic major depression (Keller et al., 2000); CBASP and nefazodone in combination did significantly better than either one in isolation.

Summary

As with MDD, there is no one treatment that is effective with all patients with DD or MD. In contrast to the efforts described previously to formulate a specific treatment for DD, there have been no specific treatments developed for MD. For DD, CBASP combines IPT's emphasis on the effects of patients' interactions with others on mood and BA's emphasis on decreasing behavioral avoidance and inactivity. However, the evidence supporting the efficacy of IPT or CT alone is mixed. Additionally, in the earlier studies (McCullough, 1984, 1991) CBASP was administered until remission, which could mean a year-long treatment. Chronic disorders intuitively argue for the need for lengthier treatments in order to effect durable change.

PST-PC appears to be a promising treatment for MD. And, although beyond the scope of this article, there is a sizable literature on how to optimally match treatments with patients, among those with MDD. In general, treatments that emphasize or draw on patients' extant skills and strengths appear to result in superior effects than treatments that address areas of relative weakness. For example, the TDCRP found that less social dysfunction predicted better response to IPT, a treatment that emphasizes relationships; fewer dysfunctional cognitions predicted better response to CT, a treatment that emphasizes identifying and modifying dysfunctional cognitions (Sotsky et al., 1991). Further treatment matching studies, and research that examines DD/MD patient characteristics that are predictors of treatment response, need to be done.

These studies emphasize the usefulness of behavioral interventions that focus on increasing activity and decreasing avoidance strategies, and whereas behavioral interventions have similar efficacy compared to antidepressant medications for reducing depressive symptoms during active treatment, they appear to be associated with longer-lasting effects than antidepressant medications. Although there are exceptions (e.g., Browne et al., 2002), the psychotherapies are generally associated with better retention in treatment than antidepressant medications. To the extent that depressive symptoms are ego-syntonic (in DD) or relatively mild (in MD), patients may be less motivated to tolerate the side effects associated with antidepressant medications or challenges inherent in psychotherapy. Motivating patients to remain in treatment, and enhancing treatment acceptability, are high priorities for future efforts to enhance treatments for DD/MD.

CONCLUDING COMMENTS

Dysthymia and minor depression are serious disorders associated with substantial morbidity and that are highly associated with the subsequent development of MDD. The distinctiveness of DPD and DD/MD needs to be further investigated. If reliable, valid, and clinically useful distinctions can be better characterized, future efforts will need to investigate treatment efficacy and effectiveness in the affected population.

REFERENCES

Abrams, K. Y., Yune, S. K., Kim, S. J., Jeon, H. J., Han, S. J., Hwang, J., et al. (2004). Trait and state aspects of harm avoidance and its implication for treatment in major depressive disorder, dysthymic disorder, and depressive personality disorder. *Psychiatry and Clinical Neurosciences, 58*(3), 240–248.

Abramson, L. Y., Metalsky, G. I., & Alloy, L. B. (1989). Hopelessness depression: A theory-based subtype of depression. *Psychological Review, 96,* 358–372.

Agosti, V., & Stewart, J. W. (2001). Atypical and non-atypical subtypes of depression: Comparison on social functioning, symptoms, course of illness, co-morbidity and demographic features. *Journal of Affective Disorders, 65*(1), 75–79.

Akiskal, H. S., Rosenthal, T. L., Haykal, R. F., Lemmi, H., Rosenthal, R. H., & Scott-Strauss, A. (1980). Characterological depressions: Clinical and sleep EEG findings separating "subaffective dysthymias" from "character spectrum disorders." *Archives of General Psychiatry, 37,* 777–783.

Alnaes, R., & Torgersen, S. (1989). Characteristics of patients with major depression in combination with dysthymic or cyclothymic disorders: Childhood and precipitating events. *Acta Psychiatrica Scandinavica, 79,* 11–18.

American Psychiatric Association. (1994). *Diagnostic and statistical manual of mental disorders* (4th ed.). Washington, DC: Author.

American Psychiatric Association. (2000). Practice guidelines for major depressive disorder in adults. *American Journal of Psychiatry, 150*(Suppl. 4), 1–26.

Bagby, R. M., & Ryder, A. G. (1999). Diagnostic discriminability of dysthymia and depressive personality disorder. *Depression and Anxiety, 10*(2), 41–49.

Beck, A. T. (1967). *Depression: Clinical, experimental, and theoretical aspects.* New York: Harper and Row.

Beck, A. T., Brown, G., Berchick, R. J., Stewart, B. L., & Steer, R. A. (1990). Relationship between hopelessness and ultimate suicide: A replication with psychiatric outpatients. *American Journal of Psychiatry, 147*(2), 190–195.

Beck, A. T., Rush, A. J., Shaw, B. F., & Emery, G. (1979). *Cognitive therapy of depression.* New York: Guilford Press.

Beck, A. T., Ward, C. H., Mendelson, M., Mock, J., & Erbaugh, J. (1961). An inventory for measuring depression. *Archives of General Psychiatry, 4,* 561–571.

Becker, J. (1974). *Depression: Theory and research.* Washington, DC: Winston-Wiley.

Beekman, A. T. F., Geerlings, S. W., Deeg, D. J. H., Smith, J. H., Schoevers, R. S., de Beurs, E., et al. (2002). The natural history of late-life depression: A 6-year prospective study in the community. *Archives of General Psychiatry, 59,* 605–611.

Bell, B., Chalklin, L., Mills, M., Browne, G., Steiner, M., Roberts, J., et al. (2004). Burden of dysthymia and comorbid illness in adults in a Canadian primary care setting: High rates of psychiatric illness in the offspring. *Journal of Affective Disorders, 78,* 73–80.

Browne, G., Steiner, M., Roberts, J., Gafni, A., Byrne, C., Bell, B., et al. (1999). Prevalence of dysthymic disorder in primary care. *Journal of Affective Disorders, 54,* 303–308.

Browne, G., Steiner, M., Roberts, J., Gafni, A., Byrne, C., Dunn, E., et al. (2002). Sertraline and/or interpersonal psychotherapy for patients with dysthymic disorder in primary care: 6-month comparison with longitudinal 2-year follow-up of effectiveness and costs. *Journal of Affective Disorders, 68,* 317–330.

Brugha, T. S., Jenkins, R., Taub, N., Meltzer, H., & Bebbington, P. E. (2001). A general population comparison of the Composite International Diagnostic Interview (CIDI) and the Schedules for Clinical Assessment in Neuropsychiatry (SCAN). *Psychological Medicine, 31,* 1001–1013.

Chambless, D. L., Baker, M. J., Baucom, D. H., Beutler, L. E., Calhoun, K. S., Crits-Christoph, P., et al. (1998). Update on empirically validated therapies II. *The Clinical Psychologist, 51*(1), 3–31.

Ciechanowski, P., Wagner, E., Schmaling, K., Schwartz, S., Williams, B., Diehr, P., et al. (2004). Community-integrated home-based depression treatment in older adults. *JAMA, 291*(13), 1569–1577.

Cloninger, C. R. (1987). A systematic method for clinical description and classification of personality variants. *Archives of General Psychiatry, 44,* 574–588.

Costa, P. T., Jr., & McCrae, R. R. (1991). *The NEO personality inventory manual.* Odessa, FL: Psychological Assessment Resources.

Coyne, J. C. (1976). Toward an interactional description of depression. *Psychiatry, 39,* 28–40.

Crum, R. M., Cooper-Patrick, L., & Ford, D. E. (1994). Depressive symptoms among general medical patients: Prevalence and one-year outcome. *Psychosomatic Medicine, 56,* 109–177.

DeLisio, G., Maremmani, I., Perugi, G., Cassano, G. B., Deltito, J., & Akiskal, J. S. (1986). Impairment of work and leisure in depressed outpatients: A preliminary communication. *Journal of Affective Disorders, 10,* 79–84.

de Mello, M. F., Myczcowisk, L. M., & Menezes, P. R. (2001). A randomized controlled trial comparing moclobemide and moclobemide plus interpersonal psychotherapy in the treatment of dysthymic disorder. *Journal of Psychotherapy Practice and Research, 10,* 117–123.

Devanand, D. P., Adorno, E., Cheng, J., Burt, T., Pelton, G. H., Roose, S. P., et al. (2004). Late onset dysthymic disorder and major depression differ from early onset dysthymic disorder and major depression in elderly outpatients. *Journal of Affective Disorders, 78,* 259–267.

Devanand, D. P., Nobler, M. S., Singer, T., Keirsky, J. E., Turret, N., Roose, S. P., et al. (1994). Is dysthymia a different disorder in the elderly? *American Journal of Psychiatry, 151,* 1592–1599.

Dimidjian, S., Hollon, S. D., Dobson, K. S., Schmaling, K. B., Kohlenberg, R. J., Addis, M., et al. (May, 2004). *Behavioral activation, cognitive therapy, and antidepressant medication in the acute treatment of major depression.* Paper presented at the annual meeting of the American Psychiatric Association, New York.

Dunner, D. L., Schmaling, K. B., Hendrickson, H., Becker, J., Lehman, A., & Bea, C. (1996). Cognitive therapy versus fluoxetine in the treatment of dysthymic disorder. *Depression, 4,* 34–41.

Elkin, I., Gibbons, R. D., Shea, M. T., Sotsky, S. M., Watkins, J. T., Pilkonis, P. A., et al. (1995). Initial severity and differential treatment outcome in the National Institute of Mental Health Treatment of Depression Collaborative Research Program. *Journal of Consulting and Clinical Psychology, 63*(5), 841–847.

Evans, S., Cloitre, M., Kocsis, J. H., Keitner, G. I., Holzer, C. P., & Gniwesch, L. (1996). Social-vocational adjustment in unipolar mood disorders: Results of the *DSM-IV* trial. *Journal of Affective Disorders, 38,* 73–80.

Ferster, C. B. (1973). A functional analysis of depression. *American Psychologist, 28,* 857–870.

First, M. B., Spitzer, R. L., Gibbon, M., & Williams, J. B. W. (1995). *Structured Clinical Interview for DSM-IV.* New York: Biometrics Research Department, New York State Psychiatric Institute.

Frank, E., Prien, R. F., Jarrett, R. B., Keller, M. B., Kupfer, D. J., Lavori, P. W., et al. (1991). Conceptualization and rationale for consensus definitions of terms in major depressive disorder. *Archives of General Psychiatry, 48,* 851–855.

Furukawa, T. A., Konno, W., Morinobu, S., Harai, H., Kitamura, T., & Takahasji, K. (2000). Course and outcome of depressive episodes: Comparison between bipolar, unipolar, and subthreshold depression. *Psychiatry Research, 96,* 211–220.

Garyfallos, G., Adamopoulou, A., Karastergiou, A., Voikli, M., Sotiropoulous, A., Donias, S., et al. (1999). Personality disorders in dysthymia and major depression. *Acta Psychiatrica Scandinavia, 99*(5), 332–340.

Griffin, D. W., & Bartholomew, K. (1994). The metaphysics of measurement: The case of adult attachment. *Advances in Personal Relationships, 5,* 17–52.

Gwirtsman, H. E., Blehar, M. C., McCullough, J. P., Kocsis, J. H., & Prien, R. F. (1997). Standardized assessment of dysthymia: Report of a National Institute of Mental Health conference. *Psychopharmacology Bulletin, 33*(1), 3–11.

Hamilton, M. (1967). Development of a rating scale for primary depressive illness. *British Journal of Social and Clinical Psychology, 6,* 278–296.

Hayden, E. P., & Klein, D. N. (2001). Outcome of dysthymic disorder at 5-year follow-up: The effect of familial psychopathology, early adversity, personality, comorbidity, and chronic stress. *American Journal of Psychiatry, 158*(11), 1864–1870.

Hays, R. D., Wells, K. B., Sherbourne, C. D., Rogers, W., & Spritzer, K. (1995). Functioning and well-being outcomes of patients with depression compared with chronic general medical illnesses. *Archives of General Psychiatry, 52,* 11–19.

Hellerstein, D. J., Kocsis, J. H., Chapman, D., Stewart, J. W., & Harrison, W. (2000). Double-blind comparison of sertraline, imipramine, and placebo in the treatment of dysthymia: Effects on personality. *American Journal of Psychiatry, 157*(9), 1436–1444.

Horwath, E., Johnson, J., Klerman, G. L., & Weissman, M. M. (1992). Depressive symptoms as relative and attributable risk factors for first-onset major depression. *Archives of General Psychiatry, 49,* 817–823.

Hunter, C. L., Hunter, C. M., West, E. T., Kinder, M. H., & Carroll, D. W. (2002). Recognition of depressive disorders by primary care providers in a military medical setting. *Military Medicine, 167*(4), 308–311.

Jacobson, N. S., & Hollon, S. D. (1996). Cognitive-behavior therapy versus pharmacotherapy: Now that the jury's returned its verdict, it's time to present the rest of the evidence. *Journal of Consulting and Clinical Psychology, 64,* 74–80.

Johnson, J., Weissman, M. M., & Klerman, G. L. (1992). Service utilization and social morbidity associated with depressive symptoms in the community. *Journal of the American Medical Association, 267*(11), 1478–1483.

Jonas, B. S., Brody, D., Roper, M., & Narrow, W. E. (2003). Prevalence of mood disorders in a national sample of young American adults. *Social Psychiatry and Psychiatric Epidemiology, 38*(11), 618–624.

Judd, L. L., Paulus, M. P., Wells, K. B., & Rapoport, M. H. (1996). Socioeconomic burden of subsyndromal depressive symptoms and major depression in a sample of the general population. *American Journal of Psychiatry, 153*(1), 1411–1417.

Katon, W., Russo, J., Frank, E., Barrett, J., Williams, J. W., Jr., Oxman, T., et al. (2002). Predictors of nonresponse to treatment in primary care patients with dysthymia. *General Hospital Psychiatry, 24*(1), 20–27.

Keller, M. B., McCullough, J. P., Klein, D. N., Arnow, B., Dunner, D. L., Gelenberg, A. J., et al. (2000). A comparison of nefazodone, the cognitive behavioral-analysis system of psychotherapy, and their combination for the treatment of chronic depression. *New England Journal of Medicine, 342*(20), 1462–1470.

Kessler, R. C., McGonagle, K. A., Zhao, S., Nelson, C. B., Hughes, M., Eshleman, S., et al. (1994). Lifetime and 12-month prevalence of *DSM-III-R* psychiatric disorders in the United States: Results from the National Comorbidity Study. *Archives of General Psychiatry, 51*, 8–19.

Klein, D., Norden, K. A., Ferro, T., Leader, J. B., Kach, K. L., Klein, L. M., et al. (1998). Thirty-month naturalistic follow-up study of early-onset dysthymic disorder: Course, diagnostic stability, and prediction of outcome. *Journal of Abnormal Psychology, 107*, 338–348.

Klein, D. N., Riso, L. P., Donaldson, S. K., Schwartz, J. E., Anderson, R. L., Ouimette, C. P., et al. (1995). Family study of early-onset dysthymia: Mood and personality disorders in relatives of outpatients with dysthymia and episodic major depression and normal controls. *Archives of General Psychiatry, 52*, 487–496.

Klein, D. N., & Santiago, N. J. (2003). Dysthymia and chronic depression: Introduction, classification, risk factors, and course. *Journal of Clinical Psychology, 59*, 807–816.

Klein, D., & Schwartz, J. E. (2002). The relation between depressive symptoms and borderline personality disorder features over time in dysthymic disorder. *Journal of Personality Disorders, 16*(6), 523–535.

Klein, D., Schwartz, J. E., Rose, S., & Leader, J. B. (2000). Five-year course and outcome of dysthymic disorder: A prospective, naturalistic follow-up study. *American Journal of Psychiatry, 157*(6), 931–939.

Klein, D., & Shih, J. H. (1998). Depressive personality: Associations with *DSM-III-R* mood and personality disorders and negative and positive affectivity, 30-month stability, and prediction of course of Axis I depressive disorders. *Journal of Abnormal Psychology, 107*(2), 319–327.

Klerman, G. L., Weissman, M. M., Rounsaville, B. J., & Chevron, E. S. (1984). *Interpersonal psychotherapy of depression.* New York: Basic Books.

Kovacs, M., Akiskal, H. S., Gatsonis, C., & Parrone, P. L. (1994). Childhood-onset dysthymia disorder: Clinical features and prospective naturalistic outcome. *Archives of General Psychiatry, 51*, 365–374.

Kuo, W. H., Gallo, J. J., & Eaton, W. W. (2004). Hopelessness, depression, substance disorder, and suicidality: A 13-year community-based study. *Social Psychiatry and Psychiatric Epidemiology, 39*(6), 497–501.

Kwon, J. S., Kim, Y., Chang, C., Park, B., Kim, L., Yoon, D. J., et al. (2000). Three-year follow-up of women with the sole diagnosis of depressive personality disorder: Subsequent development of dysthymia of major depression. *American Journal of Psychiatry, 157*(12), 1966–1972.

Lizardi, H., Klein, D. N., Ouimette, P. C., Riso, L. P., Anderson, R. L., & Donaldson, S. K. (1995). Reports of the childhood home environment in early-onset dysthymia and episodic major depression. *Journal of Abnormal Psychology, 104*, 132–139.

Lyoo, K., Gunderson, J. G., & Phillips, K. A. (1998). Personality dimensions associated with depressive personality disorder. *Journal of Personality Disorders, 12*(1), 46–55.

Martell, C. R., Addis, M. E., & Jacobson, N. S. (2001). *Depression in context: Strategies for guided action.* New York: Norton.

Mason, B. J., Kocsis, J. H., Leon, A. C., Thompson, S., Frances, A. J., Morgan, R. O., et al. (1993). Measurement of severity and treatment response in dysthymia. *Psychiatric Annals, 23*, 625–631.

McCullough, J. P. (1984). Cognitive-behavioral analysis system of psychotherapy: An interactional treatment approach for dysthymic disorder. *Psychiatry, 47*(3), 234–250.

McCullough, J. P. (1991). Psychotherapy for dysthymia: A naturalistic study of ten patients. *Journal of Nervous and Mental Disorders, 179*(12), 734–740.

McCullough, J. P. (1999). *Treatment of chronic depression: Cognitive behavioral analysis system of psychotherapy (CBASP).* New York: Guilford Press.

McCullough, J. P. (2001). *Skills training manual for diagnosing and treatment of chronic depression.* New York: Guilford Press.

McCullough, J. P., McCune, K. J., Kaye, A. L., Braith, J. A., Friend, R., Roberts, W. C., et al. (1994). Comparison of a community dysthymia sample at screening with a matched group of nondepressed community controls. *Journal of Nervous and Mental Disorders, 182*(7), 402–407.

McDermut, W., Zimmerman, M., & Chelminski, I. (2003). The construct validity of depressive personality disorder. *Journal of Abnormal Psychology, 112*(1), 49–60.

Minsky, S., Vega, W., Miskimen, T., Gara, M., & Escobar, J. (2003). Diagnostic patterns in Latino, African American, and European American psychiatric patients. *Archives of General Psychiatry, 60*, 637–644.

Murray, C. J., & Lopez, A. D. (1997). Alternative projections of mortality and disability by cause 1990–2020: The Global Burden of Disease Study. *Lancet, 349*(9064), 1498–1504.

Mynors-Wallis, L. M., Gath, D. H., Day, A., & Baker, F. (2000). Randomised controlled trial of problem solving treatment, antidepressant medication, and combined treatment for major depression in primary care. *British Medical Journal, 320*(7226), 26–30.

Mynors-Wallis, L. M., Gath, D. H., Lloyd-Thomas, A. R., & Tomlinson, D. (1995). Randomised controlled trial comparing problem solving treatment with amitriptyline and placebo for major depression in primary care. *British Medical Journal, 310*(6977), 441–445.

Oxman, T. E., Barrett, J. E., Sengupta, A., Katon, W., Williams, J. W., Jr., Frank, E., et al. (2001). Status of minor depression or dysthymia in primary care following a randomized controlled treatment. *General Hospital Psychiatry, 23*(6), 301–310.

Phillips, K. A., Gunderson, J. G., Triebwasser, J., Kimble, C. R., Faedda, G., Lyoo, I. K., et al. (1998). Reliability and validity of depressive personality disorder. *American Journal of Psychiatry, 155*(8), 1044–1048.

Pignone, M. P., Gaynes, B. N., Rushton, J. L., Burchell, C. M., Orleans, C. T., Mulrow, C. D., et al. (2002). Screening for depression in adults: A summary of the evidence for the U.S. Preventive Services Task Force. *Annals of Internal Medicine, 136*(10), 765–776.

Ravindran, A. V., Anisman, H., Merali, Z., Charbonneau, Y., Telner, J., Bialik, R. J., et al. (1999). Treatment of primary dysthymia with group cognitive therapy and pharmacotherapy: Clinical symptoms and functional impairments. *American Journal of Psychiatry, 156*(10), 1608–1617.

Riso, L. P., Miyatake, R. K., & Thase, M. E. (2002). The search for determinants of chronic depression: A review of six factors. *Journal of Affective Disorders, 70,* 103–115.

Robins, L. N., Wing, J., Wittchen, H. U., Helzer, J. E., Babor, T. F., Burke, J., et al. (1988). The Composite International Diagnostic Interview: An epidemiological instrument suitable for use in conjunction with different diagnostic systems and in different cultures. *Archives of General Psychiatry, 45*(12), 1069–1977.

Rosenstein, D. S., & Horowitz, H. A. (1996). Adolescent attachment and psychopathology. *Journal of Consulting and Clinical Psychology, 64*(2), 244–253.

Schmaling, K. B., Dimidjian, S., Katon, W., & Sullivan, M. (2002). Response styles among patients with minor depression and dysthymia in primary care. *Journal of Abnormal Psychology, 111*(2), 350–356.

Sotsky, S. M., Glass, D. R., Shea, M. T., Pilkonis, P. A., Collins, J. F., Elkin, I., et al. (1991). Patient predictors of response to psychotherapy and pharmacotherapy: Findings in the NIMH Treatment of Depression Collaborative Research Program. *American Journal of Psychiatry, 148*(8), 997–1008.

Sullivan, P. F., Neale, M. C., & Kendler, K. S. (2000). Genetic epidemiology of major depression: Review and meta-analysis. *American Journal of Psychiatry, 157*(10), 1552–1562.

Thase, M. E., Carpenter, B. A., Kupfer, D. J., & Frank, E. (1991). Clinical significance of reversed vegetative subtypes of recurrent major depression. *Psychopharmacology Bulletin, 27,* 17–22.

Watson, D., & Clark, L. A. (1984). Negative affectivity: The disposition to experience aversive emotional states. *Psychological Bulletin, 96*(3), 465–490.

Weissman, M. M., Leaf, P. J., Bruce, M. L., & Florio, L. (1988). The epidemiology of dysthymia and five communities: Rates, risks, comorbidity, and treatment. *American Journal of Psychiatry, 145*(7), 815–819.

Wells, K. B., Burnam, M. A., Rogers, W., Hays, R., & Camp, P. (1992). The course of depression in adult outcomes: Results from the Medical Outcomes Study. *Archives of General Psychiatry, 49,* 788–794.

Wells, K. B., Hays, R. D., Burnam, M. A., Rogers, W., Greenfield, S., & Ware, J. E. (1989). Detection of depressive disorder for patients receiving prepaid or fee-for-service care: Results from the Medical Outcomes Study. *Journal of the American Medical Association, 262*(23), 3298–3302.

West, M., & George, C. (2002). Attachment and dysthymia: The contributions of preoccupied attachment and agency of self to depression in women. *Attachment and Human Development, 4*(3), 278–293.

Williams, J. W., Pignone, M., Ramirez, G., & Stellato, C. P. (2002). Identifying depression in primary care: A literature synthesis of case-finding instruments. *General Hospital Psychiatry, 24,* 225–237.

World Health Organization. (1992). *The ICD-10 classification of mental and behavioural disorders: Clinical descriptions and diagnostic guidelines.* Geneva, Switzerland: Author.

CHAPTER 15

Bipolar Disorder

CORY F. NEWMAN

DESCRIPTION OF THE DISORDER AND CLINICAL PICTURE

Bipolar disorder, colloquially known as *manic depression,* comprises a spectrum of affective disorders, arguably related to unipolar depression, but involving additional symptoms that underscore the added complications and seriousness of this heterogeneous psychiatric illness. Persons who suffer from this disorder experience varying degrees of dysphoria, agitation, impulsivity, euphoria, and psychotic ideation, among other symptoms. The cognitive, emotional, behavioral, interpersonal, and physiological problems associated with bipolar disorder often appear in cyclical fashion, resulting in substantial difficulties and interruptions in a person's life.

In spite of the stereotype of manic-depressive persons who are easily spotted by their wild, frenetic, hyperenthusiastic behavior, the diagnostic signs of bipolar disorder are actually far more complex, multifaceted, and often difficult to assess. The two major subtypes are bipolar I and bipolar II, in which a single manic episode and a single hypomanic episode are necessary features respectively, with at least one depressive episode required for the diagnosis of bipolar II. As only one manic or hypomanic episode can earmark a patient for a bipolar subtype, perhaps amid numerous (and current) depressive episodes, it is very easy and potentially hazardous to misdiagnose such persons as suffering from unipolar depression (Ghaemi, Boiman, & Goodwin, 2000). For example, a fairly common scenario involves a patient who seeks therapy for his "depression," but who does not report a history of symptoms that would otherwise cue the therapist that the patient has a bipolar illness. The patient winds up being prescribed antidepressant medication, thus contributing to the precipitating of a manic episode (Goldberg & Kocsis, 1999). Such situations are a stark reminder that therapists need to conduct thorough assessments at the outset of therapy, and ideally should pursue a release of records from one of the patient's former mental health care practitioners.

Manic Episode

For a patient to meet *DSM-IV-TR* (American Psychiatric Association, 2000) criteria for a *manic episode,* he or she must have evinced an abnormally irritable or euphoric mood for a week or more, characterized by at least three of the following symptoms (four, if the primary mood problem is irritability rather than euphoria): (1) grandiosity (inflated self-esteem), (2) markedly decreased need for sleep for days at a time, (3) pressured speech, (4) flights of ideas and racing thoughts, (5) high distractibility or disorganization, (6) excessive goal-directed activity, and (7) pursuit of high stimulation, particularly hedonistic behaviors that put the patients at risk for serious life consequences but which the patients may overlook or dismiss. Occasionally, mania is typified by psychotic ideation, which can complicate the differential diagnosis between bipolar disorder and schizophrenia, especially if the patient's life situation shows a deteriorating course. When psychotic symptoms occur in the earlier context, bipolar disorder is more likely to be the appropriate diagnosis when the patients have demonstrated significantly more lucid thinking during interepisode periods, their range of mood states is broad, and the psychotic signs are relatively brief, such as only one to two weeks per year (Judd et al., 2002).

Major Depressive Episode

As noted, patients with bipolar II disorder have experienced at least one major depressive episode (MDE), and although such an episode is technically not required for a bipolar I diagnosis, most of these patients have gone through periods of major depression as well. The necessary feature for an MDE is either low mood (most of the day, every day for a period of at least two weeks), or anhedonia (lack of ability to enjoy things), also for a period of at least two weeks without relenting. If these symptoms are severe enough to result in significant interference in life functioning, then the following symptoms become relevant to assess: (1) low energy,

(2) guilt, and sense of worthlessness, (3) poor concentration and impaired decision-making, (4) sleep disturbances, (5) significant, involuntary changes in appetite and weight, (6) extremes in psychomotor activity (either retardation or agitation), (7) markedly reduced interest in sex, and (8) suicidal ideation, intentions, or actions. In order for patients to qualify for MDE, they must have at least one of the two necessary features (sad mood, or anhedonia), and a total of at least five symptoms all told. The symptoms must not be better accounted for by substance abuse, medication effects, normal bereavement, or a general medical condition.

Hypomanic Episode

Mood disturbances that are similar to a manic episode but with lesser intensity, duration (at least four days), and disruption of life activities is known as a *hypomanic* episode. Although patients in a hypomanic state often present with expansive mood, decreased need for sleep, and increased levels of goal-directed and hedonistic activities, they do not evince psychotic symptoms, generally do not require high levels of care (e.g., hospitalization), and sometimes "pass" as fun-loving and/or highly productive people who are not suffering consequences from their mood states. Nonetheless, hypomania can result in problematic life decisions, premature termination from psychosocial treatment, and may sometimes be a gateway to frank mania (Coryell, 1999). Thus, although relatively less serious than full-blown mania, hypomania is still to be considered a potentially serious clinical phenomenon.

Mixed Episodes

A particularly pernicious subtype of bipolar disorder is the *mixed episode,* involving at least a week of symptoms that meet criteria for both mania and MDE. A mixed episode is a severe manic state that involves a range of depressive symptoms including suicidality, as well as features that can be either manic or depressive, such as agitation, insomnia, and psychotic thinking. These episodes are particularly difficult to treat from a pharmacologic standpoint (Boland & Keller, 1999), are frequently complicated by substance abuse (Himmelhoch, 1986), and appear in the most suicide-prone "profile" of the bipolar patient—a young man in a mixed state who abuses alcohol (Simpson & Jamison, 1999).

Rapid Cycling

Bipolar I or II patients who display four or more "cycles" within a year are designated as *rapid cyclers,* a subtype of bipolar illness that occurs more frequently among women. Cycles are defined as involving at least four days of hypomania or mania and at least two weeks of depression (*DSM-IV;* American Psychiatric Association, 1994). A further subset of this classification is *ultrarapid cycling,* which involves shorter and more frequent occurrences of mania/hypomania and depression (Dunner, 1999). Similar to the phenomenon of the mixed state, rapid cycling is a more complicated, serious, and difficult to treat manifestation of the bipolar spectrum. For example, rapid cycling is associated with a further increase in the risk of suicide (Fawcett et al., 1987). Further, the pharmacotherapy of rapid cycling is extremely tricky in that lithium may not be the first-line medication of choice, and the titration of one or more medications is made substantially more difficult when symptoms shift rapidly (Post et al., 1999).

Cyclothymia

Cyclothymia seems to be a cross between dysthymia and a subsyndromal form of rapid cycling bipolar disorder. It is characterized by numerous affective cycles, none of which are severe, pervasive, or of sufficient duration to merit a diagnosis of bipolar disorder I or II. The symptoms must last at least two years, with no symptom-free intervals extending two months or more during this span. It can be difficult to differentiate cyclothymia from personality disorders (e.g., borderline) in which chronic mood lability is a distinguishing feature (Coryell, 1999). Like hypomania in the context of bipolar II illness, cyclothymia is considered to be in the less severe part of the bipolar spectrum. Nonetheless, cyclothymia has a long-term course, and can lead to disruptions in functioning that are clinically significant (American Psychiatric Association, 2000).

"Atypical" Bipolar Disorder

There are some manifestations of "manic depression" that do not fit neatly into the aforementioned categories, yet look suspiciously like bipolar illness. The term *atypical bipolar disorder* can be used to describe such scenarios as a patient who experiences what looks like an isolated manic episode, but for less than a week, and/or perhaps related to an episode of chemical intoxication, though this might be ambiguous and, therefore, worthy of further assessment. Another example of an atypical presentation is someone who has exhibited periods of hypomania, but without the requisite history of MDE that would indicate a diagnosis of bipolar II.

PERSONALITY DEVELOPMENT, PSYCHOPATHOLOGY, AND COMORBIDITY

The presence of comorbid disorders is a significant factor in bipolar disorder, with major implications for treatment. The following is only a sampling of some of the comorbid conditions that have been found to play an important role in the assessment and management of bipolar disorder.

Personality Disorders

Personality disorders have been estimated to occur in 33 percent to 50 percent of those patients diagnosed with bipolar disorder (Peselow, Sanfilipo, & Fieve, 1995). The Cluster B personality disorders (e.g., borderline) and the Cluster C personality disorders (e.g., avoidant) have been found to be equivalent in prevalence, each being twice as common as the Cluster A personality disorders (e.g., schizoid; Brieger, Ehrt, & Marneros, 2003). To illustrate, one can see how the affective instability, anger management problems, interpersonal strife, and propensity for self-harm of borderline personality disorder could fill even "interepisode" periods in bipolar disorder with turmoil and risk, and could exacerbate active episodes so as to accentuate the possibility of suicide. Additionally, one may predict that the person with narcissistic personality disorder may be relatively less inclined to have his or her behavior curbed or "controlled" by professionals or caring others, instead feeling entitled to do things his or her own way, including avoiding treatment and disregarding limits. Personality disorders are associated with increased levels of life crises (Beck, Freeman, & Davis, 2004), the likes of which add more stress into the lives of bipolar disordered patients for whom heightened stressors can ignite manic and other symptom episodes. Indeed, the existence of a complicating personality disorder has been associated with a poorer course, faster time to relapse, longer time to recovery, lower adherence with pharmacologic treatment, and higher risk of suicide (Dunayevich et al., 2000).

Substance Abuse

No other Axis I disorder has as high a prevalence of concurrent alcohol and other substance abuse as bipolar disorder, with lifetime estimates as high as 50 percent (Zarate & Tohen, 2001), ranking only behind antisocial personality disorder overall. Interestingly, bipolar patients have not been found to use alcohol and illicit psychoactive substance predominantly to calm their manic symptoms. Rather, they are as likely to use stimulants such as cocaine in order to enhance the high (Tohen & Zarate, 1999). Unfortunately (and predictably), this practice is likely to create a vicious cycle of biochemical dysregulation, undercontrolled behavior, increased life problems, magnified negative consequences and stressors, and further susceptibility to biochemical abnormalities (Newman, Leahy, Beck, Reilly-Harrington, & Gyulai, 2001). This is seen in cases in which alcohol and other drugs interfere with the patients' response to lithium (Albanese, Bartel, & Bruno, 1994), induce earlier onset of symptoms and more mixed states, lead to increased psychiatric hospitalizations (Sonne, Brady, & Morton, 1994), and exacerbate neuronal kindling (Tohen & Zarate, 1999).

Anxiety Disorders

Anxiety disorders also co-occur with bipolar disorder reportedly as much as in 60 percent of the cases (Himmelhoch, 1999), perhaps most prominently in mixed episodes, and when psychotic symptoms are present. Himmelhoch (1999) notes that the lifetime prevalence of panic disorder in bipolar patients is approximately 21 percent, a rate that is "26 times that found in comparison control subjects and, surprisingly, 2.1 times that found in patients with unipolar depressive illness" (p. 237).

Childhood Disorders

A further area of comorbidity—the diagnosis of childhood disorders such as attention-deficit/hyperactivity disorder (ADHD), and oppositional defiant disorder—is a controversial issue in the differential diagnosis of children and adolescents (Youngstrom, Findling, & Feeney, 2004). Much less is known about bipolar disorder in children and adolescents than in adults, partly because most of the extant assessment instruments have been developed on adult populations. Nevertheless, it is extremely important to determine the appropriate diagnosis(es), as true positives can lead to promising, early interventions (McClellan & Werry, 1997), whereas false negatives can result in a missed opportunity for treatment or, worse, an inappropriate application of stimulants for ADHD or antidepressants for childhood depression that may actually precipitate bipolar symptoms (DelBello et al., 2001; Soutullo et al., 2002). False positives are also problematic in that mistakenly diagnosed children will be placed on mood stabilizers and/or anticonvulsants, medications that have more serious side-effect profiles than typical agents for childhood psychiatric disorders (Findling, Feeny, Stansbrey, DelPorto-Bedoya, & Demeter, 2002).

EPIDEMIOLOGY

Though much less prevalent than unipolar depression, bipolar disorder nonetheless occurs in 0.8 percent to 1.6 percent of the adult population (Kessler et al., 1994). It seems to strike men and women to an equivalent degree, in contrast to unipolar depression, in which the female to male ratio is approximately 2:1 (Lam, Jones, Hayward, & Bright, 1999). Further, the data seem to indicate no appreciable differences in the prevalence of bipolar disorder across age groups or cultures (Bauer & McBride, 1996).

The available data suggest that the prevalence rate of bipolar I illness among adolescents ranges up to 1.2 percent, though it has been suggested that this figure is an underestimation (Youngstrom et al., 2004). A further complication is that some of the most commonly co-occurring conditions are also the ones most difficult and important to differentiate in children and adolescents with bipolar disorder. These disorders—including ADHD, oppositional defiant disorder, conduct disorder, and unipolar depression—all seem to be more prevalent in juvenile populations than bipolar disorder, and yet a diagnosis of bipolar disorder needs to be given due consideration in assessment.

ETIOLOGY

Among the most widely cited contributory causes of bipolar disorder are: (1) a genetic predisposition tied to biochemical vulnerabilities, (2) critical levels of life stress, including family discord, and (3) a cognitive style that adversely affects emotionality and coping. These factors interact in ways that the field is struggling to understand, toward the goal of more integrative, comprehensive, tailor-made treatments.

Hereditary and Biochemical Factors

One of the "big facts" in the research on the bipolar spectrum is that the illness runs in families (DePaolo, Simpson, Folstein, & Folstein, 1989; Miklowitz & Goldstein, 1997). Twin studies (e.g., Bertelsen, Harvald, & Hauge, 1977; Vehmanen, Kaprio, & Loennqvist, 1995) and at least one adoption study (Mendelwicz & Rainer, 1977) provide strong evidence of the prominent role of a genetic transmission in the etiology of bipolar disorder.

Although it is assumed that genetic factors play a significant role in the development of biochemical abnormalities, the specific nature of such biochemical problems has been extremely difficult to pin down. Several hypotheses have been studied extensively, though no single view stands out as being differentially substantiated by the data above all others (Bauer & McBride, 1996). Some of the major hypotheses are as follows:

1. A deficiency in norepinephrine accounts for the depressive phase in bipolar disorder, whereas dopamine is implicated in the onset of mania, especially its heightened activity level and occasional psychotic features (Goodwin & Sack, 1974);
2. Fluctuations in serotonin levels may destabilize catecholamines such as norepinephrine and dopamine, thus accounting for the abnormally wide range of mood and activity states (Goodwin & Jamison, 1990);
3. Thyroid dysfunction can produce and maintain symptoms in bipolar disorder (Bauer & Whybrow, 1990);
4. Mania is a result of dysregulation in the behavioral activating system (BAS)—a hypothesized neurobiological motivating system that modulates approach behavior in the face of cues for reward (Depue & Collins, 1998; Johnson, Sandrow, et al., 1999)—thus leading to increased intensity in noticing and pursuing opportunities for achievement, hedonic reinforcement, and other forms of stimulation;
5. Mood swings can be precipitated by significant disruptions in sleep-wake cycles and related sociobiological rhythms (Wehr, Sack, Rosenthal, & Cowdry, 1988).

Additionally, bipolar disorder seems to exhibit a "kindling effect" (Post & Weiss, 1989), in which successive episodes may recur with fewer and fewer apparent external precipitants. This hypothesis likens bipolar episodes to seizure disorders, in which fewer and less intense external stressors are required to trigger affective episodes over the course of the illness, thus emphasizing the vital importance of early intervention (Post, Rubinow, & Ballenger, 1986).

Stressful Life Events

There is a growing body of research indicating a linkage between stressful life events and affective abnormalities (e.g., Ellicott, Hammen, Gitlin, Brown, & Jamison, 1990; Hunt, Bruce-Jones, & Silverstone, 1992; Johnson & Miller, 1997; Johnson & Roberts, 1995). What remains unclear is the *valence* of the emotional dysfunction, as significant life events can trigger both depressive and manic episodes. Recent studies by Johnson and colleagues have tried to address this problem (Johnson, Meyer, Winett, & Small, 2000; Johnson, Sandrow et al., 1999; Johnson, Winett, Meyer, Greenhouse, & Miller, 1999). Their data suggest that whereas negative life events predict bipolar depression, the additive effect of a high behavioral activation system (e.g., excessive focus on goal attainment) can stimulate the onset of a manic episode. Further, low social support is related more closely to bipolar depression than mania.

Related to the previous is the research on family factors in the course of bipolar illness (e.g., Miklowitz, Goldstein, Nuechterlein, Snyder, & Mintz, 1988; Priebe, Wildgrube, & Muller-Oerlinghausen, 1989). Relapse occurs more frequently and social adjustment is poorer when bipolar patients are subject to a critical, hostile family environment on a regular basis. There seems to be a reciprocal process in which patients and their family members (one or more of whom may have affective disorders of their own) engage in aversive and coercive means of interpersonal control and countercontrol. Interventions at the family level require focusing on the behaviors and attitudes of both the patients and their family members (Miklowitz & Goldstein, 1997), as will be noted later in the chapter.

It should be stated that life events research has been vulnerable to a broad range of problems in methodology. Nevertheless, recent psychometric improvements in the area of life-stress interviews has led to findings that uphold the hypothesized relationship between life events and symptoms, even after excluding life events that are brought on by poor coping or the bipolar symptoms themselves (Johnson & Meyer, 2004).

Cognitive Styles as Vulnerability Factors

The patient's cognitive style serves as a mediating variable between life events and affective-behavioral symptoms. Negative attributional styles have been found to be related to the onset of both depressive and manic episodes following stressful life events (Reilly-Harrington, Alloy, Fresco, & Whitehouse, 1999). Further, less negative cognitive styles were predictive of greater stability in mood, whereas more negative patterns of thinking rendered patients more vulnerable to bouts of depression, and (in some cases) periods of hypomania and mania as well (Alloy, Reilly-Harrington, Fresco, Whitehouse, & Zechmeister, 1999). Interestingly, low self-esteem was related to both depression and mania, consistent with the view that hypomania and manic states may be defensive counters against patients' underlying sense of low self-worth (Winters & Neale, 1985).

The concept of *schemata*—core, fundamental negative beliefs, and negatively biased information processing—has also been posited to play a role in bipolar disorder in terms of the bipolarity of thinking styles and vulnerability to relapse (see Newman et al., 2001). These schemata, assessed by such measures as the Personality Beliefs Questionnaire (PBQ; see Beck et al., 2001) and the Young Schema Questionnaire (YSQ; see Young, 1999), purport to tap into patients' areas of cognitive bias that are most apt to play a causal role in emotional distress, and to identify significant targets for intervention. In this theoretical framework, for example, a schema of *unlovability* would put a depressed bipolar patient at risk for feeling alone, rejected, and undeserving of a relationship. In mania, the valence of the schema would shift dramatically from negative extreme to positive extreme, such that this same patient would go to great lengths to prove his lovability while manic, such as by being sexually promiscuous. Similarly, a schema of *incompetence* may be manifest in depression by a person's refusing to apply for a job, believing that she would only be turned down and humiliated. However, in mania this same person may take on tasks and projects in which she is clearly out of her depth, owing to trying too hard to overcompensate for her fundamental sense of incompetence.

COURSE, COMPLICATIONS, AND PROGNOSIS

The onset of bipolar disorder typically occurs in late adolescence or early adulthood, though more and more evidence suggests that the disorder can be found in children as well, particularly those who exhibit depression, behavioral dyscontrol, and symptoms that look like attention-deficit/hyperactivity disorder (ADHD; Bowden & Rhodes, 1996; West, McElroy, Strakowski, Keck, & McConville, 1995; Youngstrom et al., 2004). One of the most disconcerting aspects of bipolar spectrum disorders is their high propensity for repeated episodes, especially when treatment is neither early nor consistent (Tohen, Waternaux, & Tsuang, 1990). Even when a full-blown relapse is averted, many patients suffer from subsyndromal symptoms and impaired functioning (Judd et al., 2002), thus adding to their potential sense of hopelessness in ever being free of the ravages of the disorder.

Again, it must be emphasized that the course of bipolar disorder is influenced by many factors, thus it is difficult to talk about a single "natural" course of the illness. Rather, one may talk about the interactions of the course of bipolar disorder with treatment (e.g., What happens when medications are discontinued?), environmental factors (e.g., What occurs when the patients experience a significant life stressor?), and psychobiological variables (e.g., What is the impact of sleep deprivation in the context of family changes, such as childbirth, and ongoing interpersonal discord?). Add to these factors the influence of the patient's cognitive style (e.g., the patient's propensity for catastrophizing and increasing a subjective sense of stress) and coping skills (e.g., the patient's facility in recognizing early warning signs of symptom episodes and responding with appropriate measures) and it quickly becomes apparent that the course of bipolar disorder is extraordinarily difficult to predict in a specific way.

Although early and ongoing intervention can be effective in controlling the illness, it has also been found that at least half of those patients treated for bipolar disorder either do not respond sufficiently or quickly relapse after an initial response (Gitlin, Swendsen, Heller, & Hammen, 1995; Goldberg, Harrow, & Grossman, 1995). By and large, bipolar disorder typically requires lifelong treatment for patients to maximize satisfactory to optimal levels of functioning, whereas discontinuations in treatment substantially increase the likelihood of a progressively deteriorating course (Goldberg & Harrow, 1999).

IMPACT ON ENVIRONMENT

The negative effects of bipolar disorder are far reaching, adversely impacting family life, employment, schooling, and other areas of societal contribution and responsibility. For example, Dion, Tohen, Anthony, and Waternaux (1988) reported that 57 percent of their sample with bipolar disorder were unable to keep jobs six months after suffering acute depressive or manic episodes. Similarly, Coryell, Andreason, Endicott, and Keller (1987) found that a third of their bipolar patients exhibited severe occupational impairment even two years following a hospitalization. Even more sobering data were published by Gillberg, Hellgren, and Gillberg (1993), who noted that 89 percent of their sample who had been treated for bipolar disorder in adolescence were on vocational disability by age 30. Clearly, bipolar disorder is associated with significant losses in terms of productivity, financial independence, and self-sufficiency.

In the area of personal relationships, high rates of martial conflict, separation, and divorce are significantly elevated among those with bipolar disorder (Coryell et al., 1993). Family members of persons with bipolar disorder often experience a severe level of burden (Chakrabati, Kulhara, & Verma, 1992). A dramatic illustration of this finding was reported by Targum, Dibble, Davenport, and Gershon (1981), who found that 10 out of 19 spouses of persons with bipolar disorder stated that they would not have married their spouses if they had known about the bipolar disorder prior to the marriage, and 8 out of 19 added that they would not have had children with their bipolar spouses.

In light of the previous, it is troubling but not surprising that the suicide rate for this population is very high. A conservative reading of the data indicates that more than one in seven bipolar disorder sufferers will die by suicide (Goodwin & Jamison, 1990; Simpson & Jamison, 1999), and as many as half of all persons with bipolar disorder will attempt suicide at least once (Chen & Dilsaver, 1996). Clearly, the spectrum of clinical problems known collectively as bipolar disorder represents a significant public health issue that requires the field of mental health to research and develop more effective pharmacologic and psychosocial interventions.

ASSESSMENT AND DIAGNOSIS

There are a number of formal self-report measures that therapists can make available for their patients to complete before every session. For example, the Internal State Scale (Bauer et al., 1991) assesses the severity of both depressive and manic symptoms (which is especially useful if the patient is in a mixed state, or tends toward rapid cycling). Another measure is the Halberstadt Mania Inventory (Halberstadt & Abramson, 1998), a 28-item questionnaire that assesses the severity of affective, cognitive, motivational, and somatic symptoms characteristic of hypomania and mania.

A more rigorous method of assessment can be found in the form of interview-based questionnaires. For example, therapists who administer the Young Mania Rating Scale (Young, Biggs, Ziegler, & Meyer, 1978) will inquire about the patient's elevated mood, increased motor activity, sexual interest, changes in sleep patterns, speech rate, racing thoughts, irritability, new interests and plans, aggressive behaviors, degree of insight, and other variables associated with mania. Similarly, the Bech-Rafaelsen Mania Scale (Bech, Bolwig, Kramp, & Rafaelsen, 1979) is a 12-item measure in which the clinician asks the patient about such manic symptoms as euphoric mood, increased self-esteem and motor activity, reduced need for sleep, irritability, and others. The use of these assessment tools can assist therapists in making differential diagnoses between unipolar depression and bipolar disorder, between bipolar I and bipolar II illness, and additional aspects such as mixed states and rapid cycling.

A longitudinal approach to the diagnosis of disorders in the bipolar spectrum is ideal. Rather than relying largely on the patient's presentation in a given session, the clinician would do well to obtain as thorough a family history as possible (cf. DelBello & Geller, 2001) and to monitor the patient's mood (and other symptom) patterns over the course of therapy (cf. Carlson & Youngstrom, 2003). For example, when the patient's diagnosis is uncertain or ambiguous, the knowledge that two or three first-degree relatives were formally diagnosed with bipolar disorder can be invaluable information, especially when the identified patient is a child being assessed for ADHD. It can be especially useful if patients are willing to self-monitor their mood states between therapy sessions (perhaps documenting two subjective ratings per day), bringing their informal mood log to the therapist's office for evaluation as a routine part of each meeting (cf. Meaden, Daniels, & Zajecka, 2000).

TREATMENT IMPLICATIONS

Pharmacotherapy

The field of pharmacotherapy for bipolar disorder has undergone significant changes in recent years, as the range of standard medications has broadened substantially, raising both hopes and new concerns (Goldberg, 2004). As Goldberg (2004) notes, the following medications have been officially approved by the U.S. Food and Drug Administration (FDA) for the management of mania: (1) lithium (Lithobid, Eskalith, Lithonate), (2) chlorpromazine (Thorazine), (3) divalproex (Depakote, Depakene, Depakon), (4) olanzapine (Zyprexa), and (5) lamotrigine (Lamictal). Lamotrigine seems to be significant in that it was approved to delay recurrences of any symptom episodes, including depression. Of the medications mentioned previously, only chlorpromazine has fallen into relative disuse, owing primarily to the significant improvements in side-effect profiles made in the development of more recent antipsychotic medications such as olanzapine. Additional medications—not yet FDA approved specifically for the treatment of bipolar disorder—are currently being tested and have become part of the standards of practice (American Psychiatric Association, 2000; Sachs, Printz, Kahn, Carpenter, & Docherty, 2000).

Understanding the pharmacotherapy of bipolar disorder is hindered by a simple fact, as noted by Goldberg (2004): "Unlike treatments for many other medical conditions, drugs used for bipolar disorder do not ameliorate mood swings via distinctly known physiological effects" (p.114). Nonetheless, the state of the science progresses based on an accumulation of evidence about what works best, for which subtypes, under what conditions. The practice guidelines of the American Psychiatric Association (2002) identify lithium, divalproex, and olanzapine as first-line medications for acute mania, with combination therapy being recommended for more severe cases (usually involving lithium and/or divalproex, plus an atypical antipsychotic such as olanzapine). Long-term pharmacotherapy is generally advised following a single manic episode, particularly if the patient has a family history of bipolar spectrum illness (Goldberg, 2004). When and how to taper and/or discontinue adjunctive medications (that may have been necessary and effective during active episodes) remains a matter of some controversy and uncertainty. Given the long-term risk factors for recurring episodes, juxtaposed against the potential problems associated with lifelong pharmacotherapy, the goal is to provide the maximum therapeutic and prophylactic benefits, with the least amount of medication. However, this golden mean between aggressive treatment and minimization of side effects and complications remains elusive. It has been hypothesized that the implementation of concurrent, periodic, psychosocial treatments holds the key to attaining the best, most highly maintainable therapeutic outcomes, with the fewest accumulative complications (Newman et al., 2001).

Lithium

Aside from its classic, purported "mood-stabilizing" effects, there is evidence that lithium (used properly) provides an important safeguard against the risk of suicide (Isometsä, 1993; Nilsson, 1999). Additionally, for patients with liver disease, lithium is the preferred, first-line medication for bipolar disorder (Sachs et al., 2000).

That lithium has demonstrable prophylactic effects is a significant strength, and yet paradoxically a common hazard is that patients will go off their lithium because they feel normal, reasoning to themselves that they no longer need the medication. Such decisions can lead to unnecessary recurrences, serving as significant setbacks for the patients.

The efficacy of lithium alone is muted when the bipolar illness is most virulent (Maj, 1999), when there is significant comorbidity (Greil, Kleindienst, Erazo, & Muller-Oerlinghausen, 1998), and when patients exhibit mood-incongruent psychotic features (Miklowitz, 1992), mixed episodes (Himmelhoch, 1986), and rapid cycling (Dunner & Fieve, 1974). Further, even when patients experience improvements in mood state while taking lithium, they often continue to demonstrate overall problems in functioning that necessitate further intervention.

Divalproex

Initially used as an anticonvulsant, divalproex has also been prescribed as a treatment for migraines. In the 1980s and 1990s, evidence emerged suggesting its efficacy in response to bipolar disorder, particularly acute mania (Pope, McElroy, Keck, & Hudson, 1991), mixed states (Swann et al., 1997), and rapid cycling (Walden, Normann, Langosch, Berger, & Grunze, 1998). Divalproex and lithium are not typically viewed as "rival" medications. Indeed, they are often used in concert (Solomon, Keitner, Ryan, & Miller, 1998). Divalproex can be used alone in the treatment of bipolar II, and it is the preferred first-line medication for bipolar patients with heart disease, kidney dysfunction, mania as the result of stroke or head injury, and for elderly bipolar patients who suffer from dementia (Sachs et al., 2000).

Olanzapine

The strengths of olanzapine (an "atypical antipsychotic" medication) have been demonstrated in two placebo-controlled trials (Tohen et al., 1999, 2000), with one-year antimanic relapse prevention comparable to divalproex (Tohen et al., 2003), and superior to lithium (Tohen et al., 2002). Perhaps most significantly, there is early evidence that olanzapine can have therapeutic effects on bipolar patients who previously exhibited nonresponse to both lithium and divalproex (Baker et al., 2002). Additionally, olanzapine has been earmarked as an adjunctive medication when psychotic symptoms are present (Sachs et al., 2000).

Lamotrigine

A recently developed anticonvulsant, lamotrigine has had very positive effects in the treatment of refractory epilepsy (Post et al., 1999). When used in the treatment of bipolar disorder (especially when used adjunctively with first-line medications such as lithium and divalproex), lamotrigine has shown efficacy in treating treatment-refractory bipolar depression (Labbate & Rubey, 1997), rapid cycling (Calabrese et al., 1999), and mixed states (Calabrese, Rapport, Shelton, & Kimmel, 1998).

Some patients who have been on lithium long term develop renal complications. The typical medical intervention in such cases has been the use of steroids, which unfortunately can trigger the onset of manic episodes. However, when lamotrigine is used, the risk of steroid-induced mania is significantly reduced (Preda, Fazeli, McKay, Bowers, & Mazure, 1999). The most significant potential drawback of lamotrigine—serious rashes such as Stevens-Johnson syndrome and toxic epidermal necrolysis—can be largely averted through slow escalation of the dose (Kusumakar & Yatham, 1977).

Additional Commonly Used Medications

A number of drugs have become part of the clinical standard of care for bipolar disorder, especially when used as adjuncts to first-line medications. The following is a nonexhaustive review of such medications, and the initial evidence for their contributions in treating different aspects of the bipolar spectrum, under varying conditions.

Carbamazepine (Tegretol)

An antiseizure medication that predates lamotrigine in its use in the treatment of bipolar disorder, carbamazepine has demonstrated efficacy in acute mania (Post et al., 1999), but less convincing benefit as an antidepressant or in relapse prevention (Ernst & Goldberg, 2003). Denicoff et al. (1994) have found that carbamazepine, when used adjunctively with lithium, can be more beneficial to rapid cyclers than either medication used alone. Further, the authors report that a triple combination of lithium, divalproex, and carbamazepine may be helpful for highly treatment-resistant bipolar patients. Goldberg (2004) hypothesizes that carbamazepine's unattractive side-effect profile (including the risk of neurotoxicity, liver enzyme induction, and white blood-cell suppression) may be hindering its wider, more regular acceptance. Goldberg (2004) adds that a newer, "cleaner" version of carbamazepine (oxcarbazepine) is in the early stages of clinical trials, and may provide a better alternative overall.

Topiramate

In spite of a lack of support for its antimanic effects, and its potential for neurocognitive side effects, topiramate has been shown to reduce appetite in patients, possibly helping to reverse weight gain commonly associated with other medications (Goldberg, 2004). For bipolar patients whose concerns about weight gain may be sufficient to cause them to discontinue their medications, the additional use of topiramate may be a key in improving adherence and thus reducing the risk of relapse.

Risperidone

There is empirical support for this atypical antipsychotic medication as monotherapy for mania (Hirschfeld et al., 2002; Vieta et al., 2002) and as a combination drug with lithium or divalproex (Sachs, Grossman, Ghaemi, Okamoto, & Bowden, 2002). An important problem associated with risperidone is the side effect of motor restlessness, which may be difficult to differentiate from the agitation associated with mania or mixed states. As with many instances of side-effect complications, careful, conservative dosing is recommended (Goldberg, 2004).

Quetiapine

Recent data support the use of this atypical antipsychotic medication as an adjunct to lithium or divalproex in combating mania (Sachs, Mullen, et al., 2002). Significantly, this regimen has been shown to be effective with a group of adolescent inpatients experiencing mania (DelBello, Schwiers, Rosenberg, & Strakowski, 2002). Given the general dearth of empirical findings pertinent to child and adolescent bipolar populations, the support for quetiapine as an antimania medication for juveniles is a welcome development.

Antidepressants

Antidepressants can be used legitimately in the treatment of bipolar depression when combined with mood-stabilizing agents such as lithium and/or divalproex (Frances, Docherty, & Kahn, 1996). However, when such patients begin to show signs of hypomania, mania, or a mixed state, the antidepressant(s) should be discontinued (Bauer et al., 1999). The risk of patients "switching" into the manic realm of the bipolar spectrum, as well as becoming more prone to accelerate cycles, are the chief concerns about the use of antidepressants (Goldberg & Kocsis, 1999; Goldberg & Whiteside, 2002). Thus, the APA Practice Guidelines (American Psychiatric Association, 2002) advise against using antidepressants alone in the treatment of bipolar I. The issue of their appropriateness as monotherapy for bipolar II remains a topic of debate, as a limited database suggests lesser risk of switching in this population (Amsterdam, 1998).

Preliminary data have supported the use of bupropion, or paroxetine for bipolar depression, but not to a compelling degree (Goldberg, 2004). Further, whereas there is more support for the use of lithium (rather than divalproex) in combination with antidepressants (Henry, Sorbara, Lacoste, Gindrec, & Leboyer, 2001), other researchers have argued that antidepressant-induced switches are better predicted by patient variables than the specific antidepressants being used (Goldberg & Whiteside, 2002). Such variables have been hypothesized to include genetic susceptibility (Mundo, Walker, Cate, Macciardi, & Kennedy, 2001), and comorbid alcohol and other substance abuse (Goldberg & Whiteside, 2002). Furthermore, there is evidence that patients with rapid-cycling bipolar disorder are highly susceptible to switching, thus the use of antidepressants with this group must be handled delicately, if at all (Wehr et al., 1988). As a response to these difficulties, more attention is being paid to the antidepressant effects of adjunctive psychosocial treatment (Johnson & Leahy, 2004; Newman et al., 2001).

Special Considerations in the Pharmacotherapy of Bipolar Disorder

The following is a short sample of issues pertinent to the pharmacotherapy of bipolar disorder that warrant more attention than they have received to date. Unfortunately, it will take some time to acquire the empirical evidence to advance our knowledge to a more satisfactory level. Fortunately, the sensitive clinician can parlay an increasing awareness of these issues into becoming a more collaborative, thoughtful practitioner, thus increasing the quality of the patients' experience in treatment, and potentially improving adherence.

Children and Adolescents

Controlled pharmacotherapy trials for children and adolescents with bipolar illness are lacking (for exceptions, see DelBello et al., 2002; Geller et al., 1998). Open trials seem to support the use of divalproex (Papatheodorou, Kutcher, Katic, & Szalai, 1995), whereas the use of lamotrigine is discouraged because of the risk of potentially fatal skin rashes such as Stevens-Johnson syndrome. As noted earlier, the overlap between symptoms of ADHD and bipolar disorder in children and adolescents means that a differential diagnosis is both difficult and extremely important. Clinicians need to be prepared to recognize bipolar disorder in this population, so as to begin an early intervention. Nevertheless practitioners have to be mindful that medications for bipolar disorder may be particularly noxious for youngsters, and thus they must proceed with caution and care. Similarly, the diagnosis of ADHD should not automatically lead to the prescription of stimulants without first considering that these could potentiate a manic episode.

Pregnancy

According to Sachs et al. (2000), bipolar patients who are trying to get pregnant (or who are in their first trimester of pregnancy) may opt to take conventional antipsychotic medications such as haloperidol, owing to the fact that lithium, divalproex, and carbamazepine all carry some fetal teratogenic risk early in pregnancy. Later in pregnancy (second and third trimester), both conventional and atypical psychotics provide an acceptable cost-benefit ratio. Electroconvulsive therapy (ECT) may also be chosen as an alternative to drug treatment. In cases in which a mother-to-be is at risk for suicide, lithium is the best choice to keep the patient safe, even though it confers some incremental risk to the fetus. Viguera et al. (2000) note that in any case of prenatal use of bipolar medications, gradual withdrawal is best in order to reduce the risk of relapse once the patient has given birth and is breastfeeding.

Electroconvulsive Therapy (ECT)

According to Sachs et al. (2000), ECT is a viable approach in response to severe and/or psychotic depression (especially when the risk of suicide is high), though lithium would have to be discontinued prior to the administering of ECT owing to the risk of neurotoxicity (Small, Kellams, Milstein, & Small, 1980). ECT may also be recommended as a somatic treatment option when medications as a whole are contraindicated. For example, a patient in her first trimester of pregnancy may opt to eliminate all medications from her treatment regimen as a precaution against potential teratogenicity. However, a worsening of her condition that requires an intervention beyond the scope of psychosocial treatment (cf. Chor, Mercier, & Halper, 1988) may require ECT, especially if the patient is suicidal. Such instances highlight the necessity of delicately weighing the risks of ECT (as well as pharmacotherapy) to a fetus, juxtaposed against the possibility of catastrophic outcome for the mother, and the fetus by extension, if the somatic treatment is not delivered during a critical time.

Psychosocial Approaches

Although pharmacotherapeutic advances have been substantial, many patients do not reach optimal functioning on medications alone, and other patients cannot tolerate them well enough to sustain a promising regimen over time. Even the best medication-based results do not reliably meet all the patients' needs, such as the learning of vital coping skills in the face of psychosocial stressors, the likes of which may trigger symptom episodes. Thus, psychosocial models have been developed and adapted to assist in the overall treatment of bipolar disorder (Johnson & Leahy, 2004), this providing more hope for the comprehensive, long-term management of the illness.

Cognitive Therapy (and Cognitive-Behavioral Therapy)

Cognitive therapy (henceforth abbreviated interchangeably as CT or CBT) has been a widely empirically supported therapy for a plethora of disorders, most notably unipolar depression (Clark, Beck, & Alford, 1999). More recently, promising results have been obtained in the application of CBT to the treatment of bipolar spectrum disorders (including bipolar I disorder) typically in close conjunction with pharmacotherapy (Lam et al., 1999; Newman et al., 2001).

Newman (2002) has described six overarching goals of cognitive therapy with bipolar patients, all based on a positive, well-managed therapeutic alliance, and a databased case conceptualization. In order to help bipolar patients reduce their subjective sense of stress, increase their sense of efficacy, improve their problem-solving skills, make peace with medications, and feel empowered in their treatment and self-care, Newman (2002) recommends that CT therapists should pursue the following six strategies:

1. *Educate* patients about their illness, helping them to make confident, well-informed decisions about their treatment, and about how to manage the symptoms and course of the illness. This includes an exploration and explication of the early warning signs of mood episodes (prodromes), so that a coping plan can be implemented promptly to maximize interventions and avert unnecessary exacerbations (Lam & Wong, 1997). Similarly, patients are assisted in recognizing the substantive differences between normal mood variations and problematic swings that probably warrant additional treatment. This helps patients to be critical thinkers in terms of self-monitoring their moods, yet remain reasonably trustful and unfearful of their normal human reactions to life's ups and downs. Patients are encouraged to read informative accounts of the struggles and successes of others with bipolar illness (e.g., *An Unquiet Mind,* Jamison, 1995).

2. *Test* the reality of the patients' thinking, so that they become adept at catching themselves when their ideation strays outside normal limits, and becomes detached from conclusions based on evidence and consensus. In particular, patients learn to self-monitor their thoughts when they feel helpless and hopeless on the depressive side, and grandiose and overexuberant on the hypomanic or manic side. The goal is not to invalidate the patients' thinking, but rather to instruct them in the methods of sequential logic, Socratic reasoning, and utilization of cognitive checks and balances. Techniques include rational responding to maladaptive thoughts, *devil's advocacy* role-playing, and seeking further information and feedback from trusted sources (cf. Newman et al., 2001). These techniques have further applications in helping patients come to terms with their medications by helping them to be disabused of some of their more harmful, dissuasive views about being a pharmacotherapy patient. For example, therapists collaborate with the patients in eliciting and rationally evaluating such beliefs as, "Medication takes away my true personality and creativity," "If I feel better, then I no longer need medication," and "If I still don't feel well even while taking my medication, then there is no point to being on medication at all," among other problematic views. The goal is to help patients make peace with their medications, seeing their benefits and shortcomings in a nonprejudicial way.

3. *Instruct* patients in the principles and practices of problem solving so that they may develop effective ways to sidestep and/or manage real-life difficulties that require their

sober, reasoned, constructive attention. Using the CBT model of problem solving explicated by Nezu, Nezu, and Perri (1989) as a guide, therapists can have patients review the steps involved in preventing problems (e.g., weigh risks and benefits, anticipate consequences, exercise patience and caution while obtaining more information), and in containing and limiting already existing problems (e.g., identify and utilize resources, refrain from acting out of frustration, brainstorm possible solutions, examine the pros and cons, choose the best method, implement it, and evaluate the results).

4. *Control* a patient's tendency to be impulsive and/or reckless when hypomanic. Therapists give their hypomanic patients tactful, direct feedback about their behavior and ideation, and help them to use periods of reflective delay (see strategy 3) before acting on their ideation and desires. Specific techniques include consulting with at least two trusted others, waiting 48 hours before acting, using self-instructional flashcards, listening to tapes of previous therapy sessions for instruction and insight, and (in everyday social interactions) doing more sitting and listening rather than standing and talking.

5. *Modulate* the patient's extremes of affect, through modeling, role-playing, audiovisual feedback, relaxation, controlled breathing, and other techniques. The general goal is to incrementally reduce arousal, so that the patients gain some sense of control over themselves, and by extension feel more personal responsibility for their decisions and actions. Along with this goal comes a change in the patient's beliefs (see strategy 2), such that they no longer maintain that their emotions necessarily *compel* them to act, but rather are a barometer of their state of mind and physiology—states that can be observed, studied, and changed.

6. *Counteract* the patient's disorganization and distractibility by using strategies that maximize planning, focusing, repetition, and the use of "redundant systems." The structure of a CT session is helpful in keeping patients on task for maximum utilization of the session, and this serves as a model for other, important life tasks. The use of activity schedules, written reminders, visual cues, self-orienting comments (e.g., "Stay with this task 15 minutes more"), and a wide range of therapy homework assignments (drawing from the previous five principles) help patients have a better chance of succeeding in connecting meaningfully with others, and accomplishing daily goals.

One of the earliest randomized, controlled studies of the additive value of cognitive therapy in the treatment of bipolar disorder was conducted by Cochran (1984). She found that patients who went through a brief (six-week) course of cognitive therapy designed to improve medication adherence did in fact show a significant advantage over the group assigned to a treatment as usual (TAU) condition. The CT group had far fewer patients discontinuing their medications (three versus eight), and far fewer hospitalizations (two versus eight).

Recent trials of cognitive therapy have also been extremely promising and many more are in progress (Scott, 2004), including a 20-site, longitudinal study in the United States examining outcomes for bipolar disorder combining pharmacotherapy and psychosocial interventions (the Systematic Treatment Enhancement Program for Bipolar Disorder [STEP-BD]; Sachs et al., 2003). Among the completed projects in the United Kingdom is a study by Perry, Tarrier, Morriss, McCarthy, and Limb (1999), who recruited 69 active patients deemed to be at high risk for further relapse of bipolar disorder, randomly assigning the patients to CBT or TAU in addition to their pharmacotherapy. Over 18 months, the CBT group had fewer manic relapses (27 percent versus 57 percent), fewer days as an inpatient, longer duration until a manic episode, and higher levels of general adaptational functioning, all at significant levels. Scott, Garland, and Moorhead (2001) tested a 20-session module of cognitive therapy for a heterogeneous sample of bipolar patients (e.g., 12 out of 42 also met criteria for alcohol or other substance dependence). As reported by Scott (2004), ". . . results of the randomized controlled phase demonstrated that, compared with participants receiving treatment as usual, those who received additional CT experienced statistically significant improvements in symptom levels, global functioning, and work and social adjustment" (p. 234). This study currently is being followed up by a large five-center trial involving 250 patients with bipolar disorder.

The data from Lam and colleagues have also shown the efficacy of cognitive therapy relative to TAU (Lam et al., 2000, 2003). Following the initial pilot study, Lam et al. (2003) followed 103 bipolar patients who entered treatment in a euthymic state, already on medication. After controlling for gender and illness history, the CT group had fewer relapses (43 percent versus 75 percent for the control group), a lower proportion of psychiatric hospitalizations (15 percent versus 33 percent), and fewer days in symptom episodes over a 12-month period (27 days versus 88 days). The patients in the CT group also demonstrated significantly greater improvements in social adjustment and management of prodromal symptoms.

Family Focused Therapy (FFT)

This approach is derived from the empirical literature demonstrating the efficacy of family psychoeducation and skills training with neuroleptic regimens in delaying relapses, reducing symptomatology, and improving functioning in patients with schizophrenia (Miklowitz, 2004). When applied to bipolar patients, family-focused treatment (FFT; Miklowitz & Goldstein, 1997) has been tested as a nine-month, 21-session outpatient program consisting of five modules: (1) assessment of the family, (2) education about bipolar disorder, (3) communication-enhancement training, (4) problem-solving skills training, and (5) termination.

The empirical cornerstone of FFT is the repeated observation that patients with bipolar disorder are more vulnerable to relapses if their home environment is characterized by *high expressed emotion* (EE), rather than the more benign environment of low expressed emotion (e.g., Miklowitz et al., 1988; Priebe et al., 1989). High EE attitudes and behaviors in caregivers have been identified as leading indicators of family strife, particularly during the postepisode period of stabilization (Miklowitz, 2004), putting bipolar patients at risk for relapse. Characteristic of a high EE atmosphere at home are the negative, escalating cycles of verbal and nonverbal communication between the bipolar patients and their families (Simoneau, Miklowitz, & Saleem, 1998), and the attribution of these problems to personal, controllable factors (Wendel, Miklowitz, Richards, & George, 2000). FFT attempts to increase the efficacy and modulate the emotional tone of the family's communication and problem-solving styles, in addition to helping patients and their families express more tolerance for and acceptance of each other (Miklowitz, 2004).

Two randomized trials and one open study have supported FFT as an efficacious adjunct to the overall therapeutic regimen of the bipolar patient. Miklowitz and Goldstein (1990) treated nine patients (recently discharged from the hospital following manic episodes) with FFT, and compared their rates of relapse with 23 patients from an earlier study. Both groups were also treated aggressively with pharmacotherapy. Rates of relapse were significantly higher in the controls than in the FFT patients (61 percent versus 11 percent). Miklowitz et al. (2000) randomized 101 bipolar disorder patients in acute episodes to nine months of FFT, or a TAU condition known as crisis management (CM), with all patients receiving medications from community physicians. "Over two years, patients in FFT demonstrated a threefold higher rate of survival without relapse (52 percent) than patients in CM (17 percent)" (Miklowitz, 2004, p. 186). The patients in FFT also had significantly better adherence to medications than those in CM. Further, analyses of the families' interactions showed that those who received FFT were superior to those who went through CM in terms of positive verbal and nonverbal behavior. Rea et al. (2003) randomly assigned 53 patients with bipolar disorder to FFT with medication, or supportive therapy with medication. Patients in FFT experienced fewer hospitalizations and longer periods of sustained remissions during the one-year posttreatment interval, after having been statistically equivalent during the active nine-month period of treatment. It was hypothesized that the skills training needed time to be "absorbed" by the patients and their families before the apparent benefits would surface.

Interpersonal Social Rhythm Therapy (IP-SRT)

This approach is predicated on the observation that the pharmacotherapy of bipolar disorder is affected by the patients' lifestyle issues, and that psychosocial interventions are an important part of instilling regularity and stability in patients' lives, both psychologically and physiologically (Frank & Swartz, 2004). The major area of focus in IP-SRT is the patients' circadian rhythms, and the ways that their interpersonal lives potentially disturb this basic, centrally important mechanism and barometer of wellness. Life events that sufficiently upset people's personal rhythms as to trigger biological desynchrony require therapeutic intervention in order to minimize the chances of an activation of a bipolar episode (cf. Malkoff-Schwartz et al., 2000).

In addition to the attention paid to circadian rhythms, IP-SRT (as its name would suggest) is derived from interpersonal therapy (IPT; Klerman, Weissman, Rounsaville, & Chevron, 1984), a therapy originally developed for unipolar depression. IPT places great emphasis on improving the quality of the patient's interpersonal life, and on his or her comfort with his or her social roles. When patients feel largely at peace in their personal lives, and are basically contented with their attachments, social positions, and their place in the life cycle, it is likely that they will sleep well, and have dependable, reliable ways of navigating everyday life. Such a condition is hypothesized to be most conducive to maintaining a bipolar remission (Frank & Swartz, 2004). Based on the preceding principles, the IP-SRT therapist helps patients pursue three overarching goals: (1) optimizing the regularity of daily routines; (2) resolving social, interpersonal problems; and (3) understanding bipolar illness so as to minimize unnecessary provocations that might cause biopsychosocial destabilization. The social rhythm component of the treatment model helps patients develop strategies to promote regularity in their social behaviors and schedules, and to minimize the potentially harmful effects of disruptions in their personal lives. In IP-SRT, patients are asked to complete a self-monitoring instrument called the Social Rhythm Metric (SRM), a short form of which is being used in the STEP-BD multisite study (Monk, Frank, Potts, & Kupfer, 2002).

Scott (2004) has reported on the progress of a randomized treatment trial for IP-SRT, with a two-year follow-up period under current evaluation. Earlier data suggested that IP-SRT did induce more stable social rhythms (Frank et al., 1999), and patients entering the study in a major depressive episode showed a significantly shorter time to recovery with IP-SRT, as compared to intensive clinical management (21 weeks versus 40 weeks).

Group Therapy

Although most of the "group work" that pertains to illnesses such as bipolar disorder has to do with support groups such as the National Alliance for the Mentally Ill (NAMI) that are not designed as formal treatments, there have been some empirically tested group therapy methods that warrant mention. Hirshfeld et al. (1998) evaluated a cognitive-behavioral group intervention via a randomized, controlled trial. The patients who underwent the adjunctive 11-session group cognitive-behavioral therapy had significantly longer periods of euthymia and significantly fewer new symptom episodes than control patients treated with standard pharmacotherapy alone. Significantly, this finding held up at follow-up as well.

The Life Goals Program (Bauer & McBride, 2003) is a group-based psychoeducational program designed to help patients with bipolar disorder to become more active and effective collaborators in managing their illness and its comprehensive treatment. Bauer (2004) notes that early empirical tests of the Life Goals Program (at the Providence Veterans Administration Hospital and Massachusetts General Hospital) have shown that patients who remained in the groups (20 out of 29) were able to achieve a high rate of goals pertinent to knowledge about bipolar illness, and relevant to their quality of life. Median time to goal attainment was seven months. Bauer (2004) also notes that the Life Goals Program is currently being tested on a broader scale (large, multisite studies), within randomized, controlled trial paradigms.

SUMMARY

Bipolar disorder is a heterogeneous but generally serious, complicated illness that carries with it lifelong vulnerabilities. There is a strong genetic, biological causality, but the course of the disorder can be markedly influenced by life stressors, the interaction of which is moderated by psychological factors such as cognitive beliefs (and schemata), coping styles, and problem-solving skills. The phenomenon of comorbidity, from the differential diagnosis problem of ADHD in childhood to the problems of self-medication via substance abuse in adults, is a significant problem in understanding and managing bipolar disorder most effectively. Proper treatment, especially if started early and followed continuously, can greatly reduce symptom episodes, but the patients' overall levels of functioning and quality of life may still be suboptimal, and therefore need to be given greater clinical attention. Suicide has been and continues to be the most serious outcome of bipolar disorder, occurring in at least 15 percent of all cases, and putting many more people at ongoing risk.

Although significant advances in biological treatments are giving bipolar patients more hope for leading normal lives, pharmacotherapy remains far from an exact science, continues to be fraught with problems ranging from side effects to nonadherence, and does not address the critical issue of building patients' psychological skills. Psychosocial therapies are making headway in identifying and bolstering bipolar patients' areas of vulnerability (e.g., family discord, unhealthy circadian rhythms, maladaptive beliefs, sense of stigma and/or denial), but they generally need to be applied in the context of ongoing pharmacotherapy in order to be most effective and to safeguard patients in the best, most professionally responsible ways. At their nexus, pharmacotherapy can enable patients to function well enough to benefit further from ongoing, psychoeducational outpatient therapies (e.g., cognitive therapy, family-focused therapy, etc.), and psychosocial therapies can assist patients in being more vigilant and collaborative in managing their medications. Recent programs of research are shedding light on the ways that treatments can be combined so as to offer bipolar patients the best chance at an improved quality of life, with hope for maximal maintenance of therapeutic gains over the long term.

REFERENCES

Albanese, M., Bartel, R., & Bruno, R. (1994). Comparison of measures used to determine substance abuse in an inpatient psychiatric population. *American Journal of Psychiatry, 151,* 1077–1078.

Alloy, L. B., Reilly-Harrington, N. A., Fresco, D. M., Whitehouse, W. G., & Zechmeister, J. S. (1999). Cognitive styles and life events in subsyndromal unipolar and bipolar disorders: Stability and prospective prediction of depressive and hypomanic mood swings. *Journal of Cognitive Psychotherapy, 13,* 21–40.

American Psychiatric Association. (1994). *Diagnostic and statistical manual of mental disorders* (4th ed.). Washington, DC: Author.

American Psychiatric Association. (2000). *Desk reference to the diagnostic criteria from DSM-IV-TR.* Washington, DC: Author.

American Psychiatric Association. (2002). Practice guidelines for the treatment of patients with bipolar disorder (rev.). *American Journal of Psychiatry, 159,* 1–50.

Amsterdam, J. (1998). Efficacy and safety of venlafaxine in the treatment of bipolar II major depressive episode. *Journal of Clinical Psychopharmacology, 18,* 414–417.

Baker, R. W., Goldberg, J. F., Tohen, M., Milton, D. R., Stauffer, V. L., & Schuh, L. M. (2002). The impact of response to previous mood stabilizer therapy on response to olanzapine versus placebo for acute mania. *Bipolar Disorders, 4,* 43–49.

Bauer, M. S. (2004). Supporting collaborative practice management. In S. L. Johnson & R. L. Leahy (Eds.), *Psychological treatment of bipolar disorder* (pp. 203–225). New York: Guilford Press.

Bauer, M. S., Callahan, A. M., Jampala, C., Petty, F., Sajatovic, M., Schaefer, V., et al. (1999). Clinical practice guidelines for bipolar disorder from the Department of Veterans Affairs. *Journal of Clinical Psychiatry, 60,* 9–21.

Bauer, M. S., Crits-Christoph, P., Ball, W., DeWees, E., McAllister, T., Alahi, P., et al. (1991). Independent assessment of manic and depressive symptoms by self-rating scale: Characteristics and implications for the study of mania. *Archives of General Psychiatry, 48,* 807–812.

Bauer, M. S., & McBride, L. (1996). *Structured group therapy for bipolar disorder: The Life Goals Program.* New York: Springer.

Bauer, M. S., & McBride, L. (2003). *Structured group therapy for bipolar disorder: The Life Goals Program* (2nd ed.). New York: Springer.

Bauer, M. S., & Whybrow, P. C. (1990). Rapid cycling bipolar affective disorder II: Adjuvant treatment of refractory rapid cycling with high dose thyroxin. *Archives of General Psychiatry, 47,* 435–440.

Bech, P., Bolwig, T. G., Kramp, P., & Rafaelsen, O. J. (1979). The Bech-Rafaelsen Mania Scale and the Hamilton Depression Scale: Evaluation of homogeneity and inter-observer reliability. *Acta Psychiatrica Scandinavica, 30,* 330–351.

Beck, A. T., Butler, A. C., Brown, G. K., Dahlsgaard, K. K., Newman, C. F., & Beck, J. S. (2001). Dysfunctional beliefs discriminate personality disorders. *Behaviour Therapy and Research, 39,* 1213–1125.

Beck, A. T., Freeman, A., & Davis, D. (2004). *Cognitive therapy of personality disorders* (2nd ed.). New York: Guilford Press.

Bertelsen, A., Harvald, B., & Hauge, M. (1977). A Danish twin study of manic-depressive disorders. *British Journal of Psychiatry, 130,* 330–351.

Boland, R. J., & Keller, M. B. (1999). Mixed state bipolar disorders: Outcome data from the NIMH Collaborative Program on the psychobiology of depression. In J. F. Goldberg & M. Harrow (Eds.), *Bipolar disorders: Clinical course and outcome* (pp. 115–128). Washington, DC: American Psychiatric Association.

Bowden, C. L., & Rhodes, L. J. (1996). Mania in children and adolescents: Recognition and treatment. *Psychiatric Annals, 26*(7, Suppl.), S430–S434.

Brieger, P., Ehrt, E., & Marneros, A. (2003). Frequency of comorbid personality disorders in bipolar and unipolar affective disorders. *Comprehensive Psychiatry, 44,* 28–34.

Calabrese, J. R., Bowden, C. L., McElroy, S. L., Cookson, J., Andersen, J., Keck, P. E., et al. (1999). Spectrum of activity of lamotrigine in treatment-refractory bipolar disorder. *American Journal of Psychiatry, 156,* 1019–1023.

Calabrese, J. R., Rapport, D. J., Shelton, M. D., & Kimmel, S. E. (1998). Clinical studies on the use of lamotrigine in bipolar disorder. *Neuropsychobiology, 38,* 185–191.

Carlson, G. A., & Youngstrom, E. A. (2003). Clinical implications of pervasive manic symptoms in children. *Biological Psychiatry, 53,* 1050–1058.

Chakrabati, S., Kulhara, P., & Verma, S. K. (1992). Extent and determinants of burden among families of patients with affective disorders. *Acta Psychiatrica Scandinavica, 86,* 247–252.

Chen, Y.-W., & Dilsaver, S. C. (1996). Lifetime rates of suicide attempts among subjects with bipolar and unipolar disorders relative to subjects with other Axis-I disorders. *Biological Psychiatry, 39,* 896–899.

Chor, P., Mercier, M., & Halper, I. (1988). Use of cognitive therapy for treatment of a patient suffering from a bipolar affective disorder. *Journal of Cognitive Psychotherapy: An International Quarterly, 2,* 51–58.

Clark, D. A., Beck, A. T., & Alford, B. A. (1999). *Scientific foundations of cognitive therapy of depression.* New York: Wiley.

Cochran, S. (1984). Preventing medication noncompliance in the outpatient treatment of bipolar affective disorder. *Journal of Consulting and Clinical Psychology, 52,* 873–878.

Coryell, W. (1999). Bipolar II disorder: The importance of hypomania. In J. F. Goldberg & M. Harrow (Eds.), *Bipolar disorders: Clinical course and outcome* (pp. 219–236). Washington, DC: American Psychiatric Press.

Coryell, W., Andreason, N., Endicott, J., & Keller, M. (1987). The significance of past mania or hypomania in the course and outcome of major depression. *American Journal of Psychiatry, 142,* 817–821.

Coryell, W., Scheftner, W., Keller, M., Endicott, J., Maser, J., & Klerman, G. L. (1993). The enduring psychosocial consequences of mania and depression. *American Journal of Psychiatry, 150,* 720–727.

DelBello, M. P., & Geller, B. (2001). Review of studies of child and adolescent offspring of bipolar patients. *Bipolar Disorders, 3,* 325–334.

DelBello, M. P., Schwiers, M. L., Rosenberg, H. L., & Strakowski, S. M. (2002). A double-blind, randomized, placebo-controlled study of quetiapine as adjunctive treatment for adolescent mania. *Journal of the Academy of Child and Adolescent Psychiatry, 41,* 1216–1223.

DelBello, M. P., Soutullo, C. A., Hendricks, W., Niemeier, R. T., McElroy, S. L., & Strakowski, S. M. (2001). Prior stimulant treatment in adolescents with bipolar disorder: Association with age at onset. *Bipolar Disorders, 3,* 53–57.

Denicoff, K. D., Blake, K. D., Smith-Jackson, E. E., Jacob, P. A., Leverich, G., & Post, R. M. (1994). Morbidity in treated bipolar disorder: A one-year prospective study using daily life chart ratings. *Depression, 2,* 95–104.

DePaolo, J. R., Simpson, S. C., Folstein, S., & Folstein, M. (1989). The new genetics of bipolar affective disorder: Clinical implications. *Clinical Chemistry, 35*(7), B28–B32.

Depue, R. A., & Collins, P. F. (1998). Neurobiology of the structure of personality: Dopamine, facilitation of incentive motivation, and extraversion. *Behavioural and Brain Sciences, 22,* 491–569.

Dion, G. L., Tohen, M., Anthony, W. A., & Waternaux, C. (1988). Symptoms and functioning of patients with bipolar disorder six months after hospitalization. *Hospital and Community Psychiatry, 39,* 652–657.

Dunayevich, E., Sax, K. W., Keck, P. E., Jr., McElroy, S. L., Sorter, M. T., McConville, B. J., et al. (2000). Twelve-month outcome in bipolar patients with and without personality disorders. *Journal of Clinical Psychiatry, 61,* 134–139.

Dunner, D. L. (1999). Rapid-cycling bipolar affective disorder. In J. F. Goldberg & M. Harrow (Eds.), *Bipolar disorders: Clinical course and outcome* (pp. 199–217). Washington, DC: American Psychiatric Press.

Dunner, D. L., & Fieve, R. R. (1974). Clinical factors in lithium prophylactic failures. *Archives of General Psychiatry, 30,* 229–233.

Ellicott, A., Hammen, C., Gitlin, M., Brown, G., & Jamison, K. R. (1990). Life events and the course of bipolar disorder. *American Journal of Psychiatry, 147,* 1194–1198.

Ernst, C. L., & Goldberg, J. F. (2003). Antidepressant properties of anticonvulsant drugs for bipolar disorder. *Journal of Clinical Psychopharmacology, 23,* 182–192.

Fawcett, J., Scheftner, W., Clark, D., Hedeker, D., Gibbons, R., & Corell, W. (1987). Clinical predictors of suicide in patients with major affective disorders: A controlled prospective study. *American Journal of Psychiatry, 144*(1), 35–40.

Findling, R. L., Feeny, N. C., Stansbrey, R. J., DelPorto-Bedoya, D., & Demeter, C. (2002). Somatic treatment for depressive illnesses in children and adolescents. *Child and Adolescent Psychiatric Clinics of North America, 11,* 555–578.

Frances, A., Docherty, J. P., & Kahn, D. A. (1996). The expert consensus guideline series: Treatment of bipolar disorder. *Journal of Clinical Psychiatry, 57*(Suppl. 12A), 1–88.

Frank, E., & Swartz, H. A. (2004). Interpersonal and Social Rhythm Therapy. In S. L. Johnson & R. L. Leahy (Eds.), *Psychological treatment of bipolar disorder* (pp. 162–183). New York: Guilford Press.

Frank, E., Swartz, H., Mallinger, A., Thase, M., Weaver, E., & Kupfer, D. (1999). Adjunctive psychotherapy for bipolar disorder: Effect of changing treatment modality. *Journal of Abnormal Psychology, 108,* 579–587.

Geller, B., Cooper, T. B., Sun, K., Zimmerman, B., Frazier, J., Williams, M., et al. (1998). Double-blind and placebo-controlled study of lithium for adolescent bipolar disorders with secondary substance dependency. *Journal of the American Academy of Child and Adolescent Psychiatry, 37,* 171–178.

Ghaemi, S. N., Boiman, E. E., & Goodwin, F. K. (2000). Diagnosing bipolar disorder and the effect of antidepressants: A naturalistic study. *Journal of Clinical Psychiatry, 61,* 804–808.

Gillberg, I. C., Hellgren, L., & Gillberg, C. (1993). Psychotic disorders diagnosed in adolescence: Outcome at 30 years. *Journal of Child Psychology and Psychiatry and Allied Disciplines, 34,* 1173–1185.

Gitlin, M. J., Swendsen, J., Heller, T. L., & Hammen, C. (1995). Relapse and impairment in bipolar disorder. *American Journal of Psychiatry, 152,* 1635–1640.

Goldberg, J. F. (2004). Changing landscape of psychopharmacology. In S. L. Johnson & R. L. Leahy (Eds.), *Psychological treatment of bipolar disorder* (pp. 109–138). New York: Guilford Press.

Goldberg, J. F., & Harrow, M. (1999). Poor-outcome bipolar disorders. In J. F. Goldberg & M. Harrow (Eds.), *Bipolar disorders: Clinical course and outcome* (pp. 1–19). Washington, DC: American Psychiatric Press.

Goldberg, J. F., Harrow, M., & Grossman, L. S. (1995). Course and outcome in bipolar affective disorder: A longitudinal follow-up study. *American Journal of Psychiatry, 152,* 379–384.

Goldberg, J. F., & Kocsis, J. H. (1999). Depression in the course of bipolar disorder. In J. F. Goldberg & M. Harrow (Eds.), *Bipolar disorders: Clinical course and outcome* (pp. 129–147). Washington, DC: American Psychiatric Press.

Goldberg, J. F., & Whiteside, J. E. (2002). The association between substance abuse and antidepressant-induced mania in bipolar disorder: A preliminary study. *Journal of Clinical Psychiatry, 63,* 791–795.

Goodwin, F. K., & Jamison, K. R. (1990). *Manic-depressive illness.* Oxford, England: Oxford University Press.

Goodwin, F. K., & Sack, R. L. (1974). Behavioral effects of a new dopamine-beta-hydroxylase inhibitor (dusaric acid) in man. *Journal of Psychiatric Research, 11,* 211–217.

Greil, W., Kleindienst, N., Erazo, N., & Muller-Oerlinghausen, B. (1998). Differential response to lithium and carbamazepine in the prophylaxis of bipolar disorder. *Journal of Clinical Psychopharmacology, 18,* 455–460.

Halberstadt, L. J., & Abramson, L. Y. (1998). *The Halberstadt Mania Inventory (HMI): A self-report measure of manic/hypomanic symptomatology.* Madison: Department of Psychology, University of Wisconsin, Madison.

Henry, C., Sorbara, F., Lacoste, J., Gindrec, C., & Leboyer, M. (2001). Antidepressant-induced mania in bipolar patients: Identification of risk factors. *Journal of Clinical Psychiatry, 62,* 249–255.

Himmelhoch, J. M. (1986). Source of lithium resistance in mixed mania. *Psycho-pharmacological Bulletin, 22,* 613–620.

Himmelhoch, J. M. (1999). The paradox of anxiety syndromes comorbid with the bipolar illnesses. In J. F. Goldberg & M. Harrow (Eds.), *Bipolar disorders: Clinical course and outcome* (pp. 237–258). Washington, DC: American Psychiatric Press.

Hirschfeld, R. M., Keck, P. E., Jr., Karcher, K., Kramer, M., Grossman, F., & Gershon, S. (2002, December). *Rapid antimanic effect of risperidone monotherapy: A 3-week multicenter randomized double-blind placebo-controlled trial.* Paper presented at the 41st Annual Meeting of the American College of Neuropsychopharmacology, San Juan, Puerto Rico.

Hirshfeld, D. R., Gould, R. A., Reilly-Harrington, N. A., Morabito, C., Cosgrove, V., Guille, C., et al. (1998, November). *Short-term adjunctive cognitive-behavioral group therapy for bipolar disorder: Preliminary results from a controlled trial.* Paper presented at the annual meeting of the Association for the Advancement of Behavior Therapy, Washington, DC.

Hunt, N., Bruce-Jones, W., & Silverstone, T. (1992). Life events and bipolar affective disorder. *Journal of Affective Disorders, 25,* 13–20.

Isometsä, E. T., (1993). Course, outcome, and suicide risk in bipolar disorder: A review. *Psychiatria Fennica, 24,* 113–124.

Jamison, K. R. (1995). *An unquiet mind: A memoir of moods and madness.* New York: Knopf.

Johnson, S. L., & Leahy, R. L. (Eds.). (2004). *Psychological treatment of bipolar disorder.* New York: Guilford Press.

Johnson, S. L., & Meyer, B. (2004). Psychosocial predictors of symptoms. In S. L. Johnson & R. L. Leahy (Eds.), *Psychological treatment of bipolar disorder* (pp. 83–105). New York: Guilford Press.

Johnson, S. L., Meyer, B., Winett, C., & Small, J. (2000). Social support and self-esteem predict changes in bipolar depression but not mania. *Journal of Affective Disorders, 58,* 79–86.

Johnson, S. L., & Miller, I. (1997). Negative life events and time to recovery from episodes of bipolar disorder. *Journal of Abnormal Psychology, 106,* 449–457.

Johnson, S. L., & Roberts, J. (1995). Life events and bipolar disorder: Implications from biological theories. *Psychological Bulletin, 117,* 434–439.

Johnson, S. L., Sandrow, D., Meyer, B., Winters, R., Miller, I., Solomon, D., et al. (1999, November). *Life events involving goal-attainment and increases in manic symptoms.* Paper presented at the conference of the Association for the Advancement of Behavior Therapy, Toronto, Ontario.

Johnson, S. L., Winett, C., Meyer, B., Greenhouse, W., & Miller, I. (1999). Social support and the course of bipolar disorder. *Journal of Abnormal Psychology, 108,* 558–566.

Judd, L. L., Akiskal, H. S., Schettler, P. J., Endicott, J., Maser, J., Solomon, D. A., et al. (2002). The long term natural history of the weekly symptomatic status of bipolar I disorder. *Archives of General Psychiatry, 59,* 530–538.

Keller, M. B., Lavori, P. W., Kane, J. M., Gelenberg, A. J., Rosenbaum, J. F., Walzer, E. A., et al. (1992). Subsyndromal symptoms in bipolar disorder: A comparison of standard and low serum levels of lithium. *Archives of General Psychiatry, 49,* 371–376.

Kessler, R. C., McGonagle, K. A., Zhao, S., Nelson, C. B., Hughes, M., Eshleman, S., et al. (1994). Lifetime and 12-month prevalence of *DSM-III-R* psychiatric disorders in the United States: Results from the National Comorbidity Survey. *Archives of General Psychiatry, 51,* 8–19.

Klerman, G. L., Weissman, M. M., Rounsaville, B. J., & Chevron, E. S. (Eds.). (1984). *Interpersonal psychotherapy of depression.* New York: Basic Books.

Kusumakar, V., & Yatham, L. N. (1997). Lamotrigine treatment of rapid cycling bipolar disorder. *American Journal of Psychiatry, 154,* 1171–1172.

Labbate, L. A., & Rubey, R. N. (1997). Lamotrigine for treatment-refractory bipolar disorder [Letter]. *American Journal of Psychiatry, 154,* 1317.

Lam, D. H., Bright, J., Jones, S., Hayward, P., Schuck, N., Chisholm, D., et al. (2000). Cognitive therapy for bipolar illness: A pilot study of relapse prevention. *Cognitive Therapy and Research, 24,* 503–520.

Lam, D. H., Jones, S. H., Hayward, P., & Bright, J. A. (1999). *Cognitive therapy for bipolar disorder: A therapist's guide to concepts, methods, and practice.* Chichester, England: Wiley.

Lam, D. H., Watkins, E. R., Hayward, P., Bright, J., Wright, K., Kerr, N., et al. (2003). A randomized controlled study of cognitive therapy for relapse prevention for bipolar affective disorder. *Archives of General Psychiatry, 60,* 145–152.

Lam, D., & Wong, G. (1997). Prodromes, coping strategies, insight, and social functioning in bipolar affective disorders. *Psychological Medicine, 27,* 1091–1100.

Maj, M. (1999). Lithium prophylaxis of bipolar disorder in ordinary clinical conditions: Pattern of long-term outcome. In J. F. Goldberg & M. Harrow (Eds.), *Bipolar disorders: Clinical course and outcome* (pp. 21–37). Washington, DC: American Psychiatric Press.

Malkoff-Schwartz, S., Frank, E., Anderson, B. P., Hlastala, S. A., Luther, J. F., Sherrill, J. T., et al. (2000). Social rhythm disruption and stressful life events in the onset of bipolar disorder and unipolar episodes. *Psychological Medicine, 30,* 1005–1016.

McClellan, J., & Werry, J. (1997). Practice parameters for the assessment and treatment of children and adolescents with bipolar disorder: American Academy of Child and Adolescent Psychiatry. *Journal of the American Academy of Child and Adolescent Psychiatry, 36,* 157S–176S.

Meaden, P. M., Daniels, R. E., & Zajecka, J. (2000). Construct validity of life chart functioning scales for use in naturalistic studies of bipolar disorder. *Journal of Psychiatric Research, 34,* 187–192.

Mendelwicz, J., & Rainer, J. D. (1977). Adoption study supporting genetic transmission in manic-depressive illness. *Nature, 268,* 327–329.

Miklowitz, D. J. (1992). Longitudinal outcome and medication noncompliance among manic patients with and without mood-incongruent psychotic features. *Journal of Nervous and Mental Disease, 180,* 703–711.

Miklowitz, D. J. (2004). Family therapy. In S. L. Johnson & R. L. Leahy (Eds.), *Psychological treatment of bipolar disorder* (pp. 184–202). New York: Guilford Press.

Miklowitz, D. J., & Goldstein, M. J. (1990). Behavioral family treatment for patients with bipolar affective disorder. *Archives of General Psychiatry, 45,* 225–231.

Miklowitz, D. J., & Goldstein, M. J. (1997). *Bipolar disorder: A family-focused treatment approach.* New York: Guilford Press.

Miklowitz, D. J., Goldstein, M. J., Nuechterlein, K., Snyder, M., & Mintz, J. (1988). Family factors and the course of bipolar affective disorder. *Archives of General Psychiatry, 45,* 225–230.

Miklowitz, D. J., Simoneau, T., George, E., Richards, J., Kalbag, A., Sachs-Ericsson, N., et al. (2000). Family focused treatment of bipolar disorder: 1-year effects of a psycho-educational program in conjunction with pharmacotherapy. *Biological Psychiatry, 48,* 582–592.

Monk, T. H., Frank, E., Potts, J. M., & Kupfer, D. J. (2002). A simple way to measure daily lifestyle regularity. *Journal of Sleep Research, 11*(3), 183–190.

Mundo, E., Walker, M., Cate, T., Macciardi, F., & Kennedy, J. L. (2001). The role of serotonin transporter protein gene in antidepressant-induced mania in bipolar disorder: Preliminary findings. *Archives of General Psychiatry, 58,* 539–544.

Newman, C. F. (2002). Cognitive therapy of bipolar disorder. In G. Simos (Ed.), *Cognitive-behaviour therapy: A guide for the practicing clinician* (pp. 71–96). East Sussex, England: Brunner-Routledge.

Newman, C. F., Leahy, R. L., Beck, A. T., Reilly-Harrington, N. A., & Gyulai, L. (2001). *Bipolar disorder: A cognitive therapy approach.* Washington, DC: American Psychological Association.

Nezu, A. M., Nezu, C. M., & Perri, M. G. (1989). *Problem-solving therapy for depression: Theory, research, and clinical guidelines.* New York: Wiley.

Nilsson, A. (1999). Lithium therapy and suicide risk. *Journal of Clinical Psychiatry, 60*(Suppl. 2), 85–88.

Papatheodorou, G., Kutcher, S. P., Katic, M., & Szalai, J. P. (1995). The efficacy and safety of divalproex sodium in the treatment of acute mania in adolescents and young adults: An open clinical trial. *Journal of Clinical Psychopharmacology, 15,* 110–116.

Perry, A., Tarrier, N., Morriss, R., McCarthy, E., & Limb, K. (1999). Randomised controlled trial of efficacy of teaching patients with bipolar disorder to identify early symptoms of relapse and obtain treatment. *British Medical Journal, 318,* 149–153.

Peselow, E., Sanfilipo, M., & Fieve, R. (1995). Relationship between hypomania and personality disorders before and after successful treatment. *American Journal of Psychiatry, 152,* 232–238.

Pope, H. G., Jr., McElroy, S. L., Keck, P. E., Jr., & Hudson, J. L. (1991). Valproate in the treatment of acute mania: A placebo-controlled study. *Archives of General Psychiatry, 48,* 62–68.

Post, R. M., Denicoff, K. D., Frye, M. A., Leverich, G. S., Cora-Locatelli, G., & Kimbrell, T. A. (1999). Long-term outcome of anticonvulsants in affective disorders. In J. F. Goldberg & M. Harrow (Eds.), *Bipolar disorders: Clinical course and outcome* (pp. 85–114). Washington, DC: American Psychiatric Press.

Post, R. M., Rubinow, D. R., & Ballenger, J. C. (1986). Conditioning and sensitization in the longitudinal course of affective illness. *British Journal of Psychiatry, 149,* 191–201.

Post, R. M., & Weiss, S. R. (1989). Sensitization, kindling, and anticonvulsants in mania. *Journal of Clinical Psychiatry, 50* (Suppl.), 23–30.

Preda, A., Fazeli, A., McKay, B. G., Bowers, M. B., Jr., & Mazure, C. M. (1999). Lamotrigine as prophylaxis against steroid-induced mania. *Journal of Clinical Psychiatry, 60,* 708–709.

Priebe, S., Wildgrube, C., & Muller-Oerlinghausen, B. (1989). Lithium prophylaxis and expressed emotion. *British Journal of Psychiatry, 154,* 396–399.

Rea, M. M., Thompson, M., Miklowitz, D. J., Goldstein, M. J., Hwang, S., & Mintz, J. (2003). Family-focused treatment vs. individual treatment for bipolar disorder: Results of a randomized clinical trial. *Journal of Consulting and Clinical Psychology, 71,* 482–492.

Reilly-Harrington, N. A., Alloy, L. B., Fresco, D. M., & Whitehouse, W. G. (1999). Cognitive styles and life events interact to predict bipolar and unipolar symptomatology. *Journal of Abnormal Psychology, 108,* 567–578.

Sachs, G. S., Grossman, F., Ghaemi, S. N., Okamoto, A., & Bowden, C. L. (2002). Combination of a mood stabilizer with risperidone or haloperidol for treatment of acute mania: A double-blind, placebo-controlled comparison of efficacy and safety. *American Journal of Psychiatry, 159,* 1146–1154.

Sachs, G. S., Mullen, J. A., Devine, N. A., Sweitzer, D. E., & Nasrallah, H. A. (2002, December). *Quetiapine versus placebo as adjunct to mood stabilizer for the treatment of acute bipolar mania.* Paper presented at the 41st Annual Meeting of the American College of Neuropsychopharmacology, San Juan, Puerto Rico.

Sachs, G. S., Printz, D. J., Kahn, D. A., Carpenter, D., & Docherty, J. P. (2000). *Medication treatment for bipolar disorder: The Expert Consensus Guidelines Series.* New York: McGraw-Hill.

Sachs, G. S., Thase, M. E., Otto, M. W., Bauer, M., Miklowitz, D., Wisniewski, S. R., et al. (2003). Rationale, design, and methods of the Systematic Treatment Enhancement Program for Bipolar Disorder. *Biological Psychiatry, 53,* 1028–1042.

Scott, J. (2004). Treatment outcome studies. In S. L. Johnson & R. L. Leahy (Eds.), *Psychological treatment of bipolar disorder* (pp. 226–241). New York: Guilford Press.

Scott, J., Garland, A., & Moorhead, S. (2001). A pilot study of cognitive therapy in bipolar disorder. *Psychological Medicine, 31,* 459–467.

Simoneau, T. L., Miklowitz, D. J., & Saleem, R. (1998). Expressed emotion and interactional patterns in the families of bipolar patients. *Journal of Abnormal Psychology, 107,* 497–507.

Simpson, S. G., & Jamison, K. R. (1999). The risk of suicide in patients with bipolar disorders. *Journal of Clinical Psychiatry, 60*(Suppl. 2), 53–56.

Small, J. G., Kellams, J. J., Milstein, V., & Small, I. F. (1980). Complications with electroconvulsive treatment combined with lithium. *Biological Psychiatry, 15,* 103–112.

Solomon, D. A., Keitner, G. I., Ryan, C. E., & Miller, I. W. (1998). Lithium plus valproate as maintenance polypharmacy for patients with bipolar I disorder: A review. *Journal of Clinical Psychopharmacology, 18,* 38–49.

Sonne, S. C., Brady, K. T., & Morton, W. A. (1994). Substance abuse and bipolar affective disorder. *Journal of Mental and Nervous Disease, 182,* 349–352.

Soutullo, C. A.., DelBello, M. P., Ochsner, J. E., McElroy, S. L., Taylor, S. A., Strakowski, S. M., et al. (2002). Severity of bipolarity in hospitalized manic adolescents with history of stimulant or antidepressant treatment. *Journal of Affective Disorders, 70,* 323–327.

Swann, A. C., Bowden, C. L., Morris, D., Calabrese, J. R., Petty, F., Small, J., et al. (1997). Depression during mania: Treatment response to lithium or divalproex. *Archives of General Psychiatry, 54,* 37–42.

Targum, S. D., Dibble, E. D., Davenport, Y. B., & Gershon, E. S. (1981). The Family Attitudes Questionnaire: Patients' and spouses' views of bipolar illness. *Archives of General Psychiatry, 38,* 562–568.

Tohen, M. F., Jacobs. T. G., Grundy, S. L., McElroy, S. L., Banov, M. C., Janicak, P. G., et al. (2000). Efficacy of olanzapine in acute bipolar mania—A double-blind, placebo-controlled study: The Olanzapine HGGW Study Group. *Archives of General Psychiatry, 57,* 841–849.

Tohen, M. F., Ketter, T. A., Zarate, C. A., Suppes, T., Frye, M., Altshuler, L., et al. (2003). Olanzapine versus divalproex sodium for the treatment of acute mania and maintenance of remission: A 47-week study. *American Journal of Psychiatry, 160,* 1263–1271.

Tohen, M. F., Marneros, A., Bowden, C., Greil, W., Koukopolous, A., Belmaker, H., et al. (2002, December). *Olanzapine versus lithium in relapse prevention in bipolar disorder: A randomized double-blind controlled 12-month clinical trial.* Paper presented at the 41st Annual Meeting of the American College of Neuropsychopharmacology, San Juan, Puerto Rico.

Tohen, M. F., Sanger, T. M., McElroy, S. L., Tollefson, G. D., Chengappa, K. N., Daniel, D. G., et al. (1999). Olanzapine versus placebo in the treatment of acute mania: Olanzapine HGEH Study Group. *American Journal of Psychiatry, 156,* 702–709.

Tohen, M. F., Waternaux, C. M., & Tsuang, M. T. (1990). Outcome in mania: A 4-year prospective follow-up of 75 patients using survival analysis. *Archives of General Psychiatry, 47,* 1106–1111.

Tohen, M. F., & Zarate, C. A., Jr. (1999). Bipolar disorder and comorbid substance abuse disorder. In J. F. Goldberg & M. Harrow (Eds.), *Bipolar disorders: Clinical course and outcome* (pp. 171–184). Washington, DC: American Psychiatric Press.

Vehmanen, L., Kaprio, J., & Loennqvist, J. (1995). Twin studies of bipolar disorder. *Psychiatria Fennica, 26,* 107–116.

Vieta, E., Khanna, S., van Kammen, D., Lyons, B., Grossman, F., & Kramer, M. (2002, December). *Risperidone monotherapy in acute bipolar mania.* Paper presented at the 41st Annual Meeting of the American College of Neuropsychopharmacology, San Juan, Puerto Rico.

Viguera, A. C., Nonacs, R., Cohen, L. S., Tondo, L. Murray, A., & Baldessarini, R. J. (2000). Risk of recurrence of bipolar disorder in pregnant and nonpregnant women after discontinuing lithium maintenance. *American Journal of Psychiatry, 157,* 179–184.

Walden, J., Normann, C., Langosche, J., Berger, M., & Grunze, H. (1998). Differential treatment of bipolar disorder with old and new antiepileptic drugs. *Neuropsychobiology, 38,* 181–184.

Wehr, T. A., Sack, D. A., Rosenthal, N. E., & Cowdry, R. W. (1988). Rapid cycling affective disorder: Contributing factors and treatment responses in 51 patients. *American Journal of Psychiatry, 43,* 822–828.

Wendel, J. S., Miklowitz, D. J., Richards, J. A., & George, E. L. (2000). Expressed emotion and attributions in the relatives of bipolar patients: An analysis of problem-solving interactions. *Journal of Abnormal Psychology, 109,* 792–796.

West, S. A., McElroy, S. L., Strakowski, S. M., Keck, P. E., Jr., & McConville, B. J. (1995). Attention-deficit hyperactivity disorder in adolescent mania. *American Journal of Psychiatry, 152,* 271–273.

Winters, K. C., & Neale, J. M. (1985). Mania and low self-esteem. *Journal of Abnormal Psychology, 94,* 282–290.

Young, J. E. (1999). *Cognitive therapy for personality disorders: A schema-focused approach* (3rd ed.). Sarasota, FL: Professional Resource Exchange.

Young, R. C., Biggs, J. T., Ziegler, V. E., & Meyer, D. A. (1978). A rating scale for mania: Reliability, validity, and sensitivity. *British Journal of Psychiatry, 133,* 429–435.

Youngstrom, E. A., Findling, R. L., & Feeny, N. (2004). Assessment of bipolar spectrum disorders in children and adolescents. In S. L. Johnson & R. L. Leahy (Eds.), *Psychological treatment of bipolar disorder* (pp. 58–82). New York: Guilford Press.

Zarate, C. A., Jr., & Tohen, M. F. (2001). Bipolar disorder and comorbid substance use disorders. In J. R. Hubbard & P. R. Martin (Eds.), *Substance abuse in the mentally and physically disabled* (pp. 59–75). New York: Dekker.

CHAPTER 16

Schizophrenia

KIM T. MUESER, ELISA BOLTON, AND SUSAN R. MCGURK

DESCRIPTION OF THE DISORDER AND CLINICAL PICTURE

Schizophrenia is a major mental illness affecting a broad range of functioning and contributing to substantial impairment over the lifetime. The illness comprises three major groups of symptoms: psychotic symptoms, negative symptoms, and cognitive impairments (Liddle, 1987; Mueser, Curran, & McHugo, 1997). Common examples of *psychotic symptoms* include hallucinations, delusions, and bizarre behavior (e.g., maintaining a peculiar posture for no apparent reason or other odd or apparently purposeless behavior). Common delusions in schizophrenia include *persecutory delusions, delusions of control* (e.g., the belief that others can interfere with one's thoughts), *grandiose delusions* (e.g., the belief that one is Jesus Christ), and *somatic delusions* (e.g., the belief that one's brain is rotting away). For many patients, the presence of psychotic symptoms fluctuates, requiring hospitalization only if they pose a significant threat to the safety of the patient or others. However, a sizable minority of patients (30 percent to 40 percent) experience chronic psychotic symptoms that do not respond to medication and that are the cause of significant distress (Curson, Patel, Liddle, & Barnes, 1988).

Negative symptoms involve deficits in basic emotional processes and behaviors, including blunted or flattened affect, poverty of speech (i.e., diminished verbal communication), anhedonia, apathy, psychomotor retardation, and physical inertia. Negative symptoms are relatively common in schizophrenia, tend to be stable over time (Mueser, Bellack, Douglas, & Wade, 1991), and often have a pervasive impact on the ability of patients to function socially and to sustain independent living (Pogue-Geile, 1989). As negative symptoms are less obvious manifestations of a psychiatric illness, patients are often perceived by relatives and others to be lazy.

Cognitive impairments in schizophrenia are also common, including problems in attention and concentration, psychomotor speed, learning and memory, and executive functions (e.g., abstract thinking, problem solving). A decline in cognitive abilities compared with premorbid functioning is common in most patients with schizophrenia (Heaton et al., 1994). As with negative symptoms, cognitive impairments are strongly associated with functional impairments in areas such as employment (McGurk & Mueser, 2004).

Although these symptoms are critical to the diagnosis of schizophrenia, the functional impairments associated with the illness are its most striking characteristic (American Psychiatric Association, 1994). Most individuals with schizophrenia experience problems in social functioning, working or fulfilling other instrumental roles, and caring for oneself. Impairment in functioning can be profound, resulting in the need for disability entitlements and assistance in meeting basic living needs, such as housing, medical care, food, and clothing. Improving functioning remains the single most important challenge for the management of schizophrenia.

Individuals with schizophrenia are at high risk for many other disorders as well. Comorbid substance use disorders occur in approximately 50 percent of patients with schizophrenia (Regier et al., 1990). Depression, general feelings of anxiety, anger, and post-traumatic stress disorder are also common among people with schizophrenia and have been associated with poor outcomes (e.g., increased hospital use, lower employment rates) and suicidal tendencies (Mueser, Rosenberg, Goodman, & Trumbetta, 2002; Sands & Harrow, 1999). The lifetime rate of suicide for schizophrenia is approximately 4 percent, compared to 6 percent for affective disorders and 7 percent for alcohol dependence (Inskip, Harris, & Barraclough, 1998). Difficulties with anxiety, anger, and hostility are often due to psychotic symptoms (Penn, Hope, Spaulding, & Kucera, 1994), especially when the patient is paranoid (Bartels, Drake, Wallach, & Freeman, 1991).

PERSONALITY DEVELOPMENT AND PSYCHOPATHOLOGY

Poor premorbid social functioning has been found to antedate the onset of schizophrenia (Zigler & Glick, 1986). For example, people who later develop schizophrenia tend to be more socially isolated, pass fewer social-sexual developmental milestones (e.g., having a boyfriend/girlfriend), and have fewer friends in childhood and adolescence. In addition, prior to developing schizophrenia, some individuals in childhood display a maladaptive pattern, including disruptive behavior, problems in school, and impulsivity (Baum & Walker, 1995). Symptoms of conduct disorder in childhood, such as repeated fighting, truancy, and lying, have also been found to predict the later development of schizophrenia (Neumann, Grimes, Walker, & Baum 1995).

As schizophrenia frequently has an onset during early adulthood, persons with the illness are less likely to marry or remain married, particularly males (Odegaard, 1960), and are less likely to complete higher levels of education (Kessler, Foster, Saunders, & Stang, 1995). Further, it has long been known that there is an association between poverty and schizophrenia, with people belonging to lower socioeconomic classes more likely to develop the disorder (Hollingshead & Redlich, 1958). Two theories have been advanced to account for this association. The *social drift hypothesis* postulates that the debilitating effects of schizophrenia on capacity to work result in a lowering of socioeconomic means, and hence poverty (Aro, Aro, & Keskimäki, 1995). The *environmental stress hypothesis* proposes that the high levels of stress associated with poverty precipitate schizophrenia in some individuals who would not otherwise develop the illness (Bruce & Leaf, 1989). Longitudinal research on changes in socioeconomic class status and schizophrenia provide conflicting results. For example, Fox (1990) reanalyzed data from several longitudinal studies and found that after controlling for initial levels of socioeconomic class, downward drift was not evident. However, Dohrenwend et al. (1992) did find evidence for social drift, even after controlling for socioeconomic class.

Although the incidence of schizophrenia is roughly equal across different countries, the course of illness is less severe in developing countries than developed ones (Thara, Henrietta, Joseph, Rajkumar, & Eaton, 1994). For example, in a multinational World Health Organization (WHO) study, patients in 10 of 13 treatment centers in developing countries had better outcomes than those in developed countries (Craig, Siegel, Hopper, Lin, & Sartorius, 1997). The mechanisms responsible for the better outcome in developing countries are unclear, although differences in social structures, the central role of the family, and beliefs about the origins of mental illness have been postulated to be important (Kleinman, 1988).

Gender is another factor associated with a differential course of the disorder (Haas & Garratt, 1998). Women tend to have later age of onset of the illness, spend less time in hospitals, and demonstrate better social competence and social functioning than men with the illness (Goldstein, 1988). The later age of onset in women is associated with higher attainment of social role functioning before illness, which confers a better outcome (Häfner, 2000). Further, the benefits experienced by women do not appear to be explained by societal differences in tolerance for deviant behavior. A variety of different hypotheses may account for the superior outcome of women with schizophrenia (e.g., biological differences, interactions with environmental stressors; Castle & Murray, 1993), but no single theory has received strong support.

EPIDEMIOLOGY

The annual incidence of schizophrenia is 2 to 4 per 1,000. The lifetime prevalence of schizophrenia (including the closely related disorders of schizoaffective disorder and schizophreniform disorder) is approximately 1 percent (Keith, Regier, & Rae, 1991). In general, the prevalence of schizophrenia is remarkably stable across a wide range of different populations, such as gender, race, religion, and level of industrialization (Jablensky, 1999).

There are conflicting reports on potential variations in the prevalence and incidence of schizophrenia across different countries and cultural groups (U.S. Institute of Medicine, 2001). However, these differences are reduced when stricter diagnostic criteria for schizophrenia are used (Jablensky, 1999). In a WHO study, the incidence of schizophrenia was shown to be quite similar across ten countries (Jablensky et al., 1992). This research indicates that the clinical syndrome of schizophrenia is similar across a wide range of cultures and countries, including developed and developing nations. Thus, to date, the differences in incidence and prevalence reported across countries and cultural groups are not thought to be significant.

There are several sociodemographic factors that have been linked with increased risk of schizophrenia (van Os & Marcelis, 1998). Specifically, poverty and lower social class have long been linked to higher rates of schizophrenia (Bruce et al., 1991). Individuals born in urban areas are more likely to develop schizophrenia than those in rural areas (Peen & Decker, 1997). Although the incidence of the condition is similar across different ethnic groups (Jablensky, 1999), increased rates are present in some ethnic minority populations, such as second generation Afro-Caribbean people in the United Kingdom (Boydell et al., 2001), Dutch Antillean and Surinamese immigrants in Holland (Selten, Slaets, & Kahn, 1997), and African American people in the United States

(Rabkin, 1979). It is hypothesized that these differences reflect the stressful effects of being an ethnic minority, which may increase vulnerability to schizophrenia in biologically predisposed individuals.

ETIOLOGY

The etiology of schizophrenia appears to be multifactorial with evidence implicating the role of genetics, biology, and environment. In general, rates of schizophrenia are higher among relatives of patients than in the general population. The risk of a woman with schizophrenia giving birth to a child who later develops schizophrenia is approximately 10 percent, compared to only 1 percent in the general population (Gottesman, 1991). Adoption and twin studies have shown that this increased risk is genetic, with a tenfold increase in risk associated with the presence of an affected first-degree family member. This genetic risk increases with each affected relative, to nearly 50 percent when both parents are affected (McGuffin, Owen, & Farmer, 1996), and 60 percent to 84 percent when a monozygotic twin is affected (Cardno et al., 1999). There appear to be multiple susceptibility genes, each with a small effect and acting in concert with epigenetic and environmental factors (Harrison & Owen, 2003). Although there is strong evidence that genetic factors can play a role in the development of schizophrenia, there is also a growing body of evidence pointing to the influence of other biological, nongenetic factors. For example, obstetric complications, maternal exposure to the influenza virus, and other environmental-based insults to the developing fetus (e.g., rubella, malnutrition, diabetes mellitus, and smoking during pregnancy) are all associated with an increased risk of developing schizophrenia (Geddes & Lawrie, 1995; Thomas et al., 2001). Obstetric complications associated with hypoxia are particularly related to increased risk, which might be mediated by excitotoxic effects of hypoxia on the fetal neonatal brain. Because most cases of obstetric complications do not lead to schizophrenia, such complications likely interact with genetic vulnerability to increase risk of the illness (Cannon, Jones, & Murray, 2002). Furthermore, it is not yet known whether the high frequency of obstetric complications in schizophrenia is the result of abnormal brain development associated with genetic vulnerability or an additional environmental factor that contributes to the development of schizophrenia. Thus, there is a growing consensus that the etiology of schizophrenia is heterogeneous, with genetic factors playing a larger role in the development of some cases, and early environmental-based factors playing a greater function in the development of other cases. This heterogeneity could account for the fact that the genetic contribution to schizophrenia is lower than bipolar disorder (Goodwin & Jamison, 1990).

Neurochemical and structural changes in the brain have also been implicated in development of schizophrenia. The neurotransmitter most commonly associated with the onset of schizophrenia is dopamine. The dopamine hypothesis proposes that alterations in levels of dopamine are responsible for the symptoms of schizophrenia. Originally, this hypothesis was based on findings that substances that increase dopamine (e.g., levadopa used to treat Parkinson's disease) increase psychotic symptoms and substances that decrease dopamine reduce psychotic symptoms. Current versions of this hypothesis suggest that an overabundance of dopamine in certain limbic areas of the brain is responsible for psychotic symptoms whereas a lack of dopamine in cortical areas is responsible for negative symptoms (Davis, Kahn, Ko, & Davidson, 1991).

Several lines of evidence suggest that structural changes associated with schizophrenia (i.e., enlargement of the ventricular system) are likely to result from abnormal early brain development. Structural changes are apparent before the first episode and in first-degree biological relatives, indicating that such abnormalities are not restricted to the pathological process of psychosis but are a manifestation of familial risk factors, such as genes affecting neurodevelopment (McDonald et al., 2002). It has been speculated that excessive synaptic pruning occurs in schizophrenia, which leads to psychosis when it reaches a threshold (Innocenti, Ansermet, & Parnas, 2003). Substantial synaptic elimination occurs during adolescence, which may account for the onset of schizophrenia around this time (Feinberg, 1982). The age of onset may be further lowered when genetic vulnerability is compounded by neuronal loss due to hypoxia-associated obstetric complications (Cannon et al., 2000).

Further evidence that schizophrenia is a consequence of an interaction between genetic, biological, and environmental factors comes from a series of studies by Tienari (1991) and colleagues (Tienari et al., 1987). They compared the likelihood of developing schizophrenia in three groups of children raised by adoptive families. Two groups of children had biological mothers with schizophrenia, and a third group had biological mothers with no psychiatric disorder. The researchers divided the adoptive families of the children into two broad groups based on the level of disturbance present in the family: healthy adoptive families and psychologically disturbed adoptive families. Follow-up assessments were conducted to determine the presence of schizophrenia and other severe psychiatric disorders in the adopted children raised in all three groups. The researchers found that biological children of mothers with schizophrenia who were raised by adoptive families with high levels of disturbance were significantly more likely to develop schizophrenia or another psychotic disorder than either similarly vulnerable children raised in families with low levels of disturbance or children with no biological vulnerability raised in either disturbed or healthy adoptive families.

COURSE, COMPLICATIONS, AND PROGNOSIS

Course

Schizophrenia usually has an onset in late adolescence or early adulthood. Because schizophrenia usually occurs during early adulthood, many developmental tasks are disrupted, including forming close interpersonal or dating relationships, pursuing higher education, career development, separating from parents, and identity formation. It is extremely rare for the first onset of schizophrenia to occur before adolescence, with most diagnostic systems considering childhood-onset schizophrenia to be a different disorder than adolescent or adult onset (American Psychiatric Association, 1994). Late-onset schizophrenia (i.e., after age 45) is characterized by psychotic symptoms, but is less likely to involve formal thought disorder and negative symptoms (Howard, Almeida, & Levy, 1994). Furthermore, diagnosis of late-onset schizophrenia is complicated by the lack of clear distinguishing characteristics that discriminates this disorder from a variety of other disorders that develop later in life.

Typically the disorder has a gradual, insidious onset that takes place over about five years, beginning with the emergence of negative and depressive symptoms, followed by cognitive and social impairment, followed several years later by the emergence of psychotic symptoms and first psychiatric contact (Häfner et al., 2003). Psychotic symptoms tend to be episodic over time, with their emergence or exacerbation associated with some potential risk to self or others, which may require temporary hospitalization. Negative symptoms and cognitive problems tend to be more stable over time, and contribute significantly to functional impairment (McGurk, Mueser, Harvey, Marder, & LaPuglia, 2003; Mueser, 2000).

Despite the fact that most patients with schizophrenia live in the community, it is comparatively rare for patients to return to their premorbid levels of functioning between episodes. Although 21 percent to 30 percent of patients treated for a first episode have no symptom relapses over the next five years, the stability of the illness over time is moderate, with most variability occurring immediately after the onset of the disorder. In general, the course of the illness is most strongly predicted by the level of social development attained at the onset of psychosis, which is related to the age psychosis develops (Häfner, 2000). In addition, people with an acute onset of schizophrenia have a somewhat better prognosis than those with a more insidious illness (Fenton & McGlashan, 1991; Kay, Opler, & Fiszbein, 1987). There is also a growing belief that increased attention and treatment during an individual's first break may potentially avoid some of the long-term problems associated with the diagnosis (Lincoln & McGorry, 1995).

Environmental factors and participation in rehabilitation programs are important in determining the course of schizophrenia, as illustrated by the following two long-term outcome studies conducted by Harding and her associates (DeSisto, Harding, McCormick, Ashikaga, & Brooks, 1995; Harding, Brooks, Ashikaga, Strauss, & Breier, 1987a, 1987b). They studied the course of patients' schizophrenia in Vermont and Maine. At the time of the study, Vermont had a highly developed system of community-based rehabilitation programs for persons with severe mental illness. In contrast, Maine had more traditional hospital-based treatment programs. The patients in Vermont demonstrated surprisingly positive outcomes over the 20- to 40-year follow-up period, whereas the patients in Maine fared substantially worse over the long-term course of their illness. The results of this study indicate that outcome in schizophrenia is influenced by the interaction between biological and environmental factors.

The ability to predict outcome is rather poor. The primary reason for this is that symptom severity and functioning are determined by the dynamic interplay between biological vulnerability, environmental factors, and coping skills (Liberman et al., 1986). Factors such as compliance with medication (Buchanan, 1992), substance abuse (Drake, Osher, & Wallach, 1989), exposure to a hostile or critical environment (Butzlaff & Hooley, 1998), the availability of psychosocial programming (Bellack & Mueser, 1993), and assertive case management and outreach (Bond et al., 2001) all play a significant role in determining outcome.

Stress coping skills, and social support are most important factors that influence the course of schizophrenia. Stress can impinge on biological vulnerability, worsening symptoms and triggering relapses. However, coping skills (e.g., problem solving and social skills) can minimize the harmful effects of stress. Finally, social support can both reduce the effects of stress on vulnerability, and enhance the patient's ability to cope.

Complications

The presence of comorbid substance use disorders in schizophrenia is associated with a worse course of the illness, including increased vulnerability to relapses and hospitalizations, housing instability and homelessness, violence, economic family burden, and treatment noncompliance (Drake & Brunette, 1998). Furthermore, substance abuse in schizophrenia increases the chances of developing infectious diseases, including HIV, hepatitis B, and especially hepatitis C (Rosenberg et al., 2001).

Another important complicating clinical feature of schizophrenia is lack of insight (Amador, Strauss, Yale, & Gorman, 1991). Many patients with schizophrenia have little or no insight into the fact that they have a psychiatric illness, or even that they have any problems at all. This denial of illness can lead to noncompliance with recommended treatments, such as psychotropic medications and psychosocial therapies (McEvoy et al., 1989). Problems with paranoia and distrust may contribute to noncompliance, in that some patients may believe medications or treatment providers are dangerous to them. Further, medication side effects are unpleasant and can lead to noncompliance. Medication noncompliance increases the risk of relapse, and is therefore a major concern to clinical treatment providers (Buchanan, 1992).

Finally, there is growing recognition that in comparison to persons in the general population, patients with schizophrenia are more prone to experiencing traumatic events, such as physical and sexual assault and witnessing violence (Goodman, Rosenberg, Mueser, & Drake, 1997). Exposure to trauma is likely to worsen the course of schizophrenia and complicate treatment (Mueser et al., 2002) because both discrete stressors (e.g., life events) and exposure to a stressful environment can worsen psychotic disorders (Butzlaff & Hooley, 1998).

Prognosis

Once schizophrenia has developed, lifetime functional impairment is commonly observed. Several long-term studies of 20 to 40 years duration suggest that previous estimates of recovery from schizophrenia are overly conservative (Harding & Keller, 1998). Although definitions of *recovery* vary from one study to the next, some studies suggest as many as 20 percent to 50 percent of patients fully recover from schizophrenia later in life (Warner, 1985). In sum, the prognosis of schizophrenia is usually considered fair, although there is general agreement that it is worse than for other major psychiatric disorders, such as bipolar disorder or major depression.

ASSESSMENT AND DIAGNOSIS

Core Clinical Symptoms, Psychotic and Negative Symptoms

The most widely used instruments include the Brief Psychiatric Rating Scale (BPRS; Lukoff, Nuechterlein, & Ventura, 1986), the Scale for the Assessment of Negative Symptoms (SANS; Andreasen, 1984), and the Positive and Negative Syndrome Scale (PANSS; Kay, Opler, & Fiszbein, 1987), all of which are designed to be administered as semistructured clinical interviews. The BPRS was developed as a general measure of severe psychopathology in psychiatric disorders, and includes items relevant to psychotic, negative, and mood symptoms. The SANS was developed to measure the negative symptoms of schizophrenia. The PANSS incorporates all the items of the BPRS, and includes additional items tapping negative symptoms and cognitive impairment.

Cognitive Impairment

Schizophrenia is associated with deficits in attention, learning and memory, and executive functioning (MacCabe & Murray, 2004). There are no well-established relationships between specific cognitive impairments and particular deficits in adaptive functioning (Mueser, 2000). However, cognitive assessment can contribute to treatment planning as it provides information about the challenges an individual faces during reintegration into society. Identification of a deficit in verbal learning and memory, for example, may have implications for the manner in which new information is presented in a rehabilitative intervention. In addition, helping individuals develop an awareness of their cognitive difficulties will help them to develop useful compensatory strategies in performance of everyday tasks. Further, antipsychotic medications may have differential effects on specific cognitive impairments (e.g., Meltzer and McGurk, 1999). Therefore, a cognitive assessment may provide useful information about choice of medication.

Standardized measures of working memory include the Digit Span Backward subtest and the Letter-Number Sequencing of the Wechsler Adult Intelligence Scale-III (Wechsler, 1998). Other neurocognitive tests that assess working memory and also executive functioning, are the Trail Making Test (Reitan & Wolfson, 1993) and the Wisconsin Card Sorting Test (WCST; Berg, 1948). The California Verbal Learning Test (CVLT; Delis, Kramer, Kaplan, & Ober, 1987) is a widely used test of verbal learning and memory in which immediate recall, learning, time-delayed recall, and recognition may be assessed. Continuous Performance Tests are the most widely used measures of sustained attention in clinical research (Lezak, 1995).

Biological Assessment

Biological assessments may be used to rule out possible organic factors, such as a tumor, stroke, or covert substance abuse. Similarly, blood samples may be obtained in order to determine whether the patient is compliant with prescribed medication, even though the specific level of medication in the blood has not been conclusively linked to clinical response. Clozapine, an atypical antipsychotic requires ongoing blood tests to detect the rare, but potentially lethal blood disorder of agranulocytosis (Alvir, Lieberman, & Safferman, 1995).

Associated Features

The nature of schizophrenia is that the illness often pervades many aspects of an individual's life. Therefore, it is crucial to evaluate common associated features of the illness and important life domains that may contribute to impaired functioning. These include medication noncompliance, age appropriate social and role functioning, occupational functioning, issues related to sexuality, and environmental factors such as family environment.

Medication Noncompliance

Noncompliance with medication is often problematic in schizophrenia, especially early in the course of the disorder (Weiden et al., 1994). Determining level of compliance with medications is difficult. Urine and blood samples may be analyzed for presence and level of medications, but the results of these methods often are imprecise. In addition to routine blood or urine tests, there are other quantitative approaches available to evaluate compliance with medications, the simplest of which involves counting the number of pills in medication bottles and comparing this with the number that should have been taken according to the prescribed regimen (Kemp, Hayward, Applewhaite, Everitt, & David, 1996).

If noncompliance is a significant problem, a more thorough assessment should include evaluation of barriers to compliance, including: (1) unpleasant side effects, (2) complexity of medication regimens, (3) cognitive impairment, (4) poor insight or awareness of illness and the need for treatment, (5) poor alliance with mental health care providers, (6) insufficient supervision during administration, (7) family beliefs about illness and/or medications, (8) mental status or current symptoms (e.g., paranoia about medications), and (9) perceived benefit of medications (Kemp et al., 1996; Weiden et al., 1994). Standardized scales designed to evaluate compliance and attitudes toward medications may help identify targets for intervention, such as the Rating of Medication Influences Scale (Weiden et al., 1994) and the Drug Attitudes Inventory (Hogan, Awad, & Eastwood, 1983).

Family Assessment

The assessment of family functioning is highly relevant in schizophrenia. First, the presence of hostile, critical, or emotionally overinvolved attitudes and behaviors in relatives of patients is an important predictor of relapse and rehospitalization (Butzlaff & Hooley, 1998). Second, caring for a mentally ill loved one can lead to significant burden on relatives (Webb et al., 1998), which ultimately can threaten the family's ability to provide support to the patient. It is also useful to evaluate family knowledge, attributions, expectations, and beliefs about the illness (Clare & Birchwood, 1998). Before deciding whether to include family work as part of the overall treatment plan, it is important to consider the level of interest of the family and patient, the extent and quality of the family contact, and the ability of the family as a whole to identify outcomes that could serve as goals of family therapy (Dixon, Adams, & Lucksted, 2000).

A number of specific methods can be used to assess the emotional climate in the family and the burden of the illness on the family. Interviews with individual family members, including the patient, as well as with the entire family, coupled with observation of more naturalistic family interactions, can provide invaluable information about the quality of family functioning. Examples of structured interviews include the Camberwell Family Interview (Leff & Vaughn, 1985), although this instrument is primarily a research instrument, and the Family Environment Scale (Moos & Moos, 1981), a self-report instrument completed by family members (Halford, Sweitzer, & Varghese, 1991). The most comprehensive measure of family burden is the Family Experiences Interview Schedule (Tessler & Gamache, 1995), which yields information on subjective burden (e.g., emotional strain) and objective burden (e.g., economic impact).

The Relatives Assessment Interview (Barrowclough & Tarrier, 1992) is also a structured clinical interview that elicits information regarding the patient's psychiatric history and social functioning, the relatives' responses to the patient, the perceived impact of the illness, attempts at coping, and areas of difficulty and tension in the family. Family members' knowledge about schizophrenia may be assessed using the Information Questionnaire-Relative Version (McGill, Falloon, Boyd, & Wood-Siverio, 1983) or the Knowledge about Schizophrenia Interview (Barrowclough & Tarrier, 1992). Negative attitudes toward patients may be assessed with the Patient Rejection Scale (Krcisman et al., 1988).

Social Functioning

Direct interviews with patients can be used to help to identify broad areas of social dysfunction. Patient interviews are most informative when combined with interviews with significant others, such as family members and clinicians, and naturalistic observations of the patient's social interactions. There are several standardized instruments that may be helpful in structuring such interviews, including the Social Behavior Schedule (Wykes & Sturt, 1986), the Social Adjustment Scale-II (Schooler, Hogarty, & Weissman, 1979), the Social-Adaptive Functioning Evaluation (SAFE; Harvey, et al., 1997), and the Independent Living Skills Survey (Wallace, Liberman, Tauber, & Wallace, 2000).

Social skills are individual behavioral components, such as eye contact, voice loudness, and choice of words, which in combination are necessary for effective communication (Bellack, Mueser, Gingerich, & Agresta, 2004). Social skills can be assessed with interviews, naturalistic observations, and role plays. Role plays involve brief simulated social interactions between the patient and a confederate taking the role of an interactive partner. They are helpful to identify the content areas in which social and role dysfunctions occur. Role plays can be as brief as 15 to 30 seconds, to assess skill areas such as initiating conversations, or can be as long as several minutes, to assess skills such as problem solving ability. Important areas to assess include basic and complex conversational skills, history of interpersonal relationships, social problem solving, use of leisure time, grooming and hygiene, care of personal possessions, money management, and conflict resolution.

Occupational Functioning

The rates of unemployment in patients with schizophrenia are high. Competitive employment may improve overall adaptive functioning by increasing daily activity, social contact, self-esteem, involvement in other community activities, community tenure, and quality of life (Drake, McHugo, Becker, Anthony, & Clark, 1996). Therefore, desire for work should be included in a comprehensive assessment designed to inform the treatment planning process. Rather than attempting to determine whether patients are capable of work, assessment explores the types of work and patient interests most likely to result in a successful work experience. Other correlates of work may also be assessed, but more for the purposes of informing the job search and need for supports than for determining appropriateness of involvement in supported employment.

Sexuality and Family Planning

As increasing numbers of individuals with schizophrenia reside in the community rather than hospitals, the rates of HIV infection and unwanted pregnancies have likewise risen (Coverdale & Grunebaum, 1998). Studies demonstrating that many people with schizophrenia have misconceptions, misinformation, and delusional beliefs about sex and pregnancy, together with the problems of sexually transmitted diseases and the effects of psychotropic medications on the fetus, make it ethically necessary to evaluate the sexual histories and practices of all patients. After adequate therapeutic rapport has been established, an assessment should include questions regarding current sexual practices, including number and gender of partners, contraceptive use and general knowledge about contraceptive methods, desire for children, and values regarding contraception, pregnancy, and parenting.

IMPACT ON ENVIRONMENT

Family

Having a family member diagnosed with schizophrenia can have a profound effect on the family as well as the individual with the diagnosis. Family members of patients with schizophrenia typically experience a wide range of distress related to coping with the illness, such as anxiety, depression, guilt, and anger (Hatfield & Lefley, 1993). In addition, although a large majority of individuals with schizophrenia indicate that competitive employment is a primary goal, a small minority are actually working at any given time (Marwaha & Johnson, 2004). Consequently, many people with schizophrenia require supplemental income to meet their basic living needs, such as disabilities entitlements and financial support from families. The economic dependence of many patients on their relatives, combined with difficulties in independent living, leads to many patients living at home, or maintaining high levels of contact and requiring extensive assistance from relatives to live separately. The social impairments pervasive in schizophrenia create significant dependence on others that, combined with the unpredictable nature of positive symptoms, cognitive impairments, and mood problems, often lead to high levels of family burden for relatives (Baronet, 1999). Family burden may also be related to poor communication within the family, difficulties coping with the illness, and ultimately problems with the family's ability to successfully monitor and manage the schizophrenia in a family member (Mueser & Glynn, 1999).

Work

One of the most prominent effects of schizophrenia is to impair work functioning, with rates of employment ranging between 10 percent and 30 percent (Marwaha & Johnson,

2004). Fortunately, as described in the following paragraph, supported employment programs have been shown to be effective at helping many people with schizophrenia return to work and improve their lives. Consequently, increasing numbers of people with schizophrenia have been entering the workforce in recent years, which has also been supported by the Americans with Disabilities Act.

Although many people with schizophrenia are capable of working, job tenures are often relatively brief and unsuccessful job endings are common, such as being fired or quitting without another job in place (Becker et al., 1998). The characteristic impairments associated with schizophrenia are often evident at the workplace, and can interfere with optimal performance. Although psychotic symptoms such as hallucinations and delusions can make someone with schizophrenia appear strange to coworkers, negative symptoms and cognitive impairments are more strongly related to work problems (McGurk & Mueser, 2004). People with schizophrenia may show less enthusiasm, initiative, and follow-through on work tasks, and their blunted affect may make them appear less responsive to other people. Due to psychomotor speed, they may work at a slower rate. Difficulties with attention may make it more difficult to attend to work (and require more frequent breaks), whereas limited executive functions may pose a challenge for solving novel problems at work. The social impairments related to schizophrenia can also create difficulties. Impaired social cognition abilities (Penn, Corrigan, Bentall, Racenstein, & Newman, 1997) may result in people with schizophrenia being less aware of social conventions governing workplace behavior, other people's feelings, and the nature of different social roles, such as coworker, supervisor/boss, and customer. These problems can be compounded by impairments in social skills, which may be the focus of skills training programs (Wallace & Tauber, 2004). The net result is that people with schizophrenia often appear different at the workplace, and their social behavior can interfere with good work performance. Many people function best in jobs that do not require frequent social interactions and customer relations skills. Despite these challenges, people with schizophrenia are often excellent workers who are dedicated to their jobs and appreciated and accepted by their coworkers and employers.

Peer Interactions

As previously described, schizophrenia has a profound effect on social functioning, including the formation of close relationships with others. People with schizophrenia typically exhibit less social drive and are less socially skilled than others, as evident to others in behaviors such as poor eye contact, inexpressive voice tone, unassertiveness, difficulty expressing feelings and making small conversation, and less ability in resolving interpersonal conflict (Bellack et al., 2004). These problems with social skills can be compounded by negative symptoms such as poverty of thought (i.e., the person has little to say) and slowed reaction times, which can make a conversation drag and feel awkward. Thus, negative symptoms and social skill deficits can make it less rewarding for peers to interact with individuals with schizophrenia, making it more difficult for them to form close relationships. Interestingly, these deficits in social skills tend to limit the ability of males to establish intimate relationships more in Western societies, where social skills are more of a prerequisite to such relationships and marriage, than in developing countries such as India where marriages are arranged (Bhatia, Franzos, Wood, Nimgaonkar, & Deshpande, 2004).

A related factor to how people with schizophrenia impact on their environment, and peers in particular, involves the issue of stigma. Because schizophrenia is frequently inaccurately depicted in the popular media as an illness that is associated with aggression and violence (Wahl, 1995), people are often afraid of and avoid individuals with schizophrenia, thereby creating another barrier to forming relationships. Research on stigma indicates that social avoidance is most strongly determined by exaggerated fears of violence (Corrigan et al., 2002). Therefore, challenging social stereotypes about schizophrenia is crucial to overcoming the strong social stigma of the illness and the obstacles the stigma causes to social integration.

TREATMENT IMPLICATIONS

Pharmacological Treatment

Pharmacotherapy is the mainstay of treatment, without which most psychosocial treatment would not be possible. Antipsychotics are the primary medication for schizophrenia, with major effects on the reduction of psychotic symptoms and prevention of relapses (Kane & Marder, 1993). Recent evidence suggests that atypical antipsychotic medications are more clinically effective than conventional antipsychotics (Davis, Chen, & Glick, 2003), although some of this apparent benefit might be due to the relatively high dosages of conventional antipsychotics used in many studies (Lieberman et al., 2003). Atypical antipsychotics (such as clozapine, olanzapine, or risperidone) have also been found to have beneficial effects on cognitive functioning when compared with conventional antipsychotics (Harvey & Keefe, 2001).

Psychosocial Treatment

Psychosocial interventions seek to improve the management of schizophrenia (e.g., medication compliance, coping with symptoms, relapse prevention) and to enhance functioning in areas such as independent living, relationships, and work. Specific interventions that have been shown to improve outcome include assertive community treatment, family psychoeducation, supported employment, social skills training, teaching illness management skills, cognitive-behavior therapy for psychosis, and integrated treatment for comorbid substance abuse.

Medication Adherence

Several strategies exist to improve medication adherence. Injectable, long-acting (depot) medications are commonly used to bypass problems related to medication adherence due to poor memory or lack of insight. Simplifying the medication regimen and monitoring the ingestion in the patients' homes can also improve adherence. Other effective strategies include behavioral tailoring (i.e., incorporating cues for taking medication into the patient's daily routine; Boczkowski, Zeichner, & DeSanto, 1985) and exploring how medication can help people achieve personal goals (Kemp et al., 1996).

Cognitive-Behavioral Therapy

About 25 percent to 40 percent of patients experience persistent psychotic symptoms, despite optimal pharmacological treatment (Curson et al., 1988). Cognitive behavior therapy for psychosis involves developing a collaborative relationship with the patient, examining the circumstances in which delusional beliefs or hallucinations emerge, and exploring alternative interpretations that may be more adaptive and accurate, and result in less distress (Morrison, Renton, Dunn, Williams, & Bentall, 2004). Multiple controlled studies, most conducted in Great Britain, have shown that cognitive behavior therapy for persistent psychotic symptoms is effective in reducing the severity of those symptoms, with additional benefits including reduced relapse rates and negative symptoms (Gould, Mueser, Bolton, Mays, & Goff, 2001).

Social Skills Training

Social dysfunction, characterized by poor relationships with others, few friends, and lack of social reciprocity, is pervasive in schizophrenia and contributes to a poor quality of life and increased difficulty functioning in the world (Erikson, Beiser, Iacono, Fleming, & Lin, 1989). Social skills training addresses social functioning by systematically teaching patients new interpersonal skills, such as starting conversations and expressing feelings, using social learning strategies such as modeling, role-playing, and homework (Bellack et al., 2004). Social skills training has been the focus of extensive research, and the results of several controlled trials indicate that it improves social and leisure functioning of clients (Heinssen, Liberman, & Kopelowicz, 2000).

Assertive Community Treatment

Patients with severe schizophrenia often fail to follow through on outpatient treatment, which leads to frequent relapses, rehospitalizations, and housing instability (Fisher, Geller, Altaffer, & Bennett, 1992). To address this problem, multidisciplinary assertive community treatment teams have been developed for patients with the most difficulty sustaining stable community living (Stein & Santos, 1998). These teams are characterized by lower staff-to-patient ratios (1:10 instead of 1:30 or higher), provision of most services in patients' usual environments instead of the clinic, direct provision of most services by the team rather than brokering services to other providers, 24-hour coverage, and shared rather than individual caseloads. Research on this strategy, including more than 30 controlled studies performed mainly in the United States and Australia, suggests that compared with traditional approaches assertive community treatment reduces symptoms and rehospitalizations, stabilizes housing in the community, and improves subjective quality of life (Bond et al., 2001).

Integrated Dual-Disorder Treatment

The most common co-occurring disorder in schizophrenia is substance abuse (Regier et al., 1990). Previous attempts to treat substance abuse in schizophrenia by referring patients to substance use specialists were unsuccessful because of difficulties these services had in engaging and retaining patients with schizophrenia in treatment (Ridgely, Goldman, & Willenbring, 1990). Programs in which substance abuse and schizophrenia are treated simultaneously by the same individuals have shown better outcomes (Mueser, Noordsy, Drake, & Fox, 2003). Other features of effective, integrated treatment programs for substance abuse in schizophrenia include outreach to engage patients in treatment, motivation-based interventions that first instill the desire to change substance use, and efforts to minimize the negative consequences of substance abuse at the earliest possible time. Research on integrated treatment for dual disorders supports the effectiveness of integrated programs at reducing substance abuse (Drake, Mueser, Brunette, & McHugo, 2004).

Family Intervention

As many patients live with family members or have continuing contact with relatives, family programs have been developed to reduce the burden of care and family stress, and to improve the management of schizophrenia (Falloon, Boyd, & McGill, 1984; Mueser & Glynn, 1999). Family programs led by professionals focus on teaching relatives and patients about schizophrenia and the principles of its treatment, reducing stress, and improving the ability of the family to work toward individual and shared goals. Research on family psychoeducation, including more than 20 controlled studies, indicates that long-term programs are effective at reducing cumulative relapse and rehospitalization rates from about 60 percent over two years to less than 30 percent (Pitschel-Walz, Leucht, Bäuml, Kissling, & Engel, 2001).

Vocational Rehabilitation

Despite the low rate of competitive employment in individuals with schizophrenia, the majority of patients report wanting to work (Mueser, Salyers, & Mueser, 2001). To address this problem, supported employment programs have been developed that emphasize rapid job search, competitive work in integrated community settings, provision of follow-along supports, attention to patients' preferences about job type and nature of support, and integration of vocational and clinical services (Becker & Drake, 2003). Multiple controlled studies have shown that supported employment programs are more effective at improving competitive work outcomes than other approaches (Bond et al., 2001).

Cognitive Rehabilitation

Treatments aimed at improving cognitive functioning have been developed to assist in the acquisition of behaviors required for adequate social competence, medication management, and skill acquisition. The first such treatments primarily consisted of repeated practice and coaching of skills identified as deficient through formal assessment of cognitive functioning (Spaulding, Reed, Sullivan, Richardson, & Weiler, 1999). Although many individuals who received this cognitive remediation performed better on tests of particular skills, there was little evidence for generalization of skills (Hogarty & Flesher, 1999). Other cognitive rehabilitation programs, such as Cognitive Enhancement Therapy, represent more ecologically meaningful clinical approaches, using behavioral exercises in a group context to reinforce skill acquisition, with some controlled research indicating both beneficial effects on cognitive functioning as well as social adjustment (Hogarty et al., 2004). More research is currently underway in this rapidly evolving area.

Sexuality, Family Planning, and Parenting

Mothers with schizophrenia often have difficulty caring for their offspring, resulting in a significant need for social services to attend to their children, and often loosing custody of them (Howard, Thornicroft, Salmon, & Appley, 2004). Given that sexuality and family planning are only beginning to gain recognition as important areas to address in individuals with schizophrenia, empirically validated treatment interventions have yet to be developed. As referrals to separate agencies or offices for obstetrical or gynecological care increase the chance that appointments will be missed, it is necessary that mental health professionals assume some responsibility for providing information and support regarding sexuality, family planning, and parenting (Brunette & Dean, 2002). This can be accomplished by placing posters and brochures regarding these issues in waiting rooms to indicate receptiveness of staff members to discuss sexual matters, and introducing such matters in regular discussions with patients. Sexually active patients should be educated about contraception, advised of the consequences of not using protection, and taught how to address key parenting issues (Coverdale & Grunebaum, 1998).

Early Intervention

Over the past decade, interest has grown in identifying and rapidly treating schizophrenia at the earliest possible stages, specifically during the prodromal phase or immediately after the frank emergence of psychotic symptoms. Enthusiasm for early intervention has been based on ample evidence showing that individuals with a prolonged duration of untreated psychosis need a longer period of treatment to achieve a clinical remission (Lieberman et al., 2001). In addition, clinical symptoms, especially negative symptoms, tend to worsen over the first several years after the onset of the illness (McGlashan & Fenton, 1992). These data have stimulated the hope that more effective methods for detecting first-episode schizophrenia, combined with rapid pharmacological intervention and comprehensive psychosocial treatment (Birchwood, Todd, & Jackson, 1998), could improve the long-term outcome, reduce burden on relatives, and reduce the cost of treatment. To this end, several programs have been developed that target first-episode patients in Europe, Australia, and North America, with preliminary results suggesting improved outcomes for closely integrated and comprehensive pharmacological and psychosocial treatments (Penn, Waldheter, Mueser, Perkins, & Lieberman, in press).

In addition to efforts to more rapidly treat first episodes of psychosis, work has focused on identifying and treating schizophrenia before it develops during the prodromal phase. Standardized methods have been established that identify patients with prodromal symptoms who are likely to develop schizophrenia over the next 6 to 12 months (Yung et al., 2003). One study found that antipsychotic medication was more effective than placebo in reducing the severity of prodromal symptoms over six to eight weeks (Woods et al., 2003). Another study reported that the combination of antipsychotics with cognitive-behavior therapy reduced the likelihood of patients with prodromal symptoms developing schizophrenia over six months (McGorrey et al., 2002).

REFERENCES

Alvir, J. M. J., Lieberman, J. A., & Safferman, A. Z. (1995). Do white-cell count spikes predict agranulocytosis in clozapine recipients? *Psychopharmacology Bulletin, 31,* 311–314.

Amador, X., Strauss, D., Yale, S., & Gorman, J. M. (1991). Awareness of illness in schizophrenia. *Schizophrenia Bulletin, 17,* 113–132.

American Psychiatric Association. (1994). *Diagnostic and statistical manual of mental disorders* (4th ed.). Washington, DC: American Psychiatric Association.

Andreasen, N. C. (1984). *Modified scale for the assessment of negative symptoms.* Bethesda, MD: U.S. Department of Health and Human Services.

Aro, S., Aro, H., & Keskimäki, I. (1995). Socio-economic mobility among patients with schizophrenia or major affective disorder: A 17-year retrospective follow-up. *British Journal of Psychiatry, 166,* 759–767.

Baronet, A.-M. (1999). Factors associated with caregiver burden in mental illness: A critical review of the research literature. *Clinical Psychology Review, 19,* 819–841.

Barrowclough, C., & Tarrier, N. (1992). *Families of schizophrenic patients: Cognitive behavioural intervention.* London: Chapman and Hall.

Bartels, S. J., Drake, R. E., Wallach, M. A., & Freeman, D. H. (1991). Characteristic hostility in schizophrenic outpatients. *Schizophrenia Bulletin, 17,* 163–171.

Baum, K. M., & Walker, E. F. (1995). Childhood behavioral precursors of adult symptom dimensions in schizophrenia. *Schizophrenia Research, 16,* 111–120.

Becker, D. R., & Drake, R. E. (2003). *A working life for people with severe mental illness.* New York: Oxford University Press.

Becker, D. R., Drake, R. E., Bond, G. R., Xie, H., Dain, B. J., & Harrison, K. (1998). Job terminations among persons with severe mental illness participating in supported employment. *Community Mental Health Journal, 34,* 71–82.

Bellack, A. S., & Mueser, K. T. (1993). Psychosocial treatment for schizophrenia. *Schizophrenia Bulletin, 19,* 317–336.

Bellack, A. S., Mueser, K. T., Gingerich, S., & Agresta, J. (2004). *Social skills training for schizophrenia: A step-by-step guide* (2nd ed.). New York: Guilford Press.

Berg, E. A. (1948). A simple objective test for measuring flexibility in thinking. *Journal of General Psychology, 39,* 15–22.

Bhatia, T., Franzos, M. A., Wood, J. A., Nimgaonkar, V. L., & Deshpande, S. N. (2004). Gender and procreation among patients with schizophrenia. *Schizophrenia Research, 68,* 387–394.

Birchwood, M., Smith, J., Cochrane, R., Wetton, S., & Copestake, S. (1990). The Social Functioning Scale: The development and validation of a new scale of social adjustment for use in family intervention programmes with schizophrenic patients. *British Journal of Psychiatry, 157,* 853–859.

Birchwood, M., Todd, P., & Jackson, C. (1998). Early intervention in psychosis: The critical period hypothesis. *British Journal of Psychiatry, 172*(Suppl. 33), 53–59.

Boczkowski, J., Zeichner, A., & DeSanto, N. (1985). Neuroleptic compliance among chronic schizophrenic outpatients: An intervention outcome report. *Journal of Consulting and Clinical Psychology, 53,* 666–671.

Bond, G. R., Becker, D. R., Drake, R. E., Rapp, C. A., Meisler, N., Lehman, A. F., et al. (2001). Implementing supported employment as an evidence-based practice. *Psychiatric Services, 52,* 313–322.

Bond, G. R., Drake, R. E., Mueser, K. T., & Latimer, E. (2001). Assertive community treatment for people with severe mental illness: Critical ingredients and impact on clients. *Disease Management and Health Outcomes, 9,* 141–159.

Boydell, J., van Os, J., McKenzie, K., Allardyce, J., Goel, R., McCreadie, R., et al. (2001). Incidence of schizophrenia in ethnic minorities in London: Ecological study into interactions with environment. *British Medical Journal, 323,* 1336–1338.

Bruce, M. L., & Leaf, P. J. (1989). Psychiatric disorders and 15-month mortality in a community sample of older adults. *American Journal of Public Health, 79,* 727–730.

Brunette, M. F., & Dean, W. (2002). Community mental health care of women with severe mental illness who are parents. *Community Mental Health Journal, 38,* 153–165.

Buchanan, A. (1992). A two-year prospective study of treatment compliance in patients with schizophrenia. *Psychological Medicine, 22,* 787–797.

Butzlaff, R. L., & Hooley, J. M. (1998). Expressed emotion and psychiatric relapse. *Archives of General Psychiatry, 55,* 547–552.

Cannon, T. D., Jones, P. B., & Murray, R. M. (2002). Obstetric complications and schizophrenia: Historical and meta-analytic review. *American Journal of Psychiatry, 159,* 1080–1092.

Cannon, T. D., Rosso, I. M., Hollister, J. M., Bearden, C. E., Sanchez, L. E., & Hadley, T. (2000). A prospective cohort study of genetic and perinatal influences in the etiology of schizophrenia. *Schizophrenia Bulletin, 26,* 351–366.

Cardno, A., Marshall, E., Coid, B., Macdonald, A., Ribchester, T., Davies, N., et al. (1999). Heritability estimates for psychotic disorders: The Maudsley twin psychosis series. *Archives of General Psychiatry, 56,* 162–168.

Castle, D. J., & Murray, R. M. (1993). Editorial: The neurodevelopmental basis of sex differences in schizophrenia. *Psychological Medicine, 21,* 565–575.

Clare, L., & Birchwood, M. (1998). Social adjustment of patients living at home. In K. T. Mueser & N. Tarrier (Eds.), *Handbook of social functioning in schizophrenia* (pp. 79–98). Boston: Allyn & Bacon.

Corrigan, P. W., Rowan, D., Green, A., Lundin, R., River, P., Uphoff-Wasowski, K., et al. (2002). Challenging two mental illness stigmas: Personal responsibility and dangerousness. *Schizophrenia Bulletin, 28,* 293–309.

Coverdale, J. H., & Grunebaum, H. (1998). Sexuality and family planning. In K. T. Mueser & N. Tarrier (Eds.), *Handbook of social functioning in schizophrenia* (pp. 224–237). Boston: Allyn & Bacon.

Craig, T. J., Siegel, C., Hopper, K., Lin, S., & Sartorius, N. (1997). Outcome in schizophrenia and related disorders compared between developing and developed countries: A recursive partitioning re-analysis of the WHP SOSMD data. *British Journal of Psychiatry, 170,* 229–233.

Curson, D. A., Patel, M., Liddle, P. F., & Barnes, T. R. E. (1988). Psychiatric morbidity of a long stay hospital population with chronic schizophrenia and implications for future community care. *British Medical Journal, 297,* 819–822.

Davis, J. M., Chen, N., & Glick, I. D. (2003). A meta-analysis of the efficacy of second-generation antipsychotics. *Archives of General Psychiatry, 60,* 553–564.

Davis, K. L., Kahn, R. S., Ko, G., & Davidson, M. (1991). Dopamine in schizophrenia: A review and reconceptualization. *American Journal of Psychiatry, 148,* 1474–1486.

Delis, D. C., Kramer, J. H., Kaplan, E., & Ober, B. A. (1987). *California Verbal Learning and Memory Test (Manual).* San Antonio, TX: Psychological Corp.

DeSisto, M. J., Harding, C. M., McCormick, R. V., Ashikaga, T., & Brooks, G. W. (1995). The Maine and Vermont three-decade studies of serious mental illness. *British Journal of Psychiatry, 167,* 331–342.

Dixon, L., Adams, C., & Lucksted, A. (2000). Update on family psychoeducation for schizophrenia. *Schizophrenia Bulletin, 26,* 5–20.

Dohrenwend, B. R., Levav, I., Shrout, P. E., Schwartz, S., Naveh, G., Link, B. G., et al. (1992). Socioeconomic status and psychiatric disorders: The causation-selection issue. *Science, 255,* 946–952.

Drake, R. E., & Brunette, M. F. (1998). Complications of severe mental illness related to alcohol and other drug use disorders. In M. Galanter (Ed.), *Recent developments in alcoholism: Consequences of alcoholism* (Vol. 14, pp. 285–299). New York: Plenum Press.

Drake, R. E., McHugo, G. J., Becker, D. R., Anthony, W. A., & Clark, R. E. (1996). The New Hampshire Study of Supported Employment for people with severe mental illness: Vocational outcomes. *Journal of Consulting and Clinical Psychology, 64,* 391–399.

Drake, R. E., Mueser, K. T., Brunette, M. F., & McHugo, G. J. (2004). A review of treatments for clients with severe mental illness and co-occurring substance use disorder. *Psychiatric Rehabilitation Journal, 27,* 360–374.

Drake, R. E., Osher, F. C., & Wallach, M. A. (1989). Alcohol use and abuse in schizophrenia: A prospective community study. *Journal of Nervous and Mental Disease, 177,* 408–414.

Erickson, D. H., Beiser, M., Iacono, W. G., Fleming, J. A. E., & Lin, T. (1989). The role of social relationships in the course of first-episode schizophrenia and affective psychosis. *American Journal of Psychiatry, 146,* 1456–1461.

Falloon, I. R. H., Boyd, J. L., & McGill, C. W. (1984). *Family care of schizophrenia: A problem-solving approach to the treatment of mental illness.* New York: Guilford Press.

Feinberg, I. (1982). Schizophrenia: Caused by a fault in programmed synaptic elimination during adolescence? *Journal of Psychiatric Research, 17,* 319–334.

Fenton, W. S., & McGlashan, T. H. (1991). Natural history of schizophrenia subtypes: II. Positive and negative symptoms and long term course. *Archives of General Psychiatry, 48,* 978–986.

Fisher, W. H., Geller, J. L., Altaffer, F., & Bennett, M. B. (1992). The relationship between community resources and state hospital recidivism. *American Journal of Psychiatry, 149,* 385–390.

Fox, J. W. (1990). Social class, mental illness, and social mobility: The social selection-drift hypothesis for serious mental illness. *Journal of Health and Social Behavior, 31,* 344–353.

Geddes, J. R., & Lawrie, S. M. (1995). Obstetric complications and schizophrenia: A meta-analysis. *British Journal of Psychiatry, 167,* 786–793.

Goldman, H. H. (1982). Mental illness and family burden: A public health perspective. *Hospital and Community Psychiatry, 33,* 557–559.

Goldstein, J. M. (1988). Gender differences in the course of schizophrenia. *American Journal of Psychiatry, 145,* 684–689.

Goodman, L. A., Rosenberg, S. D., Mueser, K. T., & Drake, R. E. (1997). Physical and sexual assault history in women with serious mental illness: Prevalence, correlates, treatment, and future research directions. *Schizophrenia Bulletin, 23,* 685–696.

Goodwin, F. K., & Jamison, K. R. (1990). *Manic depressive illness.* New York: Oxford University Press.

Gottesman, I. I. (1991). *Schizophrenia genesis: The origins of madness.* New York: Freeman.

Gould, R. A., Mueser, K. T., Bolton, E., Mays, V., & Goff, D. (2001). Cognitive therapy for psychosis in schizophrenia: An effect size analysis. *Schizophrenia Research, 48,* 335–342.

Haas, G. L., & Garratt, L. S. (1998). Gender differences in social functioning. In K. T. Mueser & N. Tarrier (Eds.), *Handbook of social functioning in schizophrenia* (pp. 149–180). Boston: Allyn & Bacon.

Häfner, H. (2000). Onset and early course as determinants of the further course of schizophrenia. *Acta Psychiatrica Scandinavica, 102*(Suppl. 407), 44–48.

Häfner, H., Maurer, K., Löffler, W., an der Heiden, W., Hambrecht, M., & Schultze-Lutter, F. (2003). Modeling the early course of schizophrenia. *Schizophrenia Bulletin, 29,* 325–340.

Halford, W. K., Sweitzer, R. D., & Varghese, F. N. (1991). Effects of family environment on negative symptoms and quality of life on psychotic patients. *Hospital and Community Psychiatry, 42,* 1241–1247.

Harding, C. M., Brooks, G. W., Ashikaga, T., Strauss, J. S., & Breier, A. (1987a). The Vermont longitudinal study of persons with severe mental illness: I. Methodology, study sample and overall status 32 years later. *American Journal of Psychiatry, 144,* 718–726.

Harding, C. M., Brooks, G. W., Ashikaga, T., Strauss, J. S., & Breier, A. (1987b). The Vermont longitudinal study of persons with severe mental illness: II. Long-term outcome of subjects who retrospectively met *DSM-III* criteria for schizophrenia. *American Journal of Psychiatry, 144,* 727–735.

Harding, C. M., & Keller, A. B. (1998). Long-term outcome of social functioning. In K. T. Mueser & N. Tarrier (Eds.), *Handbook of social functioning in schizophrenia* (pp. 134–148). Boston: Allyn & Bacon.

Harrison, P. J., & Owen, M. J. (2003). Genes for schizophrenia: Recent findings and their pathophysiological implications. *Lancet, 361,* 417–419.

Harvey, P. D., Davidson, M., Mueser, K. T., Parrella, M., White, L., & Powchik, P. (1997). Social-Adaptive Functioning Evaluation (SAFE): A rating scale for geriatric psychiatric patients. *Schizophrenia Bulletin, 23,* 131–145.

Harvey, P. D., & Keefe, R. (2001). Studies of cognitive change in patients with schizophrenia following novel antipsychotic treatment. *American Journal of Psychiatry, 158,* 176–184.

Hatfield, A. B., & Lefley, H. P. (1993). *Surviving mental illness: Stress, coping, and adaptation.* New York: Guilford Press.

Heaton, R., Paulsen, J. S., McAdams, L. A., Kuck, J., Zisook, S., Braff, D., et al. (1994). Neuropsychological deficits in schizophrenics: Relationship to age, chronicity, and dementia. *Archives of General Psychiatry, 51,* 469–476.

Heinssen, R. K., Liberman, R. P., & Kopelowicz, A. (2000). Psychosocial skills training for schizophrenia: Lessons from the laboratory. *Schizophrenia Bulletin, 26,* 21–46.

Hogan, T. P., Awad, A. G., & Eastwood, R. (1983). A self-report scale predictive of drug compliance in schizophrenics: Reliability and discriminative validity. *Psychological Medicine, 13,* 177–183.

Hogarty, G. E., & Flesher, S. (1999). Developmental theory for a cognitive enhancement therapy of schizophrenia. *Schizophrenia Bulletin, 25,* 677–692.

Hogarty, G. E., Flesher, S., Ulrich, R. F., Carter, M., Greenwald, D., Pogue-Geile, M. F., et al. (2004). Cognitive enhancement therapy for schizophrenia: Effects of a 2-year randomized trial on cognition and behavior. *Archives of General Psychiatry, 61,* 866–876.

Hollingshead, A. B., & Redlich, F. C. (1958). *Social class and mental illness: A community study.* New York: Wiley.

Howard, L. M., Thornicroft, G., Salmon, M., & Appley, L. (2004). Predictors of parenting outcome in women with psychotic disorders discharged from mother and baby units. *Acta Psychiatrica Scandinavica, 110,* 347–350.

Howard, R., Almeida, O., & Levy, R. (1994). Phenomenology, demography and diagnosis in late paraphrenia. *Psychological Medicine, 24,* 397–410.

Innocenti, G. M., Ansermet, F., & Parnas, J. (2003). Schizophrenia, neurodevelopment and corpus callosum. *Molecular Psychiatry, 8,* 261–274.

Inskip, H. M., Harris, E. C., & Barraclough, C. (1998). Lifetime risk of suicide for alcoholism, affective disorder and schizophrenia. *British Journal of Psychiatry, 172,* 35–37.

Jablensky, A. (1997). The 100-year epidemiology of schizophrenia. *Schizophrenia Research, 28,* 111–125.

Jablensky, A. (1999). Schizophrenia: Epidemiology. *Current Opinion in Psychiatry, 12,* 9–28.

Jablensky, A., Sartorius, N., Ernberg, G., Anker, M., Korten, A., & Cooper, J. E. (1992). Schizophrenia: Manifestations, incidence, and course in different cultures: A World Health Organization ten-country study. *Psychological Medicine, Monograph Supplement, 20,* 1–97.

Kane, J. M., & Marder, S. R. (1993). Psychopharmacologic treatment of schizophrenia. *Schizophrenia Bulletin, 19,* 287–302.

Kay, S. R., Opler, L. A., & Fiszbein, A. (1987). The Positive and Negative Syndrome Scale (PANSS) for schizophrenia. *Schizophrenia Bulletin, 13,* 261–276.

Keefe, R. S. E., Seidman, L. J., Christensen, B. K., Hamer, R. M., Sharma, T., Sitskoorn, M. M., et al. (2004). Comparative effect of atypical and conventional antipsychotic drugs on neurocognition in first-episode psychosis: A randomized, double-blind trial of olanzapine versus low doses of haloperidol. *American Journal of Psychiatry, 161,* 985–995.

Keith, S. J., Regier, D. A., & Rae, D. S. (1991). Schizophrenic disorders. In L. N. Robins & D. A. Regier (Eds.), *Psychiatric disorders in America: The Epidemiologic Catchment Area Study* (pp. 33–52). New York: Free Press.

Kemp, R., Hayward, P., Applewhaite, G., Everitt, B., & David, A. (1996). Compliance therapy in psychotic patients: Randomised controlled trial. *British Medical Journal, 312,* 345–349.

Kessler, R. C., Foster, C. L., Saunders, W. B., & Stang, P. E. (1995). Social consequences of psychiatric disorders: I. Educational attainment. *American Journal of Psychiatry, 152,* 1026–1032.

Kleinman, A. (1988). *Rethinking psychiatry: From cultural category to personal experience.* New York: Free Press.

Kreisman, D., Blumenthal, R., Borenstein, M., Woerner, M., Kane, J., Rifkin, A., et al. (1988). Family attitudes and patient social adjustment in a longitudinal study of outpatient schizophrenics receiving low-dose neuroleptics: The family's view. *Psychiatry, 51,* 3–13.

Leff, J., & Vaughn, C. (Eds.). (1985). *Expressed emotion in families.* New York: Guilford Press.

Lezak, M. D. (1995). *Neuropsychological assessment* (3rd ed.). New York: Oxford University Press.

Liberman, R. P., Mueser, K. T., Wallace, C. J., Jacobs, H. E., Eckman, T., & Massel, H. K. (1986). Training skills in the psychiatrically disabled: Learning coping and competence. *Schizophrenia Bulletin, 12,* 631–647.

Liddle, P. F. (1987). The symptoms of chronic schizophrenia: A reexamination of the positive-negative dichotomy. *British Journal of Psychiatry, 151,* 145–151.

Lieberman, J. A., Perkins, D., Belger, A., Chakos, M., Jarskog, F., Boteva, K., et al. (2001). The early stages of schizophrenia: Speculations on pathogenesis, pathophysiology, and therapeutic approaches. *Biological Psychiatry, 50,* 884–897.

Lieberman, J. A., Tollefson, G., Tohen, M., Green, A. I., Gur, R. E., Kahn, R., et al. (2003). Comparative efficacy and safety of atypical and conventional antipsychotic drugs in first-episode psychosis: A randomized, double-blind trial of olanzapine versus haloperidol. *American Journal of Psychiatry, 160,* 1396–1404.

Lincoln, C. V., & McGorry, P. (1995). Who cares? Pathways to psychiatric care for young people experiencing a first episode of psychosis. *Psychiatric Services, 46,* 1166–1171.

Lukoff, D., Nuechterlein, K. H., & Ventura, J. (1986). Manual for the Expanded Brief Psychiatric Rating Scale (BPRS). *Schizophrenia Bulletin, 12,* 594–602.

MacCabe, J. H., & Murray, R. M. (2004). Intellectual functioning in schizophrenia: A marker of neurodevelopmental damage? *Journal of Intellectual Disability Research, 48,* 519–523.

Malla, A. K., Norman, R. M. G., Manchanda, R., McLean, T. S., Harricharan, R., Cortese, L., et al. (2002). Status of patients with first-episode psychosis after one year of phase-specific community-oriented treatment. *Psychiatric Services, 53,* 458–463.

Marwaha, S., & Johnson, S. (2004). Schizophrenia and employment: A review. *Social Psychiatry and Psychiatric Epidemiology, 39,* 337–349.

McDonald, C., Grech, A., Toulopoulou, T., Schulze, K., Chapple, B., Sham, P. C., et al. (2002). Brain volumes in familial and non-familial schizophrenic probands and their unaffected relatives. *American Journal of Medical Genetics: Neuropsychiatric Genetics, 114,* 616–625.

McEvoy, J. P., Freter, S., Everett, G., Geller, J. L., Appelbaum, P., Apperson, L. J., et al. (1989). Insight and the clinical outcome of schizophrenic patients. *Journal of Nervous and Mental Disease, 177,* 48–51.

McGill, C. W., Falloon, I. R. H., Boyd, J. L., & Wood-Siverio, C. (1983). Family educational intervention in the treatment of schizophrenia. *Hospital and Community Psychiatry, 34,* 934–938.

McGlashan, W. H., & Fenton, W. S. (1992). The positive-negative distinction in schizophrenia: Review of natural history validators. *Archives of General Psychiatry, 49,* 63–72.

McGorry, P. D., Yung, A. R., Phillips, L. J., Yuen, H. P., Francey, S., Cosgrave, E. M., et al. (2002). Randomized controlled trial of interventions designed to reduce the risk of progression to first-episode psychosis in a clinical sample with subthreshold symptoms. *Archives of General Psychiatry, 59,* 921–928.

McGuffin, P., Owen, M. J., & Farmer, A. E. (1996). Genetic basis of schizophrenia. *Lancet, 346,* 678–682.

McGurk, S. R., & Mueser, K. T. (2004). Cognitive functioning, symptoms, and work in supported employment: A review and heuristic model. *Schizophrenia Research, 70,* 147–174.

McGurk, S. R., Mueser, K. T., Harvey, P. D., Marder, J., & LaPuglia, R. (2003). Cognitive and clinical predictors of work outcomes in clients with schizophrenia. *Psychiatric Services, 54,* 1129–1135.

Meltzer, H. Y., & McGurk, S. R. (1999). The effects of clozapine, risperidone, and olanzapine on cognitive function in schizophrenia. *Schizophrenia Bulletin, 25,* 233–255.

Moos, R. H., & Moos, B. S. (1981). *The Family Environment Scale manual.* Palo Alto, CA: Consulting Psychologists Press.

Morrison, A. P., Renton, J. C., Dunn, H., Williams, S., & Bentall, R. P. (2004). *Cognitive therapy for psychosis: A formulation-based approach.* New York: Brunner-Routledge.

Mueser, K. T. (2000). Cognitive functioning, social adjustment and long-term outcome in schizophrenia. In T. Sharma & P. Harvey (Eds.), *Cognition in schizophrenia: Impairments, importance, and treatment strategies* (pp. 157–177). Oxford, England: Oxford University Press.

Mueser, K. T., Bellack, A. S., Douglas, M. S., & Wade, J. H. (1991). Prediction of social skill acquisition in schizophrenic and major affective disorder patients from memory and symptomatology. *Psychiatry Research, 37,* 281–296.

Mueser, K. T., Curran, P. J., & McHugo, G. J. (1997). Factor structure of the Brief Psychiatric Rating Scale in schizophrenia. *Psychological Assessment, 9,* 196–204.

Mueser, K. T., Douglas, M. S., Bellack, A. S., & Morrison, R. L. (1991). Assessment of enduring deficit and negative symptom subtypes in schizophrenia. *Schizophrenia Bulletin, 17,* 565–582.

Mueser, K. T., & Glynn, S. M. (1999). *Behavioral family therapy for psychiatric disorders* (2nd ed.). Oakland, CA: New Harbinger.

Mueser, K. T., Noordsy, D. L., Drake, R. E., & Fox, L. (2003). *Integrated treatment for dual disorders: A guide to effective practice.* New York: Guilford Press.

Mueser, K. T., Rosenberg, S. D., Goodman, L. A., & Trumbetta, S. L. (2002). Trauma, PTSD, and the course of schizophrenia: An interactive model. *Schizophrenia Research, 53,* 123–143.

Mueser, K. T., Salyers, M. P., & Mueser, P. R. (2001). A prospective analysis of work in schizophrenia. *Schizophrenia Bulletin, 27,* 281–296.

Neumann, C. S., Grimes, K., Walker, E., & Baum, K. (1995). Developmental pathways to schizophrenia: Behavioral subtypes. *Journal of Abnormal Psychology, 104,* 558–566.

Odegaard, O. (1960). Marriage rates and fertility in psychotic patients before hospital admission and after discharge. *International Journal of Social Psychiatry, 6,* 25–33.

Peen, J., & Dekker, J. (1997). Admission rates for schizophrenia in The Netherlands: An urban/rural comparison. *Acta Psychiatrica Scandinavica, 96,* 301–305.

Penn, D. L., Corrigan, P. W., Bentall, R. P., Racenstein, J. M., & Newman, L. (1997). Social cognition in schizophrenia. *Psychological Bulletin, 121,* 114–132.

Penn, D. L., Hope, D. A., Spaulding, W., & Kucera, J. (1994). Social anxiety in schizophrenia. *Schizophrenia Research, 11,* 277–284.

Penn, D. L., Waldheter, E. J., Mueser, K. T., Perkins, D. O., & Lieberman, J. A. (in press). Psychosocial treatment for first episode psychosis: A research update. *American Journal of Psychiatry.*

Pitschel-Walz, G., Leucht, S., Bäuml, J., Kissling, W., & Engel, R. R. (2001). The effect of family interventions on relapse and rehospitalization in schizophrenia: A meta-analysis. *Schizophrenia Bulletin, 27,* 73–92.

Pogue-Geile, M. F. (1989). The prognostic significance of negative symptoms in schizophrenia. *British Journal of Psychiatry, 7* (Suppl.), 123–127.

Pogue-Geile, M. F., & Harrow, M. (1985). Negative symptoms in schizophrenia: Their longitudinal course and prognostic importance. *Schizophrenia Bulletin, 11,* 427–439.

Rabkin, J. (1979). Ethnic density and psychiatric hospitalization: Hazards of minority status. *American Journal of Psychiatry, 136,* 1562–1566.

Regier, D. A., Farmer, M. E., Rae, D. S., Locke, B. Z., Keith, S. J., Judd, L. L., et al. (1990). Comorbidity of mental disorders with alcohol and other drug abuse: Results from the Epidemiologic Catchment Area (ECA) study. *Journal of the American Medical Association, 264,* 2511–2518.

Reitan, R. M., & Wolfson, D. (1993). *The Halstead-Reitan Neuropsychological Test Battery: Theory and clinical interpretation.* Tucson, AZ: Neuropsychology Press.

Ridgely, M. S., Goldman, H. H., & Willenbring, M. (1990). Barriers to the care of persons with dual diagnoses: Organizational and financing issues. *Schizophrenia Bulletin, 16,* 123–132.

Rosenberg, S. D., Goodman, L. A., Osher, F. C., Swartz, M., Essock, S. M., Butterfield, M. I., et al. (2001). Prevalence of HIV, hepatitis B and hepatitis C in people with severe mental illness. *American Journal of Public Health, 91,* 31–37.

Sands, J. R., & Harrow, M. (1999). Depression during the longitudinal course of schizophrenia. *Schizophrenia Bulletin, 25,* 157–171.

Schooler, N., Hogarty, G., & Weissman, M. (1979). Social Adjustment Scale II (SAS-II). In W. A. Hargreaves, C. C. Atkisson, & J. E. Sorenson (Eds.), *Resource materials for community mental health program evaluations* (pp. 290–303). Rockville, MD: National Institute of Mental Health.

Selten, J. P., Slaets, J., & Kahn, R. S. (1997). Schizophrenia in Surinamese and Dutch Antillean immigrants to The Netherlands: Evidence of an increased incidence. *Psychological Medicine, 27,* 807–811.

Spaulding, W. D., Reed, D., Sullivan, M., Richardson, C., & Weiler, M. (1999). Effects of cognitive treatment in psychiatric rehabilitation. *Schizophrenia Bulletin, 25,* 657–676.

Stein, L. I., & Santos, A. B. (1998). *Assertive community treatment of persons with severe mental illness.* New York: Norton.

Susser, E., Struening, E. L., & Conover, S. (1989). Psychiatric problems in homeless men: Lifetime psychosis, substance use, and current distress in new arrivals at New York City shelters. *Archives of General Psychiatry, 46,* 845–850.

Tessler, R., & Gamache, G. (1996). *Toolkit for evaluating family experiences with severe mental illness.* Amherst, MA: Evaluation Center at HSRI.

Thara, R., Henrietta, M., Joseph, S., Rajkumar, S., & Eaton, W. W. (1994). Ten-year course of schizophrenia: The Madras longitudinal study. *Acta Psychiatrica Scandinavica, 90,* 329–336.

Thomas, H. V., Dalman, C., David, A. S., Gentz, J., Lewis, G., & Allebeck, P. (2001). Obstetric complications and risk of schizophrenia: Effect of gender, age at diagnosis and maternal history of psychosis. *British Journal of Psychiatry, 179,* 409–414.

Tienari, P. (1991). Interaction between genetic vulnerability and family environment: The Finnish Adoptive Family Study of schizophrenia. *Acta Psychiatrica Scandinavica, 84,* 460–465.

Tienari, P., Sorri, A., Lahti, I., Naarala, M., Wahlberg, K., Moring, J., et al. (1987). Genetic and psychosocial factors in schizophrenia: The Finnish Adoptive Family Study. *Schizophrenia Bulletin, 13,* 477–484.

Torrey, E. F. (1995). Editorial: Jails and prisons: American's new mental hospitals. *American Journal of Public Health, 85,* 1611–1613.

U.S. Institute of Medicine. (2001). *Neurological, psychiatric, and developmental disorders: Meeting the challenges in the developing world.* Washington, DC: National Academy of Sciences.

van Os, J., & Marcelis, M. (1998). The ecogenics of schizophrenia: A review. *Schizophrenia Research, 32,* 127–135.

Wahl, O. F. (1995). *Media madness: Public images of mental illness.* New Brunswick, NJ: Rutgers University Press.

Wallace, C. J., Liberman, R. P., Tauber, R., & Wallace, J. (2000). The Independent Living Skills Survey: A comprehensive measure of the community functioning of severely and persistently mentally ill individuals. *Schizophrenia Bulletin, 26,* 631–658.

Wallace, C. J., & Tauber, R. (2004). Supplementing supported employment with workplace skills training. *Psychiatric Services, 55,* 513–515.

Warner, R. (1985). *Recovery from schizophrenia: Psychiatry and political economy* (2nd ed.). London: Routledge.

Webb, C., Pfeiffer, M., Mueser, K. T., Mensch, E., DeGirolamo, J., & Levenson, D. F. (1998). Burden and well-being of caregivers for the severely mentally ill: The role of coping style and social support. *Schizophrenia Research, 34,* 169–180.

Wechsler, D. (1998). *Wechsler Adult Intelligence Scale-Revised (WAIS III Manual).* New York: Psychological Corp.

Weiden, P., Rapkin, B., Mott, T., Zygmunt, A., Goldman, D., Horvitz-Lennon, M., et al. (1994). Rating of Medication Influences (ROMI) scale in schizophrenia. *Schizophrenia Bulletin, 20,* 297–310.

Woods, S. W., Breier, A., Zipursky, R. B., Perkins, D. O., Addington, J., Miller, T. J., et al. (2003). Randomized trial of olanzapine versus placebo in the symptomatic acute treatment of the schizophrenic prodrome. *Biological Psychiatry, 54,* 453–464.

Wykes, T., & Sturt, E. (1986). The measurement of social behaviour in psychiatric patients: An assessment of the reliability and validity of the SBS Schedule. *British Journal of Psychiatry, 148,* 1–11.

Yung, A. R., Phillips, L. J., Yuen, H. P., Francey, S. M., McFarlane, S. A., Hallgren, M., et al. (2003). Psychosis prediction: 12-month follow-up of a high-risk ("prodromal") group. *Schizophrenia Research, 60,* 21–32.

Zigler, E., & Glick, M. (1986). *A developmental approach to adult psychopathology.* New York: Wiley.

CHAPTER 17

Organic Mental Disorder

DREW GOUVIER

DESCRIPTION OF THE DISORDER AND CLINICAL PICTURE

Organic mental disorder (OMD), also known as *organic brain syndrome,* is an inclusive term used to categorize cognitive decline due to a broad range of changes in either the physical structure or physiologic functioning of the brain. The term OMD is ill defined, and the criteria for many OMD diagnoses remain unclear (Wetterling, Kanitz, & Borgis, 1996) as many of the symptoms overlap with traditional psychiatric disorders. Diminished cognition caused by long-standing or acute disorders such as depression, mania, or schizophrenia are not classified as OMD even though these disorders reflect altered brain functioning. Like Descartes's mind-body paradox, the term *organic* in OMD is not meant to exclude psychological disorders from having a biological basis. The unique difference is that OMD changes result from internally or externally inflicted disruption of brain activity. Vectors of change include, but are not limited to, neurotoxic agents, cardiovascular disorders, neurodevelopmental and neurodegenerative disorders, changes in brain metabolism, traumatic brain injury, and infections in the central nervous system. OMD is a set of conditions that bridges between medicine and psychology. The disorder is most frequently diagnosed in older populations. However, unlike milder cognitive declines in variables such as processing speed (Salthouse, 1993), OMD is not a normal developmental outcome of aging.

Core Features

Given the myriad factors leading to OMD diagnosis, it is not surprising to see OMD result in a wide range of psychological dysfunction. Although cognitive dysfunction usually occurs with OMD, other areas, such as emotion, perception, and attention may also be affected. Persons with OMD may show impairment in orientation, judgment, and memory. Affective lability may also be present. Obviously, severe impairments in cognitive ability hampers one's ability to adapt to environmental changes and even mild disruption can provide what Kurt Goldstein dubbed "catastrophic reactions" (Loring, 1999). Such problems require therapeutic intervention (Richards, 1997), and careful monitoring of the OMD individual's psychological state is warranted.

Individuals with OMD may function adequately until they are placed in more demanding or unfamiliar situations. This stress-related diminution in cognitive ability can be conceptualized as a general lowering of the individual's mental resiliency. The damaged brain is operating at less than maximum efficiency, and compared to the normal brain, the OMD brain is taxed in standard situations and becomes increasingly inefficient, and finally overloaded, as the situational demands are increased (Ewing, McCarthy, Gronwall, & Wrightson, 1980). The threshold, or margin of capability, has been lowered, sometimes permanently.

Because symptomology is so broad, differential diagnosis is sometimes difficult. OMD symptoms overlap with a large number of psychiatric disorders. An organic etiology for cognitive inefficiency should always be considered before advancing to diagnoses involving psychosis or personality disorder. In order to facilitate conceptualization of the disorder, the clinician may find it helpful to distinguish whether the mechanism of brain dysfunction is due to a primary or secondary cause. A primary source of dysfunction is one that affects the brain directly and discretely as in a stroke or traumatic injury. A secondary source affects the brain indirectly through systemic dysfunction brought about by the failure of another organ system, as in dementia associated with end-stage renal disease or psychological disorders arising as a consequence of drug use.

Clinical Features

The *International Statistical Classification of Diseases and Related Health Problems,* version 10 (*ICD-10;* World Health Organization, 1992), has specific categories for the diagnosis of OMD. Types of dementia make up the largest single grouping of OMD, including dementia in Alzheimer's disease (AD), vascular dementia, dementia in other diseases classified elsewhere, and unspecified dementia. Dementia in other diseases classified elsewhere includes neurodegenerative diseases. Other *ICD-10* categories for OMD are organic amnesic syndrome, not induced by alcohol and other psychoactive substances; delirium, not induced by alcohol and other psychoactive substances; other mental disorders due to brain damage and dysfunction and to physical disease (includes disorders of affect and perception and mild cognitive dysfunction); personality and behavioral disorders due to brain disease, damage, and dysfunction (includes postencephalitic syndrome, postconcussional syndrome, and organic personality disorder); and unspecified organic or symptomatic mental disorder.

Although the *ICD-10* lists OMD as one of its categorized disorders, the fourth edition, text revision of the *Diagnostic and Statistical Manual of Mental Disorders* (*DSM-IV-TR*), the current U.S. standard diagnostic criteria for mental disorders, no longer lists OMD as an official diagnosis (American Psychiatric Association [APA], 2000). The OMD diagnosis was, however, included in the APA's *DSM-III* and *DSM-III-R* (APA, 1980, 1987). Interestingly, cognitive impairment was not a necessary diagnostic feature of OMD in the *DSM-III*, which included three OMD diagnostic categories for symptom constellations with either no or only mild cognitive impairment: organic affective syndrome, organic delusional syndrome, and organic personality disorders. Although these diagnoses are not currently used, it is helpful to know about them when reviewing older literature.

Currently, OMDs representing acquired brain disorders would fall under the *DSM-IV-TR* categories of either mental disorders due to a general medical condition or substance induced disorders. Symptoms resembling those observed in OMD, related to acute substance abuse, are generally classified as a diagnosis distinct from OMD. However, this does not rule out chronic substance abuse as a contributor to OMD. Additionally, the presence of substance abuse should still be noted as it dramatically affects survival rates in OMD individuals (Gaitz & Baer, 1971). This exclusionary practice also holds for sleep disorders and learning disabilities that may cause impairments in domains related to OMD (Puri, Laking, & Treasaden, 2002).

This leaves mental disorders due to a general medical condition as the primary home for OMD symptomology in the *DSM-IV-TR*. The convention set by the *DSM-IV-TR* is that the medical condition responsible for the OMD, whether it is primary or secondary, is coded on both Axis I and Axis III using the *ICD-10*-CM (clinical modification) codes. There are three categories of mental disorders due to a general medical condition. These are catatonic disorder due to a general medical condition, personality change due to a general medical condition, and mental disorder not otherwise specified due to a general medical condition. Notice that these somewhat parallel the three OMD categories listed earlier in the *DSM-III*. The main considerations for the first two diagnoses are that the dysfunction cannot take place solely during a delirium and cannot be better accounted for by another mental disorder. The latter diagnosis, mental disorder not otherwise specified, is used when a physiological effect on the brain is established as the causal agent of dysfunction, but the impairment does not meet criteria for a specific mental disorder due to a general medical condition.

OMD symptomology can also fall under other diagnoses that share organic causality. These are delirium (due to a general medical condition, multiple etiologies, or not otherwise specified), dementia (Alzheimer's type, vascular, due to other general medical condition, multiple etiologies, or not otherwise specified), or cognitive disorder not otherwise specified. Delirium, primarily characterized as a confusional state, is typically marked by acute onset, altered level of consciousness, fluctuating course and disturbances in orientation, memory, thought, and behavior. A dementia diagnosis requires that the individual demonstrate impairment in both memory and at least one of the following domains: aphasia, apraxia, agnosia, or executive functioning (APA, 2000).

The deciding factors between these diagnoses are the severity and course of the symptomology. For example, significant cognitive or attentional problems that develop across the course of a few days, with the degree of impairment fluctuating at times, would be diagnosed as a delirium, whereas the same degree of impairment with a more gradual onset and observed decline across time would be characterized as dementia. Because of this, dementia is sometimes known as chronic brain syndrome and delirium as acute brain syndrome. Care should be taken with the dementia diagnosis as individuals with anxiety may subjectively report memory impairment (Philpot & Levy, 1987), and the initial symptoms of dementia may also mimic those associated with anxiety (Lindesay, 1991).

In contrast to the serious impairment associated with both dementia and delirium, mild cognitive impairment across a variety of domains would be diagnosed as cognitive disorder not otherwise specified. Other OMD-related diagnosis that could be applied for specific dysfunctions are amnestic disorder (due to a general medical condition or not otherwise specified), catatonic disorder due to a general medical condition, and personality change due to a general medical condition.

PERSONALITY DEVELOPMENT AND PSYCHOPATHOLOGY

Introductory psychology students learn of psychopathology and personality factors in OMD in the retelling of Phineas Gage and the tamping rod. Various sorts of organic events are known to contribute to developing psychopathology and/or personality changes. Thus, predispositions and the role of premorbid personality traits affecting subsequent personality changes and psychopathology in OMD are often explored. It is important to assess differences in psychological functioning across diagnostic groups to determine psychological profiles distinctly indicative of particular groups. One method to examine the presence of psychopathology and dysfunctional characterlogical traits in OMD is to contrast psychological functioning in those with OMD with other groups of diverging diagnoses. However, Furukawa et al. (1998) indicated that personality traits, according to the Five-Factor Model of personality, did not differ between groups with OMD, schizophrenic, mood, and neurotic disorders. Despite this, there is still much that has been reported pertaining to psychological functioning in those with delirium, dementias, traumatic brain injury (TBI), and other OMD.

Common symptoms associated with delirium are anxiety, depression, anger, and psychosis. With regard to palliative care, paranoid ideas can be present, as well as a high degree of anxiety in the last days of life with delirium (Barraclough, 1997). Psychiatric symptoms in organ transplant patients have been shown to vary depending on the biophysical systems affected (Trzepacz, Levenson, & Tringali, 1991). Among psychiatric patients, those with mania have been shown to be at a twelvefold risk of delirium episodes (Patten, 2001). However, delirium often goes unnoticed or is mistaken for depression in some cases when it is in its hypovariant form. Due to the normally brief course of delirium, little study has been conducted examining the interactions of personality factors and subsequent psychopathological symptoms, but the presence of psychotic/hallucinatory experience is often seen in delirium.

Patients with dementia experience a range of psychopathology and noted personality change after disease onset. Lyketsos et al. (2000) found more psychopathology in dementing individuals than those with mild cognitive impairment. Some suggest that personality changes may actually be an early sign of dementia (Persson, Berg, Nilsson, & Svanborg, 1991). Shinosaki, Nishikawa, and Masotoshi (2000) proposed that psychiatric problems have been underestimated in dementia patients and are often regarded as secondary symptoms to cognitive impairment and glimmering self-awareness of deterioration. However, they indicated the presence and severity of psychiatric symptoms in dementia is often independent of cognitive impairment. Moreover, not all with dementia show behavioral and psychiatric problems. The severity and duration of those problems also differ between individuals, which further complicates the generalizability of results.

Research investigating effects of personality and psychiatric symptoms in dementias has been a growing interest, but assessing demented patients for mood symptoms is sometimes difficult due to a loss of verbal ability and the complex cognitive demands involved in rating their moods. Therefore, measures of mood, behavior, and premorbid personality are often provided through family members or caregivers using rating scales such as the Cognitive Behavior Rating Scale (Williams, Klein, Little, & Haban, 1986) or the Neo Personality Inventory–Revised (Costa & McCrae, 1992).

Among other disorders, major depression has been particularly noted in AD, with some depressive symptoms observed in 10 percent to 50 percent of AD and prevalence of full major depressive disorder in 1 percent to 25 percent (Arnold, 2000). Gilley, Wilson, Bienias, Bennett, and Evans (2004) observed that, whereas few AD patients meet full criteria for major depression, many demonstrate depressive symptoms. This point seems lost to researchers who rely on determinations of depression caseness (yes/no) and ignore symptom levels. They suggest that depression should be viewed on a continuum in those with AD. From this perspective, they found subthreshold depression in 9 percent to 13.9 percent of patients. Orrell and Bebbington (1996) reported that anxiety and depression associated with life events disproportionately occur four to six months preceding inpatient admission for dementia, suggesting either life events are an elevating risk factor for dementia, or during the prodromal stage of dementia, coping resources are taxed to the point of being symptomatic, reflecting a decrease in coping reserve.

Others have shown psychotic symptoms to be prevalent in as many as half of AD patients, usually in the early stages after onset but before severe deterioration (Arnold, 2000). Delusional content relates to any topic, but themes of persecution (e.g., someone stealing items, thinking caregiver will abandon them, cheating spouse) are often present in AD patients. Holtzer et al. (2003) reported the rate of delusions ranges from 34 percent to 49 percent, which usually peak in the second year of the disease. They also noted that hallucinations tend to be stable during the course of AD and are relatively persistent throughout the disease course in 8 percent to 17 percent of patients. Arnold suggested that visual hallucinations are more common than auditory. People with AD also have misperceptions, such as thinking people on television are real and having conversations with people in photographs.

Wilson et al. (2004) have noted an inverse association between premorbid neurotic personality traits (i.e., distress-proneness, emotional stability) and episodic memory impairment in mild to moderate AD patients. Patients with low proneness to distress in their study, however, had episodic memory scores averaging three times the predicted value of those with high distress proneness. However, this relationship was limited only to episodic memory and no other cognitive functions. No other personality factors were associated with other memory or cognitive functions and neuroticism was not associated with disease progression.

In a prospective study of elderly persons, those with low mental energy and less degree of emotional involvement were more likely to develop dementia. Jacobs, Heberlein, Vieregge, and Vieregge (2001) reported premorbid inflexibility and a higher degree of caution in young Parkinson's Disease (PD) patients compared with normal controls. They also noted a higher degree of current depression than controls. Treat, Poon, Fozard, and Popkin (1978) have shown that complaints of memory dysfunction among the elderly were strongly correlated with depression levels but not correlated with dementia status.

High premorbid levels of neuroticism have also been associated with a propensity for depression symptoms after AD onset. Although Gilley et al. (2004) found no clear pattern between depressive symptoms and severity of cognitive decline in AD, premorbid neuroticism was significantly associated with depression symptoms. Another study has suggested the onset of AD increases preexisting neuroticism and isolation tendency (Meins & Dammast, 2000). However, Brandt et al. (1998) failed to link an association between premorbid personality and ease of adjustment to a nursing home.

In other research with AD, patients who were retrospectively rated as more hostile premorbidly were more likely to develop paranoia than those who were not (Brandt et al., 1998). Having vivid imaginations and being more open to fantasy premorbidly is related to a higher rate of hallucinations. Taken together, this research suggests there may be personality risk factors for developing specific psychiatric symptoms later in dementia, and symptoms observed in dementia patients are often exaggerations of preexisting characterlogical tendencies.

Another approach to exploring psychopathology in OMD is to examine group differences. In a comparison of TBI, stroke, and AD patients, Golden and Golden (2003) found significantly higher rates of personality dysfunction in TBI patients than stroke and AD one-year post onset of condition. Comparison between stroke and AD patients yielded few significant differences in psychopathology on the MMPI-2. However, TBI, AD, and stroke patients all manifested significant elevations on the depression scale and TBI patients averaged three standard deviations higher than the mean on the schizophrenia scale. They concluded that TBI patients had far more personality disturbances than the other two groups. TBI patients also tended to be more self-degrading, which may have resulted in higher symptom reporting. The authors suggested that TBI patients may be more reactive to their difficulties.

Psychotic, dissociative, sexually inappropriate behavior, and personality symptoms can occur after TBI (Fujii & Ahmend, 2002). Novack, Alderson, Bush, Meythaler, and Canupp (2000) reported that emotional distress was not a significant issue among those with TBI 6 to 12 months status post TBI. However, a 30-year follow-up study of TBI patients suggests enduring problems (Koponen et al., 2002). In a review, Franulic, Horta, Maturana, Scherpenisse, and Carbonell (2000) reported 32 percent of those with TBI meet criteria for organic personality disorder and nearly 66 percent of families notice changes in their TBI relative 6 to 12 months status post injury. Such personality changes include irritability, frustration, aggressiveness, egocentricity, impulsiveness, impaired judgment and insight, and inappropriate affect. Personality changes are usually attributed to direct and indirect effects of brain damage, but it is also speculated that TBI can also exacerbate previous traits.

Nevertheless, different brain areas are associated with various personality disruptions (Varney & Menefee, 1993). Cummings's (1995) conceptualization of subcortical circuits and loops attempt to explain why some individuals have frontal syndromes even though the frontal lobes remain intact. For instance, damage to orbitofrontal circuitry can result in disrupted social inhibition (e.g., inappropriate affect, impaired judgment and insight, and a lack of social tact), whereas insults to medial frontal circuitry often cause a suppression in behavior (e.g., apathy, diminished motivation and interest, psychomotor retardation, diminished social involvement, and decreased communication).

EPIDEMIOLOGY

OMD accounts for 15 percent to 17 percent of all psychiatric diagnoses (Trzepacz, Teague, & Lipowski, 1985). Because OMD is an umbrella designation, the incidence and prevalence rates discussed in this section will be drawn from a wide range of disorders and diseases. A review of 96,359 emergency room admissions from 1997 revealed that 38.8 percent of the psychiatric emergency hospitalizations in patients 65 years of age and older were attributed to dementia, delirium, or amnestic disorders (Chapman, Currier, Miller, & Anda, 2003). Dementia and delirium by themselves have been reported to account for almost 75 percent of all cases of OMD in a psychiatric setting (Lee, 1981).

Dementia

The prevalence of dementia is 7.5 percent for individuals over the age of 65 years old and 20 percent for individuals over the age of 80 years old (Zubenko, Mulsant, Sweet, Pasternak, & Tu, 1997). One study found that 67.4 percent of all new nursing home admissions have dementias of some kind (Rovner et al., 1990). AD is associated with 50 percent to 75 percent of these cases (Kawas, 2003). Dementia with Lewy bodies has been reported to account for 10 percent to 15 percent of dementia cases (Rockwell, Choure, Galasko, Olichney, & Jeste, 2000). An overall incidence rate of dementia in a rural sample composed of all ages has been reported to be 17.5 cases per 1,000 cases (Chandra et al., 2001). Given the magnitude of the problem, the contribution of environment and lifestyle to the development of dementias may be an important area of research.

Hendrie et al. (2001) reported incidence rate differences for dementia and AD between industrialized and nonindustrialized countries. They assessed African Americans in Indianapolis, Indiana, and Nigerians from the Yoruba tribe over a five-year period. All of the subjects were age 65 years or older. For the Indiana group, dementia prevalence rate was 3.24 percent per year. This included 2.52 percent who were diagnosed with AD. This contrasted with a dementia prevalence rate of 1.35 percent for the Nigerian sample, with only 1.15 percent developing AD. These findings may indicate that culture and environmental factors affect dementia prevalence rates.

After AD, vascular dementia is the second most common type of dementia in Western countries with a 1.5 percent prevalence rate after the age of 65 years (Hebert & Brayne, 1995). However, in some Asian countries, the rate of vascular dementia is as high as 2.2 percent in individuals aged 65 years or older. Vascular dementia accounts for approximately half of all dementias that occur after the age of 65 years in these Eastern countries. In Latin America, vascular dementia accounts for 15 percent of all dementias after the age of 65 years. The standardized yearly incidence of vascular dementia in individuals over the age of 70 years is estimated at 6 to 12 cases per 1,000 persons. Vascular dementia (i.e., multi-infarct dementia) occurs more commonly in certain subgroups, such as African Americans, than it does in the general population (Wallace, 1993). Individuals with developmental disabilities are also believed to have an elevated incidence rate of vascular dementia (Wherrett, 1999), and previous Down syndrome are especially prone to develop AD (Berg, Karlinsky, & Holland, 1993).

Delirium

Delirium is the most common OMD diagnosis (Trzepacz et al., 1985). Delirium has been reported to range from 9.6 percent to 51.0 percent for patients 65 years of age and older who were newly admitted to a hospital (Elie et al., 2000; Levkoff, Cleary, Liptzin, & Evans, 1991). McNicoll et al. (2003) found that 70 percent of patients over the age of 65 years met the criteria for delirium at some point during their hospital stay. Another study reported that 14.6 percent of psychiatric inpatients, regardless of age, were delirious at some time during their treatment (Ritchie, Steiner, & Abrahamowicz, 1996).

The prevalence of OMD diagnoses other than dementia and delirium is rather low (Trzepacz et al., 1985). However, as many as 13 percent of individuals are reported to have some form of a traumatic brain injury (McGuire, Burright, Williams, & Donovick, 1998), and most of those who experience lasting deficits would likely be diagnosed with *cognitive disorder not otherwise specified.* An additional diagnosis that falls under the category of OMD is mild cognitive impairment, which is a disorder for future research in the current *DSM*. Lopez et al. (2003) reported that out of a cohort of 3,608 individuals evaluated for mild cognitive impairment, the prevalence of mild cognitive impairment of all types was 22 percent. The prevalence of the amnesic type of mild cognitive impairment was 6 percent.

ETIOLOGY

Due to the breadth of the OMD categorization, the etiology of the disorder can be quite varied. Trauma, metabolic dysfunction, neurodegenerative diseases, circulatory impairment, infection, and many other factors can all result in an OMD diagnosis. A systematic review of a subset of these factors will follow.

Traumatic Brain Injury

Injury to the brain resulting in OMD can occur through a variety of methods. Such damage can be caused by a number of primary events, such as direct trauma, indirect trauma (e.g., whiplash), diffuse axonal injury (stretching and/or shearing of axonal fibers due to torque), and hypoxia. On a general level, it is understood that neuronal death after traumatic brain injury is associated with a rapid biochemical cascade that leads to a series of destructive cellular events.

Some of these events are: the release of massive amounts of excitatory neurotransmitters, unsystematic modulation of inhibitory neurotransmitters, increased free radical production and associated lipid membrane peroxidation (Sutkovoi et al., 1999), and the degradation of the blood-brain barrier (Chen, Constantini, Trembovier, Weinstock, & Shohami, 1996). These events, in turn, produce far-reaching effects on neural metabolism and morphology due to the subsequent lowering of cerebral activation levels.

Concussion is common in traumatic brain injury. A coup-contre-coup injury is often observed in a concussive incident. This occurs when the side of the brain opposite the impacted area is damaged due to the brain recoiling off the impacted side of the skull and moving directly back to collide with the area of the skull opposite the impacted region. Frequently, one can see pinpoint hemorrhages at the contre-coup site that result from cavitation and pressure changes. Concussive forces to the head can result in bleeding inside the brain or between the brain and its meninges. Bleeding inside the brain caused by ruptured blood vessels is known as an intracerebral hemorrhage or hemorrhagic stroke. The resulting loss of intracerebral blood flow can result in a hypoxic environment that is harmful to neural cells. An epidural hemorrhage between the dura and the skull produces a fast-growing space-occupying lesion that is often fatal. The presence of a "lucid interval" with an initial disturbance of consciousness followed by a brief recovery and then subsequent deterioration of consciousness marks the acute presentation of an epidural hemorrhage.

Additionally, an accumulation of blood can congeal into a mass known as a hematoma. This often occurs when the vessels between the brain and its outermost covering, the dura mater, tear and produce a subdural hematoma. The combination of a hematoma and cerebral edema (swelling due to the toxic effect of blood on brain tissue) often results in a pressured environment deleterious to brain tissue. Unrelieved, this process can lead to uncal herniation (displacement of brain or related matter outside the brain cavity) and subsequent death. A similar, but milder, mechanism of damage takes place in normal-pressure hydrocephalus when a blockage in the subarachnoid space impairs the reabsorption of cerebral spinal fluid (Puri et al., 2002) and leads to cerebral atrophy and ventricular enlargement.

Recovery from TBI and other events is tracked in clinical settings using instruments such as the Ranchos Los Amigos Levels of Cognitive Functioning Scale (LCFS) and the Disability Rating Scale (DRS). The LCFS is a 10-category scale that ranges from Level 1 (no response/total assistance) to Level 10 (purposeful, appropriate response/modified independent). Patients are matched to a scale by meeting specific criteria. In contrast, the DRS is used to numerically rate a patient on eight dimensions. The cumulative score is then used to categorize the patient into 1 of 10 disability groups ranging from no disability to death. Although both of these measures are reliable and valid instruments, the DRS has been demonstrated to be superior to the LCFS in a variety of domains (Gouvier, Blanton, LaPorte, & Nepomuceno, 1987). As patients recover, the assessment scaled used to gauge recovery change from coma scales (e.g., Glasgow Coma Scale and Comprehensive Level of Consciousness Scale; Stanczak et al., 1984) to behavior rating scales (e.g., DRS and LCFS) to neuropsychological evaluation.

Metabolic Causes of OMD

OMD often results from metabolic dysfunction and may be either reversible or irreversible. Perhaps the most well-known example of this is Korsakoff's syndrome, a profound irreversible amnesia associated with thiamine deficiency. Another disorder associated with nutrition is pellagra, which results from a diet deficient in niacin and tryptophan. Electrolytic imbalances can also negatively affect mental faculties. Endocrine disorders sometimes result in metabolic dysfunctions that affect cognitive abilities. Cushing's syndrome, which results from the excessive release of cortisol, falls into this category, as do hypothyroidism and hyperthyroidism. In addition, end-stage renal disease, liver dysfunction, and chronic toxic encephalopathy are just a few causes of metabolic dysfunction resulting in OMD symptomology.

Neurodegenerative Disorders

The neurodegenerative disorder most frequently associated with OMD is AD, also known as senile dementia/Alzheimer's type (Kawas, 2003). The cognitive impairment associated with the disease is believed to relate to formation of beta-amyloid plaques inside neurons and neurofibrillary tangles between neurons throughout the brain. The resulting neuronal death disrupts neuronal communication by affecting brain morphology and decreasing neurotransmitter levels, particularly acetylcholine.

Lewy bodies, abnormal cytoplasmic inclusions in cells, are found in both AD and Parkinson's disease. They are found in dementia with Lewy bodies, now recognized as the second most prevalent form of dementia after AD. These cell abnormalities are usually found in the brainstem, limbic, and neocortical areas (Rockwell et al., 2000). A related disorder associated with OMD symptomatology is Pick's disease, also known as focal cerebral atrophy, lobar atrophy, or frontotemporal dementia. This latter name comes from the fact that frontal and temporal lobes are the first brain areas affected. No plaques or tangles are found in Pick's disease. The causal mechanism of dysfunction instead appears to be Pick's bodies, abnormal structures inside the cell. The result of the production of these bodies is neuronal death and subsequent brain atrophy.

Creutzfeldt-Jakob disease also results in OMD. It is a disorder that results in encephalopathy due to a destructive variant of a protein called a prion. Prions are abnormally folded proteins that affect the morphology of surrounding proteins. This adversely affects neuronal functioning, resulting in cell death that gives the brain a spongelike appearance. This is the same process that occurs in the infamous "mad cow disease" or bovine spongiform encephalopathy. Some humans who ingested neural tissue from cows infected with bovine spongiform encephalopathy have developed a similar disease, known as new variant Cruetzfeldt-Jakob disease. This variant has a similar rapid progression, which also has no cure. Related prion diseases include scrapie in sheep and kuru among Pacific Island cannibals.

Huntington's disease, also known as Huntington's chorea, is a late-onset neurodegenerative genetic disorder classified as a choreiform disorder. This is due to the fact that the most pronounced symptoms manifest as an inability to inhibit motor output resulting in involuntary body movements. Cognitive impairment commensurate with OMD is observed in Huntington's disease and is believed to be related to dopaminergic dysfunction (Backman & Farde, 2001).

Cardiovascular Dysfunction

As has been previously stated, traumatic brain injury can result in an intracerebral hemorrhage that disturbs blood supply to the brain or extracerebral bleeds that exert a mass effect. An intracerebral hemorrhage, a type of stroke, does not occur exclusively during head trauma, however. It can also result from the rupturing of a blood vessel due to aneurysm, arteriovenous malformation, or high blood pressure. The resulting change in mental status may be serious enough to be classified as vascular dementia. However, most strokes are caused by blood clots blocking the arteries, a different form of cardiovascular dysfunction.

This is often precipitated by artherosclerosis, a narrowing of the arteries that augments clot formation. When the blockage occurs, the ischemia creates a hypoxic environment that can permanently damage the brain within minutes. Paradoxically, removing blockage and returning blood flow can increase the magnitude of the hypoxic damage. This is predominantly due to the creation of hydrogen peroxide and free radicals, such as nitric oxide (Cernak, Wang, Jiang, Bian, & Savic, 2001), that accompany the influx of oxygenated blood into the previously hypoxic brain tissue. Atherosclerosis is primarily responsible for multi-infarct dementia as well. This is cognitive dysfunction due to the accumulated impact of many small strokes due to the general narrowing of arteries in the brain. Brain damage resulting in OMD can also be caused by arrhythmias, which can result in such severe suppression of cardiovascular functioning that blood circulation is severely reduced.

Infection

Another common cause of OMD is infection. This category overlaps with some of the previously mentioned factors. For example, cardiac infections can adversely affect cardiovascular functioning, and infections of major organs can bring about metabolic changes that impact the brain. However, three major types of infection associated with OMD are septicemia, meningitis, and encephalitis. Septicemia is a bacterial infection of the blood that can result in septic shock. Meningitis is inflammation of the meninges. Meningitis is identified as being either purulent or aseptic depending on whether it is caused by a bacterial infection. Encephalitis is inflammation of the brain itself. The pressure caused by the resulting cerebral edema is deleterious to brain tissue. In addition to these, AIDS dementia complex (ADC), also known as HIV-related psychosis and dementia, is a form of altered mental status associated with prolonged HIV positive status (Baldeweg et al., 1997). ADC is directly related to HIV infection and is not primarily a manifestation of an opportunistic infection.

COURSE, COMPLICATIONS, AND PROGNOSIS

The range of individual disorders that make up the category of OMD implies that course, prognosis, and complications of each condition varies widely; however, they generally either follow a pattern of acute or degenerative course. The natural progression of a number of the OMD, even those with acute courses, has associated complications that adversely impact individuals in the long term. This section provides a cursory glance at the relevance of these intricately complex issues related to OMD in general, delirium, dementias, TBI, and other specific organic conditions.

Researchers have examined outcomes and length of stay in patients admitted to psychogeriatric units for OMD. Moss, Wilson, Harrigan, and Ames (1995) indicated that inpatients with OMD were more likely to enter long-term care than those with other diagnoses. Although 75 percent were eventually able to return to their preadmission living accommodations, the odds of being discharged to institutional care was significantly higher for OMD than mood disordered or psychotic patients. Similarly, the odds of having made no or worsening progress while hospitalized was higher in OMD than for mood and psychotic disorders.

Harris and Barraclough (1998) reviewed six studies on OMD mortality rate. Death rate of unspecified OMD was three times the expected rate, whereas violent causes of death, other than suicide, approached four times the expected rate. Highest excess mortality was due to infectious diseases and the greatest risk of mortality occurred in the first two years of follow-up. In other similar research, it was found that 67 percent of psychiatric patients that died of natural causes had OMD (Kamara, Person, & Dennis, 1998). Kamara et al. (1998) also revealed that 74 percent of the psychiatric patients who were 60 or older and died had an OMD. A high rate of comorbid circulatory and repertory conditions accounted for 64 percent of the diagnoses related to those deaths.

After a 5.75-year follow-up, nearly as many as half of elderly psychiatric inpatients with OMD died, compared with only one-fifth with mood and psychiatric disorders (Zubenko, Mulsant, et al., 1997). Standardized mortality rates controlling for demographics and comorbid conditions revealed a 2.5-fold increased mortality risk for OMD patients. Overall, the mortality rate was 55 percent, with delirium patients having the poorest survival rate (43 percent). A similar high mortality risk in elderly psychiatric inpatients with OMD has been shown elsewhere (Rössler, Hewer, Fätkenheuer, & Löffler, 1995).

Most strikingly, the short period after intake in the Rössler et al. (1995) study represented a very high-risk period for psychiatric patients with OMD, which is sometimes referred to as the inherent lethality of the disorder. Of the entire OMD category, cardiovascular complications were the most noted cause of death (Rössler et al., 1995). Even though other studies have shown OMD may be at risk for increased death rate, it has been suggested that OMD patients do not suffer from significantly higher rates of physical morbidity than other matched psychiatric patients (Adamis & Ball, 2000; Zubenko, Marino, et al., 1997).

Another associated feature of OMD patients is a high representation in general hospital settings. More than 17 percent of psychiatric consults from a medical center were diagnosed with OMD (Trzepacz et al., 1985). Consultation requests reflecting OMD included problems with confusion, hallucinations, agitation, bizarre behavior, combativeness, belligerence, forgetfulness, or delusions. Brayley, Lange, Baggoley, Bond, and Harvey (1994) further reported OMD patients in a general hospital accounted for 45 percent of all incident reports involving violent patients, with the majority of these patients suffering from delirium.

There is also a high death rate in delirious psychiatric patients referred from general hospitals. Delirium patients are likely referred from general hospitals to psychiatric units for psychological problems (e.g., change in emotional status) and not cognitive impairment/fluctuation (Trzepacz et al., 1985). Thus, cognitive problems (i.e., confused states) frequently go ignored for such psychiatric patients. Instead, they may be diagnosed only with psychiatric diagnoses (e.g., depression) that are unrelated to accompanying disrupted mental status.

Because OMD may not be initially recognized, physical complications spurring delirium may go unnoticed. This is particularly alarming given that the mortality rate within the first weeks of a delirium diagnosis is high. Not only that, but the presence of delirium is associated with increased length of stay in psychiatric hospitals (Patten, 2001). This suggests that rather than being treated for underlying pathophysiological conditions, the health needs of delirium patients may be compromised and neglected, which can have fatal consequences.

Delirium is also present in a number of cases in the later stages of terminal illnesses and organ transplants. Chochinov (2000) stated that this "terminal agitation" is present in as many as 40 percent of cancer patients, with degree of delirium corresponding to progression of illness. In a review, he also noted that approximately one-third of such cases are reversible. Although severity often fluctuates and tends to worsen at night (i.e., sundowners syndrome, believed to be related to fatigue-enhanced disorientation revealed when patients become understimulated), causes of such delirium are often irreversible. Complications associated with this include dehydration, neglected hygiene, and accidental self-injury, all of which may accelerate associated mental and physical deterioration (Barraclough, 1997). The course of transplant-induced delirium is suspected to subside after a matter of days, but this topic has received insufficient study (Trzepacz et al., 1991).

Delirium also presents complications for clients with concurrent progressive dementias. In a recent review of 14 studies, it has been shown that 22 percent to percent to 89 percent of dementia clients age 65 and older have had at least one episode of delirium (Frick, Agostini, & Inouye, 2002). It was also found that delirium superimposed on dementia is associated with a poor outcome (e.g., prolonged hospitalization, decline in cognitive and physical, more frequent rehospitalizations).

Most dementias are irreversible and, if progressive, eventually lead to a vegetative state and/or death (Zubenko, Mulsant, et al., 1997). The course is usually slow and progressive over several years, but varies across individuals. For example, the course of AD ranges from 1 to 20 years (Arnold, 2000). Early stages are associated with difficulties performing complex activities, employment, and other basic activities (Potkin, Anand, Hartman, Veach, & Grossberg, 2002). As the disease progresses, instrumental behaviors become problematic and Parkinsonian signs, myoclonus, bradykinesia, gait disturbance, and rigidity are more likely to occur, with about a 50 percent prevalence (Arnold, 2000). Dementia, in general, is associated with changes in eating behavior, incontinence, hoarding, reduced activity, moving and mislaying objects, aggression, and repeated requests or demands, which usually worsen as dementia progresses (Hope, Keene, Copper, Fairburn, & Jacoby, 1997).

The Mini Mental State Exam (MMSE) has been used as a marker for cognitive decline, which has been associated with increased restlessness, aggressive behavior, and other behavioral problems (Hope et al., 1997; McCarty et al., 2000). Its use has been widely criticized for being insensitive to subtle early dementias. Traditionally, the MMSE yields a possible score of 30 with lower scores signifying decreased cognitive ability (normal: ≥27, some deficits: 23–26, and widespread deficits: ≤22).

There is a wide range of behaviors and large variation in individual patterns of behavior within the course of dementia. Wandering behavior occurs in up to 63 percent of dementia patients, though recently demonstrated to be about 17 percent in a community sample (Klein et al., 1999). Such behavior often leads to falling, becoming lost, and the need for physical/chemical restraints. Klein et al. (1999) found that those with AD were more likely to wander than those with VD and unspecified dementia. There was also an increased risk for wandering as dementia progressed. Despite some of the noted behavioral changes, patients often go untreated. AIDS dementia complex (ADC) follows a similar course of steady degeneration (Navia, Jordan, & Price, 1986). Motor complications and autonomic disturbances occur at the beginning stages of HD, PD, and other subcortical dementias and are suspected to be among the most distressing symptoms (Dodel, Berger, & Wolfgang, 2001; Kostic, Marinkovic, Svetel, Stefanova, & Przedborski, 2002).

Traumatic brain injury also presents with a wide variation of course and prognosis. In this regard, it is often assumed that severity and location of injury are the most predictive indicators of recovery and/or decline in functioning. Other complications, such as posttraumatic seizures pose significant challenges to recovery in those with TBI. Those with moderate TBI have sevenfold increased risk for late seizures (Temkin, 2003). Even two years status post TBI, Temkin reported a substantial increased risk for seizure rate in the general population. However, the seizure risk decreases substantially in the first month post injury and decreases further with each passing month. Open brain injuries have an even larger seizure risk.

ASSESSMENT AND DIAGNOSIS

OMD produces dysfunction in cognitive ability as well as emotional and behavioral changes. There are a number of different mental disorders that produce a similar constellation of symptoms. The differentiation between OMD and psychiatric disorders is of critical importance in the effective diagnosis and treatment of patients. This can be a challenging task for clinicians, especially in cases in which OMD has yet to be determined. Adequate understanding of OMD can be ascertained through systematic comprehensive examination.

The initial evaluation of psychological symptoms should begin with detailed history and expanded mental status exams (Strub & Black, 1993). If OMD is suspected, further investigation via laboratory tests, neuroimaging, and neuropsychological evaluation should be conducted in searching for underlying pathology. Such investigations should be tailored to individual patients' needs (Strub & Black, 1993). For example, a neurological exam would be appropriate when extrapyramidal motor symptoms are present, whereas a CT scan could confirm multi-infarct dementia.

Neuropsychological evaluation provides a comprehensive assessment of cognitive and psychological domains to detect subtle deficits. This is useful in rehabilitation and treatment planning, progress tracking, and in determining readiness for vocational and educational reentry. The use of quantitative cutoff scores and the pathognomonic sign approach are the general strategies employed in neuropsychological assessment (Groth-Marnat, 2003). Two comprehensive neuropsychological batteries that can be utilized in the identification of brain dysfunction are the Halstead-Reitan Neuropsychological Battery (HRNB) and the Luria Nebraska Neuropsychological Battery (LNNB). Whether using an established battery or a compilation of individual tests, a thorough evaluation should include an assessment of memory, attention, language, visuospatial abilities, executive function, intelligence, mood, and personality (LaRue, 1992). Although not a comprehensive list, several well researched, psychometrically sound tests that are currently used by clinicians are highlighted in the following section.

Intelligence Testing

The current gold standard of intelligence tests for adults is the Wechsler Adult Intelligence Scale, third edition (WAIS-

III). Several studies have offered support for the use of WAIS-III subtests in the identification of brain dysfunction. For example, brain-damaged populations consistently perform lower than unimpaired populations on the Digit Symbol-Coding and Symbol Search subtests (Hawkins, 1998). The Psychological Corporation (1997) found a 10-point difference, favoring verbal over performance scores, for a group of patients with "probable" AD. Two other measures of intellectual functioning are the Leiter International Performance Scale, Revised (LIPS-R) and the Standford-Binet, fifth edition (Roid, 2003; Roid & Miller, 1997). The LIPS-R is appropriate for use individuals with hearing impairment, non-English speaking, and educationally disadvantaged patients.

Attention

Attention deficits are frequently associated with cerebral impairment (Lezak, 1995). Reaction time tests effectively detect impairments due to head trauma (Van Vomeren & Brouwer, 1990), solvent exposure (Groth-Marnat, 1993), and the early impact of dementia (Teng, Chui, & Saperia, 1990). The Trail Making Test (TMT) has been successfully used to detect early stages of dementia and track progressive decline (Rasmusson, Zonderman, Kawas, & Resnick, 1998) as well as differentiate between psychiatric, general medical, and neuropsychologically impaired patients (Lezak, 1995). Additionally, TMT-B performance of individuals with mild hypoxemia (Prigatano, 1983) and chronic toxic encephalopathy are significantly slower (Nilson, Barregard, & Baeckman, 1999) than those of normal controls. The Symbol Digit Modalities Test (SDMT, WAIS-III) has been successful in differentiating depression from dementia and in detecting head injuries. Another measure sensitive to the performance of head-injured patients is the Stroop technique (Lezak, 1995).

Memory and Learning

There is ample evidence that the Wechsler Memory Scale, third edition (WMS-III) can effectively discriminate between clinical and normal populations. Various clinical groups (Alzheimer's, Huntington's, and Parkinson's diseases, temporal lobe epilepsy, schizophrenia, chronic alcohol abuse, and multiple sclerosis) consistently score lower than the standardization sample (Groth-Marnat, 2003). The Rey Auditory Verbal Learning Test (RAVLT) can differentiate between patients with AD and those with depression (Burt, Zembar, & Niederehe, 1995). The California Verbal Learning Test (CVLT) effectively differentiates most patient groups, including those with traumatic brain injury, Alzheimer's, Parkinson's, and Huntington's diseases (Lezak, 1995). The Tactual Performance Test (TPT), a component of the HRNB, consistently shows lower scores for brain-damaged patients than for normals (Groth-Marnat, 2003).

Psychomotor

The Finger Tapping Test, a component of the HRNB, is a reliable method for detecting brain impairments due to vascular disease and head trauma (Groth-Marnat, 2003). The Hand Dynamometer Test and Grooved Pegboard Test are two other widely used methods for determining lateralization of deficit and impairments in motor skills.

Problem Solving and Executive Functioning

Leroi, O'Hearn, Lyketsos, Rosenblatt, and Brandt (2002) found that patients with degenerative cerebellar diseases appeared most impaired in executive functioning. The Porteus Maze Test is reliable in detecting the severity of brain damage (Lezak, 1995). The Wisconsin Card-Sorting Task (WCST) has received support for its sensitivity in the detection of frontal lobe lesions. The Category Test is also a sensitive measure of brain dysfunction (Strub & Black, 1993).

Language

The Boston Naming Test (BNT) is an effective measure for detecting and monitoring the progression of dementia and detecting word-finding problems associated with multiple sclerosis and traumatic brain injury (Lezak, 1995). Other commonly used measures include the Peabody Picture Vocabulary Test, Token Test, and the Animal Naming Test. There are also several comprehensive aphasia batteries, including the highly supported Boston Diagnostic Aphasia Exam and the Western Aphasia Battery (Strub & Black, 1993).

Visuospatial Ability

Differential performance of patients with OMD has been found on spatial and nonspatial tasks (Heilman & Valenstein, 1993). The greatest impairments in patients with Huntington's disease can be expected in the visuospatial domain (Leroi et al., 2002). The Bender Visual Motor Gestalt Test has received widespread usage in neuropsychological screening. Block Design and Object Assembly tasks are effective in detecting OMD, especially damage in the right parietal region (Lezak, 1995).

Personality and Mood

Instruments that assess the domains of personality and emotion, many of which are relevant to neuropsychological impairment, can effectively gauge psychosocial adjustment and rehabilitation outcome (Groth-Marnat, 2003). The Geriatric Depression Inventory is a useful instrument for assessing depression in the elderly. Other instruments designed for used with OMD patients include the Patient Competency Rating Scale, Frontal Lobe Personality Scale, Neurobehavioral Rating Scale, and the Neuropsychology Behavior and Affect Profile (Groth-Marnat, 2003).

DIAGNOSTIC CRITERIA

Diagnostic criteria for any OMD include (1) the establishment of a direct link between a general medical condition (GMC) and the presenting disturbance, (2) the disturbance is not better accounted for by a primary mental disorder or substance abuse and does not occur during the course of a dementia or delirium (except, of course, in cases for which the diagnosis is delirium or dementia), and (3) the symptoms must be sufficiently severe as to create a significant impact on the patient's ability to function (APA, 2000). In establishing a causal link, the clinician may look for a temporal association between the GMC and the mental disturbance or an atypical age of onset. When assessing clients with suspected OMD, it is important to rule out differential diagnoses that could account for the presenting pattern of disturbance (APA, 2000). For example, in patients with multi-infarct dementia (MID) memory functioning remains relatively intact, but communication abnormalities of pitch, tone, melodic qualities, with slowed speech production are present (Wymer, Lindman, & Bookish, 2002). The preservation of memory and acute onset of symptoms associated with MID distinguish it from Alzheimer's. Similarly, frontal lobe syndrome is differentiated by a change in personality, without the accompanying change in cognition. In the following section, diagnostic criteria and salient features of commonly diagnosed OMD are reviewed.

Delirium

The essential components of delirium are a disturbance in consciousness accompanied by altered cognition or perceptual disturbance that develops rapidly, fluctuating throughout the day. Delirious states are often accompanied by impaired judgment and emotional, psychomotor, and sleep disturbances. Physical examination and laboratory findings indicative of delirium may reveal tremors, asterixis, autonomic hyperactivity, and abnormal EEG readings. Additional routine investigations to rule out differential diagnoses should include full blood count, erythrocyte sedimentation rate, blood chemistry, phosphate, liver function, and glucose tests, serology for syphilis, thyroid function tests, and urea and creatinine content (APA, 2000).

Dementia

Dementia is characterized by gradual memory impairment and aphasia, apraxia, agnosia, or executive functioning deficits in an individual with previously higher functioning. Patients with dementia may also exhibit emotional and motor disturbances, poor judgment and insight, disinhibition, delusions, hallucinations, and difficulty with visuospatial functioning. Neuroimaging may reveal cerebral atrophy, focal brain lesions, hydrocephalus, or periventricular ischemic brain injury (APA, 2000). Differential diagnoses within the dementia category include dementia due to AD, vascular disease, or several other medical conditions (HIV, head trauma, Parkinson's disease, Huntington's disease, Pick's disease, Creutzfeldt-Jakob disease, and other general medical conditions).

Amnestic Disorder

Amnestic disorder is characterized by the presence of memory impairment manifested by poor ability to learn new information or inability to recall previously learned information. The impairment may be transient or chronic. Confabulation, disorientation, confusion, apathy, lack of insight, and lack of initiative are associated features that often appear in the patient with amnestic disorder (APA, 2000), but when other specific cognitive functions are affected, cognitive disorder not otherwise specified (NOS) is more appropriate.

The remaining OMDs are marked by the presence of symptoms typical of the primary mental disorders but are judged to be the direct physiological result of a medical condition. In addition, the diagnostic criteria described previously also apply to these OMDs. Other mental disorders due to a GMC include catatonic disorder due to a GMC, personality change due to a GMC, psychotic disorder due to a GMC, mood disorder due to a GMC, anxiety disorder due to a GMC, sexual disorder due to a GMC, and sleep disorder due to a GMC.

IMPACT ON ENVIRONMENT

The effect of an organic mental disorder (OMD) on the lives of the individual, family members, and caregivers can be devastating (Lezak, 1988). A formerly healthy individual, capable of fulfilling specific roles and responsibilities within the family, social circles, or community, may no longer be able to meet these expectations. These circumstances can produce frustration, depression, resentment, and many other feelings in those who interact closely with the afflicted individual. In addition to the psychological impact, health complications and safety issues add considerable burden to this issue. A multitude of psychosocial difficulties may result in those with OMD, including employment problems, family and interpersonal conflicts, and emotional and sexual difficulties.

Functional Ability

Functional status is typically measured in terms of ability to perform activities of daily living (ADL). These can be divided into two categories: (1) basic (BADL), which includes bathing, dressing, toileting, transferring, continence, and feeding; and (2) instrumental (IADL), which includes cleaning, cooking, using public transportation, handling finances, and shopping. Independent living requires successful functioning in both of these categories (Brorsson & Hulter, 1984; Katz, Ford, & Moskowitz, 1963).

A significant correlation between deterioration of functional ability and cognitive faculties has been documented, particularly as part of the dementia syndrome (Aguero-Torres, Thomas, Winblad, & Fratiglioni, 2001). Alzheimer's disease (AD), in particular, is associated with cognitive and behavioral deficits, which lead to inability to perform ADL. Declines in the cognitive and functional ability of Alzheimer's patients, especially in frontally mediated dysfunction, are associated with elevated healthcare costs, and the eventual need for institutionalization (Gutterman, Markowitz, Lewis, & Fillit, 1999, as cited in Boyle et al., 2003; Trabucci, 1999).

Several studies have found a strong association between depression and IADL deficits in individuals with dementia (Espiritu et al., 2001; Pearson, Teri, Reifler, & Raskind, 1989). Depression in AD has been linked to increased impairments in both quality of life (Gonzales-Salvador, Lyketsos, & Baker, 2000) and competence with ADL (Lyketsos, Steele, & Baker, 1997). Depression also increases the likelihood of physical aggression (Lyketsos, Steele, & Galik, 1999). Steele, Rovner, and Chase (1990) found that depression is predictive of earlier entry into assisted living facilities for individuals with AD and depression, and reduced probability of discharge from assisted living facilities for persons with depression was documented by Kopetz, Steele, and Brandt (2000).

Executive cognitive dysfunction in other neurological disorders has been shown to be an important determinant of ability to perform ADL. Cahn, Sullivan, Edith, and Shear (1998) found a positive association between the cognitive processes of Parkinson's patients and ADL abilities. In individuals with vascular dementia (VaD), executive cognitive dysfunction and behavioral manifestations of frontal symptoms (i.e., apathy) are associated with functional decline (Boyle, Cohen, Paul, Moser, & Gorden, 2002; Marin, 1991). Additionally, Boyle et al. (2003) showed an independent relationship between functional impairment and neuropathological factors (e.g., subcortical hyperintensities) in patients with VaD.

Impact on Others

An OMD not only affects the afflicted individual's independent functioning, but can cause personality and behavioral changes that significantly contribute to distress felt by family members and caretakers. Knight, Devereux, and Godfrey (1998) found behavioral and emotional changes in individuals with traumatic brain injury to be associated with caregiver distress and burden. Franulic et al. (2000) reported that caregivers often consider personality changes more stressful than actual physical disability. Problems reported by caregivers include nocturnal wandering, incontinence, inability to wash, paranoid delusions, sleep disorders, immobility, and problems with aggression. Premorbid relational difficulties between the individual and caregiver are associated with an increased likelihood of aggressive behaviors toward the caregiver (Silliman, Sternberg, & Fretwell, 1988).

Stress imposed by behavioral problems often leads to the onset of psychiatric illness in the caregiver (Gonzales-Salvador, Arango, & Lyketsos, 1999). In a study involving individuals with TBI, Franulic et al. (2000) reported a need for psychological assistance in approximately 30 percent of participating families. An added strain as the individual's condition worsens is relative abandonment by friends, family and neighbors due to these behaviors. Female caregivers, especially relatives, are more likely to experience depression and low morale (Morris, Woods, Davies, & Morris, 1992). Caregivers who are well supported experienced less strain and depression than those whose support is poor (Morris et al., 1992). In general, caregivers report feelings of anger, sadness, fatigue, as well as feeling that they have little time or energy for their own interests.

The effects of brain impairment and consequent changes in behavior and personality may also have an adverse impact on marriage quality. Spouses of individuals with head injury have reported significant feelings of tension and distress

(Levin, Grafman, & Eisenberg, 1987). In a study of individuals with Huntington's disease, Mendez (1994) found 38 percent of individuals either divorced or separated after the onset of the disease. Couples cited fears of abandonment, family conflict, and employment and sexual difficulty as contributing factors.

Sexual dysfunction and changes in sexual desire are also likely to contribute to marital discourse (Levin et al., 1987). Postinjury hypersexuality and changes in sexual preference have been reported in OMD (Miller, Cummings, McIntyre, Ebers, & Grode, 1986) and would be expected to increase the level of tension placed on an already stressed relationship.

Sexual inappropriateness not only creates a problem for caregivers, but can also impede successful rehabilitation. Bezeau, Bogod, and Mateer (2004) conducted a survey of rehabilitation professionals, documenting reports of sexual touching, use of sexual force, sexual remarks, and exhibitionism by individuals. An overwhelming 97 percent of the participants confirmed the negative impact these inappropriate behaviors had upon rehabilitation and reentry. It was suggested that impairment in executive functioning and social judgment reduces these individuals' ability to appreciate social cues and manage sexual urges.

Vocational Impact

Just as OMD-associated personality changes and behavioral problems affect individual functioning and familial relations, these changes also play a role affecting successful community and occupational reentry. Kubu et al. (1993) investigated the relationship between emotional recognition and psychosocial functioning and suggested that deficits in emotional recognition may contribute to difficulty in interpersonal relations. Impaired cognitive functioning is often manifest as impaired social interaction and social blunting, creating an obstacle to reentry into the workforce (Levin et al., 1987). This is reinforced by the fact that academic and vocational deterioration may be observed in up to one-third of brain-damaged individuals (Fujii & Ahmend, 2002).

In a study of individuals with closed head injury, Ben-Yishay, Silver, Piasetsky, and Rattock (1987) found a positive relationship between unemployment and deficits in memory and attention. In a review of previous studies involving TBI patients with anosmia, Varney and Roberts (1999) highlighted a pattern of chronic employment difficulties for approximately 60 percent to 80 percent of participants for up to five years postinjury. Most sought and successfully obtained employment but could not keep their job. Contributing factors included absentmindedness, poor planning and anticipation, indecisiveness or faulty decision making, erratic quality of work output, unreliability in work attendance, an inability to learn from errors, and an inability to get along socially with coworkers and particularly supervisors (Varney & Roberts, 1999).

Difficulties with social and occupational reintegration due to self-care deficits, impaired thought processes, and personality alterations are common in individuals with OMD. The coping abilities and premorbid relationship of the individual and his caregiver play a considerable role in rehabilitation and quality of life to be expected by both. Involved individuals must expect transformations in the role an individual with OMD will be able to fulfill in the family, workplace, and community, if they are capable of functioning in these capacities at all.

TREATMENT IMPLICATIONS

Improvements in medical care and technology have contributed to an increasing survival rate for individuals with OMD. A variety of interventions have been developed by health care professionals to treat the complications associated with OMD. Primary treatment of the underlying pathology must be combined with management of the related cognitive, emotional, and behavioral difficulties that accompany OMD. Treatment implications for individuals with an OMD, whether receiving at-home or institutional care, include consideration of individual and family education, pharmacotherapy, and psychological support.

In order to formulate an appropriate treatment strategy and provide the patient and family with suitable information, it is important to know the typical course of recovery and degree of injury related to the OMD, as well as any other factors that might influence recovery, such as premorbid intellectual abilities, age, social support, motivation to improve, and premorbid mental stability also influence an individual's recovery of function (Heilman & Valenstein, 1993). For instance, Mazaux and Richer (1998) reported that prognosis for recovery from neuromotor impairments is better for traumatic brain injury (TBI) patients than for stroke patients. Furthermore, there is a better functional outcome for neuromotor and orthopedic injury in TBI patients than for cognitive and behavioral impairments.

The treatment strategies that best serve individuals whose OMD is acute involve different components than the strategies for individuals whose OMD is chronic and progressive. A care management approach facilitating reentry and recovery of an independent lifestyle is typically the most appropriate for individuals with an acute and recoverable OMD and may involve physical, psychological, and cognitive rehabilitation. For individuals with a progressive OMD, treatment focuses on preserving the individual's current skill levels and providing resources to the family for education and patient management.

Psychosocial Intervention: Family Support

As mentioned previously, educational interventions are a necessary component in the management of OMD. A survey conducted by Gouvier, Prestholdt, and Warner (1988) indicated that the general public has many misconceptions about the recovery process after brain injury. Providing family members and individuals with adequate information about the disorder, including related symptomatology, may help reduce fears and frustrations. Increased support from external sources is related to enhanced caregiver well-being (Morris, Morris, & Britton, 1989). For example, organizations providing support for caregivers promote the use of day care and/or respite care programs that allow caregivers time for themselves during the day and even for weekends and holidays (Huckle, 1994). The importance of practical care issues (i.e., legal assistance, financial planning, long-term care) should also be emphasized (Heilman & Valenstein, 1993).

In addition to providing educational interventions, family members may also need coping skills and behavior management strategies. Caregivers are often obliged to take on this role without prior experience or appropriate knowledge to fulfill it adequately; therefore, the attainment of problem-solving skills and coping strategies is vital for success. Behavioral intervention strategies employed by family members and/or caregivers are a fundamental resource for relieving inevitable frustrations associated with caring for an individual with OMD. For example, family members may lessen emotional outbursts by eliminating stressful triggers and gradually redirecting the individual's attention to a more pleasant topic (Kermis, 1986). Family disengagement training may also be a useful intervention, especially for relatives of individuals with a chronic progressive OMD (Lezak, 1986). Both rational emotive therapy (Oliver & Block, 1990) and cognitive behavioral therapy (Levine, Daston, & Gendron, 1983) have been recommended for caregivers as a means of reducing negative emotions and improving coping ability. Perkins and Poynton (1990) found that group therapy with relatives of dementia patients increased morale and understanding of dementia among study participants.

Psychosocial Intervention: Psychological Support

The presence and severity of cognitive deficits in OMD influences an individual's potential for rehabilitation success and capability for independent living and occupational engagement. Rehabilitation programs provide remediation of cognitive, and emotional, and physical deficits. Therapeutic goals in psychology are unique to the individual and might include promotion of independence, memory retraining, improvement of self-esteem and reality coping, and alleviation of associated depression and anxiety (Ungvarski & Trzcianowska, 2000). Common psychological intervention techniques include compensation, component, and functional training.

Mackay (1994) suggested that early intervention in trauma centers decreased both the length of patient stay and providing familial stress. Although acute rehabilitation is aimed at the prevention of complications and arousal stimulation, the subacute phase of rehabilitation is typically an inpatient process and involves the initiation of recovery from physical and/or cognitive impairments. The postacute phase of rehabilitation is typically conducted at an outpatient facility with the goal of achieving independence, minimizing acquired handicaps, and facilitating reentry into the community and workplace (Mazaux & Richer, 1998). In a survey of cognitive rehabilitation centers throughout the United States, Stringer (2003) found that the majority of patients were being treated for stroke, followed by traumatic brain injury, then brain tumor, and least for anoxic brain damage. It should be noted that cognitive rehabilitation therapy may not be appropriate for some OMDs, including individuals with CNS infection, demyelinating disease, or dementia (Lincoln et al., 2002; Stringer, 2003), or for patients too obtunded to meaningfully participate or carry over new learning from session to session.

As mentioned previously, a variety of treatments may be employed to remediate and/or alleviate cognitive difficulties and emotional difficulties with organically impaired individuals. Mittenberg, Tremont, Zielinski, Fichera, and Rayls (1996) used cognitive symptom behavioral management with mild traumatic brain injury (TBI) and found a reduction in both the number of symptoms and symptom duration. Relaxation training has been shown to improve functioning for patients with severe TBI (Lysaght & Bodenhammer, 1990) and to provide symptomatic relief from postconcussive symptoms and improve cognitive functioning in patients with mild TBI (Hanna-Pladdy, Berry, Bennett, Phillips, & Gouvier, 2001). Using cognitive-behavioral therapy, Van Hout (2003) showed improvement in the dysfunctional cognitions associated with chronic fatigue disorder in chronic encephalopathy patients.

Compensation-based approaches, strategies that optimize preserved processes, tend to have greater efficacy than do rehearsal strategies in cognitive rehabilitation (Chestnut et al., 1999). Compensatory strategies typically involve environmental modification (i.e., physical alterations of space, changes in the expectations of others), the use of external aids (i.e., appointment books, checklists), or the use of internal strategies (self-instruction, rehearsal). In functional compensation, the individual learns to use substitute maneuvers where residual functioning exists, eventually forming a new system of operation. Motivational factors are essential to the success of this strategy, as a passive attitude and depression are likely to impede recovery (Robinson & Benson, 1981).

The use of cognitive prosthetics, a highly customized functional support, is a compensatory strategy used in the treatment of individuals with acquired cognitive deficits. Created to increase the individual's effectiveness in activities of daily living and assist in return to educational or vocational environments, cognitive prosthetics are capable of modifying functions based on ongoing assessment. Steele, Weinriche, and Carlson (1989) reported success in food preparation when a cognitive prosthetic was used with an aphasic head-injured individual. Major drawbacks associated with cognitive prosthetics are the individual customization required and the lack of therapists trained in the use of prosthetics (Cole, 1999).

Functional and integrative training involves the generalization and application of cognitive skills in real-life settings. Glisky, Schacter, and Tulving (1986) showed that individuals with OMD were able to acquire computer skills that could generalize to the work environment. Such training can be conducted directly at the site where it will be used or transferred from therapy to real-life settings (Cole, 1999).

Component training involves the direct remediation of deficits, usually in basic cognitive processes such as attention, memory, perceptual motor skills, linguistic skills, reasoning, and processing speed. Retraining memory deficits has received a significant amount of attention in the literature. For example, Kessels and de Hann (2003) showed the errorless learning approaches are superior to the vanishing cue method in amnestic patients. Additionally, Chiaravalloti, Demaree, and Gaudino's (2003) examination of the repetition effect in individuals with multiple sclerosis (MS) indicated that it was not a sufficient technique for use with that population.

Psychological interventions should be identified on an individual basis, as not all OMDs are appropriate for all treatments. In addition to participating in cognitive rehabilitation, patients typically work with a team of medical personnel, such as occupational, speech, and physical therapists, to overcome the acquired deficits ideally in a transdisciplinary format promoting a true rehabilitation milieu (Toglia, 1991).

Pharmacological Interventions

Pharmacological treatment in OMD is not homogeneous due to the diversity of mechanisms of impairment in the disorder. Generally, a reduction in the individual's medication regimen is advised as pharmacological agents often exacerbate cognitive impairment. Behavioral interventions are, therefore, preferred when possible. When utilized, pharmacological treatments for individuals with OMD should focus on specific symptoms, such as depression, anxiety, or psychoticism, and standard treatment should be used. One common symptom in OMD is memory impairment. Indeed, it is a necessary factor for the diagnosis of dementia. Several pharmacological interventions have been developed that, whereas they will not permanently repair memory functions, ameliorate memory impairments when taken on a regular basis. The majority of these are cholinomimetic agents. One of the first of these was tacrine (Cognex), a competitive, long-lasting cholinesterase inhibitor.

Blood-brain barrier penetration issues and side effects in the peripheral nervous system have, until recently, hampered pharmacological manipulation of ACh (Blount, Nguyen, & McDeavitt, 2002). However, newer agents have partially solved these problems and promise to offer significant improvement to individuals suffering memory deficits. One of these is donepezil (Aricept), an ACh agonist that inhibits acetylcholinesterase that has been shown to benefit individuals with cognitive impairment (Taverni, Seliger, & Lichtman, 1998). ACh precursors have been used as well (D'Orlando & Sandage, 1995). ACh affects multiple neural substrates, including the cortex, thalamus, amygdala, hypothalamus, and hippocampus (Snyder & Ferris, 2000). Theoretically, all cholinomimetic drugs should help alleviate memory impairments associated with TBI. Additionally, dopaminergic agents and psychostimulants are also used to treat post-TBI cognitive deficits. Psychostimulants act by increasing catecholamine activity by blocking the reuptake of norepinephrine and dopamine. Methylphenidate and dextroamphetamine are examples that have been shown to improve attention/arousal in patients with TBI (Whyte, Vaccaro, Grieb-Neff, & Hart, 2002).

Because psychological symptoms such as anxiety, depression, and psychosis frequently occur in individuals with OMD, other psychotropic medication appears warranted. Selective serotonin reuptake inhibitors (SSRI) and tricyclic agents (TCA) are commonly used in the treatment of depression and anxiety with this population. Atypical antipsychotics (i.e., risperidone) are effective in treating the positive and negative symptoms of psychosis and may have a reduced risk of producing extrapyramidal side effects than typical antipsychotics (Lee, Lyketsos, & Rao, 2003). The main consideration in pharmacological selection is which medications are the most effective while offering the fewest side effects for the individual.

Treatment of OMD has evolved significantly in the last few decades with increasingly effective pharmacological and behavioral interventions. Nonetheless, supportive psychotherapy and education remain key elements in the successful adjustment of patients with OMD. Ongoing investigations and product development provide the afflicted and those who care for them with hopeful expectations for the future of assistive technology and the quality of life and level of independence that can be supported through its use.

SUMMARY

Organic mental disorders encompass disturbances in cognitive functioning resulting from physical or physiological injury such as traumatic brain injury, metabolic dysfunction, neurogenerative disorders, cardiovascular dysfunction, and infection. These disorders account for approximately 15 percent of all psychiatric disorders, representing a sizable portion of patients seen by mental health professionals. However, the causes of the condition are many and the manifestation of symptoms is diverse. Thus, diagnosing OMD typically requires the acquisition of a detailed patient and family history, medical evaluation, as well as the administration of a systematic mental status exam and comprehensive cognitive assessment.

With the exception of TBI and delirium, most OMDs follow a long-term degenerative course. Nonetheless, all are often associated with personality changes (e.g., self-centeredness) and development of psychopathology (e.g., depression; Prigatano, 1986). In addition to impairment in cognitive functioning, the subsequent personality and psychological changes can have a devastating effect on social and familial relationships, employment, and community involvement. As a result, complications with complex symptom presentations may serve as roadblocks to treatment and warrant close clinical attention and interventions appropriate for individual patients and families alike. Treatment implications vary depending on the individual deficits associated with the illness or injury and have varying prognoses for recovery. These typically include components of cognitive, physical, and occupational rehabilitation, psychotherapy, and pharmacotherapy.

REFERENCES

Adamis, D., & Ball, C. (2000). Physical morbidity in elderly psychiatric inpatients: Prevalence and possible relations between the major mental disorders and physical illness. *International Journal of Geriatric Psychiatry, 15,* 248–253.

Aguero-Torres, H., Thomas, V., Winblad, B., & Fratiglioni, L. (2002). The impact of somatic and cognitive disorders on the functional status of the elderly. *Journal of Clinical Epidemiology, 55,* 1007–1012.

American Psychiatric Association. (1980). *Diagnostic and statistical manual of mental disorders,* (3rd ed.). Washington, DC: Author.

American Psychiatric Association. (1987). *Diagnostic and statistical manual of mental disorders* (3rd ed., rev.). Washington, DC: Author.

American Psychiatric Association. (2000). *Diagnostic and statistical manual of mental disorders* (4th ed., text rev.). Washington, DC: Author.

Arnold, S. E. (2000). Part II. Clinical diagnosis and course of Alzheimer's disease. *Dm-Disease-a-Month, 46*(10), 666–687.

Backman, L., & Farde, L. (2001). Dopamine and cognitive functioning: Brain imaging findings in Huntington's disease and normal aging. *Scandinavian Journal of Psychology, 42*(3), 287–296.

Baldeweg, T., Catalan, J., Pugh, K., Gruzelier, J., Lovett, E., Scurlock, H., et al. (1997). Neurophysiological changes associated with psychiatric symptoms in HIV-infected individuals without AIDS. *Biological Psychiatry, 41,* 474–487.

Barraclough, J. (1997). Depression, anxiety, and confusion. *British Medical Journal, 315*(7119), 1365–1368.

Ben-Yishay, Y., Silver, S., Piasetsky, E., & Rattock, J. (1987). Relationship between employability and vocational outcome after intensive holistic cognitive rehabilitation. *Journal of Head Trauma Rehabilitation, 2*(1), 35–48.

Berg, J. M., Karlinsky, H., & Holland, A. J. (1993). *Alzheimer disease, Down syndrome, and their relationship.* Oxford, England: Oxford University Press.

Bezeau, S. C., Bogod, N. M., & Mateer, C. A. (2004). Sexually intrusive behavior following brain injury: Approaches to assessment and rehabilitation. *Brain Injury, 18*(3), 299–313.

Blount, P. J., Nguyen, C. D., & McDeavitt, J. T. (2002). Clinical use of cholinomimetic agents: A review. *Journal of Head Trauma Rehabilitation, 17*(4), 314–321.

Boyle, P., Cohen, R., Paul, R., Moser, D., & Gorden, N. (2002). Executive and motor impairments predict functional declines in patients with vascular dementia. *International Journal of Geriatric Psychiatry, 17,* 164–169.

Boyle, P., Paul, R., Moser, D., Zawacki, T., Gorden, N., & Cohen, R. (2003). Cognitive and neurologic predictors of functional impairment in vascular dementia. *American Journal of Geriatric Psychiatry, 11,* 103–106.

Brandt, J., Campodonico, J. R., Rich, J. B., Steele, C., Ruff, T., Baker, A., et al. (1998). Adjustment to residential placement in Alzheimer disease patients: Does premorbid personality matter? *International Journal of Geriatric Psychiatry, 13,* 509–515.

Brayley, J., Lange, R., Baggoley, C., Bond, M., & Harvey, P. (1994). The violence management team: An approach to aggressive behavior in general hospital. *Medical Journal of Australia, 161,* 254–258.

Brorsson, B., & Hulter, A. K. (1984). Katz index of independence in ADL: Reliability and validity in short-term care. *Scandinavian Journal of Rehabilitation Medicine, 16,* 125–132.

Burt, D., Zembar, M., & Niederehe, G. (1995). Depression and memory impairment: A meta-analysis of the association, its pattern, and specificity. *Psychological Bulletin, 117,* 285–305.

Cahn, D., Sullivan, E., Edith, V., & Shear, P. (1998). Differential contributions of cognitive and motor component processes to physical and instrumental activities of daily living in Parkinson's disease. *Archives of Clinical Neuropsychology, 13,* 575–583.

Cernak, I., Wang, Z., Jiang, J., Bian, X., & Savic, J. (2001). Cognitive deficits involved in blast injury-induced neurotrauma: Possible involvement of nitric oxide. *Brain Injury, 15*(7), 593–612.

Chandra, V., Pandav, R., Dodge, H. H., Johnston, J. M., Belle, S. H., DeKosky, S. T., et al. (2001). Incidence of Alzheimer's disease in a rural community in India: The Indo-US Study. *Neurology, 57*(6), 985–989.

Chapman, D. P., Currier, G. W., Miller, J. K., & Anda, R. F. (2003). Medication induced emergency hospitalizations for psychiatric disorders among older adults in the U.S. *International Journal of Geriatric Psychiatry, 18,* 185–186.

Chen, Y., Constantini, S., Trembovier, V., Weinstock, M., & Shohami, E. (1996). An experimental model of closed head injury in mice: Pathophysiology, histopathology, and cognitive deficits. *Journal of Neurotrauma, 13,* 567–568.

Chestnut, R., Carney, N., Maynard, H., Mann, N., Patterson, P., & Helfand, M. (1999). Summary report: Evidence for the effectiveness of rehabilitation for persons with traumatic brain injury. *Journal of Head Trauma Rehabilitation, 14,* 277–307.

Chiaravalloti, N., Demaree, H., & Gaudino, E. (2003). Can the repetition effect maximize learning in multiple sclerosis? *Clinical Rehabilitation, 17,* 58–68.

Chochinov, H. M. (2000). Psychiatry and terminal illness. *Canadian Journal of Psychiatry, 45*(2), 143–150.

Cole, E. (1999). Cognitive prosthetics: An overview to a method of treatment. *Neurorehabilitation, 12,* 39–51.

Costa, P. T., & McCrae, R. R. (1992). *The NEO Personality Inventory–Revised Manual.* Odessa, FL: Psychological Assessment Resources.

Cummings, J. L. (1995). Anatomic and behavioral aspects of frontal-subcortical circuits. *Annals of the New York Academy of Science, 15,* 1–13.

Dodel, R. C., Berger, K., & Wolfgang, H. O. (2001). Health-related quality of life and healthcare utilization in patients with Parkinson's disease. *Pharmacoeconomics, 19*(10), 1013–1038.

D'Orlando, K. J., & Sandage, B. W. (1995). Citicoline (CDP-choline): Mechanisms of action and effects in ischemic brain injury. *Neurology Research, 17,* 281–284.

Elie, M., Rousseau, F., Cole, M., Primeau, F., McCusker, J., & Bellavance, F. (2000). Prevalence and detection of delirium in elderly emergency department patients. *Canadian Medical Association Journal, 163*(8), 977–981.

Espiritu, D., Rashid, H., Masi, B., Fitzgerald, J., Steinberg, J., & Lichtenberg, P. (2001). Depression, cognitive impairment and function in Alzheimer's disease. *International Journal of Geriatric Psychiatry, 16,* 1098–1103.

Ewing, R., McCarthy, D., Gronwall, D., & Wrightson, P. (1980). Persisting effects of minor head injury observable during hypoxic stress. *Journal of Clinical Neuropsychology, 2,* 147–155.

Franulic, A., Horta, E., Maturana, R., Scherpenisse, J., & Carbonell, C. (2000). Organic personality disorder after traumatic brain injury: Cognitive, anatomic and psychosocial factors: A 6-month follow-up. *Brain Injury, 14*(5), 431–439.

Frick, D. M., Agostini, J. V., & Inouye, S. K. (2002). Delirium superimposed on dementia: A systematic review. *Journal of the American Geriatric Society, 50,* 1723–1732.

Fujii, D., & Ahmend, I. (2002). Psychotic disorder following traumatic brain injury: A conceptual framework. *Cognitive Neuropsychiatry, 7*(1), 41–62.

Furukawa, T., Hori, S., Yoshida, S., Tsuji, M., Nakanishi, M., & Hamanaka, T. (1998). Premorbid personality traits of patients with organic (*ICD-10* F0), schizophrenic (F2), mood (F3), and neurotic (F4) disorders according to the Five-Factor Model of personality. *Psychiatry Research, 78,* 179–187.

Gaitz, C. M., & Baer, P. E. (1971). Characteristics of elderly patients with alcoholism. *Archives of General Psychiatry, 24,* 372–378.

Gilley, D. W., Wilson, R. S., Bienias, J. L., Bennett, D. A., & Evans, D. A. (2004). Predictors of depressive symptoms in persons with Alzheimer's disease. *Journal of Gerontology Series B: Psychological and Social Sciences, 59,* P75–P83.

Glisky, E., Schacter, D., & Tulving, E. (1986). Computer learning by memory-impaired patients: Acquisition and retention of complex knowledge. *Neuropsychologia, 24,* 313–328.

Golden, Z., & Golden, C. J. (2003). The differential impacts of Alzheimer's dementia, head injury, and stroke on personality dysfunction. *International Journal of Neuroscience, 113,* 869–878.

Gonzales-Salvador, M., Arango, C., & Lyketsos, C. (1999). The stress and psychological morbidity of the Alzheimer patient caregiver. *International Journal of Geriatric Psychiatry, 14*(9), 701–710.

Gonzales-Salvador, T., Lyketsos, C., & Baker, A. (2000). Quality of life in patients with dementia in long-term care. *International Journal of Geriatric Psychiatry, 15,* 181–189.

Gouvier, W. D., Blanton, P. D., LaPorte, K. K., & Nepomuceno, C. (1987). Reliability and validity of the Disability Rating Scale and the Levels of Cognitive Functioning Scale in monitoring recovery from severe head injury. *Archives of Physical Medicine and Rehabilitation, 68,* 94–97.

Gouvier, W. D., Prestholdt, P., & Warner, M. (1988). A survey of common misconceptions about head injury and recovery. *Archives of Clinical Neuropsychology, 3*(4), 331–343.

Groth-Marnat, G. (1993). Neuropsychological effects of styrene exposure: A review of current literature. *Perceptual and Motor Skills, 77,* 1139–1149.

Groth-Marnat, G. (2003). *Handbook of psychological assessment* (4th ed.). Hoboken, NJ: Wiley.

Gutterman, E. M., Markowitz, J. S., Lewis, B., & Fillit, H. (1999). Cost of Alzheimer's disease and related dementia in managed-Medicare. *Journal of the American Geriatrics Society, 47*(9), 1065–1071.

Hanna-Pladdy, B., Berry, Z., Bennett, T., Phillips, H., & Gouvier, W. (2001). Stress as a diagnostic challenge for postconcussive symptoms: Sequelae of mild traumatic brain injury or physiological stress response. *Clinical Neuropsychologist, 15*(3), 289–304.

Harris, C. E., & Barraclough, B. (1998). Excess mortality of mental disorder. *British Journal of Psychiatry, 173,* 11–53.

Hawkins, K. (1998). Indicators of brain dysfunction derived from graphic representations of the WAIS-III/WMS-III technical manual clinical sample data: A preliminary approach to clinical utility. *Clinical Neuropsychologist, 12,* 535–551.

Hebert, R., & Brayne, C. (1995). Epidemiology of vascular dementia. N*euroepidemiology, 14*(5), 240–257.

Heilman, K., & Valenstein, E. (1993). *Clinical neuropsychology.* New York: Oxford University Press.

Hendrie, H. C., Ogunniyi, A., Hall, K. S., Baiyewu, O., Unverzagt, F. W., Gureje, O., et al. (2001). Incidence of dementia and Alzheimer disease in 2 communities: Yoruba residing in Ibadan, Nigeria, and African Americans residing in Indianapolis, Indiana. *Journal of the American Medical Association, 285*(6), 739–747.

Holtzer, R., Tang, M., Devanand, D. P., Albert, S. M., Wegesin, D. J., Marder, K., et al. (2003). Psychopathological features in Alzheimer's disease: Course and relationship with cognitive status. *Journal of the American Geriatrics Society, 51,* 953–960.

Hope, T., Keene, J., Copper, S., Fairburn, C., & Jacoby, R. (1997). Behaviour changes in dementia 1: Point of entry data of a prospective study. *International Journal of Geriatric Psychiatry, 12,* 1062–1073.

Huckle, P. (1994). Review families and dementia. *International Journal of Geriatric Psychiatry, 9,* 735–741.

Jacobs, H., Heberlein, I., Vieregge, A., & Vieregge, P. (2001). Personality traits in young patients with Parkinson's disease. *Acta Neurologica Scandinavica, 103,* 82–87.

Kamara, S. G., Person, P. D., & Dennis, J. L. (1998). Prevalence of physical illness among psychiatric inpatients who die of natural causes. *Psychiatric Services, 49*(6), 788–793.

Katz, S., Ford, A., & Moskowitz, R. (1963). The index of ADL: A standardized measure of biological and psychological function. *Journal of the American Medical Association, 185,* 914–919.

Kawas, C. H. (2003). Early Alzheimer's disease. *New England Journal of Medicine, 349*(11), 1056–1063.

Kermis, M. (1986). *Mental health in late life: The adaptive process.* Boston: Jones and Bartlett.

Kessels, R., & de Hann, E. (2003). Implicit learning in memory rehabilitation: A meta-analysis on errorless learning and vanishing cues methods. *Journal of Clinical and Experimental Neuropsychology, 25*(6), 805–814.

Klein, D. A., Steinberg, M., Galk, E., Steele, C., Sheppard, J., Warren, A., et al. (1999). Wandering behaviour in community-residing persons with dementia. *International Journal of Geriatric Psychiatry, 14,* 272–279.

Knight, R., Devereux, R., & Godfrey, H. (1998). Caring for a family member with traumatic brain injury. *Brain Injury, 12*(6), 467–481.

Kopetz, S., Steele, C., & Brandt, J. (2000). Characteristics and outcomes of dementia residents in an assisted living facility. *International Journal of Geriatric Psychiatry, 15*(7), 586–593.

Koponen, S., Taiminen, T., Portin, R., Himanen, L., Isoniemi, H., Heinonen, H., et al. (2002). Axis I and II psychiatric disorders after traumatic brain injury: A 30-year follow-up study. *American Journal of Psychiatry, 159*(8), 1315–1321.

Kostic, V. S., Marinkovic, J., Svetel, M., Stefanova, E., & Przedborski, S. (2002). The effect of stage of Parkinson's disease at the onset of levodopa therapy on development of motor complications. *European Journal of Neurology, 9,* 9–14.

Kubu, C., Casey, R., Hanson, T., Campbell, D., Roberts, R., & Varney, N. (1993). An investigation of emotion recognition in patients with closed-head injury. *Journal of Clinical and Experimental Neuropsychology, 15,* 59.

LaRue, A. (1992). *Aging and neuropsychological assessment.* New York: Plenum Press.

Lee, H. B., Lyketsos, C. G., & Rao, V. (2003). Pharmacological management of the psychiatric aspects of traumatic brain injury. *International Review of Psychiatry, 15,* 359–370.

Lee, M. B. (1981). Organic brain syndromes seen in psychiatric consultation in a general hospital. *Journal of the Formosan Medical Association, 80,* 119–128.

Leroi, I., O'Hearn, E., Lyketsos, C. G., Rosenblatt, A., & Brandt, J. (2002). Psychopathology in patients with degenerative cerebellar diseases: A comparison to Huntington's disease. *American Journal of Psychiatry, 159,* 1306–1314.

Levin, H., Grafman, J., & Eienberg, H. (1987). *Neurobehavioral recovery from head injury.* New York: Oxford University Press.

Levine, N., Daston, D., & Gendron, C. (1983). Coping with dementia: A pilot study. *Journal of the Geriatric Society, 31,* 12–18.

Levkoff, S., Cleary, P., Liptzin, B., & Evans, D. (1991). Epidemiology of delirium: An overview of research issues and findings. *International Psychogeriatrics, 3*(2), 149–167.

Lezak, M. (1986). Psychological implications of traumatic brain damage for the patient's family. *Rehabilitation Psychology, 31*(4), 241–250.

Lezak, M. (1988). Brain damage is a family affair. *Journal of Clinical and Experimental Neuropsychology, 10*(1), 111–123.

Lezak, M. (1995). *Neuropsychological assessment* (3rd ed.). New York: Oxford University Press.

Lincoln, N., Dent, A., Harding, J., Weyman, N., Nicholl, C., Blumhardt, L., et al. (2002). Evaluation of cognitive assessment and cognitive intervention for people with multiple sclerosis. *Journal of Neurology, Neurosurgery, and Psychiatry, 72,* 93–97.

Lindesay, J. (1991). Delirium—The psychiatrist's perspective. In R. Jacoby & C. Oppenheimer (Eds.), *Psychiatry in the elderly* (pp. 616–626). Oxford, England: Oxford University Press.

Lopez, O. L., Jagust, W. J., DeKosky, S. T., Becker, J. T., Fitzpatrick, A., Dulberg, C., et al. (2003). Prevalence and classification of mild cognitive impairment in the Cardiovascular Health Study Cognition Study: Part 1. *Archives of Neurology, 60*(10), 1385–1389.

Loring, D. W. (1999). *INS dictionary of neuropsychology.* New York: Oxford University Press.

Lyketsos, C., Steele, C., & Baker, L. (1997). Major and minor depression in Alzheimer's disease: Prevalence and impact. *Journal of Neuropsychiatry & Clinical Neurosciences, 9*(4), 556–561.

Lyketsos, C., Steele, C., & Galik, E. (1999). Physical aggression in dementia patients and its relationship to depression. *American Journal of Psychiatry, 156*(1), 66–71.

Lyketsos, C. G., Steinberg, M., Tschanz, J. T., Norton, M. C., Steffens, D. C., & Breitner, J. C. (2000). Mental and behavioral disturbances in dementia: Findings from the Cache County Study on Memory in Aging. *American Journal of Psychiatry, 157*(5), 708–714.

Lysaght, R., & Bodenhammer, E. (1990). The use of relaxation training to enhance functional outcomes in adults with traumatic head injuries. *American Journal of Occupational Therapy, 44,* 797–802.

Mackay, L. (1994). Benefits of a formalized traumatic brain injury program within a trauma center. *Journal of Head Trauma Rehabilitation, 9,* 11–19.

Marin, R. (1991). Apathy: A neuropsychiatric syndrome. *Journal of Neuropsychiatry and Clinical Neuroscience, 3,* 243–254.

Mazaux, J. M., & Richer, E. (1998). Rehabilitation after traumatic brain injury in adults. *Disability and Rehabilitation, 20,* 435–447.

McCarty, H. J., Roth, D. L., Goode, K. T., Owen, J. E., Harrell, L., Donovan, K., et al. (2000). Longitudinal course of behavioral problems during Alzheimer's disease: Linear versus curvilinear patterns of decline. *Journals of Gerontology: Series A, Biological Sciences and Medical Sciences, 55*(4), M200–M206.

McGuire, L. M., Burright, R. G., Williams, R., & Donovick, P. J. (1998). Prevalence of traumatic brain injury in psychiatric and non-psychiatric patients. *Brain Injury, 12*(3), 207–214.

McNicoll, L., Pisani, M. A., Zhang, Y., Ely, E. W., Siegel, M. D., & Inouye, S. K. (2003). Delirium in the intensive care unit: Occurrence and clinical course in older patients. *Journal of the American Geriatrics Society, 51*(5), 591–598.

Meins, W., & Dammast, J. (2000). Do personality traits predict the occurrence of Alzheimer's disease? *International Journal of Geriatric Psychiatry, 15,* 120–124.

Mendez, M. F. (1994). Huntington's disease: Update and review of neuropsychiatric aspects. *International Journal of Psychiatry in Medicine, 24*(3), 189–208.

Miller, B., Cummings, J., McIntyre, H., Ebers, G., & Grode, M. (1986). Hypersexuality or altered sexual preference following brain injury. *Journal of Neurology, Neurosurgery, and Psychiatry, 49,* 867–873.

Mittenberg, W., Tremont, G., Zielinski, R., Fichera, S., & Rayls, K. (1996). Cognitive-behavioral prevention of postconcussive syndrome. *Archives of Clinical Neuropsychology, 11,* 139–145.

Morris, L., Morris, R., & Britton, P. (1989). Social support networks and formal support as factors influencing psychological adjustment of spouse caregivers of dementia sufferers. *International Journal of Geriatric Psychiatry, 4,* 47–51.

Morris, R., Woods, R., Davies, K., & Morris, L. (1992). Gender differences in careers of dementia sufferers. *British Journal of Psychiatry, 158*(Suppl. 10), 69–74.

Moss, F., Wilson, B., Harrigan, S., & Ames, D. (1995). Psychiatric diagnoses, outcomes and lengths of stay of patients admitted to an acute psychogeriatric unit. *International Journal of Geriatric Psychiatry, 10,* 849–854.

Navia, B. A., Jordan, B. D., & Price, R. W. (1986). The AIDS dementia complex: I. Clinical features. *Annals of Neurology, 19*(6), 517–24.

Nilson, L., Barregard, L., & Baeckman, L. (1999). Trail Making Test in chronic toxic encephalopath: Performance and discriminative potential. *Clinical Neuropsychologist, 13,* 314–327.

Novack, T. A., Alderson, A. L., Bush, B. A., Meythaler, J. M., & Canupp, K. (2000). Cognitive and functional recovery at 6 and 12 months post-TBI. *Brain Injury, 14*(11), 987–996.

Oliver, R., & Block, F. (1990). Alleviating the distress of caregivers of Alzheimer's disease patients: A rational emotive therapy model. *Journal of Rational-Emotive and Cognitive Behavior Therapy, 8*(1), 53–69.

Orrell, M., & Bebbington, P. (1996). Psychosocial stress and anxiety in senile dementia. *Journal of Affective Disorders, 39,* 165–173.

Patten, S. B. (2001). Delirium in psychiatric inpatients: A case-control study. *Canadian Journal of Psychiatry, 46*(2), 162–166.

Pearson, J., Teri, L., Reifler, B., & Raskind, M. (1989). Functional status and cognitive impairment in Alzheimer's patients with and without depression. *Journal of the American Geriatric Society, 37,* 1117–1121.

Perkins, R., & Poynton, C. (1990). Group counseling for relatives of hospitalized presenile dementia patients: A controlled study. *British Journal of Clinical Psychology, 29,* 287–295.

Persson, G., Berg, S., Nilsson, L., & Svanborg, A. (1991). Subclinical dementia—Relation to cognition, personality, and psychopathology: A nine-year prospective study. *International Journal of Geriatric Psychiatry, 6,* 239–247.

Philpot, M., & Levy, R. (1987). A memory clinic for the early diagnosis of dementia. *International Journal of Geriatric Psychiatry, 2,* 195–200.

Potkin, S. G., Anand, R., Hartman, R., Veach, J., & Grossberg, G. (2002). Impact of Alzheimer's disease and rivastignmine treatment on activities of daily living over the course of mild to moderately severe disease. *Progress in Neuro-Psychopharmacology and Biological Psychiatry, 26,* 713–720.

Prigatano, G. (1983). Neuropsychological test performance in mildly hypoxemic patients with chronic obstructive pulmonary disease. *Journal of Consulting and Clinical Psychology, 51,* 108–116.

Prigatano, G. (1986). *Neuropsychological rehabilitation after brain injury.* Baltimore, MD: Johns Hopkins University Press.

Psychological Corporation. (1997). *WAIS-III/WMS-III technical manual.* San Antonio, TX: Author.

Puri, B. K., Laking, P. J., & Treasaden, I. H. (2002). *Textbook of psychiatry.* London: Churchill Livingstone.

Rasmusson, D., Zonderman, A., Kawas, C., & Resnick, S. (1998). Effects of age and dementia on the Trail Making Test. *Clinical Neuropsychologist, 12,* 169–178.

Richards, M. (1997). Anxiety in later life. In I. Norman & S. Redfern (Eds.), *Mental health care for elderly people* (pp. 131–140). New York: Churchill Livingstone.

Ritchie, J., Steiner, W., & Abrahamowicz, M. (1996). Incidence of and risk factors for delirium among psychiatric inpatients. *Psychiatric Services, 47,* 727–730.

Robinson, R., & Benson, D. (1981). Depression in aphasic patients: Frequency, severity, and clinical-pathological correlations. *Brain & Language, 14*(2), 282–291.

Rockwell, E., Choure, J., Galasko, D., Olichney, J., & Jeste, D. V. (2000). Psychopathology at initial diagnosis in dementia with Lewy bodies versus Alzheimer disease: Comparison of matched groups with autopsy-confirmed cases. *International Journal of Geriatric Psychiatry, 15,* 819–823.

Roid, G. (2003). *Stanford-Binet Intelligence Scales* (5th ed.). Itasca, IL: Riverside.

Roid, G. H., & Miller, L. J. (1997). *Leiter International Performance Scale-Revised.* Chicago: Stoelting.

Rössler, W., Hewer, B., Fätkenheuer, B., & Löffler, W. (1995). Excess mortality among elderly psychiatric in-patients with organic mental disorder. *British Journal of Psychiatry, 167,* 527–532.

Rovner, B. W., German, P. S., Broadhead, J., Morriss, R. K., Brant, L. J., Blaustein, J., et al. (1990). The prevalence and management of dementia and other psychiatric disorders in nursing homes. *International Psychogeriatrics, 2*(1), 13–24.

Salthouse, T. A. (1993). Speed and knowledge as determinants of adult age differences in verbal tasks. *Journals of Gerontology, 48*(1), 29–36.

Shinosaki, K., Nishikawa, T., & Masatoshi, T. (2000). Neurobiological basis of behavioral and psychological symptoms in dementia of the Alzheimer's type. *Psychiatry and Clinical Neurosciences, 54,* 611–620.

Silliman, R., Sternberg, J., & Fretwell, M. (1988). Disruptive behavior in demented patients living within disturbed families. *Journal of the American Geriatric Society, 36,* 617–627.

Snyder, S. H., & Ferris, C. D. (2000). Novel neurotransmitters and their neuropsychiatric relevance. *American Journal of Psychiatry, 157,* 1738–1751.

Stanczak, D. E., White, J. G., Gouvier, W. D., Moeiile, K. A., Daniel, M., Novack, T., et al. (1984). Assessment of level of consciousness following severe neurological insult: A comparison of the psychometric qualities of the Glasgow Coma Scale and the Comprehensive Level of Consciousness Scale. *Journal of Neurosurgery, 60,* 955–960.

Steele, C., Rovner, B., & Chase, G. (1990). Psychiatric symptoms and nursing home placement of patients with Alzheimer's disease. *American Journal of Psychiatry, 147*(8), 1049–1051.

Steele, R., Weinrich, M., & Carlson, G. (1989). Recipe preparation by a severely impaired aphasic using the C-VIC 2.0 Interface. *Proceedings of the RESNA 12th Annual Conference,* 218–219.

Stringer, A. (2003). Cognitive rehabilitation practice patterns: A survey of American Hospital Association rehabilitation programs. *Clinical Neuropsychologist, 17*(1), 34–44.

Strub, R., & Black, F. (1993). *The Mental Status Examination in neurology* (3rd ed.). Philadelphia: Davis.

Sutkovoi, D. A., Pedachenko, E. G., Malyshev, O. B., Guk, A. P., Troian, A. I., Morozov, A. N., et al. (1999). The activity of free-radical lipid-peroxidative reactions in the acute and late periods of severe craniocerebral trauma. *Lik Sprava, 2,* 57–59.

Taverni, J. P., Seliger, G., & Litchman, S. W. (1998). Donepezil-mediated memory improvement in traumatic brain injury during post acute rehabilitation. *Brain Injury, 12,* 77–80.

Temkin, N. R. (2003). Risk factors for posttraumatic seizures in adults. *Epilepsia, 44*(Suppl. 10), 18–20.

Teng, E., Chui, H., & Saperia, D. (1990). Senile dementia: Performance on a neuropsychological test battery. *Recent Advances in Cardiovascular Disease, 11,* 27–34.

Toglia, J. (1991). Generalization of treatment: A multicontext approach to cognitive perceptual impairment in adults with brain injury. *American Journal of Occupational Therapy, 45,* 506–516.

Trabucchi, M. (1999). An economic perspective on Alzheimer's disease. *Journal of Geriatric Psychiatry and Neurology, 12,* 29–38.

Treat, N., Poon, L., Fozard, J., & Popkin, S. (1978). Toward applying cognitive skill training to memory problems. *Experimental Aging Research, 4,* 305–319.

Trzepacz, P. T., Levenson, J. L., & Tringali, R. A. (1991). Psychopharmacology and neuropsychiatric syndromes in organ transplantation. *General Hospital Psychiatry, 13,* 233–245.

Trzepacz, P. T., Teague, G. B., & Lipowski, Z. J. (1985). Delirium and other organic mental disorders in a general hospital. *General Hospital Psychiatry, 7,* 101–106.

Ungvarski, P., & Trzcianowska, H. (2000). Neurocognitive disorders seen in HIV disease. *Issues in Mental Health Nursing, 21,* 51–70.

Van Hout, M. (2003). Psychological treatment of patients with chronic toxic encephalopathy: Lessons from studies of chronic fatigue and whiplash. *Psychotherapy & Psychosomatics, 72*(5), 235–244.

Van Vomeren, A., & Brouwer, W. (1990). Attention deficits after closed head injury. In B. Deelman, R. Saan, & A. Van Vomeren (Eds.), *Traumatic brain injury: Clinical, social, and rehabilitation aspects* (pp. 74–107). Amsterdam: Swets & Zeitlinger.

Varney, N., & Menefee, L. (1993). Psychosocial and executive deficits following closed head injury: Implications for orbital frontal cortex. *Journal of Head Trauma Rehabilitation, 8*(1), 32–44.

Varney, N., & Roberts, R. (1999). *The evaluation and treatment of mild traumatic brain injury.* Mahwah, NJ: Erlbaum.

Wallace, G. L. (1993). Neurological impairment among elderly African-American nursing home residents. *Journal of Health Care for the Poor and Underserved, 4,* 40–50.

Wetterling, T., Kanitz, R. D., & Borgis, K. J. (1996). Comparison of different diagnostic criteria for vascular dementia (ADDTC, *DSM-IV, ICD-10,* NINDS-AIREN). *Stroke, 27*(1), 30–36.

Wherrett, J. R. (1999). Neurologic aspects. In M. P. Janicki & A. J. Dalton (Eds.), *Dementia, aging, and intellectual disabilities: A handbook* (pp. 90–102). Philadelphia: Brunner/Mazel.

Whyte, J., Vaccaro, M., Grieb-Neff, P., & Hart, T. (2002). Psychostimulant use in the rehabilitation of individuals with traumatic brain injury. *Journal of Head Trauma and Rehabilitation, 17,* 284–299.

Williams, J. M., Klein, K., Little, M., & Haban, G. (1986). Family observations of everyday cognitive impairment in dementia. *Archives of Clinical Neuropsychology, 1*(2), 103–109.

Wilson, R. S., Fleischman, D. A., Myers, R. A., Bennett, D. A., Bienias, J. L., Gilley, D. W., et al. (2004). Premorbid proneness to distress and episodic memory impairment in Alzheimer's disease. *Journal of Neurology, Neurosurgery, and Psychiatry, 75,* 191–195.

World Health Organization. (1992). *International statistical classification of diseases and related health problems* (10th rev. ed.). Geneva, Switzerland: Author.

Wymer, J. H., Lindman, L. H., & Bookish, R. L. (2002). A neuropsychological perspective of aprosody: Features, function, assessment, and treatment. *Applied Neuropsychology, 9*(1), 37–47.

Zubenko, G. S., Marino, L. J., Sweet, R. A., Rifai, A. H., Mulsant, B. H., & Pasternak, R. E. (1997). Medical comorbidity in elderly psychiatric inpatients. *Biological Psychiatry, 41*(6), 724–736.

Zubenko, G. S., Mulsant, B. H., Sweet, R. A., Pasternak, R. E., & Tu, X. M. (1997). Mortality of elderly patients with psychiatric disorders. *American Journal of Psychiatry, 154*(10), 1360–1368.

CHAPTER 18

Borderline Personality Disorder

TIMOTHY J. TRULL, STEPHANIE D. STEPP, AND MARIKA SOLHAN

DESCRIPTION OF THE DISORDER AND CLINICAL PICTURE

Borderline personality disorder (BPD) is primarily characterized by disturbances in emotional regulation, impulse control, and identity. Individuals with BPD have a maladaptive personality style that is present in a variety of contexts, emerges by early adulthood, and leads to distinct patterns of dysfunction in their behavior and relationships (APA, 2000). Table 18.1 presents the nine *DSM-IV-TR* diagnostic criteria for BPD. In order to receive a BPD diagnosis, at least five of the nine criteria must be present and the symptoms must result in significant distress or impairment (APA, 2000). In order to provide a full clinical picture of BPD, we first discuss what many consider to be the three core features of the disorder (affective instability, impulsivity, and identity disturbance) and then turn to the remaining criteria for the disorder.

One of the core features of BPD is *affective instability*. Affective instability refers to frequent affect shifts that result from one's reactivity to environmental stimuli. Individuals with BPD typically shift between different types of negative affect (e.g., anger, depression, anxiety). This distinguishes BPD from disorders such as bipolar disorder, in which a person would be expected to shift between both positive and negative affects (e.g., from depression to elation). Also, affective instability in BPD is unique in that the affect shifts occur in response to external stimuli in the person's environment. These stimuli might include interpersonal conflicts or perceived rejection. This differentiates the disorder from other affective disorders such as major depression, in which the shifts in affect may result more from internal cues.

Another core feature of borderline personality disorder is *impulsivity*. Individuals with BPD frequently engage in behaviors that are potentially harmful to themselves. Behaviors such as substance abuse, promiscuity, excessive spending, gambling, binge eating, reckless driving, and criminal activities are common. Some researchers theorize that persons with BPD engage in these behaviors as a way to cope with the intense affective shifts they experience (Linehan, 1993). For example, one might abuse alcohol and drugs or gamble large amounts of money to distract oneself from internal emotional upheaval. However, other researchers believe that such behaviors simply represent a lack of inhibition and impulse control and that the affective instability results from the chaotic environment such impulsivity creates (Links, Heslegrave, & van Reekum, 1999). In this case, one may engage in unsafe sex with numerous partners, and this behavior may create interpersonal difficulties that result in intense feelings of guilt, shame, or hopelessness.

A third core feature of BPD is *identity disturbance*. Persons with BPD frequently have unstable or poorly defined self-concepts. They may often dramatically alter career goals, personal ideals, opinions, attitudes, lifestyle, or ideas about their sexual orientation. This feature may also include unrealistic body images. Sometimes these individuals base their identity on the idea that they are inherently evil or worthless. Some researchers hypothesize that these identity issues arise from the individual's inability to integrate positive and negative aspects of the self (Wilkinson-Ryan & Westen, 2000). Often this lack of a cohesive self-image leads to intense feelings of emptiness. This emptiness is usually described as a physical sensation in one's abdomen or chest, as a feeling of a hole in oneself, and is a distinguishing characteristic of the disorder (Gunderson, 2001).

Given these three core features of BPD, it is not surprising that individuals with BPD typically experience severe *diffi-*

TABLE 18.1 *DSM-IV* Diagnostic Criteria for Borderline Personality Disorder (five or more of the following)

- Frantic efforts to avoid real or imagined abandonment
- Unstable and intense interpersonal relationships
- Persistently unstable self-image
- Impulsivity in at least two areas that are potentially self-damaging (e.g., sex and substance abuse)
- Suicidal behavior, gestures, or threats; self-mutilating behavior
- Affective instability due to a marked reactivity of mood
- Feelings of emptiness
- Inappropriate and intense anger
- Stress-related dissociative symptoms

culties in interpersonal relationships. Their relationships are often stormy and unstable. They frequently vacillate between overidealizing and devaluing friends, family, and romantic partners. New relationships quickly reach a high level of intimacy and intensity, often followed by the person with BPD feeling that the other individual is not equally committed, available, or attached. Shifting affective states, impulsive behaviors, and identity disturbances add to the chaotic nature of these relationships. Others may find it difficult to cope with an individual's dysphoria, self-damaging behavior, and inconsistency of self-concept.

In addition to frequent shifts in emotions, one common emotion in individuals with BPD is *intense and inappropriate anger.* Those with BPD may have great difficulty controlling their anger or expressing it in a productive way. Their anger may instead take the form of verbal or physical aggression, bitterness, or extreme sarcasm. Often these outbursts are triggered by interpersonal conflict or the threat of abandonment and are followed by feelings of guilt or shame.

A constant *fear of abandonment* is also common in individuals with BPD. They may constantly worry that significant caregivers in their life may leave, neglect, or reject them in some way. This feature can be thought of as a kind of separation anxiety, usually in response to a physical separation from a loved one (Gunderson, 2001). Even small events such as a friend arriving late or a romantic partner going away on a business trip can trigger this fear. This often leads to frantic efforts on the part of the individual with BPD to avoid this abandonment. A person with this feature of BPD may respond to perceived signs of abandonment with impulsive behaviors or threats of suicide or self-mutilation.

Suicidal and self-mutilating behavior is an important and distinguishing feature of BPD. Recurrent suicidal attempts, threats, or gestures are frequently displayed in these individuals and often require or result in medical care. Also, self-mutilating behavior such as cutting or burning the skin, swallowing objects, or otherwise injuring oneself is common. Suicidal behavior is believed to be a way for those with BPD to express the pain that they are experiencing. Some researchers hypothesize that these individuals use suicidal behavior to manipulate significant people in their lives, for example, to avoid abandonment. Other researchers see self-mutilating behavior as an attempt for those with BPD to distract themselves from the intense negative affect they experience (Linehan, 1993). Approximately 10 percent of those with BPD ultimately commit suicide (Work Group on Borderline Personality Disorder, 2001).

Finally, in times of stress, individuals with BPD may display *transient dissociative or paranoid symptoms.* This may include experiences such as abnormal bodily sensations, feelings of being outside one's own body, or unusual auditory or visual experiences. Also, persons with BPD may experience paranoid ideation, odd speech, and disturbed thoughts.

PERSONALITY DEVELOPMENT AND PSYCHOPATHOLOGY

BPD is frequently comorbid with Axis I disorders, especially mood disorders, substance use disorders, eating disorders (particularly bulimia), attention-deficit/hyperactivity disorder, and anxiety disorders (especially post-traumatic stress disorder; APA, 2000). This pattern of comorbidity is likely a reflection of the shared impulsivity/disinhibition and negative affect/affective instability personality traits that also underlie the BPD criteria (Pukrop, 2002; Skodol, Gunderson, Pfohl, et al., 2002; Trull, 2001).

This comorbidity is important to recognize, because a comorbid BPD diagnosis in Axis I patients predicts poorer short- and long-term outcome (Skodol, Gunderson, Pfohl, et al., 2002). Gunderson (2001) estimates that 15 percent of those with major depression, 10 percent of those with dysthymia, 15 percent of those with bipolar I disorder, 20 percent of those with bulimia or anorexia, and 10 percent of those with substance use disorder also meet criteria for BPD. Much research has focused on the comorbidity of major depression with BPD. Like BPD, major depression is characterized by dysphoric mood and suicidal thoughts or behaviors. However, several features differentiate BPD from major depression (Gunderson, 2001). Concerning personality features, BPD is characterized by impulsivity, unstable interpersonal relationships, and devaluative attitudes, whereas major depression is characterized more by anxiety, worry, and self-consciousness. The subjective experience of patients with BPD is one of anger, loneliness, and emptiness in contrast to the subjective experiences of major depression patients (hopelessness and failure).

Although most research on the comorbidity of BPD and mood disorders has focused on major depression, recent studies have explored the relationship between BPD and bipolar spectrum disorders, especially bipolar II disorder (characterized by depressive episodes and hypomanic, but not manic, episodes). BPD and bipolar II disorder share features of affective instability and impulsivity. Gunderson (2001) highlights several features that may differentiate BPD from bipolar II disorder. Concerning personality features, BPD is characterized by sensitivity to hostility and separations as well as a very negative self-image, whereas those with bipolar II disorder show interpersonal insensitivity and a grandiose self-image.

The comorbidity between BPD and substance use disorders has been well documented. For example, Trull, Sher, Minks-Brown, Durbin, and Burr (2000), based on a comprehensive literature review, estimated that approximately 57 percent of BPD patients also receive a substance use disorder diagnosis, primarily alcohol abuse or dependence. Among those with substance use disorder, it was estimated that 27 percent also meet diagnostic criteria for BPD. One reason for this high level of comorbidity is that BPD and substance use disorder share the trait of impulsivity, and many of the features of these disorders are behaviors that reflect this trait (e.g., abuse of substances, other forms of behavioral disinhibition). Further, one major theory of substance use disorder concerns attempts to regulate ones emotional state; it has been shown that those with emotional dysregulation (e.g., affective instability) are more prone to use and abuse substances presumably in order to alleviate negative affect (e.g., Dulit, Fyer, Haas, Sullivan, & Frances, 1990; Khantzian, 1985).

BPD is also frequently comorbid with other personality disorders, so much so that it rarely occurs in isolation on Axis II. As with co-occurring Axis I disorders, when an individual meets criteria for personality disorders in addition to BPD, these diagnoses should be given. However, there are some features that may help distinguish BPD from other personality disorders (APA, 2000). For example, histrionic personality disorder is also characterized by rapidly shifting emotional states and manipulativeness, but these features can typically be differentiated from BPD, which is also likely to involve self-destructiveness, angry disruptions in relationships, and chronic feelings of emptiness and loneliness. Those with BPD may report quasipsychotic experiences like paranoid ideas, illusions, and dissociation, but these experiences are more transient and reactive to the environment than what is seen in schizotypal or paranoid personality disorder. Those with antisocial personality disorder may manipulate others to gain power or profit, whereas those with BPD are more likely to engage in extreme behaviors in order to gain the concern and nurturance of others. Finally, those with dependent personality disorder fear abandonment and react with submissiveness and appeasement, whereas the fears of abandonment characterizing BPD lead to feelings of emptiness, rage, and additional demands.

EPIDEMIOLOGY

BPD is rarely a sole diagnosis, and almost all BPD patients are likely to meet criteria for one or more Axis I disorders or additional Axis II personality disorders. BPD is the most prevalent Axis II disorder in clinical settings, and it has been associated with interpersonal and occupational impairment, increased risk for suicide, and higher rates of treatment in both medical and psychiatric settings (Skodol, Gunderson, Pfohl, et al., 2002). The prevalence of BPD is estimated to be 10 percent in outpatient settings, 15 percent to 20 percent in inpatient settings, 30 percent to 60 percent among personality-disordered patients, and approximately 1 percent to 2 percent in the general population (APA, 2000; Skodol, Gunderson, Pfohl, et al., 2002). Several recent studies have focused on the prevalence of BPD outside of psychiatric settings. For example, Torgersen, Kringlen, and Cramer (2001) administered a *DSM-III-R* Axis II interview to a community sample in Norway and estimated that approximately 1 percent meets criteria for a BPD diagnosis. Using *DSM-IV* criteria, Gross et al. (2002) estimated that 6.4 percent of those in urban primary care settings meet lifetime diagnostic criteria for BPD.

In general, it is believed that more women than men will meet the criteria for BPD, but this impression is based primarily on clinical studies. We discuss this issue more fully later. It is important to distinguish BPD symptoms, which are chronic and pervasive, from borderline behaviors that may be exhibited for short periods of time in childhood or adolescence. Studies that have followed over time children and adolescents who initially received a BPD diagnosis find that only a small percentage still had a BPD diagnosis years later (e.g., see Lofgren, Bemporad, King, Lindem, & O'Driscoll, 1991). This raises the possibility that BPD may be overdiagnosed in children and adolescents.

Culture

The symptoms characteristic of BPD are observed in many cultures throughout the world (APA, 2000). Few studies have directly assessed the distribution of BPD diagnoses and symptoms across ethnic groups within the United States. One recent study in the United States (Chavira et al., 2003) reported that among 664 adults who received a personality disorder diagnosis of borderline, schizotypal, obsessive compulsive, or avoidant personality disorder, a significantly higher percentage of Hispanics received a *DSM-IV* BPD diagnosis than Caucasians or African Americans. Further, results indicated that Hispanics had significantly higher rates of the BPD criteria *intense anger, affective instability,* and *unstable relationships* than did Caucasians. Finally, African Americans had significantly higher rates of the BPD criterion *unstable relationships* than did Caucasians. As for why Hispanics were more frequently diagnosed with BPD as well as certain BPD symptoms, Chavira et al. (2003) hypothesized that the process of acculturation might make one more prone to experience many of the features of BPD including identity confusion, alienation, feelings of emptiness, abandonment, loss of control, and anxiety. However, given the paucity of research on BPD and ethnicity, these findings await replication.

Age

BPD symptoms appear by early adulthood (APA, 2000). Although one can technically be given a diagnosis in childhood and adolescence, assigning a diagnosis at these young ages is controversial. As mentioned previously, studies that have followed children and adolescents diagnosed with BPD have found that only a minority maintain this diagnosis in early adulthood; most are diagnosed with other Axis I (especially substance use disorders) or Axis II disorders in early adulthood (e.g., see Lofgren et al., 1991).

Gender

DSM-IV-TR (APA, 2000) reports that BPD is "diagnosed predominantly (about 75 percent) in females" (p. 708). However, results from previous studies on the prevalence of BPD within each gender are inconsistent (Johnson et al., 2003) and suggest that this rather pronounced gender ratio has little empirical support, especially from studies that used diagnostic interview assessments to establish BPD (Skodol & Bender, 2003). Further, most of the studies that have examined gender differences in BPD were based on clinical samples. These prevalence estimates may be biased due to selective sampling (e.g., women are more likely to present for treatment of these symptoms), and few studies have directly compared men and women with BPD to determine if there are differences in presentation.

A recent study, however, is instructive. Johnson et al. (2003) compared women (n = 175) and men (n = 65) on a number of demographic factors, as well as with respect to the prevalence of Axis I and other Axis II diagnoses and of individual BPD symptoms. Female and male BPD patients did not differ significantly on racial affiliation, marital status, or employment status. When women and men were compared for rates of lifetime Axis I diagnoses, only three differences emerged: female BPD patients were more likely to be diagnosed with post-traumatic stress disorder (50.9 percent versus 30.8 percent) and eating disorder (41.7 percent versus 18.5 percent), whereas men were more likely to receive a lifetime diagnosis of substance use disorder (84.6 percent versus 58.3 percent). Concerning Axis II disorders, BPD men had significantly higher rates of schizotypal (24.6 percent versus 10.3 percent), narcissistic (21.9 percent versus 4.6 percent), and antisocial (29.7 percent versus 10.3 percent) personality disorders. Finally, BPD women and men differed significantly only in the rate of the BPD "identity disturbance." Together, these findings suggest that the clinical presentation of BPD women and men is more similar than different.

Consistent with the proposition that the impression of a disparity of rates of BPD in men and women may be a function of a focus on clinical samples, Torgersen et al. (2001) reported that within a community sample in Norway there was no difference in BPD prevalence between men and women (both rates were approximately 1 percent). Thus, the statement in *DSM-IV-TR* that BPD is diagnosed predominantly in females seems to be based more on clinical impression than on empirical data.

ETIOLOGY

A comprehensive model of the etiology of BPD includes the influences of genetics and family history, neurobiological factors, adverse environmental conditions, and personality factors. Figure 18.1 depicts a conceptualization of how these influences may interact and lead to the development of BPD symptoms. Note that there are unidirectional effects (e.g., genetic vulnerabilities on the personality trait of disinhibition; single-headed arrow) as well as bidirectional effects (e.g., the personality trait of affective instability and attachment style may both influence each other; double-headed arrow). We discuss each posited influence in turn.

Genetics and Family History

Establishing a genetic influence on a disorder's development typically involves support from family history, twin, and adoption studies. No adoption studies have been conducted. Therefore, we focus on the available family history and twin studies of BPD probands.

A recent review of family history studies of BPD (White, Gunderson, Zanarini, & Hudson, 2003) examined the evidence supporting a link between BPD and schizophrenia spectrum disorders (schizophrenia and schizotypal personality disorder), mood disorders (major depressive disorder and bipolar disorder), or impulse spectrum disorders (substance use disorders and antisocial personality disorder). White et al. (2003) located 15 studies that assessed the prevalence of these groups of disorders in relatives of probands with BPD. Although they found no evidence linking BPD with schizophrenia spectrum disorders or (surprisingly) with mood disorders (except for some weak association with major depressive disorder), rates of impulse spectrum disorders (substance use disorders and antisocial personality disorder) were significantly elevated in relatives of BPD probands. Finally, the authors located nine studies that examined BPD in

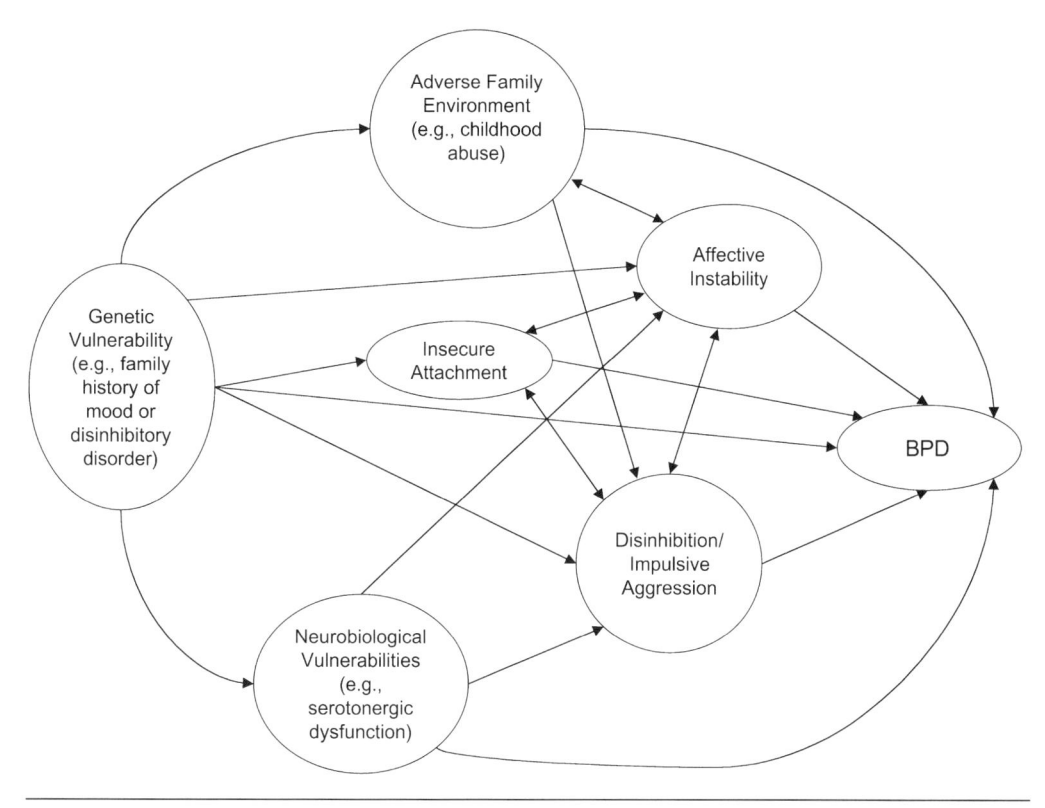

Figure 18.1 Conceptual model of putative etiological factors for borderline personality disorder.

the relatives of BPD probands and found evidence supporting a link. Taken together, these findings suggest that BPD may be associated with impulse spectrum disorders and with major depression, although more methodologically sound research is needed to establish these links. The findings are also consistent with the results of other studies that have highlighted the familial aggregation of major traits that characterize BPD, affective instability, and impulsivity (Silverman et al., 1991).

Only two twin studies on the BPD diagnosis have appeared in the literature. Torgersen (1984) conducted a small twin study of 25 BPD probands, including seven monozygotic (MZ) twins and 18 dizygotic (DZ) twins. None of the MZ pairs were concordant for BPD but two (11 percent) of the DZ pairs were. This counterintuitive finding is likely a function of the very small sample size and the lack of blind assessments. More recently, Torgersen et al. (2000) reported on a twin study of personality disorders that included 221 twin pairs, 92 MZ pairs and 129 DZ pairs. The concordance rate for definite BPD was 35 percent for MZ pairs and 7 percent for DZ pairs. Genetic modeling analyses suggested an additive genetic effect of .69 to .57 (depending on the model). Although these results suggest a strong genetic effect on the BPD phenotype, there were a number of methodological problems with this study (including sampling those who were being treated for a mental disorder, the small number of twin pairs, and the interviewers' awareness of both zygosity and diagnostic status of the co-twin). Replication with a larger twin sample will be necessary to establish such a strong genetic effect on the development of BPD.

Another approach to investigating the genetic influences on BPD is to conduct behavior genetic (twin) studies on the traits that are components of or that underlie BPD. Several studies have provided relevant data. For example, Livesley and colleagues (e.g., Jang, Livesley, Vernon, & Jackson, 1996; Livesley, Jang, & Vernon, 1998) have shown that the higher order trait "emotional dysregulation" as well as many of the lower order traits relevant to BPD like anxiousness, identity problems, affective lability, cognitive dysregulation, insecure attachment, and submissiveness appear heritable (all with heritability coefficients of .44 or higher). Further analyses examining evidence for the residual heritability of lower order traits relevant to BPD suggested that the development of BPD is influenced by multiple genetic personality trait dimensions each with differing levels of effect. This may help explain why BPD, the eventual phenotype, is such a heterogeneous diagnostic category (Skodol, Siever, et al., 2002).

Neurobiological Vulnerabilities

Several potential biological markers for BPD have been examined, and this line of research may ultimately lead to a fuller understanding of both the etiology and biological mechanism of the disorder as well as distinguishing it from other related or commonly comorbid conditions. Major areas of study include reduced serotonergic activity, related to *impulsive aggression,* and *affective instability,* related to increased responsivity in cholinergic systems (Skodol, Siever, et al., 2002). Concerning serotonergic dysfunction, research has primarily focused on either the release of serotonin or the reduced sensitivity of serotonin receptors (Siever, Koenigsberg, & Reynolds, 2003). Recent research has examined correlates of reduced serotonergic functioning (Atmaca, Kuloglu, Tezcan, Gecici, & Ustundag, 2002; New et al., 1999; Paris et al., 2004; Soloff, Kelly, Strotmeyer, Malone, & Mann, 2003) as well as imaging of brain regions that may be responsible for impulsive behaviors seen in BPD patients (e.g., Leyton et al., 2001; Soloff, Meltzer, et al., 2003). Interestingly, several studies have documented gender differences in serotonergic functioning among BPD patients, which may help explain the differences in impulsive behaviors seen in male versus female BPD patients (e.g., Soloff, Kelly, et al., 2003).

Less is known about the neurobiology of affective instability, although most research has focused on cholinergic dysregulation (Siever et al., 2003). Studies have indicated that BPD patients show more variable rapid eye movement (REM) sleep latency, which is under cholinergic control (Siever et al., 2003). Further, Steinberg et al. (1997) demonstrated that physostigmine, a cholinesterase inhibitor, produced dysphoric mood shifts in BPD patients that were more extreme than those witnessed for controls.

Finally, BPD may reflect deviations in brain structure as well as biochemical imbalances. Magnetic resonance spectroscopy revealed a significant 19 percent decrease in absolute concentration of N-acetylaspartate (NAA) in BPD patients relative to controls in the dorsolateral prefrontal cortex (van Elst et al., 2001). This may indicate disturbed neuronal metabolism, reduced neuronal density, or disturbed neuronal microstructure secondary to neurodevelopmental pathology. The last seems the most likely because BPD symptoms are present at a young age and do not worsen over time (i.e., middle age and beyond). More research is needed to clarify the pathophysiology of NAA metabolism, but there is a consensus that NAA depletion indicates neuronal dysfunction.

To this point, we have primarily discussed a variety of potential genetic and biological influences on the development of BPD. This focus has been relatively new, and much more research has been conducted (over the last several decades) on a variety of adverse family, personality, or environmental factors that are hypothesized to be relevant to the etiology of BPD. Space limitations preclude us from discussing all of the factors that have been investigated. However, we will briefly present an overview of the research on three of these, namely attachment, personality, and childhood abuse.

Attachment

For a number of years, theorists, clinicians, and researchers have noted that those suffering from BPD exhibit either a history of maladaptive attachment to caregivers or current maladaptive attachment patterns in their intimate relationships. A recent review of studies that have examined the relations between attachment styles and BPD concluded that there is a strong association between BPD and insecure attachment, especially the following three types of attachment: unresolved, preoccupied, and fearful (Agrawal, Gunderson, Holmes, & Lyons-Ruth, 2004). These attachment styles reflect a longing for closeness and intimacy but a fear of dependency or rejection. Unfortunately, it is difficult to combine or compare the studies because of the disparate methods used (e.g., some instruments focus on the relationship between patient and caregivers, whereas others focus on the relationship between patient and peers). Further, few studies demonstrated the specificity of the association to BPD. One exception was the study by Nickell, Waudby, and Trull (2002). In this study, attachment and parental bonding variables predicted a significant amount of variance in BPD above and beyond that accounted for by gender, childhood adversity variables, Axis I disorder, and non-BPD personality disorder symptoms. Therefore, based on these results, attachment seems to play an important role in the etiology of BPD, above and beyond childhood trauma, and attachment is also uniquely related to BPD features independent of other types of Axis I or II pathology. On the other hand, Fossati et al. (2001) conducted a study to distinguish between two theories of the etiology of BPD: one perspective in which extreme constellations of character traits lead to the development of personality disorders (PD), and the other in which attachment theory accounts for BPD psychopathology by disturbed caregiver-child relations. The authors found that temperament but not attachment uniquely discriminates BPD from other types of pathology. Therefore, the specificity of the link between certain attachment styles and BPD needs further investigation.

Childhood Abuse

A large number of studies have reported a link between childhood trauma (i.e., physical or sexual abuse) and BPD (for a review, see Sabo, 1997). Studies consistently demonstrate an association between BPD and physical or sexual abuse in childhood, but only rates of sexual abuse in BPD patients are reported to be significantly higher than those in depressed or other (non-BPD) personality disorder controls (Zanarini & Frankenburg, 1997). However, the relationship between BPD and sexual abuse, for example, may not be as strong as is sometimes assumed (Fossati, Madeddu, & Maffei, 1999), and most agree that childhood abuse is not the primary cause of BPD (Paris, 1997; Sabo, 1997). As noted by Paris (1997), many BPD patients do not report a history of childhood abuse, abuse histories are reported by those with other diagnoses and those with no diagnosis, and abuse histories covary with other risk factors like parental psychopathology, family conflict, and temperament or personality.

Despite these caveats, childhood abuse remains an important factor to include in etiological models of BPD, especially multivariate models. The relative importance of this factor in the context of other etiological variables has not been addressed. It is conceivable that many of the clinical features or correlates of BPD (e.g., lack of trust, dissociative experiences, affective instability) might result from the experience of physical or sexual abuse in childhood. For example, the experience of trauma may produce biological changes in the individual (e.g., noradrenergic hypersensitivity) that are consistent with neurobiological profiles of BPD patients (Figueroa & Silk, 1997). Although childhood abuse is no longer considered the major factor in the etiology of BPD, it does remain an important variable to consider. For example, even within a nonclinical sample, childhood abuse accounted for significant and unique variance in borderline features, suggesting that its relevance to BPD pathology is not limited to clinical samples (Trull, 2001).

Personality

There is a general consensus that two core, higher order personality traits, impulsivity and emotional dysregulation, underlie BPD (Gurvits, Koenigsberg, & Siever, 2000; Linehan, 1993; Paris, 2000; Siever & Davis, 1991; Silk, 2000; Trull et al., 2000). Although impulsivity and emotional dysregulation, respectively, may characterize or underlie several diagnostic syndromes (e.g., antisocial personality disorder and mood disorder), it is the combination or co-occurrence of these two traits that may uniquely characterize BPD (Siever & Davis, 1991; Trull et al., 2000).

Most contemporary work in this area has focused on lower order personality traits (i.e., traits that are components of the higher order personality dimensions) that best characterize BPD, and therefore provide even more specificity for the assessment of BPD. For example, from Livesley's model of personality pathology (Livesley et al., 1998), anxiousness, affective lability, cognitive dysregulation, identity problems, suspiciousness, insecure attachment, self-harm, stimulus seeking, rejection, and conduct problems provide a reasonable description of the traits that may underlie the symptoms associated with BPD (Bagge & Trull, 2003). Within the popular Five-Factor Model of personality (FFM), BPD may be best understood as associated with the lower order traits of anxiety, hostility, depression, impulsiveness, vulnerability, warmth, gregariousness, assertiveness, openness to fantasy, openness to feelings, low trust, low straightforwardness, low compliance, low achievement striving, and low deliberation (Trull, Widiger, & Burr, 2001; Trull, Widiger, Lynam, & Costa, 2003).

COURSE, COMPLICATIONS, AND PROGNOSIS

Course

Personality disorders are defined as stable and of long duration (APA, 2000). However, evidence suggests that the stability of a BPD diagnosis may depend on the life stage studied. For instance, Grilo, Becker, Edell, and McGlashan (2001) observed that among a cohort of 60 hospitalized adolescents, the two-year stability of BPD diagnosis was low to moderate and significantly less common at follow-up than at intake. This appears to be less stable than adult PD diagnoses over the same length of time. However, even BPD diagnoses in adults may not persist over longer periods of time, and BPD symptoms in adults appear to improve as patients get older (Paris, 2003). In one study of 64 patients initially meeting criteria for borderline personality disorder, 25 percent met criteria at 15-year follow-up, and only 7.8 percent met criteria at 27-year follow-up at an average age of 51 (Paris & Zweig-Frank, 2001). Another study found that BPD symptoms tend to remit over time with few recurrences. Zanarini, Frankenburg, Hennen, and Silk (2004) reported that among 290 inpatients with BPD, 75 percent experienced a remission over a six-year follow-up period. Impulsive symptoms, such as self-mutilation and substance abuse, were the most likely to remit. On the other hand, affective symptoms were the most likely to persist over the six-year follow-up. Even though symptoms of BPD were found to remit at high rates over the six-year period, these patients continued to experience more global psychopathology when compared to patients with other personality disorders.

In addition, BPD diagnoses may not be stable during concurrent episodes of major depression (Farabaugh et al. 2002). Eighty-three outpatients showed significant decreases in BPD comorbidity from baseline to the end point of successful eight-week treatment for depression by fluoxetine. However, in the same study, BPD diagnoses were stable for 26 weeks posttreatment for depression. The data suggest that personality disorder diagnoses in those with remitted depression are relatively stable, but diagnoses made during current depressive episodes are unstable. Another study of the stability of BPD diagnoses reported low agreement between a standardized assessment of personality and a rating made by a general practitioner one year later (Moran, Rendu, Jenkins, Tylee, & Mann, 2001). However, it is not clear whether the poor stability was due to differences in assessment methods or to the time elapsed. Finally, in a longitudinal study, Gunderson et al. (in press) found that a remission in BPD symptoms was associated with later improvements in symptoms of major depression, but not the other way around. These provocative findings suggest that clinicians should not ignore BPD symptoms in order to treat a comorbid major depression (and hope that BPD symptoms will be alleviated). Rather, BPD symptoms should be targeted for treatment from the start.

The outcome for individuals with BPD continues to draw research attention. Skodol, Gunderson, McGlashan, et al. (2002) found that patients with severe personality disorders (schizotypal and borderline) had significantly more impairment in social and occupational domains than did patients with less severe personality disorders (obsessive-compulsive and avoidant) or with major depression. Furthermore, even though BPD diagnoses themselves are somewhat unstable, impairment may continue even when the diagnosis is no longer met. As for what predicts long-term outcome in those with BPD, one study found that earlier BPD severity and global functioning scores were correlated with later functioning but that the individual's relationship with parents and childhood abuse were not associated with outcome (Zweig-Frank & Paris, 2002). One possibility is that the influence of adverse childhood events wanes over the life course. However, a recent review concluded that childhood sexual abuse (as well as other factors) was generally related to a worse outcome in adulthood (Skodol, Gunderson, McGlashan, et al., 2002).

Complications

Suicidal behavior is often a complicating feature of BPD. About 1 in 10 patients diagnosed with BPD will complete suicide and about 70 percent engage in self-injurious behaviors (for a review, see Gerson & Stanley, 2002; Paris, 2002a). Important distinctions exist between suicidal and nonsuicidal injuries, including intent to die (Gerson & Stanley, 2002). Women with BPD report different reasons for engaging in self-injurious behavior and suicidal behavior (Brown, Comtois, & Linehan, 2002). Brown et al. (2002) reported that these patients tend to engage in self-injurious behavior in order to generate feelings (when feeling numb or dissociated), express anger, and distract themselves. However, these patients engage in suicidal behavior in order to make others better off (Brown et al., 2002). Typically, these impulsive behaviors tend to "burn out" as patients age, but for the most severe cases, this may not be the case. Preliminary results suggest that inpatients with BPD continue to engage in self-harm behaviors into their fifties (Sansone, Gaither, & Songer, 2002).

Because the occurrence of chronic suicidality is common among people diagnosed with BPD, clinicians must thoroughly evaluate acute risk. Unfortunately, it is difficult to predict who will successfully complete suicide. Paris (2002a) points out that suicide completers tend to be older males who die on the first attempt. On the other hand, repeated suicide attempters tend to be younger females. The former population rarely seeks treatment, whereas the latter readily seeks treatment. In addition, researchers reported that women with BPD who endorsed few reassuring thoughts, few active coping strategies, and depressive personality traits are more likely to engage in suicidal behaviors (Rietdijk, van den Bosch, Verheul, Koeter, & van den Brink, 2001).

Paris (2002a) highlights the fact that clinicians play a role in increasing and/or decreasing the frequency of self-injurious behaviors. Hospitalization may be harmful for those patients who chronically engage in self-injurious behaviors because it provides negative reinforcement of passive coping (Gerson & Stanley, 2002; Paris, 2002a). As a result, this intervention should be reserved for those with acute psychotic symptoms and those who are acutely suicidal (Paris, 2002a). On the other hand, patients could be positively reinforced for reporting suicidal thoughts and feelings as problems to be solved (Paris, 2002a). Biological treatments may also be effective in reducing self-injurious behaviors, including antidepressants, neuroleptics, mood stabilizers, benzodiazepines, and opiate agonists (for a review, see Gerson & Stanley, 2002).

Prognosis

Several recent studies have indicated that the prognosis for those with BPD is relatively good, with relatively high remission rates occurring 10 to 15 years after initial diagnosis (Paris, 2003). As with most personality disorders, BPD symptoms seem less intense as the individual ages. Relatively few studies, however, have examined specific factors that seem to play a role in the maintenance or remission of BPD symptoms over time. Factors associated with a poorer prognosis include a history of childhood sexual abuse, early age at first psychiatric contact, aggression in relationships, magical thinking, substance abuse, antisocial features, and paranoid features (Skodol, Siever, et al., 2002).

ASSESSMENT AND DIAGNOSIS

Interviews

A number of diagnostic instruments for BPD exist. One of the most popular diagnostic instruments for BPD is the Diagnostic Interview for Borderline Patients–Revised (DIB-R; Zanarini, Gunderson, Frankenburg, & Chauncey, 1989). The DIB-R is a semistructured interview comprising 106 items for assessing the symptoms of BPD in the past two years, in addition to symptoms primarily associated with psychotic and affective disorders. This interview takes approximately one hour to administer but may vary depending on how many symptoms the patient endorses. Items include structured questions, information to be completed by multiple sources, and clinical observations. There are 22 criteria or "statements," which are categorized into four sections, representing dimensions of borderline functioning: impulse action patterns, affects, cognition, and interpersonal relations. The DIB is scored on a 3-point scale: 0 for "no," 1 for "probable," and 2 for "yes." The total score for the DIB-R is based on four sections, with two sections (i.e., interpersonal relations and impulsive action patterns) given greater weight by allowing a maximum score of 3. With these weights, the maximum total score remains at 10. The cutoff score for a DIB-R BPD diagnosis is 8 or higher.

Zanarini, Frakenburg, & Vujanovic (2002) examined the interrater and test-retest reliability of the DIB-R. Test-retest reliability was assessed using two direct interviews of 30 inpatients and interrater reliability was assessed using 45 inpatients over a four-year time frame. The researchers found excellent interrater reliability (ICC = .94) and test-retest reliability (ICC = .91). Little evidence of the criterion-related validity of the DIB-R exists. Zanarini et al. (1989) compared 95 BPD patients with 237 patients having other personality disorders to compare DIB-R scores to diagnoses based on DSM-III criteria. They reported a sensitivity of .82 and a specificity of .80 for the DIB-R when using a cutting score of ≥8. However, the modal score for the other personality disorders was very close to the cutting score (i.e., 35 percent had a score of 7).

Five semistructured instruments assess all of the *DSM-IV* personality disorders, including BPD: (1) the Structured Interview for *DSM-IV* Personality Disorders (SIDP-IV; Pfohl, Blum, & Zimmerman, 1997); (2) the Diagnostic Interview for *DSM-IV* Personality Disorders (DIPD-IV; Zanarini, Frankenburg, Chauncey, & Gunderson, 1987); (3) the International Personality Disorder Examination (IPDE; Loranger et al., 1994); (4) the Personality Disorder Interview–IV (PDI-IV; Widiger, Mangine, Corbitt, Ellis, & Thomas, 1995); and (5) the Structured Clinical Interview for *DSM-IV* Axis II Personality Disorders (SCID-II; First, Spitzer, Gibbon, & Williams, 1995). These interviews are structured so items are grouped together in sets and are organized either by personality disorder or by thematic areas (e.g., friendships and relationships). Items assess each *DSM-IV* personality disorder criterion and are rated on an ordinal scale (e.g., 0 = absent, 1 = subthreshold, and 2 = present). These assessments can then be scored categorically by counting the number of criteria met for each disorder, or dimensionally by summing the points for each criterion. The interviews are typically administered directly to the patient although significant others and family members may be consulted for additional information.

The interrater and test-retest reliabilities of semistructured interviews are far superior to that obtained by unstructured clinical interviews. Interrater reliability is consistently reported to be good to excellent for scoring the interview either dimensionally (intraclass correlations are typically in the .60 to .99 range) or categorically (kappa values range from .58 to .93). The interrater reliability for diagnosing individual personality disorders is typically good to excellent (kappa values range from .58 to 1.0). However, some studies have reported poor reliabilities for when diagnosing individual disorders (kappa values ≤.56). Test-retest reliabilities are similar to the interrater agreement values, although most studies report test-retest stabilities over relatively short periods of time (e.g., several months or less). To assess the concurrent validity of these instruments, researchers typically report their correlation to questionnaires measuring individual personality disorders and have ranged from poor to good (correlation coefficients ranging from −.32 to .78). Semistructured interviews are somewhat more strongly correlated with one another than are questionnaires.

Questionnaires

Although many questionnaires have been developed over the years to assess BPD features, here we discuss one scale that has garnered strong empirical support to date. The Personality Assessment Inventory–Borderline Features (PAI-BOR; Morey, 1991) is a subscale of the PAI, which was developed to assess clinical syndromes and personality features, and to identify possible treatment complications. The PAI-BOR is a 24-item measure that assesses major features of BPD, including affective instability, identity problems, negative relationships, and self-harm (impulsivity). In order to provide a dimensional understanding of personality functioning, items are scored on a Likert scale (0 = false, not at all true; 1 = slightly true; 2 = mainly true; 3 = very true).

This measure has demonstrated reliability and validity (e.g., Morey, 1991; Trull, 1995). An examination of the PAI-BOR's classification accuracy in a sample of female inpatients with BPD and a matched control group of college students indicated that a PAI-BOR T-score at or higher than 70 accurately classified 81.8 percent of the patients and 77.3 percent of the students (Bell-Pringle, Patte, & Brown, 1997). Additionally, Trull (1995) reported that nonclinical young adults scoring in the clinically significant range on the PAI-BOR (a raw score ≥38) differed on measures of mood, personality, coping, general psychopathology, and exhibited more BPD symptomatology than those who scored below this threshold. Further, these PAI-BOR scale classifications also predicted two-year outcomes on academic and social functioning indexes in college students, even after controlling for academic potential (Bagge et al., 2004).

IMPACT ON ENVIRONMENT

Impaired functioning is associated with all personality disorders, including BPD. In fact, the persistent and maladaptive personality styles that lead to impairment are what distinguishes personality disorders from normal personality functioning. Not surprisingly, both clinical observation and empirical research support the idea that BPD features lead to impaired functioning in all areas of a person's life. Numerous researchers have shown that BPD features contribute significantly to the difficulties these patients experience in relating to their friends, family, spouses, coworkers, and therapists (e.g., see Skodol, Gunderson, McGlashan, et al., 2002). In addition to impaired social functioning, persons with BPD often suffer negative consequences of their maladaptive behavior in the workplace or in educational settings (e.g., Bagge et al., 2004). Finally, persons with BPD typically show significant impairment on global functioning measures.

It is helpful to consider the roles of specific BPD features when examining these patterns of impairment. As mentioned previously, many researchers consider affective instability and impulsivity to be the core features of BPD. Each of these features contributes to psychosocial impairment in unique ways. Frequent and intense affect shifts make stability in relationships with friends, family, partners, and coworkers difficult to attain. For those with BPD, the constant emotional chaos can hinder one's ability to function effectively in work or school. Also, the strong negative affects (e.g., anger, depression, anxiety) frequently experienced by those with BPD can further impair one's ability to form close relationships or fulfill one's role as an employee.

The impulsivity seen in many persons with BPD can lead to similar levels of dysfunction. By definition, the impulsive behaviors in which those with BPD frequently engage are self-damaging. Substance abuse, promiscuity, or excessive spending can create long-lasting negative consequences in the lives of those with BPD. For example, impulsive behavior might prevent one from being able to fulfill his or her role as a spouse, parent, friend, or employee. One's performance in the workplace may suffer due to excessive absences or missed deadlines. Clearly, these impulsive behaviors can impact virtually every area of one's life.

One area that is particularly interesting to researchers is intimate relationships. Persons with BPD may actually be seen as attractive romantic partners because they can be exciting, emotionally expressive, and open with their partners (Paris & Braveman, 1995). However, they also typically experience many interpersonal problems that can make the selection of a compatible partner difficult. Due to their difficulties with intimate relationships, persons with BPD may also experience many difficulties in forming and maintaining a marriage. Paris and Braveman (1995) hypothesize that, in order to maintain the stability of the marriage, the spouse must assume a caretaker role and be able to effectively cope with the impulsivity and affective instability of the person with BPD. This idea is supported by Links and Stockwell (2001), who believe it may be important to differentiate between subtypes of BPD when examining the affect of the disorder on partner selection and marriage. They have found that people with BPD who are distinguished by their impulsivity are most likely to fail at marriage. The identity subtype is most likely to find success in a marriage if the spouse shares similar identity issues. Finally, the affective instability subtype is most successful in a marriage to a healthy spouse who can adequately cope with the affect shifts in the partner.

In a longitudinal study of BPD patients, Stone (1990) found that after 15 years only 52 percent of females with BPD were ever married and only 25 percent of BPD females had children. In BPD males, 29 percent had ever been married and 15 percent had children. Of those BPD patients who did marry, 33 percent were later divorced, a rate that is consistent with the general population. However, of those who divorced, only 10 percent remarried, a rate that is lower than the national average. These findings appear to support the clinical observations of other researchers who hypothesize that persons with BPD may actually learn to avoid intimate relationships (Paris, 2002d). Paris hypothesizes that these people may achieve more stability in their lives with numerous, less intimate relationships with friends, community members, or pets (2002d).

Of those who do marry and have children, the family environment may be very dysfunctional. Feldman et al. (1995) compared the family experiences of children of BPD mothers and of mothers with other personality disorders. They found that the BPD families were more chaotic and unsupportive, and less oriented toward personal growth than families of mothers with other Axis II pathology. Children in the BPD families were more likely to be aware of both their mothers' and fathers' suicide attempts. They were more likely to have been exposed to a substance-abusing parent and to have been either verbally or physically abused. The children in the BPD families also switched schools more often and 40 percent of them were living apart from their mothers, compared with only 5 percent of the control children.

Persons with BPD are also more likely than those with other Axis II disorders to experience violence in their adult lives. Zanarini et al. (1999) found that persons with BPD were significantly more likely to have an abusive partner, to be raped, to know their rapist, and to be raped repeatedly as adults. Fifty percent of the BPD females in the sample and 25 percent of the males had experienced some form of adult violence. The authors hypothesized that these findings may be due to possible childhood abuse histories or the impulsive behavior of a person with BPD that may lead to dangerous environments and relationships.

In addition to relationship difficulties, persons with BPD may also experience difficulties in work and school. In a study of college undergraduates, people with significant borderline features displayed impaired functioning at school. These people showed higher levels of social maladjustment, had a lower grade point average, and spent more semesters on academic probation (Bagge et al., 2004). These findings remained significant even after controlling for Axis I and other non-BPD Axis II psychopathology. Skodol, Gunderson, McGlashan, et al. (2002) found that BPD patients were less likely to be currently employed and more likely to be labeled as "disabled" compared to other Axis II disordered patients.

Given the significant difficulties BPD can cause in a patient's life, one might expect the societal costs to be high as well. Several studies have shown that BPD patients utilize mental health services more than patients with other Axis II pathology (Zanarini et al., 2004). This utilization includes high rates of psychiatric inpatient treatment, outpatient psychotherapy, and pharmacotherapy. Some researchers have estimated that the annual cost of such treatment per patient could be more than $50,000 (Bateman & Fonagy, 2003). Although we are not aware of any study that estimates societal costs due to lost wages or disability pay, it might be reasonable to expect that the total annual cost to society would be very high.

TREATMENT IMPLICATIONS

Mental health professionals often feel overwhelmed and frustrated when treating patients with BPD. In response to this problem, the American Psychiatric Association (APA) recently appointed a group of experts to make practice recommendations based on empirical support and clinical consensus for the treatment of BPD (APA, 2001; Oldham, 2002). Even though treatment recommendations for BPD are greatly needed, many felt the guidelines were published prematurely, failing to separate clinical lore from empirical studies (McGlashan, 2002; Paris, 2002b, 2002c; Sanderson, Swenson, & Bohus, 2002; Tyrer, 2002).

Psychological Treatment

The expert committee primarily recommends psychotherapy with psychotropic medications that target the symptoms of BPD (APA, 2001). Psychotherapy not only reduces the severity of the disorder, but researchers have found that intensive psychotherapy is cost-effective for this population (Chiesa, Fonagy, Holmes, Drahorad, & Harrison-Hall, 2002; Hall, Caleo, Stevenson, & Meares, 2001). Two psychotherapeutic approaches are recommended: psychodynamic/psychoanalytic psychotherapy and cognitive behavioral therapy, especially dialectical behavior therapy (DBT), which is discussed more fully in Chapter 29.

In randomized controlled clinical trials, DBT has proven to be more efficacious than treatment as usual for reducing parasuicidal behaviors, inpatient psychiatric days, treatment dropout rates, and self-reported anger in patients with BPD (for a review, see Koerner & Linehan, 2000; Robins & Chapman, 2004). The most recently published randomly controlled clinical trial of standard DBT was conducted in The Netherlands with 58 women diagnosed with BPD. Researchers reported that DBT patients experienced significant reductions in parasuicidal and other impulsive behaviors (Verheul et al., 2003). In addition to the efficacy of this intervention in treating women with BPD, studies suggest that mental health workers perceive DBT favorably (Alper & Peterson, 2001). With the aim to increase the internal validity of DBT, Linehan et al. (2002) evaluated the efficacy of DBT in treating patients who meet criteria for BPD and opiate addiction compared to Comprehensive Validation Therapy with 12-Step (CVT + 12-S). However, few between-group differences were found, suggesting that DBT is not more likely to reduce drug use or treatment dropout rates when compared with CVT + 12-S (Linehan et al., 2002).

Another cognitive behavioral psychotherapy, Systems Training for Emotional Predictability and Problem Solving (STEPPS), has been developed as a brief, psychoeducational program to be used in outpatient settings that involves the patient's support network (Blum, Pfohl, St. John, Monahan, & Black, 2002). The main aim of STEPPS is to teach patients specific emotion and behavioral management skills, serving as an adjunct to ongoing treatment (Blum et al., 2002). In a pilot study including 52 outpatients, Blum et al. (2002) found that symptoms associated with BPD were reduced, including scores of negative affectivity. A future study should include a randomized clinical trial to establish the efficacy of STEPPS as an adjunct treatment for BPD.

The APA also recommends *psychodynamic/psychoanalytic therapy* (APA, 2001). Although psychodynamic psychotherapy may be seen as the treatment of choice for BPD by some clinicians, few clinical trials have been done to establish its efficacy. Wildgoose, Clarke, & Waller (2001) preliminarily assessed the effectiveness of cognitive analytic therapy (CAT) in treating dissociation and personality fragmentation in patients with BPD. For the five patients included in the study, the severity of BPD was reduced at termination and at nine-month follow-up. However, findings were mixed with regards to changes in personality fragmentation, dissociation, and interpersonal adjustment (Wildgoose et al., 2001).

Mentalization-based treatment is another psychoanalytically oriented treatment for BPD that has been shown to be effective in decreasing depressive symptomatology, parasuicidal and suicidal behavior, reducing inpatient hospital stays, and increasing interpersonal functioning when compared to a treatment as usual condition in a partial hospitalization program (Bateman & Fonagy, 1999). These results occurred after 6 months of treatment and were maintained at an 18-month follow-up (Bateman & Fonagy, 2001). Mentalization-based treatment focuses on providing interventions that increase the patient's ability to think about one's self as separate from others and involves individual and group psychotherapy (for an overview, see Bateman & Fonagy, 2004a). This treatment has recently been manualized (Batemen & Fonagy, 2004b).

Transference focused psychotherapy (TFP) is a psychodynamic treatment that focuses first on containing self-injurious and treatment-interfering behaviors and then on exploring the transferential relationship between the therapist and the patient (Clarkin et al., 2001). In comparing pre-post-treatment changes, Clarkin et al. (2001) found a reduction in the severity of self-harm but not a reduction in suicide variables. In addition, there was a significant reduction in the number of hospitalizations (Clarkin et al., 2001).

Thus, CAT and TFP may be effective for treating BPD, but randomized controlled clinical trials must be conducted to better establish their efficacy. The Personality Disorders Institute/Borderline Personality Disorder Research Foundation randomized control trial was recently completed in order to investigate the effectiveness of DBT, TFP, and supportive treatment in treating BPD. Results from this study of 90 patients with BPD will be important in demonstrating the efficacy of these forms of treatment (Clarkin, Levy, Lenzenweger, & Kernberg, 2004). Regardless of the type of therapy used, the APA (2001) indicates that group therapy or skills training (like that provided by DBT) should usually be administered in adjunct to individual psychotherapy.

Pharmacotherapy

Medications are helpful for managing symptoms, such as affective lability, impulsivity or disinhibition, and cognitive perceptual disturbances (APA, 2001). The APA (2001) recommends first administering SSRIs for treating affective dysregulation and impulsive-behavioral symptoms. Several studies suggest that fluoxetine may be effective in reducing several symptoms associated with BPD including depression, anxiety, paranoia/psychoticism, obsessive-compulsive symptoms, interpersonal sensitivity, and parasuicidal behavior (Zanarini, 2004). More limited research has been conducted with other antidepressants but does suggest that sertraline and venlafaxine may be helpful in decreasing BPD symptomatology (for an overview, see Zanarini, 2004).

In addition to antidepressants, mood stabilizers may prove to be efficacious in managing mood lability (for a review, see APA, 2001). For example, BPD patients treated with divalproex sodium show improvement in global areas of functioning (Hollander, 1999). In a double-blind, placebo-controlled pilot study of divalproex sodium, the experimental group experienced a significant reduction in interpersonal sensitivity, anger/hostility, and aggression (but not depression) when compared with the placebo group (Frankenburg & Zanarini, 2002). These results are promising, and more research is needed to evaluate the efficacy of other mood stabilizers in treating BPD.

Low-dose neuroleptics are the preferred treatment for cognitive perceptual disturbances in BPD (APA, 2001). The effectiveness of atypical antipsychotics in the treatment of BPD is important to investigate because of the promising preliminary results obtained with the use of traditional antipsychotics in minimizing several symptoms associated with this disorder (for a review, see APA, 2001). In addition to managing symptoms, the administration of antipsychotics may be cost-effective (Parker, 2002). In a double-blind, placebo-controlled pilot study for olanzapine, Zanarini and Frankenburg (2001) found a significantly greater rate of change than the placebo group on measures of anxiety, interpersonal sensitivity, anger/hostility, and paranoia but not for depression. In addition to olanzapine, risperidone may be an effective treatment for symptoms of BPD. An open-label trial of risperidone found significant improvement on measures of anxiety, depression, anergia, thought disturbance, social functioning, and aggression for patients with BPD at the end of eight weeks (Rocca, Marchiaro, Cocuzza, & Bogetto, 2001). Research also suggests that clozapine may be effective in reducing BPD symptomatology and increasing psychosocial functioning (for a review, see Zanarini, 2004).

The APA (2001) guidelines for the treatment of BPD stress the importance of addressing special features when making treatment decisions, such as comorbidity with Axis I and Axis II psychopathology, substance use, violent behaviors toward self and others, PTSD, dissociative features, and cultural factors. Thus, flexibility, communication, and consultation between members of the treatment team are essential to provide optimal treatment (APA, 2001).

POSTSCRIPT

Borderline personality disorder (BPD) continues to capture the interest of both clinicians and researchers because of the intensity of the clinical presentation, the disability associated with its symptoms, and the recognition that it is relatively common in both clinical and nonclinical populations. Our knowledge about this disorder has grown tremendously, especially over the last 15 years. In addition, the National Institute of Mental Health has recognized the severe problems posed by this disorder, and this institute (along with the Borderline Personality Disorder Research Foundation) has earmarked funds for conducting research on the most pressing questions the field faces. With these funds clinical researchers are developing state of the art assessment and treatment techniques, and etiological factors are being identified. Also encouraging is the commitment and energy of several advocacy groups (e.g., Treatment and Research Advancements National Association of Personality Disorder [TARA]; National Educational Alliance for Borderline Personality Disorder [NEA-BPD]) that are calling attention to BPD and encouraging government officials to provide more funds for research on BPD. With these forms of support, we are optimistic that our knowledge about the etiology, assessment, and effective treatment of BPD will benefit in the years to come.

REFERENCES

Agrawal, H. R., Gunderson, J. G., Holmes, B. M., & Lyons-Ruth, K. (2004). Attachment studies with borderline patients: A review. *Harvard Review of Psychiatry, 12,* 94–104.

Alper, G., & Peterson, S. J. (2001). Dialectical behavior therapy for patients with borderline personality disorder. *Journal of Psychosocial Nursing, 39,* 38–45.

American Psychiatric Association. (2000). *Diagnostic and statistical manual* (4th ed., text rev.). Washington, DC: Author.

American Psychiatric Association. (2001). Practice guidelines for the treatment of patients with borderline personality disorder. *American Journal of Psychiatry, 158*(Suppl. 10), 1–52.

Atmaca, M., Kuloglu, M., Tezcan, E., Gecici, O., & Ustundag, B. (2002). Serum cholesterol and leptin levels in patients with borderline personality disorder. *Neuropsychobiology, 45,* 167–171.

Bagge, C., Nickell, A., Stepp, S., Durrett, C., Jackson, K., & Trull, T. (2004). Borderline personality disorder features predict negative outcomes 2 years later. *Journal of Abnormal Psychology, 113,* 279–288.

Bagge, C., & Trull, T. J. (2003). DAPP-BQ: Factor structure and relations to personality disorder symptoms in a non-clinical sample. *Journal of Personality Disorders, 17,* 19–32.

Bateman, A., & Fonagy, P. (1999). The effectiveness of partial hospitalization in the treatment of borderline personality disorder: A randomized controlled trial. *American Journal of Psychiatry, 156,* 1563–1569.

Bateman, A., & Fonagy, P. (2001). Treatment of borderline personality disorder with a psychoanalytically oriented partial hospitalization: An 18-month follow-up. *American Journal of Psychiatry, 160,* 169–171.

Bateman, A., & Fonagy, P. (2003). Health service utilization costs for borderline personality disorder patients treated with psychoanalytically oriented partial hospitalization versus general psychiatric care. *American Journal of Psychiatry, 160,* 169–171.

Bateman, A., & Fonagy, P. (2004a). Mentalization-based treatment of BPD. *Journal of Personality Disorders, 18*(1), 36–51.

Bateman, A., & Fonagy, P. (2004b). *Psychotherapy for borderline personality disorder: Mentalization-based treatment.* Oxford, England: Oxford University Press.

Bell-Pringle, V. J., Patte, J. L., & Brown, R. C. (1997). Assessment of borderline personality disorder using the MMPI-2 and the Personality Assessment Inventory. *Assessment, 4,* 131–139.

Blum, N., Pfohl, B., St. John, D., Monahan, P., & Black, D. W. (2002). STEPPS: A cognitive-behavioral systems-based group treatment for outpatients with borderline personality disorder: A preliminary report. *Comprehensive Psychiatry, 43,* 301–310.

Brown, M. Z., Comtois, K. A., & Linehan, M. M. (2002). Reasons for suicide attempts and nonsuicidal self-injury in women with borderline personality disorder. *Journal of Abnormal Psychology, 111,* 198–202.

Chavira, D. A., Grilo, C. M., Shea, T., Yen, S., Gunderson, J. G., Morey, L. C., et al. (2003). Ethnicity and four personality disorders. *Comprehensive Psychiatry, 44*, 483–491.

Chiesa, M., Fonagy, P., Holmes J., Drahorad, C., & Harrison-Hall, A. (2002). Health service use costs by personality disorder following specialist and nonspecialist treatment: A comparative study. *Journal of Personality Disorders, 16*, 160–173.

Clarkin, J. F., Foelsch, P. A., Levy, K. N., Hull, J. W., Delaney, J. C., & Kernberg, O. F. (2001). The development of a psychodynamic treatment for patients with borderline personality disorder: A preliminary study of behavioral change. *Journal of Personality Disorders, 15*, 487–495.

Clarkin, J. F., Levy, K. N., Lenzenweger, M. F., & Kernberg, O. F. (2004). The Personality Disorders Institute/Borderline Personality Disorder Research Foundation randomized control trial for borderline personality disorder: Rationale, methods, and patient characteristics. *Journal of Personality Disorders, 18*, 52–72.

Dulit, R. A., Fyer, M. R., Haas, G. L., Sullivan, T., & Frances, A. J. (1990). Substance use in borderline personality disorder. *American Journal of Psychiatry, 147*, 1002–1007.

Farabaugh, A., Mischoulon, D., Yeung, A., Alpert, J., Matthews, J., Pava, J., et al. (2002). Predictors of stable personality disorder diagnoses in outpatients with remitted depression. *Journal of Nervous and Mental Disease, 190*, 248–256.

Feldman, R. B., Zelkowitz, P., Weiss, M., Vogel, J., Heyman, M., & Paris, J. (1995). A comparison of the families of mothers with borderline and nonborderline personality disorders. *Comprehensive Psychiatry, 36*, 157–163.

Figueroa, E., & Silk, K. R. (1997). Biological implications of childhood sexual abuse in borderline personality disorder. *Journal of Personality Disorders, 11*, 71–92.

First, M. B., Spitzer, R. L., Gibbon, M., & Williams, J. B. W. (1995). The Structured Clinical Interview for *DSM-III-R* Personality Disorders (SCID-II): I. Description. *Journal of Personality Disorders, 9*, 82–91.

Fossati, A., Donati, D., Donini, M., Novella, L., Bagnato, M., & Maffei, C. (2001). Temperament, character, and attachment patterns in borderline personality disorder. *Journal of Personality Disorders, 15*, 390–402.

Fossati, A., Madeddu, F., & Maffei, C. (1999). Borderline personality disorder and childhood sexual abuse: A meta-analytic study. *Journal of Personality Disorders, 13*, 268–280.

Frankenburg, F. R., & Zanarini, M. C. (2002). Divalproex sodium treatment of women with borderline personality disorder and bipolar II disorder: A double-blind placebo-controlled pilot study. *Journal of Clinical Psychiatry, 63*, 442–446.

Gerson, J., & Stanley, B. (2002). Suicidal and self-injurious behavior in personality disorder: Controversies and treatment directions. *Current Psychiatry Reports, 4*, 30–38.

Grilo, C. M., Becker, D. F., Edell, W. S., & McGlashan, T. H. (2001). Stability and change of *DSM-III-R* personality disorder dimensions in adolescents followed up 2 years after psychiatric hospitalization. *Comprehensive Psychiatry, 42*, 364–368.

Gross, R., Olfson, M., Gameroff, M., Shea, S., Feder, A., Fuentes, M., et al. (2002). Borderline personality disorder in primary care. *Archives of Internal Medicine, 162*, 53–60.

Gunderson, J. G. (2001). *Borderline personality disorder: A clinical guide.* Washington, DC: American Psychiatric Publishing.

Gunderson, J. G., Morey, L. C., Stout, R. L., Skodol, A. E., Shea, M. T., McGlashan, T. H., et al. (in press). Major depressive disorder and borderline personality disorder revisited: Longitudinal interactions. *Journal of Clinical Psychiatry.*

Gurvits, I. G., Koenigsberg, H. W., & Siever, L. J. (2000). Neurotransmitter dysfunction in patients with borderline personality disorder. *Psychiatric Clinics of North America, 23*, 27–40.

Hall, J., Caleo, S., Stevenson, J., & Meares, R. (2001). An economic analysis of psychotherapy for borderline personality disorder patients. *Journal of Mental Health Policy and Economics, 4*, 3–8.

Hollander, E. (1999). Managing aggressive behavior in patients with obsessive-compulsive disorder and borderline personality disorder. *Journal of Clinical Psychiatry, 60*(Suppl. 15), 38–44.

Jang, K. L., Livesley, W. J., Vernon, P. A., & Jackson, D. N. (1996). Heritability of personality disorder traits: A twin study. *Acta Psychiatrica Scandinavica, 94*, 438–444.

Johnson, D. M., Shea, M. T., Yen, S., Battle, C. L., Zlotnick, C. Sanislow, C. A., et al. (2003). Gender differences in borderline personality disorder: Findings from the Collaborative Longitudinal Personality Disorders Study. *Comprehensive Psychiatry, 44*, 284–292.

Khantzian, E. J. (1985). The self-medication hypothesis of addictive disorders: Focus on heroin and cocaine dependence. *American Journal of Psychiatry, 142*, 1259–1264.

Koerner, K., & Linehan, M. M. (2000). Research on dialectical behavior therapy for patients with borderline personality disorder. *Psychiatric Clinics of North America, 23*, 151–167.

Leyton, M., Okazawa, H., Diksic, M., Paris, J., Rosa, P., Mzengeza, S., et al. (2001). Brain regional α-[^{11}C]methyl-L-tryptophan trapping in impulsive subjects with borderline personality disorder. *American Journal of Psychiatry, 158*, 775–782.

Linehan, M. (1993). *Cognitive-behavioral treatment of borderline personality disorder.* New York: Guilford Press.

Linehan, M. M., Dimeff, L. A., Reynolds, S. K., Comtois, K. A., Welch, S. S., Heagerty, P., et al. (2002). Dialectical behavior therapy versus comprehensive validation therapy plus 12-step for the treatment of opioid dependent women meeting criteria for borderline personality disorder. *Drug and Alcohol Dependence, 67*, 13–26.

Links, P. S., Heslegrave, R., & van Reekum, R. (1999). Impulsivity: Core aspect of borderline personality disorder. *Journal of Personality Disorders, 13*, 1–9.

Links, P. S., & Stockwell, M. (2001). Is couple therapy indicated for borderline personality disorder? *American Journal of Psychotherapy, 55*, 491–506.

Livesley, W. J., Jang, K. L., & Vernon, P. A. (1998). Phenotypic and genetic structure of traits delineating personality disorder. *Archives of General Psychiatry, 55,* 941–948.

Lofgren, D. P., Bemporad, J., King, J., Lindem, K., & O'Driscoll, G. (1991). A prospective study of so-called borderline children. *American Journal of Psychiatry, 148,* 1541–1547.

Loranger, A. W., Satorius, N., Andreoli, A., Berger, P., Buchheim, P., Channabasavanna, S. M., et al. (1994). The International Personality Disorder Examination: The World Health Organization/Alcohol, Drug Abuse, and Mental Health Administration International Pilot Study of Personality Disorders. *Archives of General Psychiatry, 51,* 215–224.

McGlashan, T. H. (2002). The borderline personality disorder practice guidelines: The good, the bad, and the realistic. *Journal of Personality Disorders, 16,* 119–121.

Moran, P., Rendu, A., Jenkins, R., Tylee, A., & Mann, A. (2001). The impact of personality disorders in UK primary care: A 1-year follow-up of attenders. *Psychological Medicine, 31,* 1447–1454.

Morey, L. C. (1991). *Personality Assessment Inventory: Professional manual.* Odessa, FL: Psychological Assessment Resources.

New, A. S., Sevin, E. M., Mitropoulou, V., Reynolds, D., Novotny, S. L., Callahan, A., et al. (1999). Serum cholesterol and impulsivity in personality disorders. *Psychiatry Research, 85,* 145–150.

Nickell, A. D., Waudby, C. J., & Trull, T. J. (2002). Attachment, parental bonding and borderline personality disorder features in young adults. *Journal of Personality Disorders, 16,* 148–159.

Oldham, J. (2002). Development of the American Psychiatric Association practice guideline for the treatment of borderline personality disorder. *Journal of Personality Disorders, 16,* 109–112.

Paris, J. C. (1997). Childhood trauma as an etiological factor in the personality disorders. *Journal of Personality Disorders, 11,* 34–49.

Paris, J. (2000). Childhood precursors of borderline personality disorder. *Psychiatric Clinics of North America, 23,* 77–88.

Paris, J. (2002a). Chronic suicidality among patients with borderline personality disorder. *Psychiatric Services, 53,* 738–742.

Paris, J. (2002b). Clinical practice guidelines for borderline personality disorder. *Journal of Personality Disorders, 16,* 107–108.

Paris, J. (2002c). Commentary on the American Psychiatric Association guidelines for the treatment of borderline personality disorder: Evidence-based psychiatry and the quality of evidence. *Journal of Personality Disorders, 16,* 130–134.

Paris, J. (2002d). Implications of long-term outcome research for the management of patients with borderline personality disorder. *Harvard Review of Psychiatry, 10,* 315–323.

Paris, J. (2003). Personality disorders over time: Precursors, course and outcome. *Journal of Personality Disorders, 17,* 479–488.

Paris, J., & Braveman, S. (1995). Successful and unsuccessful marriages in borderline patients. *Journal of the American Academy of Psychoanalysis, 23,* 153–166.

Paris, J., & Zweig-Frank, H. (2001). The 27-year follow-up of patients with borderline personality disorder. *Comprehensive Psychiatry, 42,* 482–487.

Paris, J., Zweig-Frank, H., Ng Ying Kin, N. M. K., Schwartz, G., Steiger, H., & Nair, N. P. V. (2004). Neurobiological correlates of diagnosis and underlying traits in patients with borderline personality disorder compared with normal controls. *Psychiatry Research, 121,* 239–252.

Parker, G. F. (2002). Clozapine and borderline personality disorder. *Psychiatric Services, 53,* 348–349.

Pfohl, B., Blum, N., & Zimmerman, M. (1997). *Structured Interview for DSM-IV Personality.* Washington, DC: American Psychiatric Press.

Pukrop, R. (2002). Dimensional personality profiles of borderline personality disorder in comparison with other personality disorders and healthy controls. *Journal of Personality Disorders, 16,* 135–47.

Rietdijk, E. A., van den Bosch, L. M. C., Verheul, R., Koeter, M. W. J., & van den Brink, W. (2001). Predicting self-damaging and suicidal behaviors in female borderline patients: Reasons for living, coping, and depressive personality disorder. *Journal of Personality Disorders, 15,* 512–520.

Robins, C. J., & Chapman, A. L. (2004). Dialectical behavior therapy: Current status, recent developments, and future directions. *Journal of Personality Disorders, 18,* 73–89.

Rocca, P., Marchiaro, L., Cocuzza, E., & Bogetto, F. (2001). Treatment of borderline personality disorder with risperidone. *Journal of Clinical Psychiatry, 63,* 241–244.

Sabo, A. N. (1997). Etiological significance of associations between childhood trauma and borderline personality disorder: Conceptual and clinical implications. *Journal of Personality Disorders, 11,* 50–70.

Sanderson, C., Swenson, C., & Bohus, M. (2002). A critique of the American psychiatric practice guideline for the treatment of patients with borderline personality disorder. *Journal of Personality Disorders, 16,* 122–129.

Sansone, R. A., Gaither, G. A., & Songer, D. A. (2002). Self-harm behaviors across the life cycle: A pilot study of inpatients with borderline personality disorder. *Comprehensive Psychiatry, 43,* 215–218.

Siever, L. J., & Davis, K. L. (1991). A psychobiological perspective on personality disorder. *American Journal of Psychiatry, 148,* 1647–1658.

Siever, L. J., Koenigsberg, H. W., & Reynolds, D. (2003). Neurobiology of personality disorders: Implications for a neurodevelopmental model. In D. Cicchetti & E. Walker (Eds.), *Neurodevelopmental mechanisms in psychopathology* (pp. 405–427). Cambridge, England: Cambridge University Press.

Silk, K. S. (2000). Overview of biologic factors. *Psychiatric Clinics of North America, 23,* 61–75.

Silverman, J. M., Pinkham, L., Horvath, T. B., Coccaro, E. F., Klar, H., Schear, S., et al. (1991). Affective and impulsive personality disorder traits in the relatives of patients with borderline personality disorder. *American Journal of Psychiatry, 148,* 1378–1385.

Skodol, A. E., & Bender, D. S. (2003). Why are more women diagnosed borderline than men? *Psychiatric Quarterly, 74,* 349–360.

Skodol, A. E., Gunderson, J. G., McGlashan, T. H., Dyck, I. R., Stout, R. L., Bender, D. S., et al. (2002). Functional impairment in patients with schizotypal, borderline, avoidant, or obsessive-compulsive personality disorder. *American Journal of Psychiatry, 159,* 276–283.

Skodol, A. E., Gunderson, J. G., Pfohl, B., Widiger, T. A., Livesley, W. J., & Siever, L. J. (2002). The borderline diagnosis I: Psychopathology, comorbidity, and personality structure. *Biological Psychiatry, 51,* 936–950.

Skodol, A. E., Siever, L. J., Livesley, W. J., Gunderson, J. G., Pfohl, B., & Widiger, T. A. (2002). The borderline diagnosis II: Biology, genetics, and clinical course. *Biological Psychiatry, 51,* 951–963.

Soloff, P. H., Kelly, T. M., Strotmeyer, S. J., Malone, K. M., & Mann, J. J. (2003). Impulsivity, gender, and response to fenfluramine challenge in borderline personality disorder. *Psychiatry Research, 119,* 11–24.

Soloff, P. H., Meltzer, C. C., Becker, C., Greer, P. J., Kelly, T. M., & Constantine, D. (2003). Impulsivity and prefrontal hypometabolism in borderline personality disorder. *Psychiatry Research: Neuroimaging, 123,* 153–163.

Steinberg, B. J., Trestman, R., Mitropoulou, V., Serby, M., Siverman, J., Coccaro, E., et al. (1997). Depressive response to physostigmine challenge in borderline personality disorder patients. *Neuropsychopharmacology, 17,* 264–273.

Stone, M. H. (1990). *The fate of borderline patients: Successful outcome and psychiatric practice.* New York: Guilford Press.

Torgersen, S. (1984). Genetic and nosological aspects of schizotypal and borderline personality disorders: A twin study. *Archives of General Psychiatry, 41,* 546–554.

Torgersen, S., Kringlen, E., & Cramer, V. (2001). The prevalence of personality disorders in a community sample. *Archives of General Psychiatry, 58,* 590–596.

Torgersen, S., Lygren, S., Oien, P. A., Skre, I., Onstad, S., Edvardsen, J., et al. (2000). A twin study of personality disorders. *Comprehensive Psychiatry, 41,* 416–425.

Trull, T. J. (1995). Borderline personality disorder features in nonclinical young adults: I. Identification and validation. *Psychological Assessment, 7,* 33–41.

Trull, T. J. (2001). Structural relations between borderline personality disorder features and putative etiological correlates. *Journal of Abnormal Psychology, 110,* 471–481.

Trull, T. J., Sher, K. J., Minks-Brown, C., Durbin, J., & Burr, R. (2000). Borderline personality disorder and substance use disorders: A review and integration. *Clinical Psychology Review, 20,* 235–253.

Trull, T. J., Widiger, T. A., & Burr, R. (2001). A structured interview for the assessment of the five factor model of personality: Facet level relations to the Axis II personality disorders. *Journal of Personality, 69,* 175–198.

Trull, T. J., Widiger, T. A., Lynam, D. R., & Costa, P. T., Jr. (2003). Borderline personality disorder from the perspective of general personality functioning. *Journal of Abnormal Psychology, 112,* 193–202.

Tyrer, P. (2002). Practice guidelines for the treatment of borderline personality disorder: A bridge too far. *Journal of Personality Disorders, 16,* 13–118.

van Elst, L. T., Thiel, T., Hesslinger, B., Lieb, K., Bohus, M., Hennig, J., et al. (2001). Subtle prefrontal neuropathology in a pilot magnetic resonance spectroscopy study in patients with borderline personality disorder. *Journal of Neuropsychiatry and Clinical Neuroscience, 13,* 511–514.

Verheul, R., van den Bosch, L. M. C., Koeter, M. W. J., de Ridder, M. A. J., Stijnen, T., & van den Brink, W. (2003). Dialectical behavior therapy for women with borderline personality disorder. *British Journal of Psychiatry, 182,* 135–140.

White, C. N., Gunderson, J. G., Zanarini, M. C., & Hudson, J. I. (2003). Family studies of borderline personality disorder: A review. *Harvard Review of Psychiatry, 11,* 8–19.

Widiger, T. A., Mangine, S., Corbitt, E. M., Ellis, C. G., & Thomas, G. V. (1995). *Personality Disorder Interview-IV: A semistructured interview for the assessment of personality disorders–Professional manual.* Odessa, FL: Psychological Assessment Resources.

Wildgoose, A., Clarke, S., & Waller, G. (2001). Treating personality fragmentation and dissociation in borderline personality disorder: A pilot study of the impact of cognitive analytic therapy. *British Journal of Medical Psychology, 74,* 47–55.

Wilkinson-Ryan, T., & Westen, D. (2000). Identity disturbance in borderline personality disorder: An empirical investigation. *American Journal of Psychiatry, 157,* 528–541.

Work Group on Borderline Personality Disorder. (2001). Practice guideline for the treatment of patients with borderline personality disorder. *American Journal of Psychiatry, 158,* 1–52.

Zanarini, M. C. (2004). Update on pharmacotherapy of borderline personality disorder. *Current Psychiatry Reports, 6,* 66–70.

Zanarini, M. C., & Frankenburg, F. R. (1997). Pathways to the development of borderline personality disorder. *Journal of Personality Disorders, 11,* 93–104.

Zanarini, M. C., & Frankenburg, F. R. (2001). Olanzapine treatment of female borderline personality disorder patients: A double-blind, placebo-controlled pilot study. *Journal of Clinical Psychiatry, 62,* 849–854.

Zanarini, M. C., Frankenburg, F. R., Chauncey, D. L., & Gunderson, J. G. (1987). The Diagnostic Interview for Personality Disorders: Inter-rater and test-retest reliability. *Comprehensive Psychiatry, 28,* 467–480.

Zanarini, M. C., Frankenburg, F. R., Hennen, J., & Silk, K. R. (2004). Mental health service utilization by borderline personality disorder patients and Axis II comparison subjects followed prospectively for 6 years. *Journal of Clinical Psychiatry, 65,* 28–36.

Zanarini, M. C., Frankenburg, F. R., Reich, D. B., Marino, M. F., Haynes, M. C., & Gunderson, J. G. (1999). Violence in the lives of borderline patients. *Journal of Nervous and Mental Disease, 187,* 65–71.

Zanarini, M. C., Frankenburg, F. R., & Vujanovic, A. A. (2002). Inter-rater and test-retest reliability of the Revised Diagnostic Interview for Borderlines. *Journal of Personality Disorders, 16,* 270–276.

Zanarini, M. C., Gunderson, J. G., Frankenburg, F. R., & Chauncey, D. L. (1989). The Revised Diagnostic Interview for Borderlines: Discriminating BPD from other Axis II disorders. *Journal of Personality Disorders, 3,* 10–18.

Zweig-Frank, H., & Paris, J. (2002). Predictors of outcome in a 27-year follow-up of patients with borderline personality disorder. *Comprehensive Psychiatry, 43,* 103–107.

CHAPTER 19

Other Personality Disorders

KENNETH N. LEVY AND LORI N. SCOTT

One can live magnificently in this world if one knows how to work and love.

—Leo Tolstoy

DESCRIPTION OF THE DISORDER AND CLINICAL PICTURE

Personality disorders (PDs) are among the most common forms of psychological difficulties experienced. The overall lifetime prevalence for PDs ranges between 10 percent and 14 percent in untreated adult samples (Skodol et al., 2002). People with PDs exact a heavy cost from themselves and society as well as place considerable pressure on the mental health care system (Bender et al., 2001). Most definitions of PDs stress that they are pervasive, inflexible, maladaptive, and enduring expressions of personality (APA, 2000; Rutter, 1987) and acknowledge that they exist in several forms. Nevertheless there is considerable controversy over the definition, description, and degree to which meaningful distinctions are possible and which distinctions are valid (Westen & Shedler, 1999a, 1999b). The text revision of the fourth edition of the American Psychiatric Association's (APA) *Diagnostic and Statistical Manual of Mental Disorders* (*DSM-IV-TR;* APA, 2000) is probably the most widely used diagnostic system to diagnose PD, particularly in the United States (Maser, Kaelber, & Weise, 1991); however, a number of other prominent approaches exist (*ICD-10;* Millon, 1986; Westen & Shedler, 1999a, 1999b, 2000; World Health Organization, 1992).

The *DSM-IV-TR* (APA, 2000) distinguishes between 10 PDs on Axis II that are conceptually organized into three clusters, designated Cluster A (odd-eccentric), Cluster B (dramatic-erratic), and Cluster C (anxious-fearful). Cluster A includes paranoid, schizoid, and schizotypal PDs. Cluster B includes antisocial, borderline, histrionic, and narcissistic PDs. Cluster C includes avoidant, dependent, and obsessive-compulsive PDs. In addition, *DSM* allows for the diagnosis of personality disorder not otherwise specified (PD-NOS), which is given when a person meets general criteria for a personality disorder and traits of several PDs but does not meet the criteria for any one specific disorder; alternatively, a person meets general criteria for PD, but the type of disorder is not included in the classification system (e.g., passive-aggressive or depressive PDs, which are listed in the appendix as potential diagnoses requiring further study but can be used with the PD–not otherwise specified [NOS] option).

In this chapter we will review each of the PDs listed in the *DSM-IV-TR* (APA, 2000), with the exception of borderline personality disorder (BPD), which is described in detail in Chapter 18. Our review will focus on the prevalence, comorbidity, etiology, assessment, course, and treatment of the various PDs.

Cluster A Personality Disorders (Odd-Eccentric)

Paranoid Personality Disorder

Paranoid personality disorder (PPD) has a long and diverse clinical history (Freud, 1909/1925; Kraepelin, 1904, 1921). According to *DSM-IV-TR* (APA, 2000), PPD is characterized by a consistent pattern of distrust of the motives of other people. Further, people with this disorder assume that people will intentionally exploit, harm, or deceive them, and they often feel deeply injured by another person. They are frequently reluctant to become close to others out of fear that any personal information they reveal about themselves will later be used to hurt them. An individual with this disorder is also severely sensitive to criticism and, therefore, is likely to often feel attacked, threatened, or criticized by others. He or she might read hidden meanings or malevolent intentions into innocent remarks, mistakes, or compliments. It is also very difficult for a person with PPD to forgive others for perceived insults or injuries. Prolonged hostility, aggression, reactions of anger to perceived insults, and jealousy without adequate justification are also common.

Although PPD is often thought of as a "schizophrenia spectrum" disorder (Kraepelin, 1921; Siever & Davis, 1991), it may have a stronger familial relationship with Axis I delusional disorder than with schizophrenia (Kendler, 1985). In clinical samples, about two-thirds of patients with PPD meet criteria for another PD, most frequently schizotypal, narcissistic, borderline, and avoidant PDs (Bernstein, Useda, & Siever, 1995).

Schizoid Personality Disorder

The term *schizoid* was coined by Bleuler (1929), following Hock's (1910) description of the "shut-in" personality type and Kraepelin's "autistic personality type" to describe individuals who tended to turn inwardly and away from the external world, be indifferent to relationships or pleasure, show muted emotional expressiveness, be comfortably dull, and have vague undeveloped interests. Kretschmer (1925) differentiated between two distinct subtypes of the schizoid personality: the anesthetic or insensitive type characterized as indifferent, uninterested, unfeeling, unemotional, and dull, and the hyperaesthetic or overly sensitive type. The hyperaesthetic type is the forerunner of the *DSM* avoidant personality disorder. In the 1950s the early British object relations theorists (Fairbairn, 1952/1994; Guntrip, 1969; Winnicott, 1951) began to apply the concept to describe patients with difficulties with intimacy and a broad range of behavioral peculiarities. Fairbairn focused on depersonalization, derealization, disturbances in the perception of reality, detachment, and isolation. Guntrip similarly described the traits of derealization, depersonalization, disembodiment, autistic thinking, and a fragmented self-identity. In *DSM-III* (APA, 1980) these cognitive and perceptual symptoms were tied into the schizotypal category, whereas the interpersonal difficulties were made central to its narrower conception of schizoid personality disorder (SPD).

DSM-IV-TR (APA, 2000) notes that those with SPD are characteristically detached from and uninterested in social relationships. People with SPD may choose careers or hobbies that allow them to avoid contact with other people, and they typically are uninterested in developing intimate or sexual relationships. In addition, those with SPD have a flatness of affect that leads others to experience them as cold and aloof. Not only do they derive little pleasure from sensory or interpersonal experiences, they are also usually unmoved by the disapproval of others. They might claim that they do not experience strong emotions, whether positive or negative. Further, people with SPD may fail to respond to social cues, such as a smile, leading others to perceive them as self-absorbed, socially inept, or conceited.

SPD is consistently comorbid with schizotypal and avoidant PDs (Bernstein et al., 1995). Within the Five-Factor Model, SPD is thought to reflect extremely low scores on the extraversion facets of sociability and warmth (Trull, 1992).

Schizotypal Personality Disorder

Formerly classified in *DSM-III* (APA, 1980) as a borderline spectrum disorder, schizotypal personality disorder (STPD) was later identified as a disorder independent of BPD (APA, 1987) and placed within the realm of the schizophrenia spectrum disorders. The diagnosis of STPD has its roots in research with two distinct sets of populations (clinical and familial), and therefore, may represent an especially heterogeneous category. From clinical populations, Rado (1953), Hoch and Polatin (1949), Meehl (1962), and Spitzer, Endicott, and Gibbon (1979) described patients whose symptomatology resembled that of patients with schizophrenia, yet lacked the severity and frank psychosis of schizophrenia. On the other hand, in their work with nonclinical populations in the Danish adoption studies, Kety and colleagues (e.g., Kety, Rosenthal, Wender, & Schulsinger, 1968) noted borderline schizophrenic symptoms in nonpsychotic relatives of schizophrenia patients. Several authors (e.g., Bergman, Silverman, Harvey, Smith, & Siever, 2000) have suggested that familial samples may differ from clinically selected samples by presenting with more negative symptoms (e.g., social isolation and impaired functioning), whereas clinical samples are better characterized by positive, psychoticlike symptoms (e.g., eccentricity, ideas of reference, and socially inappropriate behavior).

According to *DSM-IV-TR* (APA, 2000), STPD is characterized by a pattern of marked interpersonal deficits, discomfort with close relationships, behavioral eccentricities, and distortions in perception and thinking. The *DSM* notes that individuals with STPD will often seek treatment for anxiety, depression, or other affective dysphoria. Although persons with this disorder may experience transient psychotic episodes, they must be distinguished from those with Axis I psychotic disorders that feature more persistent delusions and hallucinations. Ideas of reference are a common feature of STPD, as are odd beliefs such as magical thinking, extreme superstition, or a preoccupation with paranormal phenomena. In addition, people with STPD might have perceptual distortions such as bodily illusions or sensory alterations, and many have odd thought and speech patterns. For example, their speech might be excessively vague, abstract, or loose, yet still maintain basic coherence. They often appear uncomfortable and act peculiar in social situations, and their affective expression is frequently constricted or inappropriate.

STPD is frequently comorbid with eating disorders and psychotic disorders on Axis I (Oldham et al., 1995) and borderline, avoidant, paranoid, and schizoid PDs (Bernstein et al., 1995) on Axis II. Marinangeli et al. (2000) found that STPD was the most frequently co-occurring PD, as it was significantly comorbid with all PDs except for avoidant and dependent in their study. There is also evidence that the concurrent diagnosis of BPD amplifies schizotypal symptoms (Jacobsberg, Hymowitz, Barasch, & Frances, 1986).

Cluster B Personality Disorders (Dramatic-Erratic)

Antisocial Personality Disorder

Traits and behaviors corresponding to antisocial personality disorder (ASPD) have been described by Pinel (1809), Maudsley (1874), Meyer (1957), Kraepelin (1921), Schneider (1923), and Rush (1827), using such terms as *sociopath, psychopath, deviant, amoral, moral insanity,* and *dissocial.* The term *antisocial personality disorder* was introduced by the American Psychiatric Association in 1980 with the publication of *DSM-III,* and represented an attempt to operationalize the much-maligned term of psychopathy. The criteria were derived from empirical research based on Robins's (1966) seminal work. As defined by *DSM-IV-TR* (APA, 2000), antisocial PD is a pervasive pattern of irresponsible behavior and disregard for the rights of others that begins by childhood or early adolescence. People with this disorder repeatedly engage in unlawful and/or reckless behavior. Frequently victimizing others and blaming their victims for their own fate, they typically lack remorse for having hurt or mistreated another person. "They had it coming" is a common rationalization for victimizing others. Alternatively, a person with this disorder might minimize the negative consequences of their actions or blame others for being weak or foolish. Those with ASPD are prone to impulsiveness, irritability, and aggressiveness that often lead to physical fights or assault, and they have a reckless disregard for the safety of themselves or others. In addition, they might repeatedly fail to honor work or financial obligations, or display other evidence of consistent and extreme irresponsibility. Manipulativeness, deceitfulness, and dishonesty are also central features of this disorder, often making collateral sources of information necessary for accurate diagnosis.

In order to be diagnosed with ASPD, the *DSM* system requires that an individual must be at least 18 years old and must have met at least some criteria for conduct disorder prior to age 15. Such criteria may include the destruction of property, theft, lying, aggressive behavior toward people and/or animals, or other serious violations of rules or the rights of others. The essential feature of ASPD is that this pattern of antisocial behavior begins during childhood and continues into adulthood. Although ASPD is the only PD in *DSM-III* (APA, 1980) to have been based on empirical research and the diagnosis has shown adequate levels of interrater reliability in routine clinical practice (Mellsop, Varghese, Joshua, & Hicks, 1982), it has been criticized for overemphasizing criminal acts and deemphasizing the general personality features of psychopathy described by Cleckley (1964/1976) in his classic book the *Mask of Sanity* (Hare, Hart, & Harpur, 1991).

In terms of comorbidity, ASPD is frequently comorbid with borderline (Becker, Grilo, Edell, & McGlashan, 2000), narcissistic (Oldham et al., 1992), histrionic (Lilienfeld, VanValkenburg, Larntz, & Akiskal, 1986), and schizotypal PDs (Marinangeli et al., 2000). On Axis I, research has demonstrated that ASPD has a particularly strong association with substance use disorders (Kessler et al., 1997).

Histrionic Personality Disorder

Histrionic personality disorder (HPD) has its early roots in Hippocrates' writings more than 2,000 years ago on "hysteria" in women, thought to be caused by a "wandering womb" (Veith, 1977). Historically, the term hysteria has been applied primarily to describe women with a range of psychological difficulties, including conversion disorders, emotional instability, anxiety, and phobias (Chodoff & Lyons, 1958). Kretschmer (1926) wrote about hysteria in the context of personality, describing the hysterical individual as theatrical and egotistical. Reich (1933) added to this characterization that hysterical individuals displayed extreme fickleness, suggestibility, a tendency toward strong reactions of disappointment, and an attitude toward others that fluctuates between compliance and derogation. Further, Lazare, Klerman, and Armor (1966) described aggression, emotionality, oral aggression, exhibitionism, egocentricity, sexual provocativeness, and the rejection of others as central traits of the hysterical personality.

Hysteria was first officially linked to the term "histrionic personality" in *DSM-II* (APA, 1968), which listed hysterical personality disorder and mentioned histrionic personality disorder parenthetically thereafter. By *DSM-III* (APA, 1980), however, hysterical personality disorder had been completely replaced by histrionic personality disorder (HPD). The core components of HPD include excessive emotionality, attention-seeking behavior, egocentricity, flirtatiousness, seductiveness, and denial of anger or hostility (Horowitz, 1991; Pfohl, 1991). Other characteristics of HPD are extreme gregariousness, manipulativeness, low frustration tolerance, suggestibility, and somatization (Andrews & Moore, 1991; Millon,

1996). In addition, according to *DSM-IV-TR* (APA, 2000), histrionic individuals consistently use their physical appearance in order to draw attention to themselves, spending excessive time, attention, and money on clothes and grooming.

The *DSM-IV-TR* (APA, 2000) notes that the emotional expression of an individual with HPD is often excessive, theatrical, shallow, and rapidly shifting. Public displays of emotion or temper tantrums are common, yet they begin and end too quickly to be perceived as genuine in feeling. In addition, the speech of a person with HPD may be overly impressionistic in style, yet lacking in detail. For instance, strong opinions might be dramatically expressed without giving adequate reasons to support them.

HPD is consistently comorbid with borderline and narcissistic PDs (Becker et al., 2000; Marinangeli et al., 2000; Oldham et al., 1992). Some studies have also found HPD to co-occur substantially with antisocial (Lilienfeld et al., 1986; Marinangeli et al., 2000; Oldham et al., 1992) and dependent (Oldham et al., 1992) PDs and with psychoactive substance use (Oldham et al., 1995).

Narcissistic Personality Disorder

The term *narcissism* derives from the commonly known Greek myth of Narcissus, who, mistaking his own image for another, falls in love with that image and dies when it fails to love him back. Clinical theorists across various orientations describe individuals diagnosed with narcissistic personality disorder (NPD) as characterized by a pervasive pattern of grandiosity, a sense of privilege or entitlement, an expectation of preferential treatment, an exaggerated sense of self-importance, and arrogant or haughty behaviors or attitudes (Westen & Shedler, 1999b). A fragile self-esteem and unconscious feelings of unworthiness are often underlying this inflated exterior.

The sense of entitlement that is central to NPD often precludes the recognition of others' abilities, needs, feelings, or concerns. Individuals with this disorder might discuss their own problems or concerns in lengthy detail, yet react with insensitivity or impatience to the problems of others. Inappropriate and hurtful remarks are frequently uttered by people with NPD, although they are typically oblivious to how these remarks affect others. They might also unconsciously exploit others and believe that the needs and feelings of other people are signs of weakness. To others these individuals appear cold, disinterested, disdainful, snobbish, or patronizing.

NPD is frequently comorbid with antisocial, histrionic, and borderline PDs (Becker et al., 2000; Oldham et al., 1992; Zanarini, Gunderson, Frankenburg, & Chauncey, 1989). In addition, a review by Ronningstam (1996) found trends of comorbidity between NPD and substance use disorders, bipolar disorder, depression, and anorexia nervosa but found no evidence of a significant relationship between NPD and any single Axis I disorder.

Cluster C Personality Disorders (Anxious-Fearful)

Avoidant Personality Disorder

Avoidant personality disorder (AVPD) was a new category added to the *DSM-III* based on Millon's (1981) evolutionary social-learning theory of PDs. According to *DSM-IV-TR* (APA, 2000), persons with AVPD are characterized by pervasive social inhibition and discomfort in social situations, feelings of inadequacy and low self-esteem, and hypersensitivity to criticism or rejection. Although they long for close relationships, they avoid activities that involve interpersonal contact and have difficulty joining group activities. Persons with this disorder assume that other people will be critical and disapproving. They act with restraint in social situations and have difficulty sharing intimate feelings for fear of criticism, disapproval, shame, or ridicule. They have a strong need for certainty and security that severely restricts their ability to become close to others, and they typically are not able to establish new friendships or intimate relationships without the assurance of uncritical acceptance.

People with AVPD frequently feel socially incompetent, personally unappealing, or inferior to others. Therefore, they are reluctant to engage in new activities and they tend to be shy, inhibited, and quiet to avoid attracting attention to themselves. In addition, they are hypervigilant about detecting subtle cues that suggest the slightest criticism or rejection. Because they expect others to disapprove of them, they quickly detect any indication of such disapproval and typically feel extremely hurt. Although AVPD has been conceptualized as linked to schizoid PD and has been found to be comorbid with schizoid PD (Oldham et al., 1992), multidimensional scaling has found AVPD can be discriminated from schizoid PD but not from dependent PD (Widiger, Trull, Hurt, Clarkin, & Frances, 1987). Avoidant PD is also frequently comorbid with dependent PD on Axis II (Oldham et al., 1992) and mood, anxiety, and eating disorders on Axis I (Oldham et al., 1995).

Dependent Personality Disorder

The history of dependent personality disorder (DPD) begins with descriptions of oral dependency by Abraham and Freud. The *DSM-I* (APA, 1952) mentioned what was called "passive-dependent personality," which was virtually synonymous with *DSM-IV* DPD. According to the *DSM-IV-TR* (APA, 2000), the central characteristic of DPD is a pervasive need to be taken care of that begins by early adulthood. People with this disorder have an exaggerated fear that they are incapable of doing things or taking care of themselves on their own, and therefore, rely on other people (usually one person) to help them. They rely heavily on advice and reassurance from others in making decisions. Because of their lack of self-confidence, it is difficult for people with DPD to begin tasks on their own without being assured that someone is supervising them. They may appear to others to be incompetent because they believe that they are inept and they present themselves as such.

DSM-IV-TR (APA, 2000) notes that because of their dependency on others, people with DPD often fail to learn basic independent living skills, and frequently find themselves in abusive or otherwise unbalanced relationships. It is not unusual for people with DPD to feel unrealistically fearful of being abandoned. They are typically passive and unwilling to disagree or become appropriately angry with the person on whom they depend. They will also go to great lengths to secure or maintain the support of another person. People with DPD usually feel highly uncomfortable being alone because of an exaggerated fear of helplessness or the inability to care for themselves. The end of an intimate relationship will often be followed by urgent efforts to replace the person with another source of closeness and support.

DPD is substantially comorbid with mood, anxiety, and psychotic disorders on Axis I (Oldham et al., 1995) and borderline and avoidant PDs on Axis II (Marinangeli et al., 2000; Oldham et al., 1992). DPD is also frequently comorbid with paranoid PD (Marinangeli et al., 2000) and obsessive-compulsive PD (Oldham et al., 1992).

Obsessive-Compulsive Personality Disorder

The modern concept of obsessive-compulsive personality disorder (OCPD) has its roots in Freud's description of the anal personality as one who is excessively orderly, obstinate, and parsimonious (Freud, 1906–1908/1959). Synonymous with anankastic personality disorder in Europe, the *DSM-IV-TR* (APA, 2000) describes OCPD as a pervasive pattern of perfectionism, orderliness, and inflexibility that begins by early adulthood. People with OCPD have an excessive need for control that interferes with their ability to maintain interpersonal relationships or employment. They are typically preoccupied with rules, lists, schedules, or other minor details (Abraham, 1921). Their rigidity, inflexibility, and stubbornness often prevent them from accepting any new ideas or alternative ways of doing things, creating difficulty in both work and personal relationships.

In addition, the *DSM* notes that individuals with OCPD often sacrifice personal relationships in favor of work, and become obsessively devoted to productivity. They hold both themselves and others to unrealistic standards of morality, ethics, or values. They are also reluctant to delegate tasks to others because they insist that everything be done their own way. Their excessive attention to trivial details, however, often interferes with their ability to complete a task (Horney, 1950).

Although individuals with obsessive-compulsive PD usually have difficulty expressing emotion (Horney, 1950), Bailey (1998) notes that they are subject to dichotomous thinking, magnification, catastrophizing, and displays of anger, frustration, and irritability. The *DSM* further notes that individuals with OCPD might be reluctant to throw away worthless and unsentimental objects for fear that they might be needed at a later date. Furthermore, people with this disorder might hoard money and tightly control their spending, believing that money should be saved for a future catastrophe.

In terms of comorbidity, the results of studies on OCPD are inconsistent. Although Marinangeli et al. (2000) found that OCPD co-occurs significantly with several other PDs, including borderline, narcissistic, histrionic, paranoid, and schizotypal PDs, Oldham et al. (1992) only found significant comorbidity with dependent PD on Axis II. Investigations of the relationship between OCPD and Axis I obsessive-compulsive disorder (OCD) have also yielded mixed results, with some researchers finding significant co-occurrence (Aubuchon & Malatesta, 1994; Baer & Jenike, 1992; Skodol, et al., 1995) and others failing to find a strong relationship between these disorders (Black, Noyes, Pfohl, Goldstein, & Blum, 1993; Joffe, Swinson, & Regan, 1988). Pfohl and Blum (1991) reviewed the literature on OCD and OCPD and concluded that the majority of patients with OCD do not meet criteria for OCPD. Further, for those with OCD with concurrent PD diagnosis, OCPD occurs no more frequently than any other PD. The authors concluded that there was not enough information to support a meaningful relationship between OCD and OCPD. Clinically, the symptoms in OCPD tend to be ego syntonic, whereas the symptoms in OCD tend to be ego dystonic.

EPIDEMIOLOGY

Prevalence rates for PDs in the general population range from approximately 6 percent to 20 percent (APA, 1994; Black et al., 1993; Bodlund, Ekselius, & Lindstrom, 1993; de Girolamo & Dotto, 2000; Drake, Adler, Vaillant, 1988; Ekselius, Tillfors, Furmark, & Fredrikson, 2001; Klein et al., 1995;

Lenzenweger, Loranger, Korfine, & Neff, 1997; Maier, Lichtermann, Klingler, Heun, & Hallmayer, 1992; Moldin, Rice, Erlenmeyer-Kimling, & Squires-Wheeler, 1994; Reich, Yates, & Nduaguba, 1989; Samuels, Nestadt, Romanoski, Folstein, & McHugh, 1994; Torgersen, Kringlen, & Cramer, 2001; Zimmerman & Coryell, 1990). There are almost no community prevalence data on PDs from countries other than the United States, the United Kingdom, Germany, Norway, and Australia.

In primary care settings, Casey and Tyrer (1990) found that about a third of the people attending general practitioners had a personality disorder. The vast majority of patients were not presenting for personality difficulties but presented as problematic medical patients (Emerson, Pankratz, Joos, & Smith, 1994). Although the whole range of PDs were present in these samples, patients with Cluster C PDs are the most common PDs to be encountered in primary care settings (Moran, Jenkins, Tylee, Blizard, & Mann, 2000).

Rates of PDs are generally much higher in clinical populations. Studies using structured diagnostic assessments have found that 20 percent to 40 percent of psychiatric outpatients and about 50 percent of psychiatric inpatients meet criteria for a personality disorder (for overviews, see de Girolamo & Reich, 1993; Dowson & Grounds, 1995; Moran, 1999). However, again PDs are rarely the primary focus of treatment.

Studies on the prevalence of specific PDs have found rates for paranoid PD ranging from 0.4 percent to 3.3 percent; schizoid, 0.5 percent to 0.9 percent; schizotypal, 0.6 percent to 5.6 percent; histrionic, 1.3 percent to 3.0 percent; narcissistic, 0 percent to 5.3 percent; antisocial, 0.2 percent to 3.7 percent; avoidant, 0 percent to 1.3 percent; dependent, 1.6 percent to 6.7 percent; and obsessive compulsive, 1.7 percent to 6.4 percent (Baron, Gruen, Asnis, & Lord, 1985; Coryell & Zimmerman, 1989; Drake & Vaillant, 1985; Kendler & Gruenberg, 1982). Nestadt et al. (1990) examined the prevalence of histrionic PD as part of the NIMH Epidemiological Catchment Area Program. Using *DSM-III-R* criteria, they found a prevalence rate of 2.1 percent for HPD in the general population. Contrary to general belief, men and women were equally affected with the disorder. The most consistently studied personality disorder in community studies has been antisocial PD, which has a lifetime prevalence of between 2 percent and 3 percent, and is more common in men, younger people, those of low socioeconomic status, single individuals, the poorly educated and those living in urban areas (Moran, 1999).

Research has generally shown that individuals diagnosed with PDs are likely to be single (Moran et al., 2000; Samuels et al., 2002). These studies have found that PDs are generally more common in younger age groups (particularly the 25 to 44 year age group) and equally distributed between men and women (one exception is that of ASPD, which is more commonly diagnosed in men). At a community level, personality disordered individuals are more likely to suffer from alcohol and drug problems. In addition, they are also more likely to experience adverse life events, such as relationship difficulties, housing problems and long-term unemployment (Moran, 1999).

Several studies have found PDs to be inversely related to age, such that younger age groups are more likely to meet diagnostic criteria than older age groups (e.g., Ekselius et al., 2001). However, Abrams and Horowitz (1996) concluded that the prevalence of PDs in the elderly (older than age 50) was approximately 10 percent across studies from 1980 to 1994, with no overall decrease in the frequency of personality disorder diagnosis with age. If PDs are indeed less common in the elderly, there are several possible explanations for this trend. Fishbain (1991) suggested that early mortality in those with PD due to impulsive and sensation-seeking behavior might lead to fewer observed cases in elderly samples. Alternatively, improvement for treated PD patients may extend over a long period of time after release. Stone, Hurt, and Stone (1987) postulated that patients improved by the second decade after discharge from treatment. Furthermore, neurodevelopmental and neurochemical changes that decrease impulsivity and aggression over the life span may be responsible for a decline in PDs in the elderly (Elliott, 1992; Morgan, May, & Finch, 1987). Supporting this theory is evidence that neuroticism and extraversion decrease with age (e.g., McCrae et al., 1999), which might suggest greater stability and impulse control as people grow older. Other authors have suggested that the current PD classifications may not be as applicable to adults older than age 50 (Clarkin, 1998), as evidenced by the predominance of PD-NOS in this age group (Abrams & Horowitz, 1996).

ETIOLOGY

The empirical data on the etiology of PDs is extremely limited and complicated by the fact that PDs are a heterogeneous group of disorders. Therefore, there is no universal agreement on their etiology. Initial etiological theories of PDs, particularly disorders like narcissistic and histrionic PDs, were mainly derived from psychodynamic object relations theorists (Kernberg, 1975; Kohut, 1971, 1977; Masterson, 1990). Most of the work in this area was based on inferences drawn in clinical settings from patients' recollections of childhood family dynamics and/or the analysis of transference. Other prominent theories include Millon's evolutionary-based social-learning theory. Recently, Fonagy (Fonagy, Gergely, Jurist, & Target, 2002) and Schore (1994), from a psychoanalytic frame, have discussed the development of PDs based on a combination of object relations theory with a more explicit integration of empirical findings from developmental psychology.

Most theories of PDs acknowledge that they are at least partially genetically determined (Siever & Davis, 1991; Torgersen et al., 2000) and that temperamental and behavioral abnormalities during childhood can precede their development (Depue & Lenzenweger, 2005; Paris, 2000; Posner et al., 2002; Rutter, 1987). These predispositions are believed to interact with environmental experience to shape personality during the early years of development (Rutter, 1987). Environmental factors are believed to range in severity and influence as a function of biological predispositions and protective factors. Traumas can include serious abuse such as physical and sexual abuse, abandonment and betrayal, emotional and physical neglect, and inconsistent emotional care. For example, Johnson et al. (1999) found that abused or neglected children were more than four times at risk of developing PD than those who were not abused or neglected. However, given the rates of abuse in PD samples and the fact that the majority of PD patients do not have histories of physical or sexual abuse, abuse is better conceptualized as a risk factor rather than as causal. These findings suggest that more subtle environmental factors may also be operating. For example, Nash et al. (1993) found that when the shared relationship between sexual abuse and pathological family environment was controlled for, only a pathological family environment accounted for increased pathology in sexually abused women. Weaver and Clum (1993) found that parental overinvolvement predicted personality pathology even after controlling for sexual abuse.

Although a number of researchers have suggested that PDs are partially genetically determined (Siever & Davis, 1991; Torgersen et al., 2000), the evidence is mixed (Nigg & Goldsmith, 1994). A number of studies have focused on the heritability of facets of personality that are relevant to PDs such as neuroticism or extroversion. Few studies have examined the heritability of specific PD diagnoses (Cadoret & Stewart, 1991; Cadoret et al., 1995; Kendler & Walsh, 1995; Torgersen et al., 1993). Findings from the few studies to date suggest that schizotypal PD has a strong genetic link to schizophrenia and that antisocial PD appears to have both genetic and environmental bases.

Using the Dimensional Assessment of Personality Problems (DAPP), Jang, Livesley, & Vernon, (1996) reported the heritability of specific traits related to personality pathology ranging from 45 percent for rejection through 56 percent for callousness. With regard to narcissism, the heritability of the specific traits ranged from 37 percent for grandiosity to 50 percent for need for approval. Torgersen et al. (2000) examined heritability in 92 MZ and 129 DZ twin pairs using the SCID-II. They found 45 percent concordance in MZ and 9 percent in DZ twins using a broad definition of the narcissistic PD (three or more criteria met). Heritability estimates were 60 percent for overall personality disorder diagnosis, 37 percent for Cluster A, 60 percent for Cluster B, and 62 percent for Cluster C. Specific PD heritability was 79 percent for narcissistic and 78 percent for obsessive-compulsive PDs. However, these estimates were determined using broadly defined diagnoses, best fitting models never included shared environmental effects, and the interviewers interviewed both twins and were not blind to zygosity status. All three of these limitations are known to inflate estimates of heritability. Another important limitation includes the absence of a clear definitive phenotype, which is a prerequisite for the establishment of inheritance. Lack of diagnostic clarity (e.g., misdiagnosis, overlap) will inevitably lead to spurious estimates of heritability (Jang & Vernon, 2001).

PDs appear to fall along a continuum of heritability, with schizotypal most strongly linked to genetic influences, antisocial linked to both environmental and genetic factors, and borderline and narcissistic typically showing the smallest estimates of heritability. Given the contradictory findings and limitations of the study designs, it is safe to say that the heritability of certain PDs like borderline and narcissistic, although reasonable to posit, is uncertain at this time and there is clearer evidence for environmental contributions to the development of these disorders. Paris (1993) suggested that the etiology of PDs is unlikely to be underpinned by simple, linear, narrow-causal processes; complex interactive processes between variables are likely to be involved in the etiology of PDs. Much work remains in order to understand the etiological significance of genetic and environmental inputs in the development of PDs.

COURSE, COMPLICATIONS, AND PROGNOSIS

PDs are thought to have an onset in late adolescence or early adulthood (APA, 2000) and are assumed to persist throughout the life span, although there is a relative paucity of empirical evidence that supports these notions (Clarkin, 1998). Recent research suggests that personality can change significantly over time (Seivewright, Tyrer, & Johnson, 2002), and PDs might not be as temporally stable as once thought (Lenzenweger, Johnson, & Willett, 2004; Shea et al., 2002). Seivewright et al. (2002) assessed a group of personality disordered patients at baseline and later at 12-year follow-up and found that whereas Cluster B traits decreased with time, Cluster A and Cluster C traits actually became more pronounced. Further, Shea and Yen (2003) concluded in their review of three longitudinal studies that PDs had higher remission rates than Axis I anxiety disorders.

Although PD diagnosis during childhood or adolescence has demonstrated short-term stability (Mattanah, Becker, Levy, Edell, & McGlashan, 1995), it is not as likely to be stable over longer periods of time (Bernstein et al., 1993; Grilo, Becker, Edell, & McGlashan, 2001; Korenblum, Marton, Golembeck, & Stein, 1990). However, Axis II pathology during childhood and adolescence increases the odds of adult PD within the same cluster (Kasen, Cohen, Skodol, Johnson, & Brook, 1999).

Generally, research has demonstrated that people with Cluster A disorders do not typically improve significantly over time (Paris, 2003). Reich et al. (1989) found that whereas those with Cluster B disorders tended to improve with age, no such age cohort effect was found for patients with Cluster A disorders. Similarly, Seivewright et al. (2002) concluded that patients with Cluster A disorders did not improve significantly at 12-year follow-up. However, some treatment gains have been documented for persons with schizotypal PD. For example, one study found that 13 patients with STPD showed marked improvement at 14-year follow-up (Plakun, Burkhardt, & Muller, 1985). In another long-term follow-up study, outcomes for patients with STPD were better than outcomes for patients with schizophrenia, yet STPD patients continued to experience interpersonal difficulties and half were unemployed at follow-up (McGlashan, 1986). There is evidence that the capacity for object relatedness, emotional warmth, and empathy in patients with STPD is related to better outcomes (McGlashan, 1986; Stone, 1983). McGlashan (1986) found that STPD patients who also had borderline PD had better outcomes than those with pure schizotypal personality disorder. McGlashan postulated that the object-seeking factor in BPD might contribute to a greater capacity for interpersonal relatedness for the schizotypal patient, and hence, contribute to better long-term outcomes.

There is evidence that many patients with antisocial and borderline PD recover as they grow older (Abrams & Horowitz, 1996), although they typically continue to experience severe interpersonal dysfunction and other forms of psychopathology (Paris, 2003). Black, Baumgard, and Bell (1995) followed antisocial patients from 16 to 45 years and found that upon long-term follow-up, most no longer met criteria for ASPD, yet the majority still experienced relationship and work-related problems.

Narcissistic PD may also remit with age, although some authors have suggested that these patients may eventually express somatic complaints (Demopoulos et al., 1996). Kernberg (1976) suggested that narcissism declines with age and older patients with NPD can become more treatable in later years of life. Supporting this hypothesis, Plakun (1991) reported close to normal functioning in narcissistic patients at 14-year follow-up. Similarly, Ronningstam, Gunderson, and Lyons (1995) found that at only a three-year follow-up with narcissistic patients, only a minority still met criteria for NPD. However, both of these studies concerned patients who were formerly hospitalized, and may not accurately represent the course of pure NPD that is normally seen in outpatient settings.

Research has generally shown that Cluster C disorders do not remit with age (Paris, 2003; Reich et al., 1989; Seivewright et al., 2002). At 12-year follow-up with Cluster C personality disordered patients, Seivewright et al. (2002) found that characteristic Cluster C traits had actually increased over time. Further, these patients showed increases in isolation and dysphoria, and developed significant Axis I mood and anxiety disorder symptomology.

ASSESSMENT AND DIAGNOSIS

Assessment

For obvious reasons, both researchers who study PDs and clinicians who treat individuals with PDs have been concerned about the assessment of PDs. However, the assessment of PDs has been highly controversial. Important conceptual issues remain unanswered. Broadly speaking there are five procedures available for PD assessment. Millon and Davis (2000) outlined these as self-report inventories, rating scales and checklists, clinical and structured interviews, projective techniques, and neurocognitive/physiological measurements (neurotransmitter or hormone levels). At this point, there is little evidence for the specificity or sensitivity of neurocognitive or psychophysiological measures for assessing or diagnosing PDs, although these types of measures are useful for studying the basic psychopathology of PDs and as concrete markers of relevant constructs (e.g., impulsivity).

With regard to self-report instruments for PDs, the most widely used in assessing PDs are the Millon Clinical Multiaxial Inventory (MCMI-III; Millon, Millon, & Davis, 1994), the fourth edition of the Personality Diagnostic Questionnaire (PDQ-4; Hyler, Kellman, Oldham, & Skodol, 1992), the Personality Assessment Inventory (PAI; Morey, 1991), and the Dimensional Assessment of Personality Pathology–Basic Questionnaire (Livesley, Jackson, & Schroeder, 1992; Livesley, Reiffer, Sheldon, & West, 1987). Other personality disorder measures include the Schedule of Nonadaptive and Adaptive Personality (SNAP; Clark, 1993), the OMNI Personality Inventory (OMNI; Loranger, 2002), the Personality Inventory Questionnaire (PIQ-II; Widiger, 1987), the Wisconsin Personality Disorder Inventory (WIPSI-IV; Klein, Benjamin, Rosenfeld, & Treece, 1993), and the Minnesota Multiphasic Personality Inventory 2–Personality Disorder Scales (MMPI 2-PD; Butcher, Dahlstrom, Graham, Tellegen, & Kraemmer, 1989).

Some theorists have recently suggested that because PDs can be conceptualized as maladaptive and inflexible expressions of basic dimensions of personality (Wiggins & Pincus, 1989), the Five-Factor Model (FFM) of personality may be relevant to assessing PDs (Widiger & Trull, 1992). Although controversial (Davis & Millon, 1993; Westen, 1996), a review of a number of studies (Widiger, Trull, Clarkin, Sanderson, & Costa, 2002) suggests that it is possible to describe PDs in terms of the FFM. However, Shedler and Westen (2004) examined the comprehensiveness of the FFM as compared to an expanded criteria set. Using the items restricted to the FFM, the factor structure could be replicated on a clinical sample. Nevertheless, they found that the expanded criteria set provided a conceptually richer factor solution that did not resemble the FFM. They concluded that the FFM was useful for layperson descriptions of personality; however, it omits important clinical constructs and does not capture the complexity of personality pathology.

Overall, self-report measures appear best suited either for assessing PDs at the dimensional level, particularly to examine multidimensional aspects of PDs, or as a screening measure for identifying individuals who might be likely to have a PD, but these measures are much less useful for diagnosing a specific personality disorder (Trull & Larson, 1994).

There are a number of structured interviews for *DSM* PDs, including the Structured Interview for *DSM* Personality Disorders–Revised (SIDP-R; Pfohl, Blum, & Zimmerman, 1997), Structured Clinical Interview for *DSM-III-R* Personality Disorders (SCID-II; First, Spitzer, Robert, Gibbon, & Williams, 1995), International Personality Disorders Examination (IPDE; Loranger, 1999), Personality Disorder Interview-IV (PDI-IV; Widiger, Mangine, Corbitt, Ellis, & Thomas, 1995), Diagnostic Interview for Personality Disorders (DIPD-IV; Zanarini, Frankenburg, Sickel, & Yong, 1996), and the Personality Assessment Schedule (PAS; Tyrer & Alexander, 1988). Diagnostic interviews exist for some specific PDs, including the Revised Diagnostic Interview for Borderlines (DIB-R; Zanarini et al., 1989), the Diagnostic Interview for Narcissistic Patients (Gunderson, Ronningstam, & Bodkin, 1990), and the Hare Psychopathy Checklist-Revised (PCL-R; Hare, 1991). There are substantial differences between the interviews, with some organized thematically (e.g., work, relationships; IPDE, SIDP-R), and others organized with respect to *DSM* categories (e.g., DIPD, SCID-II). In terms of questioning, the SCID-II is the most straightforward, the IPDE requires the interviewer to tease out the veracity of patients' reports with follow-up questions, and the PIQ-II employs vignettes and probes to elicit traits. All of these interviews emphasize that patients' self-assessments should not be taken at face value and require considerable judgment and latitude on the part of the clinician. Numerous studies have found disappointing diagnostic concordance when comparing two or more interviews (for a review, see Perry, 1992). The general finding is that the SCID-II is more liberal, whereas the IPDE is more conservative in terms of number of diagnoses given.

There are a number of checklist and rating scales that can be completed by clinicians, including the Personality Assessment Form (PAF; Shea, Glass, Pilkonis, Watkins, & Docherty, 1987), the Shedler-Westen Assessment Procedure (SWAP; Westen & Shedler, 1999a, 1999b), Personality Adjective Checklist (PACL; Strack, 1987), and the Millon Personality Diagnostic Checklist (MPDC). The PAF (Shea et al., 1987) presents a brief paragraph that describes important features of each personality disorder, which is rated on a six-point scale by an evaluator. The PAF is not a structured interview in that it does not provide systematic assessment or questions for evaluation. The SWAP (Westen & Shedler, 1999b) is a 200-item q-set of personality descriptive statements designed to quantify clinical judgment. Clinicians are directed to arrange the 200 items (presented on separate index cards) into eight categories with a fixed distribution ranging from those that are not descriptive of the patient to those that are highly descriptive of the patient. One important finding using the SWAP is a reduction of comorbidity (Westen & Shedler, 1999b). Clinician ratings on the SWAP have also been shown to be related to those of independent raters.

Rorschach and other projective tests are under renewed criticism for their alleged empirical inadequacies (Wood, Nezworski, Lilienfeld, & Garb, 2003). Although many of the criticisms levied are reasonable, the Rorschach and other projective measures are not inherently invalid as there are many valid scoring systems developed (Levy, Meehan, Auerbach, & Blatt, 2005). Nevertheless, there is no comprehensive projective measure scoring system to directly assess the *DSM* PD construct. Projective measures like the Rorschach and the Thematic Apperception Test have been used to study PDs and to clinically assess constructs related to PDs. A number of researchers have used projectives to differentiate PD patients from schizophrenic patients or to distinguish between different PDs (e.g., narcissistic versus borderline). Exner

(1969) has discussed the pair response as an indicator of narcissism, and he later developed the Egocentricity Index (EGOI) as an index of excessive self-concern. Harder (1979) constructed a projective narcissism scale for use with the Early Memory Test, the Thematic Apperception Test, and the Rorschach. The validity of the EGOI scale as a measure of narcissism is equivocal at best (Hilsenroth, Fowler, Padawer, & Handler, 1997; Nezworski & Wood, 1995), and the Harder scale has not gained widespread acceptance. A number of studies have examined Rorschach variables as they relate to the diagnosis of narcissism (Berg, Packer, & Nunno, 1993; Farris, 1988; Gacono, Meloy, & Berg, 1992; Hilsenroth, Hibbard, Nash, & Handler, 1993; Hilsenroth et al., 1997). Findings from these studies are difficult to interpret; however, consistent with the writings of Kernberg (1975) and Kohut (1971), NPD patients generally look healthier psychologically than patients with BPD.

Diagnosis

The *DSM* system purports to be atheoretical in its approach to conceptualizing PDs; however, it has been argued that it is polythetic, resulting in significant heterogeneity (Clarkin, 1998; Fong, 1995; Livesley, 2001). In addition, the evidence for the clusters is mixed with some studies providing empirical support (Widiger et al., 1987; Zimmerman & Coryell, 1990) and others failing to support this grouping (Livesley et al., 1992; Moldin et al., 1994; Plutchick, Conte, & Karasu, 1994; Widiger et al., 1991).

Numerous studies have found extensive overlap between *DSM* PDs despite the fact that these diagnostic categories were conceptualized as distinct (for review, see Blatt & Levy, 1998). The majority of patients with a personality disorder meet criteria for more than one PD, and behavioral criteria relating to different *DSM* PDs are substantially intercorrelated. Different investigators report that the average number of diagnosable PDs for an individual patient range from 2.8 to 4.6 (Blatt & Levy, 1998). It is not uncommon for patients to meet criteria for as many as seven or even more *DSM* PDs. The extensive overlap between *DSM* Axis II diagnoses suggests that the specific types of PDs based solely on symptoms and signs may not be the most efficient or meaningful way to describe PDs (Blatt & Levy, 1998; Westen, 1997). However, findings regarding the comorbidity of PDs are difficult to interpret because there are few adequate studies examining comorbidity in epidemiological samples. Most studies used convenience samples from treatment centers rather than randomly selected community samples, which introduces bias.

Many authors argue that the existing diagnostic criteria for PDs are imprecise, and some suggest a prototype approach to the classification of personality pathology (Livesley, 1986; Westen, 1997). In such an approach, the most prototypical behavioral qualities of a disorder form the center of a diagnostic category, whereas less descriptive behaviors form the periphery. Ideally, this method of classification would reduce overlap between PD criteria and lead to more precise diagnoses.

Comorbidity with Axis I disorders is also common in patients with PDs (Keown, Holloway, & Kuipers, 2002). In a study of the relationship between *DSM-III* Axis I and Axis II diagnoses, PDs were most associated with substance use disorders, anxiety disorders, and/or somatoform disorders, and were least associated with psychotic and major affective illnesses (Koenigsberg, Kaplan, Gilmore, & Cooper, 1985). At the cluster level, Oldham et al. (1995) found that those with Cluster A PDs had significantly increased odds of a concurrent Axis I psychotic disorder but did not show increased odds of having concurrent mood, anxiety, substance abuse, or eating disorders. Cluster B and C PDs were significantly associated with increased odds of anxiety, eating, and psychotic disorders. Cluster B disorders have also been shown to have a particularly strong relationship with alcohol abuse and dependence, and Cluster C disorders seem to be strongly related to anxiety and somatoform disorders (Tyrer, Gunderson, Lyons, & Tohen, 1997).

Symptomatically related Axis I and Axis II diagnoses tend to co-occur, and their comorbidity is likely to be highly relevant to clinical assessment and outcome. For instance, several researchers have found a strong relationship between social phobia and avoidant PD (Herbert, Hope, & Bellack, 1992; Skodol et al., 1995). In addition, many authors have noted that dependent, avoidant, and histrionic PDs are associated with phobic avoidance and agoraphobia (Chambless, Renneberg, Goldstein, & Gracely, 1992; Mavissakalian & Hamann, 1986; Reich, Noyes, & Troughton, 1987). Such relationships can provide clues to the etiological pathways of disorders, although it is difficult to determine the direction of causality (if there is a causal link at all). For example, dependent PDs may contribute to the development of phobias and avoidant behaviors. Alternatively, phobic avoidance may lead to dependent behavior patterns, thereby contributing to the development of dependent PDs (Reich et al., 1987).

IMPACT ON ENVIRONMENT

PDs are associated with high rates of substance abuse, impulsivity, suicidal actions, and the use of medical and psychiatric services (Brodsky, Malone, Ellis, Dulit, & Mann, 1997; Ekselius et al., 2001; Moran et al., 2000; O'Boyle &

Brandon, 1998), and thus, have a considerable impact on both individuals and society. Moran et al. (2000) found that those with PDs are more likely than those without PDs to attend their general medical practitioner on an emergency basis. Reich, Boerstler, Yates, and Nduaguba (1989) found that medical service utilization was positively correlated with the number of disordered personality traits. Saarento et al. (1998) found that PD diagnoses were the best predictor of repeated episodes of psychiatric hospitalization. In addition, Bongar, Peterson, Golann, and Hardiman (1990) found that chronically suicidal patients accounted for more than 12 percent of all emergency room visits. Even when *ICD-10* unstable PD (corresponding to BPD in the *DSM-IV*) was excluded, Ekselius et al. (2001) still found that those with PDs reported significantly more impulsive alcohol abuse and suicidal threats than those without PDs. Further, because the treatment of PD remains relatively underavailable (Keown et al., 2002), PDs put considerable strain on psychiatric resources when existing treatments fail to make lasting and significant changes. A survey of Australian psychiatrists found that although patients with PDs represented only 6 percent of the patients in treatment, they accounted for 13 percent of the psychiatrists' treatment time (Andrews & Hadzi-Pavlovic, 1988).

Research has also shown that those with PDs are significantly more psychologically impaired (Bodlund et al., 1998; Ekselius et al., 2001; Nakao, Gunderson, Phillips, & Tanaka, 1992; Reich, Boerstler, et al., 1989; Samuels et al., 1994) and more likely to lack social support (Ekselius et al., 2001) than individuals without PDs. Personality pathology has been found to predict future psychiatric hospitalization and drug abuse (Levy et al., 1999) and later psychological distress and functional impairment (Bernstein et al., 1993). Further, PDs are associated with occupational difficulties and unemployment (Bland, Stebelsky, Orn, & Newman, 1988), marital dissolution (McCranie & Kahan, 1986), violence, and criminal behaviors (Berman, Fallon, & Coccaro, 1998; Johnson et al., 2000).

TREATMENT IMPLICATIONS

Patients with PDs are notoriously difficult to treat. Improvement for patients with PDs typically consists of finding new and more adaptive ways of coping with maladaptive personality traits, rather than the complete remittance of symptoms and the achievement of normal functioning (Paris, 2003). Few controlled studies exist on treatment outcomes for specific PDs, and most have focused on BPD exclusively. A naturalistic outcome study evaluating intensive inpatient treatment for patients with various "severe" PDs (mostly borderline) yielded positive results at discharge and one-year follow-up (Gabbard et al., 2000). Most of the patients in this study received some form of psychopharmacologic treatment in addition to intensive group therapy, individual psychotherapy, and psychoeducation.

A meta-analysis by Perry, Banon, and Ianni (1999) suggests that psychotherapy is an effective treatment for PDs and may be associated with up to a sevenfold faster rate of recovery in comparison with the natural history of disorders. A recent meta-analysis examined the effectiveness of psychodynamic therapy and cognitive behavioral therapy (CBT) in the treatment of PDs (Leichsenring & Leibing, 2003). The study found that psychodynamic therapy yielded a large overall effect size of 1.46, with effect sizes of 1.08 for self-report measures and 1.79 for observer-rated measures. This contrasted with CBT in which the corresponding values were 1.00, 1.20, and .87, respectively. However, these studies are difficult to interpret because the studies differ, even within the same therapy group, in terms of therapy content, patient diagnosis, length of treatments, outcome assessments and other variables. Another finding was that the longer the treatment the greater the effect size.

There are a number of controlled studies for avoidant PD (Alden, 1989; Alden & Capreol, 1993; Marzillier, Lambert, & Kellett, 1976; Stravynski, Belisle, Marcouiller, & Lavallee-Yvon, 1994; Stravynski, Marks, & Yule, 1982; Stravynski et al., 1989). Overall, these studies suggest that improvements can be found with treatments that employ social skills training alone or in combination with exposure and cognitive techniques; however, many patients did not show clinically significant improvement or generalization to other contexts. There is one study examining antisocial PD (Woody, McLellan, Luborsky, & O'Brien, 1985), in which depressed opiate addicts with ASPD were compared to nondepressed opiate addicts with ASPD. They found that the presence of depression and the capacity to form a therapeutic alliance were good prognostic indicators in terms of outcome.

There are also a number of uncontrolled studies that suggest promising treatment approaches. Barber, Morse, Krakauer, Chittams, and Crits-Christoph (1997) found that a supportive-expressive psychodynamic psychotherapy was effective for treating both obsessive-compulsive and avoidant PDs. At the end of one year of treatment, 85 percent of OCPD patients and more than 60 percent of AVPD patients no longer met criteria for the disorders.

To date, there have been no controlled or uncontrolled outcome studies for histrionic, dependent, schizotypal, schizoid, narcissistic, passive-aggressive, or paranoid PDs. However, a number of studies have used samples that included a mixture of PDs (Diguer et al., 1993; Hellerstein et al., 1998;

Karterud et al., 1992; Monson, Odland, Faugli, Daae, & Eilertsen, 1995; Rosenthal, Muran, Pinsker, Hellerstein, & Winston, 1999; Turkat, 1990; Winston, Laikin, Pollack, & Samstag, 1994; Winston et al., 1991). Usually these studies excluded patients with BPD. Although these studies generally show improvement in treated patients, particularly with the brief psychodynamic treatments, these studies are difficult to interpret in terms of specific PDs because they do not denote specific diagnostic cohorts. Recently Svartberg, Stiles, and Seltzer (2004) reported findings from an RCT examining the treatment of Cluster C PDs. They compared a short-term psychodynamic treatment with a cognitive behavioral treatment (CBT) and found significant reduction in symptomatology for the psychodynamic group but not the CBT group (although there were no between group differences between the two groups). Hardy et al. (1995) report the outcome for a subsample of patients with Cluster C PDs who had participated in a larger study comparing interpersonal-psychodynamic psychotherapy with cognitive therapy (CT) for major depression. Findings indicated that Cluster C patients continued to show more severe symptomatology than non-Cluster C patients if they received dynamic therapy, but not if they received CT.

There is strong evidence that the presence of PD negatively affects the outcome of treatment for Axis I disorders (Hirschfeld et al., 1998; Reich & Vasile, 1993; Seivewright et al., 1998; Shea, Widiger, & Klein, 1992; Skodol, Oldham, & Gallaher, 1999). For example, researchers have repeatedly found that patients treated for major depressive disorder who also have PD have worse outcomes than those without PD (e.g., Burns and Nolen-Hoeksema, 1992; Diguer et al., 1993; Fiorot, Boswell, & Murray, 1990; Greenberg, Craighead, Evans, & Craighead, 1995; Shea et al., 1990; Sullivan, Joyce, & Mulder, 1994; Thompson, Gallagher, & Czirr, 1988; Zimmerman, Coryell, Pfohl, Corenthal, & Stangl, 1986). PDs have had similar deleterious effects on treatment outcome for anxiety disorders (e.g., Chambless et al., 1992; Hermesh, Shahar, & Munitz, 1987; Mavissakalian & Hamann, 1986; Nurnberg et al., 1989; Turner, 1987), including obsessive-compulsive disorder (Jenike, Baer, Minichiello, Schwartz, & Carey, 1986), and may worsen the severity of Axis I symptomology (Dreesen, Arntz, Luttels, & Sallaerts, 1994).[1] Recently, Westen and Morrison (2001) critiqued the external validity of controlled outcome studies, noting that the vast majority of RCTs for major depression and anxiety disorders exclude patients with comorbid PDs, even though comorbidity studies suggest that upward of 50 percent of these patients have one or more PDs. Examining the RCTs that did include PD patients indicates that the presence of PDs negatively affects the outcome of these Axis I disorders (Pilkonis & Frank, 1988; Shahar et al., 2003; Shea et al., 1990). Given these findings, clinicians who consider Axis I mood disorder diagnoses or anxiety disorder diagnoses to be primary and PDs to be less relevant for treatment planning may be seriously mistaken.

In conclusion, the classification and assessment of PDs remain controversial; issues regarding the nature of categorization or dimensionality of PDs and the extensive comorbidity between PDs and with Axis I disorders continue to be central concerns for researchers and limit the conclusions that can be drawn from outcome studies. There are a number of manualized treatments for different PDs, for specific clusters, and for mixed PDs. Uncontrolled studies suggest that psychodynamic, behavioral, and interpersonal approaches may be helpful to these patients. At present, the most conclusive evidence exists for the behavioral treatment of avoidant PD, psychodynamic and cognitive therapy treatments for Cluster C disorders, psychodynamic treatment for mixed PDs, and supportive-expressive psychotherapy for opiate-addicted antisocial patients, particularly when comorbid with depression. Little, however, is known about the specific mechanisms of action in these treatments. Studying the mechanisms of change in the treatment of PDs is of utmost importance (see Levy, Clarkin, & Kernberg, in press). Bateman and Fonagy (2004) suggest that common mechanisms of action to most tested treatments for PDs may include the provision of a coherent model in the context of a well-structured treatment, focused efforts at compliance to the treatment and connection with the therapist, and the explicit targeting of problematic symptoms.

NOTE

1. It should be noted, however, that there are a few studies that have not found personality disorders to have a negative influence on the effects of therapy for anxiety disorders (e.g., Dreessen et al., 1994). Variations in outcomes between studies can be due to several methodological differences, including assessment methods, study design, type of treatment utilized, and other procedural divergences (for a review, see Dreessen et al., 1994).

REFERENCES

Abraham, K. (1921). Contributions to the theory of the anal character (D. Byan & A. Strachey, Trans.). In E. Jones (Ed.), *Selected papers of Karl Abraham* (pp. 370–392). London: Hogarth.

Abrams, R. C., & Horowitz, S. V. (1996). Personality disorders after age 50: A meta-analysis. *Journal of Personality Disorders, 10* (3), 271–281.

Alden, L. (1989). Short-term structured treatment for avoidant personality disorder. *Journal of Consulting and Clinical Psychology, 57*(6), 756–764.

Alden, L., & Capreol, M. (1993). Avoidant personality disorder: Interpersonal problems as predictors of treatment response. *Behavior Therapy, 24,* 357–376.

American Psychiatric Association. (1952). *Diagnostic and statistical manual of mental disorders.* Washington, DC: Author.

American Psychiatric Association. (1968). *Diagnostic and statistical manual of mental disorders* (2nd ed.). Washington, DC: Author.

American Psychiatric Association. (1980). *Diagnostic and statistical manual of mental disorders* (3rd ed.). Washington, DC: Author.

American Psychiatric Association. (1987). *Diagnostic and statistical manual of mental disorders* (3rd ed., rev.). Washington, DC: Author.

American Psychiatric Association. (2000). *Diagnostic and statistical manual of mental disorders* (4th ed., text rev.). Washington, DC: Author.

Andrews, G., & Hadzi-Pavlovic, D. (1988). The work of Australian psychiatrists, circa 1986. *Australian and New Zealand Journal of Psychiatry, 22*(2), 153–165.

Andrews, J., & Moore, S. (1991). Social cognition in the histrionic/overconventional personality. In P. A. Magaro (Ed.), *Cognitive bases of mental disorders* (pp. 11–76). Newbury Park, CA: Sage.

Angus, L., & Marziali, E. (1988). A comparison of three measures for the diagnosis of borderline personality disorder. *American Journal of Psychiatry, 145,* 1453–1454.

Aubuchon, P. G., & Malatesta, V. J. (1994). Obsessive compulsive patients with comorbid personality disorder: Associated problems and response to a comprehensive behavior therapy. *Journal of Clinical Psychiatry, 5,* 448–453.

Baer, L., & Jenike, M. A. (1992). Personality disorders in obsessive compulsive disorder. *Psychiatric Clinics of North America, 15,* 803–812.

Bailey, G. R. (1998). Cognitive-behavioral treatment of obsessive-compulsive personality disorder. *Journal of Psychological Practice, 4*(1), 51–59.

Barber, J. P., Morse, J. Q., Krakauer, I. D., Chittams, J., & Crits-Christoph, K. (1997). Change in obsessive-compulsive and avoidant personality disorders following time-limited supportive-expressive therapy. *Psychotherapy, 34*(2), 133–143.

Baron, M., Gruen, R., Asnis, L., & Lord, S. (1985). Familial transmission of schizotypal and borderline personality disorders. *American Journal of Psychiatry, 142,* 927–934.

Bateman, A., & Fonagy, P. (2004). Mentalization-based treatment of BPD. *Journal of Personality Disorders, 18*(1), 36–51.

Becker, D. F., Grilo, C. M., Edell, W. S., & McGlashan, T. H. (2000). Comorbidity of borderline personality disorder with other personality disorders in hospitalized adolescents and adults. *American Journal of Psychiatry, 157*(12), 2011–2016.

Bender, D., Dolan, R., Skodol, A., Sanislow, C., Dyck, I., McGlasgan, T., et al. (2001). Treatment utilization by patients with personality disorders. *American Journal of Psychiatry 158*(2), 295–302.

Berg, J. L., Packer, A., & Nunno, V. J. (1993). A Rorschach analysis: Parallel disturbance in thought and in self/object representation. *Journal of Personality Assessment, 61,* 311–323.

Bergman, A. J., Silverman, J. M., Harvey, P. D., Smith, C. J., & Siever, L. J. (2000). Schizotypal symptoms in the relatives of schizophrenia patients: An empirical analysis of the factor structure. *Schizophrenia Bulletin, 26*(3), 577–586.

Berman, M., Fallon, A., & Coccaro, E. (1998). The relationship between personality psychopathology and aggressive behavior in research volunteers. *Journal of Abnormal Psychology, 107*(4), 651–658.

Bernstein, D. P., Cohen, P., Velez, C. N., Schwab-Stone, M., Siever, L. J., & Shinsato, L. (1993). Prevalence and stability of *DSM-III-R* personality disorders in a community-based survey of adolescents. *American Journal of Psychiatry, 150,* 1237–1243.

Bernstein, D. P., Useda, D., & Siever, L. J. (1995). Paranoid personality disorder: Review of the literature and recommendations for *DSM-IV*. *Journal of Personality Disorders, 7*(1), 53–62.

Black, D. W., Baumgard, C. H., & Bell, S. E. (1995). A 16- to 45-year follow-up of 71 men with antisocial personality disorder. *Comprehensive Psychiatry, 36*(2), 130–140.

Black, D. W., Noyes, R., Pfohl, B., Goldstein, R. B., & Blum, N. (1993). Personality disorder in obsessive-compulsive volunteers, well comparison subjects, and their first-degree relatives. *American Journal of Psychiatry, 150*(8), 1226–1232.

Bland, R., Stebelsky, G., Orn, H., & Newman, S. (1988). Psychiatric disorders and unemployment in Edmonton. *Acta Psychiatrica Scandinavica, 77*(Suppl. 338), 72–80.

Blatt, S. J., & Levy, K. N. (1998). A psychodynamic approach to the diagnosis of psychopathology. In J. W. Barron (Ed.), *Making diagnosis meaningful: Enhancing evaluation and treatment of psychological disorders* (pp. 73–109). Washington, DC: American Psychological Association.

Bleuler, E. (1929). Zeitschrift-fuer-die-Gesamte-Neurologie-und-Psychiatrie. *A contribution to biopsychology/Ein Stueck Biopsychologie, 121,* 476–486.

Bodlund, O., Ekselius, L., & Lindstrom, E. (1993). Personality traits and disorders among psychiatric outpatients and normal subjects on the basis of the SCID screen questionnaire. *Nordic Journal of Psychiatry, 47*(6), 425–433.

Bodlund, O., Ottosson, H., Ekselius, L., Grann, M., Von-Knorring, L., Kullgren, G., et al. (1998). *DSM-IV* and *ICD-10* personality disorders: A comparison of a self-report questionnaire (DIP-Q) with a structured interview. *European Psychiatry, 13*(5), 246–253.

Bongar, B., Peterson, L. G., Golann, S., & Hardiman, J. J. (1990). Self-mutilation and the chronically suicidal patient: An examination of the frequent visitor to the psychiatric emergency room. *Annals of Clinical Psychiatry, 2,* 217–222.

Brodsky, B., Malone, K., Ellis, S., Dulit, R., & Mann, J. (1997). Characteristics of borderline personality disorder associated with suicidal behavior. *American Journal of Psychiatry, 154*(12), 1715–1719.

Burns, D., & Nolen-Hoeksema, S. (1992). Therapeutic empathy and recovery from depression in cognitive behavioral therapy: A structural equation model. *Journal of Consulting and Clinical Psychology, 60*(3), 441–449.

Butcher, J. N., Dahlstrom, W. G., Graham, J. R., Tellegen, A., & Kaemmer, B. (1989). *Minnesota Multiphasic Personality Inventory-2 (MMPI-2): Manual for administration and scoring.* Minneapolis: University of Minnesota Press.

Cadoret, R., & Stewart, M. (1991). An adoption study of attention deficit/hyperactivity/aggression and their relationship to adult antisocial personality. *Comprehensive Psychiatry, 32*(1), 73–82.

Cadoret, R. J., Yates, W. R., Troughton, E., Woodworth, G., & Stewart, M. A. (1995). Genetic-environmental interaction in the genesis of aggressivity and conduct disorders. *Archives of General Psychiatry, 52*(11), 916–924.

Casey, P. R., & Tyrer, P. (1990). Personality disorder and psychiatric illness in general practice. *British Journal of Psychiatry, 156,* 261–265.

Chambless, D., Renneberg, B., Goldstein, A., & Gracely, E. (1992). MCMI-diagnosed personality disorders among agoraphobic outpatients: Prevalence and relationship to severity and treatment outcome. *Journal of Anxiety Disorders, 6,* 193–211.

Chodoff, P., & Lyons, H. (1958). Hysteria, the hysterical personality and "hysterical" conversion. *American Journal of Psychiatry, 114,* 734–740.

Clark, L. A. (1993). *Schedule for Nonadaptive and Adaptive Personality: Manual for administration, scoring and interpretation.* Minneapolis: University of Minnesota Press.

Clark, L., Livesley, W., & Morey, L. (1997). Personality disorder assessment: The challenge of construct validity. *Journal of Personality Disorders, 11,* 205–231.

Clarkin, J. F. (1998). Research findings on the personality disorders. *In Session: Psychotherapy in Practice, 4*(4), 91–102.

Cleckley, H. E. (1976). The mask of sanity. St. Louis, MO: Mosby. (Original work published 1964)

Coryell, W. H., & Zimmerman, M. (1989). Personality disorder in the families of depressed, schizophrenic, and never-ill probands. *American Journal of Psychiatry, 146*(4), 496–502.

Davis, R., & Millon, T. (1993).The Five-Factor Model for personality disorders: Apt or misguided? *Psychological-Inquiry, 4,* 104–109.

de Girolamo, G., & Dotto, P. (2000). Epidemiology of personality disorders. In M. G. Gelder, J. J. Lopez-Ibor, & N. C. Andreasen (Eds.), *New Oxford textbook of psychiatry* (pp. 959–964). New York: Oxford University Press.

de Girolamo, G., & Reich, J. H. (1993). *Personality disorders: Epidemiology of mental disorders and psychosocial problems.* Geneva, Switzerland: World Health Organization.

Demopoulos, C., Fava, M., McLean, N. E., Alpert, J. E., Nierenberg, A. A., & Rosenbaum, J. F. (1996). Hypochondriacal concerns in depressed outpatients. *Psychosomatic Medicine, 58,* 314–320.

Depue, R. A., & Lenzenweger, M. F. (2005). A neurobehavioral dimensional model of personality disturbances. In J. F. Clarkin & M. F. Lenzenweger (Eds.), *Major theories of personality disorder* (2nd ed., pp. 391–453). New York: Guilford Press.

Diguer, L., Luborsky, L., Luborsky, E., McLellan, A., Woody, G., & Alexander, L. (1993). Psychological health-sickness (PHS) as a predictor of outcomes in dynamic and other psychotherapies. *Journal of Consulting and Clinical Psychology, 61*(4), 542–548.

Dowson, J. H., & Grounds, A. T. (1995). *Personality disorders: Recognition and clinical management.* New York: Cambridge University Press.

Drake, R. E., Adler, D. A., & Vaillant, G. E. (1988). Antecedents of personality disorders in a community sample of men. *Journal of Personality Disorders, 2,* 60–68.

Drake, R. E., & Vaillant, G. E. (1985). A validity study of Axis II of *DSM-III. American Journal of Psychiatry, 142*(5), 553–558.

Dreessen, L., Arntz, A., Luttels, C., & Sallaerts, S. (1994). Personality disorders do not influence the results of cognitive behavior therapies for anxiety disorders. *Comprehensive Psychiatry, 35*(4), 265–274.

Ekselius, L., Tillfors, M., Furmark, T., & Fredrikson, M. (2001). Personality disorders in the general population: *DSM-IV* and *ICD-10* defined prevalence as related to sociodemographic profile. *Personality and Individual Differences, 30,* 311–320.

Elliott, F. (1992). Violence: The neurologic contribution: An overview. *Archives of Neurology, 49,* 595–603.

Emerson, J., Pankratz, L., Joos, S., & Smith, S. (1994). Personality disorders in problematic medical patients. *Psychosomatics, 35*(5), 469–473.

Exner, J. (1969). Rorschach responses as an index of narcissism. *Journal of Projective Techniques and Personality Assessment 33,* 324–333.

Fairbairn, W. R. D. (1994). *Psychoanalytical studies of the personality.* London: Routledge. (Original work published 1952)

Farris, M. (1988). *Differential diagnosis of borderline and narcissistic personality disorders: Primitive mental states and the Rorschach.* Madison, CT: International Universities Press.

Fiorot, M., Boswell, P., & Murray, E. (1990). Personality and response to psychotherapy in depressed elderly women. *Behavior, Health, and Aging, 1,* 51–53.

First, M., Spitzer, R., Robert, L., Gibbon, M., & Williams, J. (1995). The Structured Clinical Interview for *DSM-III-R* Personality Disorders (SCID-II): I. Description. *Journal of Personality Disorders, 9,* 83–91.

Fishbain, D. A. (1991). Personality disorder diagnosis in old age. *Journal of Clinical Psychiatry, 52,* 477–8.

Fonagy, P., Gergely, G., Jurist, E., & Target, M. (2002). *Affect regulation, mentalization, and the development of the self.* New York: Other Press.

Fong, M. L. (1995). Assessment and *DSM-IV* diagnosis of personality disorders: A primer for counselors. *Journal of Counseling and Development, 73,* 635–639.

Freud, S. (1925). *Collected papers: Case histories.* Oxford, England: Hogarth. (Original work published 1909)

Freud, S. (1959). Character and anal eroticism. In J. Strachey (Ed. & Trans.), *The standard edition of the complete psychological works of Sigmund Freud* (Vol. 9, pp. 169–175). London: Hogarth. (Original work published 1906–1908)

Gabbard, G. O., Coyne, L., Allen, J. G., Spohn, H., Colson, D. B., & Vary, M. (2000). Evaluation of intensive inpatient treatment of patients with severe personality disorders. *Psychiatric Services, 51*(7), 893–898.

Gacono, C. B., Meloy, R., & Berg, J. L. (1992). Object relations, defensive operations, and affective states in narcissistic, borderline, and antisocial personality disorder. *Journal of Personality Assessment, 59,* 32–49.

Greenberg, M., Craighead, W., Evans, D., & Craighead, L. (1995). An investigation of the effects of comorbid Axis II pathology on outcome of inpatient treatment of unipolar depression. *Journal of Psychopathology and Behavioral Assessment, 17,* 305–321.

Grilo, C., Becker, D., Edell, W., & McGlashan, T. (2001). Stability and change of *DSM-III-R* personality disorder dimensions in adolescents followed up 2 years after psychiatric hospitalization. *Comprehensive Psychiatry, 42,* 364–368.

Grilo, C. M., McGlashan, T. H., & Oldham, J. M. (1998). Course and stability of personality disorders. *Journal of Practical Psychiatry and Behavioral Health, 4,* 61–75.

Gunderson, J., Ronningstam, E., & Bodkin, A. (1990). The Diagnostic Interview for Narcissistic Patients. *Archives of General Psychiatry, 47,* 676–680.

Gunderson, J., Zanarini, M., & Kisiel, C. (1991). Borderline personality disorder: A review of data on *DSM-III-R* descriptions. *Journal of Personality Disorders, 5,* 340–352.

Guntrip, H. (1969). *Schizoid phenomena, object-relations, and the self.* New York: International Universities Press.

Harder, D. (1979). The assessment of ambitious-narcissistic character style with three projective tests: The Early Memories, TAT, and Rorschach. *Journal of Personality Assessment, 43,* 23–32.

Hardy, G., Barkham, M., Shapiro, D., Stiles, W., Rees, A., & Reynolds, S. (1995). Impact of Cluster C personality disorders on outcomes of contrasting brief psychotherapies for depression. *Journal of Consulting and Clinical Psychology, 63*(6), 997–1004.

Hare, R. D. (1991). *The Hare Psychopathy Checklist–Revised.* Toronto, Ontario: Multi-Health Systems.

Hare, R. D., Hart, S. D., & Harpur, T. J. (1991). Psychopathy and the *DSM-IV* criteria for antisocial personality disorder. *Journal of Abnormal Psychology, 100*(3), 391–398.

Hellerstein, D. J., Rosenthal, R. N., Pinsker, H., Samstag, L. W., Muran, J. C., & Winston, A. (1998). A randomized prospective study comparing supportive and dynamic therapies. *Journal of Psychotherapy Practice and Research, 7,* 261–271.

Herbert, J. D., Hope, D. A., & Bellack, A. S. (1992). Validity of the distinction between generalized social phobia and avoidant personality disorder. *Journal of Abnormal Psychology, 101*(2), 332–339.

Hermesh, H., Shahar, A., & Munitz, H. (1987). Obsessive-compulsive disorder and borderline personality disorder. *American Journal of Psychiatry, 144,* 120–121.

Hilsenroth, M. J., Fowler, C., Padawer, J. R., & Handler, L. (1997). Narcissism in the Rorschach revisited: Some reflections on empirical data. *Psychological Assessment, 9,* 113–121.

Hilsenroth, M., Hibbard, S., Nash, M., & Handler, L. (1993). A Rorschach study of narcissism, defense, and aggression in borderline, narcissistic, and Cluster C personality disorders. *Journal of Personality Assessment, 60,* 346–361.

Hirschfeld, R., Russell, J., Delgado, P., Fawcett, J., Friedman, R., Harrison, W., et al. (1998). Predictors of response to acute treatment of chronic and double depression with sertraline or imipramine. *Journal of Clinical Psychiatry, 59,* 669–675.

Hoch, A. (1910). Constitutional factors in the Dementia Praecox Group. *Review of Neurology & Psychiatry, 8,* 463–474.

Hoch, P., & Polatin, P. (1949). Pseudoneurotic forms of schizophrenia. *Psychiatric Quarterly, 23,* 248–276.

Horney, K. (1950). *Neuroses and human growth: The struggle toward self-realization.* New York: Norton.

Horowitz, M. J. (1991). *Hysterical personality style and the histrionic personality disorder.* Northvale, NJ: Aronson.

Hyler, S. E., Kellman, H. D., Oldham, J. M., & Skodol, A. E. (1992). Validity of the Personality Diagnostic Questionnaire–Revised: A replication in an outpatient sample. *Comprehensive Psychiatry, 33,* 73–77.

Jacobsberg, L. B., Hymowitz, P., Barasch, A., & Frances, A. J. (1986). Symptoms of schizotypal personality disorder. *American Journal of Psychiatry, 143*(10), 1222–1227.

Jang, K., Livesley, W., & Vernon, P. (1996). The genetic basis of personality at different ages: A cross-sectional twin study. *Personality and Individual Differences, 21*(2), 299–301.

Jang, K. L., & Vernon, P. A. (2001). Genetics. In W. J. Livesley (Ed.), *Handbook of personality disorders: Theory, research, and treatment* (pp. 177–195). New York: Guilford Press.

Jenike, M., Baer, L., Minichiello, W., Schwartz, C., & Carey, R. (1986). Concomitant obsessive-compulsive disorder and schizotypal personality disorder. *Journal of Clinical Psychiatry, 143,* 530–532.

Joffe, R. T., Swinson, R. P., & Regan, J. J. (1988). Personality features of obsessive-compulsive disorder. *American Journal of Psychiatry, 145,* 1127–1129.

Johnson, J. G., Cohen, P., Brown, J., Smailes, E., & Bernstein, D. P. (1999). Childhood maltreatment increases risk for personality disorders during early adulthood. *Archives of General Psychiatry, 56*(7), 600–606.

Johnson, J. G., Cohen, P., Smailes, E., Kasen, S., Oldham, J. M., & Skodol, A. E. (2000). Adolescent personality disorders associated with violence and criminal behavior during adolescence and early adulthood. *American Journal of Psychiatry, 157,* 1406–1412.

Karterud, S., Vaglum, S., Friis, S., Irion, T., Johns, S., & Vaglum, P. (1992). Day hospital therapeutic community treatment for patients with personality disorders: An empirical evaluation of the containment function. *Journal of Nervous and Mental Diseases, 180,* 238–243.

Kasen, S., Cohen, P., Sokdol, A. E., Johnson, J. G., & Brook, J. S. (1999). Influence of child and adolescent psychiatric disorders on young adult personality disorder. *American Journal of Psychiatry, 156,* 1529–1535.

Kendler, K. S. (1985). Diagnostic approaches to schizotypal personality disorder: A historical perspective. *Schizophrenia Bulletin, 11*(4), 538–553.

Kendler, K. S., & Gruenberg, A. M. (1982). Genetic relationship between paranoid personality disorder and the "schizophrenic spectrum" disorders. *American Journal of Psychiatry, 139,* 1185–1186.

Kendler, K., & Walsh, D. (1995). Schizotypal personality disorder in parents and the risk for schizophrenia in siblings. *Schizophrenia Bulletin, 21*(1), 47–52.

Keown, P., Holloway, F., & Kuipers, E. (2002). The prevalence of personality disorders, psychotic disorders and affective disorders amongst the patients seen by a community mental health team in London. *Social Psychiatry and Psychiatric Epidemiology, 37,* 225–229.

Kernberg, O. (1975). Further contributions to the treatment of narcissistic personalities: A reply to the discussion by Paul H. Ornstein. *International Journal of Psychoanalysis, 56*(2), 245–247.

Kernberg, O. F. (1976). *Borderline conditions and pathological narcissism.* New York: Jason Aronson.

Kessler, R. C., Crum, R. M., Warner, L. A., Nelson, C. B., Schulenberg, J., & Anthony, J. C. (1997). Lifetime co-occurrence of *DSM-III-R* alcohol abuse and dependence with other psychiatric disorder in the National Comorbidity Survey. *Archives of General Psychiatry, 54*(4), 313–321.

Kety, S. S., Rosenthal, D., Wender, P. H., & Schulsinger, F. (1968). The types and prevalence of mental illness in the biological and adoptive families of adopted schizophrenics. *Journal of Psychiatric Research, 6,* 345–362.

Klein, D. N., Riso, L. P., Donaldson, S. K., Schwartz, J. E., Anderson, R. L., Ouimette, P. C., et al. (1995). Family study of early-onset dysthymia: Mood and personality disorders in relatives of outpatients with dysthymia and episodic major depression and normal controls. *Archives of General Psychiatry, 52,* 487–496.

Klein, M., Benjamin, L., Rosenfeld, R., & Treece, C. (1993). The Wisconsin Personality Disorders Inventory: Development, reliability, and validity. *Journal of Personality Disorders, 7,* 285–303.

Koenigsberg, H. W., Kaplan, R. D., Gilmore, M. M., & Cooper, A. M. (1985). The relationship between syndrome and personality disorder in *DSM-III:* Experience with 2,462 patients. *American Journal of Psychiatry, 142,* 207–212.

Kohut, H. (1971). *The analysis of the self.* New York: International Universities Press.

Kohut, H. (1977). *The restoration of the self.* New York: International Universities Press.

Korenblum, M., Marton, P., Golembeck, H., & Stein, B. (1990). Personality status: Changes through adolescence. *Adolescence, 13,* 389–399.

Kraepelin, E. (1904). *Lectures on clinical psychiatry* (T. Johnstone, Trans.). New York: William Wood.

Kraepelin, E. (1921). Zeitschrift-fuer-die-Gesamte-Neurologie-und-Psychiatrie. *Depression/Ueber Entwurtzelung, 63,* 1–8.

Kretschmer, E. (1925). *Physique and character* (2nd ed., rev.). Oxford, England: Harcourt, Brace.

Kretschmer, E. (1926). *Hysteria.* New York: Nervous and Mental Disease Publishers.

Lazare, A., Klerman, G. L., & Armor, D. J. (1966). Oral, obsessive, and hysterical personality patterns: An investigation of psychoanalytic concepts by means of factor analysis. *Archives of General Psychiatry, 14,* 624–630.

Leichsenring, F., & Leibing, E. (2003). The effectiveness of psychodynamic therapy and cognitive behavior therapy in the treatment of personality disorders: A meta-analysis. *American Journal of Psychiatry, 160,* 1223–1232.

Lenzenweger, M., Johnson, M., & Willett, J. (2004). Individual growth curve analysis illuminates stability and change in personality disorder features: The longitudinal study of personality disorders. *Archives of General Psychiatry, 61,* 1015–1024.

Lenzenweger, M., Loranger, A., Korfine, L., & Neff, C. (1997). Detecting personality disorders in a nonclinical population: Application of a 2-stage for case identification. *Archives of General Psychiatry, 54*(4), 345–351.

Levy, K. N., Becker, D. F., Grilo, C. M., Mattanah, J. F., Garnet, K. E., Quinlan, D. M., et al. (1999). Concurrent and predictive validity of the personality disorder diagnosis in adolescent inpatients. *American Journal of Psychiatry, 156,* 1522–1528.

Levy, K. N., Clarkin, J. F., Scott, L. N., & Kernberg, O. F. (in review). Putative mechanisms of change in the treatment of borderline personality disorder with transference focused psychotherapy: What changes in the patient and how does it happen?

Levy, K. N., Meehan, K. B., Auerbach, J. S., & Blatt, S. J. (2005). Concept of the object on the Rorschach scale. The LEA series in personality and clinical psychology. In J. M. Masling & R. F.

Bornstein (Eds.), *Scoring the Rorschach: Seven validated systems* (pp. 97–133). Mahwah, NJ: Erlbaum.

Lilienfeld, S. O., VanValkenburg, C., Larntz, K., & Akiskal, H. S. (1986). The relationship of histrionic personality disorder to antisocial personality and somatization disorders. *American Journal of Psychiatry, 143,* 718–722.

Livesley, J. (1986). Trait and behavioural prototypes of personality disorder. *American Journal of Psychiatry, 143,* 728–732.

Livesley, W. J. (2001). Commentary on reconceptualizing personality disorder categories using trait dimensions. *Journal of Personality, 69*(2), 277–286.

Livesley, W., & Jackson, D. (1986). The internal consistency and factorial structure of behaviors judged to be associated with *DSM-III* personality disorders. *American Journal of Psychiatry, 143,* 1473–1474.

Livesley, W. J., Jackson, D. N., & Schroeder, M. L. (1992). Factorial structure of traits delineating personality disorders in clinical and general population samples. *Journal of Abnormal Psychology, 101*(3), 432–440.

Livesley, W. J., Reiffer, L. I., Sheldon, A. E., & West, M. (1987). Prototypicality ratings of *DSM-III* criteria for personality disorders. *Journal of Nervous and Mental Disease, 175,* 395–401.

Livesley, W. J., Schroeder, M. L., Jackson, D. N., & Jang, K. L. (1994). Categorical distinctions in the study of personality disorder: Implications for classification. *Journal of Abnormal Psychology, 103*(1), 6–17.

Loranger, A. W. (1999). *International Personality Disorder Examination (IPDE) manual.* Odessa, FL: Psychological Assessment Resources.

Loranger, A. W. (2002). *OMNI personality inventory and OMNI-IV personality disorder inventory manual.* Odessa, FL: Psychological Assessment Resources.

Maier, W., Lichtermann, D., Klingler, T., Heun, R., & Hallmayer, J. (1992). Prevalences of personality disorders *(DSM-III-R)* in the community. *Journal of Personality Disorders, 6,* 187–196.

Marinangeli, M. G., Butti, G., Scinto, A., Di Cicco, L., Petruzzi, C., Daneluzzo, E., et al. (2000). Patterns of comorbidity among *DSM-III-R* personality disorders. *Psychopathology, 33*(2), 69–74.

Marzillier, J. S., Lambert, C., & Kellett, J. (1976). A controlled evaluation of systematic desensitization and social skills training for socially inadequate psychiatric patients. *Behavioural Research and Therapy, 14,* 225–238.

Maser, J. D., Kaelber, C., & Weise, R. E. (1991). International use and attitudes toward *DSM-III* and *DSM-III-R:* Growing consensus in psychiatric classification. *Journal of Abnormal Psychology, 100,* 217–279.

Masterson, J. (1990). Psychotherapy of borderline and narcissistic disorders: Establishing a therapeutic alliance (a developmental, self, and object relations approach). *Journal of Personality Disorders, 4*(2), 182–191.

Mattanah, J., Becker, D., Levy, K., Edell, W., & McGlashan, T. H. (1995). Diagnostic stability in adolescents followed up 2 years after hospitalization. *American Journal of Psychiatry, 152,* 889–894.

Maudsley, H. (1874). *Responsibility and mental disease.* New York: Appleton.

Mavissakalian, M., & Hamann, M. (1986). Assessment and significance of behavioral avoidance in agoraphobia. *Journal of Psychopathology and Behavioral Assessment, 8*(4), 317–327.

McCrae, R., Costa, P., de Lima, M., Simoes, A., Ostendorf, F., Angleitner, A., et al. (1999). Age differences in personality across the adult life span: Parallels in five cultures. *Developmental Psychology, 35*(2), 466–477.

McCranie, E., & Kahan, J. (1986). Personality and multiple divorce: A prospective study. *Journal of Nervous and Mental Disease, 174*(3), 161–164.

McGlashan, T. H. (1986). Schizotypal personality disorder: The Chestnut Lodge follow-up study IV. Long-term follow-up perspectives. *Archives of General Psychiatry, 43,* 329–334.

Meehl, P. E. (1962). Schizotaxia, schizotypy and schizophrenia. *American Psychologist, 17,* 827–838.

Mellsop, G., Varghese, F., Joshua, S., & Hicks, A. (1982). The reliability of Axis II of *DSM-III. American Journal of Psychiatry, 139*(10), 1360–1361.

Meyer, A. (1957). *Psychobiology: A science of man.* Springfield, IL: Charles C. Thomas.

Millon, T. (1981). *Disorders of personality: DSM-III, Axis II.* New York: Wiley.

Millon, T. (1985). The MCMI provides a good assessment of *DSM-III* disorders: The MCMI-II will prove even better. *Journal of Personality Assessment, 49,* 379–391.

Millon, T. (1986). On the past and future of the *DSM-III:* Personal recollections and projections. In T. Millon and G. L. Klerman (Eds.), *Contemporary directions in psychopathology: Toward the DSM-IV* (pp. 29–70). New York: Guilford Press.

Millon, T. (1996). *Disorders of personality: DSM-IV and beyond.* New York: Wiley.

Millon, T., & Davis, R. (2000). *Personality disorders in modern life.* New York: Wiley.

Millon, T., Davis, R., Millon, C., Escovar, L., & Meagher, S. (2000). *Personality disorders in modern life.* New York: Wiley.

Millon, T., Millon, C., & Davis, R. (1994). *Millon Clinical Multiaxial Inventory-III.* Minneapolis, MN: National Computer Systems.

Moldin, S. O., Rice, J. P., Erlenmeyer-Kimling, L., & Squires-Wheeler, E. (1994). Latent structure of *DSM-III-R* Axis II psychopathology in a normal sample. *Journal of Abnormal Psychology, 103*(2), 259–266.

Monsen, J., Odland, T., Faugli, A., Daae, E., & Eilertsen, D. E. (1995). Personality disorders: Changes and stability after intensive psychotherapy focusing on affect consciousness. *Psychotherapy Research, 5,* 33–48.

Moran, P. (1999). The epidemiology of antisocial personality disorder. *Social Psychiatry & Psychiatric Epidemiology, 34*(5), 231–242.

Moran, P., Jenkins, R., Tylee, A., Blizard, R., & Mann, A. (2000). The prevalence of personality disorder among UK primary care attenders. *Acta Psychiatrica Scandinavica, 102,* 52–57.

Morey, L. C. (1991). *The Personality Assessment Inventory professional manual.* Odessa, FL: Psychological Assessment Resources.

Morgan, D., May, P., & Finch, C. (1987). Dopamine and serotonin systems in human and rodent brain: Effects of age and neurodegenerative disease. *Journal of the American Geriatrics Society, 35*(4), 334–345.

Nakao, K., Gunderson, J., Phillips, K., & Tanaka, N. (1992). Functional impairment in personality disorders. *Journal of Personality Disorders, 6*(1), 24–33.

Nash, M. R., Hulsey, T. L., Sexton, M. C., Harralson, T. L., & Lambert, W. (1993). Long-term sequelae of childhood sexual abuse: Perceived family environment, psychopathology, and dissociation. *Journal of Consulting and Clinical Psychology, 61*(2), 276–283.

Nestadt, G., Romanoski, A. J., Chahal, R., Merchant, A., Folstein, M. F., Gruenberg, E. M., et al. (1990). An epidemiological study of histrionic personality disorder. *Psychological Medicine, 20*(2), 413–422.

Nestadt, G., Romanoski, A. J., Samuels, J. F., Folstein, M. F., & McHugh, P. R. (1992). The relationship between personality and *DSM-III* Axis I disorders in the population: Results from an epidemiological survey. *American Journal of Psychiatry, 149*(9), 1228–1233.

Nezworski, T., & Wood, J. (1995). Narcissism in the Comprehensive System for the Rorschach. *Clinical Psychology: Science and Practice, 2,* 179–199.

Nigg, J., & Goldsmith, H. (1994). Genetics of personality disorders: Perspectives from personality and psychopathology research. *Psychological Bulletin, 115*(3), 346–380.

Nurnberg, H. G., Raskin, M., Levine, P. E., & Pollack, S. (1989). Borderline personality disorder as a negative prognostic factor in anxiety disorders. *Journal of Personality Disorders, 3*(3), 205–216.

O'Boyle, M., & Brandon, E. (1998). Suicide attempts, substance abuse, and personality. *Journal of Substance Abuse Treatment, 15*(4), 353–356.

O'Boyle, M., & Self, D. (1990). A comparison of two interviews for *DSM-III-R* personality disorders. *Psychiatry Research, 32,* 85–92.

Oldham, J. M., Skodol, A. E., Kellman, H. D., Hyler, S. E., Doidge, N., Rosnick, L., et al. (1995). Comorbidity of Axis I and Axis II disorders. *American Journal of Psychiatry, 152*(4), 571–578.

Oldham, J. M., Skodol, A. E., Kellman, H. D., Hyler, S. E., Rosnick, L., & Davies, M. (1992). Diagnosis of *DSM-III-R* personality disorders by two structured interviews: Patterns of comorbidity. *American Journal of Psychiatry, 149*(2), 213–220.

Paris, J. (1993). Personality disorders: A biopsychosocial model. *Journal of Personality Disorders, 7*(3), 255–264.

Paris, J. (2000). Childhood precursors of borderline personality disorder. *Psychiatric Clinics of North America, 23,* 77–88.

Paris, J. (2003). Personality disorders over time: Precursors, course, and outcome. *Journal of Personality Disorders, 17*(6), 479–488.

Perry, J. C. (1992). Problems and considerations in the valid assessment of personality disorders. *American Journal of Psychiatry, 149,* 1645–1653.

Perry, J. C., Banon, E., & Ianni, F. (1999). Effectiveness of psychotherapy for personality disorders. *American Journal of Psychiatry, 156,* 1312–1321.

Pfohl, B. (1991). Histrionic personality disorder: A review of available data and recommendations for *DSM-IV. Journal of Personality Disorders, 5,* 150–166.

Pfohl, B., & Blum, N. (1991). Obsessive-compulsive personality disorder: A review of available data and recommendations for *DSM-IV. Journal of Personality Disorders, 5*(4), 363–375.

Pfohl, B., Blum, N., & Zimmerman, M. (1997). *Structured Interview for DSM-IV Personality.* Washington, DC: American Psychiatric Press.

Pfohl, B., Coryell, W., Zimmerman, M., & Stangl, D. (1986). *DSM-III* personality disorders: Diagnostic overlap and internal consistency of individual *DSM-III* criteria. *Comprehensive Psychiatry, 27,* 21–34.

Pilkonis, P., & Frank, E. (1988). Personality pathology in recurrent depression: Nature, prevalence, and relationship to treatment response. *American Journal of Psychiatry, 145,* 435–441.

Pilkonis, P. A., Heape, C. L., Ruddy, J., & Serrao, P. (1991). Validity in the diagnosis of personality disorders: The use of the LEAD standard. *Psychological Assessment, 3*(1), 46–54.

Pinel, P. (1809). *Traite medico-philosophique sur l'alienation mentale.* Paris: Brosson.

Plakun, E. M. (1991). Empirical studies on narcissism. In S. M. Mirin, J. T. Gossett, & M. C. Grob (Eds.), *Psychiatric treatment: Advances in outcome research* (pp. 195–212). Washington, DC: American Psychiatric Press.

Plakun, E. M., Burkhardt, P. E., & Muller, J. P. (1985). 14-year follow-up of borderline and schizotypal personality disorders. *Comprehensive Psychiatry, 26*(5), 448–455.

Plutchik, R., Conte, H. R., & Karasu, T. B. (1994, June). *The circumplex structure of personality disorders.* Paper presented at the Society of Psychotherapy Research, Pittsburgh, PA.

Posner, M. I., Rothbart, M., Vizueta, N., Thomas, K., Levy, K., Fossella, J., et al. (2003). An approach to the psychobiology of personality disorders. *Development and Psychopathology, 15,* 1093–1106.

Rado, S. (1953). Dynamics and classification of disordered behavior. *American Journal of Psychiatry, 110,* 406–416.

Reich, J., Boerstler, H., Yates, W., & Nduaguba, M. (1989). Utilization of medical resources in persons with *DSM-III* personality disorders in a community sample. *International Journal of Psychiatry in Medicine, 19,* 1–9.

Reich, J., Noyes, R., & Troughton, E. (1987). Dependent personality disorder associated with phobic avoidance in patients with panic disorder. *American Journal of Psychiatry, 144*(3), 323–326.

Reich, J. H., & Vasile, R. G. (1993). Effect of personality disorders on the treatment outcome of Axis I conditions: An update. *Journal of Nervous and Mental Diseases, 181,* 475–484.

Reich, J., Yates, W., & Nduaguba, M. (1989). Prevalence of *DSM-III* personality disorders in the community. *Social Psychiatry and Psychiatric Epidemiology, 24*(1), 12–16.

Reich, W. (1933). *Charackteranalyse.* Leipzig, Germany: Sexpol Verlag.

Renneberg, B., Goldstein, A. J., Phillips, D., & Chambless, D. L. (1990). Intensive behavioral group treatment of avoidant personality disorder. *Behavior Therapy, 21,* 363–377.

Robins, L. N. (1966). *Deviant children grown up: A sociological and psychiatric study of sociopathic personality.* Baltimore: Williams and Wilkins.

Ronningstam, E., (1996). Pathological narcissism and narcissistic personality disorder in Axis I disorders. *Harvard Review of Psychiatry, 3,* 326–340.

Ronningstam, E., Gunderson, J., & Lyons, M. (1995). Changes in pathological narcissism. *American Journal of Psychiatry, 152*(2), 253–257.

Rosenthal, R. N., Muran, J. C., Pinsker, H., Hellerstein, D., & Winston, A. (1999). Interpersonal change in brief supportive psychotherapy. *Journal of Psychotherapy Practice and Research, 8,* 55–63.

Rush, B. (1827). *Medical inquiries and observations upon the diseases of the mind* (3rd ed.). Philadelphia: Kimber and Richardson.

Rutter, M. (1987). Temperament, personality and personality disorder. *British Journal of Psychiatry, 150,* 443–458.

Saarento, O., Oeiesvold, T., Sytema, S., Goestas, G., Kastrup, M., Loennerberg, O., et al. (1998). The Nordic Comparative Study on Sectorized Psychiatry: Continuity of care related to characteristics of the psychiatric services and the patients. *Social Psychiatry and Psychiatric Epidemiology, 33*(11), 521–527.

Samuels, J., Eaton, W. W., Bienvenu, O. J., III, Brown, C. H., Costa, P. T., Jr., & Nestadt, G. (2002). Prevalence and correlates of personality disorders in a community sample. *British Journal of Psychiatry, 180,* 536–542.

Samuels, J. F., Nestadt, G., Romanoski, A. J., Folstein, M. F., & McHugh, P. R. (1994). *DSM-III* personality disorders in the community. *American Journal of Psychiatry, 151*(7), 1055–1062.

Schneider, K. (1923). *Die psychipathischen Persönlichkeiten* [The Psychopathic Personalities]. Leipzig, Germany: Thieme.

Schore, A. (1994). *Affect regulation and the origin of the self: The neurobiology of emotional development.* Hillsdale, NJ: Erlbaum.

Seivewright, H., Tyrer, P., & Johnson, T. (2002). Change in personality status in neurotic disorders. *Lancet, 359,* 2253–2254.

Shea, M. T., Pilkonis, P. A., Beckham, E., Collins, J. F., Elkin, I., Sotsky, S. M., et al. (1990). Personality disorders and treatment outcome in the NIMH Treatment of Depression Collaborative Research Program. *American Journal of Psychiatry, 147,* 711–718.

Shea, M. T., Stout, R. L., Gunderson, J. G., Morey, L. C., Grilo, C. M., McGlashan, T. H., et al. (2002). Short-term diagnostic stability of schizotypal, borderline, avoidant, and obsessive-compulsive personality disorders. *American Journal of Psychiatry, 169,* 2036–2041.

Shea, M., Widiger, T., Klein, M. (1992). Comorbidity of personality disorders and depression: Implications for treatment. *Journal of Consulting and Clinical Psychology, 60*(6), 857–868.

Shea, M. T., & Yen, S. (2003). Stability as a distinction between Axis I and Axis II disorders. *Journal of Personality Disorders, 17*(5), 373–386.

Shea, T., Glass, D. R., Pilkonis, P. A., Watkins, J., & Docherty, J. P. (1987). Frequency and implications of personality disorders in a sample of depressed outpatients. *Journal of Personality Disorders, 1,* 27–42.

Shedler, J., & Westen, D. (2004). Dimensions of personality pathology: An alternative to the Five-Factor Model. *American Journal of Psychiatry, 161,* 1743–1754.

Siever, L. J., & Davis, K. L. (1991). A psychobiological perspective on the personality disorders. *American Journal of Psychiatry, 148,* 1647–1658.

Skodol, A. E., Gunderson, J. G., Pfohl, B., Widiger, T. A., Livesley, W. J., & Siever, L. J. (2002). The borderline diagnosis I: Psychopathology, comorbidity, and personality structure. *Biological Psychiatry, 51,* 936–950.

Skodol, A. E., Oldham, J. M., & Gallaher P. E. (1999). Axis II comorbidity of substance use disorders among patients referred for treatment of personality disorders. *American Journal of Psychiatry, 156*(5), 733–738.

Skodol, A. E., Oldham, J. M., Hyler, S. E., Stein, D. J., Hollander, E., Gallaher, P. E., et al. (1995). Patterns of anxiety and personality disorder comorbidity. *Journal of Psychiatric Research, 29*(5), 361–374.

Skodol, A. E., Rosnick, L., Kellman, D., Oldham, J. M., & Hyler, S. (1991). Development of a procedure for validating structured assessments of Axis II. In J. M. Oldham (Ed.), *Personality disorders: New perspectives on diagnostic validity* (pp. 43–70). Washington, DC: American Psychiatric Association.

Spitzer, R. L., Endicott, J., & Gibbon, M. (1979). Crossing the border into borderline personality and borderline schizophrenia: The development of criteria. *Archives of General Psychiatry, 36*(1), 17–24.

Stone, M. (1983). Psychotherapy with schizotypal borderline patients. *Journal of the American Academy of Psychoanalysis and Dynamic Psychiatry, 11*(1), 87–111.

Stone, M. H., Hurt, S. W., & Stone, D. K. (1987). The PI 500: Long-term follow-up of borderline inpatients meeting *DSM-III* criteria:

I. Global outcome. *Journal of Personality Disorders, 1,* 291–298.

Strack, S. (1987). Development and validation of an adjective checklist to assess the Millon personality types in a normal population. *Journal of Personality Assessment, 51,* 572–587.

Stravynski, A., Belisle, M., Marcouiller, M., & Lavallee-Yvon, J. (1994). The treatment of avoidant personality disorder by social skills training in the clinic or in real-life setting. *Canadian Journal of Psychiatry, 39,* 377–383.

Stravynski, A., Lesage, A., Marcouiller, M., & Elie, R. (1989). A test of the therapeutic mechanism in social skills training with avoidant personality disorder. *Journal of Nervous and Mental Disease, 177,* 739–744.

Stravynski, A., Marks, I., & Yule, W. (1982). Social skills problems in neurotic outpatients: Social skills training with and without cognitive modification. *Archives of General Psychiatry, 39,* 1378–1385.

Sullivan, P., Joyce, P., & Mulder, R. (1994). Borderline personality disorder in major depression. *Journal of Nervous and Mental Disease, 182*(9), 508–516.

Svartberg, M., Stiles, T., & Seltzer, M. (2004). Randomized, controlled trial of the effectiveness of short-term dynamic psychotherapy and cognitive therapy for Cluster C personality disorders. *American Journal of Psychiatry, 161*(5), 810–817.

Thompson, L., Gallagher, D., & Czirr, R. (1988). Personality disorder and outcome in the treatment of late-life depression. *Journal of Geriatric Psychiatry, 21,* 133–146.

Torgersen, S., Kringlen, E., & Cramer, V. (2001). The prevalence of personality disorders in a community sample. *Archives of General Psychiatry, 58*(6), 590–596.

Torgersen, S., Lygren, S., Oien, P. A., Skre, I., Onstad, S., Edvardsen, J., et al. (2000). A twin study of personality disorders. *Comprehensive Psychiatry, 41*(6), 416–425.

Torgersen, S., Onstad, S., Skre, I., Edvardsen, J., & Kringlen, E. (1993). "True" schizotypal personality disorder: A study of co-twins and relatives of schizophrenic probands. *American Journal of Psychiatry, 150*(11), 1661–1667.

Trull, T. J. (1992). *DSM-III-R* personality disorders and the Five-Factor Model of personality: An empirical comparison. *Journal of Abnormal Psychology, 101*(3), 553–560.

Trull, T., & Larson, S. (1994). External validity of two personality disorder inventories. *Journal of Personality Disorders, 8,* 96–103.

Turkat, I. (1990). *The personality disorders: A psychological approach to clinical management.* Elmsford, NY: Pergamon Press.

Turner, R. (1987). The effects of personality disorder diagnosis on the outcome of social anxiety symptom reduction. *Journal of Personality Disorders, 1*(2), 136–143.

Tyrer, P., & Alexander, J. (1988). Personality assessment schedule. In P. Tyrer (Ed.), *Personality disorders: Diagnosis, management and course* (pp. 43–62). London: Wright.

Tyrer, P., Casey, P., & Gall, J. (1983). Relationship between neurosis and personality disorder. *British Journal of Psychiatry, 142,* 404–408.

Tyrer, P., Gunderson, J., Lyons, M., & Tohen, M. (1997). Extent of comorbidity between mental state and personality disorders. *Journal of Personality Disorders, 11,* 242–259.

Veith, I. (1977). Four thousand years of hysteria. In M. Horowitz (Ed.), *Hysterical personality* (pp. 58–79). New York: Aronson.

Weaver, T., & Clum, G. (1993). Early family environments and traumatic experiences associated with borderline personality disorder. *Journal of Consulting and Clinical Psychology, 61*(6), 1068–1075.

Westen, D. (1996). A model and a method for uncovering the nomothetic from the idiographic: An alternative to the Five-Factor Model? *Journal of Research in Personality, 30,* 400–413.

Westen, D. (1997). Divergences between clinical and research methods for assessing personality disorders: Implications for research and the evolution of Axis II. *American Journal of Psychiatry, 154*(7), 895–903.

Westen, D., & Arkowitz-Westen, L. (1998). Limitations of Axis II in diagnosing personality pathology in clinical practice. *American Journal of Psychiatry, 155*(12), 1767–1771.

Westen, D., & Morrison, K. (2001). A multidimensional meta-analysis of treatments for depression, panic, and generalized anxiety disorder: An empirical examination of the status of empirically supported therapies. *Journal of Consulting and Clinical Psychology, 69*(6), 875–899.

Westen, D., & Shedler, J. (1999a). Revising and assessing Axis II, part I: Developing a clinically and empirically valid assessment method. *American Journal of Psychiatry, 156,* 258–272.

Westen, D., & Shedler, J. (1999b). Revising and assessing Axis II, part II: Toward an empirically based and clinically useful classification of personality disorders. *American Journal of Psychiatry, 156,* 273–285.

Westen, D., & Shedler, J. (2000). A prototype matching approach to diagnosing personality disorders: Toward *DSM-V. Journal of Personality Disorders, 14*(2), 109–126.

Widiger, T. A. (1987). *Personality Interview Questionnaire II (PIQ II).* White Plains, NY: Department of Psychiatry, Cornell Medical Center, Westchester Division.

Widiger, T. A. (2001). Official classification systems. In W. J. Livesley (Ed.), *Handbook of personality disorders: Theory, research, and treatment* (pp. 60–83). New York: Guilford Press.

Widiger, T. A., & Corbitt, E. M. (1995). Antisocial personality disorder. In W. J. Livesley (Ed.), *DSM-IV personality disorders* (pp. 103–126). New York: Guilford Press.

Widiger, T. A., Frances, A. J., Harris, M., Jacobsberg, L. B., Fyer, M., & Manning, D. (1991). Comorbidity among Axis II disorders. Progress in psychiatry, No. 20. In J. Oldham (Ed.), *Personality disorders: New perspectives on diagnostic validity* (pp. 165–194). Washington, DC: American Psychiatric Association.

Widiger, T. A., Frances, A., Spitzer, R. L., & Williams, J. B. W. (1988). The *DSM-III-R* personality disorders: An overview. *American Journal of Psychiatry, 145,* 786–795.

Widiger, T. A., Mangine, S., Corbitt, E. M., Ellis, C. G., & Thomas, G. V. (1995). *Personality Disorder Interview-IV: A semistructured interview for the assessment of personality disorders—Professional manual.* Odessa, FL: Psychological Assessment Resources.

Widiger, T., & Rogers, J. (1989). Prevalence and comorbidity of personality disorders. *Psychiatric Annals, 19,* 132–136.

Widiger, T. A., & Trull, T. J. (1992). Personality and psychopathology: An application of the Five-Factor Model. *Journal of Personality, 60*(2), 363–393.

Widiger, T. A., Trull, T. J., Clarkin, J. F., Sanderson, C., & Costa, P. T. (2002). A description of the *DSM-IV* personality disorders with the Five-Factor Model of personality. In T. A. Widiger & P. T. Costa, Jr. (Eds.), *Personality disorders and the Five-Factor Model of personality* (2nd ed., pp. 89–99). Washington, DC: American Psychological Association.

Widiger, T. A., Trull, T. J., Hurt, S. W., Clarkin, J., & Frances, A. (1987). A multidimensional scaling of the *DSM-III* personality disorders. *Archives of General Psychiatry, 44*(6), 557–563.

Wiggins, J., & Pincus, A. (1989). Conceptions of personality disorders and dimensions of personality. *Psychological Assessment, 1,* 305–316.

Winnicott, D. W. (1951). Transitional objects and transitional phenomena. In *Through pediatrics to psycho-analysis* (pp. 229–242). London: Hogarth.

Winston, A., Laikin, M., Pollack, J., & Samstag, L. (1994). Short-term psychotherapy of personality disorders. *American Journal of Psychiatry, 151*(2), 190–194.

Winston, A., Pollack, J., McCullough, L., Flegenheimer, W., Kestenbaum, R., & Trujillo, M. (1991). Brief psychotherapy of personality disorders. *Journal of Nervous and Mental Diseases, 179,* 188–198.

Wolff, S., Townshend, R., McGuire, R. J., & Weeks, D. J. (1991). "Schizoid" personality in childhood and adult life: II. Adult adjustment and the continuity with schizotypal personality disorder. *British Journal of Psychiatry, 159,* 620–629.

Wood, J. M., & Lilienfeld, S. O. (1999). The Rorschach Inkblot Test: A case of overstatement? *Assessment, 6,* 341–351.

Wood, J. M., Nezworski, M. T., Lilienfeld, S. O., & Garb, H. N. (2003). *What's wrong with the Rorschach? Science confronts the controversial inkblot test.* San Francisco: Jossey-Bass.

Woody, G., McLellan, A., Luborsky, L., & O'Brien, C. (1985). Sociopathy and psychotherapy outcome. *Archives of General Psychiatry, 42,* 1081–1086.

World Health Organization. (1992). *The ICD-10 classification of mental and behavioural disorders. Clinical descriptions and diagnostic guidelines.* Geneva, Switzerland: Author.

Zanarini, M., Frankenburg, F., Chauncey, D., & Gunderson, J. (1987). The Diagnostic Interview for Personality Disorders: Interrater and test-retest reliability. *Comprehensive Psychiatry, 28,* 467–480.

Zanarini, M., Frankenburg, F., Sickel, A. E., & Yong, L. (1996). *The Diagnostic Interview for DSM-IV Personality Disorders (DIPD-IV).* Belmont, MA: McLean Hospital.

Zanarini, M. C., Gunderson, J. G., Frankenburg, F. R., & Chauncey, D. L. (1989). The Revised Diagnostic Interview for Borderlines: Discriminating BPD from other Axis II disorders. *Journal of Personality Disorders, 3,* 110–118.

Zimmerman, M., & Coryell, W. H. (1989). *DSM-III* personality disorder diagnoses in a nonpatient sample: Demographic correlates and comorbidity. *Archives of General Psychiatry, 46*(8), 682–689.

Zimmerman, M., & Coryell, W. H. (1990). Diagnosing personality disorders in the community. A comparison of self-report and interview measures. *Archives of General Psychiatry, 47*(6), 527–531.

Zimmerman, M., & Coryell, W., Pfohl, B., Corenthal, C., & Stangl, D. (1986). The relationship between age and post-dexamethasone cortisol: A test of three hypotheses. *Journal of Affective Disorders, 11,* 185–197.

Zimmerman, M., Pfohl, B., Stangl, D., & Corenthal, C. (1986). Assessment of *DSM-III* personality disorders: The importance of interviewing an informant. *Journal of Clinical Psychiatry, 47*(5), 261–263.

CHAPTER 20

Alcohol Abuse and Dependence

MARILYN J. STRADA, JENNIFER KARMELY, AND BRAD DONOHUE

ALCOHOL ABUSE DISORDERS

The identification, assessment, and treatment of those affected by alcohol abuse and dependence have rapidly progressed since controlled treatment outcome research in this area was initiated in the early 1970s (e.g., Hunt & Azrin, 1973; Sobell & Sobell, 1973). Indeed, when empirically based treatments were first developed, many practicing addiction counselors believed the widely accepted disease concept thought to underlie "alcoholism" was inconsistent with the tenets espoused by these novel approaches. Since this time, there has been an increase in collaboration between researchers and practicing mental health professionals, leading to empirically supported diagnostic criteria, assessment and treatment in this population. For instance, controlled trials have resulted in validated treatments that have been shown to significantly reduce alcohol use and various associated problems (e.g., violence between intimate partners, antisocial conduct, drug use, underemployment, mood and anxiety disorders, family satisfaction and support, problem-solving and communication skills, inattention). Concurrently, there has been unprecedented growth in the psychometric evaluation of dozens of measures developed specifically to better understand the relative strengths and problem areas experienced in alcohol-abusing individuals and their significant others. The purpose of this chapter is to disseminate major developments in the field of alcohol abuse and dependence. In this endeavor, alcohol abuse and dependence will be fully delineated, including its personality characteristics and clinical manifestations. Premorbid personality characteristics that often contribute to the disorder, as well as epidemiology, etiology, course, complications, and prognosis for alcohol disorders, will be underscored prior to discussing empirically derived assessment and treatment methods.

DESCRIPTION OF THE DISORDER AND CLINICAL PICTURE

Alcohol abuse and dependence represent a continuum of severity, with dependence being relatively more severe. According to the text revision of the fourth edition of the *Diagnostic and Statistical Manual of Mental Disorders* (*DSM-IV-TR;* American Psychiatric Association [APA], 2000), alcohol abuse is diagnosed when one of four symptoms is present. The first symptom is predominately associated with deterioration in occupational and social functioning resulting from alcohol use. For instance, occupational tasks previously accomplished punctually and with competence are delayed or insufficiently accomplished (e.g., repeatedly coming late or missing work). Similarly, abusers of alcohol may experience significant declines in the performance of their social roles and maintenance of an appropriate domestic environment. Household activities previously completed on a regular basis (e.g., meal preparation, cleaning and organization, child care) may become increasingly neglected, or preformed by other household members. A second criterion of abuse concerns use of alcohol resulting in risky behavior (e.g., driving a vehicle or using heavy machinery while impaired due to alcohol consumption, unprotected sex, violence, or fatal overdoses resulting most commonly from mixing alcohol with other drugs). The third criterion, legal problems associated with alcohol use, includes being arrested for driving under the influence, disturbing the peace, or any other crime committed while intoxicated. A diagnosis of alcohol abuse may also be warranted when interpersonal problems result from alcohol use (the fourth criterion). Indeed, many significant others are painfully aware of the financial, legal, and emotional consequences that result from abusive drinking patterns but are unsuccessful in their attempts to convince these individuals to abstain from alcohol. Of course, this may lead to conflict between the abuser of alcohol and various family members, employees, and employers.

Alcohol dependence is essentially an exacerbation of abuse symptoms, and usually includes the development of physiological dependence. Indeed, tolerance may develop when the number of GABBA$_A$ receptors increase in response to heavy long-term consumption of alcohol, making it necessary to increase the amount of alcohol consumed per occasion to obtain the same effects that were initially achieved with lower amounts of alcohol. Conversely, the increase of GABBA$_A$ receptors can cause withdrawal symptoms when the individual abruptly ceases consumption, as there is an overabundance of receptors and a relative paucity of GABBA$_A$ neurotransmission. Moreover, as alcohol consumption opens calcium channels on GABBA$_A$ receptors, there is a calming of neural activity on related pathways, creating sedation and decreased inhibition. The abrupt elimination of alcohol creates an increase of activity along the same pathways, resulting in withdrawal symptoms (Valenzuela, 1997). Withdrawal symptoms are diverse and vary in their degree of severity. The most common and basic symptoms of alcohol withdrawal are related to an increase in sympathetic nervous system activation and include autonomic hyperactivity, hand tremors, psychomotor agitation, and general anxiety. Severe and potentially dangerous symptoms include gastric distress (i.e., severe nausea and vomiting), hallucinations, delusions, and grand-mal seizures (Faingold, Knapp, Chester, & Gonzalez, 2004). Alcohol withdrawal symptoms are rapidly alleviated by alcohol consumption, and therefore, alcohol consumption negatively reinforces continued drinking to avoid future discomfort.

The psychosocial symptoms of alcohol dependence are marked by consumption of more alcohol than originally planned during times of use, and the interval of time drinking alcohol increases. In conjunction with an increase in time spent consuming alcohol, the individual who is dependent on alcohol may spend more time recovering from its effects and less time engaged in occupational and social activities (e.g., hobbies, sports, work, family activities, social groups). In refusing to seek out professional assistance, the dependent individual often continues to use alcohol despite an increase in problems related to its use, both psychological and physiological. Along a different vein, the physiological effects of alcohol may act to reinforce the use of other drugs. For instance, Capodanno and Chavaria (1991) reported that alcohol is often used to enhance or alleviate aversive effects of other substances (e.g., cocaine-induced paranoia or anxiety). Alcohol may also be utilized as a sedative when use of stimulants or other substances disrupt the individual's circadian rhythm. Similarly, alcohol may be consumed instead of other central nervous system depressants when these substances are unavailable, mimicking their effects (e.g., alcohol may replace barbiturates as both substances result in sedation and reduce anxiety).

Alcohol disorders are also associated with problems in cognitive processing (e.g., periods of memory loss, commonly referred to as blackouts, are frequently associated with rapid and heavy episodes of alcohol consumption). Nixon (1999) notes that there has been an increasing body of literature over the past two decades indicating that individuals diagnosed with alcohol-related disorders can experience decreased cognitive and neurological functioning in the areas of "abstracting and problem solving, learning and memory, visual-spatial functions, and perceptual motor-skills" (p. 181). Moreover, individuals with an extensive history of alcohol abuse may develop a form of dementia known as Korsakoff's syndrome, which is significantly more profound than the aforementioned cognitive impairments (i.e., irreversible and severe short-term memory impairment and progressive deterioration of long-term memory; Krabbendam et al., 2002). The deterioration of cognitive abilities eventually impacts daily functioning in occupational tasks and management of domestic responsibilities.

Alcohol-related disorders can also induce or exacerbate mental disorders, particularly mood and anxiety disorders (Kessler, Nelson, & McGonagle, 1996). Indeed, chronic alcohol use acts to decrease neural activity and increase the perceived intensity of psychosocial stressors, resulting in depression, or an exacerbation of depression. Individuals with severe depression and schizophrenia are also at risk for developing comorbid alcohol disorders, as alcohol intoxication decreases aversive feelings associated with psychotic episodes that often occur in these disorders. Unfortunately, alcohol use exacerbates positive schizophrenic symptoms (Margolese, Malchy, Negrete, Tempier, & Gill, 2004). Individuals suffering from anxiety disorders are also at greater risk of developing alcohol disorders because alcohol lowers sympathetic nervous system activity (e.g., increased heart rate, sweating, hyperventilation), which is associated with anxiety. This reprieve is negatively reinforcing, and thus increases the likelihood of future alcohol consumption when anxiety is experienced.

Alcohol disorders are commonly found among individuals who evidence impulse control disorders, such as explosive disorder, kleptomania, trichotillomania, pyromania, or pathological gambling (Lejoyeux, Feuche, Loi, Solomon, & Ades, 1998). Indeed, alcohol disinhibits rational thought, and may become a barrier to activities that require effective management of impulses, such as full-time employment, academic degree completion (Paradise & Cauce, 2003), interpersonal conflict, domestic violence (Schafer, Caetano, & Clark, 1998), and violent crimes (Greenfeld, 1998).

Comorbid problems present challenges when attempting to integrate treatment for both substance abuse and mental health problems (Petrakis, Gonzalez, Rosenheck, & Krystal, 2002). Indeed, many practicing substance abuse counselors are insufficiently trained, or not licensed, to treat co-occurring mental health problems, and many mental health professionals do not consider themselves to be competent, or licensed, to treat substance abuse. Fortunately, agencies (e.g., Substance Abuse and Mental Health and Services Administration [SAMHSA], National Institute on Alcohol Abuse and Alcoholism [NIAAA]) have recognized this problem, and are now funding the development and evaluation of treatment programs that address these problems, including training programs.

PERSONALITY DEVELOPMENT AND PSYCHOPATHOLOGY

Alcohol abuse and dependence are often preceded by specific behavioral patterns, often referred to as an "alcoholic" or "alcohol abusing personality type." Cloninger and Sigvardsson (1996) arguably developed the most widely adopted view of the personality structure associated with alcohol misuse. In their dualistic model of alcoholic personality structures, a Type I personality is attributed to both genetic and environmental factors, with the central personality feature being avoidance of anxiety. These individuals tend to avoid novel situations, potential risk, and major life changes, seeking to maintain stability and routine. The onset of alcohol abuse and dependence generally occurs after the age of 25 years, and it is usually subsequent to social drinking and years of controlled use. Problematic drinking arises as a response to periods of overwhelming anxiety, and the negatively perceived biological response to abrupt alcohol cessation is a strong negative reinforcer for maintaining continued use (Stewart, Zvolensky, & Eifert, 2001). Because alcohol consumption relieves anxiety, increased frequency of alcohol use recurs. The user may also feel guilty for drinking and causing other related negative consequences, thus perpetuating the likelihood of further use to relieve resulting stress. As such, the episodes of alcohol abuse are less often a consistent lifestyle pattern than a series of sporadic but severe binges (e.g., periods of extremely heavy alcohol use lasting two or more days with inattention to basic responsibilities). Individuals with a Type I alcoholism profile (many women and some men) may have completed personality development but find that the skills associated with such maturation become subordinate to the use of alcohol as a primary coping mechanism.

Type II alcoholism is depicted as very different from Type I alcoholism. First, its origins are more genetically based, and primarily found in the male population (Jang, Vernon, & Livesley, 2000). Virkkunen and Linnoila (1990) initially noticed a reduced serotonin level in men with early onset alcohol abuse and dependence. Cloninger (1987) examined EEG responses of Type II alcoholics, and found these individuals were relatively impaired in their ability to differentiate novel from ubiquitous stimuli, which corresponded to decreased activity of monoamine oxidase (MAO). He posited that Type II alcoholics compensate for lower levels of MAO activity with spontaneity, sensory driven behavior, and extroversion. Studies involving biological parents and adoptive children have found these neurological differences are heritable primarily from father to son. The onset of Type II alcohol abuse and dependence typically occurs prior to age 25, sometimes as early as adolescence, and it rapidly becomes associated with further inhibition, socialization, and excitement. Indeed, individuals with Type II alcoholism profiles (many men and some women) may never acquire mature traits such as forethought and empathy for others when making decisions. Type II alcoholism often occurs as a part of polysubstance abuse due to ongoing need for sensory stimulation. Distorted thoughts focus on rationalization of their actions, a view of others as unreasonable and constricting, and a false sense of personal invulnerability. These cognitive patterns are reportedly antecedents to alcohol use and associated risk-taking behaviors, which are reinforced by perceived stimulation. This pattern of behavior shares common elements with, and at times coexists with, antisocial personality disorder. Indeed, both personality constructs are often associated with low impulse control, narcissistic tendencies, and profound legal and social consequences.

It should be mentioned, however, that Cloninger's (1987) theory is not without its detractors and nonconfirmatory replications. Fillmore, Leino, and Johnstone (1994), in addition to disputing the analysis utilized, questioned the emphasis placed on genetics and the ramifications that may follow for a group that already faces stigmatization in many cultures. Similarly, Sannibale and Hall (1998) found that, whereas Type II alcoholics did report more antisocial traits, Cloninger's (1987) typology primarily separated individuals by gender but not along the predicted Type I and Type II traits.

Trait theories have also been applied to alcohol abuse disorders. The five traits developed by Costa and McCrea (1989) are often used to describe the personality structure of individuals at risk for alcohol abuse disorders. Costa and McCrea's (1989) traits include emotional stability (calm versus anxious or "neurotic"), extraversion (sociable versus retiring), openness (imaginative versus practical), agreeableness (trusting versus suspicious), and conscientiousness (organized versus disorganized). In young adults, Ruiz, Pincus, and Dickinson (2003) and Loukas, Krull, Chassin, and Carle (2000) found conscientiousness was associated with alcohol abuse as well as facets of extroversion and agreeableness. Loukas and colleagues (2000) found that low levels of agreeableness and elevated levels of neuroticism partially account for the relationship between parental alcohol abuse and their young adult child's alcohol abuse. According to this model, personality structures with a suspicious and combative interpersonal communication style, or intrapersonal insecurity, leave individuals more susceptible to continuing familial patterns of alcohol abuse. This research points to both the biological heritability of traits that account for some portion of vulnerability to alcohol abuse, as well as the environmental factors that account for the rest of the relationship parent-child drinking patterns.

In addition to theories of personality, there are specific predictive factors, which are indicative of a vulnerability to developing alcohol abuse disorders in adolescence or early adulthood. For instance, stress, family conflict, and low level of parental monitoring have all been found to predict adolescent alcohol abuse, which in turn leads to greater incidence of adult alcohol abuse disorders (Bray, Adams, Getz, & Stovall, 2001). Other predictors of substance abuse include parental alcohol abuse (Loukas et al., 2000), child abuse and neglect (Mezzich et al., 1997), sibling substance use, peer substance abuse, and rejection by peers (Kirkcaldy, Siefen, Surall, & Bischoff, 2004).

EPIDEMIOLOGY

Estimates of alcohol consumption in the general population are usually generated from national surveys, often in the form of face-to-face or telephone interviews (National Institute on Alcohol Abuse and Alcoholism [NIAAA], 2000). The National Survey on Drug Use and Health (NSDUH), conducted by U.S. federal government agencies (SAMHSA, 2003), is one of the main sources of epidemiological data on alcohol consumption. In the NSDUH survey, one "drink" is equal to a can or bottle of beer, a glass of wine or wine cooler, a shot of liquor, or an alcoholic mixed drink. The various levels of drinking measured in the survey are current alcohol use (consuming at least one drink during the past 30 days), binge drinking (consuming five or more drinks per incident at least once during the past 30 days), and heavy use of alcohol (consuming five or more drinks per incident on at least 5 days during the past 30 days). The most recent NSDUH (SAMHSA, 2003) reports that alcohol consumption rates vary as a function of age, with individuals aged 21 to 25 reporting the highest rates (70 percent). Similar rates of current alcohol consumption are reported across age groups 26 and 49 years (approximately 60 percent). In addition, rates of current alcohol use vary slightly according to gender among ages 18 years or older (i.e., males 57 percent, females 44 percent). Finally, current alcohol use rates also vary to some extent across various racial/ethnic groups. Caucasian individuals report the highest rate of current alcohol use (i.e., 55 percent), and Asian Americans evidence the lowest rate (i.e., 37 percent).

Binge drinking is less prevalent, as only approximately 23 percent of individuals 12 years or older report engaging in binge drinking, with the highest rate of binge drinking occurring between 21 and 25 years (50 percent). Binge drinking tends to decrease with increased age. These rates also differ according to race/ethnicity. The highest rates of binge drinking were reported by American Indian/Alaska Native (28 percent), Native Hawaiians/Pacific Islanders (25 percent), and Hispanics/Latinos (25 percent).

Traditionally, national surveys have obtained information pertaining only to the consumption of alcohol, as opposed to the extent to which individuals meet criteria for an alcohol-related disorder (APA, 2000). However, this recent version of the NSDUH (SAMHSA, 2003) included questions based on the APA's (2000) *DSM-IV-TR* that permitted estimating the prevalence of substance abuse and dependence. Based on these criteria, it was estimated that almost 8 percent of the population age 12 years or older met criteria for alcohol abuse or dependence. This estimate is slightly higher than the 5 percent prevalence previously reported in the *DSM-IV-TR* (APA, 2000). However, due to the differences in methodology across surveys, it is difficult to ascertain whether this increase is due to actual changes in the population. In addition, it was reported that earlier onset alcohol use is associated with a higher likelihood of meeting criteria for alcohol abuse or dependence. That is, those individuals 18 years or older who had their first drink of alcohol at age 14 years or younger met criteria for an alcohol-related disorder in greater proportion than individuals of the same age who had their first drink at age 18 years or older.

Those individuals who receive treatment for alcohol-related disorders constitute a much smaller portion of the population. Estimates from the NSDUH suggest approximately 1.1 million people (less than 0.5 percent of the population) received treatment for alcohol abuse or dependence from health care programs (e.g., hospital, mental health care center, emergency room). Similarly, approximately 1.5 million individuals 12 years or older received treatment for alcohol problems at a specialty treatment facility (e.g., alcohol rehabilitation facility, inpatient or outpatient mental health care site). Therefore, whereas the prevalence rate of alcohol abuse or dependence may be on the rise, there is a considerable percentage of the population who does not receive treatment (SAMHSA, 2003).

ETIOLOGY

Despite decades of research on alcohol-related disorders, compelling evidence in support of a single underlying causal factor has not surfaced. Indeed alcohol-related disorders are thought to be complex and caused by multiple factors. Several theoretical models of etiology have been hypothesized. Some models of alcohol abuse and dependence conceptualize the disorder as having resulted from many influences. From the moral model perspective, individuals have choices and can decide not to drink. However, they lack willpower to abstain (Peterson, Nisenholz, & Robinson, 2003; Tapert, Tate, & Brown, 2001). Although support for this model via examinations of the relation between alcohol use and measures of moral strength or willpower has not been obtained empirically, there is some support for the efficacy of treatments based on the moral model (e.g., Rist & Davies-Osterkamp, 1977). Other models (i.e., spiritual model, medical or disease models) conceptualize alcohol abuse and dependence as resulting from causes beyond the individual's control. In both models individuals must rely on external forces, such as a higher power or medical treatment, to arrest the condition. However, as in the case of the moral model, the spiritual model emphasizes spiritual weakness as an underlying factor in the maintenance of this condition. Findings from recent studies that have examined the relation between alcohol abuse and dependence and measures of spirituality have yielded mixed findings, with some evidence suggesting that spirituality tends to be negatively related to alcohol drinking (e.g., Staton, Webster, Hiller, Rostosky, & Leukefeld, 2003) and other researchers finding moderate and, in some cases, no relation between these two variables (e.g., Robinson, Brower, Kurtz, 2003; Stewart, 2001).

The medical model is currently the dominant paradigm of alcohol abuse and dependence. From this perspective, physiological factors underlie this condition, much like in the case of other diseases, and recovery depends on medical treatment and absolute abstinence (Peterson et al., 2003; Tapert et al., 2001). Attempts to support this model have largely focused on examinations of family histories, twin and adoption studies to identify hereditability components relevant to family histories. Jung's (2001) and Farren and Tipton's (1999) reviews of this literature revealed mixed findings. Jung (2001), for example, reported that whereas alcohol abusing or dependent individuals were significantly more likely to have a family member who also abused or was dependent on alcohol, a large percentage of them did not have substance-abusing relatives. However, the link between hereditability and alcohol abuse and dependence was stronger among males, with fathers, brothers, and sons of alcohol abusing or dependent individuals having a higher likelihood of developing the disorder than females. Nevertheless, when cultural/societal views about males' drinking (Jung, 2001) and the possible confounding effects of the environments shared by family members are considered (Walters, 2002), it is difficult to attribute this finding solely to hereditability. The finding that male sons of individuals who abuse, or are dependent on, alcohol may be more likely to develop this condition than females was also supported by the findings presented in other comprehensive reviews of this literature (Nathan, Skinstad, & Dolan, 2001; Walters, 2002). However, Farren and Tipton (1999) concluded that the inconsistencies across studies in their definitions of what constitutes a positive family history of alcohol abuse make it difficult to resolve the mixed findings. Furthermore, gender differences, according to Walters (2002), may be the result of studies with small sample sizes, providing support for the theory that males have a stronger genetic predisposition to alcohol abuse or dependence. Indeed, findings on gender differences in genetic predisposition to alcohol abuse utilizing other methodology (twins, adoption studies) have been mixed (Heath, 1995).

Reviews of a series of twin studies conducted over the past five decades have consistently found higher concordance rates of alcohol abuse and dependence between identical twins than fraternal twins, which has provided strong support for the genetic hypothesis (Jung, 2001; Nathan et al., 2001; Rose, 1995). However, these findings can also be construed as conflicting evidence because there are many commonalities found in the life experiences and environments of twins (Jung, 2001), particularly because identical twins tend to have closer relationships than fraternal twins, which may also influence their similarities in drinking patters (Walters, 2002). Consequently, adoption studies are often thought to be a more effective method of inquiry to identify the biological influences of alcohol abuse and dependence (Nathan et al., 2001). These studies examine whether children of alcohol abusing parents who are not exposed to alcohol in their adoptive families are more likely to develop the disorder than children of nonalcohol abusing parents. Reviews of this literature have found a stronger likelihood of developing alcohol disorders among individuals whose biological parents abuse alcohol even when they are raised in nonalcohol abusing families. This has been particularly the case for sons of individuals with alcohol abuse and dependence (Heath, 1995; Nathan et al., 2001). Although these findings also support the biological basis of the alcohol-related disorders, some have pointed out the limitations of these studies, given that they are based on a population that represents a small portion of the general population (Jung, 2001).

Similarly, results from studies on biochemical factors (e.g., dopamine D2 gene) have not yielded enough evidence to conclusively support the genetic influence on alcohol abuse and dependence (Farren & Tipton, 1999). Overall, the combined findings from family history, twin, adoption, and biochemical studies suggest that genetics may, to some extent, be influential in the development and maintenance of alcohol abuse and dependence. However, it is not clear whether males have a stronger predisposition than females. In addition, researchers have yet to develop study designs that can discern between biological and environmental influences. Therefore, alcohol abuse and dependence continues to be considered a multifactorial disorder influenced by both biochemical and psychosocial factors (Farren & Tipton, 1999).

Psychosocial models have incorporated environmental factors in explaining the development of alcohol abuse and dependence. For instance, certain alcohol disorders (i.e., tolerance, withdrawal, abuse, dependence, intoxication) can, indeed, be explained by associative and learning-based models (Vogel-Sprott & Fillmore, 1999). Learning-based theorists propose that alcohol abuse and dependence develop when the tension-reducing effects of alcohol are associated with stress-related social events (e.g., tension goes away consequent to alcohol use), or when positive reinforcers are experienced consequent to alcohol use (e.g., good times with friends who drink). According to social learning theory, alcohol abuse and dependence develops by modeling others' alcohol drinking behaviors. Thus, whereas individuals may be genetically susceptible to alcohol abuse and dependence, it is the external events, past experiences, and reinforcers, that play the substantial role in its development (George & Marlatt, 1983).

COURSE, COMPLICATIONS, AND PROGNOSIS

In some societies, experimentation with alcohol and drugs during adolescence is considered an adaptational behavior and a component in adolescents' identity development process (Waldron, 1997). Indeed, for most adolescents, experimentation with substances is a phase and does not become problematic or addictive (Bukstein et al., 1997). However, given that alcohol is the most commonly used substance during adolescence and has been identified as a "gateway" to progressive drug use (Weinberg, Rahdert, Colliver, & Glantz, 1998), its consumption during adolescence may be a developmental keystone in the course of alcohol abuse and dependence. Although little is known about how experimentation develops into abuse and dependence (Waldron, 1997), early initiation and sharp increases in the levels of consumption have been identified as potential risk factors for the development of alcohol abuse and dependence (Bukstein et al., 1997; Tapert et al., 2001). In addition, the potential short-term (e.g., poor academic performance, violence, accidents) and long-term (e.g., disruption of cognitive and neuropsychological development, social skills deficits) consequences of using alcohol may contribute to the development of the disorder later in adulthood (Weinberg et al., 1998).

Although the first signs of alcohol intoxication are likely to surface during the middle of adolescence, the age of onset for the majority of alcohol abuse and dependence cases occurs between the 20s and mid-30s, rarely occurring past the late 30s (APA, 2000). Jellinek (1991), based on an analysis of more than 2,000 alcohol-drinking histories of alcohol dependent males, proposed a developmental course that occurs over four phases. The sequence of symptoms and characteristics encompassed within each phase, according to Jellinek (1991), are common among most, but not all, individuals with this disorder and are moderated by individual and environmental characteristics. During the first phase (i.e., *prealcoholic symptomatic*), drinking episodes, which may have begun in social settings, often progress from occasional consumption to drinking increased amounts for the specific purpose of feeling the effects associated with alcohol. As tolerance develops, higher amounts of alcohol may need to be ingested to achieve the desired effect. This phase may last anywhere from six months to two years before moving to the next phase.

Jellinek's (1991) second phase, *prodromal phase,* is characterized by amnesialike symptoms, preoccupation with drinking alcohol, social isolation, and feelings of guilt. While under the influence of alcohol, activities may be performed without displaying signs of intoxication. However, remembering events or conversations that take place while under the effects of alcohol may be difficult. Increased preoccupation with drinking alcohol may prompt the individual to ensure access to enough amounts of the substance, sometimes by ingesting alcohol prior to leaving the house or by gulping the first few drinks. Although heavy alcohol drinking may take place during this stage, it may not be noticeable to others. Indeed, alcohol abusing or dependent individuals may attempt to conceal their drinking behavior for fear of being judged, potentially resulting in social isolation. The duration of the prodromal phase may vary depending on various factors, such as physical and psychological characteristics and support systems, and may last approximately from six months to four or five years.

Loss of control over drinking marks the beginning of Jellinek's (1991) next phase, the *crucial phase*. During this phase, drinking episodes may begin with the intention of drinking only a few drinks, and although some control may be exerted over whether to initiate the drinking episode, the individual may be unable to stop once drinking begins. This phase is also marked by increased social isolation, interpersonal conflict with friends and family members, and occupational problems. Aggressive behavior may be displayed at others' attempts to make the individual aware of the situation. Although behavior becomes centered on alcohol, there may be some attempts to set boundaries on the amount and times of drinking.

During Jellinek's (1991) final stage, the *chronic phase*, prolonged periods of intoxication increase, occurring indiscriminately at various times of the day, or days of the week. In addition, cognitive impairments and psychomotor inhibition may be apparent; in about 10 percent of the cases alcoholic psychoses may develop. A loss of tolerance to alcohol may be observed, with less amounts of alcohol needed to reach unconsciousness. Withdrawal symptoms, such as tremors, may become more common when not under the effects of alcohol. Jellinek (1991) indicated that this developmental course of alcohol was not as well defined in women.

Although Jellinek's (1991) model has been somewhat controversial (Fingarette, 1991), it is considered seminal in the field. Several other descriptions of the course of this disorder mirror Jellinek's (1991) ideas, such as considering alcohol abuse and dependence a chronic, recurrent condition, often involving numerous episodes of remission and relapse, loss of control, and periods of abstinence alternating between low to heavy drinking (APA, 2000; Nathan et al., 2001). Jellinek's (1991) prognosis is also consistent with the prognosis presented in the *DSM-IV-TR* (APA, 2000), which involves periods of abstinence with relapses occurring after a crisis or social encounter where alcohol is available. However, this prognosis applies to more severe cases, and is not representative of the majority of cases. Indeed, most cases have a good prognosis, with about 20 percent of cases achieving long-term sobriety without ongoing treatment (APA, 2000).

The developmental course of alcohol abuse and dependence may be complicated by its comorbidity with other psychological disorders. For instance, a strong relationship has been found between depression and alcohol abuse and dependence, with up to 70 percent of individuals in treatment for alcohol-related problems meeting diagnostic criteria for a mood disorder (Gratzer et al., 2004). Whether depression is a preexisting condition, or it results as a consequence of drinking alcohol, it is likely to interfere with treatment (Nathan et al., 2001). Similarly, some researchers (e.g., Schuckit et al., 1997) have found alcohol-dependent individuals to be twice as likely to have a co-occurring anxiety disorder. Indeed, anxiety disorders may contribute to the development and/or maintenance of alcohol dependence (Kushner, Abrams, & Borchardt, 2000). Other complicating features of alcohol abuse and dependence include its detrimental effects to cognitive functioning and physical condition. Chronic consumption of alcohol has been associated with damage to neuropsychological-related systems, such as the limbic system, the diencephalons, and the frontal cerebral cortex of the brain, which may impact ability to process information, recall from short-term memory, think abstractly, problem solve, and may interfere with the acquisition of new knowledge (Secretary of Health and Human Services, 1997). Among several physical consequences associated with chronic alcohol consumption are increased risk for cardiovascular problems and diseases (e.g., hypertension, coronary heart disease, and hemorrhagic stroke, cirrhosis of the liver, cancers of the mouth, esophagus, breast and liver), with heavier drinkers exhibiting higher risks for these diseases (Rehm, Gmel, Sempos, & Trevisan, 2002).

ASSESSMENT AND DIAGNOSIS

The clinical assessment of alcohol abuse and dependence is complex, and is enhanced with collaborative input from professionals in mental health, medicine, and social services. The safety and well-being of the individual and relevant significant others should be emphasized during the initial assessment session. Medical physicians, psychiatrists, and nursing staff can conduct an initial biological assessment, including a physical examination, and signs of intoxication, withdrawal, and potential medical issues resulting from alcohol use that may impair cognitive functioning. It is especially imperative that the individual be monitored for withdrawal symptoms because serious complications (e.g., seizures, strokes, psychosis) can have long-term and potentially fatal consequences if not prevented through careful monitoring and medication. Furthermore, this evaluation assists in determining the level of care needed, as some individuals will need an inpatient detoxification prior to outpatient psychological services. Social service agencies may need to be contacted in order to assess the safety of family members. Social agencies also facilitate assistance in financial and legal issues (e.g., recent arrests, loss of employment, indigence). The mental health practitioner is chiefly responsible for assessing psychological factors and comorbid disorders that coexist in alcohol abusers and their families, and integrating the diagnostic impressions of other professionals into a unified and holistic treatment plan.

ASSESSMENT PROCEDURES

Assessment typically begins with an unstructured interview to assist in gaining rapport and understanding personality and situational variables that contribute to the development and maintenance of alcohol abuse and other problem behaviors, as well as to determine strengths that may be used to assist in ameliorating these problems. In this interview format, content and extent of questions vary to accommodate the unique needs of the interviewees. However, it should be emphasized that the general content reviewed in most unstructured interviews is fairly consistent across individuals, including assessment of basic demographic information, reasons leading to referral, current motivation to eliminate or reduce alcohol intake and other problem behaviors, background information relevant to the presenting problem (e.g., onset of alcohol and illicit substances, severity of use across time, antecedent, concurrent and consequent stimuli and circumstances associated with abstinence and severe use), family violence, suicidal ideation and intent, medication and medical history, family constellation and history, presence of mental health diagnoses, client goals for therapy, prognostic strengths and obstacles in accomplishing therapeutic goals. As alcohol abusers often provide biased or distorted information, it is very important to interview significant others, including spouses and other relatives, employers, and close friends. These interviews serve to confirm or disconfirm information so that potential incongruities or lost information can be addressed, and significant others can be recruited for later assistance in treatment.

Although the unstructured interview does not permit reliable and valid assessment of relevant problem areas, this assessment method does enable the clinician to assess specific circumstances that are relevant to alcohol disorders. Moreover, the unstructured interview acts to guide the selection of tools to be employed in the initial assessment phase. In this endeavor, there are more than 200 measures with demonstrated psychometric properties in the assessment of alcohol abuse and related clinical issues, including motivation for change, coping skills, extent of alcohol use, family relationships, conduct, and cognitive perspectives (Rotgers, 2002). Therefore, in selecting assessment measures to utilize when alcohol-related problems have been identified, the measures should be consistent with the therapeutic orientation of the mental health professional conducting treatment, and the treatment goals of the interviewee. For instance, if a therapist is cognitive-behaviorally oriented, assessment measures should be incorporated that assess relevant antecedent, concomitant, and consequent thoughts and behaviors that influence alcohol use and abstinence. If an identified goal includes enhancing motivation to abstain from alcohol, measures should be employed to assess the interviewee's current level of motivation, and measure potential future changes in motivation. It is prudent to employ standardized measures that are validated in their assessment of alcohol and drug use frequency and severity as well as other domains that are commonly indicated in alcohol abuse (e.g., family relationships, employment, comorbid diagnoses). Along these lines, the following standardized measures are specific to alcohol use and abuse.

Screening measures are typically employed to assist in identifying the presence of alcohol use problems worthy of further assessment. These instruments are sometimes utilized along with a medical evaluation, and may assist in determining the level of treatment care needed (e.g., residential, halfway house, outpatient therapy).

The Michigan Alcoholism Screening Test (MAST; Selzer, 1971) is a 25-item brief screening inventory for alcohol abuse disorders. Scores range from 0 to 53. The MAST is designed for adult use, although a version for the geriatric population is available, and an adolescent version is currently under development (Snow, Thurber, & Hodgson, 2002). The MAST contains social, physical, and problem perception domains, and it is intended only to determine potential service needs. MAST items are stated in terms of lifetime use, and, therefore, responses do not change or indicate improvement with treatment (Rotgers, 2002). Nevertheless, the MAST has been utilized for decades as a rapid screen in research, and it has been found to have good test-retest reliability, internal consistency (Thurber, Snow, Lewis, & Hodgson, 2001) and construct validity with the *DSM-IV* (Conley, 2001).

There are three frequently cited measures for alcohol dependency with good psychometric properties, including validity and adequate norm groups in adult populations. The Alcohol Dependence Scale (ADS; Skinner & Allen, 1982) is a 25-item Likert scale (0 = never, 4 = often) measuring the symptoms of alcohol dependence The ADS has demonstrated discriminative validity, convergent validity with the MAST, and it has been found to be effective at detecting alcohol dependence (Kahler, Strong, Hayaki, Ramsey, & Brown, 2003; Ross, Gavin, & Skinner, 1990). However, although it is a good diagnostic tool, the ADS does not predict future alcohol abuse or treatment outcomes (Kivlahan, Sher, & Donovan, 1989).

The Severity of Alcohol Dependence Questionnaire (SADQ; Stockwell, Murphy, & Hodgson, 1983) comprises 20 items with a total score ranging from 0 to 50. The SADQ contains five subscales related to dependence (i.e., physical withdrawal, affective withdrawal, withdrawal relief drinking, alcohol consumption, rapidity of reinstatement). Its test-retest reliability and content, criterion (predictive, concurrent, "postaddictive"), and construct validity are good (Davidson, 1987).

The Short Alcohol Dependence Data Questionnaire (SADD; Davidson & Raistrick, 1986) consists of 15 items. The SADD has demonstrated acceptable reliability (split-half, test-retest) and validity (content and construct; Davidson, Bunting, & Raistrick, 1989; Gorman, Duffy, Raine, & Taylor, 1989; Raistrick & Davidson, 1983). Although the SADD is somewhat more sensitive to dependency, all three of these instruments provide valuable information about the progression of the individual's symptoms, and are relatively brief. They also have sound psychometric support.

The Timeline Follow-Back (TLFB; Sobell & Sobell, 1996) is the most widely used standardized measure of the extent and frequency of alcohol and drug use, and it is easily adapted to assess frequency of days institutionalized, employed, and in psychiatric hospitalizations (Azrin et al., 1994). The procedure begins by presenting the patient with a calendar that usually goes back in time three months to a year. The calendar initially contains major events that are listed on their respective dates of occurrence (e.g., holidays, memorable national or local events, catastrophic weather, accidents with mass casualties, death of notable public figures, professional sports competitions). The respondent is then queried to reveal personal significant events to record on their respective dates of occurrence to assist in the enhancement of memory relevant to substance use (e.g., birthday celebrations, funerals, births, work related celebrations, attendance at local sporting events). Once this data is collected, the individual is asked to place on the form days of alcohol, including the amounts, whenever possible. Polysubstance use can be recorded in the calendar to give a complete picture of the pattern of substance use. Last, other events that are relevant to treatment goals (i.e., missed work days, days in residential settings, legal citations or arrests) can also be assessed utilizing this method. This information can be utilized to assist in diagnostic formulation, ongoing assessment of alcohol use, treatment outcome, and assessment of the relationship between alcohol use and other target behaviors that are related to treatment outcome. The TLFB has been found to be a highly reliable self-report instrument (Donohue et al., 2004).

The Structured Clinical Interview for Axis I Disorders, Version 2 (SCID-II; First, Gibbon, Williams, & Spitzer, 1994) and the Form 90 (Miller, 1996) are structured interviews for adults that may be used to assess alcohol disorders. The SCID-II is a structured interview that facilitates diagnostic examination of the major *DSM* disorders. Section E is specific to alcohol and drug abuse and dependence. Items are separated into two sections (i.e., alcohol disorders, nonalcohol substance disorders). An overall substance-use profile may be obtained, and sections are designed in a decision-tree format, permitting accurate diagnosis without extraneous questioning (i.e., screening items are employed for all major substances). The rigorous structure of the SCID-II makes it an excellent tool for forensic and research settings in which a precise and strongly substantiated diagnosis is particularly important. The items are based directly on the *DSM-IV* criteria for these disorders, and interrater reliability is excellent (Segal, Hersen, Van Hasselt, 1994).

The Form 90 (Miller, 1996) is another structured interview that focuses more exclusively on the frequency and amount of alcohol consumption to assist in assessing diagnostic criteria. It is available in long and short versions. The interview outlines the examinee's current weekly consumption, any periods of cessation of consumption, and the overall progression of the amount and frequency of alcohol use across time. This data is collected in a manner similar to the Timeline Follow-Back, with an additional "time to event" grid system used to chart alcohol use patterns, consequences of use, and a diagnostic interview based on the *DSM-IV* criterion. The Form 90 has been found to have good construct and convergent validity with other measures, as well as good interrater reliability (Tonigan, Miller, & Brown, 1997).

Biological measures are often necessary to identify alcohol use when it is denied in standardized self-report measures, and to assist in confirming or disconfirming self-report alcohol frequency data. Although the window of alcohol detection is limited (i.e., usually within a few hours of use), a variety of biological measures exist, including Breathalyzer tests, and urine, saliva, and blood screens for alcohol. Breathalyzers are the least invasive, as the individual is required to simply breathe into a tube that provides an estimate of the presence or absence of alcohol use, whereas testing blood for alcohol is more accurate, but relatively invasive as it involves the extraction of blood. Urine screening is also somewhat invasive as this procedure requires the collection of a urine specimen to examine the presence or absence of alcohol in the urine. Thus, saliva and Breathalyzer tests offer distinct advantages due to their ease in administration. However, it should be mentioned that with the exception of blood testing, all biological alcohol detection procedures now permit immediate feedback and consist of simple methods of interpreting the results (i.e., clinician or significant other can immediately test for the presence of alcohol without sending the sample to a laboratory for analysis). Given high comorbidity between alcohol and illicit substances (e.g., cocaine, marijuana, opiates, barbiturates, amphetamines), it is usually a good idea to initially conduct broad screen analyses (i.e., multipanel screens for various substances). When participants refuse to be tested, it is customary to consider these refusals positive for alcohol use. However, it should be mentioned that there are methods that may be used to increase compliance to alcohol and drug use screening procedures, such as enlisting the help of significant others to be supportive during, and after, screening. When the individual being tested is unable to provide a sample, running water while attempting to urinate or touching warm water immediately prior to attempting to urinate may be helpful. Additionally, the use of biological markers may be confounded by any of the various methods utilized to produce false negative test results, such as diluting urine with water, ingesting herbal solutions, and switching samples (see Strada & Donohue, 2004).

IMPACT ON ENVIRONMENT

Pathological patterns of alcohol consumption create a wide variety of social problems (Gmel & Rehm, 2003). Diagnostic criteria relevant to alcohol abuse and dependence inherently point to obvious problems of increased interpersonal conflict, decreased work productivity, an inability to meet domestic responsibilities, increased risk-taking behaviors, and death (due to accidents, withdrawal, or alcohol-related organ failure). These problems often exacerbate into more consistent patterns of undesired behavior culminating in divorce, termination of employment, alcohol-related medical complications, and alcohol-related accidents. Families are greatly impacted when alcohol abuse or dependence is present, including dissolution of the family through divorce (Leonard & Rothbard, 1999), domestic violence (Leonard & Roberts, 1998), and child abuse and neglect (Jacob & Johnson, 1997; Sher, Wood, Wood, & Raskin, 1996). Deteriorating occupational and domestic functioning often result in impulsive decision making by the individual who is abusing alcohol, thus exacerbating further loss of trust in those who are negatively affected by the problem drinking, such as spouses, children, and employers. Fetal alcohol syndrome (FAS; Connor & Streissguth, 1996) affects 0.33 children per 1,000 births, and the cost of treating FAS in the United States is estimated to be approximately $75 million, rising incrementally each year (Larkby & Day, 1997; NIAAA, 2000). Children are also impacted by parental alcohol abuse and dependence through loss of economic resources, an authoritarian or neglectful parenting style, exposure to marital conflict, and expectancies around alcohol use. Moreover, it is estimated that at least 16 percent of all child abuse is directly linked to alcohol consumption (Rehm et al., 2002).

The economic cost of alcohol use in the workplace is primarily felt in the loss of productivity, and the necessity of employment termination (see Strada & Donohue, 2004). Studies on alcohol-related absenteeism have found that among the male population moderate users have fewer absences than abstainers or heavy drinkers, whereas female drinkers demonstrate lower abstinence rates than nondrinking counterparts (Marmot, North, Feeney, & Head, 1993; NIAAA, 2000). However, this latter pattern is thought to be a product of the individual's desire to support the denial inherent in alcohol abuse disorder, as despite continued attendance, productivity itself is negatively impacted. A variety of negative work behaviors that decrease productivity have been found to positively correlate with alcohol consumption levels, including arriving late to the work site, falling asleep during work hours, leaving work early, and decreased productivity (Blum, Roman, & Martin, 1993; Mangione et al., 1999). Obviously, such patterns indicate an increased level of employment turnover. Thus, there is progressive economic loss in production, and further losses with an increase in retraining and hiring costs.

Use of medical resources to manage alcohol-related problems are a major cost to society, as lack of judgment and increased impulsivity associated with alcohol abuse and dependence lead to an increase in accidents and acts of violence. According to the U.S. Department of Transportation, alcohol-related car accidents cost $51 billion, and 80 percent of these accidents were directly caused by alcohol use (Blincoe et al., 2000). Alcohol intoxication increases the likelihood of a multitude of accidental injuries including burns, hypothermia, drowning, falls, gunshot wounds, poisonings, and car accidents (Smith, Branas, & Miller, 1999). Alcohol-related illnesses are less commonly diagnosed but include cirrhosis of the liver, pancreatic disease, and alcohol-related dementia (Korsakoff's syndrome).

Criminal acts of violence are another area in which alcohol abuse exacts a substantial cost to society. Greenfeld (1998) found that blood alcohol levels of at least 0.05 occurred in 90 percent of those convicted of murder and sexual assault, 86 percent of convicted robbers, and 78 percent of those convicted of nonsexual assault. In a study involving a national sample, alcohol was present in the bloodstream of as many as 57 percent of criminal assaults (Smith et al., 1999). Thus, it is clear the misuse of alcohol is a major factor in crimes perpetuated against others.

TREATMENT IMPLICATIONS

It is estimated that more than 700,000 individuals receive treatment for alcohol-related disorders on any given day (Secretary of Health and Human Services, 1997). Not surprisingly, dozens of therapy modalities have been developed to treat alcohol abuse and dependence. Therefore, this section will focus on some of the more widely utilized methods that have demonstrated efficacy or effectiveness in controlled trials.

Brief interventions are typically implemented in primary health care settings after alcohol abuse has been identified (Secretary of Health and Human Services, 1997). These interventions are typically conducted with less severe, nonchronic substance abusers to raise motivation to control their intake of alcohol. Brief interventions typically last a few sessions, and may involve motivational counseling, controlled drinking techniques (e.g., learning to drink slowly, refuse offers to drink), psychoeducation, and psychological advice or bibliotherapy to increase awareness about potentially hazardous effects of excessive alcohol use (Tapert et al., 2001). Referral to more intensive treatment is made if drinking does not decrease. One of the more popular motivational interviewing methods incorporates six factors to promote behavior change (Miller et al., 1995), including *feedback, responsibility, advice, menu, empathy,* and *self-efficacy* (FRAMES). Motivational interviewers avoid confrontation and express empathy in trying to increase the individual's awareness about the discrepancy between their current behavior and their ideal goals (Maisto, Wolfe, & Jordan, 1999). Coping skills training (e.g., Bien, Miller, & Tonigan, 1993; Wilk, Jensen, & Havighurst, 1997), an intervention that may be adapted to be brief or comprehensive, involves developing the individual's interpersonal skills, recognition and management of alcohol-related cues, management of stress, and regulation of emotions (Tapert et al., 2001). Brief interventions have been found to be effective across a number of meta-analytic studies. For example, Dunn, Deroo, and Rivara (2001) concluded that Motivational Interviewing (MI) was effective in the engagement of individuals into more intensive treatment (i.e., cognitive behavioral therapy), and coping skills training has demonstrated efficacy in reducing alcohol use when compared to other interventions in controlled trials (Dunn et al., 2001). Apodaca and Miller (2003) found bibliotherapy resulted in significant decreases in alcohol use with alcohol drinkers who did not meet criteria for alcohol dependence, and this cost-effective intervention was particularly effective for individuals who deliberately sought out these materials. However, bibliotherapy has not been evaluated in severe, chronic drinkers, nor has it been found to be more effective than intensive treatments. Therefore, bibliotherapy, similar to other brief interventions, should be utilized as a supplement to more intensive alcohol abuse treatment programs (Apodaca & Miller, 2003).

Among the several treatment modalities that have been developed for severe alcohol dependence is the Community Reinforcement Approach (CRA; Hunt & Azrin, 1973). Smith, Meyers, and Miller's (2001) comprehensive evaluation of CRA clinical trials reported that CRA is one of the most efficacious and cost-effective treatments for alcohol-related disorders in both inpatient and outpatient settings. This form of therapy utilizes cognitive behavioral components to create and increase awareness about high-risk alcohol-related situations. To this end, both therapist and client conduct functional analyses to examine the antecedents and consequences of the alcohol-related behaviors, and identify skills in need of development. CRA emphasizes the acquisition of skills to improve communication, obtain or keep a job, and control reactivity to substance use cues. The focus of CRA is to arrange circumstances in the environment that tend to influence substance use, such as social, recreational, familial, and occupational support systems in the alcohol abuser's community (Tapert et al., 2001).

A modified version of CRA, Community-Reinforcement and Family Training (CRAFT; see Smith et al., 2001) enlists the help of significant others to increase the likelihood of engaging the alcohol abusing individual in treatment. Significant others are also taught how to modify their interactions with the individual, reinforce sobriety, and maintain healthy psychosocial functioning. Interventions that involve significant others in alcohol abuse treatment, such as CRA, CRAFT, and Unilateral Family Therapy, have yielded better outcomes than traditional treatments, both in the treatment engagement phase and in the primary treatment and rehabilitation stages (see Edwards & Steinglass, 1995). As is the case with treatment engagement, attendance to aftercare programs has been higher when family members provide encouragement and support to, and attend the aftercare sessions with, the alcohol abusing or dependent individual (Edwards & Steinglass, 1995).

As indicated previously, family conflicts are a central focus in the development and maintenance of alcohol abuse and dependence. Indeed, relapse has been associated with interpersonal problems (Tapert et al., 2001). Therefore, in family therapy, family members are recruited to assist in the alcohol abuser in generating solutions to identify problems, and to provide support and reinforcement for completion of behaviors that are consistent with abstinence or controlled drinking. Family-based interventions are typically focused on improving communication and problem-solving skills training, stress reduction, behavioral contracting, scheduling activities that are incompatible with alcohol use (Walitzer, 1999). Along these lines, marital and family therapy has been found to be highly effective in the treatment of alcoholism (O'Farrell, 1995; O'Farrell & Fals-Stewart, 2003). Consistent with CRA and CRAFT, in this approach family members (usually the spouse) are recruited to assist in motivating the individual to seek treatment and support efforts to stop drinking alcohol. Accordingly, both spouses receive treatment, and their initial sessions focus on eliminating and/or reducing behaviors that may hinder abstinence, such as habitual recollection of prior drinking episodes. Additionally, couples are instructed to plan and engage in pleasant activities, utilize communication skills training, and employ conflict resolution strategies and sobriety contracts (for a detailed description of interventions and recording forms, see O'Farrell, 1995).

Several other behavioral interventions have been developed and found effective in the treatment of alcohol-related disorders. Contingency Management (Higgins & Petry, 1999) is in this group of treatments. It focuses on reinforcing behaviors conducive to sobriety and punishing behaviors that are inconsistent with the treatment goals. Other treatments in this group include traditional approaches such as aversive stimuli (e.g., electrical), and desensitization (see Childress, McLellan, & O'Brien, 1985).

One of the most widely utilized treatments for alcoholism is Twelve-Step Facilitation (TSF; Secretary of Health and Human Services, 1997). TSF programs are based on Alcoholics Anonymous's basic principles, and encourage attendance to meetings where the attendees share the detrimental impact of alcohol on their lives (Read, Kahler, & Stevenson, 2001). In this approach, complete abstinence is strongly emphasized. Recent, major quasiexperimental (Ouimette, Finney, & Moos, 1997) and controlled (Project MATCH Research Group, 1997) studies have found TSF to be comparable to Cognitive Behavior Therapy (CBT), Motivational Enhancement Therapy (Project MATCH Research Group, 1997), and a combination of CBT and TSF (Ouimette et al., 1997).

Unlike TSF, other treatment modalities have supported controlled drinking approaches (i.e., learning strategies to assist in learning to drink alcohol in moderation), as opposed to complete abstinence. These types of treatments surfaced in the early 1970s and became controversial because they challenged the traditional disease or medical model of alcoholism (Sobell & Sobell, 1995). The general conclusion has been that controlled-drinking-oriented treatments were comparable to approaches that targeted complete abstinence (Hester, 1995). However, in a review of moderation research over a 25-year period, Sobell and Sobell (1995) concluded that abstinence seems to be associated with recovery among individuals with severe alcohol dependence, whereas controlled drinking has been a central factor in the recovery of individuals with less severe drinking problems.

Some pharmacotherapeutics, such as the GABA agonist acamprosate and the opiate antagonists naltrexone and nalmefene, have been ranked among the most effective alcohol psychopharmacological treatments (Miller & Wilbourne, 2002). All three agents have demonstrated effectiveness in reducing alcohol cravings and number of drinking days (Secretary of Health and Human Services, 1997). Some (e.g., Jaffe et al., 1996) have found that pharmacotherapeutics, such as naltrexone, administered while individuals undergo behavioral therapies, such as cognitive behavioral relapse prevention, may help enhance the therapeutic effects. Although disulfiram (Antabuse) has demonstrated effectiveness for some individuals in combination with CRA (Azrin, Sisson, Meyers, & Godley, 1982), others have cautioned its use due to potential adverse physical effects (including in rare circumstances death) that may result when alcohol is consumed while disulfiram is in the body (Miller & Wilbourne, 2002). Other medications, such as the benzodiazepine aprazolam, have demonstrated effectiveness in reducing withdrawal symptoms (Secretary of Health and Human Services, 1997).

The majority of individuals who undergo alcohol treatment tend to experience lapses (ingesting alcohol after a period of abstinence occurring during treatment) and relapses (consuming alcohol after a period of abstinence occurring after treatment), and these incidents can be viewed as components intrinsic to the treatment process (Witkiewitz & Marlatt, 2004). A relapse prevention (RP) approach incorporates behavioral skills training and cognitive techniques to initiate and maintain behaviors consistent with sober living (Dimeff & Marlatt, 1995). Behavioral skills training involves helping the individual learn to identify high-risk situations, detect early physiological and psychological symptoms of lapses and relapses, regulate negative affect, manage interpersonal conflict, drug refusal skills training, and graduated exposure to increasingly risky alcohol use situations so the individual can practice newly learned coping skills that are relevant to escaping from these situations without using alcohol (Daley & Salloum, 1999). Comprehensive reviews and meta-analytic studies on RP have concurred it is superior to no treatment (Witkiewitz & Marlatt, 2004), and comparable to interpersonal therapy, nondirective counseling, interpersonal therapy, and supportive therapy (Carroll, 1996).

FUTURE DIRECTIONS

Advances in alcohol abuse and dependence treatment research are evident in our commensurate understanding of this disorder, its etiologies, and effective treatments. However, there is still much work to be done in this field. For instance, more than 40 alcohol treatment modalities have been identified to combat alcohol disorders (see Miller et al., 1995). Yet, there is a clear lack of outcome studies that have been conducted to develop, and subsequently evaluate, interventions that are specific to various diverse groups of alcohol abusers (e.g., females, adolescents, ethnic minority groups, college students). This is particularly surprising given the substantial amount of evidence to suggest these groups demonstrate unique drinking patterns. Of particular relevance to diversity, there have been no controlled treatment outcome studies to evaluate family-based therapies involving children and their substance abusing parents. Along a slightly different vein, at least 40 percent to 50 percent of child maltreatment cases are perpetrated by someone who meets diagnostic criteria for an alcohol abuse disorder, yet no outcome studies have involved concurrent treatment for alcohol disorders and child neglect or abuse. There are also relatively few studies that have been conducted to examine specific treatment components that are most relatively effective within the empirically supported comprehensive programs. Indeed, data relevant to this issue are rarely provided in treatment outcome studies.

REFERENCES

American Psychiatric Association. (2000). *Diagnostic and statistical manual of mental disorders* (4th ed., text rev.). Washington, DC: Author.

American Psychological Association. (2002). Ethical principles of psychologists and code of conduct. *American Psychologist, 57,* 1060–1073.

Apodaca, T. R., & Miller, W. R. (2003). A meta-analysis of the effectiveness of bibliotherapy for alcohol problems. *Journal of Clinical Psychology, 59,* 289–304.

Azrin, N. H., McMahon, P. T., Donohue, B., Besalel, V. A. Lapinski, K. J., Kogan, E. S., et al. (1994). Behavior therapy for drug abuse: A controlled treatment outcome study. *Behaviour Research and Therapy, 32,* 857–866.

Azrin, N. H., Sisson, R. W., Meyers, R., & Godley, M. (1982). Alcoholism treatment by disulfiram and community reinforcement therapy. *Journal of Behavior Therapy and Experimental Psychiatry, 13,* 105–112.

Bien, T. H., Miller, W. R., & Tonigan, J. S. (1993). Brief interventions for alcohol problems: A review. *Addiction, 88,* 315–335.

Blincoe, L., Seay, A., Zaloshnja, E., Miller, T., Romano, E., Luchter, S., et al. (2000). *Economic impact of motor vehicle crashes.* Washington, DC: U.S. Department of Transportation, National Highway Traffic Safety Administration (168251).

Blum, T. C., Roman, P. M., & Martin, J. K. (1993). Alcohol consumption and work performance. *Journal of Studies on Alcohol, 54,* 61–70.

Bray, J. H., Adams, G. J., Getz, G., & Stovall, T. (2001). Interactive effects of individuation, family factors, and stress on adolescent alcohol use. *American Journal of Orthopsychiatry, 71,* 436–449.

Bukstein, O., Dunne, J. E., Ayres, W., Arnold, V., Benedek, E., Benson, R. S., et al. (1997). Practice parameters for the assessment and treatment of children and adolescents with substance use disorders. *Journal of the American Academy of Child and Adolescent Psychiatry, 36,* 140–156.

Capodanno, D. J., & Chavaria, F. R. (1991). Polysubstance abuse: The interaction of alcohol and other drugs. *Federal Probation, 55,* 24–28.

Carroll, K. M. (1996). Relapse prevention as a psychosocial treatment: A review of controlled clinical trials. *Experimental and Clinical Psychopharmacology, 4,* 46–54.

Childress, A. R., McLellan, A. T., & O'Brien, C. P. (1985). Behavioral therapies for substance abuse. *International Journal of the Addictions, 20,* 947–969.

Cloninger, R. C. (1987). Neurogenetic adaptive mechanisms in alcoholism. *Science, 236,* 410–416.

Cloninger, R. C., & Sigvardsson, S. (1996). Type I and Type II alcoholism: Psychological aspects. *Alcohol Health and Research World, 20,* 18–23.

Conley, T. (2001). Construct validity of the MAST and AUDIT with multiple offender drunk drivers. *Journal of Substance Abuse Treatment, 20,* 287–295.

Connor, P. D., & Streissguth, A. P. (1996). Effects of prenatal exposure to alcohol across the life span. *Alcohol Health and Research World, 20,* 170–175.

Costa, P. T., Jr., & McCrae, R. R. (1989). Personality continuity and the changes of adult life. In M. Stroandt & G. R. VandenBros (Eds.), *The adult years: Continuity and change* (p. 134). Washington, DC: American Psychological Association.

Daley, D. C., & Salloum, I. (1999). Relapse prevention. In P. J. Ott, R. E. Tarter, & R. T. Ammerman (Eds.), *Sourcebook on substance abuse* (pp. 255–263). Boston: Allyn & Bacon.

Davidson, R. (1987). Assessment of the alcohol dependence syndrome: A review of self-report screening questionnaires. *British Journal of Clinical Psychology, 26,* 243–256.

Davidson, R., Bunting, B., & Raistrick, D. (1989). The homogeneity of the alcohol dependence syndrome: A factor analysis of the SADD questionnaire. *British Journal of Addiction, 84,* 907–915.

Davidson, R., & Raistrick, D. (1986). The validity of the short alcohol dependence data (SADD) questionnaire for the assessment of alcohol dependence. *British Journal of Addiction, 81,* 217–222.

Dimeff, L. A., & Marlatt, G. A. (1995). Relapse prevention. In R. K. Hester & W. R. Miller (Eds.), *Handbook of alcoholism treatment approaches: Effective alternatives* (pp. 176–194). Boston: Allyn & Bacon.

Donohue, B., Azrin, N. H., Strada, M. J., Silver, N. C., Teichner, G., & Murphy, H. (2004). Psychometric evaluation of self and collateral Timeline Follow-Back reports of drug and alcohol use in a sample of drug abusing and conduct disordered adolescents. *Psychology of Addictive Behaviors, 18,* 184–189.

Dunn, C., Deroo, L., & Rivara, F. P. (2001). The use of brief interventions adapted from motivational interviewing across behavioral domains: A systematic review. *Addiction, 96,* 1725–1742.

Edwards, M. E., & Steinglass, P. (1995). Family therapy outcomes for alcoholism. *Journal of Marital & Family Therapy, 21,* 475–509.

Faingold, C. L., Knapp, D. J., Chester, J. A., & Gonzalez, J. (2004) Integrative neurobiology of the alcohol withdrawal syndrome: From anxiety to seizures. *Alcoholism, Clinical and Experimental Research, 28,* 178–268.

Farren, C. K., & Tipton, K. F. (1999). Trait markers for alcoholism: Clinical utility. *Alcohol and Alcoholism, 34,* 649–665.

Fillmore, K. M., Leino, E. V., & Johnstone, B. M. (1994). The questionable foundation for a hypothesis that alcoholism is inherited. *Addiction, 89,* 1066–1068.

Fingarette, H. (1991). Alcoholism: The mythical disease. In D. J. Pittman & H. R. White (Eds.), *Society, culture, and drinking patterns reexamined* (pp. 417–439). New Brunswick, NJ: Rutgers Center of Alcohol Studies.

First, M., Gibbon, M., Williams, J., & Spitzer, R. (1994). *Structured clinical interview for Axis I DSM-IV disorders.* New York: Office of Mental Health of New York State Psychiatric Institute.

George, W. H., & Marlatt, G. A. (1983). Alcoholism: The evolution of a behavioral perspective. *Recent Developments in Alcoholism, 1,* 105–138.

Gmel, G., & Rehm, J. (2003). Harmful alcohol use. *Alcohol Research and Health, 27,* 52–62.

Gorman, D. M, Duffy, S. W., Raine, S., & Taylor, C. L. (1989). Level of agreement between questionnaire measures of alcohol dependence, alcoholism and problem drinking in a sample presenting at a specialist alcohol treatment service. *Drug and Alcohol Dependence, 24,* 227–232.

Gratzer, D., Levitan, R. D., Sheldon, T., Toneatto, T., Rector, N. A., & Goering, P. (2004). Lifetime rates of alcoholism in adults with anxiety, depression, or co-morbid depression/anxiety: A community survey of Ontario. *Journal of Affective Disorders, 79,* 209–215.

Greenfeld, L. A. (1998). *Alcohol and crime: An analysis of national data on the prevalence of alcohol involvement in crime.* Washington, DC: U.S. Department of Justice.

Heath, A. C. (1995). Genetic influences on alcoholism risk: A review of adoption and twin studies. *Alcohol Health and Research World, 19,* 166–171.

Hester, R. K. (1995). Behavioral self-control training. In R. K. Hester & W. R. Miller (Eds.), *Handbook of alcoholism treatment approaches: Effective alternatives* (pp. 148–159). Boston: Allyn & Bacon.

Higgins, S. T., & Petry, N. M. (1999). Contingency management: Incentives for sobriety. *Alcohol Research and Health, 23,* 122–127.

Hunt, G. M., & Azrin, N. H. (1973). A community-reinforcement approach to alcoholism. *Behaviour Research and Therapy, 11,* 91–104.

Jacob, T., & Johnson, S. (1997). Parenting influences on the development of alcohol abuse and dependence. *Alcohol Health and Research World, 21,* 204–209.

Jaffe, A. J., Rounsaville, B., Chang, G., Schottenfeld, R. S., Meyer, R. E., & O'Malley, S. S. (1996). Naltrexone, relapse prevention, and supportive therapy with alcoholics: An analysis of patient treatment matching. *Journal of Consulting and Clinical Psychology, 64,* 1044–1053.

Jang, K. L., Vernon, P. A., & Livesley, W. J. (2000). Personality disorder traits, family environment, and alcohol misuse: A multivariate behavioral genetic analysis. *Addiction, 95,* 873–888.

Jellinek, E. M. (1991). Phases of alcohol addiction. In D. J. Pittman & H. R. White (Eds.), *Society, culture, and drinking patterns reexamined* (pp. 403–416). New Brunswick, NJ: Rutgers Center of Alcohol Studies.

Jung, J. (2001). *Psychology of alcohol and other drugs: A research perspective.* London: Sage.

Kahler, C. W., Strong, D. R., Hayaki, J., Ramsey, S. E., & Brown, R. A. (2003). An item response analysis of the Alcohol Dependence Scale in treatment-seeking alcoholics. *Journal of Studies on Alcohol, 64,* 127–136.

Kessler, R. C., Nelson, C. B., & McGonagle, K. A. (1996). Epidemiology of co-occurring addictive and mental disorders: Implications for prevention and service utilization. *American Journal of Orthopsychiatry, 66,* 17–31.

Kirkcaldy, B. D., Siefen, G., Surall, D., & Bischoff, R. J. (2004). Predictors of drug and alcohol abuse among children and adolescents. *Personality and Individual Differences, 36,* 247–265.

Kivlahan, D. R., Sher, K. J., & Donovan, D. M. (1989). Alcohol Dependence Scale: A validation study among inpatient alcoholics. *Journal of Studies on Alcohol, 50,* 170–175.

Krabbendam, L., Visser, P. J., Derix, M., Verhey, F., Hofman, P., Verhoeven, W., et al., (2002). Normal cognitive performance in patients with chronic alcoholism in contrast to patients with Korsakoff's syndrome. *Journal of Neuropsychiatry and Clinical Neurosciences, 12,* 44–50.

Kushner, M. G., Abrams, K., & Borchardt, C. (2000). The relationship between anxiety disorders and alcohol use disorders: A review of major perspectives and findings. *Clinical Psychology Review, 20,* 149–171.

Larkby, C., & Day, N. (1997). Effects of prenatal alcohol exposure. *Alcohol Health and Research World, 21,* 192–198.

Lejoyeux, M., Feuche, N., Loi, S., Solomon, J., & Ades, J. (1998). Impulse-control disorders in alcoholics are related to sensation seeking and not to impulsivity. *Psychiatry Research, 81,* 149–155.

Leonard, K. E., & Roberts, L. J. (1998). The effects of alcohol on the marital interactions of aggressive and nonaggressive husbands and their wives. *Journal of Abnormal Psychology, 107,* 602–615.

Leonard, K. E., & Rothbard, J. C. (1999). Alcohol and the effect on the marriage. *Journal of Studies on Alcohol, 13,* 139–146.

Loukas, A., Krull, J. L., Chassin, L., & Carle, A. C. (2000). The relation of personality to alcohol abuse/dependence in a high risk sample. *Journal of Personality, 68,* 1153–1175.

Maisto, S. A., Wolfe, W., & Jordan, J. (1999). Short-term motivational therapy. In P. J. Ott, R. E. Tarter, & R. T. Ammerman (Eds.), *Sourcebook on substance abuse* (pp. 284–292). Boston: Allyn & Bacon.

Mangione, T. W., Howland, J., Amick, B., Cote, J., Lee, M., Bell, N., et al. (1999). Employee drinking practices and work performance. *Journal of Studies on Alcohol, 60,* 261–270.

Margolese, H. C., Malchy, L, Negrete, J. C., Tempier, R., & Gill, K. (2004). Drug and alcohol use among patients with schizophrenia and related psychosis: Levels and consequences. *Schizophrenia Research, 6,* 157–166.

Marmot, M. G., North, F., Feeney, A., & Head, J. (1993). Alcohol consumption and sickness absence: From the Whitehall II study. *Addiction, 88,* 369–382.

Mezzich, A. C., Tarter, R. E., Gaincola, P. R., Lu, S., Kirisci, L., & Parks, S. (1997). Substance use and risky behavior among female adolescents. *Drug and Alcohol Dependence, 44,* 157–166.

Miller, W. R. (1996). *Form 90: A structured assessment interview for drinking and related behaviors* (Vol. 5, NIH Publication No. 96-4004). Washington, DC: National Institute on Alcohol Abuse and Alcoholism.

Miller, W. R., Brown, J. M., Simpson, T. L., Handmaker, N. S., Bein, T. H., Luckie, L. F., et al. (1995). What works? A methodological analysis of the alcohol treatment outcome literature. In R. K. Hester & W. R. Miller (Eds.), *Handbook of alcoholism treatment approaches: Effective alternatives* (pp. 12–44). Boston: Allyn & Bacon.

Miller, W. R., & Wilbourne, P. L. (2002). Mesa Grande: A methodological analysis of clinical trials of treatment for alcohol use disorders. *Addiction, 97,* 265–277.

Nathan, E., Skinstad, A. H., & Dolan, S. (2001). Alcohol-related disorders: Psychopathology, diagnosis, etiology, and treatment. In P. B. Sutker & H. E. Adams (Eds.), *Comprehensive handbook of psychopathology* (pp. 595–622). New York: Kluwer Academic/Plenum.

National Institute on Alcohol Abuse and Alcoholism. (2000). Alcohol use and abuse: Where do the numbers come from? (National Institute on Alcohol Abuse and Alcoholism No. 7 PH 278, January 1990). Retrieved April 23, 2004, from http://www.niaaa.nih.gov/publications/aa07.htm

Nixon, S. J. (1999). Neurocognitive performance in alcoholics: Is polysubstance abuse important? *Psychological Science, 10,* 181–185.

O'Farrell, T. J. (1995). Marital and family therapy. In R. K. Hester & W. R. Miller (Eds.), *Handbook of alcoholism treatment approaches: Effective alternatives* (pp. 195–220). Boston: Allyn & Bacon.

O'Farrell, T. J., & Fals-Stewart, W. (2003). Alcohol abuse. *Journal of Marital and Family Therapy, 29,* 121–147.

Ouimette, P. C., Finney, J. W., & Moos, R. H. (1997). Twelve-step and cognitive-behavioral treatment for substance abuse: A comparison of treatment effectiveness. *Journal of Consulting and Clinical Psychology, 65,* 230–240.

Paradise, M. J., & Cauce, A. M. (2003). Substance use and delinquency during adolescence: A prospective look at an at-risk sample. *Substance Use and Misuse, 38,* 701–723.

Peterson, J. V., Nisenholz, B., & Robinson, G. (2003). *A nation under the influence: America's addiction to alcohol.* Boston: Allyn & Bacon.

Petrakis, I. L., Gonzalez, G., Rosenheck, R., & Krystal, J. H. (2002). Comorbidity of alcoholism and psychiatric disorders: An overview. *Alcohol Research and Health, 26,* 81–89.

Project MATCH Research Group. (1997). Matching alcoholism treatments to client heterogeneity: Project MATCH posttreatment drinking outcomes. *Journal of Studies on Alcohol, 58,* 7–29.

Raistrick, D., & Davidson, D. G. (1983). Development of a questionnaire to measure alcohol dependence. *British Journal of the Addictions, 78,* 89–95.

Read, J. P., Kahler, C. W., & Stevenson, J. F. (2001). Bridging the gap between alcoholism treatment research and practice: Identifying what works and why. *Professional Psychology: Research and Practice, 32,* 227–238.

Rehm, J., Gmel, G., Sempos, C. T., & Trevisan, M. (2002). Alcohol-related morbidity and mortality. *Alcohol Research and Health, 27,* 39–49.

Rist, F., & Davies-Osterkamp, S. (1977). An alcohol-contact program: A training aimed at increasing alcoholics' willpower in tempting situations. *Drug and Alcohol Dependence, 2,* 163–173.

Robinson, E. A. R., Brower, K. J., & Kurtz, E. (2003). Life-changing experiences, spirituality and religiousness of persons entering treatment for alcohol problems. *Alcoholism Treatment Quarterly, 21,* 3–16.

Rose, R. J. (1995). Genes and human behavior. *Annual Review of Psychology, 46,* 625–644.

Ross, H. E., Gavin, D. R., & Skinner, H. A. (1990). Diagnostic validity of the MAST and the Alcohol Dependence Scale in the assessment of *DSM-III* alcohol disorders. *Journal of Studies on Alcohol, 51,* 506–513.

Rotgers, F. (2002). Clinically useful, research validated assessments of persons with alcohol problems. *Behaviour Research and Therapy, 40,* 1425–1441.

Ruiz, M. A., Pincus, A. L., & Dickinson, K. A. (2003). NEO PI-R predictors of alcohol use and alcohol-related problems. *Journal of Personality Assessment. 81,* 226–236.

Sannibale, C., & Hall, W. (1998). An evaluation of Cloninger's typology of alcohol abuse. *Addiction, 93,* 1241–1249.

Schafer, J., Caetano, R., & Clark, C. L. (1998). Rates of intimate partner violence in the United States. *American Journal of Public Health, 88,* 1702–1704.

Schuckit, M. A., Tipp, J. E., Bucholz, K. K., Nurnberger, H. I., Hesselbrock, V. M., Crowe, R. R., et al. (1997). The lifetime rates of three major mood disorders and four major anxiety disorders in alcoholics and controls. *Addiction, 92,* 1289–1304.

Secretary of Health and Human Services. (1997). *Ninth special report to the U.S. Congress on alcohol and health* (NIH Publication No. 97–4017). Washington, DC: U.S. Department of Health and Human Services, Public Health Service, National Institute of Health, National Institute on Alcohol Abuse and Alcoholism.

Segal, D. L., Hersen, M., & Van Hasselt, V. B. (1994). Reliability of the structured clinical interview for *DSM-III-R:* An evaluative review. *Comprehensive Psychiatry, 35,* 316–327.

Selzer, M. L. (1971) The Michigan Alcoholism Screening Test: The quest for a new diagnostic instrument. *American Journal of Psychiatry, 127,* 1653–1658.

Sher, K. J., Wood, M. D, Wood, P. K., & Raskin, G. (1996). Alcohol outcome expectancies and alcohol use: A latent variable cross-lagged panel study. *Journal of Abnormal Psychology, 105,* 561–574.

Skinner, H. A., & Allen, B. A. (1982). Alcohol dependence syndrome: Measurement and validation. *Journal of Abnormal Psychology, 91,* 199–209.

Smith, G. S., Branas, C. C., & Miller, T. R. (1999). Fatal non-traffic injuries involving alcohol: A meta-analysis. *Annals of Emergency Medicine. 33,* 659–668.

Smith, J. E., Meyers, R. J., & Miller, W. R. (2001). The Community Reinforcement Approach to the treatment of substance use disorders. *American Journal of Addiction, 10,* 51–59.

Snow, M., Thurber, S., & Hodgson, J. M. (2002). An adolescent version of the Michigan Alcoholism Screening Test. *Adolescence, 37,* 835–840.

Sobell, L. C., & Sobell, M. B. (1996). Timeline Follow-Back: A technique for assessing self-reported consumption. In R. Litten & J. Allen (Eds.), *Measuring alcohol consumption* (pp. 41–72). Totowa, NJ: Humana Press.

Sobell, M. B., & Sobell, L. C. (1973). Alcoholics treated by individualized behavior therapy: One year treatment outcomes. *Behaviour Research and Therapy, 11,* 599–618.

Sobell, M. B., & Sobell, L. C. (1995). Controlled drinking after 25 years: How important was the great debate? *Addiction, 90,* 1149–1153.

Staton, M., Webster, J. M., Hiller, M. L., Rostosky, S., & Leukefeld, C. (2003). An exploratory examination of spiritual well-being, religiosity, and drug use among incarcerated men. *Journal of Social Work Practice in the Addictions, 3,* 87–103.

Stewart, C. (2001). The influence of spirituality on substance use of college students. *Journal of Drug Education, 31,* 343–351.

Stewart, S. H., Zvolensky, M. J., & Eifert, G. H. (2001). Negative-reinforcement drinking motives mediate the relation between anxiety sensitivity and increased drinking behavior. *Personality and Individual Differences, 31,* 157–171.

Stockwell, T., Murphy, D., & Hodgson, R. (1983). The Severity of Alcohol Dependence Questionnaire: Its use, reliability, and validity. *British Journal of Addiction, 78,* 145–156.

Strada, M. J., & Donohue, B. (2004). Substance abuse in the workplace. In J. C. Thomas & M. Hersen (Eds.), *Psychopathology in the workplace: Recognition and adaptation.* New York: Brunner-Routledge/Taylor & Francis.

Substance Abuse and Mental Health Services Administration (SAMHSA). (2003). *Results from the 2002 National Survey on Drug Use and Health: National findings* (Office of Applied Studies, NHSDA Series H-22, HHS Publication No. SMA 03-3836). Rockville, MD: Author.

Tapert, S. F., Tate, S. R., & Brown, S. A. (2001). Substance abuse: An overview. In P. B. Sutker & H. E. Adams (Eds.), *Comprehensive handbook of psychopathology* (pp. 559–594). New York: Kluwer Academic/Plenum.

Thurber, S., Snow, M., Lewis, D., & Hodgson, J. H. (2001). Item characteristics of the Michigan Alcoholism Screening Test. *Journal of Clinical Psychology, 57,* 139–144.

Tonigan, J. S., Miller, W. R., & Brown, J. M. (1997). The reliability of Form 90: An instrument for assessing alcohol treatment outcome. *Journal of Studies on Alcohol. 58,* 358–365.

Valenzuela, C. F. (1997). Alcohol and neurotransmitter interactions. *Alcohol Health and Research World, 21,* 144–148.

Virkkunen, M., & Linnoila, M. (1990). Serotonin in early onset, male alcoholics with violent behavior. *Annals of Medicine, 22,* 327–331.

Vogel-Sprott, M., & Fillmore, M. T. (1999). Learning theory and research. In K. E. Leonard & H. T. Blane (Eds.), *Psychological theories of drinking and alcoholism* (2nd ed., pp. 292–327). New York: Guilford Press.

Waldron, H. B. (1997). Adolescent substance abuse and family therapy outcome: A review of randomized trials. In T. H. Ollendick & R. J. Prinz (Eds.), *Advances in clinical psychology* (Vol. 19, pp. 199–234). New York: Plenum Press.

Walitzer, K. S. (1999). Family therapy. In P. J. Ott, R. E. Tarter, & R. T. Ammerman (Eds.), *Sourcebook on substance abuse* (pp. 337–349). Boston: Allyn & Bacon.

Walters, G. D. (2002). The heritability of alcohol abuse and dependence: A meta-analysis of behavior genetic research. *American Journal of Drug and Alcohol Abuse, 28,* 557–584.

Weinberg, N. A., Rahdert, E., Colliver, J. D., & Glantz, M. D. (1998). Adolescent substance abuse: A review of the past 10 years. *Journal of the American Academy of Child and Adolescent Psychiatry, 37,* 252–261.

Wilk, A. I., Jensen, M. J., & Havighurst, T. C. (1997). Meta-analysis of randomized control trials addressing brief interventions in heavy alcohol drinkers. *Journal of General Internal Medicine, 12,* 274–283.

Witkiewitz, K., & Marlatt, G. A. (2004). Relapse prevention for alcohol and drug problems: That was zen, this is tao. *American Psychologist, 59,* 224–235.

CHAPTER 21

Drug Abuse and Dependence

BRAD DONOHUE, ALISHA M. FARLEY, AND SAMANTHA L. FRENCH

DRUG ABUSE DISORDERS

Drug abuse and dependence are crippling disorders that are associated with extreme negative consequences. Indeed, health care expenses, accidents, crime, and decreased productivity resulting from drug abuse in the United States are estimated to exceed $245 billion annually (Harwood, Fountain, Livermore, & The Lewin Group, 1998). Fortunately, well-controlled applied research initiatives have led to enhanced assessment and treatment methodologies for those afflicted by drug abuse and dependence, particularly during the past two decades. Commensurate with these advancements, there has been increased recognition of various etiological factors influencing the development and progression of substance abuse and dependence. For instance, scientists have been able to identify and prevent risk factors that perpetuate this widespread problem. This chapter presents an overview of drug abuse and dependence, including its clinical presentation, prevalence, etiology, and empirically validated methods to assess and treat these disorders.

DESCRIPTION OF THE DISORDER AND CLINICAL PICTURE

The *Diagnostic and Statistical Manual of Mental Disorders* (*DSM-IV-TR;* American Psychiatric Association, 2000) recognizes 11 classes of drugs that may be abused (e.g., alcohol, amphetamines, cannabis, cocaine, hallucinogens, inhalants). With the exception of alcohol and nicotine, this chapter will underscore all of these drug classes to some extent. For each class, it is possible to receive a diagnosis for intoxication, abuse, dependence, and withdrawal. Intoxication is diagnosed when a drug-specific reaction occurs after direct contact is made with the respective drug (e.g., absorbed through exterior skin) or the drug is consumed or ingested (e.g., injected, swallowed, inhaled), and this reaction results in maladaptive behavioral or psychological changes. In general, increasing the rate at which drugs are absorbed into the bloodstream will lead to quicker and more intense drug reactions, and drugs within the same class usually result in somewhat similar intoxicating effects. For instance, Valium and Xanax (both benzodiazapines) may cause the individual to feel sedated, whereas dextroamphetamine and methamphetamine (both amphetamines) may result in decreased appetite and alertness. Concurrent use of substances within the same class may result in an increase in the intensity of intoxication effects (i.e., potentiation). In examining individuals for drug intoxication, it is imperative to rule out medical conditions and mental disorders. Indeed, apparent signs of intoxication may be due to a medical or neurological disorder that if incorrectly diagnosed and not treated immediately may lead to death.

Drug abuse involves significant problems resulting from substance use without tolerance, withdrawal or a pattern of compulsive use. Specifically, within a 12-month period repeated use of the drug results in either inability to fulfill major role obligations, use in dangerous situations, legal problems, or use despite social or interpersonal problems. *Drug dependence* is more severe and may be diagnosed if at least three of the following symptoms have been present within a 12-month period: (1) tolerance (chronic use necessitates larger amounts of the drug to experience the same effects that were obtained when the drug was first used); (2) withdrawal (a substance-specific syndrome resulting from abrupt reduction or termination of intense substance use that causes considerable distress or impairment in functioning); (3) using more of the drug than originally intended; (4) desire or unsuccessful efforts to cut down drug use; (5) spending a lot of time obtaining, taking, or recovering from the effects of the drug (e.g., prostituting oneself or selling possessions of family members to obtain drugs); (6) reduction of important social, occupational, or recreational activities; and (7) continued use of the drug even with the knowledge of the physical or psychological problems it causes.

As indicated previously, the various drugs of abuse elicit specific reactions, and each drug class presents a distinct clinical picture. For instance, while intoxicated on amphetamines (e.g., dextroamphetamine, methamphetamine or "speed," appetite suppressants or "diet pills") individuals may experience alertness, loss of weight due to loss of appetite, headaches, palpitations, rapid heart rate, rambling speech, restlessness, paranoid thoughts, repetitive stereotyped behaviors (e.g., teeth grinding), and auditory and tactile hallucinations (Schuckit, 1995). Sustained use can result in malnutrition, weight loss due to decreased appetite, and poor hygiene. Other negatively experienced symptoms include aggression, violence, theft, sexual promiscuity, and financial instability. Presenting complaints often include seizures, cardiac complaints, malnutrition, and nosebleeds (APA, 2000). Desired effects of amphetamine intoxication, as well as cocaine intoxication (which is in its own class; see following paragraph), include intense feelings of euphoria, decreased perceptions of pain, and an abundance of energy. Other substances that are commonly used in combination with these drugs include marijuana and central nervous system depressants (e.g., heroin, alcohol) because these substances act to reverse the stimulant effects. For instance, amphetamines usually cause a lack of sleep and impulsive behaviors that often get the individual in trouble (e.g., theft, initiating arguments), whereas central nervous system depressants ("downers") facilitate sleep and reduce impulsive behavior.

Cocaine is diagnosed separately from amphetamines, although its effects are similar because it is also a stimulant. As with most drugs, intensity of its effects is different depending upon the route of administration (i.e., intravenously, orally, or snorting) and extent of adulterants that are either purposely or accidentally mixed into the drug. Complications include cardiovascular problems (e.g., sinus tachycardia, ventricular tachycardia, fibrillation, heart attack), central nervous system disruptions (e.g., seizures, cerebral hemorrhage, transient ischemic attacks), respiratory paralysis, renal failure, liver dysfunction, and sudden death (see Frances & Miller, 1998).

Cannabis abuse (i.e., marijuana, bhang, ganja, hashish, sensimilla) is one of the most frequently abused drug classes. It is usually smoked, with the onset of its effects taking about a half an hour, and lasting between 5 and 12 hours. Eating these substances (e.g., "hashish brownies") will lead to delayed and less intense intoxication, as compared with other methods of use. Desired effects of cannabis include laughter, relaxation, and reduced pain. Negatively experienced symptoms of cannabis intoxication include impaired short-term memory, poor perception of time, and anxiety. Hallucinations, delusions, and delirium infrequently occur, and chronic use can lead to severe lethargy and lack of interest to perform activities. Cannabis users are often polysubstance abusers, with the other drugs usually including alcohol, nicotine, hallucinogens and cocaine (Weiss & Millman, 1998). Marijuana has been associated with depression, anxiety, and irritability in about one-third of regular users (APA, 2000), and there is some support to suggest regular use of marijuana impairs sperm production, reduces testosterone secretion, shrinks the prostate and testes in males, and blocks ovulation in females (see Tapert, Tate, & Brown, 2001).

Lysergic acid diethylamide (LSD), peyote, and methylenedioxymethamphetamine (i.e., MDMA or Ecstasy) are considered to be hallucinogens because use of these substances may result in hallucinations, enhanced or distorted perceptions, loss of contact with reality, depersonalization, paranoia, or confusion. Most hallucinogens are orally consumed, although they can be smoked, snorted, orally ingested, or intravenously injected. If injected or smoked, effects are immediate, whereas oral ingestion causes peak effects to occur approximately two hours after ingestion. The effects from these drugs usually subside within 8 to 20 hours. Symptoms of PCP use, however, may persist for several days to weeks. Frequent use leads to unusually rapid tolerance (APA, 2000), and negative effects of these drugs are usually indirectly related to the delusional beliefs experienced during intoxication. For example, a woman might attempt to jump out a second story window due to beliefs that she can fly. Other direct effects include impairment in visual-motor scanning abilities, memory deficits, and severe Parkinsonian symptoms (see Tapert et al., 2001). PCP, specifically, may result in coma and death, with individuals most often presenting to emergency rooms with extreme anxiety. Chronic prolonged use can lead to a decrease in intellectual functioning or even organic brain syndrome (Schuckit, 1995).

Inhalant abuse is particularly dangerous and includes glue, adhesives, paint, paint thinner, nail polish remover, gasoline, lighter fluid, cleaning solutions, antifreeze, correction fluid, and PVC cement (Weiss & Millman, 1998). Techniques used to inhale these substances include "ragging" (i.e., breathing a substance-soaked rag through the nose or mouth), "bagging" (i.e., inhaling gases contained in a plastic or paper bag), or inhaling after vaporizing the substances with heat. The onset of intoxication resulting from inhalant use is almost always rapid, and lasts from a few minutes to an hour. Due to its availability and low cost, disadvantaged children and adolescents abuse inhalants more often than other populations. Use of inhalants can lead to severe physical complications, including eye, nose, and throat damage, respiratory difficulty, kidney, heart, nervous system, and gastrointestinal problems. Death via heart arrhythmias or suffocation can occur (see Tapert et al., 2001). Dizziness, confusion, hallucinations, delusions, uncoordination, slurred speech, unsteady gait, lethargy, tremors, muscle weakness, blurred vision, and coma may be experienced consequent to hallucinogen use. Inhalants are usually not the primary drug of choice, but they are rather used as secondary drugs by individuals who are addicted to other substances (Weiss & Millman, 1998).

Opiates (diagnosed as *opioid abuse/dependence*) include opium, morphine, codeine, the semisynthetic drugs produced from poppy seeds (e.g., heroin, hydromorphone, and oxycodone), and the synthetic analgesics of meperidine (Demerol), propoxyphene (Darvon), and methadone (Dolophine). Methods of administration include snorting, smoking, injecting, and orally ingesting. Injection use is particularly dangerous, as it sometimes results in HIV, hepatitis, cellulites, endocarditis, and tuberculosis due to infected needles, and death from overdose is more prevalent than other illicit drugs (see Tapert et al., 2001). These substances produce analgesia and lethargy, and depression is a common side effect.

Sedatives (i.e., daytime calming drugs), hypnotics (i.e., nighttime calming drugs that promote sleep), and anxiolytics (i.e., antianxiety drugs) are often administered in conjunction with other drugs to assist in relieving stress, depression, and anxiety. Drugs in this class include benzodiazepines, carbamates, barbiturates, and other prescription sleeping and antianxiety medications. Similar to alcohol, these drugs are central nervous system depressants, and they can be lethal, particularly when combined with other substances, such as alcohol.

PERSONALITY DEVELOPMENT AND PSYCHOPATHOLOGY

The relationship between personality development and drug use behavior is complex, and not fully understood. However, personality appears to influence the development of drug disorders, and in turn, drug abusive behavior patterns influence the development of personality. Although a comprehensive review of contributing personality characteristics is beyond the scope of this chapter, some of these contributing factors will be briefly reviewed here to provide an appreciation of this process. For instance, impulsivity is a common personality trait in drug abusers, and people who act impulsively are less likely to consider negative consequences associated with drug use (see Sussman & Ames, 2001). They may engage in illicit drug use at a party while knowing little about the drug, or habitually use a substance in response to a negative emotional state without first attempting to think of alternative solutions to problem scenarios. The intoxicating effects of drugs further impair judgment and executive functioning, thus contributing to negative experiences with the environment, and higher levels of stress. Other personality traits that have been associated with drug abuse include rebelliousness (Segal, Huba, & Singer), aggressive tendencies (Krueger, Caspi, Moffitt, Silva, & McGee, 1996), and sensation seeking (i.e., willingness to take substantial risks to experience novel, complex, and intense sensations and experiences; Zuckerman, 1994). Experimentation with novel drugs often satisfy urges of most sensation seekers, particularly if the drug's effects are unpredictable, and lead to perceived insight and feelings of euphoria and energy (e.g., hallucinogens, amphetamines, cocaine). Sensation seekers pose a problem to society because these individuals are more likely than non-sensation-seeking individuals to engage in dangerous activities while intoxicated (e.g., driving while under the influence of illegal substances). Similarly, aggressive tendencies are more pronounced during periods of intoxication, resulting in potential domestic violence and child maltreatment.

EPIDEMIOLOGY

Epidemiology, as relevant to clinical psychology, is the study of the frequency and distribution of a disorder within the general population as well as within specific populations. This section will outline the prevalence and incidence of illicit drug abuse. Along these lines, selected results from the 2002 National Survey of Drug Use and Health (Office of Applied Studies, Substance Abuse and Mental Health Services Administration, 2003), which provides national estimates of drug, alcohol, and tobacco use as well as estimates of new users per year (incidence), will be underscored in this section. Accordingly, 16.6 million Americans at least 18 years of age (7 percent of the U.S. population within this age range) were identified to be current illicit drug users in 2002. An estimated 11 million (4.7 percent) Americans aged 12 years or older reported driving under the influence of an illicit drug within the past year. Approximately 9 percent of (22 million) Americans aged 12 or older were classified with substance abuse or dependence, with 7.1 million being classified with abuse or dependence of both alcohol and illicit drugs (3.2 million) or solely illicit drugs (3.9 million). Out of the 22 million persons classified with substance abuse or dependence, an estimated 19.8 million persons are adults.

In examining specific illicit drug use, National Survey on Drug Use and Health (NSDUH) investigators reported that approximately 2 million (0.9 percent) of persons aged 12 years or older were current cocaine users in 2002, with the vast majority of these individuals being adults. Of these 2 million, approximately 28 percent (i.e., 567,000) were using crack cocaine. Incidence of new users of cocaine has been slowly on the rise since the 1990s and was estimated at 1.2 million for 2001. An estimated 1.2 million were using hallucinogens in 2002. Of these 1.2 million, 676,000 (56.3 percent) were MDMA (i.e., Ecstasy) users. Use of hallucinogens seems to be on the rise since the 1990s, particularly among young adults (i.e., 18 to 25 years), increasing from 14.3 percent in 1992 to 24.2 percent in 2002. Incidence of new hallucinogen users followed a similar trend with an estimated 706,000 new users in 1992, and an estimated 1.6 million in 2001. There were 166,000 Americans at least 12 years old who were found to use heroin. Heroin use in young adults ages 18 to 25 years has doubled since the mid-1990s (i.e., 0.8 percent to 1.6 percent). The number of new heroin users, however, has remained rather steady with more than 100,000 new users each year from 1995 to 2001. According to NSDUH, marijuana is the most commonly used illicit drug with 6.2 percent, or 14.6 million, of the population at least 12 years old endorsing use within the past month. Approximately one-third (4.8 million) of these persons report using marijuana 20 or more days within a given month. The percentage of adults aged 18 to 25 years who reported ever using marijuana was essentially the same during 2001 and 2002 (i.e., 53 percent in 2001 and 54 percent in 2002). Consistent with these results, the estimation of new marijuana users for 2001 was similar to previous years since 1965, at 2.6 million. In 2002, 6.2 million (2.6 percent) individuals were estimated to abuse prescription drugs. Seventy-one percent (4.4 million) of these 6.2 million were abusing pain relievers, 29 percent (1.8 million) were abusing tranquilizers, 19.4 percent (1.2 million) were abusing stimulants, and 6.5 percent (0.4 million) were abusing sedatives. Incidence of the nonprescriptive use of pain relievers was about the same in 2000 and 2001 (i.e., 2.7 million in 2000, 2.4 million in 2001).

ETIOLOGY

What causes some individuals to use drugs and others to abstain from them? Although this question has yet to be sufficiently answered, several theories of addiction have been postulated that evidence empirical support. Consistent with the tenets espoused in these theories (see following paragraph), risk factors have been identified that increase the likelihood of drug use. Risk factors contribute to the initiation and continuation of drug use, whereas protective factors are at the other end of this continuum, acting to reduce the risk of drug abuse (e.g., strong attachment to abstinent friends and family members, lack of drug availability; see Sussman & Ames, 2001). In conceptualizing the development and maintenance of drug addiction, it is perhaps best to think of drug addiction as being influenced by various contributing factors that interact with each other throughout the progression of this disorder. Along these lines, it is very doubtful one factor will result in a drug disorder, although some factors will certainly exert greater influence than others, depending on environmental context. For instance, there appears to be a link between genetics and drug abuse and dependence, although this link is unclear due to a lack of controlled studies in this area (Erickson, 2000). Indeed, there are numerous anecdotes describing offspring of substance abusing parents who do not develop drug addiction, suggesting environmental protective factors may counteract addiction for individuals who may be genetically predisposed. However, this is speculative, as research in this area has yet to be adequately performed.

The environment contributes to the development of drug addiction in many ways, including positive and negative reinforcement for behaviors that are consistent with drug use (i.e., operant conditioning), and modeling of drug use (i.e., social learning theory; Donohue & Azrin, 2002). Positive reinforcers for drug use include pleasurable stimulating effects of the drug, and acceptance of esteemed others. Negative reinforcers for drug use (i.e., termination of an aversive stimulus consequent to drug use) include reductions in stress, fear, or anxiety. For instance, an individual who becomes anxious during social situations might get high from marijuana while attending a party. If the marijuana use resulted in a reduction in anxiety symptoms at the party, negative reinforcement would be demonstrated if future marijuana use occurred during similar social situations. Withdrawal symptoms also act to negatively reinforce future drug use (i.e., drug use eliminates aversive withdrawal symptoms that occur consequent to abrupt termination of the respective drug, thus increasing the likelihood of future drug use).

In almost all cases, drug use behavior is preceded by antecedent stimuli (e.g., offers to use drugs, drug associated friends, drug paraphernalia, streets in which drugs are sold). Through past associations with the pleasurable aspects of drug use (i.e., classical conditioning), these antecedent stimuli may result in strong cravings for drugs, or thoughts regarding the beneficial aspects of using drugs, thus increasing the likelihood of drug abuse. Teachings espoused in Narcotics Anonymous (i.e., recommendations to stay away from people and places in which drug use has been associated) are consistent with behavioral theories in this regard (Dodgen & Shea, 2000).

Along a different vein, individuals who perceive positive outcomes will result from drug use are at increased risk to use drugs (see Tapert et al., 2001). For instance, younger children often have negative outcome expectancies of drug use when their parents do not engage in drug use. However, as they grow older peers become more important, and their expectancies of drug use may become more positive if their peers are drug users. Indeed, social learning theory posits that individuals learn from the observation of others, particularly when valued or esteemed models are reinforced for the modeled behavior.

Other etiological models offer unique insights to the development of substance disorders. For instance, those who espouse the moral model of addiction believe this disorder is characterized by a lack of willpower or motivation. The individual who evidences a problem with drug abuse or dependence is solely responsible for its development and recovery (see Tapert et al., 2001). This model is in sharp contrast to the disease model, in which "alcoholism" is purportedly influenced by biological or physiological factors that are outside the control of the individual (Erickson, 2000). In addition, addicts must admit they are powerless over the disorder, and seek help from professionals to aid in the recovery process. However, many of the fundamental tenets underlying the disease model of addiction (e.g., avoidance of people, places, and situations that are associated with drug use, social encouragement for abstinence) are very compatible with behavior theory (see Tapert et al., 2001).

It has long been established that individuals are far less likely to develop drug abuse in supportive and loving families who encourage behaviors that are incompatible with drug abusive behavior (see Tapert et al., 2001). Conversely, parental conflict often contributes to poor supervision of youth because they are too focused on resolving their own problems, thus leaving less time to harmoniously spend with their children. Indeed, child neglect is a strong predictor of drug abuse (see Donohue, 2004). In understanding the relationship between child neglect victimization and later development of drug abuse, it should be emphasized that children who do not receive sufficient levels of attention are frequently unsupervised. When youth are unsupervised, they are not provided valuable opportunities to learn skills that are incompatible with drug use (e.g., study skills, social skills, empathy and compassion, work ethic, importance of being abstinent) from their parents. These skill deficits are exacerbated when neglecting parents abuse drugs due to modeling influences and there are greater opportunities to engage in drug use behavior (e.g., easy access to drugs and drug use paraphernalia, more time with antisocial peers who are more likely to encourage drug use). The desire for social acceptance becomes critical to neglected youth. Indeed, when youth are denied parental attention, they will usually seek it out from those who are willing to provide such attention and acceptance, particularly during adolescence. In these circumstances, youth may use drugs to "fit in" with their peers or let their parents know there are problems that require their attention.

Being raised in an impoverished community also contributes to drug abuse (Sussman & Ames, 2001). Indeed, poverty is associated with a lack of positive role models and financial support for drug incompatible recreational activities, frustration and stress resulting from unwanted jobs or unemployment that is influenced by a lack of education, poor supervision because single parents often must work extended hours, inferior day care, and greater exposure to crime, drugs, and psychiatric illness. Along similar lines, Mueser, Bellack, and Blanchard (1992) found 23 percent of individuals with an anxiety disorder abuse substances (particularly women), 32 percent of individuals who evidence affective disorders (e.g., major depression, dysthymia), and 47 percent of individuals with schizophrenia will abuse drugs at some point during their illness. Perhaps most striking, only 17 percent of individuals who were not found to evidence a mental health disorder were found to abuse drugs. The repeated pattern of drug use in the aforementioned disorders is brought about through negative reinforcement. The aversive experiences brought about by anxiety, depression, or delusions are temporarily eliminated consequent to the intoxicating effects of drug use. Unfortunately, drug use exacerbates the undesired mood state, and the cycle continues.

COURSE, COMPLICATIONS, AND PROGNOSIS

Complications

Physiologically induced complications of drug use were reported previously when describing substance abuse and dependence, and as indicated, these symptoms vary considerably depending on the respective drug that is being abused. However, it is certainly clear that the substance abuser is at higher risk of lethality due to (1) ingesting toxic amounts of the respective drug (i.e., "overdose"), (2) abrupt cessation of the drug (i.e., withdrawal), and (3) accidents resulting from drug intoxication (e.g., automobile accident while driving under the influence, jumping off a cliff while hallucinating). The risk of lethality is increased when two or more drugs are used at the same time. In these circumstances, lethality is possible because the interaction of various drug effects are often dangerous and unpredictable, and because drug effects may become potentiated (i.e., intensified). Therefore, it is critical to assess drug use during each therapy session, and consider hospitalization when danger is indicated.

Substance abuse and dependence is complicated by coexisting mental health conditions, most often including depressive, anxiety, bipolar, antisocial personality, eating, schizophrenia, and attention/deficit hyperactivity disorders (see Azrin et al., 1994; Ziedonis & Brady, 1997). Specifically, symptoms of drug use (e.g., lack of energy, excessive sleep) often resemble mental health symptoms, and substance abusers who are dually diagnosed with a mental health disorder frequently deny drug abuse in mental health settings (Shaner et al., 1993). Thus, drug abuse symptoms may be falsely attributed to mental health disorders, and obfuscate reliable diagnosis and monitoring of treatment outcomes. For instance, both stimulant drugs and anxiety disorders may cause palpitations, rapid heart rate, rambling speech, and restlessness, thus influencing many clinicians to erroneously overlook potential substance or anxiety disorders. This would be an important oversight because the treatments for these disorders are very different.

Relevant to treatment planning, substance abusers notoriously fail to comply with treatment protocol, as often manifested in their poor performance in attending sessions, completing therapy homework assignments, and arriving on time for scheduled sessions. Indeed, more than half of individuals in drug rehabilitation settings have been found to withdraw from treatment prematurely (McCusker, Stoddard, Frost, & Zorn, 1996). Fortunately, empirically validated interventions have been developed to improve session attendance and promptness, including session reminder calls and postcards, instructing individuals to repeat directions and the scheduled session time to assure they know how to get to the facility on time, and brainstorming solutions to anticipated problems that may occur in preventing timely session attendance (see review by Donohue et al., 1998). Behavioral techniques may also be effective in the improvement of homework compliance, such as modeling the completion of homework assignments for hypothetical days, instructing individuals to complete hypothetical homework assignments for the current day prior to leaving the office, and requiring individuals to finish incomplete homework assignments in the waiting room prior to starting the session.

Course

The course of drug abuse and dependence varies, according to many factors, including the specific drug of abuse, stressors in the environment, the age of drug use onset, and environmental factors that contribute to the development and maintenance of the disorder. However, the pattern of drug use progression is somewhat consistent for most drug abusers, as they report the onset of their first use of illicit drugs (almost always marijuana) usually occurs in their early teens, typically within a year after the onset of their first ingestion of alcohol (Azrin et al., 2001). The onset of all other drugs (i.e., often referred to as *hard drugs*) typically occurs within a year of the onset of marijuana. For this reason, marijuana and alcohol have been labeled *gateway drugs*. For most, the onset of drug use occurs during a period of experimentation, and is associated with normal healthy development (Waldron, 1997). Indeed, experimentation with substances is usually a phase, and does not become problematic or addictive (Bukstein et al., 1997). For some, however, the onset of drug use emerges into abuse and dependence, particularly when environmental stressors are present (e.g., family conflict, poor school adjustment, and lack of involvement in drug incompatible activities). Adolescent onset of drug abuse and dependence is somewhat unique to adult onset. For instance, adolescents, as compared with adults, are more likely to engage in polysubstance use and are at increased risk of drug overdose, toxic drug interaction effects, and potentiation due to a lack of knowledge of drug effects, lack of tolerance, and tendency to engage in drug experimentation. The initial stages of abuse and dependence are marked by relatively frequent use with others when onset occurs during adolescence, as compared with adult onset. Indeed, adolescents appear to be more likely to use drugs at weekend parties or "get-togethers" with friends, whereas adult onset drug abusers are more likely to use alone as a method of stress reduction. However, regardless of the time of onset, drug use frequency and quantity consumed per occasion inevitably increases as tolerance develops and the reinforcing aspects of drug use are allowed to occur.

Patterns of drug use appear to vary according to the specific drug abused. For instance, individuals who are diagnosed with cocaine and amphetamine dependence exhibit a pattern of use that is usually episodic and sometimes daily. Indeed, crack cocaine drug abusers will often "binge" shortly after being paid or obtaining money from prostitution or theft and will usually do so until they are unable to purchase more drugs. Tolerance to cocaine and other stimulants occurs quickly to protect the individual from overdose. Therefore, strong dependency can develop within a few weeks, and abusers of stimulant drugs sometimes use until serious health problems or severe detrimental consequences (e.g., terminated from employment, loss of home) force the individual to abstain. Interestingly, opiates are also abused for extended periods of time because the high is reportedly blissful, and its discontinuation is associated with severe withdrawal symptoms. A common course includes several relapses and remissions. When first using, and then again when relapsing, opioid abusers usually administer several times a day because of the short half-life of this drug. Typically, individuals initiate sedative, hypnotic, and anxiolytic use later than most other drugs, usually in their late teens, to relieve pain or assist in sleeping and leading to daily use. Given its pleasant effects and relatively nonaversive negative consequences relative to other drugs, with the exception of alcohol, marijuana is the most often co-occurring substance. Its frequency and pattern of use varies tremendously among drug abusers, as some use this substance only at occasional parties or small social gatherings, whereas others use marijuana on a daily basis, perhaps alone or with friends or family.

In general, the progression of drug abuse to drug dependence is inevitably associated with increasingly greater amounts of substance use, as tolerance develops. Although tolerance reduces the risk of overdose, other detrimental consequences (e.g., accidents, unemployment, family conflicts and violence) are drastically increased with continued use. Most drug abusers are reluctant to enter treatment initially, but may be forced to receive professional treatment by frustrated family members, court mandates, or employers when their tolerance expires. In a minority of situations, the drug abuser may appreciate the severity of the addiction, and self-refer to treatment.

Prognosis

Most drug users will not develop drug abuse or dependence (Waldron, 1997). However, when drug abuse, and particularly drug dependence, occurs the prognosis is poor, particularly when intervention is absent. Frequent lapses after short periods of abstinence, and relapses after extended periods of abstinence, are commonly encountered throughout the process of recovery, most often due to negative emotional states, peer pressure, interpersonal conflict, and drug cravings (Dimeff & Marlatt, 1995). Indeed, fewer than 50 percent of individuals who complete empirically supported substance abuse treatment programs remain abstinent after the conclusion of treatment (see review by Acierno, Donohue, & Kogan, 1994). Prognostic indicators of treatment outcome success include the implementation of intervention shortly after the onset of drug use, low severity of drug use, compliance to treatment protocol, attending regularly scheduled sessions, and absence of comorbid mental health disorders (e.g., Sharp & Getz, 1998).

ASSESSMENT AND DIAGNOSIS

The assessment and diagnosis of drug use is usually performed in medical and psychiatric hospitals and residential settings, mental health centers, halfway houses, and outpatient drug abuse clinics. Thus, collaboration between nurses, physicians, social workers, and psychologists is common (Rasmussen, 2000). Each member of the collaborative team utilizes various assessment measures and techniques to screen, diagnose, and assess individuals who are suspected to abuse drugs. Measures of substance use and abuse have been empirically developed within the context of self-report screening methods, toxicology testing, structured interviews, direct observation, and self-report measures.

Substance abusing individuals are frequently unmotivated for assessment, and notoriously poor informants. For instance, illicit drug use is known to exacerbate encoding and retrieval of memory, and substance abusers usually have a history of being scrutinized for drug use and associated problem behaviors. Therefore, significant others (i.e., family members, friends, employers) of substance abusers should always be incorporated into the assessment process to enhance accuracy of assessment findings (Donohue, Azrin, Strada, Silver, & Teichner, 2004).

Self-Report Screening Measures

Prior to being identified to abuse or neglect drugs, most individuals who are suspected of substance abuse participate in drug screening procedures, either voluntarily or involuntarily (i.e., mandated by an employer, court, or family member). The drug screening process typically involves the administration of standardized self-report instruments and/or toxicology tests. The purpose of screening is to expediently determine whether there is potentially a drug use problem for which an individual will likely benefit from drug abuse prevention or intervention services. With the exception of toxicology testing, screening measures are usually brief self-report questionnaires that are administered to individuals who are suspected of drug abuse or dependence, such as the Drug Abuse Screening Test (DAST; Skinner, 1982). Screening procedures may be implemented in a variety of settings and circumstances, including employment agencies to assist in the hiring process or determine drug use among employees, mental health settings when other disorders are present as the primary focus of treatment, and correctional facilities when inmates are admitted. Upon being identified to report symptoms that are consistent with drug abuse, the individual is usually required, or invited, to complete a comprehensive psychological assessment. Unfortunately, drug use can remain undetected unless the informant is honest and candid during the self-report screening process. In the event drug use is denied, or suspected, toxicology testing procedures may be administered to provide an objective screen for illicit drug use.

Toxicology Testing

Toxicology tests are frequently employed by physicians and mental health professionals to verify suspicions of drug use and objectively evaluate treatment. Substances can be detected through various toxicology tests involving bodily fluids (i.e., analysis of urine, blood, sweat, saliva, gastric contents) and hair testing. In general, drugs will remain in the body for up to five times the half-life of the respective drug (Williams & Baer, 1994). Half-life is considered to be the time it takes the individual to reduce the active drug in the circulation by 50 percent (see Doweiko, 2002). Hair follicle tests are relatively expensive, although the period in which drugs can be detected may be several months. Given hair growth, more recent drug use will be indicated closer to the scalp. Thus, sophisticated hair follicle analyses may assist in examining the hair follicle at different lengths, and approximate when drug use occurred. Bodily fluids may detect substance use from up to a few weeks (e.g., marijuana) to a few hours (e.g., alcohol). However, the number of days a substance may be detected subsequent to use from toxicology screens will depend on several interacting factors, including the type and amount of substance used, obesity, inactivity, and chronicity of drug use, all of which may lengthen the time in which drug use can be detected. Broad screen drug panels may be purchased from toxicology laboratories to permit the testing of multiple drugs, whereas single panel tests are available to detect only one substance. Of course, multiple panel drug tests are more costly than single panel tests, resulting in the customary practice of testing only those drugs that are suspected. To avoid the expense of testing, clinicians often forego scheduled urinalysis testing when those suspected of drug use report drug use proactively. This is probably a mistake when multiple drug use is likely. For instance, "hard drug" users (e.g., cocaine) often report marijuana and alcohol use because these substances are associated with less societal penalties than hard drugs. In these situations, relying on self-report data may result in failure to detect other targeted drugs.

Clinical Interview

Most counselors initiate comprehensive assessment of substance abuse with either an unstructured, semistructured, or structured clinical interview. In the unstructured interview, the clinical content and guidelines dictating the interviewer's method of responding are at the discretion of the interviewer. The initial stages of most unstructured interviews focus on identifying, and broadly understanding the extent and determinants of substance abuse behavior, whereas the latter stages focus on reviewing general life domains that are not directly related to drug use. Counselors typically assess reasons for the referral, substance abuse history, mental status, medical history, social and academic history, hobbies, family background, comorbid diagnoses, strengths, and goals for therapy. However, the specific domains to be assessed are at the discretion of the interviewer. The interviewer is also free to record interviewee responses that appear most relevant. Many counselors incorporate functional analysis methods into their interview format to understand the factors that maintain drug use, including the onset, frequency, intensity, and duration of drug use as well as stimuli that precede (i.e., antecedents), follow (consequences), and co-occur (concomitants) with drug use. Interviewers also assess stimuli that occur when the problem behavior is absent. In this way, interviewers are able to determine stimuli that may be incompatible with drug use, thus assisting in treatment planning. The unstructured interview is relatively unreliable because interviewers will vary in the questions they ask, and the responses they record.

Structured interviews tend to yield global indexes concerning the presence or absence of a disorder. The interviewer is usually restricted to utilizing questions that are generically applied to all interviewees. That is, the questions are predetermined, and usually focused on the assessment of substance use. The interviewer is also trained to record responses according to a prescribed response format (e.g., 1 = criterion met, 2 = unsure, 3 = criterion not met). In this manner, structured interviews tend to be reliable and valid assessment tools. The Structured Clinical Interview for Axis I Disorders, Version 2 (SCID II; First, Gibbon, Williams, & Spitzer, 1994) is an example of a structured interview that may be used to obtain diagnostic criteria for *DSM* disorders. The assessment of substance disorders (section E) is consistent with a decision-tree format, allowing accurate diagnosis without extraneous questioning. The rigorous structure of the SCID-II makes it an excellent tool in research settings. The SCID-II has demonstrated excellent reliability and validity (First et al., 1994).

Semistructured interviews often include a list of questions that are relevant to the assessment of a specific problem area. However, unlike the structured interview format, the interviewer is usually free to choose standard questions from a generic list. Similarly, guidelines are available to assist in scoring or interpreting interviewee responses. Interviewers who solely rely upon structured and semistructured interview approaches, as compared with unstructured interview formats, risk missing important idiosyncratic information that may have been absent from interview protocol. Although the prescribed nature of the semistructured and structured interviews may interfere with the establishment of rapport, this problem is usually avoided with extended training and experience. Moreover, structured interviews do not prohibit interviewers from formulating their own questions to clarify responses but rather provide detailed guidelines. Recently, there has been an increase in the use of semistructured and structured interviews in clinical practice with drug abusers due to their adaptability to computerized administration and scoring procedures.

In conducting clinical interviews in substance abuse populations, multiple informants should be interviewed separately, whenever feasible, to assess differing perspectives of drug abuse behavior, assist in understanding inconsistencies in interviewee reports, and provide additional information to assist in treatment planning.

Direct Observation

Monitoring drug use behavior is extremely valuable, as early detection is associated with enhanced outcome. Therefore, assuring familiarity with behavior patterns that typically result during intoxication and withdrawal, and monitoring behavioral changes that are consistent with these patterns, will be of great assistance in the assessment of ongoing drug use. For instance, if barbiturate use were suspected, it would be advantageous for a spouse or employer to monitor behaviors that are consistent with its intoxicating effects (e.g., slurred speech and unsteady gait). Similarly, physical side effects (e.g., red eyes consequent to marijuana use) may be observed during, or shortly after, intoxication. When substance abusers hide indications of drug use, behaviors that are associated with drug use can be monitored, including various criminal acts, prostitution, and work absenteeism. Indeed, amelioration of these behaviors is usually a good indicator of abstinence from drugs as well as goal attainment regarding the recovery process (Azrin et al., 1994).

Withdrawal symptoms may be indicators that a drug dependent individual is in need of detoxification or monitoring in a residential setting. For instance, abrupt cessation of Valium, a benzodiazapine, might result in sudden anxiety, difficulties sleeping, tremors, nausea, and irritability. Although monitoring of undesired behavior may be appropriate for pretreatment assessment, with the initiation of therapy, drug-incompatible behaviors should be monitored instead (e.g., attendance at work, sporting events, church), thus permitting performance of these behaviors to be praised and rewarded.

Self-Report Measures

Self-report measures of substance use and related problem behaviors assist in recognizing patterns of drug use, and circumstances that make drug use more likely. In the Timeline Follow-Back method (Sobell & Sobell, 1996), the substance abuser is presented with a calendar that retrospectively goes back up to one year. The calendar initially includes significant events that are commonly experienced (e.g., national holidays, memorable national or local events, catastrophic weather). The substance abuser is then instructed to record significant personal events (e.g., birthdays, social events, parties, sporting events) in the appropriate dates. The aforementioned events serve to anchor memories of past drug use. Indeed, the individual is subsequently queried to record the days in which specific drugs were used in the calendar, including the amounts whenever possible. Polysubstance use can be recorded as well as giving a complete picture of the pattern of substance use over an extended time period. Psychometric properties of the TLFB are excellent (Sobell & Sobell, 1996).

Other self-report inventories include the Severity of Dependence Scale (SDS; Gossop, Best, Marsden, & Strang, 1997), the Drug-Taking Confidence Questionnaire (DTCQ; Sklar, Annis, & Turner, 1997), the Inventory of Drug-Taking Situations (IDTS; Turner, Annis, & Sklar, 1997), and the Substance Dependence Severity Scale (SDSS; Miele et al., 2000). These empirically validated measures all provide useful, albeit unique, information that is specific to drug use behavior.

IMPACT ON ENVIRONMENT

Costs of drug abuse have been estimated to be about 1 percent of the gross domestic product (United Nations, 1998). The National Institute on Drug Abuse (NIDA) has estimated that drug abuse and dependence costs the United States about $98 billion a year in health care expenses, premature death, impaired productivity, motor vehicle crashes, crime, and social welfare.

Family

Drug abuse leads to devastating negative consequences for both the drug abuser, and those individuals who are involved in the drug abuser's life. As emphasized by Stevens (2000a), family cohesion is disrupted, communication strategies tend to be poor, and anger and hostility proliferate among household members of drug abusers. These families are wrought with secrets, and it is common for children and significant others to avoid drug-abusing loved ones due to being frequently embarrassed by them while intoxicated. In violent drug abusers, family members are sometimes hypervigilant and fearful that abusers will engage in violent tirades while intoxicated. Boundaries are also ambiguous and inconsistent, which leads to confusion in the parent-child relationship as well as in the marital relationship.

Work

Within the workplace, illicit drug use is pervasive, and destructive to productivity. For example, the 2002 NSDUH estimated that approximately 75 percent, or 12.4 million, of the 16.6 million adult drug users were employed either part-time or full-time (Substance Abuse and Mental Health Data Archive, 2003). As a result, businesses spend more than $100 billion each year on drug-related problems (Rasmussen, 2000). Indeed, substance abusing employees are "less productive than other workers, use three times as many sick days, are more likely to injure themselves or someone else, and are five times more likely to file worker's compensation claims" (Rasmussen, 2000, pp. 343–344). Moreover, many drug abusers have a difficult time maintaining employment, particularly when employers implement random toxicology drug screens (see Strada & Donohue, 2004).

In 1997, the National Center on Addiction and Substance Abuse (CASA) reported that 80 percent of the adult prison population was incarcerated due to drug- and alcohol-related crimes (see Rasmussen, 2000). Criminal activities most often include purchasing, possession, and consumption of illegal substances and driving while intoxicated, including engagement of stealing and use of forgery to obtain money for drugs (Milby, Jolly, & Beidelman, 1984). However, criminal activity is not limited to drug-related offenses, as drug-abusing individuals are often arrested for battery, both while intoxicated and sober (Rasmussen, 2000).

Peer Interactions

As mentioned earlier, drug abuse affects others involved in the drug abuser's life. Fear of violence, presence of ambiguous and inconsistent boundaries, coexisting subcultures of crime, and so forth lead to significant disruptions in peer interactions.

TREATMENT IMPLICATIONS

During the past 30 years there has been an increase in the number of controlled treatment outcome studies involving drug busers. Reflecting the unique needs of adult drug abusers, investigators have developed robust interventions that have demonstrated efficacy in both reducing drug use and ameliorating comorbid behavior problems and disorders. Commensurate with the number of outcome studies conducted, empirically based interventions have become increasingly specialized. For instance, Fals-Stewart, Kashdan, O'Farrell, and Birchler (2002) adapted behavioral couples therapy for drug-abusing patients to specifically address partner violence. Thus, if domestic violence issues were present in the drug abuser's home, this intervention would appear to be particularly warranted. In determining which interventions to employ, there are many factors that need to be considered, including the specific problems that must be addressed, utilization of treatments that have been found to be effective in ameliorating the identified problems, the extent of significant other involvement in treatment, qualifications and ability level of the therapist to implement the selected treatments, and motivational level of the drug-abusing individual.

Motivational Enhancement Interventions

Because substance abusers wax and wane in their degree of motivation, motivational enhancement interventions should be considered for implementation at the start of treatment and throughout treatment when motivation is wanting (Moyers & Waldorf, 2003). Although several motivational enhancement interventions have been developed, none have received greater empirical support than motivational interviewing (MI; Miller, & Rollinck, 1991). In this approach, feedback is first provided about the assessment results, and the substance abuser is informed about the consequences of use relative to others in the general population. Personal responsibility and choice are both emphasized, and specific recommendations are provided to assist the substance abuser in decreasing drug use. Importantly, a menu of empirically supported treatment options is provided while fostering a warm, supportive, and sympathetic environment. The therapist works to raise self-efficacy through encouragement and optimism.

In controlled trials, two individual sessions and four sessions of motivational interviewing have been shown to significantly decrease amphetamine use, as compared with bibliotherapy in 64 amphetamine users at six-month follow-up (Baker, Boggs, & Lewin, 2001). In a sample of 291 marijuana abusers, participants who were randomly assigned to motivational enhancement therapy demonstrated significantly less marijuana use than participants who were randomly assigned to a wait-list control condition at 4-month follow-up, and marijuana use reductions at 4- and 16-month follow-ups were similar between participants in motivational enhancement and participants who were randomly assigned to behavioral therapy (Stephens, Roffman, & Curtin, 2000). Motivational enhancement therapy has also demonstrated greater reductions in cocaine use as compared with participants in a detoxification only condition at 12 weeks post-detoxification, according to urinalysis results (Stotts, Schmitz, Rhodes, & Grabowski, 2001). Therefore, although much work remains to be performed in MI, this intervention is very promising. Indeed, motivational enhancement therapies have demonstrated sustained reductions in drug use across multiple settings, and relevant to its cost-effectiveness, MI appears to be as effective as behavioral therapy.

Comprehensive Behavioral Interventions

There appears to be strong support for skills-based programs that are focused on decreasing substance use and associated comorbid problems and disorders. An outstanding representation of such an approach is the Community Reinforcement Approach (CRA), which was originally developed in the early 1970s (Hunt & Azrin, 1973). In this approach, substance use is conceptualized to occur because it is reinforced. Therefore, the focus of CRA is to establish community support aimed at restricting opportunities to obtain reinforcement from drug use and teach skills that will assist the substance abuser in maintaining behaviors that are incompatible with drug use. Significant others are taught to provide social acknowledgment for abstinence and to participate in communication skills training procedures aimed at facilitating positive requests and conflict resolution strategies (i.e., conflict and poor assertion skills often influence drug use and other undesired behaviors). Alcohol and drug refusal skills are emphasized to support substance abusers in assertively denying offers to use drugs. When unemployment is indicated, the substance abuser is taught skills that are relevant to obtaining and maintaining employment. The environment is also changed to increase time spent with abstinent friends, and social activities that do not involve substances.

CRA is consistently recognized among the most cost-effective alcohol treatment programs in meta-analytic studies (Finney & Monahan, 1996; Holder, Longabaugh, Miller, & Rubonis, 1991; Miller et al., 1995). Indeed, in controlled outcome studies, CRA has convincingly demonstrated improvements in communication skills, family relationships, and reductions in alcohol use, relative to control conditions among inpatients (Azrin, 1976; Hunt & Azrin, 1973), outpatients (Azrin, Sisson, Meyers, & Godley, 1982; Mallams, Godley, Hall, & Meyers, 1982; Meyers & Miller, 2001), and the homeless (Smith, Meyers, & Delaney, 1998). Similar results have been found in outcome studies involving drug abusers (e.g., Higgins et al., 1995, 1994; Higgins, Badger, & Badger, 2000; Silverman, Higgins, et al., 1996). However, it should be mentioned that in the latter studies, CRA was augmented with an innovative incentive program. In this intervention, the substance abuser is awarded vouchers for maintaining abstinence, and these vouchers may be later exchanged for money/prizes. Indeed, this incentive program has been effective without CRA in opiate abusers (Silverman, Wong, et al., 1996) and methadone patients who abuse cocaine (Silverman et al., 1998).

CRA components have also been modified to assist in the enlistment of substance abusers through family training procedures. Specifically, Sisson and Azrin (1986) demonstrated favorable results consequent to teaching significant others of alcohol abusers to avoid behaviors that may inadvertently reinforce alcohol use and instead reinforce behaviors that are consistent with abstinence, especially methods of enlisting alcohol abusers into therapy. In a well-controlled outcome study involving drug abusers (Meyers, Miller, Hill, & Tonigan, 1999), four to five sessions of this approach (i.e., Community Reinforcement Approach and Family Training; CRAFT) was significantly more effective in the engagement of unmotivated drug users than traditional approaches (i.e., Johnson Institute of Family Intervention, Al-Anon). Moreover, Meyers, Miller, Smith, and Tonigan (2002) randomly assigned the families of individuals who refused to receive treatment to CRAFT, CRAFT plus aftercare, or Al-Anon/Nar-Anon facilitation therapy. CRAFT alone and CRAFT plus aftercare were more effective in motivating these drug users to treatment (59 percent and 77 percent, respectively) than Al-Anon/Nar-Anon (29 percent). Given the tumultuous family environment of drug abusers, the benefits of CRAFT are considerable. Indeed, the CRAFT model is certainly deserving of future expansion and evaluation in drug abuse samples, such as its psychological impact on significant others (i.e., mental health functioning, use of drugs).

Other comprehensive family-based behavioral interventions include behavioral couples therapy (BCT) and family behavior therapy (FBT). Similar to CRA and CRAFT, BCT and FBT both focus on active recruitment of significant others, management of cravings to use drugs, avoidance of drug use stimuli, relapse coping strategies, drug refusal skills training, and various communication and family enhancement skills interventions. Similar to the voucher-based CRA programs developed by Higgins and his colleagues (see earlier paragraph), FBT emphasizes written contingency contracting procedures. However, in FBT reinforcers must be derived from family members, which is sometimes difficult to arrange in drug-abusing populations. Nevertheless, both BCT and FBT intervention approaches have clearly demonstrated reductions in male and female adult drug use as well as improvements in family satisfaction and various problem behaviors (Azrin et al., 1996; Azrin et al., 1994; Fals-Stewart, Birchler, &

O'Farrell, 1996; Fals-Stewart, O'Farrell, & Birchler, 2001; Fals-Stewart et al., 2000; Winters, Fals-Stewart, O'Farrell, Birchler, & Kelley, 2001). Importantly, BCT has demonstrated the unique advantage of reducing adult partner violence in substance abusing males (Fals-Stewart et al., 2002).

12-Step Programs

Twelve-step programs for illicit drug abusers include Alcoholics Anonymous (AA, predominately for alcoholics, although all substance abusers are welcome), Narcotics Anonymous (NA; for users of any mind- or mood-altering substance, predominately other than alcohol), Cocaine Anonymous (CA; specifically for cocaine users), Al-Anon (for families and partners of alcoholics), and Nar-Anon (developed specifically for families and partners of narcotic-abusing individuals). Unique to behaviorally based programs, participants of 12-step programs espouse the belief that addiction is a disease and abstinence is a necessity. However, these approaches are consistent in their emphasis to avoid drug-associated stimuli and praise behaviors that are consistent with abstinence (see Stevens, 2000c). Attempting to progressively achieve the 12 steps is a means by which lifelong sobriety can be accomplished by focusing on spirituality, self-examination, making amends, support and guidance, awareness, and responsibility (Wallace, 2003). Twelve-step participation is often encouraged by therapists as adjunctive to individualized drug counseling programs that focus on reducing, or ideally stopping, illicit drug use. However, its effects in adult drug-abusing samples are questionable (Higgins et al., 1993).

Biologically Based Interventions

Methadone maintenance clinics were first developed in the 1960s. Methadone is a long-acting synthetic opiate (approximately 24 hours) that mimics the pleasurable effects of heroin without the rapid cycling of the intoxicating effects and withdrawal (see Tapert et al., 2001). Methadone must be administered daily to the addicted individual by a treatment professional at the methadone facility (Stevens, 2000b). Opponents of methadone maintenance feel that one addiction is being replaced by another and that this intervention does not treat the use of other illicit drugs. Along these lines, the effectiveness of methadone maintenance appears to be enhanced with behaviorally based interventions (Abbott, Weller, Delaney, & Moore, 1998) and careful administration and monitoring of appropriate dosages (i.e., significant reductions in the use of opioids, decrease in treatment attrition, reduced criminal behavior, lowers HIV risk; see Carroll, 2003; Smith, 2000).

Levomethadyl acetate, L-alpha-acetylemethadol (LAAM), has recently been approved by the U.S. Food and Drug Administration (FDA) as an alternative to methadone. The advantage of this substance is that it only needs to be administered approximately every two to three days, thus making administration more convenient and less costly than methadone. However, LAAM does not appear to be as effective in suppressing withdrawal symptoms, reducing opioid use, or decreasing attrition, as compared with methadone (see Dodgen & Shea, 2000). Buprenorphine is a partial agonist that appears promising as an alternative to methadone and LAAM. Although more studies need to be conducted in order to draw definitive conclusions, it appears to have low potential for overdose and withdrawal, while sustaining decreases in opioid use and treatment attrition similar to methadone, and potentially better than the opioid antagonist naltrexone (see Carroll, 2003).

Relapse Prevention

Relapse prevention (Marlatt & Gordon, 1985) is strongly embedded within principles of social learning theory, and includes social skills training and behavioral coping strategies relevant to preventing relapse among substance abusers. Relapse prevention strategies are intended to enhance self-control through exploration of positive and negative consequences of drug use, monitoring internal states and cues that bring about desires to use drugs, and developing strategies to avoid and escape from high-risk scenarios (Keller, 2003). Maintaining abstinence is encouraged, although individuals are taught to cope with brief "lapses" in which drug use briefly recurs (i.e., the lapse is stressed as a learning experience to prevent long-term relapses). Relapse prevention has demonstrated efficacy in maintaining abstinence from illicit drugs relative to control groups, and when significant others are unavailable, it can be combined with other individualized behavioral techniques (Carroll, Rounsaville, & Gawin, 1991; Carroll et al., 1994).

CONCLUSIONS

Although diagnostic criteria for substance abuse and dependence are consistent across the various illicit drugs, the physiological and psychological effects of these drugs are uniquely complicated. Drug abuse and dependence can have pronounced effects on the family, work unit, and peers. Similarly, drug abusers are a heterogeneous population, warranting robust treatments that are capable of addressing frequently encountered comorbid disorders and diagnoses in addition to lowering drug use frequency. Some of the treatments for adult drug abusers that appear particularly promising include motivational interviewing, the Community Reinforcement Approach and its derivatives, family behavior therapy, behavioral couples therapy, biologically based treatments (i.e., methadone maintenance combined with behavioral therapies), and relapse prevention. In adult drug-abusing populations, traditional 12-step programs are frequently employed to complement empirically based interventions, although support for the relative efficacy of this approach is undetermined at the present time.

REFERENCES

Abbott, P. J., Weller, S. B., Delaney, H. D., & Moore, B. A. (1998). Community reinforcement approach in the treatment of opiate addicts. *American Journal of Drug & Alcohol Abuse, 24,* 1998.

Acierno, R., Donohue, B., & Kogan, E. (1994). Psychological interventions for drug abuse: A critique and summation of controlled studies. *Clinical Psychology Review, 14,* 417–442.

American Psychiatric Association. (2000). *Diagnostic and statistical manual of mental disorders* (4th ed., text rev.). Washington, DC: Author.

Azrin, N. H. (1976). Improvements in the Community Reinforcement Approach to alcoholism. *Behaviour Research and Therapy, 14,* 339–348.

Azrin, N., Acierno, R., Kogan, E. S., Donohue, B., Besalel, V., & McMahon, P. T. (1996). Follow-up results of supportive versus behavioral therapy for illicit drug use. *Behaviour Research and Therapy, 34,* 41–46.

Azrin, N. H., Donohue, B., Teichner, G., Crum, T., Howell, J., & DeCato, L. (2001). A controlled evaluation and description of individual-cognitive problem solving and family-behavioral therapies in conduct-disordered and substance dependent youth. *Journal of Child and Adolescent Substance Abuse, 11,* 1–43.

Azrin, N. H., McMahon, P., Donohue, B., Besalel, V., Lapinski, K., Kogan, E., et al. (1994). Behavior therapy of drug abuse: A controlled outcome study. *Behaviour Research and Therapy, 32,* 857–866.

Azrin, N. H., Sisson, R. W., Meyers, R. J., & Godley, M. D. (1982). Alcoholism treatment by disulfiram and community reinforcement therapy. *Journal of Behavior Therapy and Experimental Psychiatry, 3,* 105–112.

Baker, A., Boggs, T. G., & Lewin, T. J. (2001). Randomized controlled trial of brief cognitive behavioural interventions among regular users of amphetamines. *Addictions, 96,* 1279–1287.

Bukstein, O., Dunne, J. E., Ayres, W., Arnold, V., Benedek, E., Benson, R. S., et al. (1997). Practice parameters for the assessment and treatment of children and adolescents with substance use disorders. *Journal of the American Academy of Child and Adolescent Psychiatry, 36*(10), 140–156.

Carroll, K. M. (2003). Integrating psychotherapy and pharmacotherapy in substance abuse treatment. In F. Rotgers, J. Morgenstern, & S. T. Walters (Eds.), *Treating substance abuse: Theory and technique* (pp. 314–342). New York: Guilford Press.

Carroll, K. M., Rounsaville, B. J., & Gawin, F. H. (1991). A comparative trial of psychotherapies for ambulatory cocaine abusers: Relapse prevention and interpersonal therapy. *American Journal of Drug and Alcohol Dependence, 17,* 229–247.

Carroll, K. M., Rounsaville, B., Nich, C., Gordon, L., Wirtz, P., & Gawin, F. (1994). One-year follow-up of psychotherapy and pharmacotherapy for cocaine dependence: Delayed emergence of psychotherapy effects. *Archives of General Psychiatry, 51,* 989–997.

Dimeff, L. A., & Marlatt, G. A. (1995). Relapse prevention. In R. K. Hester & W. R. Miller (Eds.), *Handbook of alcoholism and treatment approaches* (2nd ed., pp. 176–194). New York: Allyn & Bacon.

Dodgen, C. E., & Shea, W. M. (2000). *Substance use disorders: Assessment and treatment.* San Diego, CA: Academic Press.

Donohue, B. (2004). Co-existing child neglect and drug abuse in adolescent mothers: Specific recommendations for treatment based on a review of the outcome literature. *Behavior Modification, 28,* 206–233.

Donohue, B., & Azrin, N. H. (2002). Family behavior therapy in a conduct-disordered and substance abusing adolescent: A case example. *Clinical Case Studies, 1,* 299–323.

Donohue, B., Azrin, N. H., Lawson, H., Friedlander, J., Teichner, G., & Rindsberg, J. (1998). Improving initial session attendance in conduct disordered and substance abusing adolescents: A controlled study. *Journal of Child and Adolescent Drug Abuse, 8,* 1–13.

Donohue, B., Azrin, N. H., Strada, M. J., Silver, N. C., & Teichner, G. (2004). Psychometric evaluation of self- and collateral Timeline Follow-Back reports of drug and alcohol use in a sample of drug-abusing and conduct-disordered adolescents and their parents. *Psychology of Addictive Disorders, 18,* 184–189.

Doweiko, H. E. (2002). *Concepts of chemical dependency* (5th ed.). Pacific Grove, CA: Brooks/Cole.

Erickson, S. (2000). Etiological theories of substance abuse. In P. Stevens & R. L. Smith (Eds.), *Substance abuse counseling: Theory and practice* (pp. 77–112). Upper Saddle River, NJ: Merrill Prentice Hall.

Fals-Stewart, W., Birchler, G. R., & O'Farrell, T. J. (1996). Behavioral couples therapy for male substance-abusing patients: Effects of relationship adjustment and drug-abusing behavior. *Journal of Consulting and Clinical Psychology, 64,* 959–972.

Fals-Stewart, W., Kashdan, T. B., O'Farrell, T. J., & Birchler, G. R. (2002). Behavioral couples therapy for drug abusing patients: Effects on partner violence. *Journal of Substance Abuse Treatment, 22,* 87–96.

Fals-Stewart, W., O'Farrell, T. J., & Birchler, G. R. (2001). Behavioral couples therapy for male methadone maintenance patients:

Effects on drug-using behavior and relationship adjustment. *Behavior Therapy, 32,* 391–411.

Fals-Stewart, W., O'Farrell, T. J., & Birchler, G. R. (2003). Family therapy techniques. In F. Rotgers, J. Morgenstern, & S. T. Walters (Eds.), *Treating substance abuse: Theory and Technique* (pp. 298–313). New York: Guilford Press.

Fals-Stewart, W., O'Farrell, T. J., Feehan, M., Birchler, G. R., Tiller, S., & McFarlin, S. K. (2000). Behavioral couples therapy versus individual-based treatment for male substance abusing patients: An evaluation of significant individual changes and comparison of improvement rates. *Journal of Substance Abuse Treatment, 18,* 249–254.

Finney, J. W., & Monahan, S. C. (1996). The cost-effectiveness of treatment for alcoholism: A second approximation. *Journal of Studies on Alcohol, 57,* 229–243.

First, M., Gibbon, M., Williams, J., & Spitzer, R. (1994). *Structured clinical interview for Axis I DSM-IV disorders.* New York: Office of Mental Health of New York State Psychiatric Institute.

Frances, R. J., & Miller, S. I. (Eds.). (1998). *Clinical textbook of addictive disorders* (2nd ed.). New York: Guilford Press.

Gossop, M., Best, D., Marsden, J., & Strang, J., (1997). Test-retest reliability of the Severity of Dependence Scale. *Addiction, 92*(3), 353.

Harwood, H., Fountain, D., Livermore, G., & The Lewin Group (1998). *The economic costs of alcohol and drug abuse in the United States, 1992.* Rockville, MD: National Institute on Drug Abuse.

Higgins, S. T., Badger, G. T., & Badger, A. J. (2000). Initial abstinence and success in achieving long-term abstinence. *Experimental & Clinical Psychopharmacology, 8,* 377–386.

Higgins, S. T., Budney, A. J., Bickel, H. K., Badger, G., Foerge, F., & Ogden, D. E. (1995). Outpatient behavioral treatment for cocaine dependence: One year outcome. *Experimental & Clinical Psychopharmacology, 3,* 205–212.

Higgins, S. T., Budney, A. J., Bickel, W. K., Foerge, F., Donham, R., & Badger, G. (1994). Incentives improve outcome in outpatient behavioral treatment of cocaine dependence. *Archives of General Psychiatry, 51,* 568–576.

Higgins, S. T., Budney, A. J., Bickel, W. K., Hughes, J. R., Foerg, F., & Badger, G. (1993). Achieving cocaine abstinence with a behavioral approach. *American Journal of Psychiatry, 150,* 763–769.

Holder, H., Longabaugh, R., Miller, W., & Rubonis, A. (1991). The cost effectiveness of treatment for alcoholism: A first approximation. *Journal of Studies on Alcohol, 52,* 517–540.

Hunt, G. M., & Azrin, N. H. (1973). A Community Reinforcement Approach to alcoholism. *Behaviour Research and Therapy, 11,* 91–104.

Keller, D. S. (2003). Exploration in the service of relapse prevention: A psychoanalytic contribution to substance abuse treatment. In F. Rotgers, J. Morgenstern, & S. T. Walters (Eds.), *Treating substance abuse: Theory and technique* (pp. 82–111). New York: Guilford Press.

Krueger, R. F., Caspi, A., Moffitt, T. E., Silva, P. A., & McGee, R. (1996). Personality traits are differentially linked to mental disorders: A multitrait-multidiagnosis study of adolescent birth cohort. *Journal of Abnormal Psychology, 105,* 299–312.

Mallams, J. H., Godley, M. D., Hall, G. M., & Meyers, R. J. (1982). A social-systems approach to resocializing alcoholics in the community. *Journal of Studies on Alcohol, 43,* 1115–1123.

Marlatt, G. A., & Gordon, J. R. (Eds.). (1985). *Relapse prevention: Maintenance strategies in the treatment of addictive diseases.* New York: Guilford Press.

Maxmen, J. S., & Ward, N. G. (1995). *Essential psychopathology and its treatment* (2nd ed.). New York: Norton.

McCusker, J., Stoddard, A., Frost, R., & Zorn, M. (1996). Planned versus actual duration of drug abuse treatment. *Journal of Nervous and Mental Disease, 184,* 482–489.

Meyers, R. J., & Miller, W. R. (2001). *A Community Reinforcement Approach to addiction treatment.* Cambridge, England: Cambridge University Press.

Meyers, R. J., Miller, W. R., Hill, D. E., & Tonigan, J. S. (1999). Community reinforcement and family training (CRAFT): Engaging unmotivated drug users in treatment. *Journal of Substance Abuse, 10*(3), 291–308.

Meyers, R. J., Miller, W. R., Smith, J. E., & Tonigan, J. S. (2002). A randomized trial of two methods for engaging treatment-refusing drug users through concerned significant others. *Journal of Consulting and Clinical Psychology, 70,* 1182–1185.

Miele, G. M., Carpenter, K. M., Cockerham, M. S., Trautman, K. D., Blaine, J. D., & Hasin, D. S., (2000). Concurrent and predictive validity of the Substance Dependence Severity Scale (SDSS). *Drug and Alcohol Dependence, 59,* 77–88.

Milby, J. B., Jolly, P. A., & Beidleman, W. B. (1984). Substance abuse: Drugs. In S. M. Turner & M. Hersen (Eds.), *Adult psychopathology and diagnosis* (pp. 105–139). Toronto, Ontario: Wiley.

Miller, W. R., Brown, J. M., Simpson, T. L., Handmaker, N. S., Bein, T. H., Luckie, L. F., et al. (1995). What works? A methodological analysis of the alcohol treatment outcome literature. In R. K. Hester & W. R. Miller (Eds.), *Handbook of alcoholism treatment approaches: Effective alternatives* (2nd ed.). Needham, MA: Allyn & Bacon.

Miller, W., & Rollinck, S. (1991). Motivational interviewing: Preparing people to change addictive behavior, New York: Guilford Press.

Moyers, T. B., & Waldorf, V. A. (2003). Motivational interviewing: Destination, direction, and means. In F. Rotgers, J. Morgenstern, & S. T. Walters (Eds.), *Treating substance abuse: Theory and technique* (pp. 298–313). New York: Guilford Press.

Mueser, K. T., Bellack, A. S., & Blanchard, J. J. (1992). Comorbidity of schizophrenia and substance abuse: Implications for treatment. *Journal of Consulting and Clinical Psychology, 60,* 845–856.

National Clearinghouse for Alcohol and Drug Information. (1996). *National expenditures for mental health, alcohol and other drug abuse treatment.* Retrieved June 17, 2004, from http://www.health.org/mhoad/spending.htm

Office of Applied Studies, Substance Abuse and Mental Health Services Administration. (2003). *Results from the 2002 National Survey on Drug Use and Health: National findings* (DHHS Publication No. SMA 03–3836, NHSDA Series H-22). Rockville, MD: Author.

Rasmussen, S. (2000). *Addiction treatment: Theory and practice.* Thousand Oaks, CA: Sage.

Schuckit, M. A. (1995). *Drug and alcohol abuse: A clinical guide to diagnosis and treatment* (4th ed.). New York: Plenum Publishers.

Segal, B., Huba, G. J., & Singer, J. L. (1980). *Drugs, daydreaming, and personality: A study of college youth.* Mahwah, NJ: Erlbaum.

Shaner, A., Khalsa, E., Roberts, L., Wilkins, J., Anglin, D., & Hsieh, S. C. (1993). Unrecognized cocaine use among schizophrenic patients. *American Journal of Psychiatry, 150,* 758–762.

Sharp, M. J., & Getz, J. C., (1988). Self-process in comorbid mental health. *American Journal of Orthopsychiatry, 68,* 639–644.

Silverman, K., Higgins, S. T., Brooner, R. K., Montoya, I. D., Cone, E. J., Schuster, C. R., et al. (1996). Sustained cocaine abstinence in methadone maintenance patients through voucher-based reinforcement therapy. *Archives of General Psychiatry, 53,* 409–415.

Silverman, K., Wong, C. J., Higgins, S. T., Brooner, R. K., Montoya, I. D., Contoreggi, C., et al. (1996). Increasing opiate abstinence through voucher-based reinforcement therapy. *Drug and Alcohol Dependence, 41,* 157–165.

Silverman, K., Wong, C. J., Umbricht-Schneiter, A., Montoya, I. D., Schuster, C. R., & Preston, K. L. (1998). Broad benefits of cocaine abstinence reinforcement among methadone patients. *Journal of Consulting and Clinical Psychology, 66,* 811–824.

Sisson, R. W., & Azrin, N. H. (1986). Family-member involvement to initiate and promote treatment of problem drinkers. *Journal of Behavior Therapy and Experimental Psychiatry, 17,* 15–21.

Skinner, H. A. (1982). The drug abuse screening test. *Addictive Behaviors, 7,* 363–371.

Sklar, S. M., Annis, H. M., & Turner, N. E. (1997). Development and validation of the Drug-Taking Confidence Questionnaire: A measure of coping self-efficacy. *Addictive Behaviors, 22,* 655–670.

Smith, J. E., Meyers, R. J., & Delaney, H. D. (1998). The Community Reinforcement Approach with homeless alcohol-dependent individuals. *Journal of Consulting and Clinical Psychology, 66,* 541–548.

Smith, R. L. (2000). Research and contemporary issues. In P. Stevens & R. L. Smith (Eds.), *Substance abuse counseling: Theory and practice* (pp. 322–347). Upper Saddle River, NJ: Merrill Prentice Hall.

Sobell, L. C., & Sobell, M. B. (1996). Timeline Follow-Back: A technique for assessing self-reported consumption. In R. Litten & J. Allen (Eds.), *Measuring alcohol consumption* (pp. 41–72). Totowa, NJ: Humana Press.

Stephens, R. S., Roffman, R. A., & Curtin, L. (2000). Comparison of extended versus brief treatments for marijuana use. *Journal of Consulting and Clinical Psychology, 68,* 898–908.

Stevens, P. (2000a). Family therapy in substance abuse treatment. In P. Stevens & R. L. Smith (Eds.), *Substance abuse counseling: Theory and practice* (pp. 201–226). Upper Saddle River, NJ: Merrill Prentice Hall.

Stevens, P. (2000b). Individual and group treatment. In P. Stevens & R. L. Smith (Eds.), *Substance abuse counseling: Theory and practice* (pp. 179–200). Upper Saddle River, NJ: Merrill Prentice Hall.

Stevens, P. (2000c). Maintaining behavior change: Relapse prevention strategies. In P. Stevens & R. L. Smith (Eds.), *Substance abuse counseling: Theory and practice* (pp. 277–297). Upper Saddle River, NJ: Merrill Prentice Hall.

Stotts, S. L., Schmitz, J. M., Rhodes, H. M., & Grabowski, J. (2001). Dextroamphetamine for cocaine-dependence treatment: A double-blind randomized clinical trial. *Journal of Consulting and Clinical Psychology, 69,* 858–862.

Strada, M. J., & Donohue, B. (2004). Substance abuse. In J. Thomas & M. Hersen (Eds.), *Psychopathology in the workplace: Recognition and adaption.* New York: Brunner-Routledge.

Substance Abuse and Mental Health Data Archive. (2003). *National Household Survey on Drug Abuse (NHSDA) series.* Retrieved May 25, 2004, from http://www.icpsr.umich.edu/SAMHDA/ and http://www.oas.samhsa.gov/

Sussman, S., & Ames, S. L. (2001). The social psychology of drug abuse. In S. Sutton (Ed.), *Applying social psychology.* Philadelphia: Open University Press.

Tapert, S. E., Tate, S. R., & Brown, S. A. (2001). Substance abuse: An overview. In P. B. Sutker & H. E. Adams (Eds.), *Comprehensive handbook of psychopathology* (3rd ed., pp. 559–594). New York: Kluwer/Plenum.

Turner, N. E., Annis, H. M., & Sklar, S. M. (1997). Measurement of antecedents to drug and alcohol use: Psychometric properties of the Inventory of Drug-Taking Situations (IDTS). *Behaviour Research and Therapy, 35,* 465–483.

United Nations. (1998). United Nations Chronicle: Social and economic costs of illicit drugs. Retrieved May 10, 2004, from http://www.un.org/Pubs/chronicle/1998/issue2/0298p7.html

Waldron, H. B. (1997). Adolescent substance abuse and family therapy outcome: A review of randomized trials. In T. H. Ollendick & R. J. Prinz (Eds.), *Advances in clinical psychology* (Vol. 19, pp. 199–234). New York: Plenum Press.

Wallace, J. (2003). Theory of 12-step-oriented treatment. In F.

Rotgers, J. Morgenstern, & S. T. Walters (Eds.), *Treating substance abuse: Theory and technique* (pp. 31–66). New York: Guilford Press.

Weiss, C. J., & Millman, R. B. (1998). Hallucinogens, phencyclidine, marijuana, inhalants. In R. J. Frances & S. I. Miller (Eds.), *Clinical textbook of addictive disorders* (2nd ed., pp. 202–232). New York: Guilford Press.

Williams, B. R., & Baer, C. L. (1994). *Essentials of clinical pharmacology in nursing* (2nd ed.). Springhouse, PA: Springhouse.

Winters, J., Fals-Stewart, W., O'Farrell, T. J., Birchler, G. R., & Kelley, M. L. (2002). Behavioral couples therapy for female substance abusing patients: Effects on substance use and relationship adjustment. *Journal of Consulting and Clinical Psychology, 70,* 344–355.

Ziedonis, D., & Brady, K. (1997). Dual diagnosis in primary care. *Medical Clinics of North America, 81,* 1017–1036.

Zuckerman, M. (1994). *Behavioral expressions and biosocial bases of sensation seeking.* New York: Cambridge University Press.

CHAPTER 22

Gambling and Impulse Disorders

ALEX BLASZCZYNSKI AND LIA NOWER

DESCRIPTION OF THE DISORDER AND CLINICAL PICTURE

The *DSM-IV-TR* (American Psychiatric Association [APA], 2000) category of *impulse control disorders not elsewhere classified* includes five disorders characterized by recurrent behaviors that result in harm either to the self or to others: *pathological gambling, trichotillomania, kleptomania, intermittent explosive disorder,* and *pyromania.* Impaired control is defined by the recurrent failure to resist an urge to carry out a behavior that is, on the one hand, appetitive in that it provides positive or negative reinforcement but, on the other, is associated with severe deleterious consequences in personal, social, familial, employment, and/or legal functioning. Clinically, individuals describe an increasing tension or arousal prior to the commission of an act, a sense of gratification, and/or tension reduction on its completion, followed by an immediate sense of guilt or remorse.

Pathological Gambling

Gambling involves risking an item of value (usually monetary) on the outcome of a chance event. Primary forms of gambling include wagering (betting on horses), lotteries, electronic gaming machines (slot machines), and sports betting.

Epidemiological studies indicate that most individuals gamble responsibly within financial limits. The terms *pathological, problem, compulsive,* or *disordered gambling* are all used to describe the minority of individuals who exhibit impaired control over their behavior as evidenced by the presence of persistent and recurrent maladaptive gambling behaviors that disrupts personal, social, family, or vocational pursuits (APA, 2000, p. 671). To meet a formal psychiatric diagnosis, individuals must endorse 5 of 10 symptoms of disorder: (1) a *preoccupation* with gambling; (2) need to gamble increasing amounts to achieve desired excitement (*tolerance*); (3) repeated, unsuccessful efforts to reduce or cease gambling (*loss of control*); (4) restlessness or irritability attempting to reduce or cease (*withdrawal*); (5) gambling to escape problems or relieve dysphoric mood (*escape*); (6) continued gambling to recoup losses (*chasing*); (7) lying to conceal involvement in gambling; (8) commission of illegal acts to finance gambling; (9) jeopardizing significant relationships, employment, or educational opportunities; and/or (10) relying on money from others to relieve desperate financial circumstances caused by gambling (*bailouts*). The behavior cannot be accounted for by a manic episode.

The evolution of the *DSM* criteria highlights the paradoxical nature of the disorder, which is typically compared to substance abuse but otherwise classified with other nonsubstance use disorders that are characterized primarily by impulse dyscontrol. Unlike the other disorders "not elsewhere classified," which require endorsement of all criteria, pathological gamblers are required to endorse only 5 of 10 symptoms. Those symptoms are unweighted, though studies have shown that only some of the indicators are able to differentiate pathological gamblers from those with gambling problems (e.g., betting increasing amounts of money, lying about gambling; Stinchfield, 2003). As a result, an individual may endorse five symptoms that do not, individually, indicate pathology yet receive the same diagnosis as another gambler who endorses the most severely predictive symptoms. Accordingly, Stinchfield (2003) has cautioned that clinicians should be careful in classifying individuals who endorse three or four symptoms because tests of reliability, validity, and classification accuracy of the *DSM-IV* criteria indicate there is only a 50/50 probability that those individuals may require treatment. The clinical picture is further confounded by the fact that gamblers may meet diagnostic criteria at one point and not another, gambling in "binges" or fluctuating between subclinical and clinical levels of disorder (Nower & Blaszczynski, 2003).

Clinical studies suggest that 90 percent of pathological gamblers in treatment commence gambling prior to age 20 (mean age around 12 to 15 years), maintain control for 1 to 10 years, before losing control and gambling excessively for a similar length of time prior to entering treatment at an average age of 35 to 39 (Blaszczynski & McConaghy, 1986; Petry, 2005). Rapidity of onset of pathological gambling varies extensively, however females reported shorter periods than males of intense (1.0 years versus 4.6 years) and problem gambling (1.8 years versus 8.6 years; Tavares, Zilberman, Beites, & Gentil, 2001). Electronic gaming devices account for a disproportionate percentage of problem gamblers, particularly among females. Although life events are considered important precipitants, factors that contribute to the transition from controlled to pathological gambling remain poorly understood.

The gender distribution for pathological gamblers seeking treatment is 60 percent males and 40 percent females (Petry, 2005). Females show a tendency to gamble predominantly as a means of escaping emotional distress in contrast to males who are motivated for factors related to winning, excitement, and chasing losses (Custer & Milt, 1985; Mark & Lesieur, 1992).

Trichotillomania

Trichotillomania or repetitive hair pulling, first identified by the French dermatologist Hallopeau, is a chronic, neglected psychiatric disorder, characterized by the failure to resist impulses to pull out one's hair, resulting in noticeable hair loss. A diagnosis of trichotillomania requires: (1) recurrent, episodic hair pulling resulting in noticeable hair loss; (2) increased tension immediately prior to hair pulling or when trying to resist hair pulling; (3) pleasure, gratification, or relief when hair pulling; (4) the absence of another mental health disorder or medical condition to better account for the behavior; and (5) clinically significant distress or impairment in social, occupational, or other important areas of functioning (APA, 2000). Though classified as an impulse control disorder, some have argued that trichotillomania would be better classified as an affective (Christenson, MacKenzie, & Mitchell, 1991) or obsessive-compulsive spectrum disorder (Swedo & Leonard, 1992).

Compared to earlier versions of the diagnostic criteria, *DSM-IV* added the requirement that hair pulling result in clinically significant distress (Criterion E) and included "pleasure" (Criterion C) as an emotion that accompanies the act of hair pulling.

Despite a high degree of individual variation in those with the disorder, there are some phenomenological consistencies among clients (for a review, see Diefenbach, Reitman, & Williamson, 2000). Hair pulling occurs at sites throughout the body, though the most common sites are the scalp, followed by lashes, brows, and pubic hair (Christenson, Mackenzie, et al., 1991; Schlosser, Black, Blum, & Goldstein, 1994). Episodes, lasting a few minutes to a few hours, are often prompted by negative affective states and sedentary activities like reading, watching television, driving, or talking on the phone (Christenson, MacKenzie, et al., 1991; Schlosser et al., 1994). In addition, the behavior can be automatic or result from focused intention (Christenson, MacKenzie, et al., 1991). Du Toit, van Kradenburg, Niehaus, and Stein (2001) have suggested that hair pulling varies with clinical subtypes, characterized by the presence or absence of automatic/focused hair pulling, comorbid self-injurious habits, and/or oral habits. In addition, comorbid obsessive-compulsive disorder and negative versus positive affective cues may reflect greater severity in symptomatology. Following hair pulling behavior, about 48 percent of individuals with trichotillomania will perform oral behaviors such as chewing or eating the hair, which can lead to dental erosion and medical complications (Christenson, MacKenzie, et al., 1991; Diefenbach et al., 2000).

Kleptomania

Kleptomania (Greek for "stealing madness") is characterized by (1) a recurrent failure to resist impulses to steal objects that are not needed for personal use or their monetary value. Individuals with the disorder experience (2) an increasing sense of tension immediately before the theft and (3) pleasure, gratification, or relief during the theft. In addition, (4) the stealing is not merely an expression of anger or vengeance or a response to a delusion or hallucination and (5) is not better accounted for by conduct disorder, a manic episode, or antisocial personality disorder (APA, 2000).

Initially introduced in the first edition of the American Psychiatric Association's *Diagnostic and Statistical Manual of Mental Disorders,* kleptomania was omitted from the second version only to return in 1980 in *DSM-III* and its subsequent versions. Revisions of the criteria in *DSM-IV* in 1994 added "gratification" to the sense of pleasure and relief that accompanies stealing and added as exclusionary criteria theft that occurs in response to a delusion, hallucination, or manic episode. However, despite its long tenure among psychiatric disorders, kleptomania is a poorly understood and underdiagnosed disorder. Because it often presents in comorbidity with other psychiatric disorders, it is conceptually unclear whether the disorder presents in clusters with different symptomalogical expressions or, rather, whether it is merely a nonspecific symptom of alternate, underlying, primary psychopathology (Presta et al., 2002).

Intermittent Explosive Disorder

Individuals with intermittent explosive disorder characteristically report (1) several discrete episodes of the failure to resist aggressive impulses that result in serious assaultive acts (e.g., physical assaults, verbal threats) or property destruction (e.g., purposefully breaking an object of value; APA, 2000). In addition, (2) the level of aggressiveness during episodes must be grossly out of proportion to any precipitating psychosocial stressors and (3) is not better accounted for by other mental disorders (e.g., antisocial or borderline personality disorder, psychotic disorder, and bipolar disorder). The current criteria eliminated the requirement in *DSM-III-R* of an absence of generalized impulsiveness or aggressiveness between episodes.

The current diagnosis is primarily one of exclusion, as aggressive or explosive behavior is also symptomatic of psychotic, conduct, and personality disorders, as well as a variant of panic disorder and a possible feature of depression (Opdyke & Rothbaum, 1998). *DSM-IV-TR* (APA, 2000) cautions that the diagnosis should be made only if other diagnostic possibilities are ruled out. Accordingly, there is little consensus as to whether the disorder should be an independent diagnostic category related to mood disorders or a nonspecific group of symptoms that often presents in a wide range of psychiatric and medical conditions (McElroy, 1999; McElroy, Soutullo, Beckman, Taylor, & Keck, 1998). In addition, the current criteria have been criticized for lacking an emphasis on the concept of an irresistible impulse and the highly ego-dystonic and largely uncontrollable nature of the range of outbursts (McElroy, 1999).

Though reliable data are lacking, onset for the disorder, between childhood and early 20s, is typically abrupt and absent a prodromal period; it is most prevalent in children who exhibit temper tantrums, impaired attention, hyperactivity, and other behavioral difficulties like stealing and fire setting (APA, 2000). Individuals with narcissistic, obsessive, paranoid, or schizoid traits are the most likely to exhibit episodic explosive outbursts (APA, 2000). In addition, the course of the disorder varies from chronic to episodic. First-degree relatives of individuals with intermittent explosive disorder are more likely than others in the general population to suffer from mood, substance use, intermittent explosive, and other impulse control disorders (APA, 2000).

Prior to aggressive outbursts, individuals with the disorder report experiencing physiological symptoms such as tingling, tremor, palpitations, chest tightness, head pressure, or hearing an echo (APA, 2000). They often feel (1) intense urges toward aggression prior to initiating the act; (2) irritability or rage, increased energy, and/or racing thoughts during the acts; and (3) depressed mood and fatigue when the aggressive acts are completed (APA, 2000; McElroy et al., 1998).

Neurological symptoms might include nonspecific EEG findings or evidence of abnormalities on neuropsychological testing, such as difficulty with letter reversal (APA, 2000). In addition, altered serotonin metabolism (e.g., low mean 5-hydroxindoleacetic [5-HIAA]) has been noted in the cerebrospinal fluid of some aggressive individuals, but studies have yet to clarify the nature of the relationship of these findings to intermittent explosive disorder (APA, 2000).

Pyromania

Pyromania is characterized by (1) deliberate and purposeful fire setting, preceded by a feeling of (2) tension or affective arousal and accompanied by (3) a fascination with, interest in, curiosity about, or attraction to fire and its situational contexts. Individuals with pyromania report (4) pleasure or gratification when setting fires or when witnessing or participating in their aftermath. Fire setting cannot be undertaken (5) for monetary gain, as an expression of sociopolitical ideology, to conceal criminal activity, to express anger or vengeance, to improve one's living circumstances, in response to a delusion or hallucination, or as a result of impaired judgment. Nor may the fire setting be (6) better accounted for by conduct disorder, a manic episode, or antisocial personality disorder, an exclusionary criterion added in *DSM-IV* (APA, 1994).

Historically, the term *pyromania* preceded its classification as an impulse control disorder. Lewis and Yarnell (1951) were the first to explore the disorder using psychiatric and police records of 1,300 arsonists and enumerated five classification types: accidental or unintentional, delusional, erotically motivated, revenge-motivated, and children who light fires. Under the current diagnostic criteria, only the "erotically motivated" offenders would qualify for diagnosis if they met other criteria for the disorder.

Accordingly, pyromania is particularly difficult to diagnose because of the numerous exclusionary symptoms such as alcohol abuse, retaliatory motives, or delusional thinking that typically accompany fire-setting behavior. Accordingly, the majority of research into fire setting or arson either fails to differentiate between offenders who meet the diagnostic criteria for pyromania or applies the label colloquially to individuals who would not meet criteria in a clinical setting. The latter may be due, in part, to the fact that the diagnostic label is applied infrequently by psychiatrists but commonly by law enforcement officers who actually have a poor understanding of the parameters of the disorder. Laubichler and Kuhberger (1997) have also theorized that diagnostic criteria are unnecessarily limited by the exclusion of single fire settings, comorbid alcohol usage, and aggressive motives, which often characterize adolescent fire setters who act out of anger against peers or family members.

PERSONALITY DEVELOPMENT AND PSYCHOPATHOLOGY

Pathological Gambling

A number of scientific studies have reported that a significant percentage of pathological gamblers demonstrate evidence of mood or personality disorders (Blaszczynski & McConaghy, 1989; Vitaro, Arseneault & Tremblay, 1999), neurobiological dysfunction (Potenza & Winters, 2003), and/or genetic abnormalities (Comings, Rosenthal, Lesieur, & Rugle, 1996) that predispose them to pleasure seeking. They may also exhibit high levels of impulsivity (Vitaro, Arseneault, & Tremblay, 1997), sensation seeking (Powell, Hardoon, Derevensky, & Gupta, 1999), substance use (Ladouceur, Boudreault, Jacques, & Vitaro, 1999; Stinchfield, Cassuto, Winters, & Latimer, 1997), compulsive eating and/or working (Shaffer, LaBrie, LaPlante, Kidman & Korn, 2002), sexual risk taking (Petry, 2000), and attention deficit (Rugle & Melamed, 1993). In a majority of individuals, these disorders may preexist problem gambling behavior; however, in other cases they may result from stress caused by problem gambling (for a discussion of pathways leading to problem gambling, see Blaszczynski & Nower, 2002).

Developmentally, it is theorized that a large proportion of individuals who become problem gamblers have experienced deprivation or abuse in childhood and premorbid substance abuse and symptoms of depression or anxiety (Gupta & Derevensky, 1998a, 1998b; Jacobs, 1986; Nower & Blaszczynski, 2003). In addition, they often score higher than their nonproblem gambling counterparts on measures of impulsivity and sensation seeking, report parents who gamble problematically or abuse substances, and, particularly among males, use gambling as an avoidant stress coping strategy (Nower, Derevensky, & Gupta, 2004).

A substantial percentage of disordered gamblers have comorbid mood disorders, including depression (Becona, Del Carmen Lorenzo, & Fuentes, 1996), bipolar disorder (McCormick, Russo, Ramirez, & Taber, 1984), anxiety (Black & Moyer, 1998), and severe insomnia (Bergh & Kuehlhorn, 1994). In addition, several studies have suggested that gamblers are particularly vulnerable to suicide because of high levels of comorbid depression coupled with the severe financial, legal, and psychosocial consequences of problem gambling (Bergh & Kuehlhorn, 1994; MacCallum & Blaszczynski, 2002; Nower, Gupta, Blaszczysnki, & Derevensky, 2004). Reported rates of suicidality in these studies vary widely from 17 percent to 80 percent for suicidal ideation and 4 percent to 24 percent for reported suicide attempts, depending on the population sampled and methodology employed. However, it is important to note that studies have failed to clarify whether affective symptoms, officially diagnosed or not, predated the onset of problematic gambling behavior.

In addition to comorbid affective disorders, up to 50 percent of disordered gamblers also report a substance use disorder (MacCallum & Blaszczynski, 2002). Petry (2001b) has suggested that pathological gambling and substance abuse have an additive effect, manifesting in a preference for immediate gains with higher levels of punishment and overall net losses than either substance abusers alone or subjects with no addictions.

Trichotillomania

Though no single diagnosis is consistently associated with the disorder, a number of studies have found higher rates of personality, affective, and eating disorders in individuals with trichotillomania as compared to the general population (Christenson, MacKenzie, et al., 1991; Diefenbach et al., 2000; Schlosser et al., 1994; Swedo & Leonard, 1992). For example, prevalence estimates suggest 25 percent to 55 percent of clients with trichotillomania also have a personality disorder such as histrionic, borderline, or obsessive-compulsive personality disorder (Christenson, Chernoff-Clementz, & Clementz, 1992; Swedo & Leonard, 1992). Similarly, Christenson, Pyle, and Mitchell (1991) noted a 20 percent lifetime prevalence rate for eating disorders and an 82 percent lifetime prevalence of Axis I disorders.

Kleptomania

Though kleptomania has long been recognized as a disorder, there is relatively little research into its nature and course. Most of the published reports in the area are either derived from case studies and/or family histories of a small number of individuals in treatment or provide merely demographic information about the client population. For example, Sarasalo, Bergman, and Toth (1996) sought to explore personality characteristics, psychiatric disorders, and somatic illness among 37 individuals with kleptomania recruited through newspaper ads. As a whole, the participants scored extremely low on measures of socialization. More than half of the sample reported receiving treatment for another psychiatric disorder, most commonly depressive, anxiety, and sleep disorders, and had a family history of psychiatric illness. Nearly half of the sample reported a history of chronic somatic diseases, including asthma/allergy, lower back and neck pain, hearing deficiency, heart disease, Crohn's disease, and other neurological disorders. In addition one-third of subjects reported either an alcohol problem or a need to cut back on alcohol consumption.

Another study compared individuals with kleptomania (n = 11), alcohol abuse/dependence (n = 60), and psychiatric disorders other than impulse control or substance-related disorders (n = 29) on various psychopathological dimensions (Bayle, Caci, Millet, Richa, & Olie, 2003). Findings indicated that those with kleptomania reported significantly higher rates of impulsivity and sensation seeking, comorbid psychiatric disorders (particularly mood disorders), other impulse-control disorders, and substance abuse or dependence (mainly nicotine) as compared to other groups.

Other studies have also found a high prevalence of both unipolar and bipolar mood disorders and obsessive-compulsive disorder in individuals with kleptomania (Presta et al., 2002), suggesting possible inclusion of the disorder with so-called obsessive-compulsive spectrum disorders (OCSD). Presta and colleagues (2002) noted that about 60 percent of the 20 participants met diagnostic criteria for bipolar I or II disorder, however the participants reported feeling distinct subjective differences between kleptomanic impulses and abnormal behaviors occurring exclusively in the course of mood polarity. In addition, unlike individuals with obsessive-compulsive disorder, participants in the study reported a variable degree of resistance to the stealing behavior, despite the pleasurable deriving action (Presta et al., 2002).

Limited evidence from studies with small, nonrepresentative samples exists to suggest a familial link between kleptomania and other psychiatric disorders, including mood disorders, obsessive-compulsive disorder, and substance use disorders. Presta et al. (2002) found that 35 percent of first-degree relatives of individuals diagnosed with kleptomania suffered from a mood disorder, 25 percent had obsessive-compulsive disorder, and 15 percent reported a substance use disorder. McElroy, Pope, Hudson, Keck, and White (1991) likewise reported a significant prevalence of mood, anxiety, and eating disorders in first-degree relatives of participants with kleptomania. A third study, which compared self-reported individual and familial psychiatric histories of 31 clients with "stealing behavior" with unmatched controls, failed to find any relationship between mood disorders and stealing, though subjects were not required to meet diagnostic criteria for kleptomania (Grant, 2003). The study did, however, note a correlation between stealing and both comorbid impulse control disorders and the presence of a first-degree relative with alcoholism and/or another psychiatric disorder.

Intermittent Explosive Disorder

Little is known about the developmental history of individuals with intermittent explosive disorder. In one study, childhood histories were notable for hyperactivity, impaired attention, attention-deficit/hyperactivity disorder, problematic temper tantrums, stealing, and fire setting (McElroy et al., 1998). The study also found that 96 percent (n = 26) of individuals surveyed met criteria for one or more and 70 percent (n = 19) for three or more comorbid Axis I disorders, most commonly a mood disorder (e.g., bipolar disorder), anxiety disorders (panic disorder, post-traumatic stress disorder, phobias, and obsessive-compulsive disorder), substance use disorder (alcohol abuse), eating disorders (binge eating), and/or other impulse-control disorders (McElroy et al., 1998).

Pyromania

Most of the research in the area focuses on individuals charged with arson or children and adolescent fire setters who may or may not meet criteria for pyromania. The *DSM-IV-TR* (APA, 2000) indicates that more than 40 percent of those arrested for arson-related offences are younger than 18, but most of those offenders do not suffer from pyromania; rather, the fire setting is associated with conduct disorder, attention-deficit/hyperactivity disorder, or adjustment disorder. Impulsive fire setters (with or without pyromania) often have a current or past history of alcohol dependence or abuse (APA, 2000). In addition, authors have noted that fire setting often bears a complex and complementary relationship with sexuality, which may serve as an additional motive for the behavior (Fras, 1997). Lejoyeux, Arbaretaz, McClaughlin, & Ades (2002) also found a significant history of depression among clients with pyromania as compared to subjects with other impulse control disorders.

Developmentally, research in the area of adolescent fire setting (without regard to pyromania) has reported a high correlation between fire setting and shyness and aggression as a reaction to perceived rejection by peers (Chen, Arria, & Anthony, 2003); extreme drug use and antisocial and suicidal behavior (Martin, Bergen, Richardson, Roeger, & Allison, 2004); and depression, alienation and poor reality testing (Moore, Thompson-Pope, & Whited, 1996). Most of these findings would preclude diagnosis for pyromania.

EPIDEMIOLOGY

Pathological Gambling

A variety of studies internationally have attempted to estimate the lifetime prevalence rate for adult pathological gambling, though it should be noted that findings often vary widely depending on location, survey methods, classification schemes, and ease of accessibility to gambling over time. A meta-analysis of 120 prevalence studies in the United States and Canada found that an average of 1.6 percent of adults met criteria for pathological and 5.5 percent for problem gambling disorder (Shaffer, Hall, & Vander Bilt, 1997). For other countries, reported rates vary between 1.2 percent for Australia, 1.7 to 3.2 percent for Spain, 0.8 percent for Switzerland, 1.8 percent for Hong Kong, 0.6 percent for Norway, and 2.7 percent for New Zealand. Rates of subthreshold problem gambling are generally double those for pathological gambling; however, there is significant conceptual uncertainty regarding the actual status of gamblers "in transition," who may be moving toward or away from pathology (Shaffer & Hall, 1996) or "binge gamblers" who may meet clinical criteria at some times but not at others (Nower & Blaszczysnki, 2003).

Rates of disordered gambling may also vary by geographical location and by socioeconomic status. Volberg (1996) has noted that U.S. states with a long history of legalized gambling reported higher rates of pathological gambling with a propensity for more pathological gambling to come from lower socioeconomically disadvantaged groups.

Adolescents characteristically report higher rates of both problem and pathological gambling than adults, due in large part to phases of development that correlate with heightened risk taking and disinhibition. Studies have reported that 24 percent to 40 percent of adolescents gamble weekly, 10 percent to 14 percent are at risk for gambling problems, and 2 percent to 9 percent meet diagnostic criteria for pathological gambling (for reviews of youth gambling, see Hardoon & Derevensky, 2002; Shaffer & Hall, 1996). The mean prevalence rate for adolescent pathological gambling is estimated at 5 percent—three times the 1.5 percent average for adults (National Research Council, 1999).

Trichotillomania

There have been no epidemiological studies to determine the prevalence of trichotillomania in the general population. One study of more than 2,500 college students reported that 1.5 percent of males and 3.4 percent of females reported chronic hair pulling though only 0.6 percent of either gender met diagnostic criteria for disorder (Christenson, Pyle, et al., 1991). Another study found that 10 percent to 13 percent of college students surveyed in the United States reported chronic hair pulling, though only 1 percent resulted in clinically significant hair loss and/or distress (Diefenbach et al., 2000).

The majority of diagnosed hair pullers are female, though studies suggest males also suffer from the disorder and present with similar phenomenological features though they may be less likely to seek treatment (Christenson, MacKenzie, & Mitchell, 1994; Christenson, Pyle, et al., 1991; Swedo et al., 1989).

There have been no longitudinal studies to detail the progression of trichotillomania over time. However, it is clinically accepted that symptoms may manifest in benign form in early childhood then remit with little or no therapeutic intervention (Swedo & Rapoport, 1991) or present in adolescence around the age of 13 years in a late-onset form that is more resistant to treatment and associated with comorbid psychopathology (Christenson, Pyle, et al., 1991; Diefenbach et al., 2000; Swedo & Leonard, 1992).

Kleptomania

Kleptomania is rarely diagnosed, occurring in fewer than 5 percent of identified shoplifters (APA, 2000). The overall prevalence rate in the general population is unknown, though evidence from clinical samples suggests that two-thirds of individuals with the disorder are female.

Intermittent Explosive Disorder

In the absence of prevalence studies, *DSM-IV-TR* (APA, 2000) notes that the disorder is "rare" and more common in males as compared to females. The disorder needs to be adequately differentiated from aggression linked to other causes such as an organic brain damage, drug-induced aggression, other psychiatric disorder or in response to deliberate provocation by others.

Pyromania

Little is known about the actual prevalence of pyromania except that it occurs more frequently in males and is "rare" (APA, 2000). In one unconventional study designed to ascertain the prevalence of the disorder in a small number of arsonists, a group of Canadian psychiatrists evaluated 236 arson cases and determined that only 2.9 percent (n = 7) met the clinical criteria (Crossley & Guzman, 1985). In another study, Ritchie and Huff (1999) examined the mental health records and/or prison files of 283 arsonists and found that, whereas most had psychiatric histories, only three offenders were diagnosed with pyromania. The authors indicated that the majority of fire setters were either angry or delusional, two criteria that would exclude them from a diagnosis of pyromania. Of note, 36 percent of the sample had been diagnosed with schizophrenia or bipolar disorder and 64 percent were abusing alcohol at the time of the fire setting.

ETIOLOGY

Pathological Gambling

It is generally agreed that the etiology of gambling disorder is multifactorial, dependent on a variety of biopsychosocial and environmental risk factors. Blaszczynski and Nower (2002) have proposed that all gamblers are initiated into gambling as a result of common ecological factors such as accessibility, availability, and accessibility of gambling. In addition, subsequent exposure to a variable ratio reinforcement schedule and other cues in the gambling environment provide behavioral conditioning needed to habituate and maintain the behavior. However, despite these commonalities, the pathways that lead certain individuals to progress toward the disorder while protecting others depends on a variety of factors including age of onset, childhood experiences, familial exposure to addictive behaviors, sensation-seeking and impulsivity traits, gender, ethnicity and socioeconomic status, age, and biobehavioral abnormalities (Blaszczynski & Nower, 2002).

Early onset and familial participation in gambling behavior are significant risk factors for future problems in youth. A number of studies have found that adolescents with gambling problems began gambling before the age of 11 (Griffiths, 1990; Gupta & Derevensky, 1998a). In addition, a significant percentage of youth problem gamblers report they first gambled with parents or other relatives or had parents with gambling problems (Gupta & Derevensky, 1998b). A recent meta-analysis of 17 family and 2 twin studies found a stronger familial effect for sons of problem gambling fathers and daughters of problem gambling mothers—strongest for high severity problem gambling in males (Walters, 2001).

Problem gambling behavior is also common in individuals with high levels of intensity seeking and impulsivity. Because gambling involves a high degree of mental and sensory stimulation, it is not surprising that a majority of studies have noted a strong empirical association in both youth and adults between problem gambling and the pursuit of intense stimulation, one form of sensation seeking (Anderson & Brown, 1984; Coventry & Brown, 1993; Kuley & Jacobs, 1988; Nower et al., 2004). Findings have been mixed (see, Blaszczysnki, Wilson, & McConaghy, 1986; Dickerson, Hinchy, & Fabre, 1987) due in large part to sampling bias and other methodological inconsistencies.

Severe gambling problems have also been noted in highly impulsive individuals (Nower et al., 2004; Petry, 2001a, 2001b; Steel & Blaszczynski, 1996; Vitaro, Brendgen, Ladouceur, & Tremblay, 2001). With few exceptions (Allcock & Grace, 1988; Petry, 2000), studies with both adult and youth gamblers have consistently noted a positive relationship between problem gambling and high levels of impulsivity, particularly the subtype associated with an inability to act with forethought and deliberation.

Male gender has long been a strong predictor of gambling problems. The majority of early studies on pathological gambling focused on men from Gamblers Anonymous and the Veterans Administration hospital system, limiting the number of women sampled (Mark & Lesieur, 1992). But recent surveys have noted that an increasing number of women are developing gambling problems due in part to a preference for gaming machines that prolong play while offering a highly addictive reinforcement schedule and low rate of monetary return. Recent studies comparing male and female gamblers have reported that females prefer lower denomination slot machines and longer sessions of play (Hing & Breen, 2001); a later age of onset (mean age 34.2 years versus 20.4 years) and shorter periods of intense (1.0 years versus 4.6 years) and problem gambling (1.8 years versus 8.6 years; Tavares, Zilberman, Beites, & Gentil, 2001); fewer problems with drugs or gambling-related arrests (Potenza et al., 2001); and higher rates of affective disorders and histories of physical abuse (Ibanez, Blanco, de Castro, Fernandez-Piqueras, & Saiz-Ruiz, 2003). A majority of those studies found similar rates of gambling severity, overall psychiatric comorbidity, and indebtedness in both males and females.

Though research is limited, it appears that gambling problems may be more prevalent in ethnic cultures that sanction the behavior. Zitzow (1996) has reported that American Indian adolescents, who also report higher rates of substance abuse than their non-Indian peers, also endorsed an earlier onset of gambling problems. Similarly, Blaszczynski, Huynh, Dumlao, and Farrell (1998) found that 2.9 percent of individuals in the Chinese community in Sydney were pathological gamblers. Among African Americans in the United States, Welte, Barnes, Wieczorek, Tidwell, and Parker (2002) noted lower overall past-year rates of gambling participation, however, those who did gamble bet more frequently and reported larger wins and losses than other groups. Likewise, another study reported that nearly 17 percent of 80 elderly African Americans living in senior centers with bus trips to casinos were "heavy to pathological" gamblers (Bazargan, Bazargan, & Akanda, 2001).

Increasingly, researchers are concerned that advanced age is an additional risk factor for problem gambling, particularly when individuals live in residential facilities that provide transportation to gambling venues. As indicated in the Bazargan et al. (2001) study, elderly African American gamblers surveyed reported a prevalence rate of pathological gambling about 15 percent higher than that of the adult population in general. McNeilly and Burke (2000) have also reported that 24 percent of seniors who actively gambled frequented casinos, 17 percent played the numbers, and 41 percent played bingo once a week or more.

Finally, an increasing number of studies have indicated abnormalities in biobehavioral functioning and genetic mechanisms that may contribute to the development or maintenance of gambling disorder (for a comprehensive review, see Goudriaan, Oosterlaan, de Beurs, & van den Brink, 2004). Neuropsychological studies indicate deficits in executive functioning, such as delay discounting, fluency and interference control, and impulsiveness/disinhibition. Neuroimaging studies have identified abnormalities in braining functioning, including decreased hemispheric lateralization and/or temporal lobe function, and abnormal activation in specific subcortical frontal regions. Research into neurochemistry has likewise identified deficits in neurotransmitter mechanisms in pathological gamblers, particularly dopamine, serotonin and norepinephrine in reward-pathway areas. Finally, genetic studies have identified allele variants of dopamine receptors (DRD2, DRD3, DRD4), deficits in the serotonin transporter (5-HTTLPR) and monoamine oxidase A (MAO-A) genes, and shared genetic factors that suggest a heritable vulnerability to factors that contribute to the development of pathological gambling disorder.

Trichotillomania

A variety of approaches have attempted to explain the etiology of trichotillomania: psychoanalytic, biological, and behavioral (see Diefenbach et al., 2000). However, to date, none is comprehensive and supported by a large body of empirical evidence. Psychoanalytic theorists suggested that the disorder is a symbolic expression of unconscious conflicts, or the result of childhood trauma or poor object relationships (Singh & Maguire, 1989). In contrast, biological theories maintain that trichotillomania is an obsessive-compulsive spectrum disorder (OCSD), characterized by intrusive and obsessive thoughts and/or uncontrollable, repetitive behaviors (Hollander, Skodol, & Oldham, 1996; Swedo & Leonard, 1992). Studies to test this association have been largely unsuccessful, reporting instead significant phenomenological, neuropsychological, and neurological differences between the two disorders (see for review, Diefenbach et al., 2000). Some recent studies have noted a possible overlap with Tourette's syndrome, also an OCSD (Diefenbach et al., 2000). Both disorders are characterized by repetitive behaviors prompted by sensory cues and urges, share structurally similar morphometric findings, and respond well to neuroleptic drugs, and the presence of comorbid Tourette's syndrome appears to amplify hair-pulling behavior (Diefenbach et al., 2000; Stein & Hollander, 1992).

Finally, several potentially complementary theories have attempted to explain the etiology and maintenance of trichotillomania from a behavioral perspective. One theory proposes that hair-pulling behavior is initiated in response to stress, reinforced by its capacity for tension reduction, and, ultimately, maintained by association with environmental cues by virtue of operant conditioning (Diefenbach et al., 2000). A second theory maintains that hair pulling results from modeling, as children imitate the behavior of their caregivers (Christenson, MacKenzie, & Reeve, 1992; Diefenbach et al., 2000). Other models assert an integrative approach, suggesting that a combination of biological, cognitive, affective, behavioral, and environmental factors serve to initiate and maintain pathological hair-pulling behavior over time (Diefenbach et al., 2000).

Kleptomania

Historically, kleptomania was initially viewed as a "feminine sickness," resulting from hysteria, insanity, menstruation, and pelvic and uterine diseases (for a review of early theories on etiology, see Murray, 1992) These theories were later replaced by psychoanalytic interpretations, which viewed the act of stealing as an ego defense against anxiety and a manifestation of sexuality in which a female, out of desire to obtain a penis, stole objects that represented the symbolic byproducts of anal fixation.

Subsequent conceptualizations of the disorder have viewed kleptomania as an adaptive response to underlying depression in which an individual adopts the stealing behavior in response to aversive mood (Presta et al., 2002). During these periods, individuals experience a sense of elation concurrently with the kleptomanic urge, relieving the ego-dystonic nature of the behavior. The behavior is often followed by feelings of depression, guilt, and fatigue, though individuals report that, overall, the act of stealing has a therapeutic effect on the severity of depressive symptoms (Presta et al., 2002). Most patients do not exhibit other antisocial behavior (Goldman, 1991).

Intermittent Explosive Disorder

Few studies have explored the etiology of individuals who meet criteria for intermittent explosive disorder apart from other psychiatric conditions with aggressiveness as an associated feature. Commonalities in one early study included a history of coma-producing conditions (e.g., meningitis, febrile convulsions, head injuries), a high incidence of family violence and alcoholism, aggressive eruptions with alcohol usage, and comorbid pyromania (Bach-y-rita, Lion, Climent, & Ervin, 1971). In addition, clients in that study reported chronic anxiety and insecurity, poor coping skills, and childhood deprivation (Bach-y-rita et al., 1971). Other researchers have asserted that PTSD symptoms, precipitated by early childhood exposure to violence, are subsequently triggered by situations that evoke feelings of being trapped, criticized or rejected. One study found that individuals with intermittent explosive disorder had at least one first-degree relative with a mood disorder (56 percent, n = 14), another impulse-control disorder (56 percent, n = 14), a substance use disorder (80 percent, n = 20), and an anxiety (8 percent, n = 2) or eating disorder (8 percent, n = 2; McElroy et al., 1998).

Mounting evidence suggests that the disorder may be related to mood disorders and a form of affective spectrum disorders (for summary, see McElroy et al., 1998). First, mood disorders are common in alcoholic violent offenders and impulsive fire setters, who also commonly meet criteria for intermittent explosive disorder. Second, studies have reported abnormalities in central serotonergic neurotransmission and circadian rhythm disturbances common to individuals with mood disorders. Third, individuals with intermittent explosive disorder have been found to respond to treatment with antidepressants, mood stabilizers, and antiepileptic drugs with mood stabilizing properties (McElroy et al., 1998).

Pyromania

The etiology of pyromania is unknown. Limited information from case histories suggests a possible familial tendency toward fire setting and frontal lobe dysfunction (Calev, 1995) and/or varying degrees of mental retardation (Geller, 1987). Adolescent fire setters, not necessarily diagnosed with pyromania, have also reported families characterized by absent fathers, parental drug and alcohol abuse, physical abuse, and neglect (Showers & Pickrell, 1987).

COURSE, COMPLICATIONS, AND PROGNOSIS

Pathological Gambling

Pathological gambling is commonly viewed as a spectrum disorder, progressing from social gambling for entertainment to pathological gambling that meets clinical criteria for disorder. The majority of problem gamblers report participation in adolescence with fluctuating degrees on involvement over adulthood. Problem gamblers who exhibit some gambling-related difficulties may be in transition, moving either toward or away from the serious end of the spectrum (Shaffer & Hall, 1996). Gambling disorder progresses through three or four stages (for discussions of gambling stages, see Custer & Milt, 1985; Rosenthal, 1992). During the *winning phase,* gamblers play for fun and excitement, however an early big win or other accomplishment fuels a desire to gamble more frequently for greater profit. Heightened preoccupation with gambling, increases in gambling frequency and mounting losses herald the *losing phase,* in which gamblers increase the frequency and amount of bets in a frantic attempt to win back lost funds. As losing continues, gamblers begin lying, borrowing, ignoring bills, begging for financial bailouts, and exploiting relationships to hide the extent of gambling losses. This behavior leads ultimately to the *desperation phase,* a period characterized by engaging in previously inconceivable behaviors like embezzlement, fraud, and stealing as a necessary means of financial and psychological survival. Some gamblers progress to the *hopelessness phase,* in which they abandon all hope of winning to gamble frantically for excitement alone (Rosenthal, 1992). As gambling increases in severity and frequency, pathological gamblers find themselves with an increasingly limited spiral of options (Lesieur, 1979), leading to serious adverse financial, legal, and psychosocial consequences.

The primary complications of pathological gambling are the development of major depressive symptoms including risk of suicidality and marital problems. The direction of causality is varied with some cases in which depression leads to gambling and vice versa.

Trichotillomania

Trichotillomania manifests itself in infancy, childhood, and early adolescence and runs a chronic and debilitating course of variable intensity through adulthood. As noted by Swedo (1993a), the onset of trichotillomania in early infancy, that is, prior to age 5 may constitute a separate group and represent a habit disorder that is benign, relatively self-limiting and remits by school age following maturation. The behavior occurs when the infant is tired or bored and increases during separation. Accordingly, it is viewed as a self-soothing behavior comparable to rocking or thumb sucking. In early as compared to later onset cases, there is a greater proportion of males; almost twice as many.

Males tend to have a slightly earlier onset in the prepubescent phase of maturation as compared to females who display hair-pulling behaviors in early adolescents. Symptoms may be exacerbated during menstruation and under conditions of emotional stress taking on a focused and ritualistic form of repetitive behavior that is associated with tension reduction. In about three-quarters of sufferers, there does not appear to be any perceptible relationship between trichotillomania and stresses; the behavior appearing to be entirely habitual or automatic, and associated with sedentary conditions such as reading, watching television and use of computers. Individuals attempt to conceal the disorder from family and others, for example, through use of scarfs, hats, wigs, or concealing hairstyles or, if limited to eyebrows or lashes, may tolerate the social opprobrium that may emanate from peers or family members. Given the embarrassment, shame, and lowered self-esteem associated with the cosmetic effects of unseemly bald patches or thinning hair, patterns of social avoidance and isolation are common. Typically, the behavior persists into adulthood before presentation for treatment in the late 20s and early 30s.

Physical complications may arise from secondary behaviors associated with trichotillomania. Slightly fewer than a half of people with trichotillomania show a tendency to chew and/or swallow the hair (trichophagia). This behavior presents risk of dental erosion or serious medical complications caused by the development of hair balls (trichobezoar) in the stomach and intestines (Diefenbach et al., 2000).

With respect to comorbid disorders, there is no single psychiatric diagnosis or personality traits inherently linked to trichotillomania, although affective and anxiety disorders are commonly present, with 50 percent to 65 percent reporting mood disturbances, 23 percent current major depression, and 32 percent history of major depression. Approximately half experience lifetime anxiety and 18 percent current/past panic. A small percentage (10 percent) report a current obsessive-compulsive disorder, 5 percent a history of such, and 18 percent to 27 percent have obsessive-compulsive symptoms that do not meet criteria for the diagnosis of the disorder.

Addictive behaviors and eating and body dysmorphic disorders have been reported in 20 percent of cases in addition to a range of Axis II personality disorders including the dramatic Cluster B, histrionic and borderline, obsessive-compulsive, and passive-aggressive disorders (Diefenbach et al., 2000). The casual relationship between these disorders and trichotillomania remains open to speculation. Concurrent self-cutting/harm occurs in approximately 3 percent to 5 percent of cases.

Methodological problems and mixed results reported in treatment outcome studies preclude any definitive comment on prognosis (Diefenbach et al., 2000). However, pharmacological and behavioral treatments do lead to symptomatic improvement in the short term but there are difficulties maintaining gains in the long term with high rates of relapse occurring.

Kleptomania

There is little published information or systematic study on the course of the disorder. Presta et al. (2002) note this is due in large part to two factors: (1) the secretive nature of the disorder and associated shame that dissuades individuals from seeking treatment until they are arrested or in treatment for a comorbid psychiatric disorder and (2) the lack of sophisticated, widely used assessment instruments resulting in underdiagnosis and small sample sizes for research.

The *DSM* suggests the course is variable, beginning in childhood, adolescence, or adulthood and, in rare cases, in late adulthood and may continue for years despite multiple convictions for shoplifting (APA, 2000). The typical course is thought to follow one of three patterns: (1) sporadic with brief episodes and long periods of remission; (2) episodic with protracted periods of stealing and periods of remission; or (3) chronic, with some degree of fluctuation (APA, 2000). Limited information from empirical research suggests individuals with the disorder tend to be older (mean age 35 to 40) when sampled, evade diagnosis for years, and report a stealing history that exceeds 10 years in duration and an age of onset in late teens or early 20s (McElroy, Hudson, Pope, & Keck, 1991; Sarasalo et al., 1996).

Intermittent Explosive Disorder

The nature of the disorder suggests that aggressive behaviors are intermittent and, therefore, unpredictable, largely determined by eliciting events that trigger rageful internal states. This is further complicated by the fact that triggers for explosive behaviors are often undetectable by direct observation (Opdyke & Rothbaum, 1998). The course of an explosive episode begins with perceived threats, rejections or criticisms, which produce aversive stimulation in the form of internal unrest. This, in turn, precipitates a need for escape through erupting in a violent outburst, which serves to dissipate the pool of negative emotion (Opdyke & Rothbaum, 1998). Furthermore, the number of perceived threats, rejections, or criticisms may accrue, increasing the reoccurrence of outbursts or increasing the overall level of volatility.

Subjects in a study by McElroy et al. (1998) reported that their aggressive acts were very brief, lasting an average of 22 to 23 minutes. Most indicated that outbursts were precipitated by psychosocial stressors, typically conflicts with other people, though a majority of the subjects also reported they also had spontaneous aggressive outbursts. Aggressive impulses began with an urge to attack or defend themselves or, simply, with an "adrenaline rush," were often accompanied by autonomic symptoms and associated with some degree of loss or change in awareness, and were followed by a sense of relief and/or pleasure (McElroy et al., 1998). Most of the individuals in the study indicated they also experienced difficulty with chronic anger and frequent subthreshold episodes, which they managed to either suppress or channel into less aggressive behaviors such as screaming or punching walls with no damage.

Pyromania

There are no longitudinal or other empirical studies investigating the course of the disorder or the relationship between fire setting in childhood and adulthood (APA, 2000). It is generally accepted that fire setting is episodic and may wax and wane in frequency (APA, 2000).

ASSESSMENT AND DIAGNOSIS

Pathological Gambling

The South Oaks Gambling Screen (SOGS; Lesieur & Blume, 1987) is the most widely utilized screening instrument in treatment and research with adults. Based on the *DSM-III-R* (APA, 1987), the SOGS categorizes individuals who endorse five or more items as pathological gamblers. Despite its popularity, the SOGS has been criticized for generating a high number of false positives in general population samples, diagnosing based on outdated criteria for pathological gambling, providing only lifetime estimates of pathological gambling behavior, and failing to discriminate adequately between subclinical and pathological gambling groups (see, e.g., Stinchfield, 2002).

Other adult screening instruments include the Canadian Problem Gambling Index (CPGI; Ferris & Wynne, 2001), a 31-item measure used for general population surveys; the two-item Lie/Bed Questionnaire (Johnston, O'Malley, & Backman, 1997), a two-item screen measuring two *DSM-IV*-based questions found particularly sensitive in identifying pathological gamblers; and the NODS (NORC, 1999), a *DSM-IV*-based measure used in U.S. prevalence studies. Adolescent studies typically administer the adolescent version of the SOGS, called the SOGS-RA (Winters, Stinchfield, & Fulkerson, 2003), or the *DSM-IV*-based measures by Fisher, *DSM-IV*-J (Fisher, 1992), or, more recently, the *DSM-IV*-MR-J (Fisher, 2000).

In addition to formal screening measures, 20 questions devised by members of Gamblers Anonymous, the GA 20 Questions, have long been utilized as an informal self-screening mechanism, and some clinicians merely adapt the 10 *DSM-IV-TR* criteria to question format. Despite the variety of screening tools, it is important to note that few treatment programs routinely screen for gambling disorder, and many treatment providers know little, if anything, about pathological gambling (Rowan & Galasso, 2000; Volberg, 2002). Shepherd (1996) suggested that some professionals may resist screening for gambling because they are reluctant to accept changes in protocol, have inadequate education and training to administer instruments properly, are unaware that gambling can serve as a relapse trigger for substance abuse, or perceive screening as "intrusive to the therapeutic agenda" (p. 27). Medical professions may also lack resources and training to encourage proper implementation of screening tools (Rowan & Galasso, 2000).

Trichotillomania

The diagnosis is typically established through clinical interview and scalp examination and biopsy to rule out organic factors. Accurate scalp examination and biopsy are critical, though the process is often complicated by patient and family denial or a lack of knowledge about the disorder in general (Walsh & McDougle, 2001). Characteristic scalp biopsies for the disorder feature trichomalacia, pigment clumps, peribulbar hemorrhage, and hair canal pigment casts; a lack of lymphocytic infiltrates is typically observed in individuals with alopecia areata (Walsh & McDougle, 2001). Methods of clinical assessment include: (1) clinical interview (e.g., Minnesota Trichotillomania Assessment Inventory-II [MTAI-II]; Christenson, Mackenzie, et al., 1991); (2) clinical rating scales (e.g., Yale-Brown Obsessive-Compulsive Scale modified for trichotillomania [Y-BOCS TM]; Stanley, Prather, Wagner, Davis, & Swann, 1993); Psychiatric Institute Trichotillomania Scale (PITS; Winchel, Jones, Molcho, Parsons, & Stanley, 1992); (3) self-report measures such as the Massachusetts General Hospital (MGH) Hair-Pulling Scale (Keuthen et al., 1995); (4) self-monitoring; and (5) collateral report.

Kleptomania

Diagnosis is typically made through self-report, according to *DSM-IV-TR* criteria. Care must be taken to differentiate the disorder from behaviors associated with an antisocial personality and where theft is motivated for personal economic gain or due to peer-group pressure or deviant subculture membership.

Intermittent Explosive Disorder

There is no empirical research on the assessment and diagnosis of intermittent explosive disorder as defined by the *DSM-IV-TR* (APA, 2000) criteria, though there are studies that examine episodic dyscontrol and explosive rage. In one study, McElroy (1999) recruited subjects with self-reported rage outbursts that resulted in serious assaultive acts or destruction of property. The participants were assessed using a combination of measures including a structured interview based on the *DSM* criteria, a semistructured interview to elicit demographic data, phenomenology and course of the disorder, and the Structured Clinical Interview of *DSM-IV* Axis I Disorders (SCID-I/P; First, Spitzer, Gibbon, & Williams, 1996) to rule out outbursts that resulted solely from another mood or psychotic disorder.

Pyromania

Diagnosis is primarily made through exclusion, using the *DSM-IV-TR* (APA, 2000) criteria. Assessment instruments for general child and adolescent fire-setting behavior are also available (for a review, see Wilcox & Kolko, 2002).

IMPACT ON ENVIRONMENT

Pathological Gambling

Though estimating the actual social costs of pathological gambling is problematic due to the multifactorial nature of the disorder and difficulty in establishing causality, it is generally accepted that pathological gamblers are at increased risk for committing crimes, accruing debts and filing for bankruptcy, and defrauding employers (NRC, 1999). In addition, they are at high risk for separation or divorce, unemployment, mental and physical health problems, and are likely to pass on intergenerational patterns of addictive behavior to their children (NRC, 1999).

It is estimated that 21 percent to 85 percent of pathological gamblers commit crimes like fraud, stealing, embezzlement, forgery, robbery, assault, and blackmail, and 25 percent to 39 percent are convicted and may serve prison terms for those offenses (for a review of the social cost literature, see Nower, 2003). In a national study in the United States, one-third of problem and pathological gamblers reported arrests, compared to 10 percent of social gamblers and only 4 percent of nongamblers (NORC, 1999). In addition, about 23 percent of pathological gamblers and 13 percent of problem gamblers had been imprisoned, compared to 4 percent of social gamblers and 0.3 percent of nongamblers (NORC, 1999). Another study found that one in five identified callers to a gambling helpline admitted to committing illegal acts to finance their gambling, and those gamblers were more likely to be younger, report suicidality secondary to gambling, use alcohol or drugs, and require mental health treatment (Potenza et al., 2000).

Several investigators have attempted to estimate the relative costs of gambling-related crimes, though methodologies differ and fail to clarify the causal relationship between gambling and crime (Shaffer & Korn, 2002). Derived from studies in the United States and depending upon location and survey methodology employed, estimates of gambling-related theft and misappropriation range from $6,000 to $61,000, suggesting a total annual cost of about $1.7 million in police, probation, incarceration, and judicial administration costs (NORC, 1999; Thompson, Gazel, & Rickman, 1996b).

A high percentage of gamblers will also face bankruptcy, defaulting on financial obligations at alarming rates. The Gambling Impact Behavior Study (GIBS), a national survey of gambling in the United States, estimated that 19 percent of pathological gamblers, compared to 5.5 percent of social gamblers and 4.2 percent of nongamblers, filed for bankruptcy in 1998 and owed an estimated $1.80 for every $1 of income (NORC, 1999). Similarly, a Canadian study reported that one-third of problem gamblers had either filed for bankruptcy or owed debts ranging from $75,000 to $150,000 each (Ladouceur, Boisvert, Pepin, Loranger, & Sylvain, 1994).

Burdened with pressure from creditors, escalating rates of debt, mounting social stressors, and interaction with the court system, pathological gamblers also typically experience serious problems in the workplace. In a survey of the social cost literature, Lesieur (1998) reported that 69 percent to 76 percent of pathological gamblers were often late to work or absent in order to gamble. Others gambled on company time, reported moodiness and irritability, borrowed from fellow employees, stole from employers, and arranged for advances on their paychecks. In addition, 25 percent to 30 percent of pathological gamblers were likely to lose their jobs due to gambling—one-third due to theft—costing employers indirectly in unemployment or severance benefits, extended health benefits, and retraining costs (Ladouceur et al., 1994; Lesieur, 1998). The GIBS study in the United States found that pathological gamblers reported nearly triple the rates of unemployment of social and nongamblers (NORC, 1999). Additional job-related social costs also include search and training costs to employers as well as health and welfare payments (Thompson, Gazel, & Rickman, 1996).

Most pathological gamblers require mental health treatment and, possibly, medical attention for a range of stress-related medical problems at a cost of $722 to $1,000 per gambler for outpatient (NORC, 1999; Thompson et al., 1996) and $20,000 to $28,000 for inpatient treatment services (Vatz & Weinberg, 1995). Studies have found that, even after discontinuing gambling, adverse medical and psychological symptoms persist, including depression, ulcers and heartburn, bowel disorders, insomnia, excessive weight gain, high blood pressure, back or neck pain, and headaches (Ladouceur et al., 1994; Lorenz & Yaffee, 1986).

Other environmental consequences include the long-term adverse effects on the gambler's family system. Discord between gamblers and their partners are common. Studies have reported that 23 percent of pathological gamblers engaged in affairs, 33 percent separated from their spouses, and 54 percent divorced (Lorenz & Yaffee, 1986; NORC, 1999).

Family turmoil may have dire implications for children. Jacobs et al. (1989) theorized that certain family environments breed "intergenerational effects wrought by highly stressed, preoccupied, inconsistent, and often absent parents who have provided seriously flawed parenting, sex, social and occupational role models for children" (p. 266). As a result, children of disordered gamblers reported feeling angry, hurt, isolated, depressed, and abandoned as a result of their parent's gambling problems (Lesieur & Rothschild, 1989). They are also more likely to develop dependencies on gambling, food, cigarettes, alcohol, and drugs. In addition, children of problem gamblers may experience physical abuse resulting from the displaced anger of one or both parents (see Darbyshire, Oster, & Carrig, 2001; Lesieur & Rothschild, 1989).

Trichotillomania

Embarrassment caused by hair-pulling behavior may lead to social isolation. Other environmental consequences are in need of further exploration.

Kleptomania

Little is known about the environmental impact of kleptomania, except that individuals typically enter treatment only after one or more arrests for shoplifting. In one study, more than 80 percent of participants reported they had been arrested, many on several occasions (Sarasalo et al., 1996).

Intermittent Explosive Disorder

Due to the nature and unpredictability of aggressive behavior, the disorder often results in job loss, school suspension, divorce, difficulties with interpersonal relationships or other impairments in social and occupational functioning, accidents (e.g., in vehicles), hospitalization (e.g., due to fights or accidents), financial problems, incarcerations, and other legal problems (APA, 2000). In one study of 27 individuals diagnosed with the disorder, 41 percent (n = 11) admitted to attempting homicide during an episode, and most had both destroyed property and seriously assaulted another person in the past, 37 percent (n = 10) with a weapon (McElroy et al., 1998). In addition, most of the subjects viewed their outbursts as highly problematic, resulting in distress as well as social, vocational, legal, and financial problems.

Pyromania

Individuals with pyromania are often indifferent to the personal or economic consequences caused by the fire or may derive satisfaction from the results of their behavior. Fire setting may lead to property damage, legal consequences, or injury or loss of life to the fire setter or to others (APA, 2000).

TREATMENT IMPLICATIONS

Pathological Gambling

Treatment for pathological gambling disorder typically includes some combination of attendance at GA support groups, counseling, hotline services, cognitive and behavioral therapies, and/or pharmacological interventions (for a review, see Petry & Armentano, 1999). Early therapeutic interventions involved psychodynamic treatment, attendance at GA and nonspecific professional treatment services. Studies found that the combination of GA attendance and therapy (Russo, Taber, McCormick, & Ramirez, 1984) were more effective than GA alone (Stewart & Brown, 1988), though abstinence rates for the combination were still only 50 to 60 percent.

The few controlled studies currently available have evaluated the efficacy of cognitive behavioral therapy and imaginal desensitization, a form of visualization combined with relaxation. Three studies found that imaginal desensitization was more effective than other behavioral treatments at decreasing gambling urges in treatment-seeking gamblers from one month to nine years following treatment (McConaghy, Blaszczynski, & Frankova, 1991).

Several studies have provided empirical support for cognitive behavioral therapy, particularly when combined with social skills training and cognitive restructuring that targets the notion of randomness (Bujold, Ladouceur, Sylvain, & Boisvert, 1994), though studies are traditionally hampered by small, nongeneralizable sample sizes, insufficient data on dropouts, and inconsistent administration of treatments (i.e., variability in treatment time; for reviews see Blaszczysnki & Silove, 1995; Toneatto & Ladouceur, 2003).

Similarly, an increasing number of studies are demonstrating promising results using pharmacological agents, including carbamazepine, naltrexone, clomipramine, paroxetine, fluvoxamine, and lithium (for a review, see Grant, Kim, & Potenza, 2003).

It is important to note that drop-out rates in treatment programs for pathological gambling approach 50 percent, due largely to the fact that individuals miss the thrill of gambling or gain increased confidence they could win and relieve their financial burdens (Grant, Kim, & Kushwoski, 2004). Predictors of treatment completion include a positive response to treatment within eight weeks and having a supportive environment (Grant et al., 2004). Another study found the level of impulsivity to be the single biggest predictor of drop-out rates (Leblond, Ladouceur, & Blaszczynski, 2004).

Trichotillomania

Until the 1990s, trichotillomania received little interest from the research community apart from case studies or descriptive reports of hair pulling and associated disorders and behaviors. Treatment consists primarily of pharmacotherapy combined with behavioral interventions. Case studies have reported mixed results using a variety of medications including lithium, chlorpromazine, amitriptyline, buspirone, isocarboxazid, fensluramine, progestin, and selective serotonin reuptake inhibitors (SSRIs; for a review, see Diefenbach et al., 2000). The tricyclic antidepressant clomipramine has proven the most efficacious in controlled studies. However, it is often difficult for clients to tolerate the medication at adequate doses, which severely limits compliance (Walsh & McDougle, 2001). More benign medications are generally ineffective, though topical preparations and psychotropic medication may help some clients who are experiencing difficulties with treatment or relapse (Walsh & McDougle, 2001). Studies suggest that long-term success of pharmacotherapy alone may be limited, reporting a significant reduction in symptoms for the first few months followed by a high rate of relapse long term, particularly when dosages are lowered or the drugs are discontinued (Alexander, 1991; Iancu, Weizman, Kindler, Sasson, & Zohar, 1996; Swedo, 1993b).

Increasingly, optimal treatment includes a combination of pharmaco- and behavioral therapies. Clinicians have attempted to treat the disorder with therapies including biofeedback, covert sensitization, aversion therapy, positive practice, extinction, overcorrection, and response prevention (Diefenbach et al., 2000). However, one treatment—habit reversal training (HRT; Peterson, Campsie, & Azrin, 1994)—has received the strongest empirical support. HRT, initially formulated with nine components, is designed to identify conditioned cues associated with hair pulling, interrupt hair-pulling behavior, and replace the behavior with adaptive coping strategies (Diefenbach et al., 2000). It is most effective when combined with cognitive therapy (Rothbaum, 1992). However, HRT is a highly specialized and intensive treatment modality, practiced by a limited number of therapists, thereby limiting accessibility to many clients (Walsh & McDougle, 2001).

Kleptomania

The few reports that address effective treatment for kleptomania consist of case studies or small clinical samples, often to ameliorate shoplifting behavior rather than to address kleptomania as a disorder. Studies utilizing covert, systematic, and imaginal desensitization (see Opdyke & Rothbaum, 1998) have reported moderate success. In addition, other studies have noted a remission of symptoms in patients treated with regular pharmacological treatment, including antidepressants (most commonly SSRIs), benzodiazepines, mood stabilizers, thymoleptic, and opioid receptor antagonists, often as adjuvants to cognitive behavioral therapy (Durst, Katz, Teitelbaum, Zislin, & Dannon, 2001; McElroy et al., 1991; Sarasalo et al., 1996).

Intermittent Explosive Disorder

No protocol exists for the treatment of intermittent explosive disorder. Individuals in one study indicated they received the most help from insight-oriented psychotherapy, which assisted them in increasing control over aggressive impulses (McElroy et al., 1998). Other subjects in the study reported undergoing behavior modification or couples, group or family therapy with little success.

Preliminary investigations have suggested that individuals with explosive disorder benefit from treatment with tricyclic antidepressants, serotonin specific reuptake inhibitors (SSRIs), and mood stabilizers such as lithium or carbamazepine (see McElroy, 1999; McElroy et al., 1998). In one study, subjects with a highly compulsive or impulsive presentation with a unipolar component were given SSRIs, whereas patients with affective instability or bipolarity were administered the mood stabilizer, divalproex (McElroy, 1999). The researchers noted that 60 percent of the subjects receiving pharmacotherapy reported a moderate response to SSRIs and a marked response to mood stabilizers, as measured by a reduction in aggressive impulses and explosive acts.

Opdyke and Rothbaum (1998) have suggested adapting therapeutic strategies used for other forms of behavioral outbursts as treatment for intermittent explosive disorder. One treatment, commonly used with mentally retarded inpatients, involves blocking violent sequelae with the use of physical restraint while simultaneously presenting escape-provoking stimuli. In theory, this procedure should extinguish aggressive behavior by removing the negative reinforcement that often encourages the behavior (i.e., to avoid the explosive outburst, the "victim" complies with the client's wishes). Alternatively, the differential reinforcement of other behaviors (DRO) approach, successful in treating self-injurious behavior, could be adapted so that clients are differentially reinforced or rewarded for failing to display explosive outbursts during a designated time period until the behavior is extinguished.

Pyromania

There are no existing treatment interventions for pyromania in the literature, though several authors have suggested optimal treatment strategies for adolescent fire setting behavior (for a review, see Soltys, 1992). Those interventions include parenting training, overcorrection/satiation/negative practice with corrective consequences, behavior contracting/token reinforcement, special problem-solving skills training, relaxation training, overt sensitization, cognitive behavioral therapy, fire safety and prevention education, individual and family therapy, and medication. It is, however, important to note that adolescent fire setting behavior typically differs from the idiosyncratic nature of pyromania, which would arguably require greater emphasis on pharmacological interventions, cognitive behavioral therapy, social skills, covert sensitization, relaxation and response cost (Opdyke & Rothbaum, 1998). Treatments to diffuse the buildup of tension, increase awareness of negative consequences of the behavior, and substitute healthy stress coping strategies should prove most effective.

REFERENCES

Alexander, R. C. (1991). Fluoxetine treatment of trichotillomania [Letter to editor]. *Journal of Clinical Psychiatry, 52,* 88.

Allcock C., & Grace, D. M. (1988). Pathological gamblers are neither impulsive nor sensation-seekers. *Australian and New Zealand Journal of Psychiatry, 22,* 307–311.

American Psychiatric Association. (APA). (1987). *Diagnostic and statistical manual of mental disorders* (3rd ed., rev.). Washington, DC: Author.

American Psychiatric Association. (APA). (1994). *Diagnostic and statistical manual of mental disorders* (4th ed.). Washington, DC: Author.

American Psychiatric Association. (APA). (2000). *Diagnostic and statistical manual of mental disorders* (4th ed., text rev.). Washington, DC: Author.

Anderson, G., & Brown, I. F. (1984). Real and laboratory gambling, sensation seeking and arousal: Towards a Pavlovian component in general theories of gambling and gambling addictions. *British Journal of Psychology, 75,* 401–411.

Bach-y-rita, G., Lion, J. R., Climent, C. E., & Ervin, F. R. (1971). Episodic dyscontrol: A study of 130 violent patients. *American Journal of Psychiatry, 127,* 1473–1478.

Bayle, F. J., Caci, H., Millet, B., Richa, S., & Olie, J. P. (2003). Psychopathology and comorbidity of psychiatric disorders in patients with kleptomania. *American Journal of Psychiatry, 160,* 1509–1513.

Bazargan, M., Bazargan, S., & Akanda, M. (2001). Gambling habits among aged African Americans. *Clinical Gerontologist, 22,* 51–62.

Becona, E., Del Carmen Lorenzo, M., & Fuentes, M. J. (1996). Pathological gambling and depression. *Psychology Report, 78,* 635–640.

Bergh, C., & Kuehlhorn. E. (1994). Social, psychological, and physical consequences of pathological gambling in Sweden. *Journal of Gambling Studies, 10,* 275–285.

Black, D. W., & Moyer, T. (1998). Clinical features and psychiatric comorbidity of subjects with pathological gambling behaviour. *Psychiatric Services, 49,* 1434–1439.

Blaszczynski, A., Huynh, S., Dumlao, V. J., & Farrell, L. (1998). Problem gambling within a Chinese speaking community. *Journal of Gambling Studies, 14,* 359–380.

Blaszczynski, A., & McConaghy, N. (1986). Demographic and clinical data on compulsive gambling. In M. Walker (Ed.), *Faces of gambling* (pp. 263–272). Sydney, Australia: National Association for Gambling Studies.

Blaszczynski, A., & McConaghy, N. (1989). Anxiety and/or depression in the pathogenesis of addictive gambling. *International Journal of Addiction, 24,* 337–350.

Blaszczynski, A., & Nower, L. (2002). A pathways model of problem and pathological gambling. *Addiction, 97,* 487–499.

Blaszczynski, A., & Silove, D. (1995). Cognitive behavioural therapies for pathological gambling. *Journal of Gambling Studies, 11,* 195–220.

Blaszczynski, A., Wilson, A. C., & McConaghy, N. (1986). Sensation seeking and pathological gambling. *British Journal of Addictions, 81,* 113–117.

Brown, R. I. F. (1986). Arousal and sensation-seeking components in the general explanation of gambling and gambling addictions. *International Journal of Addiction, 21,* 1001–1016.

Bujold, A., Ladouceur, R., Sylvain, C., & Boisvert, J.-M. (1994). Treatment of pathological gamblers: An experimental study. *Journal of Behavior Therapy and Experimental Psychiatry, 25,* 275–282.

Calev, A. (1995). Pyromania and executive/frontal dysfunction. *Behavioural Neurology, 8,* 163–167.

Chen, Y., Arria, A., & Anthony, J. (2003). Firesetting in adolescence and being aggressive, shy and rejected by peers: New epidemiological evidence from a national sample survey. *Journal of the American Academy of Psychiatry and the Law, 31,* 44–52.

Christenson, G., Chernoff-Clementz, E., & Clementz, B. A. (1992). Personality and clinical characteristics in patients with trichotillomania. *Journal of Clinical Psychiatry, 53,* 407–413.

Christenson, G. A., MacKenzie, T. B., & Mitchell, J. E. (1991). Characteristics of 60 adult chronic hair pullers. *American Journal of Psychiatry, 148,* 365–370.

Christenson, G., MacKenzie, T. B., & Mitchell, J. E. (1994). Adult men and women with trichotillomania: A comparison of male and female characteristics. *Psychosomatics, 35,* 142–149.

Christenson, G., MacKenzie, T. B., & Reeve, E. A. (1992). Familial trichotillomania [Letter to editor]. *American Journal of Psychiatry, 149,* 283.

Christenson, G., Pyle, R. L., & Mitchell, J. E. (1991). Estimated lifetime prevalence of trichotillomania in college students. *Journal of Clinical Psychiatry, 52,* 415–417.

Comings, D. E., Rosenthal, R. J., Lesieur, H. R., & Rugle, L. (1996). A study of dopamine D2 receptor gene in pathological gambling. *Pharmacogenetics, 6,* 73–79.

Coventry, K. R., & Brown, R. L. (1993). Sensation seeking, gambling and gambling addictions. *Addiction, 89,* 541–554.

Crossley, T., & Guzman, R. (1985). The relationship between arson and pyromania. *American Journal of Forensic Psychology, 3,* 39–44.

Custer, R., & Milt, H. (1985). *When luck runs out: Help for compulsive gamblers and their families.* New York: Facts on File.

Darbyshire, P., Oster, C., & Carrig, H. (2001). The experience of pervasive loss: Children and young people living in a family where parental gambling is a problem. *Journal of Gambling Studies, 17,* 23–45.

Dickerson, M., Hinchy, J., & Fabre, J. (1987). Chasing, arousal and sensation seeking in off-course gamblers. *British Journal of Addiction, 82,* 673–680.

Diefenbach, G. J., Reitman, D., & Williamson, D. A. (2000). Trichotillomania: A challenge to research and practice. *Clinical Psychology Review, 20,* 289–309.

Durst, R., Katz, G., Teitelbaum, A., Zislin, J., & Dannon, P. N. (2001). Kleptomania: Diagnosis and treatment options. *CNS Drugs, 15,* 185–195.

du Toit, P. L., van Kradenburg, J., Niehaus, D., & Stein, D. J. (2001). Comparison of obsessive-compulsive disorder patients with and without comorbid putative obsessive-compulsive spectrum disorders using a structured clinical interview. *Comprehensive Psychiatry, 42,* 291–300.

Ferris, J., & Wynne, H. (2001). *The Canadian Problem Gambling Index: Final report.* Ottawa, Ontario: Canadian Centre on Substance Abuse.

First, M. B., Spitzer, R. L., Gibbon, M., & Williams, J. B. W. (1996). *Structured Clinical Interview for DSM-IV Axis I Disorders–Patient Edition (with psychotic screen; SCID-I/P, version 2.0).* New York: Biometric Research, New York State Psychiatric Institute.

Fisher, S. (1992). Measuring pathological gambling in children: The case of fruit machines in the U.K. *Journal of Gambling Studies, 8,* 263–285.

Fisher, S. (2000). Developing the *DSM-IV* criteria to identify adolescent problem gambling in non-clinical populations. *Journal of Gambling Studies, 16,* 253–273.

Fras, I. (1997). Fire setting (pyromania) and its relationship to sexuality. In L. B. Schlesinger & E. Revitch (Eds.), *Sexual dynamics of anti-social behaviour* (2nd ed., pp. 188–196). Springfield, IL: Charles C. Thomas.

Geller, J. L. (1987). Firesetting in the adult psychiatric population. *Hospital and Community Psychiatry, 38,* 501–506.

Goetestam, K., & Johansson, A. (2003). Characteristics of gambling and problematic gambling in the Norwegian context: A *DSM-IV*-based telephone interview study. *Addictive Behaviors, 28,* 189–197.

Goldman, M. J. (1991). Kleptomania: Making sense of the nonsensical. *American Journal of Psychiatry, 148,* 986–996.

Goudriaan, A. E., Oosterlaan, J., de Beurs, E., & van den Brink, W. (2004). Pathological gambling: A comprehensive review of biobehavioral findings. *Neuroscience and Biobehavioral Reviews, 28,* 123–141.

Grant, J. E. (2003). Family history and psychiatric comorbidity in persons with kleptomania. *Comparative Psychiatry, 44,* 437–441.

Grant, J. E., Kim, S. W., & Kushwoski, M. (2004). Retrospective review of treatment retention in pathological gambling. *Comparative Psychiatry, 45,* 83–87.

Grant, J. E., Kim, S. W., & Potenza, M. N. (2003). Advances in the pharmacological treatment of pathological gambling. *Journal of Gambling Studies, 19,* 85–109.

Griffiths, M. D. (1990). The cognitive psychology of gambling. *Journal of Gambling Studies, 6,* 31–42.

Gupta, R., & Derevensky, J. (1998a). Adolescent gambling behavior: A prevalence study and examination of the correlates associated with problem gambling. *Journal of Gambling Studies, 14,* 319–345.

Gupta, R., & Derevensky, J. (1998b). An empirical examination of Jacob's General Theory of Addictions: Do adolescent gamblers fit the theory? *Journal of Gambling Studies, 16,* 315–342.

Hardoon, K. K., & Derevensky, J. (2002). Child and adolescent behaviour: Current knowledge. *Clinical Child Psychology and Psychiatry, 7,* 263–281.

Hing, N., & Breen, H. (2001). Profiling lady luck: An empirical study of gambling and problem gambling amongst female club members. *Journal of Gambling Studies, 17,* 47–69.

Hollander, E., Skodol, A., & Oldham, J. (Eds.). (1996). *Impulsivity and compulsivity.* Washington, DC: American Psychiatric Press.

Iancu, I., Weizman, A., Kindler, S., Sasson, Y., & Zohar, J. (1996). Serotonergic drugs in trichotillomania: Treatment results in 12 patients. *Journal of Nervous and Mental Disease, 184,* 641–644.

Ibanez, A., Blanco, C., de Castro, I. P., Fernandez-Piqueras, J., & Saiz-Ruiz, J. (2003). Genetics of pathological gambling. *Journal of Gambling Studies, 19,* 11–22.

Jacobs, D. F. (1986). A general theory of addictions: A new theoretical model. *Journal of Gambling Behavior, 2,* 15–31.

Jacobs, D. F., Marston, A. R., Singer, R. D., Widman, K., Little, T., & Veizades, J. (1989). Children of problem gamblers. *Journal of Gambling Studies, 5,* 261–268.

Johnston, L. D., O'Malley, P. M., & Backman, J. G. (1997). *National survey results on drug use from the Monitoring the Future Study 1975–1995: Vol. 2. College students and young adults* (NIH Publication No. 98-4140). Washington, DC: U.S. Department of Health and Human Services.

Keuthen, N. J., Riccaiardi, J. N., Shera, D., Savage, C. R., Borgmann, A. S., Jenike, M. A., et al. (1995). The Massachusetts General Hospital (MGH) Hairpulling Scale: I. Development and factor analyses. *Psychotherapy and Psychosomatics, 64,* 141–145.

Kuley, N. B., & Jacobs, D. F. (1988). The relationship between dissociative-like experiences and sensation seeking among social and problem gamblers. *Journal of Gambling Behavior, 4,* 197–207.

Ladouceur, R., Boisvert, J.-M., Pepin, M., Loranger, M., & Sylvain, C. (1994). Social cost of pathological gambling. *Journal of Gambling Studies, 10,* 399–409.

Ladouceur, R., Boudreault, N., Jacques, C., & Vitaro, F. (1999). Pathological gambling and related problems among adolescents. *Journal of Child and Adolescent Substance Abuse, 8,* 55–68.

Laubichler, W., & Kuhberger, A. (1997). A critique of pyromania and arson in the modern nomenclature. *Krankenhauspsychiatrie, 8,* 160–164.

Leblond, J., Ladouceur, R., & Blaszczynski, A. (2004). Which pathological gamblers will complete treatment? *British Journal of Clinical Psychology, 42,* 205–209.

Lejoyeux, M., Arbaretaz, M., McClaughlin, M., & Ades, J. (2002). Impulse control disorders and depression. *Journal of Nervous and Mental Disease, 190,* 310–314.

Lesieur, H. R. (1979). The compulsive gambler's spiral of options and involvement. *Psychiatry, 42,* 79–87.

Lesieur, H. R. (1998). Cost and treatment of pathological gambling. *Annals of the American Academy of Political and Social Sciences, 556,* 153–171.

Lesieur, H. R., & Blume, S. B. (1987). The South Oaks Gambling Screen (SOGS): A new instrument for the identification of pathological gamblers. *American Journal of Psychiatry, 9,* 1184–1187.

Lesieur, H. R., & Rothschild, J. (1989). Children of Gamblers Anonymous members. *Journal of Gambling Behavior, 5,* 269–281.

Lewis, N., & Yarnell, H. (1951). Pathological firesetting (pyromania). *Nervous and Mental Disorders Monographs, 82,* 437.

Lorenz, V. C., & Yaffee, R. A. (1986). Pathological gambling: Psychosomatic, emotional and marital difficulties as reported by the gambler. *Journal of Gambling Behavior, 2,* 40–49.

MacCallum, F., & Blaszczynski, A. (2002). Pathological gambling and co-morbid substance use. *Australian and New Zealand Journal of Psychiatry, 36,* 411–415.

Mark, M. E., & Lesieur, H. R. (1992). A feminist critique of problem gambling research, *British Journal of Addiction, 87,* 549–565.

Martin, G., Bergen, H. A., Richardson, A. S., Roeger, L., & Allison, S. (2004). Correlates of firesetting in a community sample of young adolescents. *Australian and New Zealand Journal of Psychiatry, 38,* 148–154.

McConaghy, N., Blaszczynski, A., & Frankova, A. (1991). Comparison of imaginal desensitisation with other behavioural treatments of pathological gambling: A two to nine year follow-up. *British Journal of Psychiatry, 159,* 390–393.

McCormick, R. A., Russo, A. M., Ramirez, L. F., & Taber, J. I. (1984). Affective disorders among pathological gamblers seeking treatment. *American Journal of Psychiatry, 141,* 215–218.

McElroy, S. L. (1999). Recognition and treatment of *DSM-IV* intermittent explosive disorder. *Journal of Clinical Psychiatry, 60*(Suppl. 15), 12–16.

McElroy, S. L., Hudson, J. I., Pope, H. G., & Keck, P. E. (1991). Kleptomania: Clinical characteristics and associated psychopathology. *Psychological Medicine, 21,* 93–108.

McElroy, S. L., Keck, P. E., & Phillips, K. A. (1995). Kleptomania, compulsive buying and binge-eating disorder. *Journal of Clinical Psychiatry, 56*(Suppl. 4), 14–26.

McElroy, S. L., Pope, H. G., Hudson, J. I., Keck, P. E., & White, K. L. (1991). Kleptomania: A report of 20 cases. *American Journal of Psychiatry, 148,* 652–657.

McElroy, S. L., Soutullo, C. A., Beckman, D., Taylor, P., & Keck, P. E. (1998). *DSM-IV* intermittent explosive disorder: A report of 27 cases. *Journal of Clinical Psychiatry, 59,* 203–210.

McNeilly, D., & Burke, W. (2000). Late life gambling: The attitudes and behaviors of older adults. *Journal of Gambling Studies, 16,* 393–415.

Moore, J. K., Thompson-Pope, S. K., & Whited, R. M. (1996). MMPI-A profiles of adolescent boys with a history of fire setting. *Journal of Personality Assessment, 67,* 116–126.

Murray, J. B. (1992). Kleptomania: A review of the literature. *Journal of Psychology, 126,* 131–137.

National Opinion Research Center (NORC). (1999). *Gambling Impact and Behavior Study: Report to the National Gambling Impact Study Commission.* Chicago: Author.

National Research Council (NRC). (1999). *Pathological gambling: A critical review.* Washington, DC: National Academy Press.

Nower, L. (2003). Pathological gambling in the workplace: A primer for employers. *Employee Assistance Quarterly, 18,* 55–72.

Nower, L., & Blaszczynski, A. (2003). Binge gambling: A neglected concept. *International Journal of Gambling Studies, 3,* 23–36.

Nower, L., Derevensky, J., & Gupta, R. (2004). The relationship of impulsivity, sensation seeking, coping, and substance use in youth gamblers. *Psychology of Addictive Behaviors, 18,* 49–55.

Nower, L., Gupta, R., Blaszczynski, A., & Derevensky, J. (2004). Suicidality and depression among youth gamblers: A preliminary examination of three studies. *International Gambling Studies, 4,* 69–81.

Opdyke, D., & Rothbaum, B. (1998). Cognitive-behavioural treatment of impulse control disorders. In V. E. Caballo (Ed.), *International handbook of cognitive and behavioural treatments for psychological disorders* (pp 417–439). Oxford, England: Pergamon/Elsevier Science.

Peterson, A. L., Campsie, R. L., & Azrin, N. H. (1994). Behavioral and pharmacological treatments for tic and habit disorders: A review. *Journal of Developmental and Behavioral Pediatrics, 15,* 430–441.

Petry, N. M. (2000). Gambling problems in substance abusers are associated with increased sexual risk behaviours. *Addiction, 95,* 1089–1100.

Petry, N. M. (2001a). Pathological gamblers, with and without substance use disorders, discount delayed rewards at high rates. *Journal of Abnormal Psychology, 110,* 482–487.

Petry, N. M. (2001b). Substance abuse, pathological gambling, and impulsiveness. *Drug and Alcohol Dependence, 63,* 29–38.

Petry, N. M. (2005). *Pathological gambling: Etiology, comorbidity and treatment.* Washington, DC: American Psychological Association.

Petry, N. M., & Armentano, C. (1999). Prevalence, assessment and treatment of pathological gambling: A review. *Psychiatric Services, 50,* 1021–1027.

Potenza, M. N., Steinberg, M. A., McLaughlin, S. D., Wu, R., Rounsaville, B. J., & O'Malley, S. S. (2000). Illegal behaviors in problem gambling: Analysis of data from a gambling helpline. *Journal of the American Academy of Psychiatry and the Law, 28,* 389–403.

Potenza, M. N., Steinberg, M. A., McLaughlin, S. D., Wu, R., Rounsaville, B. J., & O'Malley, S. S. (2001). Gender-related differences in the characteristics of problem gamblers using a gambling helpline. *American Journal of Psychiatry, 158,* 1500–1505.

Potenza, M. N., & Winters, K. C. (2003). The neurobiology of pathological gambling: Translating research findings into clinical advances. *Journal of Gambling Studies, 19,* 7–10.

Powell, J., Hardoon, K., Derevensky, J., & Gupta, R. (1999). Gambling and risk-taking behaviour among university students. *Substance Use & Misuse, 34,* 1167–1184.

Presta, S., Marazziti, D., Dell'Osso, L., Pfanner, C., Pallanti, S., & Cassano, G. (2002). Kleptomania: Clinical features and comorbidity in an Italian sample. *Comprehensive Psychiatry, 43,* 7–12.

Ritchie, E. C., & Huff, T. G. (1999). Psychiatric aspects of arsonists. *Journal of Forensic Sciences, 44,* 733–740.

Rosenthal, R. (1992). Pathological gambling. *Psychiatric Annals, 22,* 72–78.

Rothbaum, B. O. (1992). The behavioural treatment of trichotillomania. *Behavioural Psychotherapy, 20,* 85–89.

Rothbaum, B. O., Shaw, L., Morris, R., & Ninan, P. T. (1993). Prevalence of trichotillomania in a college freshman population. *Journal of Clinical Psychiatry, 54,* 72.

Rowan, M. S., & Galasso, C. S. (2000). Identifying office resource needs of Canadian physicians to help prevent, assess and treat patients with substance use and pathological gambling disorders. *Journal of Addictive Diseases, 19,* 43–58.

Rugle, L., & Melamed, L. (1993). Neuropsychological assessment of attention problems in pathological gamblers. *Journal of Nervous and Mental Disease, 181,* 107–112.

Russo, A. M., Taber, J. I., McCormick, R. A., & Ramirez, L. F. (1984). An outcome study of an inpatient treatment program for pathological gamblers. *Hospital and Community Psychiatry, 35,* 823–827.

Sarasalo, E., Bergman, B., & Toth, J. (1996). Personality traits and psychiatric and somatic morbidity among kleptomaniacs. *Acta Psychiatrica Scandinavica, 94,* 358–364.

Schlosser, S., Black, D. W., Blum, N., & Goldstein, R. B. (1994). The demography, phenomenology, and family history of 22 persons with compulsive hair pulling. *Annals of Clinical Psychiatry, 6,* 147–152.

Shaffer, H. J., & Hall, M. N. (1996). Estimating prevalence of adolescent gambling disorders: A quantitative synthesis and guide toward standard gambling nomenclature. *Journal of Gambling Studies, 12,* 193–214.

Shaffer, H. J., Hall, M. N., & Vander Bilt, J. (1997). Estimating the prevalence of disordered gambling behavior in the Unite States and Canada: A research synthesis. *American Journal of Public Health, 89,* 1369–1376.

Shaffer, H. J., & Korn, D. (2002). Gambling and related mental disorders: A public health analysis. *Annual Review of Public Health, 23,* 171–212.

Shaffer, H. J., LaBrie, R., LaPlante, D., Kidman, R., & Korn, D. A. (2002). *Evaluating the Iowa Gambling Treatment Program.* Boston: Harvard Medical School, Division on Addictions.

Shepherd, R. B. (1996). Clinical obstacles in administering the South Oaks Gambling Screen in methadone and alcohol clinic. *Journal of Gambling Studies, 12,* 21–32.

Showers, J., & Pickrell, E. (1987). Child firesetters: A study of three populations. *Hospital and Community Psychiatry, 38,* 495–501.

Singh, A. N., & Maguire, J. (1989). Trichotillomania and incest. *British Journal of Psychiatry, 155,* 108–110.

Soltys, S. M. (1992). Pyromania and firesetting behaviors. *Psychiatric Annals, 22,* 79–83.

Stanley, M. A., Prather, R. C., Wagner, A. L., Davis, M. L., & Swann, A. C. (1993). Can the Yale-Brown Obsessive-

Compulsive Scale be used to assess trichotillomania? A preliminary report. *Behaviour Research and Therapy, 31,* 171–177.

Steel, Z. P., & Blaszczynski, A. (1996). Factorial structure of pathological gambling. *Journal of Gambling Studies, 12,* 3–20.

Stein, D. J., & Hollander, E. (1992). Low-dose pimozide augmentation of serotonin reuptake blockers in the treatment of trichotillomania. *Journal of Clinical Psychiatry, 53,* 123–126.

Stewart, R. M., & Brown, R. I. F. (1988). An outcome study of gamblers anonymous. *British Journal of Psychiatry, 152,* 284–288.

Stinchfield, R. (2002). Reliability, validity, and classification accuracy of the South Oaks Gambling Screen (SOGS). *Addictive Behaviors, 27,* 1–19.

Stinchfield, R. (2003). Reliability, validity, and classification accuracy of a measure of *DSM-IV* diagnostic criteria for pathological gambling. *American Journal of Psychiatry, 160,* 180–182.

Stinchfield, R., Cassuto, N., Winters, K., & Latimer, N. (1997). Prevalence of gambling among Minnesota public school students in 1992 and 1995. *Journal of Gambling Studies, 13,* 25–38.

Swedo, S. E. (1993a). Trichotillomania. In E. Hollander (Ed.), *Obsessive-compulsive related disorders.* Washington, DC: American Psychiatric Press.

Swedo, S. E. (1993b). Trichotillomania. *Psychiatric Annals, 23,* 402–407.

Swedo, S. E., & Leonard, H. L. (1992).Trichotillomania: An obsessive compulsive spectrum disorder? *Psychiatric Clinics of North America, 15,* 777–790.

Swedo, S. E., Leonard, H. L., Rapoport, J. L., Leanne, M. C., Goldberger, E. L., & Cheslow, D. L. (1989). A double-blind comparison of clomipramine and desipramine in the treatment of trichotillomania (hairpulling). *New England Journal of Medicine, 321,* 497–502.

Swedo, S. E., & Rapoport, J. L. (1991). Annotation: Trichotillomania. *Journal of Child Psychology and Psychiatry, 32,* 401–409.

Sylvain, C., Ladouceur, R., & Boisvert, J. M. (1997). Cognitive and behavioral treatment of pathological gambling: A controlled study. *Journal of Consulting and Clinical Psychology, 65,* 727–732.

Tavares, H., Zilberman, M. L., Beites, F. J., & Gentil, V. (2001). Gender difference in gambling progression. *Journal of Gambling Studies, 17,* 151–159.

Thompson, W. N., Gazel, R., & Rickman, D. (1996a). Casinos and crime in Wisconsin. *Wisconsin Policy Research Institute Report, 9*(9), 1–20.

Thompson, W. N., Gazel, R., & Rickman, D. (1996b). The social costs of gambling in Wisconsin. *Wisconsin Policy Research Institute Report, 9*(6), 1–44.

Toneatto, T., & Ladouceur, R. (2003). Treatment of pathological gambling: A critical review of the literature. *Psychology of Addictive Behaviors, 17,* 284–292.

Vatz, R. E., & Weinberg, L. S. (1995). Refuting the myths of compulsive gambling. In A. Riconda (Ed.), *Gambling: The reference shelf* (pp. 167–192). New York: Wilson.

Vitaro, F., Arseneault, L., & Tremblay, R. E. (1997). Dispositional predictors of problem gambling in male adolescents. *American Journal of Psychiatry, 154,* 1769–1770.

Vitaro, F., Arseneault, L., & Tremblay, R. E. (1999). Impulsivity predicts problem gambling in low SES adolescent males. *Addiction, 94,* 565–575.

Vitaro, F., Brendgen, M., Ladouceur, R., & Tremblay, R. E. (2001). Gambling, delinquency, and drug use during adolescence: Mutual influences and common risk factors. *Journal of Gambling Studies, 17,* 171–190.

Volberg, R. (1996). *Gambling and problem gambling in New York: A 10 year replication survey, 1986 to 1996.* Albany: New York Council on Problem Gambling.

Volberg, R. A. (2002). The epidemiology of pathological gambling. *Psychiatric Annals, 32,* 171–178.

Walsh, K. H., & McDougle, C. J. (2001). Trichotillomania: Presentation, etiology, diagnosis and therapy. *American Journal of Clinical Dermatology, 2,* 327–333

Walters, G. D. (2001). Behavior genetic research on gambling and problem gambling: A preliminary meta-analysis of available data. *Journal of Gambling Studies, 17,* 255–271.

Welte, J. B., Barnes, G. M., Wieczorek, W. F., Tidwell, M.-C., & Parker, J. (2002). Gambling participation rates in the US: Results from a national survey. *Journal of Gambling Studies, 18,* 313–337.

Wilcox, D., & Kolko, D. J. (2002). Assessing recent firesetting behaviour and taking a firesetting history. In D. Kolko (Ed). *Handbook on firesetting in children and youth* (pp. 161–175). San Diego, CA: Academic Press.

Winchel, R. M., Jones, J. S., Molcho, A., Parsons, B., & Stanley, M. (1992). The Psychiatric Institute Trichotillomania Scale (PITS). *Psychopharmacology Bulletin, 28,* 463–476.

Winters, K. C., Stinchfield, R., & Fulkerson, J. (2003). Toward the development of an adolescent gambling problem severity scale. *Journal of Gambling Studies, 9,* 63–84.

Zitzow, D. (1996). Comparative study of problematic gambling behaviours between American Indian and non-Indian adolescents within and near a Northern Plains reservation. *American Indian and Alaska Native Mental Health Research, 7,* 14–26.

CHAPTER 23

Eating Disorders

ERIC STICE, JOANNE PEART, HEATHER THOMPSON-BRENNER, ERIN MARTINEZ, AND DREW WESTEN

An array of cognitive, behavioral, emotional, and motivational disturbances characterizes individuals with eating disorders (EDs). The diagnostic criteria for each disorder vary with regard to the cognitive and behavioral features of the disorder, which include abnormal eating behaviors, maladaptive weight control efforts, and distorted perceptions or self-evaluations involving weight or shape. We begin by discussing the central features of the major forms of eating pathology.

DESCRIPTION OF THE DISORDER AND CLINICAL PICTURE

Anorexia Nervosa

The diagnostic criteria specified by the *DSM-IV* (American Psychiatric Association, 1994) for anorexia nervosa (AN) include (1) body weight less than 85 percent expected for height and age; (2) unreasonable fear of gaining weight or becoming overweight despite extreme thinness; (3) disturbances in perception of weight and shape, undue influence of weight and shape on self-evaluation, or denial of the gravity of severe underweight; and (4) amenorrhea in postmenarcheal females. The *DSM-IV* makes a further diagnostic distinction between restricting and binge-eating/purging subtypes of the disorder based on the absence or presence of binge-eating or purging behaviors. Some research suggests that the binge-purge type of AN, compared to the restricting type, is associated with higher levels of psychopathology, such as elevated risk of suicidality, stealing, drug abuse, emotional distress (e.g., Garner, 1993), self-injury (Favaro & Santonastaso, 1996), and family and personal histories of obesity (Garner, Garfinkel, & O'Shaughnessy, 1985). However, other findings call this subtyping scheme into question (Strober, Freeman, & Morrell, 1997). A recent prospective study with a lengthy follow-up period did not find significant differences between the current diagnostic subtypes on measures of impulsivity (kleptomania, substance abuse, suicide attempts, or borderline personality diagnosis), course, or outcome (Eddy et al., 2002), an issue to which we return in addressing subtyping based on personality characteristics.

The clinical features of AN include a relentless pursuit of thinness and overvaluation of body shape. This typically results in a state of semistarvation via severe dietary restriction and/or high levels of physical activity, accompanied by mood disturbances, preoccupation with food, and ritualistic and stereotyped eating (Fairburn & Harrison, 2003). Physical symptoms of the disorder, aside from emaciation, may include lanugo (a light growth of hair covering the body), skin discoloration, and cardiac irregularities (Gupta, Gupta, & Haberman, 1987; Kreipe & Harris, 1992; Pomeroy, 2004; Schulze et al., 1999). Theoretical and empirical work also implicate interpersonal dysfunction as characteristic of the disorder, particularly with regard to family functioning (Leung, Schwartzman, & Steiger, 1996; Minuchin, Rosman, & Baker, 1978; Slade, 1982), a point to which we also return.

The pursuit of thinness that characterizes AN poses challenges with regard to treatment. Because patients often perceive the ED as a personal accomplishment rather than a psychiatric disorder in need of treatment, individuals with AN are typically very resistant to treatment, which invariably involves weight restoration.

Bulimia Nervosa

The diagnostic criteria specified by the *DSM-IV* (American Psychiatric Association, 1994) for bulimia nervosa (BN) include (1) recurrent episodes (at least two days per week for previous three months) of uncontrollable consumption of large amounts of food, (2) recurrent use (at least twice weekly for previous three months) of compensatory behavior to prevent consequent weight gain (e.g., vomiting, laxative abuse, diuretic abuse, fasting, or excessive exercise), and (3) undue influence of weight and shape on self-evaluation. If these symptoms occur exclusively during a period of time in which the individual satisfies diagnostic criteria for AN, this latter diagnosis is given precedence. Individuals with BN (and binge-eating disorder) typically consume between 1,000 and 2,000 kilocalories per binge episode, usually consisting of foods with high fat and sugar content (Walsh, 1993; Yanovski et al., 1992). These individuals often experience marked feelings of guilt and shame regarding their secretive eating behaviors (Wilson, Becker, & Heffernan, 2003) and are thus typically less resistant to treatment than their anorexic counterparts (Fairburn & Harrison, 2003).

The clinical presentation of BN, as in AN, is characterized by disturbances in eating behaviors and an overvaluation of thinness. However, the commonly observed physical characteristics associated with BN differ from those associated with AN. Bulimic individuals are often of normal weight (or are overweight, rather than underweight), and a host of physiological symptoms are common but not necessary for the diagnosis of the disorder, including dorsal scarring on the hand, swelling of the parotid (salivary) glands in the face, cardiac irregularities, and varying degrees of enamel damage (Kreipe & Harris, 1992; Metzger, Levine, McArdel, Wolfe, & Jimerson, 1999; Pomeroy, 2004; Schulze et al., 1999).

Eating Disorder Not Otherwise Specified and Binge-Eating Disorder

In addition to the two widely recognized EDs noted previously, *DSM-IV* also allows for the diagnosis of EDs not otherwise specified, or EDNOS (American Psychiatric Association, 1994). Like other NOS categories in *DSM-IV*, EDNOS is an artifact of a categorical diagnostic system that needs a classification for patients with clinically meaningful or subthreshold symptomatology who fall through the cracks of established diagnoses. This is particularly problematic because the majority of patients seeking treatment for EDs receive an EDNOS diagnosis (Fairburn & Harrison, 2003; Herzog, Hopkins, & Burns, 1993), with possible implications for insurance coverage and the quality of treatment they may receive given the relatively sparse research on subthreshold or atypical presentations (Franko, Wonderlich, Little, & Herzog, 2004).

This EDNOS diagnosis is used for a variety of subthreshold conditions (Fairburn & Harrison, 2003). For example, an individual who meets all the criteria for BN except for the requisite frequency of compensatory behaviors (e.g., only once a week) would have to be diagnosed using *DSM-IV* with EDNOS rather than BN. The EDNOS category also includes partial syndrome EDs. For instance, an individual who engages in weekly compensatory behaviors in the absence of uncontrollable binge eating would probably receive a diagnosis of EDNOS. The EDNOS category also includes other atypical EDs, such as rumination or pica exhibited during adulthood.

Researchers are paying increasing attention to one condition currently included under EDNOS and under consideration for "elevation" to its own diagnosis in *DSM-V*, namely binge-eating disorder (BED; American Psychiatric Association, 2000). The proposed diagnostic criteria for BED include (1) repeated episodes (at least twice weekly for previous six months) of uncontrollable binge eating characterized by certain features (e.g., rapid eating, eating until uncomfortably full, eating large amounts of food when not physically hungry, eating alone because of embarrassment, and feeling guilty or depressed after overeating); (2) marked distress regarding binge eating; and (3) the absence of compensatory behaviors. If these symptoms occur exclusively during a period of time in which the individual satisfies diagnostic criteria for AN, this latter diagnosis is given precedence. If the symptoms of BED occur exclusively during a period of time in which the individual satisfies diagnostic criteria for BN, this latter diagnosis is given precedence.

BED is associated with overweight and obesity, with interview-based prevalence estimates ranging from just more than 2 percent in the general population (Stunkard et al., 1996) to nearly 19 percent (Brody, Walsh, & Devlin, 1994) in treatment-seeking obese populations. Compared to non-bingeing obese persons, those with BED evidence increased weight and shape concerns and higher levels of psychopathology, particularly affective disorders (Eldredge & Agras, 1996; Marcus et al., 1996; Mitchell & Mussell, 1995; Telch & Stice, 1998; Wilfley, Schwartz, Spurrell, & Fairburn, 2000). Although obesity is characterized by a disturbance in eating, wherein caloric intake exceeds the caloric expenditure (Rosenbaum, Leibel, & Hirsch, 1997), it is not considered a psychiatric disorder. This is in large part due to the variation in eating behaviors and psychological characteristics among the obese. The two EDs most closely associated with obesity are the aforementioned BED and night-eating syndrome, the latter having yet to appear in an edition of the *DSM* (Stunkard, 2002).

As suggested previously, numerous questions remain with respect to the classification of EDs, notably the validity of diagnostic subtypes, the problem of subthreshold diagnoses, and the utility of a widely diagnosed by heterogeneous NOS diagnosis. In addition, unlike the criteria for other disorders, the current diagnostic system does not include significant functional impairment among the requisite criteria for ED diagnoses.

PERSONALITY DEVELOPMENT AND PSYCHOPATHOLOGY

Characterizing the links between personality and disordered eating presents a number of challenges. Personality could predispose individuals to EDs, EDs could affect personality (e.g., patients with AN could become more rigid or obsessional while starving), or personality and eating pathology could mutually influence each other (see Lilenfeld, Wonderlich, Riso, Crosby, & Mitchell, 2004). Although personality and ED variables appear to influence each other, the evidence seems clear that personality variables represent diatheses for EDs (e.g., they often predate eating pathology, persist after treatment of ED symptoms, and aggregate in families of ED probands; see Gillberg, Rastam, & Gillberg, 1995; Nilsson, Gillberg, Gillberg, & Rastam, 1999; Rastam, Gillberg, & Gillberg, 1995; Sunday, Reeman, Eckert, & Halmi, 1996).

Personality researchers have approached PDs using several different models. In this section we examine four ways researchers have studied personality in EDs: (1) assessment of salient personality dimensions originally identified through clinical observation; (2) application of omnibus trait models, largely derived from personality psychology; (3) assessment of *DSM-IV* Axis II pathology (personality disorders; PDs); and (4) identification of personality subtypes in ED patients.

Clinically Observed Personality Dimensions

Three clinically observed traits have received substantial empirical attention, two originally identified in AN (perfectionism and obsessionality) and one in BN (impulsivity). Perfectionism has been consistently identified as a salient trait in AN patients (e.g., Bastiani, Rao, Weltzin, & Kaye, 1995; Halmi et al., 2000; Strober, 1980), although it is common in BN patients as well (Vitousek & Manke, 1994). Indeed, perfectionism appears to be a significant risk factor for the development of both disorders (Fairburn, Cooper, Doll, & Welch, 1999; Fairburn, Welch, Doll, Davies, & O'Connor, 1997) and persists after weight restoration and/or recovery from EDs (Bastiani et al., 1995; Srinivasagam et al., 1995). Research has also found elevated levels of perfectionism in parents of individuals with AN, especially mothers (Woodside et al., 2002), suggesting that perfectionism is a diathesis for EDs or a phenotypic marker of a genetic vulnerability to EDs.

Closely related to the concept of perfectionism is obsessionality. As many as 30 percent of individuals with AN have marked obsessional features upon first presentation (Thornton & Russell, 1997), and obsessive-compulsive personality traits in childhood are highly predictive of subsequent ED development (Anderluh, Tchanturia, Rabe-Hesketh, & Treasure, 2003). Obsessionality also appears to persist in patients with AN after treatment, although obsessive-compulsive symptoms generally decrease as preoccupation with food and rituals surrounding food intake subside (Strober, 1980). Further, studies have consistently reported significant comorbidity between EDs and obsessive compulsive disorder (OCD; Fahy, 1991; Hsu, Kaye, & Weltzin, 1993; Rubenstein, Altemus, Pigott, Hess, & Murphy, 1995). Estimates of co-occurrence range from 25 percent to 79 percent for AN (Halmi et al., 1991, 2003; Hudson, Pope, Jonas, & Yurgelun-Todd, 1983; Rothenberg, 1986) and 25 percent to 36 percent for BN (Braun, Sunday, & Halmi, 1994; Hudson, Pope, Jonas, Yurgelun-Todd, & Frankenburg, 1987). Although the data are not yet conclusive as to the causal sequence linking obsessionality and EDs, a number of studies strongly suggest that obsessionality predates and is a significant risk factor for eating pathology (Anderluh et al., 2003; Smart, Beumont, & George, 1976; Thornton & Russell, 1997).

As early as 1980, researchers found impulsivity to be significantly more descriptive of bulimic anorexics than restricting anorexics (Casper, Eckert, Halmi, Goldberg, & Davis, 1980; Garfinkel, Modlofsky, & Garner, 1980). Subsequent research has consistently found heightened impulsivity in bulimic subjects compared to both restricting anorexics (e.g., Casper, Hedeker, & McClough, 1992; Vervaet, van Heeringen, & Audenaert, 2004) and normal controls (e.g., Casper et al., 1992; Diaz-Marsa, Carrasco, & Saiz, 2000). In a study of the long-term prognosis of patients with AN and BN, Sohlberg and colleagues (Sohlberg, Norring, Holmgren, & Rosmark, 1989) found impulsivity to be the strongest predictor of negative outcome. Like perfectionism, impulsivity is a multidimensional construct (Barratt, 1993). For example, one study found that lack of planning was not associated with bulimic symptomatology, but the tendency to act rashly during episodes of negative affect was (Fischer, Smith, & Anderson, 2003).

A widely studied distinction is between "multi-impulsive" versus "uni-impulsive" bulimia (Lacey & Evans, 1986). Multi-impulsive individuals with BN display several impulsive behaviors (e.g., stealing, substance abuse) in addition to binge eating, whereas uni-impulsive patients have binge eating as their only symptom or behavior that could be described as impulsive. Empirically, multi-impulsive bulimic individuals tend to have significantly more pathology than uni-impulsive patients, with greater rates of borderline PD (BPD) and mood disorders (Fichter, Quadflieg, & Rief, 1994). Data on impulsivity appear to be particularly important in light of research linking impulsivity to early dropout rates from psychotherapy (Agras, Crow, et al., 2000).

Omnibus Personality Trait Models

Several researchers have examined the personality correlates of EDs using omnibus personality measures. A handful of studies have examined individuals with EDs using Eysenck's (1990) three-factor model of personality (neuroticism, extraversion, and psychoticism) or the Five-Factor Model (FFM; McCrae & Costa, 1999; neuroticism, extraversion, agreeableness, conscientiousness, and openness to experience). Studies using the Eysenck Personality Questionnaire (EPQ; Eysenck & Eysenck, 1975) have found neuroticism to correlate with AN (e.g., Geller, Cockell, & Goldner, 2000; Walters & Kendler, 1995). The limited number of studies applying the FFM to EDs has also consistently found increased levels of neuroticism in ED samples (Ghaderi & Scott, 2000; Heaven, Mulligan, Merrilees, Woods, & Fairooz, 2001; Podar, Hannus, & Allik, 1999; Tylka & Subich, 1999). Studies comparing subgroups of ED patients (e.g., AN with and without binge-purging) are rare but tend to find purging anorexics to be both higher in neuroticism and higher in extraversion (Ben-Tovim, Marilov, & Crisp, 1979; Gomez & Dally, 1980).

Several studies have used Cloninger's psychobiological trait model, which identifies four temperamental dimensions (novelty seeking, harm avoidance, reward dependence, and persistence) and three character dimensions (self-directedness, cooperativeness, and self-transcendence). Consistent with the clinical portrait of patients with (restricting) anorexia, AN individuals tend to be characterized by high harm avoidance and low novelty seeking (Brewerton, Hand, & Bishop, 1993; Cloninger, Przybeck, Svrakic, & Wetzel, 1994; Fassino et al., 2002; Klump et al., 2000). Researchers have obtained conflicting results on reward dependence, with most finding AN patients to be low on this dimension but some finding them to be high (e.g., Bulik, Sullivan, Weltzin, & Kaye, 1995). Other studies find AN individuals to be low on self-directedness and high on persistence (Diaz-Marsa et al., 2000; Fassino et al., 2002).

Much like their anorexic counterparts, individuals with BN tend to be high in harm avoidance (e.g., Fassino et al., 2002; Waller et al., 1993), reflecting the tendency of most ED patients to be prone to negative affect states. BN patients tend, however, to be higher on novelty seeking (Bulik, Sullivan, Joyce, & Carter, 1995; Bulik, Sullivan, Weltzin, et al., 1995; Fassino et al., 2002) and RD (Brewerton et al., 1993) and lower on self-directedness than BN patients (Diaz-Marsa et al., 2000; Klump et al., 2000; Vervaet, Audenaert, & van Heeringen, 2003). Fassino et al. (2002) found that patients with both anorexic and bulimic features tend to have personality profiles falling midway between those of "pure" cases.

In general, studies using omnibus trait measures have tended to produce a similar portrait to that painted by studies of clinically observed traits: AN patients tend to be high in negative affectivity or neuroticism (anxious, fearful, and harm-avoidant) and obsessional (persistent), whereas BN patients do not seem to fit any single profile. Although BN patients tend, like those with AN, to be high in negative affectivity, some studies have shown them to resemble AN patients in other respects, whereas other studies have found them to be more extraverted, impulsive, novelty-seeking, and reward dependent.

Axis II Comorbidity

Studies assessing the comorbidity between EDs and PDs have yielded highly disparate estimates, ranging from 21 percent to 97 percent depending on samples and measures (Skodol et al., 1993; Vitousek & Manke, 1994). Cluster A (odd-eccentric) diagnoses are infrequent in ED samples (Sunday et al., 2001). Cluster B (dramatic-erratic) diagnoses are the PDs most frequent observed in BN patients (e.g., Rosenvinge, Martinussen, & Ostensen, 2000), whereas Cluster C (anxious-fearful) disorders are the PDs most frequently observed in AN patients (Gartner, Marcus, Halmi, & Loranger, 1989; Herpertz-Dahlmann et al., 2001; Herzog, Keller, Sacks, Yeh, & Lavori, 1992; Nilsson et al., 1999).

Patients with AN are more likely than other ED patients to have obsessive-compulsive and avoidant features (Gartner et al., 1989; Herzog et al., 1992; Rastam, 1992; Skodol et al., 1993). Studies comparing restricting and binge-purging anorexics tend to find elevated OCPD only in patients with restricting AN, however; patients with both anorexic and bulimic symptoms tend to display more pervasive personality pathology (see Herzog et al., 1992; Wonderlich, Swift, Slotnik, & Goodman, 1990). Borderline PD (BPD) is common in both binge-purging AN and BN (Braun et al., 1994; Skodol et al., 1993; Vitousek & Manke, 1994). Little research has addressed the incidence of personality pathology in patients with ED not otherwise specified (EDNOS), which is probably the most prevalent ED diagnosis (Andersen, Bowers, & Watson, 2001; Grilo, Devlin, Cachelin, & Yanovski, 1997). However, a large longitudinal study of women with BPD found that 33 percent had a lifetime history of ED-NOS (Marino & Zanarini, 2001).

Personality Subtypes in Eating Disorders

Research on Axis II comorbidity in EDs thus tends to echo both the consistencies and inconsistencies in the literature using other personality constructs. Patients with AN, particularly restricting AN, tend to be avoidant (i.e., higher in negative affectivity and harm avoidance, and lower in extraversion) and obsessional (higher on rigidity, constraint, and compulsivity). Patients with BN, and AN patients with binge-purging symptoms, are more likely to have borderline features (including negative affectivity, impulsivity, extraversion), although in some samples they are distinguished from other ED patients by their relative freedom from personality pathology.

These findings raise two questions. First, what accounts for the inconsistency in findings for BN and for the tendency of binge-purging AN patients sometimes to resemble AN patients and sometimes to resemble BN patients? Second, given that many patients cross over from AN to BN or vice versa at some point in their lives (Eddy et al., 2002), how can patients with different EDs show such different personality profiles?

One promising explanation lies in the hypothesis that patients with similar ED diagnoses may be heterogeneous vis-à-vis personality styles but that this heterogeneity is systematic (i.e., patterned) rather than random. To put it another way, patients may be vulnerable to EDs by virtue of personality styles that only imperfectly map onto *DSM-IV* ED diagnoses.

Several research groups have in fact attempted to cluster ED patients empirically based on personality patterns, and a convergence among different methods and measures has begun to emerge (Goldner, Srikameswaran, Schroeder, Livesley, & Birmingham, 1999; Pryor & Wiederman, 1996; Rybicki, Lepkowsky, & Arndt, 1989; Strassberg, Ross, & Todt, 1995; Strober, 1981; Vitousek & Manke, 1994; Westen & Harnden-Fischer, 2001). For example, using a dimensional self-report personality pathology measure, Goldner et al. (1999) identified three personality subtypes within an ED sample, including a "rigid" group, a borderlinelike group, and a third group with differences from a normal comparison group.

Using a Q-sort measure of personality pathology, Westen and Harnden-Fischer (2001) similarly identified three personality subtypes that have now replicated across instruments and samples (Thompson-Brenner & Westen, 2004), which they labeled high-functioning/perfectionistic, constricted/overcontrolled, and emotionally dysregulated/undercontrolled. Constricted/overcontrolled patients were most likely to have AN, with or without bulimic symptoms, whereas and emotionally dysregulated/undercontrolled patients were likely to have BN, with or without AN symptoms (classified in *DSM-IV* as AN, binge-purging subtype). High-functioning/perfectionistic patients were not limited to any single diagnosis but were most common among BN patients without AN symptoms. Across samples, the three subtypes differ in frequency of various Axis II symptoms in ways that make sense of the consistencies and inconsistencies in the literature. Constricted patients, who are likely to have a diagnosis of restricting AN, tend to receive diagnoses of avoidant PD and OCPD. Dysregulated patients, who are likely to have either BN or binge-purging AN, are most likely to have a diagnosis of BPD. High-functioning/perfectionistic patients, who are most likely to have BN, are least likely to receive a PD diagnosis. These findings make sense of the consistent finding of constricted personality traits in restricting anorexics, borderline and impulsive traits in a subset of patients with BN and binge-purging AN, and negative affectivity without a PD diagnosis in a subset of patients with both BN and restricting AN.

EPIDEMIOLOGY

Findings from large community-recruited studies that used diagnostic interviews suggest that the lifetime prevalence of AN is between 0.5 percent and 1.0 percent for females and between 0.0 percent and 0.3 percent for males, the lifetime prevalence for BN is between 1.5 percent and 4.0 percent for females and between 0.1 percent and 0.5 percent for males, and the lifetime prevalence for BED is between 1.5 percent and 3.0 percent for females and is 0.5 percent and 2.0 percent for males (Garfinkel et al., 1995; Johnson, Cohen, Kasen, & Brook, 2002; Lewinsohn, Hops, Roberts, Seeley, & Andrews, 1993; Newman et al., 1996). Including subthreshold cases, however, makes clear the prevalence of eating pathology in the population. Community-recruited samples indicate that for females, the rates of subthreshold or partial syndrome AN range between 1.1 percent and 3.0 percent, that the rates of subthreshold or partial syndrome BN range between 2.0 percent and 5.4 percent, and that the rate of subthreshold BED is 1.6 percent (Garfinkel et al., 1995; Lewinsohn, Striegel-Moore, & Seeley, 2000; Spitzer et al., 1992; Stice, Presnell, & Bearman, 2004). Although less attention has focused on subthreshold EDs among males, the available evidence suggests that the rates appear to be consistently lower for males than females (e.g., Garfinkel et al., 1995).

Research suggests that the incidence of new cases of AN and BN ranges between 1.3 percent and 2.8 percent during adolescence for females and that the risk for onset of these disorders peaks between 16 and 17 years of age (Lewinsohn et al., 2000; Stice, Killen, Hayward, & Taylor, 1998; Stice,

Presnell, et al., 2004). These incidence estimates suggest a relatively narrow developmental window for the emergence of the majority of cases of AN and BN, a factor that distinguishes EDs from many psychiatric disorders.

ETIOLOGY

There are numerous theories regarding the etiologic processes that promote the development of AN, implicating a wide variety of risk factors for AN, including norepinephrine abnormalities, serotonergic abnormalities, childhood sexual abuse, low self-esteem, perfectionism, need for control, disturbed family dynamics, internalization of the thin-ideal, dietary restraint, and mood disturbances (Fairburn & Harrison, 2003; Kaye, Klump, Frank, & Strober, 2000; Wilson et al., 2003). However, there have been very few prospective investigations of factors that predict subsequent onset of anorexic pathology or increases in anorexic symptoms and no prospective tests of multivariate etiologic models. The paucity of prospective studies is of concern, as these tests are essential to determining whether a putative risk factor is a precursor, concomitant, or consequence of eating pathology.

The only prospective study that tested predictors of subsequent onset of threshold or subthreshold AN found that girls with the lowest relative weight and those with very low scores on a dietary restraint scale at baseline were at increased risk for future onset of anorexic pathology over a five-year period (Stice, Presnell, et al., 2004). In contrast to hypotheses, early puberty, perceived pressure to be thin, thin-ideal internalization, body dissatisfaction, depressive symptoms, and deficits in parental and peer support did not predict onset of anorexic pathology; however, these null findings should be interpreted with care because of the low base rate of this outcome. Unfortunately, the four additional studies we were able to locate collapsed across anorexic and bulimic pathology (e.g., McKnight Investigators, 2003; Patton, Johnson-Sabine, Wood, Mann, & Wakeling, 1990; Santonastaso, Friederici, & Favaro, 1999). Thus, surprisingly little is known about the risk factors for anorexic pathology or how they work together to promote this pernicious eating disturbance.

In contrast to the dearth of prospective research in anorexic pathology, greater progress has been made regarding our understanding of the risk factors for bulimic pathology. According to the sociocultural model, an internalization of the socially sanctioned thin-ideal for females interacts with direct pressures for female thinness (e.g., weight-related teasing) to promote body dissatisfaction, which in turn is thought to increase the risk for the initiation of dieting and for negative affect and consequent bulimic pathology (Cattarin & Thompson, 1994; Garner, Olmstead, & Polivy, 1983; Polivy & Herman, 1985; Stice et al., 1998). Body dissatisfaction may lead to dietary restraint, a behavioral manifestation of the desire to conform to the thin-ideal, which paradoxically increases the likelihood of onset of binge eating. Dieting also entails a shift from a reliance on physiological cues to cognitive control overeating behaviors, the disruption of which may lead to overeating. Body dissatisfaction is also theorized to contribute to negative affect, which increases the risk of binge eating to provide comfort and distraction from these negative emotional states.

Consistent with this general etiologic model, thin-ideal internalization, perceived pressure to be thin, body dissatisfaction, dietary restraint, and negative affect have been consistently found to increase the risk for future onset of bulimic symptoms and bulimic pathology (Field, Camargo, Taylor, Berkey, & Colditz, 1999; Killen et al., 1994, 1996; Stice et al., 1998; Stice, Presnell, et al., 2004). Support for this model derives from experimental evidence that a reduction in thin-ideal internalization, body dissatisfaction, and negative affect produce decreases in bulimic symptoms; however, these studies have failed to provide support for the role of dietary restraint as a risk factor for future onset of bulimic pathology (for a review, see Stice, 2002). Other risk factors, such as deficits in social support, substance abuse, and elevated body mass, have received limited empirical support, but these effects have not been consistently replicated (Stice, 2002). Interestingly, several hypothesized risk factors for bulimic pathology have not received support in prospective studies, including early menarche and temperamental impulsivity (Stice, 2002).

There has been comparatively little theoretical work regarding the etiologic processes that promote BED, but extant models display conceptual overlap with etiologic theories of bulimic pathology (Vogeltanz-Holm et al., 2000). Prospective studies have provided evidence that initial elevations in body mass, body dissatisfaction, dietary restraint, negative affect and emotional eating increase the risk for future onset of binge eating (Stice et al., 1998; Stice, Presnell, & Spangler, 2002; Vogeltanz-Holm et al., 2000).

Genetic factors likely contribute to the development of EDs, though the findings in this area are inconsistent. Twin studies have produced conflicting results, with heritability estimates ranging from 0.0 percent to 70 percent for AN and from 0.0 percent to 83 percent for BN (Bulik, Sullivan, & Kendler, 1998; Fairburn, Cowen, & Harrison, 1999; Kaye et al., 2000). Concordance rates are also inconsistent, as one study found that the rate for monozygotic twins was greater than for dizygotic twins (Treasure & Holland, 1989), but another observed findings in the opposite direction (Walters &

Kendler, 1995). Similarly, studies that have tried to identify specific receptor genes that are associated with EDs have produced inconsistent results that have not replicated (e.g., Hinney et al., 1998, 1999). The large range in parameter estimates suggests fundamental problems with sampling error resulting from small samples, the reliability of diagnostic procedures, or statistical models used to estimate genetic effects.

There are several important considerations regarding the interpretation of the etiologic findings. First, we were unable to locate any prospective study testing whether any biological variable, including structural or functional abnormalities in the brain or neurotransmitter abnormalities, predicted onset of any ED. This dearth of prospective research renders a determination of the causal relation between biological factors and eating pathology difficult. Second, there have been very few studies that predicted onset of anorexic pathology, bulimic pathology, or BED or compared and differentiated the risk factors for these three classes of EDs. In the absence of this type of research, it is not possible to distinguish among the etiologic processes that give rise to EDs. Third, given the focus on adolescence, very little is known about risk factors for adult onset eating pathology. Fourth, as with other disorders, research into etiology may need to focus on subcomponents or endophenotypes of the disorders (e.g., negative affect in BN) rather than on complete syndromes, given that syndromes are likely to have more complex and multifaceted etiologies than specific features or deficits. Finally, as described in the following section, another avenue for exploring etiology focuses on personality vulnerabilities or subtypes that may map only imperfectly onto particular disturbances in eating behavior.

COURSE, COMPLICATIONS, AND PROGNOSIS

Anorexia nervosa appears to have a highly variable course. Some individuals recover after a single episode, others show a chronic course marked by fluctuating patterns of weight restoration and relapse, and still others may go on to develop other EDs (Wilson et al., 2003). Severe medical complications also result from the disorder, including permanent organ damage, cerebral atrophy, and osteoporosis, which necessitates close medical monitoring during periods of low body weight. Anorexia nervosa is also associated with the highest rates of suicidal ideation and mortality of any psychiatric condition (Herzog et al., 2000; Newman et al., 1996).

Findings from community-recruited samples suggest that BN typically shows a chronic course that is characterized by periods of recovery and relapse, although subthreshold bulimic pathology shows less chronicity (Fairburn, Cooper, Doll, Norman, & O'Connor, 2000; Stice, Burton, & Shaw, 2004). Bulimia nervosa typically results in marked subjective distress and functional impairment (Lewinsohn et al., 2000). Serious medical complications may arise in the most severe cases, some requiring hospitalization (e.g., esophageal tears) or even causing death (e.g., electrolyte imbalances that result in cardiac arrest). Community recruited samples indicate that BN is also associated with an increased risk for suicide attempt and elevated rates of comorbid affective disorders, anxiety disorders, and substance abuse (Johnson, Cohen, Kotler, Kasen, & Brook, 2002; Lewinsohn et al., 1993; Newman et al., 1996). Threshold and subthreshold BN increase the risk for future onset of depression, suicide attempts, anxiety disorders, substance abuse, obesity, and health problems (Johnson, Cohen, Kotler, et al., 2002; Stice, Cameron, Killen, Hayward, & Taylor, 1999; Striegel-Moore, Seeley, & Lewinsohn, 2003). The treatment prognosis for BN is fair, as lasting symptom remission typically occurs for only 30 percent to 40 percent of patients who are provided with the treatment of choice (Agras, Walsh, Fairburn, Wilson, & Kraemer, 2000; Fairburn et al., 1995).

Community-recruited natural history studies suggest that BED shows a high autoremission rate over time, with fewer than 20 percent of cases meeting diagnostic criteria over long follow-up periods (Fairburn et al., 2000; Wilson et al., 2003), although the majority appear to meet criteria for EDNOS. Another noteworthy finding is that a large portion of individuals with binge ED show onset of obesity (Fairburn et al., 2000). Binge-eating disorder is associated with elevated major depression and slight elevations in Axis I and Axis II psychiatric disorders, as well as obesity and the consequent elevated morbidity and mortality associated with this health problem (Striegel-Moore, Wilfley, Pike, Dohm, & Fairburn, 2000; Telch & Stice, 1998). The prognosis for the treatment of BED may be hopeful, with psychotherapeutic interventions showing abstinence rates of approximately 60 percent at one-year follow-up (Wilson et al., 2003) and evidence that low-calorie behavioral weight loss interventions can be effective (Goodrick, Poston, Kimball, Reeves, & Foreyt, 1998; Reeves et al., 2001).

ASSESSMENT AND DIAGNOSIS

There are a variety of self-report questionnaires and structured diagnostic interviews for the assessment of eating pathology (Anderson & Paulosky, 2004). The following is a brief overview of the evidence for the reliability and validity of the most widely researched assessment strategies. With the exception of the Eating Disorders Diagnostic Scale (Stice, Telch, & Rizvi, 2000), however, it is important to note that self-report eating disorder measures generally provide dimensional assessments and cannot be used to make *DSM-IV* categorical diagnoses.

The Eating Attitudes Test (EAT; Garner & Garfinkel, 1979) is a 40-item questionnaire designed to assess the symptoms of AN, but various adaptations of this scale exist, including a 26-item short form and forms for children and adolescents (Anderson & Paulosky, 2004). There is considerable evidence that the EAT possesses internal consistency, test-retest reliability, and discriminant validity with adolescents and adults.

The Eating Disorder Inventory (EDI; Garner et al., 1983) is a multi-item scale that assesses the symptoms and features of AN and BN. The current version (EDI-2; Garner, 1991) includes 11 scales, such as the bulimia, body dissatisfaction, drive for thinness, perfectionism, and impulse regulation subscales. Research suggests that the EDI possesses adequate internal consistency and test-retest reliability, and good discriminant and predictive validity with adolescents and adults.

The Bulimia Test–Revised (BULIT-R; Thelen, Farmer, Wonderlich, & Smith, 1991) and its predecessor the BULIT were designed to assess the symptoms of BN. Research has found that the BULIT-R possesses good internal consistency, test-retest reliability, discriminant validity, and predictive validity with adolescents and adults (Anderson & Paulosky, 2004; Thelen et al., 1991).

The Eating Disorder Examination–Questionnaire (EDE-Q; Fairburn & Beglin, 1994) is a questionnaire version of the Eating Disorder Examination interview (EDE; Fairburn & Cooper, 1993), a validated measure of eating pathology. This scale assesses the diagnostic symptoms of AN and BN, and contains subscales assessing features that are commonly associated with these EDs, such as dietary restraint and eating concern. Research has found that this scale possesses good internal consistency and test-retest reliability with adolescents and adults (Black & Wilson, 1996; Fairburn & Beglin, 1994; Luce & Crowther, 1999; Stice, 2001).

The Questionnaire for Eating Disorder Diagnoses (QEDD; Mintz, O'Halloran, Mulholland, & Schneider, 1997) is a questionnaire assessing the diagnostic criteria for AN, BN, and BED. Research has found that this scale showed good test-retest reliability and criterion validity (Mintz et al., 1997).

The Eating Disorder Diagnostic Scale (Stice et al., 2000) is a brief self-report scale assessing the *DSM-IV* diagnostic criteria for AN, BN, and BED. Research has found that the continuous symptom composite shows good internal consistency, test-retest reliability, and predictive validity, and that the ED diagnoses made with this scale also possess good test-retest reliability and show good criterion validity with interview-based diagnoses (mean k = .81; Stice, Fisher, & Martinez, 2004; Stice et al., 2000).

There are structured psychiatric interviews for arriving at *DSM-IV* (American Psychiatric Association, 1994) diagnoses of AN, BN, and BED (e.g., the Eating Disorder Examination [EDE]; Fairburn & Cooper, 1993; Spitzer, Williams, Gibbon, & First, 1990; Structured Clinical Interview for *DSM* [SCID]).

The Eating Disorder Examination (EDE; Fairburn & Cooper, 1993) is a semistructured psychiatric interview assessing the diagnostic criteria for AN and BN. This interview also contains subscales assessing features that are commonly associated with these EDs, such as dietary restraint and eating concern. Research has found that the continuous scales from this interview possess good internal consistency, test-retest reliability, and discriminant validity, and that the diagnoses show good interrater reliability and test-retest reliability (Fairburn & Cooper, 1993; Rizvi, Peterson, Crow, & Agras, 2000; Stice, Burton, et al., 2004; Williamson, Anderson, Jackman, & Jackson, 1995).

The SCID (Spitzer et al., 1990) is a standardized interview that assesses current and lifetime psychiatric status for major Axis I psychiatric disorders using criteria in accordance with the *DSM*. The reliability and validity of the SCID I have been well documented, with interrater reliability agreement (k) ranging from .70 to 1.00 (Segal, Hersen, & Van Hasselt, 1994; Williams et al., 1992). However, we were unable to locate information concerning the test-retest reliability for specific ED diagnosis with the SCID.

IMPACT ON ENVIRONMENT

Research on PDs in general would suggest that individuals with the kinds of pathology to which ED patients are vulnerable would likely suffer substantial social and occupational problems. A large body of research suggests that social functioning is worse across all categories of PD than in non-PD comparison groups (Casey & Tyrer, 1986), and that PD traits predict poor social functioning above and beyond variance accounted for by Axis I symptoms such as depression and anxiety (Oltmanns, Melley, & Turkheimer, 2002; Seivewright, Tyrer, & Johnson, 2004). Indeed, interpersonal dysfunction, or personality traits or dynamics that render individuals vulnerable to such dysfunction, comprises many PD criteria in *DSM-IV*. For example, the *DSM-IV* criteria for BPD characterize these patients' interpersonal functioning as unstable and intense, with alternating patterns of idealization and devaluation, inappropriate rage, and desperate fears of rejection and fears of aloneness. Work histories of patients with BPD are also frequently impaired, with many losing jobs for interpersonal reasons (Zittel & Westen, in press).

Interpersonal pathology also characterizes the other most frequent PDs seen in ED patients, avoidant PD and OCPD. Avoidant PD, which by definition disrupts social functioning, involves a pervasive pattern of social inhibition and fears of becoming close to others. The work and interpersonal functioning of patients with OCPD is characterized by the sacrifice of friendships and leisure activity to excessive devotion to productivity and difficulty delegating tasks to others unless they submit to the patient's often critical standards. The *ICD-10* adds to this list excessive pedantry and adherence to social conventions (World Health Organization, 1993). Recent research finds, in fact, that OCPD patients can be socially aversive because of their self-righteousness, often couched in moral terms (Shedler & Westen, 2004).

The available research on comorbid personality pathology in patients with EDs suggests that personality pathology has a strong impact on the patient's environment—particularly through social and work functioning—above and beyond the considerable problems that EDs alone can cause. Cluster B personality problems in ED patients are associated with suicide attempts, self-destructiveness, and substance abuse, as in other patients with Cluster B (particularly borderline) pathology (Johnson, Tobin, & Enright, 1989; Milos, Spindler, Hepp, & Schnyder, 2004). These problems in turn are associated with significant disruptions in social and occupational functioning. For example, studies comparing patients with BN and BPD to those with BN without BPD have found that the borderline patients showed significantly more disturbed psychosocial adaptation and family environment (Johnson et al., 1989). As a result, these patients may appear more often for treatment than ED patients without significant personality pathology.

Similarly, several studies have found that the subtypes of patients with both dysregulated/undercontrolled and rigid/overcontrolled personality disturbances show substantially lower global functioning scores than patients without these profiles (Thompson-Brenner & Westen, 2004; Westen & Harnden-Fischer, 2001). ED patients matching these personality-disturbed profiles also show higher rates of psychiatric hospitalization (Thompson-Brenner & Westen, 2004; Westen & Harnden-Fischer, 2001). In another study, individuals characterized by a dietary-depressive subtype identified in other research and associated with considerable personality pathology showed more symptom persistence and social impairment over a five-year follow-up period (Stice & Fairburn, 2003).

TREATMENT IMPLICATIONS

Clinicians have treated EDs in the community for more than three decades (see Bruch, 1973; Fairburn, 1997; Minuchin et al., 1978), employing a range of therapies, mostly cognitive behavioral (CBT), psychodynamic, family systems (particularly for adolescents with the disorder), biological, and eclectic or integrative. With the exception of some promising early studies using family therapy to treat adolescents with AN (Dare, Eisler, Russell, & Szmukler, 1990; Eisler et al., 1997; Le Grange, Eisler, Dare, & Russell, 1992), a recent study employing CBT after hospitalization (Pike, Walsh, Vitousek, Wilson, & Bauer, 2003), and some limited data on medication response (Kaye et al., 2001), data from controlled trials are limited for AN. In part this reflects the refractoriness of AN to randomized controlled trials (RCTs) methods, given that many patients require hospitalization, even in the midst of outpatient treatments that are ultimately successful. Even less data are available regarding treatment of the substantial numbers of patients in clinical practice who receive a diagnosis of EDNOS, and research on the treatment of BED is just beginning, although promising (see National Institute for Clinical Excellence guidelines, 2004).

In contrast, a substantial empirical literature exists using RCTs to assess treatments for BN, particularly CBT, with some studies also testing alternative behavioral treatments and interpersonal psychotherapy (IPT). A recent meta-analysis of these trials, analyzing not only effect size but additional variables bearing on outcome and generalizability, indicates that CBT (18 to 19 sessions on average), IPT, and various behavior therapies produce substantial reductions in BN symptomatology (Thompson-Brenner, Glass, & Westen, 2003). Additional treatments with promise for treating EDs include guided self-help (Bailer et al., 2004) and dialectical behavior therapy (Safer, Telch, & Agras, 2001). Meta-analytic data suggest that individual CBT produces substantially better outcomes than group CBT and slightly better outcomes than other therapies tested on some indexes. Even the most successful treatments, however, produce only a 50 percent recovery rate among treatment completers, and approximately 40 percent among those who begin treatment, including those who do not complete it (intent to treat analyses). Furthermore, approximately 40 percent of patients seeking inclusion in RCTs are ruled out of the average study for meeting one or more of a long list of exclusion criteria (Thompson-Brenner et al., 2003).

Before examining data on the relation between personality and treatment, we briefly describe three treatments for BN, which have implications for the treatment of all EDs given their theoretical postulates and intervention strategies that are readily adapted to other EDs: CBT, IPT, and psychodynamic psychotherapy. We focus on CBT and IPT because they have been most often tested in clinical trials. We include psychodynamic therapy because it is frequently practiced or integrated with CBT techniques in the community (Arnow, 1999; Thompson-Brenner & Westen, in press b).

Cognitive Behavioral Therapy

CBT for BN was first developed and tested by Christopher Fairburn and colleagues in the 1980s, and the 19-session manual produced for a treatment-comparison study in 1993 remains the standard for CBT in the field (Fairburn, Marcus, & Wilson, 1993). CBT has recently been compared with nutrition management in AN patients following weight restoration (Pike et al., 2003), and Fairburn's latest CBT manual is designed to treat patients with any ED diagnosis (Fairburn, Cooper, & Shafran, 2003). CBT is based on the premise that patients with EDs are overly concerned with their shape and weight that they too closely link their self-esteem to shape and weight concerns. The CBT model proposes that overconcern with shape and weight leads to particular behaviors (such as rigid dietary rules, overall calorie restriction, and driven exercise) that leave patients vulnerable to subjective overeating and objective binge eating. Overeating and binge eating, in the context of shape and weight concerns, in turn lead to purging behavior, increased restriction, and other forms of calorie and weight elimination. In addition, the low self-esteem produced by overeating, binge eating, and purging also may produce additional motivation to raise self-esteem through weight loss.

This vicious cycle is hypothesized to lie at the core of ED behavior, although the CBT model has recently begun to expand to emphasize other behaviors that contribute to the maintenance of the disorder, such as avoidance of looking at one's appearance and weight (Shafran, Fairburn, Robinson, & Lask, 2004). This avoidance in turn contributes to the maintenance of the association between shape and weight and anxiety and prevents more accurate appraisal of appearance and weight. Similarly, patients may engage in body checking, producing selective information that reinforces the belief that their body or a body part is too large. CBT researchers view these core cognitive and behavioral processes as central to the development and maintenance of pathological eating behaviors in patients with and without personality pathology (Wilson & Fairburn, 1998).

Cognitive behavioral treatment for EDs (Fairburn, Marcus, et al., 1993; Pike et al., 2003) consists of multiple interventions arranged in a phased sequence. The interventions include psychoeducation regarding the model and the symptoms; self-monitoring of eating and symptom behavior; prescription of regular eating, including three meals and two snacks at regular intervals; reintroduction to feared foods and loosening of dietary rules; and cognitive and behavioral interventions for shape and weight concerns (as well as mood and interpersonal problems and other issues that require problem solving). The early phase of treatment is highly focused on behavior change and self-monitoring; later phases of treatment focus on addressing obstacles to behavior change and vulnerabilities to relapse. Fairburn and colleagues have recently proposed a flexible transdiagnostic version of CBT that may include modules even more directly targeting interpersonal and mood regulation issues as well as certain aspects of personality (notably perfectionism and self-esteem) using CBT interventions such as cognitive restructuring (Shafran et al., 2004).

Interpersonal Psychotherapy

Interpersonal psychotherapy was originally developed for use with major depressive disorder and was chosen as a short-term treatment comparison for later trials of CBT (Fairburn, Jones, Peveler, Hope, & O'Connor, 1993). Since then, however, it has demonstrated efficacy for reducing the symptoms of BN in two trials (Agras, Walsh, et al., 2000; Fairburn et al., 1991; Fairburn, Jones, et al., 1993). IPT focuses on four general domains of interpersonal functioning believed to contribute to the development or maintenance of depression, BN, and other psychiatric disorders, called interpersonal deficits, grief, conflict, and role transitions (Fairburn, 1997; Wilfley, Dounchis, & Welch, 2000).

IPT includes an initial extended assessment period, which links the onset and development of ED symptoms to important interpersonal events. Following the assessment, the interpersonal problem is formulated, and strategies to solve it are proposed, with the goal of resolving the problem or problems in roughly 20 sessions. Reflecting its origins as a credible control condition for CBT that does not overlap substantial with CBT in intervention strategies (Westen, Novotny, & Thompson-Brenner, 2004), IPT therapists do not focus on eating symptoms themselves, focusing instead on current interpersonal problems in the patient's life.

Psychodynamic Psychotherapy

Psychodynamic treatments for EDs assume that eating symptoms typically arise in the broader context of personality patterns, such as difficulty identifying and regulating emotions; conflicts about, or difficulties in, the self-regulation of impulses (either undercontrol or overcontrol); problematic ways of viewing the self and others and interacting with significant others, particularly in meaningful relationships such as attachment relationships ("object relations"; Westen, 1991); and deficits in the consolidation of a sense of self or identity (Waller, Dickson, & Ohanian, 2002). Psychodynamic approaches do not assume that all patients with the same ED diagnosis have the same underlying problems, and although contemporary dynamic theorists acknowledge the substantial roles of culture and biology in symptom generation and maintenance, they tend to view eating symptoms and body image distortions as symptomatic expressions of broader personality patterns that may manifest in other realms of the patient's life as well, such as impulse and emotion regulation in situations not involving food (e.g., the literature on multi-impulsive bulimics; Waller et al., 2002; Waller, Ohanian, Meyer, & Osman, 2000), relationships, or sexuality (e.g., Eddy, Novotny, & Westen, in press).

Psychodynamic practice with ED patients is nowhere presented in a manual, and probably its most definitive statement remains Bruch's (1973, 1978) conceptualization of the nature and treatment of ED pathology, although several others have contributed as well (e.g., Tobin & Johnson, 1991). In a recent naturalistic study of treatments for BN in the community (Thompson-Brenner & Westen, in press a), although most clinicians self-reporting a primary psychodynamic orientation reported using a range of strategies, including relatively directive strategies targeting specific symptoms typically associated with CBT, the following interventions were among those with high loadings on an identifiable psychodynamic factor: encouraging exploration of feelings the patient found uncomfortable or unacceptable; focusing on the similarities between the patient's relationships and perceptions of relationships repeated over time, settings, or people; focusing on the patient's conflicting feelings or desires; helping the patient come to terms with her relationships with and feelings about significant others from the past; addressing the patient's avoidance of important subjects and shifts in mood; identifying maladaptive interpersonal patterns and the thoughts, feelings, and motives underlying them; focusing on ways the patient deals with anger or aggression; encouraging the patient to experience and express feelings in the session; using the therapeutic relationship to offer the patient a different model for relationships than she had previously experienced; linking the patient's current feelings or perceptions to experiences from the past; encouraging the discussion of the patient's wishes, fantasies, dreams, and so forth; exploring issues of sexuality; focusing on the relationship between the therapist and patient; encouraging the patient to assert herself or get her needs met in relationships; and helping the patient regulate intense emotions. Many of these interventions were among those identified by Hilsenroth and colleagues (Hilsenroth, Ackerman, Blagys, Baity, & Mooney, 2003) as distinguishing psychodynamic from CBT treatments for other disorders, notably depression.

Personality, Treatment Interventions, and Outcome

Data from a number of studies indicate that personality pathology has a negative influence on ED treatment outcome. Debate exists over inconsistencies in these findings, however, such as differences in the personality variables associated with negative outcome and failures to replicate. Some of these inconsistencies likely reflect limitations of sample size for detecting moderators in most outcome studies. A number of common exclusion criteria—such as suicidality, upper weight limits, and other comorbidity—may also inadvertently rule out patients with the most personality disturbance from inclusion in major trials and hence prevent definitive conclusions on personality pathology as a moderator of outcome (Thompson-Brenner & Westen, in press a). Application of four common RCT exclusion criteria to a naturalistic BN sample suggested that 40 percent of all patients—including 66 percent of patients with BPD—would likely have been excluded, and as reported in the following paragraph, these patients in fact fared considerably worse and required different intervention strategies (Thompson-Brenner & Westen, in press a). Given that the average treatment group in an RCT has 30 patients (Thompson-Brenner & Westen, 2003), a third or less of the sample is likely to show the same form of significant personality pathology, and as much as 60 percent may be ruled out by other exclusion criteria, at present little can be said with certainty about the relation between personality pathology and outcome.

The majority of studies investigating associations between assorted personality variables (e.g., BPD, Cluster B PDs, any PD) and assorted outcome variables have, in fact, found significant negative association (or strong trend) in RCTs for BN (e.g., Davis, Olmsted, & Rockert, 1992; Fahy & Russell, 1993; Fairburn, Jones, et al., 1993; Garner et al., 1990; Johnson, Tobin, & Dennis, 1990; Rossiter, Agras, Telch, & Schneider, 1993; Steiger & Stotland, 1996; Wonderlich, Fullerton, Swift, & Klein, 1994), although such findings are not universal (e.g., Bossert, Schmolz, Wiegand, Junker, & Krieg, 1992; Bulik, Sullivan, Joyce, Carter, & McIntosh, 1998; Grilo et al., 2003). Multiple studies suggest that personality variables such as perfectionism, obsessive compulsive personality disorder, and asceticism predict poor outcome in AN (e.g., Bizeul, Sadowsky, & Rigaud, 2001; Fassino et al., 2001; Rastam, Gillberg, & Wentz, 2003; Sutandar-Pinnock,

Blake Woodside, Carter, Olmsted, & Kaplan, 2003; for a review, see Steinhausen, 2002).

To what extent each of the treatments described previously is likely to address personality or to show moderation of outcome by personality variables is speculative. The effort to broaden CBT for BN to include interventions targeted at particular aspects of personality (i.e., perfectionism and self-esteem) and problems often associated with personality disorders (i.e., interpersonal problems and mood dysregulation) may increase its applicability to the range of problems typically presented by patients with personality disturbance, although this is not likely to be accomplished in the brief manualized version of the treatment. Indeed, in a recent naturalistic study of treatments for BN in the community (Thompson-Brenner & Westen, in press a, in press b), the average length of treatment for CBT was 69 sessions, and treatment length was associated with degree of personality pathology. Because of the flexible nature of IPT treatment planning, it could conceivably be adapted to the needs of patients with personality pathology, particularly those with dysregulated pathology, which has substantial interpersonal components. To what extent it can address personality problems such as obsessionality, perfectionism, or rigidity, which are more internalizing, or the noninterpersonal problems of dysregulated patients (such as deficits in emotion regulation), is unclear. In either case, there is no evidence suggesting that enduring personality pathology is likely to change in 20 weeks (see Westen et al., 2004), suggesting that adaptations of IPT to patients with substantial personality pathology would likely need to be significantly extended. Psychodynamic therapy is unique in its focus on personality as a diathesis for EDs; unfortunately, however, it has not been subjected to empirical test (except as an "intent to fail" condition in one study, in which therapists were forbidden to talk with the patient about eating or weight concerns; see Westen et al., 2004).

A naturalistic study of treatment in the community may shed some preliminary light on personality as a moderator of outcome and of the kinds of interventions that may prove useful to test in future studies of treatment of ED patients with significant personality pathology (Thompson-Brenner & Westen, in press a, in press b). A national sample of 145 experienced MD and PhD clinicians provided data concerning their most recently terminated (successful or unsuccessful) treatment of a patient with bulimic symptomatology (including mixed ED diagnoses). The sample was roughly evenly split by theoretical orientation, with most clinicians reporting a primary psychodynamic or CBT orientation (about 40 percent each), although the majority described themselves as drawing heavily from other approaches (which was apparent in the interventions they reported using). Personality pathology was the norm rather than the exception and did not vary by clinicians' theoretical orientation: Clinicians diagnosed almost 60 percent of patients with a personality disorder, with approximately one in four meeting criteria for BPD and one in four for dependent PD. Clinicians classified 41.7 percent as high-functioning/perfectionistic, 30.9 percent as constricted, and 27.3 percent as dysregulated. Pretreatment global functioning and posttreatment outcome were both significantly related to personality style, with dysregulated patients faring most poorly, followed by constricted patients, followed by high-functioning patients. In multiple regression analyses, both dysregulation and constriction significantly predicted poor outcome, above and beyond variance accounted for by severity of eating symptoms and comorbid Axis I disorders.

CONCLUSIONS

Researchers have made substantial inroads into the understanding of EDs over the last 25 years, providing increasing knowledge about their nature, prevalence, course, and treatment. Controversies remain, however, about the classification and etiology of EDs and about the complex relations between symptoms of disordered eating and personality.

REFERENCES

Agras, W. S., Crow, S. J., Halmi, K. A., Mitchell, J. E., Wilson, G. T., & Kraemer, H. C. (2000). Outcome predictors for the cognitive behavior treatment of bulimia nervosa: Data from a multisite study. *American Journal of Psychiatry, 157,* 1302–1308.

Agras, W. S., Walsh, B. T., Fairburn, C. B., Wilson, G. T., & Kraemer, H. C. (2000). A multicenter comparison of cognitive-behavioral therapy and interpersonal psychotherapy for bulimia nervosa. *Archives of General Psychiatry, 57,* 459–466.

American Psychiatric Association. (1994). *Diagnostic and statistical manual of mental disorders* (4th ed.). Washington, DC: Author.

American Psychiatric Association. (2000). *Diagnostic and statistical manual of mental disorders* (4th ed., text rev.). Washington, DC: Author.

Anderluh, M., Tchanturia, K., Rabe-Hesketh, S., & Treasure, J. L. (2003). Childhood obsessive-compulsive personality traits in adult women with EDs: Defining a broader ED phenotype. *American Journal of Psychiatry, 160*(2), 242–247.

Andersen, A., Bowers, W., & Watson, T. (2001). A slimming program for EDs not otherwise specified: Reconceptualizing a confusing, residual diagnostic category. *Psychiatric Clinics of North America, 24,* 271–280.

Anderson, D. A., & Paulosky, C. A. (2004). Psychological assessment of eating disorders and related features. In J. K. Thompson (Ed.), *Handbook of eating disorders and obesity* (pp. 112–129). Hoboken, NJ: Wiley.

Arnow, B. A. (1999). Why are empirically-supported treatments for bulimia nervosa underutilized and what can we do about it? *Journal of Clinical Psychology, 55,* 769–779.

Bailer, U., de Zwaan, M., Leisch, F., Strnad, A., Lennkh-Wolfsberg, C., El-Giamal, N., et al. (2004). Guided self-help versus cognitive-behavioral group therapy in the treatment of bulimia nervosa. *International Journal of Eating Disorders, 35,* 522–537.

Barratt, E. S. (1993). Impulsivity: Integrating cognitive, behavioral, biological, and environmental data. In W. G. McCown & J. L. Johnson (Eds.), *The impulsive client: Theory, research, and treatment* (pp. 39–56). Washington, DC: American Psychological Association.

Bastiani, A., Rao, R., Weltzin, T., & Kaye, W. (1995). Perfectionism in anorexia nervosa. *International Journal of Eating Disorders, 17,* 147–152.

Ben-Tovim, D., Marilov, V., & Crisp, A. (1979). Personality and mental state (P.S.E.) within anorexia nervosa. *Journal of Psychosomatic Research, 23,* 321–325.

Bizeul, C., Sadowsky, N., & Rigaud, D. (2001). The prognostic value of initial EDI scores in anorexia nervosa patients: A prospective follow-up study of 5–10 years. *European Psychiatry, 16,* 232–238.

Black, C. M., & Wilson, G. T. (1996). Assessment of eating disorders: Interview versus questionnaire. *International Journal of Eating Disorders, 20,* 43–50.

Bossert, S., Schmolz, U., Wiegand, M., Junker, M., & Krieg, J. (1992). Predictors of short-term treatment outcome in bulimia nervosa inpatients. *Behaviour Research and Therapy, 30,* 193–199.

Braun, D., Sunday, S., & Halmi, K. (1994). Psychiatric comorbidity in patients with eating disorders. *Psychological Medicine, 24,* 859–867.

Brewerton, T., Hand, L., & Bishop, E. (1993). The Tridimensional Personality Questionnaire in eating disorder patients. *International Journal of Eating Disorders, 14,* 213–218.

Brody, M. L., Walsh, B. T., & Devlin, M. J. (1994). Binge eating disorder: Reliability and validity of a new diagnostic category. *Journal of Consulting and Clinical Psychology, 62,* 381–386.

Bruch, H. (1973). *Eating disorders: Obesity, anorexia nervosa, and the person within.* New York: Basic Books.

Bruch, H. (1978). *The golden cage: The enigma of anorexia nervosa.* New York: Vintage.

Bulik, C., Sullivan, P., Joyce, P., & Carter, F. (1995). Temperament, character, and personality disorder in bulimia nervosa. *Journal of Nervous & Mental Disease, 183,* 593–598.

Bulik, C., Sullivan, P., Joyce, P., Carter, F., & McIntosh, V. (1998). Predictors of 1-year treatment outcome in bulimia nervosa. *Comprehensive Psychiatry, 39,* 206–214.

Bulik, C., Sullivan, P., Weltzin, T., & Kaye, W. (1995). Temperament in eating disorders. *International Journal of Eating Disorders, 17,* 251–261.

Bulik, C. M., Sullivan, P. F., & Kendler, K. S. (1998). Heritability of binge-eating and broadly defined bulimia nervosa. *Biological Psychiatry, 44,* 1210–1218.

Casey, P., & Tyrer, P. (1986). Personality, functioning and symptomatology. *Journal of Psychiatric Research, 20,* 363–374.

Casper, R., Eckert, E., Halmi, K., Goldberg, S., & Davis, J. (1980). Bulimia: Its incidence and clinical importance in patients with anorexia nervosa. *Archives of General Psychiatry, 37,* 1030–1035.

Casper, R., Hedeker, D., & McClough, J. (1992). Personality dimensions in EDs and their relevance for subtyping. *Journal of the American Academy of Child & Adolescent Psychiatry, 31,* 830–840.

Cattarin, J. A., & Thompson, J. K. (1994). A 3-year longitudinal study of body image, eating disturbance, and general psychological functioning in adolescent females. *Eating Disorders: The Journal of Treatment and Prevention, 2,* 114–125.

Cloninger, C. R., Przybeck, T. R., Svrakic, D. M., & Wetzel, R. D. (1994). *The Temperament and Character Inventory (TCI): A guide to its development and use.* St. Louis, MO: Washington University, Center for Psychobiology of Personality.

Dare, C., Eisler, I., Russell, G., & Szmukler, G. (1990). Family therapy for anorexia nervosa: Implications from the results of a controlled trial of family and individual therapy. *Journal of Marital and Family Therapy, 16,* 39–57.

Davis, R., Olmsted, M. P., & Rockert, W. (1992). Brief group psychoeducation for bulimia nervosa: II. Prediction of clinical outcome. *International Journal of Eating Disorders, 11,* 205–211.

Diaz-Marsa, M., Carrasco, J., & Saiz, J. (2000). A study of temperament and personality in anorexia and bulimia nervosa. *Journal of Personality Disorders, 14,* 352–359.

Eddy, K., Novotny, C., & Westen, D. (in press). Sexuality, personality, and eating disorders. *Eating Disorders: The Journal of Treatment and Prevention.*

Eddy, K. T., Keel, P. K., Dorer, D. J., Delinsky, S. S., Franko, D. L., & Herzog, D. B. (2002). A longitudinal comparison of anorexia nervosa subtypes. *International Journal of Eating Disorders, 31,* 191–201.

Eisler, I., Dare, C., Russell, G., Szmukler, G., Le Grange, D., & Dodge, E. (1997). A five-year follow-up of a controlled trial of family therapy in severe eating disorders. *Archives of General Psychiatry, 54,* 1025–1030.

Eldredge, K. L., & Agras, W. S. (1996). Weight and shape overconcern and emotional eating in binge eating disorder. *International Journal of Eating Disorders, 19,* 73–82.

Eysenck, H., & Eysenck, S. (1975). *Manual of the Eysenck Personality Questionnaire.* San Diego, CA: Educational and Industrial Testing Service.

Eysenck, H. J. (1990). Biological dimensions of personality. In L. A. Pervin (Ed.), *Handbook of personality: Theory and research* (pp. 244–276). New York: Guilford Press.

Fahy, T. A. (1991). Obsessive-compulsive symptoms in eating disorders. *Behaviour Research and Therapy, 29,* 113–116.

Fahy, T. A., & Russell, G. F. M. (1993). Outcome and prognostic variables in bulimia nervosa. *International Journal of Eating Disorders, 14,* 135–145.

Fairburn, C., Cooper, Z., Doll, H., & Welch, S. (1999). Risk factors for anorexia nervosa: Three integrated case-control comparisons. *Archives of General Psychiatry, 56,* 468–476.

Fairburn, C., Cooper, Z., & Shafran, R. (2003). Cognitive behaviour therapy for eating disorders: A "transdiagnostic" theory and treatment. *Behaviour Research and Therapy, 41,* 509–528.

Fairburn, C., Welch, S., Doll, H., Davies, B., & O'Connor, M. (1997). Risk factors for bulimia nervosa: A community-based case-control study. *Archives of General Psychiatry, 54,* 509–517.

Fairburn, C. G. (1997). Interpersonal psychotherapy for bulimia nervosa. In D. M. Garner & P. E. Garfinkel (Eds.), *Handbook of treatment for eating disorders* (2nd ed., pp. 278–294). New York: Guilford Press.

Fairburn, C. G., & Beglin, S. J. (1994). Assessment of eating disorders: Interview or self-report questionnaire? *International Journal of Eating Disorders, 16,* 363–370.

Fairburn, C. G., & Cooper, Z. (1993). The eating disorder examination. In C. Fairburn & G. Wilson (Eds.), *Binge eating: Nature, assessment, and treatment* (12th ed., pp. 317–360). New York: Guilford Press.

Fairburn, C. G., Cooper, Z., Doll, H. A., Norman, P. A., & O'Connor, M. E. (2000). The natural course of bulimia nervosa and binge eating disorder in young women. *Archives of General Psychiatry, 57,* 659–665.

Fairburn, C. G., Cowen, P. J., & Harrison, P. J. (1999). Twin studies and the etiology of eating disorders. *International Journal of Eating Disorders, 26,* 349–358.

Fairburn, C. G., & Harrison, P. J. (2003). Eating disorders. *Lancet, 361,* 407–416.

Fairburn, C. G., Jones, R., Peveler, R., Carr, S. J., Solomon, R. A., O'Connor, M., et al. (1991). Three psychological treatments for bulimia nervosa: A comparative trial. *Archives of General Psychiatry, 48*(5), 463–469.

Fairburn, C. G., Jones, R., Peveler, R. C., Hope, R. A., & O'Connor, M. E. (1993). Psychotherapy and bulimia nervosa: Longer-term effects of interpersonal psychotherapy, behavior therapy, and cognitive behavior therapy. *Archives of General Psychiatry, 50,* 419–428.

Fairburn, C. G., Marcus, M. D., & Wilson, G. T. (1993). Cognitive behaviour therapy for binge eating and bulimia nervosa: A comprehensive treatment manual. In C. G. Fairburn & G. T. Wilson (Eds.), *Binge eating: Nature, assessment, and treatment* (pp. 361–404). New York: Guilford Press.

Fairburn, C. G., Norman, P. A., Welch, S. L., O'Connor, M. E., Doll, H., & Peveler, R. (1995). A prospective study of outcome in bulimia nervosa and the long-term effects of three psychological treatments. *Archives of General Psychiatry, 52,* 304–312.

Fassino, S., Abbate-Daga, G., Amianto, F., Leombruni, P., Boggio, S., & Rovera, G. (2002). Temperament and character profile of eating disorders: A controlled study with the Temperament and Character Inventory. *International Journal of Eating Disorders, 32,* 412–425.

Fassino, S., Abbate-Daga, G., Amianto, F., Leombruni, P., Garzaro, L., & Rovera, G. (2001). Nonresponder anorectic patients after 6 months of multimodal treatment: Predictors of outcome. *European Psychiatry, 16*(8), 466–473.

Favaro, A., & Santonastaso, P. (1996). Purging behaviors, suicide attempts, and psychiatric symptoms in 398 eating disordered subjects. *International Journal of Eating Disorders, 20,* 99–103.

Fichter, M., Quadflieg, N., & Rief, W. (1994). Course of multi-impulsive bulimia. *Psychological Medicine, 24,* 591–604.

Field, A. E., Camargo, C. A., Taylor, C. B., Berkey, C. S., & Colditz, G. A. (1999). Relation of peer and media influences to the development of purging behaviors among preadolescent and adolescent girls. *Archives of Pediatric Adolescent Medicine, 153,* 1184–1189.

Fischer, S., Smith, G., & Anderson, K. (2003). Clarifying the role of impulsivity in bulimia nervosa. *International Journal of Eating Disorders, 33,* 406–411.

Franko, D. L., Wonderlich, S. A., Little, D., & Herzog, D. B. (2004). Diagnosis and classification of eating disorders. In J. K. Thompson (Ed.), *Handbook of eating disorders and obesity.* Hoboken, NJ: Wiley.

Garfinkel, P., Modlofsky, H., & Garner, D. (1980). The heterogeneity of anorexia nervosa: Bulimia as a distinct subgroup. *Archives of General Psychiatry, 37,* 1036–1040.

Garfinkel, P. E., Lin, E., Goering, P., Spegg, C., Goldbloom, D. S., Kennedy, S., et al. (1995). Bulimia nervosa in a Canadian community sample: Prevalence and comparison of subgroups. *American Journal of Psychiatry, 152,* 1052–1058.

Garfinkel, P. E., & Newman, A. (2001). The Eating Attitudes Test: Twenty-five years later. *Eating and Weight Disorders, 6,* 1–24.

Garner, D., Olmstead, M., & Polivy, J. (1983). Development and validation of a multidimensional eating disorder inventory for anorexia nervosa and bulimia. *International Journal of Eating Disorders, 2,* 15–34.

Garner, D. M. (1991). *Eating Disorder Inventory-2 manual.* Odessa FL: Psychological Assessment Resources.

Garner, D. M. (1993). Binge eating in anorexia nervosa. In C. G. Fairburn & G. T. Wilson (Eds.), *Binge eating: Nature, assessment, and treatment* (pp. 50–76). New York: Guilford Press.

Garner, D. M., & Garfinkel, P. (1979). The Eating Attitudes Test: An index of the symptoms of anorexia nervosa. *Psychological Medicine, 9,* 273–279.

Garner, D. M., Garfinkel, P. E., & O'Shaughnessy, M. (1985). The validity of the distinction between bulimia with and without anorexia nervosa. *American Journal of Psychiatry, 142,* 581–582.

Garner, D. M., Olmsted, M. P., Davis, R., Rockert, W., Goldbloom, D., & Eagle, M. (1990). The association between bulimic symptoms and reported psychopathology. *International Journal of Eating Disorders, 9,* 1–15.

Gartner, A., Marcus, R., Halmi, K., & Loranger, A. D. (1989). *DSM-III-R* PDs in patients with eating disorders. *American Journal of Psychiatry, 146,* 1585–1591.

Geller, J., Cockell, S. J., & Goldner, E. M. (2000). Inhibited expression of negative emotions and interpersonal orientation in anorexia nervosa. *International Journal of Eating Disorders, 28,* 8–19.

Ghaderi, A., & Scott, B. (2000). The Big Five and eating disorders: A prospective study in the general population. *European Journal of Personality, 14,* 311–323.

Gillberg, I. C., Rastam, M., & Gillberg, C. (1995). Anorexia nervosa 6 years after onset: 1. Personality disorders. *Comprehensive Psychiatry, 35,* 61–69.

Goldner, E., Srikameswaran, S., Schroeder, M., Livesley, W. J., & Birmingham, C. L. (1999). Dimensional assessment of personality pathology in patients with eating disorders. *Psychiatry Research, 85,* 151–159.

Gomez, J., & Dally, P. (1980). Psychometric rating in the assessment of progress in anorexia nervosa. *British Journal of Psychiatry, 136,* 290–296.

Goodrick, G. K., Poston, W. S., Kimball, K. T., Reeves, R. S., & Foreyt, J. P. (1998). Nondieting versus dieting treatments for overweight binge-eating women. *Journal of Consulting and Clinical Psychology, 66,* 363–368.

Grilo, C., Devlin, M., Cachelin, F., & Yanovski, S. (1997). Report of the National Institutes of Health (NIH) workshop on the development of research priorities in eating disorders. *Psychopharmacology Bulletin, 33,* 321–333.

Grilo, C. M., Sanislow, C. A., Shea, M. T., Skodol, A. E., Stout, R. L., Pagano, M. E., et al. (2003). The natural course of bulimia nervosa and eating disorder not otherwise specified is not influenced by personality disorders. *International Journal of Eating Disorders, 34,* 319–330.

Gupta, M. A., Gupta, A. K., & Haberman, H. F. (1987). Dermatologic signs in anorexia nervosa and bulimia nervosa. *Archives of Dermatology, 123,* 1386–1390.

Halmi, K., Eckert, E., Marchi, P., Sampugnaro, V., Apple, R., & Cohen, J. (1991). Comorbidity of psychiatric diagnoses in anorexia nervosa. *Archives of General Psychiatry, 48,* 712–718.

Halmi, K., Sunday, S., Klump, K., Strober, M., Leckman, J., Fichter, M., et al. (2003). Obsessions and compulsions in anorexia nervosa subtypes. *International Journal of Eating Disorders, 33,* 308–319.

Halmi, K., Sunday, S., Strober, M., Kaplan, A., Woodside, D., Fichter, M., et al. (2000). Perfectionism in anorexia nervosa: Variation by clinical subtype, obsessionality, and pathological eating behavior. *American Journal of Psychiatry, 157,* 1799–1805.

Heaven, P., Mulligan, K., Merrilees, R., Woods, T., & Fairooz, Y. (2001). Neuroticism and conscientiousness as predictors of emotional, external, and restrained eating behaviors. *International Journal of Eating Disorders, 30,* 161–166.

Herpertz-Dahlmann, B., Müller, B., Herpertz, S., Heussen, N., Hebebrand, J., & Remschmidt, H. (2001). Prospective 10-year follow-up in adolescent anorexia nervosa: Course, outcome, psychiatric comorbidity, and psychosocial adaptation. *Journal of Child Psychology and Psychiatry, 42,* 603–612.

Herzog, D., Keller, M., Sacks, N., Yeh, C., & Lavori, P. (1992). Psychiatric comorbidity in treatment-seeking anorexics and bulimics. *Journal of the American Academy of Child & Adolescent Psychiatry, 31,* 810–818.

Herzog, D. B., Greenwood, D. N., Dorer, D. J., Flores, A. T., Ekeblad, E. R., Richards, A., et al. (2000). Mortality in eating disorders: A descriptive study. *International Journal of Eating Disorders, 28,* 20–26.

Herzog, D. B., Hopkins, J., & Burns, C. D. (1993). A follow-up study of 33 subdiagnostic eating disordered women. *International Journal of Eating Disorders, 14,* 261–267.

Hilsenroth, M., Ackerman, S., Blagys, M., Baity, M., & Mooney, M. (2003). Short-term psychodynamic psychotherapy for depression: An evaluation of statistical, clinically significant, and technique specific change. *Journal of Nervous and Mental Disease, 191,* 349–357.

Hinney, A., Bornscheuer, A., Depenbusch, M., Mierke, B., Tolle, A., Middeke, K., et al. (1998). No evidence for involvement of the leptin gene in anorexia nervosa, bulimia nervosa, underweight or early onset extreme obesity: Identification of two novel mutations in the coding sequence and a novel polymorphism in the leptin gene linked upstream region. *Molecular Psychiatry, 3,* 539–543.

Hinney, A., Schmidt, A., Nottebom, K., Heibult, O., Becker, I., Ziegler, A., et al. (1999). Several mutations in the melanocortin-4 receptor gene including a nonsense and a frameshift mutation associated with dominantly inherited obesity in humans. *Journal of Clinical Endocrinology and Metabolism, 84,* 1483–1486.

Hsu, L., Kaye, W., & Weltzin, T. (1993). Are the eating disorders related to obsessive compulsive disorder? *International Journal of Eating Disorders, 14,* 305–318.

Hudson, J., Pope, H., Jonas, J., & Yurgelun-Todd, D. (1983). Family history study of anorexia nervosa and bulimia. *British Journal of Psychiatry, 142,* 133–138.

Hudson, J., Pope, H., Jonas, J., Yurgelun-Todd, D., & Frankenburg, F. (1987). A controlled family history study of bulimia. *Psychological Medicine, 17,* 883–890.

Johnson, C., Tobin, D. L., & Dennis, D. L. (1990). Differences in treatment outcome between borderline and nonborderline bulimics at one-year follow-up. *International Journal of Eating Disorders, 9*(6), 617–627.

Johnson, C., Tobin, D. L., & Enright, A. (1989). Prevalence and clinical characteristics of borderline patients in an eating disordered population. *Journal of Clinical Psychiatry, 50,* 9–15.

Johnson, J., Cohen, P., Kotler, L., Kasen, S., & Brook, J. (2002). Psychiatric disorders associated with risk for the development of eating disorders during adolescence and early adulthood. *Journal of Consulting Clinical Psychology, 70,* 1119–1128.

Johnson, J. G., Cohen, P., Kasen, S., & Brook, J. S. (2002). Eating disorders during adolescence and the risk for physical and mental disorders during early adulthood. *Archives of General Psychiatry, 59,* 545–552.

Kaye, W., Nagata, T., Weltzin, T., Hsu, L. K., Sokol, M. S., McConaha, C., et al. (2001). Double-blind placebo-controlled administration of fluoxetine in restricting and restricting-purging-type anorexia nervosa. *Biology of Psychiatry, 49,* 644–652.

Kaye, W. H., Klump, K. L., Frank, G. K., & Strober, M. (2000). Anorexia and bulimia nervosa. *Annual Review of Medicine, 51,* 299–313.

Killen, J., Taylor, C., Hayward, C., Wilson, D., Haydel, F., Hammer, L., et al. (1994). Pursuit of thinness and onset of eating disorder symptoms in a community sample of adolescent girls: A three-year prospective analysis. *International Journal of Eating Disorders, 16,* 227–238.

Killen, J. D., Taylor, C. B., Hayward, C., Haydel, K. F., Wilson, D. M., Hammer, L., et al. (1996). Weight concerns influence the development of eating disorders: A 4-year prospective study. *Journal of Consulting and Clinical Psychology, 64,* 936–940.

Klump, K., Bulik, C., Pollice, C., Halmi, K., Fichter, M., Berrettini, W., et al. (2000). Temperament and character in women with anorexia nervosa. *The Journal of Nervous and Mental Disease, 188,* 559–567.

Kreipe, R. E., & Harris, J. P. (1992). Myocardial impairment resulting from eating disorders. *Pediatric Annals, 21,* 760–768.

Lacey, J., & Evans, C. (1986). The impulsivist: A multi-impulsive personality disorder. *British Journal of Addiction, 81,* 641–649.

Le Grange, D., Eisler, I., Dare, C., & Russell, G. (1992). Evaluation of family treatments in adolescent anorexia nervosa: A pilot study. *International Journal of Eating Disorders, 12,* 347–357.

Leung, F., Schwartzman, A., & Steiger, H. (1996). Testing a dual-process family model in understanding the development of eating pathology: A structural equation modeling analysis. *International Journal of Eating Disorders, 20,* 367–375.

Lewinsohn, P. M., Hops, H., Roberts, R. E., Seeley, J. R., & Andrews, J. A. (1993). Adolescent psychopathology: I. Prevalence and incidence of depression and other *DSM-II-R* disorders in high school students. *Journal of Abnormal Psychology, 102,* 133–144.

Lewinsohn, P. M., Striegel-Moore, R. H., & Seeley, J. R. (2000). Epidemiology and natural course of eating disorders in young women from adolescence to young adulthood. *Journal of the American Academy of Child & Adolescent Psychiatry, 39,* 1284–1292.

Lilenfeld, L. R. R., Wonderlich, S. A., Riso, L. P. L., Crosby, R. D., & Mitchell, J. E. (2004). Eating disorders and personality: A methodological and empirical review. Manuscript submitted for publication.

Luce, K. H., & Crowther, J. H. (1999). The reliability of the Eating Disorder Examination–Self-Report Questionnaire version (EDE-Q). *International Journal of Eating Disorders, 25,* 349–351.

Marcus, M. D., Wing, R. R., Ewing, L., Kern, E., Gooding, W., & McDermott, M. (1996). Psychiatric disorders among obese binge eaters. *International Journal of Eating Disorders, 9,* 69–77.

Marino, M., & Zanarini, M. (2001). Relationship between EDNOS and its subtypes and borderline PD. *International Journal of Eating Disorders, 29,* 349–353.

McCrae, R. R., & Costa, P. T. (1999). A Five-Factor Theory of personality. In L. A. Pervin & O. P. John (Eds.), *Handbook of personality: Theory and research* (2nd ed., pp. 139–153). New York: Guilford Press.

McKnight Investigators. (2003). Risk factors for the onset of eating disorders in adolescent girls: Results of the McKnight Longitudinal Risk Factor Study. *American Journal of Psychiatry, 160,* 248–254.

Metzger, E. D., Levine, J. M., McArdel, C. R., Wolfe, B. E., & Jimerson, D. C. (1999). Salivary gland enlargement and elevated serum amylase in bulimia nervosa. *Biological Psychiatry, 45,* 1520–1522.

Milos, G., Spindler, A., Hepp, U., & Schnyder, U. (2004). Suicide attempts and suicidal ideation: Links with psychiatric comorbidity in eating disorder subjects. *General Hospital Psychiatry, 26,* 129–135.

Mintz, L. B., O'Halloran, M. S., Mulholland, A. M., & Schneider, P. A. (1997). Questionnaire for eating disorder diagnoses: Reliability and validity of operationalizing *DSM-IV* criteria into a self-report format. *Journal of Counseling Psychology, 44,* 63–79.

Minuchin, S., Rosman, B., & Baker, I. (1978). *Psychosomatic families: Anorexia nervosa in context.* Cambridge, MA: Harvard University Press.

Mitchell, J. E., & Mussell, M. P. (1995). Comorbidity and binge eating disorder. *Addictive Behaviors, 20,* 725–732.

National Collaborating Centre for Mental Health. (2004). *Eating disorders: Core interventions in the treatment and management of anorexia nervosa, bulimia nervosa and related eating disorders. Clinical guideline 9.* London: National Institute for Clinical Excellence.

National Institute for Clinical Excellence. (2004). Eating Disorders: Core interventions in the treatment and management of anorexia nervosa, bulimia nervosa, and related eating disorders. Retrieved

October 21, 2004, from http://www.nice.org/uk/cg009NICE guideline

Newman, D. L., Moffitt, T. E., Caspi, A., Magdol, L., Silva, P. A., & Stanton, W. R. (1996). Psychiatric disorder in a birth cohort of young adults: Prevalence, comorbidity, clinical significance, and new case incidence from ages 11 to 21. *Journal of Consulting and Clinical Psychology, 64,* 552–562.

Nilsson, E., Gillberg, C., Gillberg, I., & Rastam, M. (1999). Ten-year follow-up of adolescent-onset anorexia nervosa: Personality disorders. *Journal of the American Academy of Child & Adolescent Psychiatry, 38,* 1389–1395.

Oltmanns, T. F., Melley, A. H., & Turkheimer, E. (2002). Impaired social functioning and symptoms of personality disorders assessed by peer and self-report in a nonclinical population. *Journal of Personality Disorders, 16*(5), 437–452.

Patton, G. C., Johnson-Sabine, E., Wood, K., Mann, A. H., & Wakeling, A. (1990). Abnormal eating attitudes in London schoolgirls—A prospective epidemiological study: Outcome at twelve month follow-up. *Psychological Medicine, 20,* 383–394.

Pike, K., Walsh, B., Vitousek, K., Wilson, G., & Bauer, J. (2003). Cognitive behavior therapy in the posthospitalization treatment of anorexia nervosa. *American Journal of Psychiatry, 160,* 2046–2049.

Podar, I., Hannus, A., & Allik, J. (1999). Personality and affectivity characteristics associated with eating disorders: A comparison of eating disordered, weight-preoccupied, and normal samples. *Journal of Personality Assessment, 73,* 133–147.

Polivy, J., & Herman, C. P. (1985). Dieting and binge eating: A causal analysis. *American Psychologist, 40,* 193–204.

Pomeroy, C. (2004). Assessment of medical status and physical factors. In K. Thompson (Ed.), *Handbook of eating disorders and obesity.* Hoboken, NJ: Wiley.

Pryor, T., & Wiederman, M. W. (1996). Use of the MMPI-2 in the outpatient assessment of women with anorexia nervosa or bulimia nervosa. *Journal of Personality Assessment, 66,* 363–373.

Rastam, M. (1992). Anorexia nervosa in 51 Swedish adolescents: Premorbid problems and comorbidity. *Journal of the American Academy of Child & Adolescent Psychiatry, 31,* 819–829.

Rastam, M., Gillberg, C., & Wentz, E. (2003). Outcome of teenage-onset anorexia nervosa in a Swedish community-based sample. *European Child and Adolescent Psychiatry, 12,* 178–190.

Rastam, M., Gillberg, I. C., & Gillberg, C. (1995). Anorexia nervosa 6 years after onset: II. Comorbid psychiatry problems. *Comprehensive Psychiatry, 35,* 70–76.

Reeves, R. S., McPherson, R. S., Nichaman, M. Z., Harrist, R. B., Foreyt, J. P., & Goodrick, G. K. (2001). Nutrient intake of obese female binge eaters. *Journal of the American Dietetic Association, 101,* 209–215.

Rizvi, S. L., Peterson, C. B., Crow, S. J., & Agras, W. S. (2000). Test-retest reliability of the eating disorder examination. *International Journal of Eating Disorders, 28,* 311–316.

Rosenbaum, M., Leibel, R., & Hirsch, J. (1997). Obesity. *New England Journal of Medicine, 337,* 396–407.

Rosenvinge, J., Martinussen, M., & Ostensen, E. (2000). The comorbidity of eating disorders and personality disorders: A meta analytic review of studies published between 1983 and 1988. *Eating and Weight Disorders, 5,* 52–61.

Rossiter, E. M., Agras, W. S., Telch, C. F., & Schneider, J. A. (1993). Cluster B personality disorder characteristics predict outcome in the treatment of bulimia nervosa. *International Journal of Eating Disorders, 13,* 349–357.

Rothenberg, A. (1986). Eating disorder as a modern obsessive-compulsive syndrome. *Journal for the Study of Interpersonal Processes, 49,* 45–53.

Rubenstein, C., Altemus, M., Pigott, T., Hess, A., & Murphy, D. (1995). Symptom overlap between OCD and bulimia nervosa. *Journal of Anxiety Disorders, 9,* 1–9.

Rybicki, D., Lepkowsky, C., & Arndt, S. (1989). An empirical assessment of bulimic patients using multiple measures. *Addictive Behaviors, 14,* 249–260.

Safer, D., Telch, C., & Agras, W. (2001). Dialectical behavior therapy for bulimia nervosa. *American Journal of Psychiatry, 158,* 632–634.

Santonastaso, P., Friederici, S., & Favaro, A. (1999). Full and partial syndromes in eating disorders: A 1-year prospective study of risk factors among female students. *Psychopathology, 32,* 50–56.

Schulze, U. M. E., Pettke-Rank, C. V., Kreienkamp, M., Hamm, H., Bröcker, E. B., Wewetzer, C., et al. (1999). Dermatologic findings in anorexia and bulimia nervosa of childhood and adolescence. *Pediatric Dermatology, 16,* 90–94.

Segal, D. L., Hersen, M., & Van Hasselt, V. B. (1994). Reliability of the structured clinical interview for *DSM-III-R:* An evaluative review. *Comprehensive Psychiatry, 35,* 316–327.

Seivewright, H., Tyrer, P., & Johnson, T. (2004). Persistent social dysfunction in anxious and depressed patients with personality disorder. *Acta Psychiatrica Scandinavica, 109,* 104–109.

Shafran, R., Fairburn, C., Robinson, P., & Lask, B. (2004). Body checking and its avoidance in eating disorders. *International Journal of Eating Disorders, 35,* 93–101.

Shedler, J., & Westen, D. (2004). Refining *DSM-IV* personality disorder diagnosis: Integrating science and practice. *American Journal of Psychiatry, 161,* 1–16.

Skodol, A., Oldham, J., Hyler, S., Kellman, H., Doidge, N., & Davies, M. (1993). Comorbidity of *DSM-III-R* eating disorders and personality disorders. *International Journal of Eating Disorders, 14,* 403–416.

Slade, P. (1982). Towards a functional analysis of anorexia nervosa and bulimia nervosa. *British Journal of Clinical Psychology, 14,* 167–179.

Smart, D., Beumont, P., & George, G. (1976). Some personality characteristics of patients with anorexia nervosa. *British Journal of Psychiatry, 128,* 57–60.

Sohlberg, S., Norring, C., Holmgren, S., & Rosmark, B. (1989). Impulsivity and long-term prognosis of psychiatric patients with anorexia nervosa/bulimia nervosa. *Journal of Nervous & Mental Disease, 177,* 249–258.

Spitzer, R. L., Devlin, M., Walsh, B. T., Hasin, D., Wing, R., Marcus, M., et al. (1992). Binge eating disorder: A multisite field trial of the diagnostic criteria. *International Journal of Eating Disorders, 11,* 191–203.

Spitzer, R. L., Williams, J. B., Gibbon, M., & First, M. B. (1990). *Structured Clinical Interview for DSM-III-R (SCID).* Washington, DC: American Psychiatric Press.

Srinivasagam, N., Kaye, W., Plotnicov, K., Greeno, C., Weltzin, T., & Rao, R. (1995). Persistent perfectionism, symmetry, and exactness after long-term recovery from anorexia nervosa. *American Journal of Psychiatry, 152,* 1630–1634.

Steiger, H., & Stotland, S. (1996). Prospective study of outcome in bulimics as a function of Axis-II comorbidity: Long-term responses on eating and psychiatric symptoms. *International Journal of Eating Disorders, 20,* 149–161.

Steinhausen, H. (2002). The outcome of anorexia nervosa in the 20th century. *American Journal of Psychiatry, 159,* 1284–1293.

Stice, E. (2001). A prospective test of the dual pathway model of bulimic pathology: Mediating effects of dieting and negative affect. *Journal of Abnormal Psychology, 110,* 124–135.

Stice, E. (2002). Risk and maintenance factors for eating pathology: A meta-analytic review. *Psychological Bulletin, 128,* 825–848.

Stice, E., Burton, E. M., & Shaw, H. (2004). Prospective relations between bulimic pathology, depression, and substance abuse: Unpacking comorbidity in adolescent girls. *Journal of Consulting and Clinical Psychology, 72,* 62–71.

Stice, E., Cameron, R., Killen, J. D., Hayward, C., & Taylor, C. B. (1999). Naturalistic weight reduction efforts prospectively predict growth in relative weight and onset of obesity among female adolescents. *Journal of Consulting and Clinical Psychology, 67,* 967–974.

Stice, E., & Fairburn, C. (2003). Dietary and dietary-depressive subtypes of bulimia nervosa show differential symptom presentation, social impairment, comorbidity, and course of illness. *Journal of Consulting and Clinical Psychology, 71,* 1090–1094.

Stice, E., Fisher, M., & Martinez, E. (2004). Eating disorder diagnostic scale: Additional evidence of reliability and validity. *Psychological Assessment, 16,* 60–71.

Stice, E., Killen, J. D., Hayward, C., & Taylor, C. B. (1998). Age of onset for binge eating and purging during adolescence: A four-year survival analysis. *Journal of Abnormal Psychology, 107,* 671–675.

Stice, E., Presnell, K., & Bearman, S. K. (2004). *Risk factors for onset of threshold and subthreshold bulimia nervosa: A 4-year prospective study of adolescent girls.* Manuscript submitted for publication.

Stice, E., Presnell, K., & Spangler, D. (2002). Risk factors for binge eating onset: A prospective investigation. *Health Psychology, 21,* 131–138.

Stice, E., Telch, C. F., & Rizvi, S. L. (2000). A psychometric evaluation of the Eating Disorder Diagnostic Screen: A brief self-report measure for anorexia, bulimia, and binge eating disorder. *Psychological Assessment, 12,* 123–131.

Strassberg, D., Ross, S., & Todt, E. (1995). MMPI performance among women with bulimia: A cluster analytic study. *Addictive Behaviors, 29,* 137–140.

Striegel-Moore, R. H., Seeley, J. R., & Lewinsohn, P. M. (2003). Psychosocial adjustment in young adulthood of women who experience an eating disorder during adolescence. *American Academy of Child and Adolescent Psychiatry, 42,* 587–593.

Striegel-Moore, R. H., Wilfley, D. E., Pike, K. M., Dohm, F. A., & Fairburn, C. G. (2000). Recurrent binge eating in Black American women. *Archives of Family Medicine, 9,* 83–87.

Strober, M. (1980). Personality and symptomological features in young, nonchronic anorexia nervosa patients. *Journal of Psychosomatic Research, 24,* 353–359.

Strober, M. (1981). The significance of bulimia in juvenile anorexia nervosa: An exploration of possible etiologic factors. *International Journal of Eating Disorders, 1,* 28–43.

Strober, M., Freeman, R., & Morrell, W. (1997). The long-term course of severe anorexia nervosa in adolescents: Survival analysis of recovery, relapse, and outcome predictors over 10–15 years in a prospective study. *International Journal of Eating Disorders, 22,* 179–186.

Stunkard, A. J. (2002). Binge-eating disorder and the night-eating syndrome. In T. A. Wadden & A. J. Stunkard (Eds.), *Handbook of obesity treatment.* New York: Guilford Press.

Stunkard, A. J., Berkowitz, R., Wadden, T., Tanrikut, C., Reiss, E., & Young, L. (1996). Binge eating disorder and the night eating syndrome. *International Journal of Obesity, 20,* 1–6.

Sunday, S., Peterson, C., Andreyka, K., Crow, S., Mitchell, J., & Halmi, K. (2001). Differences in *DSM-III-R* and *DSM-IV* diagnoses in eating disorder patients. *Comprehensive Psychiatry, 42,* 448–455.

Sunday, S. R., Reeman, I. M., Eckert, E., & Halmi, K. A. (1996). Ten-year outcome in adolescent onset anorexia nervosa. *Journal of Youth and Adolescence, 25,* 533–544.

Sutandar-Pinnock, K., Blake Woodside, D., Carter, J., Olmsted, M., & Kaplan, A. (2003). Perfectionism in anorexia nervosa: A 6–24-month follow-up study. *International Journal of Eating Disorders, 33,* 225–229.

Telch, C., & Stice, E. (1998). Psychiatric comorbidity in a nonclinical sample of women with binge eating disorder. *Journal of Consulting and Clinical Psychology, 66,* 768–776.

Thelen, M., Farmer, J., Wonderlich, S., & Smith, M. (1991). A revision of the Bulimia Test: The BULIT-R. *Psychological Assessment, 3,* 119–124.

Thompson-Brenner, H., Glass, S., & Westen, D. (2003). A multidimensional meta-analysis of psychotherapy for bulimia nervosa. *Clinical Psychology: Science and Practice, 10,* 269–287.

Thompson-Brenner, H., & Westen, D. (2003). *Mediators and moderators of outcome in a naturalistic study of bulimia nervosa: Therapeutic interventions, psychopathology, and personality.* Unpublished manuscript, Emory University.

Thompson-Brenner, H., & Westen, D. (2004). *Accumulating evidence for personality subtypes in eating disorders: Differences in comorbidity, adaptive functioning, treatment response, and treatment interventions in a naturalistic sample.* Manuscript submitted for publication.

Thompson-Brenner, H., & Westen, D. (2005). Personality subtypes in eating disorders: Validation of a classification in a naturalistic sample. *British Journal of Psychiatry, 186,* 516–524.

Thompson-Brenner, H., & Westen, D. (in press a). A naturalistic study of psychotherapy for bulimia nervosa, Part 1: Comorbidity and therapeutic outcome. *Journal of Nervous and Mental Disease.*

Thompson-Brenner, H., & Westen, D. (in press b). A naturalistic study of psychotherapy for bulimia nervosa, Part 2: Therapeutic interventions in the community. *Journal of Nervous and Mental Disease.*

Thornton, C., & Russell, J. (1997). Obsessive compulsive comorbidity in the dieting disorders. *International Journal of Eating Disorders, 21,* 83–87.

Tobin, D. L., & Johnson, C. L. (1991). The integration of psychodynamic and behavior therapy in the treatment of eating disorders: Clinical issues versus theoretical mystique. In C. L. Johnson (Ed.), *Psychodynamic treatment of anorexia nervosa and bulimia* (pp. 374–397). New York: Guilford Press.

Treasure, J., & Holland, A. (1989). Genetic vulnerability to eating disorders: Evidence from twin and family studies. In H. Remschmidt & M. H. Schmidt (Eds.), *Child and youth psychiatry: European perspectives* (pp. 59–68). New York: Hogrefe & Huber.

Tylka, T., & Subich, L. (1999). Exploring the construct validity of the eating disorder continuum. *Journal of Counseling Psychology, 46,* 268–276.

Vervaet, M., Audenaert, K., & van Heeringen, C. (2003). Cognitive and behavioural characteristics are associated with personality dimensions in patients with eating disorders. *European Eating Disorders Review, 11,* 363–378.

Vervaet, M., van Heeringen, C., & Audenaert, K. (2004). Personality-related characteristics in restricting versus bingeing and purging eating disordered. *Comprehensive Psychiatry, 45,* 37–43.

Vitousek, K., & Manke, F. (1994). Personality variables and disorders in anorexia nervosa and bulimia nervosa. *Journal of Abnormal Psychology, 103,* 137–147.

Vogeltanz-Holm, N. D., Wonderlich, S. A., Lewis, B. A., Wilsnack, S. C., Harris, T. R., Wilsnack, R. W., et al. (2000). Longitudinal predictors of binge eating, intense dieting, and weight concerns in a national sample of women. *Behavior Therapy, 31,* 221–235.

Waller, D. A., Gullion, C. M., Petty, F., Hardy, B. W., Murdock, M., & Rush, J. (1993). Tridimensional Personality Questionnaire and serotonin in bulimia nervosa. *Psychiatry Research, 48,* 9–15.

Waller, G., Dickson, C., & Ohanian, V. (2002). Cognitive content in bulimic disorders: Core beliefs and eating attitudes. *Eating Behaviors, 3,* 171–178.

Waller, G., Ohanian, V., Meyer, C., & Osman, S. (2000). Cognitive content among bulimic women: The role of core beliefs. *International Journal of Eating Disorders, 28,* 235–241.

Walsh, B. T. (1993). Binge eating in bulimia nervosa. In C. G. Fairburn & G. T. Wilson (Eds.), *Binge eating: Nature, assessment, and treatment* (pp. 37–49). New York: Guilford Press.

Walters, E., & Kendler, K. (1995). Anorexia nervosa and anorexic-like syndromes in a population-based female twin sample. *American Journal of Psychiatry, 152,* 64–71.

Westen, D. (1991). Social cognition and object relations. *Psychological Bulletin, 109,* 429–455.

Westen, D., & Harnden-Fischer, J. (2001). Personality profiles in eating disorders: Rethinking the distinction between Axis I and Axis II. *American Journal of Psychiatry, 165,* 547–562.

Westen, D., Novotny, C., & Thompson-Brenner, H. (2004). The empirical status of empirically supported therapies: Assumptions, methods, and findings. *Psychological Bulletin, 130,* 631–663.

Wilfley, D. E., Dounchis, J. Z., & Welch, R. R. (2000). Interpersonal psychotherapy. In K. J. Miller & J. S. Mizes (Eds.), *Comparative treatments for eating disorders* (pp. 128–282). New York: Springer.

Wilfley, D. E., Schwartz, M. H., Spurrell, E. B., & Fairburn, C. G. (2000). Using the eating disorder examination to identify specific psychopathology of binge eating disorder. *International Journal of Eating Disorders, 27,* 259–269.

Williams, J. B., Gibbon, M., First, M. B., Spitzer, R. L., Davies, M., Borus, J., et al. (1992). The Structured Clinical Interview for *DSM-III-R* (SCID) II: Multisite test-retest reliability. *Archives of General Psychiatry, 49,* 630–363.

Williamson, D. A., Anderson, D. A., Jackman, L. P., & Jackson, S. R. (1995). Assessment of eating disordered thoughts, feelings, and behaviors. In D. B. Allison (Ed.), *Handbook of assessment methods for eating behaviors and weight-related problems: Measures, theory, and research* (pp. 347–386). Thousand Oaks, CA: Sage.

Wilson, G., Becker, C. B., & Heffernan, K. (2003). Eating disorders. In E. J. Mash & R. A. Barkley (Eds.), *Child psychopathology* (2nd ed., pp. 687–715). New York: Guilford Press.

Wilson, G., & Fairburn, C. G. (1998). Treatments for eating disorders. In P. E. Nathan & J. M. Gorman (Eds.), *A guide to treatments that work* (pp. 501–530). London: Oxford University Press.

Wonderlich, S., Swift, W., Slotnik, H., & Goodman, S. (1990). *DSM-III-R* personality disorders in eating-disorder subtypes. *International Journal of Eating Disorders, 9,* 607–616.

Wonderlich, S. A., Fullerton, D., Swift, W. J., & Klein, M. H. (1994). Five-year outcome from eating disorders: Relevance of personality disorders. *International Journal of Eating Disorders, 15,* 233–243.

Woodside, D., Bulik, C., Halmi, K., Fichter, M., Kaplan, A., Berrettini, W., et al. (2002). Personality, perfectionism, and attitudes towards eating in parents of individuals with eating disorder. *International Journal of Eating Disorders, 31,* 290–299.

World Health Organization. (1993). *The ICD-10 Classification of Mental and Behavioural Disorders: Diagnostic criteria for research.* Geneva, Switzerland: Author.

Yanovski, S. Z., Leet, M., Yanovski, J. A., Flood, M., Gold, P. W., Kissileff, H. R., et al. (1992). Food selection and intake of obese women with binge eating disorder. *American Journal of Clinical Nutrition, 56,* 975–980.

Zittel, C., & Westen, D. (in press). Borderline personality disorder as seen in clinical practice: Implications for *DSM-V. American Journal of Psychiatry.*

CHAPTER 24

Psychophysiological Disorders: Headache as a Case in Point

FRANK ANDRASIK

DESCRIPTION OF THE DISORDER AND CLINICAL PICTURE

A number of medical conditions can be triggered, exacerbated, or maintained by various psychological factors. That this is so was first acknowledged in the third edition of the *Diagnostic and Statistical Manual of Mental Disorders* (*DSM-III;* American Psychiatric Association, 1980), when the diagnosis of "psychophysiological disorders" was subsumed under the descriptor *psychological factors affecting medical conditions* (Williamson, Barker, & Lapour, 1994). It remains so designated in the text revision of the fourth edition (*DSM-IV-TR;* American Psychiatric Association, 2000). The defining feature of psychological factors affecting medical condition is the presence of one or more identifiable psychological or behavioral factors that adversely affect the condition. These factors may come into play in various ways. The factors (1) can influence the course of the condition, as evidenced by a close temporal association between the factor and the development, exacerbation, or delayed recovery from the condition; (2) may interfere with appropriate treatment; (3) may constitute an additional health risk (e.g., chronic overeating in someone whose diabetes is weight related); and (4) may precipitate or exacerbate symptoms by creating stress-related physiological responses (e.g., causing bronchospasms in asthmatics). The psychological or behavioral factors that influence the general medical condition may be a diagnosable Axis I or Axis II disorder. In many situations, however, they do not meet the full criteria for a specific mental disorder, are maladaptive health behaviors, or are physiological reactions to varied stressors (environmental or social).

It could be argued that psychological or behavioral factors are present in nearly every medical condition or major category of disease (cardiovascular, dermatologic, endocrinologic, gastrointestinal, neoplastic, neurological, pulmonary, renal, and rheumatologic conditions). This category is reserved, however, for use when there is reasonable evidence that these factors have a pronounced clinical effect on the outcome or course of the condition or place the person at significantly elevated risk for an untoward outcome.

The psychological factor affecting medical condition is coded on Axis I, whereas the medical condition is coded on Axis III. More descriptive specifiers are chosen from the following: (1) mental disorder affecting [indicate the general medical condition; e.g., the Axis I or Axis II disorder]; (2) psychological symptoms affecting . . . (e.g., symptoms of anxiety contribute to the severity of irritable bowel syndrome); (3) personality traits or coping style affecting . . . (e.g., the type A behavior pattern and coronary artery disease); (4) maladaptive health behaviors affecting . . . (e.g., unsafe sexual practices, sedentary lifestyle, excessive use of illicit substances); (5) stress-related physiological response affecting . . . (e.g., stressors precipitate chest pain or heart rate fluctuations in a patient diagnosed with coronary artery disease); and (6) other or unspecified factors affecting . . . (i.e., a factor that is significant but is not addressed in the preceding). Conditions to rule out consist of substance use disorders and the varied somatoform disorders.

This chapter addresses psychophysiological disorders and focuses on recurrent headache as an exemplar because it is the most common disorder in this diagnostic grouping and has been the focus of extensive investigations. The major thrust will be the primary headache types of migraine and tension-type (Headache Classification Subcommittee of the International Headache Society, 2004). Among all diseases worldwide that cause disability, migraine is ranked 19th by the World Health Organization. Migraine consists of two major subtypes: with and without aura. Migraine without aura is the most common, having a higher attack frequency and a greater level of disability. The prototypical migraine consists of a unilateral pain that is sudden in onset, pulsating in nature, and that fairly quickly reaches a pain intensity that is judged to be moderate to severe. It is often accompanied by gastrointestinal distress, photophobia (light sensitivity), and phonophobia (sound sensitivity). The attack may be brief (4 hours or so) or extended (72 hours if untreated or unsuccessfully treated). Some individuals experience a premonitory phase that can occur hours or days before the headache attack and a resolution phase. Symptoms experienced during the premonitory and resolution phases include hyper- or hypoactivity, depression, craving for particular foods, and repetitive yawning, among others. In younger children, the symptom presentation may depart from that described previously (headache may be more frequent but the duration is briefer; headache may be experienced bilaterally instead of unilaterally).

The auras that precede the other subtype of migraine typically develop gradually over 5 to 20 minutes and last for less than 60 minutes. The aura is a complex of fully reversible neurological symptoms, including visual (e.g., flickering lights, gaps in the visual field), sensory (i.e., numbness and feelings of pins and needles), and dysphasic speech disturbances. Additional premonitory symptoms may include fatigue, difficulty concentrating, neck stiffness, photo- and phonophobia, nausea, blurred vision, and pallor. The auras occur in about 10 percent to 15 percent of migraines.

Tension-type is the most common primary headache type, with a lifetime prevalence ranging from 30 percent to 78 percent. Surprisingly, it has received less research attention in the literature. The prototypical tension-type headache occurs frequently, in episodes lasting minutes to days. The pain is typically bilateral, pressing or tightening in nature, and of mild to moderate intensity. Nausea is absent, but photo- or phonophobia may be present. Current classification schemes distinguish between (1) infrequent (at least 10 episodes occurring on less than 1 day per month or 12 days per year on average), (2) frequent (at least 10 episodes occurring on 1 or more but less than 15 days per month for at least 3 months), and (3) chronic forms (occurring on 15 or more days per month on average for more than 3 months) of tension-type headache, and each of these is further subdivided for the presence or absence of pericranial tenderness (identified by manual palpation). The frequency distinction is important because, all things remaining equal, the greater the frequency the poorer the treatment response.

PERSONALITY DEVELOPMENT AND PSYCHOPATHOLOGY

Associations between headache and a variety of personality characteristics and somatic and psychiatric conditions have been described in the literature since headaches were first recognized as distinct syndromes. These associations were based primarily on anecdotal or uncontrolled observations from clinical case series. Persons with migraine and tension headache were thusly described as being rigid, obsessional, hostile, ambitious, perfectionistic, compulsive, angry (primarily repressed), anxious, socially fearful, depressed, and dependent, with unresolved psychosexual conflicts (Adler, Adler, & Packard, 1987; Anderson, 1980; Packard, 1987). Harold G. Wolff (1937), one of the pioneers in headache research, coined the term *migraine personality,* a term that went unchallenged for decades. More well-controlled studies have failed to find a specific headache-prone personality type. However, there are important associations between various medical disorders and anxiety and depressive disorders.

Merikangas and Rasmussen (2000) extensively reviewed the literature investigating the comorbidity of migraine and a number of medical disorders. They rated the strength of the evidence on a scale of + (low) to + + + (high). The strongest associations were found for migraine and allergies, depression, anxiety, and stroke. Intermediate in strength were the relationship between migraine and asthma, mitral valve prolapse, hypotension, hypertension, colitis, irritable bowel, ulcers, and epilepsy. Only a weak association was found between migraine and myocardial infarction.

The relationship between migraine and anxiety and depression merits further discussion. To date, a number of well-controlled examinations have been conducted in both clinical and community settings, both with migraine serving as the index disorder for which participants sought treatment and the converse (anxiety or depression were the index disorder). Merikangas and Rasmussen (2000), upon reviewing these studies, note a fairly remarkable consistency of findings, despite the studies using varied participant characteristics, geographical sites, and assessment criteria; suggesting that sampling is not a source of bias. Odds ratios have ranged from 2.2 to 3.6 between migraine and depression and from 1.9 to 5.3 between migraine and anxiety. The evidence for an association between migraine and bipolar spectrum disorder (major depression with either manic or hypomanic episodes), these authors note, is particularly strong.

Two longitudinal studies have examined order of onset of migraine, depression, and anxiety. From data obtained with a cohort of young adults in Zurich, Switzerland, onset of anxiety preceded that of migraine in approximately 80 percent of cases that were comorbid, whereas onset of depression followed that of migraine in about 75 percent of cases that were comorbid (Merikangas, Angst, & Isler, 1990). A follow-up investigation of children and adolescents in Detroit, Michigan, revealed associations of similar magnitude as well as the same order of onset: anxiety appearing first, migraine second, followed by depression in adulthood (Breslau, Merikangas, & Bowden, 1994). A subsequent investigation revealed a bidirectional relationship between migraine and depression; the presence of each increased the risk for first onset of the other (Breslau et al., 1994). These findings have led researchers to speculate that migraine, anxiety, and depression may result from a partially shared diathesis (disturbances in the same neurochemical systems; Merikangas & Rasmussen, 2000).

The literature examining associations between tension-type headache and personality and psychopathology, although perhaps not as comprehensive as that for migraine, has taken a different path. Here the chief focus has been upon the role of stress, which has been a focus for many decades. The hypothesis that stress is casually related to pain is plausible based on pain theories. Melzack (1999) has discussed the integrated relationship between stress and pain in detail. Prolonged activation of the stress system, resulting in high levels of cortisol, is related to a number of physiological changes that can produce pain. Stress is also directly linked to negative affect, which in turn influences pain, including headache (Fernandez, 2002). Therefore, there are strong arguments for closely investigating the link between stress and varied pain syndromes. Wittrock and Myers (1998) and more recently Andrasik, Wittrock, and Passchier (2005) have systematically examined the literature bearing on the role of stress in tension-type headache. These reviews have been guided by a model that incorporates the transactional model of stress (Lazarus & Folkman, 1984) and adds to it the role that pain itself plays in the experience of headache, especially when it is of a chronic, unremitting nature. Briefly, the model begins with the occurrence of an event that is potentially stressful. Emphasis is on *potential* because stress is experienced in an idiosyncratic manner; it rests within an individual's cognitive interpretive framework. If an event is judged to be both relevant and a threat, then a coping response is required. Unsuccessful attempts at coping lead to physiological arousal and pain. Onset of pain can lead to further negative appraisals, which then intensify attendant pain, promote further, perhaps more desperate, efforts to cope, and ultimately exacerbate headache.

This model suggests five possible roles that stress might play with respect to tension-type headache: (1) people with headache may be exposed more frequently to stressful events; (2) people with headache may be more likely to appraise situations as stressful; (3) people with headache may show increased physiological reactivity to stress; (4) people with tension-type headache may have an increased sensitivity to pain and/or a decreased threshold for pain; and (5) people with headache may cope with stress in a way that increases its impact. The most consistent support to date is for hypotheses 2, 4, and 5.

EPIDEMIOLOGY

Carefully designed, large-scale investigations of the epidemiology of pain conditions were relatively scarce until the 1990s (Chojnowska & Stannard, 2003). Recognition of this led the International Association for the Study of Pain (IASP) to appoint a task force to conduct a systematic, critical, interdisciplinary review of the extant literature and to identify problems and pitfalls, with the hopes of improving future investigations. The published report of the IASP Task Force (Crombie, Croft, Linton, LeResche, & Von Korff, 1999) reviewed a diverse array of acute and recurrent pain conditions: phantom limb, chronic postsurgical, fibromyalgia, central poststroke, facial, temporomandibular disorder, neck, shoulder, knee, low back, and headache—the focus of this chapter.

Headache is a clinical syndrome affecting more than 90 percent of the population at some time during their life, resulting in it being considered a major public health issue (Mannix, 2001). It is the seventh leading presenting complaint in ambulatory care in the United States, accounting for about 18 million office visits a year (Barret, 1996). The two most common forms of headache are migraine, experienced by about 18 percent of females and 7 percent of males, and tension-type headache, experienced by about 40 percent of the population at any point in time (Mannix, 2001). Migraine incidence is higher among women than men at every age, except in the very young (Bille, 1962; Lipton, Diamond, Reed, Diamond, & Stewart, 2001). Migraine peaks in the third and fourth decades of life (Lipton et al., 2001). Tension-type headache, as noted previously, is far more common than migraine, with a lifetime prevalence of nearly 80 percent (Jensen, 1999). As with migraine, tension-type headache peaks in the third and fourth decades, and females reveal higher rates of occurrence. The female preponderance is greater for chronic than for episodic forms of tension-type headache (Schwartz, Stewart, Simon, & Lipton, 1998).

Although most headaches are relatively benign, for 1 percent to 3 percent of patients the etiology can be life threatening (Evans, 2001). Consequently, nonphysician practitioners are urged to refer all headache patients to a physician who is experienced with evaluating headache, then to maintain a close collaboration during treatment as necessary. Even after arranging a medical evaluation, the nonphysician therapist must be continually alert for evidence of a developing underlying physical problem.

ETIOLOGY

The prevailing model accounting for all forms of chronic pain, including headache, is best termed as the *biomedical model,* and it is characterized as viewing pain as a direct transmission of impulses from the periphery to structures within the central nervous system (Turk & Flor, 1999). This model has led to a number of important insights into pathophysiological mechanisms and development of medical procedures and pharmacological agents designed to modify identified aberrant aspects. This model, at the same time, has a number of limitations and has difficulty explaining observations like the following: (1) pain that continues when pathology cannot be identified, (2) pathology that exists in the absence of pain, (3) the varied individual responses to seemingly identical treatments, (4) the failure of potent medications to provide consistent levels of pain relief, and (5) the lack of a strong relationship between pain, impairment, and disability. Some dismiss the previous unresolved observations of the biomedical model to a lack of technology and claim that, with time, these issues will be resolved. Yet, an alternative viewpoint is that varied psychological factors are playing an equally important role in the genesis and maintenance of recurrent pain conditions and a proper explication of these factors is needed for a more complete understanding.

Early psychological models of pain and headache were unidirectional, oversimplified (e.g., pain in the absence of identifiable pathology was judged to be consciously motivated for secondary gain, believed to be maintained because of reinforcement contingencies, or was due to an underlying mental disorder), and had minimal impact upon the field (Turk & Flor, 1999). These views, like the biomedical model, also perpetuated an artificial dichotomy, that pain was either somatogenic or psychogenic. A model that is more fruitful and heuristic is that which has been labeled the *biopsychosocial* or *biobehavioral* model (in the latter case, behavioral subsumes psychological and social factors). This model views pain (and any chronic illness, for that matter) as emanating from a complex interaction of biological, psychological, and social variables. From this perspective (Turk & Flor, 1999) the diversity in illness expression (including severity, duration, and consequences to the individual) can be accounted for by the complex interrelationships among predispositional, biological, and psychological characteristics (e.g., genetics, prior learning history), biological changes, psychological status, and the social and cultural contexts that shape the individual's perceptions and response to illness. This model stands in sharp contrast to the traditional biomedical perspective that conceptualizes illness in terms of more narrowly defined physiochemical dimensions. This alternative model differs in other key ways, as it is dynamic and recognizes reciprocal multifactorial influences over time. Andrasik, Flor, and Turk (2005) have applied this model to recurrent headache disorders, pointing out the role of behavioral, affective, and cognitive influences.

Of course, biological aspects play a critical role in both forms of headache. For migraine, chief among the biological etiological factors are biochemical imbalances, neurotransmitter/receptor dysfunction, neuronal suppression (Olesen & Goadsby, 2000), allodynia and sensitization (Goadsby, 2005), and inflammation (Waeber & Moskowitz, 2005). For tension-type headache, increased attention is being given both to peripheral sensitization (primarily for infrequent, more recent onset of headaches) and to central sensitization (as headaches evolve into chronic forms; Jensen, 2003; Milanov & Bogdanova, 2004).

COURSE, COMPLICATIONS, AND PROGNOSIS

Headaches can onset at an early age (preschool to just beginning school), and the prevalence gradually increases throughout adolescence (Bille, 1962). Prior to puberty, headache occurrence is fairly similar among males and females. Around the time of puberty, migraine prevalence increases in females, suggesting that hormones are etiologically important to its occurrence. Larsson (2002), upon completing a comprehensive review of the literature examining the course and prognosis of childhood headache, arrived at the following conclusions. About one-third of child headache sufferers become headache free (for periods up to 25 years), 40 percent to 54 percent reveal some level of improvement, but about 20 percent continue their headaches with some revealing deterioration. These figures are confounded as the majority of children have received some form of treatment during this time. Thus, the natural history (untreated state) is unknown. Available evidence suggests the following have the poorest outcome: headaches that are more frequent (with about one-third continuing to have significant headache activity), migraines that occur in prepubescent boys, early presence of behavioral problems, and headache present in the mother.

Guidetti et al. (1998) investigated how comorbid conditions interact with childhood headache over time in an eight-year longitudinal study. At time one, all patients (mean age = 11.4 years; range = 4 to 18 years of age) were carefully examined for the presence of the following disorders, in addition to headache: anxiety disorders (separation anxiety disorder, overanxious disorder, and social phobia), sleep disorders (sleep terror disorder, dream anxiety disorder, difficulties in initiating or maintaining sleep, early awakenings,

TABLE 24.1 Evolution of Headaches in Relation to Comorbid Disorder Status at Time 1

Cormorbid disorders present at time 1	Headache-free	Improvement	Unvarying or worse
None	40.0%	52.5%	7.5%
One	38.5%	46.1%	15.4%
Two or more	14.3%	28.6%	57.1%

Note. Adapted from Guidetti et al. (1998).

and sleepwalking disorder), adjustment disorder, elimination disorders (enuresis and encopresis), eating disorders (anorexia nervosa and bulimia nervosa), mood disorders, and school disorder. Table 24.1 presents the primary findings for the 100 patients randomly selected for follow-up eight years later. When headache was unaccompanied by a comorbid disorder, nearly all children and adolescents were found to be headache-free or improved. The presence of a single comorbid disorder had a slight effect over the time period investigated. When two or more comorbid disorders accompanied headache, the outcome at eight years was markedly different. Nearly 60 percent retained their headaches in their present or worsened state, suggesting such persons are particularly in need of attention.

Although it had long been suspected that two types of medication commonly prescribed for headache patients, namely analgesics and ergotamine preparations, could lead to "rebound" headache if overused (Horton & Macy, 1946), it was not until the 1980s that researchers began to take serious note of this fact (Kudrow, 1982; Saper, 1987). Kudrow (1982) first described this condition for tension-type headache patients. He noted that such patients gradually took increasing amounts of analgesics, which subsequently increased pain symptomatology, and then rendered the headache refractory to treatments that formerly would have been of benefit. Saper (1987) described a similar phenomenon for migraineurs taking abortive medication. The classification system for headache acknowledges that consumption or withdrawal of varied substances can induce headache, with caffeine being the most common. More importantly, the following substances, when taken in excess, can lead to a condition that is now labeled medication-overuse headache: ergotamine, triptans, analgesics, and opioids. It is believed that medication overuse accounts for a number of headaches evolving from episodic to chronic, becoming more resilient to treatment.

Patients whose headaches occur following trauma can experience a multitude of problems and significant disability that make treatment particularly challenging (Andrasik & Wincze, 1994; Ham, Andrasik, Packard, & Bundrick, 1994; Marcus, 2003; Martelli, Grayson, & Zasler, 1999; Ramadan & Keidel, 2000). Furthermore, approximately one-third develop chronic forms of headaches, adding to the treatment challenge (Ramadan & Keidel, 2000).

ASSESSMENT AND DIAGNOSIS

Clinical Interview

A clinical interview and select laboratory tests, to rule out underlying organic pathology (it has been said that headache is a diagnosis by exclusion), are the primary means for diagnosing the primary headache types and the presence of medication overuse, which complicates treatment. The diagnostic criteria for migraine and tension-type headache are presented in Table 24.2. Readers are referred to the headache classifications system prepared by the International Headache Society (2004) for criteria for other forms of headache and for the criteria used to diagnose medication overuse headache.

The primary assessment tools consist of the headache diary (Andrasik, 2001a; Andrasik, Lipchik, McCrory, & Wittrock, 2005), the psychophysiological profile (Andrasik, Thorn, & Flor, in press; Flor, 2001), and measures of quality of life/headache impact (Andrasik, Lipchik, et al., 2005). When comorbid conditions are suspected, they are diagnosed and assessed in the typical manner, as covered elsewhere in this volume. The three basic approaches are discussed in brief here. Table 24.3 summarizes the ideal assessment battery, as recommended by the AHS Behavioral Clinical Trials Workgroup (Penzien et al., 2005). This document discusses other pertinent considerations when designing clinical trails employing behavioral treatments.

Headache Diary

Pain is a private event and no method yet exists that can reliably objectify any of the important parameters of headache. Subjective ratings of head pain, sampled daily (preferably multiple times per day), have come to be regarded as the "gold standard" in both behavioral and medical research. Initially, patients were asked to provide ratings of head pain on an hourly basis, using a graded intensity scale (0 to 5 or 0 to 10, with 0 representing the absence of headache and 5 or 10 representing the maximal value). Because headache improvement can occur in varied ways, data from these diary entries were summarized in multiple ways: (1) frequency; (2) duration; (3) intensity (either average or peak to assess whether the "edge" was being taken off of the headache, or both); (4) headache index/activity, a composite measure that incorporated the key dimensions (summation of the intensity of each headache); and (5) responder rate (achieving a reduction of a certain percentage, typically 50 percent relative

TABLE 24.2 Headache Diagnostic Criteria

1.1 Migraine without aura
  A. At least five attacks fulfilling criteria B–D
  B. Headache attacks lasting 4–72 hours (untreated or unsuccessfully treated)
  C. Headache has at least two of the following characteristics:
    1. unilateral location
    2. pulsating quality
    3. moderate or severe pain intensity
    4. aggravation by or causing avoidance of routine physical activity (e.g., walking or climbing stairs)
  D. During headache at least one of the following:
    1. nausea and/or vomiting
    2. photophobia and phonophobia
  E. Not attributed to another disorder

1.2 Migraine with aura
  A. At least two attacks fulfilling criterion B
  B. Migraine aura fulfilling criteria B and C for one of the subforms 1.2.1–1.2.6
  C. Not attributed to another disorder

1.2.1 Typical aura with migraine headache
  A. At least two attacks fulfilling criteria B–D
  B. Aura consisting of at least one of the following but no motor weakness:
    1. fully reversible visual symptoms including positive features (e.g., flickering lights, spots, or lines) and/or negative features (i.e., loss of vision)
    2. fully reversible sensory symptoms including positive features (i.e., pins and needles) and/or negative features (i.e., numbness)
    3. fully reversible dysphasic speech disturbance
  C. At least two of the following:
    1. homonymous visual symptoms and/or unilateral sensory symptoms
    2. at least one aura symptom develops gradually over ≥5 minutes and/or different aura symptoms occur in succession over ≥5 minutes
    3. each symptom lasts ≥5 and ≤60 minutes
  D. Headache fulfilling criteria B–D for 1.1 migraine without aura begins during the aura or follows aura within 60 minutes
  E. Not attributed to another disorder

2.1 Infrequent episodic tension-type headache
  A. At least 10 episodes occurring on <1 day per month on average (<12 days per year) and fulfilling criteria B–D
  B. Headache lasting from 30 minutes to 7 days
  C. Headache has at least two of the following pain characteristics:
    1. bilateral location
    2. pressing/tightening (nonpulsating) quality
    3. mild or moderate intensity
    4. not aggravated by routine physical activity such as walking or climbing stairs
  D. Both of the following:
    1. no nausea or vomiting (anorexia may occur)
    2. no more than one of the photophobia or phonophobia
  E. Not attributed to another disorder

2.2 Frequent episodic tension-type headache
  A. At least 10 episodes occurring on ≥1 but <15 days per month for at least 3 months (≥12 but <180 days per year) and fulfilling criteria B–D
  B. Headache lasting from 30 minutes to 7 days
  C. Headache has at least two of the following characteristics:
    1. bilateral location
    2. pressing/tightening (nonpulsating) quality
    3. mild or moderate intensity
    4. not aggravated by routine physical activity such as walking or climbing stairs
  D. Both of the following:
    1. no nausea or vomiting (anorexia may occur)
    2. no more than one of the photophobia or phonophobia
  E. Not attributed to another disorder

2.3 Chronic tension-type headache
  A. Headache occurring on ≥15 days per month on average for >3 months (≥180 days per year) and fulfilling criteria B–D
  B. Headache lasts hours or may be continuous
  C. Headache has at least two of the following characteristics:
    1. bilateral location
    2. pressing/tightening (nonpulsating) quality
    3. mild or moderate intensity
    4. not aggravated by routine physical activity such as walking or climbing stairs
  D. Both of the following:
    1. no more than one of photophobia, phonophobia, or mild nausea
    2. neither moderate or severe nausea nor vomiting
  E. Not attributed to another disorder

Note. From the International Headache Society (IHS) Headache Classification Committee (2004). Reprinted by blanket permission.

---

to baseline). Committees tasked by the IHS to develop guidelines for conducting and evaluating pharmacological agents (International Headache Society Committee on Clinical Trials in Migraine, 1999; International Headache Society Committee on Clinical Trials in Tension-Type Headache, 1999) have argued against using the headache index, as it is seen as weighting severity and duration in an arbitrary manner, rendering it of little value when making comparisons across research participants. Nevertheless, this later composite measure has continued to serve as one of the key indexes in behavioral investigations and its utility (as a secondary measure) has been reaffirmed by the behavioral guidelines committee of the American Headache Society (Penzien et al., 2005). Other approaches for assessing head pain include attending to multiple dimensions (affective/reactive in addition to the sensory/intensity dimension), social validation, and pain behavior or behavior motivated by pain (such as pill taking; Andrasik, 2001a; Andrasik, Lipchik, et al., 2005).

Psychophysiological Assessment

Prior to physiologically based treatment (i.e., biofeedback), a psychophysiological stress profile is sometimes used. This assessment is designed to identify the physiological dysfunc-

TABLE 24.3 Assessment and Outcome Measures Recommended by the AHS Behavioral Clinical Trials Guidelines Committee

Headache pattern	Baseline headache frequency	Primary outcome measure	Secondary headache measures	Secondary disability/QOL measures**	Secondary nonheadache measures
Episodic	3–4 to 14 days/month	attack frequency (#/mo)* HA days/month*	HA index HA duration peak HA severity	HA-specific QOL* QOL (generic) missed work/school	medication use patient preferences psychological symptoms
Chronic	15 + days/month	HA days/month*	HA index severe HA days/month HA duration peak HA severity	(same as previous)	(same as previous)

Note. Adapted from Penzien et al. (2005).
* requisite measure.
** standardized instruments.

tion or response modalities assumed to be relevant to the pain condition and to do so under varied stimulus conditions, psychological and physical, that mimic real life, work, and rest (operating at a keyboard, simulated stressors) in order to guide treatment efforts and gauge progress. Further details go beyond the scope of this chapter, so interested readers are referred to Andrasik, Thorn, et al. (in press), Arena and Schwartz (2003), and Flor (2001).

Quality of Life/Headache Impact

The World Health Organization (WHO; 1948) long ago defined health as "a state of complete physical, mental and social well-being, and not merely the absence of disease," thus laying the groundwork for a focus on quality of life. In the more than 50 years that have passed, *quality of life* remained an ill-defined term with a loose definition for quite some time. Absent of an agreed-upon formal definition, researchers typically describe what quality of life means to them; definitions must be inferred back from the item content. Item contents are typically drawn from the following categories: general or overall health, physical functioning, physical symptoms and toxicity, emotional functioning, cognitive functioning, role functioning, social well-being and functioning, sexual functioning, and existential issues (Fayers & Machin, 2000).

Within the area of migraine headache, for example, interest in quality of life is a relatively recent phenomenon. A Medline search of *migraine* and *quality of life* revealed sporadic interest in this topic until 1994, with a rapid growth thereafter (Andrasik, 2001b). This research has proceeded much as it has for other medical conditions: awareness that aspects beyond physical symptoms are important, a focus that first concerns general health measures, which is then followed by exploration of specific or tailored measures. Both approaches have value. General assessments provide health status overviews, they permit comparisons across diverse patient groups, and they may identify unexpected findings worthy of continued pursuit. Condition-specific measures, on the other hand, can be customized and, as a result, they may be more sensitive to detecting small but important differences (Andrasik, 2001b; Andrasik, Lipchik, et al., 2005).

More recently, WHO defined functional consequences of an illness in terms of (1) impairment or primary manifestations of the illness (such as pain, limitations in range of motion, and effects on other sensations), (2) functional limitations (the effects of the illness on an individual's activities, such as walking or climbing stairs), and (3) disability (the consequences of an illness on one's ability to work and function in various roles; National Academy of Sciences/Institute of Medicine, 1991). The degree of disability is known to be the most important indicator of the severity of the disease and the social impact of migraine, at least in economic terms (de Lissovoy & Lazarus, 1994). Attention has thus been devoted to the development of measures to assess disability or the psychosocial impact of headache disorders.

Tools for assessing headache impact or disability are increasingly being recommended as part of generalized headache management guidelines to produce individualized treatment plans (Dowson, 2001). We (Andrasik, Lipchik, et al., 2005) expect increasing attention will be paid to the ability of treatments to ameliorate the psychosocial impact of headaches as well as to reduce pain and associated symptoms in future clinical trials evaluating pharmacological and nonpharmacological therapies.

The numerous available measures of disability vary in their specificity (for migraine, for headache in general, or for medical conditions in general), in the dimensions they assess (primarily disability, or other impact dimensions as well), in the time frame they address (a single migraine episode, or a month or longer period of time), and in the availability of supportive psychometric data (Andrasik, Lipchik, et al., 2005).

In the following paragraph one of most commonly used measures is discussed in greater detail. (Readers seeking further information are referred to Andrasik, Lipchik, et al., 2005; Holroyd, 2002; Holroyd, Penzien, & Lipchik, 2001.)

The Migraine Disability Assessment (MIDAS) questionnaire is a five-item self-administered questionnaire that sums the number of productive days lost over the past three months in two settings: the workplace and the home, as these settings are most important in the 20- to 50-year-old age group in which migraine is most prevalent (Stewart et al., 2001). The MIDAS also assesses disability in family, social, and leisure activities. All questions are asked about either missed activity or days when productivity was reduced by at least half. The MIDAS score is the sum of missed days due to a headache from paid work, housework, and nonwork (family, social, leisure) activities, and days at paid work or housework when productivity was reduced by at least half. (Two additional questions, which are not included in the MIDAS score, assess frequency and severity of head pain.) The MIDAS score has been found to have solid psychometric support (Stewart, Lipton, Kolodner, Liberman, & Sawyer, 1999; Stewart, Lipton, Whyte, et al., 1999). It has been shown to predict treatment needs in a randomized trial (Lipton, Stewart, Stone, Lainez, & Sawyer, 2000) and scores on it were highly correlated with physicians' judgments regarding patients' pain, disability, and need for medical care. Further, it has been shown to be responsive to treatment (Grazzi et al., 2004).

Like most measures, it is not without criticism (Pryse-Phillips, 2002). Inability to work is likely to be closely correlated with inability to do anything else, such as effectively managing a home or family, but the MIDAS treats them as separate items. A 50 percent reduction in capacity is scored the same as complete inability to perform. The nature of the questions appears best suited for more severely affected headache sufferers. The 90-day assessment period could make this instrument difficult to use in some situations (Andrasik, Lipchik, et al., 2005).

IMPACT ON ENVIRONMENT

Solomon and Dahlöf (2000) reviewed the impact of migraine at both the individual and familial level and identified key investigations on this topic. As regards effects on the family unit, the following were identified. In a sample of more than 100 migraineurs (Edmeads et al., 1993), 50 percent stated their headaches affected their families, 45 percent worried about driving because of headache, 40 percent feared headache would onset at a future event, and 35 percent stated their headaches affected their social plans. A portion of these patients maintained diary records for several months, which showed that social or family activities were cancelled approximately 20 percent of the time because of migraine. An investigation by Smith (1996), including a national sample of 4,000 U.S. households (which included 350 migraine sufferers and 77 nonsufferer spouses), revealed similar findings. Approximately 60 percent of migraine sufferers noted migraine to have an impact on the family; 21 percent rated this impact as very or extremely serious. About one-third stated that migraines negatively affected the relationship with their children, and more than 70 percent reported missing activities with their children as a result of migraine. Finally, nearly 40 percent of those interviewed felt that migraine had a negative impact on their marriage. Thus, spousal and child relationships were affected to a significant degree, likely increasing the overall suffering from migraine.

Osterhaus, Gutterman, and Plachetka (1992) assessed for impairments in leisure-time activities. Their sample of migraineurs reported losing an average of 5.6 leisure days per year to migraine, with 1.1 leisure days being impacted per year.

Dahlöf and Dimenäs (1995), comparing migraine patients to carefully matched controls, found the former to report an overall diminished sense of well-being, as reflected by disturbed contentment, vitality, and sleep, and greater emotional distress.

Clarke, MacMillan, Sondhi, and Wells (1996) examined the impact both during and between attacks. As expected, effects during a migraine attack were pronounced: 90 percent had to delay household tasks, 76 percent had to lie down for a period, and 50 percent reported missing work. Between attacks, approximately 50 percent reported they had difficulty interacting with family, friends, and coworkers. Repeated attacks of migraine can elevate levels of fear and anxiety (of having a tumor, losing time at work, and the intensity of pain; Blau, 1984).

In a more recent investigation of migraine, 90 percent reported functional impairment with their headaches and 53 percent exhibited impairment sufficient to require bed rest (Lipton et al., 2001). Nearly one-third of all migraineurs had missed at least one day of work or school in the three months preceding the survey, and 51 percent reported productivity was reduced by at least one-half due to headache. Household, family, and social activities were even more often disrupted than work.

Michel (2000) similarly comprehensively reviewed the socioeconomics of headache, focusing on the direct (those incurred by the health care system in diagnosing and treating headache), indirect (days of lost or diminished productivity), and intangible (pain, suffering) costs. In all categories, costs were substantial.

Migraine results in 112 million bedridden days each year (Hu, Markson, Lipton, Stewart, & Berger, 1999). The cost of migraine to the total U.S. workforce would be an estimated $13 billion a year in missed workdays and lost productivity. Direct medical costs (i.e., physician office visits, prescription medication claims, hospitalizations) for migraine care average $1 billion annually. Notably, migraineurs generate twice the medical claims and 2.5 times the pharmacy claims as other comparable patients without migraine in a health maintenance organization (Clouse & Osterhaus, 1994).

In comparison to migraine, much less is known about the impact of tension-type headache (Penzien, Rains, & Andrasik, 2002). In a sample of tension-type headache patients, Schwartz et al. (1998) found that 8.3 percent of those with episodic forms lost days at work (average 9 per year), with 44 percent reporting reduced effectiveness at work, home, and school as a result of headache. For those with chronic forms of headache, 11.8 percent lost days at work (average 20 per year) and 47 percent reported reduced productivity due to headache. Given the markedly increased prevalence of tension-type headache, the total societal impact of lost workdays and decreased productivity may well rival that for migraine (Penzien et al., 2002).

TREATMENT IMPLICATIONS

Pharmacological Approaches

Most individuals will experience a headache from time to time, yet few of these individuals seek regular treatment from a health care provider, even when headaches are severe and disabling (Mannix, 2001; Michel, 2000). More typically, headaches are tolerated, treated symptomatically with over-the-counter analgesics, or managed by "borrowing" prescribed medications from friends and family members. When recurrent headache sufferers do present to a health care practitioner, their headaches are most commonly managed with a combination of medication and advice. For example, among primary care headache patients, more than 80 percent reported the use of over-the-counter medications and more than 75 percent reported the use of some form of prescription-only medications for management of their headaches (Von Korff, Galer, & Stang, 1995). A number of effective pharmacologic options are available to treat headaches and they fall within three broad categories: symptomatic, abortive, and prophylactic.

Symptomatic medications are pharmacologic agents with analgesic or pain relieving effects. These include over-the-counter analgesics (i.e., aspirin, acetaminophen), nonsteroidal anti-inflammatory agents (i.e., ibuprofen), opioid analgesics, muscle relaxants, and sedative/hypnotic agents. Von Korff et al. (1995) report, for example, that ibuprofen accounted for 84 percent of all use of nonsteroidal anti-inflammatory consumption in a sample of more than 600 primary care headache patients. The most commonly consumed opioid analgesics were acetaminophen with codeine (33 percent), meperidine (also known as Demerol; 21 percent), and percocet (15 percent). Midrin (33 percent), cyclobenzaprine (28 percent), and methocarbonal (10 percent) were the most commonly consumed sedative/hypnotic medications.

Abortive medications are pharmacologic agents that are consumed at the onset of a migraine headache, in an effort to terminate or markedly lessen an attack. Ergotamine tartrate preparations were the mainstays of abortive care until the early 1990s when triptans, designed to act on specific serotonin receptor subtypes, were introduced. Multiple triptan formulations are now available, differing with respect to potency, delivery mode (oral versus other, for patients likely to vomit during attacks), time of peak onset, duration of sustained headache relief, rate of headache recurrence, improvement in associated symptoms, safety, and tolerability (Rapoport & Tepper, 2001; Silberstein, 2000; Tepper, 2001).

Prophylactic medications are consumed daily in an effort to prevent headaches or reduce the occurrence of attacks in the chronic sufferer. Beta-blockers, calcium channel antagonists, antidepressants (e.g., tricyclics, serotonin-specific reuptake inhibitors), and anticonvulsants are used most frequently as prophylactic medications for migraine headache, but many other agents are being explored (Chronicle & Mulleners, 2004; Rapoport & Bigal, 2005; Silberstein, 2000). Recent meta-analyses comparing various prophylactic medications, conducted with child as well as adult patients, have shown them to be superior to varied control conditions (waiting list, medication placebo, etc.; Hermann, Kim, & Blanchard, 1995; Holroyd, Penzien, & Cordingley, 1991). One of these analyses (Hermann et al., 1995), along with an additional meta-analysis (Holroyd & Penzien, 1990), found various behavioral treatments achieved outcomes similar to those for varied prophylactic medications.

For tension-type headache, the most commonly administered medications include tricyclic and newer generation antidepressants, muscle relaxants, nonsteroidal anti-inflammatory agents, and miscellaneous drugs (Mathew & Bendtsen, 2000). A recent, large-scale randomized controlled trial found stress management and drug prophylaxis to be equivalent in effectiveness (although time to response was quicker for medication). The combination of the two treatments was more effective than either treatment by itself (Holroyd, O'Donnell, et al., 2001). Combined care is probably the most common treatment in clinical practice.

Although a number of medications are effective in the treatment of recurring headache, concern exists regarding the risks of frequent, long-term use of certain medications. Major risks associated with pharmacological management include the potential for misuse and dependency (Mathew, 1987), rebound headache, development of drug-induced chronic headache, reduced efficacy of prophylactic headache medications, potential side effects, and acute symptoms associated with the cessation of headache medication (such as increased headache, nausea, cramping, gastrointestinal distress, sleep disturbance, and emotional distress). Chronic use of prescription-only medication has been reported by 10 percent of primary care headache patients and chronic use of over-the-counter medications has been reported by almost 20 percent of primary care headache patients (Von Korff et al., 1995). These potential risks, combined with the growing interest in self-management and alternative approaches, warrant the consideration of nonpharmacological treatments, to which our attention is now turned.

Nonpharmacological Approaches

The primary nonpharmacological approaches are designed (1) to promote general overall relaxation either by therapist instruction alone (e.g., progressive muscle relaxation, autogenic training, meditation, etc.) or therapist instruction augmented by feedback of various physiological parameters indicative of autonomic arousal or muscle tension to help fine tune relaxation (e.g., temperature, electromyographic, or electrodermal biofeedback); (2) to control, in more direct fashion, those physiological parameters assumed to underlie headache (e.g., blood flow and electroencephalographic biofeedback primarily); and (3) to enhance abilities to manage stressors and stress reactions to headache (e.g., cognitive and cognitive behavior therapy). With the exception of EEG biofeedback these nonpharmacological approaches have been the subject of extensive research. In assessing efficacy, the available literature has been examined from two perspectives: qualitative (evidence-based review panels evaluating level of design sophistication) and quantitative (via meta-analysis).

Evidence-based reviews have been conducted by multiple groups, including the Division 12 of the American Psychological Society (Task Force on Promotion and Dissemination of Psychological Procedures, 1995), the U.S. Headache Consortium (composed of eight medical societies: American Academy of Family Physicians, American Academy of Neurology, American Headache Society, American College of Emergency Physicians, American College of Physicians, American Society of Internal Medicine, American Osteopathic Association, and National Headache Foundation; Campbell, Penzien, & Wall, 2000), Canadian Headache Society (Pryse-Phillips et al., 1998), the Task Force of the Society of Pediatric Psychology (Holden, Deichmann, & Levy, 1999), and the Association for Applied Psychophysiology and Biofeedback (Yucha & Gilbert, 2004).

The U.S. Headache Consortium's recommendations pertaining to behavioral interventions for migraine are as follows: (1) relaxation training, thermal biofeedback combined with relaxation training, electromyographic biofeedback, and cognitive behavioral therapy may be considered as treatment options for prevention of migraine (Grade A Evidence); (2) behavioral therapy may be combined with preventive drug therapy to achieve additional clinical improvement for migraine (Grade B Evidence); and (3) evidenced-based treatment recommendations are not yet possible regarding the use of hypnosis (Campbell et al., 2000). This consortium concluded that behavioral treatments may be particularly well suited for patients having one or more of the following characteristics: (1) the patient prefers such an approach; (2) pharmacological treatment cannot be tolerated or is medically contraindicated; (3) the response to pharmacological treatment is absent or minimal; (4) the patient is pregnant, has plans to become pregnant, or is nursing; (5) there is a long-standing history of frequent or excessive use of analgesics or acute medications that can exacerbate headache; and (6) the patient is faced with significant stressors or has deficient stress-coping skills.

The consortium also drew the following conclusions, which identify areas for further study: (1) too few studies provide head-to-head comparisons of nondrug and drug treatments; (2) the integration of drug and nondrug treatments not adequately addressed; (3) behavioral therapies are effective as sole or adjunctive therapy, but it is not yet established which specific patients are likely to be most responsive to specific behavioral modalities; (4) component analysis is needed to determine extent various elements of multimodal regimens contribute to efficacy; and (5) additional studies treating patients from primary care settings are needed.

Finally, the various meta-analyses that have been conducted for tension-type and migraine headaches, some of which concern comparisons of pharmacological and nonpharmacological treatments, have been summarized in Andrasik and Walch (2003) and Penzien et al. (2002), among other sources. The major conclusions that can be drawn are the following: (1) these treatments (relaxation, biofeedback, and cognitive behavioral) produce significant improvements in headache activity, although a sizeable number of patients remain unhelped; (2) improvements are similar among the treatments, including those obtained for pharmacological treatment; (3) improvements exceed those obtained by various control conditions; and (4) effects appear to endure well over time. From a recent investigation, there is some evidence to suggest that biofeedback can enhance medication treatment effects over time, particularly with difficult to treat patients (Grazzi et al., 2002).

SUMMARY

Migraine and tension-type headaches are among the most common psychophysiological disorders, accounting for a great deal of pain, suffering, lost productivity, and direct medical costs for the individual sufferer. Effects extend to the family and social environment as well. These forms of headache reveal a significant association with anxiety and depressive disorders and with psychosocial stress. The early presence of these conditions contributes to the continuation of headaches over time. The biopsychosocial model is most useful for gaining understanding and guiding treatment efforts with headache patients. The clinical interview, headache diary, and measures of impact are the primary diagnostic and assessment tools, with psychophysiological assessment being used on occasion. A number of palliative, abortive, and prophylactic medications have been shown to be useful, as have various nonpharmacological approaches (chiefly relaxation, biofeedback, and cognitive stress-coping training), either separately or in combination.

REFERENCES

Abenheim, L., & Suissa, S. (1987). Importance and economic burden of occupational back pain: A study of 2,500 cases representative of Quebec. *Journal of Occupational Medicine, 29,* 670–674.

Adler, C. S., Adler, S. M., & Packard, R. C. (1987). *Psychiatric aspects of headache.* Baltimore: Williams and Wilkins.

American Psychiatric Association. (1980). *Diagnostic and statistical manual of mental disorders* (3rd ed.). Washington, DC: Author.

American Psychiatric Association. (2000). *Diagnostic and statistical manual of mental disorders* (4th ed., text rev.). Washington, DC: Author.

Anderson, R. W. (1980). The relation of life situations, personality features, and reactions to the migraine syndrome. In D. J. Dalessio (Ed.), *Wolff's headache and other head pain* (4th ed., pp. 403–417). New York: Oxford University Press.

Andersson, G. B. (1999). Epidemiological features of chronic low-back pain. *Lancet, 354,* 581–585.

Andrasik, F. (2001a). Assessment of patients with headache. In D. C. Turk & R. Melzack (Eds.), *Handbook of pain assessment* (2nd ed., pp. 454–474). New York: Guilford Press.

Andrasik, F. (2001b). Migraine and quality of life: Psychological considerations. *Journal of Headache and Pain, 2,* S1–S9.

Andrasik, F., Flor, H., & Turk, D. C. (2005). An expanded view of psychological aspects in head pain: The biopsychosocial model. *Neurological Sciences, 26*(Suppl. 2), S87–S91.

Andrasik, F., Lipchik, G. L., McCrory, D. C., & Wittrock, D. A. (2005). Outcome measurement in behavioral headache research: Headache parameters and psychosocial outcomes. *Headache, 45,* 429–437.

Andrasik, F., Thorn, B. E., & Flor, H. (in press). Psychophysiological assessment of pain. In R. F. Schmidt & W. D. Willis (Eds.), *Encyclopedic reference of pain.* Heidelberg, Germany: Springer-Verlag.

Andrasik, F., & Walch, S. E. (2003). Headaches. In A. M. Nezu, C. M. Nezu, & P. A. Geller (Eds.), *Handbook of psychology: Vol. 9. Health psychology* (pp. 245–266). New York: Wiley.

Andrasik, F., & Wincze, J. P. (1994). Emotional and psychological aspects of mild head injury. *Seminars in Neurology, 14,* 60–66.

Andrasik, F., Wittrock, D. A., & Passchier, J. (2005). Psychologic mechanisms of tension-type headache. In J. Olesen, P. Tfelt-Hansen, K. M. A. Welch, P. Goadsby, & N. Ramadan (Eds.), *The headaches* (3rd ed., pp. 661–665). Philadelphia: Lippincott Williams & Wilkins.

Arena, J. G., & Schwartz, M. S. (2003). Psychophysiological assessment and biofeedback baselines for the front-line clinician: A primer. In M. S. Schwartz & F. Andrasik (Eds.), *Biofeedback: A practitioner's guide* (3rd ed., pp. 128–158). New York: Guilford Press.

Barrett, E. J. (1996). Primary care for women: Assessment and management of headache. *Nurse Midwifery, 41,* 117–124.

Bille, B. (1962). Migraine in school children. *Acta Paediatrica Scandinavica, 51*(Suppl. 136), 1–151.

Blau, J. N. (1984). Fears aroused in patients by migraine. *British Medical Journal, 288,* 1126.

Breslau, N., Merikangas, K., & Bowden, C. L. (1994). Comorbidity of migraine and major affective disorders. *Neurology, 44,* 17–22.

Campbell, J. K., Penzien, D. B., & Wall, E. M. (2000). *Evidence-based guidelines for migraine headaches: Behavioral and physical treatments.* Retrieved February 14, 2005, from http://www.aan.com/professionals/practice/guideline/index.cfm

Chojnowska, E., & Stannard, C. (2003). Epidemiology of chronic pain. In T. S. Jensen, P. R. Wilson, & A. S. C. Rice (Eds.), *Chronic pain: Clinical pain management* (pp. 15–26). London: Arnold.

Chronicle, E., & Mulleners, W. (2004). Anticonvulsant drugs for migraine prophylaxis. *Cochrane Database Systematic Review,* (3). Retrieved June 27, 2005, from http://www.cochrane.org/reviews/en/ab003226.html

Clarke, C. E., MacMillan, L., Sondhi, S., & Wells, N. E. J. (1996). Economic and social impact of migraine. *Quarterly Journal of Medicine, 89,* 77–84.

Clouse, J. C., & Osterhaus, J. T. (1994). Healthcare resource use and costs associated with migraine in a managed healthcare setting. *Pharmacoeconomics, 28,* 659–664.

Crombie, I. K., Croft, P. R., Linton, S. J., LeResche, L., & Von Korff, M. (Eds.). (1999). *Epidemiology of pain.* Seattle, WA: IASP Press.

Cypress, B. K. (1983). Characteristics of physician visits for back symptoms: A national perspective. *American Journal of Public Health, 73,* 389–395.

Dahlöf, C., & Dimenäs, E. (1995). Migraine patients experience poorer subjective well being/quality of life even between attacks. *Cephalalgia, 15,* 31–36.

de Lissovoy, G., & Lazarus, S. S. (1994). The economic cost of migraine: Present state of knowledge. *Neurology, 44*(Suppl. 4), 56–62.

Dowson, A. J. (2001). Assessing the impact of migraine. *Current Medical Research and Opinion, 17,* 298–309.

Edmeads, J., Findlay, H., Tugwell, P., Pryse-Phillips, W., Nelson, R. F., & Murray, T. J. (1993). Impact of migraine and tension-type headache on life-style, consulting behaviour, and medication use: A Canadian population survey. *Canadian Journal of Neurological Sciences, 20,* 131–137.

Evans, R. W. (2001). Diagnostic testing for headache. *Medical Clinics of North America, 85,* 865–886.

Fayers, P. M., & Machin, D. (2000). *Quality of life: Assessment, analysis and interpretation.* New York: Wiley.

Fernandez, E. (2002). *Anxiety, depression, and anger in pain: Research findings and clinical options.* Dallas, TX: Advanced Psychological Resources.

Flor, H. (2001). Psychophysiological assessment of the patient with chronic pain. In D. C. Turk & R. Melzack (Eds.), *Handbook of pain assessment* (2nd ed., pp. 76–96). New York: Guilford Press.

Goadsby, P. J. (2005). Migraine, allodynia, sensitization and all of that.... *European Neurology, 53*(Suppl. 1), 10–16.

Grazzi, L., Andrasik, F., D'Amico, D., Leone, M., Usai, S., Kass, S. J., et al. (2002). Behavioral and pharmacologic treatment of transformed migraine with analgesic overuse: Outcome at 3 years. *Headache, 42,* 483–490.

Grazzi, L., Andrasik, F., D'Amico, D., Usai, S., Kass, S., & Bussone, G. (2004). Disability in chronic migraine patients with medication overuse: Treatment effects at 1-year follow-up. *Headache, 44,* 678–683.

Guidetti, V., Galli, R., Fabrizi, P., Giannantoni, A. S., Napoli, L., Bruni, O., et al. (1998). Headache and psychiatric comorbidity: Clinical aspects and outcome in an 8-year follow-up study. *Cephalalgia, 18,* 455–462.

Ham, L. P., Andrasik, F., Packard, R. C., & Bundrick, C. M. (1994). Psychopathology in individuals with post-traumatic headaches and other pain types. *Cephalalgia, 14,* 118–126.

Hart, L. G., Deyo, R. A., & Cherkin, D. C. (1995). Physician office visits for low back pain: Frequency, clinical evaluation, and treatment patterns from a U.S. national survey. *Spine, 20,* 11–19.

Headache Classification Subcommittee of the International Headache Society. (2004). The international classification of headache disorders: 2nd edition. *Cephalalgia, 24*(Suppl. 1), 1–160.

Hermann, C., Kim, M., & Blanchard, E. B. (1995). Behavioral and prophylactic pharmacological intervention studies of pediatric migraine: An exploratory meta-analysis. *Pain, 60,* 239–256.

Holden, E. W., Deichmann, M. M., & Levy, J. D. (1999). Empirically supported treatments in pediatric psychology: Recurrent pediatric headache. *Journal of Pediatric Psychology, 24,* 91–109.

Holroyd, K. A. (2002). Assessment and psychological management of recurrent headache disorders. *Journal of Consulting and Clinical Psychology, 70,* 656–677.

Holroyd, K. A., O'Donnell, F. J., Stensland, M., Lipchik, G. L., Cordingley, G. E., & Carlson, B. W. (2001). Management of chronic tension-type headache with tricyclic antidepressant medication, stress management therapy, and their combination. *Journal of the American Medical Association, 285,* 2208–2215.

Holroyd, K. A., & Penzien, D. (1990). Pharmacological versus non-pharmacological prophylaxis of recurrent migraine headache: A meta-analytic review of clinical trials. *Pain, 42,* 1–13.

Holroyd, K. A., Penzien, D. B., & Cordingley, G. E. (1991). Propanolol in the management of recurrent migraine: A meta-analytic review. *Headache, 31,* 333–340.

Holroyd, K. A., Penzien, D. B., & Lipchik, G. L. (2001). Behavioral management of headache. In S. D. Silberstein, R. B. Lipton, & D. J. Dalessio (Eds.), *Wolff's headache and other head pain* (7th ed., pp. 562–598). New York: Oxford University Press.

Horton, B. T., & Macy, D., Jr. (1946). Treatment of headache. *Medical Clinics of North America, 30,* 811–831.

Hu, X. H., Markson, L. E., Lipton, R. B., Stewart, W. F., & Berger, M. L. (1999). Burden of migraine in the United States: Disability and economic costs. *Archives of Internal Medicine, 159,* 813–818.

International Headache Society Committee on Clinical Trials in Migraine. (1999). *Guidelines for controlled trials of drugs in migraine: Members' handbook 2000* (pp. 111–133). Oslo, Norway: Scandinavian University Press.

International Headache Society Committee on Clinical Trials in Tension-Type Headache. (1999). *Guidelines for trials of drug treatments in tension-type headache: Members' handbook 2000* (pp. 134–160). Oslo, Norway: Scandinavian University Press.

Jensen, R. (1999). Pathophysiological mechanisms of tension-type headache: A review of epidemiologic and experimental studies. *Cephalalgia, 19*(6), 602–621.

Jensen, R. (2003). Peripheral and central mechanisms in tension-type headache: An update. *Cephalalgia, 23*(Suppl. 1), 49–52.

Kudrow, L. (1982). Paradoxical effects of frequent analgesic use. In M. Critchley, A. Friedman, S. Gorini, & F. Sicuteri (Eds.), *Head-*

ache: Physiopathological and clinical concepts. Advances in neurology (Vol. 33, pp. 335–341). New York: Raven Press.

Larsson, B. (2002). Prognosis of recurrent headaches in childhood and adolescence. In V. Guidetti, G. Russell, M. Sillanpää, & P. Winner (Eds.), *Headache and migraine in childhood and adolescence* (pp. 203–214). London: Martin Dunitz.

Lazarus, R. S., & Folkman, S. (1984). Coping and adaptation. In W. D. Gentry (Ed.), *The handbook of behavioral medicine* (pp. 282–325). New York: Guilford Press.

Lipton, R. B., Diamond, S., Reed, M. L., Diamond, M. L., & Stewart, W. F. (2001). Migraine diagnosis and treatment: Results from the American Migraine Study II. *Headache, 41*(7), 638–645.

Lipton, R. B., Stewart, W. F., Stone, A. M., Lainez, M. J., & Sawyer, J. P. (2000). Stratified care vs. step care strategies for migraine. The Disability in Strategies of Care (DISC) Study: A randomized trial. *Journal of the American Medical Association, 294,* 2599–2605.

Mannix, L. K. (2001). Epidemiology and impact of primary headache disorders. *Medical Clinics of North America, 85,* 887–895.

Marcus, D. A. (2003). Disability and chronic posttraumatic headache. *Headache, 43,* 117–121.

Martelli, M. F., Grayson, R. L., & Zasler, N. D. (1999). Posttraumatic headache: Neuropsychological and psychological effects and treatment implications. *Journal of Head Trauma Rehabilitation, 14,* 49–69.

Mathew, N. (1987). Drugs and headache: Misuse and dependency. In C. S. Adler, S. M. Adler, & R. C. Packard, *Psychiatric aspects of headache* (pp. 289–297). Baltimore: Williams and Wilkins.

Mathew, N. T., & Bendtsen, L. (2000). Prophylactic pharmacotherapy of tension-type headache. In J. Olesen, P. Tfelt-Hansen, & K. M. A. Welch (Eds.), *The headaches* (2nd ed., pp. 667–673). Philadelphia: Lippincott Williams & Wilkins.

Melzack, R. (1989). Phantom limbs, the self and the brain. *Canadian Psychology, 30,* 1–16.

Melzack, R. (1999). Pain and stress: A new perspective. In R. J. Gatchel & D. C. Turk (Eds.), *Psychosocial factors and pain: Critical perspectives* (pp. 89–106). New York: Guilford Press.

Merikangas, K. R., Angst, J., & Isler, H. (1990). Migraine and psychopathology: Results of the Zurich cohort study of young adults. *Archives of General Psychiatry, 47,* 849–853.

Merikangas, K. R., & Rasmussen, B. K. (2000). Migraine comorbidity. In J. Olesen, P. Tfelt-Hansen, & K. M. A. Welch (Eds.), *The headaches* (2nd ed., pp. 235–240). Philadelphia: Lippincott Williams & Wilkins.

Michel, P. (2000). Socioeconomic costs of headache. In J. Olesen, P. Tfelt-Hansen, & K. M. A. Welch (Eds.), *The headaches* (2nd ed., pp. 33–40). Philadelphia: Lippincott Williams & Wilkins.

Milanov, I., & Bogdanova, D. (2004). Pain and tension-type headache: A review of the possible pathophysiological mechanisms. *Journal of Headache and Pain, 5,* 4–11.

National Academy of Sciences/Institute of Medicine (NAS/IOM). (1991). *Disability in America: Toward a national agenda for prevention.* Washington, DC: NAS Press.

Olesen, J., & Goadsby, P. J. (2000). Synthesis of migraine mechanisms. In J. Olesen, P. Tfelt-Hansen, & K. M. A. Welch (Eds.), *The headaches* (2nd ed., pp. 331–336). Philadelphia: Lippincott, Williams, & Wilkins.

Osterhaus, J. T., Gutterman, D. L., & Plachetka, J. R. (1992). Healthcare resource and lost labour costs of migraine headaches in the US. *Pharmacoeconomics, 2,* 67–76.

Packard, R. C. (1987). Life stress, personality features, and reactions to the migraine syndrome. In D. J. Dalessio (Ed.), *Wolff's headache and other head pain* (5th ed., pp. 370–387). New York: Oxford University Press.

Penzien, D. B., Andrasik, F., Lake, A. E., III, Lipchik, G. L., Holroyd, K. A., Lipton, R. B., et al. (2005). Guidelines for trials of behavioral treatments for recurrent headache, first edition: American Headache Society Behavioral Clinical Trials Workgroup. *Headache, 45*(Suppl. 2), S110–S132.

Penzien, D. B., Rains, J. C., & Andrasik, F. (2002). Behavioral management of recurrent headache: Three decades of experience and empiricism. *Applied Psychophysiology and Biofeedback, 27,* 163–181.

Pryse-Phillips, W. (2002). Evaluating migraine disability: The Headache Impact Test instrument in context. *Canadian Journal of Neurological Sciences, 29*(Suppl. 2), S11–S15.

Pryse-Phillips, W. E., Dodick, D. W., Edmeads, J. G., Gawel, M. J., Nelson, R. F., Purdy, R. A., et al. (1998). Guidelines for the nonpharmacologic management of migraine in clinical practice: Canadian Headache Society. *Canadian Medical Association Journal, 159,* 47–54.

Ramadan, N. M., & Keidel, M. (2000). Chronic posttraumatic headache. In J. Olesen, P. Tfelt-Hansen, & K. M. A. Welch (Eds.), *The headaches* (2nd ed., pp. 771–780). Philadelphia: Lippincott Williams & Wilkins.

Rapoport, A. M., & Bigal, M. E. (2005). Migraine preventive therapy: Current and emerging treatment options. *Neurological Sciences, 26*(Suppl. 2), S111–S120.

Rapoport, A. M., & Tepper, S. J. (2001). All triptans are not the same. *Journal of Headache and Pain, 2*(Suppl. 1), S87–S92.

Sander, R. A., & Meyers, J. E. (1986). The relationship of disability to compensation status in railroad workers. *Spine, 11,* 141–143.

Saper, J. R. (1987). Ergotamine dependency: A review. *Headache, 27,* 435–438.

Schwartz, B. S., Stewart, W. F., Simon, D., & Lipton, R. B. (1998). Epidemiology of tension-type headache. *Journal of the American Medical Association, 279*(5), 381–383.

Silberstein, S. D. (2000). Practice parameter: Evidence-based guidelines for migraine headache. Report of the Quality Standards Subcommittee of the American Academy of Neurology. Retrieved February 14, 2005, from http://www.aan.com/professionals/practice/guideline/index.cfm

Smith, R. (1996). Impact of migraine on the family. *Headache, 36,* 278.

Solomon, G. D., & Dahlöf, C. G. H. (2000). Impact of headache on the individual sufferer. In J. Olesen, P. Tfelt-Hansen, & K. M. A. Welch (Eds.), *The headaches* (2nd ed., pp. 25–31). Philadelphia: Lippincott Williams & Wilkins.

Spitzer, W. B., LeBlanc, F. E., Dupuis, M., et al. (1987). Scientific approach to the assessment and management of activity-related spinal disorders: A monograph for clinicians. Report of the Quebec Task Force on Spinal Disorders. *Spine, 12*(Suppl.), S1–S59.

Stewart, W. F., Lipton, R. B., Dawson, A. J., & Sawyer, J. (2001). Development and testing of the Migraine Disability Assessment (MIDAS) Questionnaire to assess headache-related disability. *Neurology, 56*(Suppl. 6), S20–S28.

Stewart, W. F., Lipton, R. B., Kolodner, K., Liberman, J. N., & Sawyer, J. (1999). Reliability of the Migraine Disability Assessment (MIDAS) score in a population-based sample of headache sufferers. *Cephalalgia, 19,* 107–114.

Stewart, W. F., Lipton, R. B., Kolodner, K., Sawyer, J., Lee, C., & Liberman, J. N. (2000). Validity of the Migraine Disability Assessment (MIDAS) score in comparison to a diary-based measure in a population-based sample of migraine sufferers. *Pain, 88,* 41–52.

Stewart, W. F., Lipton, R. B., Whyte, J., Dowson, A., Kolodner, K., Liberman, J. N., et al. (1999). An international study to assess reliability of the Migraine Disability Assessment (MIDAS) score. *Neurology, 53,* 988–994.

Task Force on Promotion and Dissemination of Psychological Procedures. (1995). Training in and dissemination of empirically-validated psychological treatments: Report and recommendations. *Clinical Psychologist, 48,* 3–23.

Tepper, S. J. (2001). Safety and rational use of the triptans. *Medical Clinics of North America, 85,* 959–970.

Turk, D. C., & Flor, H. (1999). Chronic pain: A biobehavioral perspective. In R. J. Gatchel & D. C. Turk (Eds.), *Psychosocial factors in pain.* New York: Guilford Press.

Von Korff, M., Galer, B. S., & Stang, P. (1995). Chronic use of symptomatic headache medications. *Pain, 62,* 179–186.

Waeber, C., & Moskowitz, M. A. (2005). Migraine as an inflammatory disorder. *Neurology, 64*(Suppl. 2), S9–S15.

Williamson, D. A., Barker, S. E., & Lapour, K. J. (1994). Psychophysiological disorders. In M. Hersen & S. M. Turner (Eds.), *Diagnostic interviewing* (2nd ed., pp. 257–273). New York: Plenum Press.

Wittrock, D. A., & Myers, T. C. (1998). The comparison of individuals with recurrent tension-type headache and headache-free controls in physiological response, appraisal, and coping with stressors: A review of the literature. *Annals of Behavioral Medicine, 20,* 118–134.

Wolff, H. G. (1937). Personality features and reactions of subjects with migraine. *Archives of Neurology and Psychiatry, 37,* 895–921.

World Health Organization. (1948). *Constitution of the World Health Organization.* Geneva, Switzerland: World Basic Documents.

Yucha, C., & Gilbert, C. (2004). *Evidence-based practice for biofeedback-assisted behavioral therapy.* Wheatridge, CO: Association for Applied Psychophysiology and Biofeedback.

CHAPTER 25

Sexual Dysfunction

ERIC W. CORTY

DESCRIPTION OF THE DISORDER AND CLINICAL PICTURE

Sexual activity is considered one of the most pleasurable activities in which humans can engage and is very important to us. One measure of its importance comes from sex as an entertainment industry for which, in 2001, Americans spent $10 billion to $14 billion on pornography. Sex, as an entertainment industry, generates more profits than professional baseball, basketball, and football combined (Rich, 2001).

Clearly, when something is such a focus of our interest and a defining aspect of our lives, we are concerned when malfunctions occur. Prime-time advertising for the treatment of sexual dysfunctions, starting with Viagra in 1998, has further increased expectations for flawless sexual functioning.

Sexual dysfunctions are disturbances in the processes through which sexual behavior unfolds. Much of how we conceptualize the natural unfolding of human sexual behavior comes from the work of Masters and Johnson (1966) who studied about 300 men and almost 400 women who engaged in sexual behaviors in their laboratory. From their study of more than 10,000 orgasms, Masters and Johnson derived the sexual response cycle in which men and women move from a state of quiescence to arousal, from arousal to a state of maximal arousal (the plateau phase), from plateau to orgasm, and then from orgasm back to quiescence (the resolution phase). These four phases are marked primarily by changes in the genitalia and reproductive organs, but there are also changes that occur in other systems (e.g., changes in heart rate, respiration, and skin). Most simply, Masters and Johnson's sexual response cycle can be thought of as two distinct phases: arousal and orgasm. The primary physiological process underlying the arousal phase is vasocongestion, increased blood flow. It is vasocongestion that causes both the penis to become erect and the vagina to become lubricated. Myotonia, or muscular contraction, is the physical process underlying orgasm.

Kaplan (1974) added a psychological dimension to the sexual response cycle with the addition of sexual desire to the two components of vasocongestion (arousal) and myotonia (orgasm). This three-part model is commonly used to organize sexual dysfunctions into problems of sexual desire, problems of arousal, and problems of orgasm. Not fitting neatly into this typology, the sexual dysfunctions also include sexual pain disorders in which sexual activity causes physical pain.

Problems of desire are appetitive disorders in which the appetite for sexual activity is inhibited or lacking. There are two sexual desire disorders that are classified by the *DSM-IV-TR* (American Psychiatric Association, 2000): hypoactive sexual desire disorder and sexual aversion disorder. Hypoactive sexual desire disorder involves a recurrent and persistent deficiency in sexual fantasy and desire for sexual activity. A person with hypoactive sexual desire disorder does not think about trying to engage in sex. He or she may find sex pleasurable when it is engaged in, but it is just not something that he or she thinks about or plans on doing. Clearly, the judgment of lack of interest is a subjective one, and the *DSM-IV-TR* notes that the clinician making the judgment must take into account factors, such as age and the context of the person's life, that may affect sexual functioning. In addition, in order to qualify as a disorder, the absence of interest in sexual activity must cause marked distress or interpersonal difficulty and it must not be caused by another psychological or physical disorder. (These provisos—that the disorder must cause marked distress or interpersonal difficulty and that the disorder is not caused by another physical or psychological disorder—apply to all the sexual dysfunctions.) The second desire disorder, sexual aversion disorder, involves more than a lack of interest in sex; it involves an aversion to sex. People with sexual aversion disorder find sex unpleasant and actively try to avoid genital sexual contact.

Turning from desire to arousal, there are two *DSM-IV* diagnoses of sexual arousal disorders, one for women (female sexual arousal disorder) and one for men (male erectile disorder). Female sexual arousal disorder refers to a persistent or recurrent inability to attain or maintain adequate vaginal lubrication or swelling until the completion of sexual activity. Male erectile disorder refers to a persistent or recurrent inability to attain or maintain an adequate erection until the completion of sexual activity.

There are three *DSM-IV* orgasmic disorders, one that relates to women and two for men. Female orgasmic disorder, what used to be called inhibited female orgasm, refers to a persistent or recurrent absence of orgasm following a normal phase of sexual arousal. The corollary to this in men is male orgasmic disorder, sometimes called retarded ejaculation, in which there is a persistent or recurrent delay in or absence of orgasm following a normal phase of sexual arousal. The third diagnosis in this category, rapid ejaculation, involves achieving orgasm too quickly and applies only to men. The *DSM* definition of rapid ejaculation involves persistent or recurrent ejaculation with minimal sexual stimulation and before the man wishes it. Though rapid ejaculation is diagnosed only in men, reaching orgasm too quickly may be a problem for women also. In a national probability sample in the United States (Laumann, Gagnon, Michael, & Michaels, 1994), 12 percent of women reported that they had a problem with reaching orgasm too quickly.

Sexual pain disorders—dyspareunia and vaginismus—are typically classified as sexual dysfunctions, though recently, it has been suggested that in women it may be more fruitful to classify these as pain disorders that interfere with sexual functioning (Binik et al., 2002). Vaginismus, obviously, occurs only in women and refers to recurrent or persistent involuntary spasms of the muscles at the entrance to the vagina, spasms that are severe enough to make penetration of the vagina painful or impossible. Dyspareunia can occur in either sex and refers to genital pain associated with sexual intercourse.

PERSONALITY DEVELOPMENT AND PSYCHOPATHOLOGY

Though since Freud we have thought of children as erogenous beings, it is not until puberty that interest in sexual activity surges and the normative sexual response cycle—desire, arousal, orgasm—occurs. Though boys can have erections before puberty, it is not until puberty that ejaculation occurs; for girls, puberty brings about increased blood supply to the clitoris and thickening of the walls of the vagina (Hyde & DeLamater, 2003).

Thus, sexual dysfunction is unusual among the topics covered in this handbook as it is not diagnosed in children. Children may exhibit behaviors that are corollary to adult disorders of mood, anxiety, or thought but children are not recognized as exhibiting impairments of sexual desire, arousal, or orgasm. Children certainly do engage in erogenous behavior, but behavior imitative of adults is rare.

For example, Friedrich, Grambsch, Broughton, Kuiper, and Beilke (1991) studied 880 2- to 12-year-olds in a North American city, excluding from their sample children with a known or suspected history of sexual abuse. The mothers of the children completed questionnaires about their child's behavior. Though there were some differences based on sex (boy versus girl) and age (2- to 6-year-olds versus 7- to 12-year-olds) the overall rate in these children of imitating adult sexual behaviors was low with only 1.1 percent imitating intercourse at least once in the past six months. Only 0.1 percent of the sample was reported as putting their mouth on someone else's sexual parts, 0.4 percent as asking to engage in sexual acts, 0.8 percent as masturbating with objects, and 0.9 percent as inserting objects into their vaginas or anuses. Friedrich et al. (1991) conclude that sexual behaviors that are more aggressive and that are more imitative of adult sexual behavior are unusual in children. This conclusion is tempered by the observation that children who have been sexually abused exhibit a greater frequency of sexual behaviors (Friedrich et al., 2001).

Trauma in childhood can increase the risk of psychopathology, whether a sexual dysfunction or some other form, in adulthood. Sexual abuse, in particular, has negative, long-term, psychological sequelae. The best studies in this area are twin studies as they control, to some degree, genetic and environmental variables that may influence psychopathology. Nelson et al. (2002) studied almost 2,000 Australian twins and found that both women and men who reported childhood sexual abuse were at increased risk for a variety of psychopathologies (e.g., conduct disorder, major depression, alcohol dependence).

Looking at the effects of childhood sexual abuse on adult sexual functioning, Laumann et al. (1994), in their national probability sample, found that women who reported childhood sexual contact with an adult or adolescent were more likely to report current problems in their sexual functioning. In a review article looking specifically at the effects of childhood sexual abuse on sexual functioning, Loeb et al. (2002) concluded that though we do not yet know how and to what extent it affects sexual functioning, deleterious effects occur with sexual experiences that occur too early in life, against the child's will, or when the child does not have the cognitive capacity to understand what is happening.

Even sexual behavior that may be apparently consensual may have negative psychological sequelae if it occurs too early and if there is an age discrepancy between partners. Leitenberg and Saltzman (2000) report on a representative sample of adolescent girls in the state of Vermont. The younger the age at first intercourse, the greater the likelihood of suicide attempts, use of alcohol, illegal drug use, truancy, and pregnancy in the subsequent teen years. Interestingly, there was an interaction between age discrepancy and age of first intercourse such that having an older partner had a greater impact the younger the girl was at first intercourse. These results mirror the conclusions drawn by Loeb et al. (2002): Sexual experiences that occur too early, against the child's will, or when the child lacks the cognitive/emotional capacity to understand what is happening can have negative consequences.

With regard to adult personality and sexual functioning, a number of different types of studies have been completed. One type of study links a personality variable to some sexual behavior or attitude. For example, Eysenck (1972) found that extroverts engaged in more sexual behavior than introverts. With regard to studies examining the relationship between sexual dysfunction and personality, most studies are descriptive, not hypothesis driven. In some studies many sexual dysfunctions are lumped together. For example, Fagan et al. (1991) administered a five-factor measure of personality to 51 men with sexual dysfunctions and compared their scores to the norms for the five-factor measure. They found the men with dysfunctions comparable to the normative sample except for an elevation in neuroticism. But, as the sample consisted of a heterogeneous group of men with sexual dysfunctions (about half had erectile disorder, about one-quarter had rapid ejaculation, and about 15 percent had desire problems), it is hard to draw conclusions about personality factors for specific disorders.

Of more interest are studies that examine personality characteristics for specific sexual dysfunctions. The Minnesota Multiphasic Personality Inventory (MMPI) has been used frequently in this regard. Munjack, Oziel, Kanno, Whipple, and Leonard (1981) had two samples of men in the United States seeking treatment for erectile disorder. One sample showed a mean MMPI score higher than 70 on scale 5 (Mf) and the other showed mean scores higher than 70 on scales 4 (Pd) and 8 (Sc). Tondo et al. (1991) had samples of Italian men with erectile dysfunction and rapid ejaculation. For none of the MMPI scales for either of the samples was a mean score higher than 70. Safir and Almagor (1991), with an Israeli sample consisting of men with erectile disorder, women with a sexual desire disorder, and women with an orgasm disorder, found that the only MMPI scale elevated higher than 70 was scale 8 (Sc) for the women with sexual desire disorders. In a Dutch sample of 38 women with a sexual pain disorder, VanLankveld, Weijenborg, and TerKuile (1996) administered a short form of the MMPI and found that the women differed from a comparison group on subscales measuring somatization and shyness. In a more recent paper with a non-MMPI measure, Hartmann, Heiser, Rueffer-Hesse, and Kloth (2002), with a sample of women in Germany with sexual desire disorders compared on a five-factor measure of personality to a control group, found that the women with desire disorders scored higher on neuroticism and lower on extroversion and openness to experience. Using an additional measure of narcissism, they found that the women with desire disorders felt threatened, unprotected, and defenseless.

It seems fair to say that no clear picture of a personality style associated with a particular dysfunction emerges from these studies and that research with larger and more representative samples is advisable. In addition, hypothesis driven, not descriptive, research is advisable. For example, I am in the midst of a study collecting personality data from men with rapid ejaculation in order to determine if, as predicted, they have higher than normative levels of introversion. There are two reasons to expect men with rapid ejaculation to be introverted. First, Eysenck's (1967) conceptualization of introversion/extroversion maintains that introverts have overaroused nervous systems, making them more sensitive to stimuli. This increased sensitivity should result in sexual stimuli being perceived as more intense, leading to more rapid ejaculation. Secondly, antidepressant medications that have been shown to be effective in increasing ejaculatory latencies have also been shown to lead to decreased levels of introversion (Knutson et al., 1998).

EPIDEMIOLOGY

The frequency with which sexual dysfunction occurs in the general population is not definitively established. The best data in the United States come from the National Health and Social Life Survey (NHSLS; Laumann et al., 1994), a representative, national probability sample of 3,432 18- to 59-year-olds who were interviewed over a seven-month period starting on Valentine's Day, 1992. The consent rate was quite high, with almost 79 percent of potential participants agreeing to participate. In the survey there were seven questions that asked about sexual problems. The stem for the questions was, "During the past 12 months has there ever been a period of several months or more when you . . . ," and the questions went on to ask about lacking interest in sex, having difficulty climaxing, climaxing too quickly, experiencing pain during intercourse, not finding sex pleasurable, feeling anxious about one's ability to perform sexually, and either having erectile problems (men) or lubrication problems (women). Though a response to one of these questions does not warrant a clinical diagnosis of a sexual dysfunction as it fails to take into ac-

TABLE 25.1 Percentages of Men and Women in the United States and United Kingdom Reporting Sexual Problems in the Past Year for Several Months (U.S.) or for at Least One Month (U.K.)

	Men		Women	
	U.S.	U.K.	U.S.	U.K.
Lack of interest in sex	16	17	33	41
Erection or lubrication problem	10	6	19	9
Unable to orgasm	8	5	24	14
Rapid orgasm	28	12	10	1
Painful intercourse	3	2	14	12
Sex not pleasurable	8	NR	21	NR
Anxious about performance	17	9	12	7

Note. NR = not reported.
U.S. data from Laumann et al. (1994); U.K. data from Mercer et al. (2003).

count, as *DSM-IV* requires it should, the degree to which the disturbance causes marked distress or interpersonal difficulty, the percentages who responded yes give some idea of the upper bound of 18- to 59-year-old adults in the United States who may have some sexual dysfunction. In Table 25.1, I have arrayed the percentages of men and women, ordered in terms of the sexual response cycle, who reported these problems.

Table 25.1 also includes similar data from the United Kingdom, based on a national probability sample survey of 11,161 16- to 44-year-old men and women (Mercer et al., 2003). The response rate to this survey was slightly higher than 65 percent, and the questions were similar to those posed by Laumann et al. (1994). Mercer et al. (2003) report, for men and women who had at least one heterosexual partner in the past year, the percentages who had these sexual problems for at least one month or for six months or longer.

Except for lack of interest in sex, the percentages reporting problems are higher in the United States than in the United Kingdom. There is a fair amount of similarity between the two countries with the top three problems for men, in both countries, being rapid ejaculation, lack of interest in sex, and anxiety about performance. For women in both countries the number one problem was lack of interest in sex, with difficulty achieving orgasm being the second most common problem.

Laumann, Paik, and Rosen (1999), in a secondary analysis of the Laumann et al. (1994) data, calculated that about 43 percent of U.S. women and about 31 percent of U.S. men had sexual dysfunctions. (Remember, these numbers are overestimates as they do not take into account the degree of distress or interpersonal difficulty caused by the disturbance.) Specifically, they concluded that the most common dysfunction in U.S. women was low sexual desire (22 percent), followed by arousal problems (14 percent), and sexual pain disorders (7 percent). In case you are wondering about the lack of orgasmic disorders as a specific difficulty, their clustering technique did not yield that as a unique factor. Orgasm problems were associated with arousal problems as 84 per-

cent of the women in this category also reported orgasmic problems and it was associated with low sexual desire as 49 percent of women in this category also reported orgasm problems; it was not associated with sexual pain disorders as only 4 percent of women in this category reported problems with orgasm (A. Paik, personal communication, April 13, 2001). The most common problem for U.S. men was rapid ejaculation (21 percent), followed by erectile dysfunction (5 percent), and low sexual desire (5 percent).

Laumann et al. (1994) and Mercer et al. (2003) may overestimate the prevalence of sexual dysfunction as they did not ask about the degree to which the sexual problems experienced caused distress and causing either marked distress or interpersonal difficulty is necessary to meet criteria for a sexual dysfunction diagnosis. Bancroft, Loftus, and Long (2003) conducted a study in which a probability sample of almost 1,000 White or Black/African American women in the United States were interviewed by phone. The women were between the ages of 20 and 65 and had to be living for at least six months in a heterosexual relationship. The participation rate was lower than in the Laumann study, 53 percent. The women were asked about the frequency of sexual experiences over the past month and, among other questions, on how many of those occasions they had experienced arousal, vaginal lubrication, orgasm, or pain. Following this, they were asked two questions about sexual distress over the past four weeks: (1) how much distress or worry their sexual relationships had caused them and (2) how much distress or worry their own sexuality had caused them.

Almost 20 percent reported moderate or a great deal of distress about their sexual relationship and almost 15 percent reported moderate or a great deal of distress about their own sexuality. Combining these two questions, about a quarter of the respondents (24.4 percent) indicated that in the past month they had had moderate or more distress about either their sexual relationship or their own sexuality. This number is lower than the figure reported by Laumann et al. (1999) that 43 percent of U.S. women have a sexual dysfunction. The difference may be methodological (the two studies queried about different time frames, had different consent rates, were conducted at different points in time, etc.) or may reflect that sexual problems are not necessarily sexual dysfunctions. In either event, the differences serve to remind us that our estimates of prevalence are just that—estimates.

ETIOLOGY

Views on the causes of sexual dysfunction have shifted over the years as theories have given way to empirical research and pharmacotherapy has become a first-line treatment modality. Etiological theories rely upon either organic or psychological factors and within psychological theories they focus either on distal factors (e.g., childhood sexual abuse) or proximal factors (e.g., relationship problems or anxiety over sexual performance). Of course, a more nuanced view of etiology calls for the interaction of organic and psychological factors.

Organic, or physical, factors certainly can account for sexual dysfunctions. For example, physical illness (e.g., diabetes), physical trauma (e.g., prostatectomy), prescription drugs (e.g., antihypertensives), and substance abuse (e.g., alcoholism) are all associated with male erectile disorder. A common side effect of drugs used to treat psychiatric disorders is a decrease in sexual desire and an interference with orgasm in both men and women (Crenshaw & Goldberg, 1996).

An organic etiology can also involve constitutional factors. Fischer et al. (2004) conducted a twin study of erectile dysfunction. Using more than 1,500 twin pairs from the Vietnam Era Twin Registry, they calculated concordance rates for difficulty in having and in maintaining an erection for both monozygotic and dizygotic twin pairs. Adjusting the concordance rates for physical risk factors (e.g., age, diabetes, hypertension, alcohol consumption, cigarette smoking), they found a correlation between monozygotic twins of .32 for difficulty in having an erection compared to a correlation of .18 in dizygotic twins. Using these correlations, they calculated a heritability coefficient of 29 percent. In other words, they estimate that about 29 percent of the variability in self-reported presence/absence of an erection problem is due to genetic factors. They speculate that these genetic factors play their role through impact on such things as the production of a neurotransmitter involved in the relaxation of smooth muscles in the penis.

Prior to the work of Masters and Johnson (1970) much of the psychological theorizing about sexual dysfunction focused upon the psychodynamic meaning of the symptoms. The classic psychoanalytic interpretation of premature ejaculation, for example, viewed rapid ejaculation as an expression of a man's unconscious hostility toward his partner (Abraham, 1949). Masters and Johnson brought a behavioral and cognitive focus to sexual dysfunction. They viewed sex as a process that should unfold naturally (à la their sexual response cycle) and sexual dysfunction as occurring when something interfered with this natural unfolding. In their view the interference could be due to a failure to engage in effective sexually stimulating behavior, due to ignorance or communication problems, or due to anxiety.

Masters and Johnson (1970) used the term *spectatoring* to describe a specific type of anxiety/cognitive interference. Imagine a man or a woman who experiences a transient disturbance in his or her normal sexual functioning during sexual activity. The next time he or she engages in sexual activity, he or she is likely to be anxious about sexual performance ("Will this problem happen again?") and thus is likely to be standing back in order to view, or judge, his or her sexual functioning. This being a judge, or spectator, of one's own performance interferes with the flow of behavior, making a reoccurrence of the dysfunction more likely and engendering a vicious cycle.

Barlow (1986) developed a model showing how anxiety and cognitive interference affect sexual functioning and sexual desire. Compared to people who are sexually functional, when people with sexual dysfunctions are placed in situations in which there is an opportunity for sexual performance, they respond with negative emotions like fear and anxiety and underestimate their degree of sexual arousal. Both the negative emotions and the misperception of arousal level lead to cognitive interference via nonerotic thoughts such as fear of failure. This leads to further anxiety and further interfering cognitions, resulting in a sexual dysfunction. Fear of the sexual dysfunction can then inhibit sexual desire.

With the advent of Viagra for the treatment of erectile dysfunction in men (Goldstein et al., 1998), there has been an increased focus on the physiology of sexual functioning for both men and women. This approach treats sexual dysfunctions as a physical problem that may be rectified by pharmacology. If a pharmacological treatment works one should not necessarily conclude that it is a lack of the externally supplied biochemical that caused the sexual dysfunction just as one should not conclude, if aspirin removes a headache, that the headache was caused by lack of salicylic acid. Additionally, Basson (2000) posits that the sexual response is more contextual in women than men and thus sexual dysfunction is less likely to be redressed pharmacologically in women. In fact, in 2004 Pfizer, the makers of Viagra, gave up on eight years of research on more than 3,000 women and stopped testing Viagra as a treatment for sexual dysfunction for women. The head of Pfizer's sex research team concluded that the brain, not the genitals, was the crucial sexual organ for women (Harris, 2004).

This more contextual approach is captured in the concept of the sexual equilibrium developed by Levine (1988). The sexual equilibrium recognizes that in intimate relationships sexual behavior is a dynamic, interactive balance between a person's sexual desires and behaviors, his or her partner's responses to these, and his or her perceptions of his or her partner's responses to these.

COURSE, COMPLICATIONS, AND PROGNOSIS

Sexual dysfunctions can be classified as lifelong or acquired and as generalized or situational (American Psychiatric Association, 2000). A lifelong, or primary, sexual dysfunction is one that has been present for a person's whole sexual life, for example a man who has never had or maintained an erection satisfactory for intercourse would be classified as having a lifelong male erectile disorder. The term *acquired,* or *secondary,* is used when a person has had a period of normal sexual functioning and now has developed a sexual dysfunction. For example, Waldinger (2003) reports the case of a 43-year-old man who had had normal ejaculatory latencies until one year before consultation. During evaluation Waldinger learned that the man's rapid ejaculation started about the same time that he had learned that his wife had been having an affair. In this instance the secondary dysfunction appears to be psychogenic, but in other situations organic factors could be the cause of a change in sexual functioning.

The generalized versus situational distinction refers to how pervasive the sexual dysfunction is in a person's sexual life. Generalized dysfunctions occur in all situations and with all partners whereas situational dysfunctions are limited to certain situations, partners, or stimulation. Many sex therapists report cases in which a man or a woman exhibits a sexual dysfunction with his or her spouse but not with his or her extramarital partner. This dysfunction would be termed *situational* and the etiology in such a case is almost always psychological.

Longitudinal data on the course of sexual dysfunctions are rare. Ernst, Földényi, and Angst (1993) report on 10 years worth of data following a sample of 591 young, Swiss adults at four points in time from age 20. At each interview the participants were asked if they had experienced any difficulties in their sexual life over the past 12 months. The overall percentage of women reporting any dysfunction over the past year remained stable over time (ranging from 24 percent to 27 percent), whereas the percentage for the men climbed over the 10 years from 11 percent to 26 percent. Limiting analyses to the 356 participants who completed all four interviews, Ernst et al. (1993) examined the chronicity with which sexual dysfunction was reported. Fifty-five percent of the men and 45 percent of the women in this subset of 356 never reported a sexual dysfunction; 29 percent and 24 percent (men and women, respectively) reported a dysfunction at one point in time; 13 percent and 18 percent, respectively, reported a dysfunction at two points in time; 3 percent and 10 percent, respectively, reported dysfunctions at three points in time; and 0 percent and 3 percent, respectively, reported dysfunctions at four points in time. Thus, about a quarter of the men and women reported a transitory, one-time period of sexual dysfunction. Ernst et al. (1993) considered anyone who reported a dysfunction at two or more points in time to have a more chronic disturbance and the women were significantly more likely to meet criteria for this (16 percent for the men versus 31 percent for the women). Comparing participants with "chronic" problems to those with "temporary" problems on other variables measured, Ernst et al. found that men with chronic problems tended to report more childhood externalizing problems and women reported more childhood emotional difficulties. Mirroring an association reported earlier, women with chronic problems also reported more traumatic sexual experiences before age 16. Looking at personality variables and symptoms clusters at age 30, in general men and women with chronic problems looked like men and women with temporary problems and differed from those with no reported sexual dysfunctions. That is, having a more chronic problem rather than a more time-limited problem was not an indication of more severe psychopathology.

It is generally accepted that depression is associated with disturbances in sexual function (Araujo, Durante, Feldman, Goldstein, & McKinlay, 1998) and a loss of interest in pleasurable activities, like sex, is one of the hallmarks of depression. Nofzinger et al. (1993) in a longitudinal study of 40 depressed men treated with cognitive behavior therapy found that successful treatment did not lead to increased sexual activity but did lead to greater satisfaction with the sexual activity experienced. They conclude that loss of sexual interest is a cognitive symptom of depression.

In one study based on data from the Massachusetts Male Aging Study, the longitudinal relationship between baseline risk factors, measured when the men were between ages 40 and 70, and the development of erectile disorder almost nine years later was studied (Araujo, Johannes, Feldman, Derby, & McKinlay, 2000). Though Araujo et al. (2000) measured physical risk factors (e.g., weight, alcohol use, cigarette smoking) their focus was on the psychological risk factors of depression, dominance, and anger. They found that the presence of depressive symptoms at Time 1 was not related to the development of erectile dysfunction and neither was the degree to which anger was experienced or expressed at Time 1. Dominance, however, was a statistically significant factor; men who were most submissive to their environment at Time 1 were about two times more likely to develop erectile dysfunction nine years later.

ASSESSMENT AND DIAGNOSIS

As a person's sexual life is private and may be an emotionally charged topic, assessing sexual dysfunction requires rapport and tact. Even small and apparently inconsequential changes in how a question is asked can affect how it is answered. Turner et al. (1998) asked teenagers about the frequency with which they engaged in high risk sexual behaviors either via a paper and pencil questionnaire or via a computer. The teens were randomly assigned to the two groups and significantly higher percentages reported high risk behaviors on the computer-based administration. How questions are delivered can determine the information gathered.

Risen (2003), in detailing how to obtain a sexual history, addresses clinicians' discomfort and awkwardness in asking about their clients' sexual functioning. She points out that though sexual problems often manifest themselves as the problems brought to treatment (e.g., depression, anxiety, or marital dissatisfaction), clients are unlikely to bring up a sexual issue on their own and need to be asked about it. Risen suggests that except in moments of crisis counseling and unless the presenting complaint is so focused as to preclude a sexual problem, that every client should be given the opportunity to address sexual concerns. Asking questions about sexual development should be a natural part of an initial inquiry about developmental history and significant life events.

An inquiry into sexual dysfunction should have some structure and should address the dimensions of desire, arousal, orgasm, and pain (Risen, 2003). In addition, an inquiry into gender identity and paraphilias should be made as problems in these areas can affect sexual functioning. Risen suggests having a structure but not being a slave to a structured interview. Rather, she conceptualizes the taking of a sexual history as helping people tell their "sexual story" while attending to the themes that emerge.

Often it is useful to have a paper and pencil measure of sexual functioning in order to collect consistent, comparative data. The Golombok Rust Inventory of Sexual Satisfaction (GRISS) was developed by Rust and Golombok (1985) as a short (28-item) measure of sexual dysfunction for heterosexual couples. There are two main scales, one for men and one for women, that measure the overall quality of sexual functioning within a relationship. In addition there are subscales that measure impotence, premature ejaculation, anorgasmia, vaginismus, infrequency, noncommunication, male dissatisfaction, female dissatisfaction, male nonsensuality, female nonsensuality, male avoidance, and female avoidance. Questions on the GRISS (e.g., "Do you have sexual intercourse as often as you would like?" "Do you fail to reach orgasm during intercourse?") are answered on a five-point Likert scale ranging from *never* to *always*. Among the strengths of the GRISS are its brevity, its coverage, and its psychometric adequacy. A problem, however, is that it is meant to be used by heterosexual couples, making it inappropriate for people who are homosexual or not in a relationship.

The rise of pharmacological treatments for specific sexual dysfunctions has increased interest in having focused outcome measures for clinical trials. As medications for erectile dysfunction have been around for the longest time, assessment in this area is most developed. Rosen et al. (1997) developed the International Index of Erectile Function (IIEF) based on interviews with men from five countries. The IIEF was originally translated into 10 languages, and the translations were checked via back translations into English. The final version of the IIEF has 15 items that fall into five factors: erectile function, orgasmic function, sexual desire, intercourse satisfaction, and overall satisfaction.

Realizing that the subjective evaluation of the level of satisfaction with treatment can have as large an impact on treatment continuation as more objectively measurable treatment efficacy, Althof et al. (1999) developed the Erectile Disorder Inventory of Treatment Satisfaction (EDITS). Rather than measure whether erections are adequate for intercourse and the frequency with which intercourse occurs, the EDITS has 11 questions that focus on factors such as whether the treatment has met the client's expectations and how confident the treatment has made the client feel about his ability to engage in sexual activity. In addition, as the partner's satisfaction with treatment can determine whether treatment continues, Althof et al. (1999) also developed a five-item partner version of the EDITS.

The most commonly used measure for evaluating female sexual functioning is the Female Sexual Function Index (FSFI), developed by Rosen et al. (2000). The FSFI is a 19-item self-report scale that yields subscale scores in the domains of sexual desire, arousal, lubrication, orgasm, satisfaction, and sexual pain. Items are scored on 5- and 6-point scales for which higher scores indicate better functioning. The FSFI, as well as directions about administration and scoring, is available online at www.fsfiquestionnaire.com.

IMPACT ON ENVIRONMENT

Family

Sexual dysfunctions occur in the context of sexual activity between people and both people can be affected. Levine's (1988) concept of the sexual equilibrium, that there is a balance between a person's sexual behavior and his or her partner's responses is relevant here. That is, a person will respond to a sexual dysfunction with thoughts about his or her own sexual abilities and the implications of this for his or her value as a person and a partner, filtered through his or her experiences and expectations. This will lead to changes in the person's sexual behavior or changes in other aspects of interactions with the partner. The partner will respond to these changes based upon her or his experiences and expectations and these responses will affect the other person as well. This equilibrium is dynamic, not static.

Carroll and Bagley (1990), in interviews with female partners of men with erectile dysfunction, present some data relevant to this. About half of the women reported that they felt that their partner was withdrawing as a result of the sexual difficulties and about 60 percent reported that they felt that their partners were not sexually pleased with them. One woman reported: "It has created a lot of tension and I feel extremely angry at my husband's lack of physical contact" (p. 75). It is very easy to imagine that this man would be aware that his wife was angry, making it less likely that he would approach her sexually, increasing her anger, increasing the distance between them, ad infinitum. Thus problems that are initially sexual can spill over into nonsexual aspects of relationships.

The study by Bancroft et al. (2003), in which a sample of women was surveyed about sexual distress in heterosexual relationships, provides some interesting data about how one partner's dysfunction can affect the other partner. Not significant in predicting a woman's level of distress about her sexual relationship with her partner was the presence of lubrication problems for her or the frequency with which she had orgasms. Instead, a variable that was a significant predictor of her distress about the sexual relationship with her partner was whether her partner had premature ejaculation. Distress was specifically related to ejaculation problems and not to male dysfunction in general as a partner having erection problems was not a significant predictor of the woman's level of distress. Thus for the women in this study, and the women made up a probability sample from the United States, a sexual dysfunction *in her partner* was more relevant to her distress about the sexual relationship than was her own level of sexual functioning. It is possible, of course, that her distress was caused by her partner's inability to provide adequate sexual stimulation, but this interpretation is mitigated by the fact that having a partner with an erection problem did not have an impact on distress. One reasonable interpretation of these data is that the sexual equilibrium is at play here, that a man with rapid ejaculation behaves differently with regard to sexual activity with his partner, likely withdrawing from it or curtailing it in some way, and that this has a negative effect on the partner's level of satisfaction.

Symonds, Roblin, Hart, and Althof (2003) present data that show that when sexual function is not smooth it has an impact on nonsexual self-perceptions. They conducted qualitative interviews with 28 men with rapid ejaculation. The most commonly reported concern, reported by almost 70 percent, was that rapid ejaculation had negative effects on their self-esteem and confidence. Half the men reported relationship problems, either being reluctant to establish a new relationship if they were not in a relationship at present or, if in a relationship, having distress over not satisfying a partner.

McCabe (1997) compared perceptions of degree of intimacy in the relationship between men and women with and without sexual dysfunctions. In every measured dimension of intimacy (emotional, social, sexual, recreational, and intellectual) men with dysfunctions reported less intimacy in their relationships than did men without dysfunctions. Interestingly, the picture was more complex for women. Though the total intimacy score was lower for women with dysfunctions than without, there were no significant differences between the two groups for emotional intimacy and intellectual intimacy. That is, though women with sexual dysfunctions reported less social intimacy, less sexual intimacy, and less recreational intimacy with their partners than did women without sexual dysfunctions, they did not differ in terms of how emotionally or intellectually intimate they found the relationship. This seems anomalous to me and in need of replication, but McCabe posits that as long as the woman is committed to the continuation of the relationship, emotional intimacy and sharing of ideas may remain unchanged from the woman's perspective.

Laumann et al. (1994), using NHSLS data, examined cross-sectionally the relationship between sexual problems and happiness. They found that for both men and women as their ratings of general level of happiness decreased on a five-point scale from *extremely happy* to *unhappy most times* that the percentage of respondents reporting sexual problems increased. For example, as happiness decreased there was almost a fourfold increase, for both men and women, in the percentages reporting a lack of interest in sex. Ten percent of the men who reported being extremely happy reported a lack of interest in sex compared to 37 percent of men who reported being unhappy most of the time; for women the percentages were 19 percent and 76 percent.

These data are cross-sectional and thus do not address whether it is a sexual problem that leads to unhappiness or unhappiness that leads to a sexual problem. Obviously, compelling arguments can be made for either interpretation.

In their analysis of the NHSLS data, Laumann et al. (1999) found more of a relationship between sexual problems and marital status for men than for women. Laumann et al. examined six sexual problems (lacking interest in sex, being unable to achieve an orgasm, experiencing pain during sex, not finding sex pleasurable, feeling anxious about one's sexual performance, or arousal problems (trouble lubricating for women, erection problems for men) and divided subjects into three marital status categories (never married, currently married, or divorced/separated/widowed). Only for two sexual problems for women (unable to achieve orgasm and being anxious about one's sexual performance) was this problem more prevalent among never married and divorced/separated/widowed than among married women. For men there were four sexual problems (lack of interest in sex, anxiety about sexual performance, not finding sex pleasurable, and having trouble maintaining or achieving an erection) that were more common among never-married and divorced/separated/widowed men than among married men. These data are correlational and, though one cannot definitively conclude that sexual problems increase the probabilities of being unpartnered, this certainly seems like a reasonable interpretation.

It is worthwhile to spend a little time pondering why more sexual problems seem to have an impact on men's marital status more than women's. This may relate both to romantic/sexual roles/expectations and to the relative importance of sexual functioning in defining one's identity. As men are, traditionally, expected to be more active in initiating relationships and are, traditionally, more concerned with their sexual prowess, it is easy to consider that a man whose sexual functioning is problematic may be more likely to be restrained in initiating relationships. In contrast, a woman with sexual problems may still be pursued by a man and may, passively, end up in a relationship.

All the research I have examined regarding the impact of sexual dysfunctions on the family environment has focused on the impact on the relationship of the dysfunctional person with his or her partner. Though, it stands to reason that the sequelae of a sexual dysfunction could devolve. I am not aware of any research that examines the impact of a sexual dysfunction on children or other family members.

Work, School, and Peer Interactions

Just as I am not aware of research examining the impact of sexual dysfunctions on family members other than partners, I am aware of little to no research that directly examines the impact of sexual dysfunctions on work, school, or peers. It is clinical wisdom that when taking a history of a man with erectile dysfunction one should explore business setbacks as a possible cause. Thus, it seems reasonable to posit an influence in the other direction, that a man who is having erection problems may feel less "manly" and thus may be less confident in a business or social setting. Such an effect is speculative and, I suspect, if it exists not very strong.

The only research that I am aware of that addresses the impact on nonsexual and nonrelationship domains is the already cited study by McCabe (1997). Not only did she measure intimacy in men and women with and without sexual dysfunctions, but she also measured quality of life. The quality of life scale she used measured both objective and subjective quality of life on seven domains: material well-being, health, productivity, intimacy, safety, place in the community, and emotional well-being. The subjective domains measure satisfaction and the objective domains provide more objective data (e.g., how satisfied are you with your material possessions versus how many material possessions do you have). I am going to focus on select, relevant, objective measures.

Though men and women with sexual dysfunctions reported, overall, a significantly lower objective quality of life, there were interesting differences between the two sexes. (In a personal communication, McCabe [March 7, 2005] points out that though the means reported in one of her tables are wrong, the reported F statistics are correct.) The women, but not the men, showed a decrement in material well-being (e.g., income) and productivity (e.g., productive hours spent per week) and both groups showed a decrement in community involvement. These data are correlational and their meaning hinges on the degree to which the dysfunctional and functional groups differ only in terms of sexual dysfunctions. However, they certainly suggest that the impact of sexual dysfunctions extends beyond the sexual arena. I find it curious that the impact seems less for men than for women and look forward to more research that directly assesses the impact of sexual dysfunctions.

TREATMENT IMPLICATIONS

Though potentially high percentages of men and women suffer from a sexual dysfunction, relatively low percentages seek treatment for it. Laumann et al. (1999) present data from the United States showing that of those who reported sexual problems, only about 10 percent of men and 20 percent of women sought consultation. The arrival of Viagra in 1998 brought about an increased awareness that treatment options existed for sexual dysfunctions and so the Laumann et al. (1999) data, which were collected in 1992, may underestimate the current rate of help seeking. Interestingly, data from Mercer et al. (2003), which, though collected from a different country (United Kingdom) and collected post-Viagra, show similar percentages of men (10 percent) and women (21 percent) seeking treatment for their sexual problems.

Laumann et al. (1999) report that they conducted an analysis of help-seeking behavior that was not included in their article but that is available upon request. An examination of the available table shows some variables that are associated with seeking help for sexual dysfunctions. Women in their 30s are more likely to seek help for a sexual dysfunction than are 18- to 29-year-old women, and White women are more likely to seek help than are Black or Hispanic women. With regard to specific disorders, women with arousal disorders and sexual pain disorders are more likely to seek treatment than are women with desire disorders. (Remember, there was no specific category, in this analysis for orgasmic disorders, though almost 85 percent of women with arousal disorders experienced orgasm difficulties.) The odds ratios for the specific disorders are quite high; compared to women with desire disorders, those with arousal disorders are 3.6 times as likely to seek treatment and those with pain disorders are 6.3 times as likely to seek treatment. Marital status and education had no impact on treatment seeking.

The picture for men is different, with only two variables being significantly related to help seeking: men who have never been married are significantly less likely to seek help than are married men and men who are Catholic are significantly less likely to seek help than are men of mainline Protestant denominations. No other variable is significantly related to help seeking for men, not age, marital status, or race/ethnicity and not type of sexual problem.

The most interesting thing in this data set to me are the dramatic differences in help seeking for women based upon the type of problem they have and the lack of differences for men. No matter the problem they have—desire, erection, or rapid ejaculation—men are equally unlikely to seek treatment, whereas women are almost four to six times more likely to seek treatment if they have an arousal or a pain problem over low sexual desire. Understanding this disparity merits further attention.

Masters and Johnson (1970) offered the first comprehensive treatment for sexual dysfunctions. Their treatment protocol conceptualized a sexual dysfunction as involving both members of a couple and necessitated the couple traveling to the Masters and Johnson clinic in St. Louis, Missouri, for a two-week stay. During this time there was an intensive evaluation involving sexual histories from both members of the dyad, medical and physical examinations, a roundtable discussion of the information obtained, training in sensate focus techniques, and specification of behaviorally focused treatment goals dependent upon the specific dysfunction. All of this was conducted under the supervision of a team of male and female therapists for each couple. Couples would be given sexual homework assignments to be completed away from the clinic and then discussed and troubleshot during treatment sessions. The homework assignments were graded in the sense that the final behavior was shaped by successive approximations to more sexually stimulating endpoint activities.

Such intensive and expensive treatment led to a select and highly motivated clientele, which may be partially responsible for the high success rates reported by Masters and Johnson. There was variability in success from dysfunction to dysfunction with, for example, Masters and Johnson reporting initial treatment success in 98 percent of men with rapid ejaculation and 77 percent of women with situational orgasmic dysfunction. Such high success rates have not been the norm since.

Since Masters and Johnson's time, psychologically based treatment has become of shorter duration, almost always involves only one therapist, and is less likely to involve both members of the couple. Nonetheless, the basic idea that the sexual response cycle is a natural process that will unfold if barriers are removed and education is given remains. To this end the removal of performance pressure, often via an increase in nondemand pleasuring and the use of gradual approximations to more complex and more sexually stimulating activities remain important aspects of therapy. Heiman and Meston (1997), in a review of empirically validated treatments for sexual dysfunctions, found evidence that treatments incorporating Masters and Johnson elements were effective for primary orgasmic dysfunction in women, vaginismus, and rapid ejaculation.

Heiman and Meston (1997) did find that mechanical treatments for male erectile dysfunction were effective. Their review was completed before the arrival of Viagra as a treatment for erectile dysfunction (Goldstein et al., 1998). The effectiveness of pharmacotherapy for this sexual dysfunction—it improves erectile function in 56 percent to 84 percent of the men who take it—has changed the treatment landscape for both men and women. Medications are now the front line treatment for male erectile disorder and, though no medication has been officially approved by the U.S. Department of Agriculture for the treatment of rapid ejaculation, some medications are effective (Althof et al., 1995) and this has become a first-choice treatment option. Ease of use is clearly a driving force behind treatment selection.

There are no pharmacological treatments that are approved for any of the female sexual disorders, though this arena is being hotly pursued by pharmaceutical companies. The pursuit is controversial as some are concerned that the economics of large potential profits have led pharmaceutical companies to co-opt researchers to medicalize sexual problems, defining the range of normative sexual functioning and classifying anything out of that range as in need of treatment (Moynihan, 2003).

Relevant to this controversy, recently there has been increased focus on male/female differences in their sexual response cycles. Basson (2000) has proposed a *female* sexual response model in contrast to the *human* response cycle of Kaplan (1974) and Masters and Johnson (1966, 1970). She points out that Masters and Johnson based their conclusions about women's sexual functioning from a group of women who were willing to be observed while engaging in sexual behavior in a laboratory setting and who were orgasmic with intercourse and that this subset of women may not be representative of the larger population of women. The traditional Masters and Johnson sexual response cycle is focused on genital responses and ignores relationship issues that tend to be more important to women.

Women's sexual response is more likely to be due to a desire for intimacy and men's is more likely to be due to a desire for sexual release. For example, in a 1985 study, Carroll, Volk, and Hyde asked college students why they wanted or needed sex. The most common answer from men was "horniness" and the most common answer from women was for "emotional reasons." Women's motivations to engage in sexual behavior certainly do and may include biological drive but often more important are relationship based goals such as establishing or maintaining intimacy. That genital vasocongestion may not lead to a subjective sense of sexual arousal in women as it does in men (Meston, 2000) and that orgasmic release is not as important to women as to men for sexual satisfaction (Basson, 2000) has implications for the efficacy of pharmacological treatments for sexual dysfunction in women. A recent cartoon (Gregory, 2004) neatly sums this up; it shows a man and a woman lying on their backs in bed, with some physical distance between them. The woman has turned to the man and is lamenting that it is unfortunate that no pill exists that stimulates conversation.

It may be that pills are not adequate for men either. Althof and Wieder (2004) report that helping men achieve erections—thanks to pharmacotherapy—is an easy process, but that getting them to engage in regular lovemaking after a period of dysfunction-related abstinence is more complex. They argue that psychotherapy still has a role in the treatment of sexual dysfunctions and point out four goals it may help meet. Just because a medical treatment is initially effective does not mean that it will be used or if it is used that the use will continue. Thus, psychotherapy can be used to identify and work through resistances to medical interventions. Althof and Wieder point out that factors such as how long a couple was asexual before seeking treatment, how one partner approaches the other about resuming a sexual life, and how each partner feels about using a medical intervention may be obstacles to effective treatment that came be overcome through a talk therapy.

Klotz, Mathers, Klotz, and Sommer (2005) present some data relevant to this. They followed 234 men who had been prescribed Viagra for the treatment of erectile dysfunction and for whom the medication had been effective. Although the Viagra had been effective for all the men, 31 percent did not refill their prescriptions within six months and were operationally defined as having abandoned treatment. Klotz et al. conducted a telephone survey of the 73 men who had abandoned treatment and found that 23 percent reported that they had stopped treatment because their partners showed no interest in sexual activity. An additional 43 percent reported that they had stopped treatment because either a lack of desire for sexual intercourse or a lack of opportunity for sexual intercourse. Though psychotherapy may not, directly, provide opportunity (i.e., a partner) for sexual intercourse, it can help address issues of lack of desire or interest whether on the part of the patient or the partner.

Second, performance anxiety may still play a role. Even though a medication may make sexual performance more reliable, the existence of past problems will likely lead to increased focus on the adequacy of one's sexual performance, which leads to increased concern about failure, which makes failure more likely. Performance anxiety is difficult to overcome without addressing it and most primary care physicians are not prepared to do so.

Third, couples make love in a context and the quality of the nonsexual relationship does affect the sexual relationship. As Althof and Wieder (2004) point out, relationships in which couples feel disconnected, resentful, or angry impede good sexual functioning, as may employment, financial, or family concerns. Psychotherapy, individual or couples, can help show the connection between these issues and sexual functioning and can help resolve or ameliorate these issues.

Finally, talk therapy can address sexual misconceptions and change sexual scripts. Couples can learn ways to have a satisfying sexual life even if arousal is not always reliable or long lasting or orgasm does not occur as or when desired. The primary definition of intercourse in most dictionaries is communication between people and psychotherapy can help restore this in both sexual and nonsexual aspects of a relationship.

REFERENCES

Abraham, K. (1949). Ejaculatory praecox. In E. Jones (Ed.), *Selected papers of Karl Abraham*. London: Hogarth.

Althof, S. E., Corty, E. W., Levine, S. B., Levine, F., Burnett, A. L., McVary, K., et al. (1999). The EDITS: The development of questionnaires for evaluating satisfaction with treatments for erectile dysfunction. *Urology, 53,* 793–799.

Althof, S. E., Levine, S. B., Corty, E. W., Risen, C. B., Stern, E. B., & Kurit, D. M. (1995). A double blind crossover trial of clomipramine for rapid ejaculation in 15 couples. *Journal of Clinical Psychiatry, 56,* 402–407.

Althof, S. E., & Wieder, M. (2004). Psychotherapy for erectile dysfunction. *Endocrine, 23,* 131–134.

American Psychiatric Association. (2000). *Diagnostic criteria from DSM-IV-TR.* Washington, DC: Author.

Araujo, A. B., Durante, R., Feldman, H. A., Goldstein, I., & McKinlay, J. B. (1998). The relationship between depressive symptoms and male erectile dysfunction: Cross-sectional results from the Massachusetts Male Aging Study. *Psychosomatic Medicine, 60,* 458–465.

Araujo, A. B., Johannes, C. B., Feldman, H. A., Derby, C. A., & McKinlay, J. B. (2000). Relation between psychosocial risk factors and incident erectile dysfunction: Prospective results from the Massachusetts Male Aging Study. *American Journal of Epidemiology, 152,* 533–541.

Bancroft, J., Loftus, J., & Long, J. S. (2003). Distress about sex: A national survey of women in heterosexual relationships. *Archives of Sexual Behavior, 32,* 193–208.

Barlow, D. H. (1986). Causes of sexual dysfunction: The role of cognitive interference. *Journal of Consulting and Clinical Psychology, 54,* 140–148.

Basson, R. (2000). The female sexual response: A different model. *Journal of Sex and Marital Therapy, 26,* 51–65.

Binik, Y. M., Reissing, E., Pukall C., Flory, N., Payne, K. A., & Khalife, S. (2002). The female sexual pain disorders: Genital pain or sexual dysfunction? *Archives of Sexual Behavior, 31,* 425–429.

Carroll, J., Volk, K., & Hyde, J. S. (1985). Differences between males and females in motives for engaging in sexual intercourse. *Archives of Sexual Behavior, 141,* 131–139.

Carroll, J. L., & Bagley, D. H. (1990). Evaluation of sexual satisfaction in partners of men experiencing erectile failure. *Journal of Sex and Marital Therapy, 16,* 70–78.

Crenshaw, T. L., & Goldberg, J. P. (1996). *Sexual pharmacology: Drugs that affect sexual function.* New York: Norton.

Ernst, C., Földényi, M., & Angst, J. (1993). The Zurich Study: XXI. Sexual dysfunctions and disturbances in young adults: Data of a longitudinal epidemiological study. *European Archives of Psychiatry and Clinical Neuroscience, 243,* 179–188.

Eysenck, H. J. (1967). *The biological basis of personality.* Springfield, IL: Charles C. Thomas.

Eysenck, H. J. (1972). Personality and sexual behavior. *Journal of Psychosomatic Research, 16,* 141–152.

Fagan, P. J., Wise, T. N., Schmidt, C. W., Ponticas, Y., Marshall, R. D., & Costa, P. T., Jr. (1991). A comparison of five-factor personality dimensions in males with sexual dysfunction and males with paraphilia. *Journal of Personality Assessment, 57,* 434–448.

Fischer, M. E., Vitek, M. E., Hedeker, D., Henderson, W. G., Jacobsen, S. J., & Goldberg, J. (2004). A twin study of erectile dysfunction. *Archives of Internal Medicine, 164,* 165–168.

Friedrich, W. N., Fisher, J. L., Dittner, C A., Acton, R., Berliner, L., Butler, J., et al. (2001). Child Sexual Behavior Inventory: Normative, psychiatric, and sexual abuse comparisons. *Child Maltreatment, 6,* 37–49.

Friedrich, W. N., Grambsch, P., Broughton, D., Kuiper, J., & Beilke, R. L. (1991). Normative sexual behavior in children. *Pediatrics, 88,* 456–464.

Goldstein, I., Lue, T. F., Padma-Nathan, H., Rosen, R. C., Steers, W. D., Wicker, P., et al. (1998). Oral sildenafil in the treatment of erectile dysfunction. *New England Journal of Medicine, 338,* 1397–1404.

Gregory, A. (2004, May 24). Cartoon. *The New Yorker, 80,* 92.

Harris, T. G. (2004, February 28). Pfizer gives up testing Viagra in women [Electronic version]. *The New York Times.*

Hartman, U., Heiser, K., Rueffer-Hesse, C., & Kloth, G. (2002). Female sexual desire disorders: Subtypes, classification, personality factors and new directions for treatment. *World Journal of Urology, 20,* 79–88.

Heiman, J. R., & Meston, C. M. (1997). Empirically validated treatment for sexual dysfunction. *Annual Review of Sex Research, 8,* 148–194.

Hyde, J. S., & DeLamater, J. D. (2003). *Understanding Human Sexuality* (8th ed.). New York: McGraw-Hill.

Kaplan, H. S. (1974). *The new sex therapy.* New York: Brunner/Mazel.

Klotz, T., Mathers, M., Klotz, R., & Sommer, F. (2005). Why do patients with erectile dysfunction abandon effective therapy with sildenafil (Viagra)? *International Journal of Impotence Research, 17,* 2–4.

Knutson, B., Wolkowitz, O. M., Cole, S. W., Chan, T., Moore, R. A., Johnson, R. C., et al. (1998). Selective alteration of personality and social behavior by serotonergic intervention. *American Journal of Psychiatry, 155,* 373–379.

Laumann, E. O., Gagnon, J. H., Michael, R. T., & Michaels, S. (1994). *The social organization of sexuality.* Chicago: University of Chicago Press.

Laumann, E. O., Paik, A., & Rosen, R. C. (1999). Sexual dysfunction in the United States: Prevalence and predictors. *Journal of the American Medical Association, 281,* 537–544.

Leitenberg, H., & Saltzman, H. (2000). A statewide survey of age at first intercourse for adolescent females and age of their male partners: Relation to other risk behaviors and statutory rape implications. *Archives of Sexual Behavior, 29,* 203–215.

Levine, S. B. (1988). *Sex is not simple.* Columbus: Ohio Psychology Publishing.

Loeb, T. B., Williams, J. K., Carmona, J. V., Rivkin, I., Wyatt, G. E., Chin, D., et al. (2002). Child sexual abuse: Associations with the sexual functioning of adolescents and adults. *Annual Review of Sex Research, 13,* 307–345.

Masters, W. H., & Johnson, V. (1966). *Human sexual response.* Boston: Little Brown.

Masters, W. H., & Johnson, V. (1970). *Human sexual inadequacy.* Boston: Little Brown.

McCabe, M. P. (1997). Intimacy and quality of life among sexually dysfunctional men and women. *Journal of Sex and Marital Therapy, 23,* 276–290.

Mercer, C. H., Fenton, K. A., Johnson, A. M., Wellings, K., Macdowall, W., McManus, S., et al. (2003). Sexual function problems and help seeking behaviour in Britain: National probability sample survey. *British Medical Journal, 327,* 426–427.

Meston, C. M. (2002). The psychophysiological assessment of female sexual function. *Journal of Sex Education and Therapy, 25*(1), 6–16.

Moynihan, R. (2003). The making of a disease: Female sexual dysfunction. *British Medical Journal, 326,* 45–47.

Munjack, D. J., Oziel, L. J., Kanno, P. H., Whipple, K., & Leonard, M. D. (1981). Psychological characteristics of males with secondary erectile failure. *Archives of Sexual Behavior, 10,* 123–131.

Nelson, E. C., Heath, A. C., Madden, P. A. F., Cooper, L., Dinwiddie, S. H., Bucholz, K. K., et al. (2002). Association between self-reported childhood sexual abuse and adverse psychosocial outcomes. *Archives of General Psychiatry, 59,* 139–145.

Nofzinger, E. A., Thase, M. E., Reynolds, C. F., III, Frank, E., Jennings, J. R., Garamoni, G. L., et al. (1993). Sexual function in depressed men: Assessment by self-report, behavioral, and nocturnal penile tumescence measures before and after treatment with cognitive behavior therapy. *Archives of General Psychiatry, 50,* 24–30.

Rich, F. (2001, May 20). Naked capitalists [Electronic version]. *New York Times Magazine.*

Risen, C. B. (2003). Listening to sexual stories. In S. B. Levine, C. B. Risen, & S. E. Althof, *Handbook of clinical sexuality for mental health professionals.* New York: Brunner-Routledge.

Rosen, R., Brown, C., Heiman, J., Leiblum, S., Meston, C., Shabsigh, R., et al. (2000). The Female Sexual Function Index (FSFI): A multidimensional self-report instrument for the assessment of female sexual function. *Journal of Sex and Marital Therapy, 26,* 191–208.

Rosen, R. C., Riley, A., Wagner, G., Osterloh, I. H., Kirkpatrick J., & Mishra, A. (1997). The international index of erectile function (IIEF): A multidimensional scale for assessment of erectile dysfunction. *Urology, 49,* 822–830.

Rust, J., & Golombok, S. (1985). The Golombok-Rust Inventory of Sexual Satisfaction (GRISS). *British Journal of Clinical Psychology, 24,* 63–64.

Safir, M. P., and Almagor, M. (1991). Psychopathology associated with sexual dysfunction. *Journal of Clinical Psychology, 47,* 17–27.

Symonds, T., Roblin, D., Hart, K., & Althof, S. (2003). How does premature ejaculation impact a man's life? *Journal of Sex and Marital Therapy, 29,* 361–370.

Tondo, L., Cantone, M., Carta, M., Laddomado, A., Mosticoni, R., & Rudas, N. (1991). An MMPI evaluation of male sexual dysfunction. *Journal of Clinical Psychology, 47,* 391–396.

Turner, C. F., Ku, L., Rogers, S. M., Lindberg, L. D., Pleck, J. H., & Sonenstein, F. L. (1998). Adolescent sexual behavior, drug use, and violence: Increased reporting with computer survey technology. *Science, 280,* 867–873.

VanLankveld, J. J. D. M., Weijenborg, P. T. M., & TerKuile, M. M. (1996). Psychologic profiles of and sexual function in women with vulvar vestibulitis and their partners. *Obstetrics and Gynecology, 88,* 65–70.

Waldinger, M. (2003). Rapid ejaculation. In S. Levine, C. B. Risen, & S. E. Althof (Eds.), *Handbook of clinical sexuality for mental health professionals.* New York: Brunner-Routledge.

CHAPTER 26

Sexual Deviation

WILLIAM D. MURPHY AND I. JACQUELINE PAGE

DESCRIPTION OF THE DISORDER AND CLINICAL PICTURE

There are a variety of ways individuals seek sexual pleasure, and human sexual behavior many times meets other than sexual needs, such as the need for intimacy, to relieve stress, to gain power, and so forth. *Sexual deviation* is a term that society and professionals use to denote certain sexual behaviors, and the term has a number of connotations and definitions. It may be interpreted in terms of psychopathology, deviation from a statistical norm, being illegal, and many times has moral or religious connotations. Often what is considered morally unacceptable can change over time, as can what we label as psychopathology or criminal. The changes in mental health professionals', and to some extent society's, views of homosexuality are good examples of changes in attitudes over time.

The psychopathology approach to sexual deviations is codified in the fourth edition of the *Diagnostic and Statistical Manual of Mental Disorders* (*DSM-IV*; American Psychiatric Association, 1994) in the section on paraphilias. The essential features of paraphilias are "intense sexually arousing fantasies, sexual urges or behaviors generally involving (1) nonhuman objects, (2) the suffering or humiliations of one's self or one's partner, or (3) children or other nonconsenting persons" (pp. 522–523). A second feature of the paraphilias is that they must "cause clinically significant distress or impairment in social, occupational, or other important areas of functioning" (p. 523). The common paraphilias and their core features, as defined by the *DSM-IV*, are described in Table 26.1.[1] In addition, many working in the area of paraphilias would also include a subset of rapists generally referred to as preferential rapists (Freund & Seto, 1998) or paraphilic rapists (Abel & Rouleau, 1990). However, this diagnosis has been controversial, and feminist scholars (Brownmiller, 1975) view sexual aggression against women as related to broader sociological factors and male socialization rather than to individual psychopathology. However, because rapists have been included in many of the studies we will review, they will be covered in this chapter.

Although the *DSM-IV* would seem to describe the core features of the paraphilias, the empirical data would suggest that, in fact, individuals engaging in the paraphilias vary on some of the core features, and there are questions regarding whether paraphilias actually represent forms of psychopathology.

Some paraphilias are criminal and victimize others (exhibitionism, voyeurism, pedophilia, frotteurism, and a small number of sadists). However, other paraphilias (fetishism, transvestitic fetishism, masochism, and probably most sadists) do not necessarily victimize others, have been decriminalized over the years and are viewed by some as a nonpathological alternative sexual lifestyle by many professionals (Baumeister & Butler, 1997; Docter & Prince, 1997).[2]

The study of the nonvictimizing paraphilias has a history similar to the study of homosexuality. Early studies of homosexuality focused on clinical samples, whereas later studies began to focus on nonclinical samples, and, as might be expected, these two groups differed in terms of psychological disturbance. Similarly, early studies of the nonvictimizing paraphilias also were clinical samples whose focus was on defining the psychopathology and treatment needs of this population (Wise, 1985). However, studies that are more recent have attempted to recruit nonclinical populations by sampling from social organizations, such as transvestite or sadomasochistic clubs, alternative lifestyle conferences, or publications geared to specific nonvictimizing paraphilias (Baumeister & Butler, 1997; Docter & Prince, 1997). Although these samples do not represent a random sample, they do present a different picture of these paraphilias than early clinical studies. These studies do not suggest severe concomitant psychopathology and individuals studied tended to show relatively healthy current social functioning.

The *DSM-IV* states that the fantasies, urges, and behaviors are recurrent and intense. Although the *DSM-IV* allows it to be episodic, it does suggest certain compulsiveness and a more than normal drive to engage in paraphilic behavior.

TABLE 26.1 Common Paraphilias and Descriptions from the *DSM-IV*

Exhibitionism	Recurrent, intense, sexually arousing fantasies, sexual urges, or behaviors involving the exposure of one's genitals to an unsuspecting stranger.
Fetishism	Recurrent, intense, sexually arousing fantasies, sexual urges, or behaviors involving the use of nonliving objects (e.g., female undergarments).
Frotteurism	Recurrent, intense, sexually arousing fantasies, sexual urges, or behaviors involving touching and rubbing against a nonconsenting person.
Pedophilia	Recurrent, intense, sexually arousing fantasies, sexual urges, or behaviors involving sexual activity with a prepubescent child or children (generally age 13 years or younger). The person is at least age 16 and at least 5 years older than the child or children.
Sexual masochism	Recurrent, intense, sexually arousing fantasies, sexual urges, or behaviors involving the act (real, not stimulated) of being humiliated, beaten, bound, or otherwise made to suffer.
Sexual sadism	Recurrent, intense, sexually arousing fantasies, sexual urges, or behaviors involving acts (real, not stimulated) in which psychological or physical suffering of the victim is sexually exciting to the person.
Transvestism	Recurrent, intense, sexually arousing fantasies, sexual urges, fetishism, or behaviors involving cross-dressing.
Voyeurism	Recurrent, intense, sexually arousing fantasies, sexual urges, or behaviors involving the act of observing an unsuspecting person who is naked, in the process of disrobing, or engaging in sexual activity.

However, this is probably not supported by the literature or clinical experience and not all paraphilics will report intense, recurrent drives. In fact, paraphilics tend to range on how "compulsive" their sexual urges and behavior are. Some paraphilics may be quite compulsive and preoccupied with their sexual interest, whereas for others the intensity and frequency of their paraphilic interest and behavior may be no different from individuals who prefer consenting sexual activities with mature, adult partners. In fact, individuals who prefer mature, adult partners also vary on the intensity of their sexual urges and behavior and a percentage of nonparaphilic individuals are very compulsive in their sexual behavior (Kafka, 2003). From a purely practical standpoint, many individuals engaging in illegal sexually deviant behavior will not self-report urges or fantasies making it impossible to "officially" apply a *DSM-IV* diagnosis.

In addition, many individuals who engage in what is viewed as paraphilic behavior are not distressed by the behavior. Many individuals engaging in nonvictimizing paraphilias view their behavior as nondeviant and as an alternative way of obtaining sexual pleasure. Some pedophiles do not experience distress (Marshall, 1997) or do not perceive their behavior as wrong, viewing it instead as more of a societal nonacceptance of their behavior.

One might draw from the preceding discussion that the paraphilias or sexual deviations do not belong in a book on adult psychopathology. However, our position is not to argue whether paraphilias represent mental disorders but to look at issues of consent and harm. A number of the paraphilias (pedophilia, frotteurism, exhibitionism, voyeurism, and some sadists) and rape are behaviors that occur without consent, at times involve significant force, and risk causing both physical and psychological harm to other human beings.[3] For this reason, this set of "disorders" deserves professional attention and intervention. Mental health professionals' approach to the other paraphilias is somewhat more complicated. Although, as we will see in later sections, many of the treatment approaches to both sets of paraphilias have a similar goal of stopping the paraphilic behavior, one can question whether this is always an appropriate goal with the nonvictimizing paraphilias.

PERSONALITY DEVELOPMENT AND PSYCHOPATHOLOGY

In general, paraphilias have an early onset. Abel and Rouleau (1990) report that more than 50 percent of their clinical sample of voyeurism, frottage, exhibitionism, and nonincest pedophilia had an onset before age 18. Breslow, Evans, and Langley (1985) report that more than 70 percent of a nonclinical sample of self-identified male sadomasochists had onset before age 18, whereas approximately 42 percent of self-identified female sadomasochists had onset before age 18. Bullough, Bullough, and Smith (1983) reported that 90 percent of a nonclinical sample of individuals self-identified as transvestites had cross-dressed by age 15, and fetishes have been reported to have an early onset (Mason, 1997).

Although adults engaging in paraphilias or sex-offending behavior report an early onset of their behavior, this does not mean that most adolescents, who engage in sex-offending behavior and probably other paraphilic behavior, continue into adulthood. For adolescents identified as sex offenders, recidivism rates across studies suggest only 8 percent to 12 percent recidivism rates. Even though recidivism rates only reflect those caught, the data still suggest that many adolescents, whose behavior is labeled as sex offending, desist before adulthood. There is less data on nonvictimizing paraphilias. However, it would not be unusual for an adolescent to use female underwear to masturbate and to have this behavior stop as the adolescent moves into adulthood.

Most of the data we have on the personality development of sexually deviant behavior is based on studies of adolescent sex offenders or are retrospective reports of adults. In recent years, there has been some increased focus on what are termed children with sexual behavior problems (Chaffin, Letourneau, & Silvosky, 2002). These are children who engage in aggressive sexual behavior, sexual behavior directed toward much younger children, or various compulsive sexual behaviors such as compulsive masturbating or inserting objects in their rectum or vagina. However, there is little evidence these children are similar to adults engaging in paraphilic behavior and, therefore, will not be covered in this chapter.

Murphy, Page, and Hoffmann (2004) reviewed the literature on individual factors that have been studied or proposed to be specific risk factors or characteristics of adolescents engaging in sexual offending behavior, some of which would be considered paraphilic in nature. Those related to personality development included factors such as impulsivity, social competence, emotional management, deviant sexual interest, sexual preoccupation, the development of attitudes supportive of offending, and the development of empathy. Various reviews, including those by Murphy et al. (2004), Weinrott (1996) and Chaffin et al. (2002), all concluded that adolescent offenders are heterogeneous in terms of personality characteristics. That is, we have identified no single developmental pathway for paraphilic or sex-offending behavior. Although some differences in personality development and social functioning do emerge when one looks at different types of sexual offending or paraphilic behavior, there is significant overlap. Adolescents who molest children, and a mixed group engaging in obscene phone calls, exhibitionism, and toucherism (similar to frotteurism), show more deficits in social competence (Richardson, Kelly, Bhate, & Graham, 1997; Saunders, Awad, & White, 1986) when compared to those who assault peers/adults. Hunter, Figueredo, Malamuth, and Becker (2003) applied path analytic techniques to investigate factors that predicted offenses against children versus offenses against peers. They found that a number of psychosocial deficits, such as anxiety and depression, social problems, social withdrawal, and poor self-esteem, predicted offenses against children. In terms of factors related to delinquent type behavior, adolescent offenders are again heterogeneous. Butler and Seto (2002) have shown that adolescent offenders can be divided into those with and without additional delinquent behavior. It is not surprising that those adolescent sex offenders who had engaged in delinquent behavior were much more similar to delinquent peers than those who had not.

Worling (2001) took a somewhat different approach and applied cluster analysis to the California Personality Inventory of 112 adolescent offenders, which included both offenders against children and those against peers and adults. Results indicated that subjects were classified into four groups, which included (1) the antisocial/impulsive, (2) unusual isolated, (3) overanxious and reserved, and (4) competent/anxious. The antisocial/impulsive and unusual isolated groups had higher rates of violent reoffending than the other groups. These groups varied on amount of delinquent behavior and amount of what appears to be psychological/psychiatric disturbance.

For adult offenders, especially those offending against extrafamilial children, deviant sexual arousal as measured by penile plethysmography (Murphy & Barbaree, 1994) has generally separated this group from other paraphilic groups and normals. However, there is limited data on the degree of sexual deviation in adolescents and what data there is suggests that this may only be relevant for a subgroup of adolescents who abuse young males (Murphy, DiLillo, Haynes, & Steere, 2001).

Although some studies of adolescents showing paraphilic type behaviors suggest certain characteristics such as internalizing disorders or delinquent characteristics, it is not clear that these characteristics would differ from other clinical groups. For example, many youth seen in mental health systems show similar types of personality characteristics, and many individuals seen in correctional settings also show disturbances in conduct and emotional control.

When attempting to study the psychopathology of adults engaging in sex-offending behavior, the findings are very similar to those found with adolescents. Adult offenders vary on most of the characteristics outlined, such as impulsivity, social competence, emotional management, and deviant sexual arousal (Chaffin et al., 2002).

Wise, Fagan, Schmidt, Ponticas, and Costa (1991) studied personality functioning in a clinical sample of transvestites comparing their results to another paraphilic group, which was not clearly defined, but in general, there was no difference between the transvestite group and the other paraphilic group. The study did report that compared to the normative sample for the NEO Personality Inventory, transvestites were high in neuroticism and vulnerability to stress and low in agreeableness and conscientious. However, this was a group of adults being seen by mental health professionals and may not be representative of transvestites as a group. Many of the characteristics described could be secondary to having a sexual attraction pattern that society in general does not accept.

There are also questions as to whether gender identity disturbance may be a precursor to transvestitic behavior. A retrospective study (Doorn, Poortinga, & Verschoor, 1994) compared normal heterosexual males to transvestites to early and late onset transsexuals. They found that transvestites reported less preference for female toys and games and for female friends than the transsexual groups, although they had a slight preference for feminine related activities and friends than the heterosexual group. The overall literature suggests that there is a subgroup of transvestites (Docter & Prince, 1997) for whom gender identity disturbance may contribute to transvestitic behavior, and this is reflected in *DSM-IV* criteria that allows specification of the presence of gender dysphoria. However, for most individuals engaging in transvestitic behavior, gender identity is primarily masculine.

EPIDEMIOLOGY

There are limited data on the actual incidents or prevalence of any of the paraphilias. Most estimates are biased by the samples chosen and response rates. In addition, data are at times based on individuals who may have engaged in a paraphilic behavior on only a few occasions and are not representative of individuals for whom the paraphilia represents the individual's usual sexual functioning. Given these limitations, we will review different estimates of the frequency of sexually deviant behavior.

One way of looking at frequency of paraphilic behavior is to look at the rates of victimization. Finkelhor (1994) reviewed a number of studies of adults reporting on the frequency of child abuse and found that 20 percent to 25 percent of women and 5 percent to 15 percent of men had been sexually abused as children. Cox and MacMahon (1978) report that 30 percent of college-age females had been victims of exhibitionists.

A second method of looking at the possible incidence or prevalence is to look at the number of victims per offenders. The most extensive data on this topic is by Abel et al. (1987), who presented self-reports of sex crimes by nonincarcerated paraphilics. This study was unique in that it was conducted under a federal certificate of confidentiality. The data are presented in Table 26.2 for paraphiliacs with victims. Offenders under conditions of confidentiality reported a significant and surprising numbers of victims. It is possible that the clinic directed by the senior author, who was one of the early practitioners in the field, may have been referred more difficult cases and, therefore, these numbers may not represent sex offenders in general. However, the numbers still raise concerns about the frequency at which victimization occurs.

A third approach is to collect data from the general population. As one can imagine, this is somewhat difficult as people may be reluctant to talk about sexual behavior that others

TABLE 26.2 Number of Victims for Selected Paraphilias

Paraphilia	Number of subjects	Number of victims
Extrafamilial pedophilia female target	224	4,435
Extrafamilial pedophilia male target	153	22,981
Intrafamilial pedophilia female target	159	286
Intrafamilial pedophilia male target	44	75
Exhibitionism	142	72,974
Voyeurism	62	26,648
Frottage	62	55,887
Rape	126	882
Sadism	28	132

Note. From Abel et al., 1987.

may consider deviant and illegal. In a college sample, Briere and Runtz (1989) found that 21 percent reported some sexual attraction to children and that 7 percent reported some likelihood that they would sexually involve themselves with a child if they thought they would not be caught. Fromuth, Burkhart, and Jones (1991) surveyed 582 college males from two universities and found that 16, or 3 percent, reported that they had sexually molested children. Templeman and Stinnett (1991), in a sample of 60 college students, found that 2 percent self-reported a history of exhibitionism.

In terms of sadomasochistic behavior, Kinsey, Pomeroy, Martin, and Gebhard (1953) found that 3 percent to 12 percent of women and 10 percent to 20 percent of men admitted to responding sexually to sadomasochistic themes. Hunt (1974), in a survey of *Playboy* readers, found that 4.8 percent of men and 2.1 percent of women reported obtaining pleasure from inflicting pain, whereas 2.5 percent of men and 4.6 percent of women reported sexual arousal to receiving pain. Baumeister and Butler (1997), in summarizing a number of studies, reported that 5 percent of people may enjoy some masochistic sex play, but probably fewer than 1 percent engage in masochistic sexual behavior on a regular basis.

Gosselin and Wilson (1980) report that 18 percent of a nonparaphilic sample reported having some fetish fantasies. Bullough and Bullough (1993) estimated that 1 percent of individuals engage in cross-dressing. However, Zucker and Blanchard (1997) severely criticized this number and indicate that it is not based on any reliable data.

ETIOLOGY

Unfortunately, there has been much more theorizing about the etiology of the sexual deviations than empirical investigations. There have been attempts to explain sexual deviations from psychoanalytic, behavioral, and biological perspectives and to look at the role of early childhood victimization in the etiology of sexual deviation.

There have also been attempts to develop more integrated theories, primarily in the area of rape and pedophilia (Finkelhor, 1984; Hall & Hirschman, 1992; Marshall & Marshall, 2000; Ward & Sorbello, 2003). Because the vast majority of those paraphilics who victimize others are male, there has also been a focus by feminist-oriented scholars (Brownmiller, 1975) and researchers (Stermac, Segal, & Gillis, 1990) to focus on cultural causes of rape. These include factors such as males' socialization to be dominant, to engage in sexual stereotyping, to be dominant in relationships, to perceive women as objects, and society's reinforcement of rape myths. Given the limitations of a single chapter, it will be impossible to give detailed attention to the various etiological theories. Therefore, we will try to highlight the evolution of thinking regarding etiology.

Like many psychological/psychiatric disorders, initial explanations of etiology tended to be from psychoanalytic theory. Early psychoanalytic theory (Karpman, 1954) focused on the role of maternal relationships, the Oedipus complex, and castration anxiety as being causative of paraphilias. Paraphilias were hypothesized as being the means in which the individual attempted to resolve castration anxiety and fear of adult women. As is generally the case, psychoanalytic theory is difficult to prove.

Learning and behavioral therapies began to dominate thinking in the 1960s (McGuire, Carlisle, & Young, 1965). The early theorizing was that paraphilic behavior developed through conditioning, such as the pairing of fantasies of a paraphilic behavior with masturbation and orgasm. There were a number of problems with simple conditioning models, one being that not all paraphilic subjects showed deviant sexual arousal in a laboratory (Murphy & Barbaree, 1994). For example, it is generally found that incest cases do not show deviant sexual arousal patterns (Murphy & Barbaree, 1994). From an empirical perspective, there were also serious questions of whether there is adequate scientific evidence that human sexual arousal could be conditioned and such conditioning maintained over time (O'Donohue & Plaud, 1994). Therefore, behavioral theories of sexual offending began to expand (Marshall & Laws, 2003) to include factors related to social competence, including relationship skills, and to cognitions that supported offending such as rape-myth acceptance or perceiving children as being interested in sex and not hurt by sexual involvement with adults. Although cognitive/behavioral models, as will be seen later, have guided treatment, it is not clear how well they explain etiology. As noted, not all paraphilics show deviant sexual preferences and not all show deficits in social competence and relationship skills. Many of the attitudes or what are referred to as cognitive distortions or minimizations may be post hoc excuses for the behavior and, although they may be involved in the maintenance of paraphilic sexual behavior, it is not clear they are involved in the etiology.

There have been a number of attempts to link abnormalities in brain functioning to paraphilic behavior (Langevin, 1990). One focus has been on temporal lobe abnormalities, and in case studies there have been reports of temporal dysfunctions in paraphilics, primarily fetishes (Blumer, 1970). Since that time, there have been a number of other studies using electroencephalogram (EEG) or neuropsychological testing that suggest temporal lobe problems in a variety of paraphilias (for a review of these studies, see Langevin, 1990). The data suggests that although there may be a small percentage of individuals engaging in paraphilic behavior that have findings suggestive of temporal lobe problems, the vast majority do not. Conversely, the vast majority of people with temporal lobe disorders do not engage in deviant sexual behavior.

Given the large gender differences in paraphilic behaviors, especially in those that involve victims, there has also been an interest in the study of androgens, specifically testosterone. However, there has been limited support for testosterone differences between paraphilic subjects, especially those engaging in sexual aggression and nonparaphilic subjects (for a review, see Hucker & Bain, 1990).

A popular belief is that being a victim of childhood sexual abuse has a causative role especially for pedophilia. However, it is not clear that data support this notion. First, Hanson and Slater (1988), in a comprehensive review, found that approximately 30 percent of adult sex offenders, which primarily included child molesters and rapists, reported a history of being victims of sexual abuse, although this may be closer to 50 percent for those who abuse young males. Deitz, Hazelwood, and Warren (1990), in a study of sadistic sexual offenders, found that approximately 23 percent had histories of sexual abuse and approximately 47 percent had histories of being physically abused. There is little evidence exhibitionists, voyeurs, or nonvictimizing paraphilias have higher rates of being sexually abused than the general population.

Lee, Jackson, Pattison, and Ward (2002) looked at developmental risk factors for sexual abuse in groups of adult paraphilics (pedophiles, exhibitionists, rapists, and multiple paraphilics) and a comparison group of nonsexual offenders. Childhood sexual abuse was predictive of pedophilia versus the comparison group and predictive of the multiparaphilic group (which included some of the pedophilic subjects who had other paraphilias) but not predictive of exhibitionism or rape. Childhood sexual abuse may increase risk for some subgroups of paraphilias but it clearly does not explain most paraphilic behavior. In addition, we also know that sexual abuse is a general risk factor for many psychiatric disorders (Burman et al., 1988) and that most young males who have been sexually abused do not go on to engage in sex-offending behavior (Slater et al., 2003).

There are a number of multifactor theories that have been proposed (Finkelhor, 1984; Hall & Hirschman, 1992; Ward & Sorbello, 2003). These theories propose that there are multiple pathways to sexually deviant behavior. For example, offending may occur because of deviant sexual attraction, deficits in relationship skills, inability to meet emotional needs with adults, or a general antisocial orientation. However, these theories do not answer the question of how deviant sexual arousal actually develops or why the other factors lead to deviant sexual behavior rather than other psychopathology.

Some have proposed that sexually deviant behavior may be related to deficits in parental attachment (Burk & Burkhart, 2002). Marshall and Marshall (2000) have integrated attachment theory into an extensive theory of the etiology of sex offending. Marshall proposes that poor parent-child attachment bonds increases the child's vulnerability and leads to poor self-esteem and poor relationship skills. These combined factors increase the child's risk to be sexually abused. Sexual abuse, low self-esteem, and poor relationship skills can lead to inappropriate juvenile sexual behavior and poor coping skills and the offender may learn to cope by turning to sex. This early inappropriate sexual behavior and using sex as a coping style can, through conditioning, increase the predisposition for adult offending. If the individual experiences disinhibiting influences, such as attitudes condoning offending, and the opportunity arises, offending may occur that is reinforced by further conditioning processes. Although the model is comprehensive and, as Marshall notes, there are studies that may support individual components of the model, there are no studies of the overall model. In addition, not all offenders have been abused and not all offenders show attachment deficits.

COURSE, COMPLICATIONS, AND PROGNOSIS

As noted, paraphilias tend to have an early onset. Although we have limited information on the life course of these disorders, we do have more knowledge regarding sexual offending behavior versus the paraphilias that do not involve victims.

Recidivism rates for adolescents engaging in sexual offending behavior, as noted, tend to be low, although general criminal recidivism tends to be much higher in the 20 percent to 25 percent range (Weinrott, 1996). Due to this, Becker and Kaplan (1988) proposed that there might be different developmental pathways: (1) the dead end path, (2) the delinquent path, and (3) the sexual interest path. Becker and Kaplan propose that most adolescent offenders will desist, as do many adolescents who engage in general delinquent behavior. A subgroup will desist sexual offending behavior but will demonstrate ongoing antisocial behavior, whereas a third, and probably the smallest group, will continue a pathway of sexually deviant behavior.

Another way of looking at life course is to look at recidivism rates based on age. Hanson (2002) has provided the most extensive data for individuals convicted of rape, extrafamilial child molesting, and incest. Rapists show a steady decline in recidivism rates with age, similar to that observed in nonsexual criminal behavior. Incest cases show a precipitous decline after age 30. Extrafamilial child offenders, on the other hand, show only small reductions in recidivism until after age 50, and none of the groups showed offending after age 60. This suggests, at least based on recidivism, that rapists' and intrafamilial child molesters' behavior desist over time, but this does not seem true for extrafamilial child molesters. Murphy (1997), in a review of the literature on exhibitionists, suggests that their behavior also tends to decline with age with few reports of exhibitionists being identified after age 40.

In addition to questions regarding the life course of paraphilic activity, a second question is whether there is progression from either less intrusive sexual offending behavior or nonvictim oriented paraphilias to more serious sexual offending behavior. This issue is complicated by the fact that many individuals display multiple paraphilias and, therefore, it is not clear that it is actually one paraphilia leading to another. For example, cross-dressing is sometimes found in the history of sexually sadistic criminals (Deitz et al., 1990). However, there are no data that indicate that most individuals who engage in cross-dressing behavior go on to be sadistic murderers.

In a study of 128 incarcerated child molesters and 170 incarcerated rapists, Longo and Groth (1983) reported that 28 percent of the child molesters and 15 percent of the rapists had histories of exposing as juveniles. Freund (1990), in a study of exhibitionists, found that 15 percent had raped. Abel, Mittelman, and Becker (1985) indicated that voyeurism was the initial paraphilic behavior for 9 percent of their rapists and 3 percent of their child molesters. The results suggest that for some more serious sexually deviant behavior, such as rape and child molestation, a percentage have engaged in less intrusive behaviors in the past. However, it still appears that most individuals engaging in exhibitionism or voyeurism do not proceed on to intrusive sexual behaviors. Currently there are little data to assist in identifying those who may be at more risk for more serious sex-offending behaviors.

COMPLICATING FACTORS

For those paraphilias involving victims, the most significant complicating factor is the presence of antisocial personality disorder, or more specifically psychopathy as measured by the Hare Psychopathy Checklist (Hare, 1991). Psychopathic individuals engage in a variety of antisocial behaviors and are very exploitive, callous, and self-centered. The literature is quite clear that the presence of psychopathy significantly increases not only risk for general criminal offending but sex offending (Hanson & Morton-Bourgon, 2004). In addition, their manipulative style and disregard for others make this group very difficult to manage in treatment programs.

PROGNOSIS

Most of the knowledge regarding prognosis is based on recidivism studies of those individuals engaging in sex-offending behavior, which generally includes rapists, child molesters and exhibitionists. As is well known, recidivism is a poor outcome measure and it is generally defined as rearrest and/or reconviction. Unfortunately, many sex offenses are never reported, resulting in many offenders never being apprehended. Therefore, recidivism rates will always be an underestimate of true reoffending. For those paraphilic behaviors that do not involve victims, recidivism rates, of course, have little to no meaning. Issues that are more important are quality of life, adjustment to the paraphilia over time, and impact of the paraphilia on intimate relationships.

In the largest meta-analytic study in the field, Hanson et al. (2002) reviewed 43 studies with a combined sample of 9,454 offenders. Most of the subjects were incarcerated rapists and child molesters. Those studies that used contemporary treatments (cognitive behavioral) and had credible designs showed a significant reduction in recidivism rates, with the treatment group showing a 9.9 percent rate of sexual recidivism and the control group displaying a 17 percent recidivism rate. Unfortunately, most of the creditable designs were not randomized clinical trials, and the strongest randomized clinical trial in the sex offender field (Marques & Day, 1998) has failed to find significant differences between groups. Therefore, the determination of whether sex offender treatment reduces recidivism is still unanswered, although the meta-analytic studies are encouraging.

ASSESSMENT AND DIAGNOSIS

Diagnostic criteria for the major paraphilias are included in Table 26.1, and, as noted, many in the field feel that there is at least a subgroup of rapists who meet criteria for a paraphilia (Abel & Rouleau, 1990; Freund & Seto, 1998). Some in the field of sex offender evaluation and treatment find the *DSM-IV* diagnoses to have limited relevance to either assessment or treatment planning (Marshall, 1997; Murphy, 1997) with paraphilic diagnoses providing little guidance to the assessment of relevant treatment targets. In addition, the two major criteria—recurrent sexual fantasies and urges and/or the behavior being distressing—are not found in all offenders (Marshall, 1997). Therefore, the sex offender treatment field has adopted an assessment model that focuses on principles drawn from the general correctional rehabilitation literature (Andrews & Bonta, 1998). These principles are referred to as the risk, need, and responsivity principles.

Assessment of sexually deviant behavior that is sexual offending requires assessment of risk to reoffend. During the last 10 years, there have been significant developments in our ability to predict recidivism, at least for those engaging in pedophilic behavior and those engaging in rape (Doren, 2002). The field has a number of validated, actuarial risk-assessment instruments that significantly improve risk prediction over clinical judgment (Hanson & Morton-Bourgon, 2004).

Frequently used instruments include the Rapid Risk Assessment of Sex Offender Recidivism (RRASOR; Hanson, 1997), the STATIC-99 (Hanson & Thornton, 2000), the Minnesota Sex Offender Screening Tool–Revised (MNSOST-R; Epperson et al., 1999), the Violence Risk Appraisal Guide (VRAG; Webster, Harris, Rice, Cormier, & Quinsey, 1994), and the Sex Offender Risk Appraisal Guide (SORAG; Quinsey, Harris, Rice, & Cormier, 1998). The reliability and validity data associated with these instruments has been thoroughly reviewed by Doren (2002), and a number of studies have compared the various instruments (Barbaree, Seto, Langton, & Peacock, 2001; Hanson & Morton-Bourgon, 2004; Hanson & Thornton, 2000). Whereas there is some variation across studies, the various instruments generally perform equally in predicting sexual recidivism, although the VRAG is thought to be a better predictor of general violent reoffending. These scales basically assess deviant sexual interest and general criminality and primarily assess static variables, that is, past history that cannot change.

These scales are most valuable for determining the intensity of treatment needed and the degree of external supervision needed. However, because they are primarily static, they do little to guide choice of treatment targets. Therefore, the second aspect of the assessment model is the assessment of need or what is generally referred to as dynamic risk factors. These are factors that have been shown to relate to recidivism and are changeable. The specific factors have generally been determined by meta-analysis (Hanson & Morton-Bourgon, 2004). Assessment approaches have included structured clinical rating scales such as the Sex Offender Need Assessment Rating (SONAR; Hanson & Harris, 2001) or the Sexual Violence Risk–20 (Boer, Hart, Kropp, & Webster, 1997). Other assessment models have used a variety of psychological tests to measure dynamic risk factors (Beech, Fisher, & Thornton, 2003).

Although there have been different approaches, they all tend to assess similar constructs. Those most relevant to psychological assessment are (1) significant social influences, (2) intimacy deficits/relationship deficits, (3) sexual self-regulation, (4) attitudes supportive of offending, and (5) general self-management, which includes both behavior and emotional management skills (Hanson & Harris, 2002).

The offender's social network can assist an offender in avoiding relapse or can increase risk to reoffend. Offenders who have social networks that encourage their denial, minimizations, and distortions are more likely to reoffend than those who have a social network that encourages prosocial behavior. When assessing offenders, it is important to attempt to identify those who are important in their lives, the attitudes these individuals have toward the offending, and the extent to which the individual's social network itself is involved in criminal behavior.

There has been increased attention focused on offenders' relationship skills and possible intimacy deficits. Under this general category, Hanson and Harris (2002) have identified a number of factors to be assessed, such as (1) stability of any current relationships; (2) the offender's emotional identification with children, that is, an attempt to meet emotional needs through children; (3) hostility toward women; (4) general feeling of social rejection and loneliness; and (5) a general lack of concern for others.

Those sex offenders who are more likely to reoffend also show deficits in sexual self-regulation, which include such factors of sexual compulsivity or preoccupation, using sex as a coping mechanism, and specific deviant sexual arousal. Offenders need to be assessed regarding their degree of sexual preoccupation, which may be reflected by frequency of masturbation, involvement in interpersonal sex, use of prostitutes, and involvement in pornography. In addition, Cortoni and Marshall (2001) have shown that many sex offenders use sex as a way to cope with a variety of stressors in their lives. They have described and presented some psychometric data on a specific scale to measure this factor. Deviant sexual arousal is many times measured by direct assessment of penile tumescence in the laboratory (Murphy & Barbaree, 1994) and more recently by viewing time (Abel, Jordan, Hand, Holland, & Phipps, 2001).

It has long been recognized that many offenders possess attitudes that seem to be supportive of their sexual assault, and Hanson and Harris (2002) have identified that factors such as sexual entitlement, rape supportive attitudes, and attitudes supporting child molesting may relate to recidivism risk. Many times these sexual attitudes are referred to as minimizations, distortions, or justifications. There are a variety of scales available that measure such attitudes (Beech et al., 2003).

High-risk sex offenders tend to not only show problems with sexual self-regulation but also show problems with what Hanson and Harris (2001, 2002) have labeled general self-regulation and Beech et al. (2003) have labeled self-management skills. This refers to individuals who are very impulsive with poor problem-solving skills. Such individuals tend to experience negative emotionality and tend to feel hostile, victimized, and resentful.

The final factor that guides assessment is responsivity (Andrews & Bonta, 1998). The basic concept is that for treatment to be effective, the treatment must match the learning style of the offender. Although there are a number of factors that impact an individual's ability to respond to treatment, some common factors that need to be assessed are cultural background, intellectual deficits or severe learning disorders, the presence of major psychiatric disorders or chronic mental illness, and the presence of severe personality disorders such as psychopathy. For individuals with intellectual deficits or severe learning disorders cognitively oriented programs will have to be adapted. Those with major psychiatric disorders need their disorders stabilized, and those who are more chronically mentally ill may not function well in the typical sex offender group. As we have noted, those with psychopathy can be quite disruptive in programs and there is some suggestion that they may need to be managed in separate programs, although the data on this are not clear.

Although the model is primarily geared toward individuals who sexually offend, much of the model may apply to other paraphilics who wish to change their behavior. However, as we have noted, many consider the nonvictim paraphilias as alternative sexual lifestyles rather than problems to be treated. Therefore, in addition to the assessment previously outlined, there are some specific considerations in assessing the nonvictim paraphilics. The first is assessing whether the individual is seeking help because of his own distress or whether the behavior is distressing others in their environment. For some, the treatment target may not be changing their behavior but working with the individual's social network to assist acceptance of the behavior. Factors to consider in terms of whether treatment should be geared toward reducing the behavior in the nonvictim paraphilias are the compulsivity of the behavior, the extent to which the behavior interferes with interpersonal relationships, the individual's own distress with the behavior, and whether the behavior may be dangerous to the individual. For example, one form of masochistic behavior (autoerotic asphyxiation) has a risk of death (Hucker & Blanchard, 1992). Autoerotic asphyxiation is a paraphilia in which sexual arousal is enhanced by self-strangulation and deprivation of oxygen to the brain.

IMPACT ON ENVIRONMENT

Like other sections of this chapter, one has to separate those sexually deviant behaviors that constitute sex offending, especially child molesting and rape, and those paraphilic behaviors that do not include victims. As we have previously noted, sexual abuse may affect at least 20 percent of women and probably more than 10 percent of males. There were more than 103,000 substantiated cases of child abuse in 1998 (Jones & Finklehor, 2001) and 248,000 rapes of persons older than age 12 (Rennison, 2002), based on the National Crime Data Survey.

Sexual victimization has a significant impact on the emotional and physical functioning of victims. Berliner and Elliott (2002) describe the multiple problems secondary to sexual abuse, such as emotional distress, post-traumatic stress disorder, acting out behaviors, and internalizing difficulties. Burman et al. (1988), as part of the Los Angeles Epidemiological Catchment Area study, found that histories of sexual abuse significantly increased risk for most psychiatric disorders and substance-abuse problems. Experiences of sexual assault also increase health care use (Walker et al., 2000).

In addition to the cost in terms of victimization, the actual handling of individuals apprehended for sex offending is extremely costly. In 1995, there were 240,000 sex offenders under the care or custody of correctional systems, with approximately 40 percent of these being in prison (Greenfeld, 1997), and this number has most likely increased. Aos, Phipps, Barnoski, and Lieb (1999), using cost data from Washington, found that in 1998 it cost the criminal justice system approximately $79,800 for one felony conviction for a sex offense; this includes the cost of investigation, prosecution, and the cost of incarceration. One can see if we multiply these numbers by the large numbers of offenders in the criminal justice system, the dollar cost for managing sex offenders is enormous.

Although there have been several studies on the impact of sexual abuse on victims, there has been limited data collected on the impact sexual abuse has on the larger system in which the offender lives. However, from clinical experience, especially when there are within family victims, there is significant cost to the family unit. First, in most jurisdictions, either the offender will have to leave the home or unfortunately, in some cases, the victim will be removed and placed in foster care. The foster care placement for the child has a number of possible negative impacts. The offender moving from the home can have an impact on the victim's siblings and affects the offender's partner. In addition, it many times leads to financial stress due to the reality that the family is now supporting two households. Finally, for any sexual offense, there is a risk that the offender will be incarcerated. Although most individuals in society feel that this is an appropriate response, it does clearly have a significant impact on the offender's family. Again, the offender's children, who may not be victims, have to deal with their parent's incarceration and the stigma associated with that. In addition, family income is likely to decrease creating additional stress.

Federal regulations that all states have community notification laws can also impact the offender's employment and family. These laws require that states have procedures in place to inform the community when sex offenders return to the community. At this point, more than half the states place this information on a Web site available to the public. In other states, a tier approach is used, with the general public only being notified regarding highest risk offenders, whereas for moderate-risk offenders notification would be on a need-to-know basis, such as to schools or day care centers, and for low-risk offenders only the police would be provided information.

A recent study of the community notification process in Wisconsin (Zevitz & Farkas, 2000) suggested, at least by offender reports, some significant negative impacts of community notification. The offenders interviewed were ones for whom their return to the community was presented in community meetings, a more active notification than placement on a public Web site. The offenders reported that 57 percent had lost employment, 83 percent reported they had been excluded from residence, and 67 percent reported emotional harm to family members. Examples were given of offenders' children being targeted for harassment.

For the nonvictim paraphilics, the impact of the paraphilia on the environment seems to be largely dependent on whether clinical samples are studied or nonclinical samples are studied. In our experience, individuals presenting for treatment may be having significant family disruption or may be finding themselves more isolated from social groups because of increased focus on the paraphilic behavior.

However, when one looks at nonclinical samples, such as the Docter and Prince's (1997) study of more than 1,000 transvestites, it appears that their paraphilic behavior does not necessarily impact marital relationships. They found that 60 percent of their sample was currently married, 23 percent divorced, and 17 percent never married. Twenty-eight percent of this nonclinical sample reported that their wives were completely accepting of their cross-dressing, 47 percent reported they had mixed views, and 19 percent were described as being antagonistic. It appears that most individuals in this sample were employed, and in fact many were employed in what would be considered upper-middle-class professions. Baumeister and Butler (1997) also observed that masochistic subjects tend to come from higher SES levels.

The nonvictim paraphilics may appear in clinical situations with significant distress, disruption of family relationships and potentially disruption of other social relationships because of obsessive focus on the paraphilia. However, for many of the nonvictim paraphilics there is limited disruption of their lives and many individuals find a way of integrating the paraphilia into their everyday functioning.

TREATMENT IMPLICATIONS

Within the context of this chapter, it is not possible to describe in detail treatment techniques used in the treatment of sexually deviant behavior, paraphilias, and/or sex-offending behavior and, therefore, we will try to outline a model of treatment. Treatment is guided by the risk, need, and responsivity principles described in the assessment section (Andrews & Bonta, 1998). Meta-analytic studies suggest that the general correctional rehabilitation programs following these principles show reduced recidivism (Bonta, 1997).

In designing treatment, the first question is intensity of treatment in terms of length and frequency. The risk principle states that intensity should be matched to risk. The literature also clearly indicates that placing low-risk offenders in long-term intensive programs either has no effect on recidivism or actually can increase risk (Andrews & Bonta, 1998; Bonta, 1997), and placing high-risk individuals in short-term, limited treatment will have no impact on recidivism. Because of society's and the legal system's understandable reaction to sexual offending, there has been a tendency to place all offenders in long-term treatment, which unfortunately may actually lead to increased reoffending for low-risk offenders.

Treatment is also most effective when interventions focus on treatment targets or dynamic risk factors that relate to

TABLE 26.3 Relevant Treatment Goals

Improving intimacy and relationship skills
Decreasing deviant sexual interest/arousal
Decreasing sexual preoccupation
Decreasing attitudes supportive of offending
Improving behavioral management skills
Improving emotional management skills
Developing prosocial support groups

recidivism (Bonta, 1997). Broad areas have been outlined in the assessment section and treatment goals derived from these broad areas are included in Table 26.3. At times, clinicians focus on targets that research has found not relevant to actually changing the frequency of future sexually deviant behavior. Examples are focusing on the individual's personal victimization or focusing on victim empathy. Although we may want individuals to recognize the impact their behavior has on others, and there may be clinical reasons to address an individual's history of trauma, there is no evidence that a focus on these areas will lead to a reduction in sexually deviant behavior (Hanson & Morton-Bourgon, 2004).

As noted in the responsivity principle (Bonta, 1997), effective treatment requires that treatment is delivered in a way that the individual can learn from the therapeutic experience. Therefore, treatment needs to be sensitive to the cultural background of the individual, learning difficulties, and/or psychiatric difficulties that may impact treatment delivery. In addition, style of treatment delivery is also a critical factor. Early treatment of sex offenders was often quite confrontational, with the offender being viewed as always being manipulative. However, the meta-analytic literature (Bonta, 1997) suggests that therapists who are warm and empathetic yet firm produce the best results. This information has been integrated in the sex-offender treatment research, including an increased use of motivational interviewing approaches (Mann, 2000) and attending to process variables may improve treatment outcome (Marshall & Serran, 2000).

The most effective programs also appear to be those that are structured, cognitive behavioral, and focus on behavioral skills training (Bonta, 1997; Hanson & Harris, 2002). Therefore, the treatment of sexually deviant behavior is cognitive behavioral and skill based. It is also recognized that there is no "cure" and treatment is embedded in a relapse prevention format (Pithers, 1990). Relapse prevention recognizes that interventions must focus not only on initial change but also on maintenance of change. When applied to sexually deviant behavior, this requires the therapist to identify individual factors that increase the individual's risk to return to deviant behavior (e.g., stress, anger, access to children, etc.) and help the individual recognize these risk factors and either learn to avoid them or to develop skills to cope with them.

Treatment is generally delivered in a group format. Many in the field feel that groups lessen the chance that individual patients can manipulate therapists, allow individuals with similar problems to confront other offenders, and that groups are clearly more cost-effective. However, there are no data that would indicate whether individual therapy or group therapy is more effective. The actual treatment methods used in many ways do not differ significantly from cognitive therapy techniques for other behavioral/psychiatric problems. These include procedures such as cognitive restructuring, role-playing to build skills, use of self-talk or relaxation to manage emotions, anger management training, teaching problem-solving skills, and impulse management skills.

In cases involving interfamily sexual abuse, family therapy is sometimes recommended, especially if families are to reunite. A general approach in some cases is for the various members of the family to receive treatment, including the offender, victim, and spouse, which may be followed by marital therapy and then followed by family therapy. Many treatment providers also work with the offender's social network, at least in educating them about the offender's risk and eliciting them as individuals to support a nonoffending and noncriminal lifestyle.

When dealing with deviant sexual interests, there are some conditioning techniques that are more specific to the treatment of paraphilias. For offenders who show deviant sexual interest, there are a number of behavioral procedures that are frequently used to assist the offender in managing their arousal and sexual urges. The most frequently used techniques are (1) satiation therapies, (2) covert sensitization, and (3) odor aversion.

There are two forms of satiation, masturbatory satiation and verbal satiation. Masturbatory satiation requires an offender to masturbate to nondeviant sexual fantasies until he ejaculates and then to switch to deviant fantasies and to continue masturbating to deviant fantasies. The underlying principle is the pairing of deviant fantasies with nonarousal that occurs during the refractory state. A more simplified version that appears to be just as effective is not to require the offender to masturbate following ejaculation but to just verbalize the deviant fantasies for 30 to 60 minutes. Covert sensitization is a technique that pairs deviant sexual fantasies with aversive imagery. Finally, odor aversion is similar to covert sensitization except the deviant imagery or the presentation of deviant stimuli is paired with a noxious odor, typically ammonia. Although all the techniques will tend to reduce arousal in a laboratory situation, the extent to which it generalizes outside the laboratory and the extent to which it maintained over time is not known. However, in most programs, techniques are presented as self-control techniques and not techniques that permanently reduce arousal.

Medications to reduce deviant sexual arousal are increasingly being used as adjuncts to cognitive behavioral programs (Bradford, 1997). The two most common classes of drugs are the selective serotonin reuptake inhibitors (SSRIs) and anti-androgens. Given that SSRIs appear to be effective for obsessive-compulsive disorders, it was felt that they also would be effective for those individuals who are most sexually preoccupied and/or sexually compulsive. There are no well-controlled trials, but clinical reports suggest these drugs can be an important part of an overall treatment program (Bradford, 1997). Antiandrogens work to reduce testosterone levels, which theoretically would reduce sexual drive. Again, clinical studies and experience suggest they should be considered for high-risk offenders with significant deviant arousal and compulsive sexual behavior.

NOTE

1. There are a number of other paraphilias listed under the *DSM-IV* category of *paraphilias NOS*. Because limited data exists on these more infrequent paraphilias, they will not be covered in the current chapter. However, those interested can find an excellent overview of paraphilias NOS in Milner and Dopke (1997).
2. We will refer to these as nonvictimizing paraphilias.
3. In this chapter we at times refer to these behaviors as sex offending. Most of the research literature on these sexual behaviors do not usually follow *DSM-IV* criteria but instead report on individuals engaging in child molestation, rape, exhibitions, etc.

REFERENCES

Abel, G. G., Becker, J. V., Mittelman, M. S., Cunningham-Rathner, J., Rouleau, J.-L., & Murphy, W. D. (1987). Self-reported sex crimes of nonincarcerated paraphiliacs. *Journal of Interpersonal Violence, 2,* 3–25.

Abel, G. G., Jordan, A. D., Hand, C. G., Holland, L. A., & Phipps, A. (2001). Classification models of child molesters utilizing the Abel Assessment for Sexual Interest. *Child Abuse and Neglect, 25,* 703–718.

Abel, G. G., Mittelman, M., & Becker, J. (1985). Sexual offenders: Results of assessment and recommendations for treatment. In M. M. Ben-Aaron, S. I. Huckers, & C. D. Webster (Eds.), *Clinical criminology: Current concepts* (pp. 191–205). Toronto, Ontario: M & M Graphics.

Abel, G. G., & Rouleau, J.-L. (1990). The nature and extent of sexual assault. In W. L. Marshall, D. L. Laws, & H. E. Barbaree

(Eds.), *Handbook of sexual assault: Issues, theories, and treatment of the offender* (pp. 9–21). New York: Plenum Press.

American Psychiatric Association. (1994). *Diagnostic and statistical manual of mental disorders* (4th ed.). Washington, DC: Author.

Andrews, D. A., & Bonta, J. (1998). *The psychology of criminal conduct* (2nd ed.) Cincinnati, OH: Anderson.

Aos, S., Phipps, P., Barnoski, R., & Lieb, R. (1999). *The comparative costs and benefits of programs to reduce crime: A review of national research findings with implications for Washington State.* Olympia: Washington State Institute for Public Policy.

Barbaree, H. E., Seto, M. C., Langton, C. M., & Peacock, E. J. (2001). Evaluating the predictive accuracy of six risk assessment instruments for adult sex offenders. *Criminal Justice and Behavior, 28,* 490–521.

Baumeister, R. F., & Butler, J. L. (1997). Sexual masochism: Deviance without pathology. In D. R. Laws & W. O'Donohue (Eds.), *Sexual deviance: Theory, assessment, and treatment* (pp. 225–239). New York: Guilford Press.

Becker, J. V., & Kaplan, M. S. (1988). The assessment of sexual offenders. *Advances in Behavioral Assessment of Children and Families, 4,* 97–118.

Beech, A. R., Fisher, D. D., & Thornton, D. (2003). Risk assessment of sex offenders. *Professional Psychology: Research and Practice, 4,* 339–352.

Berliner, L., & Elliott, D. M. (2002). Sexual abuse of children. In J. E. B. Myers, L. Berliner, J. Briere, R. T. Hendrix, C. Jenny, & T. A. Reid (Eds.), *The APSAC handbook on child maltreatment* (2nd ed., pp. 55–78). Thousand Oaks, CA. Sage.

Blumer, D. (1970). Changes in sexual behavior related to temporal lobe disorders in man. *Journal of Sex Research, 6,* 173–180.

Boer, D. P., Hart, S. D., Kropp, P. R., & Webster, C. D. (1997). *Manual for the Sexual Violence Risk–20: Professional guidelines for assessing risk of sexual violence.* Vancouver: British Columbia Institute against Family Violence and the Mental Health, Law, and Policy Institute.

Bonta, J. (1997). *Offender rehabilitation: From research to practice.* Ottawa, Ontario: Public Works and Government Services.

Bradford, J. (1997). Medical interventions in sexual deviance. In D. R. Laws & W. O'Donohue (Eds.), *Sexual deviance: Theory, assessment, and treatment* (pp. 449–464). New York: Guilford Press.

Breslow, N., Evans, L., & Langley, J. (1985). On the prevalence and roles of females in the sadomasochistic subculture: Report of an empirical study. *Archives of Sexual Behavior, 14,* 303–317.

Briere, J., & Runtz, M. (1989). University males' sexual interest in children: Predicting potential indices of "pedophilia" in a nonforensic sample. *Child Abuse and Neglect, 13,* 65–75.

Brownmiller, S. (1975). *Against our will: Men, women, and rape.* New York: Simon & Schuster.

Bullough, V. L., & Bullough, B. (1993). *Crossdressing, sex and gender.* Philadelphia: University of Pennsylvania.

Bullough, V. L., Bullough, B., & Smith R. (1983). A comparative study of male transvestites, male to female transsexuals, and male homosexuals. *Journal of Sex Research, 19,* 238–257.

Burk, L. R., & Burkhart, B. R. (2002). Disorganized attachment as a diathesis for sexual deviance: Developmental experience and the motivation for sexual offending. *Aggression and Violent Behavior, 8,* 487–511.

Burman, M. A., Stein, J. A., Golding, J. M., Siegel, J. M., Sorenson, S. B., Forsythe, A. B., et al. (1988). Sexual assault and mental disorders in a community population. *Journal of Consulting and Clinical Psychology, 56,* 843–850.

Butler, S. M., & Seto, M. C. (2002). Distinguishing two types of adolescent sex offenders. *Journal of American Academy of Clinical and Adolescent Psychiatry, 41,* 83–90.

Chaffin, M., Letourneau, E., & Silvosky, J. F. (2002). Adults, adolescents, and children who sexually abuse children: A developmental perspective. In J. E. B. Myers, L. Berliner, J. Briere, R. T. Hendrix, C. Jenny, & T. A. Reid (Eds.), *The APSAC handbook on child maltreatment* (2nd ed., pp. 205–232). Thousand Oaks, CA. Sage.

Cortoni, F., & Marshall, W. L. (2001). Sex as a coping strategy and its relationship to juvenile sexual history and intimacy in sexual offenders. *Sexual Abuse: A Journal of Research and Treatment, 13,* 27–43.

Cox, D. J., & MacMahon, B. (1978). Incidence of male exhibitionism in the United States as reported by victimized female college students. *National Journal of Law and Psychiatry, 1,* 453–457.

Deitz, P. E., Hazelwood, R. R., & Warren, J. (1990). The sexually sadistic criminal and his offenses. *Bulletin of the American Academy of Psychiatry and the Law, 18,* 163–178.

Docter, R. F., & Prince, V. (1997). Transvestism: A survey of 1,032 cross-dressers. *Archives of Sexual Behavior, 26,* 589–605.

Doorn, C. D., Poortinga, J., & Verschoor, A. M. (1994). Cross-gender identity in transvestites and male transsexuals. *Archives of Sexual Behavior, 23,* 185–201.

Doren, D. M. (2002). *Evaluating sex offenders: A manual for civil commitments and beyond.* Thousand Oaks, CA: Sage.

Epperson, D. L., Kaul, J. D., Huot, S., J., Hesselton, D., Alexander, W., & Goldman, R. (1999). *Minnesota Sex Offender Screening Tool–Revised (MnSOST-R): Development, performance, and recommended risk level cut scores.* Retrieved May 1, 2004, from http://www.psychology.iastate.edu/faculty/epperson/mnsost_download.htm

Finkelhor, D. (1984). *Child sexual abuse: New theory and research.* New York: Free Press.

Finkelhor, D. (1994). Current information on the scope and nature of child sexual abuse. *Future of Children, 4,* 31–53.

Freund, K. (1990). Courtship disorders. In W. L. Marshall, D. R. Laws, & H. E. Barbaree (Eds.), *Handbook of sexual assault: Issues, theories, and treatment of the offender* (pp. 195–207). New York: Plenum Press.

Freund, K., & Seto, M. C. (1998). Preferential rape in the theory of courtship disorder. *Archives of Sexual Behavior, 27,* 433–443.

Fromuth, M. E., Burkhart, B. R., & Jones, C. W. (1991). Hidden child molestation: An investigation of adolescent perpetrators in a nonclinical sample. *Journal of Interpersonal Violence, 6,* 376–384.

Gosselin, C., & Wilson, G. (1980). *Sexual variations.* New York: Simon & Schuster.

Greenfeld, L. A. (1997). *Sex offenses and offenders: An analysis of data on rape and sexual assault.* Washington, DC: U.S. Department of Justice, Bureau of Justice Statistics.

Hall, G. C. N. (1995). Sexual offender recidivism revisited: A meta-analysis of recent treatment studies. *Journal of Consulting and Clinical Psychology, 63,* 802–809.

Hall, G. C. N., & Hirschman, R. (1992). Sexual aggression against children: A conceptual perspective of etiology. *Criminal Justice and Behavior, 19,* 8–23.

Hanson, R. K. (1997). *The development of a brief actuarial risk scale for sexual offense recidivism.* Ottawa, Ontario: Department of the Solicitor General of Canada. Retrieved May 1, 2004, from www.psepc-sppcc.gc.ca/publications/corrections/199704_e.pdf

Hanson, R. K. (2002). Recidivism and age: Follow-up data from 4,673 sexual offenders. *Journal of Interpersonal Behavior, 17,* 1046–1062.

Hanson, R. K., Gordon, A., Harris, A. J. R., Marques, J. K., Murphy, W., Quinsey, V. L., et al. (2002) First report of the collaborative outcome data project on the effectiveness of psychological treatment for sex offenders. *Sexual Abuse: A Journal of Research and Treatment, 14,* 169–194.

Hanson, R. K., & Harris, A. J. R. (2001). A structured approach to evaluating change among sexual offenders. *Sexual Abuse: A Journal of Research and Treatment, 13,* 105–122.

Hanson, R. K., & Harris, A. (2002). *STABLE scoring guide: Developed for the Dynamic Supervision Project. A collaborative initiative on the community supervision of sexual offenders.* Available from author.

Hanson, R. K., & Morton-Bourgon, K. (2004). *Predictors of sexual recidivism: An updated meta-analysis.* Ottawa, Ontario: Public Works and Government Services.

Hanson, R. K., & Slater, S. (1988). Sexual victimization in the history of sexual abusers: A review. *Annals of Sex Research, 1,* 485–499.

Hanson, R. K., & Thornton, D. (2000). Improving risk assessments for sex offending: A comparison of three actuarial scales. *Law and Human Behavior, 24,* 119–136.

Hare, R. D. (1991). *Manual for the Hare Psychopathy Checklist–Revised.* Toronto, Ontario: Multi-Health Systems.

Hucker, S. J., & Bain, J. (1990). Androgenic hormones and sexual assault. In W. L. Marshall, D. R. Laws, & H. E. Barbaree (Eds.), *Handbook of sexual assault: Issues, theories, and treatment of the offender* (pp. 93–102). New York: Plenum Press.

Hucker, S. J., & Blanchard, R. (1992). Death scene characteristics in 118 fatal cases of autoerotic asphyxia compared with suicidal asphyxia. *Behavioral Sciences and the law, 10,* 509–523.

Hunt, M. (1974). *Sexual behavior in the 1970s.* Chicago: Playboy Press.

Hunter, J. A., Figueredo, A. J., Malamuth, N. M., & Becker, J. V. (2003). Juvenile sex offenders: Toward the development of a typology. *Sexual Abuse: A Journal of Research and Treatment, 15,* 27–48.

Jones, L., & Finkelhor, D. (2001). *The decline in child sexual abuse cases.* Washington, DC: U.S. Department of Justice, Office of Juvenile Justice and Delinquency Prevention.

Kafka, M. P. (2003). Sex offending and sexual appetite: The clinical and theoretical relevance of hypersexual desire. *International Journal of Offender Therapy and Comparative Criminology, 47,* 439–451.

Karpman, B. (1954). *The sexual offender and his offenses: Etiology, pathology, psychodynamics and treatment.* New York: Julian.

Katz, R. C. (1990). Psychosocial adjustment in adolescent child molesters. *Child Abuse and Neglect, 14,* 567–575.

Kinsey, A. C., Pomeroy, W. B., Martin, C. E., & Gebhard, P. H. (1953). *Sexual behavior in the human female.* New York: Simon & Schuster.

Langevin, R. (1990). Sexual anomalies and the brain. In W. L. Marshall, D. R. Laws, & H. E. Barbaree (Eds.), *Handbook of sexual assault: Issues, theories, and treatment of the offender* (pp. 93–102). New York: Plenum Press.

Lee, J. K. P., Jackson, H. J., Pattison, P., & Ward, T. (2002). Developmental risk factors for sexual offending. *Child Abuse and Neglect, 26,* 73–92.

Longo, R. E., & Groth, A. N. (1983). Juvenile sexual offenses in the histories of adult rapists and child molesters. *International Journal of Offender Therapy and Comparative Criminology, 27,* 150–155.

Mann, R. E. (2000). Managing resistance and rebellion in relapse prevention intervention. In D. R. Laws, S. M. Hudson, & T. Ward (Eds.), *Remaking relapse prevention with sex offenders: A sourcebook* (pp. 187–200). Thousand Oaks, CA: Sage.

Marlatt, G. A., & Gordon, J. R. (1985). *Relapse prevention: Maintenance strategies in the treatment of addictive behaviors.* New York: Guilford Press.

Marques, J. K., & Day, D. M. (1998). *Sex offender treatment evaluation project: Progress report.* Sacramento, CA: California Department of Mental Health.

Marshall, W. L. (1997). Pedophilia: Psychopathology and theory. In D. R. Laws & W. O'Donohue (Eds.), *Sexual deviance: Theory, assessment, and treatment* (pp. 152–174). New York: Guilford Press.

Marshall, W. L., & Laws, D. R. (2003). A brief history of behavioral and cognitive behavioral approaches to sexual offender treatment: Part 2. The modern era. *Sexual Abuse: A Journal of Research and Treatment, 15,* 93–120.

Marshall, W. L., & Marshall, L. E. (2000). The origins of sexual offending. *Trauma, Violence, and Abuse, 1,* 250–265.

Marshall, W. L., & Serran, G. A. (2000). Improving the effectiveness of sexual offender treatment. *Trauma, Violence, and Abuse, 1,* 203–222.

Mason, F. L. (1997). Fetishism: Psychopathology and theory. In D. R. Laws & W. O'Donohue (Eds.), *Sexual deviance: Theory, assessment, and treatment* (pp. 75–91). New York: Guilford Press.

McGuire, R. J., Carlisle, J. M., & Young, B. G. (1965). Sexual deviations as conditioned behaviour: A hypothesis. *Behaviour Research and Therapy, 2,* 185–190.

Milner, J. S., & Dopke, C. A. (1997). Paraphilia not otherwise specified: Psychopathology and theory. In D. R. Laws & W. O'Donohue (Eds.), *Sexual deviance: Theory, assessment, and treatment* (pp. 394–423). New York: Guilford Press.

Murphy, W. D. (1997). Exhibitionism: Psychopathology and theory. In D. R. Laws & W. O'Donohue (Eds.), *Sexual deviance: Theory, assessment, and treatment* (pp. 22–39). New York: Guilford Press.

Murphy, W. D., & Barbaree, H. E. (1994). *Assessments of sexual offenders by measures of erectile response: Psychometric properties and decision making.* Brandon, VT: Safer Society.

Murphy, W. D., DiLillo, D., Haynes, M. R., & Steere, E. (2001). An exploration of factors related to deviant sexual arousal in juvenile sex offenders. *Sexual Abuse: A Journal of Research and Treatment, 13,* 91–103.

Murphy, W. D., Page, I. J., & Hoffmann, M. L. (2004). Adolescent sex offenders: Characteristics, prevention, and treatment. In P. Allen-Meares & M. W. Fraser (Eds.), *Intervention with children and adolescents: An interdisciplinary perspective* (pp. 477–492). Boston: Pearson.

O'Donohue, W., & Plaud, J. J. (1994). The conditioning of human sexual arousal. *Archives of Sexual Behavior, 23,* 321–344.

Pithers, W. D. (1990). Relapse prevention with sexual aggressors: A method for maintaining therapeutic gain and enhancing external supervision. In W. L. Marshall, D. R. Laws, & H. E. Barbaree (Eds.), *Handbook of sexual assault: Issues, theories, and treatment of the offender* (pp. 343–361). New York: Plenum Press.

Quinsey, V. L., Harris, G. T., Rice, M. E., & Cormier, C. A. (1998). *Violent offenders: Appraising and managing risk.* Washington, DC: American Psychological Association.

Rennison, C. (2002). *Criminal victimization 2001: Changes 2000–01 with trends 1993–2001* (NCJ 194610). Washington, DC: U.S. Department of Justice, Bureau of Justice Statistics.

Richardson, G., Kelly, T. P., Bhate, S. R., & Graham, F. (1997). Group differences in abuser and abuse characteristics in a British sample of sexually abusive adolescents. *Sexual Abuse: A Journal of Research and Treatment, 9,* 239–257.

Saunders, E., Awad, G. A., & White, G. (1986). Male adolescent sexual offenders: The offender and the offense. *Canadian Journal of Psychiatry, 31,* 542–549.

Slater, D., McMillan, D., Richards, M., Talbot, T., Hodges, J., Bentovim, A., et al. (2003). Development of sexually abusive behaviour in sexually victimized males: A longitudinal study. *Lancet, 361,* 471–476.

Stermac, L. E., Segal, Z. V., & Gillis, R. (1990). Social and cultural factors in sexual assault. In W. L. Marshall, D. R. Laws, & H. E. Barbaree (Eds.), *Handbook of sexual assault: Issues, theories, and treatment of the offender* (pp. 143–160). New York: Plenum Press.

Templeman, T. L., & Stinnett, R. D. (1991). Patterns of sexual arousal and history in a "normal" sample of young men. *Archives of Sexual Behavior, 20,* 137–150.

Walker, E. A., Unutzer, J., Rutter, C., Gelfand, A., Saunders, K., VonKorff, M., et al. (2000). Costs of health care use by women HMO members with a history of childhood abuse and neglect. *Archives of General Psychiatry, 56,* 609–613.

Ward, T., & Sorbello, L. (2003). Explaining child sexual abuse: Integration and elaboration. In T. Ward, D. R. Laws, & S. M. Hudson (Eds.), *Sexual deviance: Issues and controversies* (pp. 3–20). Thousand Oaks, CA: Sage.

Webster, C. D., Harris, G. T., Rice, M. E., Cormier, C., & Quinsey, V. L. (1994). *The violence prediction scheme: Assessing dangerousness in high risk men.* Toronto, Ontario: University of Toronto, Centre of Criminology.

Weinrott, M. R. (1996). *Juvenile sexual aggression: A critical review.* Boulder, CO: Center for the Study and Prevention of Violence.

Wise, T. N. (1985). Fetishism—Etiology and treatment: A review from multiple perspectives. *Comprehensive Psychiatry, 26,* 249–257.

Wise, T., Fagan, P., Schmidt, C., Ponticas, Y., & Costa, P. (1991). Personality and sexual functioning of transvestic fetishists and other paraphilics. *Journal of Nervous and Mental Disease, 179,* 694–698.

Worling, J. R. (2001). Personality-based typology of adolescent male sexual offenders: Differences in recidivism rates, victim-selection characteristics, and personal victimization histories. *Sexual Abuse: A Journal of Research and Treatment, 13,* 149–166.

Zevitz, R. G., & Farkas, M. A. (2000). *Sex offender community notification: Assessing the impact in Wisconsin.* Washington, DC: U.S. Department of Justice, National Institute of Justice.

Zucker, K. J., & Blanchard, R. (1997). Transvestic fetishism: Psychopathology and theory. In D. R. Laws & W. O'Donohue (Eds.), *Sexual deviance: Theory, assessment, and treatment* (pp. 253–279). New York: Guilford Press.

CHAPTER 27

Marital Dysfunction

STEVEN R. H. BEACH, CHARLES KAMEN, AND FRANK FINCHAM

Despite considerable progress in defining and understanding marital discord, there is still no widespread agreement on the key issue of whether marital discord is best viewed as a *disorder,* defined by several distinct criteria and having categorical properties (e.g., Heyman, Feldbau-Kohn, Ehrensaft, Langhinrichsen-Rohling, & O'Leary, 2001), or whether it should be viewed as a *dimension,* defined primarily in terms of varying degrees of marital satisfaction. Nonetheless, available research identifies likely indicators of marital discord and suggests a number of generalizations about key aspects of etiology and consequences as well as treatment.

DESCRIPTION OF THE DISORDER AND CLINICAL PICTURE

Clinical Characteristics

Maritally discordant couples presenting for treatment are often caught up in a cycle of mutual vilification, polarization, and feelings of being trapped (Jacobson & Christensen, 1996), suggesting that they highlight rather than downplay their differences, and view these differences as indications of stable, global, and blameworthy deficits or failings in the partner (Fincham & Bradbury, 1993). As a result, discordant couples often find themselves with relatively low problem-solving efficacy and limited ability to work together as a team.

It has also been observed clinically that discordant couples may express anger rather than expressing feelings of hurt or that they may withdraw rather than express their disappointment in their partner's behavior, suggesting that discordant couples often display emotional reactions that short circuit the couple's ability to identify and respond effectively to the source of the distress. As a result, the reaction to the problem becomes a source of difficulty in its own right, leading to a vicious cycle of increasingly intractable difficulties over time (Kobak, Ruckdeschel, & Hazan, 1994).

When couples find themselves unable to break out of persistent conflict, this can initiate a cascade of changes in other areas of the relationship, leading to observable shifts in behavior and arousal, self-reported shifts in cognition, and a dramatic change in the goals that guide and structure interaction with the partner (Fincham & Beach, 1999). As a result, the pattern of marital discord becomes more entrenched. These considerations suggest a wide range of potential interpersonal and intraindividual indicators of marital discord, many of which have been examined in the empirical literature.

INTERPERSONAL INDICATORS OF MARITAL DISCORD

Increased Negativity

Distressed couples emit more negative statements, tend to make fewer positive statements, and reciprocate negative behaviors at a higher rate during problem-solving interactions (Weis & Heyman, 1997). Elevated negative affect reciprocity is a consistent feature of the interactions of distressed couples and is viewed as the best overt signature of marital discord. Elevated rates of negative communication behaviors, negative reciprocity, and patterns of escalation, lead to protracted sequences of negative behavior during the conflict episodes of distressed couples (Weiss & Heyman, 1997). Because discordant couples do not easily hide negative affect, an elevated rate of observed negative affect is especially useful as a potential indicator of marital discord.

Inability to Repair

When discordant couples attempt to repair problematic interactions, they often engage in metacommunication delivered with negative affect (e.g., irritation, sadness). This increases the likelihood of a negative response from the partner, thereby continuing and perhaps escalating the negative interaction. The result is a rigid and highly predictable interaction pattern (Gottman 1994; Weiss & Heyman, 1997). As a result, distressed couples have difficulty exiting from periods of negative exchange except through withdrawal, suggesting that an inability to repair negative interactions through metacommunication or other means is another potentially useful indicator of marital discord (Weiss & Heyman, 1997).

Decreased Forgiveness and Accommodation

All partners engage in hurtful behavior toward one another. However, as each partner's commitment decreases, the likelihood of accommodating the spouse's negative behavior also decreases (Rusbult, Johnson, & Morrow, 1986), as does the likelihood of forgiveness (Finkel, Rusbult, Kumashiro, & Hannon, 2002). Accordingly, low levels of accommodation and forgiveness may serve as useful indicators of marital discord. Because forgiveness reduces the propensity to engage in verbally aggressive behavior toward the partner (Fincham, Beach, & Davila, 2004) and is one of the most important factors contributing to marital longevity and satisfaction (Fenell, 1993), it may be a useful indicator of marital discord.

Increased Withdrawal and Increased Demand

Another pattern used by couples in dealing with difficult problems, or in response to negative partner behavior, is to avoid interaction with the partner. Within marital communication studies, statements suggestive of withdrawal, such as not responding and making irrelevant comments, are more common among men than women (Schaap, Buunk, & Kerkstra, 1988). Roberts and Krokoff (1990) found that male withdrawal followed by female hostility accounted for 20 percent of the variance in marital dissatisfaction above that accounted for by overall affective tone. In addition, it appears that it is possible to assess withdrawal either through observational ratings or spouse reports of partner typical behavior, with each providing a useful index of marital discord. However, results obtained from observational ratings vary as a function of whose issue is being discussed during conflict (e.g., Sagrestano, Christensen, & Heavey, 1998).

Elevated Level of Violence

Among discordant couples seeking marital therapy, the percentage who have experienced physical aggression with their partner in the last year may be as high as 60 percent to 70 percent even though fewer than 5 percent report physical aggression as a problem in the relationship (Cascardi, Langhinrichsen, & Vivian, 1992). This suggests that presence of intimate partner violence is associated with marital discord, or, at a minimum, will be a complicating factor present among many discordant couples.

Lower Level of Supportive Behavior

There are differences in spousal support between distressed and nondistressed couples (Acitelli & Antonucci, 1994). Lower support is only weakly related to conflict and predicts later marital distress independently of conflict behavior. It may be, however, that perceptions of spousal support within marriage are more strongly related to the general well-being of wives than husbands (Acitelli & Antonucci, 1994; Julien & Markman, 1991). In addition, because current definitions of social support are focused on behaviors that may be more salient for and explicitly valued by women (Acitelli & Antonucci, 1994), the strength of the association between some types of perceived spousal support and marital discord may vary by gender.

Lower Level of Other Positive Behavior

Reported frequency of positive instrumental behavior may be more closely related to satisfaction in husbands than in wives, whereas positive affectional behavior may be more closely related to satisfaction in wives than in husbands (Wills, Weiss, & Patterson, 1974). Therefore, it may be necessary to utilize different types of positive behavior for husbands and wives when developing indicators of marital discord.

INTRAINDIVIDUAL INDICATORS OF MARITAL DISCORD

In addition to interpersonal manifestations of marital discord, there are also promising intraindividual indicators.

Attributions

Attributions for relationship problems are strongly related to marital discord (Sabourin, Lussier, & Wright, 1991); however, attributions for hypothetical partner behavior have the psychometric advantage of standardization and are also robustly related to marital discord (Fincham, Bradbury, & Scott, 1990). Accordingly, negative causal and responsibility attributions either for ongoing problems or for hypothetical partner behavior may provide a sensitive and valid index of ongoing or developing marital discord.

Expectations, Beliefs, and Standards

Generalized positive efficacy expectations covary with level of marital satisfaction, as do efficacy expectations relating to specific upcoming interactions (e.g., Fincham, Garnier, Gano-Phillips, & Osborne, 1995). Likewise, particular relationship assumptions such as "disagreement is destructive," "partners cannot change," and "the sexes are different" have been shown to account for unique variance in marital satisfaction (Epstein & Baucom, 2002), but relationship standards focusing on the expectation that relationships should be particularly positive have proven to be less useful as indicators of marital discord.

Commitment

Commitment is important for many aspects of couple functioning and low levels of commitment are common among discordant spouses (Rusbult & Buunk, 1993; Van Lange, Rusbult, Drigotas, & Arriaga, 1997). Interestingly, couples are not very good at estimating their partners' levels of commitment to their marriage (Nock, 1995). However, the perceived level of partner commitment is strongly related to one's own reported commitment, suggesting that both own commitment and perceived partner commitment might be useful, and correlated indicators of marital discord. It is important, however, to distinguish between *personal dedication*, focused on rewards and intrinsic motivations, and *constraint commitment*, based on psychological costs associated with potential termination of a relationship (Stanley, 1998). The distinction is critical in the context of identifying indicators of marital discord because low "personal dedication" but not low "constraint commitment" is characteristic of discordant couples.

Communal versus Exchange Orientation

A shorter term perspective and a preference for a quid pro quo or exchange orientation (Clark, Graham, & Grote, 2002) are associated with marital discord. Accordingly, endorsement of a communal versus an exchange orientation vis-à-vis the spouse may also provide a useful index of marital discord (Murstein, Cerreto, & MacDonald, 1977). The adoption of an exchange orientation toward the spouse may also capture a fundamental shift from more accommodative to less accommodative tendencies in the dyad.

Conflicting Goals

The preceding discussion of cognitive variables associated with marital discord suggests that discordant couples may differ from nondiscordant couples in the extent to which their behavior toward their partner reflects different intentions and interpretations as well as different emergent goals during interaction and conflicts (Fincham & Beach, 1999). Whereas nondiscordant couples are able to transform conflict of interest or disagreement into opportunities for advancing long-term goals and so foster accommodation, a communal orientation, and forgiveness (see Rusbult, Verette, Whitney, & Slovik, 1991), discordant couples find themselves pulled toward short-term and avoidance goals, leading to heightened negative affect reciprocity, increased negative intent, and increased willingness to engage in negative behaviors should the occasion arise.

Summary

At a behavioral level, there are several characteristics that serve as useful indicators of marital discord. These include greater negativity, greater reciprocity of negative behavior, more sustained negative interaction, more escalation of negative interactions, more withdrawal from the partner, and more difficulty with relationship repair and de-escalation of conflict. At the same time, a reduction in positive, supportive behavior and of positive interactions in general, is also associated with marital discord. However, amount of conflict or amount of positive behavior may not be as good an indicator of level of discord as the combination of decreased positive and increased negative behavior (Gottman, 1993). Greater perceived severity of problems, as well as problems in specific areas, may also be useful markers of marital discord. At an intraindividual level, attributions, efficacy expectations, particular assumptions and an orientation that focuses on a shorter time frame and the potential for goal conflict with the partner may be particularly characteristic of discordant couples.

PERSONALITY DEVELOPMENT AND GENETIC INFLUENCES

Personality factors are cited by approximately 10 percent of divorced individuals as the cause of their marital problems (Amato & Previti, 2003). But the exact role of personality factors in the development of marital discord remains elusive.

Personality Disorders and Marital Dysfunction

When one or both partners in a marriage meet criteria for a personality disorder diagnosis, the resulting maladaptive interpersonal behaviors are likely to affect the marital relationship in direct and profound ways. Borderline personality, for example, may occasion serious conflict in close relationships. However, it appears that all Axis II diagnoses are associated to some extent with increased likelihood of relationship dysfunction (Flick, Roy-Byrne, Cowley, 1993), and that diagnosis with any personality disorder increases an individual's risk of being divorced, separated, or single. However, the high comorbidity among Axis II diagnoses makes isolating the unique contribution of any one personality disorder difficult. Nonetheless, the so-called dramatic personality cluster (e.g., borderline, histrionic, antisocial, and narcissistic personalities; Cluster B) appears to be more strongly associated with marital dysfunction, partner abuse and partner dissatisfaction than are other personality disorders (Daley, Burge, & Hammen, 2000).

An alternative strategy, and one that has been more widely used to date, is to examine one or more of the broad dimensions of personality that are reflected in the dramatic personality disorders, such as high neuroticism or low conscientiousness. However, it is possible that the association between personality processes and the development of marital discord may be complex, with different characteristics exerting an effect at different points in the life of the marriage. If so, the connection between personality and marital outcomes may be difficult to capture in cross-sectional designs and this may account for some of the difficulty in identifying a consistent pattern of relationships between specific personality dimensions and marital outcomes across studies. One way to summarize a large number of different traits of potential interest to marital researchers is to utilize the Big Five personality factors of neuroticism, extraversion, impulsivity, agreeableness, and conscientiousness (e.g., McCrae, Costa, & Busch, 1986). Although results are inconsistent for several factors, high conscientiousness is correlated with relationship satisfaction (for both men and women; Engel, Olson, & Patrick, 2002), as is low neuroticism or negative affectivity (Karney & Bradbury, 1995).

Conscientiousness

Conscientiousness comprises a sense of personal competency, responsibility, and ambition, and plays a role, particularly for men, in marital adjustment (Bouchard, Lussier, & Sabourin, 1999). Antisocial personality, in contrast, is defined as a lack of social responsibility and thus involves a lack of conscientiousness that can, in many cases, lead to marital discord. Men diagnosed with antisocial personality tend to respond to marital stress with alcoholism and physical abusiveness, and promote increased levels of conflict in the relationship through their use of the same destructive behaviors (e.g., Hart, Dutton, & Newlove, 1993). For wives, low conscientiousness is predictive of elevated risk of divorce (Kurdek, 1993). Accordingly low conscientiousness appears to be associated with patterns implicated in declining relationship satisfaction over time.

Neuroticism

Neuroticism is defined as the tendency "to report distress, discomfort, and dissatisfaction over time and regardless of the situation" (Watson & Clark, 1984, p. 483). One might suspect, therefore, that elevated neuroticism would be associated with self-reports of lower marital satisfaction on a concurrent basis and elevated risk of divorce (Kurdek, 1993). Although data confirm that there is a concurrent association between neuroticism and marital satisfaction, neuroticism is unrelated to rate of change in relationship quality (Karney & Bradbury, 1997).

Sex Differences

There may also be sex differences in the relationship between a partner's personality and marital dysfunction. Husbands' reports of marital distress may be more strongly focused on their partners' tendency to express negative affect (Engel et al., 2002), whereas women may use information about both negative and positive expressions of emotion, as well as emotional constraint, in arriving at their judgments of marital satisfaction (Robins, Caspi, & Moffitt, 2000). Thus, somewhat different personality characteristics in partners may influence the satisfaction of men and women.

Intergenerational Transmission and Heritability

In recent years there has been increased interest in the possibility that marital conflict may be transmitted across generations, and may have a heritable component. Supporting this possibility, parental divorce increases the odds of offspring divorce by 70 percent for daughters (Bumpass, Martin, & Sweet, 1991). In addition, odds may increase further if the parents of both partners were divorced. For example, Amato (1996) found a 69 percent increase in odds of divorce if the wife's parents had been divorced but a 189 percent increase in odds of divorce if both the wife's and the husband's parents had been divorced. One possible explanation is that there is a strong social transmission of commitment to marriage between generations (Amato, 1996). However, it may also be that some of the effect is attributable to heritable factors, possibly reflecting personality, temperament, or other characteristics relevant to marital success.

Suggesting the possibility of a genetic effect on propensity to marry, Johnson, McGue, and Krueger (2004) examined a sample of 4,225 women and 2,869 men, including 2,527 twin pairs. Monozygotic twins were substantially more concordant for marital status than were dizygotic twins, suggesting that marital status does in fact have a strong heritable component. Using a similar genetically informed design, McGue and

Lykken (1992) found evidence for a genetic component in the propensity to divorce, with monozygotic twin pairs demonstrating significantly greater concordance for divorce status than dizygotic twins.

Attachment Style

Originally developed to describe an infant's response to a caregiver, attachment styles in adults are moderately stable characteristics (Hazan & Shaver, 1994) associated both with global appraisals of relationship quality and specific relational behaviors. A secure attachment is associated with an individual's feelings of relationship satisfaction, ability to communicate, capacity to handle problems in the relationship, and sense of social support from one's partner (e.g., Cobb, Davila, & Bradbury, 2001). Securely attached individuals are able to maintain a positive perception of the relationship despite conflict (Treboux, Crowell, & Waters, 2004). Interestingly, the effect of attachment style does not appear to work through the personality style variables reflected in the Big Five scheme described previously. Attachment and caregiving mechanisms may, therefore, account for differences in marital trajectories that are not well accounted for by traditional personality variables.

Summary

Although the available data do not produce a picture that is entirely coherent with regard to the role of particular personality disorders or personality characteristics, in broad brush they conform to the expectation that personality scores (e.g., neuroticism scores) predict reports of poorer marital relationships (cf. Kelly & Conley, 1987) and that intergenerational transmission of risk for marital discord is mediated by family of origin experiences, learning, and genetic factors. Consistent with this view, Caspi and Elder (1988) found parental divorce conferred greater risk for offspring displaying an abrasive interpersonal style that negatively affected the quality of their marriages. Likewise, Amato (1996) found that parental divorce conferred on offspring a risk for problems such as frequent criticism of the spouse or showing anger easily, which in turn conferred increased risk of their own divorce.

EPIDEMIOLOGY

The lack of a consensual definition of marital discord hinders the collection of sound epidemiological data regarding incidence and prevalence of marital discord. However, there is relatively good information about the distribution of marriage and various problematic outcomes in marriage. We discuss the available research and call for needed research that would provide a better picture of the epidemiology of marital discord.

Prevalence of Marriage and Divorce

Marriage remains very common, with the large majority of people marrying at some point in their lives. The divorce rate increased dramatically during the 1970s, peaked around 1980, and has since stabilized or declined, with approximately half of first marriages ending in divorce. Remarriage is also common, leading to a substantial decrease in percentage of children raised in households with two biological parents. Second marriages are characterized by somewhat lower marital quality on average and have a greater likelihood of ending in divorce. Age at first marriage has increased from a median of 24.7 in 1980 to 26.7 in 1998 among men and increased for women from 22.0 to 25.0. There has been an increase in the practice of cohabitation as well, which nearly trebled between 1980 and 1997, climbing from 1.6 million to 4.5 million couples, leading to increased interest in possible effects of premarital cohabitation. When cohabitation occurs with more than one partner (i.e., serial cohabitation), it is associated with lower marital happiness, more arguments, and higher likelihood of future divorce (Bumpass et al., 1991).

Prevalence of Marital Discord

The level of marital quality decreased between 1960 and 1990 (Glenn, 1991; Rogers & Amato, 1997), but there is little evidence of a continuing decrease in overall marital quality since 1990 (Amato, Johnson, Booth, & Rogers, 2003). Although average amount of time spent with the spouse declined from 1980 to 2000, probably due to increased time at work, an increased percentage of wives employed outside the home, and increased amount of time spent on children's activities, this negative change was offset by other positive changes including increased personal income (Amato et al., 2003). In addition, partners in the most recent marital cohort report greater support for lifelong marriage and higher levels of religious influence than those of a decade before. This suggests relative stability in prevalence of marital discord over the past decade or longer.

Spontaneous Recovery

There is little information about rates of spontaneous recovery from marital discord. However, understanding spontaneous recovery, and the conditions under which it may occur, is integral to understanding the epidemiology of marital discord. Waite and Luo (2002) reported that nearly two-thirds (62 percent) of unhappily married spouses who stayed married reported that their marriages were happy five years later and that 77 percent of unhappily married spouses remained married. In addition, the most unhappily married spouses reported the most dramatic turnarounds: among those who rated their marriages as very unhappy, almost 8 out of 10 who avoided divorce were happily married five years later. Accordingly, there appear to be some couples that can be identified as "unhappy" at one point in time but who will exit from that status over time. Conversely, across 20 outcome studies of marital therapy, there is no evidence of an appreciable level of spontaneous recovery among couples on the waitlist for marital therapy (Baucom, Shoham, Mueser, Daiuto, & Stickle, 1998). The apparent divergence between the stability of discord among treatment-seeking couples and community couples has yet to be well explained.

The divergence between the Waite and Luo (2002) report and the results obtained in marital outcome research may be the result of widely differing methodology and measurement strategies. However, the divergence also suggests the possibility that there are two groups of "unhappy" couples, that is, those who are *transiently distressed* and those who have more complex or interlocking problems and should be considered *maritally discordant*. If so, finding a method for distinguishing between couples that are transiently distressed only versus those who are truly maritally discordant will be of pivotal practical and theoretical importance in clarifying a range of issues related to the description, epidemiology, and etiology of marital discord.

Distinguishing Distressed Couples from Discordant Couples

One way to approach the problem of distinguishing between couples who are merely "distressed" and those who are "discordant," or to examine whether any such distinction is warranted, is to use a technique developed by Paul Meehl to identify types versus continua. Taxometric procedures (Waller & Meehl, 1998) have been developed to address the question of whether psychological constructs are best characterized as being dimensional only or whether there is evidence of a latent categorical structure superimposed on the dimension of interest. Taxometric procedures applied in the marital area (Beach, Kim, Cercone-Keeney, & Brody, in press) suggest that there is a point of discontinuity consistent with threshold, or categorical, models of marital discord (e.g., Gottman, 1994), indicating that it should be possible to develop categorical criteria for distinguishing between "discordant" and "nondiscordant" couples (Heyman et al., 2001). This has important implications for the epidemiology of marital discord. If there is a categorical entity, "marital discord," it should be possible to provide precise estimates of its prevalence in the general population and increase the precision of claims about its relationship to divorce and health outcomes.

In sum, we can say with some confidence that overall level of marital failure, as indexed by reported marital unhappiness or by divorce has stabilized over the past two decades. At the same time, available data suggest that marital discord has a moderately high base rate in the community (e.g., Ren, 1997) and can be assessed as a categorical variable (Beach et al., in press). Due to selection out of marriage through divorce as well as cohort differences in rates of marital success, however, it may be that the percentage of maritally discordant couples will vary somewhat as a function of years married or age of the couples sampled (Glenn, 1998). Similarly, it may be that optimal indicators of marital discord will vary as a function of cohort or community context.

ETIOLOGY

The absence of a well-established criterion measure of marital discord makes it difficult to confidently present an integrated etiological model for marital discord. Currently, we are best equipped to describe the variables that forecast declines in marital satisfaction and/or divorce. However, because somewhat different processes may operate in the context of relatively mild relationship distress compared to more severe marital discord, and because divorce may not always result from severe marital discord, we cannot be certain about the extent to which variables found to forecast declines in satisfaction or increased probability of divorce also forecast marital discord. Despite its limitations, however, the available research may provide insight into the etiology of marital discord. Accordingly, we review the literature on change in marital satisfaction as the best available window on etiology of marital discord.

Models of Change in Marriage

Longitudinal data suggest that a linear decline in marital happiness as a function of years married provides a relatively good approximation to the shape of change in satisfaction over the early years of marriage (Karney & Bradbury, 1997), with the possibility of slightly steeper linear declines early and late in marriage (Van Laningham, Johnson, & Amato, 2001). However, there is considerable individual variability in change over time, with some couples showing relatively little change and others showing steep declines in satisfaction. Indeed, in one study, approximately 10 percent of couples showed increases in satisfaction over the first four years of marriage (Karney & Bradbury, 1997).

Prediction of Intercepts (or Average Level)

As discussed earlier, neuroticism appears to exert its effect by creating a lower overall level of satisfaction across time rather than by changing the slope of change in satisfaction (Karney & Bradbury, 1997). Accordingly, it seems likely that other characteristics linked to negative affectivity may also be predictors of different set points for marital satisfaction rather than different trajectories of change. Consistent with this expectation, high levels of negative emotional expression were also found to be associated with lower concurrent satisfaction but not greater decline in satisfaction over time (Smith, Vivian, & O'Leary, 1990). It remains possible, however, that having a lower set point for marital satisfaction interacts with other processes or contextual variables to place the couple at risk for decline in satisfaction over time.

Predictors of Differential Linear Change

Negative marital communication, one of the most studied factors in predicting marital decline, predicts degree of linear decline in relationship satisfaction over time (Karney & Bradbury, 1995) and can result in a more steeply sloped downward trend for a couple. Likewise, intimate partner violence is another potent predictor of decline in satisfaction in early marriage. Lawrence and Bradbury (2001) found that marital dysfunction was more common among aggressive than among nonaggressive couples (70 percent versus 38 percent) and among severely aggressive than among moderately aggressive couples (93 percent versus 46 percent). Aggression remained a reliable predictor of marital outcomes after the authors controlled for stressful events and negative communication. Finally, less emotional engagement in a problem-solving discussion predicted greater decline in marital satisfaction over the first 30 months of marriage (Smith et al., 1990), suggesting that withdrawal is also problematic over time.

Level of positive behavior may also predict change in marital satisfaction, and supportive behavior moderates the association between conflict behavior and marital deterioration. Poorer support in the context of poorer conflict management skills is associated with greater risk of marital deterioration. In addition, for newlyweds, wives' supportive behavior predicted marital distress 12 months later (Cutrona, 1996, Davila, Bradbury, & Cohan, 1997) and positive affective reactions during conflict discussions early in marriage predicted both lower likelihood of divorce and greater marital happiness (Gottman et al., 1998).

Intraindividual processes are also useful predictors of marital outcomes. Conflict promoting attributions for partner behavior have predicted declines in satisfaction across a number of studies (Fincham, 2003). Recent work suggests that stressful experiences may also be associated with the trajectory of marital quality over time. However, stressful events and circumstances exert their influence on satisfaction indirectly by influencing *relationship* cognitions. That is, stress influences the nature of spouses' marital perceptions as well as their interpretations, and these changes in intraindividual processes account for the association of stress with decline in marital satisfaction (Neff & Karney, 2004).

AN INTEGRATIVE ETIOLOGICAL/MAINTENANCE MODEL

Karney and Bradbury (1995) offer a model that organizes three major sources of influence on marital quality over time, incorporating important elements from major theoretical statements in the marital area. Using their framework as a foundation, we offer a dynamic, nonlinear model that may capture the nature of individual change in marital satisfaction over time (cf. Gottman, Swanson, & Swanson, 2002). However, it should be understood that the model is meant to be heuristic rather than fully descriptive of the intricacies of marital change (see Figure 27.1).

Karney and Bradbury (1995)

The Karney and Bradbury model incorporates traditional behavioral models of the etiology of marital change by specifying a reciprocal relationship between the responses partners make to each other (i.e., the interpersonal transactions in the marital relationship) and the intrapersonal processes that both guide and are influenced by those transactions. Accordingly, spousal interaction is expected to influence and be influenced by changes occurring within each partner. In addition, incorporating key aspects of crisis theory, the model highlights the important role played by stressful life events and the ecological context in which the marital relationship is embedded. Thus, the model indicates that an accumulation of stressors and difficulties external to the relationship can influence both the way spouses respond to each other, but also that spouses can engage in behaviors that may lessen the impact of these events on each other and the relationship. Finally, the model emphasizes the potential importance of fixed risk factors such as history of parental divorce, or personality and attachment

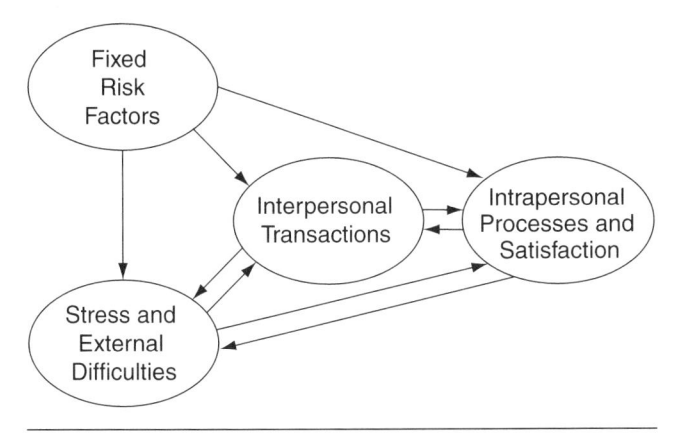

Figure 27.1 The Stress, Risk, Interaction, Intrapersonal processes model.

processes that may contribute to change in the relationship by occasioning stressful events, or giving rise to important differences in the way couples interact or think about their relationships. The bidirectional relationships illustrated in Figure 27.1 create a series of potential positive and negative feedback mechanisms that could give rise to nonlinear, systemic dynamics.

Nonlinear Dynamics

This model portrayed in Figure 27.1 captures several key aspects of the correlates and etiology of marital discord, including key empirical results that have been reviewed previously. In addition, it highlights the possibility that links between stress, interaction, and intraindividual processes may form a dynamic system. This raises the possibility that the model might predict a variety of nonlinear effects over time. In particular, the structure of the relationships portrayed in Figure 27.1 allows for the emergence of "vicious cycles," "set points," and "splitting variables." Each of these may be important in better describing the processes leading to marital discord.

Vicious cycles could emerge if a negative change were amplified over time by positive feedback loops. An example might be if external stress produced a change in thoughts about the partner, which in turn led to negative changes in one or both partners' interpersonal behavior (Neff & Karney, 2004). If such changes accumulated, they might pass the point at which each spouse would continue to accommodate the other's negative behavior, producing a shift in relationship dynamics that could, in turn, amplify the stressfulness of the original experience. A positive feedback loop, once initiated, could maintain and perhaps amplify itself without further external input. As can be seen in Figure 27.1, nonlinear systems have an inherent potential for a series of interconnected effects of this sort, creating a situation in which a small initial change could result in a much larger change that feeds on itself over time.

Conversely, *set points* could emerge if negative (i.e., counteracting) feedback loops were initiated by the external stress, dampening the effect of stress over time. For example, if a substantial and salient external stressor were to prompt supportiveness and solidarity in the dyad, this could result in more effective coping with the external stressor, compensatory benefits to the dyad, and a dampening or even reversal of the negative effects of stress on the relationship (Tesser & Beach, 1998). Similarly, if husbands de-escalate in response to low-level negative partner affect (Gottman et al., 2002), this could dampen any negative effect of wives' negative affect on the relationship. Because these sequences reflect cases in which negative behavior prompts effective repair efforts, and so reduce rather than amplify negative interaction, they are examples of negative feedback loops that could help maintain a "set point" even in the face of significant external challenges. Couples displaying evidence of "set points" should be more likely to experience stable, happy marriages (Gottman et al., 2002).

Finally, *splitting variables* are those that may change the nature of the relationship between a relationship stressor and the outcome. Of particular interest are variables that shift a couple from entering a vicious cycle to maintaining a set point. For example, commitment to the relationship might be a splitting variable. At high levels of commitment, the probability of an accommodative response to negative partner behavior should be high. This should set in motion dampening, negative feedback loops as described previously. In such cases negative partner behavior is likely to lead to no change or even increases in satisfaction over time. At low levels of commitment, however, there is decreased likelihood of accommodation and increased likelihood of withdrawal or reciprocation of negative behavior (Finkel et al., 2002) potentially triggering a vicious cycle. This suggests that at relatively high levels of commitment, negative partner behavior might initiate a cycle that leads to no change or even a stronger relationship over time, whereas at lower levels of commitment negative partner behavior could initiate an escalating cycle that leads to decay in marital quality over time. At some intermediate level of commitment there should be a "tipping point." Above the tipping point the effect of spousal negative behavior or an external stressor will be qualitatively different than its effect below the tipping point. Splitting variables are of particular interest because, if they are amenable to intervention, a small change could produce a big difference in relationship outcomes, such as differentiating between a relationship characterized by vicious cycles or, alternatively, a relationship regulated by effective repair.

These examples suggest that attention to nonlinear systems models may lead to a range of predictions that will help advance the field. To the extent that couples form an interactive system with each other and with their immediate context (Karney & Bradbury, 1995), it seems likely that at least some of the concepts of nonlinear systems modeling will be necessary if we are to adequately describe the development of marital discord (cf. Gottman et al., 2002). Of particular interest is the potential for these models to help researchers clarify potential vicious cycles, set points, and "splitting variables" that may set couples on different relationship trajectories.

COURSE, COMPLICATIONS, AND PROGNOSIS

There are potentially serious consequences of prolonged marital discord. A rich research literature informs our understanding of the likely complications of prolonged marital discord on individual mental and physical health, areas that account for much of the morbidity associated with marital discord.

Individual Mental Health in Adulthood

Marital happiness contributes considerable variance in psychological well-being, and appears to exert a greater influence than does satisfaction in other areas of life (Glenn & Weaver, 1981). Serious marital dissatisfaction predicts increased risk for a major depressive episode in the subsequent year, even after controlling for history of depression (Whisman, 1999) or comorbidity (Whisman & Bruce, 1999), and both marital conflict and physical abuse predict subsequent increases in depressive symptoms among women (Beach et al., in press). Conversely, improvement in marital satisfaction mediates the effect of marital intervention on improvements in mental health (Christensen et al., 2004) and depression (Beach & O'Leary, 1992). Likewise, the effect of humiliating marital events on depression has been shown to be substantial (Cano & O'Leary, 2000).

There is also an association between the severity/chronicity of marital conflicts and subsequent exacerbation of problem drinking, even after controlling for earlier alcohol problems. Moreover, patients whose spouses are highly negative and critical are not only more likely to relapse but also to drink on a greater percentage of days in the year following treatment of alcoholism than are patients whose spouses engaged in low levels of negative behaviors (O'Farrell, Hooley, Fals-Stewart, & Cutter, 1998).

Physical Health and Illness

Although married individuals are healthier and live longer on average than the unmarried, marital conflict is associated with poorer health (Burman & Margolin, 1992) and with specific illnesses such as cancer, cardiac disease, and chronic pain. Marital interaction studies suggest possible mechanisms that may account for these links by showing that hostile behaviors during conflict are associated with alterations in immunological (Kiecolt-Glazer et al., 1997; Kiecolt-Glazer, Malarkey, Chee, & Newton, 1993), endocrine (Kiecolt-Glaser et al., 1997; Malarkey, Kiecolt-Glazer, Pearl, & Glaser, 1994), and cardiovascular functioning. In particular, marital discord is associated with increases in catecholamines and corticosteroids, the "stress hormones" (Kiecolt-Glaser et al., 1994). Marital discord is consequential for both husbands and wives, but has more pronounced health consequences for wives (Kiecolt-Glaser et al., 1993, 1997; Malarkey et al., 1994). Thus, marital discord appears to confer a substantial health burden and may be particularly consequential in the context of other acute or chronic conditions.

ASSESSMENT AND DIAGNOSIS

There are several assessment approaches in the marital area and each has amassed considerable support for its validity. At the same time, none has been specifically validated with regard to the assessment of "marital discord" per se (Heyman et al., 2001). Accordingly, we next briefly review self-report, observational, quasi-observational, physiological, and interview approaches.

Self-Report Approaches

A number of self-report measures of marital satisfaction, marital adjustment, and marital cognition are readily available (for a review, see Fincham & Bradbury, 1987). The most comprehensive of the individual measures is the Marital Satisfaction Inventory (MSI; Snyder, 1997). The MSI comprises a number of descriptive subscales in addition to global distress, making it a potentially useful clinical tool. It is not clear, however, to what extent the different subscales would serve as independent indicators of "marital discord." However, at a minimum, the MSI has the advantage of assessing inconsistent responding and unrealistic responding, potentially identifying false negatives and false positives. In addition, the MSI uses nongendered language that may make it useful in assessing nontraditional couples.

Another widely available self-report measure of marital adjustment is the Dyadic Adjustment Scale (DAS; Spanier, 1976), which is a 32-item measure with good internal consistency and good test-retest reliability. The DAS can also be used to assess nontraditional relationships. Likewise, the older and somewhat shorter 15-item Marital Adjustment Scale (Locke & Wallace, 1959) has shown good internal consistency and test-retest reliability. There are also several shorter measures of relationship functioning that focus specifically on satisfaction. Thus, there are a number of potential approaches to assessment of marital adjustment or the highly related construct of marital satisfaction.

One disadvantage of all the self-report approaches at present is that the "cutoffs" used to identify marital discord are based on statistical rather than clinical criteria. For example, the cutoff of 97 on the DAS was adopted because it was one standard deviation below the mean in the original sample. In addition, when the DAS or MAT is used to establish "marital discord," it is possible to define "marital discord" either in terms of one partner's score or in terms of both partners' scores. Given the dyadic nature of the construct of "marital discord," the latter approach seems preferable (Beach et al., in press). Finally, the "optimal" cutoff point on any of the scales will also vary depending on the relative importance of avoiding false positives and false negatives. Accordingly, even when widely used cutoffs are found to be approximately correct, they will need to be tailored depending on research or clinical priorities.

Observational Approaches

A number of coding systems for quantifying marital problem-solving interaction have been developed during the past 30 years (for a comprehensive review, see Gottman & Notarius, 2000). The Marital Interaction Coding System (MICS) and its offspring, the rapid MICS (Heyman & Vivian, 1993), have been among the most widely used. However, the Couples Interaction Scoring System (CISS; see Gottman & Notarius, 2000) and the Kategoriensystem fur Partnerschaftliche (KPI; Hahlweg, Kaiser, Christensen, Fehm-Wolfsdorf, & Groth, 2000) have also been shown to discriminate well between distressed and nondistressed couples (Weiss & Heyman, 1990). The advantage of these observational coding systems is that they are known to yield reliable indexes of marital interaction that are related to marital discord. Accordingly, they have good potential to provide indicators of marital discord that share only limited method variance with self-report indexes. However, if observational strategies are to be used in the assessment of marital discord it will be necessary to develop clinically useful, generally applicable, and well-standardized stimuli that can be used to evoke interaction samples. In addition, given the independence of positive and negative interactions (Fincham, Beach, Kemp-Fincham, 1997), it will also be important to develop different standardized situations and specific codes to allow adequate assessment of positive (e.g., support) and negative (e.g., recent conflict) dimensions. Heyman (2001) provides a useful and comprehensive review of a number of coding systems.

As with self-report measures of satisfaction, it will also be necessary to develop cutoff scores that can be used to indicate the presence of marital discord. Accordingly, considerable parametric work remains to create optimally informative observational indexes of martial discord.

Quasi-Observational Approaches

Partners may also be asked to report on each other's marital behavior. This approach has led to the development of several variations of the Spouse Observation checklist (Weiss, Hops, & Patterson, 1973). Difficulty in obtaining spouse agreement on checklist measures led to a decline in the use of this approach in recent years. Lack of spousal agreement on particular items does not, however, invalidate the assessment as a measure of marital discord. Accordingly, as a way of identifying martially discordant couples brief, quasi-observational methods may provide a useful supplementary approach (O'Leary, 1987).

Physiological Assessment

Although not widely used for clinical purposes, there are a number of reports suggesting that physiological, hormonal, or immunological assays might differentiate satisfied and discordant couples (Gottman, 1994; Kiecolt-Glazer et al., 1993, 1997). If further validated, such approaches offer an interesting alternative to currently used assessment methods. As with observational methods, such approaches would require the use of generally applicable, standardized stimuli that could be used to evoke interaction and set the stage for data collection in order to make comparisons across couples possible. Although the technical expertise and equipment for such assessments is not generally available, these approaches have the advantage of sharing little method variance with other approaches and so could complement self-report or behavioral observation methods.

Interview Approaches

One suggestion for providing a better criterion measure of marital discord is to develop an interview procedure that would allow for a diagnosis of "marital discord" (First et al., 2002; Heyman et al., 2001). This approach would bring the identification of marital discord more in line with current methods for identifying other categories of dysfunction. In addition, it directly confronts the problem of identifying a nonarbitrary cutoff for designating a couple as "maritally discordant." Heyman et al. (2001) tested the reliability of an interview measure for marital discord. Agreement on the diagnosis of marital distress was 96 percent (kappa = .92). They also found that the interview measure was somewhat less likely to trigger a diagnosis compared to using a cut point of 97 on the DAS or a cut point of 49 on the RSAT. The interview assesses feelings of unhappiness in the relationship, thoughts of separation, each partner's belief that the couple is in need of therapy, as well as patterns of escalation and withdrawal, attributions for the partner's behavior, and low sense of efficacy to improve the relationship. Spouses were diagnosed as distressed if they met at least one criterion for overall dissatisfaction (perceived unhappiness, pervasive thoughts of divorce, or perceived need for professional help) and at least one criterion for key symptoms (one symptom of significant behavioral, cognitive, or affective impairment). Although the interview may be revised in future uses, it suggests the potential of this approach and indicates that reliable diagnosis of marital discord is possible.

IMPACT ON ENVIRONMENT

Marital discord not only affects the members of the dyad in terms of their individual mental and physical health outcomes, it also affects outcomes for children. Accordingly, an understanding of the impact of marital discord on the family as well as its potential developmental effects is necessary for a full appreciation of the impact of marital discord on the broader family system.

Family Effects

Marital discord is associated with important family outcomes, including poorer parenting (see Erel & Burman, 1995), poorer child adjustment (see Grych & Fincham, 2001), problematic attachment to parents (e.g., Owen & Cox, 1997), increased likelihood of parent-child conflict, and conflict between siblings (e.g., Brody, Stoneman, & McCoy, 1994). Marital discord is also associated with negative health and mental health outcomes for children, including depression, poorer health, poorer academic performance, and increased problems with aggression (Fincham, 1998). Aspects of marital conflict that have a particularly negative influence on children include more frequent, intense, physical, unresolved, child-related conflicts and conflicts attributed to the child's behavior. In addition, parental marital discord is associated with increased risk of future marital discord for offspring (Amato, 1996).

Developmental Effects

Conflict between parents or between offspring and their parents also may exert important developmental effects. For example, women who were adopted soon after birth and who were at high genetic risk for depression showed no evidence of the disorder if the rearing parents were free of marital difficulties or psychopathology (Cadoret et al., 1996). Similar findings have been reported for schizophrenia (Tienari et al., 1994). One possible mechanism for a gene-environment interaction in the expression of genetic effects may be the effect of parental conflict on increased CNS activity among children. That is, observed parental conflict may lead to heightened insecurity and autonomic arousal among children at critical phases of their development. Supporting this conjecture, animal data suggest that there may be critical periods in which poor maternal care may lead to enhanced glucocorticoid feedback sensitivity and to increased lifetime sensitivity to stress (Liu et al., 1997).

TREATMENT IMPLICATIONS

Several treatments for marital discord have demonstrated efficacy. These include traditional behavioral couple therapy, cognitive behavioral couple therapy, and emotion focused couple therapy (Baucom et al., 1998). In addition, strategic couple therapy, insight-oriented couple therapy, and integrative couple therapy all have some evidence of efficacy in relieving episodes of marital discord (Baucom et al., 1998; Christensen et al., 2004; Christensen & Heavey, 1999). However, there have been no replicated demonstrations of the superiority of any efficacious treatment for marital discord relative to other treatments shown to be efficacious for marital discord. At present it appears that the overall effect size for couple therapy using Cohen's d is .60 (Shadish, Montgomery, Wilson, & Wilson, 1993), and fewer than half of treated couples experience a change that moves both partners from the distressed range into the nondistressed range after treatment (Christensen & Heavey, 1999). In addition, although treatment effects tend to be well maintained at one-year follow-up, longer term follow-ups have suggested considerable potential for relapse, with relapse being predicted by life stressors that may occur in the interim period. There is also good evidence for the efficacy of premarital programs designed to change problematic marital behavior (e.g., Hahlweg, Markman, Thurmaier, Engl, & Eckert, 1998), but effect sizes are smaller for marital satisfaction. For both marital therapy and prevention programs, therefore, there appears to be considerable room to enhance outcomes.

Can Marital Interventions Be Improved?

Key to future efforts to improve marital interventions will be the recognition that the central targets of prevention versus treatment may be quite different (Karney & Bradbury, 1995). In each case, researchers will need to focus on the intraindividual, interpersonal, and contextual processes that are most amenable to change and that produce the greatest potential for sustained change. In this effort, the potential for some variables to emerge as "splitting variables," that can shift couples from a trajectory dominated by vicious cycles to one protected by self-regulating, constructive feedback loops is likely to be key. At the same time, it is precisely these key variables that may differ for prevention versus intervention efforts. To the extent that "splitting" variables can be identified and influenced, they represent important targets for enhancing prevention and treatment efforts.

Commitment

For marital discord prevention programs, the literature reviewed previously suggests that dedication commitment, communal orientation, and tendency to forgive may be powerful "splitting variables." Accordingly, developing methods to sustain and enhance these key intraindividual processes may be an appropriate target for the enhancement of prevention programs. These might also be viewed as important targets for intervention with discordant couples. At a minimum, however, efforts to enhance these intraindividual processes are likely to require a rather different approach when couples are already maritally discordant. Once couples have passed a "tipping point" in dedication commitment and perceived partner commitment, change may require additional indirect approaches or additional contextual supports that would not be required in a prevention program. From the standpoint of a nonlinear systems framework, the likely need for a different approach for discordant couples illustrates the property of hysteresis, meaning, the likelihood that one cannot simply "retrace one's steps" to exit from a vicious cycle, particularly one that has produced a discontinuous shift in marital quality.

An example of an intervention strategy that might work efficiently for nondiscordant couples is suggested by the literature on couple commitment. Given the close connection between own and partner perceived commitment, a potential approach for increasing perceived partner commitment would be to enhance one's own positive intentions and willingness to benefit the spouse. That is, if partners engage in activities that increase their own positive intentions and willingness to support and nurture their partners, they should experience an increase in their own dedication commitment and a corresponding increase in perceived partner commitment. Given the importance of dedication commitment as a likely "splitting variable," exercises and activities of this sort have the potential to exert effects that far exceed the size of the initial intervention. Accordingly, this could be a powerful addition to current prevention programs. Conversely, once powerful vicious cycles are already in play, as is likely for discordant couples, it is likely that these efforts could be easily overwhelmed.

Genetic Effects

The research reviewed previously suggests that genetic contributions to marital discord have been insufficiently integrated into models of the development and maintenance of marital discord. The data suggest that people bring genetic predispositions to their marriage. These genetic predispositions, in turn, may influence level of satisfaction, vulnerability to discord, vulnerability to stress, and possibly response to marital intervention. Genetic effects will be critical as research progresses regarding the connection between marital discord and mental and physical health consequences. Accordingly, better understanding of the role of genetic predispositions on response to prevention of marital discord and intervention for marital discord should have a high priority in future research on marital discord and its treatment.

Violence

Recent marital research also strongly suggests that marital outcomes are influenced by the occurrence of intimate partner violence, and that this pattern is too widespread to be ignored in marital prevention and marital intervention programs. Because many couples engaging in marital aggression do not define it as a problem, intimate partner violence has the potential to slip through current prevention programs undetected. At the same time, it may be that prevention programs designed to prevent discord in general are the most practical approach to eliminating intimate partner violence. Finding ways to discuss intimate partner violence and its prevention in a manner that is not off-putting for nondistressed couples is, therefore, one avenue for further developing the potential of prevention programs.

Policy and Social Change

Contextual variables are included in the Karney and Bradbury (1995) integrative model, but the research reviewed previously suggests that broad societal changes and other contextual processes need to be better incorporated into etiological models of marital discord. For example, decreases in the amount of time couples and families spend together have been occurring at a societal level, not just at an individual level. Examining the role of societal or community level variables that might support couples' efforts to increase shared activities, recurring relationship rituals, or family time together may lead researchers to better examine the nature of healthy social contexts and the role they can play in supporting resilient dyads. A shift toward greater appreciation of contextual effects will also highlight that marriage is embedded in a changing cultural context, and so optimal prevention and intervention efforts may change somewhat over time as couples face different sets of contextual challenges and expectations.

CONCLUSIONS

The study of marital discord has made tremendous progress in the past 20 years. There is currently a set of potential indicators of marital discord that can be proposed with some confidence. Indicators can be drawn from multiple domains including self-report, observation, quasi-observation, and physiology. In addition, there has been a marked increase in research suggesting that marital discord confers substantial burden through its impact on mental and physical health outcomes. As a result, it is clear that marital discord often confers considerable morbidity on sufferers. Success in treatment and prevention provide grounds for optimism with regard to intervention. Likewise, new integrative models of marital discord suggest considerable potential for enhancing the efficacy of intervention efforts. However, it is critical that integrative models incorporate a nonlinear, dynamic systems perspective and better incorporate genetic contributions, attention to intimate partner violence, and contextual contributions to the development of marital discord. Doing so has the potential to suggest new avenues for intervention that build on the success that has been achieved in treating and preventing marital discord to date.

REFERENCES

Acitelli, L. K., & Antonucci, T. C. (1994). Gender differences in the link between marital support and satisfaction in older couples. *Journal of Personality and Social Psychology, 67*(4), 688–698.

Amato, P. R. (1996). Explaining the intergenerational transmission of divorce. *Journal of Marriage and the Family, 58*(3), 628–640.

Amato, P. R., Johnson, D. R., Booth, A., & Rogers, S. J. (2003). Continuity and change in marital quality between 1980 and 2000. *Journal of Marriage and the Family, 65,* 1–22.

Amato, P. R., & Previti, D. (2003). People's reasons for divorcing: Gender, social class, the life course, and adjustment. *Journal of Family Issues, 24,* 602–626.

Baucom, D. H., Shoham, V., Mueser, K. T., Daiuto, A. D., & Stickle, T. R. (1998). Empirically supported couple and family interventions for marital distress and adult mental health problems. *Journal of Consulting & Clinical Psychology, 66*(1), 53–88.

Beach, S. R. H., Kim, S., Cercone-Keeney, J., & Brody, G. (in press). Physical aggression and depression: Gender asymmetry in effects? *Journal of Social and Personal Relationships.*

Beach, S. R. H., & O'Leary, K. D. (1992). Treating depression in the context of marital discord: Outcome and predictors of response for marital therapy versus cognitive therapy. *Behavior Therapy, 23,* 507–528.

Bouchard, G., Lussier, Y., & Sabourin, S. (1999). Personality and marital adjustment: Utility of the Five-Factor Model of personality. *Journal of Marriage and the Family, 61*(3), 651–660.

Brody, G. H., Stoneman, Z., & McCoy, J. K. (1994). Contributions of family relationships and child temperaments to longitudinal variations in sibling relationship quality and sibling relationship styles. *Journal of Family Psychology, 8*(3), 274–286.

Bumpass, L. L., Martin, T. C., & Sweet, J. A. (1991). The impact of family background and early marital factors on marital disruption. *Journal of Family Issues, 12*(1), 22–42.

Burman, B., & Margolin, G. (1992). Analysis of the association between marital relationships and health problems: An interactional perspective. *Psychological Bulletin, 112*(1), 39–63.

Cadoret, R. J., Winokur, G., Langbehn, D., Troughton, E., Yates, W. R., & Stewart, M. A. (1996). Depression spectrum disease: I. The role of gene-environment interaction. *American Journal of Psychiatry, 153,* 892–899.

Cano, A., & O'Leary, K. D. (2000). Infidelity and separations precipitate major depressive episodes and symptoms of nonspecific depression and anxiety. *Journal of Consulting and Clinical Psychology, 68,* 774–781.

Cascardi, M., Langhinrichsen, J., & Vivian, D. (1992). Marital aggression: Impact, injury, and health correlates for husbands and wives. *Archives of Internal Medicine, 152,* 1178–1184.

Caspi, A., & Elder, G. H., Jr. (1988). Childhood precursors of the life course: Early personality and life disorganization. In E. M.

Hetherington & R. M. Lerner (Eds.), *Child development in lifespan perspective* (pp. 115–142). Hillsdale, NJ: Erlbaum.

Christensen, A., Atkins, D. C., Berns, S., Wheeler, J., Baucom, D. H., & Simpson, L. E. (2004). Traditional versus integrative behavioral couple therapy for significantly and chronically distressed married couples. *Journal of Consulting & Clinical Psychology, 72*(2), 176–191.

Christensen, A., & Heavey, C. L. (1999). Interventions for couples. *Annual Review of Psychology, 50*, 165–190.

Clark, M. S., Graham, S., & Grote, N. (2002). Bases for giving benefits in marriage: What is ideal? What is realistic? What really happens? In P. Noller & J. A. Feeney (Eds.), *Understanding marriage: Developments in the study of couple interaction* (pp. 150–176). Cambridge: Cambridge University Press.

Cobb, R. J., Davila, J., & Bradbury, T. N. (2001). Attachment security and marital satisfaction: The role of positive perceptions and social support. *Personality & Social Psychology Bulletin, 27*, 1131–1143.

Cutrona, C. E. (1996). *Social support in couples: Marriage as a resource in times of stress.* Thousand Oaks, CA: Sage.

Daley, S. E., Burge, D., & Hammen, C. (2000). Borderline personality disorder symptoms as predictors of 4-year romantic relationship dysfunction in young women: Addressing issues of specificity. *Journal of Abnormal Psychology, 109*(3), 451–460.

Davila, J., Bradbury, T. N., & Cohan, C. L. (1997). Marital functioning and depressive symptoms: Evidence for a stress generation model. *Journal of Personality and Social Psychology, 73*, 849–861.

Engel, G., Olson, K. R., & Patrick, C. (2002). The personality of love: Fundamental motives and traits related to components of love. *Personality & Individual Differences, 32*(5), 839–853.

Epstein, N. B., & Baucom, D. H. (2002). *Enhanced cognitive-behavioral therapy for couples: A contextual approach.* Washington, DC: American Psychological Association.

Erel, O., & Burman, B. (1995). Interrelatedness of marital relations and parent child relations: A meta-analytic review. *Psychological Bulletin, 118*(1), 108–132.

Fenell, D. L. (1993). Characteristics of long-term first marriages. *Journal of Mental Health Counseling, 15*, 446–460.

Fincham, F. D. (1998). Child development and marital relations. *Child Development, 69*, 543–574.

Fincham, F. D. (2003). Marital conflict: Correlates, structure, and context. *Current Directions in Psychological Science, 12*, 23–27.

Fincham, F. D., & Beach, S. R. H. (1999). Conflict in marriage: Implications for working with couples. *Annual Review of Psychology, 50*, 47–77.

Fincham, F. D., Beach, S. R. H., & Davila, J. (2004). Forgiveness and conflict resolution in marriage. *Journal of Family Psychology, 18*, 72–81.

Fincham, F. D., Beach, S. R. H., & Kemp-Fincham, S. I. (1997). Marital quality: A new theoretical perspective. In R. J. Sternberg & M. Hojjat (Eds.), *Satisfaction in close relationships* (pp. 275–304). New York: Guilford Press.

Fincham, F. D., & Bradbury, T. N. (1987). The assessment of marital quality: A reevaluation. *Journal of Marriage and the Family, 49*, 797–809.

Fincham, F. D., & Bradbury, T. N. (1993). Marital satisfaction, depression, and attributions: A longitudinal analysis. *Journal of Personality and Social Psychology, 64*(3), 442–452.

Fincham, F. D., Bradbury, T. N., & Scott, C. K. (1990). Cognition in marriage. In F. D. Fincham & T. N. Bradbury (Eds.), *Psychology of marriage: Basic issues and applications* (pp. 118–149). New York: Guilford Press.

Fincham, F. D., Garnier, P. C., Gano-Phillips, S., & Osborne, L. N. (1995). Preinteraction expectations, marital satisfaction, and accessibility: A new look at sentiment override. *Journal of Family Psychology, 9*(1), 3–14.

Finkel, E. J., Rusbult, C. E., Kumashiro, M., & Hannon, P. A. (2002). Dealing with betrayal in close relationships: Does commitment promote forgiveness? *Journal of Personality and Social Psychology, 82*(6), 956–974.

First, M. B., Bell, C. C., Cuthbert, B., Krystal, J. H., Malison, R., Offord, D. R., et al. (2002). Personality disorders and relational disorders: A research agenda for addressing crucial gaps in *DSM*. In D. J. Kupfer (Ed.), *A research agenda for DSM-V* (pp. 123–199). Washington, DC: American Psychiatric Association.

Flick, S. N., Roy-Byrne, P. P., & Cowley, D. S. (1993). *DSM-III-R* personality disorders in a mood and anxiety disorders clinic: Prevalence, comorbidity, and clinical correlates. *Journal of Affective Disorders, 27*, 71–79.

Floyd, F. J. (1989). Segmenting interactions: Coding units for assessing marital and family behaviors. *Behavioral Assessment, 11*(1), 13–29.

Glenn, N. D. (1991). The recent trend in marital success in the United States. *Journal of Marriage and the Family, 53*, 261–270.

Glenn, N. D. (1998). The course of marital success and failure in five American 10-year marriage cohorts. *Journal of Marriage and the Family, 60*(3), 569–576.

Glenn, N. D., & Weaver, C. N. (1981). The contribution of marital happiness to global happiness. *Journal of Marriage and the Family, 43*, 161–168.

Gottman, J. M. (1993). A theory of marital dissolution and stability. *Journal of Family Psychology, 7*, 57–75.

Gottman, J. M. (1994). *What predicts divorce?* Hillsdale, NJ: Erlbaum.

Gottman, J. M., & Notarius, C. I. (2000). Decade review: Observing marital interaction. *Journal of Marriage and the Family, 62*(4), 927–947.

Gottman, J. M., Swanson, C., & Swanson, K. (2002). A general systems theory of marriage: Nonlinear difference equation modeling of marital interaction. *Personality & Social Psychology Review, 6*(4), 326–340.

Grych, J. H., & Fincham, F. D. (Eds.). (2001). *Interparental conflict and child development: Theory, research, and applications.* New York: Cambridge University Press.

Hahlweg, K., Kaiser, A., Christensen, A., Fehm-Wolfsdorf, G., & Groth, T. (2000). Self-report and observational assessment of couples' conflict: The concordance between the Communication Patterns Questionnaire and the KPI observation system. *Journal of Marriage and the Family, 62*(1), 2422–2445.

Hahlweg, K., Markman, H. J., Thurmaier, F., Engl, J., & Eckert, V. (1998). Prevention of marital distress: Results of a German prospective longitudinal study. *Journal of Family Psychology, 12*(4), 543–556.

Hart, S. D., Dutton, D. G., & Newlove, T. (1993). The prevalence of personality disorder among wife assaulters. *Journal of Personality Disorders, 7*(4), 329–341.

Hazan, C., & Shaver, P. R. (1994). Attachment as an organizational framework for research on close relationships. *Psychological Inquiry, 5,* 1–22.

Heyman, R. E. (2001). Observation of couple conflicts: Clinical assessment applications, stubborn truths, and shaky foundations. *Psychological Assessment, 13,* 5–35.

Heyman, R. E., Feldbau-Kohn, S. R., Ehrensaft, M. K., Langhinrichsen-Rohling, J., & O'Leary, K. D. (2001). Can questionnaire reports correctly classify relationship distress and partner physical abuse? *Journal of Family Psychology, 15*(2), 334–346.

Heyman, R. E., & Vivian, D. (1993). *Rapid Marital Interaction Coding System (RMICS): Training manual for coders.* Stony Brook, NY: Marital Therapy Clinic. Retrieved June 15, 2004, from http://www.psychology.sunysb.edu/marital-/

Jacobson, N. S., & Christensen, A. (1996). *Integrative couple therapy: promoting acceptance and change.* New York: Norton.

Johnson, W., McGue, M., & Krueger, R. F. (2004). Marriage and personality: A genetic analysis. *Journal of Personality and Social Psychology, 86,* 285–294.

Julien, D., & Markman, H. J. (1991). Social support and social networks as determinants of individual and marital outcomes. *Journal of Social and Personal Relationships, 8,* 549–568.

Karney, B. R., & Bradbury, T. N. (1995). The longitudinal course of marital quality and stability: A review of theory, methods, and research. *Psychological Bulletin, 118*(1), 3–34.

Karney, B. R., & Bradbury, T. N. (1997). Neuroticism, marital interaction, and the trajectory of marital satisfaction. *Journal of Personality and Social Psychology, 72*(5), 1075–1092.

Kelly, E. L., & Conley, J. J. (1987). Personality and compatibility: A prospective analysis of marital stability and marital satisfaction. *Journal of Personality and Social Psychology, 52*(1), 27–40.

Kiecolt-Glaser, J. K., Glaser, R., Cacioppo, J. T., MacCallum, R. C., Snydersmith, M., Kim, C., et al. (1997). Marital conflict in older adults: Endocrinological and immunological correlates. *Psychosomatic Medicine, 59*(4), 339–349.

Kiecolt-Glaser, J. K., Malarkey, W. B., Cacioppo, J. T., & Glaser, R. (1994). Stressful personal relationships: Immune and endocrine function. In R. Glaser & J. K. Kiecolt-Glaser (Eds.), *Handbook of human stress and immunity* (pp. 321–339). New York: Academic Press.

Kiecolt-Glaser, J. K., Malarkey, W. B., Chee, M., & Newton, T. (1993). Negative behavior during marital conflict is associated with immunological down-regulation. *Psychosomatic Medicine, 55*(5), 395–409.

Kobak, R., Ruckdeschel, K., & Hazan, C. (1994). From symptom to signal: An attachment view of emotion in marital therapy. In S. M. Johnson & L. S. Greenberg (Eds.), *Heart of the matter: Perspectives on emotion in marital therapy* (pp. 46–71). Philadelphia: Brunner/Mazel.

Kurdek, L. A. (1993). Predicting marital dissolution: A 5-year prospective longitudinal study of newlywed couples. *Journal of Personality and Social Psychology, 64,* 221–242.

Lawrence, E., & Bradbury, T. N. (2001). Physical aggression and marital dysfunction: A longitudinal analysis. *Journal of Family Psychology, 15,* 135–154.

Liu, D., Diorio, J., Tannenbaum, B., Caldji, C., Francis, D., & Freedman, A. (1997). Maternal care, hippocampal glucocorticoid receptors, and hypothalamic-pituitary-adrenal responses to stress. *Science, 277,* 1659–1662.

Locke, H. J., & Wallace, K. M. (1959). Short marital adjustment and prediction tests: Their reliability and validity. *Marriage and Family Living, 21,* 251–255.

Malarkey, W. B., Kiecolt-Glaser, J. K., Pearl, D., & Glaser, R. (1994). Hostile behavior during marital conflict alters pituitary and adrenal hormones. *Psychosomatic Medicine, 56*(1), 41–51.

McCrae, R. R., Costa, P. T., & Busch, C. M. (1986). Evaluating comprehensiveness in personality systems: The California Q-Set and the Five-Factor Model. *Journal of Personality, 54*(2), 430–446.

McGue, M., & Lykken, D. T. (1992). Genetic influence on risk of divorce. *Psychological Science, 3,* 368–373.

Murstein, B. I., Cerreto, M., & MacDonald, M. G. (1977). A theory and investigation of the effect of exchange-orientation on marriage and friendship. *Journal of Marriage and the Family, 39*(3), 543–548.

Neff, L. A., & Karney, B. R. (2004). How does context affect intimate relationships? Linking external stress and cognitive processes within marriage. *Personality & Social Psychology Bulletin, 30*(2), 134–148.

Nock, S. L. (1995). Commitment and dependency in marriage. *Journal of Marriage and the Family, 57*(2), 503–514.

O'Farrell, T. J., Hooley, J., Fals-Stewart, W., & Cutter, H. S. (1998). Expressed emotion and relapse in alcoholic patients. *Journal of Consulting and Clinical Psychology, 66*(5), 744–752.

O'Leary, K. D. (Ed.). (1987). *Assessment of marital discord: An integration for research and clinical practice.* Hillsdale, NJ: Erlbaum.

Owen, M. T., & Cox, M. J. (1997). Marital conflict and the development of infant-parent attachment relationships. *Journal of Family Psychology, 11*(2), 152–164.

Ren, X. S. (1997). Marital status and quality of relationships: The impact on health perception. *Social Science & Medicine, 44*(2), 241–249.

Roberts, L. J., & Krokoff, L. J. (1990). A time-series analysis of withdrawal, hostility, and displeasure in satisfied and dissatisfied marriages. *Journal of Marriage and the Family, 52*(1), 95–105.

Robins, R. W., Caspi, A., & Moffitt, T. E. (2000). Two personalities, one relationship: Both partners' personality traits shape the quality of their relationship. *Journal of Personality and Social Psychology, 79,* 251–259.

Rogers, S. J., & Amato, P. R. (1997). Is marital quality declining? The evidence from two generations. *Social Forces, 75,* 1089–1100.

Rusbult, C. E., & Buunk, B. P. (1993). Commitment processes in close relationships: An interdependence analysis. *Journal of Social and Personal Relationships, 10*(2), 175–204.

Rusbult, C. E., Johnson, D. J., & Morrow, G. D. (1986). Determinants and consequences of exit, voice, loyalty, and neglect: Responses to dissatisfaction in adult romantic involvements. *Human Relations, 39*(1), 45–63.

Rusbult, C. E., Verette, J., Whitney, G. A., & Slovik, L. F. (1991). Accommodation processes in close relationships: Theory and preliminary empirical evidence. *Journal of Personality and Social Psychology, 60*(1), 53–78.

Sabourin, S., Lussier, Y., & Wright, J. (1991). The effects of measurement strategy on attributions for marital problems and behaviors. *Journal of Applied Social Psychology, 21,* 734–746.

Sagrestano, L. M., Christensen, A., & Heavey, C. L. (1998). Social influence techniques during marital conflict. *Personal Relationships, 5,* 75–89.

Schaap, C., Buunk, B., & Kerkstra, A. (1988). Marital conflict resolution. In P. Noller & M. A. Fitzpatrick (Eds.), *Perspectives on marital interaction* (pp. 203–244). Clevedon, England: Multilingual Matters.

Shadish, W. R., Montgomery, L. M., Wilson, P., & Wilson, M. R. (1993). Effects of family and marital psychotherapies: A meta-analysis. *Journal of Consulting and Clinical Psychology, 61,* 992–1002.

Smith, D. A., Vivian, D., & O'Leary, K. D. (1990). Longitudinal prediction of marital discord from premarital expressions of affect. *Journal of Consulting and Clinical Psychology, 58,* 790–798.

Snyder, D. K. (1997). *Manual for the Marital Satisfaction Inventory–Revised (MSI-R).* Los Angeles: Western Psychological Services.

Spanier, G. B. (1976). Measuring dyadic adjustment. *Journal of Marriage and the Family, 38,* 15–28.

Stanley, S. (1998). *The heart of commitment.* Nashville, TN: Thomas.

Tesser, A., & Beach, S. R. H. (1998). Life events, relationship quality, and depression: An investigation of judgment discontinuity in vivo. *Journal of Personality and Social Psychology, 74,* 36–52.

Tienari, P., Wynne, L. C., Moring, J., Lathi, I., Naarala, M., & Sorri, A. (1994). The Finnish adoptive family study of schizophrenia: Implications for family research. *British Journal of Psychiatry, 164*(Suppl. 23), 20–26.

Treboux, D., Crowell, J. A., & Waters, E. (2004). When "new" meets "old": Configurations of adult attachment representations and their implications for marital functioning. *Developmental Psychology, 40*(2), 295–314.

Van Lange, P. A. M., Rusbult, C. E., Drigotas, S. M., & Arriaga, X. B. (1997). Willingness to sacrifice in close relationships. *Journal of Personality and Social Psychology, 72*(6), 1373–1395.

Van Laningham, J., Johnson, D. R., & Amato, P. (2001). Marital happiness, marital duration, and the U-shaped curve: Evidence from a five-wave panel study. *Social Forces, 79,* 1313–1341.

Waite, L., & Luo, Y. (2002, August). *Marital happiness and marital stability: Consequences for psychological well-being.* Paper presented at the meeting of the American Sociological Association, Chicago.

Waller, N. G., & Meehl, P. E. (1998). *Multivariate taxometric procedures: Distinguishing types from continua.* Thousand Oaks, CA: Sage.

Watson, D., & Clark, L. A. (1984). Negative affectivity: The disposition to experience aversive emotional states. *Psychological Bulletin, 96*(3), 465–490.

Weiss, R. L., & Heyman, R. E. (1990). Observation of marital interaction. In F. D. B. Fincham & N. Thomas (Eds.), *The psychology of marriage: Basic issues and applications* (pp. 87–117). New York: Guilford Press.

Weiss, R. L., & Heyman, R. E. (1997). A clinical-research overview of couples interactions. In W. K. Halford & H. J. Markman (Eds.), *Clinical handbook of marriage and couples interventions* (pp. 13–41). New York: Wiley.

Weiss, R. L., Hops, H., & Patterson, G. R. (1973). A framework for conceptualizing marital conflict, a technology for altering it, some data for evaluating it (pp. 309–342). In L. O. Handy & E. L. Nash (Eds.), *Behavioral change: Methodology, concepts, and practice.* Champaign, IL: Research Press.

Whisman, M. A. (1999). Marital dissatisfaction and psychiatric disorders: Results from the National Comorbidity Survey. *Journal of Abnormal Psychology, 108,* 701–706.

Whisman, M. A., & Bruce, M. L. (1999). Marital dissatisfaction and incidence of major depressive episode in a community sample. *Journal of Abnormal Psychology, 108,* 674–678.

Wills, T. A., Weiss, R. L., & Patterson, G. R. (1974). A behavioral analysis of the determinants of marital satisfaction. *Journal of Consulting and Clinical Psychology, 42,* 802–811.

PART THREE
TREATMENT APPROACHES

CHAPTER 28

Psychodynamic Psychotherapy

STEVEN K. HUPRICH AND RACHEL A. KEASCHUK

INTRODUCTION

To write a chapter on psychodynamic psychotherapy in a manner in which it can be comprehensively represented is a daunting, and probably impossible, task. Many outstanding (Brenner, 1973; Fenichel, 1941; Ferenczi, 1953; Gill, 1954; Greenson, 1967; Guntrip, 1971; Kohut, 1971; Langs, 1973, 1974; Luborsky, 1984; Menninger, 1958; Schafer, 1983; Stone, 1961) and contemporary (e.g., Gabbard, 2000; Goldstein, 1998; Kernberg, 1993; McWilliams, 1994, 1999; Moore & Fine, 1995; Usher, 1993; Wallerstein, 1989) books and papers have addressed this topic in far greater detail and depth than what we can in this chapter.[1] These writings address the importance of understanding psychological drives and drive derivatives, ego functions and the mechanisms of defense, object relations, the development of the self, the workings and prominence of the inner world, resistances to therapy, transference, countertransference, interpretation, free association, and dream interpretation. Nevertheless, it is our goal to present an overview of the basic principles of psychodynamic theory and psychotherapy that are commonly practiced today as well as to provide an empirical review of the studies published on psychodynamic therapy and its related constructs. In doing so, we assert that the contribution of Freud and his followers to the understanding of personality provides invaluable and empirically supported knowledge when treating individuals within a psychotherapy framework. We conclude that, to understand personality and psychopathology, conceptualization from a psychodynamic framework will enhance the clinician's effectiveness and ability to provide useful assistance to his or her patient.

BASIC PREMISES OF PSYCHODYNAMIC THEORY

Despite controversies about the utility of psychodynamic and psychoanalytic theory (e.g., Grunbaum, 1984, 1993), recent reviews have found broad support for the basic principles of psychodynamic theory. Westen (1998) identifies five major domains that seem to characterize psychodynamic theory and are supported within the empirical literature:

1. The existence and centrality of unconscious processes, which includes unconscious thoughts, memories, affective processes, defensive operations, and motivation.
2. The presence of psychic conflict, ambivalence, and various mechanisms by which this conflict and ambivalence is expressed. In other words, compromise formations exist as ways in which conflicted thoughts, feelings, drives, and motives can be expressed behaviorally.
3. The continuity of personality and the role of childhood experiences in shaping personality and subsequent psychopathology. Within this context, it is understood that there is an interactive effect of genetic predispositions and childhood experience.
4. The role of mental representations of the self, others, and relationships. This complex relationship, commonly referred to as an individual's object relations, helps clinicians understand personality and psychopathology.
5. There are developmental trajectories that individuals follow. That is, biogenetic and experiential factors combine to create the typical thoughts, feelings, motivations, and behaviors of the person.

Fisher and Greenberg (1977, 1996) have presented perhaps the most exhaustive review of empirical studies of Freud's ideas. Having reviewed decades of research, they make several conclusions about what appear to be the most fundamental and empirically supported components of psychoanalytic and psychodynamic theory. First, "oral" and "anal" character types appear to be empirically supported in many, methodologically sound studies. Second, "the studies that have been reviewed affirm the underlying Oedipal notion of positive attraction between opposite-sex parent and child and of negative tension between the same-sex pair" (Fisher & Greenberg, 1996, p. 258). However, "Freud's ideas concerning the role of oedipal factors in sexual dysfunction have not stood up well to empirical testing" (p. 259). More specifically, "Freud's theory of homosexuality, while partially supported, was still largely either untested or equivocal with reference to evidence" (p. 259). Third, dreaming does not appear to occur the way Freud suggested. That is, dreams have greater functions than just as ways to express unconscious wishes. Finally, Freud's ideas about the development of paranoia and depression seem supported. Paranoia seems to be related, at times, to a defense against aggressive and/or homosexual impulses, and depression seems to be related to current and past loss experiences, ambivalent parenting styles, inclinations to being passive and dependent, and self-criticism and attack.

Developmental Stages

From the early writings of Freud, psychodynamic theory has asserted that psychological development proceeds through a series of stages that are the result of biological/physiological processes coupled with early experience. Throughout the evolution of Freud's ideas, the role of drive, affects, and interpersonal relationships has changed in the magnitude with which they influence the resulting personality and psychopathology. This evolution, for instance, may be detected in what is considered "psychoanalytic" theory versus "psychodynamic" theory (Gabbard, 2000; Mitchell & Black, 1995). Gabbard (2000), for instance, suggests that dynamic theory and therapy are broader than what Freud originally envisioned. A dynamic therapist is interested in understanding a patient's conflicts, psychic/psychological deficits and distortions, and internalized object relations. For a more fine-tuned analysis of these distinctions, the interested reader is directed toward the following sources: Kernberg (1993, 1995, 2001), Mitchell and Black (1995), and Moore and Fine (1995).

The earliest of Freud's developmental stages, the oral stage (see Table 28.1), is of importance in at least three domains. First, it provides the framework with which the very young child begins to develop a sense of relatedness to the world, thereby allowing him/her to establish a basic sense of trust. Second, it is the time in life when self and other begin to become differentiated, thereby setting down the psychic template upon which experience may be evaluated as originating from within or without. Third, as self-other differentiation occurs, one develops a sense of the inner world of drives, fantasies, impulses, affects, and wishes. As Edith Jacobson (1964) has explained, and expanded upon by Kernberg (2001), experience is organized around internal experiences of affect, that is, what feels generally good and bad, pleasurable and unpleasurable.

Psychodynamic theorists have long observed that the oral stage provides a basic groundwork upon which the person becomes aware of his or her inner experience and begins to receive attention and direction from others. The world begins to be understood as a safe, trustworthy place, or as dangerous and frustrating. As neurological development and perception develops, sensory experience (as it was first described by Freud) becomes a world of people and objects, which are capable of soothing, comforting, and amusing. Oral stimulation and gratification serve as a basic filter for experience, although as object and person representation becomes more developed, mental representation and evocation of sensory, episodic, and semantic memory ensues. McClelland, Koestner, and Weinberg (1989) also note that preverbal, affective experience is established, whereby the young child "implicitly" learns rules of behavior that shape his burgeoning sense of self and other. Not surprisingly, overgratification or unfulfilled oral needs may lead to later problems with dependency, as can problems with depressed mood if loss of the object's love and support occurs.

The oral stage has been the subject of much discussion by psychoanalytic and psychodynamic theorists. Some have elaborated upon the role of fantasy, aggression, and defenses throughout most of this stage (e.g., Melanie Klein), whereas others have indicated that behavior of the parents/caregiver plays a more prominent role in the resolution of this stage. For instance, developmental theorists (i.e., Ainsworth, Bowlby, Mahler) explained how children around one year of age develop separation anxiety from caregivers and experience a need to return to them for comfort and soothing. This type of caregiving behavior is important for the young child in developing his sense of initiative and curiosity in the world, his desire to relate and interact in the world, while at the same time, providing a sense of comfort from the fear and anxiety that arises from novel situations.

The second stage, the anal stage, is known for its emphasis on control, orderliness, regulation, separation, and independence. This stage derives its name from the child's increased awareness of anal functions, his or her ability to control or regulate these functions, and his or her interactions with parents or caregivers to master this bodily function. Pleasure is experienced and recognized in anal expulsion and retention. Conflict is also consciously felt and experienced when bodily impulses and tensions and appropriate means of relieving these do not readily coexist. Not surprisingly, this stage can lead to obsessive-compulsive and/or perfectionistic tendencies.

This stage is also understood as a time of increasing self-awareness and the deliberate exercising of one's desire to act upon his or her wishes. Conflict with the caregiver occurs regularly, as the willful and curious child seeks to learn about

TABLE 28.1 Basic Themes in Development

Psychosexual stage	Predominant issues and themes	Important outcomes
Oral (0–18 months)	Beginning to separate inner and outer worlds Predominant absorption in the inner world Establishing trust with the caregiver Being dependent upon a caregiver Gratifying physiological and relational needs quickly; expressing frustration when needs are not met Emphasis on oral eroticism Language and motor activity develop	Basic trust in the caregiver and the environment Use of language to begin to express needs Expectation of caregiving from parent Ability to act on impulses with parental care, oversight, and protection Beginning recognition of ambivalence toward others
Anal (18 months–3 years)	Further differentiation of self and others Cognitive distinctions between self and others Taking in rule-governed behavior Developing internalized controls of behavior Emphasis on separation and independence Emphasis on control, orderliness, regulation Emphasis on anal eroticism Guilt and distress when acting outside of internalized controls	Developing sense of autonomy and mastery A growing sense of distinction between that which is from within and that which is not Growing sense of self-regulation Capacity to use volition without guilt Ability to act cooperatively Growing sense of ambivalence toward others Beginning to recognize the intentions of others
Phallic (3 years–5 years)	Triadic relationship of mother-father-child Recognition of one's sex and sexual differences Recognition of sex roles and values Desire for opposite-sex parent Competition, shared desires, jealousy Fears over harm and loss because of desire Guilt over one's sexual impulses and wishes Emphasis on genital eroticism	Repression of sexualized and aggressive feelings toward parents Recognition of competition, jealousy, and shared desires that minimizes potential for loss and harm Growing recognition of complexity of others' thoughts, feelings, wishes, and desires
Latent (5 years–puberty)	De-emphasis on sexual interest Tendency to play with same sex Further refinement of self and other representations Further development of empathy Further development of analytic reasoning	Repression or redirection of interests toward other activities Expanded ability to use various types of reasoning Good mastery of impulses and drives Further consolidation of sex-role identification Further consolidation of mastering skills, activities Broadened social contact, social interest Quality of relationships matures, other represented in more holistic ways
Genital (puberty–young adulthood)	Onset of menses in girls and expression of secondary sex characteristics in both sexes Interest in sexual activities, relationships Psychological separation from parents Developing sense of self-identity	Ability to both love and work successfully Ability to manage conflicts that evoke earlier psychosexual themes Acceptance of societal standards and capacity to operate within these parameters

Note. Some have made reference to a urethral stage of psychosexual development. For further discussion of this issue, see Meissner (2000). This table was developed with reference to Blatt, Wein, Chevron, and Quinlan (1979), Brenner (1973), Compton (1995), and Meissner (2000).

the world and the parent/caregiver sets rules, guidelines, and even prohibitions about what the child may or may not do. Self and object/other representations become more defined and articulated, although the tendency exists (as it did in the oral stage) for the child to split his mental representation into positive or negative experience. An internal struggle exists with understanding and accepting ambivalence toward others and life's experience.

Inherent in this stage are the child's representation of experience and his or her judgment of it as positive or negative. In slightly different words, as the superego develops during this stage, the child comes to evaluate his or her experience in moral terms. This evaluation may originate from a direct pronouncement from the parent, such as, "You may not hit your sister," or from an identification process with the caregiver; that is, acting and being like the caregiver who is admired and respected. Ideally, a child near the end of this stage will come to act upon his desires and intentions without guilt, while at the same time, have a rudimentary sense of what is right and wrong and a belief that the caregiver can and will provide him/her with guidance and instruction.

The third stage, the phallic stage, is fraught with the most controversy both within psychodynamic and psychoanalytic theory, as well as the psychological community in general. Nevertheless, important themes and ideas have emerged from the clinical experience of many that are commonly accepted in the context of conducting psychodynamically oriented psychotherapy. The phallic stage presents the child with new awareness and psychological challenges. Recognition of one's own sex and sex differences becomes a preoccupying theme. Culture, society, and values introjected by parents all play a predominant role in beginning to shape the sexual role and identification the child assumes. Also in this stage, the child becomes aware of his or her own needs and wishes to have a relationship with the opposite-sex parent, but that the same-sex parent shares his or her affections for the desired parent. In fact, the child becomes most aware that eventually he or she cannot win the parent's affection away from the other parent and must come to accept the loss and disappointment he or she feels.

Related to the preceding, desires of competition and jealousy become predominant in the psychic life of the child. Competition elicits aggressive feelings and impulses, and the delicate balance begins between a shared and dyadic relationship with the desired parent. An overly strict superego at this point may lead the child to feel guilt for having pleasurable and/or aggressive feelings toward his or her parents; whereas, id impulses that operate with forcefulness and with relatively lower levels of restraint lead the child toward pursuing that which he or she wants. Consequently, aggressive themes and behaviors may emerge. Because the child is ultimately frustrated in achieving the kind of relationship he or she desires with the opposite-sex parent, angry, hostile, or competitive affect may come to characterize the object relations of the child and the same sex parent. To the extent that this frustration is successfully repressed and other relationships later come to take the place of the parental relationship is the extent to which jealousy, competition, and desire make up the inner life of the person as an adult. Not surprisingly, narcissistic and antisocial tendencies may be observed in adulthood when the aforementioned feelings are not resolved.

Latency, the fourth psychosexual stage, is a relatively docile stage. Here, the child enters into primarily same-sex relationships, engaging regularly in play and other shared activities. Cognitive and intellectual abilities quickly expand, and thinking moves to formal operational and abstract levels in the analytic and moral domains (Kohlberg, 1981; Piaget, 1990). Impulses and drives by this point should be well managed, and greater awareness of the thoughts, needs, and desires of others occurs. Social interest and investment in social relationships should occur, as should mutually gratifying peer and family relationships.

The final period of psychosexual development, the genital stage, begins with the onset of puberty. Secondary sexual characteristics begin to develop, and hormonal and physiological processes prepare the young person for physical reproduction. Consequently, interest in sexual relationships reappears, and latent sexual interest now is expressed. At this time, like in any other time, conflicts from past stages may shape or influence behavior. For instance, strong needs to control may lead the individual to press for definition and greater control of the interpersonal dynamics of a new relationship.

Although the previous paragraphs offer a brief overview of psychosexual development, it is by no means complete. There are at least three other elements that are associated with most expansions of Freud's theory that are important to understand. First, it is important to acknowledge that there are defense mechanisms employed by the ego that are used to ward off anxiety and distress that come from conflicts over wishes, impulses, and needs and how they are expressed and manifested. The most basic defense is repression. Freud (1915/1957) thought that repression served to block impulses that could not be brought to awareness and acted upon. His original conception of repression has been modified somewhat to account for how impulses are expressed in everyday life without a compromise to one's well-being (Brenner, 1982), and other mechanisms of defense have also been proposed (A. Freud, 1936/1966). Thus, when conducting psychodynamic therapy, psychotherapists are interested in: (1) an understanding of the defense mechanisms being utilized is crucial; (2) understanding what impulse is being blocked from expression is central to understanding the person's symptom; and (3) examining and challenging the use of maladaptive defenses is considered essential in helping the person overcome his or her difficulties.

Related to this is the concept of compromise formation. Brenner (1982) writes:

> The essential components of psychic conflict are drive derivative, anxiety and/or depressive affect, and defense. Its consequence is a *compromise formation* [italics added] among its

several components. ... Compromise formations are the data of observation when one applies the psychoanalytic method and observes and/or infers a patient's wishes, fantasies, moods, plans, dreams, and symptoms. (p. 109)

Pathology results when any of the following occur: (1) there is too much restriction of gratification of drives, impulses, or affect; (2) there is too much inhibition of functional capacity; (3) there is too much displeasure, such as anxiety or depression; (4) there is too much of a tendency to injure or destroy oneself; or (5) there is too much conflict with one's environment (Brenner, 1982). Thus, when conducting psychodynamic psychotherapy, the therapist considers how the resulting behavior (observed in word, affect, overt and nonverbal behavior) is the product of these impulses and defenses and a reflection of the rich inner life of the patient that is now leading him/her to harm, conflict, or distress.

Finally, the concept of fixation is important when conducting psychodynamic therapy. Fixation results from unresolved issues that occur in early development, whereby unresolved psychic conflicts persist between unexpressed feelings or impulses and guilt that may accompany such feelings and impulses. Fixation may be relatively circumscribed or pervasive. For instance, a man with unresolved issues surrounding oedipal competition may become timid when competing in sporting events with friends, fearing that he will be perceived as weak and powerless, but under most other circumstances, is comfortable in discussing his flaws or weaknesses with others. In contrast, an individual may develop overtly narcissistic qualities that protect his self-esteem by symbolically conquering potential challengers, being pervasively critical of others, belittling or indirectly hurting those with whom he works when they frustrate him, and seeking positions of power and authority so that he may not be vulnerable. Regardless of the pervasiveness of the fixation, psychodynamic therapists are interested in how these psychosexual issues may play themselves out in the patient's presenting problems and overall structure of personality and character.

BASIC PREMISES OF PSYCHODYNAMIC PSYCHOTHERAPY

Alliance

One of the most widely documented factors that affect the outcome of psychotherapy is the nature of the therapeutic alliance (Norcross, 2002). This alliance is the understanding between patient and therapist that the therapist is invested in assisting the patient to reach his or her therapeutic goals in effective, caring, and compassionate ways. Alliance is not to be confused with likeability, although the two concepts overlap. A therapist may make statements that are uncomfortable for the patient, perhaps even challenging the patient to make difficult changes. Although a patient may find temporary dislike, or even hatred, of the therapist at these times, a patient who has a positive therapeutic alliance will come to evaluate, accept, and enact the suggestions of the therapist. This acceptance and action, however, occurs because the relationship has been established and a sense of trust and safety between the patient and therapist has been developed. As such, attending to the therapeutic alliance in the outset and duration of treatment is essential for good psychodynamic therapy to occur.

Gabbard (2000) has elaborated upon important concepts related to the therapeutic alliance. First, he describes the concept of "neutrality," which is the notion that therapists are to reveal nothing about themselves to their patients. Although such ideas originated from Freud's papers on analytic technique, Gabbard (2000) notes that there is evidence demonstrating how Freud did not abide by such principles. Neutrality, according to Gabbard, is "the assumption of a nonjudgmental stance regarding the patient's behaviors, thoughts, wishes, and feelings" (p. 95). Anna Freud (1936/1966) suggested that this means the therapist maintain an equal distance from the patient's id, ego, and superego, whereas Greenberg (1986) considered neutrality to be the development of a relationship with the patient that reflects both elements of the new object relationship (with the therapist) and the old object relationship (revealed in the transference with the therapist). Although these definitions seem somewhat idealized and difficult to operationalize in the therapy process, neutrality is perhaps best considered to be an attitude of nonjudgment toward the patient (as discussed by Gabbard) while at the same time maintaining the appropriate psychological distance from the patient's subjective experience so as to think in more objective and theoretically informed ways about the patient in order to plan and act in therapeutically beneficial ways.

Second, Gabbard (2000) describes the concept of anonymity, which is the "mythical construct" that personal effects, self-disclosure, and the "blank screen" approach are not to be utilized in dynamic psychotherapy. Gabbard dissuades therapists from acting out of this position, noting that it is technically impossible not to reveal oneself in the therapy process. He notes that whenever the therapist speaks, his or her personal subjectivity impacts what is communicated. Nonverbal communication acts in the same fashion. More specifically, McWilliams (1999) suggests that it is impossible for the personal, idiosyncratic interpretative processes of the therapist not to impact therapy. She writes, "the term implies that patient and therapist have created together, from their combined subjectivities and quality of the relationship that evokes between them, a narrative that makes sense of the client's background and predicament—a narrative truth rather than a historical one (Levenson, 1972; Spence, 1982; Atwood & Stolorow, 1984; Schafer, 1992; Gill, 1994)" (p. 15). Nonetheless, anonymity is an important therapeutic construct, in that therapists are cautioned to screen their words carefully, especially those words that knowingly involve self-revelation.

Finally, Gabbard (2000) describes the construct of abstinence, which is the "deliberate withholding of gratification wishes so that those wishes could be analyzed rather than satisfied" (p. 96). Unlike many psychotherapies, dynamic and analytic approaches to treatment are interested in the wishes and fantasies of patients and the means by which these fantasies and wishes are gratified. Systematic exploration and analysis of these wishes is a defining feature of analytic and dynamic treatment. Gabbard notes that partial gratification of these wishes occurs simply by nature of the therapy process, whereby the therapist listens empathically to the patient, or by simple responses to the patient's behaviors, such as laughing at a joke or acknowledging a comment from the patient not related to the therapy (e.g., "It sure is cold outside today"). Yet, to practice from a psychodynamic perspective, a therapist must be able to withhold or carefully select his or her words to the patient instead of responding immediately to the demands or solicitations of the patient. For many beginning therapists, this task is difficult to master, given the countertransference wishes to help, save, rescue, or even cure the patient.

Ideation, Fantasy, and Wishes

Just as behavior therapy is identified by its focus on identifying precipitants of problematic behavior in the individual's environment, so is psychodynamic therapy identified by its focus on the internal mental processes of the patient, or the rich inner subjective life of the patient. These processes include an understanding of the person's ideas, fantasies, and wishes. The patient is asked to verbalize whatever content comes to mind, so that clues may be identified as to the unconscious determinants of behavior. The importance of these mental processes has been articulated by almost all psychoanalytic and psychodynamic writers and serves as the groundwork upon which psychodynamic therapy is conducted.

For example, Brenner (1982) states that the data upon which psychoanalytic treatment is conducted is "the wishes, fears, fantasies, dreams, physical sensations, and so on, expressed in words and gestures. It is the *range* [italics added] and content of psychoanalytic data that are unique [to this science]. Their *nature* [italics added] is not unique at all. They are commonplace psychological data" (p. 4). Recently, Acklin, Li, and Tyson (2005) eloquently noted that "the raw material and aboriginal language of human subjectivity is fantasy." In fact, they observed that many theoretical and contemporary concepts embrace these ideas—imagoes, complexes, object representations, internalized working models, and schemata. In other words, psychological science is increasingly recognizing the importance of the workings of internal mental life in understanding psychopathology and behavior change.

For instance, consider the case of a man in his late 20s entering psychotherapy. He is in training to obtain a degree in a helping profession and seeks treatment because he wants to know what therapy is like, as he will be conducting counseling as part of his profession. He cannot identify any particular area of concern and speaks somewhat tangentially about his current activities. Although some may view this individual as inappropriate for therapy, given his lack of goals and relative lack of distress, careful attention to the patient's words reveals three important issues in this patient's psychic life. First, the patient has *ideas* about his need to be morally superior to others (despite the fact that he reports accepting flaws in others). He finds it difficult to relinquish his goal of having a morally impeccable character, despite knowing that he could be happier by being more accepting of himself. Second, he continues to have sporadic contact with a female friend in which they engage in sexual activities. Although he *wishes* to be married someday, he does not think that his friend is one whom he could marry because of her neediness. This activity produces much guilt and the idea that he should restrain his impulses even further. Finally, as therapy continues, he *fantasizes* that, if he does not curb his impulses and develop greater control of his impulses, he will be discovered by those whom he helps and will lose credibility.

In this case, attention to the patient's ideas reveals (among other things) an overly developed superego, strong, unrealistic standards for himself, and the belief that he can contain his impulses by restraining them more. His ideation also suggests that his self-representation consists of ideas of perfection, flawlessness, and help giving, whereas his representation of others seems to consist of weakness and neediness. Attention to the patient's wishes indicates that he desires to have a sexualized relationship and that he indeed acts upon these wishes, in spite of tremendous conscious efforts to resist sexual activity. His self and other representations seem to be somewhat disconnected, as sexualized experiences are kept separate from other components of the relationship. It also seems as if he wishes for a perfect spouse, whom he is not likely find. Finally, by evaluating the patient's fantasy, it appears that he fears embarrassment and ridicule from others were he to be caught having a sexual relationship with this woman. Here, strong introjected values in the superego produce conscious feelings of remorse and guilt, along with beliefs about being punished for his activities. His self-representation seems to be diminished and infantilized when he acts upon these desires, and his representation of others seems to be that of persecutors.

In listening to these ideas, wishes, and fantasies, the therapist was able to see a narcissistic character structure that was highly vulnerable to both internal and external threats. His desire to appear morally impeccable was foiled by his giving way to sexualized impulses. Despite wanting to be in a helping role, the patient found it difficult to view himself as those whom he helped, that is, as being someone who had wants and needs. He also seemed to anticipate punishment from others were they to see him as one who has needs and acts upon them. This information subsequently assisted in treatment planning. Specifically, the therapist paid close attention to his demonstration of empathy, so as not to damage or challenge the patient's fragile esteem. However, as the therapeutic relationship continued, the therapist challenged the patient's beliefs more often, making comparisons between the patient and others as having impulses and desires and not always being perfect or flawless. The therapist challenged the patient's use of repression and intellectualization as a means of avoiding psychic conflict. As the patient's awareness grew, he became more accepting of himself and began to see a relationship between his internalized expectations and the demanding standards of his father. He also began to see a relationship between his caretaking role for women and his mother, who had struggled with some addiction when the patient was younger, thereby leading the patient to assume a more caretaking role in the family. Finally, the therapist began to explore with the patient how underlying feelings of aggression toward his parents may play a role in his current functioning.

Interpretation

Interpretation in the context of psychotherapy is a speculation or hypothesis provided by the therapist about the nature of the patient's problem of which the patient is not currently aware. It is an explanation with the intent of providing insight and meaning to the patient. To make an interpretation meaningful, the timing and process by which the interpretation is made is crucial. Weiner (1998) states that interpretation must be made when the patient is ready to accept a new understanding of his or her problems. This best occurs when the therapeutic relationship has been well established and the patient is low in his or her resistance to treatment. Weiner (1998) also notes that interpretation of therapy process should occur before the content, as a focus on the here-and-now exchange between patient and therapist that is observed by the therapist will lay the foundation for the patient to hear a content-oriented explanation.

By the nature of the act itself, interpretation is a challenge to the patient's current way of thinking, feeling, and behaving. Although it provides a new understanding for the patient, an interpretation explicitly suggests that the patient's current way of managing his or her situation is maladaptive. Thus, interpretations can be met with resistance and may require time to work through and understand. It is for this reason that the stereotypical response of, "Aha, now I see it all!" is infrequently observed with an interpretation. Rather, interpretations are worked through, often many times.

Resistance

One of the ironies of psychotherapies is that patients resist making changes for their own good. This is often observed in psychodynamic and psychoanalytic treatment. Weiner (1998) proposes several important mechanisms that account for resistance. These include resistance emanating from a secondary gain of being a patient, resistance to changing the relationship patterns with others, resistance to specific content, resistance to being in the patient role, and self-criticism the person experiences because of his or her psychological growth. Although written more than 40 years ago, Menninger (1958) astutely noted that resistance may also be observed in acting out and erotization of the therapy process.

Resistance can also be rooted in one's personality, as Reich (1949), Shapiro (1965), and McWilliams (1994) readily observed. These characterological resistances are tied into the stereotypical use of defense mechanisms (discussed in the following section) and tend to be difficult to overcome.

Defenses

Defenses are psychic processes that protect the individual from experiencing psychological pain or turmoil. Understanding defense mechanisms and their utility is often the focus of ego psychological perspectives. Anna Freud (1936/1966) is attributed with differentiating these mechanisms of defense, and as just noted previously, certain defenses have been understood as components of different character structures. For instance, obsessive-compulsive personalities tend to use intellectualization, repression, and isolation of affect as common defenses. Many therapists view defense mechanisms as evidence of one's ego maturity sophistication. The more the ego has developed in its capacity to process information from the external world and respond accordingly to it, the more mature the defense is generally believed to be. Less-developed defenses, in contrast, rely more on internal impulses, feelings, or states and protect the individual by involving the ego less in processing information in the world and testing reality by more reason-based processes. As compiled by Meissner (2000), narcissistic and immature defenses consist of denial, projection, gross distortion, acting out, blocking, hypochondriasis, introjection, passive-aggressive behavior, regression, schizoid fantasy, somatization, and splitting. Neurotic defenses consist of controlling, displacement, dissociation, externalization, inhibition, intellectualization, isolation, rationalization, reaction formation, repression, and sexualization. Mature defenses consist of altruism, anticipation, asceticism, humor, sublimation, and suppression.

Transference

Transference is a distortion. It is an inaccurate perception, representation, and interaction the patient experiences with the therapist, often reflecting the patient's experience with someone similar in his or her past. Transference is considered a fundamental process that needs to occur in psychoanalytic and psychodynamic treatment in order to trace the psychosexual origins of the patient's conflicts. Thus, transference is fostered, usually by the therapist being "like a projective test" (Weiner, 1998), wherein the therapist minimizes what parts of him- or herself that are shared with the patient. Gabbard (2000) writes that transference may be generated when therapists act out of anonymity and, at times, abstinence. Thus, when fostering transference and considering its impact on the therapy hour, therapists must carefully and delicately evaluate what may and may not be considered transference.

Transference may be either positive or negative toward the therapist. It may also be relatively short-lived or circumscribed in its scope, as well as long-lived or pervasive. Weiner (1998) provides three guidelines for when to interpret transference: (1) when it is producing resistance; (2) when it is of moderate intensity and interferes with treatment; and (3) significant information is believed to come from the exploration. Despite its importance, however, transference sometimes takes time to develop, and depending upon the length of therapy, it may not be examined and worked through for the patient's benefit.

Countertransference

Countertransference has traditionally been considered a distortion made by the therapist about a patient. When it occurs, countertransference is traditionally viewed as inappropriate or irrational, needing careful scrutiny by the therapist so as to prevent it from interfering with the therapist's ability to be objective.

Alternative views of countertransference also have been posited. Racker (1968) boldly stated, "if the analyst is well identified with the patient and he has fewer repressions than the patient, then the thoughts and feelings which emerge in him (i.e., the analyst) will be, precisely, those which did emerge in the patient, i.e., the repressed and the unconscious" (p. 17). Racker's ideas stem from the concepts of concordant and complementary identifications. In the former, the therapist identifies with the thoughts, feelings, and desires (i.e., id and ego) of the patient. In the latter, the therapist identifies with internalized objects or relationship roles that are assigned to him or her. Eagle (2000) writes that Racker's statement about countertransference reflects an overemphasis on complementary identifications, thereby reinforcing the idea that the therapist can truly function as a blank slate without projecting any of his or her wishes or ideas onto the patient. As such, Eagle (2000) recommends that countertransference be viewed from a more balanced perspective; that is, therapist feelings and thoughts may reflect *either* the therapist or the patient's inner life. Most psychodynamic therapists today tend to view countertransference in this balanced manner.

Expressive-Supportive Continuum and Indicators for Treatment

Contrary to popular belief, not all psychodynamic therapy is structured so that the patient sits across from the therapist (or lies on a couch) and associates freely about his problems as the therapist explores the origins of the patient's difficulties and makes interpretations about these origins. Rather, psychodynamic therapy is structured in large part by the level of the patient's adaptive function, the nature of the presenting problem (e.g., crisis), and his or her level of ego development and functioning. Gabbard (2000) has developed a continuum of treatment, which is presented in Table 28.2. Patients with poorer levels of functioning and more poorly developed ego functions (e.g., impulse control, ability to tolerate frustration and delay gratification, reality testing, self-definition) are best suited for supportive therapy. These patients regularly engage in self-destructive behavior and/or act in impulsive and dangerous ways. This approach is aimed toward assisting patients in managing day-to-day activities and crises or problems in more adaptive ways than they are currently capable. Maintaining and/or attaining stability are important therapeutic goals, as is the development of psychosocial support. Such

TABLE 28.2 Indications for Expressive or Supportive Emphasis in Psychotherapy

Expressive	Supportive
Strong motivation to understand	Significant, chronic ego defects
Significant suffering	Severe life crisis
Ability to regress in service of ego	Low anxiety tolerance
Tolerance for frustration	Poor frustration tolerance
Capacity for insight (psychological mindedness)	Lack of psychological mindedness
Intact reality testing	Poor reality testing
Meaningful object relations	Severely impaired object relations
Good impulse control	Poor impulse control
Ability to sustain a job	Low intelligence
Capacity to think in terms of analogy and metaphor	Little capacity for self-observation
Reflective responses to trial interpretations	Organically based cognitive dysfunction
	Tenuous ability to form alliance

Note. From Gabbard (2000), p. 108, Table 4-1. Reprinted by permission.

patients often need to be taught basic social skills and/or rationally based thinking.

Patients with higher levels of adaptive functioning and ego development are best suited for expressive forms of therapy. These forms are sometimes known as insight-oriented approaches. Here the patient must have the ability to step outside of him or herself (i.e., possess an observing ego), an ability to tolerate frustration, explore painful or difficult topics, and be open to the interpretations and guidance of the therapist. Of course, it is unusual to find therapy that functions just at one end of the continuum. Many patients have an admixture of ego strengths and weaknesses, and given the nature of what brought them to therapy (e.g., a crisis vs. a desire to further explore problematic areas), a supportive or expressive stance would be utilized. A more specific discussion of level of ego organization and functioning and treatment planning is provided by Trimboli and Farr (2000).

Convergence and Divergence in Technique

As psychoanalytic and psychodynamic theory has evolved, so have the techniques used by therapists who are proponents of the theories. Classical psychoanalytic technique has given way to psychoanalytically oriented and psychodynamically oriented psychotherapy. Such differences in technique are primarily guided by the theory itself. For instance, self-psychology emphasizes the active role of therapeutic empathy in technique, as it is needed for the patient's ongoing development of the self.

Kernberg (1993) recently evaluated trends in technique from writers of drive theory, ego psychology, self-psychology, Kleinian, and interpersonal perspectives. He describes nine areas of convergence in technique. These consist of the following: a trend toward earlier interpretations of transference (with particular interest in unconscious meanings of the transference; an interest in identifying and interpreting character defenses; an emphasis on understanding here-and-now unconscious meanings of events; the translation of unconscious conflicts over impulse and defense into an understanding of the object relations aspect of the conflict; understanding countertransference as the total emotional reaction of the therapist to the patient; understanding the patient's affective experience (rather than exploring the drive derivative); utilizing mechanisms other than dreams to learn about the unconscious, including daydreams, metaphors within the patient's language, and jokes; greater concern about patients' use of analytic and dynamic language at the expense of working through their transference and other related conflicts; and finally, a greater questioning of the developmental time line and its relationship to psychopathology as proposed originally by Freud.

Just as there have been convergences in technique, Kernberg (1993) describes seven dimensions in which opinions on technique are highly varied. These consist of: varying opinion about what is transference and what is a "real relationship"; discussion about the role of regression in therapy; ongoing differences about the distinction between traditional psychoanalysis and psychoanalytic therapy; a distinction between self-psychology and other psychodynamic approaches in the extent to which the therapist demonstrates empathy; controversy about the extent to which historical truth and narrative truth are derived; growing interest in the extent to which culture and political ideas influence the treatment process; and finally, the extent to which preverbal, early experience may be recovered and reconstructed.

EMPIRICAL SUPPORT FOR PSYCHODYNAMIC PSYCHOTHERAPY

Does Psychodynamic Treatment Work?

In a review of 18 quantitative meta-analyses, Luborsky et al. (2003) found nonsignificant differences among commonly practiced psychotherapies. Further, when these differences were corrected for the researcher's allegiance to the form of psychotherapy being studied, the differences between treatments decreased. Results of this nature have led to what has been considered the "Dodo Bird Verdict," that is all treatments are equally effective. Yet, psychodynamic therapy offers a distinctive approach to treatment that is not found in other forms of therapy. An examination of the empirical literature on psychodynamic treatment suggests that there is good evidence to support its clinical utility. Thus, the purpose of this section is to provide a general review of research on the efficacy and process of psychodynamic therapies including length of treatment, therapeutic alliance, defenses, transference, countertransference, and patient characteristics that affect outcome.

Length of Treatment

Traditionally psychodynamic forms of therapy have been long term and high frequency. Dose-response relationship studies that evaluate long-term therapies suggest that longer term treatment may benefit a higher proportion of patients (Shapiro et al., 2003). Research on long-term therapies has suggested that there also may be a tendency for long-term therapies to show more lasting benefits, especially with regards to posttreatment maintenance of gains (Luborsky, 2001; Sandell et al., 2000; Shapiro et al., 2003). In addition, significant differences in patient's perception of the effectiveness of therapy have been found between patients receiving 6 months or 24 months of psychotherapy, with patients in therapy longer viewing their therapy as more effective (Freedman, Hoffenberg, Vorus, & Frosch, 1999).

In the current state of managed care there has been a drive to decrease cost and the length of treatment and, as such, there has been an increase in research investigating the efficacy of short-term psychodynamic therapy. In short, meta-analyses have shown that short-term psychodynamic treatments are as efficacious as other forms of treatment, slightly better than minimal treatments, and are significantly better than control treatments (Anderson & Lambert, 1995; Crits-Christoph, 1992). The question of necessary "doses" of psychotherapy has also been raised. Studies on the stages of psychotherapy (i.e., a phase model) have demonstrated a negatively accelerating positive growth curve, suggesting that clinical improvement is apparent after relatively few sessions and that increases in gain tend to diminish after a certain number of sessions (Hilsenroth, Ackerman, & Blagys, 2001; Howard, Lueger, Maling, & Martinovich, 1993). Although few studies of the phase model have deliberately used short-term modalities, changes consistent with the phase model have been found in short-term psychodynamic treatment (Hilsenroth et al., 2001). Additionally, the fact that improvement in subjective well-being, symptoms, and relational functioning can occur in relatively few sessions generally demonstrated by phase model research can be seen as lending further support to short-term therapies.

In contrast, Sandell, Blomberg, and Lazar (2002) have proposed that there is no set effective dose of psychotherapy, and that session frequency and duration interact in determining eventual treatment outcome. Research has supported these ideas. In a review comparing short- and long-term therapies, Luborsky (2001) found that both forms of treatment show positive benefits for some patients. Patient characteristics and diagnostic classification appear to differentially impact response to treatment in both short- and long-term therapies. For example, patients with personality disorders have been found to have a slower positive response to short-term dynamic therapies (Barber, Morse, Krakauer, Chittams, & Crits-Christoph, 1997; Hardy et al., 1995), and it has been suggested that characterological changes will occur more slowly than changes in acute and chronic distress (Kopta, Howard, Lowry, & Beutler, 1994).

Therapeutic Alliance

The therapeutic alliance has recently been identified as a common treatment factor that mediates psychotherapy outcomes across theoretical orientations (Norcross, 2002). However, the majority of the research on therapeutic alliance has primarily been undertaken by investigators supporting a psychodynamic orientation. Reviews of the research on therapeutic alliance consistently demonstrate a positive relationship between alliance and psychotherapy outcome across various studies and measures of alliance (Gaston, 1990; Horvath, Gaston & Luborsky, 1993; Horvath & Greenberg, 1994; Horvath & Luborsky, 1993; Horvath & Symonds, 1991; Luborsky, 1990, 1996). In particular, initially positive alliances have been consistently related to positive psychotherapy outcomes (Luborsky, 1996). Measures of alliance also appear to be more predictive of a positive outcome when outcome is measured as change in the patient's target complaint, rather than symptoms (Horvath et al., 1993). Alliances that are initially more negative do not seem to share this same relationship, as it appears that initial negativity in the alliance is a relatively irregular predictor of outcome (Luborsky, 1996).

Empirical evidence also lends support to the concept that the therapeutic alliance will undergo change throughout treatment duration, a result of a cycle of relationship rupture and repair. These changes may impact the predictive validity of a positive therapeutic alliance. Some have suggested that positive early alliances occur because strain has not yet been placed on the therapeutic relationship (Safran, Muran, & Samstag, 1994). Accordingly, it is possible that a more accurate prediction of outcome would occur if alliance measures were averaged across sessions. Krupnick et al. (1996) found stronger associations between outcome and alliance when measures of alliance were averaged across several sessions than when measured during early sessions. However, one potential confound in measuring alliance during later sessions is that an improved therapeutic relationship may actually be an early indicator of positive treatment effects, which would decrease the predictive value of these measurements.

The therapeutic alliance is interactional in nature. As such, research has investigated the attributes of both patients and therapists that contribute to positive therapeutic alliances. In-session investigation has identified some of the personal qualities of therapists and techniques employed in the therapy process that have been positively related to the formation of alliance and the repair of relationship disturbance during the course of treatment. A review of 25 studies identified therapist personal attributes that contribute positively to the alliance, including flexibility, trustworthiness, experience, confidence, clear communication, enthusiasm, warmth, and interest (Ackerman & Hilsenroth, 2003). This same analysis identified therapeutic techniques that positively contribute to the alliance including clear communication, accurate interpretation, exploration, affirmation, understanding, facilitation of affect expression, and attention to the patient's experience. These techniques focus primarily on therapist activities in session and may be described as common factors across modalities of treatment as they were present in different modalities of psychotherapy. Although active therapists can utilize the preceding information to develop (and repair) alliances, the client's participation in this relationship cannot be ignored. The mental health (Luborsky, 1975), quality of interpersonal relations (Piper, Azim, Joyce, & McCallum, 1991), and initial object relations (Piper & Duncan, 1999) of a patient have been correlated with their ability to form an alliance and to positive outcomes in psychodynamic psychotherapy. Clinician ratings of a patient's capacity for dynamic process, as measured by the Capacity for Dynamic Process Scale (CDPS; Thackrey, Butler, & Strupp, 1993), also have been positively associated with the therapeutic alliance.

Defenses

Defenses have received considerable attention compared to other aspects of psychodynamic psychotherapy. Defensive functioning, which can be described as an individual's automatic psychological response to stressors or conflict, has been shown to differentiate healthy from mentally ill individuals (Bond, Gardner, & Christian, 1983). Defenses have also been found to be organized hierarchically, from immature to mature, according to adaptive ability (Perry, 1993). In a review of five clinical studies, Perry (1993) found consistent trends and support for the hierarchical relationship between defenses and global functioning. In general, less-adaptive defenses were negatively related to levels of mental health and global functioning, whereas more-adaptive defenses were associated with higher levels of mental health and global functioning. Psychotic level defenses (defined here as delusional projection, psychotic denial, and distortion) had a large negative relationship to global functioning (median $r = -.57$). Immature level defenses (e.g., avoidance, acting out, neurotic denial, fantasy, projection, hypochondriasis, and passive aggression) similarly had a negative association with global functioning, which was slightly less than that seen for psychotic level defenses (median $r = -.28$). Borderline and narcissistic defenses, or image-distorting defenses (e.g., splitting, projective identification, and devaluation), also had a negative correlation with global functioning (median $r = -.12$), whereas neurotic level defenses did not (median $r = .04$); however, it was noted that most individuals in these studies utilized some of the neurotic level defenses in addition to other defenses. Mature defenses had an overall median correlation of .33 with global functioning, which indicates they were related to better overall mental health and global functioning. This is not surprising, given the more adaptive and socially acceptable nature of these defenses.

Maturity of defenses has also been associated with specific disorders and change in dynamic psychotherapy. In a study of patients with personality disorders, Perry (2001) found a higher proportion of immature defenses (46.3 percent; e.g., avoidance, projection) compared to nonclinical controls. Within this sample, higher overall defensive functioning (more adaptive defenses) was found to predict continuance in psychotherapy at one-year follow-up, whereas lower defensive functioning (less adaptive defenses) predicted dropout. In another study, patients with major depressive disorder who possessed higher defensive functioning showed more positive treatment outcomes at six months than patients with lower defensive functioning, even after controlling for severity and the presence of a personality disorders (Høglend & Perry, 1998). The hypothesis that defensive functioning improves over the course of therapy also has been empirically supported in the literature. Clinician ratings of patient defensive function have been shown to become significantly more adaptive during the course of time-limited dynamic therapy, although the effect size of this result was moderate (Hersoug, Sexton, & Høglend, 2002).

Transference

The concept of transference has been examined in both laboratory and clinical settings and has been found to impact both clinical relationships and social functioning. Analogue laboratory studies of transference within social relationships have found that fictional characters that activate subjects' representations of a significant other will likely be misremembered as possessing characteristics of the significant other (Andersen & Cole, 1990). This finding suggests that the perception of new people is influenced by representations of meaningful others from one's past. In addition to influencing perceptions, representations of significant others have also been found to influence affective responses to new people when representations of significant others are activated (Andersen & Baum, 1994).

Within the context of psychotherapy, Luborsky et al. (1985) used the Core Conflictual Relationship Theme (CCRT) method to examine narratives relating to the therapist and significant others of eight patients at different points in psychodynamic treatment. The CCRT identifies a transference pattern based on the patient's wishes, needs, and intentions toward another person, the responses of the other person to these wishes, and the responses of the patient. The most frequent pattern found is labeled as being the CCRT. The results of these case studies supported nine of Freud's hypothesizes about transference. In particular, individual patients were found to have one specific core transference pattern (but may possess other patterns as well), which is repeated in a relationship with the therapist and is also carried out in outside relationships.

Further empirical investigation of the specificity and pervasiveness of the transference pattern as measured with the CCRT in larger samples has yielded more generalizable results than the previous case study. Investigation of the pervasiveness of relationship themes found that 66.3 percent of patient narratives ($n = 33$ patients) contained the patient's main wishes as determined using the CCRT (Crits-Christoph & Luborsky, 1990). When looking at transference in the therapeutic relationship in particular, Fried, Crits-Christoph, and Luborsky (1992) compared the patients' CCRTs derived from relationships with significant others to narratives about the therapist. They found that the patient's own CCRT was similar to their narratives about the therapist. In addition, the transference toward the therapist appeared to be patient specific, as a patient's narratives about the therapist were found to be more closely related to their CCRT than to the CCRTs of other patients.

Connolly et al. (1996) further investigated transference relationships in psychotherapy using the Quantitative Assessment of Interpersonal Themes (QUAINT). The authors proposed that the QUAINT controls for rater bias in the rating narratives and allows for the extraction of more than one prevalent transference pattern. Connolly et al. (1996) examined the narratives of 35 male opiate addicts seeking dynamic and cognitive therapy. They found that patients generally displayed repetitive patterns of interaction with significant others in their lives; however, patients appeared to have several different interpersonal patterns with specific subsets of people in their lives. In addition, the most pervasive pattern may not be the one that is transferred onto the therapist. However, the majority (60 percent) of patients who give a narrative about the therapist early in treatment report similar interactions with others in their lives. Despite the strong findings in this study that authors caution about generalizing these results to other patient groups and treatments.

Countertransference

Research in the area of countertransference was rarely done prior to the 1980s. Until recently, this area has primarily been investigated using analogue research, which has raised questions about the generalizability of these findings to clinical settings. Despite this, analogue research has contributed to the operationalization of countertransference and has improved in measurement methodology (Rosenberger & Hayes, 2002). Analogue research has lent support to several hypotheses including the following: self-integration and anxiety management on the part of the clinician can beneficially impact the management of countertransference behavior (Gelso, Fassinger, Gomez, & Latts, 1995); clinician gender is a moderator of countertransference—in particular, male therapists have a tendency to withdraw when they are anxious (Gelso et al., 1995); and clinician awareness of countertransference feelings in concert with adherence to a theoretical orientation decreases countertransference behavior (Latts & Gelso, 1995).

In an effort to provide a framework of countertransference that could be used to direct empirical research, Hayes (1995) proposed a structural model of countertransference consisting of five factors: origins, triggers, manifestations, effects, and management. In a qualitative field study, Hayes et al. (1998) examined postsession interview data from eight clinicians involved in brief psychodynamic treatment with eight patients. These authors found support for the first three elements of the model (origins, triggers, and manifestations) and for relationships between these three elements. Countertransference was defined as therapist reactions identified (by the therapist) as being related to unresolved personal intrapsychic conflict. They found that countertransference was present in 80 percent of the sessions.

Based on this data Hayes et al. (1998) were able to identify common origins of countertransference including family issues (family of origin, parenting, and partnering), therapist needs and values, issues related to the role of the therapist (competence and termination), and cultural issues (gender and race). Common triggers of countertransference behavior were identified as including the content of patient material, the therapist comparing the patient to others, a change in therapy structure, the progress of therapy, the therapist's perception of the patient, and emotional arousal on the part of the therapist and the patient. The relationship between origins and triggers was found to be a strong predictor of whether countertransference will be experienced by a particular therapist with a particular patient. In general, an incident in session will trigger countertransference only if that incident is related to relevant origins for the specific therapist. More specifically, countertransference has been found to be more prevalent when the patient reminds the therapist of significant people in the therapist's life (including the therapist's identification with the client), when the patient's therapy content is similar to the therapist's unresolved issues, and when the therapist positively or negatively evaluates the clients progress in therapy (Hayes et al., 1998; Williams, Judge, Hill, & Hoffman, 1997).

Using the interview data from therapists, Hayes et al. (1998) were able to categorize therapist manifestations of countertransference behavior into four categories: approach (thoughts, feelings, and behaviors on the part of the therapist that decrease distance between therapist and patient), avoidance (thoughts, feelings, and behaviors on the part of the therapist that increase distance between therapist and patient), negative feelings (uncomfortable therapist emotions), and treatment planning (therapist decisions relating to the therapy process). All of the therapists reported countertransference manifestations that included the categories of approach, avoidance, and negative feelings. The type of countertransference manifestation that occurred was found to be related to specific origins and triggers. For example, when the therapist's family of origin issues were stirred the therapist tended to identify with the patient; when the trigger of countertransference was the patient discussing their family of origin issues the therapist tended to respond with compassionate understanding.

Few empirical studies have examined the relationship between countertransference and therapy outcome, and results from these investigations have been mixed. Yet, it appears that countertransference can interfere with the therapist's ability to be maximally effective (Williams et al., 1997), and that countertransference behavior is inversely related to treatment outcome in cases with poor outcome (Hayes, 1995). For this reason, the management of countertransference is an important issue. In fact, studies have found that therapists who possess better self-integration appear to have fewer countertransference reactions (Gelso et al., 1995; Hayes, Riker, & Ingram, 1997). Therapist personal qualities including empathy, self-insight, and the ability to manage anxiety have also been related to better management of countertransference (Hayes et al., 1997; Van Wagoner, Gelso, Hayes, & Diemer, 1991).

Patient Characteristics

Psychodynamic therapy requires engagement on the part of both the therapist and the patient. A significant amount of empirical research has been directed toward identifying patient characteristics that can positively impact treatment outcome in psychodynamic therapy. Patient characteristics have also been applied to outcome in different forms of psychodynamic therapy. Several of these characteristics, including motivation, health-sickness, ego integration, object relations, and interpersonal relations, have been found to consistently impact therapy outcome.

Motivation has consistently been emphasized in empirical research. Measures of motivation have examined the patient's ability to recognize the psychological nature of symptoms, tendency toward introspection, willingness to participate in treatment process, ability to become emotionally involved in treatment, willingness to understand oneself, willingness to change, willingness to make reasonable sacrifices, realistic expectations of therapy outcome, and the degree of autonomy in seeking therapy (Keithly, Samples, & Strupp, 1980; Sifneos, 1978). In general, early ratings of patient motivation have a significant, positive relation to participation and outcome in psychodynamic therapy (Frayn, 1992; Keithly, Samples, & Strupp, 1980; Sifneos, 1978).

Initial psychological "health" and "sickness" of a patient can be generally described as emotional stability and mental health. Luborsky et al.'s (1993) review of health-sickness research found that higher initial levels of psychological health were related to more positive treatment outcomes (mean predictive $r = .27$). The authors note, however, whereas this is a significant correlation it does not directly imply that psychodynamic therapy should be avoided for patients with less favorable ratings of health-sickness.

Psychodynamic therapy involves a significant relational element. For this reason the impact of the patient's initial quality of interpersonal relations and object relations have been investigated. A history of good interpersonal relations has not been associated with symptomatic change, but has been related to improvement in dynamic processes (e.g., improved interpersonal relations and self-understanding) during the course of psychotherapy (Høglend, 1993). Quality of object relations has been significantly related to the patient's ability to form a therapeutic alliance and to positive treatment outcomes (Piper, Joyce, McCallum, & Azim, 1998). Prediction of treatment outcome from quality of object relations was found to be particularly relevant when evaluating patients who were in interpretative psychodynamic therapy but not significant for patients in supportive psychotherapy (Piper, McCallum, Joyce, Azim, & Ogrodniczuk, 1999). This implies that the match between patient characteristics and treatment process may be of particular importance.

Further support for the proposition that treatment outcomes may be related to matching treatment with patient variables (i.e., treatment congruence with patient variables) comes from Blatt's (1992) reanalysis of the data from the Menninger Psychotherapy Research Project (MPRP). Kernberg (1973) had reported that patients in the MPRP with higher levels of initial ego strength appeared to improve regardless of the treatment modality. Results from the MPRP, however, demonstrated negligible differences between the outcomes of patients in psychoanalysis and in psychotherapy (Wallerstein, 1986). In Blatt's (1992) reanalysis, he distinguished between anaclitic patients, whose pathology is related to interpersonal disruptions, and introjective patients, whose pathology is related to self-definition and autonomy. His analysis found that anaclitic patients have better outcome in psychotherapy, possibly because of the relational nature of this form of treatment. In contrast, introjective patients had more positive outcome in psychoanalysis, which may be related to the focus on insight and understanding in this modality. Although this congruence appears related to treatment outcomes, Blatt suggests that both types of patients require integration of the needs for integration and relatedness and, as such, both processes need to be addressed during the course of treatment (Blatt, 1992).

The abilities of the patient to engage in the process of dynamic therapy has been investigated using the Capacity for Dynamic Process Scale (CDPS; Thackrey et al., 1993), which is a clinician-rated scale that combines measurement of patient characteristics across several domains. There are nine basic patient skills that are assessed by the CDPS: appears introspective, integrates affect, manifests verbal fluency, manifests insight, perceives affective aspects of problems, differentiates affect, differentiates interpersonal events, and therapeutic collaboration (Thackrey et al., 1993). Baumann et al. (2001) found the CDPS to effectively discriminate patients' persistence in treatment. In particular, patients with higher CDPS scores were more likely to remain in psychodynamic treatment and to continue their involvement in the psychotherapy process.

SUMMARY

This chapter has provided an overview of the basic premises of psychoanalytic and psychodynamic theory and treatment. Attention has been directed toward psychodynamic models about the development of personality and essential components that guide the provision of psychodynamic treatment.

We have provided an overview of research that supports many psychodynamic concepts that are associated with positive treatment outcome. From this data, it appears that psychodynamically oriented treatment has much to offer and that therapists interested in those factors related to positive psychotherapy outcome may wish to pay special attention to the contributions of psychodynamic theory.

NOTE

1. The interested reader is directed toward "Highlights of the Psychoanalytic Literature: A Topical Reading List," prepared by Robin Render, PhD, and Lisa Mellman, MD, members of the Fellowship Committee of the American Psychoanalytic Association.

While the terms *psychoanalytic* and *psychodynamic* are not synonymous and can have important implications about one's theoretical orientation, they are used interchangeably here in those cases for which ideas borne out of psychoanalytic theory are relevant to conducting psychodynamic psychotherapy.

REFERENCES

Ackerman, S. J., & Hilsenroth, M. J. (2003). A review of therapist characteristics and techniques positively impacting the therapeutic alliance. *Clinical Psychology Review, 23,* 1–33.

Acklin, M. W., Li, S. H. S., & Tyson, J. (2005). Rorschach assessment of personality disorders: Applied clinical science and psychoanalytic theory. In S. K. Huprich (Ed.), *Rorschach assessment of the personality disorders* (pp. 423–443). Mahwah, NJ: Erlbaum.

Andersen, S. M., & Baum, A. (1994). Transference in interpersonal relations: Inferences and affect based on significant other representations. *Journal of Personality, 62,* 459–497.

Andersen, S. M., & Cole, S. W. (1990). "Do I know you?": The role of significant others in general social perception. *Journal of Personality and Social Psychology, 59,* 384–399.

Anderson, E. M., & Lambert, M. J. (1995). Short-term dynamically oriented psychotherapy: A review and meta-analysis. *Clinical Psychology Review, 15,* 503–514.

Atwood, G. E., & Stolorow, R. D. (1984). *Structures of subjectivity: Explorations in psychoanalytic phenomenology.* Hillsdale, NJ: Analytic Press.

Barber, J. P., Morse, J. Q., Krakauer, I. D., Chittams, J., & Crits-Christoph, P. (1997). Change in obsessive compulsive and avoidant personality disorders following time limited supportive expressive therapy. *Psychotherapy, 34,* 133–143.

Baumann, B. D., Hilsenroth, M. J., Ackerman, S. J., Baity, M. R., Smily, C. L., Smith, S. R., et al. (2001). The capacity for dynamic process scale: An examination of reliability, validity, and relation to therapeutic alliance. *Psychotherapy Research, 11,* 275–294.

Blatt, S. J. (1992). The differential effect of psychotherapy and psychoanalysis with anaclitic and introjective patients: The Menninger psychotherapy research project revisited. *Journal of Personality Assessment, 40,* 691–724.

Blatt, S. J., & Shichman, S. (1983). Two primary configurations of psychopathology. *Psychoanalysis and Contemporary Thought, 6,* 187–254.

Blatt, S. J., Wein, S. J., Chevron, E. S., & Quinlan, D. M. (1979). Parental representations and depression in normal young adults. *Journal of Abnormal Psychology, 88,* 388–397.

Bond, M., Gardner, S. T., & Christian, J. (1983). Empirical study of self-rated defense styles. *Archives of General Psychiatry, 40,* 333–338.

Bornstein, R. F. (2001). The impending death of psychoanalysis. *Psychoanalytic Psychology, 18,* 2–20.

Brenner, C. (1973). *An elementary textbook of psychoanalysis: Revised and expanded edition.* New York: Doubleday.

Brenner, C. (1982). *The mind in conflict.* Madison, CT: International Universities Press.

Compton, A. (1995). Objects and relationships. In B. E. Moore & B. D. Fine (Eds.), *Psychoanalysis: The major concepts* (pp. 433–449). New Haven, CT: Yale University Press.

Connolly, M. B., Crits-Christoph, P., Demorest, A., Azarian, K., Muenz, L., & Chittams, J. (1996). Varieties of transference patterns in psychotherapy. *Journal of Consulting and Clinical Psychology, 64,* 1213–1221.

Crits-Christoph, P. (1992). The efficacy of brief dynamic psychotherapy: A meta-analysis. *American Journal of Psychiatry, 149,* 151–158.

Crits-Christoph, P., & Luborsky, L. (1990). Changes in CCRT pervasiveness during psychotherapy. In L. Luborsky & P. Crits-Christoph (Eds.), *Understanding transference: The Core Conflictual Relationship Theme method* (pp. 133–146). New York: Basic Books.

Eagle, M. N. (2000). A critical evaluation of current conceptions of transference and countertransference. *Psychoanalytic Psychology, 17,* 24–37.

Fenichel, O. (1941). *Problems of psychoanalytic technique.* New York: Psychoanalytic Quarterly.

Ferenczi, S. (1953). *First contributions to psychoanalysis.* London: Hogarth.

Fisher, S., & Greenberg, R. P. (1977). *The scientific credibility of Freud's theories and therapy.* New York: Basic Books.

Fisher, S., & Greenberg, R. P. (1996). *Freud scientifically reappraised: Testing theories and therapy.* New York: Wiley.

Frayn, D. H. (1992). Assessment factors associated with premature psychotherapy termination. *American Journal of Psychotherapy, 46,* 250–261.

Freedman, N., Hoffenberg, J. D., Vorus, N., & Frosch, A. (1999). The effectiveness of psychoanalytic psychotherapy: The role of treatment duration, frequency of sessions and the therapeutic relationship. *Journal of Personality Assessment, 47,* 741–772.

Freud, A. (1966). *The ego and mechanisms of defense.* New York: International Universities Press. (Original work published 1936)

Freud, S. (1957). Repression. In J. Strachey (Ed. & Trans.), *The standard edition of the complete psychological works of Sigmund Freud* (Vol. 14, pp. 141–158). London: Hogarth. (Original work published 1915)

Fried, D., Crits-Christoph, P., & Luborsky, L. (1992). The first empirical demonstration of transference in psychotherapy. *The Journal of Nervous and Mental Disease, 180,* 326–331.

Gabbard, G. O. (2000). *Psychodynamic psychiatry in clinical practice* (3rd ed.). Washington, DC: American Psychiatric Association.

Gaston, L. (1990). The concept of the alliance and its role in psychotherapy: Theoretical and empirical considerations. *Psychotherapy, 27,* 143–153.

Gelso, C. J., Fassinger, R. E., Gomez, M. J., & Latts, M. G. (1995). Countertransference reactions to lesbian clients: The role of homophobia, counselor gender and countertransference management. *Journal of Counseling Psychology, 42,* 356–364.

Gill, M. (1954). Psychoanalysis and exploratory psychotherapy. *Journal of the American Psychoanalytic Association, 2,* 771–797.

Gill, M. (1994). *Psychoanalysis in transition: A personal view.* Hillsdale, NJ: Analytic Press.

Goldstein, W. N. (1998). *A primer for beginning psychotherapy.* New York: Brunner/Mazel.

Greenberg, J. R. (1986). Theoretical models and the analyst's neutrality. *Contemporary Psychoanalysis, 22,* 87–106.

Greenson, R. (1967). *The technique and practice of psychoanalysis.* New York: International Universities Press.

Grunbaum, A. (1984). *The foundations of psychoanalysis: A philosophical critique.* Berkeley: University of California Press.

Grunbaum, A. (1993). *Validation in the clinical theory of psychoanalysis: A study in the philosophy of psychoanalysis.* Madison, CT: International Universities Press.

Guntrip, H. (1971). *Psychoanalytic theory, therapy, and the self.* New York: Basic Books.

Hardy, G. E., Barkham, M., Shapiro, S. A., Stiles, W. B., Rees, A., & Reynolds, S. (1995). Impact of Cluster C personality disorders on outcomes of contrasting brief psychotherapies for depression. *Journal of Consulting and Clinical Psychology, 63,* 997–1004.

Hayes, J. A. (1995). Countertransference in group psychotherapy: Waking a sleeping dog. *International Journal of Group Psychotherapy, 45,* 521–535.

Hayes, J. A., & Gelso, C. J. (2001). Clinical implications of research on countertransference: Science informing practice. *In Session: Psychotherapy in Practice, 57,* 1041–1051.

Hayes, J. A., McCracken, J. E., McClanahan, M. K., Hill, C. E., Harp, J. S., & Carozzoni, P. (1998). Therapist perspectives on countertransference: Qualitative data in search of a theory. *Journal of Counseling Psychology, 45,* 468–482.

Hayes, J. A., Riker, J. R., & Ingram, K. M. (1997). Countertransference behavior and management in brief counseling: A field study. *Psychotherapy Research, 7,* 145–153.

Hersoug, A. G., Sexton, H. C., & Høglend, P. (2002). Contribution of defensive functioning to the quality of working alliance and psychotherapy outcome. *American Journal of Psychotherapy, 56,* 539–554.

Hilsenroth, M. J., Ackerman, S. J., & Blagys, M. D. (2001). Evaluating the phase model of change during short-term psychodynamic psychotherapy. *Psychotherapy Research, 11,* 29–47.

Høglend, P. (1993). Suitability for brief dynamic psychotherapy: Psychodynamic variables as predictors of outcome. *Acta Psychiatrica Scandinavica, 88,* 104–110.

Høglend, P., & Perry J. C. (1998). Defensive functioning predicts improvement in major depressive episodes. *Journal of Nervous and Mental Disease, 186,* 283–243.

Horvath, A. O., Gaston, L., & Luborsky, L. (1993). The therapeutic alliance and its measures. In N. E. Miller, L. Luborsky, J. P. Barber, & J. P. Docherty (Eds.), *Psychodynamic treatment research: A handbook for clinical practice* (pp. 247–273). New York: Basic Books.

Horvath, A. O., & Greenberg, L. S. (Eds.). (1994). *The working alliance: Theory, research, practice.* New York: Wiley.

Horvath, A. O., & Luborsky, L. (1993). The role of the therapeutic alliance in psychotherapy. *Journal of Consulting and Clinical Psychology, 61,* 561–573.

Horvath, A. O. & Symonds, B. D. (1991). Relation between working alliance and outcome in psychotherapy: A meta-analysis. *Journal of Counseling Psychology, 38,* 139–149.

Howard, K. I., Kopta, S. M., Krause, M. S., & Orlinsky, D. E. (1986). The dose-effect relationship in psychotherapy. *American Psychologist, 41,* 159–164.

Howard, K. I., Lueger, R. J., Maling, M. S., & Martinovich, Z. (1993). A phase model of psychotherapy: Causal mediation of outcome. *Journal of Consulting and Clinical Psychology, 61,* 678–685.

Jacobson, E. (1964). *The self and the object world.* New York: International Universities Press.

Keithly, L. J., Samples, S. J., & Strupp, H. H. (1980). Patient motivation as a predictor of process and outcome in psychotherapy. *Psychotherapy and Psychosomatics, 33,* 87–97.

Kernberg, O. F. (1970). A psychoanalytic classification of character pathology. *Journal of the American Psychoanalytic Association, 18,* 800–822.

Kernberg, O. F. (1973). Summary and conclusions of "psychotherapy and psychoanalysis, final report of the Menninger Foundation's psychotherapy research project." *International Journal of Psychiatry, 11,* 62–77.

Kernberg, O. F. (1993). Convergences and divergences in contemporary psychoanalytic technique. *International Journal of Psycho-Analysis, 70,* 659–673.

Kernberg, O. F. (1995). Psychoanalytic object relations theories. In B. E. Moore & B. D. Fine (Eds.), *Psychoanalysis: The major concepts* (pp. 450–462). New Haven, CT: Yale University Press.

Kernberg, O. F. (2001). Object relations, affects, and drives: Toward a new synthesis. *Psychoanalytic Inquiry, 21,* 604–619.

Kohlberg, L. (1981). *The philosophy of moral development: Moral stages and the idea of justice. Essays on moral development* (Vol. 1). New York: Harper and Row.

Kohut, H. (1971). *The analysis of the self: A systematic approach to the psychoanalytic treatment of narcissistic personality disorders.* New York: International Universities Press.

Kopta, S. M., Howard, K. E., Lowry, J. L., & Beutler, L. E. (1994). Patterns of symptomatic recovery in time-unlimited psychotherapy. *Journal of Consulting and Clinical Psychology, 62,* 1009–1016.

Krupnick, J. L., Sotsky, S. M., Simmens, S., Moyer, J., Elkin, I., Watkins, J., et al. (1996). The role of the therapeutic alliance in psychotherapy and pharmacotherapy outcome: Findings in the National Institute of Mental Health Treatment of Depression Collaborative Research Program. *Journal of Consulting and Clinical Psychology, 64,* 532–539.

Langs, R. L. (1973). *The technique of psychoanalytic psychotherapy* (Vol. 1). Northvale, NJ: Aronson.

Langs, R. L. (1974). *The technique of psychoanalytic psychotherapy* (Vol. 2). Northvale, NJ: Aronson.

Latts, M. G., & Gelso, C. J. (1995). Countertransference behavior and management with survivors of sexual assault. *Psychotherapy, 32,* 405–415.

Levenson, E. A. (1972). *The fallacy of understanding: An inquiry into the changing structure of psychoanalysis.* New York: Basic Books.

Luborsky, L. (1975). Clinician's judgments of mental health: Specimen case descriptions and forms for the Health-Sickness Rating Scale. *Bulletin of the Menninger Clinic, 35,* 448–480.

Luborsky, L. (1984). *Principles of psychoanalytic psychotherapy: A manual for supportive and expressive treatment.* New York: Basic Books.

Luborsky, L. (1990). Theory-based research for understanding the process of dynamic psychotherapy. *Journal of Consulting and Clinical Psychology, 58,* 281–287.

Luborsky, L. (1996). Theories of cure in psychoanalytic psychotherapies and the evidence for them. *Psychoanalytic Inquiry, 16,* 257–264.

Luborsky, L. (2001). The meaning of empirically supported treatment research for psychoanalytic and other long-term therapies. *Psychoanalytic Dialogues, 11,* 583–604.

Luborsky, L., Diguer, L., Luborsky, E., McLellan, A. T., Woody, G., & Alexander, L. (1993). Psychological health-sickness (PHS) as a predictor of outcomes in dynamic and other psychotherapies. *Journal of Consulting and Clinical Psychology, 61,* 542–548.

Luborsky, L., Mellon, J., Cohen, K. D., van Ravenswaay, P., Hole, A. V., Childress, A. R., et al. (1985). A verification of Freud's grandest hypothesis: The transference. *Clinical Psychological Review, 5,* 231–246.

Luborsky, L., Rosenthal, R., Diguer, L., Andrusyna, T. P., Levitt, J. T., Seeligman, D. A., et al. (2003). Are some psychotherapies much more effective than others? *Journal of Applied Psychoanalytic Studies, 5,* 455–460.

McClelland, D. C., Koestner, R., & Weinberg, J. (1989). How do self-attributed and implicit motives differ? *Psychological Review, 96,* 690–702.

McWilliams, N. (1994). *Psychoanalytic diagnosis.* New York: Guilford Press.

McWilliams, N. (1999). *Psychoanalytic case formulation.* New York: Guilford Press.

Meissner, W. M. (2000). *Freud and psychoanalysis.* South Bend, IN: Notre Dame University Press.

Menninger, K. A. (1958). *Theory of psychoanalytic technique.* New York: Basic Books.

Mitchell, S. A., & Black, M. J. (1995). *Freud and beyond.* New York: Basic Books.

Moore, B. E., & Fine, B. D. (1995). *Psychoanalysis: The major concepts.* New Haven, CT: Yale University Press.

Norcross, J. C. (2002). Empirically supported therapy relationships. In J. C. Norcross (Ed.), *Psychotherapy relationships that work* (pp. 3–16). New York: Oxford University Press.

Perry, J. C. (1993). Defenses and their effects. In N. E. Miller, L. Luborsky, J. P. Barber, & J. P. Docherty (Eds.), *Psychodynamic treatment research: A handbook for clinical practice* (pp. 247–273). New York: Basic Books.

Perry, J. C. (2001). A pilot study of defenses in adults with personality disorders entering psychotherapy. *Journal of Nervous and Mental Disease, 189,* 651–660.

Piaget, J. (1990). *The child's conception of the world.* New York: Littlefield Adams.

Piper, W. E., Azim, H. F., Joyce, A. S., & McCallum, M. (1991). Quality of object relations versus interpersonal functioning as predictors of therapeutic alliance and psychotherapy outcome. *Journal of Nervous and Mental Disease, 179,* 432–438.

Piper, W. E., & Duncan, S. C. (1999). Object relations theory and short-term dynamic psychotherapy: Findings from the Quality of Object Relations Scale. *Clinical Psychology Review, 19,* 669–685.

Piper, W. E., Joyce, A. S., McCallum, M., & Azim, H. F. (1998). Interpretive and supportive forms of psychotherapy and patient personality variables. *Journal of Consulting and Clinical Psychology, 66,* 558–567.

Piper, W. E., McCallum, M., Joyce, A. S., Azim, H. F., & Ogrodniczuk, J. S. (1999). Follow-up findings for interpretive and supportive forms of psychotherapy and patient personality variables. *Journal of Consulting and Clinical Psychology, 67,* 267–273.

Racker, H. (1968). *Transference and countertransference.* Madison, CT: International Universities Press.

Reich, W. (1949). *Character analysis.* New York: Farrar, Straus, & Giroux.

Rosenberger, E. W., & Hayes, J. A. (2002). Therapist as subject: A review of the empirical countertransference literature. *Journal of Counseling and Development, 80,* 264–270.

Safran, J. D., Muran, J. C., & Samstag, L. W. (1994). Resolving therapeutic alliance ruptures: A task analytic investigation. In A. O. Horvath & L. S. Greenberg (Eds.), *The working alliance: Theory, research, and practice* (pp. 38–50). New York: Wiley.

Sandell, R., Blomberg, J., & Lazar, A. (2002). Time matters: On temporal interactions in long-term follow-up of long-term psychotherapies. *Psychotherapy Research, 12,* 39–58.

Sandell, R., Blomberg, J., Lazar, A., Carlsson, J., Broberg, J., & Schubert, J. (2000). Varieties of long-term outcome among patients in psychoanalysis and long-term psychotherapy: A review of findings in the Stockholm Outcome of Psychoanalysis and Psychotherapy Project (STOPP). *International Journal of Psychoanalysis, 81,* 921–942.

Schafer, R. (1983). *The analytic attitude.* New York: Basic Books.

Schafer, R. (1992). *Retelling a life.* New York: Basic Books.

Shapiro, D. (1965). *Neurotic styles.* New York: Basic Books.

Shapiro, D. A., Barkham, M., Stiles, W. B., Hardy, G. E., Rees, A., Reynolds, S., et al. (2003). Time is of the essence: A selective review of the fall and rise of brief therapy research. *Psychology and Psychotherapy, 76,* 211–235.

Sifneos, P. E. (1978). Motivation for change: A prognostic guide for successful psychotherapy. *Psychotherapy and Psychosomatics, 29,* 293–298.

Spence, D. P. (1982). *Narrative truth and historical meaning: Meaning and interpretation in psychoanalysis.* New York: Norton.

Stiles, W. B., Agnew-Davis, R., Hardy, G. E., Barkham, M., & Shapiro, D. A. (1998). Relations of the alliance with psychotherapy outcome: Findings in the Second Sheffield Psychotherapy Project. *Journal of Consulting and Clinical Psychology, 66,* 791–802.

Stone, L. (1961). *The psychoanalytic situation.* New York: International Universities Press.

Thackrey, M., Butler, S. F., & Strupp, H. H. (1993). The Capacity for Dynamic Process Scale (CDPS). In M. L. Canfield & J. E. Canfield (Eds.), *A collection of psychological scales* (pp. 57–63). Bartlesville, OK: Research, Evaluation & Statistics.

Trimboli, F., & Farr, K. L. (2000). A psychodynamic guide for essential treatment planning. *Psychoanalytic Psychology, 17,* 336–359.

Usher, S. F. (1993). *Introduction to psychodynamic psychotherapy technique.* Madison, WI: International Universities Press.

Vaillant, G. E. (1971). Theoretical hierarchy of adaptive ego mechanisms. *Archives of General Psychiatry, 24,* 107–118.

Vaillant, G. E. (1992). *Ego mechanisms of defense: A guide for clinicians and researchers.* Washington, DC: American Psychiatric Press.

Van Wagoner, S., Gelso, C. J., Hayes, J. A., & Diemer, R. (1991). Countertransference and the reputedly excellent therapist. *Psychotherapy, 28,* 411–421.

Wallerstein, R. S. (1986). *Forty-two lives in treatment: A study of psychoanalysis and psychotherapy.* New York: Guilford Press.

Wallerstein, R. S. (1989). Psychoanalysis and psychotherapy: An historical perspective. *International Journal of Psycho-Analysis, 70,* 563–591.

Weiner, I. B. (1998). *Principles of psychotherapy.* New York: Wiley.

Westen, D. (1998). The scientific legacy of Sigmund Freud: Toward a psychodynamically informed psychological science. *Psychological Bulletin, 124,* 333–371.

Williams, E. N., Judge, A. B., Hill, C. E., & Hoffman, M. A. (1997), Experiences of novice therapists in prepracticum: Trainees', clients', and supervisors' perceptions of therapists' personal reactions and management of strategies. *Journal of Counseling Psychology, 44,* 390–399.

CHAPTER 29

Cognitive Behavioral Treatment

ALISA R. SINGER AND KEITH S. DOBSON

INTRODUCTION

Although cognitive behavioral theory and therapy (CBT) were initially developed for the treatment of depression (Beck, Rush, Shaw, & Emery, 1979) and anxiety disorders (Beck, Emery, and Greenberg, 1985), CBT has expanded to address a vast range of mental disorders (Dobson & Pusch, 1993), including substance abuse (Beck, Wright, Newman, & Leise, 1993), eating disorders (Fairburn, Marcus, & Wilson, 1993), personality disorders (Linehan, 1993; Young, Klosko, & Weishaar, 2003), and, more recently, psychosis (Rector & Beck, 2002). Cognitive behavioral treatment has become widely practiced and is generally considered to be an empirically supported psychotherapeutic approach (Chambless & Ollendick, 2001).

This chapter will introduce the cognitive behavioral formulation and treatment for a variety of mental disorders, with a focus on the evidence that supports the proposed models rather than treatment outcome. The historical and general philosophical bases for CBT are described. Following this introduction of the basic principles, the CBT model and interventions for the treatment of depression, anxiety disorders, substance abuse, eating disorders, schizophrenia, and personality disorders will be outlined. The chapter concludes with suggestions for future research developments in CBT.

CBT: HISTORY AND PHILOSOPHICAL BASES

One of the difficulties in describing cognitive behavioral therapy is that it is a broad term that encompasses several forms of treatment, all of which target cognitive and behavioral change. Although there is some variation across approaches to treatment, all cognitive behavioral therapies share the theoretical assumption that internal covert processes called *thinking* or *cognition* occur and that these cognitive events mediate behavior change (Dobson & Dozois, 2001). These cognitions are assumed to be knowable through direct observation and as such are also subject to change in the service of improving both the cognitive and behavioral experience of clients in therapy.

The historical roots of CBT can be traced to the 1960s with the advent of Albert Ellis's rational emotive therapy that emphasized the relationship between thinking and feeling (RET; Ellis, 1962). CBT only emerged in a more varied form in the 1970s with the publication of pivotal texts (Mahoney, 1974; Meichenbaum, 1977) and the establishment of the journal *Cognitive Therapy and Research* in 1977. It is likely not coincidental that the 1970s have been described as the period of the "cognitive revolution" in psychology, and it certainly is the case that information-processing models of basic processes were a major influence in emerging models of clinical disorders (Dobson & Dozois, 2001). Researchers began to challenge the radical behavioral theorists because behavioral models failed to account for the role of cognitive phenomena in human behavior.

The second developmental pathway for CBT emerged from an emerging cynicism about the value of the psychodynamic model, primarily due to the rather unimpressive reviews of clinical outcome (Dobson, Backs-Dermott, & Dozois, 2000). Discouraged with the limitations of the psychoanalytic method, Beck and Ellis both rejected the principles and practices of their earlier psychoanalytic training and developed models of disorders that emphasized internal cognitive and emotional processes. Rather than focusing on the motivational-affective conceptualizations that were the hallmarks of the psychoanalytic tradition, these theorists began focusing on the thematic content of the cognitions of neurotic patients (cf. Beck, 1967).

CBT is based on a rationalist philosophy, and assumes that the world may be either perceived accurately or misperceived (Dobson et al., 2000). Distortion, bias, and irrationality reflect the extent to which a person's perceptions are not in line with reality. Thus, one focus of CBT is on the accurate perception of events. Another assumption of CBT is that emotional experience and behavior follow from a person's cognitive appraisal of different situations (i.e., that cognition is what mediates the emotional and behavioral reactions to different situations) and that extreme emotions and maladaptive behaviors are the result of misperceptions of reality.

Current cognitive behavioral therapies fall within three major classes: problem solving therapy, coping skills therapy, and cognitive restructuring therapy (Dobson & Dozois, 2001). These therapy classes orient themselves to different degrees of cognitive versus behavioral change. Problem solving therapy, for example, emphasizes behavioral change through teaching clients to identify, examine, and find adaptive solutions to life problems. Coping skills therapies are largely focused on dealing with problems in life and focus on identifying and altering the ways in which a person may exacerbate or reduce the influence of negative events. Thus, coping skills training often involves the learning of adaptive behavioral repertoires through use of cognitive mechanisms such as coping statements or distraction. Cognitive restructuring therapies focus on cognitive change by promoting optional functioning through the examination and change of unrealistic or dysfunctional thought processes.

One of the innovative features of the CBT therapies is that a number of them have been written into treatment manuals, which are available for the purposes of treatment outcome studies, and structuring clinical treatments. Treatment manuals provide guidelines for the structure and content of therapy. One concern that has been raised regarding manuals, however, is their potential lack of flexibility; for many therapists, CBT needs to be tailored to the individual client's needs. The ultimate utility of treatment manuals continues to be debated (Addis, Wade, & Hatgis, 1999), even while they are being developed and disseminated.

At present, there are several specific CBT approaches, including rational emotive behavior therapy (Ellis, 1962), cognitive therapy (Beck, 1967), problem solving therapy (D'Zurilla & Goldfried, 1971), and self-control therapy (Rehm, 1977). They all share the assumption that cognitive processes mediate the stimulus-response relationship and that clients have control over their thoughts and actions. The therapy is either implicitly or explicitly educational, with the ultimate goal of teaching clients to develop their own therapeutic skills and to deal with the problems themselves (Dobson & Dozois, 2001). Another commonality across the CBT approaches is that they are time limited, with many of the manuals recommending 12 to 16 sessions (Dobson & Dozois, 2001).

In the sections that follow, the breadth of the cognitive behavioral approach will be highlighted through a discussion of the conceptualization and treatment of several disorders. In some cases, such as anxiety and depression, the research to support the models is extensive, whereas for other disorders the empirical support for the cognitive behavioral formulation is preliminary. This issue will be addressed in each section.

DEPRESSION

Cognitive therapy (CT) for the treatment of depression was one of the earliest cognitive behavioral formulations. The cognitive theory of Aaron Beck (1967) proposed that the vulnerability to depression lies in the content of cognitive structures—later called schemata—that become activated during negative experiences. Schemata are viewed as stable cognitive structures for screening, coding, evaluating, and creating meaning from the external world; individuals who are vulnerable to depression are those who hold negative schemata or views of the world, the self, and the future. In times of negative experience, these schemata become activated, leading to a negative bias in the processing of information, distortions of reality, and patterns of illogical errors. Beck posited that these negative schemata and affective structures are involved in a circular feedback loop, whereby negative cognition results in increased feelings of depression and increased depressive feelings lead to more negative thinking. In addition, he hypothesized that interpretations of events are consistently distorted in depression so that they maintain their negative valence. For example, individuals with depression are susceptible to cognitive distortions such as emotional reasoning, all-or-nothing thinking, and mind reading.

There is a large body of research to support the cognitive theory of depression (Clark, Beck, & Alford, 1999), and the varied predictions that derive from it. For example, research has shown that when formerly depressed individuals (who in theory have a depression-related schema) are put in a negative mood state, they exhibit increased negative bias in their recall of past experiences, in their perceptions and interpretations of current situations, and in their predictions about the future (Teasdale, 1988) as well as increased dysfunctional attitudes (Miranda, Gross, Persons, & Hahn, 1998).

CT is based on a collaborative relationship between the therapist and client in which they work together to reach mutually agreed upon goals. The cognitive therapist regularly shares the treatment rationale and plan with the client, and feedback is elicited from the client regarding whether he or she accepts these formulations. CT is also based on the notion of collaborative empiricism, meaning that the client and therapist act as a team to investigate the client's automatic thoughts and beliefs as well as to gather evidence to support or refute the content of the client's cognitions. Behavioral experiments are employed to test the validity and utility of specific cognitions.

A typical CT therapy session begins with the collaborative establishment of an agenda, including the order of topics to discuss. Throughout the session, the therapist asks questions designed to gather the facts regarding the problem and to reveal any schemata, misinterpretations, or expectations that are involved. Once a target problem has been selected, the therapist chooses appropriate cognitive or behavioral techniques to apply to the problem. It has been suggested that a typical course of standard CT for depression lasts from 15 to 25 weekly sessions, followed by 4 to 5 booster sessions after termination (Young, Weinberger, & Beck, 2001).

The early phase of CT includes techniques designed to reduce symptoms. In this first phase of therapy, a number of techniques are used to elicit and test the validity of automatic thoughts such as asking the client what went through their mind in response to particular events or reviewing a daily record of situations, emotion, and automatic thoughts. Automatic thoughts are challenged by discussing the evidence for and against the thoughts, reattribution of self-blaming, the identification of cognitive distortions, and the generation of alternative rebuttals. Behavioral techniques are also used including scheduling mastery and pleasurable activities, role-playing, and role reversal.

In the second phase of therapy, schemata are identified, assessed, and challenged. A development in CT has been Young's elaboration of early maladaptive schemata (Young et al., 2001). Young has elaborated Beck's model by proposing that early maladaptive schemata develop during childhood but that these schemata are elaborated throughout a person's lifetime, and if they are maladaptive, they place particular individuals at risk for depression. Young's model includes 18 early maladaptive schemata, and he has developed a number of techniques for the identification and amelioration of each of these early maladaptive schemas, using a range of cognitive, experiential, and behavioral strategies (Young et al., 2003).

Questions remain as to how CT produces its effects (Hollon, Haman, & Brown, 2002). For example, the behavioral component of CT may be more valuable for the amelioration of depression than originally thought. A component analysis of CT revealed that individuals treated with only the behavioral component of CT faired as well as individuals treated with the full CT treatment package, suggesting that the behavioral component of CT has a major value in the treatment of depression (Gortner, Gollan, Dobson, & Jacobson, 1998; Jacobson et al., 1996). It is also not clear at present whether the long-term benefits of CT that have been found are due to change in the accessibility of dysfunctional schemata or if they are due to change in the attitudes toward these beliefs (metacognition). Some recent research suggests that changes in attitudes toward dysfunctional schemata may mediate long-term effects of CT (Sheppard & Teasdale, 2004), although further research within the context of a CT trial is needed to understand this process.

A provocative development in the treatment of depression has been the emergence of mindfulness-based cognitive therapy (MBCT; Segal, Williams, & Teasdale, 2002) for the prevention of relapse to depression. The MBCT approach teaches individuals who have recovered from depression to disengage from rumination by increasing their awareness and acceptance of negative thoughts and feelings at times of potential relapse (Teasdale et al., 2000). Early results of MBCT with formerly depressed persons suggest a preventative effect, particularly with individuals with a longer history of depression (Segal et al., 2002).

To summarize, one of the first cognitive behavioral developments was in the treatment of depression. There is an extensive body of research to support the cognitive model and treatment of depression (Ingram, Miranda, & Segal, 1998). Researchers have investigated the mediating mechanisms and components of the CT package. The application of mindfulness and behavioral approaches to the treatment of depression is also being investigated. The scientific knowledge base for depression has assisted in the development of CBT for other mental disorders.

ANXIETY DISORDERS

Several cognitive behavioral models have been developed to explain the onset and maintenance of the spectrum of anxiety disorders (Clark, 1986; Rapee & Heimberg, 1997; Salkovskis, 1985). Each of these models proposes a cognitive behavioral formulation for the unique features of the specific anxiety disorders. However, across most of the models there are several conceptual similarities. The common features of the CBT models for anxiety disorders are discussed here, and CBT interventions for anxiety will be highlighted.

One of the most influential and earliest behavioral approaches to understanding the development of phobic disorders was Mowrer's (1939) two-stage model (see also Chapter 3). According to this model, the first stage in which phobias develop occurs through classical conditioning, the process in which a neutral stimulus is paired with an aversive stimulus, which subsequently becomes a trigger for fear. The second stage concerns the maintenance of fear through operant conditioning. By avoiding or escaping the feared situation, individuals reduce their discomfort and fear, which negatively reinforces their desire to avoid the feared situation. Rachman (1977) extended this model by proposing that vicarious acquisition (by seeing someone else behave fearfully in presence of an object) and information and instruction (reading or hearing that an object or situation is dangerous) are two other pathways to developing fear.

Cognitive theorists have proposed that cognitive vulnerability to anxiety disorders consists of distorted beliefs regarding the dangerousness of certain situations, sensations, and/or mental events. The content of each disorder is associated with specific negative beliefs (Clark, 1999). Specific phobias are associated with perceived dangerousness of the particular phobic object and/or its consequences (Antony & Swinson, 2000). Social phobia arises from a desire to make a favorable impression on others in social situations, combined with dysfunctional beliefs that when one encounters a social situation they will behave in a way that is embarrassing or humiliating (Antony & Swinson, 2000). There is also evidence that individuals with social phobia overestimate the degree to which their anxiety is visible to others (Rapee & Heimberg, 1997).

In contrast to specific and social phobias, which include cognitions about external stimuli, panic disorder is thought to arise from the tendency to view the state of anxiety itself and the accompanying bodily sensations as being harmful (Clark, 1999; Craske & Barlow, 2001). This tendency to view anxiety as harmful may derive from life experiences (such as personal history of illness or injury), vicarious observations (family member illness), observing family member distress over body sensations, or informational processes (family members' warnings or overprotectiveness; Craske & Barlow, 2001). Panic disorder is maintained by catastrophic interpretations of the bodily sensations as not easily escapable and uncontrollable, leading to the elevation of general anxiety about upcoming adverse events and chronic high levels of anxious apprehension. Agoraphobia is based on an elevated concern about the social consequences of panic; the anticipation of panic in specific situations predicts the extent of avoidance (Craske & Barlow, 2001).

By definition, post-traumatic stress disorder (PTSD) is the result of a traumatic event in which the individual felt helpless, threatened or terrified. However, cognitive theorists have postulated that as opposed to trauma, persistent PTSD is also the result of negative appraisals of the traumatic event and its sequelae, which leads to a sense of recurrent threat. It has been proposed that PTSD sufferers hold dysfunctional external beliefs (the world is a dangerous place) and internal beliefs (the view that one's capability, acceptability, or survivability has been threatened). In addition, PTSD patients may overgeneralize from the original event and consequently, perceive a range of normal events as more dangerous than they really are (Ehlers & Clark, 2000).

In addition to the specific cognitive content of the anxiety disorders, it has been recognized that most anxiety disorders involve a process of attentional bias, which is thought to maintain the disorder (Clark, 1999). In the case of panic disorder, individuals have heightened awareness and ability to detect bodily sensations of arousal. Ehlers and colleagues have conducted a number of experiments that demonstrate a heightened awareness and accurate perception of heartbeat in panic disorder (Ehlers & Breuer, 1996). In addition, increased awareness and accuracy of heart rate perception predicted the reoccurrence of panic attacks in a one-year longitudinal study (Ehlers, 1995). Also consistent with the cognitive model, individuals with specific phobias demonstrate stronger attention to threat-related stimuli than non-threat-related stimuli (Antony & Swinson, 2001).

Memory dysfunction is also apparent in anxiety disorders. In the case of PTSD, for example, the process of memory encoding and retrieval is puzzling (Clark, 1999). On the one hand, patients have difficulty retrieving a complete memory of the trauma; however, they also involuntarily experience recurrent thoughts and images, experiencing the memory of the event in a very vivid and emotional way. It has been proposed that PTSD arises from the poor elaboration and incorporation of the memory into autobiographical memory, leading to poor voluntary recall and cuing of intrusions by stimuli that may be temporarily associated with the trauma. Thus, one target of treatment for PTSD is in the "reliving" of the event through recall of the memory with a therapist (Ehlers & Clark, 2000).

Behavioral avoidance is also a common feature across anxiety disorders. Most cognitive behavioral approaches conceptualize avoidance as negatively reinforcing because it maintains the fear and prevents its extinction. In panic disorder, for example, avoidance behaviors, such as avoiding situations in which a panic attack might occur, are thought to maintain the negative beliefs about bodily sensations.

Avoidance can also take the form of safety behaviors, which prevent or minimize the feared catastrophe (Clark, 1999). Negative beliefs about feared bodily sensations in panic disorder are maintained through avoidance or safety behaviors, such as holding onto objects or persons for fear of fainting, moving slowly, or searching for an escape (Craske & Barlow, 2001). Individuals with social phobia might avoid eye contact, have reduced verbal output or voice tone, stand on the periphery of a group (Rapee & Heimberg, 1997), keep conversations superficial, wear certain items of clothing to hide anxiety symptoms, or hide the face with long hair (Clark, 1999). PTSD sufferers also engage in avoidance strategies such as suppressing thoughts about the trauma and avoiding reminders of the trauma. They also engage in safety behaviors. For example, a car accident survivor might be extremely vigilant for possible dangerous situations when driving by driving slowly or avoiding crowded streets (Ehlers & Clark, 2000).

The cognitive behavioral formulation of anxiety disorders leads to a consistent treatment model. Treatment begins with an explanation of the rationale for intervention and a cognitive behavioral model tailored to the individual's problem. Education about anxiety is an important component. For example, in the case of panic disorder, psychoeducation regarding the nature of panic attacks and cognitive restructuring are used to target misappraisals of bodily sensations. Because cognitive interventions are designed to target the misappraisals and catastrophic interpretations of perceived threat, CBT for anxiety next involves the identification and examination of the negative beliefs. The therapist's goal is to show patients how the specific triggers to their anxiety produce negative automatic thoughts related to feared outcomes (Clark, 1999).

Systematic behavioral exposure is used to target anxiety-related avoidance, and it also is used to obtain data to disconfirm the misappraisals. The individual is systematically taught to enter the feared situations. Relaxation training and breathing retraining might be employed to reduce the arousal and physiological symptoms of anxiety while entering the feared situations. Unique to panic disorder is the use of interoceptive exposure to lessen fear of specific bodily cues through repeated and systematic exposure to those cues (Craske & Barlow, 2001). In the case of PTSD, the individual is exposed systematically to the memory of the traumatic event by recalling it in detail. In vivo exposure is also used to target avoidance of the current life triggers of PTSD symptoms (Ehlers & Clark, 2000). Therapy can also target safety behaviors by teaching the patient to enter the feared situation while purposefully not using the safety behaviors.

Although there appear to be cognitive and behavioral features that are common across the anxiety disorders, generalized anxiety disorder (GAD) and obsessive-compulsive disorder (OCD) have several unique characteristics. GAD is characterized by persistent worry that is difficult to control. Borkovec (1994) formulated a model of GAD worry as a conceptual verbal/linguistic attempt to avoid future averse events and imagery. GAD patients are thought to overestimate potential threat and underestimate their ability to cope with or control future negative events. The worry is negatively reinforced because it is associated with avoidance and escape from more threatening imagery. Although worry might lead to short-term relief from anxiety, the long-term consequences include inhibited emotional processing and maintenance of anxiety producing cognition and behavior (Brown, O'Leary, & Barlow, 2001). Worry also hinders effective problem solving of true-life circumstances. Thus, the cognitive behavioral targets for intervention are the excessive uncontrollable worry and persistent overarousal.

GAD, like other anxiety disorders, begins with psychoeducation followed by identification and examination of negative automatic thoughts. In addition, the cognitive distortions that are common to GAD are identified such as *probability overestimation* and *catastrophic thinking*. To counter catastrophic thoughts, the clients are asked to imagine the worst possible feared outcome actually happening and then to critically evaluate the severity of the impact of the event. An intervention known as *worry exposure* is also used that involves identifying two or three spheres of worry ordered hierarchically. Clients are then instructed to imagine the worst possible scenario while using relaxation methods and to generate as many alternative outcomes as possible. Problem-solving methods are also employed in which clients examine and apply solutions to their life problems.

The cognitive behavioral approach to OCD also has special considerations. Patients with OCD suffer from recurrent obsessions and/or compulsions that interfere with daily functioning. Obsessions produce anxiety or distress and are in the form of persistent ideas, thoughts, impulses, or images. Compulsions are repetitive behaviors or mental acts to reduce the anxiety associated with the obsessions (American Psychiatric Association, 2000). Mowrer's (1939) two-stage theory was originally used to explain the development of OCD, proposing that a neutral event (thought) becomes associated with fear by being paired with a stimulus that by its nature provokes anxiety. In the second stage, active avoidance patterns in the form of compulsions are developed and maintained because they alleviate the distress.

It now appears that the content of normal intrusive thoughts and obsessional thoughts are comparable and that intrusions occur in at least 90 percent of the general population (Salkovskis & Harrison, 1984). It thus appears that dysfunction in obsessional intrusive cognitions lies not in their content or uncontrollability but, rather, in the interpretation of the content and the occurrence of intrusive thoughts (Salkovskis, 1999). Salkovskis (1985) has suggested that intrusive obsessive thoughts are stimuli that provoke certain types of negative automatic thoughts that arise from dysfunctional belief systems (i.e., only bad people have sexual thoughts). Thus, an intrusive thought will lead to mood disturbances only if it triggers automatic thoughts through the interaction between the unacceptable intrusion and the individual's belief system. Salkovskis proposed that an exaggerated sense of responsibility and self-blame are central themes in the belief systems of individuals with OCD. In support of the cognitive theory, Foa, Admir, Bogert, Molnar, and Przeworski (2001) examined perceptions of responsibility for harm in individuals with OCD, generalized social phobia, and nonanxious controls. They found that compared to social phobia and normal controls, patients with OCD demonstrated an inflated sense of responsibility for low-risk situations and obsessive-compulsive relevant situations. In addition, unlike the other groups, the degree of perceived responsibility was highly correlated with the degree of OCD responsibility.

Other cognitive theorists have emphasized information-processing biases in OCD (Foa & Franklin, 2001). They propose that individuals with OCD tend to make conclusions that situations are dangerous based on the absence of evidence for safety but tend to fail at making interpretations about safety from information about the absence of danger. Thus, rituals are performed to reduce the likelihood of harm but can never really provide safety and must be repeated (Foa & Franklin, 2001).

The cognitive behavioral treatment for OCD includes prolonged exposure to obsessional cues, coupled with procedures to prevent rituals (Foa & Franklin, 2001). It is believed that repeated prolonged exposure to the feared thoughts and situations provides information that disconfirms the mistaken associations and promotes habituation. Exposure is conducted gradually as the client tackles situations that are increasingly more distressing. The efficacy of exposure plus response prevention has been demonstrated in treatment outcome studies (for a review, see Chambless & Ollendick, 2001).

To summarize, cognitive behavioral models for anxiety disorders are elaborate and compelling. There has been a movement toward microscopic theories to explain the unique features of specific anxiety disorders (Rachman, 2002). Most interventions combine both cognitive and behavioral interventions for the amelioration of anxiety, although treatments for disorders such as OCD and specific phobia incorporate more behavioral strategies (exposure) relative to cognitive interventions, than for some of the other anxiety disorders.

SUBSTANCE ABUSE

Substance abuse disorders are generally considered a set of heterogeneous problems, both with respect to the abused substance, and the severity of abuse (McCrady, 2001). Interventions are tailored to the individual after considering a number of dimensions, including these issues, concomitant life problems, motivation for treatment, and the individual's social support (McCrady, 2001). A number of CBT approaches have been described specifically for alcoholism (Monti, Kadden, Rohsenow, Cooney, & Abrams, 2002) and cocaine dependence (Higgins, Budney, & Sigmon, 2001), whereas other models have been developed for the treatment of addictions more generally (Beck et al., 1993).

Beck et al. (1993) developed a primarily cognitive model of addiction, suggesting that the sociological, interpersonal, and psychological dimensions of abuse need to be considered. They proposed that individuals engage in substance abuse initially to experience pleasure, the physiological effects of the drugs, and to participate with friends. The maintenance of drug use is postulated to occur by way of both external influences (i.e., peers) and internal problems (i.e., transient relief of depression, anxiety, and tension). Similar to depression, their model proposes that erroneous thinking and maladaptive beliefs underlie the emotional reactions and self-defeating behavior that leads to chronic substance abuse. Vulnerable individuals are postulated to have negative beliefs about the self, the world, and others. When activated, these beliefs lead to emotions such as anger or sadness. When these emotions occur, addictive beliefs are activated (i.e., attitudes about the positive effects of the drug, substance use as relief or escape), which then lead to the craving and use of the drug.

In addition, the model explains the relationship between urges and control. An urge is defined as internal pressure or mobilization to act on the craving (doing). The cognitive model proposes that dysfunctional beliefs in addictions are expectations of the positive effects of drugs. These beliefs fall into six factors: beliefs that the drug will increase experiences in a positive way, enhance social and physical pleasure, increase sexual performance and satisfaction, increase power and aggressiveness, increase social assertiveness, and/or decrease tension. The process of stimulus generalization leads to the individual responding to the craving to an increasingly broader range of stimulus situations.

Cognitive therapy for substance abuse aims to reduce the negative emotional reactions and self-defeating behavior by modifying dysfunctional thinking and maladaptive beliefs that underlie these reactions. In the case of urges and craving, the therapist helps the client to examine trigger events and to evaluate beliefs about the value of the substance. The individual is taught to reflect and decide whether to indulge in the craving or to resist and increase the sense of self-control. Therapy techniques include evaluating the short- and long-term consequences of using the substance and helping the patient to develop more healthy ways of coping with problems and negative emotions. Interpersonal difficulties are targeted through training in skills such as assertiveness. To further increase self-control, the stimulus conditions that elicit the craving are recreated in therapy and control behaviors are rehearsed.

There is partial empirical support for CT of addiction. Chambless and Ollendick (2001) identify CT as probably efficacious for cocaine dependence. They also identify components of CT such as urge-coping skills and social skill training as efficacious for the treatment of alcohol abuse. However, CT has not yet been empirically validated as a stand-alone model for addictions.

A more specific model aimed at alleviated alcohol abuse is Monti et al.'s (2002) cognitive social learning approach that incorporates both cue exposure treatment (CET) and coping skills training (CST). The model proposes that addictive behavior is a habitual, maladaptive way of coping with stress, which is influenced by a biological/genetic vulnerability to stressors and behavioral deficits or excesses. Social learning theory proposes that addiction is the result of an interaction between genetic influences and psychosocial factors and thus implies that changes in social attitudes and behavior can alter the occurrence and course of the disorder. The major assumption of the model is that if clients take responsibility for learning new behavior they can learn to better manage their genetic and social vulnerabilities.

The coping skills approach is predicated on the idea that individuals who are at risk for alcohol dependence and abuse are those who have deficits in skills for coping with a number of life situations. Thus, they turn to alcohol use to cope with life's problems and hold dysfunctional expectancies about alcohol's effects. These expectancies are learned through growing up in a culture with certain social influences of family, peers, and media. In addition, alcohol use is influenced by positive reinforcement from direct drug effects and social reinforcement, such as terminating unpleasant social experiences or release from social inhibitions. It is also postulated that environmental stimuli or cues can play an important role in eliciting drinking behavior or setting the occasion for drinking through classical conditioning mechanisms.

Cue exposure treatment (CET) was developed to help clients reduce the strength of internal reactions, to reduce their reactivity to environmental cues, and to provide an opportunity to practice coping skills in a state of arousal that these cues generate. The treatment is based on the notion that gradual exposure to increasingly difficult situations combined with the successful use of coping and avoidance of drinking in these situations help individuals to develop confidence in their ability to successfully cope without drinking. The treatment uses a variety of techniques, including psychoeducation, didactic instruction, behavioral rehearsal, modeling, cognitive restructuring, and cue exposure. It is thought that through the repeated, unreinforced exposure to drinking cues, individuals will habituate and reduce alcohol cue reactivity (Monti et al., 2002). In addition, practicing skills in the presence of alcohol cues should increase their real-life effectiveness in the presence of alcohol cues and increase individuals' expectancies that they can respond to these cues without drinking (Monti et al., 2002).

Empirical evidence to support the coping skills model is promising. For example, Moser and Annis (1996) found that continued abstinence was related to use of coping strategies and that individuals who relapsed were more likely to use avoidant coping strategies. Chung, Langenbucher, Labouvie, Pandina, and Moos (2001) also found that increased behavioral approach coping predicted lower severity of alcohol problems after 12 months. They also found that a decline in cognitive avoidance coping predicted fewer alcohol dependence symptoms and psychosocial difficulties at 12 months. Finally, the efficacy of CET plus coping skills is well established (Chambless & Ollendick, 2001).

Another approach to alcoholism is relapse prevention (RP), which combines cognitive and behavioral techniques to help individuals maintain abstinence (Dimeff & Marlatt, 1995). The goals of RP are to enhance patients' ability to anticipate and prevent relapses from occurring, to cope effectively with relapse to reduce the negative consequences and maximize learning, and to change lifestyles so that behavioral change can be maintained. RP assumes that most individuals view relapse in dichotomous terms (i.e., "Either I am sober or I have failed") but argues that this view of relapse is detrimental because even one lapse may be viewed as a total loss of control and send a person into a complete relapse. Thus, RP begins by challenging this dichotomous thinking by taking the approach that relapse is a mistake or error in new learning. The RP treatment emphasizes problem solving, learning from experience, and active coping strategies. Intervention strategies include self-monitoring, behavioral assessment, relaxation training, stress management, contract to limit use, skill training, education, and cognitive restructuring.

Although the RP approach seems clinically relevant, its efficacy has yet to be demonstrated. One reason for the lack of empirical support may be due to the fact that RP incorporates a number of different strategies, making it difficult to compare to more established treatments such as coping skills or cue exposure. In addition, RP is considered an idiographic approach, which makes it difficult to conduct in a group format (Dimeff & Marlatt, 1995). Nonetheless, the RP approach is intriguing and awaits further empirical support.

EATING DISORDERS

CBT was initially developed for the treatment of bulimia nervosa (BN; Fairburn, 1981), and a treatment manual for BN was published in 1993 (Fairburn et al., 1993; see also Wilson, Fairburn, & Agras, 1997). More recently, the CBT models have been expanded to account for anorexia nervosa (AN; Garner, Vitousek, & Pike, 1997) and psychopathology that underlies the full range of eating disorders (Fairburn, Cooper, & Shafran, 2003).

The model underpinning CBT for BN is best conceptualized as a maintenance model. According to the original cognitive behavioral theory of BN—a belief system that overvalued eating, shape and weight, and their control—is the primary cognitive vulnerability for the maintenance of the disorder (Wilson et al., 1997). The other clinical features, such as extreme attempts at weight control, restricted food intake, self-induced vomiting, body checking, and avoidance, as well as the preoccupation, are thought to directly stem from this overevaluation of eating, weight, body, and their control. Binge eating is viewed as the result of individuals' extreme rigid and extreme dietary rules and attempts to overly restrict their eating. Thus, even small dietary slips are interpreted as evidence of their lack of control, leading to purging behavior in attempts to regain control.

CBT for BN addresses the cycle of binge eating and purging, dietary restraint, and dysfunctional thoughts about the personal significance of body weight and shape (Wilson et al., 1997). The manualized treatment consists of 19 weekly sessions that incorporate a number of cognitive and behavioral techniques (Wilson et al., 1997). Initially, therapy aims at establishing regular eating behaviors and reducing the frequency of binging and purging. Strategies include self-monitoring, education about weight and eating, and prescription of regular eating strategies. Later stages attempt to develop cognitive and behavioral coping skills to resist binge eating. Problems solving skills, eliminating dieting, and cognitive restructuring are used to promote cognitive and behavioral change.

Cognitive behavioral theory has also been applied to explain the maintenance of AN. Fairburn, Shafran, and Cooper (1998) proposed that an extreme need to control eating is the central feature of the disorder. They postulate that individuals vulnerable to anorexia are those who have a need for control in general and begin to primarily focus their self-control on eating. The need for self-control of eating may be reinforcing for the individual. For example, self-control may have a potent effect on dysfunctional relationships in the immediate environment. Alternatively, restricted eating may provide a means of arresting or reversing puberty, which may constitute a threat to self-control. Finally, self-control and restricted eating may be reinforced in societies that place value on control of shape and weight.

Fairburn et al. (1998) postulated that dietary restriction is maintained by three mechanisms. First, dietary restriction may enhance the sense of being in control, which positively reinforces further dietary restriction. Second, individuals' interpretations of symptoms of starvation may also maintain the dietary restriction. Symptoms such as abnormal eating attitudes and behaviors, mood fluctuations, cognitive impairments, and physiological changes may be perceived as threats to control over eating and so encourage continued dietary restraint. Dietary restriction is also maintained in a societal context in which thinness is encouraged. Thus, the person's sense of self-control is enhanced by the actual weight loss that is associated with extreme dietary restraint. Fairburn et al. (1998) hypothesized that an information processing bias also operates in anorexia. When in a high state of arousal, individuals with anorexia tend to engage in hypervigilant checking of their shape, which magnifies their perception of bodily imperfection and increases their arousal and anxiety, encouraging further monitoring. The result of this vicious cycle is that these individuals come to think that they are failing to control their shape and thus persist in dietary restriction. Overall, the cognitive behavioral conceptualization of anorexia implies that treatment should focus on the core maintaining mechanisms and on the issue of self-control (Fairburn et al., 1998).

Garner et al. (1997) have developed a three-stage treatment procedure for anorexia. The first phase involves mainly behavioral interventions focused on prescribing normalized eating patterns, increasing motivation for change, and challenging cultural values regarding body shape and weight. An "experimental" model of change is explicitly utilized in which the client and therapist carefully plan to gather and evaluate evidence to test the impact of weight gain. Therapy techniques include self-monitoring and meal planning. The second phase of treatment involves increased use of cognitive interventions such as identifying dysfunctional thoughts and schemata, developing cognitive restructuring skills, modifying self-concept, and addressing the personal meaning that thinness has acquired for the individual. The final phase of therapy involves summarizing the gains made during treatment and reviewing the fundamentals for continued progress and prevention of relapse. Although CBT for anorexia and bulimia have features in common, there are differences. In particular, individuals with anorexia may be reluctant to commit to therapy and refuse to gain weight, particularly in a social context that rewards thinness. Thus, the initial stages of treatment often focus on cultivating motivation for change (Garner et al., 1997). In addition, anorexia clients may be reluctant to gain weight out of fear of becoming overweight. This fear needs to be recognized and addressed throughout the therapy.

The findings from the efficacy research suggest that between 40 percent and 50 percent of patients who complete

CBT will cease binge eating and purging and maintain progress over the long term (Fairburn, Cooper, et al., 2003). CBT has also been found to be more effective than delayed treatment and pharmacotherapy for bulimia nervosa (Fairburn, Cooper, et al., 2003). In addition, to test the cognitive behavioral formulation, Shafran, Fairburn, Nelson, and Robinson (2003) investigated whether individuals with eating disorders were more likely to interpret symptoms of dietary restraint in terms of control compared to noneating disordered controls. They were presented with ambiguous scenarios, some of which described symptoms of starvation. They were asked to complete a sentence of what they would think in each scenario. The responses were then coded in terms of control, positive, negative, and neutral. In partial support for the CBT formulation, they found that the clinical group was more likely to interpret the symptoms of dietary restraint in terms of control over eating, shape, weight, or themselves in general. There were, however, no significant differences between groups on positive interpretations of symptoms of dietary restraint. Finally, in another study, Fairburn, Stice, et al. (2003) studied the predictors of persistent bulimia in a five-year period. Consistent with cognitive behavioral theory, they found that greater overevaluation of shape and weight predicted persistent binge eating and that this relationship was mediated by dietary restraint.

Recently, the original theory has been extended to address the 50 percent to 60 percent of patients who fail to make recovery (Fairburn, Cooper, et al., 2003). The new theory proposes that, in certain patients, one or more additional maintaining mechanisms serve as an obstacle to change. These additional components include perfectionism, unconditional and pervasive low self-esteem, difficulty coping with intense mood states (mood intolerance), and interpersonal difficulties. Perfectionism is marked by fear of failure, frequent and selective attention to performance (e.g., frequent shape and weight checking, repeated caloric counting), and self-criticism. Unconditional and pervasive low self-esteem refers to the clinical observation that some patients hold a pervasive negative view of themselves, which is seen as part of their permanent identity. Despite a reduction in eating disorder symptomatology, they still hold a perpetuating, negative view of the self. Mood intolerance refers to an inability to cope appropriately with intense mood states such as anxiety, depression, and anger. These patients engage in dysfunctional mood modulation behavior, including self-harm and substance use. Finally, dysfunctional interpersonal processes involving family members (i.e., family tensions, adverse interpersonal events) may also serve to maintain the eating disorder for several patients.

Fairburn, Cooper, et al. (2003) argue that this model addresses the common features of BN, AN, and eating disorder not otherwise specified. Based on clinical observations, they argue that these disorders share the same psychopathology and that some patients move between diagnostic states over time. They postulate that, irrespective of type of eating disorder, the central pathology is a core cognitive disturbance characterized by overevaluation of eating, shape, and weight. One or more of the four additional mechanisms may serve to maintain the disorder. They also recommend that treatment focus on the four additional processes that may be operating in the maintenance of the disorder. A transdiagnostic perspective to the theory and treatment of anorexia is an interesting development. The expansion of treatment strategies to target the features of the transdiagnostic model, and further efficacy research, are needed.

SCHIZOPHRENIA

Although psychopharmacology remains the mainstay of the treatment of patients with psychotic disorders, as many as 50 percent of patients will continue to experience psychotic symptoms, even when adhering to medication regimens (Rector & Beck, 2002). Cognitive models have been developed to explain the development and maintenance of delusions (Freeman, Garety, Kuipers, Fowler, & Bebbington, 2002) and hallucinations (Birchwood & Chadwick, 1997). These models draw on the CBT principles from anxiety and depressive disorders and incorporate a diathesis-stress framework in which the emergence of symptoms depends upon an interaction between vulnerability (genetic, biological, psychological) and stress (biological, psychological, or social; Birchwood & Chadwick, 1997). Cognitive behavioral strategies have also been applied to the treatment of negative symptoms such as emotional withdrawal and anhedonia, but the cognitive model and research to support this work is still preliminary (Rector & Beck, 2002).

CBT theorists propose that delusions share similarities with nonpsychotic beliefs and that the content of delusions reflect everyday concerns and the patient's predelusional beliefs (Rector & Beck, 2002). Dimensions that are common to both delusions and nonpsychotic beliefs include pervasiveness (the degree to which the patient's consciousness is controlled by the belief), conviction (the degree to which the patient believes it), significance (the importance in the patient's overarching meaning system), intensity (the degree to which it prevents more realistic beliefs), and inflexibility.

Similar to the model for anxiety and depression, the cognitive model for persistent psychosis suggests that cognitive biases may distort the way the patient interprets reality. Psychotic patients are prone to jump to conclusions and fail to consider alternative explanations for their interpretations. Research suggests that there are three common biases in psychotic thinking: an egocentric bias (construe irrelevant events as self-relevant), an externalizing bias (internal sensations are attributed to external agents), and an intentionalization bias (attribute malevolent and hostile intentions to other people's behavior; Rector & Beck, 2002).

The CBT approach involves cognitive and behavioral strategies aimed at undermining the rigidity and conviction of delusions. The development of a strong therapeutic alliance, as can be achieved through exploring and understanding the patient's life context including their past life events and appraisal, is seen as a critical precursor to intervention (Rector & Beck, 2002). Assessment also involves understanding the proximal events critical to the formation of delusions and the current events that trigger the delusion. Once an understanding of the patient's delusional system and the past and current events that are interpreted as supporting the delusion is reached, the evidence is gently questioned. As in the case of anxiety and depression, the approach is collaborative and Socratic. In addition to cognitive strategies, the therapist can also set up behavioral strategies that test the accuracy of different interpretations or delusional beliefs.

The cognitive model of auditory hallucinations proposes that hallucinations result from difficulties in discriminating between internally generated and externally generated events. Research has shown that individuals with hallucinations are prone to assuming that a voice is present when in fact it is not (Bentall & Slade, 1985). In addition, Birchwood and Chadwick (1997) found that the emotional and behavioral disturbances associated with hallucinatory voices are predicted more by the beliefs regarding the voice, rather than the frequency, duration, or form of the voice per se. Thus, cognitive and behavioral interventions can be used to help clients identify, test, and challenge cognitive distortions in the cognitive content of the voices, with the assumption that the voice content is similar to their own negative view of themselves. Second, therapy can aim at identifying, questioning, and developing alternative beliefs about the voices' identity, purpose, and meaning (Rector & Beck, 2002).

As in the case of delusions, CBT for hallucinations begins with a thorough assessment of the past events that led to the initial formation of the hallucination as well as the current stressors that maintain them. The therapist gently questions the evidence to support the interpretation of voices, and through collaboration the client and therapist attempt to generate alternative explanations for the voices. Using knowledge from the assessment phase, beliefs about uncontrollability of the voice can be addressed by demonstrating to the client that they can initiate, diminish, or terminate the voices. The client learns that particular cues activate the voices (e.g., imagining an upsetting event) and that they can engage in an activity to terminate the voice (e.g., a conversation). Beliefs about omnipotence and omniscience can be addressed by setting up behavioral experiments that ignore the demands of the voice. Finally, the therapist guides the client to recognize that the voices simply reflect their own beliefs.

A number of other therapeutic strategies have been used for the management of schizophrenia. Psychoeducation may be helpful for individuals with psychosis and their families as an adjunct to medical treatment. Social skills training have also been developed to help people regain social skills, improve their quality of life, and reduce symptomatology. A recent review cautions that psychoeducation and social skills training are of limited effectiveness when implemented on their own but may be useful when applied in addition to CBT for delusions and hallucinations (Turkington, Dudley, Warman, & Beck, 2004).

Research to support CBT for psychosis is preliminary but promising. A recent meta-analysis of seven outcome studies found that patients who received CBT in addition to routine medical care demonstrated better outcomes on overall schizophrenia symptomatology when compared to patients who received routine care only and those who received supportive counseling in addition to routine care (Rector & Beck, 2001). Research also suggests that CBT for schizophrenia can reduce overall symptoms and depression and improve insight (for a review, see Turkington et al., 2004). In addition, patients who received CBT reported feeling very satisfied with the treatment, suggesting that CBT may be useful in reducing medication noncompliance (Rector & Beck, 2001). Although these results are intriguing, more research is needed to understand the active ingredient in CBT for psychosis.

PERSONALITY DISORDERS

Although the pervasive nature of personality disorders (PD) have posed a number of challenges to theorists and clinicians, several cognitive behavioral approaches for the treatment of personality disorders (PD) have been developed (Linehan, 1993; Young et al., 2003). A cognitive model of PD has been proposed in which the characteristic rigid patterns of behaviors are seen as "strategies" with the ultimate goal of survival and reproduction (Beck et al., 2004). From this view, the behavioral strategies seen in PD are adaptive in some situations but grossly maladaptive when the situational context changes. These strategies are thought to arise from dysfunctional beliefs, which develop from the combination of innate predisposition and environmental influences. For example, some individuals may be particularly sensitive to rejection or abandonment by others, leading to the development of strong fears about the catastrophic meaning of social loss. They are then predisposed to overreact to any sort of rejection in childhood, even if relatively mild, leading to the development of a negative self-image that is reinforced, particularly if rejection is repeated over time (Beck et al., 2004).

According to Beck, maladaptive schemata are the central dysfunction in PD. However, schemata in PD differ from depression or anxiety in that they are more persistent and more global. Schemata are consistently activated when a problematic situation arises for the PD client; for example, schemata such as "I am helpless" or "people are dangerous" become activated when negative situations occur, leading to strategies such as the dependence on or the avoidance of others. Individuals with borderline PD (BPD), for example, are proposed to hold beliefs regarding the self as bad, vulnerable, and helpless and that other people are malevolent, abusing, and rejecting. Emotions are viewed as dangerous, and these individuals may hold expectations of pending abuse and abandonment.

Another distinction between Axis I and Axis II conceptualizations is the control system in individuals with PD. Unlike in Axis I disorders, individuals with PD are thought to have a rigid internal control system based on dysfunctional beliefs regarding appropriate and inappropriate behavior. In addition, it is proposed that individuals with PD show both "overdeveloped" and "underdeveloped" behavioral patterns. For example, individuals with dependent PD have overdeveloped patterns of help seeking and clinging but underdeveloped behaviors such as self-sufficiency and mobility.

Beck et al. (2004) have developed specific models for the treatment of different PDs. For individuals with comorbid Axis I and Axis II disorders, they recommend using "standard" cognitive behavioral treatment (behavioral activation, elicit, and challenge automatic thoughts and beliefs) for the treatment of the Axis I disorder, followed by a shift to treatment of the Axis II disorder by examining the more deeply ingrained core schemata.

Incorporating many of the principles of CT, Young et al. (2003) have developed a treatment approach for maladaptive core schema that they call *schema therapy*. Young et al. (2003) elaborated the term *early maladaptive schema*, which they defined as, "a broad pervasive theme or pattern comprised of memories, emotions, cognitions and bodily sensations regarding oneself and one's relationships, which is developed during childhood or adolescence, elaborated throughout one's lifetime, and dysfunctional to some degree." Like in CT, maladaptive behaviors are considered responses to the schema and driven by the schema, not part of the schema itself. As earlier mentioned, Young et al. (2003) have defined 18 schemata that fall within 5 broad categories: disconnection and rejection, impaired autonomy and performance, impaired limits, other-directness, and overvigilance and inhibition.

One conceptual difference between the cognitive model and Young et al.'s schema model is the emphasis that they place on maladaptive coping styles. Although CT acknowledges the use of maladaptive coping strategies, Young et al. proposed that coping styles play a central role in perpetuating schema (Young et al., 2003). Young proposed three main coping responses in PD: schema surrender, schema avoidance, and schema overcompensation. An individual is thought to surrender to the schema when he or she accepts that the schema is true and act in ways that confirm the schema. For example, an individual with a defectiveness schema will consistently choose critical and rejecting friends as well as engage in self-deprecating remarks. When individuals use an avoidance coping style, they try to arrange their lives so that the schema is never activated. For example, an individual with a mistrust schema may become socially isolated and withdrawn, avoiding intimacy and the potential abuse from others. Schema overcompensation refers to the tendency to fight the schema by thinking, feeling, behaving, and relating as though the opposite of the schema were true. For example, an individual with a dependence schema might overcompensate by becoming so self-reliant that he or she does not ask anyone for anything. Although overcompensation coping styles may be viewed as partial attempts to fight the schemata, individuals tend to overshoot so the schema is perpetuated rather than healed (Young et al., 2003).

Cognitive therapy for PD can begin by using data from a self-report inventory such as the Personality Beliefs Questionnaire (PBQ; Beck & Beck, 1991), the Young Schema Questionnaire (YSQ; Young & Brown, 1990, 2001), or the Young-Rygh Avoidance Inventory (YRA-I; Young & Rygh, 1994), a measure of coping styles. The therapist can also use verbal reports or information learned over the course of treatment to identify the schemata, assumptions, and strategies that are most operative in the client's life. Evidence to support the schema can also be discovered through examining the therapeutic relationship, or the historical roots of the belief system. Guided imagery may also be used to activate the traumatic events that led to the negative self-image (Beck et al., 2004).

The efficacy of either standard CT for PD or Young's schema therapy has not been demonstrated in randomized treatment outcome studies. Although Young et al.'s (2003) model has generated much interest and appears to be clinically relevant, there is, at present, very limited research to support the model. Preliminary support for the cognitive model of PD is scarce but promising. For example, Beck et al. (2001) used the Personality Beliefs Questionnaire (PBQ) to assess dysfunctional beliefs in 756 individuals who also received an Axis II diagnosis on a structured interview. Patients with avoidant, dependent, obsessive compulsive, narcissistic, and paranoid personality disorders differentially endorsed sets of beliefs that were consistent with their disorder. Although these findings offer support for the association between certain beliefs and certain disorders, the findings do not reveal any conclusions regarding the influence of beliefs on behavior (Beck et al., 2001).

Arntz, Dietzel, and Dressen (1999) investigated the association between beliefs such as "I am inherently bad," childhood trauma, and borderline PD. Participants included individuals with a borderline PD, Cluster C PD (as assessed on a structured interview), and normal controls. All participants rated the strength of beliefs on a belief questionnaire. They also assessed retrospective accounts of childhood trauma, hypothesizing that the relationship between childhood trauma and BPD would be mediated by borderline beliefs. They found that patients with BPD scored significantly higher than the Cluster C patients and normal controls on borderline beliefs. Using regression analysis and structural equation modeling, they also found that retrospective report of sexual, emotional, and physical abuse predicted BPD and that this relationship was mediated by borderline beliefs. Although these results are consistent with cognitive theory, the limitations of this study include the questionable validity and reliability of retrospective reporting. In addition, the results do not allow for any conclusions regarding whether the trauma or beliefs play a causal role in the development of borderline PD.

Cognitive and behavioral interventions are integrated within a dialectical framework in dialectical behavior therapy (DBT; Linehan, 1993), which is considered to be a well-established treatment for BPD. According to Linehan, dysfunctional emotional regulation, resulting from biological irregularities or difficult temperament combined with invalidating environments during childhood (erratic, inappropriate, and extreme responses or punishment of the expression of private experiences), is at the core of BPD. The behavioral patterns associated with BPD, such as difficulty regulating emotions, failure to recognize one's emotional responses, inhibited grieving, active passivity in relationships, and unrelenting crises, are thought to be consequences of this core dysregulation.

DBT is predicated on the principles of dialectics. A dialectical perspective stresses interrelatedness, wholeness, and process as fundamental principles of reality. Reality comprises internal opposing forces (thesis and antithesis), and change within the system is produced by tension between the two. BPD is thought to be the result of failure of dialectics, resulting from the tendency to see only the polarized categories (either-or) rather than the "all." This rigid cognitive style limits the ability to entertain ideas for future change and thus leads the patient to get "stuck" in either thesis or antithesis. Its resolution requires the recognition of the polarities and the ability to come to "synthesis." For example, Linehan (1993) proposes that BPD clients are confused about their own identity, leading them to constantly scan the environment for guidelines on how to be and what to think and feel. They fail to experience their whole relatedness with other people. Thus, one incident of interpersonal tension (a part) is interpreted as infinite interpersonal conflict (the whole).

DBT is designed to treat individuals through a set of four stages (Linehan, Cochran, & Kehrer, 2001). In the first stage, the primary focus is on attaining a life pattern that is reasonably functional and stable. Therapy specifically targets the reduction of the suicidal behaviors, therapy-interfering behaviors, quality-of-life-interfering behaviors (substance abuse, eating disorders, high-risk behaviors), and increasing behavioral skills. In the second stage, the goal is to reduce posttraumatic stress associated with early childhood trauma. The third stage involves synthesizing one's early experience in an evolving healthy sense of self and increasing respect for this self. To achieve this goal, the individual learns to evaluate one's own behavior, to trust one's own responses, and to hold onto self-evaluations independent of others' opinions. The final stage of treatment targets the resolution of a sense of incompleteness and the development of a capacity for sustaining joy through incorporation of experientially oriented techniques.

The DBT approach balances core strategies of acceptance and problem solving. The therapist uses supportive acceptance to emphasize the continual process of synthesis. The targets of therapy include decreasing dichotomous and rigid thinking as well as behavioral avoidance. Emotional regulation, interpersonal effectiveness, distress tolerance, core mindfulness, and self-management skills are taught. As opposed to more mainstream CBT approaches, DBT emphasizes increased acceptance and validation of behavior as it is in the moment. In addition, there is greater emphasis on the process of dialectical change, which is also in contrast to more mainstream CBT approaches.

The first randomized clinical trial of DBT demonstrated that compared to treatment as usual, DBT reduced the frequency and medical risk of parasuicidal behavior. However, no differences were observed between groups for patients' depression, hopelessness, suicidal ideation, or reasons for living (Linehan, Armstrong, Suarez, Allmoon, & Heard, 1991). These results suggest that although DBT is effective in reducing behaviors common to borderline patients, it does not appear to ameliorate the underlying cognitive symptoms such as hopelessness and suicidal ideation. Using a less behaviorally extreme sample, a more recent study (Koons et al., 2001) found that in addition to reducing suicidal behaviors, DBT was superior to treatment as usual on improving depression, hopelessness, and suicidal ideation. Although these results are promising, the field awaits further validation of the DBT approach.

SUMMARY AND FUTURE DEVELOPMENTS

CBT theory and interventions have been developed for the treatment of a broad range of mental disorders, and they continue to evolve (Dobson & Dozois, 2001). Several specific models have been proposed that theoretically explain the development and maintenance of mental disorders. Although empirical support for the cognitive and behavioral vulnerabilities postulated to be at the core of psychopathology is preliminary, the research base is steadily growing. However, several conceptual and research questions remain unanswered. In this final section, these questions are posed as challenges to the field.

On a conceptual level, a number of approaches have been developed that all share the assumption that cognition and behavior are at the core of emotional difficulties. However, what remains unclear is whether the different CBT approaches represent a single conceptual approach to psychotherapy, several related approaches, or different sets of techniques (Dobson & Dozois, 2001). In addition, a number of concepts, such as *schema* and *beliefs* are defined in different ways by different theorists, which can potentially lead to confusion. For example, there are several conceptual differences between Aaron Beck's and Jeffrey Young's notions of schemata. To be clinically useful and subject to replicable investigation, theoretical terms need to be defined precisely (Dobson & Dozois, 2001).

One issue with cognitive behavioral theories is that they identify dysfunctional thinking as the central problem across several disorders. These models offer limited explanation of why an individual will develop one particular disorder but not another. For example, CBT theory is limited in its explanation of why an individual might develop bulimia versus anorexia, or anxiety versus depression. Fairburn et al.'s (2003) transdiagnostic model is a complex and intriguing new development in the field of eating disorders and has implications for new therapeutic interventions in this area that are both generic to all eating disorders but also specific to unique disorders. It is also possible that transdiagnostic models may be developed to explain the development and maintenance of anxiety and mood disorders, substance use disorders, or schizophrenia spectrum disorders.

Another conceptual issue concerns comorbidity. For example, many individuals will present for treatment with both anxious and depressive disorders. Comorbidity between Axis I and Axis II disorders is also common, as individuals with personality disorders will often seek treatment for depression or anxiety (Beck et al., 2004). As most of the extant theory and research in CBT addresses distinct disorders, further theory and research to explain comorbid states and to establish CBT efficacy with comorbid disorders are warranted.

There are a number of specific issues with CBT models and treatments for several disorders. For example, in the area of substance abuse, the theory is limited in its explanation of why individuals will abuse different substances and the possible cognitive and behavioral implications of abusing a stimulant versus a depressant drug. In the area of eating disorders, it appears that interventions and clinical trials need to be elaborated to catch up to the models that have recently been proposed. Further research is also needed to investigate the eating disorder models, which have largely been derived from clinical observations (Fairburn, Cooper, et al., 2003). The CBT of personality disorders is limited by a lack of sensitivity and specificity of the Axis II diagnosis. There is conceptual overlap in symptoms across the disorders, which limits the reliability and validity of diagnoses and thus makes it difficult to formulate CBT treatment plans and study CBT efficacy.

In terms of research issues, empirical support is becoming increasingly important for establishing the use of psychotherapy (cf. Chambless & Ollendick, 2001). However, one issue is whether the methodology associated with clinical trials can provide evidence for the effectiveness of cognitive therapy in the real world. Thus, it remains unclear whether there are conceptual and practical differences between CBT in manualized form versus idiosyncratic practice (Addis et al., 1999). In addition, CBT comprises several different treatment interventions designed to target both cognitive and behavioral change. Further research is needed to determine the active ingredients for CBT efficacy with respect to the treatment of a variety of disorders (Clark, 1999; Rector & Beck, 2001). Furthermore, the addition of acceptance and mindfulness approaches to the CBT model has also generated interest, particularly in depression relapse and with personality disorders (Teasdale et al., 2000). Further research is needed to understand the role of mindfulness in other diagnostic states, such as the spectrum of anxiety disorders and eating disorders. The return of interest to a more behavioral, contextual focus in the treatment of depression (Jacobson, Martell, & Dimidjian, 2001) also needs further empirical validation. Finally, randomized clinical outcome trials will be required to validate the efficacy of schema therapy for the treatment of Axis II personality disorders.

In summary, the last 40 years has witnessed a veritable explosion of cognitive behavioral approaches in clinical psychology. The research to support the fundamental assumptions of the CBT model is continually expanding as studies are conducted to understand in detail the cognitive processes that are postulated to underlie psychopathology. The body of scientific evidence has been and continues to be incorporated into the development of CBT interventions. CBT approaches to disorders are now widely taught in graduate schools for mental health professionals, and they are seen as a critical feature of training for the next decade (Norcross, Hedges, & Prochaska, 2002). Despite these advances, further validation of both the cognitive behavioral models for different disorders and for the CBT interventions that are associated with these models are needed. Surely, the next decade will generate continued interest in the scientific and practical applications of CBT.

REFERENCES

Addis, M. E., Wade, W. A., & Hatgis, C. (1999). Barriers to dissemination of evidence-based practices: Addressing practitioners' concerns about manual-based psychotherapies. *Clinical Psychology, Science & Practice, 6,* 430–441.

American Psychiatric Association. (2000). *Diagnostic and statistical manual of mental disorders* (4th ed., text rev.). Washington, DC: Author.

Antony, M. M., & Swinson, R. P. (2000). *Phobic disorders and panic in adults: A guide to assessment and treatment.* Washington, DC: American Psychological Association.

Arntz, A., Dietzel, R., & Dressen, L. (1999). Assumptions in borderline personality disorder: Specificity, stability, and relationship with etiological factors. *Behaviour Research and Therapy, 37,* 545–557.

Beck, A. T. (1967). *Depression: Clinical, experimental, and theoretical aspects.* New York: Harper and Row.

Beck, A. T., & Beck, J. S. (1991). *The Personality Beliefs Questionnaire.* Unpublished assessment instrument, Beck Institute for Cognitive Therapy and Research, Bala Cynwyd, PA.

Beck, A. T., Butler, A. C., Brown, G. K., Dahlsgaard, K. K., Newman, C. F., & Beck, J. S. (2001). Dysfunctional beliefs discriminate personality disorders. *Behaviour Research and Therapy, 39,* 1213–1225.

Beck, A. T., Emery, G., & Greenberg, R. (1985). *Anxiety disorders and phobias: A cognitive perspective.* New York: Basic Books.

Beck, A. T., Freeman, A., & Davis, D. D. (2004). *Cognitive therapy of personality disorders* (2nd ed.). New York: Guilford Press.

Beck, A. T., Rush, A. J., Shaw, B. F., & Emery, G. (1979). *Cognitive therapy of depression.* New York: Guilford Press.

Beck, A. T., Wright, F. D., Newman, C. F., & Liese, B. S. (1993). *Cognitive therapy of substance abuse.* New York: Guilford Press.

Bentall, R. P., & Slade, P. D. (1985). Reality testing and auditory hallucinations: A signal detection analysis. *British Journal of Clinical Psychology, 24,* 159–169.

Birchwood, M., & Chadwick, P. (1997). The omnipotence of voices: Testing the validity of a cognitive model. *Psychological Medicine, 27,* 1345–1353.

Borkovec, T. D. (1994). The nature, functions, and origins of worry. In G. Davey & F. Tallis (Eds.), *Worrying: Perspectives on theory, assessment, and treatment* (pp. 5–33). New York: Wiley.

Brown, T. A., O'Leary, T. A, & Barlow, D. H. (2001). Generalized anxiety disorder. In D. H. Barlow (Ed.), *Clinical handbook of psychological disorders* (pp. 154–208). New York: Guilford Press.

Chambless, D. L., & Ollendick, T. H. (2001). Empirically supported psychological interventions: Controversies and evidence. *Annual Review of Psychology, 5,* 685–716.

Chen, Y. P., Ehlers, A., Clark, D. M., & Mansell, W. (2002). Patients with generalized social phobia direct their attention away from faces. *Behaviour Research and Therapy, 40,* 677–688.

Chung, T., Langenbucher, J., Labouvie, E., Pandina, R. J., & Moos, R. H. (2001). Changes in alcoholic patients' coping responses predict 12-month treatment outcomes. *Journal of Consulting and Clinical Psychology, 69,* 92–100.

Clark, D. A., Beck, A. T., & Alford, B. A. (1999). *Scientific foundations of cognitive theory and therapy of depression.* New York: Wiley.

Clark, D. M. (1986). A cognitive approach to panic. *Behaviour Research and Therapy, 24,* 461–470.

Clark, D. M. (1999). Anxiety disorders: Why they persist and how to treat them. *Behaviour Research and Therapy, 37*(Suppl. 1), S5–S27.

Craske, M. G., & Barlow, D. H. (2001). Panic disorder and agoraphobia. In D. H. Barlow (Ed.), *Clinical handbook of psychological disorders* (pp. 1–59). New York: Guilford Press.

Dimeff, L. A., & Marlatt, G. A. (1995). Relapse prevention. In R. K. Hester & W. R. Miller (Eds.), *Handbook of alcoholism treatment approaches* (pp. 176–194). Needham Heights, MA: Allyn & Bacon.

Dobson, K. S., Backs-Dermott, B. J., & Dozois, D. (2000). Cognitive and cognitive-behavioral therapies. In C. R. Snyder & R. E. Ingram (Eds.), *Handbook of psychological change: Psychotherapy process and practices for the 21st century* (pp. 409–428). New York: Wiley.

Dobson, K. S., & Dozois, D. J. A. (2001). Historical and philosophical bases of the cognitive-behavioral therapies. In K. S.

Dobson (Ed.), *Handbook of cognitive-behavioral therapies.* (2nd ed., pp. 3–39). New York: Guilford Press.

Dobson, K. S., & Pusch, D. (1993). Towards a definition of the conceptual and empirical boundaries of cognitive therapy. *Australian Psychologist, 28,* 137–144.

D'Zurilla, T. J., & Goldfried, M. R. (1971). Problem solving and behavior modification. *Journal of Abnormal Psychology, 78,* 107–126.

Ehlers, A. (1995). A 1-year prospective study of panic attacks: Clinical course and factors associated with maintenance. *Journal of Abnormal Psychology, 104,* 164–172.

Ehlers, A., & Breuer, P. (1996). How good are patients with panic disorder at perceiving their heartbeats? *Biological Psychology, 42,* 165–182.

Ehlers, A., & Clark, D. M. (2000). A cognitive model of posttraumatic stress disorder. *Behaviour Research and Therapy, 38,* 319–345.

Ellis, A. (1962). *Reason and emotion in psychotherapy.* New York: Stuart.

Fairburn, C. G. (1981). A cognitive behavioral approach to the management of bulimia. *Psychological Medicine, 11,* 701–711.

Fairburn, C. G., Cooper, Z., & Shafran, R. (2003). Cognitive behavioral therapy for eating disorders: A "transdiagnostic" theory and treatment. *Behaviour Research and Therapy, 41,* 509–528.

Fairburn, C. G., Marcus, M. D., & Wilson, G. T. (1993). Cognitive behavioral therapy for binge eating and bulimia nervosa: A comprehensive treatment manual. In C. G. Fairburn & G. T. Wilson (Eds.), *Binge eating: Nature, assessment, and treatment* (pp. 361–404). New York: Guilford Press.

Fairburn, C. G., Shafran, R., & Cooper, Z. (1998). A cognitive behavioral theory of anorexia nervosa. *Behaviour Research and Therapy, 37,* 1–13.

Fairburn, C. G., Stice, E., Cooper, Z., Doll, H. A., Norman, P. A., & O'Connor, M. E. (2003). Understanding the persistence in bulimia nervosa: A 5-year naturalistic study. *Journal of Consulting and Clinical Psychology, 71,* 103–109.

Foa, E. B., Amir, N., Bogert, K. V. A., Molnar, C., & Przeworski, A. (2001). Inflated perception of responsibility for harm in obsessive-compulsive disorder. *Journal of Anxiety Disorders, 15,* 259–275.

Foa, E. B., & Franklin, M. E. (2001). Obsessive-compulsive disorder. In D. H. Barlow (Ed.), *Clinical handbook of psychological disorders* (pp. 209–263). New York: Guilford Press.

Freeman, D., Garety, P. A., Kuipers, E., Fowler, D., & Bebbington, P. E. (2002). A cognitive model of persecutory delusions. *British Journal of Clinical Psychology, 41,* 331–347.

Garner, D. M., Vitousek, K. M., & Pike, K. M. (1997). Cognitive behavioral therapy for anorexia nervosa. In D. M. Garner & P. E. Garfinkel (Eds.), *Handbook of treatment for eating disorders* (2nd ed., pp. 94–144). New York: Guilford Press.

Gortner, E. T., Gollan, J. K., Dobson, K. S., & Jacobson, N. S. (1998). Cognitive behavioral treatment for depression relapse prevention. *Journal of Consulting and Clinical Psychology, 66,* 377–384.

Higgins, S. T., Budney, A. J., & Sigmon, S. C. (2001). Cocaine dependence. In D. H. Barlow (Ed.), *Clinical handbook of psychological disorders* (pp. 434–469). New York: Guilford Press.

Hollon, S. D., Haman, K. L., & Brown, L. L. (2002). Cognitive-behavioral treatment of depression. In I. H. Gotlib & C. L. Hammen (Eds.), *Handbook of depression* (pp. 383–403). New York: Guilford Press.

Ingram, R. E., Miranda, J., & Segal, Z. V. (1998). *Cognitive vulnerability to depression.* New York: Guilford Press.

Jacobson, N. S., Dobson, K. S., Truax, P. A., Addis, M. E., Koerner, K., Gollan, J. K., et al. (1996). A component analysis of cognitive-behavioral treatment for depression. *Journal of Consulting and Clinical Psychology, 64,* 295–304.

Jacobson, N. S., Martell, C. R., & Dimidjian, S. (2001). Behavioral activation treatment for depression: Returning to contextual roots. *Clinical Psychology: Science and Practice, 8,* 255–270.

Koons, C. R., Robins, C. J., Tweed, J. L., Lynch, T. R., Gonzalez, A. M., Morse, J. Q., et al. (2001). Efficacy of dialectical behavior therapy in women veterans with borderline personality disorder. *Behavior Therapy, 332,* 371–390.

Linehan, M. M. (1993). *Cognitive behavioral treatment of borderline personality disorder.* New York: Guilford Press.

Linehan, M. M., Armstrong, H. E., Suarez, A., Allmoon, D., & Heard, H. L. (1991). Cognitive behavioral treatment of chronically parasuicidal borderline patients. *Archives of General Psychiatry, 48,* 1060–1064.

Linehan, M. M., Cochran, B. N., & Kehrer, C. A. (2001). Dialectical behavior therapy for borderline personality disorder. In D. H. Barlow (Ed.), *Clinical handbook of psychological disorders* (pp. 470–522). New York: Guilford Press.

Mahoney, M. J. (1974). *Cognition and behavior modification.* Cambridge, MA: Ballinger.

Martell, C. R., Addis, M. E., & Jacobson, N. S. (2001). *Depression in context: Strategies for guided action.* New York: Norton.

McCrady, B. S. (2001). Alcohol use disorders. In D. H. Barlow (Ed.), *Clinical handbook of psychological disorders* (pp. 376–433). New York: Guilford Press.

Meichenbaum, D. H. (1977). *Cognitive behavioral modification.* New York: Plenum Press.

Miranda, J., Gross, J. L., Persons, J. B., & Hahn, J. (1998). Mood matters: Negative mood induction activates dysfunctional attitudes in women vulnerable to depression. *Cognitive Therapy and Research, 22,* 363–376.

Monti, P. M., Kadden, R. M., Rohsenow, D. J., Cooney, N. L., & Abrams, D. B. (2002). *Treating alcohol dependence: A coping skills training guide.* New York: Guilford Press.

Moser, A. E., & Annis, H. M. (1996). The role of coping in relapse crisis outcome: A prospective study of treated alcoholics. *Addiction, 91,* 1101–1114.

Mowrer, O. H. (1939). Stimulus response theory of anxiety. *Psychological Review, 46,* 553–565.

Neimeyer, R. A., & Raskin, J. D. (2001). Varieties of constructivism in psychotherapy. In K. S. Dobson (Ed.), *Handbook of cognitive-behavioral therapies* (2nd ed., pp. 393–430). New York: Guilford Press.

Norcross, J. C., Hedges, M., & Prochaska, J. O. (2002). The face of 2010: A Delphi poll on the future of psychotherapy. *Professional Psychology: Research and Practice, 33,* 316–322.

Rachman, S. (1977). The conditioning theory of fear-acquisition: A critical examination. *Behaviour Research and Therapy, 15,* 375–387.

Rachman, S. (2002). A cognitive theory of compulsive checking. *Behaviour Research and Therapy, 40,* 625–640.

Rapee, R. M., & Heimberg, R. G. (1997). A cognitive-behavioral model of anxiety in social phobia. *Behaviour Research and Therapy, 35,* 741–756.

Rector, N. A., & Beck, A. T. (2001). Cognitive behavioral therapy for schizophrenia: An empirical review. *Journal of Nervous and Mental Disease, 189,* 278–287.

Rector, N. A., & Beck, A. T. (2002). Cognitive therapy for schizophrenia: From conceptualization to intervention. *Canadian Journal of Psychiatry, 47,* 39–48.

Rehm, L. (1977). A self-control model of depression. *Behavior Therapy, 8,* 787–804.

Salkovskis, P. M. (1985). Obsessional-compulsive problems: A cognitive-behavioral analysis. *Behaviour Research and Therapy, 23,* 571–583.

Salkovskis, P. M. (1999). Understanding and treating obsessive-compulsive disorder. *Behaviour Research and Therapy, 37* (Suppl. 1), S29–S52.

Salkovskis, P. M., & Harrison, J. (1984). Abnormal and normal obsessions: A replication. *Behaviour Research and Therapy, 22,* 549–552.

Segal, Z. V., Williams, J. M. G., & Teasdale, J. D. (2002). *Mindfulness-based cognitive therapy for depression.* New York: Guilford Press.

Shafran, R., Fairburn, C. G., Nelson, L., & Robinson, P. H. (2003). The interpretation of symptoms of severe dietary restraint. *Behaviour Research and Therapy, 41,* 887–894.

Sheppard, L. C., & Teasdale, J. D. (2004). How does dysfunctional thinking decrease during recovery from major depression? *Journal of Abnormal Psychology, 113,* 64–71.

Teasdale, J. D. (1988). Cognitive vulnerability to persistent depression. *Cognition and Emotion, 2,* 247–274.

Teasdale, J. D., Segal, Z. V., Williams, J. M. G., Ridgeway, V. A., Soulsby, J. M., & Lau, M. A. (2000). Prevention of relapse/recurrence in major depression by mindfulness-based cognitive therapy. *Journal of Consulting and Clinical Psychology, 68,* 615–623.

Turkington, D., Dudley, R., Warman, D. B., & Beck, A. T. (2004). Cognitive behavioral therapy for schizophrenia: A review. *Journal of Psychiatric Practice, 10,* 5–16.

Wilson, G. T., Fairburn, C. G., & Agras, W. S. (1997). Cognitive behavioral therapy for bulimia nervosa. In D. M. Garner & P. E. Garfinkel (Eds.), *Handbook of treatment for eating disorders* (2nd ed., pp. 67–93). New York: Guilford Press.

Young, J. E. (1994). *Young Parenting Inventory.* New York: Cognitive Therapy Center of New York.

Young, J. E. (1995). *Young Compensation Inventory.* New York: Cognitive Therapy Center of New York.

Young, J. E., & Brown, G. (1990). *Young Schema Questionnaire: Special edition.* New York: Schema Therapy Institute.

Young, J. E., & Brown, G. (2001). *Young Schema Questionnaire: Special edition.* New York: Schema Therapy Institute.

Young, J. E., Klosko, J. S., & Weishaar, M. E. (2003). *Schema therapy: A practitioner's guide.* New York: Guilford Press.

Young, J. E., & Rygh, J. (1994). *Young-Rygh Avoidance Inventory.* New York: Cognitive Therapy Center of New York.

Young, J. E., Weinberger, A. D., & Beck, A. T. (2001). Cognitive therapy for depression. In D. H. Barlow (Ed.), *Clinical handbook of psychological disorders* (pp. 264–308). New York: Guilford Press.

CHAPTER 30

Psychopharmacological Interventions

TIMOTHEY C. DENKO AND MICHAEL E. THASE

The past 20 years have witnessed many important developments in psychopharmacology, with the advent of a new class of "atypical" antipsychotics, serotonin selective reuptake inhibitors (SSRIs) and other newer antidepressants, cholinesterase inhibitors for dementia, and new uses for a host of anticonvulsants. In fact, new indications for established pharmacologic agents are blurring the historic taxonomy of *antipsychotic, antidepressant,* and *anxiolytic.* Debate likewise continues as to what in fact constitutes a *mood stabilizer.*

This chapter will present psychopharmacologic agents class by class. The classes presented will include drugs called antipsychotics (despite their myriad of uses), antidepressants (although many of them are also first-line maintenance treatments for anxiety disorders), lithium, the anticonvulsants (although epilepsy will not be discussed), and a section on the benzodiazepines and nonbenzodiazepine hypnotics and anxiolytics will also be presented. This latter class remains the most commonly prescribed psychotropic in the world, and such popularity continues to generate controversy among prescribing clinicians and academics. Finally, cognitive enhancers will be presented, both relating to dementia as well as attention-deficit disorder.

Let us begin by noting that, for almost all of the conditions included in this handbook, with the exception of mania and psychosis, different types of psychotherapies have evidence for efficacy comparable to medication, and when combined with medication they offer the individual the best chance for a favorable outcome.

ANTIPSYCHOTICS

In 1952, the first antipsychotic medication, chlorpromazine (Thorazine), was shown to be an effective treatment for schizophrenia and soon revolutionized the treatment of severe and persistent mental illness. Over the next decade, a number of other antipsychotics were introduced, including thioridizine (Mellaril), trifluoperazine (Stellazine), fluphenazine (Prolixin), and perphenazine (Trilafon). Later nonphenothiazine antipsychotics such as haloperidol (Haldol), thiothixine (Navane), loxapine (Loxitane), molindone (Moban), and pimozide (Orap) were added to the armamentarium of agents for the treatment of psychosis. These agents all antagonize the dopamine D2 receptor, which is believed to be necessary for the treatment of psychosis (see Table 30.1 for additional information on first-generation antipsychotics). Although these medications were a major advancement in the treatment of schizophrenia and other psychotic disorders, they did have a significant side effect burden including sedation, weight gain, tremor, stiffness, dystonia (severe muscle contraction), cognitive dulling, galactorrhea (milk leaking from breasts), gynecomastia (enlarged breasts), restlessness, and potentially tardive dyskinesia. Neuroleptic malignant syndrome (NMS) is a particularly serious adverse effect related to the use of these "first-generation" antipsychotics, characterized by hyperthermia (increased body temperature), rigidity, mental status changes, and muscle breakdown with subsequent elevations in serum creatine phosphokinase (CPK) levels and possible renal failure and death.

Tardive dyskinesia (TD) is an involuntary movement disorder associated with the use of antipsychotic medication. TD was a major complication from treatment with the original antipsychotics, can remit after discontinuation of the antipsychotic, but at times is permanent. The most common form of TD is involuntary movement of the lips or tongue, but any muscle group can be affected. The incidence of TD has greatly diminished with the advent of the "atypical" antipsychotic.

The treatment of schizophrenia and psychosis has changed dramatically in the past decade. The first "atypical" antipsychotic, clozapine, introduced in the 1970s in Europe and in 1990 in the United States, demonstrated that treatment of psychosis did not automatically necessitate extrapyramidal side effects (tremor, dystonia, TD). Unfortunately, the propensity of clozapine to suppress the production of white blood cells has limited its use.

Subsequently, other less toxic "second-generation" antipsychotics, different from typical or first-generation anti-

TABLE 30.1 Antipsychotics

First-generation antipsychotics	Class	Dose	Comments
Chlorpromazine (Thorazine)	Phenothiazine	100–1,000 mg	Preferred when heavy sedation desired
Perphenazine (Trilafon)	Phenothiazine	6–64 mg	Reasonably well tolerated
Trifluoperazine (Stelazine)	Phenothiazine	4–30 mg	FDA approved for anxiety (not recommended)
Thioridazine (Mellaril)	Phenothiazine	100–800 mg	Can prolong QTc; avoid in people with arrythmia
Fluphenazine (Prolixin)	Phenothiazine	1–40 mg	Available in depot injection
Haloperidol (Haldol)	Butyrophenone	1–20 mg	Historically dosed much higher than necessary; available as depot
Loxapine (Loxitane)	Dibenzoxazepine	10–100 mg	Rare blood dyscrasias
Pimozide (Orap)	Diphenylbutylpiperidine	0.5–10 mg	FDA indicated for Tourette's disorder
Molindone (Moban)	Dihydroindolone	5–200 mg	TID or QID dosing limits utility
Second-generation (atypical) antipsychotics	Class	Dose	Comments: All patients on these agents should have periodic metabolic monitoring (lipids, glucose, weight, abdominal girth)
Clozapine (Clozaril, Leponex)	Dibenzodiazepine	250–450 mg	In U.S., weekly or semiweekly CBCs required to monitor for agranulocytosis; serious interaction with fluvoxamine, avoid this combination; excellent efficacy
Olanzapine	Thienobenzodiazepine	10–20 mg	Good evidence for efficacy in psychosis and mania
Risperidone (Risperidal)	Benzisoxazole	0.25–2 mg (nonpsychotic) 4/5/6 mg for psychosis	Historically dosed too high, resulting in EPS; hyperprolactinemia may be a problem
Quetiapine (Seroquel)	Dibenzodiazepine	500–800 mg for psychosis	Start at 100 mg qhs, increase by 100 mg q night to target dose
Ziprasidone (Geodon)	Benzisothiazolyl	120–160 mg for psychosis	Must be taken with food for proper absorption; avoid low doses in bipolar disorder
Aripiprazole (Abilify)		15–30 mg (higher doses for mania)	"Mixed" dopamine agonist/antagonist; very little sedation; akithesia can be significant
Sertindole (Serdolect)	Arylpiperidylindole	12–24 mg	Not available in the United States

psychotics by their antagonism of 5-hydoxytriptamine 2A (5-HT2A) receptors in addition to weaker antagonism of the dopamine D2 receptors, have been introduced (see Table 30.1 for additional information on atypical antipsychotics). Dopamine D2 receptors are thought to be responsible for positive symptoms of schizophrenia and active psychosis and are located in the mesolimbic pathway. However, dopamine receptors located in different areas of the brain affect mood and cognition, as well as movement and prolactin release, and are not as markedly affected by these second-generation drugs—hence, their "atypical" profile. 5-HT2 antagonism in some areas of the brain actually potentiates the release of dopamine in areas not associated with psychosis and diminishes some of the troubling side effects of tremor, galactorrhea, and cognitive dulling associated with the first-generation antipsychotics. Furthermore, the risk of tardive dyskinesia is much lower with the second-generation antipsychotics than with the first generation.

Today clozapine is reserved as a third-line agent for the treatment of schizophrenia (Miller et al., 2003). Clozapine appears to have a unique mechanism of action, with very high affinity for the dopamine D4 receptor, in addition to its affinity for the 5-HT2 receptor. It has been shown to be effective for treatment-resistant schizophrenia (Kane, Honigfeld, Singer, & Meltzer, 1988). Clozapine has been associated with agranulocytosis (very low white blood cell count), with an estimated frequency of 1 percent per year (*Physicians' Desk Reference*, 2002), and weekly or semiweekly monitoring of blood counts is required in the United States for all people taking clozapine. Hyperlipidemia (high cholesterol or triglyceride), hyperglycemia (high blood sugar), siallorhea (excessive salivation), and weight gain can also be significantly problematic with the use of clozapine.

Risperidone was the next atypical antipsychotic available in the United States. It has a potent affinity for the 5-HT2A and 5-HT2C receptors and some affinity for the 5-HT1A and 5-HT1D receptors. Risperidone is indicated for the treatment of schizophrenia, and there is evidence supporting its efficacy in the treatment of acute mania (Hirshfeld et al., 2004). Risperidone appears to have moderately negative influence on lipids, glycemia, and weight.

Olanzapine (Zyprexa) is structurally similar to clozapine, but it has no affinity for the dopamine D4 receptor. It has intermediate affinity for the 5-HT2A and 5-HT2C and dopamine D2 receptors. Olanzapine has been shown to be significantly efficacious in the treatment of schizophrenia (Tollefson & Sanger, 1997) and has been shown to be effective in the treatment of acute mania (Tohen et al., 2000), and there is reasonable evidence as to its utility in bipolar maintenance (Tohen et al., 2003). Olanzapine has a poor metabolic side effect profile, with weight gain, hyperlipidemia, and hyperglycemia associated with its use. Other side effects include somnolence, dry mouth, and occasionally orthostasis (low blood pressure after standing or rising from sitting.

Quetiapine (Seroquel) is a much less potent antagonist of dopamine D2 and 5-HT than any of the other atypical antipsychotics. It is indicated for the treatment of schizophrenia and has recently performed as well as lithium in a large double-blind, placebo-controlled study in acute mania (Bowden et al., 2005). Quetiapine has intermediate effects on lipids, weight, and glycemia. The major side effect of quetiapine is sedation, and some clinicians favor its use as a hypnotic at very low doses.

Ziprasidone (Geodon) differs significantly from its predecessors in that it has potent affinity for dopamine D2, 5-HT 2A, 2C, 1A, and 1D receptors (Stahl & Shayegan, 2003). It is indicated for the treatment of schizophrenia and acute mania. There has been some concern with prolongation of the QTc (a measurement of cardiac conduction that, if greatly prolonged, can increase the possibility of sudden death) associated with ziprasidone, but the clinical significance of this appears to be quite small. Ziprasidone should not be combined with other drugs that can prolong the QTc, nor should it be given to people with congenital long QTc syndrome (*Physicians' Desk Reference,* 2002). Ziprasidone performed well in a double-blind, placebo-controlled study as monotherapy in acute mania, with separation from placebo by day 3 (Keck, Versiani, et al., 2003). Adverse metabolic effects tend to be low with ziprasidone.

Aripiprazole, the most recent addition to the atypical antipsychotics, is unique in that it is a partial dopamine agonist in addition to having some antagonism of the dopamine D2 receptor. It is indicated for the treatment of schizophrenia, has recently performed well in a double-blind study of acute mania (Keck, Marcus, et al., 2003), and has shown evidence of efficacy in bipolar maintenance. It has U.S. Food and Drug Administration (USFDA) indication for both of these purposes. Adverse metabolic effects tend to be low with aripiprazole. Common side effects include akathisia (inner feeling of restlessness) and nausea.

ANTIDEPRESSANTS

All of the medications used to treat depression at this time affect one or more of the monoamine neurotransmitters. These neurotransmitters are serotonin (5-HT), norepinephrine (NE), and dopamine (DA). There are numerous subtypes of 5-HT receptors in different locations, performing different functions (see Table 30.2 for antidepressants organized by mechanism of action, dosing, and unique characteristics).

Since 1950 the pharmacologic treatment of depression has been marked by both major advances and ongoing challenges. The first antidepressant discovered was iproniazid, a monoamine oxidase inhibitor (MAOI) that was developed for the treatment for tuberculosis. Soon after the discovery of iproniazid, imipramine (Tofranil), a tricyclic antidepressant (TCA), was synthesized and found to be efficacious in the treatment of depression. For the next 20 years these two classes of antidepressant were the mainstays of the psychopharmacology of depression, but each had its drawbacks. The MAOIs require patients to avoid food and beverages high in tyramine or risk a sudden, potentially dangerous elevation of blood pressure called a hypertensive crisis. The TCAs have, for some, an onerous side effect profile of somnolence, weight gain, constipation, and urinary retention. Additionally, the TCAs were potentially lethal in overdose, due to their effects on cardiac conduction.

The TCAs also affect monoamine neurotransmitters, inhibiting either serotonin reuptake, norepinephrine reuptake, or both. They are metabolized in the liver, principally, by the cytochrome 2D6 and have the potential for numerous drug interactions and commonly have unpleasant side effects. Anticholinergic side effects such as dry mouth, urinary retention, constipation, blurred vision, and dulled cognition all limit the tolerability of these agents. Cardiovascular effects, such as orthostatic hypotension, increased pulse, and conduction delay can all complicate treatment with TCAs. Despite these drawbacks, TCAs have excellent antidepressant activity and remain a reasonable treatment option if a trial of a more benign class of antidepressant fails to achieve desired effects.

TABLE 30.2 Antidepressants

SSRIs	Starting dose	Target dose	Comments
Fluoxetine (Prozac)	20 mg	40–60 mg	Some patients activated by 20 mg starting dose; starting at 5 or 10 mg acceptable
Sertaline (Zoloft)	25 or 50 mg	100–200 mg	Most dopaminergic of the SSRIs
Fluvoxamine (Luvox)	50 mg	150–300 mg	FDA approved for OCD, not MDD; in Europe used for depression
Paroxetine (Paxil, Pexeva)	20 mg	40–80 mg	Can have problematic withdrawal syndrome
Citalopram (Celexa)	20 mg	40–60 mg	Considered the most "selective"
Escitalopram (Lexapro)	10 mg	20–30 mg	Isomer of citalopram

Serotonin norepinephrine reuptake inhibitors

Venlafaxine (Effexor XR)	37.5 mg	150–375 mg	Once daily dosing with XR formulation at doses ≤225 mg
Duloxetine (Cymbalta)	30 mg	40–120 mg	Also approved for treatment of neuropathic pain

Antidepressants with other mechanisms of action

Bupropion (Wellbutrin SR, Wellbutrin XL)	150 mg	300–450 mg	Once daily dosing with XL; seizure risk comparable to SSRIs when SR or XL used correctly
Mirtazapine (Remeron)	15 mg	45–60 mg	Sedation may decrease with higher doses
Nefazodone	50 mg bid	150 mg bid–300 mg bid; some clinicians dose all at bedtime	Brand name (Serzone) withdrawn from U.S. market due to rare cases of hepatic failure
Trazodone (Desyrel)	50 mg	200–300 mg	More commonly used as hypnotic
Amoxapine (Asendin)	50 mg bid or 50 mg tid	150–300 mg	Neuroleptic malignant syndrome and bone marrow suppression have been reported
Maprotiline (Ludiomil)	25 mg bid or tid	100–225 mg	Rare cases of agranulocytosis

Tricyclic antidepressants	Starting dose	Target dose	Comments: All TCAs are metabolized through CYP2D6, and drugs that inhibit this enzyme will increase TCA levels.
Imipramine (Tofranil)	75–100 mg; may be given in single or divided doses	150–300 mg	Serum levels higher than 200 ng/mL considered therapeutic
Amitriptilline (Elavil)	75–100 mg in single or divided doses	150–300 mg	Active metabolite is nortriptilline
Clomipramine (Anafranil)	25 mg TID	150–300 mg	FDA approved for OCD
Doxepin (Sinequan)	75 mg	150–300 mg	Has norepinephrine reuptake inhibition
Trimipramine (Surmontil)	75 mg in divided doses	50–150 mg	Strong affinity for histamine H1 receptor
Desipramine (Norpramin)	25–50 mg	100–300 mg	High norepinephrine reuptake inhibition; fewer adverse effects than most TCAs
Nortriptilline (Pamelor)	25 mg	50–150 mg	Fewer Adverse effect than most TCAs
Protriptyline (Vivactil, Concordin)	5 mg tid	15–60 mg	Can be quite activating; very long half-life

Monoamine Oxidase Inhibitors — Dietary restrictions of tyramine required

Phenelzine (Nardil)	15 mg tid	60–90 mg in three divided doses	Irreversible MAO-A and MAO-B
Tranylcypromine (Parnate)	10 mg tid	20 mg tid	Irreversible MAO-A and MAO-B
Isocarboxazid (Marplan)	10 mg bid	15–20 mg bid	Irreversible MAO-A and MAO-B
Moclobemide (Aurorix, Manerix)	100 mg tid	100–600 mg in three divided doses after meals	Reversible MAO-A inhibitor; no tyramine restrictions; not available in the U.S.

In the early 1980s, trazodone (Desyrel) was introduced, marking the first of the second-generation antidepressants. This compound was chemically and functionally distinct from its predecessors. Trazodone functions as a 5-HT2 antagonist and as a serotonin reuptake inhibitor. Despite its side effect of somnolence, trazodone became quite popular until the introduction of the serotonin selective reuptake inhibitors (SSRIs). A rare but serious adverse effect from trazodone is priapism, a prolonged painful erection that can induce impotence. Patients starting this drug should be warned of this possibility.

The name *selective serotonin reuptake inhibitor* (SSRI) describes the relative pharmacologic simplicity of this class of antidepressants. Fluoxetine (Prozac) was introduced in the mid-1980s as the first SSRI. It had significantly fewer side effects than the TCAs, did not require dietary restrictions as did the MAOIs, and was much safer in overdose. Soon thereafter, fluvoxamine (Luvox), sertraline (Zoloft), paroxetine (Paxil), citalopram (Celexa), and most recently escitalopram (Lexapro) became available. Although these drugs quickly supplanted the TCAs as first- and second-line treatments for depression, they did not demonstrate improved efficacy as compared to the TCAs or MAOIs. Common side effects from the SSRIs include dry mouth, gastrointestinal distress, sedation, and sexual dysfunction. Abrupt discontinuation from any of these agents can be unpleasant, with a flulike, highly anxious discontinuation syndrome being linked to paroxetine.

The SSRIs are also considered first-line treatments for obsessive-compulsive disorder, generalized anxiety disorder, panic disorder, post-traumatic stress disorder, and social anxiety, although not all of the SSRIs have an indication from the USFDA for all of these disorders.

Bupropion (Wellbutrin) first became available in 1986 but was quickly withdrawn after reports of seizures were associated with its use. It was reintroduced in 1989, and newer sustained- and extended-release formulations became available in 1996 and 2003. The sustained-release formulation did not have an increased risk of seizures, as compared to the SSRIs, when dosing guidelines were followed. The mechanism of action of bupropion remains unclear, and it is thought to enhance dopamine as well as norepinephrine activity. It offers a dramatically different side effect profile from the SSRIs. Sexual dysfunction is much less frequent with bupropion, as is sedation. Side effects from bupropion include headache and excessive activation. Bupropion has also been shown to be effective in helping cigarette smokers become abstinent and has received a USFDA indication for this purpose. Bupropion is marketed as Zyban for this purpose.

Mirtazapine (Remeron) is a unique compound that is thought to exert its antidepressant effect through stimulation of norepinephrine release as well as antagonism of some subtypes of serotonin receptors. In numerous controlled studies mirtazapine was found to be as efficacious as TCAs and SSRIs in moderate to severe depression (Fawcett & Barkin, 1998). Somnolence and weight gain can be problematic with mirtazapine.

Nefazodone, chemically related to trazodone, is another antidepressant with unique activity. Nefazodone functions primarily as a postsynaptic 5-HT2 antagonist but also has some serotonin and norepinephrine reuptake inhibition. Side effects associated with nefazodone include somnolence and, like trazodone, rare instances of priapism. Nefazodone appears to lack many of the sexual side effects associated with the SSRIs. Nefazodone is no longer commonly prescribed due to an extremely rare risk of hepatic failure associated with this compound.

The newest class of antidepressant is the serotonin-norepinephrine reuptake inhibitor (SNRI). These include venlafaxine (Effexor) and duloxetine (Cymbalta). A meta-analysis of eight controlled studies of more than 2,000 patients treated for depression (Thase, Entsuah, & Rudolph, 2001) concluded that remission rates, as defined by a HAM-D score of 7 or lower, are significantly higher with venlafaxine than with any of the standard SSRIs. Furthermore, this same study reported a significantly shorter time to remission in the venlafaxine group as compared to the SSRI group.

Duloxetine is the second drug in the SNRI class to be approved by the USFDA. Although it would be expected to be more similar to venlafaxine than to the SSRIs, it has neither been available for general use for long enough nor studied sufficiently in comparison to others to draw definitive conclusions.

The therapeutic potential of lithium, which was used in some patent medicines in the nineteenth century, was rediscovered by John Cade, an Australian psychiatrist, in 1949. Lithium became popular in Europe in the 1950s but was not approved by the FDA until 1970. Because lithium is an element, and elements can not be patent-protected, there has been little enthusiasm for continued marketing of lithium.

Lithium appears to affect the neurotransmitters serotonin, dopamine, norepinephrine, acetylcholine, as well as gamma-aminobutyric acid (GABA). Lithium has also been shown to affect intracellular second messengers such as cyclic AMP, phosphoinositide metabolism, and protein kinase C.

Efficacy of lithium for acute mania has been demonstrated in numerous trials dating back to the 1960s. As monotherapy, lithium continues to compare well to valproate and the atypical antipsychotics. Lithium excels in the prophylaxis of affective relapse, primarily in bipolar disorder but perhaps unipolar depression as well.

Lithium has demonstrated efficacy in the prophylaxis of mania. Tondo, Baldessarini, Hennen, and Floris (1998) followed 317 bipolar I and bipolar II patients for an average of 6.3 years and compared mood episode frequency before lithium treatment and after lithium treatment. Fifty percent survival time was extended from a mean of 8 months to a mean of 17 months in the bipolar I patients and from a mean of 8 months before lithium to 100 months after lithium for bipolar II patients. Most of this improvement in survival in bipolar II disorder was in the prophylaxis of depression. Efficacy in mania prophylaxis was again reported recently, lithium being an active comparator, and found in 184 patients randomized to lithium a decrease of 64 percent in risk of relapse into mania (Goodwin et al., 2004). They did not, however, find lithium to be significantly protective of relapse into depression.

This finding was somewhat unexpected because lithium continues to be considered a first-line treatment for bipolar depression by numerous international panels (APA Steering Committee on Practice Guidelines, 2004; Calabrese et al., 2004). Baldessarini, Tondo, Hennen, and Viguera (2002) performed a meta-analysis of lithium and bipolar disorder and pooled 28 studies, encompassing 2,985 patients and 23,263 person-years of data. Data were analyzed using a number of different criteria: only blinded studies, only placebo-controlled studies, and only studies with randomized parallel group design. All of these analyses revealed a decrease of affective relapse of approximately 60 percent to 65 percent, with little difference in the subcategories. Finally, five studies were identified with a minority of patients having bipolar disorder, the majority unipolar depression, and lithium was found to be similarly protective of affective relapse.

Lithium appears to have a significant advantage over valproate in prevention of suicide and reduction of suicide attempts (Goodwin et al., 2003). Data from 20,000 people in a large integrated health care plan in California and Washington were examined. Patients were identified with a diagnosis of bipolar I or II and had received at least one prescription for lithium, valproate, or carbamazepine. After adjusting for numerous independent variables, risk of suicide death was 2.7 times higher during treatment with valproate than with treatment with lithium.

Despite the benefits of lithium, it can be difficult for patients to take doses sufficient to prevent mania, both in the short term and the long term. Side effects of lithium include increased thirst, polyuria (increased production of urine), sedation, mental dulling, acne, psoriasis, hair loss, tremor, gastrointestinal distress, and weight gain. Goiter (an enlarged thyroid gland) and hypothyroidism can also occur due to lithium. Additionally, over time lithium can have a negative impact on kidney function, although the proportion of patients who experience this is moderate, recently estimated to be approximately 20 percent of long-term lithium patients (Lepkifker et al., 2004).

Lithium has a narrow therapeutic index, which means the difference between a therapeutic dose and a toxic dose is small. Lithium blood levels and periodic monitoring of kidney and thyroid function is required in all patients taking lithium.

Lithium also has an abundance of evidence for its efficacy in augmenting antidepressants in treatment-resistant depression and has performed well in placebo-controlled, double-blind conditions (Austin, Souza, & Goodwin, 1991; Heninger, Charney, & Sternberg, 1983). It should be considered strongly as an option for this condition.

ANTICONVULSANTS

Table 30.3 summarizes anticonvulsants commonly used in psychiatry. Valproic acid, or in the enterically coated formulation divalproex (Depakote), is an anticonvulsant approved for absence seizures in 1978 by the USFDA. It has been used to treat mania since the late 1960s in Europe and more recently in the United States and was approved by the USFDA for the treatment of acute mania in 1996. Divalproex is frequently used "off-label" for the prophylaxis of mania, despite lack of data from long-term, placebo-controlled trials demonstrating efficacy for this purpose.

Valproate has extensive data supporting its efficacy in treating acute mania (Bowden et al., 1994), with response rates usually reported to be approximately 50 percent. Evidence for the efficacy of divalproex in mania prophylaxis is less robust. Bowden and colleagues (2000), in a placebo-controlled divalproex/lithium/placebo 52-week maintenance study, found no difference between divalproex or lithium and placebo in the primary outcome time to any mood episode.

Divalproate has long held a reputation as the preferred first-line maintenance drug for rapid-cycling bipolar disorder. However, a double-blind, 20-month randomized parallel group study of lithium and divalproate in people with rapid-cycling bipolar disorder reported comparable time to any mood episode between the two groups (Calabrese et al., 2005).

An additional potential niche for divalproex sodium in bipolar disorder involves those individuals who are additionally dependent on ethanol. A recent study by Salloum et al. (2005) randomized 59 individuals with bipolar I disorder and ethanol dependence to valproate or placebo in a double-blind trial. These patients were maintained openly on their "treatment as usual" pharmacotherapy for bipolar disorder, usually lithium or carbamazepine, and all were continued in psycho-

TABLE 30.3 Anticonvulsants

Agent	Function	Dosing	Comments
Valproate (Depakote)	Acute mania; used for mania prophylaxis with reasonable data for efficacy	20–30 mg/kg in two or three divided doses	Blood levels of 50–125 generally the target; platelets, CBC, liver function to be monitored
Carbamazepine (Tegretol, Equetro)	Acute mania; used for mania prophylaxis with reasonable data for efficacy	Usually 200 mg bid, increased as tolerated to 400 mg or 600 mg bid	Blood levels in the 6–10 range generally the target CBC with platelets and liver function to be monitored
Oxcarbazepine (Trileptal)	Acute mania, mania prophylaxis	Start at 150–300 mg bid, target dose up to 2,100 mg daily	APA second-line agent, data not robust; associated with hyponatremia
Lamotrigine (Lamictal)	Maintenance treatment of bipolar depression; some efficacy for mania	Start at 25 mg daily × 2 weeks, may be doubled q 2 weeks to target of 200 mg po q d. Half-dosing with concomitant valproate, double dosing with concomitant carbamzepine	Benign rash common (10%), severe rash rare (0.1%); valproate inhibits metabolism, carbamazepine induces metabolism
Topiramate (Topamax)	Failed in placebo controlled trials for acute mania	Start with 25 mg q d, increase by 25 mg q week	Used to treat weight gain primarily; data unclear as to efficacy
Gabapentin (Neurontin)	Failed in placebo-controlled trials for mania and depression	Can be as little as 100 tid or as much as 1,200 tid	May have utility targeting anxiety, although failed in placebo-controlled trials for panic disorder, social phobia

social interventions. Those patients assigned valproate had a significant reduction in heavy drinking days, and those compliant with valproate also had significantly lower drinks per heavy drinking day. Because the rate of ethanol abuse in individuals with bipolar I disorder has been estimated to be six to eight times that of the general population (Levin & Hennessy, 2004), interventions that are effective in reducing alcohol abuse in patients being treated for bipolar I disorder may significantly reduce medical and psychiatric morbidity related to ethanol.

Valproate can be difficult to tolerate. Side effects of weight gain, hair loss, and gastrointestinal distress are common. Valproate can suppress bone marrow and irritate the liver, with rare cases of hepatic failure reported. Periodic monitoring of blood counts and liver function is required for all patients maintained on valproate.

Carbamazepine (Tegretol) was first synthesized in the late 1950s in Switzerland. It is structurally similar to imipramine and was formulated to be used to treat depression. Carbamazepine did not prove to be an efficacious antidepressant but was found to be an effective treatment for seizure disorder and was approved by the USFDA for this use in 1974. The mechanism of action either as an anticonvulsant or as an antimanic agent is unknown. Rare but serious effects of carbamazepine include aplastic anemia and agranulocytosis as well as, more frequently, thrombocytopenia. Periodic blood monitoring is required.

Evidence of efficacy for carbamazepine in acute mania and mania prophylaxis continues to accumulate (Weisler et al., 2005), and the USFDA has approved an extended-release formulation of carbamazepine (Equetro) for the treatment of acute mania. In a maintenance study comparing carbamazepine to lithium in patients with bipolar II and bipolar not otherwise specified (NOS) disorders, no difference was found over two years in the rate of rehospitalization, use of concomitant medication, or subsyndromal relapse (Greil & Kleindienst, 1999).

Oxcarbazepine (Trileptal) is structurally very similar to carbamazepine and has been approved by the USFDA as an anticonvulsant. Interest in oxcarbazepine as a treatment for mania has recently reemerged because it appears to have a more favorable adverse effect profile than carbamazepine and is not associated with thrombocytopenia. Electrolyte monitoring is still required because clinically significant hyponatremia (low sodium in the blood) can occur with this agent.

Although the American Psychiatric Association recommends oxcarbazepine as a second-line agent in the treatment of acute mania, equivalent to carbamazepine (APA Steering Committee on Practice Guidelines, 2004), the lack of randomized, blinded data for the utility of oxcarbazepine does not appear to warrant such an endorsement. An open study, using on-off-on design, reports 3 of 12 patients responded within two weeks of starting oxcarbazepine, and 4 were considered responders by the end of the 35-day trial (Hummel et al., 2002). Ghaemi, Berv, Klugman, Rosenquist, and Hsu (2003) performed a chart review of 42 outpatients who received oxcarbazepine either as monotherapy or as an augmenting agent and found roughly half of these patients responded at least moderately, although half of the patients stopped oxcarbazepine due to intolerable side effects.

Oxcarbazepine also was found to have similar efficacy in blinded trials with comparator controls of lithium (n = 52) and valproate (n = 12; Emrich, 1990; Emrich, Dose, & von Derssen, 1985), but these studies lacked placebo controls. The role of oxcarbazepine in the treatment of mania requires additional study.

Lamotrigine (Lamictal) was approved by the USFDA for the treatment of epilepsy in 1994 and for the maintenance treatment of bipolar disorder in 2003. Lamotrigine has fared well in double-blind, placebo-controlled trials for bipolar I depression with 51 percent of patients responding at 200 mg (Calabrese et al., 1999). Recently, a study using pooled data from two studies comparing different doses of lamotrigine to lithium and placebo revealed significant benefit for lamotrigine in the prophylaxis of mania as compared to placebo, although not nearly as robust an effect as was found in the lithium-treated group. Additionally, lamotrigine was clearly superior to placebo and lithium in the prophylaxis of depression (Goodwin et al., 2004).

Lamotrigine is generally well tolerated, with headache, dizziness, diplopia (double vision), nausea, and skin rash being the most common causes for discontinuation. Lamotrigine is labeled with a black box warning of rare but potentially fatal skin reactions including toxic epidermal necrolysis and Stevens-Johnson syndrome, which is estimated to occur at a rate of approximately 0.3 percent (*Physicians' Desk Reference,* 2002). Current recommendations are, in the presence of any rash, to withdraw lamotrigine in an effort to prevent progression to a more severe skin reaction. However, a group of neurologists rechallenged 40 individuals in treatment for epilepsy who had experienced a skin rash associated with lamotrigine at a much lower dose and slower rate of increase. Only 3 of these 40 patients were unable to be titrated to therapeutic levels of lamtrigine due to a recurrence of skin rash (P-Codrea Tigaran, Sidenius, & Dam, 2005).

Gabapentin (Neurontin) was synthesized for the purpose of functioning as a gamma-amino-butyric acid (GABA) analogue, but in practice it appears to exert anticonvulsant actions through a different mechanism (*Physicians' Desk Reference,* 2002). It is approved by the USFDA as an adjunctive treatment for complex partial seizure disorder. In the mid- to late 1990s there was a lot of excitement in psychiatry at the possibility that gabapentin could be effective as an antimanic agent, effective for bipolar depression, or both. Open-label studies and case series reported impressive preliminary results. Unfortunately, the two placebo-controlled trials of gabapentin, one using gabapentin/placebo to augment lithium or valproate (Pande, Crockatt, Janney, Werth, & Tsaroucha, 2000) and the other using lamotrigine/gabapentin/placebo monotherapy in a double-crossover design study (Frye et al., 2000), demonstrated efficacy for gabapentin in mania and depression to be no better than placebo.

Gabapentin does appear to have some anxiolytic properties but has not convincingly outperformed placebo in double-blind studies of social phobia (Pande et al., 1999) or panic disorder (Pande, Pollack, et al., 2000). Gabapentin should not be considered a primary treatment of bipolar disorder.

Topiramate (Topamax) was approved by the USFDA in 1996 as an adjunctive agent in the treatment of partial-onset seizure disorder. Its mechanism of action is believed to involve activity as a sodium channel blocker as well as potentiating GABA (*Physicians' Desk Reference,* 2002). Since it has become available, psychiatrists have been searching for a role for topiramate in the management of bipolar disorder. Open studies have yielded favorable results (Calabrese, Keck, McElroy, & Shelton, 2001; Chengappa et al., 1999), but there is an absence of positive results in more rigorous studies.

Topiramate does have, for some, powerful anorectic properties. A randomized, double-blind, placebo-controlled study of topiramate in a group of obese nonpsychiatric patients yielded impressive results in regard to weight loss (Wilding, Van Gaal, Rissanen, Vercruysse, & Fitchet, 2004). Randomized controlled studies of topiramate, added to zyprexa, targeting weight have also yielded promising results, with patients in the active treatment arm losing 5-plus kilograms in the 10-week study (Nickel et al., 2005).

Currently available data concerning topiramate and bipolar disorder do not support its use as a primary antimanic agent, although it may have some role in ameliorating psychotropic-induced weight gain.

ANXIOLYTICS AND HYPNOTICS

Many antidepressants have USFDA indications for the treatment of anxiety disorders. This section will present non-antidepressant anxiolytics (Table 30.4 summarizes benzodiazepines, nonbenzodiazepine hypnotics, and buspirone).

Chlordiazepoxide (Librium), the first benzodiazepine (BZD), was synthesized in 1959 and represented a dramatic improvement in terms of safety and tolerability in anxiolytics as compared to the pharmacologic agents available at the

TABLE 30.4 Anxiolytics and Hypnotics

Benzodiazepine anxiolytics	Absorption/half-life	Dosing	Comments: BZDs should not be co-administered with azole antifungals (Diflucan) as BZD metabolism is inhibited
Alprazolam (Xanax, 60 other preparations)	Fast/short	0.25–2 mg 3–4× daily	The most prescribed psychotropic drug in the U.S.
Alprazolam XR	Fast/medium-long	0.5–6 mg once daily	Believed to reduce rebound/interdose anxiety
Lorazepam (Ativan, 40 other preparations)	Fast/short	1–3 mg 3× daily	Favored in hospital settings
Chlordiazepoxide (Librium, Librax, 48 other preparations)	Medium/long	5–25 mg 3× daily, up to 300 mg/day in ethanol detoxification	First BZD, good for ethanol detoxification
Clonazepam (Klonopin Rivotril)	Medium/long	0.25–4 mg	Popular high potency, long acting maintenance BZD; also FDA-approved for seizure disorder
Diazepam (Valium, Calmpose, Anxicalm, 50 other preparations)	Fast/long	2–10 mg, 2–4× daily	Long half-life, used in ethanol detoxification, quite reinforcing
Halazepam (Paxipam)	Intermediate/long	20–40 mg 3 or 4× daily	Has active metabolite with long half-life
Prazepam (Centrax, 10 others)	Fast/slow	10 mg 3× daily to 20 mg 3× daily	Active metabolite, oxazepam
Oxazepam (Serax, Tranquo, Anxiolit, Sobril, 59 others)	Intermediate/long	10 mg 3× daily to 30 mg 4× daily	FDA-approved for ethanol withdrawal
Chlorazepate	Fast/long	15–60 mg	Has long half-life metabolites
Midazolam (Versed)	Ultra fast (IV)/short	0.3–0.6 mg/kg	Used IV in anesthesia
Nitrazepam (Insoma, Mogadon, Numbon, Serenade, 40 other preparations)	Fast/long	5–20 mg	24-hour half-life makes for some hangover effect when used as hypnotic
Triazolam (Halcion, Somese)	Fast/short	0.25–0.5 mg	When introduced was dosed too high and associated with psychosis
Temazepam (Restoril)	Fast/short	7.5–30 mg	Popular in the U.S.
Lormetazepam (Loramet, Noctamid, 13 other preparations)	Fast/medium	0.5–2.0 mg	May have less amnestic properties than most BZDs
GABA A/ BZD receptor agonists			
Zolpidem (Ambien)	Fast/short	5–20 mg	Still has rebound anxiety with long-term (4 weeks) use
Zaleplon (Sonata)	Fast/short	5–20 mg	Maybe less physiologic dependence with chronic administration
Zopiclone (Imovane)	Fast/short	3.75–7.5 mg	Not available in the U.S.
Eszopiclone (Lunesta)	Fast/short	1–3 mg	Isomer of zopiclone
Non-benziodiazepine anxiolytic			
Buspirone (Buspar)	N/A	5–15 mg 3× daily	Excellent maintenance medication for GAD

time: meprobamate (Miltown) and the barbiturates. Diazepam (Valium) was introduced in 1963 and became immensely popular, and alprazolam (Xanax) became one of the most frequently written prescriptions in the United States in the 1980s and continues to be the most frequently prescribed psychotropic targeting mood or anxiety in the United States (Stahl, 2002).

Benzodiazepines act as agonists at a GABA-BZD receptor, making chloride ions enter the neuron, resulting in anxiolysis as well as sedation. Some of the BZDs are also effective as anticonvulsants. The basic differences between the various BZDs on the market relate to rapidity of onset of action as well as rapidity of clearance from the body. Short-acting, rapid-onset BZDs such as alprazolam (Xanax) are thought to be more reinforcing for the individual to take as well as more difficult to discontinue following long-term use. Conversely, the longer acting, slower onset BZDs such as chlordiazepoxide (Librium) and clonazepam (Klonopin) appear to be less reinforcing as well as less problematic to discontinue. Efficacy for anxiolysis of each individual agent appears to be similar, assuming comparable dosing.

Although zolpidem (Ambien), zaleplon (Sonata), and zopiclone (Imovane)—the "z drugs," colloquially—technically are not benzodiazepines, they do act as agonists at the GABA-A/Benzodiazepine receptor and have therapeutic and side effects similar to the BZDs. Additionally, they have similar drawbacks, such as physiologic dependence and tolerance to therapeutic effect.

Benzodiazepines have been proven to be efficacious as monotherapy in placebo-controlled trials in the treatment of numerous anxiety disorders, including panic disorder (Tesar et al., 1991), generalized anxiety disorder (Rickels, Downing, Schweizer, & Hassman, 1993), as well as social phobia (Davidson, Ford, Smith, & Potts, 1991), although antidepressants remain first-line agents for maintenance treatment of these disorders. In the 1990s there was an unfortunate perception that alprazolam was a treatment for major depressive disorder. Alprazolam was studied against desipramine in a double-blind study of moderately depressed outpatients and inpatients and found equivalent in reduction of Hamilton Rating Scale for Depression (HAM-D) scores (Remick et al., 1985). It should be noted that the HAM-D has three questions pertaining to insomnia as well as three questions pertaining to anxiety and agitation. If one were to completely resolve a person's insomnia and anxiety and use the HAM-D to rate improvement in "depression," one could detect an improvement of 18 points on the HAM-D, which is a very sizable treatment effect, although none of it specific to the treatment of depression. There appears to be no evidence supporting the use of alprazolam monotherapy for the management of depression.

Debate continues as to the advisability of long-term maintenance treatment of anxiety and sleep disorders with benzodiazepines. Tolerance to the hypnotic or anxiolytic effect, physiologic dependence, cognitive dulling, and increased risk of falls or accidents are all concerns regarding chronic benzodiazepine use.

Rickels, Schweizer, Case, and Greenblatt (1990) examined the effect of discontinuing long-term BZD treatment in 57 patients abruptly and again in 63 patients using a gradual taper (Schweizer, Rickels, Case, & Greenblatt, 1990). These studies are interesting for some incidental findings. Baseline HAM-A (anxiety rating scale) scores were 17.0 and 12.7, respectively; 14 is generally considered a cutoff for clinically significant anxiety, and someone in remission is closer to a 6 or 7, the implication being that these people remained significantly anxious despite maintenance BZD therapy. The second incidental finding in these studies is that for people able to discontinue successfully their BZD, HAM-A scores decreased significantly, as did HAM-D in the gradual-taper study (not reported in the abrupt discontinuation study).

This finding was reproduced nine years later by Rickels, Lucki, Schweizer, Garcia-Espana, and Case (1999), who again tapered BZD from 96 people treated long term with BZDs. Data collected included an analog scale used for patients to report symptoms of mental sedation, physical sedation, tranquilization, as well as HAM-A and HAM-D. HAM-A scores decreased from 11 to 7 in the successful taper group. Mental sedation and physical sedation scores also significantly decreased in the successful taper group, and tranquilization scores increased in those no longer receiving BZD. These differences were less pronounced 12 weeks post taper than 5 weeks post taper.

Tolerance to the hypnotic effect of BZDs, as well as to at least some of the new "z drugs," can also be problematic. A large study of zaleplon (Sonata), an open-label 12-month extension with subsequent taper, revealed some interesting findings (Ancoli-Israel et al., 2005). Total time slept at the end of the 11-month open phase (people on zaleplon) averaged 358 minutes, whereas total time slept after taper (same people, off zaleplon) averaged 351 minutes. Average number of awakenings were also unchanged, 1.56 and 1.53, comparing the end of the treatment phase (on) with the end of the taper phase (off). Time to fall asleep went from 42 minutes to 52 minutes, on average, from treated to untreated. In fact, Britain's Health Technology Assessment issued an executive summary stating that there is not enough evidence of improved safety or efficacy with the "z drugs" as compared to standard BZDs to warrant the additional cost and recommended against including them in the national formulary of covered medication (Dundar et al., 2004).

Physiologic dependence to benzodiazepines, defined as withdrawal symptoms upon discontinuation, is common with BZDs and usually develops within a few weeks of continuous treatment. Shorter half-life agents and higher doses are more likely to be associated with withdrawal than with longer acting agents (Rickels et al., 1990). In Rickels et al.'s (1990) gradual-taper study, reducing at 25 percent in BZD per week, only 60 percent of the patients were able to become benzodiazepine-free (Schweizer et al., 1990). Withdrawal symptoms reported by this study at a rate of 20 percent or more included anxiety, sweating, restlessness, agitation, anorexia, irritability, fatigue, dysphoria, lethargy, light-headed-ness, dizziness, difficulty concentrating, tremor, weakness, insomnia, diarrhea, and headaches.

Zolpidem (Ambien) was found to be no better than temazepam (Restoril) with regard to rebound insomnia following discontinuation after four weeks of treatment in a randomized, double-blind study of 159 patients (Voshaar, van Balkom, & Zitman, 2004). Zolpidem and temazepam users were abruptly discontinued after four weeks of nightly treatment; 50 percent of each group reported significantly worse sleep-onset latency following discontinuation, as compared to prewithdrawal levels, and 25 percent of each group reported a decreased total sleep time, again compared to prewithdrawal levels. Poyares, Guilleminault, Ohayon, and Tufik (2004) performed sleep studies on 25 chronic BZD-hypnotic users before taper immediately after BZD was withdrawn and 15 days after BZD was withdrawn. In the 19 who were able to tolerate being tapered, Poyares et al. (2004) found significant improvement in percentage of slow-wave sleep as well as patients' reported "sleep quality" 15 days after BZD had been removed as compared to when these patients were maintained on their BZD hypnotic.

Cognitive decline has long been a concern with BZD use. Barker, Greenwood, Jackson, and Crowe (2004) performed a meta-analysis of studies of cognition in long-term BZD users and found 13 studies comprising 386 patients. The results, as compared to controls, showed that chronic BZD users were statistically significantly impaired in all domains tested: sensory processing, psychomotor speed, nonverbal memory, visuospacial, speed of processing, attention and concentration, problem solving, verbal memory, general intelligence, motor control/performance, working memory, and verbal reasoning.

Benzodiazepines have also been implicated in increasing the likelihood of a motor vehicle accident. In fact, two of the subjects in the desipramine/alprazolam study for depression (Remick et al., 1985) were involved in such accidents during the acute phase of their study. Neutel (1995) performed a case control study in Canada of 78,000 people recently prescribed a BZD hypnotic, 148,000 people recently started on a BZD anxiolytic, and 98,000 control subjects. Within the first week of the index prescription, the odds ratios of being involved in an accident were 9.1 and 13.5 for hypnotics and anxiolytics, respectively.

The safety of BZDs in the geriatric population remains controversial. Maxwell, Neutel, and Hirdes (1997) in a prospective study in Saskatchewan estimated the relative risk of falls to be 2.8 in elderly patients receiving a new prescription for a BZD hypnotic. In Europe, it is estimated that BZD-related falls in the elderly cost 1.6 billion euros (Panneman, Goettsch, Kramarz, & Herings, 2003).

An alternative to the BZDs is buspirone. Buspirone is chemically unrelated to the BZDs and does not interact at the GABA-BZD receptor. It has affinity for the 5-HT1A receptor, but its mechanism of action is unclear. Buspirone 5–10 mg tid has been shown to be as effective as oxazepam (Strand et al., 1990), and as well as diazepam (Pecknold et al., 1989), in double-blind, randomized, placebo-controlled studies. One drawback of buspirone treatment is that it usually requires two to three weeks to achieve clinical response. The benefits include lack of physiologic dependence and lack of tolerance.

COGNITIVE ENHANCERS I: MEMORY ENHANCERS

Prior to 1993 when the first cholinesterase inhibitor (CEI), tacrine (Cognex), was approved by the USFDA, ergoloid mesylates (Gerinal, Hydergine) were the generally unsatisfactory treatment for cognitive decline in the elderly. Tacrine, although representing an important advance in the pharmacologic treatment of dementia, carried a high side effect burden and did not achieve widespread popularity. Donepezil (Aricept) soon surpassed tacrine due to a markedly more favorable side effect profile and has become the world's most prescribed centrally acting CEI. More recently, two additional CEIs, galantamine (Reminyl) and rivastigmine (Exelon), have become available. Finally, memantine (Namenda, Exiba), an NMDA-receptor antagonist, has been added to the pharmacopoeia of agents with utility as cognitive enhancers (see Table 30.5 for summaries of these agents).

The cholinesterase inhibitors inhibit the breakdown of acetylcholine in the brain, increasing concentrations of this neurotransmitter and enhancing cognition. This reverses to some degree cognitive impairment, as well as delays the progression of cognitive decline, but does not appear to alter underlying pathophysiology. In the case of Alzheimer's disease, the dementia progresses. Lopez et al. (2005), in a cross-sectional longitudinal analysis of people with dementia treated with CEIs compared to matched controls never on CEIs, report both a significantly higher likelihood that those on CEIs will have a slower progression of their dementia and will be less likely to have nursing home placement than those never on a CEI.

All of the cholinesterase inhibitors have been FDA approved for the treatment of Alzheimer's disease, and there is growing evidence, in randomized, placebo-controlled studies, of their efficacy in the treatment of vascular dementia as well (Black et al., 2003). These agents are also being tested in traumatic brain injury, with some suggestion of benefit in preliminary studies (Tenovuo, 2005).

TABLE 30.5 Cholinesterase Inhibitors and Memantine

Name	Class	Starting/target dose	Comments
Tacrine (Cognex)	Cholinesterase inhibitor	10 mg qid/40 mg qid	Basically no longer prescribed due to side effect burden and qid dosing
Donepezil (Aricept)	Cholinesterase inhibitor	5 mg qd/10 mg qd	Demonstrated efficacy alone or coadministered with memantine
Rivastigmine	Cholinesterase inhibitor	1.5 mg bid/6 mg bid	Also inhibits butyrlcholinesterase
Galantamine	Cholinesterase inhibitor	4 mg bid/12 mg bid	Also affects nicotininic receptors
Memantine	NMDA receptor antagonist	10 mg qd/20 mg qd	Indicated for moderate to severe dementia; can be used with donepezil for additional response

Rivastigmine differs from donepezil in that it is an inhibitor of butyryl-cholinesterase in addition to acetylcholinesterase. This additional activity may be of some benefit in more advanced states of Alzheimer's disease. Side effects include nausea, vomiting, and diarrhea, and they tend to be mild.

Galantamine differs from donepezil in that it modulates nicotinic receptor activity in addition to inhibiting acetylcholinesterase. It tends to be less well tolerated than donepezil and rivastigmine. Head-to-head comparisons of the cholinesterase inhibitors have design flaws making it difficult to reach definitive conclusions as to the possible superiority of one over another.

Memantine, an NMDA antagonist, has a number of biochemical effects, including the blockade of glutamate, which is believed to be neuroprotective, and increases levels of brain-derived neurotrophic factor. Memantine has been shown to delay deterioration in moderate to severe dementia. Memantine can add benefit to patients already receiving donepezil, as was demonstrated in a randomized, double-blind, placebo-controlled study, of people with moderate to severe dementia (Tariot et al., 2004). Primary outcome measures, the Severe Impairment Battery (SIB) and the Alzheimer's Disease Cooperative Study Activities of Daily Living Inventory, favored dual treatment, and the differences were statistically significant. Whether these differences are clinically significant has been hotly debated.

In fact, the National Institute for Clinical Excellence (NICE), which reviews prescription medication for the United Kingdom's National Health Service, has recommended that memantine and the cholinesterase inhibitors should no longer be prescribed because of concerns about limited efficacy and an unfavorable cost-effectiveness ratio (Kmietowicz, 2005).

COGNITIVE ENHANCERS II: STIMULANTS AND OTHER ADHD MEDICATIONS

Amphetamine was first used to treat "hyperkinesis" in 1937, and methylphenidate (Ritalin) was approved by the USFDA in 1968 for the treatment of what is now known as attention-deficit/hyperactivity disorder (ADHD). Although ADHD is commonly considered an illness of childhood, significant symptomatology can continue to adulthood.

Two basic molecules, methylphenidate (Ritalin) and amphetamine (Dexedrin, Adderall), make up the first-line treatments for ADHD, both in children and adults. Differences in delivery system with varying pharmacokinetics differentiate the available preparations.

Methylphenidate and amphetamine have superior efficacy for the treatment of ADHD. Side effects from these agents can include anorexia (decreased appetite), irritability, and insomnia. There are wide variations in absorption of these agents with unpredictable clinical response, so dosing needs to be dictated by clinical effects. Methylphenidate has been demonstrated efficacious in the treatment of adult ADHD (Spencer et al., 2005).

Pemoline (Cylert) is an older stimulant with an unknown mechanism of action. It is FDA-approved for the treatment of ADHD and is considered a distant third-line agent due to its association with hepatic failure and death.

Atomoxetine (Strattera) is a norepinephrine reuptake inhibitor that has been demonstrated to be efficacious also in the treatment of ADHD, in both children (Kelsey et al., 2004) and adults (Adler, Spencer, Milton, Moore, & Michelson, 2005). Advantages of atomoxetine include once-daily dosing as well as lower risk of anorexia.

Bupropion has also been demonstrated to be efficacious in the treatment of ADHD (Wilens et al., 2005), although the treatment effect does not rival that of the original stimulants. Advantages of bupropion include the possibility of treating comorbid depression, which is common in people with ADHD.

Modafinil (Provigil) is a recent addition to the class of cognitive enhancers. Its mechanism of action is unclear, but it does alter dopamine neurotransmission, although not as a direct agonist (*Physicians' Desk Reference*, 2005). Preliminary evidence is accumulating as to its efficacy in the treat-

TABLE 30.6 Treatments for ADHD

Stimulant	Category	Dosing	Comments
Methylphenidate (Ritalin)	Amphetamine	10–60 mg (divided into 2 or 3 daily doses)	Ritalin SR actually more just "delayed release"; Ritalin LA preferred
Dextroamphetamine plus amphetamine (Adderall)	Amphetamine	5–60 mg	Adderall XR good delivery system
Methylphenidate HCl (Concerta)	Amphetamine	18–54 mg daily	Once daily dosing
Other medications			
Modafinil	Nonamphetamine stimulant	100–400 mg	Indicated for narcolepsy
Bupropion	Antidepressant	300–450 mg	Less robust response for ADHD than amphetamines
Pemoline (Cylert)	Stimulant, distinct from the amphetamines	37.5–112.5 mg	FDA-approved for ADHD; associated with liver failure

ment of ADHD for children (Rugino & Samsock, 2003) and adults (Turner, Clark, Dowson, Robbins, & Sahakian, 2004). Modafinil may have some abuse liability, at least in non-human primates (*Physicians' Desk Reference,* 2005) (Table 30.6 summarizes treatments for ADHD).

SUMMARY

Despite the advances of the past 20 years, a need remains for improved treatments of all the major psychiatric disorders. Efforts continue to clarify how best to use agents that are currently available. Novel compounds, with novel mechanisms of action, are in development. Ideally, the next 20 years will bring as much advancement as the last 20 so that in the future we may again reflect, "The past 20 years have witnessed many important developments in psychopharmacology."

REFERENCES

Adler, L. A., Spencer, T. J., Milton, D. R., Moore, R. J., & Michelson, D. (2005). Long-term, open-label study of the safety and efficacy of atomoxetine in adults with attention-deficit/hyperactivity disorder: an interim analysis. *Journal of Clinical Psychiatry, 66*(3), 294–299.

Ancoli-Israel, S., Richardson, G. S., Mangano, R. M., Jenkins, L., Hall, P., & Jones, W. S. (2005). Long-term use of sedative hypnotics in older patients with insomnia [Electronic version]. *Sleep Medicine, 6*(2), 107–113.

APA Steering Committee on Practice Guidelines. (2004). *Practice guidelines for the treatment of psychiatric disorders compendium 2004.* Washington, DC: American Psychiatric Association.

Austin, M. P., Souza, F. G., & Goodwin, G. M. (1991). Lithium augmentation in antidepressant-resistant patients: A quantitative analysis. *British Journal of Psychiatry, 159,* 510–514.

Baldessarini, R. J., Tondo, L., Hennen, J., & Viguera, A. C. (2002). Is lithium still worth using? An update of selected recent research. *Harvard Review of Psychiatry, 10*(2), 59–75.

Barker, M. J., Greenwood, K. M., Jackson, M., & Crowe, S. F. (2004). Cognitive effects of long-term benzodiazepine use: A meta-analysis. *CNS Drugs, 18*(1), 37–48.

Black, S., Roman, G. C., Geldmacher, D. S., Salloway, S., Hecker, J., Burns, A., et al. (2003). Efficacy and tolerability of donepezil in vascular dementia: Positive results of a 24-week multicenter, international, randomized placebo-controlled clinical trial. *Stroke: A Journal of Cerebral Circulation, 34,* 2323–2332.

Bowden, C. L., Brugger, A. M., Swann, A. C., Calabrese, J. R., Janicak, P. G., Petty, F., et al. (1994). Efficacy of divalproex vs lithium and placebo in the treatment of mania. *Journal of the American Medical Association, 271*(12), 918–924.

Bowden, C. L., Calabrese, J. R., McElroy, S. L., Gyulai, L., Wassef, A., Petty, F., et al. (2000). A randomized, placebo-controlled 12-month trial of divalproex and lithium in treatment of outpatients with bipolar I disorder. *Archives of General Psychiatry, 57*(5), 481–489.

Bowden, C. L., Grunze, H., Mullen, J., Brecher, M., Paulsson, B., Jones, M., et al. (2005). A randomized, double-blind, placebo-controlled efficacy and safety study of quetiapine or lithium as monotherapy for mania in bipolar disorder. *Journal of Clinical Psychiatry, 66*(1), 111–121.

Calabrese, J. R., Bowden, C. L., Sachs, G. S., Ascher, J. A., Monaghan, E., & Rudd, G. D. (1999). A double-blind placebo-controlled study of lamotrigine monotherapy in outpatients with bipolar I depression. *Journal of Clinical Psychiatry, 60*(2), 79–88.

Calabrese, J. R., Kasper, S., Johnson, G., Tajima, O., Vieta, E., Yatham, L. N., et al. (2004). International Consensus Group on Bipolar I Depression Treatment Guidelines. *Journal of Clinical Psychiatry, 65*(4), 571–579.

Calabrese, J. R., Keck, P. E., Jr., McElroy, S. L., & Shelton, M. D. (2001). A pilot study of topiramate as monotherapy in the treatment of acute mania. *Journal of Clinical Psychopharmacology, 21*(3), 340–342.

Calabrese, J. R., Rapport, D. J., Youngstrom, E. A., Jackson, K., Bilali, S., & Findling, R. L. (2005). New data on the use of lithium, divalproate, and lamotrigine in rapid cycling bipolar disorder. *European Psychiatry, 20*(2), 92–95.

Chengappa, K. N., Rathore, D., Levine, J., Atzert, R., Solai, L., Parepally, H., et al. (1999). Topiramate as add-on treatment for patients with bipolar mania. *Bipolar Disorders, 1*(1), 42–53.

Davidson, J. R., Ford, S. M., Smith, R. D., & Potts, N. L. (1991). Long-term treatment of social phobia with clonazepam. *Journal of Clinical Psychiatry, 52*(Suppl. 11), 16–20.

Dundar, Y., Boland, A., Strobl, J., Dodd, S., Haycox, A., Bagust, A., et al. (2004). Newer hypnotic drugs for the short-term management of insomnia: A systematic review and economic evaluation. *Health Technology Assessment, 8*(24), 1–125

Emrich, H. M. (1990). Studies with oxcarbazepine (Trileptal) in acute mania. *International Clinical Psychopharmacology, 5*(Suppl. 1), 83–88.

Emrich, H. M., Dose, M., & von Derssen, D. (1985). The use of sodium valproate, carbamazepine and oxcarbazepine in patients with affective disorders. *Journal of Affective Disorders, 8*, 243–250.

Fawcett, J., & Barkin, R. L. (1998). Review of the results from clinical studies on the efficacy, safety and tolerability of mirtazapine for the treatment of patients with major depression. *Journal of Affective Disorders, 51*(3), 267–285.

Frye, M. A., Ketter, T. A., Kimbrell, T. A., Dunn, R. T., Speer, A. M., Osuch, E. A., et al. (2000). A placebo-controlled study of lamotrigine and gabapentin monotherapy in refractory mood disorders. *Journal of Clinical Psychopharmacology, 20*(6), 607–614.

Ghaemi, S. N., Berv, D. A., Klugman, J., Rosenquist, K. J., & Hsu, D. J. (2003). Oxcarbazepine treatment of bipolar disorder. *Journal of Clinical Psychiatry, 64*(8), 943–945.

Goodwin, F. K., Fireman, B., Simon, G. E., Hunkeler, E. M., Lee, J., & Revicki, D. (2003). Suicide risk in bipolar disorder during treatment with lithium and divalproex. *Journal of the American Medical Association, 290*(11), 1467–1473.

Goodwin, G. M., Bowden, C. L., Calabrese, J. R., Grunze, H., Kasper, S., White, R., et al. (2004). A pooled analysis of 2 placebo-controlled 18-month trials of lamotrigine and lithium maintenance in bipolar I disorder. *Journal of Clinical Psychiatry, 65*(3), 432–441.

Greil, W., & Kleindienst, N. (1999). Lithium versus carbamazepine in the maintenance treatment of bipolar II disorder and bipolar disorder not otherwise specified. *International Clinical Psychopharmacology, 14*(5), 283–285.

Heninger, G. R., Charney, D. S., & Sternberg, D. E. (1983). Lithium carbonate augmentation of antidepressant treatment: An effective prescription for treatment-refractory depression. *Archives of General Psychiatry, 40*(12), 1335–1342.

Hirschfeld, R. M., Keck, P. E., Jr., Kramer, M., Karcher, K., Canuso, C., Eerdekens, M., et al. (2004). Rapid antimanic effect of risperidone monotherapy: A 3-week multicenter, double-blind, placebo-controlled trial. *American Journal of Psychiatry, 161*(6), 1057–1065.

Hummel, B., Walden, J., Stampfer, R., Dittmann, S., Amann, B., Sterr, A., et al. (2002). Acute antimanic efficacy and safety of oxcarbazepine in an open trial with an on-off-on design. *Bipolar Disorders, 4*(6), 412–417.

Kane, J., Honigfeld, G., Singer, J., & Meltzer, H. (1988). Clozapine for the treatment-resistant schizophrenic: A double-blind comparison with chlorpromazine. *Archives of General Psychiatry, 45*(9), 789–796.

Keck, P. E., Jr., Marcus, R., Tourkodimitris, S., Ali, M., Liebeskind, A., Saha, A., et al. (2003). A placebo-controlled, double-blind study of the efficacy and safety of aripiprazole in patients with acute bipolar mania. *American Journal of Psychiatry, 160*(9), 1651–1658.

Keck, P. E., Jr., Versiani, M., Potkin, S., West, S. A., Giller, E., & Ice, K. (2003). Ziprasidone in the treatment of acute bipolar mania: A three-week, placebo-controlled, double-blind, randomized trial. *American Journal of Psychiatry, 160*(4), 741–748.

Kelsey, D. K., Sumner, C. R., Casat, C. D., Coury, D. L., Quintana, H., Saylor, K. E., et al. (2004). Once-daily atomoxetine treatment for children with attention-deficit/hyperactivity disorder, including an assessment of evening and morning behavior: A double-blind, placebo-controlled trial. *Pediatrics, 114*(1), 1–8.

Kmietowicz, Z. (2005). NICE proposes to withdraw Alzheimer's drugs from NHS. *British Medical Journal, 330*(7490), 495.

Lepkifker, E., Sverdlik, A., Iancu, I., Ziv, R., Segev, S., & Kotler, M. (2004). Renal insufficiency in long-term lithium treatment. *Journal of Clinical Psychiatry, 65*(6), 850–856.

Levin, F. R., & Hennessy, G. (2004). Bipolar disorder and substance abuse. *Biological Psychiatry, 56*(10), 738–748.

Lopez, O. L., Becker, J. T., Saxton, J., Sweet, R. A., Klunk, W., & DeKosky, S. T. (2005). Alteration of a clinically meaningful outcome in the natural history of Alzheimer's disease by cholinesterase inhibition. *Journal of the American Geriatrics Society, 53*(1), 83–87.

Maxwell, C. J., Neutel, C. I., & Hirdes, J. P. (1997). A prospective study of falls after benzodiazepine use: A comparison of new and repeat use. *Pharmacoepidemiology and Drug Safety, 6*(1), 27–35.

Miller, A. L., Hall, C. S., Buchanan, R. W., Buckley, P. F., Chiles, J. A., Conley, R. R., et al. (2003). The Texas Medication Algorithm Project antipsychotic algorithm for schizophrenia: 2003 update. *Journal of Clinical Psychiatry, 65*(4), 500–508.

Neutel, C. I. (1995). Risk of traffic accident injury after a prescription for a benzodiazepine. *Annals of Epidemiology, 5*(3), 239–244.

Nickel, M. K., Nickel, C., Muehlbacher, M., Leiberich, P. K., Kaplan, P., Lahmann, C., et al. (2005). Influence of topiramate on olanzapine-related adiposity in women: A random, double-blind, placebo-controlled study. *Journal of Clinical Psychopharmacology, 25*(3), 211–217.

Pande, A. C., Crockatt, J. G., Janney, C. A., Werth, J. L., & Tsaroucha, G. (2000). Gabapentin in bipolar disorder: A placebo-controlled trial of adjunctive therapy. *Bipolar Disorders, 2*(3, Pt. 2), 249–255.

Pande, A. C., Davidson, J. R., Jefferson, J. W., Janney, C. A., Katzelnick, D. J., Weisler, R. H., et al. (1999). Treatment of social phobia with gabapentin: A placebo-controlled study. *Journal of Clinical Psychopharmacology, 19*(4), 341–348.

Pande, A. C., Pollack, M. H., Crockatt, J., Greiner, M., Chouinard, G., Lydiard, R. B., et al. (2000). Placebo-controlled study of gabapentin treatment of panic disorder. *Journal of Clinical Psychopharmacology, 20*(4), 467–471.

Panneman, M. J., Goettsch, W. G., Kramarz, P., & Herings, R. M. (2003). The costs of benzodiazepine-associated hospital-treated fall injuries in the EU: A pharmo study. *Drugs & Aging, 20*(11), 833–839.

P-Codrea Tigaran, S., Sidenius, P., & Dam, M. (2005). Lamotrigine-induced rash—Worth a rechallenge. *Acta Neurologica Scandinavica, 111*(3), 191–194.

Pecknold, J. C., Matas, M., Howarth, B. G., Ross, C., Swinson, R., Vezeau, C., et al. (1989). Evaluation of buspirone as an antianxiety agent: Buspirone and diazepam versus placebo. *Canadian Journal of Psychiatry, 34*(8), 766–771.

Physicians' Desk Reference (56th ed.). (2002). Montvale, NJ: Medical Economics.

Physicians' Desk Reference (59th ed.). (2005). Montvale, NJ: Thompson PDR.

Poyares, D., Guilleminault, C., Ohayon, M. M., & Tufik, S. (2004). Chronic benzodiazepine usage and withdrawal in insomnia patients. *Journal of Psychiatric Research, 38*(3), 327–334.

Remick, R. A., Fleming, J. A., Buchanan, R. A., Keller, F. D., Hamilton, P., Loomer, F., et al. (1985). A comparison of the safety and efficacy of alprazolam and desipramine in moderately severe depression. *Canadian Journal of Psychiatry, 30*(8), 597–601.

Rickels, K., Downing, R., Schweizer, E., & Hassman, H. (1993). Antidepressants for the treatment of generalized anxiety disorder: A placebo-controlled comparison of imipramine, trazodone, and diazepam. *Archives of General Psychiatry, 50*(11), 884–895.

Rickels, K., Lucki, I., Schweizer, E., Garcia-Espana, F., & Case, W. G. (1999). Psychomotor performance of long-term benzodiazepine users before, during, and after benzodiazepine discontinuation. *Journal of Clinical Psychopharmacology, 19*(2), 107–113.

Rickels, K., Schweizer, E., Case, W. G., & Greenblatt, D. J. (1990). Long-term therapeutic use of benzodiazepines: I. Effects of abrupt discontinuation. *Archives of General Psychiatry, 47*(10), 899–907.

Rugino, T. A., & Samsock, T. C. (2003). Modafinil in children with attention-deficit hyperactivity disorder. *Pediatric Neurology, 29*(2), 136–142.

Salloum, I. M., Cornelius, J. R., Daley, D. C., Kirisci, L., Himmelhoch, J. M., & Thase, M. E. (2005). Efficacy of valproate maintenance in patients with bipolar disorder and alcoholism: A double-blind placebo-controlled study. *Archives of General Psychiatry, 62*(1), 37–45.

Schweizer, E., Rickels, K., Case, W. G., & Greenblatt, D. J. (1990). Long-term therapeutic use of benzodiazepines: II. Effects of gradual taper. *Archives of General Psychiatry, 47*(10), 908–915.

Spencer, T., Biederman, J., Wilens, T., Doyle, R., Surman, C., Prince, J., et al. (2005). A large, double-blind, randomized clinical trial of methylphenidate in the treatment of adults with attention-deficit/hyperactivity disorder. *Biological Psychiatry, 57*(5), 456–463.

Stahl, S. M. (2002). Don't ask, don't tell, but benzodiazepines are still the leading treatments for anxiety disorder. *Journal of Clinical Psychiatry, 63*(9), 756–757.

Stahl, S. M., & Shayegan, D. K. (2003). The psychopharmacology of ziprasidone: Receptor-binding properties and real-world psychiatric practice. *Journal of Clinical Psychiatry, 64*(Suppl. 19), 6–12.

Strand, M., Hetta, J., Rosen, A., Sorensen, S., Malmstrom, R., Fabian, C., et al. (1990). A double-blind, controlled trial in primary care patients with generalized anxiety: A comparison between buspirone and oxazepam. *Journal of Clinical Psychiatry, 51*(Suppl.), 40–45.

Tariot, P. N., Farlow, M. R., Grossberg, G. T., Graham, S. M., McDonald, S., & Gergel, I. (2004). Memantine treatment in patients with moderate to severe Alzheimer disease already receiving donepezil: A randomized controlled trial. *Journal of the American Medical Association, 291*(3), 317–324.

Tenovuo, O. (2005). Central acetylcholinesterase inhibitors in the treatment of chronic traumatic brain injury: Clinical experience in 111 patients. *Progress in Neuropsychopharmacology and Biological Psychiatry, 29,* 61–67.

Tesar, G. E., Rosenbaum, J. F., Pollack, M. H., Otto, M. W., Sachs, G. S., Herman, J. B., et al. (1991). Double-blind, placebo-controlled comparison of clonazepam and alprazolam for panic disorder. *Journal of Clinical Psychiatry, 52*(2), 69–76.

Thase, M. E., Entsuah, A. R., & Rudolph, R. L. (2001). Remission rates during treatment with venlafaxine or selective serotonin reuptake inhibitors. *British Journal of Psychiatry, 178,* 234–241.

Tohen, M., Jacobs, T. G., Grundy, S. L., McElroy, S. L., Banov, M. C., Janicak, P. G., et al. (2000). Efficacy of olanzapine in acute bipolar mania: A double-blind, placebo-controlled study. *Archives of General Psychiatry, 57*(9), 841–849.

Tohen, M., Ketter, T. A., Zarate, C. A., Suppes, T., Frye, M., Altshuler, L., et al. (2003). Olanzapine versus divalproex sodium for the treatment of acute mania and maintenance of remission: A 47-week study. *American Journal of Psychiatry, 160*(7), 1263–1271.

Tollefson, G. D., & Sanger, T. M. (1997). Negative symptoms: A path analytic approach to a double-blind, placebo- and haloperidol-controlled clinical trial with olanzapine. *American Journal of Psychiatry, 154*(4), 466–474.

Tondo, L., Baldessarini, R. J., Hennen, J., & Floris, G. (1998). Lithium maintenance treatment of depression and mania in bipolar I and bipolar II disorders. *American Journal of Psychiatry, 155*(5), 638–645.

Turner, D. C., Clark, L., Dowson, J., Robbins, T. W., & Sahakian, B. J. (2004). Modafinil improves cognition and response inhibition in adult attention-deficit/hyperactivity disorder. *Biological Psychiatry, 55*(10), 1031–1040.

Voshaar, R. C., van Balkom, A. J., & Zitman, F. G. (2004). Zolpidem is not superior to temazepam with respect to rebound insomnia: A controlled study. *European Neuropsychopharmacology, 14*(4), 301–306.

Weisler, R. H., Keck, P. E., Jr., Swann, A. C., Cutler, A. J., Ketter, T. A., & Kalali, A. H. (2005). Extended-release carbamazepine capsules as monotherapy for acute mania in bipolar disorder: A multicenter, randomized, double-blind, placebo-controlled trial. *Journal of Clinical Psychiatry, 66*(3), 323–330.

Wilding, J., Van Gaal, L., Rissanen, A., Vercruysse, F., & Fitchet, M. (2004). A randomized double-blind placebo-controlled study of the long-term efficacy and safety of topiramate in the treatment of obese subjects. *International Journal of Obesity and Related Metabolic Disorders, 28*(11), 1399–1410.

Wilens, T. E., Haight, B. R., Horrigan, J. P., Hudziak, J. J., Rosenthal, N. E., Connor, D. F., et al. (2005). Bupropion XL in adults with attention-deficit/hyperactivity disorder: A randomized, placebo-controlled study. *Biological Psychiatry, 57*(7), 793–801.

Author Index

Abbott, P. J., 365
Abe, J. S., 71, 80
Abe-Kim, J., 75, 80
Abel, G. G., 436–437, 441–443
Abel, J. L., 102–104, 108, 111
Abene, M. V., 163
Abraham, K., 319–320, 427
Abrahamowicz, M., 282
Abramowitz, J. S., 169, 177–180
Abrams, D. B., 492
Abrams, K. Y., 233, 343
Abrams, R. C., 321, 323
Abramson, L. Y., 45, 212, 235, 249
Acierno, R., 360
Acitelli, L. K., 451
Ackerman, S. J., 399, 478–479
Acklin, M. W., 474
Adair, R., 75
Adamis, D., 285
Adams, C., 267
Adams, G. J., 340
Addis, M. E., 235, 488, 499
Adèr, H., 196
Ader, R., 37
Ades, J., 338, 374
Adler, C. S., 410
Adler, D. A., 320
Adler, L. A., 514
Adler, S. M., 410
Adolfsson, R., 54
Aggarwal, A. K., 69
Aggen, S. H., 211
Aghajanian, G. K., 193
Agosti, V., 232
Agostini, J. V., 285
Agras, W. S., 390, 392, 395–399, 493
Agrawal, H. R., 304
Agresta, J., 268
Ahlner, J., 221
Ahmad, S., 142
Ahmend, I., 281, 290
Akanda, M., 377
Akande, A., 155
Akiskal, H. S., 214, 232, 234, 318
Albanese, M., 246
Albano, A. M., 102
Alcaine, O., 106
Alden, L. E., 75, 104, 326
Alderson, A. L., 281
Alegria, M., 75
Alexander, J., 324
Alexander, R. C., 383
Alford, B. A., 253, 488
Allan, T., 108
Allcock, C., 376
Allen, B. A., 344
Allen, G. J., 163
Allen, J. J., 174, 175
Allen, N. B., 90
Allik, J., 392
Allison, S., 374
Allmoon, D., 499
Alloy, L. B., 45, 235, 248
Allsworth, J., 130
Alm, T., 162
Almagor, M., 425
Almeida, O., 265
Alnaes, R., 237

Alper, G., 309
Alpert, A., 31
Al-Sadir, J., 122
Altaffer, F., 270
Altemus, M., 391
Alterman, I. S., 172
Althof, S. E., 429–430, 432–433
Altman, B., 191
Alvidrez, J., 72
Alvir, J. M. J., 267
Amador, X., 266
Amato, P. R., 452–455, 460
American Psychiatric Association, 4–5,
  27, 108–109, 121, 138, 154, 169,
  189–190, 207–209, 213, 218, 221–223,
  231, 244–245, 250, 252, 262, 265, 279,
  309, 318, 337, 354, 370, 389–390, 396,
  409, 423, 436, 491, 509
Ameringen, M., 148
Ames, D., 284
Ames, S. L., 356–358
Amick-McMullan, A., 190
Amir, N., 47, 139, 142, 172, 174
Amsterdam, J., 252
Anand, R., 286
Ananth, J., 174
Ancoli-Israel, S., 515
Anda, R. F., 281
Andberg, M. M., 5
Andenberg, U. M., 140
Anderluh, M., 391
Andersen, A., 392
Andersen, S. M., 480
Anderson, B. P., 214
Anderson, C. A., 40
Anderson, D. A., 395–396
Anderson, D. J., 105, 107
Anderson, E. M., 478
Anderson, G., 376
Anderson, I. M., 221
Anderson, J. C., 107
Anderson, K., 391
Anderson, P. L., 162
Anderson, R. W., 410
Anderson, W. P., 43
Andrasik, F., 409, 411–418
Andrea, H., 159
Andreasen, N. C., 12, 94, 266
Andreski, P., 175, 189
Andrews, B., 190–191, 195
Andrews, D. A., 442–443, 445
Andrews, G., 121, 141, 171, 173, 175,
  177, 326
Andrews, J., 318
Andrews, J. A., 393
Andrews, V. H., 101, 103, 110
Angst, J., 410, 428
Annas, P., 154
Annis, H. M., 362, 493
Ansermet, F., 264
Anthony, J., 374
Anthony, W. A., 249, 268
Antonucci, T. C., 451
Antony, M. M., 123, 154–157, 159–163,
  172, 490
Aos, S., 444
APA Steering Committee on Practice
  Guidelines, 508–509

Apodaca, T. R., 347
Applewhaite, G., 267
Appley, L., 271
Arana, G., 12
Arango, C., 289
Araujo, A. B., 181, 428
Arbaretaz, M., 374
Arcus, D., 104, 122
Arena, J. G., 415
Armenian, H. K., 122
Armentano, C., 382
Armor, D. J., 318
Armstrong, H. E., 499
Arndt, S., 393
Arnold, S. E., 280, 286
Arnon, I., 190
Arnow, B. A., 398
Aro, H., 263
Aro, S., 263
Arria, A., 374
Arriaga, X. B., 452
Arrindell, W. A., 129, 157, 159
Arseneault, L., 373
Ashby, D., 221
Asher, R. H., 126
Ashikaga, T., 265
Asmundson, G. J., 64, 123, 142
Asnis, L., 321
Astin, M. C., 198
Atchison, M., 193
Atkinson, L., 159
Atmaca, M., 304
Atwood, G. E., 474
Aubuchon, P. G., 320
Audenaert, K., 391–392
Auerbach, J. S., 324
Aufdembrinke, B., 112
Austin, M. P., 508
Avenevoli, S., 11
Awad, A. G., 267
Awad, G. A., 438
Ayllon, T., 105
Azim, H. F., 479, 481
Azrin, N. H., 337, 345, 347–348,
  357–360, 362, 364, 383

Bach-y-rita, G., 378
Backman, J. G., 380
Backman, L., 284
Backs-Dermott, B. J., 487
Bacoworowski, A., 47
Badger, A. J., 364
Badger, G. T., 364
Baeckman, L., 287
Baer, C. L., 361
Baer, L., 172, 175, 180–181, 320, 327
Baer, P. E., 279
Bagby, R. M., 233
Bagge, C., 305, 308–309
Baggoley, C., 285
Bagley, D. H., 430
Bailer, U., 397
Bailey, G. R., 328
Bailey, M., 29
Bain, J., 440
Bair, M. J., 211

Baird, A. D., 90
Baity, M. R., 399
Baker, A., 289, 363
Baker, F., 221, 239
Baker, I., 389
Baker, L., 289
Baker, R. W., 251
Baker, S. L., 144
Baker, T. B., 21
Bakker, C., 91
Baldacci, H. B., 40
Baldessarini, R. J., 12, 508
Baldeweg, T., 284
Ball, C., 285
Balla, J. R., 24
Ballenger, J. C., 112, 129, 247
Balon, R., 163
Balslev-Olesen, T., 176
Baltazar, P. L., 122
Bancroft, J., 426, 430
Bandura, A., 39, 103, 105
Banon, E., 326
Barasch, A., 318
Barbaree, H. E., 438, 440, 442–443
Barber, J. P., 212, 326, 478
Barker, L., 37–39
Barker, M. J., 513
Barker, S. E., 409
Barlow, D. H., 27, 101–105, 107–111,
  121, 123, 125, 127, 129–130, 144,
  154–155, 159–161, 163, 427, 490–491
Barnes, G. M., 376
Barnes, T. R. E., 262
Barnoski, R., 444
Baron, M., 321
Baronet, A. M., 268
Barraclough, B., 218, 285
Barraclough, C., 262
Barraclough, J., 280, 285
Barratt, E. S., 391
Barregard, L., 287
Barrowclough, C., 267
Barry, R., 192
Bartel, R., 246
Bartels, S. J., 262
Barth, J. T., 94
Bartholomew, K., 237
Bartko, J. J., 74
Barton, K. A., 194
Basco, M. R., 219
Basoglu, M., 68, 125, 181, 190
Basson, R., 427, 432, 433
Basten, C., 198
Bastiani, A., 391
Bateman, A., 309–310, 327
Battaglia, M., 104, 122
Baucom, D. H., 452, 455, 460
Bauer, J., 397
Bauer, M. S., 247, 249, 252, 256
Baum, A., 480
Baum, K. M., 263
Baumann, B. D., 482
Baumeister, R. F., 47, 436, 439, 445
Baumgard, C. H., 323
Baumgardner, J., 40
Baxter, L. R., 86
Bayle, F. J., 374
Bayon, C., 211

519

Bazargan, M., 377
Bazargan, S., 377
Beardslee, W. R. G., 41
Bearman, S. K., 393
Beattie, A. D., 87
Beaulieu, J., 193
Bebbington, P. E., 67, 236, 280, 495
Bech, P., 249
Beck, A. T., 5, 8, 11, 44–47, 102–103, 107, 122, 125, 219–220, 235–236, 238, 240, 246, 253, 487, 488, 489, 492, 495–499
Beck, J. C., 74
Beck, J. G., 146
Beck, J. S., 248, 495–497
Becker, C. B., 175, 390
Becker, D. F., 7, 305, 318–319, 323
Becker, D. R., 90, 142, 212, 268–269, 271
Becker, J. T., 235
Becker, J. V., 438, 441
Becona, E., 373
Bedoya, D., 246
Beebe, K. L., 197
Beech, A. R., 443
Beech, H. R., 172
Beekman, A. T. F., 235
Beglin, S. J., 396
Behan, P. O., 5
Behar, E. S., 106
Beidel, D. C., 103, 139–140, 145
Beilke, R. L., 424
Beiser, M., 270
Beites, F. J., 371, 376
Belisle, M., 326
Bell, B., 125, 237
Bell, S. E., 323
Bellack, A. S., 262, 265, 268–270, 325, 358
Bellodi, L., 104
Bell-Pringle, V. J., 308
Belluardo, P., 221
Beloch, E., 146–147
Bemporad, J., 301
Bender, D., 316
Bender, D. S., 287, 302
Bendtsen, L., 417
Benjamin, J., 163
Benjamin, L., 324
Benkelfat, Jr., C., 125
Bennett, D. A., 280
Bennett, M. B., 270
Bennett, T., 291
Ben-Noun, L., 104, 110
Benson, D., 292
Bentall, R. P., 269–270, 496
Bentler, P. M., 23–24
Ben-Tovim, D., 392
Ben-Yishay, Y., 290
Ben-Zion, I. Z., 163
Berah, E. F., 194
Berchick, R. J., 235
Berg, E. A., 266
Berg, J. L., 325
Berg, J. M., 282
Berg, S., 280
Bergen, H. A., 374
Berger, K., 286
Berger, M., 250, 417
Berger, P. A., 139
Bergh, C., 373
Berglund, P., 6, 107, 123
Bergman, A. J., 317
Bergman, B., 373
Berkey, C. S., 394
Berlin, B., 3, 15
Berliner, L., 444
Berman, J. A., 211
Berman, J. J., 77
Berman, M., 326
Berndt, E. R., 220

Bernstein, D. P., 317–318, 323, 326
Bernstein, S. E., 173, 186
Berry, J. W., 68, 75–78
Berry, Z., 291
Bertelsen, A., 247
Berwick, D. M., 12
Besag, F. M. C., 221
Best, C. L., 64
Best, D., 362
Best, S. R., 190
Betancourt, H., 72
Betz, F., 103, 122
Beumont, P., 391
Beutler, L. E., 72, 478
Bezeau, S. C., 290
Bhate, S. R., 438
Bhatia, T., 269
Bhaumik, D. K., 221
Bian, X., 284
Bickel, K., 130
Biederman, J., 122, 140, 158, 212
Bien, T. H., 347
Bienias, J. L., 280
Bierer, L. M., 196
Biever, J. L., 138
Bigal, M. E., 417
Biggs, J. T., 249
Bille, B., 411–412
Billings, A. G., 78
Binder, J. L., 103
Binder-Brynes, K., 196
Binik, Y. M., 424
Birchall, H. M., 156
Birchler, G. R., 363–365
Birchwood, M., 267, 271, 495–496
Birmingham, C. L., 393
Bischoff, R. J., 340
Bishop, E., 392
Bizeul, C., 399
Black, D. W., 104, 173, 176, 310, 320, 323, 371
Black, F., 286–287
Black, M. J., 470
Black, S., 5
Blacker, D., 122
Blagys, M., 399
Blagys, M. D., 478
Blake, D. D., 195
Blake Woodside, D., 400
Blanchard, E. B., 107–108, 190, 193–194, 198, 417
Blanchard, J. J., 358
Blanchard, R., 439, 444
Blanco, C., 148, 376
Bland, R., 326
Blanton, P. D., 283
Blashfield, R. K., 3, 6, 103
Blaszczynski, A., 106, 370–371, 373, 376, 382–383
Blatt, S. J., 324–325, 471, 482
Blau, J. N., 416
Blazer, D. G., 104, 107, 143, 212
Blehar, M. C., 231
Blendell, K. A., 147
Bleuler, E., 317
Blincoe, L., 346
Blizard, R., 321
Block, F., 291
Blomberg, J., 478
Blouin, J. L., 54
Blount, P. J., 292
Blum, N., 173, 307, 310, 320, 324, 371
Blum, T. C., 346
Blume, S. B., 380
Blumer, D., 440
Boczkowski, J., 270
Bodden, D., 160
Bodenhammer, E., 291
Bodkin, A., 324
Bodlund, O., 320, 326
Boer, D. P., 443

Boerstler, H., 326
Bogdanova, D., 412
Bogert, K. V. A., 492
Bogetto, F., 311
Boggs, T. G., 363
Bogod, N. M., 290
Bohus, B., 193
Bohus, M., 309
Boiman, E. E., 244
Boisvert, J. M., 381–382
Boland, R. J., 208, 217–218, 245
Bolger, N., 25
Bollen, K. A., 22–23
Bolte, M. C., 159
Bolton, E., 262, 270
Bolwig, T. G., 249
Bond, G. R., 265, 270, 271
Bond, M. H., 77, 285, 479
Bongar, B., 48, 326
Bonta, J., 442–443, 445
Bonte, F. J., 125
Book, S. W., 196
Booker, K., 72
Bookish, R. L., 288
Boomsma, D. I., 55
Boone, E., 215
Booth, A., 454
Borchardt, C., 343
Borden, J. W., 103, 139
Borges, A., 190
Borgis, K. J., 278
Borkovec, M., 111
Borkovec, T. D., 26, 101–104, 106–112, 491
Borod, J. C., 92
Borus, J. F., 12
Borzi, M. G., 147
Boscarino, J. A., 191, 194–195
Boshuisen, M. L., 125
Bossert, S., 399
Bostwick, J. M., 218
Boswell, P., 327
Bouchard, G., 453
Bouchard, S., 162
Bouchard, T. J., Jr., 57
Boudreault, N., 373
Boulougouris, J. C., 171
Bouton, M. E., 125, 127
Bowden, C. L., 248, 251, 411, 505, 508
Bowers, M. B., Jr., 251
Bowers, W., 392
Bowlby, J., 105, 470
Boyd, J. L., 267, 271
Boydell, J., 263
Boyer, R., 104
Boyle, P., 289
Bradbury, T. N., 450–451, 453–456, 458, 461–462
Bradford, J., 446
Bradley, B. P., 103
Bradley, S., 122
Brady, K. T., 197, 246, 359
Brailey, K., 190
Bramsen, I., 191, 196
Branas, C. C., 346
Brandes, D., 190
Brandon, E., 12
Brandt, J., 281, 287, 289
Braun, D., 391–392
Braveman, S., 308
Brawman-Mintzer, O., 103, 107–108, 129
Bray, J. H., 340
Brayley, J., 285
Brayne, C., 282
Breedlove, D. E., 3, 15
Breen, H., 376
Breen, L. J., 41
Breier, A., 265
Breiter, H. C., 172
Breitholtz, E., 46, 103

Bremner, J. D., 189, 191, 194
Brendgen, M., 376
Brennan, P. A., 220
Brenner, C., 469, 471–474
Brenner, H., 389, 393, 397–400
Brent, D. A., 221
Breslau, N., 175, 189, 192, 411
Breslow, N., 437
Bressi, C., 176
Broatch, J., 176
Breuer, P., 490
Brewerton, T., 392
Brewin, C. R., 190–191, 195
Brieger, P., 246
Briere, J., 439
Bright, J. A., 247
Bright, P., 128
Brigidi, B., 47
Britton, P., 291
Broatch, J., 176
Brodsky, B., 193, 325
Brody, A. L., 86, 92
Brody, D., 234
Brody, G. H., 455, 460
Brody, M. L., 390
Bromet, E., 6, 192
Brook, J. S., 9, 40, 323, 393, 395
Brooks, G. W., 265
Brooks, R. B., 122
Brorsson, B., 289
Brosschot, J. F., 159
Brothers, A. J., 157
Broughton, D., 424
Brouwer, W., 287
Brower, K. J., 241
Brown, D. R., 155
Brown, G., 90, 235, 247, 497
Brown, G. K., 219
Brown, G. W., 214
Brown, H. D., 172
Brown, I. F., 376
Brown, J. M., 75, 345
Brown, L. L., 44, 489
Brown, M., 123
Brown, M. T., 72, 123
Brown, M. Z., 306
Brown, R. A., 344
Brown, R. C., 308
Brown, R. I. F., 382
Brown, R. L., 376
Brown, S. A., 341, 355
Brown, T., 87
Brown, T. A., 9, 21, 26–27, 30–31, 101, 103–105, 107–111, 121, 123, 127, 139, 144, 154–160, 175, 491
Brown, V., 41
Browne, G., 234, 238, 240
Brownell, K. D., 41
Brownmiller, S., 436, 440
Bruce, M. L., 234, 263, 458
Bruce, S. E., 107–108, 126
Bruce, T. J., 130
Bruce-Jones, W., 247
Bruch, H., 397
Bruch, M. A., 139, 147
Brugha, T. S., 236
Brunette, M. F., 266, 270–271
Bruno, R., 246
Bryant, B., 198
Bryant, R. A., 189–198
Bryntwick, S., 174
Buchanan, A., 265–266
Buckley, T. C., 194
Buddeberg, C., 190
Budney, A. J., 492
Bujold, A., 382
Buka, S. L., 74
Bukstein, O., 342, 359
Bulik, C., 392, 394, 399
Bullock, R., 92
Bullough, B., 437, 439
Bullough, V. L., 437, 439

Bumpass, L. L., 453–454
Bundrick, C. M., 413
Bunting, B., 345
Burge, D., 453
Burk, L. R., 441
Burke, J. D., 14, 16
Burke, K. C., 14, 16
Burke, W. J., 221, 377
Burkhardt, P. E., 323
Burkhart, B. R., 439, 441
Burman, B., 458, 460
Burman, M. A., 171, 232, 441, 444
Burnett, J. W., 43
Burns, C. D., 390
Burns, D., 327
Burr, R., 301, 305
Burrell, R. D., 147
Burright, R. G., 282
Burt, D., 287
Burton, E. M., 395–396
Busch, C. M., 453
Bush, B. A., 281
Bushman, B., 47
Bushnell, W. D., 178
Butcher, J. N., 324
Butera, F., 214
Butler, F. K., 125
Butler, G., 101–102
Butler, J. L., 436, 439, 445
Butler, S. F., 479
Butler, S. M., 438
Butterman, J., 157
Butzlaff, R. L., 265–267
Buunk, B., 451
Buunk, B. P., 452
Bux, D. A., Jr., 179
Byrne, B. M., 30

Cachelin, F., 392
Caci, H., 374
Cacioppo, J. T., 464
Caddell, J. M., 198
Cadoret, R. J., 322, 460
Caetano, R., 339
Cahill, L., 193, 197
Cahn, D., 289
Calabrese, J. R., 251, 508, 510
Caldwell, F., 96
Caleo, S., 309
Calev, A., 378
Calvocoressi, L., 176
Camargo, C. A., 394
Cameron, R., 395
Camp, P., 232
Campbell, D. T., 27, 29
Campbell, J. K., 418
Campbell, L. A., 9, 107–108, 127, 139, 144, 154, 175
Campbell-Sills, L., 21
Campsie, R. L., 383
Canales, G., 71
Cancienne, J., 193
Candilis, P. J., 129
Canetti, L., 190
Canino, G. J., 10
Cannon, T. D., 264
Cano, A., 458
Cantor, N., 3, 15
Canupp, K., 281
Caplan, P. J., 10
Capodanno, D. J., 338
Capreol, M., 326
Caputo, G. C., 128
Capuzzo, N., 110
Cara, M., 10
Caraveo-Poortinga, Y. H., 69, 75
Carbonell, C., 281
Cardeña, E., 194, 196
Cardno, A., 264
Carey, G., 159
Carey, R., 327

Carle, A. C., 340
Carlisle, J. M., 440
Carlson, G. A., 249, 292
Carmelli, D., 210
Carnagey, N. L., 40
Carney, M., 193
Carpenter, B. A., 236
Carpenter, D., 177, 250
Carpenter, W. T., 74
Carr, A. T., 171
Carrasco, J., 391
Carrig, H., 382
Carroll, B. J., 12
Carroll, D. W., 237
Carroll, J. L., 430, 433
Carroll, K. M., 348, 365
Carson, R. C., 10
Carter, F., 392, 399
Carter, J., 400
Carter, K., 46
Carter, R. M., 110
Carter, W. R., 106
Cartwright-Hatton, S., 110
Cascardi, M., 451
Case, W. G., 512
Casey, P. R., 321, 396
Casey, T., 196
Cashman, L., 195
Cashman-McGrath, L., 144
Casper, R., 391
Caspi, A., 61, 122, 215–216, 356, 453–454
Cassiday, K. L., 192
Cassidy, F., 12
Cassidy, J. A., 106
Cassuto, N., 373
Castle, D. J., 263
Castonguay, L. G., 110–112
Catchment Area study, 6, 10, 104, 107, 110, 155, 234, 444
Cate, T., 252
Cattarin, J. A., 394
Catts, S. V., 95
Cauce, A. M., 338
Cavanagh, K., 160
Cawson, D. A., 21
Cedarbaum, J. M., 193
Cercone-Keeney, J., 455
Cernak, I., 284
Cerreto, M., 452
Chadwick, P., 495–496
Chaffin, M., 438
Chakrabati, S., 249
Chambless, D. L., 122, 125, 128–129, 173, 176, 238, 325, 327, 487, 492–493, 499
Champagne, D., 193
Chandra, V., 282
Chapman, A. L., 309
Chapman, D. P., 233, 281
Charney, D. S., 189, 193, 508
Chartier, M., 157
Chartier, M. J., 54
Chase, G., 289
Chassin, L., 340
Chatterjee, S., 140
Chauncey, D. L., 307, 319
Chavaria, F. R., 338
Chavira, D. A., 139–140, 142, 301
Chavoya, G. A., 191
Chee, M., 458
Chelminski, I., 233
Chen, N., 269
Chen, R., 12
Chen, Y. P., 249, 283, 374
Cheng, S. K., 43
Chernoff-Clementz, E., 373
Cheslow, D. L., 171
Chester, J. A., 338
Chestnut, R., 291
Cheung, F. M. C., 80

Chevron, E. S., 220, 238, 255, 471
Chiaravalloti, N., 292
Chiesa, M., 309
Chilcoat, H. D., 189
Childress, A. R., 96, 348
Chin, D., 67, 74, 76
Chittams, J., 326, 478
Chiu, W. T., 212
Cho, Y., 123
Chochinov, H. M., 285
Chodoff, P., 211, 318
Chojnowska, E., 411
Chor, P., 253
Chorpita, B. F., 102, 105, 109–110
Chou, S. P., 211
Choure, J., 282
Christ, M. A., 103
Christensen, A., 450–451, 458–460
Christenson, G. A., 371, 373, 375, 377, 380
Christian, J., 479
Chronicle, E., 417
Chui, H., 287
Chung, T., 13. 493
Cicchetti, P., 193
Ciechanowski, P., 239
Claiborn, J. M., 194
Clancy, S. A., 193
Clare, L., 267
Clark, C. L., 339
Clark, D., 191–192, 197
Clark, D. A., 253
Clark, D. M., 46–47, 125–127, 129, 139, 141–142, 147, 191, 488–491, 499
Clark, L., 515
Clark, L. A., 52, 105, 158–159, 211, 233, 324, 453
Clark, M. S., 452
Clark, R. E., 268
Clarke, C. E., 416
Clarke, J. C., 105, 145–146, 157–158, 160, 162
Clarke, S., 310
Clarkin, J. F., 310, 319, 321–322, 324–325, 327
Clarkson, C., 105
Clary, C., 130
Classen, C., 194, 196
Clausen, J. A., 74
Clayton, P. J., 6
Cleary, P., 282
Cleckley, H. E., 318
Clementz, B. A., 373
Climent, C. E., 378
Cloitre, M., 193
Clomipramine Collaborative Group, 178
Cloninger, C. R., 54, 211, 233, 240, 392
Cloninger, R. C., 339
Clouse, J. C., 417
Clum, G., 129, 322
Clum, G. A., 43, 129
Cobb, J., 178
Cobb, R. J., 454
Coccaro, E. F., 88, 326
Cochran, B. N., 498
Cochran, S., 254
Cockell, S. J., 392
Cocuzza, E., 311
Cohan, C. L., 456
Cohen, D. C., 161
Cohen, H., 197
Cohen, J., 6
Cohen, M., 101
Cohen, N., 37
Cohen, P., 9, 40, 105, 323, 393, 395
Cohen, R., 289
Colditz, G. A., 394
Coldwell, S. E., 163
Cole, D. A., 12
Cole, E., 292

Cole, S. W., 480
Coles, M. E., 138–139, 142, 146–147, 174
Collins, C. C., 74, 78
Collins, N. L., 110
Collins, P. F., 247
Collins, T. M., 139
Colliver, J. D., 342
Comings, D. E., 373
Compton, A., 471
Compton, W. M., 12, 78
Comtois, K. A., 306
Condray, R., 78
Conley, J. J., 454
Conley, T., 344
Connolly, J., 174
Connolly, M. B., 480
Connor, P. D., 346
Constans, J., 172
Constans, J. I., 190
Constantine, R., 159
Constantini, S., 283
Constantino, M. J., 144
Conte, H. R., 325
Conti, S., 221
Cook, M., 158
Cooney, N. L., 492
Cooper, A. M., 325
Cooper, J., 174
Cooper, J. E., 70
Cooper, M. J., 160
Cooper, Z., 391, 396, 398, 494–495, 499
Cooper-Patrick, L., 234
Coplan, J. D., 124
Copper, S., 286
Corbitt, E. M., 10, 307, 324
Cordingley, G. E., 417
Corenthal, C., 327
Corey-Bloom, J., 88
Corley, R. P., 59
Cormier, C. A., 442
Corr, P. J., 159
Corrigan, P. W., 269
Corsini, R. J., 75
Cortoni, F., 443
Corty, E. W., 423
Coryell, W., 245, 249, 321, 325, 327
Costa, P. T., 57, 233, 280, 305, 324, 339, 392, 438, 453
Costello, E., 109, 112
Cottraux, J., 174, 178
Coventry, K. R., 376
Coverdale, J. H., 268, 271
Cowan, W. M., 67
Cowdry, R. W., 247
Cowen, P. J., 394
Cowley, D. S., 126, 130, 452
Cox, B. J., 177–178
Cox, D. J., 439
Cox, D. R., 13
Cox, M. J., 460
Coyne, J. C., 212, 235, 237
Crago, M., 73
Craig, I. W., 54
Craig, T. J., 263
Craighead, L. W., 36, 38, 327
Craighead, W. E., 36, 38, 327
Cramer, V., 301, 321
Craske, M. G., 101–102, 125, 130–131, 162–163, 490–491
Creamer, M. C., 195
Crenshaw, T. L., 427
Crino, R. D., 173, 177
Crits-Christoph, K., 326
Crits-Christoph, P., 112, 478, 480
Croft, P. R., 411
Crombie, I. K., 411
Cronkite, R. C., 78
Crosby, R. D., 391
Crossley, T., 375

Crothers, L., 72
Croughan, J., 6
Crow, S. J., 392, 396
Crowe, R. R., 105, 107
Crowe, S. F., 513
Crowell, J. A., 454
Crowther, J. H., 396
Crum, R. M., 234
Csernansky, J. G., 88
Cuellar, I., 76
Cuesta, M. J., 12–13
Cuijpers, P., 220
Cuk, M., 160
Cummings, J., 290
Curran, P. J., 31, 262
Currier, G. W., 281
Curry, J. F., 180
Curson, D. A., 262, 270
Curtin, L., 363
Curtis, G. C., 155–156
Custer, R., 371, 378
Cuthbert, B. N., 106
Cutrona, C. E., 456
Cutter, H. S., 458
Czirr, R., 327

Daae, E., 327
Dahlen, E. R., 47
Dahlöf, C., 416
Dahlstrom, W. G., 324
Daiuto, A. D., 455
Daley, D. C., 348
Daley, S. E., 453
Dally, P., 392
Damasio, A. R., 94
Damasio, H., 94
Dammast, J., 281
da Motta, W. R., 155
Dancu, C. V., 195
Dang, S. T., 192, 196, 198
Daniels, B. A., 41
Daniels, R. E., 250
Dannon, P., 163
Dannon, P. N., 383
Darbyshire, P., 382
Dare, C., 397
Dasen, P. R., 75
Daston, D., 291
Davenport, Y. B., 249
Davey, G., 155, 160
Davey, G. C. L., 106, 110, 157–158
David, A., 267
Davidson, A. C., 196
Davidson, A. R., 69
Davidson, D. G., 345
Davidson, J., 189
Davidson, J. R., 130, 143, 146–147, 195, 512
Davidson, J. R. T., 148, 196–197
Davidson, M., 264
Davidson, R., 345
Davies, B., 391
Davies, K., 289
Davies-Osterkamp, S., 341
Davila, J., 146, 451, 454, 456
Davis, D., 246
Davis, G. C., 175, 189
Davis, J. M., 269, 391
Davis, K. L., 264, 305, 317, 322
Davis, M. L., 193, 380
Davis, R., 323–324, 399
Davis, T. E., III, 161
Day, A., 221, 239
Day, D. M., 442
Day, N., 346
Dean, W., 271
de Araujo, L. A., 181, 428
de Beurs, E., 128, 377
de Bono, J., 103
de Castro, I. P., 376
Deffenbacher, J. L., 47, 101

DeFries, J. C., 54, 61
de Girolamo, G., 320–321
DeHaan, E., 292
Deichmann, M. M., 418
Deitz, P. E., 440–441
de Jong, P. J., 157–160, 194
Delahanty, D. L., 191, 193
DeLamater, J. D., 424
Delaney, H. D., 364–365
DelBello, M. P., 246, 249, 252
Del Carmen Lorenzo, M., 373
Delgado, P. L., 88, 178
Delis, D. C., 266
DeLisio, G., 237
de Lissovoy, G., 415
DelPorto-Bedoya, D., 246
Demaree, H., 292
DeMartinis, N., 112
de Mello, M. F., 238
Demeter, C., 246
Demler, O., 212
Dempster, C., 221
Demyttenaere, K., 212
den Boer, J. A., 125, 443
Denicoff, K. D., 251
Dennis, D. L., 399
Dennis, J. L., 285
Denys, D. A. J. P., 173
DePaolo, J. R., 247
DePree, J. A., 101
Depression Guideline Panel, 213, 218, 220–221, 223
Depue, R. A., 247, 322
Derby, C. A., 428
Derevensky, J., 373, 375–376
Derogowski, J. B., 70
Deroo, L., 347
DeRubeis, R. J., 44
Desai, R. A., 75
DeSanto, N., 270
Deshpande, S. N., 269
de Silva, P., 105, 122, 175, 189, 356
DeSisto, M. J., 265
Desjarlais, R., 79
Detera-Wadleigh, S. D., 54
Deutsch, R., 138
Devanand, D. P., 234
DeVeaugh-Geiss, J., 178
Devereux, R. A., 289
Devlin, M. J., 390, 392
Devous, M. D., Sr., 125
Dewick, H., 101
Dewis, L. M., 162
DeWit, D. J., 143
Dey, S., 85
Diaferia, G., 104
Diamond, M. L., 411
Diamond, S., 411
Diaz, M. L., 102
Diaz-Guerrero, R., 69
Diaz-Marsa, M., 391–392
Dibble, E. D., 249
DiCiano, P., 92
Dick, D. M., 62–63
Dickinson, K. A., 340
Dickerson, M., 376
Dickson, C., 399
Diefenbach, G. J., 371, 373, 375, 377, 379, 383
Diehl, L., 106
Diemer, R., 481
Dietzel, R., 498
Difede, J., 190, 195
DiGiuseppe, R., 147
Diguer, L., 326, 327
DiLillo, D., 438
Dilsaver, S. C., 12, 249
Dimeff, L. A., 348, 360, 493
Dimenäs, E., 416
Dimidjian, S., 238–239, 500

Di Nardo, P. A., 9, 127, 144, 155, 157, 160
Dindia, K., 110
Dion, G. L., 249
Dirkzwager, A. J. E., 191, 196
Dishman, R. K., 191, 196
Dixon, L., 267
Dixon, W. A., 43
Dobson, K. S., 42, 45, 487–489, 499
Docherty, J. P., 250, 252, 324
Docter, R. F., 436, 439, 445
Doddi, S., 122
Dodel, R. C., 286
Dodge, C. S., 148
Dodge, K. A., 47
Dodgen, C. E., 357, 365
Dohm, F. A., 395
Dohrenwend, B. P., 71, 74
Dohrenwend, B. R., 263
Dohrenwend, B. S., 71, 74
Dolan, S., 341
Doll, H. A., 391, 395
Dollard, J., 171
Dollfus, S., 12
Donnell, C. D., 123
Donohue, B., 337, 345–346, 354, 357–360, 363
Donovan, D. M., 344
Donovick, P. J., 282
Doorn, C. D., 438
Doren, D. M., 442
D'Orlando, K. J., 292
Dotto, P., 320
Douban, J., 109
Doucet, C., 103
Dougherty, D. D., 178
Douglas, M. S., 262
Dounchis, J. Z., 398
Dovey, T. M., 41
Dowd, E. T., 43
Doweiko, H. E., 361
Dowson, S. N., 269
Dowson, J. H., 321, 515
Dozois, D., 487–488, 499
Draguns, J. G., 3, 68, 70, 72, 76
Drahorad, C., 341
Drake, R. E., 262, 265–266, 268, 270–271, 320–321
Dressen, L., 180–181, 327, 446, 498
Drevets, W. C., 209–210
Drigotas, S. M., 452
Drolet, G., 193
Dryman, A., 155
Duane, S., 176
Dubbert, B., 173
Dudley, R., 496
Duffy, S. W., 345
Dugas, M. J., 103, 106
Dulcan, M. K., 103
Dulit, R. A., 193, 301, 325
Duman, R. S., 214
Dumlao, V. J., 376
Dunayevich, E., 246
Duncan, S. C., 31, 479
Duncan, T. E., 31
Dunham, H. W., 74
Dunmore, E., 191
Dunn, C., 347
Dunn, H., 270
Dunner, D. L., 233, 238, 245, 250
DuPont, R. L., 107
Dupuis, G., 124
Durante, R., 428
Durbin, J., 301
Durham, R. C., 108
Durkheim, E., 79
Durst, R., 383
du Toit, P. L., 371
Dutton, D. G., 453
Dutton, S. S., 103, 110
Duvdevani, T., 196

Dyck, D. G., 41
Dyck, I. R., 103, 107–108, 126, 128, 143, 180
D'Zurilla, T. J., 42–43, 488

Eagle, M. N., 476
East, M. P., 106
Eastin, M. K. D., 41
Eastwood, R., 267
Eaton, W. W., 11, 103, 121–122, 124, 141, 155–156, 235, 263
Eaves, L. J., 61–62, 105, 211, 215
Ebers, G., 290
Eckert, E., 391
Eckert, V., 461
Eddy, K. T., 389, 393, 399
Edell, W. S., 7, 305, 318, 323
Edelmann, R. J., 140, 142
Edgerton, R. B., 70
Edith, V., 289
Edmeads, J., 416
Edwards, M. E., 347
Egeland, B., 105
Ehlers, A., 47, 190–192, 197–198, 490–491
Ehrensaft, M. K., 450
Ehrt, E., 246
Eid, M., 29
Eifert, G. H., 126, 339
Eilertsen, D. E., 327
Eisen, J. L., 171–173, 176, 180
Eisenberg, L., 79, 290
Eisler, I., 397
Ekselius, L., 57, 140, 320–321, 325–326
Elder, G. H., Jr., 454
Eldredge, K. L., 390
Elie, M., 282
Elkin, I., 221, 238
Ellicott, A., 212, 247
Elliott, D. M., 321
Elliott, F., 321
Ellis, A., 45, 487–488
Ellis, B. J., 220
Ellis, C. G., 324
Ellis, S. P., 221, 325
Embretson, S. E., 14
Emerson, J., 321
Emery, G., 44–45, 102, 125, 220, 238, 487
Emery, R. E., 71, 73
Emmelkamp, P. M., 129, 162, 176, 179
Endicott, J., 6, 11, 219, 249, 317
Eng, W. E., 146
Engel, C. C., Jr., 189
Engel, G., 453
Engel, R. R., 271
Engelhard, I., 191
Engl, J., 461
Ennis, N. E., 78
Enright, A., 397
Entsuah, A. R., 221, 507
Epperson, D. L., 442
Epstein, N. B., 176, 452
Erazo, N., 250
Erbaugh, J. K., 5, 11, 219, 236
Erel, O., 460
Erickson, S., 357–358
Erickson, T., 103, 112
Eriksson, C. B., 41
Erlenmeyer-Kimling, L., 321
Ernberg, G., 72
Ernst, C. L., 251, 428
Eron, L. D., 40
Ervin, F. R., 378
Escobar, J. O., 234
Espiritu, D., 289
Essau, C. A., 212
Estes, L. S., 73
Etienne, M. A., 106
Eubanks, J., 40
Evans, C., 391

Evans, D., 280, 282, 327
Evans, L., 145, 437
Evans, M. D., 220
Evans, R. W., 411
Evans, S., 237
Everitt, B., 267
Ewing, R., 278
Exner, J., 324
Eysenck, H. J., 37, 125, 392, 425
Eysenck, M., 101–103
Eysenck, S., 392

Faberm, J., 91
Fabre, J., 376
Fabrega, H., Jr., 75
Fabrigar, L. R., 32
Fagan, P. J., 425, 438
Fahlen, T., 140
Fahy, T. A., 391, 399
Faingold, C. L., 338
Fairbairn, W. R. D., 317
Fairbank, J., 191
Fairbank, J. A., 198
Fairburn, C. G., 286, 389–391, 394–399, 487, 493–495, 499
Fairooz, Y., 392
Fallon, A., 326
Fallon, M., 147
Falloon, I. R. H., 267, 271
Fals-Stewart, W., 177, 180–181, 348, 363–365, 458
Farabaugh, A., 305
Faraone, S. V., 7
Faravelli, C., 155
Farb, C. R., 193
Farde, L., 284
Farkas, M. A., 444
Farkas, T., 70
Farmer, A. E., 215, 264
Farmer, J., 396
Farr, K. L., 477
Farrell, L., 376
Farren, C. K., 341–342
Farris, M., 325
Farvolden, P., 174
Fassinger, R. E., 480
Fassino, S., 392, 399
Fauerbach, J. A., 64
Faugli, A., 327
Fava, G. A., 221
Fava, M., 211
Favaro, A., 389, 394
Favilla, L., 103
Fawcett, J., 245, 507
Fayers, P. M., 415
Fazeli, A., 251
Fecteau, G., 198
Feeney, A., 246, 346
Feeny, N. C., 179, 246
Fehm, L., 141, 143, 146
Fehm-Wolfsdorf, G., 459
Fehr, F. S., 106
Feighner, J. P., 6, 16
Feinberg, I., 264
Feinstein, A. R., 52, 87, 194
Feldbau-Kohn, S. R., 450
Feldman, H. A., 428
Feldman, J. M., 37
Feldman, R. B., 309
Fenell, D. L., 451
Fenichel, O., 469
Fennig, S., 7
Fenton, W. S., 265, 271
Ferenczi, S., 469
Fernandez, E., 411
Fernandez, R., 79
Fernandez-Cordoba, E., 177
Fernandez-Piqueras, J., 376
Ferris, C. D., 292
Ferris, J., 380
Ferro, T., 7

Ferster, C. B., 235, 238
Feske, U., 192
Feuche, N., 338
Fichera, S., 291
Fichter, M., 391
Field, A. E., 394
Fieve, R. R., 246, 250
Fifer, S. K., 110
Figueredo, A. J., 438
Figueria, I., 148
Figueroa, E., 305
Fillit, H., 289
Fillmore, K. M., 339
Fillmore, M. T., 342
Filsinger, E. E., 146
Finch, C., 321
Fincham, F. D., 450–452, 456, 458–460
Fincham, S. I., 459
Findling, R. L., 246
Fine, B. D., 469
Fingarette, H., 343
Finkel, E. J., 451, 457
Finkelhor, D., 439–441
Finkelstein, S. N., 12, 219
Finney, J. W., 348, 364
Fiorot, M., 327
Fischer, H., 154
Fischer, J., 393, 397
Fischer, M. E., 427
Fischer, S., 391
Fishbain, D. A., 321
Fisher, D. D., 443
Fisher, M., 396
Fisher, S., 380, 469
Fisher, W. H., 270
Fiske, D. W., 27
Fiszbein, A., 265–266
Fitzgibbon, M. L., 73
Fitzmaurice, G. M., 74
Flament, M. F., 171, 176
Flay, B., 41
Fleiss, J. L., 6
Fleming, J. A. E., 270
Flesher, S., 271
Flick, S. N., 130, 452
Flor, H., 412–413, 415
Florio, L., 234
Foa, E. B., 39, 106, 139, 142, 162, 169, 172, 174–181, 189, 192, 194–195, 197–198, 492
Folkman, S., 411
Folstein, M. F., 103, 247, 321
Folstein, S., 247
Fonagy, P., 309–310, 322, 327
Fong, M. L., 325
Ford, A., 289
Ford, D. E., 234
Ford, S. M., 512
Foreyt, J. P., 196, 395
Forgas, J. P., 77
Forgue, D. F., 194
Forsyth, J. P., 27
Fossati, A., 304–305
Foster, B. M., 176
Foster, C. L., 263
Fountain, S. B., 354
Fournier, S., 103
Fowler, C., 325
Fowler, D., 495
Fox, J. W., 263
Fox, L., 270
Foy, D. W., 41, 189
Fozard, J., 281
Fram, C. L., 103
Frances, A. J., 8, 177, 190, 252, 301, 318–319
Frances, R. J., 355
Frank, E., 214, 236, 255, 327
Frank, G. K., 394
Frank, R. G., 94, 220
Franke, P., 124

Frankenburg, F. R., 305, 307, 310–311, 319, 324, 391
Franklin, M. E., 39, 139, 169, 172, 174, 177–179, 180, 492
Franko, D. L., 390
Frankova, A., 382
Franulic, A., 281, 289
Franzos, M. A., 269
Fras, I., 374
Frayn, D. H., 481
Fredrikson, M., 140, 154–155, 320
Freedman, N., 478
Freedman, R., 190
Freeman, A., 44, 246
Freeman, D. H., 262, 495
Freeman, R., 389
Freemantle, N., 221
Freeston, M. H., 103, 106, 110, 179
Freinkel, A., 194
French, R., deS, 3
French, S. L., 354
Fresco, D. M., 26, 106, 111, 142, 144, 248
Freshman, M., 47
Fretwell, M., 289
Freud, A., 472–473, 475
Freud, S., 316, 320
Freund, B., 174
Freund, K., 436, 440, 442
Freyberger, H. J., 110
Frick, D. M., 285
Frick, P. J., 40, 103–104
Fridman, R. B., 112
Fried, D., 480
Friederici, S., 394
Friedman, B. H., 102
Friedman, M. J., 191, 196–197, 310
Friedman, S., 103, 110
Friedrich, W. N., 424
Friend, R., 145
Frijda, N., 69
Frodl, T., 210
Fromuth, M. E., 439
Frosch, A., 478
Frost, R., 359
Frye, A. A., 43
Frye, M. A., 510
Fuentes, M. J., 373
Fuetsch, M., 146
Fujii, D., 281, 290
Fujino, D. C., 70
Fulkerson, J., 380
Fullerton, C. S., 195
Fullerton, D., 399
Funk, J. B., 40
Furmark, T., 57, 140, 320
Furukawa, T. A., 232, 280
Fyer, A. J., 124, 154
Fyer, M. R., 301

Gabbard, G. O., 326, 469–470, 473–474, 476–477
Gabel, J., 176
Gacono, C. B., 325
Gado, M. H., 210
Gaffney, G. R., 176
Gafni, A., 340
Gagnon, J. H., 424
Gaither, G. A., 306
Gaitz, C. M., 279
Galaburda, A. M., 94
Galasko, D., 282
Galasso, C. S., 380
Galea, S., 194
Galer, B. S., 417
Galik, E., 289
Gallagher, D., 327
Gallagher, R., 128
Gallaher, P. E., 327
Gallo, J. J., 235
Galovski, T., 193

Gamache, G., 267
Gano-Phillips, S., 451
Gansicke, M., 110
Gara, M., 234
Garb, H. N., 324
Garber, J., 212, 220
GarciaColl, C., 122
Garcia-Espana, F., 512
Gardenswartz, C., 131
Gardiner, M., 41
Gardner, C. O., 211–212, 214–215
Gardner, F., 147
Gardner, S. T., 479
Garety, P. A., 495
Garfinkel, P. E., 73, 389, 391, 393, 396
Garland, A., 254
Garlow, S. J., 215
Garmezy, N., 8
Garner, D. M., 73, 389, 391, 394, 396, 399, 494
Garnier, P. C., 451
Garratt, L. S., 263
Gartner, A., 392
Garyfallos, G., 234
Gasperini, M., 104, 110
Gaston, L., 478
Gath, D. H., 221, 239
Gatsonis, C., 232
Gavin, D. R., 344
Gawin, F. H., 365
Gazel, R., 381
Gebhard, P. H., 439
Gecici, O., 304
Geddes, J. R., 264
Geert-Jorgensen, E., 176
Gelder, M. G., 126
Gelernter, C. S., 148
Geller, A. M., 112
Geller, B., 249, 252
Geller, D. A., 178
Geller, J. L., 270, 378, 392
Gelpin, E., 194
Gelso, C. J., 480–481
Gemar, M., 212
Gendron, C., 291
Gentil, V., 371, 376
George, E. L., 255
George, G., 391
George, L. K., 104, 143
Gerardi, R. J. T. P., 193
Gergely, G., 322
German, P. S., 4
Gershon, E. S., 54, 279
Gershuny, B. S., 172, 175
Gerson, J., 306
Getz, G., 340
Getz, J. C., 360
Ghaderi, A., 392
Ghaemi, S. N., 244, 251, 510
Giardinelli, L., 155
Giardino, N. D., 37
Gibbon, M., 11, 109, 127, 144, 160, 219, 236, 307, 317, 324, 345, 361, 381, 396
Gibbons, R. D., 221
Gilbert, C., 418
Gilbertson, M. W., 191
Gilboa, A., 194
Gill, K., 338
Gill, M., 469, 474
Gillberg, C., 249, 258, 391, 399
Gillberg, I. C., 249, 258, 391
Gillespie, J., 41
Gilley, D. W., 280–281
Gillis, R., 440
Gilman, S. E., 74
Gilmore, M. M., 325
Gindrec, C., 252
Gingerich, S., 268
Giovino, G., 41
Girgus, J. S., 212

Gitlin, M. J., 212, 247, 249
Glantz, M. D., 342
Glanville, J., 221
Glaser, R., 458, 464
Glass, C. R., 138
Glass, D. R., 324
Glass, R. M., 122
Glass, S., 397
Glassman, A. H., 210–211
Glenn, N. D., 454–455, 458
Glick, I. D., 269
Glick, M., 74, 262
Glidden, R. A., 94
Glisky, E., 292
Glynn, S. M., 198, 268, 271
Gmel, G., 343, 346
Goadsby, P. J., 412
Godfrey, H., 289
Godley, M. D., 348, 364
Goering, P., 103
Goff, D., 270
Goisman, R. M., 107, 121, 126, 143, 155–156
Golann, S., 326
Goldberg, J. F., 244, 249–252
Goldberg, J. P., 427
Goldberg, S., 122, 391
Goldenberg, I., 107, 143
Goldfried, M. R., 112, 488
Golding, J. M., 171
Goldman, H. H., 11, 270
Goldman, M. J., 377
Goldman, M. S., 41
Goldner, E., 393
Goldner, E. M., 392
Goldsmith, H., 322
Goldstein, A. J., 125, 129, 325
Goldstein, I., 427–428, 432
Goldstein, J. M., 263
Goldstein, M. J., 247–248, 255
Goldstein, R. B., 173, 320, 371
Goldstein, W. N., 469
Golembeck, H., 323
Gollan, J. K., 489
Golombok, S., 429
Gomez, J., 392
Gomez, M. J., 480
Gonzales-Salvador, T., 289
Gonzalez, G., 339
Gonzalez, J., 338
Gonzalez, M. E., 214
Good, B., 79
Goodman, L. A., 262, 266
Goodman, S. H., 43, 215, 392
Goodman, W. K., 174, 178
Goodnow, J. J., 74
Goodrick, G. K., 395
Goodwin, A. H., 172
Goodwin, F. K., 244, 247, 249, 264, 508
Goodwin, G. M., 508, 510
Goodwin, R. D., 122–123
Gorden, N., 289
Gordon, E., 192
Gordon, J. R., 365
Gorman, D. M., 345
Gorman, J. M., 124, 130, 266
Gorsky, J. M., 139
Gorsuch, R. L., 11, 41, 110
Gortner, E. T., 489
Gosselin, C., 439
Gossop, M., 362
Gotlib, I. H., 215, 220
Goto, S. G., 75
Gottesman, I. I., 53, 57, 264
Gottman, J. M., 450, 452, 455–459
Goudriaan, A. E., 377
Gould, R. A., 112, 127, 129–131, 270
Gouvier, W. D., 278, 283, 291
Goveas, J. S., 88
Gowensmith, W. N., 47
Grabowski, J., 364

Grabowski, R., 94
Grace, D. M., 376
Gracely, E. J., 122, 128, 325
Grafman, J., 290
Graham, F., 438
Graham, J. R., 324
Graham, S., 452
Graham, Y. P., 215
Grambsch, P., 424
Grandi, S., 221
Grant, B. F., 210–211
Grant, J. E., 374, 383
Gratzer, D., 343
Gray, J. A., 159
Gray, T., 193
Grayson, D., 29
Grayson, J. B., 174
Grayson, R. L., 413
Grazzi, L., 416, 419
Green, A. I., 211
Greenberg, B. S., 41
Greenberg, J. R., 473
Greenberg, L. S., 478
Greenberg, M., 327
Greenberg, P. E., 156–157, 219, 220
Greenberg, R. L., 45, 102, 125
Greenberg, R. P., 469, 487
Greenberg, T., 221
Greenblatt, D. J., 112, 512
Greenfeld, L. A., 339, 346, 444
Greenhouse, W., 247
Greenson, R., 469
Greenwald, A. G., 160
Greenwood, K. M., 513
Gregg, A. P., 160
Gregg, S. F., 130
Gregory, A., 433
Greil, W., 250, 509
Greist, J. H., 172, 178–180
Grieb-Neff, P., 292
Grieger, T. A., 195
Griez, E., 159
Griez, E. J. L., 124
Griffin, D. W., 237
Griffiths, M. D., 376
Grilo, C. M., 305, 318, 323, 392, 399
Grimes, K., 263
Grisham, J. R., 107, 139, 154, 175
Grode, M., 290
Gronwall, D., 278
Groom, C., 103
Gross, J. L., 488
Grossberg, G., 286
Grossman, F., 251
Grossman, L. S., 249
Grote, N., 452
Groth, A. N., 441
Groth, T., 459
Groth-Marnat, G., 286, 287, 288
Grounds, A. T., 321
Grove, W. M., 56
Gruen, R., 321
Gruenberg, A. M., 321
Grunbaum, A., 469
Grunebaum, H., 268, 271
Grunebaum, M. F., 221
Grunze, H., 250
Grych, J. H., 460
Guarnaccia, P. J. J., 72
Gudanowski, D. M., 189–190
Guerrini Degl'Innocenti, B., 155
Guggeri, G., 176
Guidetti, V., 412, 414
Gullion, C. M., 219
Gunderson, J. G., 233, 299–302, 304, 306–309, 319, 323–326
Gunnell, D., 221
Guntrip, H., 317, 469
Gupta, A. K., 389
Gupta, M. A., 389
Gupta, R., 373, 376

Gupta, S., 130
Gurland, B. J., 70
Gursky, D. M., 123
Gurvits, I. G., 305
Gusman, F. D., 199
Guthrie, G., 79
Guthrie, R. M., 192–193, 196, 198
Gutterman, D. L., 416
Gutterman, E. M., 289
Guze, S., 12, 16
Guze, S. B., 12, 218
Guzman, R., 375
Gwirtsman, H. E., 231, 236
Gyulai, L., 246

Haas, G. L., 263, 301
Haban, G., 280
Haberman, H. F., 389
Hackett, C. A., 108
Hackmann, A., 139, 160
Hadzi-Pavlovic, D., 106, 326
Haen, E., 92
Hafner, H., 129
Hafner, R. J., 129
Hahlweg, K., 459, 461
Hahn, J., 488
Haidt, J., 161
Halberstadt, L. J., 249
Halford, J. C., 41
Halford, W. K., 267
Hall, E. T., 79
Hall, G. C. N., 440–441
Hall, G. M., 364
Hall, J., 309
Hall, M. N., 375, 378
Hall, W., 171, 339
Halligan, S. L., 196
Hallman, R. S., 174
Hallmayer, J., 321
Halmi, K., 391–392
Halper, I., 253
Ham, L. P., 413
Haman, K. L., 44, 489
Hamann, M., 325, 327
Hambleton, R. K., 14
Hambrick, R. K., 14
Hamilton, J. D., 163
Hamilton, K. E., 45
Hamilton, M., 219, 236
Hamilton, P., 512
Hammen, C., 212, 220, 247, 249, 253
Hammer, L., 404
Hammett, E., 189
Hammond, C., 146
Hand, C. G., 443
Hand, L., 392
Handler, L., 325
Hanna, G. L., 171
Hanna-Pladdy, B., 291
Hannon, P. A., 451
Hannus, A., 392
Hanson, R. K., 440–443, 445
Harder, S., 325
Hardiman, J. J., 326
Harding, C. M., 265–266
Hardoon, K. K., 373, 375
Hardy, G. E., 327, 478
Hare, R. D., 318, 324, 442
Hariri, A. R., 215
Harnden-Fischer, J., 393, 397
Harold, G., 215, 410
Harp, J. S., 126
Harpur, T. J., 318
Harrigan, S., 284
Harrington, P. J., 128
Harris, A., 443, 445
Harris, E. C., 218, 262, 285
Harris, G. T., 442
Harris, J. P., 389–390
Harris, S. L., 5
Harris, T. G., 427

Harris, T. O., 214
Harrison, J., 491
Harrison, P. J., 264, 389–390, 394
Harrison, W., 233
Harrison-Hall, A., 309
Harrow, M., 249, 262
Hart, K., 430
Hart, S. D., 318, 443, 453
Hart, T. A., 146, 292
Hartman, R., 286
Haruki, Y., 77
Harvald, B., 247
Harvey, A. G., 190–198
Harvey, P. D., 265, 268–269, 317, 385
Harwood, H., 354
Hasin, D. S., 11, 211
Haslam, N., 8
Hatfield, A. B., 268
Hatgis, C., 488
Hauge, M., 247
Havighurst, T. C., 347
Hawk, L. W., 161
Hawkins, K., 287
Hayaki, J., 344
Hayden, E. P., 233
Hayes, J. A., 480–481
Haynes, M. C., 438
Haynes, M. R., 438
Hays, R. D., 232
Hayward, C., 123, 140, 393, 395
Hayward, P., 247, 267
Hazaleus, S. L., 101
Hazan, C., 450, 454
Hazelwood, R. R., 440
Hazlett-Stevens, H., 102, 107, 111
Head, J., 346
Headache Classification Subcommittee of the International Headache Society, 409
Headache Society Committee on Clinical Trials in Tension-Type Headache, 414
Heard, H. L., 499
Heath, A. C., 11, 62, 105, 211, 215, 341–342
Heatherington, E. M., 55
Heatherington, M., 61
Heaton, R., 262
Heaven, P., 392
Heavey, C. L., 451, 460
Heberlein, I., 281
Hebert, R., 282
Heckelman, L. R., 138–139
Hecker, J., 4
Hedegaard, K. B., 178
Hedeker, D., 391
Hedges, M., 500
Heffernan, K., 390
Hegel, M. T., 130
Hegeman, I. M., 122
Heide, F. J., 110
Heilman, K., 287, 290–291
Heim, C., 215
Heiman, J. R., 432
Heimberg, R. G., 26, 46, 106, 111, 138–139, 141–142, 144, 146–148, 489–490
Heinrichs, N., 139, 144
Heinssen, R. K., 270
Heiser, K., 425
Heiser, N. A., 139
Heller, T. L., 249
Heller, W., 106
Hellerstein, D., 327
Hellerstein, D. J., 233, 326
Hellgren, L., 249
Hellström, K., 162
Helzer, J. E., 6, 219
Hemami, S., 12
Hemnani, T., 92
Henderson, J., 176
Henderson, S., 171

Hendrie, H. C., 282
Heninger, G. R., 508
Hennen, J., 305, 508
Henrietta, M., 263
Henry, C., 252
Henry, J. L., 195
Hepp, U., 397
Heppner, P. P., 43
Hepworth, C., 214
Herbert, J. D., 139, 325
Herman, C. P., 395
Hermann, C., 417
Hermesh, H., 327
Herpertz-Dahlmann, B., 392
Herscovitch, P., 125
Hersen, M., 345, 396
Hershberger, S. L., 33
Herskovits, M., 72
Hersoug, A. G., 479
Herz, L. R., 194
Herzog, D. B., 390, 392, 395
Heslegrave, R., 299
Hess, A., 391
Hester, C., 73
Hester, R. K., 348
Hettema, J. M., 124, 210, 214
Heun, R., 321
Hewer, B., 285
Hewitt, J. K., 59
Heyman, M., 309
Heyman, R. E., 450–451, 455, 458–460
Hibbard, S., 325
Hickling, E. J., 193–194
Hicks, A., 318
Higgins, S. T., 348, 364–365, 492
Hill, C. E., 481
Hill, D. E., 364
Hiller, M. L., 341
Hillman, R. G., 194
Hilsenroth, M. J., 325, 399, 478–479
Himelstein, J., 88
Himmelhoch, J. M., 245–246, 250
Hinchy, J., 376
Hing, N., 376
Hinney, A., 395
Hipsley, P., 112
Hirsch, J., 390
Hirschfeld, R., 327
Hirschfeld, R. M., 214, 251
Hirschfeld, R. M. A., 211
Hirschman, R., 440–441
Hirshfeld, D. R., 104, 256
Hirshfeld-Becker, D. R., 90, 142, 212, 505
Hiss, H., 176
Hladek, D., 162
Hobfoll, S. E., 78
Hoch, P., 317
Hodges, L. F., 162
Hodgson, J. H., 344
Hodgson, J. M., 344
Hodgson, R., 171–172, 174, 177, 345
Hoehn-Saric, R., 102, 106–107, 112
Hoekstra, R., 180
Hoekstra, R. J., 179
Hoenk, P. R., 194
Hoffart, A., 46
Hoffenberg, J. D., 478
Hoffman, M. A., 481
Hoffmann, M. L., 438
Hofmann, S. G., 138–139, 144, 154
Hofschire, L., 41
Hogan, T. P., 267
Hogarty, G. E., 268, 271
Hohagen, F., 178, 180
Hoke, S., 41
Holborn, S. W., 160
Holden, E. W., 418
Holder, H., 364
Holeva, V., 195
Holland, A. J., 282, 394

Holland, L. A., 443
Hollander, E., 176, 310, 377
Hollingshead, A. B., 10, 74, 263
Hollon, S. D., 44, 220, 238, 489
Holloway, F., 325
Holmes, B. M., 304, 309
Holmes, M., 101
Holmgren, P., 221
Holmgren, S., 391
Holroyd, K. A., 416–417
Holsboer, F., 214
Holt, C. S., 113, 147
Holtzer, R., 280
Holzer, C. E., 75
Hood, J., 122
Hoogduin, C. A. L., 180
Hoogduin, K. A. L., 176
Hoogstraten, J., 157
Hooley, J. M., 193, 215, 265–267, 458
Hope, D. A., 138–139, 147, 262, 325
Hope, R. A., 398
Hope, T., 286
Hopkins, J., 390
Hopkins, M., 108
Hopper, K., 263
Hops, H., 393, 459
Horney, K., 320
Hornig, C. D., 139, 159
Hornsveld, R. H., 171
Horowitz, H. A., 237
Horowitz, J. H., 212
Horowitz, M. J., 318
Horowitz, S. V., 321, 323
Horta, E., 281
Horvath, A. O., 478
Horwath, E., 235
Houts, A. C., 8
Howard, K. E., 478
Howard, K. I., 478
Howard, L. M., 271
Howard, R., 265
Howland, R. H., 214
Hsu, D. J., 510
Hsu, L., 391
Hu, L. T., 23–24, 70
Hu, S., 101, 106, 108, 111
Hu, X. H., 417
Huba, G. J., 356
Huckle, P., 291
Hucker, S. J., 440, 444
Hudson, J., 142, 379, 391
Hudson, J. I., 302, 374, 386
Hudson, J. L., 250
Huesmann, L. R., 40
Huff, T. G., 375
Hugdahl, K., 125
Hughes, D. C., 104
Hughes, D. L., 143, 146–147
Hughes, M., 6, 192
Huijding, J., 160
Hulter, A. K., 289
Hunt, C., 103–105, 110
Hunt, G. M., 337, 347, 364
Hunt, M., 439
Hunt, N., 247
Hunter, C. L., 237
Hunter, C. M., 237
Hunter, J. A., 438
Hunter, K., 129
Huot, R. L., 214
Huppert, J. D., 175
Hur, K., 221
Hurt, S. W., 319, 321
Hussong, A. M., 31
Huston, L., 105
Huta, V., 172
Hutchinson, G., 74
Huynh, S., 376
Hyde, J. S., 424, 433
Hyler, S. E., 323
Hyman, S. E., 67

Hymel, S., 142
Hymowitz, P., 318
Hynd, G. W., 103
Hypericum Depression Trial Study Group, 223

Iacono, W. G., 58, 270
Iancu, I., 383
Ianni, F., 326
Ibach, B., 92
Ibanez, A., 376
Illardi, S. S., 36
Imperator, P. J., 90
Ingman, K. A., 155
Ingram, K. M., 481
Ingram, R. E., 489
Innis, R. B., 86, 90
Innocenti, G. M., 264
Inouye, S. K., 285
Insel, T. R., 172
Inskip, H. M., 218, 262
International Headache Society Committee on Clinical Trials in Migraine, 414
Inz, J., 102, 106, 111
Isacsson, G., 221
Isler, H., 410
Isometsä, E. T., 250
Issakidis, C., 103, 141
Ito, L. M., 181
Iwata, J., 193

Jablensky, A., 9, 72, 263
Jaccard, J., 23–24
Jaccard, J. J., 69
Jack, M. S., 138
Jackel, L., 101
Jackman, L. P., 396
Jackson, A. P., 78, 129
Jackson, C., 271
Jackson, D. N., 303, 323
Jackson, H. J., 440
Jackson, M., 513
Jackson, R. J., 123
Jackson, S. R., 396
Jackson, S. W., 207, 211
Jacob, R. A., 103
Jacob, R. G., 139
Jacob, T., 346
Jacobi, F., 122
Jacobs, D. F., 373, 376, 382
Jacobs, G. A., 110
Jacobs, H., 281
Jacobs, R. J., 130
Jacobsberg, L., 190
Jacobsberg, L. B., 318
Jacobson, E., 470
Jacobson, K. C., 211
Jacobson, N. S., 235, 238, 450, 489, 500
Jacoby, R., 286
Jacques, C., 162, 373
Jacquin, K. M., 123, 128
Jaffe, A. J., 348
Jahoda, G., 69
Jaimez, T. L., 128
Jamani, N., 172
Jameson, J. S., 162
Jamison, K. R., 212, 245, 247, 249, 253, 264
Janet, P., 202
Jang, K., 322
Jang, K. L., 52, 55–57, 64, 124, 142, 303, 322, 339
Järeskog, K. G., 12, 23, 25, 27
Jarrett, R. B., 218–219
Jasin, S. E., 128
Jaycox, L., 195
Jaynes, G. D., 75
Jefferson, J. W., 172
Jeffery, S., 157
Jellinek, E. M., 342–343

Jenike, M. A., 181, 320, 327
Jenkins, J. H., 79–80
Jenkins, R., 236, 306, 321
Jensen, M. J., 347
Jensen, R., 411–412
Jeste, D. V., 282
Jilek-Aall, L., 79
Jimerson, D. C., 390
Jindal, R. D., 214
Joffe, R. T., 173, 320
Johannes, C. B., 428
Johansson, B., 103
Johnson, C. L., 397, 399
Johnson, D. J., 451
Johnson, D. R., 189, 454–455
Johnson, J., 139, 234–235, 393, 395
Johnson, J. G., 9, 40, 323
Johnson, M. C., 106, 268, 322
Johnson, R. J., 78
Johnson, S. L., 247, 346
Johnson, T., 322, 396
Johnson, W., 453
Johnson-Sabine, E., 394
Johnston, L. D., 380
Johnstone, B. M., 339
Johnstone, K. A., 162
Joiner, T. E., 220
Jolly, P. A., 363
Jonas, B. S., 234
Jonas, J., 391
Jones, D. J., 221
Jones, H. J., 194
Jones, J., 380
Jones, P. B., 264
Jones, R., 398–399
Jones, S., 247
Joos, S., 321
Jordan, A. D., 443
Jordan, B. D., 286
Jordan, B. K., 196
Jordan, J., 347
Joshua, S., 318
Joyce, A. S., 479, 481
Joyce, P., 327, 392, 399
Judd, L. L., 128, 237, 244, 248
Judge, A., 481
Julien, D., 451
Julien, R. M., 89
Jung, J., 341–342
Junker, M., 399
Jurist, E., 322

Kachin, K. E., 144
Kadden, R. M., 492
Kaelber, C., 316
Kafka, M. P., 437
Kagan, J., 104, 122, 123, 140, 212
Kagitcibasi, C., 77
Kahan, J., 326
Kahler, C. W., 344, 348
Kahn, D. A., 177, 250, 252
Kahn, R. S., 263–264
Kaiser, A., 459
Kalmar, K., 43
Kamara, S. G., 285
Kameoka, V. A., 67, 69, 80
Kaminer, D., 157
Kane, J. M., 269, 504
Kane, P., 220
Kangas, M., 195
Kanitz, R. D., 278
Kanno, P. H., 425
Kaplan, A., 400
Kaplan, B., 266
Kaplan, R. D., 325
Kaplan, Z., 197
Kaprio, J., 62–63, 247
Karajgi, B., 122
Karasu, T. B., 325
Karbofsky, E., 163
Karcher, K., 259

Karkowski, L. M., 142, 158, 215
Karkowski-Shuman, L., 63
Karlinsky, H., 282
Karney, B. R., 456–457
Karno, M., 79–80, 155, 171, 176
Karoly, P., 38
Karpman, B., 440
Karterud, S., 327
Kasen, S., 9, 40, 323, 393, 395
Kashdan, T. B., 363
Kashy, D. A., 25, 29
Kasper, S., 178
Kaspi, S. P., 192
Kasvikis, Y., 181
Katic, M., 252
Katon, W., 211, 239
Katz, G., 383
Katz, R., 178, 212, 215
Katz, S., 289
Katzelnick, D. J., 148, 172
Kaufman, E. R., 122
Kaufman, P., 26
Kawachi, I., 74
Kawas, C. H., 282–283, 287
Kay, S. R., 265–266
Kaye, W. H., 391–392, 394
Kazdin, A. E., 103
Kean, Y. M., 146
Keane, T. M., 191, 195, 198
Keck, P. E., 248, 250, 372, 374, 379, 505, 510
Keefe, R., 269
Keene, J., 286
Keeney, J., 455
Kehrer, C. A., 498
Keidel, M., 413
Keijsers, G. P. J., 180–181
Keith, S. J., 263
Keitner, G. I., 176, 250
Kellams, J. J., 253
Keller, A. B., 266
Keller, D. S., 365
Keller, M. B., 104, 107–108, 110, 126, 129–130, 143, 217–218, 245, 392
Kellett, J., 326
Kelley, M. L., 365
Kellman, D., 323
Kelly, H. S., 7
Kelly, T. M., 47, 304
Kelly, T. P., 438
Kemp, R., 267, 270
Kemp-Fincham, S. I., 459
Kendall, R. E., 9, 70
Kendler, K. S., 7, 8, 10, 58, 60–61, 63, 105, 124, 142, 157, 158, 209–212, 214–215, 234, 317, 321–322, 392, 394–395
Kenna, D., 145
Kennedy, B. L., 104
Kennedy, J. L., 54, 252
Kennedy, S. H., 209, 211, 220
Kenny, D. A., 25, 29
Kent, G., 160
Kent, J. M., 124
Kenwright, M., 163
Keown, P., 325–326
Kerkstra, A., 451
Kermis, M., 291
Kernberg, O. F., 310, 321, 327, 469
Keskimäki, I., 263
Kessler, R. C., 6, 11, 103, 105, 107, 110–111, 121–123, 141, 155–156, 189, 192, 211–213, 215, 263, 292, 338
Kestler, L. P., 86, 90
Kety, S. S., 317
Keuthen, N. J., 380
Khanna, S., 140
Khantzian, E. J., 301
Kidman, R., 373
Kiecolt-Glaser, J. K., 458
Killen, J. D., 123, 140, 393, 394–395

Kilpatrick, D. G., 64, 190
Kim, H., 138, 144
Kim, J., 75
Kim, M., 417
Kim, S. W., 383, 455
Kim, U., 75
Kimball, K. T., 395
Kimble, M. O., 175
Kim-Cohen, J., 9
Kimmel, S. E., 251
Kinder, M. H., 237
Kindler, S., 383
Kindt, M., 159
King, D. W., 189–190, 196
King, J., 301
King, L. A., 189–190, 196
King, M. E., 122
King, N., 54, 160
King, R. A., 53
Kinsey, A. C., 439
Kinyon, J., 111
Kinzie, J. D., 69
Kirk, M., 191, 195
Kirk, S. A., 8, 10
Kirkby, K. C., 41
Kirkcaldy, B. D., 340
Kirkeby, L., 176
Kirkpatrick, D. R., 155
Kirmayer, L. J., 12, 68
Kirsch, I., 163
Kissling, W., 271
Kitayama, S., 77
Kivlahan, D. R., 344
Kjernisted, K. D., 146–148, 157
Klaghofer, R., 190
Klein, D., 235
Klein, D. N., 7, 233
Klein, E., 190
Klein, J. F., 139
Klein, K., 280
Klein, M. H., 211, 324, 327, 399
Kleindienst, N., 41, 156
Kleinknecht, R. A., 41, 156, 158–159, 161
Kleinman, A., 68–69, 71–72, 79, 263
Klerman, G. L., 8, 122, 213, 220, 234–235, 238, 255, 318
Kletti, R., 194
Klieger, D. M., 161
Klingler, T., 321
Klosko, J. S., 487
Kloth, G., 425
Klotz, R., 433
Klotz, T., 433
Klump, K. L., 392, 394
Knapp, D. J., 338
Knapp, M., 91, 176
Knauper, B., 213
Knight, R., 289
Knutson, B., 425
Ko, G., 264
Kobak, K. A., 172, 180
Kobak, R., 450
Koch, W. J., 123, 130
Kocsis, J. H., 231, 233, 244, 252
Koenen, K. C., 64
Koenigsberg, H. W., 9, 304–305, 325
Koerner, K., 309
Koestner, R., 470
Koeter, M. W. J., 306
Kogan, E., 360
Kohlbeck, P. A., 172
Kohlberg, L., 472
Kohn, M. L., 74, 450
Kohut, H., 321, 325, 469
Kolb, L. C., 193
Kolko, D. J., 381
Koller, K., 87
Kolli, R., 122
Kolodner, K., 416
Koolhaas, J. M., 193

Koons, C. R., 499
Koopman, C., 194, 196
Kopelowicz, A., 270
Kopetz, S., 289
Kopnisky, K. L., 67
Koponen, S., 281
Kopta, S. M., 478
Koren, D., 190
Korenblum, M., 323
Korfine, L., 193, 321
Korn, D., 373, 381
Korotitsch, W., 110
Korten, A., 72
Koskenvuo, M., 62
Kosslyn, S. M., 172
Kostic, V. S., 286
Kotler, L., 9, 395
Kotler, M., 196–197
Kovacs, M., 232
Kozak, M. J., 162, 169, 172, 174, 177, 179–180, 192
Kozak, M. V., 54
Kraaimaat, F. W., 171
Krabbendam, L., 338
Kraemer, H. C., 123, 140, 210, 395
Kraepelin, E., 4, 6, 15, 68, 316–318
Krakauer, I. D., 326, 478
Kramer, J. H., 266
Kramp, P., 249
Krauter, K. S., 59
Kreipe, R. E., 389–390
Kreisman, D., 267
Kretschmer, E., 317–318
Krieg, J., 399
Krijn, M., 162
Kringlen, E., 158, 176, 301, 321
Krishnan, K. R., 215
Krishnan, R. R., 189
Krishnappa, U., 174
Kroenke, K., 211, 214
Krokoff, L. J., 451
Kropp, P. R., 443
Krueger, R. F., 52, 57–58, 356, 453
Kruh, I., 40
Krull, J. L., 340
Krupnick, J. L., 478
Krystal, J. H., 193, 339
Kubu, C., 290
Kucera, M., 262
Kuehlhorn, E., 373
Kuhberger, A., 372
Kuhn, J. W., 211
Kuiper, J., 424
Kuipers, E., 325, 495
Kuley, N. B., 376
Kulhara, P., 269
Kuloglu, M., 304
Kumari, V., 159
Kumashiro, M., 451
Kuo, W. H., 235
Kuperman, S., 194
Kupfer, D. J., 209, 214, 217, 221, 236, 255
Kurdek, L. A., 453
Kurtz, E., 341
Kushner, M. G., 343
Kushwoski, M., 383
Kusumakar, V., 251
Kutcher, S. P., 252
Kutchins, H., 8, 10
Kwon, J. H., 176
Kwon, J. S., 233

Labbate, L. A., 251
Labouvie, E., 493
LaBrie, R., 373
Lacey, J., 391
Lachlan, K., 41
Lachner, G., 143
Lacoste, J., 252

Ladd, C. O., 214
Ladouceur, R., 103, 106, 112, 373, 376, 381–383
Lahey, B. B., 103
Laikin, M., 327
Lainez, M. J., 416
Laje, R. P., 211
Laking, P. J., 279
Lam, D. H., 247, 253–254
Lam, R. W., 209
Lambert, C., 326
Lambert, M. J., 478
Lamparski, D. M., 191
Lampe, L., 141, 143
Lance, C. E., 29
Landau, P., 178
Lane, L., 125
Lang, A. J., 141–142, 162
Lang, P. J., 106, 161
Lange, A., 128
Lange, R., 285
Langenbucher, J. W., 8, 13, 34, 493
Langer, T. S., 10
Langevin, R., 440
Langhinrichsen, J., 451
Langhinrichsen-Rohling, J., 450
Langley, J., 437
Langs, R. L., 469
Langton, C. M., 442
LaPlante, D., 373
LaPorte, K. K., 283
Lapour, K. J., 409
LaPuglia, R., 265
Larkby, C., 346
Larntz, K., 318
Larsen, K. H., 138
Larsson, B., 412
LaRue, A., 286
Lasch, K. H., 157
Lask, B., 398
Lasko, N. B., 192–194
Last, C. G., 40, 103, 345
Latimer, N., 373
Latimer, P., 174
Latts, M. G., 480
Laubichler, W., 372
Laumann, E. O. M., 424–426, 430–431
Lavallee-Yvon, J., 326
Lavori, P., 392
Lavy, E., 159
Lawrence, E., 456
Lawrie, S. M., 264
Laws, D. R., 440
Lax, T., 181
Lazar, A., 478
Lazare, A., 318
Lazarus, R. S., 411
Lazarus, S. S., 415
Leader, J. B., 235
Leaf, P. J., 234, 263
Leahy, R. L., 246, 252–253
Leary, M. R., 145
Lease, C. A., 103
Leblond, J., 383
Leboyer, M., 252
LeDoux, J. E., 124, 193
Ledwidge, B., 138
Lee, H. B., 292
Lee, J. H., 162
Lee, J. K. P., 440
Lee, J. S., 106
Lee, L. C., 122
Lee, M. B., 282
Lee, P. S., 177
Lee, R., 26
Lee, S., 33
Lee, T. C., 159
Leeuw, I., 162
Leff, J. P., 68, 79, 267
Lefley, H. P., 268
LeGrange, D., 397

Lehman, C. L., 9, 39, 108, 127, 144, 154, 175
Lehrer, P. M., 37
Leibel, R., 390
Leiber, E., 76
Leibing, E., 326
Leichsenring, F., 326
Leighton, A. H., 78
Leino, E. V., 339
Leitenberg, H., 424
Lejoyeux, M., 338, 374
Lelliott, P., 180
LeMare, L., 142
Lemming, O. M., 178
Lenane, M., 171
Lenz, J., 156
Lenzenweger, M. F., 310, 321–322
Leon, A. C., 129, 176
Leonard, H. L., 171, 173, 371, 373, 375, 377
Leonard, K. E., 346
Leonard, M. D., 425
Lepkowsky, C., 393
LeResche, L., 411
Lerew, D. R., 123
Leroi, I., 287
Lesieur, H. R., 371, 373, 376, 378, 380–382
Letarte, H., 106
Letourneau, E., 438
Leucht, S., 271
Leukefeld, C., 341
Leung, F., 389
Levenson, E. A., 474
Levenson, J. L., 280
Levin, H., 290, 509
Levine, J. L., 221
Levine, J. M., 390
Levine, N., 291
Levine, S. B., 427
Levitan, C., 95
Levitan, R. D., 209
Levitt, J., 177
Levitt, K., 126
Levkoff, S., 282
Levy, J. D., 418
Levy, K. N., 7, 310, 316, 323–327
Levy, L., 87
Levy, R., 177, 265, 279
Lewin, M. R., 130
Lewin, T. J., 363
Lewin Group, 354
Lewinsohn, P. M., 90, 212, 393, 395
Lewis, B., 289
Lewis, D., 344
Lewis, N., 372
Lewis-Fernandez, R., 79
Leyton, M., 107, 304
Lezak, M., 287, 289, 291
Lezak, M. D., 266
L'Heureux, F., 173
Li, F., 31
Li, S., 221
Li, S. H. S., 474
Li, W., 215
Li, X. F., 193
Liberman, J. N., 416
Liberman, R. P., 265, 268, 270
Liberthson, R., 122
Liberzon, I., 194
Lichtermann, D., 124, 321
Licinio, J., 221
Liddle, P. F., 262
Lieb, M., 122
Lieb, R., 142, 444
Lieberman, J. A., 267, 269, 271
Liebowitz, M. R., 101, 138–139, 144, 146, 148
Lightcap, P. E., 194
Lilenfeld, L. R. R., 391
Lilienfeld, S. O., 3, 324, 318, 319

Lilly, R. S., 155
Lim, L., 139, 142
Limb, K., 254
Lin, S., 263
Lin, T. Y., 77, 270
Lincoln, C. V., 265
Lincoln, N., 291
Lincoln, T. M., 147
Lindem, K., 301
Lindesay, J., 279
Lindman, L. H., 288
Lindsay, M., 177
Lindstrom, E., 320
Linehan, M. M., 299–300, 305–306, 309–310, 487, 496, 498–499
Links, P. S., 299
Linnoila, M., 172, 339
Linton, S. J., 411
Lion, J. R., 378
Liotti, M., 209
Lipchik, G. L., 413–416
Lipowski, Z. J., 281
Lipsey, T. L., 190
Lipsitz, J., 154
Lipton, R. B., 411, 416–417
Liptzin, B., 282
Lischetzke, T., 29
Lish, J. D., 122
Little, D., 390
Little, M., 280
Little, R. J. A., 11
Litz, B. T., 192
Liu, D., 460
Livanou, M., 198
Livermore, G., 354
Livesley, J., 325
Livesley, W. J., 56–57, 64, 124, 303, 305, 322–323, 325, 339, 393
Livingston-van Noppen, B., 176
Lizardi, H., 237
Lloyd-Thomas, A. R., 239
Löffler, W., 285
Locke, H. J., 459
Loeb, T. B., 424–425
Loehlin, J. C., 61
Loennqvist, J., 247
Lofgren, D. P., 301–302
Loftus, J., 426
Lohr, J. M., 159, 161
Loi, S., 174, 338
Lombardo, E. R., 36–38, 48
Long, P. J., 103
Longabaugh, R., 364
Longo, R. E., 441
Lopatka, C., 126
Lopez, A. D., 219, 236
Lopez, O. L., 282, 513
Lopez, S. R., 70, 72, 79
Lopez-IborAlino, J., 177
Loranger, A. D., 392
Loranger, A. W., 307, 321, 324
Loranger, J., 381
Lord, S., 321
Lorenz, V. C., 382
Loring, D. W., 278
Loukas, A., 340
Lousberg, H., 124
Lovell, K., 198
Lovibond, P. F., 110
Lovibond, S. H., 110
Lowry, J. L., 478
Luborsky, L., 326, 469, 477–481
Lucas, J. A., 128
Luce, K. H., 396
Lucente, S., 180–181
Lucki, I., 112, 512
Lucksted, A., 267
Lucock, M. P., 139
Lukoff, D., 266
Luo, Y., 455
Luscombe, D. K., 172

Lushene, R., 110
Lushene, R. E., 11
Lussier, Y., 451, 453
Luterek, J. A., 106
Luttels, C., 327
Lydiard, R. B., 112, 129
Lygren, S., 158
Lyketsos, C., 280, 289
Lyketsos, C. G., 287, 292
Lykken, D. T., 454
Lynam, D. R., 305
Lynch, K. G., 47
Lynch, R. S., 47
Lyonfields, J. D., 102, 106
Lyons, D. M., 210
Lyons, H., 318
Lyons, M., 323, 325
Lyons-Ruth, K., 304
Lyoo, K., 233
Lysaght, R., 291
Lytle, R., 109

MacCabe, J. H., 266
MacCallum, F., 373
MacCallum, R. C., 25, 32–33
Macciardi, F., 252
MacDonald, K., 143
MacDonald, M. G., 452
MacDonald, P. A., 172
Machan, J. T., 107
Machin, D., 415
Machin, M. A., 55
Mackay, L., 291
MacKenzie, T. B., 371, 373, 375, 377, 380
Macklin, M. L., 191–192
MacLeod, C. M., 102–103, 112, 172
MacMahon, B., 439
MacMillan, L., 416
Madeddu, F., 305
Maffei, C., 305
Magee, W. J., 121–122, 141, 143, 146, 155–157
Magnuson, D., 193
Maguire, J., 377
MaguthNezu, M., 36, 219
Mahoney, M. J., 41, 487
Maier, W., 110, 124, 215, 321
Maisto, S. A., 347
Maj, M., 250
Mak, W. S., 76
Maki, K. M., 123, 131
Malamuth, N. M., 438
Malarkey, W. B., 458
Malatesta, V. J., 320
Malcarnem, V. L., 139
Malchy, L., 338
Malhi, G. S., 215
Malkoff-Schwartz, S., 255
Mallack, M., 90
Mallams, J. H., 364
Maller, R. G., 123
Malone, K., 325
Malone, K. M., 304
Maltby, N., 163
Manassis, K., 122
Mancill, R. B., 139, 154, 175
Mancini, C., 147–148
Mangine, S., 307, 324
Mangione, T. W., 346
Manicavasagar, V., 106
Manke, F., 391–393
Mann, A. H., 306, 321, 394
Mann, E. M., 70
Mann, J. J., 221, 304, 325
Mann, R. E., 445
Mannix, L. K., 411, 417
Mannuzza, S., 138, 154
Marcelis, M., 263
March, J. S., 177–178, 189–190
Marchand, A., 124

Marchiaro, L., 311
Marcouiller, M., 326
Marcus, D. A., 413
Marcus, M. D., 390, 398, 487
Marcus, R., 392, 505
Marcus, S. C., 221
Mardekian, J., 130
Marder, J., 265
Marder, S. R., 269
Margolese, H. C., 338
Margolin, G., 458
Margraf, J., 129
Marilov, V., 392
Marin, R., 289
Marinangeli, M. G., 318–320
Marinkovic, J., 286
Marino, L. J., 3
Marino, M. F., 285, 392
Markman, H. J., 451, 461
Markon, K. E., 57
Markowitz, J. C., 122, 220
Markowitz, J. S., 289
Marks, A. P., 177
Marks, I. M., 125, 163, 172, 174, 177–178, 180–181, 198, 326
Marks, M., 175
Markus, H. R., 77
Marlatt, G. A., 342, 348, 360, 365, 493
Marmot, M. G., 346
Marneros, A., 246
Marques, C., 148
Marques, J. K., 442
Marsden, J., 362
Marsella, A. J., 67–69, 71–72, 76–78
Marsh, H. W., 24, 26–27, 29
Marshall, G. N., 191
Marshall, L. E., 440–441
Marshall, R. D., 197
Marshall, W. L., 437, 440–443, 445
Marteinsdottir, I., 140
Martell, C. R., 235, 238, 500
Martelli, M. F., 413
Marten, P. A., 108
Martin, C. E., 439
Martin, G., 374
Martin, J. A., 346
Martin, N. G., 55
Martin, T. C., 453
Martinez, E., 389, 396
Martinussen, M., 392
Marton, P., 323
Marwaha, S., 268
Marzillier, J. S., 326
Maser, J. D., 127, 316
Masi, G., 103
Mason, B. J., 236
Mason, F. L., 243
Massion, A. O., 104, 110, 111, 129, 130, 143
Masters, W. H., 423, 427, 432–433
Masterson, J., 321
Mataix-Cols, D., 9, 163, 180–181
Matar, M., 197
Matchett, G., 106
Mateer, C. A., 290
Mathe, A. A., 61, 211
Mathers, H., 433
Mathew, N., 417–418
Mathews, A. M., 101–103, 112, 128, 172
Mattanah, J. J. F., 7, 323
Mattick, R. P., 145–146
Maturana, R., 281
Matuzas, W., 122
Maudsley, H., 318
Mavissakalian, M., 128–129, 325, 327
Mawson, D., 172, 178
May, J., 102
May, P., 321
Mayberg, H. S., 209
Maydeu-Olivares, A., 42
Mayerovitch, J. I., 173

Mayers, M., 163
Mayou, R. A., 190
Mays, V., 270
Mazaux, J. M., 290–291
Mazure, C. M., 174, 214, 251
McArdel, C. R., 390
McBride, L., 247, 256
McCabe, M. P., 430–431
McCabe, R. E., 154, 160–162
McCallum, M., 479, 481
McCann, I. L., 47
McCanna, M., 145
McCarthy, D., 278
McCarthy, E., 254
McCarthy, P. R., 179, 192
McCarty, H. J., 286
McCauley, C., 161
McChesney, C. M., 105
McClaughlin, M., 374
McClay, J., 61
McClellan, J., 246
McClelland, D. C., 270
McClough, J., 391
McClure, K. S., 219
McConaghy, N., 371, 373, 376, 382
McConville, B. J., 248
McCool, R. E., 189, 194
McCormick, R. A., 382
McCormick, R. V., 265
McCoy, J. K., 460
McCrady, B. S., 492
McCrae, R. R., 57, 280, 321, 392, 453
McCranie, E., 326
McCrory, D. C., 413
McCullough, J. P., 209, 231, 233, 237, 239
McCusker, J., 359
McCutcheon, A. L., 12
McDeavitt, J. T., 292
McDermut, W., 233
McDonald, C., 264
McDonald, R. P., 24, 178
McDonough, M., 163
McDougle, C. J., 380, 383
McElroy, S. L., 248, 250, 372, 374, 378–383, 510
McEvoy, J. P., 266
McFall, M. E., 171
McFarlane, A. C., 191, 193
McGaugh, J. L., 193, 197
McGee, R., 105, 356
McGhee, D. E., 160
McGill, C. W., 267, 271
McGlashan, T., 318, 323
McGlashan, T. H., 7, 265, 305–306, 308–309, 323
McGlashan, W. H., 271
McGonagle, K. A., 121, 141, 156, 212, 338
McGorry, P., 265
McGowan, L., 147
McGrath, P. J., 209
McGue, M., 58, 453
McGuffin, P., 53–54, 215, 264
McGuire, L. M., 282
McGuire, R. J., 440
McGurk, S. R., 262, 265–266, 269
McHugh, P. R., 103, 321
McHugo, G. J., 262, 268, 270
McIntosh, V., 399
McIntyre, H., 290
McKay, B. G., 251
McKenzie, K., 74
McKinlay, J. B., 428
McKinney, W. T., Jr., 214
McKnight Investigators, 394
McLean, P. D., 130, 179
McLean, R. Y., 127
McLellan, A. T., 348
McLeod, D. R., 102, 106–107, 112
McLeod, J. D., 103, 110

McManus, F., 139, 142
McNally, R. J., 123, 125, 128, 158–159, 172, 189, 191–193
McNeil, D. W., 144, 146
McNeilly, D., 377
McNicoll, L., 282
McWilliams, N., 469, 473, 475
Meaden, P. M., 250
Meadows, E. A., 197
Meares, R., 309
Mechanic, M. B., 189
Meehan, K. B., 324
Meehl, P. E., 317, 455
Meesters, C., 105
Meichenbaum, D. H., 487
Meijer, J., 159
Meins, W., 281
Meissner, W. M., 471, 476
Melamed, L., 373
Melley, A. H., 396
Mellman, T. A., 196, 482
Mellor, D. J., 196
Mellsop, G., 318
Meloy, J. R., 325
Meltzer, C. C., 304
Meltzer, H. Y., 176, 236, 266, 504
Melzack, R., 411
Mendelson, M., 5, 11, 219, 236
Mendelwicz, J., 247
Mendez, M. F., 290
Mendlowicz, M., 148
Menefee, L., 281
Menezes, P. R., 238
Menlove, F. L., 105
Mennin, D. S., 26, 106, 111, 138
Menninger, K. A., 469, 475, 482
Menzies, R. G., 41, 105, 157, 160, 162
Mercer, C. H., 426, 431
Mercier, M., 253
Merckelbach, H., 105, 157–160
Merikangas, K. R., 11, 121–122, 212, 410–411
Merluzzi, T. V., 138
Merrilees, R., 392
Meston, C. M., 432–433
Metalsky, G. I., 45, 235
Metzger, E. D., 390
Metzger, L. J., 193
Metzger, R. L., 26, 101, 109
Meyer, A., 318
Meyer, B., 247–248
Meyer, C., 399
Meyer, D. A., 249
Meyer, T. J., 26, 109–110
Meyer, V., 177
Meyerhoff, A. S., 130
Meyers, R. J., 347–348, 364
Meythaler, J. M., 281
Mezzich, A. C., 340
Michael, S. T., 10, 424
Michaels, M., 424
Michel, P., 416–417
Michels, R., 8
Michelson, D., 514
Michelson, L., 128
Mick, M. A., 140
Miele, G. M., 362
Miklowitz, D. J., 247–248, 250, 255
Mikulincer, M., 196
Milanov, I., 412
Milby, J. B., 363
Millar, N., 103
Miller, A. H., 215
Miller, A. L., 504
Miller, B., 390
Miller, G. A., 106
Miller, I. W., 176, 247, 250
Miller, J. K., 281
Miller, L. C., 110
Miller, L. J., 287
Miller, M. L., 26, 101, 109

Miller, N. E., 171
Miller, P. P., 125
Miller, S. I., 355
Miller, W. R., 345–349, 363–364
Millet, B., 173, 374
Millman, R. B., 355–356
Millon, C., 323
Millon, T., 316, 318, 323–324
Milner, A. D., 172
Milner, T. A., 193
Milos, G., 397
Milstein, V., 253
Milt, H., 371, 378
Milton, D. R., 514
Mineka, S., 40, 52, 105, 125, 158–159, 162
Miner, R. C., 43
Minge, P. J., 129
Minges, J., 124
Minichiello, W. E., 181, 327
Mink, I. T., 76
Minks-Brown, C., 301
Minsky, S., 10, 234
Mintz, J., 248
Mintz, L. B., 396
Mintzer, O., 103, 107–108, 129
Minuchin, S., 289, 297
Miranda, J., 72, 488–489
Miskimen, T., 10, 234
Mitchell, J. E., 371, 375, 391
Mittelman, M., 441
Mittenberg, W., 291
Miyatake, R. K., 235
Mock, J. E., 5, 11, 219, 236
Modlofsky, H., 391
Moergeli, H., 190
Moffitt, T. E., 61, 122, 356, 453
Mogg, K., 102–103
Mogotsi, M., 157
Moise-Titus, J., 40
Molcho, A., 380
Moldin, S. O., 321, 325
Molina, S., 101, 109
Moller, H. J., 112
Molnar, C., 110–111, 172, 492
Monahan, P., 310
Monahan, S. C., 364
Monk, T. H., 255
Monroe, S., 147
Monteiro, W., 180
Montgomery, L. M., 460
Montgomery, S. A., 110, 178
Monti, P. M., 492–493
Mooney, M., 399
Moore, B. A., 365
Moore, B. D., 469–470
Moore, R. J., 215, 374
Moore, R. J., 380
Moore, S., 514
Moore, S., 318
Moorhead, S., 254
Moos, B. S., 267
Moos, R. H., 78, 348, 493
Morales, M. J., 69
Moran, P., 306, 321, 325–326
Moras, K., 108
Morey, L. C., 12, 307, 308, 323
Morgan, D., 321
Morrell, W., 389
Morris, C. D., 47
Morris, L., 289, 291
Morris, R., 289, 291
Morris, T. L., 140
Morrison, A. P., 270
Morrison, B., 177
Morrison, K., 327
Morriss, R., 254
Morrow, G. D., 451
Morse, J. Q., 326, 478
Morton, W. A., 246
Morton-Bourgon, K., 442–443, 445
Moscovitch, D. A., 138

Moseley, M. E., 210
Moser, A. E., 493
Moser, D., 289
Moser, J., 174
Moskowitz, M. A., 412
Moskowitz, R., 289
Moss, F., 284
Mota, V. L., 12
Moulds, L. M., 192–193, 196, 198
Moutier, C. Y., 140–141, 143
Mowrer, O. H., 39, 105, 125
Moyer, T., 373
Moynihan, R., 432
Mucci, M., 103
Mueller, E. A., 172
Muenz, L. R., 212
Mueser, K. T., 262, 265–266, 268–271, 358, 455
Mueser, P. R., 271
Mulder, R., 327
Mulholland, A. M., 396
Mullen, J., 251
Mulleners, W., 417
Muller, H., 146
Muller, J. P., 323
Muller-Oerlinghausen, B., 248, 250
Mulligan, K., 392
Mulsant, B. H., 208, 282, 285
Mundo, E., 252
Munitz, H., 327
Munjack, D. J., 122, 425
Muran, J. C., 327, 478
Murdock, T. B., 192, 194, 197
Muris, P., 105, 159, 160–161
Murphy, D. L., 172–173, 345, 391
Murphy, G. E., 221
Murphy, J. M., 12
Murphy, W. D., 436, 438, 440–443
Murphy-Berman, V., 77
Murray, C. J., 219, 236
Murray, E., 327
Murray, J. B., 190–191, 195, 377
Murray, M. L., 221
Murray, R. M., 67, 74, 263–264, 266
Murstein, B. I., 452
Musgni, G., 190
Mussell, M. P., 390
Muthen, B. O., 14, 23, 30
Muthen, L. K., 14, 23
Myczcowisk, L. M., 238
Myers, J., 58, 157
Myers, J. K., 75
Myers, T. C., 411
Mynors-Wallis, L. M., 221, 239
Mystkowski, J. L., 162

Nakao, K., 326
Narang, R. L., 69
Nardi, A. E., 148
Narikiyo, T. A., 80
Narrow, W. E., 141, 234
Nash, M., 322, 325
Nasrallah, H. A., 90
Nathan, E., 341, 343
Nathan, P. E., 8, 45
National Academy of Sciences/Institute of Medicine (NAS/IOM), 415
National Institute for Clinical Excellence (NICE), 397, 514
National Institute on Alcohol Abuse and Alcoholism (NIAAA), 339–340
National Research Council (NRC), 375
Navia, B. A., 286
Nduaguba, M., 321, 326
Neal, A. M., 155
Neale, J. M., 140, 142, 248
Neale, M. C., 7, 58, 61, 105, 124, 157, 209, 211, 215, 234
Neary, E., 47
Neff, C., 321
Neff, L. A., 456–457

Negrete, J. C., 338
Neiderhiser, J. M., 61
Neiger, S., 159
Neighbors, H. W., 75
Nelson, A. H., 178
Nelson, B. S., 41, 196
Nelson, C. B., 6, 11, 192, 212, 338
Nelson, E. C., 7, 424
Nelson, G. B., 143
Nelson, L., 495
Nemeroff, C. B., 214–215
Nemeroff, C. J., 38
Nepomuceno, C., 283
Nestadt, G., 103, 321
Neumann, C. S., 263
Newlove, T., 453
Newman, C. F., 244, 246, 248, 250, 252–253, 487
Newman, D. L., 122, 393, 395
Newman, L., 269
Newman, M. G., 101–103, 106, 108–112, 144
Newman, S., 326
Newton, T., 458
Nezu, A. M., 36–38, 42–43, 48, 219, 254
Nezu, C. M., 36–38, 42–43, 48, 219, 254
Nezworski, M. T., 324
Nezworski, T., 325
Nguyen, C. D., 292
Nichter, M., 41
Nickell, A. D., 304
Nicki, R., 198
Niederehe, G., 287
Niehaus, D., 371
Nigg, J., 322
Nihara, K., 76
Nilson, L., 287
Nilsson, A., 250
Nilsson, E., 391–392
Nilsson, L., 280
Nimgaonkar, V. L., 269
Nisenholz, B., 341
Nishith, P., 189, 198
Nitschke, J. B., 106
Nixon, R. D. V., 198
Nixon, S. J., 338
Noble, C. L., 29
Nock, S. L., 452
Nofzinger, E. A., 428
Nolen-Hoeksema, S., 212, 327
Noordsy, D. L., 270
Norcross, J. C., 473, 478, 500
Nordahl, T. E., 125
Norman, P. A., 395
Normann, C., 250
Norring, C., 391
North, C. S., 194
North, F., 346
Norton, G. R., 123
Noshirvani, H., 180, 198
Notarius, C. I., 459
Novack, T. A., 281
Novaco, R. W., 47
Novotny, C., 398–399
Nower, L., 370, 373, 375–376, 381
Noyes, J., 107–108
Noyes, R., 104–105, 107, 138, 173, 194, 320, 325
Nuechterlein, K., 248, 266
Nunno, V. J., 325
Nurnberg, H. G., 327
Nussbeck, F. W., 29
Nutt, D. J., 209
Nuzzarello, A., 130

Oakes, D., 13
Ober, B. A., 266
Oberklaid, F., 139
O'Boyle, M., 325
O'Brien, C. P., 326, 348
O'Brien, G. T., 108

O'Connor, M. E., 391, 395, 398
Odegaard, O., 263
Odejide, A. O., 73
Odland, T., 327
O'Donnell, F. J., 417
O'Donnell, M. L., 195
O'Driscoll, G., 301
Oehrlein, A., 124
Oei, T. P., 145
Oerlinghausen, B., 248, 250
O'Farrell, T. J., 348, 363, 365, 458
Office of Applied Studies, Substance Abuse and Mental Health Services Administration, 356
Offord, D. R., 356
Ogborne, A., 143
Ogrodniczuk, J. S., 481
O'Halloran, M. S. S., 396
Ohanian, V., 399
O'Hearn, E., 287
Okamoto, A., 251
Okasha, A., 107
Okazaki, S., 75
Okiguji, T., 37
Oldham, J. M., 27, 309, 318–320, 323, 325, 377
Oldham, M., 197
O'Leary, K. D., 450, 456, 458–459
O'Leary, T. A., 491
Olesen, J., 412
Olfson, M., 129, 221
Olichney, J., 282
Olie, J. P., 374
Oliver, A., 26–27
Oliver, R., 291
Ollendick, T. H., 142, 155, 160–161, 487, 492–493, 499
Olmstead, M., 394
Olmsted, M., 399
Olmsted, M. P., 400
Olson, K. R., 453
Oltmanns, T. F., 396
O'Malley, P. M., 380
Omi, M., 72
Onstad, S., 158
Oosterlaan, J., 377
Opdyke, D., 372, 379, 383–384
Opler, L. A., 265–266
Opler, M. K., 10
Oquendo, M. A., 221
Orn, H., 326
Orr, S. P., 191, 193–194
Orrell, M., 280
Orsillo, S. M., 145–146
Ortega, A. N., 75
Osborne, L. N., 451
Osher, F. C., 265
Osman, S., 399
Öst, L. G., 46, 103, 125–126, 154–156, 161–162
Ostensen, E., 392
Oster, C., 382
Osterhaus, J. T., 416–417
O'Sullivan, G., 180–181
Otto, M. W., 112, 121, 123, 126–131, 147
Ouellette, R., 122
Ouimette, P. C., 7, 348
Overmeier, B., 38
Owen, M. J., 53, 264
Owen, M. T., 460
Owens, M. J., 215
Oxman, T. E., 233
Ozdemir, O., 173
Ozer, E. J., 190
Oziel, L. J., 425
Ozmen, E., 190

Paans, A. M., 125
Packard, R. C., 410, 413, 419

Packer, A., 325
Padawer, J. R., 325
Pagani, L., 157
Page, A. C., 156, 162
Page, I. J., 436, 438
Paivio, A., 106
Paker, M., 190
Pallmeyer, T. P., 193
Panasetis, P., 193
Pandina, R. J., 493
Panico, S., 76
Pankratz, L., 321
Pankratz, V. S., 218
Papageorgiou, C., 101
Papart, P., 212
Papp, L. A., 123–124
Paptheodorou, G., 252
Paradise, M. J., 338
Parihar, M. S., 92
Paris, J., 70–71, 79, 304–309, 322–323, 326
Parker, G. F., 105–106, 209, 310
Parker, J., 376
Parker, L., 157
Parnas, J., 264
Parrone, P. L., 232
Parsons, B., 380
Pasold, T., 40
Passchier, J., 411
Pasternak, R. E., 282
Patch, V. D., 5
Pate, J. E., 73
Patel, A., 176
Patel, M., 262
Patrick, C., 453
Patte, J. L., 308
Patten, S. B., 280, 285
Patterson, G. R., 451, 459
Pattison, P., 195, 440
Patton, G. C., 394
Paul, R., 289
Paulhus, D. L., 75
Paulosky, C. A., 395–396
Paulus, M. P., 237
Pavlov, I. P., 36, 125
Pavlovic, D., 106, 326
Paykel, E. S., 68, 221
Payne, L. P., 162
Peacock, E. J., 442
Pearl, D., 458
Pearlman, L. A., 47
Pearlstein, T., 196
Pearson, J., 289
Peasley-Miklus, C., 106, 111
Pedersen, N. L., 61, 211
Peen, J., 263
Pelissolo, A., 140
Penava, S. A., 127
Penava, S. J., 123
Penn, D. L., 262, 269, 271
Pennanen, C., 95
Penzien, D. B., 413–418
Pepin, M., 381
Peralta, V., 12–13
Perel, J. M., 129
Peri, T., 190, 194
Perkins, D. O., 271
Perkins, R., 291
Perri, M. G., 43, 254
Perry, A., 254
Perry, J. C., 324, 326, 479
Perry, K. J., 139, 195
Perry, S. W., 190, 193
Person, P. D., 285
Persons, J. B., 44, 106, 237, 278, 299, 308–309, 410, 413, 488
Persson, G., 280
Peselow, E., 246
Peters, M., 159
Peterson, A. L., 383

Peterson, C. B., 396
Peterson, E., 175, 189
Peterson, J. V., 341
Peterson, L. G., 326
Peterson, R. A., 123, 128, 159, 161
Peterson, S. J., 309
Petrakis, I. L., 339
Petruzzi, D. C., 159
Petry, N. M., 348, 371, 373, 376, 382
Peveler, R., 398
Pfefferbaum, A., 210
Pfeiffer, W., 69
Pfister, H., 110, 122
Pfohl, B., 173, 300–301, 307, 310, 318, 320, 324, 327
Phillips, H., 291
Phillips, K. A., 326, 233
Phillips, S., 451
Philpot, M., 279
Philpott, R., 174
Phinney, J. S., 76
Phipps, A., 443
Phipps, P., 444
Piaget, J., 472
Piasetsky, E., 290
Pickrell, E., 378
Pierce, K. A., 155
Pignone, M. P., 237
Pigott, T. A., 173, 391
Pike, K. M., 395, 397–398, 494
Pilkonis, P., 327
Pilkonis, P. A., 324, 327
Pincus, A. L., 104, 109–110, 324, 340
Pincus, H. A., 8
Pinel, P., 4, 318
Pinnock, K., 399
Pinsker, H., 327
Piper, W. E., 479, 481
Pithers, W. D., 445
Pitman, R. K., 169, 175, 191–194, 197
Pitschel-Walz, G., 271
Plachetka, J. R., 416
Plakun, E. M., 323
Plant, E. A., 78
Plaud, J. J., 440
Plochg, I., 179
Plomin, R., 54–55, 61, 63
Plotsky, P. M., 214–215
Podar, I., 392
Podolski, C. L., 40
Pogue-Geile, M. F., 262
Polat, A., 173
Polatin, P., 317
Poli, P., 103
Polivy, J., 394
Pollack, J., 327
Pollack, M. H., 112, 123, 126–127, 129–131, 510
Pomeroy, C., 389–390
Pomeroy, W. B., 439
Ponticas, Y., 438
Pontin, E. E., 41
Poon, L., 281
Poortinga, J., 438
Poortinga, Y. H., 69, 75
Pope, H., 391
Pope, H. G., 250, 374, 379
Popkin, S., 281
Porges, S. W., 102
Portera, L., 129, 176
Posner, M. I., 322
Post, R. M., 193, 215, 245, 247, 251
Poston, W. S., 395
Potenza, M. N., 373, 376, 381, 383
Potkin, S. G., 286
Potts, J. M., 255
Potts, N., 148, 512
Poulton, R., 157–158
Pourmotabbed, T., 112
Powell, J., 373
Powers, M. B., 123, 162

Poynton, C., 291
Prassas, A., 192
Prather, R. C., 380
Pratt, D., 160
Pratt, L. A., 122
Pratt, P., 172
Preda, A., 251
Prescott, C. A., 58, 142, 157–158, 210–212, 214–215
President's Commission on Mental Health, 196
Presnell, K., 393–394
Presta, S., 371, 374, 377, 379
Prestholdt, P., 291
Previti, D., 452
Price, J. M., 47
Price, L. H., 174, 162, 178
Price, R. W., 286
Priebe, S., 248, 255
Prien, R. F., 231
Priester, M. J., 43
Prigatano, G., 287, 293
Prigerson, H. G., 12
Prince, R. H., 68–69, 72–73
Prince, V., 436, 439
Prins, B., 197
Printz, D. J., 250
Prior, M., 139
Prochaska, J. O., 500
Project MATCH Research Group, 348
Pruyn, N. A., 176
Pruzinsky, T., 101
Pryor, T., 393
Pryse-Phillips, W. E., 416, 418
Przedborski, S., 286
Przeworski, A., 108, 492
Przybeck, T. R., 54, 392
Psychological Corporation, 287
Pugh, K. H., 30
Pukrop, R., 300
Pulkkinen, L., 63
Pumariega, A. J., 73
Puri, B. K., 279, 283
Pusch, D., 487
Pyle, R. L., 373, 375

Quadflieg, N., 391
Quarrington, B., 159
Quinlan, D. M., 471
Quinsey, V. L., 442
Quitkin, F. M., 209

Rabavilas, A. D., 171
Rabe-Hesketh, S., 391
Rabkin, J. G., 209, 264
Racenstein, J. M., 269
Rachman, S., 125–126, 157, 160, 171–172, 174, 177–178, 180, 490, 492
Rack, P. H., 174
Racker, H., 476
Rado, S., 317
Radomsky, A. S., 172, 175
Rae, D. S., 14, 141, 263
Rafaelsen, O. J., 249
Rafanelli, C., 221
Rahdert, E., 342
Raichle, M. E., 125
Raimonde, A. J., 193
Raine, A., 67
Raine, S., 345
Rainer, J. D., 247
Rains, J. C., 417
Raistrick, D., 345
Rajkumar, S., 263
Ralph, J., 176
Ramadan, N. M., 413
Ramirez, G., 237
Ramirez, L. F., 373, 382
Ramsey, B., 47
Ramsey, S. E., 344
Randall, P. K., 159

Rao, R., 391
Rao, V., 292
Rapaport, M. H., 130
Rapee, R. M., 40, 46, 101–102, 107–108, 123, 138–139, 141–142, 155, 192, 489–490
Rapoport, A. M., 417
Rapoport, J. L., 171, 173, 375
Rapoport, M. H., 237
Rapport, D. J., 251
Rasinski, K. A., 26
Raskin, G., 346
Raskin, S. A., 92
Raskind, M., 289
Rasmussen, B. K., 410–411
Rasmussen, S. A., 171–174, 176, 178, 180, 360, 363
Rasmusson, D., 287
Rastam, M., 391–392, 399
Ratcliff, K. S., 6, 219
Rattock, J., 290
Rauch, S. L., 178, 194, 212
Raven, P. H., 3, 10, 15
Ravindran, A. V., 238
Rayls, K., 291
Raynor, R., 37
Rea, M. M., 255
Read, J. P., 348
Rector, N. A., 44, 487, 495–496, 499
Redlich, F. C., 10, 74, 263
Reed, D., 271
Reed, G. F., 172
Reed, M. L., 411
Reeman, I. M., 391
Reese, H. E., 130
Reeve, E. A., 377
Reeves, R. S., 395
Regan, J. J., 173, 320
Regier, D. A., 6, 14, 74, 141, 210–211, 262–263, 270
Rehm, J., 343, 346
Rehm, L., 488
Reich, J., 103, 138, 143, 211, 321, 323, 325–327
Reich, W., 318, 475
Reiffer, L. I., 323
Reifler, B., 289
Reilly-Harrington, N. A., 246, 248
Reiman, E. M., 125
Reinders, A. A., 125
Reis, D. J., 193
Reise, S. P., 14, 30
Reiss, D., 55, 61
Reiss, R. S., 128
Reiss, S., 123, 159, 161
Reitan, R. M., 266
Reitman, D., 371
Ren, X. S., 455
Rendu, A., 306
Renneberg, B., 122, 325
Rennie, T. A., 10
Rennison, C., 444
Renton, J. C., 270
Resick, P. A., 47, 189, 197–198
Resnick, H. S., 64, 194
Resnick, J. S., 212
Resnick, S., 287
Resnik, S., 106
Rettew, D. C., 139–140
Reynolds, C. F. III, 214
Reynolds, D., 304
Reznick, J. S., 122
Rezutek, P. E., 160
Rheaume, J., 106
Rhodes, H. M., 364
Rhodes, L. J., 248
Rice, J. P., 7, 321
Rice, M. E., 442
Rich, F., 423
Richa, S., 374
Richards, J. A., 255

Richards, J. E., 102
Richards, M., 278
Richardson, A. S., 374
Richardson, C., 271
Richardson, G., 438
Richer, E., 290–291
Richter, M. A., 172
Rickels, K., 112, 512
Rickman, D., 381
Riddle, M. A., 178
Ridgely, M. S., 270
Rief, W., 391
Riemann, B. C., 192
Ries, B. J., 144
Rietbroek, H., 160
Rietdijk, E. A., 306
Rifkin, A., 122
Rigaud, D., 399
Riggs, D. S., 169, 175–176, 189, 194–195, 197
Riker, J. R., 481
Risen, C. B., 429
Riso, L. P., 7, 235
Riso, L. P. L., 391
Rist, F., 341
Ritchie, E. C., 375
Ritchie, J., 282
Ritenour, A., 214
Rivara, F. P., 347
Rivzi, S. L., 396
Robbins, J. M., 12, 515
Robert, L., 324
Robert, P., 88
Roberts, J., 247
Roberts, L. J., 346, 451
Roberts, R. E., 290, 393
Robins, C. J., 309
Robins, E., 6, 12, 16, 125, 218
Robins, L. N., 6, 10, 141, 219, 236
Robins, R. W., 453
Robins, S., 47
Robinson, E. A., 101
Robinson, G., 341
Robinson, P. H., 398, 495
Robinson, R. L., 211, 292
Roblin, D., 430
Rössler, W., 285
Rocca, P., 311
Rockert, W., 399
Rockwell, E., 282–283
Rodriguez, B. I., 162
Roeger, L., 374
Roemer, L., 101–103, 106, 111
Roffman, R. A., 363
Rogers, H. J., 14
Rogers, M. P., 105, 122
Rogers, S. J., 454
Rogers, W., 232
Rohling, J., 450
Rohsenow, D. J., 492
Roid, G., 287
Roid, G. H., 287
Rollnick, S., 363
Roman, P. M., 346
Romano, E., 157
Romano, R., 103
Romanoski, A. J., 103, 321
Ronan, G. F., 42–43
Ronningstam, E., 319, 323–324
Roose, S. P., 210–211, 220
Roozendaal, B., 193
Roper, G., 171
Roper, M., 234
Rosch, E. R., 3, 10, 15
Rose, R. J., 62–63, 341
Rose, S., 191, 195, 235
Rosen, R. C., 426, 429
Rosenbaum, J. F., 105, 122–123, 126, 158, 212
Rosenbaum, M., 390
Rosenberg, H. L., 252

Rosenberg, M., 26
Rosenberg, S. D., 191, 262, 266
Rosenberger, E. W., 480
Rosenblatt, A., 287
Rosenfeld, R., 324
Rosenhan, D. L., 5–6, 15
Rosenheck, R., 75, 339
Rosenstein, D. S., 237
Rosenthal, D., 317
Rosenthal, N. E., 247
Rosenthal, R. J., 373, 378
Rosenthal, R. N., 327
Rosenvinge, J., 392
Rosman, B., 389
Rosmark, B., 391
Ross, H. E., 344
Ross, S., 393
Rossiter, E. M., 399
Rostosky, S., 341
Rotgers, F., 344
Rothbard, J. C., 346
Rothbaum, B. O., 162, 177, 189, 194–195, 197, 372, 379, 383–387
Rothenberg, A., 391
Rothschild, A. J., 208, 382
Rotter, J. I., 53
Rouleau, J. L., 436–437, 442
Rounsaville, B. J., 220, 238, 255, 365
Rovner, B. W., 282, 289
Rowan, M. S., 380
Rowden, L., 142
Rowe, D. C., 55
Rowe, M. K., 162–163
Roy, M. A., 8, 61, 211
Roy-Byrne, P. P., 104, 121, 126, 130, 452
Rozin, P., 161
Rubenstein, C., 391
Rubey, R. N., 251
Rubin, K. H., 142
Rubinow, D. R., 247
Rubonis, A., 364
Ruckdeschel, K., 450
Rudolph, R. L., 221, 507
Rueffer-Hesse, C., 425
Ruggiero, D. A., 193
Rugle, L., 373
Ruiz, M. A., 340, 376
Runtz, M., 439
Rusbult, C. E., 451–452
Ruscio, A. M., 109, 195–196
Ruscio, J., 109
Rush, A. J., 44, 125, 219–220, 223, 238, 487
Rush, B., 318
Russell, G. F. M., 397, 399
Russell, J., 391
Russo, A. M., 373, 382
Rust, J., 429
Rutherford, J., 215
Rutter, M., 54, 316, 322
Ryan, C. E., 250
Ryan, P., 193
Ryan, T., 299
Rybicki, D., 393
Ryder, A. G., 75, 233
Rye, P., 11
Rygh, J., 497

Saarento, O., 326
Sabo, A. N., 304–305
Sabourin, S., 451, 453
Sachs, G. S., 126, 250–252, 254
Sachs-Ericsson, N., 78
Sack, D. A., 247
Sack, R. L., 247
Sackeim, H. A., 223
Sacks, N., 392
Sackville, T., 196, 198
Sadowsky, N., 399

Safer, D., 397
Safferman, A. Z., 267
Safir, M. P., 425
Safran, J. D., 103, 478
Safren, S. A., 146–147
Sagrestano, L. M., 451
Sahar, T., 190
Sahin, O., 190
Saiz, J., 391
Saiz-Ruiz, D. F., 376
Saleem, R., 255
Salkovskis, P. M., 46–47, 126, 139, 159, 162, 171–172, 174, 179, 489, 491
Sallaerts, S., 327
Salloum, I., 348, 508
Salmon, M., 271
Salter, M. W., 86–87
Salthouse, T. A., 278
Saltzman, H., 424
Salvador, S., 289
Salvador, T., 289
Salyers, M. P., 271
Salzman, D. G., 147
Sam, D., 76
Samstag, L. W., 327, 478
Samuels, J. F., 103, 173, 321, 326
Sanathara, V. A., 212
Sanavio, E., 174
Sandage, B. W., 292
Sandell, R., 478
Sanderson, C., 309, 324
Sanderson, K., 110
Sanderson, W. C., 103, 107, 110, 122, 155
Sandrow, D., 247
Sands, E., 76
Sands, J. R., 262
Sanfilipo, M., 246
Sanislow, C. A., 12
Sannibale, C., 339
Sano, N., 162
Sanson, A., 139
Sansone, R. A., 306
Santiago, N. J., 233, 234, 237
Santonastaso, P., 389, 394
Santos, A. B., 270
Santosh, P. J., 221
Saper, J. R., 413
Saperia, D., 287
Saperia, J., 221
Sapolsky, R. M., 210
Sarasalo, E., 373, 379, 382, 383
Saraydarian, L., 43
Sartorius, N., 70, 72, 78, 263
Sasson, Y., 171, 173, 383
Saunders, B. E., 64, 190
Saunders, E., 438
Saunders, W. B., 263
Savic, J., 284
Sawchuk, C. N., 159
Sawyer, J. P., 416
Sawyer-Glover, A. M., 210
Saxena, S., 86, 92
Schaap, C., 180, 451
Schachar, R. J., 12
Schacht, T. E., 8
Schacter, D., 292
Schafer, J., 177, 339
Schafer, R., 469, 474
Schatzberg, A. F., 208, 210
Schell, T. L., 191
Scherpenisse, J., 281
Schlenger, W. E., 41
Schlosser, S., 104, 176, 371, 373
Schmaling, K. B., 37, 231, 239
Schmeidler, J., 196
Schmidt, C., 438
Schmidt, N. B., 123, 128–130
Schmitz, J. M., 364
Schmolz, U., 399
Schnaier, J. A., 110

Schneider, J. A., 399
Schneider, K., 5, 318
Schneider, P. A., 396
Schneider, T., 215
Schneier, F. R., 138–141, 143, 146–147
Schnicke, M. K., 47, 197–198
Schnurer, A., 177
Schnurr, P. P., 191
Schnyder, U., 190, 195, 397
Schoevers, R. A., 220
Schonfeld, W. H., 157
Schooler, N., 268
Schoonfeld, M., 91
Schotte, C. K. W., 173
Schouten, E., 159
Schreiber, S., 190
Schroeder, K. E. E., 78
Schroeder, M. L., 323, 393
Schuckit, M. A., 9, 343, 355
Schulberg, H. C., 213–214
Schulsinger, F., 317
Schultz, R. T., 95
Schulze, U. M. E., 389–390
Schwab, J. J., 75, 104
Schwartz, B. S., 411, 417
Schwartz, C. E., 122, 140, 212, 327
Schwartz, J. E., 234–235
Schwartz, J. L. K., 160
Schwartz, J. M., 86
Schwartz, M. H., 390
Schwartz, M. S., 415
Schwartz, S., 255
Schwartzman, A., 389
Schweder, R. A., 79
Schweizer, E., 112, 512
Schwiers, M. L., 252
Scott, B., 392
Scott, C. K., 451
Scott, J., 254, 256
Scott, L. N., 316
Scott, W. O., 191
Scullen, S. E., 29
Seabrook, M. K., 72
Secretary of Health and Human Services, 343, 347–348
Seeley, J. R., 90, 393, 395
Segal, B., 356
Segal, D. L., 345, 396
Segal, Z. V., 103, 212, 440, 489
Segall, M. H., 75
Segrin, C., 220
Seidman, S. N., 210
Seivewright, H., 322, 323, 327, 396
Seliger, G., 292
Seligman, M. E. P., 38, 158
Selten, J. P., 263
Seltzer, M., 327
Selzer, M. L., 344
Sempos, C. T., 343
Sengun, S., 125
Serlin, R. C., 172
Serran, G., 445
Seto, M. C., 436, 438, 442
Sexton, H. C., 479
Shader, R. I., 112
Shadick, R. N., 108
Shadish, W. R., 460
Shaffer, D., 221
Shaffer, H. J., 373, 375, 378, 381
Shafran, R., 176, 398, 494–495
Shahar, A., 327
Shahar, F., 177
Shalev, A. Y., 190–191, 193–194
Shaner, A., 359
Shapiro, D. A., 475, 478
Shapiro, F., 197
Sharp, C., 360
Sharpley, M., 74
Sharrock, R., 159
Shatz, M. W., 90
Shavelson, R. J., 30

Shaver, P. R., 106, 454
Shaw, B. F., 44, 87, 212, 220, 238
Shaw, H., 395
Shea, J. M., 189
Shea, M. T., 9, 130, 211, 221, 322–323, 327
Shea, T., 324
Shea, W. M., 357, 365
Shear, M. K., 127, 130
Shear, P., 289
Shedler, J., 316, 319, 324, 397
Sheehan, D. V., 122, 219
Sheldon, A. E., 323
Sheldon, C. T., 103
Sheline, Y. I., 210
Shelton, M. D., 251, 510
Shelton, R. C., 223
Shepherd, R. B., 380
Sheppard, L. C., 489
Sher, K. J., 105, 172, 301, 344, 346
Sherbourne, C. D., 128, 232
Shermis, M. D., 128
Shih, J. H., 220, 233
Shin, L. M., 189, 192, 194, 212
Shinosaki, K., 280
Shisslak, C. M., 73
Shoaib, A. M., 12
Shoham, V., 455
Shohami, E., 283
Showers, J., 378
Sickel, A. E., 324
Siefen, G., 340
Siegel, C., 263
Siever, L. J., 303–305, 307, 317, 322
Sifneos, P. E., 481
Sigmon, S. C., 492
Sigvardsson, S., 339
Silberstein, S. D., 417
Silk, K. R., 305
Silliman, R., 289
Silove, D., 106, 383
Silva, P. A., 105, 122, 175, 356
Silva, R. R., 189
Silver, N. C., 360
Silver, S., 290
Silverman, J. M., 33, 317
Silverman, K., 364
Silverman, W. K., 105
Silverstone, T., 417
Silverthorn, P., 104
Silvia, E. S., 25
Silvosky, J. F., 438
Simon, D., 411
Simon, G. E., 220
Simon, N. M., 122–123, 128
Simoneau, T. L., 255
Simons, A. D., 221
Simpson, P. E., 214
Simpson, S. C., 247
Simpson, S. G., 245, 249
Singer, A. R., 487
Singer, J. L., 13, 356, 504
Singer, K., 70
Singh, A. N., 377
Singh, P., 77
Sinha, S., 124
Sirovatka, P., 11
Sisson, R. W., 348–349, 364
Skinner, B. F., 38
Skinner, H. A., 344, 360
Skinstad, A. H., 341
Sklar, S. M., 362
Skodol, A. E., 4, 300–304, 306–309, 316, 320, 323, 325, 327, 377, 392
Skre, I., 158
Slade, P. D., 389, 496
Slade, T., 121, 141, 175
Slaets, J., 263
Slater, A., 41
Slater, D., 441
Slater, S., 440

Sloan, P., 194
Slotnik, H., 392
Slovik, L. F., 452
Slymen, D. J., 194
Smailes, E. M., 40
Small, I. F., 253
Small, J. G., 247, 253
Smart, D., 139, 391
Smith, C. J., 317
Smith, D. A., 105, 221, 456
Smith, E. E., 3
Smith, E. M., 189, 194
Smith, G. S., 346, 391
Smith, J. E., 96, 347, 364
Smith, K. L., 41, 191
Smith, M., 193, 396
Smith, R., 416, 437
Smith, R. D., 512
Smith, R. L., 365
Smith, S., 162, 321
Smits, J. A. J., 121, 123, 130, 159
Smukler, M., 79
Snidman, N., 102, 104, 122, 140, 212
Snow, M., 344
Snowden, L. R., 73
Snyder, D. K., 458
Snyder, M., 248
Snyder, S. H., 292
Soares, J. C., 86, 90
Sobell, L. C., 337, 345, 348, 362
Sobell, M. B., 337, 345, 348, 362
Sörbom, D., 12, 23
Sofka, M., 101
Sohlberg, S., 391
Sokolof, M., 75
Soloff, P. H., 47, 304
Solomon, D. A., 250
Solomon, G. D., 416
Solomon, J., 338
Solomon, Z., 196
Soltys, S. M., 384
Solyom, C., 138
Solyom, L., 138, 174
Sommer, F., 433
Sondhi, S., 416
Songer, D. A., 306
Sonne, S. C., 246
Sonnega, A., 6, 192
Sonntag, H., 146
Sorbara, F., 252
Sorbello, L., 440–441
Sorensen, C. B., 176
Sorenson, S. B., 171, 176
Sotsky, S. M., 239
Soutullo, C. A., 246, 372
Souza, F. G., 508
Spangler, D., 394
Spanier, G. B., 459
Spaulding, W. D., 262, 271
Speilberger, C. S., 11
Spence, D. P., 474
Spencer, T. J., 514–515
Spiegel, D. A., 130, 194–196
Spielberger, C. D., 110
Spindler, A., 397
Spinelli, M. G., 209
Spitzer, R. L., 4–8, 11, 16, 109, 127, 144, 160, 219, 236, 307, 317, 324, 345, 361, 381, 393, 396
Spoonster, E., 193
Spritzer, K., 232
Spurgeon, A., 87
Spurrell, E. B., 390
Squires-Wheeler, E., 321
Srikameswaran, S., 393
Srinivasagam, N., 391
Srole, L., 10
Sroufe, L. A., 105
Staab, J. P., 123, 195
Staak, M., 106

Staats, A. W., 36
Staats, C. K., 36
Stallings, M. C., 59
Stanczak, D. E., 283
Stang, P. E., 111, 263, 417
Stangl, D., 327
Stanley, B., 306, 380
Stanley, M. A., 103, 139, 380
Stanley, S., 452
Stannard, C., 411
Stansbrey, R. J., 426
Staton, M., 341
Stebelsky, G., 326
Steel, Z. P., 376
Steele, C., 289, 292
Steer, R. A., 219, 235
Steere, E., 438
Steerneman, P., 105
Stefanis, C., 171
Stefanova, E., 286
Steffens, D. C., 215
Steiger, H., 389, 399
Stein, B., 323
Stein, D. J., 110, 157, 176, 178, 371, 377
Stein, L. I., 270
Stein, M. B., 6, 54, 57, 64, 111, 124, 138–143, 146
Steinberg, B. J., 304
Steiner, M., 178
Steiner, W., 282
Steinglass, P., 347
Steinhauer, S. R., 78
Steinhausen, H., 400
Steketee, G. S., 173–174, 176, 179–181
Stellato, C. P., 237
Stelzl, I., 33
Stephens, R. S., 363
Stepp, S., 299
Stermac, L. E., 440
Stern, J. A., 106
Stern, R. S., 101, 172, 178
Sternberg, J., 289, 508
Stevens, H., 102, 111
Stevens, P., 362, 365
Stevenson, J., 309
Stevenson, J. F., 348
Stewart, B. L., 235
Stewart, C., 341
Stewart, J. W., 209, 232–233, 240
Stewart, M., 322
Stewart, M. A., 458
Stewart, R. M., 382
Stewart, R. S., 125
Stewart, S. H., 41, 339
Stewart, W. F., 411, 416–417
Stice, E., 389–390, 393–397, 495
Stickle, T. R., 455
Stiglin, L. E., 219
Stiles, T., 327
Stinchfield, R., 370, 373, 380
Stinnett, R. D., 439
Stinson, F. S., 211
St. Jacques, J., 162
St. John, D., 310
Stober, J. B., 106
Stockhorst, U., 37
Stockwell, M., 308
Stockwell, T., 345
Stoddard, A., 359
Stolorow, R. D., 474
Stone, A. M., 416
Stone, D. K., 321
Stone, L., 469
Stone, M. H., 308, 321, 323
Stoneman, Z., 460
Stopa, L., 139, 142
Storck, M., 189
Stotland, S., 399
Stotts, S. L., 364
Stovall, T., 340

Strack, S., 324
Strada, M. J., 337, 346, 360, 363
Strakowski, S. M., 242, 252
Strang, J., 362
Strassberg, D., 393
Strauss, C. C., 103
Strauss, D., 266
Strauss, J. S., 3, 74, 78, 265
Stravynski, A., 326
Street, G. P., 180, 194
Streissguth, A. P., 346
Striegel-Moore, R. H., 393, 395
Stringer, A., 291
Strober, M., 389, 391, 393–394
Strong, D. R., 344
Strotmeyer, S. J., 304
Strub, R., 286–287
Strupp, H. H., 103, 479, 481
Strycker, L. A., 31
Stuart, G. L., 131
Stunkard, A. J., 390
Sturt, E., 268
Stutzmann, G. E., 193
Suarez, A., 499
Subich, L., 392
Substance Abuse and Mental Health Data Archive, 363
Substance Abuse and Mental Health Services Administration (SAMHSA), 356
Sue, D. W., 76
Sue, S., 70, 73–74
Sullivan, E., 289
Sullivan, E. V., 210
Sullivan, G. M., 124
Sullivan, M., 239, 271
Sullivan, P. F., 209, 215, 324, 327, 392, 394, 399
Sullivan, T., 301
Summerfeldt, L. J., 160, 172
Sunday, S. R., 391–392
Sunitha, T. A., 140
Surall, D., 340
Surls, R., 129
Sussman, L., 155
Sussman, S., 356–358
Sutandar-Pinnock, K., 399
Sutker, P. B., 190
Sutkovoi, D. A., 283
Sutton-Simon, K., 147
Svanborg, A., 280
Svartberg, M., 280
Svetel, M., 286
Svrakic, D. M., 211, 392
Svrakic, N. M., 54
Swaminathan, H., 14
Swan, G. E., 210
Swan, N., 96
Swann, A. C., 12, 250, 380
Swanson, C., 456
Swanson, K., 456
Swartz, H. A., 255
Swartz, K. L., 122
Swartz, M. S., 104, 189, 212
Swedo, S. E., 171, 173, 371, 373, 375, 377–378, 383
Sweet, J. A., 453
Sweet, R. A., 282
Sweitzer, R. D., 267
Swendsen, J., 249
Swenson, C., 112, 309
Swift, W. J., 392, 399
Swinson, R. P., 122, 162, 172, 173, 177, 320, 490
Sylvain, C., 381–382
Symonds, B. D., 478
Symonds, T., 430
Szalai, J. P., 252
Szasz, T. S., 5, 15
Szmukler, G., 397
Szymanski, J., 161

Taber, J. I., 373, 382
Takeuchi, D. T., 70–71, 75, 79
Tallis, F., 101, 110, 172, 176
Tanaka, N., 326
Tanaka-Matsumi, J., 68–70, 72, 76
Tanco, P. P., 79
Tang, T. Z., 44
Tapert, S. E., 355–365
Tapert, S. F., 341–342, 347, 352
Tapscott, M., 40
Target, M., 322
Targum, S. D., 249
Tarrier, N., 195, 197–198, 254, 267
Tasdemir, O., 190
Task Force on Promotion and Dissemination of Psychological Procedures, 418
Tata, P., 130
Tate, S. R., 341, 355
Taub, N., 236
Tauber, R., 268–269
Tavares, H., 371, 376
Taverni, J. P., 292
Taylor, C. B., 123, 140, 393–395
Taylor, C. L., 345
Taylor, M., 372
Taylor, S., 64, 130, 148, 159, 162, 174
Taylor, W. D., 215
Tchanturia, K., 391
Teachman, B. A., 159–160
Teague, G. B., 281
Teasdale, J. D., 212, 488–489, 499
Teichner, G., 360
Teitelbaum, A., 383
Teja, J. S., 69
Telch, C. F., 390, 395–397, 399
Telch, M. J., 123, 128–130, 140, 159
Tellegen, A., 324
Temkin, N. R., 286
Tempier, R., 338
Templeman, T. L., 439
TenBerge, M., 157
Teng, E., 287
Tenney, N. H., 173
Tepper, S. J., 417
Tepperwien, S., 106
TerHorst, G. J., 125
Teri, L., 289
TerKuile, M. M., 425
Tesser, A., 457
Tessler, R., 267
Tezcan, E., 304
Thackrey, M., 479, 482
Thapar, A., 215
Thara, R., 263
Thase, M. E., 207–209, 214, 218, 220–221, 223, 235–236, 503, 507
Thayer, J. F., 102
Thefeld, W., 122
Thelen, M., 396
Thomas, D. R., 71–72
Thomas, G. V., 307, 324
Thomas, V., 289
Thompson, J. K., 394
Thompson, L., 327
Thompson, P., 67
Thompson, W. N., 381–382
Thompson-Brenner, H., 389, 393, 397–400
Thompson-Pope, S. K., 374
Thomsen, P. H., 176, 178
Thorn, B. E., 85, 413, 415
Thorndike, E. L., 38
Thorndike, R. M., 156
Thornicroft, G., 271
Thornton, C., 391
Thornton, D., 442–443
Thornton, L. M., 215
Thorpe, S. J., 159
Thrasher, S., 198

Thrivikraman, K. V., 214
Thurber, S., 344
Thurmaier, F., 461
Thyer, B. A., 156
Tidwell, M. C., 376
Tienari, P., 61, 264, 460
Tiggemann, M., 41
Tillfors, M., 57, 140, 320
Tillmanns, A., 169
Tipton, K. F., 341–342
Tobin, D. L., 397, 399
Todd, P., 271
Todt, E., 393
Toglia, J., 292
Tohen, M. F., 246, 248–249, 251, 325, 505
Tolin, D. F., 159, 161, 172, 195
Tollefson, G. D., 178, 505
Tomäs, J. M., 26–27
Tomarken, A. J., 21, 33
Tomlinson, D., 239
Tondo, L., 425, 508
Toneatto, T., 383
Tonigan, J. S., 345, 347, 364
Torgersen, S., 158, 237, 301–303, 321–322
Torgrud, L. J., 138
Toth, J., 373
Townsley, R. M., 139
Tracey, S. A., 109
Trakowski, J. H., 123
Tran, G. Q., 173
Treasaden, I. H., 279
Treasure, J. L., 391, 394
Treat, N., 281
Treat, T. A., 131
Treboux, D., 454
Treece, C., 324
Tremblay, R. E., 157, 373, 376
Trembovier, V., 283
Tremont, G., 291
Trevisan, M., 343
Trezise, L., 159
Triandis, H. C., 69, 72, 77
Trierweiler, L. I., 29
Trimboli, F., 477
Tringali, R. A., 280
Trivedi, M. H., 219, 223
Troisfontaines, B., 212
Troughton, E., 325
True, W. R., 191
Trull, T. J., 8, 10, 105, 299–301, 304–305, 308, 317, 319, 324
Trumbetta, S. L., 262
Trzcianowska, H., 191
Trzepacz, P. T., 280–282, 285
Tsao, J. C., 130
Tseng, W. S., 77
Tsuang, M. T., 7, 171, 173, 248
Tu, X. M., 282
Tuby, K. S., 127
Tucker, D. M., 106
Tucker, P., 197
Tukel, R., 173
Tulving, E., 292
Tune, G. S., 174
Turgeon, L., 124
Turk, C. L., 26, 106, 111, 142, 144, 146–147
Turkat, I., 327
Turkheimer, E., 61, 396
Turkington, D., 496
Turksoy, N., 173
Turner, C. F., 428
Turner, D. C., 515
Turner, N. E., 362
Turner, R. M., 162, 174, 327
Turner, S. M., 103, 139–140, 145
Tweedy, J., 92
Tylee, A., 306, 321
Tylka, T., 392

Tyrer, P., 309, 321–322, 324–325, 396
Tyson, J., 474

Uchino, B. N., 32
Uehara, E., 71, 79
Uhlenhuth, E. H., 122
UKECT Review Group, 223
Ulusahin, A., 68
Ungvarski, P., 291
United Nations, 362
Ursano, R. J., 195
Useda, D., 317
Usher, S. F., 469
U.S. Institute of Medicine, 263, 415
Ustundag, B., 304

Vaccaro, M., 292
Vagg, P. R., 110
Vaillant, G. E., 8, 320–321
Vaiva, G., 197
Valenstein, E., 287, 290–291
Valent, P., 194
Valentine, J. D., 190
Valentiner, D. P., 159
Valenzuela, C. F., 338
Valk, J., 91
Valleni-Basile, L. A., 171
VanAmeringen, M. A., 148
vanBalkom, A. J. L. M., 177–179, 513
van Dam-Baggen, R. M., 171
VandeKemp, H., 41
vandenBosch, L. M. C., 306
vandenBrink, W., 57, 306, 377
vandenHout, M., 124, 159, 160, 191, 291
Vander Bilt, J., 375
Vanderhallen, I., 159
vanderHart, O., 195
vanderHelm, M., 179
VanderKnapp, M., 91
vanderKolk, B. A., 195, 197
vanderPloeg, H. M., 191, 196
VandeVijver, F. J., 69
VanDyck, R., 128
van Elst, L. T., 304
Van Gaal, L., 510
Van Hasselt, V. B., 345, 396
van Heeringen, C., 391–392
VanHout, M., 291
van Kradenburg, J., 371
Van Lange, P. A. M., 452
Van Laningham, J., 455
Van Lankveld, J. J. D. M., 425
van Megan, H. J. G. M., 173
van Os, J., 263
van Reekum, R., 299
Van Valkenburg, C., 318
Van Vomeren, A., 287
Van Wagoner, S., 481
van Zanten, B. L., 179
Varghese, F. N., 267, 318
Varney, N., 281, 290
Vasey, M., 101
Vasile, R. G., 107, 143, 327
Vasterling, J. J., 190
Vatz, R. E., 382
Vaughn, C. E., 79, 267
Veach, J., 286
Veazey, C., 193
Veerkamp, J. S. J., 157
Vega, E. M., 86
Vega, W. A., 10, 75, 234
Vehmanen, L., 247
Veith, I., 318
Velayudhan, A., 140
Veljaca, K. A., 142
Vella, D. D., 212
Ventura, J., 266
Verburg, C., 159
Verette, J., 452

Verheul, R., 57, 306, 309
Verma, S. K., 249
Vermilyea, B. B., 107
Vermilyea, J. A., 107
Vernon, L. L., 162
Vernon, P. A., 56–57, 303, 322, 339
Versage, E. M., 41
Versiani, M., 148, 505
Vervaet, M., 391–392
Vieregge, A., 281
Vieregge, P., 281
Vieta, E., 251
Viguera, A. C., 252, 508
Viken, R. J., 62–63
Virkkunen, M., 339
Visser, S., 179
Vitaro, F., 157, 373, 376
Vitousek, K. M., 391–393, 397, 494
Vivian, D., 451, 456, 459
Vlahov, D., 194
Vogel-Sprott, M., 342
Vogeltanz-Holm, N. D., 394
Volans, P. J., 172
Volberg, R. A., 373, 380
Volk, K., 433
Vollebergh, W. A. M., 58
von Frenckell, R., 212
Von Korff, M., 411, 417–418
Vorus, N., 478
Vrana, S. R., 106, 111
Vreven, D. L., 190
Vujanovic, A. A., 307
Vulcano, B., 41

Wachtel, P. L., 103
Waddell, M., 108
Wade, J. H., 262
Wade, T. D., 215
Wade, W. A., 131, 488
Wadleigh, S. D., 54
Waeber, C., 412
Waelde, L. C., 196
Wagner, A. L., 380
Waite, L., 455
Wakeling, A., 394
Wakfield, M., 41
Walch, S. E., 418
Wald, J., 162
Walden, J., 250
Waldheter, E. J., 271
Waldinger, M., 428
Waldorf, V. A., 363
Waldron, H. B., 342, 359–360
Waldron, M., 61
Walitzer, K. S., 348
Walker, E., 86, 263
Walker, E. A., 444
Walker, F. R., 263
Walker, J. R., 146–148, 157
Walker, M., 252
Walker, V. J., 172
Wall, E. M., 418
Wallace, C. A., 75
Wallace, C. J., 268–269
Wallace, G. L., 282
Wallace, J., 215, 268, 365
Wallace, K. M., 459
Wallach, M. A., 262, 265
Waller, D. A., 392
Waller, G., 310, 399
Waller, N. G., 33, 455
Wallerstein, R. S., 469, 482
Walsh, B., 397
Walsh, B. T., 390, 395, 398
Walsh, C., 67
Walsh, D., 7, 322
Walsh, K. H., 380, 383
Walsh, W., 194
Walters, E., 392, 394
Walters, E. E., 111, 212

Walters, G. D., 341, 376
Wan, C. K., 23–24
Wang, P. S., 123, 220
Wang, Z., 284
Ward, C. H., 5, 11, 219, 236
Ward, J. H., 12
Ward, P. B., 95
Ward, T., 440–441
Warda, G., 191–192
Ware, J. E., 128
Warman, D. B., 496
Warner, L. A., 122
Warner, M., 291
Warner, R., 266
Warren, J., 440
Warren, S. L., 105
Warshaw, M. G., 104, 108, 110, 129–130, 180
Waternaux, C. M., 248–249
Waters, E., 454
Watkins, J., 324
Watson, D., 52, 105, 145, 158–159, 211, 233, 453
Watson, J. B., 37
Watson, T., 392
Watts, F. N., 106, 159
Waudby, C. J., 304
Weathers, F. W., 192, 195–196
Weaver, C. N., 458
Weaver, T., 198, 322
Webb, C., 267
Weber, M., 197
Webster, C. D., 442–443
Webster, J. M., 341
Wechsler, D., 266
Weeks, J. W., 145
Weems, C. F., 123
Wegener, D. T., 32
Wehr, T. A., 247, 252
Weiden, P., 267
Weijenborg, P. T. M., 425
Weiler, R., 271
Wein, S. J., 471
Weinberg, J., 470
Weinberg, L. S., 382
Weinberg, N. A., 342
Weinberger, A. D., 489
Weinberger, D. R., 93
Weiner, I. B., 475–476
Weinman, J., 102
Weinrott, M. R., 438, 441
Weinstein, M. C., 12
Weinstock, M., 283
Weise, R. E., 316
Weishaar, M. E., 487
Weiss, C. J., 355–356
Weiss, D. S., 190
Weiss, J. M., 214
Weiss, R. L., 450–451, 459
Weiss, R. D., 263
Weiss, S. R., 247
Weiss, S. R. B., 193
Weissenburger, J. E., 209
Weissman, M. M., 68, 75, 122, 125, 139, 155, 176, 212–213, 215, 220, 234–235, 237–238, 255, 268
Weizman, A., 46, 172, 383
Welch, R. R., 398
Welch, S., 391
Weller, S. B., 365
Wells, A., 101, 110, 142, 195
Wells, K. B., 128, 220, 232, 237
Wells, N. E. J., 416
Welte, J. B., 376
Weltzin, T., 391–392
Wendel, J. S., 255
Wender, P. H., 317
Wentz, E., 399
Werry, J., 246
Wessel, I., 160
West, E. T., 237
West, J., 26

West, M., 323
West, S. A., 248
Westen, D., 299, 316, 319, 324, 325, 327
Westenberg, H. G. M., 173
Westling, B. E., 126
Wetterling, T., 278
Wetzel, R. D., 392
Wetzler, S., 103, 122
Weyman, A. E., 122
Wheadon, D. E., 178
Wherrett, J. R., 282
Whiffen, V. E., 212, 220
Whipple, K., 425
Whisman, M. A., 103, 108, 110, 458
White, C. N., 302
White, G., 438
White, J., 103
White, K. L., 374
White, K. S., 27
Whited, R. M., 374
Whitehouse, W. G., 248
Whiteside, J. E., 252
Whitney, G. A., 452
Whittaker, M., 163
Whybrow, P. C., 247
Whyte, J., 292, 416
Widaman, K. F., 29–30
Widiger, T. A., 8–10, 57, 211, 305, 307, 319, 324–325, 327
Wieczorek, W. F., 376
Wieder, M., 433
Wiederman, M. W., 393
Wiegand, M., 399
Wiggins, J. S., 104, 324
Wik, G., 154
Wilbourne, P. L., 348
Wilcox, D., 381
Wilcox, J. A., 90
Wildes, J. E., 71, 73
Wildgoose, A., 310
Wildgrube, C., 248
Wilfley, D. E., 390, 395, 398
Wilk, A. I., 347
Wilkins, V. M., 43
Wilkinson-Ryan, T., 299
Willenbring, M., 270
Willett, J., 13, 322
Williams, B. R., 361
Williams, C., 128
Williams, D. R., 74–75, 78
Williams, E. N., 481
Williams, J., 144, 324, 345, 361
Williams, J. B., 127, 219, 396
Williams, J. B. W., 4, 6, 8, 11, 16, 109, 160, 236, 307, 381
Williams, J. M., 212, 280, 489
Williams, J. W., 237
Williams, R. M., Jr., 75, 282
Williams, S. M., 105, 270
Williamson, D. A., 371, 396, 409
Willis, K. E., 90
Willner, P., 214
Wills, T. A., 451
Wilson, A. C., 376
Wilson, B., 284
Wilson, G. D., 159
Wilson, G. T., 171, 390, 394–396, 398, 439, 487, 494
Wilson, J. P., 195
Wilson, K. A., 175
Wilson, M. R., 146, 460
Wilson, P., 460
Wilson, R. S., 280–281
Winant, H., 72
Winchel, R. M., 380
Winett, C., 247
Wing, J. K., 74
Winnicott, D. W., 317
Winston, A., 327
Winters, J., 265

Winters, K. C., 248, 373, 380
Wise, T. N., 436, 438
Wiser, S. L., 106
Witkiewitz, K., 348
Wittchen, H. U., 11, 103–104, 107, 110–111, 121–122, 141, 143, 146–147, 155–156, 213
Wittrock, D. A., 411, 413
Wolfe, B. E., 390
Wolfe, W., 347
Wolff, H. G., 410
Wolfgang, H. O., 286
Wolfson, D., 266
Wolkow, R., 130
Wollersheim, J. P., 171
Wolpe, J., 37, 161, 197
Wonderlich, S. A., 390–392, 396, 399
Wong, C. J., 364
Wong, D. F., 106
Wong, G., 353
Wong, I. C., 221
Wong, M. L., 221
Wood, J., 325
Wood, J. A., 269
Wood, J. M., 324
Wood, K., 394
Wood, M. D., 346
Wood, P. K., 43, 346
Woodman, C. L., 104, 107–108
Woodruff-Borden, J., 157
Woods, R., 289
Woods, S. W., 122, 125, 130, 272
Woods, T., 392

Woodside, D., 391, 400
Wood-Siverio, C., 267
Woody, G., 326
Woody, S. R., 130, 159–160
Woolaway-Bickel, K., 130
Woolf, C. J., 86–87
Wootton, J., 40
Work Goup on Borderline Personality Disorder, 300
World Health Organization (WHO), 68, 77, 219, 231, 263, 278, 316, 397, 415
Worling, J. R., 438
Wothke, W. A., 25
Wright, C. I., 212
Wright, D. W., 41, 196
Wright, F. D., 487
Wright, J., 451
Wright, L. M., 160
Wrightson, P., 278
Wykes, T., 268
Wymer, J. H., 288
Wynne, H., 380

Yaffee, R. A., 382
Yagla, S. J., 104
Yale, S., 266
Yamada, A. M., 76
Yamas, K., 111
Yang, C., 210
Yanovski, S. Z., 390, 392
Yap, L., 112
Yarnell, H., 372
Yartz, A. R., 161

Yates, W., 138, 321, 326
Yates, W. R., 105
Yatham, L. N., 251
Yee, E., 77
Yeh, C., 392
Yehuda, R., 189, 191–193, 196
Yen, S., 9, 323
Yong, L., 324
Yonkers, K. A., 104, 107–108, 124, 126, 143
Young, B. G., 440
Young, J. E., 44, 47, 248, 487, 489, 496–497
Young, R. C., 249
Young, S. E., 59
Youngstrom, E. A., 246–249
Yucha, C., 418
Yule, W., 326
Yung, A. R., 272
Yurgelun-Todd, D., 391

Zajecka, J., 250
Zakis, S., 155
Zanarini, M. C., 302, 305, 307, 309–311, 319, 324, 392
Zane, N. W., 70–71
Zaninelli, R., 197
Zarate, C. A., 246
Zasler, N. D., 413
Zechmeister, J. S., 248
Zeichner, A., 270
Zeitlin, S. B., 192
Zembar, M., 287

Zevitz, R. G., 444
Zhang, A. Y., 73
Zhao, S., 11, 103
Ziedonis, D., 359
Ziegler, V. E., 249
Zielinski, R., 291
Zigler, E., 74, 262
Zilberman, M. L., 371, 376
Zilboorg, G., 4
Zillmer, E. A., 94
Zimering, R. T., 198
Zimmerli, W. D., 102
Zimmerman, M., 233, 307, 321, 324–325, 327
Zimmermann, P., 122
Zinbarg, R. E., 40, 105, 162
Zislin, J., 383
Zittel, C., 397
Zitterl, W., 172
Zitzow, D., 376
Zoccolillo, M., 157
Zoellner, L. A., 179
Zohar, J., 172, 383
Zonderman, A., 287
Zorn, M., 359
Zubenko, G. S., 215, 282, 285
Zubin, J., 5, 78
Zucker, K. J., 439
Zuckerman, M., 78, 356
Zuellig, A. R., 109, 144
Zvolensky, M. J., 126, 339
Zweig-Frank, H., 305–306
Zwick, M. L., 43, 219

Subject Index

Abecaranil, 112
Absolute fit, 23–24
Acetaminophen, 417
Acetylcholine (ACh), 88, 92, 283, 292, 507, 513
Acetylcholinesterase (AChE), 92, 292, 514
Acrophobia Questionnaire, 161
Activities of daily living (ADL), 289
Acute stress disorder (ASD), 191–196, 198
Acute Stress Disorder Interview (ASDI), 196
Acute Stress Disorder Scale (ASDS), 196
Adderall, 514
Adjusted Goodness of Fit Index (AGFI), 24
Adjustment disorder with depressed mood, 207
Adoption studies
  on adopted-away children and biological parents, 54
  alcohol use and dependence, 341–342
  bipolar disorder, 247
  BPD, 302
  gene-environment interaction, 61–62
  schizophrenia, 264, 317
African Americans, 10, 70, 155, 212, 234, 263, 282, 301, 376–377, 426
Agnosia, 288
Agoraphobia. *See* Panic disorder and agoraphobia (PDA)
AIDS, 170, 284, 286
AIDS dementia complex (ADC), 284, 286
Al-Anon, 365
Albany Panic and Phobia Questionnaire, 31
Alcohol abuse and dependence, 9, 11, 337–349
  assessment/diagnosis, 343–346
  associated disorders, 337
  course, complications, prognosis, 342–343
  description/clinical picture of, 337–339
  DSM-IV diagnosis, 14–15
  environmental impact of, 346
  epidemiology, 340–341
  etiology, 341–342
  future directions, 348–349
  Korsakoff's syndrome, 338, 346
  personality development and psychopathology, 339–340
  traits theories, 339–340
  treatment implications, 347–348
    interventions, 347
    psychopharmacological, 348
    relapse prevention, 348
    Twelve-Step Facilitation, 348
  Type II alcoholism, 339
Alcohol Dependence Scale (ADS), 344
Alcoholics Anonymous (AA), 365
Alienation, 76–77, 79, 302, 374
Alprazolam, 148, 511–512
Alzheimer's disease, 67, 88, 92, 95, 279–283, 286–289, 513–514

Alzheimer's Disease Cooperative Study Activities of daily Living Inventory, 514
Ambien, 512–513
American Headache Society (AHS), 414
  Behavioral Clinical Trials Workgroup, 413
American Psychiatric Association (APA), 5, 309–310, 509
American Psychiatric Association/New York Academy of Medicine, 4
American Psychological Society, 418
Amitriptyline, 223, 239, 383
Amnestic disorder, 279, 288
Amphetamines, 354–355, 514
Amygdala, 92, 124, 193–194, 209, 292
Analgesics, 413
Analysis of variance (ANOVA), 22, 31, 33
Anankastic personality disorder. *See* Obsessive-compulsive disorder (OCD)
The Anatomy of Melancholia (Burns), 207
Anger problems, 37, 47
Anhedonia, 68, 208–209, 231, 244–245, 262, 495
Animal Naming Test, 287
Animal phobia, 154, 156
Anomie, 77, 79
Anorexia nervosa (AN), 389. *See also* Eating disorders
Anosmia, 290
Antabuse, 348
Anterograde amnesia, 112
Antiandrogens, 446
Antidepressants, 112, 505–508
  benefits of, 221
  for bipolar disorder, 252
  Saint-John's-wort, 223
  tricyclic (TCAs), 129–178, 209, 221, 292, 383, 417, 505
Antipsychotic medications, 89, 221, 250–252, 310, 507
  atypical, 223, 267, 292
  nonphenothiazine, 503
  for schizophrenia, 266–267
    noncompliance, 267, 270
    prodromal phase, 272
  second generation, 503–504
Antipsychotics, 503–505
Antisocial personality disorder (ASPD), 10, 40, 318
Anxiety disorders. *See also* Generalized anxiety disorder (GAD); Social anxiety disorder
  Anxiety Schedule for *DSM-IV* (ADIS-IV), 109
    Lifetime Version (ADIS-IV-L), 109
  Axis I disorders, 7
  in bipolar disorder, 246
  classical conditioning, 37
  cognitive behavioral treatment, 489–492
  cognitive theory, 125–126
  depression, 42–43, 144, 158, 212, 280, 291–292, 327, 356, 396, 410, 438, 473, 488, 495–496
  depression and, 280

DSM diagnostic reliability for, 7
general medical conditions as causative factor, 288
migraine and, 410–411
modeling of, 40
social, 46
Anxiety Disorders Interview Schedule (ADIS), 174
  Revised (ADIS-R), 127
Anxiety Schedule for *DSM-IV* (ADIS-IV), 109, 160
  Lifetime Version (ADIS-IV-L), 109, 144
Anxiety Schedule for *DSM-IV*-Lifetime Version, 144
Anxiety sensitivity, 122–123, 159
Anxiety Sensitivity Index (ASI), 123, 128, 159, 161
Anxiolytics, 356
Anxious misery, 58–59
Aphasia, 288
Applied relaxation (AR), 111–112
Apraxia, 288
Area postrema, 87
Aricept, 292, 513
Aripiprazole, 505
Arthritis, 220
Asians and Asian Americans, 70–71, 73, 75, 78–79, 212, 340
Aspirin, 417
Assessment of Negative Symptoms (SANS), 266
Association for Applied Psychophysiology and Biofeedback, 418
Associative learning, 36–39, 105, 125, 157, 193, 357, 489, 493
Asthma, 37, 195, 374, 409–410
Asylums, 4
Ataque de nervios, 80
Atomoxetine, 514
Attention-deficit/hyperactivity disorder (ADHD), 12, 246–249, 252, 514–515
Australian National Survey, 104–105
Autonomic nervous system, 89–90
  arousal, 139, 194, 418, 460
  classical conditioning of, 37
  dysregulation, 197
  higher order conditioning of, 37
  hyperactivity, 288, 338
  inflexibility, 102
  reactivity, 102, 108, 379
Avoidance behavior, 42, 171, 194
Avoidant personality disorder (AVPD), 9, 57, 122, 139–140, 143, 147, 316, 319
Axis I disorders, 7
  alcohol and drug disorders, 121–122
  antisocial personality disorder, 318
  anxiety disorders, 144
  avoidant personality disorder, 319
  binge eating disorder, 395
  bipolar disorder, 246
  borderline personality disorder, 300–302, 304, 309, 311
  Cluster A disorders, 325
  Cluster C disorders, 323

comorbidity, 108, 122, 173, 210, 325, 374, 497, 499
dependent personality disorder, 320
depressive disorders, 173, 233
dysthymia disorder, 232, 234
GAD, 108–109
narcissistic personality disorder, 319
obsessive-compulsive disorder, 173, 176
obsessive-compulsive personality disorder, 320
organic mental disease, 279
panic disorder, 121
paranoid personality disorder, 317
psychophysiological disorders, 409
schizotypal personality disorder, 318
SCID, 109, 219, 345, 361, 381, 396
social phobia, 56–57, 139–140
substance use disorders, 325
treatment outcomes, 327
trichotillomania, 373
Axis II disorders
  avoidant personality disorder, 57, 122, 139–140
  comorbidity, 130, 173, 210, 392–393, 497, 499
  diagnosis of, 409, 452–453, 498
  GAD, 103
  panic disorder, 122
  psychophysiological disorders, 409
  schema therapy efficacy, 500
Axis III disorders, 7, 210, 279, 409
Axis IV disorders, 7, 218
Axis V disorders, 7, 218
Azapirones, 112

Barbiturates, 356, 511
Basal ganglia, 92
Basic activities of daily living (BADL), 289
Bech-Rafaelsen Mania Scale, 249
Beck Depression Inventory (BDI), 11, 219, 236
BDI-II, 219
Behavioral activation (BA), 238–239
Behavioral and cognitive influences, 36–48
  associative learning, 36–38
    nonassociative learning, 37–38
    psychosomatics, 37
  associative pain, 36–37
  autoshaping, 38–39
  cognitive vulnerability factors, 41–47
    biased cognitive schemata, 43–45
    attributions, 45
    cognitive therapy, 43–44
    irrational beliefs, 44–45
    negative thoughts and cognition, 45–47
  problem solving, 42–43
  decision making, 42
  disconnection and rejection, 44
  generation of alternatives, 42
  instrumental learning, 38–39
    autoshaping/automaintenance, 38–39
    two-factor theory of, 39
  irrational beliefs, 44–45
  negative affect, 43

Behavioral and cognitive influences
    (continued)
  negative thoughts, 45
  other-directedness, 44
  overgeneralization, 44
  overvigilance and inhibition, 44
  social learning, 39–41
    modeling and, 39–40
    observational learning and adult
      psychopathology, 40–41
  telencephalon, 91
Behavioral Approach Test (BAT), 161
Behavioral Assessment Tests (BATs), 146
Behavioral avoidance, 102, 239, 490
Behavioral Avoidance Tests (BATs), 128
Behavioral couples therapy (BCT),
    364–365
Behavioral inhibition (BI), 122–123, 212
Bender Visual Motor Gestalt Test, 287
Benzodiazepine aprazolam, 348
Benzodiazepines (BDZs), 112, 129–130,
    148, 354, 356, 383, 511–513
Bereavement, 207
Bicêtre Hospital (Paris), 4
Binge eating disorder (BED), 390. *See
    also* Eating disorders
Biological influences, 85–96. *See also*
    Mental health and illness
  cellular anatomy and physiology,
    86–87
    blood-brain barrier, 87
    cell body, 86
    neuroglia, 87
    neuron, 86–88
  methodology, 93–96
    brain lesions, 93–94
    CT scan, 94–95
    MRI, 95
    PET, 95–96
  nervous system, 89–93
    neuroanatomy, 91–93
    neurodevelopment, 90–91
    neurochemical transmission, 87–89
    neurotransmitters, 88–89
Biosocial Model of Personality, 54
Bipolar disorder, 4, 244–256
  assessment/diagnosis, 249–250
  bipolar II, 9, 244–245, 249–252, 300,
    508–509
  course, complications, prognosis,
    248–249
  depression, 54, 247–248, 251–252,
    508–510
  description/clinical picture of, 244–245
    atypical bipolar disorder, 245–246
    cyclothymia, 245
    hypomanic episode, 245, 249
    major depressive episode, 244–245
    manic episode, 244, 249
    mixed episodes, 245
    rapid cycling, 245
  DSM diagnosis, 7
  environmental impact of, 249
  epidemiology, 247
  etiology, 247–248
  manic episode, 244
  personality development,
    psychopathology, comorbidity,
    246
  schemata, 248
  treatment implications, 250–256
    cognitive-behavioral therapy,
      253–254
    electroconvulsive therapy, 252–253
    family focused therapy, 254–255
    group therapy, 256
    interpersonal social rhythm therapy,
      255–256
    pharmacotherapy, 250–252
      antidepressants, 221
      children/adolescents, 252

    electroconvulsive therapy (ECT),
      252–253
    pregnancy, 252
    psychosocial approaches, 253
Bipolar spectrum disorder, 410
Blocjk Design and Object Assembly, 287
Blood-brain barrier, 87
Blood-injection-injury phobia (BII), 154,
    156, 159
Body dysmorphic disorder (BDD), 175
Body Sensations Questionnaire (BSQ),
    128
Borderline personality disorder (BPD), 9,
    12, 299–311
  assessment/diagnosis, 307–308
    interviews, 307
    questionnaires, 307–308
  behavioral and cognitive influences, 47
  complications, 306
  course, 305–306
  description/clinical picture of, 299–300
  dialectical behavior therapy (DBT),
    309–310
  eating disorders and, 392–393,
    396–397
  effective instability, 299
  environmental impact of, 308–309
  epidemiology, 301–302
    age/gender, 302
    culture, 301–302
  etiology, 302–305
    attachment, 304
    childhood abuse, 304–305
    genetics and family history, 302–303
    neurobiological vulnerabilities,
      303–304
    personality, 305
  fear of abandonment, 300
  identity disturbances, 299
  impulsivity, 299–301, 303, 305,
    307–308, 310
  interpersonal relationship difficulties,
    300–301
  metallization-based treatment, 310
  paranoia, 300–301, 307, 310–311
  personality development and
    psychopathology, 300–301
  prognosis, 306–307
  psychodynamic/psychoanalytic therapy,
    310
  self-mutilating behavior, 299–300, 305
  substance use disorders, 301
  suicidal behavior, 300
  transferenced focused psychotherapy
    (TFP), 310
  transient dissociative symptoms, 300
  treatment implications, 309–311
    pharmacological, 310–311
    psychodynamic/psychoanalytic
      therapy, 310
    psychological, 309–310
Borderline Personality Disorder Research
    Foundation, 311
Boston Diagnostic Aphasia Exam, 287
Boston Naming Test (BNT), 287
Bovine spongiform encephalopathy, 284
Brain
  composition of, 91–93
  lesions of, 93–94, 287–288
  methodology, 93
Brain-behavior relationships, 85, 93–94,
    96
Brain derived neurotropic factor (BDNF),
    214
Brain fag, 69
Brief Fear of Negative Evaluation Scale,
    145
Brief Fear of Negative Evaluation Scale
    (BFNE), 145
Brief Psychiatric Rating Scale (BPRS),
    266

Brofaromine, 148
Bromazepam, 148
Bulimia nervosa (BN), 389–390. *See also*
    Eating disorders
Bulimia Test-Revised (BULIT-R), 396
Buprenorphine, 365
Bupropion, 221, 507, 514
Buspirone, 223, 383

California Personality Inventory, 438
California Verbal Learning Test (CVLT),
    266, 287
Camberwell Family Interview, 267
Canadian Headache Society, 418
Canadian Problem Gambling Index
    (CPGI), 380
Cannabis, 355
Capacity for Dynamic Process Scale
    (CDPS), 482
Carbamates, 356
Carbamazepine, 250–251, 383, 508–509
Cardiovascular dysfunction, 284
Catatonia, 209
Catatonic disorder, 279, 288
Category Test, 287
Caucasians, 69, 155, 301, 340
Caudate nucleus, 92
Celexa, 221, 507
Center for Epidemiological Studies
    Depression Scale (CES-D), 219
Central nervous system (CNS), 86–87,
    89–91, 291
Central sensitization, 87
Cerebellum, 91
Cerebral atrophy, 288
Cerebral cortex, 92
Cerebrospinal fluid (CSF), 90
Cerebrovascular accident (CVA), 90
Childhood and adolescent disorders
  ADHD, 246–249, 252
  bipolar, 246–248, 252
  BPD, 304–305, 308–309
  depressive disorders in, 9, 11
  DSM diagnostic reliability, 7
  headache, 412
  overanxious disorder, 109
Chlordiazepoxide, 510–511
Chlorpromazine, 383, 503
Cholesky decomposition, 55
Cholinesterase inhibitor (CEI), 292, 304,
    503, 513–514
Chronic brain syndrome. *See* Delirium
Chronic psychopathology. *See* Organic
    mental disorder (OMD)
Cingulate gyrus, 92
Cingulotomy, 92
Citalopram, 178, 221, 507
Classical conditioning. *See* Associative
    learning
Classical test theory (CTT), 12, 14
Classic categorization, 3
Classification systems, 4. *See also*
    Diagnosis and classification
Clinical depression. *See* Major depressive
    disorder (MDD)
Clinician-Administered PTSD Scale
    (CAPS), 195
Clomipramine (CMI), 172, 178–179, 383
Clonazepam, 148
Clozapine, 267, 269, 504–505
Cluster analysis, 12, 438
Cocaine, 355, 357
Cocaine Anonymous (CA), 365
Codeine, 356
Cognex, 292, 513
Cognitive-behavioral analysis system of
    psychotherapy (CBASP), 239
Cognitive-behavioral treatment (CBT),
    326–327, 487–500, 496–499
  for alcohol abuse and dependence, 348
  for anxiety disorders, 489–492

  for bipolar disorder, 253–254
  for BPD, 497–498
  cognitive therapy and, 112
  for depression, 238–239, 488–489
  for dysthymic disorder and, 238–239
  for eating disorders, 397–398, 493–495
  future developments in, 499–500
  for GAD, 111–112, 491
  history/philosophical bases of, 487–488
  for MDD, 220–221
  for OCD, 179–180, 491–492
  for OMD, 291
  for panic disorder, 127, 129–131
  for pathological gambling, 382
  for PTSD, 197–198, 490–491
  for pyromania, 384
  for schizophrenia, 495–496
  for sexual deviation, 445
  for social phobia, 147–149
  for substance abuse, 492–493
  for trichotillomania, 383
Cognitive Behavior Rating Scale, 280
Cognitive deficiencies, 42
Cognitive distortions, 42
Cognitive dysfunction, 278–279, 284,
    289, 477
Cognitive Enhancement Therapy, 271
Cognitive impairments, 262
Cognitive influences. *See* Behavioral and
    cognitive influences
Cognitive processing therapy (CPT), 198
Cognitive theory, 125–126, 192
Cognitive therapy (CT). *See* Cognitive-
    behavioral treatment (CBT)
Cognitive Therapy Research (journal),
    487
Cognitive vulnerability factors, 36, 41–42,
    48
Columbia University College of
    Physicians and Surgeons (New
    York), 6
Community mental health center,
    (CMHC), 131
Community-Reinforcement and Family
    Training (CRAFT), 347–348,
    364
Community Reinforcement Approach
    (CRA), 347–348, 364
Comorbidity
  alcohol abuse and dependence, 343,
    346
  antisocial personality disorder, 318
  anxiety disorder, 154
  Axis I and Axis II disorders, 108, 130,
    173, 392–393, 449
  bipolar disorder, 246, 250, 256
  BPD, 300–301, 305, 311
  defined, 52
  dysthymia disorder, 234
  eating disorders, 391–393, 399
  GAD, 103–104, 107–108, 110–112
  genetic, 54
  kleptomania, 346
  major depressive disorder, 210–211,
    217, 458
  migraines, 410
  narcissistic personality disorder, 319
  National Comorbidity Study (NCS), 6,
    10–11, 104, 107, 121, 124, 129,
    140–141, 155, 234
  obsessive-compulsive disorder,
    173–175, 179, 391
  obsessive-compulsive personality
    disorder, 320
  panic disorder, 121–122, 124, 130
  pathological gambling, 376
  personality disorders, 324–325, 327,
    392, 453, 499
  PTSD, 192
  Shedler-Westen Assessment Procedure,
    324

Subject Index

social anxiety disorder, 139–140, 143, 147
specific phobias, 154–155
structure of, 58–61
Comparative Fit Index (CFI), 24
Composite International Diagnostic Interview (CIDI), 10–11, 15, 236
-SAM, 15
-UM, 11
Comprehensive Level of Consciousness Scale, 283
Compulsive Activity Checklist (CAC), 174
Computed transaxial tomography (CAT or CT scan), 94
Computerized tomography (CT), 93
Concentration deficits, 194
Conditional growth models, 32
Conditioned response (CR), 36, 125, 193
Conditioned stimulus (CS), 125
Conduct disorder, 9, 43, 56, 58–59, 64, 247, 263, 274, 318, 371–372, 424
Confirmatory factor analysis (CFA), 12, 25–30, 26, 32–33
exploratory factor analysis, (E/CFA), 27
Congressional Public Health Summit, 40
Consequences of Worrying Questionnaire (CWQ), 110
Constructs
anxiety disorder etiology, 142
Five-Factor Model and, 324
individual levels, 76
latent, 21, 26–27, 455
measurement errors in, 22
mediational, 41
negative, 160
overlapping, 30, 72
personality, 339, 393
sociocultural levels, 67, 74–75, 78
validation, 21, 27, 29, 69
verbal measurement of, 79
Contingency Management, 348
Continuous Performance Tests, 266
Core Conflictual Relationship Theme (CCRT), 480
Cornell Dysthymia Scale, 236
Corpus callosum, 92
Corticotrophin releasing factor (CRF), 214
Couples Interaction Scoring System (CISS), 459
Covariance matrices, 22–24, 32
Crack cocaine, 357
Creatine phosphokinase (CPK), 503
Creutzfeldt-Jakob disease, 284, 288
Crisis management (CM), 255
Criterion
of abuse, 337
BPD, 301
clinical significance, 141
distress, 371
DSM-IV, for alcohol consumption, 345
eating disorders, validity, 307, 345, 396
hair pulling, 371
impairment, 157
marital discord, measure of, 460
overlap, 52
personality disorder, 307
pyromania, 372
stressor, 189
symptom, 109
Critical/conflictual, 62
Crohn's disease, 374
Cue exposure treatment, 493
Cyclophosphamide, 37
Cyclothymia, 245
Cylert, 514
Cymbalta, 221, 507

Darvon, 356
Davidson Trauma Scale, 196
Dementia, 4, 278–279
AIDS dementia complex, 284, 286
in alcohol abuse (Korsakoff's syndrome), 338, 346
in Alzheimer's disease, 513
diagnostic history of, 4
differential diagnosis of, 288
in elderly bipolar patients, 251
end stage renal disease, 278
in OMD, 278–289, 291–292
pharmacologic treatment of, 503, 513–514
vascular, 279, 282, 284, 289, 513, 515
Dementia praecox, 4, 68. *See also* Schizophrenia
Demerol, 356
Demyelinating disease, 91, 95, 291
Dendrite, 86
Depakene, 250
Depakon, 250
Depakote, 250, 508
Dependent personality disorder (DPD), 319–320
Depersonalization, 194
Depression. *See also* Major depressive disorder (MDD)
in Alzheimer's disease, 289
and anxiety, 42–43, 144, 158, 212, 280, 291–292, 327, 356, 396, 410, 438, 473, 488, 495–496
atypical, 209
in bipolar disorder, 54, 247–248, 251–252, 508–510
in children/adolescents, 11, 41
chronic, 209, 211, 239
comorbid, 112, 122, 130, 173, 180, 373, 514
cultural conception of, 68–69
family history of, 85, 210, 212, 215–216, 374, 458, 489
geriatric, 43, 288
maternal, 41
migraines and, 411
mood disorder and, 41
relapse, 499
subthreshold depression, 232, 280
treatment of, 221, 292, 487–489, 500, 505, 512
for chronic, 239
resistance to, 223, 508
unipolar, 14, 43, 208, 244, 247, 249, 253, 255, 507–508
Depression, Anxiety and Stress Scales, 110
Depressive personality disorder, 9, 231–233, 237, 240
Derealization, 194
Desensitization, 111–112, 163, 177, 197, 348, 382–383
Desyrel, 507
Developmental disorders, 4
Dexedrin, 514
Dextroamphetamine, 292, 354–355
DIAGNO/DIAGNO-II, 6
Diagnosis and classification
hazard function, 14
manifest variables, 12
natural categories, 3, 15
subtyping research, 13
Diagnostic and Statistical Manual of Mental Disorders. See DSM
Diagnostic Interview for Borderline Patients-Revised (DIB-R), 307
Diagnostic Interview for *DSM IV* Personality Disorders (DIPD-IV), 307
Diagnostic Interview for Narcissistic Patients, 324

Diagnostic Interview for Personality Disorders (DIPD-IV), 324
Diagnostic Interview Schedule (DIS), 10, 14, 219
CIDI-UM, 11
NIMH, 6
Diagnostic systems
categorization
classic, 3
natural, 3
nature of, issues regarding, 327
OMD, 282
prototype, 3–4
consistency, 5
decision trees, 6
diagnostic consistency, 5
history of, 4–5
neo-Kraepelinian research, 6
psychiatric, 3–6, 9, 12, 15, 39, 139, 236, 281, 285, 370
syndromal diagnosis, 4, 6, 15
validation models, 12
Dialectical behavior therapy (DBT), 309–310, 498–499
Diazepam, 112, 511
Diencephalon, 91
Digit Span Backward subtest, 266
Digit Symbol-Coding and Symbol Search subsets, 287
Dimensional Assessment of Personality Pathology-Basic Questionnaire, 323
Dimensional Assessment of Personality Problems (DAPP), 322
Dimensional model of personality disorder, 57
Direct conditioning, 157
Disability Rating Scale (DRS), 283
Disgust Emotion Scale, 161
Disgust Scale, 161
Disgust sensitivity, 159, 161
Disulfiram, 348
Divalproate, 508
Divalproex, 250–251, 508
Dolophine, 356
Donepezil, 292, 513
Dopamine
D4 receptor, 505
D2 receptor, 342, 503–505
for mania, 247
neurotransmission, 86, 88–93, 221
pathological gambling, 377
receptor up-regulation, 86, 90
for schizophrenia, 264
for traumatic brain injuries, 292
Dopamine theory of schizophrenia, 89
Dorsolateral prefrontal cortex, 20
Driving phobia, 156, 163
Drug abuse and dependence, 354–366
abuse versus dependence, 354
assessment/diagnosis, 360–362
clinical interview, 361–362
direct observation, 362
self-report screening measures, 360, 362
toxicology testing, 361
complications, 358–359
course, 359–360
description of, 354–356
drug abuse disorders, 354
environmental impact of, 362–363
on family, 362–363
on peer interactions, 363
on work, 363
epidemiology, 356–357
etiology, 357–358
inhalant abuse, 355–356
marijuana, 346, 355, 357, 359–363
opioid abuse/dependence, 356
personality development and psychopathology, 356

prognosis, 360
sedatives, 356
treatment, 363–365
biologically based interventions, 365
comprehensive behavioral interventions, 364–365
motivational enhanced interventions, 363–364
relapse prevention, 365
12-step programs, 365
Drug Abuse Screening Test (DAST), 360
Drug Attitudes Inventory, 267
Drug-Taking Confidence Questionnaire (DTCQ), 362
DSM, 4–8, 319. *See also individual Axis disorders*
DSM-V, 390
DSM-IV, 3
ADHD conceptualization, 27
agoraphobia, definition of, 121
alcohol disorders
construct validity, 344
dependence, 14–15
diagnosis, 345
BPD, 299, 301
brain fag, 69
criticism of, 10
dependent personality disorder, 319
depressive personality disorder, 233
dysthymic disorder
diagnosis, 233
lifetime prevalence of, 234
specifiers, 231–232, 235
eating disorders, 389, 393
anorexia nervosa, 389
bulimia nervosa, 389
eating disorders not otherwise specified, 390
GAD
diagnosis, 102, 107–109
prevalence rate statistics, 104
social phobia, 138
gender/cultural bias, 10
goals of, 8–9
kleptomania, 371
major depressive disorder
diagnosis, 207, 218–219
multiaxial case formulation of, 208
NOS, 232
severity coding of, 208, 218
minor depression, 232
mood disorder, 9, 231
OCD
characteristics of, 169
classification schemes, 170
definition of, 169
orgasmic disorders, 424
panic disorder, 127
pathological gambling
diagnosis, 370
DSM-IV-J and *DSM-IV-MR-J*, 380
NODS and U.S. prevalence style, 380
personality disorders assessment material, 307, 396
PTSD
acute stress disorder, 194
criteria for, 189
severity/frequency definition, 195
pyromania, exclusionary criterion for, 372
reliability/validity of, 9–10
sexual desire disorders classification, 423, 426
sexual deviations, diagnostic criteria, 436–437, 442
social phobia, prevalence criteria for, 141
syndromal criteria, 219
Task Force, 10
trichotillomania, 371

538 Subject Index

DSM-IV-TR, 154, 160, 244, 279, 299, 302, 316–319
  alcohol abuse
    diagnosis, 337
    prognosis, 343
  antisocial personality, 318
  avoidant personality disorder, characteristics, 319
  Axis II personality disorders, 316
  BPD
    diagnosis, 299
    gender predominance, 302
  dependent personality disorder, 319–320
  drug abuse and dependence
    drug classes, recognition of, 354
  histrionic personality disorder, 318–319
  impulse control disorders not elsewhere specified, 370
  intermittent explosive disorder, 372, 375, 381
  kleptomania, 380
  manic episode, 244
  obsessive-compulsive personality disorder, 320
  OMDs representing acquired brain disorders, 279
  paranoid personality disorder, 316
  pathological gambling, criteria and question format, 380
  psychological factors affecting medical conditions, 409
  pyromania
    children/adolescent fire setters and, 374
    diagnosis, 381
  schizoid personality disorder, 317
  schizotypal personality disorder, 317
  sexual desire disorders classification, 423
  specific phobia
    central feature of, 160
    types of, 154
  substance abuse and dependence/ estimating prevalence, 340
DSM-IV-J, 380
DSM-IV-MR-J, 380
DSM-III, 3
  advantages of, 7
  antisocial personality disorder, 318
  avoidant personality disorder, 319
  criticism of, 8
  diagnostic criteria/decision tress in, 6
  Feighner criteria, 6
  GAD prevalence estimates, 104
  histrionic personality disorder, 318
  kleptomania, diagnosis, 371
  melancholia, introduction of, 209
  neo-Kraepelinian diagnostic research, 6
  OMD diagnostic categories, 279
  psychological factors affecting medical conditions, 409
  PTSD, introduction to, 189
  reliability/stability studies of, 7–8
  schizotypal personality disorder, 317
DSM-III-R, 3, 6
  advantages of, 7
  BPD, 301
  criticism of, 8
  GAD
    diagnosis, 102, 107
    prevalence rates, 104
  histrionic personality disorder, 321
  intermittent explosive disorder, 372
  OCD, functional relationship of obsessions and compulsions, 169
  OMD, 279
  pathological gambling and South Oaks Gambling Screen, 380
  reliability/stability studies of, 7
  social phobia, 141
  subthreshold GAD, 110
DSM-II, 5–7, 11, 318
Duloxetine, 221, 223, 507
Dyadic Adjustment Scale (DAS), 459–460
Dysphoric mood, 68, 171, 231, 300, 304, 370
Dysthymia and minor depression, 231–240
  course, complications, prognosis, 235–236
  depressive personality disorder, 231–233, 237, 240
  description/clinical picture of, 231
  DSM-IV and *ICD-10* diagnosis, 231
  dysthymic disorder specifiers, 232
  environmental impact of, 237
  epidemiology, 234
  etiology, 234–235
    biological-genetic factors, 234–235
    cognitive behavioral models, 235
    interpersonal/psychodynamic factors, 235
  hopelessness, 235–236
  minor depressive disorder, 232–233
    differential diagnosis, 232
    functional status, 232–233
  neuroticism, 233
  personality development and psychopathology, 233–234
    Five-Factor-Model, 233
  suicidal tendencies, 235
  treatment implications, 237–239
    behavioral treatments versus medications, 238–239
    for chronic depression, 239
    cognitive-behavioral analysis system of psychotherapy, 239
    cognitive/interpersonal treatments versus medications, 238

Early maladaptive schema, 44, 497
Early Memory Test, 325
Eating Attitudes Test (EAT), 396
Eating Disorder Diagnostic Scale, 396
Eating Disorder Examination (EDE), 396
Eating Disorder Examination-Questionnaire (EDE-Q), 396
Eating Disorder Inventory (EDI and EDI-2), 396
Eating disorders, 389–400
  assessment/diagnosis, 395–396
  course, complications, prognosis, 395
  description/clinical picture of, 389–390
    anorexia nervosa, 389
    binge eating, 390
    bulimia nervosa, 389–390
    eating disorders not otherwise specified, 390, 393
  environmental impact of, 396–397
  epidemiology, 393–394
  etiology, 394–395
  modeling of, 41
  overeating, 41
  personality development and psychopathology, 391–393
    Axis II comorbidity, 392
    personality dimensions, clinically observed, 391–392
    personality subtypes, 393
  treatment implications, 397–400
    cognitive behavioral treatment, 398, 493–495
    interpersonal psychotherapy, 398
    personality/treatment interventions outcomes, 399–400
    psychodynamic psychotherapy, 398–399
Eating Disorders Diagnostic Scale, 396
Ecstasy, 355, 357

Effective instability, 299
Effexor, 507
Egocentricity Index (EGOI), 325
Electroconvulsive therapy (ECT), 209, 223, 252–253
Electroencephalogram (EEG), 288, 372, 418, 440
Electromyogram (EMG), 191, 194
Emic perspectives, 67–69, 71, 73, 80
Emotional numbing, 194
Encephalitis, 284
Endocarditis, 356
Endocrine system, 91
Environmental stress hypothesis, 262
Epidemiological Catchment Area Program (ECA), 14, 234
  development of, 10–11
  DSM diagnosis and, 6
  emotional health characterizations, 110–111
  GAD
    prevalence estimates, 104, 107
  of histrionic personality disorder, 321
  of OCD patients, 7
  purpose of, 73–74
  social phobia
    lifetime prevalence rate of, 141
    onset of, 142–143
    with other lifetime psychiatric diagnosis, 139
  specific phobias, lifetime prevalence of, 155
Epinephrine, 197
EQS software program, 24
Equal-precise test, 15
Equivalence, 69
Erectile Disorder Inventory of Treatment Satisfaction (EDITS), 419
Ergoloid mesylates, 513
Ergotamine tartrate, 417
Escitalopram, 221
Eskalith, 250
Ethanol, 508
Ethnicity, 10, 67, 72–76, 80, 302, 340, 376, 432
Etic perspectives, 67–69, 71, 73, 80
European Americans, 10
Event-history analyses, 13–14
Excitatory postsynaptic potential (EPSP), 86
Executive cognitive dysfunction, 289
Executive functioning deficit, 288
Exelon, 513
Exiba, 513
Existential despair, 77–78
Expected parameter change (EPC), 25
Exploratory factor analysis (EFA), 26–27
Exposure and ritual prevention (EX/RO), 177–180
Expressed emotion (EE), 79, 255
Externalizing disorder, 58–59
Eye Movement Desensitization and Reprocessing (EMDR), 163
Eysenck Personality Questionnaire (EPQ), 292

Family behavior therapy (FBT), 364
Family Environment Scale, 267
Family Experiences Interview Schedule, 267
Family focused therapy (FFT), 254–255
Fear, 58–59, 124, 127, 157, 160–161
Fear of Negative Evaluation Scale, 145
Fear of Negative Evaluation Scale (FNE), 145
Fear of Spiders Questionnaire, 161
Fear Questionnaire (FQ), 128
Fear Survey Schedule III (FSS-III), 161
Feedback, responsibility, advice, menu, empathy, and self-efficacy (FRAMES), 347

Feighner criteria, 6
Female sexual Function Index, 429
Fensluramine, 383
Fetal alcohol syndrome, 346
Fight-or-flight system, 91
Finger Tapping Test, 287
5-HT, 214–215, 505
5-HT2A, 504–505
5-HT2C, 505
5-HTTLPR, 56, 64, 377
Five-Factor-Model (FFM), 233, 305, 324, 392
Fluoxetine, 178, 197, 221, 238, 507
Fluphenazine, 503
Fluvoxamine (FLU), 148, 163, 178, 221, 383, 507
Folk taxonomy, 3, 10, 15
Forebrain, 91
Form 90, 345
Frontal cortex, 89–90
Frontal lobe, 92
Frontal Lobe Personality Scale, 288
Functional magnetic resonance imaging (fMRI), 93, 95, 209

GABA agonist acamprosate, 348
Gabapentin, 89, 510
GABBA$_A$ receptors, 338
Galantamine, 513–514
Gamblers Anonymous, 376, 382
  20 Questions, 380
Gambling, pathological
  advanced age and, 377
  as alcohol-related disorder, 338
  assessment/diagnosis, 380
  BPD and, 299
  course, complications, prognosis, 378
  description/clinical picture of, 370–371
  diagnosis of, formal psychiatric criteria, 370
  environmental impact of, 381–382
  epidemiology, 375
  in ethnic cultures, 376
  etiology, 376–377
  gender statistics, 371, 376
  personality development and psychopathology, 373
  phases of, 378
  treatment implications, 382–383
Gambling Impact Behavior Study (GIBS), 381
Gamma-amino-butyric acid (GABA), 89, 507, 510
GASBA-BZD receptor, 511–512
Gene-environment interaction, 61–64
Generalized anxiety disorder (GAD), 101–113. *See also* Anxiety disorders
  assessment, diagnosis, 108–110
  behavioral and cognitive influences, 46, 111
  course, complications, prognosis, 107–108
  description/clinical picture of, 101–103
  environmental impact of, 110–111
  epidemiology, 104
  etiology, 105–106
  OCD and, 175
  onset of, 107
  overanxious disorder, in children, 109
  personality development and psychopathology, 103–104
  prevalence rates, 104–105
  role-reversed/enmeshed relationships, 106
  treatment implications, 111–112
  vagal tone, 102
  worry and, 46, 101–104, 106, 108–113
    trait, 103
    Type 1/Type 2 worry, 46
    worrisome thoughts, 106

Generalized Anxiety Disorder
    Questionnaire IV (GADQ-IV),
    109, 113
Genetic influences. *See also* Adoption
    studies; Twins
  alleles, 52–53, 56, 377
  behavioral geneticists, methods of,
      53–64
    gene-environment, 61–64
      correlation (r_{ge}), 63–64
      interplay/interaction, 61–63
    pleiotropy, genetic, 53–54
      association methods, 53–54
      comorbidity, 54
      linkage methods, 53
    pleiotropy, statistical, 54–61
      applications of, recent, 56–57
      behavior, normal/abnormal,
          57–58
      comorbidity, structure of, 58–61
  boundary problems, 62
  c^2, 55, 61–64
  candidate genes, 54
  common pathway model, 58–59, 64
  constriction, 62
  e^2, 55, 62–64
  experience by environmental
      interaction (E [X] E), 62
  h^2, 52, 55, 57, 62–64
  h^2_A, 62–63
  M_a, 62–63
  r_G, 55–58, 63–64
Geodon, 505
Geriatric Depression Inventory, 288
Gerinal, 513
Glia, 87
Global Assessment of Functioning, 218
Globus pallidus, 92
Golombok Rust Inventory of Sexual
    Satisfaction (GRISS), 429
Goodness of Fit Index (GFI), 24
Grooved Pegboard Test, 287
Gyri, 92

Habit reversal training (HRT), 383
Habituation, 37–38, 106, 177, 492
Haldol, 503
Hallucinogens, 355, 357
Haloperidol, 503
Halstead-Reitan Neuropsychological
    Battery (HRNB), 286–287
Hamilton Depression Rating Scale
    (HAM-D), 219, 236, 512
Hand Dynamometer Test, 287
Hare Psychopathy Checklist-Revised
    (PCL-R), 324, 442
Harvard Anxiety Research Program
    (HARP), 126
Headache. *See* Psychophysiological
    disorders and headache
Heritability coefficient (h_2). *See* Genetic
    influences
Heroin, 355–356
Higher order conditioning, 36–37
Hindbrain, 91
Hippocampus, 92, 124, 191, 209–210,
    292
Hispanics, 73–75, 301, 340
Histrionic personality disorder (HPD),
    318–319
HIV, 43, 266, 268, 284, 288, 356, 365
HIV-related psychosis, 284
Hopelessness, 29, 43, 45, 79, 231,
    235–236, 299–300, 498–499
Hopelessness phase, 378
Hopelessness theory, 45
Human Genome Project, 67
Huntington's disease, 284, 287–288
Hydergine, 513
Hydrocephalus, 90, 288
Hydromorphone, 356

Hypericum Depression Trial Study
    Group, 223
Hypnosis, 198
Hypnotics, 356
Hypochondriasis, 191
Hypofrontality, 90, 93
Hypoglycemia, 37
Hypomania, 245, 249
Hypomanic episode, 245
Hypothalamic-pituitary-adrenocortical
    axis (HPA), 214–215
Hypothalamus, 91, 292

Ibuprofen, 417
Identity disturbances, 299
Idiotism, 4
Imipramine, 130, 238, 505
Imitative learning, 36, 39–40. *See also*
    Modeling
Imovane, 512
Implicit Associations Test (IAT), 160
Impramine, 112
Impulse disorders, 370–384. *See also*
    individual listings
  assessment/diagnosis, 380–381
  course, complications, prognosis,
      378–380
  description/clinical picture of, 370–373
  environmental impact of, 381–382
  epidemiology, 375–376
  etiology, 376–378
  personality development and
      psychopathology, 373–374
  treatment implications, 382–384
Impulsivity, 21, 27–28, 42, 70, 244, 263,
    299–308, 310, 373–376,
    391–394
Incremental fit indexes, 24
Independent Living Skills Survey, 268
Independent pathways model, 58–60, 64
Information Questionnaire-Relative
    Version, 267
Inhalant abuse, 355–356
Inhibitory postsynaptic potential (IPSP),
    86
Instrumental activities of daily living
    (IADL), 289
Instrumental learning, 36, 38–39, 105,
    157, 177, 357, 377, 489
Interclinician agreement, 5
Intermittent explosive disorder
  as alcohol-related disorder, 338
  assessment/diagnosis, 381
  course, complications, prognosis,
      379–380
  description/clinical picture of, 372
  environmental impact of, 382
  epidemiology, 375
  etiology, 378
  personality development and
      psychopathology, 374
  treatment implications, 383–384
International Association for the study of
    Pain Task Force (IASP), 411
International Classification of Diseases,
    13
  ICD-8, 5, 70
  ICD-9, 70
  ICD-10, 9, 13, 52, 231, 236, 278–279,
      326, 397
  ICD10-CM, 279
International Headache Society (IHS),
    413
  Committee on Clinical Trials in
      Migraine/Tension type
      Headaches, 414
International Index of Erectile Function
    (IIEF), 429
International Personality Disorders
    Examination (IPDE), 307, 324
Interoceptive conditioning, 125

Interpersonal social rhythm therapy
    (IP-SRT), 255–256
Interpersonal therapy, (IPT), 220–221,
    238, 398
Intolerance of Uncertainty Scale (IU), 110
Inventory of Depressive Symptoms (IDS),
    219
  quick version of (Q-IDS), 218
Inventory of Drug-Taking Situations
    (IDTS), 362
Inventory of Interpersonal Problems
    Circumplex Scales, 104
In vivo exposure, 38, 129, 162, 177–178,
    197–198, 491
Isocarboxazid, 383
Item information curve (IIC), 15
Item response curve (IRC), 15
Item Response Theory (IRT), 14–16

Journal of Abnormal Psychology, 21
*Journal of Personality and Social
    Psychology*, 32

Karney and Bradbury model of marital
    change, 456–457
Kategoriensystem fur Partnerschaftliche
    (KPI), 459
Kleptomania, 338
  as alcohol-related disorder, 338
  assessment/diagnosis, 380
  course, complications, prognosis, 379
  description/clinical picture of, 371
  environmental impact of, 382
  epidemiology, 375
  etiology, 377
  obsessive-compulsive spectrum
      disorder, 374
  personality development and
      psychopathology, 373–374
  treatment implications, 383
Knowledge about Schizophrenia
    Interview, 267
Koro, 69
Korsakoff's syndrome, 338, 346

Labeling, psychiatric, 5, 8
Lamictal, 250, 510
Lamotrigine, 250–251, 510
Latent class analysis (LCA), 12–13, 16
Latent profile analysis, 12
Latent trait, 14–15
Latent trajectory modeling (LTM), 31–33
Latinos, 10, 234
Law of effect, 38
Learned helplessness, 41, 214
Learned responses (CRs), 125
Leiter International Performance Scale,
    Revised (LIPS-R), 287
Letter-Number Sequencing of the
    Wechsler Adult Intelligence
    Scale-III, 266
Levomethadyl acetate, 365
Lexapro, 221
Leyton Obsessional/Compulsive
    Questionnaire (LOCQ), 174
Leyton Obsessional Inventory (LOI), 174
Librium, 510–511
Lie/Bed Questionnaire, 380
Liebowitz Social Anxiety Scale (LSAS),
    144–145
Life Goals Program, 256
Limbic cortex, 92
Limbic system, 92
LISREL software program, 17, 23–25
Lithium, 33, 223, 250, 507–508
Lithobid, 250
Lithonate, 250
Lobotomies, 94
Log probability ratio score (LOD), 53
Loxapine, 503
Loxitane, 503

LSD (lysergic acid diethylamide), 355
Luria Nebraska Neuropsychological
    Battery (LNNB), 286
Luvox, 221, 507
Lysergic acid diethylamide (LSD), 355

Mad cow disease, 284
Magnetic resonance imaging (MRI), 87,
    93, 95
Magnification and minimization, 44
Major depressive disorder, treatment
    implications, psychotherapy,
    220–221
Major depressive disorder (MDD), 7,
    207–223. *See also* Depression
  adjustment disorder with depressed
      mood, 207
  assessment/diagnosis, 218–219
  atypical depression, 209
  bereavement, 207
  BPD and, 300
  chronic, 208–209
  cognitive therapy, 44
  comorbidity, 210–211
  course, complications, prognosis,
      217–218
    length of, 217
    outcomes of, 217
  description/clinical picture of, 207–208
  DSM diagnostic categories for, 7–8
  environmental impact of, 219–220
  epidemiology, 212–213
  episode sensitization, 215
  etiology, 214–216
  heritability, 215
  melancholia, 4, 207, 209
  neuroticism, 211–212
  obsessionality, 212
  personality development and
      psychopathology, 211–212
  postpartum onset, 209
  psychotic episodes, 208
  regional cerebral metabolism changes,
      209–210
  stress factor, 214–215
  subtypes of, 8, 208–209
  treatment implications, 220–223
    cognitive behavioral treatment,
        488–489
    pharmacotherapy, 221–223
    psychotherapy, 220–221
Major depressive episode (MDE), 231,
    244–245
Mania, 12, 249
  acute, 250
  with delirium, 4
Manic depression. *See* Bipolar disorder
Manic episode, 244
Marijuana, 346, 355, 357, 359–363
Marital Adjustment Scale, 459
Marital dysfunction, 426, 450–462
  assessment/diagnosis, 458–460
    interview approaches, 460
    observational approaches, 459
    physiological assessment, 459
    quasi-observational approaches, 459
    self-report approaches, 458–459
  attachment style, 454
  clinical characteristics, 450
  conscientiousness, 453
  course, complications, prognosis, 458
  discord
    distressed couples, distinguishing,
        455
    GAD and, 103
    interpersonal indicators of, 450–451
    intraindividual indicators of,
        451–452
  prevalence of, 454
  prevention programs, 461
  spontaneous recovery from, 454–455

540 Subject Index

Marital dysfunction *(continued)*
 divorce rate, 454
 environmental impact of, 460
 epidemiology, 454–455
 etiology, 455–456
  integrative maintenance model, 456–458
   Karney and Bradbury, 456–457
   nonlinear dynamics, 457–458
  models of change in marriage, 455–456
  predictors, 456
 genetic influences, 453–454, 461
 neuroticism, 453
 personality disorders and, 452–453
 sex differences, 453
 treatment implications, 460–462
  commitment to, 461
  improvements in, 461
  policy/social change, 462
 violence and, 461–462
Marital Interaction Coding System (MICS), 459
Marital Satisfaction Inventory (MSI), 458–459
Mask of Sanity (Cleckley), 318
Massachusetts General Hospital Hair-Pulling Scale (MGH), 380
Massachusetts General Hospital Longitudinal Study of Panic Disorder, 126
Massachusetts Male Aging Study, 428
Maudsley Obsessive-Compulsive Inventory (MOCI), 174
Maximum likelihood (ML), 22–23, 30
MDMA, 355, 357
Medial forebrain bundle, 92
Medically unexplained symptoms, 37
Medical Outcomes Study Short Form-36, 232
Medical Outcome Study Short Form-36 (SF-36), 128
Medulla oblongata, 91
Melancholia, 4, 207, 209
Mellaril, 503
Memantine, 513–514
Mendel's law of genetics, 53
Meningitis, 284
Menninger Psychotherapy Research Project (MPRP), 482
Mental health and illness. *See also* Biological influences
 attitudes and beliefs about, 79–80
 brain-behavior relationships, 85, 93–94, 96
 care, 71, 79, 244, 267, 316, 340–341
 facilities, 5, 104
 professionals, 5, 10, 70, 271, 293, 309, 337, 339, 361, 436–438, 500
Metallization-based treatment, 310
Mental Status Schedule, 6
Meperidine, 356
Meprobamate, 511
Mesencephalon, 91
Meta-Cognitions Questionnaire (MCQ), 110
Metencephalon, 91
Methadone, 356, 365
Methamphetamine, 354–355
Methylenedioxymethamphetamine, 355
Methylphenidate, 292, 514
Michigan Alcoholism Screening Test (MAST), 344
Midbrain, 91
Midlife Development in the U.S. survey, 107, 123
MIDMA, 355
Midtown Manhattan Study, 10
Migraine. *See* Psychophysiological disorders and headache

Migraine Disability Assessment (MIDAS), 416
Millon Clinical Multiaxial Inventory (MCMI-III), 323
Millon Personality Diagnostic Checklist (MPDC), 324
Miltown, 511
Mindfulness-based cognitive therapy (MBCT), 489
Mini International Neuropsychiatric Interview (MINI), 174
Mini Mental State Exam (MMSE), 286
Minnesota Multiphasic Personality Inventory 2-Personality Disorder Scale (MMPI 2-PD), 324
Minnesota Multiphasic Personality Inventory (MMPI), 57, 219, 425
Minnesota Sex Offender Screening Tool-Revised (MNSOST-R), 442
Minnesota Trichotillomania Assessment Inventory-II (MTAI-II), 380
Minor depressive disorder (MD). *See* Dysthymia and minor depression
Mirtazapine, 221, 507
Mixed episode, 245
Mobility Inventory (MI), 128
Moban, 503
Moclobemide, 148
Modafinil, 514–515
Modeling, 36, 39–40
 of antisocial behavior, 40
 of anxiety, 40–41
 biomedical, 412
 cognitive, 42–45, 126, 191
  of auditory hallucinations, 496
  Beck's, 45, 212
   of addiction, 492
   of emotional disorders, 43
  of depression, 235, 489
  of delusions, 495
  of emotional disturbance, 42
  of persistent psychosis, 495
  of personality disorders, 496–498
  of PTSD, 191–192
  rational emotive behavior therapy, 45
  schemata, 44
 common pathways, 58–59, 64
 of depression, 41, 235
 of eating disorders, 41
 effects of, 40
 of fear development, 157
 independent pathways, 58–60, 64
 of marriage, changes in, 455–456
 omnibus personality model, 392
 of pain and headache, 412
 principles of, 39–40
 of problem solving and stress, 43
 of PTSD, 192
 of stress-diathesis relationships, 211
 of substance abuse, 41
 tripartite, of anxiety and depression, 158–159
Moderator variables, 30, 32, 63
Modification indexes (MIs), 24–25
Molindone, 503
Monoamines
 function changes and depression, 214
 for major depressive disorder, 223
 neurotransmitter systems, 54, 505
 oxidase inhibitors (MAOIs)
  for atypical depression, 209
  moclobemide, 238
  for panic disorder, 129
  reversible/irreversible, for social phobia, 148
  for tuberculosis, 505
 oxidase (MAO), 339
  alcoholics and, 339

 pathological gambling and MAO-A, 61, 377
 serotonin, (5-HT), 214–215, 505
Mood disorder
 alcohol use and dependence, 343
 Axis I diagnosis, 327
 BPD, and 305
 depression and, 41
 DSM-IV diagnosis of, 9
 general medical conditions and, 208, 288
 intermittent explosive disorder and, 374, 378
 kleptomania and, 374
 social phobia and, 147
 substance-induced, 208
Morphine, 356
Motivational Enhancement Therapy, 348, 363–364
Motivational Interviewing (MI), 347, 363–364
Mplus, 14–15
Multidimensional Personality Questionnaire, 57
MULTILOG, 14–15
Multiple-Groups Solutions (MGS), 30–31
Multiple Indicators Multiple Indicator Causes models (MIMIC), 30–31
Multiple sclerosis (MS), 87
Multitrait-multimethod matrix (MTMM), 27, 29
Myelencephalon, 91
Myelin, 87
Myocardial infarction, 220
Myotonia, 423

N-acetylaspartate (NAA), 304
Nalmefene, 348
Naltrexone, 348, 383
Namenda, 513
Narcissism, 319
Narcissistic personality disorder (NPD), 10, 319
Narcotics Anonymous (NA), 357, 365
Nar-Non, 365
National Academy of Sciences/Institute of Medicine, 415
National Alliance for the Mentally Ill (NAMI), 256
National Center on Addiction and Substance Abuse (CASA), 363
National Commission on Mental Hygiene/Committee on Statistics of the American Medico-Psychological Association, 4
National Comorbidity Survey (NCS), 6, 10–11, 234
 GAD prevalence estimates, 104, 107
 panic disorder
  annual rate of, 124
  sufferers experiencing anxiety disorders, 121
  utilization of medical services, 129
 social phobia diagnosis, 140–141, 143
 specific phobia, lifetime prevalence of, 155
 traumatic stressor exposure in PTSD, 192
National Educational Alliance for Borderline Personality Disorder (NEA-BPD), 311
National Health and Social Life Survey (NHSLS), 425, 430
National Institute for Clinical Excellence (NICE), 514
National Institute of Mental Health (NIMH), 221, 236. *See also* Epidemiological Catchment Area Program (ECA)
 BPD, research funds for, 311

 Diagnostic Interview Schedule, 74
 dysthymic disorder assessment conference of, 236
 Treatment of Depression Collaborative Research Program (TDCRP), 238
National Institute on Alcohol Abuse and Alcoholism (NIAAA), 339–340
National Institute on Drug Abuse (NIDA), 362
National Survey on Drug Use and Health (NSDUH), 340–341, 356, 363
National Vietnam Veterans Readjustment Study, 196
Natural environment phobia, 154
Navane, 503
Nefazodone, 239, 507
Negativism, 191
Neo-Kraepelinian school of U.S. psychiatry, 6, 12
NEO Personality Inventory, 438
NEO Personality Inventory-Revised (NEO-PI-R), 57, 280, 438
Neuroanatomy, 91–92
Neurobehavioral Rating Scale, 288
Neurochemical transmission, 87–89
Neurochemistry, 86
Neurodegenerative disorders/diseases, 279, 283–284
Neurodevelopment abnormalities, 90–91
Neuroglia, 87
Neurohormones, 86–87
Neuroimaging, 21, 93, 286, 288
Neuroleptic malignant syndrome (NMS), 503
Neuromodulators, 86–87
Neurontin, 510
Neuropsychological Behavior and Affect Profile, 288
Neuroticism, 55, 57, 63, 105, 158–159, 211–212, 223, 233, 281, 321–322, 392, 453–456
Neurotransmitters, 86, 88–89
New Haven Study, 10
New York State Psychiatric Institute, 5–6
NODS, 380
Nomenclature, 209–211, 232
 asylums and, 4
 categorical, establishment of, 3
 common U.S., 5
 consensual, 3
 empirically based, 8–10, 15
  criticisms of, 10
  gender/cultural bias and, 10
  reliability/validity of, 9–10
 war casualties, psychological, 5, 15
Non-Normed Fit Index, 24
Norepinephrine (NE), 54, 88–89, 193, 214, 221, 247, 292, 377, 394, 505–507, 514
Nucleus accumbens, 89, 91

Objective epistemic orientations, 78
Observational learning. *See* Modeling
Obsessionality, 212, 391, 400
Obsessive-compulsive disorder (OCD), 9–10, 169–181
 assessment/diagnosis, 173–176
  complications, 170–171
  issues, 174–176
 avoidant personality disorder and, 140
 behavioral and cognitive influences, 46–47
 course, complications, prognosis, 172–173
  associated disorders, 173
 description/clinical picture of, 169
 subtypes, 170–171
 DSM-III lifetime diagnoses of, 7
 environmental impact of, 176
 epidemiology, 171

Subject Index 541

etiology, 171–172
GAD and, 175
pediatric, 171
PTSD comorbidity, 175
repeating and counting, 170
shyness, 139–140
social phobias and, 139
treatment implications, 176–181
   cingulotomy, 92
   cognitive therapy, 179–180
   EX/RP, 177–180
   outcomes and gains predictors, 180–181
   pharmacotherapy, 178
   SRIs, EX/RP versus pharmacotherapy and, 178–179
Obsessive-Compulsive Inventory (OCI), 174
Obsessive-compulsive personality disorder (ACPD), 320, 392–393, 396–397
Obsessive-compulsive spectrum disorder (ACSD), 374, 377
Obsessive Thoughts Questionnaire (OTQ), 174
Occipital lobe, 92
Olanzapine, 250–251, 269, 311, 505
Omnibus personality trait models, 392
OMNI Personality Inventory (OMNI), 324
Operant conditioning. *See* Instrumental learning
Opiate antagonists receptors, 348, 383
Opiates, 356, 365
Opioid abuse/dependence, 356
Opioid analgesics, 417
Opium, 356
Orap, 503
Organic brain syndrome. *See* Organic mental disorder (OMD)
Organic mental disorder (OMD), 4, 278–293. *See also* Dementia
Alzheimer's disease, 279–283, 286–289
amnestic disorder, 288
assessment/diagnosis, 286–288
   attention deficit, 287
   intelligence testing, 286–287
   language, 287
   memory and learning, 287
   personality and mood, 288
   problem solving and executive functioning, 287
   psychomotor, 287
   visuospatial ability, 287
course, complications, prognosis, 284–286
   long-term care, 284–285
   mortality rate, 285
   for psychiatric patients, 285
delirium, 279–280, 282, 288
delusions, 262
description/clinical picture of, 278–279
   core features, 278
   features, 278–279
diagnosis, 288
environmental impact of, 288–290
   functional ability, 289
   on others, 289–290
   vocational, 290
epidemiology, 281–282
etiology, 282–284
   cardiovascular dysfunction, 284
   infection, 284
   metabolic causes, 283
   neurodegenerative disorders, 283–284
   traumatic brain injury, 282–283
   general medical conditions, conditions caused by, 288
personality change, 288

personality development and psychopathology, 280–281
traumatic brain injury, 280, 282–283, 286
treatment implications, 290–293
   pharmacological, 292–293
   psychosocial intervention, 291–292
Overanxious disorder, in children, 109
Oxcarbazepine, 509–510
Oxycodone, 356

Padua Inventory (PI), 174
Pain, 36–37, 87
Panic disorder and agoraphobia (PDA), 45–46, 121–132
agoraphobia
   agoraphobic avoidance, 128–129
   defined, 121
   without panic disorder (AWOPD), 121
anxiety disorders
   most common, 126
   sensitivity, 122–123
assessment and diagnosis, 127–129
   panic disorder, 127
      diagnosis of, 127
      frequency of, 127
      related fears, 127–128
behavioral inhibition, 122–123
course, complications, prognosis, 126–127
environmental impact of, 128–129
epidemiology, 123–124
etiology, 124–126
   cognitive theory, 125–126
   learning theory, 125
   neurobiology, 124–125
   neuroimaging studies, 124
mental/physical catastrophes, 125–126
personality development and psychopathology, 122–123
remission/relapse, 126
treatment implications, 129–131
   approaches to, 129
   clinical response predictors, 130–131
   cognitive behavioral treatment, 129–131
   efficacy, 129–131
   pharmacotherapy, 129–131
   quality of life, effects on, 130
Paranoia, 4, 10, 191, 262, 266, 280–281, 289, 300–301, 307, 310–311, 355, 470
Paranoid personality disorder, 10, 316–317
Parasympathetic nervous system, 89
Parietal lobe, 92
Parkinson's disease, 92, 264, 283, 286–289, 355
Paroxetine, 112, 148, 163, 178, 221, 238–239, 383, 507
Passive-avoidance strategies, 171
Passive-dependent personality. *See* Dependent personality disorder (DPD)
Patient Competency Rating Scale, 288
Patient Rejection Scale, 267
Pavlovian conditioning. *See* Associative learning
Paxil, 221, 507
Paxil CR, 221
PCP, 355
Peabody Picture Vocabulary Test, 287
Pediatric autoimmune neuropsychiatric disorders (PANDA), 173
Pemoline, 514
Penn State Worry Questionnaire (PSWQ), 26, 109
Peripheral nervous system (PNS), 89
Periventricular ischemic brain injury, 288
Perphenazine, 503

Personality Objective Checklist (PACL), 324
Personality Beliefs Questionnaire (PBQ), 497–498
Personality Assessment Form (PAF), 324
Personality Assessment Inventory-Borderline features (PAI-BOR), 307
Personality Assessment Inventory (PAI), 2323
Personality Assessment Schedule (PAS), 324
Personality Beliefs Questionnaire (PBQ), 248
Personality Diagnostic Questionnaire (PDQ), 323
Personality Disorder Interview-IV (PDI-IV), 307, 324
Personality disorder not otherwise specified (PD-NOS), 316
Personality disorders. *See also individual listings*
assessment, 323–325
basic traits of, 57–58
course, complications, prognosis, 322–323
diagnosis, 325
description/clinical picture of, 316–320
   cluster A (odd-eccentric), 316–318
      paranoid personality disorder, 316–317
      schizoid personality disorder, 246, 317
      schizotypal personality disorder, 317–318
   cluster B (dramatic-erratic), 318–319
      antisocial personality disorder, 318
      histrionic personality disorder, 318–319
      narcissistic personality disorder, 319
      paranoid, 246
   cluster c (anxious-fearful), 319–320
      avoidant, 246
      dependent personality disorder, 319–320
      obsessive-compulsive personality disorder, 320
DSM diagnostic reliability for, 7
environmental impact of, 325–326
epidemiology, 320–321
etiology, 321–322
personality disorder not otherwise specified (PD-NOS), 316
subtype manifestations, research and, 12
treatment implications, 326–327
   cognitive behavioral treatment, 496–499
Personality Inventory Questionnaire (PIQ-II), 324
Peyote, 355
Pharmacological treatments, 503–515. *See also* Antidepressants; Antipsychotic medications; Dopamine; Monoamines; Selective serotonin reuptake inhibitors (SSRIs)
for ADHD, 514–515
for agoraphobia, 129–130
for alcohol abuse and dependence, 348
allergic reactions, 37
analgesics, 417
antiandrogens, 446
anticonvulsants, 417, 508–510
for anxiety disorders, 512
anxiolytics and hypnotics, 510–513
benefits of, 221
beta-blockers, 417
for bipolar disorder, 250–252, 508
for BPD, 310–311

calcium channel antagonists, 417
cholinomimetic drugs, 292
cognitive enhancers
   I (memory), 513–514
   II (stimulants/ADHD medications), 514–515
for dysthymic disorder and minor depression, 238
electroconvulsive therapy, 223
for GAD, 112
for headaches, 417–418
   abortive medications, 413, 417
   ergotamine preparations, 413, 417
immunosuppressant drugs, 37
for intermittent explosive disorder, 383
for kleptomania, 383
for major depressive disorder, 221–223
mood stabilizers, 246, 306, 310, 378, 383
muscle relaxants, 417
nonsteroidal anti-inflammatory agents, 417
for OCD, 178
for OMD, 292–293
opioid analgesics, 417
for panic disorder, 129–130, 512
for pathological gambling, 382–383
pill placebo, 129–130, 147, 172, 177–179
prophylactic medications, 417–418
psychoactive (psychotropic) drugs, 88–89
psychostimulants, 292
for PTSD, 196–197
for pyromania, 384
for schizophrenia, 266–267, 269, 503–505
sedatives/hypnotic agents, 417
for sexual deviation, 446
for sexual dysfunction, 432–433
or social phobia, 148
for specific phobia, 163
symptomatic medications, 417
thymoleptic, 383
for trichotillomania, 383
Pharmacotherapeutics, 253, 348
Phenelzine, 148
Pick's disease, 288
Pill placebo (PBO), 129–130, 147, 172, 177–179
Pimozide, 503
Pleiotropy, 52–55
Pneuma psychikon, 4
Pons, 91
Positive affectivity, 211–212
Positive and Negative Syndrome Scale (PANSS), 266
Positron-emission tomography (PET), 93, 95–96, 209
Post-Traumatic Stress Diagnostic Scale (PDS), 195
Post-traumatic stress disorder (PTSD), 189–198
acute stress disorder, 191–196, 198
assessment/diagnosis, 195–196
behavioral and cognitive influences, 47
cognitive behavioral treatment, 197–198
cognitive theory, 192
course, complications, prognosis, 194–195
description/clinical picture, 189
environmental impact of, 196
epidemiology, 191–192
etiology, 192–194
   biological theories of PTSD, 193–194
   cognitive models of PTSD, 192–193
holocaust survivors, 191, 196
intrusive thoughts, 194
maternal, 196

542   Subject Index

Post-traumatic stress disorder (PTSD) *(continued)*
  OCD comorbidity and, 175
  personality development and psychopathology, 189–191
    risk factors, 190–191
      peritraumatic, 190–191
      postrauma, 191
      pretrauma, 189–190
    rape victims, 192, 194, 198
    trauma, without direct encounter with, 41
  treatment implications, 196–197
    cognitive behavioral treatment, 197–198
    hypnosis, 198
    pharmacological, 196–197
    psychological therapy, 197–198
  Vietnam veterans, 191–194, 196
Prefrontal cortex, 92–93, 124
President's Commission on Mental Health, 196
Prions, 284
Problem solving, 42–43
  efficacy of, 43
  as moderator of stress, 43
  and negative affect, 43
  stress and psychopathology, 42–43
Problem-solving style, 42
Problem-solving therapy (PST), 239
  for primary care (PST-PC), 239
Progestin, 383
Progressive muscle relaxation (PMR), 111–112
Prolixin, 503
Propoxyphene, 356
Propranolol, 197
Prototype categorization, 3–4, 15
Providence Veteran's Administration Hospital, 256
Provigil, 514–515
Proxy variable, 76–77
Prozac, 221, 507
Psyche, 85
Psychiatric diagnosis, 3–6, 9, 12, 15, 39, 139, 236, 281, 285, 370
Psychiatric Institute Trichotillomania Scale (PITS), 380
Psychiatric research interview for substance and mental disorders (PRISM), 11
Psychiatric Status Schedule, 6
Psychoneuroimmunology, 37
Psychobiology. *See* Brain-behavior relationships
Psychodynamic psychotherapy, 469–482
  for acute mania, 250
  basic premises, 469–477
    fixation, 473
      of psychodynamic psychotherapy, 473–477
    alliance, 473–474
    convergence/divergence in technique, 477
    defenses, 475–476
    expressive-supportive continuum and inductors for treatment, 476–477
    ideation, fantasy, wishes, 474–475
    interpretation, 475
    resistance, 475
    transference/counter transference, 476
  of psychodynamic theory, 469–473
    anal, 470–472
    developmental stages, 470–473
    genital, 472
    latency, 472
    oral, 470
    phallic, 472
    drug tolerance, 37

  for eating disorders, 398–399
  empirical support, 477–482
    counter transference, 480–481
    defenses, 479
    effectiveness of, 477–478
    patient characteristics, 481–482
    therapeutic alliance, 478–479
    transference, 479–480
    treatment length, 478
  for personality disorders, 326
Psychological Corporation, 287
Psychomotor dysfunction, 112
Psychopharmacological intervention. *See* Pharmacological treatments
Psychophysiological disorders and headache, 409–419
  assessment/diagnosis, 413–416
    clinical interview, 413
    headache diary, 413–414
    psychophysiological assessment, 414–415
    quality of life, headache impact on, 415–416
    tools, 415–416
  associated disorders, 412–413
  course, complications, prognosis, 412–413
  description/clinical picture of, 409–410
  environmental impact of, 416–417
  epidemiology, 411
  etiology, 412
  migraines, 122, 250, 409–419
    anxiety and, 410–411
    aura, 409–410
    comorbidity of, 410
    depression and, 411
    diagnosis, 413–414
    environmental impact of, 416
    migraine personality, 410
    socioeconomic costs of, 416–417
    subtypes of, 409–410
  personality development and psychopathology, 410–411
  prevalence of, 411
  rebound headaches, 413
  tension-type headaches, 409–414, 417–419
    described, 410
    diagnosis, 413–414
    environmental impact of, 417
    stress and, 411
  treatment implications, 417–419
    nonpharmacological approaches, 418–419
    pharmacological approaches, 413, 417–418
Psychosis
  antipsychotic drug treatment, 292
  DSM-III-R, diagnostic stability of, 7
  LCA, 13
  mixed, 13
  nonaffective, 7–8
Psychosocial treatments
  for bipolar disorder, 245, 249–250, 252–255
  for OCD, 177–178
  for OMD, 291–292
  for schizophrenia, 269–271
  versus pharmacological, 8
Psychosomatics, 37
Psychotic affective illness, 7
Psychotic disorder, 288, 372, 381, 265327
Psychopathic deviate, 191
PTSD Checklist, Civilian Version (PCL-C), 196
PTSD Symptom Scale-Interview (PSS-I), 195
Putamen, 92
Pyromania
  as alcohol disorder, 338
  assessment/diagnosis, 381

  course, complications, prognosis, 380
  description/clinical picture of, 372–373
  environmental impact of, 382
  epidemiology, 375–376
  etiology, 378
  personality development and psychopathology, 374
  treatment implications, 384
Quantitative Assessment of Interpersonal Themes (QUAINT), 480
Quantitative trait loc (QTL), 54
Questionnaire for Eating Disorder Diagnosis (QEDD), 396
Quetiapine, 250–252, 505
Ranchos Los Amigos Levels of Cognitive Functioning Scale (LCFS), 283
Randomized controlled trials (RCTs), 177, 327, 397, 399
Rapid cycling, 245
Rapid Risk Assessment of Sex Offender Recidivism (RRASOR), 442
Rating of Medication Influences Scale, 267
Ratio chi-square, 12
Rational emotive therapy (RET), 45, 179, 291, 487
Rational problem solving, 42
Reactions to Relaxation and Arousal Questionnaire (RRAQ), 110
Receptor up-regulation, 86
Receiver/operator characteristic analysis (ROC), 12, 16
Relapse prevention (RP)
  alcohol abuse and dependence, 348, 493
  bipolar disorder, 251
  drug abuse and dependence, 365–366
  PTSD, 197
  schizophrenia, 270
  sexual deviation, 445
Relatives Assessment Interview, 267
Remeron, 507
Reminyl, 513
Research considerations, 21–33. *See also* Structural equation modeling (SEM)
  animal, 36, 94, 214
  of BPD, 311
  clinical, 3, 6, 11, 60–61, 193, 266, 311
  comorbidity, 52
  cross-cultural, 69, 77
  depression onset and life stress factors, 214
  diagnostic, 6, 12–14
    temporal, 13
  efficacy, 494–495
  genetics, 64
  linkage, 53
  longitudinal, 31, 123, 263
  moderation, 348
  of personality disorders, 57, 61, 122, 326, 391
  psychopathology
    comorbidity, 52
    construct validation, 27
    culture and nationality/ethnicity, 72
    descriptive, 15
    evaluating measurement invariance and population heterogeneity and, 30
    personality development and, 158–160
  PSWQ, 26
  r_{ge}, 63
  SEM, 21–22, 27, 33
  SES, 26, 74
  on serotonergic dysfunction, 304

  subtyping, 13
  tools, for validation models, 12–15
    IRT analysis, 14–15
    LCA, 12–13
    survival/hazard analysis, 13–14
Research Diagnostic Criteria (RDC), 6
Restori, 513
Reversible monoamine oxidase inhibitors (RIMAs), 148
Revised Diagnostic Interview for Borderlines (DIB-R), 324
Rey Auditory Verbal Learning Test (RAVLT), 287
Risperidone, 250–251, 269, 311, 505
Ritalin, 514
Rivastigmine, 513–514
Robins and Guze validation model, 12
Root mean square error of approximation (RMSEA), 24
Rorschach Test, 324–325
Saccharine, 37
Saint-John's-wort, 223
Salpêtrière Hospital (Paris), 4
Sampling, 71
Scalar invariance analysis, 31
Schedule of Nonadaptive and Adaptive Personality (SNAP), 324
Schedules for Clinical Assessment in Neuropsychiatry, 236
Schemata, 248
  biased cognitive, 43–45
Schema therapy, 497
Schizoaffective disorder, 7–8, 73
Schizodepression, 13
Schizoid, 317
Schizoid personality disorder, 10, 317
Schizomanic/schizobipolar disorder, 13
Schizophrenia, 4, 262–272. *See also* Antipsychotic medications
  biological assessment, 266–267
  chronic nonparanoid, 90
  cognitive impairments, 262, 266
  complications, 265–266
  course, 265
  delusions, 262
  description/clinical picture of, 262
  DSM diagnostic categories of, 7–8
  environmental impact of, 268–269
  epidemiology, 263–264
  etiology, 264–265
  family involvement/intervention, 268, 271
  gender factors, 263
  hallucinations, 5, 262
  hypofrontality, 93
  LCA, 13
  negative symptoms, 262
  occupational functioning, 268–269
  onset of, 262–263
  peer interactions, 269
  personality development and psychopathology, 262–263
  prevalence of, 263
  prognosis, 266
  psychotic symptoms of, 262
  sexuality, family planning, parenting, 268, 271
  social drift hypothesis, 262
  social functioning, 267–268
  stress hypothesis, environmental, 262
  subtype manifestations, research and, 12
  symptoms, 266
  treatment implications, 269–272
    pharmacological, 269
      medication noncompliance/ adherence, 267, 270
    psychosocial, 270–272
      assertive community treatment, 270

Subject Index   543

cognitive-behavioral therapy, 270–271, 495–496
early intervention, 271–272
integrated dual-disorder treatment, 270
medication adherence, 270
social skills training, 270
vocational rehabilitation, 271
Schizophreniform disorder, 73, 263
Schizotypal personality disorder (STPD), 7–10, 317–318
Science, 3, 5
Sedatives, 356
Selective abstract, 44
Selective serotonin reuptake inhibitors (SSRIs)
for BPD, 310–311
fluoxetine, 178, 197, 221, 238
for intermittent explosive disorder, 383
for kleptomania, 383
for major depressive disorder, 221
side effects of, 221, 223
for migraines, 417
for OCD, 178
for OMD, 292
for panic disorder, 127, 129
for PTSD, 197
sertraline, 148, 197, 221, 238
for sexual deviation, 446
for social phobia, 148
for specific phobia, 163
for trichotillomania, 383
Self-control desensitization (SCD), 112
Self-depreciation, 41, 68
Self-Esteem Scale (SES), 26
Self-mutilating behavior, 299–300, 305
Sensation seeking, 56, 63–64, 321, 356, 373–374, 376
Sensitization, 37–38, 87, 177, 193, 215, 383–384, 412, 446
Septicemia, 284
Seroquel, 505
Serotonergic dysfunction, 304
Serotonin, 54–55, 88–89, 172, 221, 233, 235, 247, 377, 507
Serotonin-norepinephrine reuptake inhibitors (SNRIs), 221, 507
Sertraline, 148, 197, 221, 238, 507
Severe Impairment Battery (SIB), 514
Severity of Alcohol Dependence Questionnaire (SADQ), 345
Severity of Dependence Scale (SDS), 362
Sex Offender Need Assessment Rating (SONAR), 443
Sex Offender Risk Appraisal Guide (SORAG), 442
Sexual deviation, 436–446
assessment/diagnosis, 442–444
behavioral theories, 440
childhood sexual abuse, 440–441
complicating factors, 442
course, 441–442
description/clinical picture of, 436–437
environmental impact of, 444–445
epidemiology, 439
etiology, 439–441
exhibitionism, 436–442
frotteurism, 436–438
gender differences, 440
paraphilias, 429, 436–449
pedophiles, 437, 440
personality development and psychopathology, 43–439
prognosis, 442
rape, 437, 439–444
recidivism rates, 441–442, 445
sadists, 436–437
sadomasochists, 436–437, 439
sex-offending behavior, 437–438, 441–442

transvestites, 436–439, 445
treatment implications, 445–446
cognitive behavioral treatment, 445
intensity/length of, 445
pharmacological, 446
satiation, masturbatory/verbal, 446
voyeurism, 436–437, 439–442
Sexual disorder, 288
Sexual dysfunction, 423–433
acquired/secondary, 428
assessment/diagnosis, 428–429
course, complications, prognosis, 427–428
description/clinical picture of, 423–424
environmental impact of, 429–431
community notification, 444
on family, 429–431
victimization, 444
on work, school, peer interactions, 431
epidemiology, 425–426
etiology, 426–427
female sexual arousal disorder, 423, 432
male erectile disorder, 423–424, 427–428, 432
OMD and, 290
orgasmic disorders, 424, 426, 432
personality development and psychopathology, 424–425
rapid ejaculation, 424–428, 430, 432
sexual pain disorders, 424
treatment implications, 431–433
Masters and Johnson clinic, 432
mechanical, for erectile dysfunction, 432
pharmacological, 432–433
treatment seeking percentages, 431–432
Viagra, 427
Sexual Violence Risk-20, 443
Shedler-Westen Assessment Procedure (SWAP), 324
Shenjing shuaiuro, 68
Short Alcohol Dependence Data Questionnaire (SADD), 345
Shyness, 139–140
Situational phobia, 154, 156
Skinnerian conditioning. *See* Instrumental learning
Sleep disorders, 52, 69, 245, 288
Smoking
of cigarettes, 427–428
modeling, 41
opiates, administering by, 356
during pregnancy, 264
Social-Adaptive Functioning Evaluation (SAFE), 268
Social Adjustment Scale-II, 268
Social anxiety disorder, 138–149. *See also* Anxiety disorders
assessment and diagnosis, 144–146
behavioral and cognitive influences, 46
course, complications, prognosis, 142–143
description/clinical picture of, 138–139
environmental impact of, 146–147
epidemiology, 140–141
etiology, 141–142
OBCD and, 139
personality development and psychopathology, 139–140
remission of, 143
treatment implications, 147–148
Social Avoidance and Distress Scale (SADS), 145
Social Behavior Schedule, 268
Social disintegration, 79
Social drift hypothesis, 262

Social Interaction Anxiety Scale (SIAS), 145–146
Social isolation, 40, 79, 142, 317, 342–343, 382
Social learning theory, 36, 39, 319, 342, 357–358, 365, 493
Social phobia. *See* Social anxiety disorder
Social Phobia Diagnostic Questionnaire (SPDQ), 144
Social Phobia Scale (SPS), 145–146
Social Rhythm Metric (SRM), 255
Social stress, 78–79
Sociocultural influences, 67–80
culture/subculture, 71–73
defining/articulating, 71–76
ethnic identity, acculturation and, 75–76
race, culture, ethnicity, nationality, 72–73
SES/minority status, 73–75
derived etic, 68
elucidating mechanisms, 76–80
characteristic variable, 77
communication style, 79
individual/collectivism, 77–78
mental health/illness, attitudes and beliefs about, 79–80
social stress/support, 78–79
epistemological/methodological issues, 67–71
assessment, 69–70
diagnosis, 70–71
etic versus emic perspectives, 67–69, 73, 80
sampling, 71
feature variable, 77
nationality, 72–73
race, 30, 67, 71–75, 104, 263, 340, 432, 480
rapid social change, 79
Sociocultural level, 76
Sociocultural influences, support, 78–79
Socioeconomic status (SES), 71–78, 445
Sociotropy, 212
Solution implementation and verification, 42
Soma, 86
Somatization, 12
Sonata, 512
Sourcebooks (Widiger, et al.), 9
South Oaks Gambling Screen (SOGS), 380
SOGS-RA (adolescent version), 380
Specific phobia, 45, 154–163
animal, 154, 156
anxiety sensitivity, 159
assessment, 160–161
behavioral, 161
clinical overview, 160–161
diagnostic features, 160
self-report measures, 161
blood-injection-injury phobia, 154, 156, 159
comorbidity, 154–155
course, complications, prognosis, 156
cues, physiological responses to, 156
disgust sensitivity, 159, 161
environmental impact of, 156–157
epidemiology, 155–156
etiology, 157–158
functional impairment, 156–157
gender, age, cultural differences, 155
height, 156
informational pathways, 157
neuroticism, 158–159
onset of, 156
personality development and psychopathology, 158–160
prevalence rates of, 155–156
situational, 154, 156
spider phobia, 40, 159–160, 162

treatment, 161–163
medications and, 163
other options of, 163
technology in, 162–163
types of, 154, 156
Spider phobia, 40, 159–160, 162
S polymorphism, 215
Spouse Observation checklist, 459
Standardized Clinical Interview for *DSM-IV* (SCID), 174
Standardized root mean square residual (SRMR), 23
Standford-Binet, fifth edition, 287
Stanford Acute Stress Reaction Questionnaire (SASRQ), 196
State-Trait Anxiety Inventory (STAI), 11, 110
Stellazine, 503
Stevens-Johnson syndrome, 252
Storm phobia, 163
Strattera, 514
Stress-diathesis relationships, 211
Stroke, 220, 284
Stroop technique, 287
Structured Clinical Interview for *DSM-IV* Axis II Personality Disorders (SCID-II), 307
Structural equation modeling (SEM), 21–33
advantages/benefits of, 21–23
applied, 32–33
covariance matrices, 22–24, 32
psychopathology research, 27–32
CFA and construct validity assessment, 27–30
correlated models, 28–29
inclusion of background variables, 29–30
MTMM matrices, 27
latent trajectory modeling, 31–32
measurement invariance/population heterogeneity tests, 30–31
strengths of, maximizing, 22–27
error specification in, 26–27
goodness-of-fit statistics, 22–27, 32
fitting function, 22–23
localized points of ill fit, 24–25
maximum likelihood, 22–23, 30
overall fit, 23–24
parameter estimates, evaluating strength and interpretability, 25–26
proper application of, 22
Structured Clinical Interview for Axis I Disorders, Version 2 (SCID-II), 345, 361
Structured Clinical Interview for *DSM-III-R* Personality Disorders (SCID-II), 324
Structured Clinical Interview for *DSM-III* (SCID), 6, 11, 14, 396
-IV, 109, 160
for panic disorder, 127
in randomized surveys, 11
-II, 307, 322, 324, 345, 361
Structured Clinical Interview for *DSM-IV* (SCID-IV), 109, 160, 219, 236
Structured Clinical Interview of *DSM-IV* Axis I Disorders (SCIP-I/P), 381
Structured Interview for *DSM-IV* Personality Disorders (SIDP-IV), 307
Structured Interview for *DSM* Personality Disorders-Revised (SIDP-R), 324
Subcortical vascular disease, 215
Subjective epistemic orientations, 78
Substance abuse
in bipolar disorder, 246

Substance abuse *(continued)*
  in BPD, 301
  cognitive behavioral treatment, 492–493
  and dependence
    DSM diagnostic categories for, 7
  modeling of, 41
Substance Abuse and Mental Health and Services Administration (SAMHSA), 339–341
Substance Dependence Severity Scale (SDSS), 362
Substantia nigra, 92
Subthresholds
  depression, 232, 280
  eating disorders, 393
    AN, 393–394
    BED, 393
    BN, 395
    EDNOS diagnoses and, 390
  intermittent explosive disorder, 380
  pathological gambling, 375
Suicide, 9, 235, 300
Sulci, 92
Survival/hazard analysis, 13–14, 16
Susto, 69
Symbol Digit Modalities Test (SDMT), 287
Sympathetic nervous system (SNS), 89–90
Synapse, 86
Syndromal diagnosis, 4, 6, 15
Systematic Treatment Enhancement Program for Bipolar Disorder (STEP-BD), 254–255
Systems Training for Emotional Predictability and Problem Solving (STEPPS), 310

Tacrine, 292, 513
Tactual Performance Test (TPT), 287
Tardive dyskinesia (TD), 503–504
Task Force of the Society of Pediatric Psychology, 418
Tectum, 91
Tegmentum, 91–92
Tegretol, 250–251, 383, 508–509
Telencephalon, 91
Temazepam, 513
Temporal lobe, 92

Tension-type headache. *See* Psychophysiological disorders and headache
Terminal button(s), 86
Test information curve (TIC), 15
Thalamus, 91, 292
Thematic Apperception Test, 324–325
Thioridizine, 503
Thiothixine, 503
Thorazine, 250, 503
Thought-action fusion, 47
Threat-relevant information, 159–160
Thresholds. *See also* Subthresholds
  clinical, 12, 148
  criterion, 14–15
  diagnostic, 9, 11–12, 108
  item difficulty in CTT, 14
Thyroid hormone, 223
Timeline Follow-Back (TLFB), 345, 362
Tofranil, 505
Token Test, 287
Topamax, 510
Topiramate, 250–251, 510
Tracts, 89
Trail Making Test (TMT), 266, 287
Transferenced focused psychotherapy (TFP), 310
Traumatic brain injury (TBI), 280, 282–283, 286, 289–291
Trazodone, 507
Treatment and Research Advancements National Association of Personality Disorder (TARA), 311
Treatment as usual condition (TAU), 254–255
Treatment for Adolescents with Depression Study (TADS), 221
Triangular decomposition, 55
Trichotillomania
  as alcohol-related disorder, 338
  assessment/diagnosis, 380
  course, complications, prognosis, 378–379
  description/clinical picture of, 371
  environmental impact of, 382
  epidemiology, 375
  etiology, 377

  habit reversal training (HRT), 383
  hair-pulling, 371, 375, 377–379, 382–383
  obsessive-compulsive spectrum disorder, 377
  personality development and psychopathology, 373
  scalp biopsies, 380
  treatment implications, 383
Trifluoperazine, 503
Trilafon, 503
Trileptal, 509
Triptans, 417
Tuberculosis, 356
Tucker-Lewis Index (TL), 24
Twelve-Step Facilitation (TSF), 348
Twins
  genetic influences, 53, 55–56, 58–64
    alcohol abuse, 341
    BPD, 303
    depression, 215
    divorce status, 454
    eating disorders, 394
    erectile dysfunction, 427
    marriage propensity, 453
    panic disorder, 124
    personality disorders, 322
    PTSD, 191
    sexual abuse, 424
Two-factor theory of learning, 39, 125
Two-parameter model, 14

Unconditioned response (UR), 125
Unconditioned stimulus (UCS), 105
Unilateral Family Training, 347
Univariate Lagrange multipliers, 24–25
U.S. Food and Drug Administration (FDA), 197, 221, 223, 250, 365, 505, 507–508, 510, 513–514
U.S. Headache Consortium, 418
U.S.–U.K. Diagnostic Project, 70
U.S. War Department, 5

Vagal tone, 102
Valium, 354, 511
Valproate, 507, 509–510
Valproic acid, 508
Vascular dementia (VaD), 279, 282, 284, 289, 513, 515

Vascular disease, 215, 287–288
Venlafaxine, 221, 223, 507
Veterans Administration, 5, 376
  Providence Veteran's Administration Hospital, 256
Viagra, 427
Vicarious acquisition, 157
Vicarious learning. *See* Modeling
Violence Risk Appraisal Guide (VRAG), 442

Washington University School of Medicine (Saint Louis), 6
Wechsler Adult Intelligence Scale, third edition (WAIS-III), 286–287
Wechsler Memory Scale, third edition (WMS-III), 287
Wellbutrin, 507
Western Aphasia Battery, 287
Why Worry Scale, 110
Wisconsin Card Sorting Test (WCST), 266, 287
Wisconsin Personality Disorder Inventory (WIPSI-IV), 324
World Health Organization (WHO), 5, 68, 70–72, 263, 415
World War II, 4–5, 194

X_2 statistic, 23–24, 30
Xanax, 354, 511–512
X-ray, 94

Yale-Brown Obsessive Compulsive Scale (Y-Bocs), 174, 178–179
  for trichotillomania (Y-BOCS TM), 380
Young Mania Rating Scale, 249
Young-Rygh Avoidance Inventory (YRA-I), 497
Young Schema Questionnaire (YSQ), 248, 497

Zaleplon, 512
Ziprasidone, 505
Zoloft, 221, 507
Zolpidem, 512–513
Zopiclone, 512
Zung Depression Rating Scale, 219
Zyban, 507
Zyprexa, 250, 505